THE WESTMINSTER DICTIONARY
OF WORSHIP

THE WESTMINSTER
DICTIONARY
OF WORSHIP

Edited by
J. G. DAVIES

THE WESTMINSTER PRESS
Philadelphia

© SCM Press Ltd. 1972

First published in Great Britain in 1972
(second impression, 1974; third impression, 1976)
under the title *A Dictionary of Liturgy and Worship*

Published by The Westminster Press®
Philadelphia, Pennsylvania

PRINTED IN THE UNITED STATES OF AMERICA

9 8 7 6 5 4 3 2 1

Library of Congress Cataloging in Publication Data

Main entry under title:

The Westminster dictionary of worship.

   First ed. entered under: Davies, John Gordon,
1919–   A dictionary of liturgy and worship.
   1. Liturgies — Dictionaries. I. Davies,
John Gordon, 1919–   II. Davies, John Gordon,
1919–   A dictionary of liturgy and worship.
BV173.D28 1979   264'.003   78-25582
ISBN 0-664-21373-1

PREFACE

Ritual would appear to be natural to man. When even birds and animals engage in it, as for example in sex play, it is not surprising to discover that human beings practise it almost universally. This formalization of natural actions lies at the basis of worship, which is the expression in corporate gatherings of adoration, praise and thanksgiving to God in response to his activity in the world. This response precedes doctrinal formulation, so that one may say that worship is primary and theology secondary. In Christian terms, this means that the early church worshipped Christ long before it had reached an intellectual understanding of his person and work. It is this sequence that explains the Latin tag *lex orandi, lex credendi,* i.e. what is to be believed is derived from the practice of worship. Consequently, worship has always been regarded as the living heart of any religion. Because of this centrality, a knowledge of worship is essential for a sympathetic appreciation of all religious movements.

Worship can be either 'free' or formal. In the latter case it is offered according to fixed rites and it is customary to use the term 'liturgy' in reference to these. Liturgy also bears a narrower sense in that it can refer in particular to the eucharist as the church's corporate and official act of worship.

As a reference book, this present volume is intended to provide background knowledge about worship for those who are regularly involved in it or would learn something about it. It seeks to concentrate upon the information that Christians today need in order to participate with understanding in the worship of the traditions to which they belong. At the same time, it aims to assist them to appreciate traditions and contemporary practices other than their own, familiarity with which is required to further the cause of ecumenical cooperation.

The separate articles are not confined to simple definitions, but give the historical background to the subject treated and seek to relate this to the contemporary scene. However, while a reliable factual content is essential, emphasis is laid upon its interpretation, with particular reference to the principles upon which the practice, object, etc. is founded or used. In this way the reader will be enabled to understand not only what has been or is done but why it has been or is done. Hence, the *Dictionary* is concerned not only with the structures but also with the rationale of worship, the tracing of patterns and influences, and the underlying basis.

The entries relate not only to the historic Christian churches, such as the Anglican, the Lutheran, the Presbyterian and the Roman Catholic, but also to those bodies which have intimate links with the biblical and Christian inheritance, such as the

Pentecostals and the Unitarians. In addition, accounts are given of the worship of other major world religions, e.g. Judaism and Islam.

In order to ensure representative accounts, the contributors to the *Dictionary* have been chosen from recognized liturgical experts within the different churches, so that, for example, Eastern Orthodox scholars have written on subjects pertaining to their own church, similarly Old Catholics, etc. The result of this is that some of the major articles are composite. The accounts of baptism, matrimony, liturgies, etc., are divided into sections, each one detailing the practice of a major denomination. The opening three sections of each composite article are in historical sequence, so that the first is devoted to the patristic period, the second to Eastern Orthodoxy, and the third to Roman Catholicism, medieval and modern; the remainder follow in alphabetical order, beginning with Anglicanism.

One consequence of this composite authorship is that different viewpoints are expressed, so that, e.g. in the entry on 'Ordination', varied and sometimes conflicting understandings of the subject are to be found. This lack of uniformity is inevitable if the positions of the several Christian churches are to be presented faithfully. Not only has each contributor been left free to give his own denominational interpretation, but no attempt has been made to achieve a consensus on matters of minor importance; e.g. the date of the *Apostolic Tradition* of Hippolytus is variously given, according to the predilection of the individual writers, as *c.*215, *c.*217 or even *c.*222.

While the majority of entries are devoted to the principal aspects of liturgy and worship, others treat of its ancillaries, e.g. its architectural setting, vestments, etc.

Worship today is, of course, not simply a matter of history. The Liturgical Movement, to which a major article is devoted, and the many revisions that are currently being produced witness to a desire to formulate patterns of worship relevant to contemporary man. But to say this is to recognize that worship is undergoing a crisis. To some it has lost its meaning. Hence the need, which is emphasized in several entries, for experimental forms, for attention to the problems of indigenization, to secularization, to the relation of liturgy and culture and liturgy and mission.

It is hoped that the *Dictionary* will be found useful by several types of reader. It is intended to appeal to church leaders, clergy and ministers, to laity and to students who wish to increase their understanding of the history and contemporary practice of worship and liturgy.

The selection of topics is always a difficult task. What one would include, another would omit. The existence of companion volumes, such as the *Theological Word Book of the Bible* (1950) and *A Dictionary of Christian Theology* (1969), has enabled the editor to have a greater latitude than would otherwise have been the case, for it has seemed unnecessary to repeat what is to be found in these works of reference. While he must bear the responsibility for the final choice, he is grateful to those who have given their advice and to all the contributors, without whose ready cooperation this project could not have been completed.

J. G. DAVIES

CONTRIBUTORS

The Rev. Dr Henry Ashworth, OSB
Books, Liturgical 3. Medieval and Roman Catholic

The Rev. Dr Frank Baker
Love Feast

The Rev. Dr John M. Barkley
Baptism; Burial 12. Reformed; Ordination 13. Reformed

Dr B. B. Beach
Baptism 15. Seventh-day Adventist; Books, Liturgical 15. Seventh-day Adventist; Burial 13. Seventh-day Adventist; Liturgies 15. Seventh-day Adventist (Communion Service); Matrimony 13. Seventh-day Adventist; Ordination 14. Seventh-day Adventist; Seventh-day Adventist Worship

The Rev. Dr Eugene Brand
Liturgies 9. Lutheran; Lutheran Worship

Dr F. F. Bruce
Baptism 13. Plymouth Brethren; Burial 11. Plymouth Brethren; Liturgies 13. Plymouth Brethren; Matrimony 11. Plymouth Brethren; Plymouth Brethren

The Rev. C. O. Buchanan
Burial 4. Anglican; Liturgies 4. Anglican

Dr H. Ellsworth Chandlee
Baptism 4. Anglican; Liturgical Movement, The

The Rev. Joseph Connelly
All Saints; All Souls; Ember Days; Fast Days; Ferial; Mariological Feasts; Rogation Days; Saints' Days

The Rev. Dr Gilbert Cope
Colours, Liturgical; Gestures; Postures; Vestments

General Frederick Coutts
Salvation Army

Dr Maurice A. Creasey
Quaker Worship

The Rev. J. D. Crichton
Altar, Stripping of; Altar, Washing of; Ashes; Asperges; Baptism 3. Medieval and Roman Catholic; Bible Services; Books, Liturgical 2. Roman Catholic; Liturgies 3. Medieval and Roman Catholic; Mass, High; Mass, Low; Matrimony 3. Medieval and Roman Catholic; New Fire; Ordination 3. Medieval and Roman Catholic; Paschal Vigil; Roman Catholic Worship; Tenebrae; Unction

The Rev. Canon G. J. Cuming
Books, Liturgical 4. Anglican; Churching of Women; Commination; Matrimony 4. Anglican; Sick, Visitation of the

The Rev. Dr Horton Davies
Baptism 7. Congregational; Books, Liturgical 7. Congregationalist; Burial 6. Congregationalist; Congregationalist Worship; Liturgies 7. Congregationalist; Matrimony 6. Congregationalist; Ordination 7. Congregationalist

The Rev. Professor J. G. Davies (Editor)
Ablutions; Absolution; Aisle; Alms; Amen; Apse; Architectural Setting; Atrium; Baptistery; Basilica; Bible, Use of in Worship; Blessing; Books, Liturgical 1. The Early Church; Books, Liturgical 9. Lutheran (2) United States; Burial 1. The Early Church; Calendar; Canticles; Cathedral; Centralized Building; Ceremonial; Chancel; Chapel; Choir (Architectural); Commixture; Communion; Consecration of Churches; Crucifix; Dedication; Dismissal; Disposal of Eucharistic Remains; Easter Garden or Sepulchre; Eucharist; Font; Fraction; Gallery; Invocation; Lavabo; Lord's Supper; Martyrium; Matrimony 1. The Early Church; Mission and Worship; Mixed Chalice; Narthex; Nave; Office Hymn; Ordination 1. The Early Church; Orientation; Rite; Ritual; Rubrics; Sacristy; Sanctuary; Secularization and Worship; Sentences; Tract; Transept; Vestry; Words of Administration

The Rev. F. Debuyst
Architectural Setting (Modern)

Peter Dickinson
Music, Modern; Organ

The Rev. Dr C. W. Dugmore
Canonical Hours

The Rev. Canon J. D. C. Fisher
Baptism 1. Patristic; Catechumen, Catechumenate; Insufflation

The Rev. P. V. Fisher
Culture and Worship

The Rt. Rev. J. H. Foy
Moravian Worship

The Rev. Dr R. H. Fuller
Lectionary; Sermon

The Rt. Rev. T. S. Garrett
Church of South India Worship

The Rev. A. Raymond George
Anniversary; Baptism 10. Methodist; Books, Liturgical 10. Methodist; Burial 9. Methodist; Extempore Prayer; Methodist Worship; Ordination 10. Methodist; Prayer Meeting

W. Jardine Grisbooke
Agnus Dei; Anaphora; Antidoron; Baptism 2. Orthodox; Books, Liturgical 2. Orthodox; Cathedral Office; Collect; Consecration Prayer; Diptychs; Doxology;

Enarxis; Entrance, Great; Entrance, Little; Incense; Intercession; Kyrie; Litany; Liturgies 2. Orthodox; Lord's Prayer; Oblation; Ordinary; Orthodox Worship; Presanctified Mass; Proper; Prothesis; Sanctus; Shinto Worship; Silent Prayer; Suffrages; Super Oblata; Synaxis; Trisagion

The Rev. Dr E. R. Hardy
Coptic Worship

Andrew Heley
Baptism 8. Jehovah's Witnesses; Books, Liturgical 8. Jehovah's Witnesses; Burial 7. Jehovah's Witnesses; Jehovah's Witnesses' Worship; Liturgies 8. Jehovah's Witnesses; Matrimony 7. Jehovah's Witnesses; Ordination 8. Jehovah's Witnesses

The Rev. Dr Peter Hinchcliff
Acolyte; Bishop; Cantor; Celebrant; Chairman of District; Crucifer; Deacon; Deaconness; Elder; Lay Preacher; Lector; Local Preacher; Presbyter; Reader; Server; Superintendent; Thurifer

Dr W. J. Hollenweger
Camp Meeting; Experimental Forms of Worship; Liturgies 12. Pentecostal; Open-Air Meeting; Ordination 12. Pentecostal; Pentecostal Worship; Spirituals

The Rev. Clifford Howell, SJ
Vernacular

The Rev. Dr E. Bolaji Idowu
Indigenization

The Rev. R. C. D. Jasper
Anglican Worship; Canon; Ordination 4. Anglican; Procession

The Rev. Dr F. Kalb
Books, Liturgical 9. Lutheran

Archdale A. King
Benediction; Concelebration; Exposition; Forty Hours Devotion; Reservation; Rosary; Sacred Heart; Stations of the Cross; Veneration of the Cross

The Rev. Dr J. A. Lamb
Books, Liturgical 14. Reformed; Liturgies 14. Reformed; Matrimony 12. Reformed

The Rev. Paul Lazor
Burial 2. Orthodox; Matrimony 2. The Orthodox Church; Ordination 2. Orthodox

The Rev. Dr Allan A. McArthur
Advent; Ascension Day; Ash Wednesday; Christmas; Corpus Christi; Easter; Epiphany; Good Friday; Holy Saturday; Holy Week; Lent; Low Sunday; Octave; Palm Sunday; Pentecost; Quinquagesima; Sunday; Transfiguration; Trinity Sunday

The Rev. Dr Kilian McDonnell
Baptism 12. Pentecostal; Books, Liturgical 12. Pentecostal

The Rev. Dr W. D. Maxwell
Reformed Worship

The Rev. Brian A. Newns
Burial 3. Medieval and Roman Catholic; Epistle; Exorcism; Gospel; Last Gospel; Lesson

Dr Alfred Niebergall
Burial 8. Lutheran; Matrimony 8. Lutheran

The Rev. Dr Geoffrey Parrinder
Buddhist Worship; Hindu Worship

The Rev. A. E. Peaston
Unitarian Worship

The Rev. Thomas Phelan
Offertory

The Rev. Canon Ronald Pilkington
Papal Rites

The Rev. Dr C. E. Pocknee
Alms-Dish; Altar; Altar Hangings; Altar Rails; Ambo; Aumbry; Baldachin; Bells; Candles, Lamps and Lights; Cathedra; Chalice and Paten; Chrismatory; Ciborium; Corporal; Cross; Cruet; Fan; Frontal; Iconostasis; Lectern; Monstrance; Pall; Paschal Candle; Pew; Piscina; Pulpit; Purificator; Pyx; Reredos; Rostrum; Screen; Stoup; Tabernacle; Thurible; Tower; Veil

Dr Jacob Posen
Jewish Worship

The Rev. Kurt Pursch
Baptism 11. Old Catholic; Books, Liturgical 11. Old Catholic; Burial 10. Old Catholic; Liturgies 11. Old Catholic; Matrimony 10. Old Catholic; Old Catholic Worship; Ordination 11. Old Catholic

Bernarr Rainbow
Carol; Chants; Choir (Musical); Hymns 2. Vernacular

The Very Rev. Dr Alan Richardson
Creed, Creeds

The Rev. Alec Robertson
Antiphon; The Chants of the Proper of the Mass; Church Modes; The Divine Office: Gregorian Chant; Hymns 1. Latin; Motet; Music in the Mass of the Roman Rite; Notation and Rhythm; Polyphony; Psalmody; Psalm Tones; Responsorial Psalmody and Responsories

Dr Albert E. Rüthy
Baptism 11. Old Catholic; Books, Liturgical 11. Old Catholic; Burial 10. Old Catholic; Liturgies 11. Old Catholic; Matrimony 10. Old Catholic; Old Catholic Worship; Ordination 11. Old Catholic

The Rev. Peter Selby
Prayer

Dr E. J. R. H. S. von Sicard
Baptism 9. Lutheran; Ordination 9. Lutheran

The Rev. Dr John E. Skoglund
Baptist Worship; Burial 5. Baptist; Liturgies 5. Baptist; Ordination 5. Baptist

John B. Taylor
Islamic Worship

The Rev. C. Tol
Baptism 11. Old Catholic; Books, Liturgical 11. Old Catholic; Burial 10. Old Catholic; Liturgies 11. Old Catholic; Matrimony 10. Old Catholic; Old Catholic Worship; Ordination 11. Old Catholic

The Rev. David Tripp
Covenant Service; Watch Night

The Rev. Paul Verghese
East Syrian Worship; Ethiopian Worship; Mar Thoma Church Worship; West Syrian Worship

Dr Keith Watkins
Baptism 6. Christian Church (Disciples of Christ); Books, Liturgical 6. Christian Church (Disciples of Christ); Christian Church (Disciples of Christ) Worship; Liturgies 6. Christian Church (Disciples of Christ); Ordination 6. Christian Church (Disciples of Christ)

The Rev. Canon E. C. Whitaker
Ante-Communion; Bidding Prayer; Confirmation; Harvest Thanksgiving; Three-hours Service

Dr James F. White
Baptism 10. Methodist; Liturgies 10. Methodist; Matrimony 9. Methodist; Methodist Worship 2. USA

The Rev. Stephen Winward
Baptism 5. Baptist; Books, Liturgical 5. Baptist; Matrimony 5. Baptist

Dr Thomas F. Zimmerman
Assemblies of God Churches' Worship

ACKNOWLEDGMENTS

We are grateful to the following for permission to reproduce copyright illustrations: A.C.L., Brussels, *Plate 35; L'Art Sacré*, Paris, *Fig. 10;* James Austin, *Plate 5;* Bernsen's International Press Service Ltd., *Plate 41;* D. X. Botte, *Plate 15;* James Brooks, *Plate 10;* Courtauld Institute of Art, *Plates 7 & 8;* Graphion, London, *Plate 31;* Louis Grossé Ltd. *Fig. 25;* C. V. Hancock, *Plates 6 & 27;* The Mansell Collection, *Plates 1 & 3;* Fritz Metzger, Zürich, *Plate 13;* National Gallery, London, *Plate 39;* Pax House, Ipswich, Suffolk, *Plate 22;* Otto Pfeifer, Lucerne, *Plates 14, 42 & 43;* Poppe, Bad Kissingen, *Plate 11;* Rheinisches Bildarchiv, *Plate 12;* Victoria & Albert Museum, Crown Copyright, *Plates 34 & 40;* Colin Westwood, *Plate 23;* C. D. & A. Willmott, *Plate 2.*

ABBREVIATIONS

AV	Authorized Version (King James Version) of the Bible
BCP	*Book of Common Prayer*
DCT	*Dictionary of Christian Theology*, ed. Alan Richardson, 1969
DTC	*Dictionnaire de Théologie Catholique*, ed. A. Vacant, E. Mangenot and E. Amann, 1903-50
ET	English translation
IKZ	*Internationale Kirchliche Zeitschrift*
NEB	New English Bible
NT	New Testament
OT	Old Testament
RV	Revised Version of the Bible
TDNT	*Theological Dictionary of the New Testament*, ET of *TWNT*, trans. and ed. Geoffrey W. Bromiley, 1964 ff.
TWNT	*Theologisches Wörterbuch zum Neuen Testament,* ed. Gerhard Kittel, 1933 ff.
WCC	World Council of Churches

Ablutions

The ceremonial cleansing of the eucharistic vessels and of the minister's fingers after communion. In the patristic period this took place in the sacristy (q.v.) when the service was ended (*see* **Disposal of Eucharistic Remains**). But in the tenth and eleventh centuries it became customary to do this immediately after the act of communion itself, i.e. before the end of the service proper. This transference of the ablutions to a position within the mass was realized in two stages. The first stage comprised the washing of the priest's hands, the water being poured down the piscina (q.v.). The second stage involved the cleaning of the chalice with the consumption of the liquid used. The ablutions as finally evolved were the product of the fusion of these two, and so the Roman practice, regulated by the missal of Pope Pius V, requires the cleansing of the chalice with wine and then of the fingers and chalice with wine and water.

W. Lockton, *The Treatment of the Remains at the Eucharist after Holy Communion and the Time of the Ablutions*, 1920.

EDITOR

Absolution

A formal act of pronouncing the forgiveness of sins. In the early church this was a public event, in the sense that sinners were reconciled in the presence of the congregation, after they had previously made private confession; the church leaders were thus acting upon the commission of Christ to 'bind' and 'loose' (Matt. 16.19; 18.18). By the side of this public system of discipline, there was also the practice of confessing one's sins privately to a spiritual director without absolution. In the Celtic monasteries of the sixth century these two systems were amalgamated, the absolution, in front of the congregation, being transferred to private confession. The confession (q.v.) of sin entered the liturgy soon after the year 1000 and the accompanying absolution was either declaratory or precatory, i.e. God's forgiveness was either declared or prayed for. In the thirteenth century the indicative form was adopted, i.e. 'I absolve you'.

Absolution continues to be given privately, e.g. in the Anglican, Lutheran, Orthodox and Roman Churches. Liturgically it is included in most services, such as the daily offices (q.v.) or in the eucharist.

EDITOR

Acolyte

Strictly one of the minor orders of the ministry, the office existed in the church in Rome by the middle of the third century. It was subsequently introduced into the other parts of Western Christendom and is still one of the stages through which aspirants to the priesthood in the Roman Catholic Church pass. In this sense it is part of the ordained ministry. The acolyte's functions were originally similar to those of the modern server (q.v.) and included the carrying of ceremonial lights. The term is commonly used by Anglicans to denote anyone who carries a torch or candle in liturgical processions.

P. HINCHLIFF

Adoration *see* Prayer (1)

Advent

The word 'Advent' is derived from a Latin root which means 'coming' or 'arrival', and the season was developed in the Western Church as a preparation for the festival of the Nativity. Councils held in Gaul in the sixth century refer to a penitential period of six weeks before Christmas. There was fasting on Mondays, Wednesdays and Fridays. But the season was already known to Gregory of Tours in the latter part of the preceding century. It may be affirmed that fifth-century Gaul was the place of origin of the fully-organized period of six Sundays, and that the structure of Advent, with regard to its length, was modelled on Lent. Various lectionaries dating from the seventh and eighth centuries, or representing the use of that time, show the six-Sunday pattern in Gaul and north-west Italy. At a greater distance from Gaul, that is, in Spain, northeast Italy and south Italy, we find five Sundays, clearly representing a modification of the original structure. One of the lectionaries noted above is derived from *Reginensis 9*, a seventh-century manuscript, containing a complete table of lessons from the Pauline epistles, an early witness to the Ambrosian liturgy of Milan. The table begins with the Christmas vigil and lists the lessons of a six-Sunday Advent at the end of the lectionary. Similarly, with reference to a lectionary not taken into account above, it is evident that also at Rome liturgical conservatism ensured that the inclusion of Advent, a practice introduced from elsewhere, did not at that stage succeed in disturbing the pattern of a lectionary which traditionally began with Christmas. For the Würzburg manuscript, *Mp.th. fol.62*, containing in a table of epistles the oldest Roman lectionary and the usage of the early seventh century, commences with Christmas and places a five-Sunday Advent at the end. The logic of the invention of Advent had not been completely accepted. Eventually at Rome Advent was reduced from five to four Sundays. As the Roman rite gradually triumphed over the native uses of the West the four-Sunday Advent became the norm, and the original structure of six Sundays was almost completely obscured.

A. A. McArthur, *The Evolution of the Christian Year*, 1953; A. A. McArthur, *The Christian Year and Lectionary Reform*, 1958.

A. A. MCARTHUR

Adventist Worship
see Seventh-day Adventist Worship

Agape *see* Love Feast

Agnus Dei

The anthem *Agnus Dei*, for many centuries sung between the fraction (q.v.) and communion in the Roman mass, has recently been restored to its original purpose as a *confractorium*, i.e. anthem to be sung during the fraction. It appears to have been introduced into the Roman rite in the seventh century, perhaps during the pontificate of Sergius I (687-701), for it is clearly of Eastern origin – the word 'lamb' is commonly used in the Eastern liturgies to designate both Christ and the consecrated bread of the eucharist, and the West Syrian liturgy contains *confractoria* which speak of 'the Lamb of God who takes away the sins of the world' – and this was a period of considerable Eastern, and especially Syrian, influence at Rome: Syria had recently been overrun by the Moslems, and many Syrian clergy found their way to Rome, among them Pope Theodore I (642-9), while Sergius I was a Syrian by descent.

A prayer addressed specifically to Christ present in the eucharist as a sacrificial offering, the anthem originally comprised simply as many repetitions as necessary of the single sentence 'O Lamb of God, that takest away

the sins of the world, have mercy upon us'. When the fraction was shortened through the introduction of unleavened bread, the number of repetitions was fixed at three, probably about the middle of the ninth century, and during the tenth and eleventh centuries, when the fraction had all but disappeared, and the anthem in practice therefore accompanied the kiss of peace (q.v.) immediately following, the third clause was given the appropriately variant ending it has had ever since – '. . . of the world, grant us peace'. As early as the eleventh century, too, a further variant appears, which has also persisted: at requiem masses, the first and second petitions end '. . . grant them rest', and the third 'grant them rest everlasting'.

J. A. Jungmann, *The Mass of the Roman Rite*, II, 1955, pp. 332-40.

W. JARDINE GRISBROOKE

Aisle

The lateral division of a church, being the part on either side of the nave (q.v.). In the patristic period in certain areas it was customary to assign the south aisle to the men and the north to the women. The application of this word to the gangways up the centre of a nave or elsewhere is of course incorrect, and the expression 'centre aisle' is a contradiction in terms.

EDITOR

Alb *see* Vestments (1*a*)

All Saints

Many martyrs and non-martyrs were unrecorded and therefore unhonoured on earth. On the other hand, places like Antioch and Rome had more known martyrs than there were days of the year. So a common feast for all martyrs was instituted, and this is the origin of the later All Saints feast. A feast of All Martyrs was observed on Easter Friday in Syria at the beginning of the fifth century, and the octave day of Pentecost was the day for a similar feast in the Byzantine liturgy. In Rome, Boniface IV had the relics of many martyrs moved from the catacombs to the Pantheon, and on 13 May 610, he consecrated the building as *St Maria ad Martyres*. This became known as the feast of All Martyrs and All Saints and of Our Lady. These three feasts, especially the Syrian one, were closely connected with the Easter season and therefore with Christ's victory. This paschal connection was broken and eventually rather lost sight of after the Roman feast of 13 May was transferred in 835 to 1 November, with the title of All Saints.

J. CONNELLY

All Souls

Most Christians who were remembered each year were neither martyrs nor confessors – people not distinguished by their death or by their way of life. At such anniversaries the eucharist was offered, not in thanksgiving as for the martyrs, but in petition to God and in the hope that God would give the departed to share in the victory of the risen Christ. The funeral service is a glowing testimony to Christian hope in a 'blessed resurrection' and to Christian love for departed relatives and friends.

Besides the funeral or anniversary rites, a general commemoration or *memento* of the dead is found in the eucharistic prayer of liturgies. There has also been for centuries a day set apart for the general commemoration of the dead. Easter Saturday was designated in the Syrian rite as a 'memorial day of all priests and monks and of all the faithful departed'. This shows the connection between Easter and the liturgy of the dead, and between All Saints and All Souls.

There is evidence of many local 'memorial days' in the West in earlier centuries, but All Souls, as now observed, is due to Odilo of Cluny. This solemn 'memorial day', first kept in Cluniac houses (from about 1000), eventually became an official part of the Roman rite.

During the 1914-18 war Benedict XV allowed priests to celebrate the eucharist three times on All Souls' Day (2 November). This permission was given partly because of the 'useless slaughter' of the war and also because the confiscation of church property at, and since, the Reformation had made it impossible to carry out the obligations for anniversary masses which had been the conditions of so many gifts and legacies.

J. CONNELLY

Alleluia *see* Chants of the Proper of the Mass

Alms

Ultimately derived from the Greek word *eleemosune* meaning 'mercy', the term alms refers to charitable gifts. The necessity for generous giving was recognized by the first Christians as the right response to Christ's own self-giving (II Cor. 8.9). The presentation of these gifts early became an integral part of worship, especially at the eucharist associated with the offertory (q.v.), and they were a portion of the offerings made either in kind or in money.

At the present day the tendency is to speak of the 'collection' and the word 'alms' has a certain archaic character. In liturgical usage, however, the correct phrase would be 'the collection of alms'.

EDITOR

Alms-dish

The duty of sharing material things with those less fortunately placed occupies a prominent place in the teaching of the OT and NT (Matt. 6.3-4; Acts 11.27-30), and the subject is often mentioned by early Christian writers, such as Justin Martyr and Cyprian. In earlier times the method was sometimes to collect alms (q.v.) for the poor outside the church; in many English medieval churches there was an alms-chest with a slot in the lid, as at Heckfield, Yorkshire. Pope Innocent III ordered such chests to be placed in English churches in the time of King John for collections for the Crusades. In the time of King Edward VI many of the alms-chests disappeared, but there remained the poor men's box.

Some commentators have wrongly concluded that the alms-dish or basin was entirely an innovation of the post-Reformation rites introduced in the English prayer book; but this is incorrect, as there are fifteenth-century examples still extant, and there are references to such dishes in the fourteenth century (*Test. Ebor.* i. 114, Surtees Soc.).

It is, however, interesting to notice the changes that have taken place in the method of collecting alms in the various editions of the English prayer book. That of 1549 says, 'While the clerks do sing the Offertory, so many as are disposed shall offer to the poor men's box, everyone according to his ability.' But in the 1552 book the rubric was altered thus, 'Then shall the Churchwardens or some other by them appointed gather the devotion of the people, and put the same into the poor men's box.' It was not until 1662 that the present custom appeared, following the Scottish Liturgy of 1637, 'The deacon or (if no such be present) one of the churchwardens shall receive the devotions of the people there present, in a bason provided for that purpose. And when all have offered, he shall reverently bring the said bason, with the oblations therein, and deliver it to the presbyter, who shall humbly present it before the Lord, and set it upon the Holy Table.'

This was a return in principle to the custom of earlier centuries when the elements of bread and wine as well as other offerings in kind were brought up by the people and received on tray-shaped patens (*see* **Chalice and Paten**).

C. E. POCKNEE

Almuce *see* Vestments (2*e*)

Altar

Derived from the Latin *altare*, the word means a place or structure where sacrifice is offered. In Christian worship it is associated with the chief act of Christian worship, the Lord's Supper, the eucharist, the holy communion or the mass.

There can be little doubt that at the institution of the sacrament of the Lord's body and blood in the Upper Room Jesus presided at a wooden table; and that structures of this kind were used in the house-churches when the eucharist was celebrated on the first day of the week during the first three centuries of the Christian era. References to the eucharist in the NT are not frequent since it was the normal function of the Christian assembly on Sundays.

It has been mistakenly supposed that the term 'altar' can only be applied to a structure of stone rather than wood. Paul, referring to the disorders at Corinth in connection with the eucharist, speaks of 'the Lord's table' (I Cor. 10.21); but this is an oblique reference to the sacrament itself rather than to the structure of the table. The writer of the Epistle to the Hebrews says, 'We have an altar from which those who serve the tent have no right to eat' (Heb. 13.10). There can be little doubt that the writer is referring to the eucharist in distinction from the sacrifices of the old covenant. It is important to take note that he refers not simply to an altar in the new dispensation but to a place where eating takes place, a sacrificial act. In the Greek text of this passage the term for altar is the normal term used to describe both Jewish and pagan altars of sacrifice in the

Septuagint, e.g. Lev. 6.9 and Judg. 6.25. The fact that this term is applied to the eucharist is of considerable significance. The reference to the eucharist as 'a pure sacrifice' by the writer of the *Didache*, ch. 14, about AD 100, also underlines this fact. Ignatius of Antioch in his epistles, written about 107, also makes numerous references to the altar (the same term) and the eucharist, thus 'Be careful to use one eucharist, for there is one flesh of our Lord Jesus Christ, and one cup for union with his blood, one altar, as there is one bishop' (*Ep. Phil.* 4.1). The Greek fathers during the first four centuries sometimes use the term 'table' and sometimes 'altar' for the structure upon which the eucharist is celebrated. The Latin fathers, such as Tertullian and Cyprian in the third century, also use the terms *mensa* and *altare* for the eucharistic table. Augustine of Hippo (d. 430) uses the term *altare* in connection with a wooden table (*Ep.* 185), thus disproving the idea that a distinction was drawn between a communion table of wood and a sacrificial altar of stone. Wooden altars seem to have been of various shapes, square, round and semi-circular.

There can be little doubt that the custom of having stone altars is directly connected with the celebration of the eucharist at or near the tomb of a saint in the catacombs, thus linking altar with tomb. With the building of permanent churches in the fourth century at Rome, Jerusalem and elsewhere, the idea was carried a step further and the altar was built over the martyr's or confessor's tomb or shrine. Hence the words *martyrium* (q.v.) or *confessio*. In the more important churches the body of a celebrated saint was buried under the altar, but in the smaller churches which were used simply as a place of assembly for public worship it became the custom to require that some kind of relic associated with a saint should be buried in a cavity in the top of the altar. In some instances a consecrated host was used instead. Thus eventually it became the more usual custom to require that no altar was used without such relics.

While in the first three centuries the mere fact of celebrating the eucharist on an altar-table was considered to be sufficient to hallow it, it gradually came to be the custom that no altar should be used without its formal consecration by a bishop. This consisted in the placing of relics in the altar, to which we

Plate 1
Altar with ciborium
c. 1000, Castel S. Elia,
Italy

have alluded; in addition, the altar-top had five crosses engraved on it and these were anointed with chrism by the bishop (*see* **Consecration of Churches**). Nevertheless, it is possible to produce evidence for the use of altars which had received no such consecration. Also, we know that wooden altars were in use in England until quite late in the Middle Ages.

In the earlier centuries the altar was of equal dimensions, i.e. it was cube-shaped. Prominence was given to this type of altar by surmounting it with a canopy mounted directly on four columns, and known as a ciborium (*see* Plate 1). This kind of canopy and its columns were made of wood, stone, or precious metal. In the West, as the centuries went on, the altar tended to be lengthened,

until in the late Middle Ages we find very long altars such as that at Tewkesbury Abbey (13 ft) and that of the Lady Chapel at Ely (over 16 ft). The result was that the ciborium resting on its four columns became dismembered; the posts or columns remained round the ends of the lengthened altar, while the canopy became suspended as a separate tester hanging from the roof. Sometimes the posts were surmounted by carved angels holding candles. This type of altar was more prevalent in northern Europe, and it has been mistakenly termed an 'English altar', as though it was something peculiar to the Church of England.

Another development in Western Christendom in the Middle Ages was the multiplication of altars in churches associated with guilds and fraternities, in contrast to the primitive era when there was only one altar and one celebration of the eucharist in any one church on any one day. In this respect the Eastern Orthodox Church, with its one altar and one eucharist on any one day, has remained closer to the primitive church.

For many centuries, too, except possibly in churches of the East Syrian rite, the altar was normally free-standing and accessible on all sides. In the West, however, the altar came to be placed against a wall or screen. In the greater churches such as abbeys and cathedrals, this screen often separated the altar from the reliquary containing the body of the patron saint, as we can still see at Westminster Abbey and St Albans Cathedral. The separation of the altar from the saint's reliquary in the later Middle Ages was to permit the crowds to pray at the shrine of the saint without interrupting the service in progress at the high altar.

The placing of candlesticks (*see* **Candles, Lamps and Lights**) and a cross (q.v.) on the altar was also a very late innovation in the West, the candlesticks and cross originally being used in processions and placed on the pavement around the altar. Only at the end of the Middle Ages did these ornaments sometimes come to be set upon the altar. The idea that all altars must have a cross standing on them is an error of the nineteenth-century ecclesiologists. Also, the custom of having precisely six candlesticks on the altar was a development that arose from the Counter-Reformation movement in the Roman Church in the sixteenth century. Nor did flower vases find a place on the holy table in olden times, but flowers were thrown on the pavement before the altar and not crammed into vases to decline in a state of putrefaction.

At the Reformation many stone altars were destroyed and replaced by wooden tables because stone altars had become associated with a particular view of the eucharistic sacrifice. Through a revived biblical theology and the wider study of comparative religion we realize that both medievalists and Reformers were too limited in their conception of sacrifice which they associated exclusively with death or immolation. Today we should prefer to say that the sacrifice of Christ recalled in the eucharist is the whole of his atoning work culminating in the cross, resurrection and ascension.

J. Braun, *Der Christliche Altar*, 2 vols, 1924; D. R. Dendy, *The Use of Lights in Christian Worship*, 1959; C. E. Pocknee, *The Christian Altar*, 1963.

C. E. POCKNEE

Altar Hangings

In the first two centuries of the Christian era it is unlikely that the table at which the eucharist was celebrated was regarded as a permanent feature and ornament. But in the third century, rooms came to be adapted permanently in the larger houses as the eucharistic room, and the altar-table was looked upon as the focal point of Christian worship (*see* **Architectural Setting**). Over the table was thrown a cloth of silk, damask or brocade which enveloped it on all sides, the altar (q.v.) being cube-shaped in structure at that time. As time went on, this cloth was decorated with emblems in embroidery and with jewels; John Chrysostom in the fourth century had to give a warning that too much attention should not be paid to this kind of thing. We can see, in a sixth-century mosaic in the church of San Vitale, Ravenna, a depiction of an altar arrayed in this kind of altar-cloth or pall.

Over the decorated cloth there was spread at the time of the offertory (q.v.) the fair linen cloth upon which the eucharist was celebrated. The altar arrayed in this vesture was regarded as the symbol of Christ in the midst of his church.

This type of throw-over altar cloth was revived in the Church of England in the seventeenth century and has somewhat misleadingly come to be termed a 'Jacobean' altar frontal; but it is, as we have stated, a revival of the vesture of the early Christian centuries.

In the second part of the Middle Ages in the West, when altars came to be placed close to screens and walls, the throwover cloth was abandoned for a frontal (q.v.), a flat silk cloth which was suspended on the side of the altar visible to the congregation.

In the earlier centuries there were also silk or damask curtains suspended on rods between the columns or posts that supported the ciborium (*see* **Baldachin**). These curtains were also embroidered and decorated with jewels in the larger and more affluent churches. In the later Middle Ages, when the altar came to be lengthened, these curtains were hung between the riddel-posts that enclosed the ends of the altar, while at the back of the altar, if there was not a reredos (q.v.) of wood or stone, a cloth with embroidered figures and emblems was hung. This back-cloth is properly termed a *dorsal* or *super-frontal*.

A fair linen cloth is spread on the top of the altar at the time of the celebration of the eucharist. As the shape of the altar has changed over the course of the centuries, this cloth has had to be adapted in form to meet such changes. (*See* Plate 2.)

P. Dearmer, *The Linen Ornaments of the Church*, [2]1950; C. E. Pocknee, *The Christian Altar*, 1963; The Warham Guild, *The Warham Guild Handbook*, rev. ed., 1963.

C. E. POCKNEE

Altar Rails

Altar rails were unknown in England before the Reformation and they began to come into use in the last part of the reign of Queen Elizabeth I. But a considerable impetus was given to their use by William Laud who, first as Dean of Gloucester in 1616, and later as Bishop of Bath and Wells and then Bishop of London, and finally as Archbishop of Canterbury in 1634, insisted that the altar should be placed in the traditional position in the sanctuary (q.v.) and fenced off with rails to protect it from irreverence. The purpose of these rails was to protect the altar from profanity. They were provided with a gate in the middle and the closeness of the balusters to one another was to prevent dogs from getting into the sanctuary. To quote the words of Bishop Wren of Norwich, 'the Rayle be made before the Communion Table reaching crosse from the north wall to the south wall, neere one yarde in height, so

Plate 2   Altar with carved reredos and riddel posts, vested with frontal and frontlet, Tring, England

thick with pillars that doggs may not gett in'. The purpose of these rails, therefore, was not to provide a support for the communicants to lean against when they received holy communion. Indeed, the height of these seventeenth century rails makes them inconvenient for the kneeling communicant.

During the Commonwealth period some of these rails were destroyed and had to be replaced at the Restoration of 1660. Many of the rails erected in the nineteenth century are of poor design. In the present century some of these have been replaced by kneeling benches for the communicants. But liturgical reforms now taking place seem to indicate that both rails and benches alike may become obsolete with the increasing custom of standing to receive holy communion. It should be realized that for over a thousand years throughout Christendom the normal posture for receiving holy communion was that of standing; only in the thirteenth century did the custom of kneeling come into fashion in connection with the introduction of the ceremony of the elevation of the host. Standing at the holy communion has never been abandoned in the Eastern Orthodox rite.

C. E. POCKNEE

Altar, Stripping of

A rite that took place at the end of the liturgy on Maundy Thursday. The altar cloth(s) and frontal were removed during the recitation of Ps. 21 (22).

From a very early time altars which were simple and unpretentious structures were covered with a single cloth, for such was the custom of the Roman empire at the time. Of this we have probably the first witness in the Gnostic *Acts of Thomas* (5th act, ch. 49), and by the fourth century Optatus of Milevis certainly refers to the linen cloth. This was removed without ceremony at the end of the eucharist and the altar stood bare throughout the week. This remained the custom for centuries, although by the sixth century, at least in some places (e.g. Ravenna), the altar was richly clothed. This practice, together with the later allegorizing tendencies, led to a symbolic interpretation of the rite.

There were two factors that led to the development of the rite summarily described above. (1) The altar itself came to signify Christ's body and the cloth(s) and frontal or pallium the members of Christ's body, namely Christians. (2) The place in the

Passion according to St John (which was and is still sung on Good Friday) where Ps. 21 (22) is quoted (John 19. 23, 24) led to a *dramatization* of the rite. By the second half of the eighth century (*Ordo Romanus* XXVII), two deacons standing at either end of the altar took away the cloth 'in the manner of thieves', furtively. Later still (*Ordo Romanus* XXXI – *c*. 850-900), the cloth was taken from the altar at the words 'They divided my vesture among them'. In the tenth century the rite was associated with the rending of the veil in the Temple, and two cloths were prepared which at the appropriate moment were parted and taken away.

The rite then signified the stripping of Christ before his crucifixion and the separation of Christ from his members, the church. All this was summed up in the (allegorical) commentaries of Beleth (d. 1165) and Durandus of Mende (d. 1296), with sundry additions. For the former, the rite signified the kenosis of Christ who in the passion was stripped of his glory, his stripping by the soldiers before crucifixion and the abandonment of him by the apostles. The rite reminds Durandus of Isa. 53 and of the rending of the Temple veil. The ancient action, then, of removing the cloth from the altar after every eucharist and then on Maundy Thursday without ceremony was now transferred to that day with the significance that it symbolized the stripping of Christ before his crucifixion. Combined with the washing of the altar (q.v.), it ultimately signified the church's mourning for its dead Lord.

In the revision of the Holy Week liturgy of 1970, there has been a return to the earliest tradition. Both on Maundy Thursday and Good Friday the cloth is removed without ceremony.

J. D. CRICHTON

Altar, Washing of

A rite now observed only at St Peter's, Rome, on Maundy Thursday, it was, in the Middle Ages, practised very generally (e.g. Spain, France, England) at least in cathedrals and larger churches on the same day.

Originally it was a utilitarian rite whose purpose was to clean the whole church in preparation for the celebration of the Easter festival. Thus Isidore of Seville (*De Ecclesiasticis Officiis*, I, 29) speaks of the altars, walls, floors and vessels being washed on Maundy Thursday. This statement is juxtaposed to one referring to the Lord's washing of his disciples' feet, thus discreetly suggesting a symbolism: the church in the person of the disciples is washed, cleansed from sin.

A Gallic writer, St Eloy or Eligius of Noyon (588-659), repeats this statement, which would seem to indicate that the custom was common at this time to Spain and Gaul. It does not appear in the Roman books until the tenth-century *Romano-Germanic Pontifical* (ed. C. Vogel, 1963, vol. II, p. 57) where Isidore's words are reproduced almost *verbatim*. It would seem to be a clear inference that the custom came from Spain through France to Rome under German influence. Thence it spread throughout Europe. It is found in J. Beleth (d. 1165) and in Durandus of Mende (d. 1296), the Sarum books and in the English writer John Myrc (fl. 1400), who provides a commentary on the Sarum use.

Symbolism. As can be seen from the origin of the observance (*see above*), its meaning is partly suggested by its place in the Holy Week liturgy. It was associated with the commemoration of the Last Supper and of the Passion. But during all the Middle Ages the altar acquired an ever richer symbolism and became more and more the focus of attention. It became the principal symbol of Christ. At its consecration, five crosses were carved in the table (*mensa*) to represent the five wounds of Christ, and the cloths and covering (frontal or *antependium*) were regarded as the members of Christ's (mystical) body. The stripping of the altar (q.v.) was a sign of death and, as the present rite (*see below*) indicates, the washing with wine and water signifies the mourning over the dead Christ. In other words, it is a funeral rite.

But the medieval writers, after their fashion, allegorized the rite. Thus for Beleth, the washing with wine and water signifies the blood of redemption and the water, the water of regeneration. There is naturally a reference to the water and blood that flowed from Christ's side, and there is the comment that the church washes the altar because his body was sprinkled with blood and water on the cross. The branches or sprigs with which the wine and water were spread over the altar suggest the crown of thorns, and therefore the branches must have rough leaves. But he also refers to the cleaning of the floor with similar branches, and this symbolizes our being cleansed from vice. Durandus repeats much of this, sometimes using the very words

of Beleth, and offering very little of his own. In the Sarum use we note that it was the five crosses themselves that were washed, thus emphasizing that it was a funeral rite. John Myrc repeats Beleth and Durandus.

The twigs or branches were scattered upon the altar after the washing, and even in recent times, the palms from the previous Palm Sunday were put on the (now unwashed) altars (*see* Herbert Thurston, *Lent and Holy Week*, 1904, pp. 302f.).

The present rite. It is performed by seven canons of St Peter's after the last office of Maundy Thursday. With the other clergy of the basilica, they go in procession to the Altar of the Confession, Ps. 21 (22) is intoned and the canons then pour wine mixed with water on the altar. The cardinal archpriest approaches and with a branch of yew spreads it over the altar and the canons do likewise. Afterwards, they dry the altar with sponges and towels. All now retire from the altar and kneel while the responsory *Christus factus est* (Phil. 2.8) is sung. The rite concludes with a silent recitation of the Lord's Prayer and the collect used at the day's office (*see* Mario Righetti, *Storia Liturgica*, [2]1955, vol. II, p. 168).

J. D. CRICHTON

Ambo

Also spelt ambon, a Greek term in origin. A structure often approached by a flight of steps and surrounded by a parapet, and made of wood, stone or marble. It was used for the reading of the gospel at the eucharist and was usually larger than the medieval pulpit (q.v.) as its platform not only accommodated the reader of the gospel but also the attendant taperers or candle-bearers. The ambo was used also on the eve of Easter by the deacon who sang the *exsultet* at the blessing of the Paschal candle. In the larger basilicas (q.v.) the ambo was often decorated with carved or tessellated designs, a frequent one being Jonah and the whale, a type of Christ's resurrection (Matt. 12.40).

There were sometimes lesser ambos, as at St Clement's, Rome, from which the other lessons at the eucharist were read. All these structures usually had a desk upon which the liturgical book was placed.

From the steps of the ambo a portion of psalmody was sung by the chanters in between the reading of the epistle and the gospel. Hence this chant came to be known as the *gradual* (q.v.), from the Latin *gradus*, a step. The ambo was not primarily designed as the place from which a sermon was delivered, as this was done by the bishop from his throne or *cathedra* (q.v.). *See* Plate 3.

C. E POCKNEE

Amen

A Hebrew word meaning 'firm' or 'established', and then, as an adverb, 'certainly' or 'assuredly'. It is used often in the OT as an acknowledgment that a saying is valid and binding and constitutes a claim which is accepted. In synagogue worship it served as a community response of assent and confirmation.

In the NT it is frequent on the lips of Jesus, being translated in the AV by 'verily' and in more recent versions by 'truly'. It stands, however, at the beginning and not the end of Jesus' sayings to show that the words are reliable and true and are so because he acknowledges them as his own and hence makes them valid.

Following the example of Jesus and the practice of the synagogue, it was adopted into Christian liturgical usage, and so Paul speaks of the amen of the assembly at the giving of thanks (I Cor. 14.16). According to Justin Martyr the people say amen after prayer and thanksgiving and 'this word amen answers in the Hebrew language to *genoito*, i.e. so be it'. Cyril of Jerusalem states that the Lord's Prayer is 'sealed' with an amen.

In the eucharist the amen is especially noticeable as the people's response to the prayer of consecration and, in many liturgies, to the words of administration. It is, however, not only an assent but also a proclamation of faith, for Jesus himself is 'the amen' (Rev. 3.14), i.e. he himself is the response to the divine Yes in him. So the worshippers proclaim their belief that in Christ the faithfulness of God has been vindicated.

TDNT, I, pp. 335-8.   EDITOR

Amice *see* Vestments (1*b*)

Anamnesis *see* Anaphora (7)

Anaphora

A Greek word, meaning 'offering', from the verb *anaphero*, 'I carry up', 'I offer up (in sacrifice)', 'I offer up (to God on high)', which has from a very early date been the normal Greek name for the eucharistic prayer, commonly called in English the prayer of consecration (q.v.), and is universally the name most widely used by liturgical scholars. The oldest name for this

Plate 3   Ambo, thirteenth century, Ravello cathedral, Italy

prayer is probably *eucharistia* (Gk. and thence Lat. 'thanksgiving'); other ancient names are *actio sacrificii* (Lat. 'the act of sacrifice'), *oratio oblationis* (Lat. 'the prayer of offering'), and simply *oratio* or *prex* (Lat. '*the* prayer'). In the Roman rite for many centuries this prayer has been entitled *canon* (q.v.) (Lat. 'rule', the exact sense of which in this application is uncertain); in the revised *Ordo Missae* of 1969 it is entitled *prex eucharistica* (Lat. 'eucharistic prayer').

The common opinion of earlier generations of liturgists, that there was originally a single basic pattern of the eucharistic prayer, has fallen increasingly out of favour in the present century, partly as a result of the greater number of early documents now available, and partly as a result of the more scientific detailed study both of these and of documents previously known, to such an extent that there are some writers who deny that there was even an approximation to such a pattern. This assertion, however, appears to rest upon an inability to see the wood for the trees, as well as, in some cases, speculations belonging to the realm of fantasy rather than to that of sober scientific scholarship, and sometimes involving positive mishandling of the evidence. A serious study of all the available evidence, and of the work done upon it, suggests that the earlier opinion may be right after all, in principle although not in detail.

For the apparently considerable differences between the anaphorae of the historic rites, and between all of them and such primitive evidence as is available, all reveal themselves, when carefully examined, to be the consequence of secondary elements added to the primitive structure or elaborated from it – secondary elements which were added or elaborated in different ways and at different points in the common basic structure. That common basic structure appears to be preserved in the oldest actual text of an anaphora which, so far as is at present known, survives, that in the *Apostolic Tradition* of Hippolytus of Rome, written *c*.215. The integrity of the textual tradition of this document has been disputed, notably by Dix and Ratcliff (in different ways and with different, and mutually incompatible, implications), but it has been established beyond reasonable doubt by the editor of the definitive critical edition, Bernard Botte, who has also vindicated the authorship and date of it.

The eucharistic prayer of the *Apostolic Tradition* may be divided into the following parts (the definition and description of which we leave to a later point): introductory dialogue; thanksgiving; narrative of the institution; anamnesis; epiclesis; concluding doxology. With one exception (apart from certain Hispano-Gallican and Ethiopic documents which are in such a manifest state of textual confusion that no reliance can be placed upon them), there is no known anaphora in any of the historic rites which does not contain, or has not contained at some time, all these parts in this order. The one exception is the mid-fourth-century Egyptian Anaphora of St Serapion, in which the narrative of the institution and the anamnesis are conflated; a second apparent exception, the East Syrian Anaphora of the Holy Apostles Addai and Mari, from the existing text of which the institution narrative is missing, has been conclusively proved once to have included it, on both internal and external grounds, by Dom Botte.

Absent from the anaphora of the *Apostolic Tradition* are three elements, two of which are all but universal, and one of which is not uncommon, in the historic anaphorae: the anthem *Sanctus*, which occurs in the course of the thanksgiving or at its close in almost every other complete anaphora at present known, with the single significant exception of that in a fourth-century (?) Syrian document, the *Testament of our Lord Jesus Christ*, closely dependent on the *Apostolic Tradition*; the intercessory prayers technically called the diptychs (q.v.), which occur in every other anaphora but those of the ancient Hispano-Gallican rites, where they are placed between the offertory (q.v.) and the anaphora; and a preliminary epiclesis before the institution narrative, which occurs in the Alexandrine and Roman rites. The varying arrangement of these elements, in itself a strong indication of their addition to an original common structure which did not include them, is the principal means by which the anaphorae of the historic rites are classified, and the great liturgical families distinguished one from another.

In order to clarify the issue, we will first enumerate the possible component parts of a developed anaphora of classical structure, and then examine their disposition in the anaphorae of the great liturgical families. The possible component parts are as follows: (1) introductory dialogue; (2) preface (q.v.)

or first part of the thanksgiving; (3) *Sanctus*; (4) post-*Sanctus* or second part of the thanksgiving; (5) preliminary epiclesis (alternative or additional post-*Sanctus*); (6) narrative of the institution; (7) anamnesis; (8) epiclesis; (9) diptychs or intercessions, which may be divided; (10) concluding doxology.

The expansion of the postulated original common structure in the anaphorae of the Antiochene or West Syrian family of liturgies (which includes the second most widespread of the great historic rites, the Byzantine, commonly called, through the anachronistic application of denominational labels to the ancient liturgies, 'Orthodox') is clear from a comparison of the anaphora in the *Apostolic Tradition*, that in the *Testament of our Lord*, and those of the developed Antiochene type. The order of the first of these is: 1 2 6 7 8 10. The order of the second is: 1 2 6 7 8 9 10. All the developed anaphorae of this family follow the order: 1 2 3 4 6 7 8 9 10. (Some of them conclude 8 10 9 10, a variant which clearly reveals the way in which 9 was added to an existing complete structure.) The distinguishing features of the Antiochene anaphora are (*a*) the absence of any preliminary epiclesis (5), together with the continuation of the thanksgiving, often indeed the greater part of it, in the post-*Sanctus* (4), and (*b*) the insertion of the diptychs between the epiclesis and the doxology.

The anaphorae of the East Syrian family follow the order: 1 2 3 4 6 (absent, as already noted, from the existing text of one of them, but undoubtedly originally present) 7 9 8 10.

The anaphorae of the Alexandrine family exhibit a number of internal variants (although many of these are due to the textual confusion of the Ethiopic anaphorae, which constitute the majority of the family). The normal order appears to be that found in the Liturgy of St Mark, the principal liturgy of the family: 1 2a 9 2b 3 5 6 7 8 10. This exhibits the principal distinctive features of this type of anaphora: (*a*) the insertion of the diptychs (9) in the middle of the thanksgiving, and (*b*) the presence of a preliminary epiclesis (5) before the institution narrative, together with the absence of any further thanksgiving (4) after the *Sanctus*. Certain variants deserve notice. The conflation of the institution narrative and the anamnesis in the Anaphora of St Serapion has already been noted; the same anaphora has no intercessory insertion in the preface, but a brief one after the epiclesis, in

the position characteristic of the Antiochene type. Some liturgists suggest, on fragmentary evidence and technical grounds, that originally the Alexandrine diptychs may have been divided, like those of the Roman rite (*see below*). A feature common to a number of the Ethiopic anaphorae is the substitution of a post-*Sanctus* thanksgiving (4) for a post-*Sanctus* preliminary epiclesis (5), but this probably originated in direct borrowing from Antiochene liturgies; one ancient Alexandrine liturgical fragment, however, has a post-*Sanctus* succinctly combining 4 and 5.

The surviving texts of the ancient Hispano-Gallican liturgies of the West are in a state of evident confusion similar to that of the Ethiopic texts in the East. It is, however, possible to reconstruct from them a normal form of their anaphora (which was almost entirely composed of variable prayers appropriate to the day or season). The diptychs (9) were recited between the offertory and the anaphora, and the structure of the latter appears to have originally been that of the *Apostolic Tradition* with the sole addition of the *Sanctus* with a post-*Sanctus* continuation of the thanksgiving: 1 2 3 4 6 7 8 10; in the extant texts the anamnesis (7) is often reduced to a minimal form and combined with the epiclesis (8).

The most distinctive feature of the historic Roman canon is the division of the diptychs, half being placed before and half after the central prayers. Its order is as follows: 1 2 3 9a 5 6 7 8 9b 10. The new eucharistic prayers of the Roman rite abandon this particular distinctive feature, being structured thus: 1 2 3 4 5 6 7 8 9 10. Like the Roman canon itself, therefore, their structure falls midway between those of the Antiochene and Alexandrine types, although they have moved a stage nearer the former.

From this consideration of the structure of the anaphorae in the primitive and historic liturgies, we pass to a more detailed examination of its component parts.

1. *The Introductory Dialogue.* Like the Jewish forms of thanksgiving from which it is derived, the Christian thanksgiving begins with a dialogue inviting the participants to remembrance of God and thanksgiving for his mercies. That still in use in the Roman rite and its derivatives is the basic form, closely resembling that preserved in the *Apostolic Tradition* of Hippolytus; most of the Eastern

rites elaborate it to a greater or lesser extent, as did the ancient Hispano-Gallican rites in the West. But in all the Christian forms the basic content remains the same: mutual greeting; an invitation to lift up the heart to God, with a response declarative of doing so; an invitation to give thanks, with a response declaring the propriety and duty of doing so. It is the third versicle, 'Let us give thanks', and response, which explain the universality and necessity of the dialogue: before he may proceed with the thanksgiving, the president of the assembly must receive the assembly's authority to do so in the name of all, and its assent to what he is about to say. (This is even more clearly marked in the otherwise very different Jewish forms of the dialogue.)

2. *The Preface or (First Part of the) Thanksgiving.* The significance of the word 'preface' in this context is explained elsewhere (*see* **Preface**). The thanksgiving is the foundation of all that follows it in the anaphora: the church gives thanks for God's mighty works in the past, in creation and redemption, and thereby proclaims its faith in their continuance in the future, the faith which is the source and spring of the prayers which follow.

During the formative centuries of the liturgy a clear distinction arose between two types of this thanksgiving: the one variable, stressing from day to day one part or aspect after another of the saving work of Christ, and the other fixed, longer, and presenting a general view of the whole history of salvation at each celebration of the eucharist. The first type came to predominate in the West, and the second in the East. Each has its advantages and disadvantages: the variable thanksgiving, or 'proper preface', makes it possible to think more deeply and appositely of the mystery appropriate to the day or season than does the invariable type, while the latter enables thanksgiving to be made at one eucharist for the whole action of God in creation and redemption more fully than does the variable type. The proper preface has the advantage of comparative brevity, the invariable thanksgiving that of maintaining a better balance between thanksgiving and prayer in the anaphora. It is perfectly possible to have both types of thanksgiving in one rite, either by providing a full general thanksgiving into which proper clauses or paragraphs can be inserted when appropriate, or by including one or more such general thanksgivings among a full range of proper prefaces, for use either on certain occasions or at will. It is also possible to have a number of alternative forms of the full internally invariable thanksgiving, as is common in the Eastern rites.

The content of the preface is also affected by the insertion of the anthems *Sanctus* and *Benedictus* in the anaphorae of all the historic liturgies. In certain rites, notably the Roman, these anthems conclude the thanksgiving; in others, including most of the great Eastern liturgies, they divide the thanksgiving, and in the latter case it is common either for the preface to be essentially no more than a formal ascription of praise, the detailed thanksgiving for the works of creation and redemption being postponed until after the *Sanctus* (*see below*), or alternatively for the greater part of the thanksgiving to be made in the preface, leaving only, e.g., a specific reference to Christ's passion to be made after the *Sanctus*, as an introduction to the institution narrative. Other divisions of the thanksgiving matter are also found, and in some anaphorae there is a considerable amount of repetition. Further reference to this question will be found below, in the consideration of the post-*Sanctus*.

3. *The Sanctus.* In all the great historic liturgies the preface ends with the singing or saying of the anthem *Sanctus*, to which is added in all but the Alexandrine anaphorae the anthem *Benedictus qui venit*. In the oldest surviving texts these anthems are either missing or evidently interpolated. This interpolation, while it provides for the congregation to join vocally in the climax of the thanksgiving, has not been an unmixed blessing: it has done as much as anything to confuse the clarity of structure which ought to be apparent in the anaphora. Whether, as in most rites, the thanksgiving originally led directly to the narrative of the institution as the account of the divinely-given means of making the thanksgiving truly effective, or, as in the Roman and Alexandrine rites, to a prayer for the acceptance or hallowing of the offerings within which the narrative was set, the transition from the thanksgiving by word to the thanksgiving by act was clear: we thank God . . . and therefore we *offer*. Once the *Sanctus* and *Benedictus* are interpolated, this sequence is obscured: it is all too easy for the thanksgiving (especially the first part of it,

when it is divided) to be seen as a mere preliminary, concluding with these anthems – we thank God . . . and therefore we *sing* . . .

For these reasons some have suggested the suppression of these anthems in contemporary liturgical revision. This, however, is unnecessary; it is perfectly possible so to integrate them into the thanksgiving that the sequence of thought is clear and uninterrupted. It is also undesirable; they provide a valuable opportunity for the whole assembly to join its voice with that of the celebrant at this climactic point. Moreover, the question of the date and circumstances of their introduction into the anaphora is a far from simple one, and those who argue that in some places they may have formed part of it from the beginning are not without evidence which may reasonably be held to support their thesis, not least the presence of markedly similar passages in certain Jewish thanksgivings of this type. Nor is there sufficient reason for dividing them, or suppressing the *Benedictus*, or transferring *Sanctus* and *Benedictus*, or *Benedictus* alone, to the end of the anaphora: the arguments which have been put forward for these courses all rest on debatable hypotheses based on evidence carefully selected and interpreted for the purpose, and while they may be of great interest to liturgical scholars, they are not an adequate foundation for practical liturgical reform.

4, 5. *The Post-*Sanctus *and Preliminary Epiclesis.* Whether the *Sanctus* was inserted in the middle or at the end of the thanksgiving, its insertion necessitated the provision of a passage linking it with what follows. It has already been noted that the post-*Sanctus* may take one of two forms, so far as its content is concerned: it may be either a continuation of the thanksgiving, or a prayer consequent upon the thanksgiving called for convenience the preliminary epiclesis; it may comprise both, as in the new Roman anaphorae. In most of the historic liturgies in which it is a continuation of the thanksgiving, it is linked to the *Sanctus* by the device of opening it with some such phrase as 'Holy in truth and blessed in truth . . .', thus taking up the themes of the divine holiness and blessedness from the *Sanctus* and *Benedictus* respectively. In the Alexandrine anaphorae, in which the post-*Sanctus* takes the form of a preliminary epiclesis, the theme of fullness is taken up from the preceding anthem, the prayer asking

that as the heaven and earth are full of God's glory, so the gifts now offered in sacrifice may be filled with his blessing, or some equivalent petition. Only in the historic Roman canon is any link of this kind all but absent, and the sequence of thought obscured by the insertion of the diptychs of the living at this point.

In liturgical revision, the form and content of the post-*Sanctus* should be determined by two principal considerations: first, the content and structure of the thanksgiving, and in particular by whether the preface is variable (in which case an invariable thanksgiving is desirable in the post-*Sanctus* making mention of the whole economy of creation and thanksgiving, however briefly) or invariable (with or without variable insertions, in which case the post-*Sanctus* needs to be so worded as to make a smooth transition from the verbal thanksgiving to the ritual thanksgiving with the bread and cup); second, the theology of consecration which the rite is intended to embody, a preliminary epiclesis being required in the post-*Sanctus* if the theory of consecration by the recitation of the words of institution is held, although the presence of a preliminary epiclesis does not necessarily imply such a theory of consecration. This issue will be considered further in connection with the epiclesis.

6. *The Narrative of the Institution.* The recital of the narrative of the institution of the eucharist at the Last Supper is universal in the primitive and historic anaphorae (the one apparent exception being, as already remarked, due to demonstrable textual corruption). It appears always to have been held necessary, whether or not the recitation of our Lord's words in it is regarded (as in the West from quite early in the Middle Ages) as itself constituting the whole consecration. In almost every anaphora the narrative is elaborated to a greater or lesser extent; in many, congregational responses are provided in the course of it or at the close of it, an enrichment which has been introduced into the new eucharistic prayers of the Roman rite, the historic Roman canon having none. Theologically, in those traditions which do not regard the recitation of the words of institution as by themselves operating the consecration, their essentiality is understood in the sense that they are the authority for proceeding to the anamnesis and the epiclesis, an authority which must be invoked in order that the

anamnesis and epiclesis may be effectual.

7. *The Anamnesis.* A Greek word expressing a Semitic concept, *anamnesis* is all but untranslatable into English. Memorial, commemoration, remembrance – all these suggest that the person or deed commemorated is past and absent, whereas anamnesis signifies exactly the opposite: it is an objective act, in and by which the person or event commemorated is actually made present, is brought into the realm of the here and now. And the eucharist, as the early church understood it, is 'the "re-calling" before God of the one sacrifice of Christ in all its accomplished fullness so that it is here and now operative by its effects in the souls of the redeemed' (Dix, *Shape of the Liturgy*, p. 243: so far as the doctrine of the early church is concerned, he ought to have written 'bodies and souls').

As a liturgical term, then, the anamnesis signifies that part of the anaphora in which it is explicitly stated that the church is offering the bread and cup with this meaning and for this purpose, in obedience to Christ's command so to do. The normal form of the anamnesis, which is all but universal in the primitive and historic liturgies, comprises a statement of the memorial and a statement of the offering, inseparably linked by making the former grammatically dependent on and relative to the latter. The former always mentions at least the passion, resurrection and ascension of our Lord; other aspects of the mystery of redemption, such as the incarnation, the burial, and the mediation of the ascended Christ at the right hand of the Father are added in some anamneses, and most contain also a reference to the second coming which sets the eucharist in its eschatological perspective. The statement of offering in the ancient liturgies always explicitly offers the bread and cup, either using those words or some elaborated equivalent; certain anaphorae, notably those of the Byzantine rite and the historic Roman canon, contain clauses emphasizing that in this offering the whole of the created order is representatively offered, but all make it clear that the offering is dependent upon its identification, in virtue of Christ's institution, with his own offering of himself. The anamneses in the new eucharistic prayers III and IV of the Roman rite carry this to lengths unprecedented in expression although not in content in the ancient anaphorae, a con-

sequence of the formal embodiment in these prayers of the medieval and post-medieval Western doctrine that the consecration is effected solely by the recitation of the words of institution.

8. *The Epiclesis.* Though the Greek word *epiclesis* simply means 'invocation', it has long been commonly used only of the prayer for the consecration of the bread and cup in the anaphora, and it is usually restricted to that form of it which asks the Father to send the Holy Spirit upon them to change them into the body and blood of Christ. This restriction appears, when the evidence is examined with care and without *a priori* presuppositions, to have little or no historical or theological justification, and to be partly the result of, and partly responsible for, the unfortunate controversies which have raged about this prayer, notably that which arose between East and West in the Middle Ages concerning the 'moment of consecration'.

A prayer at this point in the anaphora is universal, and the essential content of it, as distinct from its formulation and elaboration of the content, is also universal: it asks for the divine response to the church's obedience to Christ's command in the preceding anamnesis. The epiclesis in the anaphora of the *Apostolic Tradition* comprises a petition for the descent of the Holy Spirit on the elements and a statement of the ends for which this is sought, the fruits of communion. It does not specify the change of bread and cup into body and blood (although this is clearly implied throughout the prayer), and has therefore been called by some a 'communion epiclesis' as distinct from a 'consecration epiclesis'. This distinction is anachronistic, in that it implies a later and more sophisticated theology of the eucharistic action. It is also inaccurate, in so far as it is the prayer for the descent of the Spirit which is the actual petition for consecration in later and more elaborate Spirit-epicleses, the specification of the effect of this descent as the change of bread and cup into body and blood being essentially no more than a descriptive elaboration of it. The first certain evidence for the fuller form is the Greek Alexandrine Anaphora of St Basil, the basis of the Byzantine Anaphora of St Basil (which has been proved to be the work of Basil), and a document which cannot date from later than the first half of the fourth century and may well be older. From the middle of the fourth century the fuller form, comprising (1) the petition for the operation of the Spirit, (2) the description of the effects of this operation as the change of the bread and cup into the body and blood of Christ, and (3) the statement of the ends for which this is sought, the fruits of communion, has been universal in the Eastern liturgies. The Anaphora of St Serapion has an epiclesis asking for the descent of the Logos or Word instead of that of the Spirit, but this is an isolated theological variant, as there is evidence of an epiclesis of the Spirit in Egypt before it as well as after it. Some Eastern epicleses ask for the descent of the Spirit on the people as well as on the elements, a prayer clearly related to that for the fruits of communion with which they conclude.

In the West the epiclesis asking for the descent of the Spirit to effect the consecration appears to have been common in the ancient Hispano-Gallican rites. It has commonly been asserted that the historic Roman canon contains no epiclesis, but this assertion is based on the *a priori* presupposition that the epiclesis must ask for the descent of the Spirit, and specify the effect of this as the change of the elements, in so many words. In fact, so far from not containing an epiclesis at all the Roman canon contains one of an unusually rich and elaborate kind: it comprises two paragraphs (not one as in most anaphorae), the first (*supra quae* . . .) praying for the acceptance of the gifts, with profound typological scriptural references, and the second (*supplices te* . . .) asking for their translation to the heavenly altar (i.e. Christ himself), followed by the statement of the ends for which this is sought. A more explicit, or theologically more precise, petition for consecration than the latter of these two prayers would be difficult to conceive.

The issue has been confused both by the development in the West of the doctrine of consecration by the recitation of the words of institution and by the presence of the clause describing the change of the elements in a preliminary epiclesis (*quam oblationem*). The Alexandrine anaphorae, as previously noted, also have such a preliminary epiclesis, the division of the epicletic material between this and the epiclesis after the anamnesis varying somewhat from one anaphora to another, and in some involving considerable repetition. The origin of this division or duplication of the epiclesis is by no means clear, for there is

no adequate evidence for supposing that either is a later interpolation in those anaphorae in which they occur.

In the new eucharistic prayers of the Roman rite the preliminary epiclesis is definitely 'consecratory' in content, introducing the institution narrative, while the second epiclesis is specifically a prayer for the fruits of the eucharist: the operation of the Spirit is invoked in both. This arrangement is clearly designed to embody a particular doctrine of the moment of consecration; and this is true of the arrangement of the epicletic material in most modern eucharistic prayers. But it would be anachronistic to regard the double epicleses of the ancient Roman and Alexandrine traditions as the result of considerations of this kind. On the other hand, it is not now possible to eliminate them from the mind in the work of contemporary liturgical revision; given that the issue of a 'moment of consecration' has been raised, even the attempt to abandon such a concept by saying that the whole prayer consecrates merely results, in practice, in regarding the conclusion of the prayer as that moment.

In the Antiochene tradition, which has no preliminary epiclesis, as well as in the Alexandrine tradition which has, the conclusion of the epiclesis after the anamnesis has from a very early date been regarded as 'the moment of consecration'. This should not, however, be understood as an exact parallel to the developed Western doctrine of consecration by the recitation of the words of institution, although in controversy some Eastern writers have themselves tended so to regard it; the classical Eastern position is that the epiclesis is necessary to the consecration, and therefore that its conclusion is the moment when the latter is complete, but this insistence on the necessity of the epiclesis is not exclusive – the narrative of the institution and the anamnesis are equally so.

9. *The Diptychs*. The origins of the diptychs (q.v.), or eucharistic intercessions, in the historic anaphorae are considered in the article devoted to them, and it has been pointed out both in that and earlier in the present article that their insertion at different points in the prayer is one of the principal structural distinctions between the anaphorae of different traditions. A word must be added on the theological rationale of intercessory prayers in the anaphora, in view of the current

tendency in some quarters to eliminate such prayers from the eucharist proper altogether, which appears to owe more to liturgical archaeologizing (and that on a rather slender basis) than to serious theological and pastoral consideration. To remove all intercessory prayer from the memorial of Christ's one all-sufficient sacrifice cannot but obscure the fact that we can offer this, like any other prayer, only as members of Christ, redeemed through that sacrifice, and in the power of that sacrifice. Nothing can make this clearer, nor more effectively express the co-inherence of all redeemed humanity in Christ, than placing the intercessions in the anaphora, in the context of the offering of the eucharistic sacrifice, and of the prayer for the supreme gift of God which we ask for ourselves and for all men, the fruits of unity with Christ in communion. This is most clearly apparent when the intercessions are placed, as in the Antiochene anaphorae and the new Roman eucharistic prayers, after the central prayers of the anaphora as a continuance of the prayer for the fruits of communion. In the words of Alexander Schmemann:

. . . before we partake of the heavenly food there remains one last, essential and necessary, act: the *intercession*. To be in Christ means to be like him, to make ours the very movement of his life. And as he 'ever liveth to make intercession' for all 'that come unto God by him' (Heb. 7.25), so we cannot help accepting his intercession as our own. The Church is not a society for escape – corporately or individually – from this world to taste of the mystical bliss of eternity. Communion is not a 'mystical experience': we drink of the chalice of Christ, and he gave himself for the life of the world. The bread on the paten and the wine in the chalice are to remind us of the incarnation of the Son of God, of the cross and death. And thus it is the very joy of the Kingdom that makes us *remember* the world and pray for it. It is the very communion with the Holy Spirit that enables us to love the world with the love of Christ. The Eucharist is the sacrament of unity and the *moment of truth*: here we see the world in Christ, as it really is, and not from our particular and therefore limited and partial points of view. Intercession begins here, in the glory of the messianic banquet, and this is the only true beginning for the

Church's mission. It is when, 'having put aside all earthly care', we seem to have left *this world*, that we, in fact, recover it in all its reality. Intercession constitutes, thus, the only real preparation for communion (*The World as Sacrament* [1966], p. 53).

10. *The Doxology.* The anaphora ends as it begins with praise and thanksgiving, all but universally in the form of a particularly solemn Trinitarian doxology (q.v.). The concluding *amen* by the people is of equal importance with their responses to the introductory dialogue, expressing their assent to, and participation in, all that the president has said in their name.

Further reading: So many works have been devoted to this subject that it is impossible to recommend even an adequate representative selection, and any less adequate selection would tend to reflect the personal preferences of the present writer to an undesirable extent. Two books should, however, be mentioned: the first, *Prex Eucharistica*, by A. Hänggi and I. Pahl (1968), contains the most complete documentation of the subject available, together with an extensive bibliography; the second, *On the Epiclesis of the Eucharistic Liturgy and in the Consecration of the Font*, by E. G. C. F. Atchley (1935), is the most fully documented treatment of the epiclesis.

                                    W. JARDINE GRISBROOKE

Anglican Worship

Anglican worship was a unique product of the Reformation, in that it is a development from the traditional Western Christian cultus and not merely another variant of continental Protestantism. Its base was a liturgy whose use was obligatory and whose contents conformed to what was believed in the sixteenth century to be a truly primitive pattern. Its principles were set out in the 1549 *BCP* in the preface and in the tract entitled *Of Ceremonies*.

First, instead of a series of local variations of the medieval Roman rite, there was now to be a single 'use' for the whole country. Furthermore, the ceremonies connected with it were essential to the rite and conducive to order, reverence and intelligibility. Secondly, all services were to be in English instead of Latin, in the interests of intelligibility and lay participation. Thirdly, there was an emphasis on edification, particularly through scripture, whereby men might profit in the knowledge of God and 'be the more inflamed with the love of his true religion'. To this end there was a daily office of morning and evening prayer – a unique Anglican feature among the worship of the Reformed Churches – involving the systematic recitation of the psalter and the reading of the Bible in accordance with a drastically simplified calendar. Fourthly, the central act of public worship was to be the eucharist, to be celebrated at least on Sundays and holy days, and possibly even daily. Finally, the liturgy was to be loyal to scripture and loyal to tradition – it was to contain nothing repugnant to the word of God and was to be expressive of the mind and purpose of the early fathers.

With the passage of time these basic principles have been modified, either by law or by common consent. Strict uniformity is no longer recognized as tenable: a church as comprehensive as the Church of England must make provision for differing attitudes – the sacramental and the prophetic, the corporate and the individual, simple austerity and rich splendour, the other-worldly and the this-worldly. It now attempts to have 'a tendency to conservatism in respect of the past; a passion for freedom in respect of the present; a reverence for the institution which incorporates its life; and an inveterate individualism in living that life'. Anglican worship has therefore moved away from a rigid and universal adherence to a single 'use' towards a conformity to a general pattern within fairly wide but nevertheless prescribed limits. This was recognized in the report of the Royal Commission on Ecclesiastical Discipline in 1906: 'The *law* of public worship in the Church of England is too narrow for the religious life of the present generation.' The report therefore recommended that this law should be modified in the light of the comprehensiveness of the Church of England and its existing needs. A great part of the twentieth century has been occupied in attempting to implement that recommendation, and the operation still continues.

Secondly, although English is still the language of liturgy, it has remained unchanged since 1662; in consequence it is now increasingly thought to be irrelevant and unintelligible. Only in the present day has the task of creating a truly contemporary liturgical language been undertaken, and this task is far from completion.

Thirdly, the system of public daily worship shared by both clergy and laity has never really worked, because the practising Christian layman has never been more than a Sunday worshipper. Broadly speaking, corporate worship of the entire community of clergy and laity is now a weekly event, while the daily round of worship is largely maintained by clergy and the members of certain institutions – religious communities, theological colleges, college chapels and cathedrals. But this in itself has produced another element in worship which is unique in the Church of England, the choral daily office, and around this has developed a corpus of church music such as no other church possesses.

Fourthly, it is now recognized that worship cannot be static; it is affected not only by developments in theology but also by the changing pattern of life in the world. The church today cannot be committed to the precise doctrinal positions of Anglican reformers and revisers of the sixteenth and seventeenth centuries. It can only be committed to their general appeal to scripture and the early church, and it must take into account fresh and contemporary understanding of the gospel. It is true that the ideal of the eucharist as the basic act of public worship has become generally accepted, but the way in which that rite is celebrated and the circumstances in which it is celebrated are beginning to change. Anglican worship has begun to combine with the sense of order and tradition a greater degree of freedom and spontaneity, largely under the influence of the Ecumenical and Liturgical Movements (q.v.). This is particularly evident in those acts of worship which now take place outside the traditional church building. There is a growing recognition of the connection between worship and the mission (q.v.) of the church, and of the need to relate worship to a variety of situations.

Nowhere has this been seen more clearly than in the developing worship of the Anglican Church overseas. Until the twentieth century, with relatively few exceptions, the 1662 prayer book was the basis of all public worship throughout the whole Anglican Communion. But the Lambeth Conference of 1920 sounded the note of reform with the assertion that the development of self-conscious and indigenous churches had created a demand for new forms of worship and for local adaptations of the prayer book. The principle of uniformity as expressed in the preface to the prayer book was not applicable to Anglican churches overseas, nor was it necessary as a bond of union between churches which possessed a unity of faith. This note was repeated by the Lambeth Conferences of 1930 and 1948, while the Conference of 1958 urged that each part of the Anglican Communion must be free to order its worship in ways which were real and meaningful in its own area. Anglican worship is therefore now beginning to assume different forms in different parts of the world, although the basic appeal to scripture, to the primitive church and to reason is maintained.

F. E. Brightman, *The English Rite*, 1915; Church of England Liturgical Commission, *Prayer Book Revision in the Church of England*, 1957; P. Dearmer, *The Parson's Handbook* (revised by C. Pocknee, 1966); C. Dunlop, *Anglican Public Worship*, 1953; E. Underhill, *Worship*, 1936.

R. C. D. JASPER

Anniversary

An annual celebration in the life of a church. A church or chapel anniversary is the Free Church equivalent of what others call a dedication festival (q.v.). It usually commemorates so many years of worship in the building, but sometimes the continuous history of a congregation, even though the building is not that which was used originally. Particular departments of church life also have anniversaries, e.g. choir anniversary, sisterhood anniversary. Anniversaries are often divorced from the original starting-date of the department; they are simply annual festivals. The chief of these is the Sunday school anniversary usually held in the spring. At these services Sunday school scholars sing hymns and anthems during the services. Sunday school anniversaries have been held, especially in Methodist churches, since at least the early part of the nineteenth century. Many local customs attached themselves to them, e.g. the building of a special platform for the scholars, the wearing of white dresses, the holding in the afternoon of a 'demonstration' of the work of the Sunday school. They were for long the best-attended services of the year. They are still held, but are not as popular as formerly.

A. RAYMOND GEORGE

Annunciation
see Mariological Feasts

Ante-communion

The *BCP* provides that 'if there is no communion' the communion service shall be said to the end of the prayer for the church and concluded with a collect and the blessing. Such a service is known as ante-communion, and this name was preserved in the Series 2 experimental Order of Holy Communion in the Church of England for that part of the service which included the introduction, the ministry of the word, and the intercessions. The name is a relatively recent innovation. From the seventeenth century until the nineteenth both the communion service and the ante-communion were commonly called the second service; during this period of infrequent communion the ante-communion was more frequently observed for the second service. It was 'second' in relation to mattins (q.v.) and the litany (q.v.) which came before it, since the strict observance of the Act of Uniformity required mattins, litany, and holy communion every Sunday morning.

This service is comparable to the mass of the catechumens of the patristic age, when catechumens (q.v.) were dismissed after the lessons and sermon (but before the prayers of the faithful), and also to the dry mass of the Middle Ages, which consisted at the least of the epistle, gospel, Lord's Prayer and blessing, and at the most of the whole rite of the mass except the canon and the use and presence of the elements and their vessels. The dry mass came to be associated with superstitious notions and practices, and came to be regarded as quasi-sacramental in character, and so incurred the disapproval of the reformers. Another name for the dry mass was *memoria*, and it is noteworthy that Archbishop Grindal and others described the ante-communion as 'a commemoration of the holy communion'.

The position from which the priest read the ante-communion was a matter of contention in the seventeenth century. The Puritans read it from the reading desk, and their 'exceptions' included a demand that the rubric should require it. The high churchmen read it from the altar, 'the church thereby keeping her ground, visibly minding us of what she desires and labours towards, our more frequent access to that Holy Table' (Sparrow, *Rationale*). It was one of the charges against

Laud at his trial that he 'read the Second Service at the Communion Table or Altar'.

W. E. Scudamore, *Notitia Eucharistica*, 1876, pp. 814 ff.

E. C. WHITAKER

Anthem

Although various alternative derivations for the term anthem have been suggested, it is almost certainly an anglicization of the word antiphon (q.v.). Traditionally a musical setting of words drawn from the psalms or from scripture, the anthem may be regarded as a vernacular equivalent of the Latin motet (q.v.), authority for its place in the liturgy being conferred by the rubric in the *BCP: In choirs and places where they sing, here followeth the anthem.* Regarded in that light, to justify its place in a service, an anthem should be chosen not only for its musical excellence but as making a valuable and relevant contribution to an act of worship. When selected on a seasonal or *de tempore* basis, and when the words are made known to the listening congregation, that result becomes possible; but the precarious performance of an anthem beyond the choir's abilities must inevitably cause distraction to the listener, thus contradicting its true function.

Anthems may be accompanied or unaccompanied, for 'single' or 'double' choir, and with or without soloists, a particular type in which the full choir is employed alternately with a soloist or group of soloists being known as a 'verse anthem'. The wide repertoire is perhaps best considered chronologically:

1. *Tudor, Elizabethan and Jacobean.* Tallis and Tye, who were active as composers both before and after the Reformation, provide a direct link between motet and anthem, the Latin or English of their texts, rather than questions of musical style, frequently marking the distinction. Other representative composers of the period are Tomkins, Byrd, Farrant, Morley, Mundy, Weelkes, Orlando Gibbons, Bevin and Batten. Characteristic of the period is a general absence of independent organ accompaniment – though many sixteenth-century anthems sung unaccompanied today probably received light organ support in contemporary performance.

2. *Restoration.* The type of anthem written for the Chapel Royal under Charles II was influenced by the French idiom made familiar to the monarch during his exile at Versailles. Accompanied by a string band and organ, such anthems were often lightly rhythmic and contained solo passages and sections in recitative. Perhaps most familiar in Purcell's 'Bell Anthem' (Rejoice in the Lord alway), the style was first introduced by Pelham Humphrey, to be continued by Blow, Wise and Turner – all of whom, like Purcell himself, had been Chapel Royal choristers.

3. *Hanoverian.* Representative of the English Baroque manner, and recalling Handelian conventions, the anthems of Boyce, Croft, Greene, Battishill, and Handel himself are marked by a dignity which sometimes approaches ponderousness; but which fades into dullness with Nares and Kent.

4. *Late Georgian and Early Victorian.* Sometimes influenced by Mozart and Mendelssohn, the best anthems of Crotch, Attwood, Goss and Walmisley yet preserve an integrity of their own. Those of S. S. Wesley introduce a new emotional content coloured by the chromaticism of Spohr, but avoiding excess. S. S. Wesley and Walmisley were the first to write the important independent organ accompaniments at this time which became a feature of most later anthems.

5. *Later Victorian and Edwardian.* Few of the multitude of anthems produced during the age of 'fashionable' church-going have earned a lasting place in the repertoire, the emotionalism and lack of dignity of much of Stainer, Sullivan, Barnby, and their successors proving unacceptable to modern tastes. Recovery began with Stanford, whose anthems include several masterpieces, and Parry, whose coronation anthem, 'I was glad', in particular, affords luxurious harmonies and sonorities without offending propriety. Charles Wood continued the new tradition to produce several rich anthems which still satisfy.

6. After the founding of the Motett Society in 1841, the anthem repertoire was further widened and enriched by the inclusion of works by Catholic composers such as Palestrina, Victoria, and their successors, often with an English paraphrase of the original texts. In the present century, the

advent of radio brought about a general rise in musical awareness which stimulated the revival after 1920 of many sixteenth-century compositions hitherto regarded as merely archaic. The same development encouraged a new astringency in composers as diverse as Vaughan Williams and John Joubert. There is today no shortage of modern anthems written by English composers of international standing who have managed to discipline their writing successfully so as to avoid making impossible demands upon the church choirs anxious to perform their works. It is perhaps in that direction that the biggest challenge to the modern anthem composer is presented.

C. Dearnley, *English Church Music, 1650-1750*, 1970; E. H. Fellowes, *English Cathedral Music*, rev. Westrup, 1969; M. B. Foster, *Anthems and Anthem Composers*, 1901; P. le Huray, *Music and the Reformation in England*, 1967; C. H. Phillips, *The Singing Church*, rev. Hutchings, 1968; E. Routley, *The Church and Music*, 1970.

BERNARR RAINBOW

Antidoron

Antidoron (Gk lit. 'instead of the gift') is the name given to the blessed bread which is distributed to the congregation after the eucharistic liturgy in the Byzantine rite.

The purpose of this distribution is threefold: (1) to consume what remains of the bread offered by the faithful for the eucharist but not used for it (*see* **Prothesis; Oblation**), (2) to provide immediate sustenance for communicants who have been fasting at least since midnight, and (3) to provide an additional element of participation in the service for non-communicants. It is from the third of these that the name 'antidoron' is derived: for non-communicants it to some extent takes the place of *the* gift, the eucharistic elements themselves. In recent years, with the spread of ecumenical contacts, this third purpose of the antidoron has been extended to provide an additional element of participation, and of fellowship with the congregation, for non-Orthodox visitors.

Similar usages have existed, and in some places still exist, outside the Byzantine rite: the distribution of blessed bread after the liturgy is a feature also of the Armenian and Syrian rites in the East, and it was once common in many parts of the West as well,

surviving in France until recent years and still in certain parts of that country.

W. JARDINE GRISBROOKE

Antiphon

This word has several liturgical meanings. The most familiar is the ancient practice of antiphonal singing, that is the two sides of the choir alternately singing in psalms or canticles. This is the Christian adoption of the Greek word *antiphonos*. The term antiphon was, however, applied later on to texts taken either from the psalms or from scriptural or other sources. Such antiphons were sung before and after the psalms or canticles of the divine office (q.v.) and provided matter relevant to the Sunday or feast day, or feria. The mode of the antiphon determined which of the psalm tones should follow, and so the final of the mode is to be sought in the concluding note of the antiphon, not of the psalm tone. Another use of the term applies to the four songs addressed to Mary, known as Marian antiphons, and also to other chants, as at the blessing of the palms on Palm Sunday and the exquisite 'In Paradisum' in the absolution after the mass for the dead.

ALEC ROBERTSON

Apse

An architectural term denoting a semi-circular structure roofed with a half dome. It was the standard form of the sanctuary in the early Christian basilica (q.v.), and could either project beyond the east end, as in the Latin or Roman type, or be enclosed by a wall, thus providing side chambers, as in the Hellenistic form found in Syria.

EDITOR

Architectural Setting

The nature of Christian worship is such that it does not of itself require any particular architectural setting. It does not centre in a cult object, such as an image, that has to be protected within a shrine. It does not require a large item of liturgical furniture, such as a stone altar (q.v.), that has to be housed in a special way. It can be and has been celebrated in a dining room, a hospital ward or an open field. Nevertheless, throughout the centuries, it has had an architectural setting, which has expressed the Christian understanding of worship. Hence the study of worship historically cannot be divorced from a knowledge of the buildings in which it was conducted.

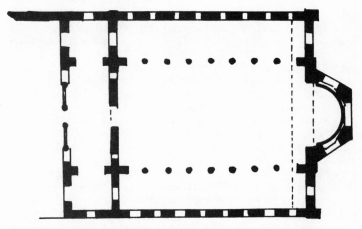

Fig. 1   Basilica of St John of Studion, Constantinople, Turkey

Yet, it has to be recognized that the minutiae of liturgical change can have little architectural effect. The addition of a prayer here or a petition there is not reflected in the buildings. New ideas only produce alterations if they are related to (1) new concepts of the nature of worship and of the church; (2) movement; (3) different ways of doing things. The development of Christian architecture in its connection with the liturgy is in part an account of the operation of these three 'laws'.

Primitive Christian worship, centring in the eucharist (q.v.), was essentially domestic and so was celebrated in the private house. The shape and location of these house-churches differed therefore according to the several forms of domestic architecture throughout the empire. In the east, where one-family buildings up to four storeys high were the norm, worship took place in the dining room which was usually on the top floor. In Rome, on the other hand, tenement dwellings were general, with apartments horizontally across them, and not necessarily having a dining room, so that the largest chamber available would have been used.

In time, houses were bought by or given to the church and these were then specially adapted to the needs of the cult. So the one at Dura Europos, built shortly after 200, had two rooms made into one, by removing a wall, and a dais was set up, while, to the right of the entrance, a small chamber was transformed into a baptistery, complete with font and wall decorations.

After the victory of Constantine, with Christianity replacing the pagan cults as the state religion, worship ceased to be a family gathering and became a public occasion. Its architecture accordingly was made to correspond with civic and imperial forms, and so the basilica became general in both east and west. The basilica (q.v.) was a large meeting hall, belonging to a recognizable class of public buildings, with nave (q.v.) and aisles (q.v.), possibly galleries (q.v.) and clerestories. These pagan forms were given religious overtones by the presence of the emperor's image. The Christian basilica was a similar monumental place of public gathering with religious associations, devotion to God as emperor of heaven being substituted for the imperial cult. Here, then, is an example of the operation of 'law' (1) above, i.e. a new concept of worship, public instead of private, being embodied in fresh architectural forms. Since the genus basilica did not have a uniform plan, the early Christian examples differed, but by the end of the fourth century they had assumed a recognizable identity.

Its general aspect was that of a single room, its horizontal perspective being emphasized by parallel colonnades which seemed to converge on the altar standing towards one end on the middle axis. This was the focal point of the building, and around it priesthood and laity gathered for the celebration of the liturgy, each section having its prescribed place. In the centre of the semi-circular apse (q.v.), roofed by a half-dome, the bishop had his throne, on either side of which were the seats of the presbyters. The superior clergy were separated from the rest of the congregation by the altar (q.v.) around which

Plate 4   The Christian basilica, Abbey of Pomposa, Italy

the deacons were grouped. It could stand on the chord of the apse or even in the body of the church, well down the central nave. The rectangular hall was divided by parallel rows of columns into areas of which there was always an odd number. The centre one, the nave, corresponded to the apse in width and was equivalent to the sum of the side aisles. Its walls rose above them and were pierced with windows to form a clerestory and allow the access of light (*see* Fig. 1 and Plate 4).

In the eighth and ninth centuries in western Europe, the operation of 'law' (2) above, i.e. movement, produced a new type of church, known as the porch-church or *Vollwestwerk*. In effect this was still a basilica but with its west end completely transformed and composed of two elements: a crypt at ground level and, above it, an upper church with aisles and galleries. Externally this was provided with a central tower and two smaller ones on each side gave access to the upper church. This porch-church was in fact to provide for the services of Holy Week and was modelled in part on the Holy Sepulchre complex at Jerusalem; it allowed for the many processions, i.e. movement, as well

as for the celebration of the eucharist, the adoration of the cross, etc. The first examples, from *c*.775, include St Riquier near Abbeville. In the tenth century there was a change in liturgical observance – the operation of (1) above – which immediately had an architectural effect. Whereas in the heyday of the porch-church, worship was something in which all actively participated, it gradually became a spectacle at which the people were passive onlookers. This meant that the plan could be simplified, circulation space being no longer required, and so the porch-church steadily atrophied, first losing its crypt, as in St Pantaleon, Cologne, then being transformed into a western apse, e.g. the cathedral of Paderborn, and finally only surviving as a decorative feature of the western facade, as in the triple towers of Maria-Laach in the twelfth century or the twin towers which appear on the front of so many Gothic buildings (*see* Plate 5).

The passivity of the congregation, which played so important a part in the decline of the porch-church, had, as its obverse, the increasing importance of the clergy who now ceased to conduct the liturgy 'on behalf of'

Plate 5   The porch-church, Jumièges, France

and celebrated it 'instead of' the congregation. The architectural result of this was that the place of the clergy, which had usually occupied the east end of the nave together with the apse, was removed out of the body of the church to create a second room (*see* Fig. 2). Hence the two-room plan of the Middle Ages – the sanctuary (q.v.) being for the ordained ministers, the nave for the laity (*see* Plate 6). In terms of the eucharist, this had involved a shift of emphasis from the communion to the consecration with the elevation as its climax – all that was needed therefore, since non-communicating attendance was widespread, was a distant view of the raised host, dimly glimpsed through the chancel screen beneath the rood at the far end of the choir. The priest had also moved from facing the people across the altar to standing with his back to them and so looking towards the east – here 'law' (3) is in operation.

The medieval church plan was not only the product of a different concept of worship – primarily a sacrifice in the presence of an audience – and of the church – an hieratically structured institution rather than an organism with interdependent functions – nor just of a new concept of the eucharist – centred in the consecration – but also of the developed cult of the saints. For this we have to go back to the fifth century and to recognize the existence of a building type other than the basilica.

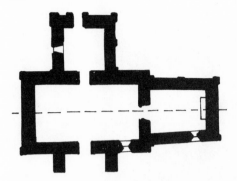

Fig. 2   St Laurence, Bradford-on-Avon,
England

With the cessation of persecution, the period of the martyrs came to be looked upon as a golden age with the martyrs themselves as the heroes of the faith. Christians then began to enclose their remains in *martyria* (q.v.). These copied the form of pagan tombs and were roofed with domes, the symbol of heaven and the bliss of eternal life. The domes were supported by round or octagonal structures and in some cases abutted at all four points of the compass to pro-

duce the shape of a cross (*see* Plate 7). This so-called centralized architecture was in origin a type of funerary monument and it provided for the cult of the saints side by side with the Jesus-cult in the congregational basilicas. The fusion of the two cults in the east brought the two building types into relation and the result was a new form which perpetuated that of the *martyria* but modified it, sometimes by the addition of a basilican east end, to create centralized churches. This became the standard plan for Eastern Orthodoxy. One had only to add side chambers to the apse and an iconostasis (q.v.) with its doors, and the type which has remained traditional to the present day had been created (*see* Fig. 3). In this instance a developed understanding of the eucharist – 'law' (1) – relating it to the intercession of the saints, has had long lasting architectural effects. In the West, however, this cult did not have the same result; there the relics were placed in direct association with the main altar, either enclosed therein or connected by a shaft. Nevertheless the translation of relics did leave its mark on the internal arrangement of churches in Western Christendom, in so far

Plate 6   Two-roomed medieval plan, Heath chapel, Shropshire, England

Plate 7   Centralized cruciform church, Djivari, Georgia, USSR

as each and every relic had its own altar. This, together with the practice of votive masses and the belief that every priest must celebrate every day – further instances of 'law' (1) – led to the multiplication of altars which was such a feature of the medieval cathedrals and, to a lesser degree, of the parish churches.

The Reformation inevitably marked a watershed in the architectural setting of worship, since the Protestants had their own ideas about the cult, which differed radically from those embodied in the medieval buildings. Within the Roman Catholic Church, however, there was no such break with the immediate past, although the Renaissance initiated a new phase in church design. The Renaissance was a rebirth of classical culture, based upon a careful study of the writings and ruins of ancient Rome coupled with an imaginative re-creation of that past era as a golden age in which consolation and refreshment could be sought. For centuries a

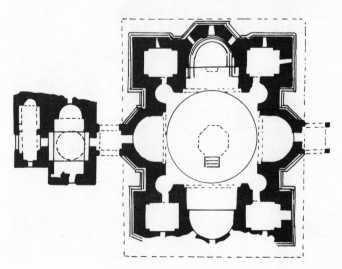

Fig. 3 Typical Eastern Orthodox plan, Djivari, Georgia, USSR

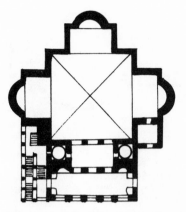

Fig. 4 Centralized Renaissance plan,
S. Sebastiano, Mantua, Italy

church had been regarded as a sacred edifice, and the effect of this concept within the Renaissance context was to equate churches and temples, and so the temples of pagan Rome served as models for Christian buildings. The result was twofold: first, a centralized plan (q.v.) was favoured, e.g. S. Sebastiano, Mantua; and, second, aisles were suppressed, since these had no place in pagan temples, and were replaced by side chapels (*see* Fig. 4 and Plate 8).

Out of Renaissance classicism grew the baroque – an exuberant proclamation of the triumph of the Counter-Reformation. Here the prototype was no longer the temple but the theatre which, through the opera, had become the cultural focus of the period. Churches were now erected to provide distant vistas, with a scenic progression along

Plate 8
The Renaissance
temple, Maser, Italy

the horizontal axis. The church was now a place for an occasion, similar to a *soirée* at court complete with a *divertissement* by Lully. The focal point of worship became the exposition (q.v.) of the reserved sacrament – 'law' (1) above was operative – and in this divine presence a kind of heavenly grand opera was performed, with the high altar, profusely decorated and housing the sacrament, providing the centre piece (*see* Fig. 5 and Plate 9).

The further operation of 'law' (1) is nowhere better to be observed than in the churches of Protestantism. Many of the Reformers rejected the sacrificial interpretation of the mass and emphasized its communion aspect; they laid stress on the ministry of the word and denied a rigid dichotomy of ordained and lay. The circumstances of the time – wars, religious strife – precluded any large-scale new building programme, and consequently Protestants reused or re-ordered the existing medieval churches that they had taken over. Anglicans may serve as an example of the first and Calvinists of the second.

The Church of England authorities re-

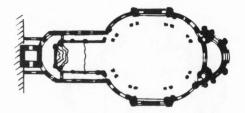

Fig. 5   Baroque theatrical architecture, Die Wies, Germany

cognized that the medieval plan did indeed consist of two rooms; it was therefore decided to use them as such for different functions. So the nave was the place for the ministry of the word and the sanctuary became the scene for the celebration of the eucharist, the altar (q.v.) being moved forward into the middle of the choir and the worshippers arranging themselves around it. This was a different way of doing things – 'law' (3) – under the influence of new concepts of worship and of the church – 'law' (1).

The Calvinists replanned the interior of their churches, as illustrated by St Pierre, Geneva. The medieval building, oblong with

Plate 9   Baroque theatrical architecture, Wallfahrtskirche, Innen, Germany

transepts, had the bishop's throne in the eastern apse, the altar in the choir and the pulpit at the same level as the rood screen separating the priest from the congregation. In 1541 rood screen and choir were demolished; the pulpit was moved to the first pillar on the left and the congregation was arranged in the form of a star at the front of the nave, in the transepts and the ancient choir. A table was brought in only on communion days and baptism was administered from a basin.

Within Anglicanism 'law' (1) continued to operate during the seventeenth century and is particularly noticeable during the Laudian controversy. The mobility of the altar under the Elizabethan settlement – being carried forward into the centre of the choir – led on occasion to its being treated with lack of reverence and even profaned. To prevent this, William Laud initiated a policy of protecting it with rails and fixing it permanently against the east wall. Although the archbishop's ideal was repudiated by the Puritans, it came back into favour at the Restoration and by the end of the century the majority of churchmen were shocked when they found an altar not so placed and fenced in. Laud and his later imitators had to deal with the two-room plan, but with Sir Christopher Wren a new type was introduced, usually referred to as the auditory church, and this was in effect a one room design. Wren was convinced that Anglicanism, unlike Catholicism, required its worship to be both visible and audible. His stress therefore was not only on the sermon but on the services as a whole. This involved, according to his calculations, small churches with galleries to seat not more than 2000 people. He suppressed the projecting chancels, dispensed with the screens, and produced a single volume with three liturgical centres instead of well-defined places. So he sited the font by the door; he installed pulpit and reading-pew, and finally the altar (*see* Fig. 6).

A similar concern to stress the importance of both the auditory and visual aspects of worship resulted within Lutheranism in the *Prinzipalstück*. The declared ideal was that of an oblong building, minus Gothic chancel, with a single space at the east end in which were combined all the principal liturgical acts. Altar, font and pulpit (q.v.) were thus assembled together – 'law' (3) operating under the influence of (1). This concept was first advocated by Joseph Fürttenbach, writing in 1649, and was taken up by L. C.

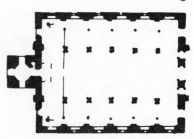

Fig. 6   The Wren auditory church, Christ Church, Newgate Street, London

Sturm in two works of 1712 and 1718. Influenced by the plan of the classical theatre, Sturm supported the adoption of the *Zentralbau*, or centralized auditorium, with *Prinzipalstück*.

A somewhat similar concept of the place of assembly as an auditorium, with the emphasis on the sermon – 'law' (1) – was embodied in the chapels built by the English Nonconformists, first licensed after the Declaration of Indulgence of 1671-72. Most of these were of a modest and domestic nature, without spires or obvious ecclesiastical features on the exterior. The design was rectangular, without chancel or transepts. Galleries (q.v.) were introduced into the larger buildings, mainly to provide greater accommodation, and the pulpit was big and prominent.

There was, therefore, a general tendency within the Protestant church to affirm both the visual and auditive elements in worship, to favour a single room design and even, especially within Calvinism, to adopt a centralized plan. This tendency was completely reversed by the Gothic Revival which was to affect all Christian communions.

To the adherents of the Gothic Revival each religion produces its own supreme architectural form that best expresses its ethos and spirit. Renaissance architecture, in so far as it sought inspiration from the heathen temples of ancient Rome, was to be dismissed as pagan. Only Gothic represented the full flowering and ideal embodiment of the Christian faith. The pioneers of this movement within Anglicanism were influenced to no small degree by the Tractarians, whose teaching about the church and the sacraments was meant to be both biblical and patristic but frequently did not achieve more than an echo of the medieval understanding. The same ideas were shared on the Catholic side by another great leader of the movement,

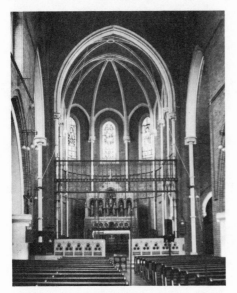

Plate 10 Gothic revival, two-roomed plan,
St Chad, Nicholas Square, London

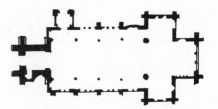

Fig. 7 Gothic revival, two-roomed plan,
Privett church, England

design and it was only when the Liturgical
Movement (q.v.) had sufficiently come of age
and had wedded itself to the modern movement in architecture that any liberation
from the dead hand of the past was achieved
and new forms began to emerge. These
embodied new concepts of the nature of
worship (e.g. that it is corporate), and of the
church (e.g. that it is an organic whole with
interdependent functions), different movements (e.g. offertory processions) and different
ways of doing things (e.g. celebration facing
the people) – so 'laws' (1), (2), and (3) were
once again stimulating a development of
Christian architecture in relation to the
liturgy (*see also* **Architectural Setting [Mod-
ern] and the Liturgical Movement**).

A.W.N. Pugin. 'Law' (1) now came into its
own. The emphasis upon the nature of the
ministry and the sacrificial character of the
eucharist required the two-room plan which
had originally expressed these same ideas.
The ecclesiologists therefore advocated and
secured the all but universal adoption of the
medieval church design with elongated
chancel; the tyranny of an architectural
orthodoxy was imposed (*see* Plate 10 and
Fig. 7).

Wherever British influence extended,
thither the Gothic plan and elevation was
exported, so that churches of the period,
whether in the USA, in Australia or even in
India, followed the same revivalist norm. No
church escaped this mixture of antiquarianism
and romanticism. Roman Catholic buildings
were frequently indistinguishable from Anglican, apart from certain details of the
furnishings. Even the Free Churches submitted themselves to the prevailing fashion,
but more under the pressure of social considerations than of theological ideas. Anxious
to demonstrate that they were as socially
respectable as the Established Church, Methodists, Congregationalists, Baptists, all vied
with one another in adopting the full medieval
plan with nave, aisles, transepts and chancels.
For a hundred years, from approximately
1850 to 1950, revivalism dominated church

G. W. O. Addleshaw and F. Etchells, *The
Architectural Setting of Anglican Worship*,
1948; A. Biéler, *Architecture in Worship*,
1965; J. G. Davies, *The Secular Use of
Church Buildings*, 1968; C. Heitz, *Recherches
sur les rapports entre architecture et liturgie à
l'époque carolingienne*, 1963; R. Krautheimer,
Early Christian and Byzantine Architecture,
1965; T. F. Mathews, *The Early Churches of
Constantinople: Architecture and Liturgy*,
1971.   EDITOR

Architectural Setting (Modern) and the Liturgical Movement

To guide us amidst the stupendous and almost
chaotic diversity of forms and structures
which are characteristic of modern church
architecture, we have two main criteria: the
human consistency of the architectural setting,
and its intrinsic relation to the needs of the
Christian community, in other words, hospitality and celebration.

Modern architecture and the Liturgical
Movement (q.v.) are very complex phenomena. Their parallel evolution, and in our case
their interaction, depend upon a great variety
of factors. To avoid overcomplication, we

shall concentrate upon a few particularly significant examples. They alone are able to give us insight into the principles (theological, liturgical, functional, etc.) which inspired the evolution of modern church-building. These architectural facts cover a period of almost half a century of continual change, stretching from approximately 1925 to the present day.

1. *From 1925 to 1945.* Many authors take as the starting point for modern church architecture the church at Le Raincy near Paris, by A. Perret (1923), both for its thoroughly honest reinforced-concrete structure and for its one-room plan, which foreshadows in a measure the liturgical spaces of the German and Swiss churches of the following decade. But Le Raincy had only a slight influence upon subsequent church building, and one has to remember that the Liturgical Movement was still almost non-existent in France at that time.

Therefore it is preferable to start with something more decisive, a real and living *centre* of liturgical and architectural renewal.

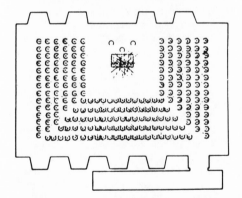

Fig. 8   The main hall, Schloss Rothenfels, Germany

The obvious choice is Schloss Rothenfels-am-Main, the castle which served as head-quarters to the Catholic Youth movement in Germany between 1927 and the Second World War. (Other centres, like Maria-Laach or Klosterneuburg, had only slight contact with modern architecture.)

Castle Rothenfels was remodelled in 1928 under the direction of its chaplain, the already famous liturgist Romano Guardini, and of the architect Rudolf Schwarz, who was to become later one of the greatest church

builders in Europe. It possessed a regular chapel, but the most interesting feature was the main hall, occasionally used for the eucharist.

This hall was a large rectangular space, with pure white walls, deep windows and a stone pavement. It was void of decoration. The only furniture was a hundred little black cuboid stools. The disposition of these stools could be easily changed according to the different functions of the room and the nature of the assembly. For example, it was different for a discussion, a recital, a conference, or for a festive occasion. On the days of liturgical celebration, a provisional altar was set up in the hall and the faithful surrounded it on three sides. On the fourth side, facing them from behind the altar, the celebrant closed the circle. In the autobiographical book which Schwarz wrote many years later about his own churches, we find a description of these celebrations and a record of the extraordinary climate of active unity which characterized them (R. Schwarz, *Kirchenbau*, 1960, pp. 37-46). Rothenfels was frequented by an *élite*. Its influence on the Liturgical Movement in Germany and in Switzerland has been enormous, even if we

Plate 11   S. Christophorus, Köln-Niehl, Germany

Plate 12 Corpus Christi, Aachen, Germany

had to wait almost thirty years to find a really consistent application of its principles to parish churches. We can say that the liturgical arrangement at Schloss Rothenfels was probably 'optimal', the best possible solution for an active participation of the faithful in word and sacrament. The liturgy was celebrated and understood as a totally corporate affair, to be expressed with the greatest possible simplicity and flexibility. This included celebration facing the people, a free grouping of the faithful and an overall interpretation of the place of worship where the interior symbol (the living community itself) took precedence over the exterior, the world of persons over that of objects, and hospitality (the pluri-functional room) over monumentality.

Some of these principles were refounded in a measure in the first parish church planned by Schwarz, Böhm and Guardini shortly after Rothenfels: Corpus Christi at Aachen (1928–30) (*see* Plate 11). Aesthetically, its relation to the *Bauhaus* is unmistakable. The plain cubic exterior fits perfectly into its industrial surrounding. The interior, with its white walls and colourless windows, is, a rectangular space of absolute geo-metrical strictness. It unites in a single space the space for the altar and that for the faithful. But this space is still a *Langbau*, i.e. a narrow rectangle at the end of which the altar remains somewhat isolated. The architect has clearly concentrated on *visual* participation, and thus primarily on the visibility of the altar, which dominates the room with almost dictatorial power. It has almost no connection with the pulpit (q.v.) situated at the centre of the nave (q.v.). Schwarz insisted on the fact that his church was not 'christocentric' (as the hall at Rothenfels) but 'theocentric' and even 'trinitarian', having, so to speak, three 'regions': first the area of the faithful with its black pavement and long rows of benches, image of this earth, realm of the Holy Spirit; then the space of transition with the steps leading to the altar, region of Jesus Christ, the Mediator; finally the great white void of the back wall, image of heaven, the region of the Eternal and Invisible Father, and of the glorified Lord.

There is no doubt that, notwithstanding its concentration on essentials and its functional honesty, the lofty, over elevated interior of Corpus Christi still kept a strong symbolic expressivity (which was to be carried even farther in the great post-war 'theological' churches of Rudolf Schwarz). It is interesting to note that this symbolism was explicitly sanctioned by Romano Guardini, who related it to the 'theocentric' movement of liturgical prayer itself.

The influence of Corpus Christi was instrumental in the planning of some of the best churches of the early thirties, particularly the church at Norderney by Dominikus Böhm (1930), St Theresa at Zürich by Fritz Metzger (1932) and the delightful little country church of Leversbach by Schwarz himself (1932). The first two look literally like smaller 'sisters' of the great geometrical church of Aachen. At the same time, their more human scale points already (and this is even more true of Leversbach) towards the *domus ecclesiae*, i.e. a church building considered primarily as the 'house' of the local community.

The two leading Swiss architects in Switzerland, Metzger and Baur, had been in direct contact with Schwarz, Guardini and the Rothenfels movement. This was to prove a very happy circumstance. The coming to power of Hitler put an end to almost any further development of church building in Germany. From now on, and at least until

1945, the new spirit was, so to speak, a Swiss responsibility. Northern Switzerland became the only place in Europe where one could find authentically modern churches. Most of them were one-room, rectangular spaces, well lighted, and in some cases, of beautiful human proportions. But they kept, as a rule, the over-elevated altar at the far end of their elongated plan. One hesitates to speak here of 'free-standing' altars, because in all these churches, the altar remains rather away from the people, hardly detached from the back wall and much too broad or too monumental to allow the assistants any kind of enveloping movement. Even the most progressive liturgists of that time still considered the church as a building to house primarily an altar and only secondarily the community. Therefore, the altar *had to be* a big static object, the visual and monumental focus of the whole space.

A memorable exception to this situation was provided by three projects for a diaspora church by the German architect Emil Steffann. They show us: (*a*) exteriors which are much closer to a barn, a farm house or a simple family house than to a religious building in the then accepted meaning of the word; (*b*) an organization of the area of celebration which (at least for projects 1 and 3) is that of the main hall at Rothenfels, i.e. a free-standing altar surrounded on three sides by the faithful; (*c*) an extension of the function of the church to other needs of the community than mere worship. (The drawings were published in *Die Schildgenossen*, 1938, pp. 279–81. *See* Fig. 9.)

These plans, however, could not be realized at the moment. The first one foreshadows the famous barn church arranged by Steffann at Bust near Thionville (1942–45). The third is a very close anticipation of one of the most interesting churches of the late fifties: Maria-in-den-Benden at Düsseldorf-Wersten (1958), an almost perfect example of a *domus ecclesiae*.

Before closing this short review of the pre-war period, we must remember that the really authentic modern churches of that time were an extremely small minority. Between 1925 and 1945, the concept of the church remained by and large the old traditional and monu-mental concept, or at best a compromise between this concept and the new vision of things. All the examples given above are Roman Catholic. This does not mean that the Reformation did not sponsor any good church buildings before 1945. The experi-ments of Otto Bartning (project for the 'Star church' in 1924; 'Steel church' in 1928; 'Round church' at Essen in 1930), and later, in the Swiss context, the *Johanneskirche* at Basel by Egender and Burckhardt (1936) or the beautiful church of Zürich-Altstetten by Werner Moser (1941), had a real influence on contemporary religious architecture. But their liturgical inspiration remained some-what ambiguous. One of the reasons for this limitation is that the Reformed theology of the first part of the century pointed less in the direction of a more active participation of the congregation in the liturgy than towards a re-integration of the symbolic values of the church building itself ('The Evangelical place of worship is not only a meeting-place, it is a "Word in stone" – "*ein gebautes Wort*"', Paul Girkon). One may add that the churches at Basel and Altstetten were too close to the

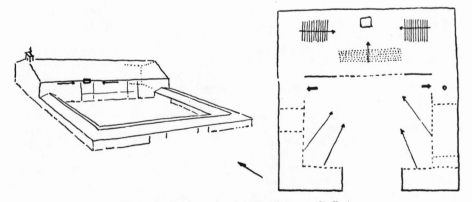

Fig. 9   Project for a church in the diaspora (Steffan)

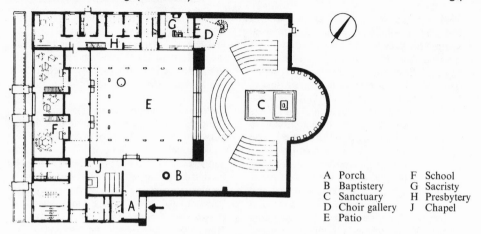

A	Porch	F	School
B	Baptistery	G	Sacristy
C	Sanctuary	H	Presbytery
D	Choir gallery	J	Chapel
E	Patio		

Fig. 10   S. Maria-in-den-Benden, Düsseldorf- Wersten, Germany

passive *auditorium* to be representative of the Liturgical Movement.

2. *From 1945 to 1963*.   After the interruption of the war, a new period opened and stretched from 1945 (or rather 1950) to Vatican II, i.e. at least until 1963.

The main characteristic of this new period was the progressive abandonment of the rectangular plan and of the traditional symmetry. This process was realized by two very different, and almost opposite, groups of churches.

The best examples of the first group present in general a very rational vision of space, an interior which is simple, functional, of human scale and of good proportions. Their plan is most of the time based on the *square* (or on a broad rectangle), where the assembly has a real chance to approach the altar and to surround it on three sides. This is not yet the case in the Illinois Institute of Technology chapel of Chicago, by Mies van der Rohe (1952), nor in the church of Maria Königin at Köln, the last work of Dominikus Böhm (1954), two classical examples of the early fifties. But we find this arrangement fully realized (with even the presidential seat and the possibility of celebrating the eucharist facing the people) in a remarkable series of churches by Emil Steffann: St Laurentius at München (1955), St Elisabeth at Opladen (1957), St Maria-in-den-Benden at Düsseldorf-Wersten (1958) (*see* Fig. 10) and St Laurentius at Köln-Lindenthal (1962). Their architecture is not pointedly modern (some

critics call them heavy and slightly 'archaeological') but they have a deep human quality and their liturgical synthesis, with the accent on the living community, is probably the best of the whole period, better even than that proposed as 'ideal' in a famous text of the German Liturgical Commission, the 'Guiding Principles for the design of churches according to the spirit of the Roman liturgy' (1947 and 1955). Together with excellent proposals, this text remains somewhat prone to exalt monumentality. It speaks of objects more than of persons and still insists, in the case of large churches, on a distinct sanctuary (two-room building).

To these churches, we must add some other sober, hospitable, liturgically very sound buildings, for instance, the lovely little Episcopalian church of St James the Fisherman at Cape Cod, Connecticut, by Olav Hammerstrom and the then priest-in-charge, James A. Pike. In this wooden structure, the central, square altar is entirely surrounded by *four* groups of pews – an arrangement which would probably be dangerous in a big church, but which works perfectly in a fifty-eight feet square space. As other good examples, we may recall here St Paul at Bow Common, by Maguire and Murray (1960), the prefabricated churches of Rainer Senn in Eastern France, the churches of Le Donné at Marienau (1955), Mulhouse (1956), Vitry-sur-Seine (1964), and the last churches by Rudolf Schwarz, particularly St Christophorus at Köln-Niehl (1962). In drastic contrast with the 'theological' schemes developed in his book *Vom Bau der Kirche*, Schwarz allowed this small, unassuming church no other symbolism than the fundamental one of the *domus ecclesiae*. Its climate of simplicity, of tranquil harmony, of plain and radiant humanity, is the very kind of architectural setting which points towards the future of the liturgy. (*See* Plate 12.)

The second, very different direction taken by church-building after 1950 is by way of a much more organic vision of space and symbol. The typical examples, here, are of course strongly individualized. Their forms become more and more lyric. All the elements of architecture: walls, ceilings, floors, etc., become parts of each other. Continuity is everywhere, in the materials and the furnishing as well as in the functions. Applied to the space of worship, this organic character becomes the symbol of the organic, hierarchized body of the faithful.

One of the first experiments in this direction is the church of St Franziskus at Basel-Riehen, by Fritz Metzger (1950) (*see* Plate 13). Its sanctuary and the nave (an ellipse and trapezium) blend in one symbolic form, whose meaning is to express, and at the same time to activate, the participation in the celebration. The floor of the nave follows a slight declivity, where the benches are disposed in a segment of a circle. Everything is organically concentrated on the sanctuary and particularly on the altar. This kind of direct, quasi-physical symbolism is always dangerous in architecture. We must admit that in the case of Riehen, it remained rather discreet.

But directly after 1955, the impact of Le Corbusier's chapel at Ronchamp accelerated the normal pace of the evolution to the point of almost changing its nature. It led to a complete break away from the axial symmetry and other rules which had governed Christian churches since Constantine. Not a bad thing in itself, this liberation unfortunately resulted in the attempt to infuse into every new country church the lyrical creativity of Ronchamp. Many German and practically all Swiss architects were intoxicated by this. It is evident that in this unhealthy, competitive atmosphere, it was difficult to avoid overdoing things, and to escape a touch of

Plate 13   S. Franziskus, Basel-Riehen, Switzerland

megalomania. And what is true of the Swiss churches could be repeated of a large number of 'organic' churches designed between 1955 and 1965 all over the world. From our point of view in the 1970s, we realize that there was little more in this movement than a new metamorphosis of the old temptation to monumentality – a climate in which the liturgical functions were either swallowed up in the *décor* (the form of the space, the dazzling rhythm of the lighting, the heavy fixation of the liturgical poles, etc.) or stressed in a one-sided way.

One has to remember that Ronchamp, the most famous of all 'modern' churches, had been the embodiment of a very special programme (a pilgrimage chapel at the top of a hill). It had only little to do with normal, everyday worship. It had almost no connection with the Liturgical Movement in France, which had become at that time the thinking and living *milieu* which laid the basis for the liturgical revolution of Vatican II.

This does not mean that the organic direction in church building is necessarily to be condemned. It is not lyricism as such which is wrong, but lack of coherence, of human scale, of ecclesiastical and functional fitness. However, when trying to point out the churches which really anticipated the 'post-conciliar' church, we see that the examples are generally found in the other group, illustrated by the works of Steffann, Le Donné, etc. They are the best churches liturgically, and also architecturally, in so far as they unite strictness with poetry, and architectural seriousness with a sufficient amount of creative liberty.

3. *From 1963 to 1970.* We have now reached the period of Vatican II. Its importance in the realm of church building does not depend only upon the 'Constitution on the Sacred Liturgy' (1963), but also upon other later texts and statements such as the 'Constitution on the Church and the World' (1965) and the 'Declaration on Religious Liberty' (1965). Even more important was the general climate of freedom, research and the need for authenticity.

Strictly speaking, the 'Constitution on the Liturgy' did not do much more than 'officialize' the major tenets of the Liturgical Movement of the post-war period, particularly the principle of *assembly* worship (considered as the living sign of the universal body of the faithful) and the close link which unites liturgy and mission. But this was enough to suggest a new image of the church building, completely at the 'service' of the assembly. It meant a break with the image still familiar to the great majority of Christians, the 'monumental' image which came from the beginning of the Middle Ages and remained ours even – as we have seen – in the most recent metamorphoses of organic architecture. This break could not be achieved in a single day.

It seemed easier to start from the *functional* modifications implied by the new liturgy and to comply with the demands of the Constitution by a simple readjustment of the poles of celebration.

Before the Council, many liturgists still arranged everything in church in strict subordination to *one pole*: the altar. The new emphases on the liturgy of the word, celebration facing the people and concelebration (q.v.), obliged them now to give prominence also to the chair of the celebrant and to the pulpit, i.e. to the two poles of the liturgy of the word, and to find a distinct location for the tabernacle (for example, against the wall or on a pillar). These three or four poles have to be at the same time clearly differentiated and formed into a living synthesis. The liturgical arrangements of the years immediately following 1963 display an extraordinary variety of solutions. But these arrangements have one thing in common: the *fixity* of all the liturgical furniture. Chair, pulpit, and altar remain firmly bound in stone, concrete and marble. In the organic climate of the Swiss churches, for example, one is confronted with a sanctuary full of huge stones, themselves over-activated by the talent of the sculptor. We are still very far from the place of *interpersonal* communion supposed by the new liturgy of word and eucharist.

The same is true for the liturgy of baptism. In the earlier stages of the Liturgical Movement, the baptismal font (q.v.) was still located in its traditional chapel, or elsewhere near the entrance area. A special stress was thus given to the initial rite of entry into the church. But the act of incorporation into the community, which is the *living* image of the church, is far more important. Therefore, some liturgists looked for other solutions. They located, for instance, the font in one of the lateral spaces of the church, largely open to the assembly (*see* **Baptistery**). We find examples of this arrangement in some churches by Rudolf Schwarz, like St Anna at Düren (1955) and St Christophorus at Köln-Niehl (1962) (*see* Plate 12).

Other liturgists think that baptism should normally be celebrated facing the assembly; thus the best position for the baptismal font is in a symmetrical relation to the ambo (q.v.). Apart from its communal value, this position emphasizes the close tie that binds baptism to the liturgy of the word and to the eucharist. The danger of this new location is of overcrowding the area of celebration, and this is exactly what happened in the Swiss churches mentioned above (*see* Plate 14). The baptismal font added one huge stone to others.

Real progress in the general arrangement of the church and especially of the sanctuary was to be found by way of more suppleness, simplicity and movement. Paradoxically, this was first realized in countries like Austria or Belgium, where the movement of modern churches had remained, at least up to 1960, practically sterile. It is these countries, too, which offered the first truly post-conciliar churches – completely and uncompromisingly so.

The idea coming to life in these churches can be summed up in one phrase: the serving of the assembled community in the simplest possible form. Beyond the limited perspective of pure liturgical functionalism, this means humility, limpidity, and above all a great opening to a living dialogue. But dialogue excludes any kind of rigid confrontation between the celebrant and the faithful, and thus also rigidity in the form, material and location of the liturgical objects. The Belgian architect Marc Dessauvage was probably the first to accept this evolution and to draw the consequences. In the parish churches he built after 1963, the altar, the pulpit, the chair and the font are generally *mobile* (*see* Plate 15).

An even more important change, introduced by the Austrian architect Ottokar Uhl, was the possibility of movement for the assembly itself. In his students' chapel of the Peter Jordanstrasse at Vienna (1965), the single space is divided into two distinct areas. The first is furnished by benches and occupied by the assembly during the liturgy of the word. The second is an open, free space for the eucharist. The faithful enter this space after the sermon and stand in a semi-circle around the altar. Provision for movement is carried even farther in another chapel by Uhl, arranged at the Benedictine abbey of Melk (1967) (*see* Plate 16).

Plate 14 S. Pankratius, Oberkirch, Lucerne, Switzerland (Fritz Metzger)

The question of movement in church is related to the question of number and to other fundamental problems. At the New York Congress on Religion, Architecture and the Visual Arts (1967), which is another major milestone in the evolution of modern church building, the main theme in discussion was not any more the liturgical fitness of the church, but the very question of still building churches in a situation of acute mobility, anonymity, urbanization and secularization. The parochial system, i.e. the frame of Christian life and worship which the faithful had known for centuries, and until a very recent time, appeared now clearly to be in the process of crumbling away. The question was: how to replace it? In the conclusions of the Congress, Prof. Houtart demonstrated the need to develop the new solutions on three levels: the small group (a homogeneous meeting of no more than twenty people), the congregation (a flexible, not strictly territorial adaptation of the parochial assembly) and the large community (an occasional grouping of many hundreds or even thousands of faithful). These three levels of ecclesial belonging and

expression have to be simultaneously ordered for several functions: not only the liturgy, but also communication, social action, etc. (*Revolution, Place and Symbol*. Journal of the New York Congress, 1969, pp. 57-9).

The small group is characterized by the openness and simplicity of its contacts, and, in the liturgy, by the reduction of external rites. It does not need any specialized space for worship. Because the centres of life and worship coincide, everything can normally take place in the homes of individuals. For the large community, there is no architectural problem either: it will use great, pre-existing spaces (a cathedral, a theatre, a cultural centre, a stadium, etc.). Only the group called 'congregation' will still need and ask for specialized church buildings.

The problem is to adapt these buildings fully to the new situation. It is evident that the majority of the churches built between 1967 and 1970 do not differ very much from the churches of the early 'sixties. In a few cases, however, we find a real attempt to integrate the new values. Good examples are the Church of St Paul at Waterloo, Belgium

Plate 15   S. Rochur, Aarschot, Belgium

Plate 16   Chapel for students, Melk, Austria

(1968) and the church at Neuville near Liège (1970), both by Jean Cosse. In the second of these buildings, especially, which has a demountable podium and movable furniture, the space for worship is occasionally used for conferences, concerts, etc. It can be extended towards the reception room (with open fire-hearth, adjacent kitchen, cloak room and other facilities). The dominant character of the main space remains thus that of a place of worship, but it is flexible enough to accommodate other functions. Although at least 150 people take part in worship, the liturgy in this church has a real family climate: it is a *domestic* liturgy, thanks to the very hospitable setting. (*See* Fig. 11.)

Neuville is thus a kind of multi-purpose church. This new concept, elaborated between 1965 and 1967, will certainly gain more and more attention and probably dominate the church building of the 'seventies. It supposes

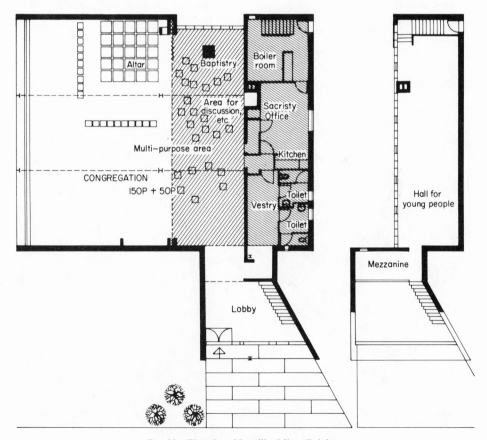

Fig. 11   Church at Neuville, Liège, Belgium

a real synthesis, and not only a juxtaposition, of the liturgical and the secular functions. In his important book on *The Secular Use of Church Buildings* (1968), Prof. J. G. Davies has demonstrated that the union of liturgical and secular functions is deeply traditional and corresponds to the very nature of Christianity. In the modern context, the experiments of multi-purpose churches point towards a plurality of solutions. The church at Neuville is a timid, but quite acceptable one. Another possibility is to keep a *fixed* sanctuary, and to screen it off when using the nave for other purposes. This solution is best known, probably because it is the easiest to put into practice, but its future is very uncertain if only because it is not really honest, and is better defined as dual-purpose rather than multi-purpose.

The Institute for the Study of Worship and Religious Architecture of the University of Birmingham, and Prof. Davies himself, have inspired multi-purpose churches of another type, where the worship area includes a fixed and defined space for the sanctuary, choir

and the font, but without any screen to shield them during secular use (*see* Fig. 12). This enables the unity of the functions 'to be demonstrated and to be lived' (*The Secular Use of Church Buildings*, pp. 243-8).

A fourth kind could be illustrated by the new pastoral centre at Kessel-Loo near Louvain, in Belgium, by Dessauvage (1970). The very flexible main space, which offers pluri-dimensional possibilities, serves for worship on Sundays and feast days only, and has no permanent liturgical furniture. Normally, it is used for secular purposes (like the hall at Rothenfels). However, in the quietest part of the centre, a much smaller room, liturgically fully equipped, is reserved for daily worship and personal meditation. This could seem a regressive arrangement. But in 1970, 'secularization' is no longer the only problem. One has to take into account the rediscovery of meditation and intense personal prayer. The same can be said of the need for new and vital forms of festivity and celebration. The Liturgical Movement will have to integrate better these two, almost opposite, forms of

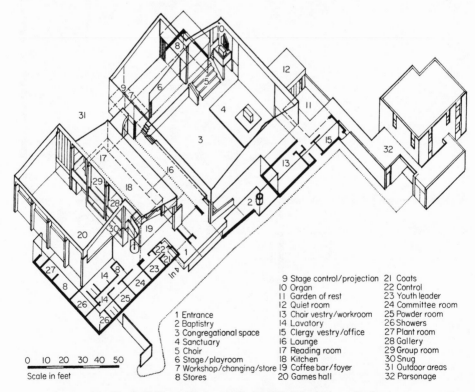

	9 Stage control/projection
	10 Organ
	11 Garden of rest
	12 Quiet room
1 Entrance	13 Choir vestry/workroom
2 Baptistry	14 Lavatory
3 Congregational space	15 Clergy vestry/office
4 Sanctuary	16 Lounge
5 Choir	17 Reading room
6 Stage/playroom	18 Kitchen
7 Workshop/changing/store	19 Coffee bar/foyer
8 Stores	20 Games hall

21 Coats
22 Control
23 Youth leader
24 Committee room
25 Powder room
26 Showers
27 Plant room
28 Gallery
29 Group room
30 Snug
31 Outdoor areas
32 Parsonage

0 10 20 30 40 50
Scale in feet

Fig. 12   St Philip and St James, Hodge Hill, Birmingham, England

worship; and so will the church building, if it is to remain faithful to its never-ending quest for adaptation and authenticity.

F. Debuyst, *Modern Architecture and Christian Celebration*, 1968; P. Hammond, *Liturgy and Architecture*, 1960; R. Maguire and K. Murray, *Modern Churches of the World*, 1965.

F. DEBUYST

Ascension Day

The commemoration of the ascension of Christ on the fortieth day after Easter (q.v.). Late in the fourth century, Etheria's description of worship at Jerusalem includes an account of a service held in the Church of the Nativity at Bethlehem on the fortieth day after Easter, the preaching being related to the place and the occasion. At first sight it seems that this can hardly be other than a festival of the Ascension. But when we consider the sense of appropriateness which was so characteristic of the worship of the Jerusalem church, it seems incredible that there would be a celebration of Ascension Day at Bethlehem. Further, Etheria immediately goes on to speak of the arrangements for the Day of Pentecost, which was a unitive festival commemorating the ascension of the Lord and the descent of the Holy Spirit. The unitive commemoration was still in existence at Jerusalem early in the eighth century. The problem disappears when we examine the ancient lectionary of the Jerusalem church preserved in the *Rituale Armenorum*. The entry preceding that for Whitsunday runs – 'May 18, in holy Bethlehem, of the children slain by King Herod' (F. C. Conybeare, *Rituale Armenorum*, 1905, p. 525). One of the passages read was Matt. 2. 16-18, which recounts the massacre of the innocents. This is clearly the commemoration to which Etheria refers, held appropriately at Bethlehem, in the Church of the Nativity. It must be emphasized that Etheria does not testify to a festival of the Ascension on the fortieth day after Easter. In the *Apostolic Constitutions*, deriving from the region of Antioch towards the end of the fourth century, the festival is definitely prescribed in the context of regulations concerning the liturgical year. It may be stated that the evolution of Ascension and Pentecost was probably taking place during the last quarter of the fourth century, and that in all likelihood the theatre of this evolution was the region Constantinople-Asia Minor-Antioch.

A. A. McArthur, *The Evolution of the Christian Year*, 1953.

A. A. MCARTHUR

Ash Wednesday

At Rome in the middle of the fifth century the Station days of Wednesday and Friday, in the week preceding the first Sunday in Lent, were transformed into full liturgical days with their own services. Then the Thursday and Saturday would be included in a preliminary penitential period. As Lent came to be more rigidly observed, so the difference between Sundays and fasting days became more marked, and it was noted that only thirty-six days were actually fasted. But already it was customary for the Church to keep a preliminary fast of four days beginning on the Wednesday. The Quadragesima was reconstituted by the incorporation of these four days. This was the situation early in the eighth century. The emergence of Wednesday as the commencement of the Quadragesima was a deformation of the original Lent. (*See also* **Commination**.)

A. A. MCARTHUR

Ashes

Ashes are a symbol of (1) purification (*cf.* Num. 19.9, 17f.; Heb. 9.13); (2) penitence (*cf.* Judith 9.1; Jonah 3.6; Luke 10.13; Matt. 11.21).

The former symbolism is seen in the consecration of a church (q.v.) according to the Roman rite. Water, called Gregorian water, is mingled with wine, salt and ashes, and with this mixture the bishop sprinkles the altar and the walls of the church in different places. It is an exorcistic rite intended to purify the building before it is consecrated by the anointing with chrism (*see* **Chrismatory**).

The latter symbolism, common to many religions and part of the common stock of OT and NT religion (*cf.* texts quoted), is to be found in the rite of the imposition of ashes on Ash Wednesday. In the earlier centuries of the church, when the discipline of public penitence was in force, penitents sometimes sprinkled ashes on their heads or alternatively received from the bishop a rough garment on which ashes had been sprinkled. In the tenth to eleventh century when the primitive discipline had become obsolete, Christians generally associated themselves with the modified discipline and came to church on the Wednesday before the first Sunday in Lent (subsequently called Ash Wednesday) to have blessed ashes (made of the palm branches of the previous year) put on their foreheads (*see* **Commination**). The prayer(s) used indicate that the rite is a penitential one and one formula used for the imposition of the ashes suggests the necessary abasement before God if forgiveness is to be achieved: 'Remember, man, that you are dust and into dust you shall return' (*cf.* Gen. 3.19).

Formerly the rite took place before the mass. Since 1970 it takes place within it, after the homily.

J. D. CRICHTON

Asperges

The word comes from Ps. 50.9 in the Vulgate Psalter: 'Thou shalt *sprinkle* me with hyssop and I shall be cleansed: thou shalt wash me and I shall be made whiter than snow', which in the Roman rite is recited when holy water is sprinkled over the people, before mass, when holy communion is given in the home and on some other occasions. Formerly other verses of the psalm were sung or said during the sprinkling, which took place usually in a procession of celebrant, ministers and servers around the church before the principal mass on Sunday. The rite (now to be performed after the entrance chant) is no longer of obligation in parish churches.

Originally, it would seem, an exorcistic rite (though there is a reference to sprinkling of the people in the ancient prayer of the blessing of baptismal water of the Paschal Vigil [q.v.]) for the cleansing of a building or place where a liturgical service was to take place, and also more strictly so when fields were sprinkled, it has become in the course of centuries connected with baptism. It is seen both as a reminder of baptism and as a means of renewing its grace. This is indicated both by the sprinkling of the people after the renewal of their baptismal promises at the Paschal Vigil and by the change of text for the Sunday sprinkling in Paschal time. The *Asperges* is replaced by a text based on Ezek. 47.1, 8, 9: 'I saw water coming out from the temple on the right side and all whom this water touched were saved.'

The rite of the Sunday *Asperges* probably had its origin in the monastic custom of sprinkling the monastery on that day. In the Middle Ages in some parts of Europe the procession for the sprinkling with holy water went through the whole village.

In modern Roman Catholic churches the rite is replaced for ordinary masses by the custom of taking holy water from stoups placed at the entrance to the church. The people are supposed to recite the *Asperges* while doing so.

J. D. CRICHTON

Assemblies of God Churches' Worship

The Assemblies of God, with international headquarters in Springfield, Missouri, was organized in 1914, and ten years later the Assemblies of God, Great Britain and Ireland was constituted by about seventy independent Assemblies agreeing to form a recognized fellowship. It is one of the denominations brought into existence as a result of the Pentecostal (q.v.) revival of the late nineteenth and early twentieth centuries. In addition to being a church of the evangelical tradition, the Assemblies of God is known for an emphasis on the manifestation of the gifts of the Holy Spirit as described in I Cor. 12-14.

In many ways the architecture of Assemblies of God churches is similar to that of other non-liturgical churches. Almost invariably the pulpit (q.v.) is in the centre of the platform, indicating the emphasis placed on the centrality and authority of the scriptures. Ordinarily a communion table is directly in front of the pulpit at the level of the congregation; altar rails (q.v.) or benches are either made a part of the platform or placed between the congregation and the platform, symbolizing the direct access man has to God through Jesus Christ. A baptistery (q.v.) is usually located behind the platform.

The Assemblies of God considers the mission of the church to be threefold. The ministry of the church towards God involves worship and obedience (Acts 13.2). Its ministry towards its members provides for edification and maturation (Eph. 4.11-16). Its ministry towards unbelievers emphasizes the need of personal regeneration (John 3.3). The Assemblies of God ministry to unbelievers includes a missionary programme built on indigenous principles which reaches around the world.

Assemblies of God services are informal and non-liturgical. Vestments (q.v.) are not worn by officiating clergy. In expression of the threefold mission of the church, regular services may have one of three major emphases. The Sunday morning service usually emphasizes worship, but it is also designed for the edification of the worshippers. The Sunday evening service usually emphasizes the need of regeneration and is intended to bring unbelievers to a personal commitment to Christ. A mid-week service is most often thought of as a time for Bible study and prayer. Special services of the local congregation include evangelistic meetings, Bible conferences, mission conventions, and training courses. Because the Assemblies of God has a basic congregational polity, there are variations of the emphases mentioned, and the degree of informality varies.

The order of the services usually includes congregational singing of hymns and gospel songs, often accompanied by a variety of musical instruments, public prayer, ministry of music by a choir and/or individuals, receiving of tithes and offerings, and the ministry of the word. Quite often opportunities are given for members of the congregation to share personal testimonies concerning scripture portions which have been especially meaningful to them or experiences in which they feel God has helped them in a special way. The testimonies may be interspersed with the singing of choruses by the congregation. Enthusiastic congregational participation is an important aspect of worship in Assemblies of God churches.

Ways in which an Assemblies of God service differs from other non-liturgical evangelical services include times of united audible prayer and worship; manifestations of the gifts of the Holy Spirit, such as speaking in tongues, interpretation of tongues, and prophecy; and prayer for the sick, including anointing with oil. In many instances, especially in smaller congregations, opportunity is given in a service for members of the congregation to mention needs which they feel should be remembered during public prayer. Most services end with an invitation for those present to kneel at the altar rail or at their seats for a time of prayer.

The Assemblies of God recognizes two ordinances and considers both symbolic rather than being inherently efficacious.

Baptism (q.v.) by total submersion is considered essential as an act of obedience and outward sign of the believer's identification with Christ in his death, burial, and resurection. Baptism is administered only on profession of faith in Christ, and for this reason infants are dedicated to God rather than baptized. Baptismal services are conducted either in a church baptistery or in an outside natural body of water.

The Lord's Supper (q.v.), usually celebrated monthly, is considered a memorial of Christ's substitutionary death and a reminder of Christ's second coming. Faith in Christ, rather than membership in an Assemblies of God church, is the basis upon which worshippers are invited to participate in this ordinance. Communicants partake of both elements, usually at their seats, served by laymen.

The churches of the Assemblies of God without exception accept the Bible as the infallible and authoritative rule of faith and conduct.

THOMAS F. ZIMMERMAN

Assumption
see Mariological Feasts

Atrium
The entrance or fore-court of a basilica (q.v.). It was usually open in the centre and surrounded by covered colonnades.

EDITOR

Aumbry
A cupboard or recess in the wall of a church or the sacristy (q.v.) in which the sacred vessels and books, and sometimes also reliquaries, were kept. Aumbries were also used to house the three oils used in certain sacramental rites; these were stored in a chrismatory (q.v.). They were also used with a locked door for the reservation (q.v.) of the blessed sacrament usually in a wall near the altar, but sometimes in the sacristy. This method of reserving the consecrated elements has been revived in the Church of England during the last hundred years, and the door and surround of the aumbry sometimes have elaborate decoration, as we can see in the examples at St Mary-le-Bow, London, and St Philip and St James, Oxford. But an even longer standing tradition for this method of reservation exists in the Scottish Episcopal Church, to which reference is made in the 1929 Scottish prayer book as 'the long standing custom in the Scottish Church'; this custom is to be traced back to the Liturgies of the Nonjurors in the eighteenth century, where we

are told 'that some of the consecrated Elements be constantly reserved in the vestry or some other convenient place in the church under a safe lock'.

While the wall-aumbry does not appear to have been used very much in medieval English churches as the place of reservation, it was undoubtedly employed in pre-Reformation Scottish churches. The wall-aumbry was also in use for reservation in Sweden, Germany and Italy. With the post-Tridentine legislation in the sixteenth century the use of such cupboards was abandoned in Italy and some of these were converted to housing the oil for the sick, as at St Egidio, Florence, by having the legend *Oleum Infirmorum* inscribed on the plinth; but the original sculpture displays a chalice and host with adoring angels.

The wall-aumbry was also termed 'sacrament house' in Germany; but there and in the Low Countries this term came to be applied at the end of the Middle Ages to a large spire-like structure standing on a pedestal in which the reserved sacrament was housed.

A. A. King and C. E. Pocknee, *Eucharistic Reservation in the Western Church*, 1965; E. Maffei, *La Réservation Eucharistique jusqu'à la Renaissance*, 1942.

C. E. POCKNEE

Baldachin

Also spelt balddachino, baldachinum or baldaquin. This term is often used rather loosely to describe any kind of canopy over an altar (q.v.), but it should only be applied to a canopy of woven fabric and not to wooden, stone or metal canopies. Baldachin is derived from the Italian *Baldacco*, meaning Baghdad, where woven textiles of silk woof and metal thread were first made. Canopies made from such textiles first appear in the Renaissance period, and particularly where the altar was near or attached to a wall or screen. Fabric canopies known as baldachins were also placed over the thrones of kings and princes. A canopy resting directly on four columns and made of wood, stone or metal is more correctly described as a ciborium (q.v.). Sometimes the reserved sacrament was suspended in a pyx (q.v.) hanging from under the canopy.

In the return to the more cube-shaped altar that is now being made under modern liturgical reforms, such an altar tends to appear insignificant and the provision of a ciborium over the holy table will give an emphasis that is likely to be otherwise lacking in the focal point of Christian worship.

C. E. Pocknee, *The Christian Altar*, 1963.

C. E. POCKNEE

Baptism

The rite whereby a person is made a member of the church. From the Greek *baptizo*, to dip, baptism has especial reference to the water rite, but it can be used of Christian initiation as a whole and may therefore, on occasion, include both the water rite and confirmation (q.v.).

1. *Patristic*. The principal authorities for the patristic rite of baptism are: in Africa, Tertullian, Cyprian and Augustine; in Rome, Hippolytus and John the Deacon; in North Italy, Ambrose; in Spain, Isidore and Hildephonsus; in the East, Cyril of Jerusalem, Chrysostom, Theodore of Mopsuestia and Pseudo-Dionysius Areopagiticus.

In the West baptism was normally administered at Easter, Pentecost being an alternative season. The font (q.v.) was blessed by the bishop with a prayer invoking the Holy Spirit upon the water so that baptism should not be a mere physical washing. Anointed with the oil of exorcism (q.v.), the candidates renounced Satan. Asked successively whether they believed in the Father, the Son and the Holy Spirit, they replied in the affirmative to each question and were dipped in the water, this threefold series of question, answer and dipping constituting baptism in the name of the Trinity. Emerging from the font, they were anointed on the head by a presbyter to signify their incorporation into the royal and priestly body of Christ. During this period it became customary for them to be vested in white robes after their baptism. From the privacy of the baptistery (q.v.) they were led into the church, where all the faithful were assembled with the bishop, who then prayed over them, invoking the sevenfold Spirit upon them, laid his hand upon them and signed them with chrism on the forehead. Finally, regenerated by water and the Spirit and sealed with the Spirit of adoption, they took part in the corporate prayers and received communion for the first time, never before having been allowed to see the last part of the eucharist, or even know what happened at it. There was no strict uniformity throughout the West, the African church, for instance, having only one unction (q.v.) after baptism and placing more emphasis on the episcopal hand-laying, and the Gallican churches including the ceremony of washing the candidates' feet.

In the East there were some notable differences. The negative renunciation of Satan was followed by a positive declaration of adhesion to Christ. The Trinitarian formula of baptism, 'N. is baptized in the name . . .', goes back at least to Chrysostom's time, thus anticipating by several centuries the appearance of the formula 'N., I baptize thee in the name . . .' in the West. There was only one anointing after baptism, a sealing with chrism not only of the forehead, as in the West, but also of the breast and organs of sense. At an early date hand-laying disappeared from Eastern usage. In some Syrian rites from the third to the seventh centuries the gift of the Holy Spirit was associated with the unction before baptism, in the opinion of some scholars the original sequence of events.

The rite was essentially corporate, presided over by the bishop (q.v.), assisted by his clergy, and with all the faithful involved. Candidates might be of any age from infancy upwards, the rite itself, though not the catechumenate, remaining unchanged long after infant candidates began to outnumber all others. There was as yet no question of infants being prevented by their age from receiving the grace conveyed by one part of the rite as opposed to another. Liturgically and theologically the patristic rite possessed far more unity than modern Western students can easily appreciate. Everything from the renunciation of Satan to the final episcopal unction could be covered by the word *baptisma*, Tertullian describing baptism, anointing and hand-laying under the heading *De Baptismo*. The episcopal unction was the moment when the candidates received the Pentecostal gift of the Spirit, and were anointed with chrism, or christened with the same Spirit with whom Christ, the anointed One, was endowed at his baptism. What is now called confirmation (q.v.) was that part of baptism which signified and conferred the baptismal gift of the Holy Spirit.

The rite could be administered in its entirety only if a bishop were present. This was impossible in the case of adult catechumens (q.v.) suddenly taken ill, or newborn infants not expected to survive, as soon as it became generally accepted that they must not be allowed to die unbaptized. While the Eastern Church solved this problem by delegating the whole rite to presbyters when a bishop was not available, in the West the rule was gradually established that the post-baptismal unction and hand-laying must be reserved to the episcopate, a decision for which scriptural justification was claimed in the apostolic laying on of hands in Acts 8.17. Consequently, where this rule was in force and baptism was required in haste, presbyters, being instantly available, gave baptism and communion, hand-laying and anointing being, in the case of those who recovered, deferred until the next episcopal visitation.

Thus, while the Eastern Church has been able to keep the unity of the patristic rite of initiation intact even to the present day, the Western Church allowed it gradually to be divided into the seemingly independent rites of baptism and confirmation. So arose the need to define the activity of the Holy Spirit in each of these rites. A sermon preached by Faustus of Riez in the late fifth century, in which he said that the Holy Spirit restores to innocence at the font and in confirmation confers an increase in grace, was one of the main sources on which medieval theologians based their solution of this theological problem.

J. D. C. FISHER

2. *Orthodox*. More correctly, Byzantine. The baptismal service of the historic rites, like those of the other Byzantine rites, is a conflation of a number of short services designed to be spread over a period of time – originally Lent (q.v.), leading to baptism at Easter – but now celebrated together, one after another. Its shape and content have changed remarkably little for at least eleven hundred years, and probably very much longer, even to the extent that although it is, and has been throughout that time, used far more often for the baptism of infants than for that of adults, the rubrics for the most part still seem to presuppose the latter.

The service falls into two halves, the order for the making of a catechumen (q.v.), and the order of holy baptism, and this division is still clearly retained in the service-books, the two halves being printed separately, each with its own title.

The order for the making of a catechumen comprises four separate acts: (*a*) the prayer for the admission of a catechumen; (*b*) the exorcisms; (*c*) the renunciations; (*d*) the profession of faith.

The prayer for the admission of a catechumen asks for the deliverance of the candidate from error, and the bestowal upon him of the gifts of faith, hope and love, that he may come to know God, to follow his commandments, and to be united to God's flock, that in him God's name may be glorified; it is preceded by a triple breathing upon the candidate by the priest (*see* **Insufflation**), and a triple signing of him with the sign of the cross (q.v.) on brow and breast, and commences with a laying-on of hands in the name of the Trinity.

The exorcisms (q.v.), four in number (although the modern Greek books print the third and fourth together), all beseech the expulsion from the catechumen of all evil spirits and their influence, while the fourth beseeches also the gift of the guardian angel. Each was originally accompanied by the laying on of hands, but this is no longer customary now that they are all said together immediately after the admission of the catechumen, with the laying on of hands at the beginning; at an appropriate point in the fourth the priest breathes upon the brow, mouth and breast of the catechumen.

The renunciations follow the exorcisms. The catechumen, turned towards the west, and with arms upraised, three times renounces Satan, all his works, all his angels, all his worship, and all his pomp; confirms the renunciation; and then blows and spits as an expression of his contempt for all that he has renounced.

The profession of faith follows at once; its inclusion in the order for the making of a catechumen rather than in that of holy baptism may occasion surprise, in the light of the intimate connection between the profession and the baptism in the early liturgy, but it is probably due to an historical accident in the arrangement of the books, an issue too involved to go into here, consequent upon the conflation of the several baptismal rites into one service and their celebration at times other than Easter. The essential element of the profession of faith, to which are added various decorative questions and answers, is the recitation of the Nicene-Constantinopolitan Creed, the candidate facing east. The order for the making of a catechumen is then concluded with a prayer for the grace of baptismal renewal and enlightenment.

The order of holy baptism comprises: (*a*) the hallowing of the baptismal water; (*b*) the pre-baptismal anointing: (*c*) the baptism itself.

The hallowing of the font (q.v.) is introduced by a litany, based on the common greater litany (*see* **Litany**) with several appropriate additional petitions – for the hallowing of the water by the coming of the Holy Spirit, for the descent upon it of the grace of redemption, for illumination by the power of the Holy Spirit, for the averting of every device of evil spirits, and six petitions for the candidate, that he may truly acquire all the benefits of baptism. During this litany, sung by the deacon, the celebrant prays secretly for the divine assistance in the administration of the sacrament. The litany concluded, he proceeds to bless the font, with a very lengthy prayer, following the pattern of the eucharistic prayer or anaphora (q.v.), commencing with a thanksgiving for God's manifestations of himself in creation and redemption, continuing with a prayer for the hallowing of the water by the descent of the Holy Spirit, and concluding with a petition for the effects of this hallowing to be operative in him who is to be baptized, with a closing doxology. The ceremonial accompanying this prayer is of the simplest, the essential act being a triple breathing on the water in the form of the cross at an appropriate point.

The pre-baptismal anointing is preceded by the blessing of the 'oil of gladness' corresponding to the Western 'oil of catechumens', and a triple signing of the water with this oil – a typical early medieval addition to the blessing of the water, paralleled in the other historic rites, which adds nothing to the clarity of the liturgical structure of the rite. The candidate is then anointed on brow, breast and back (*see* **Unction**).

The baptism itself then follows immediately. Orthodox theology and canon law require total immersion, except in emergency; the candidate is held upright in the font, with his face towards the east, and is immersed three times, at the naming of each person of the Trinity, with the formula: 'The servant of God N. is baptized in the Name of the Father, Amen; and of the Son, Amen; and of the

Holy Spirit, Amen.' Psalm 31 (32) is then sung (while the newly-baptized is dried), after which the new white clothing is put on the newly-baptized, with appropriate formulae.

The administration of the sacrament of chrismation (the Byzantine name of what is called confirmation in the West) follows at once, for infants as well as adults. The administration, like that of baptism and the eucharist, is of course delegated to the priest, although he uses episcopally consecrated (in modern practice patriarchally or·primatially consecrated) chrism (see **Unction**). The celebrant says a prayer giving thanks for baptism, beseeching the gifts of the seal of the Holy Spirit and participation in the eucharist (which anciently also followed without a break). He then anoints the newly-baptized with the chrism, making the sign of the cross on the brow, the eyes, the nostrils, the mouth, the ears, the breast, the hands and the feet, saying at each anointing 'The seal of the gift of the Holy Spirit, Amen.'

The baptismal rites are concluded by a brief form of the synaxis (q.v.) with an appropriate epistle and gospel; originally, of course, this was the synaxis of the baptismal eucharist. It is still the custom in many Greek churches, unless the celebration of the eucharist is to follow shortly, to give the newly-baptized and confirmed (especially if he is an infant) communion from the reserved sacrament at the end. With the spread of liturgical reform it is reasonable to hope that before long the restoration of the baptismal eucharist will be achieved at least in some places, in which case the Byzantine baptismal liturgy will again manifest the integrity of the rites of Christian initiation as they were celebrated in the early church; as it is, it has for many centuries done so more fully than has any of its Western counterparts.

W. JARDINE GRISBROOKE

3. *Medieval and Roman Catholic.* In Rome from the sixth century, since adult baptism had become rare, the custom of baptizing infants became general. The *ritual* of the catechumenate (q.v.) was retained and even elaborated, but the adult catechumenate became obsolete.

The child was necessarily passive, and, as it were to compensate for this, the scrutinies (examinations) were increased to seven; since instruction could not be given to unconscious children, a rite of the 'tradition' of the gospels was substituted for it. The questions about faith formerly put to the candidate during the action of baptism were now anticipated and addressed to the parents and godparents. The formula, said by the priest, 'I baptize you, in the name of the Father, etc.', is attested in eighth-century Rome. Gradually, too, the traditional liturgical days of scrutiny and the giving back (*redditio*) of the Lord's Prayer and the creed (q.v.) were separated from the traditional days of Lent when these acts had taken place. By the eighth century there were only two assemblies in church, the first for the enrolment and giving of salt (indicating that the child was now a catechumen) and the 'tradition' of the gospels which consisted of no more than the reading of the first phrases of each of the four gospels. Neither of these observances required the response of the candidate. With the compilation of the Romano-German pontifical of the tenth century, the ceremony of the giving of the white garment was accompanied with a prayer giving its sense, a prayer that passed into the Roman rite of baptism of a later age, and the giving of the lighted candle, a symbol of Christ the light of the world, was added. This, too, has survived in the Roman rite. Later still, in the fourteenth century, baptism by 'infusion', the pouring of the water on the head, replaced the ancient custom of immersion, though immersion was still known in the thirteenth century (witness Thomas Aquinas, *Summa Theologica*, III,66.7) and the practice of baptism by immersion has never been forbidden in the Roman Catholic Church.

All traces of a catechumenate as a separate ceremony were finally wiped out by the ever more prevalent custom of baptizing infants as soon after birth as possible, a custom that became general from the tenth century onwards. By the thirteenth century all the pre-baptismal ceremonies of catechumenate, renunciation of Satan and the anointing with the oil of catechumens had been combined into one service which is first found in the *Ordo ad cathecumium* (sic) *faciendum* of the Pontifical of the Roman Curia of the same century. The books of the local churches, e.g. the *Manuale* of Salisbury, merely endorsed this situation. But local usages remained, and in the post-Tridentine period, it became necessary to introduce order into the administration of baptism. The *Rituale Romanum*, issued by Pope Paul V in 1614, tidied up the situation and this book remained in force until the new order of baptism of 1969. Unfortunately, it was no more than a work of compilation. No effort was made to construct an order of infant baptism that would meet the changed conditions of the church. The compiler merely took two orders found in the tradition, one longer and one shorter: the longer, which comprises all the ancient rites of the catechumenate in one service, was destined for adults and the other, shorter, for infants.

The new order for the baptism of infants was promulgated on 15 May 1969 and came into force on 8 September of the same year.

It was issued with two introductions, one on baptism in general and the second on the baptism of infants. This order, then, is part of a fuller document, still awaited, which will contain the rites of the (restored) catechumenate and of adult baptism. Both introductions are documents of considerable theological importance, a summary of which would, however, take up a good deal of space. It may be noted, however, that the faith of the parents, who play a central role in the service, is the crucial factor in accepting infants for baptism. They, with the gathered community, profess the faith of the church which they represent, a faith they are required to communicate to the child as it grows up.

A brief description of the rite. Baptisms are to be celebrated normally on Sundays in the presence of the local community whether at mass or at some other time of the day.

The celebrant welcomes the baptismal party at the church door and asks the first questions establishing the willingness of the parents to bring their child up in the Christian faith. He then signs the child on the forehead with the cross and the parents and godparents are invited to do likewise. This is a relic of the ancient enrolment ceremony.

There follows 'the celebration of God's word', consisting of one or two passages from scripture, a homily, intercessions for the child, the family and all baptized persons.

There is a single prayer of exorcism (q.v.) and the anointing on the breast (only) with the oil of catechumens. Local conferences of bishops may allow, for good reasons, the omission of the whole of this rite.

'The celebration of the sacrament' follows with the blessing of the water (three forms provided, to be used at choice), the parents'

renunciation of evil (two forms given) and profession of faith with the gathered community, the act of baptism (either by immersion or affusion), the anointing with chrism, the giving of the white garment, and of the candle.

The service concludes before the altar where a blessing is given to the mother (replacing churching), to the father and the assembled congregation.

The new order is both new and traditional. It is adapted to circumstances of infant baptism, it addresses itself to the parents and their friends and it requires a genuine commitment. Traditional elements will be found in the ministry of the word, parallel to the ancient vigil, the anointings and the ceremonies after the act of baptism. In one respect it fails to keep the ancient order: the renunciation of evil is separated from the exorcism (q.v.).

J. D. CRICHTON

4. *Anglican.* After it had separated from the Roman Communion, the teaching and practice of the Church of England in respect to the sacrament of baptism remained largely those which had become commonly accepted in Western Catholicism. The attention of the English Reformers was occupied chiefly with the presentation of a strong apologetic for continuing the practice of infant baptism, the provision of instructional material, and the revision of the baptismal service. The order for baptism in the first English *BCP* of 1549 was a combination of materials drawn from the pre-Reformation Latin service and early Lutheran sources. It followed closely the structure of the Latin rite, but abridged the catechumenal introduction which had become prefixed to the baptismal rite in the Middle Ages. The traditional ceremonies of signing with the cross, exorcism, unction (qq.v.), and bestowal of the white baptismal dress were all retained. Many of the words translated or paraphrased the Latin. There were a number of new compositions, chiefly prayers and exhortations; in these the influence of the Reformation is the most apparent. Reformed influences, however, were much more evident in the second *BCP* of 1552. The baptismal order in this book reduced the introductory section still more, made a number of changes in the words of the service, and added a thanksgiving section. With the exception of signing with the cross, which was transferred

to follow the baptism, all the traditional ceremonies were omitted. Without significant alteration, the 1552 baptismal rite passed eventually into the 1662 *BCP*. All of the orders for baptism in the various Anglican prayer books derive from the 1662 order, and all follow it closely, while differing from it and each other in details.

The Anglican baptismal rite begins with an introductory section consisting of prayers, addresses, and a reading from the gospel. The baptismal vows or promises follow. These are made personally in the case of adult candidates, by sponsors in the case of infants. The promises are in the form of a series of questions and answers involving a set of renunciations, a promise of adherence to the Christian faith as stated in the Apostles' Creed, and a promise to follow the Christian way of life. The baptismal water is then consecrated according to a form adapted from that prescribed for monthly use in the first *BCP*. The baptism then takes place. Water is poured upon the candidate or he is dipped into water – the latter rarely in actual practice – while the Trinitarian baptismal formula is recited. The newly-baptized are then signed with the cross and declared received into the church. A thanksgiving and address to the sponsors or a blessing concludes the service. The Anglican prayer books design baptism as a public liturgy, and make provision for the insertion of the baptismal service into the regular services of worship. However, in common practice, baptisms have been more generally held before or after regular services or at specially arranged times, with only those immediately concerned present.

Anglican teaching about baptism has changed but little since the Reformation, and is very much the same in all of the churches which make up the Anglican Communion. Most of its baptismal doctrine Anglicans hold in common with other parts of the Christian church, and it is difficult to discern anything distinctively Anglican about it. Anglicans have always regarded baptism as a sacrament instituted by Christ and, except in the presence of most unusual conditions, necessary for salvation. The sacramental sign is water, poured upon an unbaptized person, or into which he is dipped. The form of words which must accompany this action are: 'N., I baptize thee in the Name of the Father, and of the Son, and of the Holy Ghost.' Any baptism carried out by means of this sign and formula Anglicans regard as true baptism, and all persons thus baptized are accounted members of the Christian church. While it is baptism which Anglicans hold to be necessary for admission into the Christian church, the Anglican churches have generally required confirmation (q.v.) as well as baptism for admission to communion and full participating membership in the church, thus in effect regarding baptism by itself as incomplete; some Anglicans have taught that this is the case. The spiritual gifts of baptism may be summed up in the words: 'A death unto sin, and a new birth unto righteousness'. Repentance and faith are the necessary requirements for the effective reception of the sacrament. Baptism is to Anglicans a mystical washing away of sin both original and actual. It is a sharing in the death and resurrection of Christ, a rebirth into the saving community of the church. By means of it one is incorporated into Christ's mystical body, made a child of God, and an inheritor of the Kingdom of Heaven. While Anglicanism has always taught that the baptism is of water and of the Spirit, and that the Holy Spirit is active and in some way given in baptism, it has never clearly defined the activity and gift of the Spirit in baptism in relation to those in confirmation. Everywhere in Anglicanism, from the Reformation to the present day, infant baptism has continued to be defended and to be the norm of practice.

During the last three decades there has been a debate about baptism which has gathered force and has spread to all parts of the Anglican Communion. The present pastoral situation, insights gained from the Liturgical Movement (q.v.), and increasing ecumenism have all combined to produce a growing dissatisfaction with traditional Anglican teaching and practice. A Baptismal Reform Movement has been started and is doing much to further investigation of baptism in relation to the modern situation of the church and to awaken the church to the needs for change and revision. A major point in the discussion has been the practice of baptizing all infants presented for baptism, and the relevance of infant baptism in the contemporary pastoral scene. It is also evident that the rites of baptism in use at present are but one part of Christian initiation; a re-integration of baptism, confirmation, and first communion into a single rite of

Christian initiation is necessary to a full appreciation of the meaning of the sacrament in the life of the church. At the present time there are before the Anglican churches a number of proposed revisions of the baptismal rites which attempt this re-integration. There is also a deep need for a re-statement of the traditional theology in a manner understandable by our contemporary world. The debate is by no means resolved, and will doubtless increase as Anglicans examine more deeply their mission in the present-day world.

H. ELLSWORTH CHANDLEE

5. *Baptist.* The use of the title *Baptist* may account for the belief, now widespread, that the baptism of believers by immersion is the basic principle of that denomination. It is, in fact, secondary and derivative. Believers' baptism rests on three primary convictions about authority, faith, and the church. The source of authority is God manifest in Christ, and the medium of his authority is scripture. The only baptism found in the NT is the baptism of believers. On the authority of scripture, baptism is administered only to those who have professed repentance towards God and faith in Jesus Christ. Conversion must precede baptism. This personal response to the activity of the Holy Spirit is essential for membership in the body of Christ. For the Christian society consists of those who have heard the gospel with faith; it is the fellowship of believers. It follows from these three convictions that it is not the *mode* but the *subject* of baptism which is of primary importance. The mode is immersion; the subject is the believer. The Anabaptists and the early English Baptists baptized by affusion or pouring. When circumstances, such as sickness or extreme age, make it advisable, baptism is occasionally administered in that way today. It was to exhibit the full meaning of the rite that immersion was eventually adopted. The actions of going down into, of being buried beneath, and raised up from the water, proclaim the death, burial, and resurrection of Christ. The mode has importance because of what it signifies, but what really matters is *who* is baptized, not *how* the rite is administered. The emphasis on personal response is characteristic of the teaching and practice of all Baptists. The candidate is said to be following the example and obeying the command of Christ, making a confession of faith in him, pledging allegiance to him. This stress on the human response has been and is accompanied by a widespread tendency to ignore or deny the activity of God, not prior to, but in the sacrament. To many Baptists, baptism is represented as a purely symbolic rite, a dramatic portrayal of what has already taken place in the experience of the candidate. It would be misleading to generalize on this matter, and among Baptists today, as in the past, there are marked differences of teaching. Recent Baptist scholarship has emphasized the relationship between baptism, the Holy Spirit, and the church. On the question of when baptism should be administered to a believer, there are two conflicting points of view. On the one hand, since conversion and baptism belong together, there is a desire to minimize the period between the initial response and the administration. On the other hand, especially on the mission field, the need for an adequate period of preparation is recognized. Candidates are usually, though not always, taught before baptism. Baptists have no prescribed liturgy, but administer the rite in the threefold context of the fellowship, the word, and the prayers. Baptism is not regarded as a private or domestic occasion, but is administered in the setting of the congregation at worship, and of the reading and preaching of the word. There is a marked evangelistic quality about the service. The candidates bear witness, sometimes verbally, and always in the act of baptism, and it is expected that this witness, together with the preaching of the gospel, will be used to make disciples from among those present. Baptism is regarded as a converting ordinance, and the service often concludes with an appeal for others also to respond. After the preaching it is the usual, though not invariable custom, to put questions to the candidates. Typical answers include a confession of faith in the Holy Trinity, the acceptance of Jesus Christ as Lord and Saviour, and a pledge to follow and serve him. The occasion is often preceded by prayer meetings, and in the service itself a prayer for the candidates precedes or follows the questions and answers. In the baptistery, the names of the candidate, and words indicative of personal response, often precede the traditional Trinitarian formula. 'N., on thy profession of repentance towards God and of faith in our Lord Jesus Christ, I baptize thee in the name of the Father, and

of the Son, and of the Holy Spirit.' Immersion takes place in one of three ways. The candidate stands in the water, and is lowered backwards into it until submerged, and is then lifted up again. The candidate may kneel in the baptistery, and then be immersed forwards. When the rite is administered in a river or pool, as often in Africa, Asia, or Latin America, the candidate is led out into the water until it reaches the neck, and then, after the formula, the head is pressed under. In many churches, the Aaronic blessing (q.v.) is said or sung after each immersion. The baptisms may be followed by an appeal for decisions; the service then concludes with a hymn and the blessing. In some churches, the laying on of hands after baptism, practised by the early General Baptists of Britain, and always adhered to by a small minority of Baptist communities, has been restored. The practice of baptizing at the Lord's Supper is also on the increase. The desire to enrol the candidates as members of the church at the baptismal service itself is one outcome of the new emphasis upon baptism as initiation into the body of Christ.

S. WINWARD

6. *Christian Church (Disciples of Christ)*. Although the major founders of the Christian Church (Disciples of Christ) stood in the Reformed tradition, they early set aside the practice of infant baptism in favour of the baptism of believers by immersion. Alexander Campbell (1788-1866) took the lead in the examination of the NT that led to the conclusion that the 'one baptism' mentioned in scripture required a specific action, upon certain candidates, with a particular meaning. The action was defined as immersion, to the exclusion of other modes, and that mode was single immersion as contrasted with trine immersion practised by people in the various Brethren churches. The proper candidate was a penitent believer. The meaning ascribed to the act was phrased in this way by Campbell: 'Baptism is, then, designed to introduce the subjects of it into the participation of the blessings of the death and resurrection of Christ.'

In his writings Campbell regularly translated the Greek terms into immerse and related words instead of into baptize and its related words. Yet his discourses clearly indicate that he was talking about the Christian sacrament of baptism rather than merely

a water rite. Furthermore, his views constituted a high doctrine of baptism. He claimed that regeneration and conversion were both equivalent terms to immersion (by which he meant the sacrament of baptism). Therefore wherever the scripture discusses regeneration or conversion that teaching must be applied to baptism. The scripture, said Campbell, calls for 'an actual coming' to the Lord Jesus. But 'Where shall we find him? Where shall we meet him? Nowhere on earth but in his institutions, the first of which is the institution for remission of sins – the sacrament of baptism.'

It is clear in early writings of the Disciples that salvation was seen as the free gift of God; in this way they stood firmly in orthodox Christianity as interpreted by the churches of the Reformation. The new element in their view was the emphasis upon man's active participation. Faith was considered to be a requisite of baptism, faith understood as trust in Christ and therefore an act of complete obedience to Christ. Repentance was to follow from faith and was understood to be a complete turning around of life. Then would come immersion, death and resurrection with Christ, the first act signifying complete surrender to Christ's will. The result was that a person was changed to a new relationship with God.

This careful synthesis has suffered from abuse through the years since it was first articulated. Some have stressed the active participation of the baptizand to the degree that the free gift of God has been compromised. Some have stressed the idea of obedience to the degree that divine grace and the imperative to lead a new life have been neglected. Some have emphasized the mode of the act so much that the equivalence of regeneration, conversion, and baptism has not been recognized.

At first Disciples admitted only persons immersed as penitent believers into membership in their churches. If there had been previous baptism in some other mode, baptism by immersion would be administered anew, under the rubric of 'completing one's obedience to Christ'. The severity of this closed membership policy has been moderated by open admission to communion, so that persons from other denominations may share freely in the liturgical and congregational life of a Disciple church even when not admitted to formal membership because of irregular baptism. An increasing number of congregations have, since about 1900, received by transfer of membership Christians from churches who baptize by other modes. Furthermore, there is a growing resistance in the denomination to what is now widely recognized to be rebaptism.

There has been a widespread custom in Disciple congregations for a simple act of blessing and dedication to be ministered shortly after a baby is born into one of the families of the church. This rite has sometimes included the naming of the child. More characteristic has been the practice of asking parents to pledge that they will rear the child in the Christian faith. The congregation is asked to share in this responsibility and a prayer of dedication concludes the service.

The baptismal rite, as commonly practised, has two parts which may be separated in time and place. The first is called *confession of faith* and always takes place in a regular service of worship. During an *invitation hymn*, usually following a sermon, the believer walks to the front of the church where he is met by the minister. The minister, usually drawing upon Peter's confession in Matt. 16, asks him: 'Do you believe that Jesus is the Christ, the son of the Living God; and do you accept him as your Lord and Saviour?' The person answers affirmatively, after which the minister speaks a brief word of commendation, usually drawing upon some appropriate passage of scripture. At some later date, again at a regular service of worship, the baptism takes place. Although the rite is occasionally performed in running water, it is ordinarily administered in a baptistery constructed so as to be visible to people in the main worship room of the church. The minister may read a passage of scripture dealing with baptism. Then he pronounces: 'By the authority of our Lord Jesus Christ, in whom you have confessed your faith, I baptize you (N) in the name of the Father and of the Son and of the Holy Spirit. Amen.' Single immersion, the baptizand leaned backwards into the water, then takes place.

Current discussions among Disciples indicate that the theological position first developed continues to be widely supported. There is somewhat less emphasis now upon the absolute necessity of immersion, although that mode continues to be the only one practised. There is ambivalence about the appropriate age of baptism. As a general rule children from church families are received for instruction and baptism at about the age of twelve; only then are they received at the communion table.

KEITH WATKINS

7. *Congregationalist.* The early Congregationalists (or Independents, as they were then known) held the same views about baptism as the English Presbyterians. Both groups dissented from three characteristics of the Anglican administration of the sacrament according to the *BCP*. First, they objected to signation with the cross as an additional ceremony for which there was no biblical warrant. Secondly, they disliked the godparents taking the role of the parents in making the promises that the child should be brought up as a Christian, since this was the duty of the parents. Thirdly, they objected to private baptism. In their view baptism was a sacrament of the gospel, giving assurance of forgiveness of sins and of eternal life, which ought to be celebrated in the church.

John Cotton's *The True Constitution of a Particular Visible Church* (1642) describes the classical Independent administration of baptism:

As for Baptism, it is to be dispensed by a Minister of the Word unto a Believer professing his Repentance, and his Faith, being a member of the same Church Body as also unto his seed, presented by the Parent unto the Lord and his Church at which time the Minister in God's roome calleth upon the Parent to renew his Covenant with God for himselfe and his seed and calleth upon God as the nature of the Ordinance requireth, for the pardon of originall sinne, and for the sin of the Parents and for a blessing upon the Sacrament and Infant and then calling the Childe by the name, which the Parent hath given it for his owne edification, and the Childes, he baptizeth it either by dipping or sprinkling into the name of the Father, the Son, and the Holy Ghost (pp. 6f.).

Plainly, early Congregational baptism was the claiming of the covenant promise of God to be with his children and his children's children, a solemn inclusion of the child of believing parents within the company of the elect, by baptism in the triune name, and accompanied by the parental promise to bring up the child in the nurture and admonition of the Lord, until this promise should be honoured by the child when he reaches physical and spiritual maturity. The only point of difference between Independent and Presbyterian usage was that the latter used to require the parent to recite the Apostles' Creed as a test of orthodoxy in belief, whereas the Independents insisted that a covenant (or affirmation of loyalty) was more appropriate than a creed, which was a historical summary which could be recited with 'the top of the mind'.

In the early and middle part of the twentieth century, when theology had become increasingly more immanental, there was a tendency for baptismal orders of worship to stress the human profession of faith rather than the divine initiative in baptism. This meant that baptism came to look increasingly like infant dedication. *A Manual for Ministers* (1936) in its baptismal order affirms that there are three purposes in baptism: to acknowledge God as the source of all good; to affirm the divine fatherhood of all children; and that 'we solemnly re-dedicate ourselves in the presence of God, and ask for His help worthily to fulfil these new and sacred duties' (p. 73).

A richer theological exposition of the meaning of baptism will be found in the 'Order for the Baptism of Children' in *A Book of Public Worship* (1948). It reads:

This Sacrament is a sign and seal of the covenant of grace, of union with Christ in his body, of remission of sins in his blood, of resurrection unto eternal life through him, and of our calling and engagement to be his for ever. It declares that the children of Christian parents belong, with us who believe, to the membership of the Church; and that Christ claims them as his own . . . (p. 159).

Surveying contemporary Congregational baptismal practice in Britain and the USA, it could be stated with confidence that a typical administration of baptism would comprise the following elements, though not necessarily in the order given:

1. Warrant for baptism (usually Matt. 28.18-20; occasionally Mark 10.13-16).
2. Exhortation on the meaning of baptism.
3. Questions to the parents to elicit solemn promises from them.

4. Prayers for the sanctification of the child to be baptized.
5. The act of baptism by sprinkling of water on the child's head, mentioning the child's name, and saying, 'N., I baptize thee in the name of the Father, and of the Son, and of the Holy Ghost.' The Aaronic blessing (q.v.) follows.
6. A declaration by the minister, with the congregation as witnesses, that the child is now received into the congregation of Christ's flock.
7. A concluding prayer for the child, parents and congregation, that they may be protected and guided by God to fulfil their vows and to recall their own baptism, and finally attain to everlasting life.

A similar service, with the necessary adaptation, is used for the baptism of believers.

In recent times Congregationalists, like other Christians, have been disturbed by the relatively small percentage of infants baptized who come to confirmation or full church membership at maturity. They have attempted to meet this problem in two ways. They have made the explanatory section of the rite fuller and more clear. In England they have made considerable use of the Rev. H. A. Hamilton's book *The Family Church*, which is an attempt to cross the abyss between church and Sunday school (which previously had met in different buildings). He insisted on including children in the beginning of common worship in the sanctuary on Sundays and throughout the service for the four major festivals of the year. He also advocated the provision of 'church friends' with whom the children might sit if their own parents took no interest in their spiritual progress. Imaginative as this suggestion is, the problem is still of major proportions.

HORTON DAVIES

8. *Jehovah's Witnesses.* (*a*) Water baptism marks the initiate's entry into the family of God, with consequential privileges and responsibilities, including ordination to public Christian ministry.

Water does not wash away sins: 'The blood of Jesus [God's] Son cleanses us from all sin' (I John 1.7). However, baptism performed in faith is with the consciousness of God's forgiveness, and is therefore a 'request made to God for a good conscience'. It is also 'now saving you' since withdrawal from the world's course, presupposed to be antagonistic to God's righteousness, has necessarily preceded it (I Peter 3.21-4.6).

Jehovah's Witnesses have always practised total immersion (*Zion's Watch Tower*, 15 June 1893). Not only do the lexicographers show *baptizo* to mean 'to dip in or under water' (Liddell and Scott), but scriptural usage demands total immersion. Jesus, baptized in Jordan River, came 'up out of the water'; Philip and the Ethiopian 'went down into the water' (Mark 1.10; Acts 8.38).

Only adults are baptized. The Lord's command was to baptize 'disciples'; 'teach all the nations, making them your pupils' (K. S. Wuest's translation), and *then* baptize them (Matt. 28.19,20). They were old enough to be 'pupils'. Acts 10.48; 18.8 and others speak of whole households being baptized, but only 'those hearing the word' (Acts 10.44) and 'believer(s) in the Lord' (18.8), hence at an age of understanding.

A preparatory course, usually at least six months long, is undertaken by each candidate. He should consider what he is doing soberly and with a clear mind (Eccles. 5.2-6). The 190-page Bible study aid *The Truth That Leads to Eternal Life* is currently being used for this pre-baptismal course. It summarizes fundamental Bible doctrine and practice in uncompromising terms. Worldwide Jehovah's Witnesses immersed 434,906 adults in the period 1969–71, a substantially increased rate over previous years.

(*b*) John's baptism (Acts 19.3) was 'in symbol of repentance for forgiveness of sins' against the Mosaic law covenant (Luke 3.3). Jesus was baptized, not in repentance over sins (I Peter 2.22), but as 'presenting himself to his Father Jehovah to do his Father's "will"' (*Aid to Bible Understanding*, 'Baptism'; Heb. 10.5-7). Christ's disciples are baptized similarly, hence not with John's baptism, superseded by (a) and (c).

(*c*) A baptism which can be performed only by Jehovah God is that by holy spirit into Christ and his death (Rom. 6.3). Christ understood he was to be plunged into death but raised out of it on the third day, and he likened the experience to a baptism into death (Luke 12.50). His disciples were to experience a like baptism (Mark 10.39; Col. 3.3,4). At their anointing by holy spirit, Christ's footstep followers and joint heirs become united to him, their Head (I Cor.

12.12, 13). They belong to him. Baptism 'into his death' is climaxed by a willing sacrificial death like his and the reward of unity with him in resurrected heavenly glory.

(*d*) The baptism 'with fire' of Matt. 3.11 is understood to refer to Jerusalem's destruction in AD 70 (vv. 10-12).

A. HELEY

9. *Lutheran.* Baptism, according to the Lutheran confessional writings, is an ordinance commanded by God and instituted by Jesus Christ, through which a special promise of inward grace, regeneration and incorporation into Christ's body the church, is offered in conjunction with an outward material sign, water. It is therefore one of the true sacraments and normally necessary for salvation (*Large Catechism* IV; *Apol. der Conf. Aug* XIII, 3 ff., *Smalcaldic Articles* III, 4; *Augsburg Confession* = *CA* IX). It summons the baptized to lifelong trust and obedience and the expectation of perfect renewal at the last day.

The Lutheran doctrine of baptism developed during the Reformation period both as a reform of the Roman Catholic view and as a defence against more radical teachings, e.g. those of the Anabaptists.

The main points emphasized were:

1. That the effective working of baptism is *by faith*, not by the objective performance of the rite. Faith is not just an outward profession but is the fruit of God's grace growing within man until it is manifested outwardly. Faith is not proved empirically (*CA* IV, 57).

2. That since baptism is God's act, infant baptism is the clearest demonstration of this (Luther, *Werke*, Weimar, 1883 ff. = WA 26, 157; American edition, 1958 ff., 40,244). Luther held that baptism calls forth faith in infants, though he agreed that we do not understand how (WA 26,157; Amer. ed. 40,243). Child faith is inferred from child baptism, not vice versa.

3. The relationship of baptism to sin. Baptism is seen as a continuing work of God, preparing a Christian for the last day. The entire Christian life with its struggle against sin is a constant return to one's baptism. This eschatalogically oriented view of baptism helps to establish a tone of trust and prayerful responsibility and offers a key to the Christian quest for sanctification.

4. The responsibility of all who are baptized to the word of God and to the people of

God.

5. The exaltation of the baptismal vow of faithfulness to Christ in all walks of life.

Luther's interpretation generally set the pattern for the Lutheran church. Lutheran orthodoxy, however, as it developed in the sixteenth or seventeenth centuries transformed Luther's flexible, paradoxical view into a more fixed and institutionalized conception. In the background was what eventually became a complex and rigid analysis of the 'order of salvation' with a sharp distinction between justification and sanctification. The rise of rigid state-church systems also helped to externalize baptism.

The rite. At the Reformation, Luther conservatively simplified the traditional rite and laid the emphasis on earnest prayer for the child (WA 12,38 ff.). In the *Taufbüchlein* of 1523 he retained the medieval practices. In his revised order of 1526, which attained great popularity in Germany, he made some editorial revisions and omitted a number of symbolic features, such as the two anointings (*see* sections 1–3 above, and **Unction**). His positive contribution was a collect known as the 'Flood prayer'. For the mode of baptism he preferred immersion as more adequate to signify the drowning of sin, but he did not insist on this mode. Lutherans have agreed that immersion is not essential; pouring and sprinkling have become the most common modes in Lutheran churches.

During the eras of pietism and rationalism exorcism (q.v.) and renunciation generally dropped out of the Lutheran rite, though the latter has returned in many orders.

In Scandinavia the admonition to the sponsors and the salutation were added to the liturgy. In many of the churches the custom of signing the child with a cross (*see* **Cross, Sign of**) was retained or has reappeared. The renunciation of the devil is retained in most liturgies except that of the Church of Sweden.

The German churches experienced a proliferation of baptismal liturgies, basically on the lines of either Luther's rite of 1526 or Bugenhagen's of 1535. Since 1961 they all have a common one which closely follows Luther's.

In view of Luther's doctrine of the priesthood of all believers any Christian may in an emergency perform baptism according to the order laid down for such situations. Such a baptism, which is to be reported to the authorities of the church, is considered a proper function of the church (WA 12,181; 31,211).

The place of baptism in the worship of the church is less prominent in Europe, where the practice of private baptism in homes or at the church after public worship has developed, than in the American tradition, where there is a strong tendency to administer baptism at a public service to emphasize the communal significance of the sacrament.

E. J. R. H. S. VON SICARD

10. *Methodist.* John Wesley's *Sunday Service of the Methodists in North America*, 1784, is the foundation for subsequent initiation rites in Methodism. Its baptismal services were adopted from the *BCP*, 1662, of the Church of England, but with some drastic alterations.

The private baptism of infants was omitted. All references to godparents were omitted, though the 'Friends of the Child' were asked to give the name; consequently the vows of renunciation, belief and obedience in the name of the infant were omitted. In 1784 two references to regeneration were removed, but that in the prayer 'Almighty and Immortal God' was retained, as was the phrase 'that he may be born again' in the prayer 'Almighty and Everlasting God, Heavenly Father'. These prayers were both omitted, among other changes, in 1786; the prayer for the sanctification of the water was then still retained, but the central petition was in some editions modified and in the others wholly omitted. In 1784 Wesley added to the modes of baptism 'or sprinkle', but omitted the possibility of pouring water. A few of the 1784 copies retained the signing with the cross and the reception, but the others omitted them. Other changes were aimed at shortening the service.

In Great Britain there were further changes in the Wesleyan Church in 1846, 1864 and 1882 (in *Public Prayers and Services*), as well as in very different services produced in the non-Wesleyan Churches. After the union, *The Book of Offices*, 1936, produced a further revision, in which a leading feature of the service was the promises made by the parents.

In America the Methodist Episcopal Church (MEC) in 1864 and the Methodist Episcopal Church South (MECS) in 1866 added reference to others than parents, and the term 'sponsors' appeared in MEC in 1916 and is retained in the *Book of Worship (BW)*,

1964. The prayer for the sanctification of the water lasted till 1858 in MECS and 1916 in MEC. The 1792 *Discipline* allowed sprinkling, pouring or immersing, all of which are provided for in the 1964 rite, though sprinkling is almost always used.

In American Methodism today baptism is almost always performed in the presence of a congregation. Baptized children are regarded as 'preparatory members' in the United Methodist Church. The current rite has moved away from mention of OT precedents, from reference to washing from sin, and neglects the sense of incorporation into the church evident in Wesley. It stresses more the vows the parents or sponsors take for themselves in promising to rear the child as a Christian. The congregation also joins in this. The service is very brief, because of its insertion in the midst of the Sunday service.

An office for the 'Baptism of Children and Youth' appeared in 1914 (MECS) and remained till 1964.

Wesley's treatment of the ministration of baptism to such as are of 'riper years' was, in general, similar to his treatment of infant baptism. Several references to baptismal regeneration disappeared, rubrics and exhortations were dropped, and, in this case, the sign of the cross was definitely omitted in all editions of the Sunday service. The renunciation, creed and vow of obedience were retained, though the 1786 editions dropped the phrase in the creed (put interrogatively): 'that he went down into hell', and the same editions dropped the petition for the sanctification of the water. The British books made various changes, in the same years as for infants, though the changes did not always correspond. In America, Wesley's version remained remarkably intact until twentieth century revisions began pushing in the direction of brevity. Alternate gospel lessons were provided, four choices appearing in the *BW*, 1944. The American service of 1964 for baptism of 'youth and adults' remains brief, but represents a move away from the watering down of sacramental doctrine of the recent past with more emphasis on remission of sins and the reception of the Holy Spirit.

Wesley's most significant change was the omission of a confirmation rite (q.v.). Not till 1864 did MEC add an office for the reception of members and MECS followed in 1870. In 1886 MECS added a rubric to adult baptism to allow the minister to 'lay his hands on the subject . . . with suitable invocation'. Today baptism of youth and adults is often (but not always) followed by confirmation, though as yet most United Methodists are more familiar with the designation of this rite as 'reception into the church'. In Britain the Wesleyan Conference did not adopt a service for the 'Public Recognition of New Members' till 1894. There was a new form in 1936.

In general, the black Methodist churches have done less pruning of the Wesleyan services than the predominantly white churches, though the African Methodist Episcopal and the Christian Methodist Episcopal churches have alternate brief orders for infant baptism.

The British Conference of 1967 authorized a booklet 'Entry into the Church' for experimental use. The service for the baptism of infants has an entirely fresh structure: gospel, homily, the great prayer of baptism, promises by the congregation, the parents, the sponsors (the sponsors are optional), Apostles' Creed, presentation of the child by the parents, baptism, signation, reception, Aaronic blessing, final prayers, grace. The booklet then contains 'Public Reception into Full Membership, or Confirmation'; and then finally 'The Baptism of those who are able to answer for themselves with the Public Reception into Full Membership, or Confirmation'. This proceeds as follows: hymn, prayer, OT lesson, epistle, hymn, gospel, sermon, hymn, homily, the great prayer of baptism, promises by the congregation and the candidates, Apostles' Creed, further question to the candidates, baptism, homily when there are others to be confirmed who have been baptized previously, confirmation and reception, prayer, hymn, Lord's Supper, with alternative ending 'if, in exceptional circumstances and for good reason, Confirmation does not immediately follow the baptism of those who are able to answer for themselves'.

A. RAYMOND GEORGE
JAMES F. WHITE

11. *Old Catholic*. The teaching of the Old Catholic churches of the Utrecht Union on baptism is that of holy scripture and the catholic church. Baptism is administered with water 'in the name of the Father and of the Son and of the Holy Spirit', usually by affusion. The baptismal water is blessed in the liturgy of Easter night and kept in the

font. Infant baptism is generally practised.

Grace received at baptism is completed and developed by the sacrament of confirmation (q.v.), bestowed on children by the bishop, after the children have received instruction in the Christian faith. In the Old Catholic Church of the Netherlands confirmation is brought into closer connection with baptism by the renewal of baptismal vows. In other countries, this takes place on receiving first communion. In the Polish National Catholic Church in America, baptism and confirmation together are regarded as a single sacrament: 'The Word of God, heard and preached', is regarded as the seventh (or second) sacrament.

The baptismal rite of the Old Catholic churches is based on the *Ordo Baptismi Parvulorum* of the *Rituale Romanum* of Paul V; it is partly an exact translation and partly a free revision. In the German and Swiss rites of baptism there is a clear concern to explain the sacred actions by accompanying words.

Taking over the order of baptism from the old *Rituale Romanum* raises a number of difficult problems: (1) This rite is not made for infant baptism, but is an abbreviation of the rite for adult baptism. In some Old Catholic rites of baptism, therefore, attempts have long been made to adapt the content of the prayers to the normal situation (infant baptism!), for example, with the addition of the reading of the 'children's gospel' (Mark 10.13-16). On the rare occasions when adults are baptized, John 3.1-21 or Rom. 6.3-11 are substituted. Mark 10.13-16 (for adults, John 3.1-8) together with the command to baptize (Matt. 28.18-20) stand at the beginning of the Swiss rite as a biblical foundation for baptism and especially infant baptism. (2) The first part of the earlier Roman, and so also Old Catholic, baptismal rite contains the rites of the catechumenate (q.v.), which were originally spread over a considerable length of time; here, however, they are compressed into a single celebration. The significance of some of these rites is no longer immediately recognizable, as they are no longer connected with their original situation. (3) Individual rites seem strange and incomprehensible to men of today, e.g. touching the candidate's ears and nose (*cf.* Mark 7.34) with spittle to the accompaniment of the word 'ephphatha'. In the Old Catholic rites, however, this has long been replaced by a simple touching (without spittle) of mouth and ears. The repeated exorcisms (q.v.), too, have a distressing effect at the baptism of small children and seem unjustified. They are therefore either omitted from the ritual of Old Catholic churches or replaced by other texts. The custom of breathing on the person baptized is retained in part, but more stress is laid on the idea of insufflation (q.v.), i.e. the breathing in of the Holy Spirit, than on the 'exsufflation' (the breathing out of evil spirits).

In the context of liturgical renewal which is also taking place in Old Catholic churches, new formulae for baptism, too, are being worked out, in which the difficulties of the earlier rite, mentioned above, are taken into account.

In the Netherlands, baptism was administered in Dutch as early as the eighteenth century, according to formulae which were a complete literal translation of the *ordo baptismi parvulorum* from the *Rituale Romanum*. In 1902 the bishops introduced a revised text. Though they kept to the old Roman pattern for the most part, the exsufflation and the exorcisms disappeared. After the threefold renunciation of Satan the promise 'to love the Lord your God with all your heart and with all your soul, and with all your strength, and with all your mind, and your neighbour as yourself' is required. At the first anointing a prayer for Christ's grace was added, for strength to fight the good fight.

Between World War I and World War II it became the practice more and more to baptize the child in the presence of the mother, and therefore after a few weeks rather than immediately after birth, as the strict Dutch practice had been before. Also, increasingly, baptism took place immediately after the eucharist, in the presence of the congregation. For the past few years there has been a tendency to baptize during the eucharist, after the gospel and the sermon.

As an example of an Old Catholic order of baptism, there follows here a short description of baptism in the Old Catholic Church in Germany. After an address, the priest assures himself of the willingness of the sponsors or the person to be baptized, and informs him of the chief commandment (Luke 10.27). The *exsufflatio* is hardly used any more. The exorcisms have been replaced by a single formula, entirely in accord with the spirit of the Bible. Thereupon the priest signs the person to be baptized on the forehead and chest with the sign of the cross, and salt, which has previously been blessed, is placed on his lips. The reading of a passage from the gospels (Mark 10.13-16 or John 3.1-21) has been taken from the ritual of Cologne, but it has its roots in the *traditio evangeliorum* from earliest times.

The repetition of the creed and Lord's Prayer no longer has its original form of question and answer, but the two are said together. The renunciation of Satan, which occurs in the earliest baptismal formulae of East and West, and has also been preserved in Anglican and Protestant forms of service, is summed up in a single clear question. There follows the anointing of the breast with oil. After a threefold question about belief, the priest pours the baptismal water three times on the head of the person to be baptized, in the form of a cross, and says, 'N, I baptize you in the name of the Father and of the Son and of the Holy Spirit.'

The baptism is followed by the anointing of the head with chrism (see **Unction**), the bestowal of a white baptismal garment and a lighted candle. The priest dismisses the person baptized and his sponsors with the blessing.

KURT PURSCH
A. E. RÜTHY
C. TOL

12. *Pentecostal.* In classical Pentecostalism (*cf.* **Pentecostal Worship**), many churches have no given rite of baptism but improvise a a ceremony according, as it is said, to the movement of the Spirit. A rite of baptism which the author observed in the Bahama Islands consisted of a procession from the church to the sea, accompanied with singing, hand clapping, ejaculatory prayers. On the beach the pastor addressed the faithful, admonishing them to repent of their sins and to accept Christ as their personal Saviour. Baptism was by immersion. The spontaneity of the people and deep sense of prayer and celebration made it evident that the participants were not going through a prescribed rite, but were deeply involved in prayer. In many classical Pentecostal groups the baptismal rite is accompanied with tongues, prophecies, and in one African church, the rite is accompanied with a prayer for healing. In the Church of the

Twelve Apostles (Nackabah), an African church, the baptismal candidates are properly soaped and bathed (W. Hollenweger, *The Pentecostals*, 1971, p.391). Within classical Pentecostalism one can also find baptismal rites written down and printed in a disciplinary book or a minister's manual. These would include prayers, exhortations, and either the Trinitarian baptismal formula or a formula mentioning only the name of Jesus. These rites would be used with great freedom by the ministers.

Most classical Pentecostals (e.g. Assemblies of God) follow a Baptist conception of baptism, that is, for adults who have made a personal commitment to Christ. But there is a sizeable minority of classical Pentecostals who use sprinkling: the majority of Chilean Pentecostals, the largest of the German churches, a Yugoslav group, and in the beginning, the Finnish and Norwegian movements (Hollenweger, *The Pentecostals*, p.392). Often the pastor dips his hand in a bowl of water and rubs the head of the candidate. One American directory says that 'the candidate shall have the right to choose whatever mode of baptism he prefers' (*Discipline of the Pentecostal Holiness Church*, 1961, p.78). The Quaker Pentecostals think the whole baptismal controversy peripheral. Both a Chilean and a German church allow adult baptism *and* infant baptism and therefore have baptism by immersion or sprinkling. In addition to these groups, all of which are Trinitarian, there are the Pentecostal modalists, or 'Jesus only' groups, which take Acts 2.38 to mean that the Trinitarian formula is not to be used, but rather candidates should be baptized only in the name of Jesus. Among some of the Churches of God (USA) there are groups which baptize only in the name of the Father (E. Clark, *The Small Sects in America*, 1949, p.105).

Neo-Pentecostals (*cf.* **Pentecostal Worship**) would tend to follow the rite of their respective churches. Some Lutheran Pentecostals have taken over the patterns of classical Pentecostals and have been re-baptized by immersion, not necessarily because their baptism by pouring was thought invalid. When a Catholic priest who is involved in the charismatic renewal baptizes a child of a Catholic neo-Pentecostal couple, the rite of the Roman Catholic Church would be followed but there can, in addition, be quiet praying in tongues, interpretation, prophecy, and free prayer.

In Chile men and women admitted that they were deeply moved the first time they attended a Pentecostal service: 'Not because of the beauty of the ceremonial – oh, no, it is not as beautiful as with Catholics – but because people spoke to me, the pastor shook my hand, and I was able to sing and pray with them' (C. Lalive d'Epinay, *Haven of the Masses*, 1969, p. 49).

At their worst, Pentecostal baptismal liturgies can be theologically impoverished and too subjectivistic. At their best, Pentecostal baptismal liturgies are successful because each individual is a participant, because their liturgies are essentially oral rather than printed (and usually oral even when printed), because they are simple, direct, and personal, because baptism is more immediately a prayer act than an external ritual, because whether dealing with a pre-literate or post-literate culture they know how to elicit a personal commitment through involvement in an experience which is self-explanatory, because the baptismal rite is itself an instrument of evangelization.

Finally, their rites are not techniques and are not separable from their spirituality, which is fullness of life in the Spirit and the exercise of the gifts of the Spirit. (For bibliography *see under* **Pentecostal Worship**.)

KILIAN MCDONNELL

13. *Plymouth Brethren*. The Open Brethren almost without exception practise the baptism of believers only, on personal confession of faith, and the accepted mode is, almost invariably, total immersion. If immersion is impracticable for reasons of health or age, such token baptisms as affusion or sprinkling are not employed; the will is simply accepted for the deed. In these respects they closely resemble the Baptists; they do not, however, treat their baptismal doctrine and practice as so essential a feature of their church life that they could properly be described as Baptists.

Baptism is commonly understood among them as an act of public confession and Christian obedience, not as a vehicle of grace or as necessary to salvation. Probably the majority of those baptized among them are young people who have either grown up in the fellowship with their families or have become attached to it through various departments of its youth work; but one finds people of all age-groups asking for it and receiving it. It is normally administered before a congregation; most of the Open Brethren's meeting-places have suitable baptisteries sunk in the floor and boarded over when not in use.

Open Brethren do not, for the most part, treat baptism as an indispensable condition for admission to the communion table or to church membership; this would unfairly exclude Christians who have been baptized in infancy and cannot conscientiously recognize any obligation to receive 'responsible' baptism. But the baptismal teaching given at their meetings is uniformly that connected with believers' baptism.

Among the Exclusive Brethren the situation is much less uniform. Those who adhere most closely to the Darbyite tradition follow J. N. Darby in baptizing the infant children of their church members; this practice is commonly called 'household' baptism' (on the basis of Acts 16.15, 31-34; I Cor. 1.16, etc.). In the Taylorite connection such baptized children are regularly admitted to church fellowship at the age of twelve, if not earlier. Some of Darby's closest associates who disagreed with infant baptism found it expedient not to press their views: when an argumentative lady once asked him what his principal lieutenant, George Vicesimus Wigram (1805-1879), held about baptism, he is said to have replied, 'Madam, he holds his tongue.' And when the first major division took place within the Exclusive ranks (1881), although the issue had nothing to do with baptism, practically all those who held 'Baptist' views seceded with William Kelly (1820-1906), while the paedobaptists went 'nearly solid' for Darby (W. B. Neatby, *A History of the Plymouth Brethren*, 1901, pp. 237f.).

An interesting situation arises when reunions take place (as they happily do from time to time) between groups or congregations which have incidentally differed from each other in baptismal doctrine or practice; there proves in practice to be no obstacle to the peaceful coexistence of the two ways (believers' baptism and infants' baptism). Tension is perhaps prevented by the fact that among the paedobaptist Exclusives infants are in any case baptized at home whereas Open Brethren and others who baptize believers do so in public.

F. F. BRUCE

14. *Reformed*. The baptismal rites in the Western church at the eve of the Reformation show that many ceremonies had been added to the practice of the early church, but these were not essential to the sacrament and their omission in cases of emergency did not affect its validity. This led to revision. In 1523, Luther published his *Das Taufbüchlein verdeutscht* (*Works*, Weimar XII, 42-48), which with minor alterations was a German translation of the medieval order in use at Wittenberg. When Diebold Schwarz translated the order in use at Strasbourg in 1524, he drew heavily on this. This was revised in 1525 (Hubert, *Die Stras. lit.*, 37-52), but it was now more than a translation, for the whole rite was re-cast. Under the influence of Bucer, further revisions were carried out during the years 1525-33, and it was on these Farel based his *La Manière et façon*. To Farel and Bucer, Calvin was much indebted for his Strasbourg rite. This later was simplified for use in Geneva (*Op.*, VI, 184-191) and became the determining influence in the *Form of Prayers* (*FP*, 1556) of the English exiles there and the Scottish *Book of Common Order* (*BCO*, 1564).

Calvin's Strasbourg order, as found in the 1545 edition published by Paul Garnier, is:

1. Scripture sentence (Ps. 124.8).
2. Question: Do you present this child to be baptized, earnestly desiring that he may be engrafted in the mystical body of Christ?
3. Long exposition and exhortation.
4. Prayer for grace and reception of the child into the Kingdom of Christ.
5. The Lord's Prayer.
6. Question: Do you wish this child baptized in the name of the Father and of the Son, and of the Holy Spirit?
7. Apostles' Creed, said by parents.
8. Exhortation to parents.
9. Baptism with water in the triune name.
10. Declaration that the child is a member of Christ's church.

In *FP* and *BCO* the order is altered to 2 3 7 4 5 9 and a concluding prayer of thanksgiving and for the blessing of the Holy Spirit.

In the Reformed Church baptism was always placed in the setting of the worship of the people of God, the rite following the reading and preaching of the word. It was to be administered only 'in the face of the congregation'. Baptism, being a sacrament of the gospel, could only be administered by a minister of the word. For this reason also, the font (q.v.) was removed from the church-door and placed near the pulpit.

The Reformed Church sought to remove all non-scriptural elements from the rite and to make it relevant to the baptism of infants. Whereas some other traditions superimpose a baptismal order upon the existing medieval rite, which was designed in the first place for the baptism of adult believers, in Reformed rites no vicarious profession of faith is required of the parents or godparents, the children being admitted to baptism on the grounds of the covenant of grace. For this reason also, exorcisms (q.v.) and renunciations are laid aside as being inappropriate to the baptism of children of Christian parents. The Creed is repeated by the parents as the faith which they themselves believe as members of the church of Christ and into which they wish their children baptized, they taking a vow to bring them up therein. While there is no objection to godparents, the chief sponsor is, generally speaking, the father of the child.

In the early Reformed rites there is no epiclesis in the baptismal prayer. The reason for this could be that in the medieval church the consecration of the font had become a separate rite, or perhaps it was held that the declaration of intention of baptism was sufficient. Baptism is normally by affusion, but nothing is prescribed as to whether it should be single or triple. The latter has always been the practice of the Reformed churches in France, Switzerland, Germany and Hungary.

The order in *FP* (1556) and *BCO* (1564) remained the practice in the Reformed churches in Britain until it was replaced by that in the Westminster *Directory for the Public Worship of God* in 1645. Its order is:

Exhortation.
Prayer, including epiclesis.
Inquiry as to name.
Baptism with water in the triune name.
Prayer of thanksgiving and for the blessing of the Holy Spirit.

Here no profession of faith is required of the sponsors, but the adopting Act of the General Assembly of the Church of Scotland shows that the same requirement was continued. This is also true of Irish Presbyterianism. The

Directory, being really only one extended rubric, resulted in a period of decadence. Renewal did not begin until the Church Service Society published the first edition of its *Euchologion* in 1867.

(*a*) *Rites in English*. The editors of *Euchologion* (1867) said concerning the baptismal order: 'The following Service is based upon the Baptismal Service in John Knox's *Book of Common Order*. It is condensed and considerably curtailed; but may be regarded as presenting the original and genuine doctrine of the Scottish Church regarding the sacrament of Baptism.' Several revisions followed, and the fifth (1884) may be said to have become normative. It is:

Scripture sentence (Ps. 124.8).
Scripture readings: Matt. 28.18-20; Mark 10.13-16; Acts 2.38-39.
Vows: Apostles' Creed, or alternative, answered by parents; upbringing of child.
Prayer: based on Greek, *BCP* and Catholic Apostolic rites with epiclesis from Westminster *Directory*.
Baptism with water in the triune name.
Apostolic or Aaronic blessing (optional).
Declaration that the child is received into the church: from 'Savoy Liturgy' (1661).
Prayer: from *BCO* (1564) and 'Larger Catechism'.
The Lord's Prayer.
Apostolic benediction.

This rite won its way into most of the English Reformed rites, and became almost universally accepted, remaining substantially unaltered in the Scottish *BCO* (1940) and American *Book of Common Worship* (*BCW*, 1946). In recent years, however, revision has taken place as a result of continental, Scottish and Irish research.

The Irish *Book of Public Worship* (*BPW*, 1965) may be taken as representing a transitional stage between the old and the new, (1) having references in the scripture readings to God's covenant with Abraham and the baptism of Jesus, (2) requiring the congregation to take a specific vow; and (3) departing from the traditional wording of the parents' vow to bring up the child in the Christian faith by adopting the form in *BCW* of the Church of South India.

Good examples of the new rites are *BCO* (Presbyterian Church, Canada, 1964), *Public Service Book* (*PSB*, England and Wales, 1968)

and the Scottish 'Order for Holy Baptism' (1969). While there are variations in these orders the last may be outlined. It is:

Liturgy of the word.
Scripture readings: Matt. 28.18-20 (reference to baptism of Jesus), Acts 2.38-39 (statement on end of baptism), Mark 10.13-16.
Vows of parents, added first in Calvin's rite.
Congregation accepts responsibility by reciting Apostles' Creed.
Prayer: *Sursum corda*, adoration, epiclesis.
Baptism with water in the triune name.
Aaronic blessing.
Declaration that the child is received into the church.
Matt. 18.5, 6, 10 may be read.
Prayer: supplication and intercession.
The Lord's Prayer.
Psalm or hymn.
Benediction: 'The peace of God . . .'

The English-Welsh and Canadian rites both open with Ps. 124.8. In the former the reference to the baptism of Jesus is omitted, but in the latter Mark 1.9-11 is read. In both the Apostles' Creed is said by the congregation before the parents take their vows. The Scottish rite, in 1963, re-introduced Calvin's first question to the parents. The other two do not do so. The English-Welsh rite adds a vow for godparents, if there are any. In the baptismal prayer the *Sursum corda* is omitted by both, the Canadian also omitting the epiclesis. Both conclude with the apostolic benediction.

While theologically these rites add nothing new to what was always the doctrine of baptism in the Reformed Church, they do give fuller expression to it.

The Presbyterian Churches in America used the 1788 revision of the Westminster *Directory*, and this practice, apart from the experiments of individuals, continued until the formation of a Church Service Society, on the Scottish model, in 1897. Its instigators and leaders were Henry van Dyke and Louis Benson. This led eventually to the *BCW: Prepared by the Committee of the General Assembly of the Presbyterian Church in the USA for Voluntary Use* (1906), in which the baptismal rite was firmly based on a 'covenant theology', but rather defective structurally. This was revised in 1932, when it was also adopted by the Southern Presbyterians 'for the optional and selective use of our ministers'. The impetus for a third edition came from the publication of the *BCO* (1940) by the Church of Scotland, and this appeared in 1946. The new baptismal rite was considerably influenced by the Scottish and it reveals a more careful handling of the theological implications of baptism.

In 1955, the Presbyterian Church in the USA set up a committee to revise the *BCW*, and in this work three things are of note: (1) the United Presbyterian Church of North America and the Presbyterian Church in the United States (Southern) decided to participate together in the project; (2) in 1961 a revision of the old *Directory* was published setting out basic principles; and (3) before issuing a revised *BCW*, a *BCW: Provisional Services* (1966) was prepared for use and report. This is the baptismal rite now in use, and is noteworthy for three distinctive features: (1) 'the service is designed to be used both for the baptism of adults and for the baptism of infants'; (2) opportunity is provided for an elder representing the session to take a part in the service; and (3) 'the service includes opportunity for the whole congregation to renew baptismal vows in a unison prayer'.

(*b*) *Rites in French*. The liturgical movement in the Reformed Church in France begins with *La Liturgie d'Eugène Bersier* (1874). This work was destined to exercise a wide influence not only in France but in French-speaking Switzerland and elsewhere. The result of this movement may be illustrated by the Genevan rite (1945):

Scripture sentence: (Ps. 124.8).
Declaration of intention.
Scripture readings: Ezek. 36.25-28; Matt. 28.18-20; Acts 2.38-39.
Baptismal instruction.
Vows.
Exhortation to parents.
Baptism with water in the triune name.
Prayer of supplication and intercession.
The Lord's Prayer.
Benediction (Phil. 4.7; Rom. 15.33).

Here, as in the English-speaking rites, recent research has exercised a great influence. While they differ structurally, good examples of the new rites are those in the Canton de Vaud (1962) and in France (1963). The order for the latter is:

Welcome based on Mark 10.13 and Ezek.

36.24-27.
Invocation and adoration.
Apostles' Creed said by congregation.
Institution: Matt. 28.18-20.
Prayer.
Baptismal instruction.
Exhortation to parents.
Desire of parents.
Involvement of congregation.
Baptism with water in the triune name.
Vows of parents, may be placed before baptism.

The rite for Vaud adds Mark 1.9-11 and Acts 2.38-39 to the readings, which are followed by the creed and a prayer based on Geneva (1542) and *La Liturgie des Églises du Pays de Vaud* (1725). Then come the vows, institution, and a prayer from the Roman rite. Neither rite contains an epiclesis, although the Vaud rite has a petition that the child may be 'baptized with water and the Spirit'. The baptismal instruction (omitted in Vaud) is based on Strasbourg (1536) and Geneva (1542). In the French rite the vows are presented as laid upon the parents by the church, which itself is a 'witness' to the baptism and required to take upon itself 'responsibility' for the baptized. Baptism is always with water 'in the name of the Father, and of the Son, and of the Holy Spirit'. The concluding prayer is based upon Genevan, French or Vaudoise sources. The Vaud rite ends with a declaration, 'We receive you into the family of God, the church of Jesus Christ.'

(*c*) *Rites in German*. The baptismal order in the German rites, broadly speaking, is:

Scripture readings: Matt. 28.18-20, Mark 10.13-16.
Baptismal instruction.
Prayer: supplication and intercession.
Apostles' Creed, sometimes said by the congregation.
Vows of parents and godparents.
Baptism with water in the triune name.
Exhortation to parents and congregation.
Prayer of thanksgiving.

This may be taken as representative, even though some service-books in addition include the form in *Der Taufordnung der Pfälzischen Kirchenordnung* (1563).

The scripture readings from Matthew and Mark are always included as the warrant for baptism. The baptismal instruction is drawn from many sources – Strasbourg (1524), a'Lasco (1550), Geneva (1542), Pfalz (1563) and Basle (1572), as are the questions to the parents. The words introducing the Apostles' Creed are drawn from Micronius (1554), Pfalz (1563), or Basle (1572). Baptism is with water 'in the name of the Father, and of the Son, and of the Holy Spirit'. The exhortation is based on Zurich (1529) and Pfalz (1563). The supplications and intercessions have a common content but vary considerably in different rites, according to whether or not they are derived from Zurich (1525), Strasbourg (1536), Geneva (1542), a'Lasco (1550), Scottish *BCO* (1564), Basle (1572), Bern (1598), Cassel (1657), or St Gallen (1699). None includes an epiclesis. Generally speaking several thanksgivings are provided, but they almost always include a'Lasco (1550) and Pfalz (1563).

(*d*) *Confirmation, Baptism of the Sick, Baptism of Believers.* All these rites contain an order for confirmation (*see* **Confirmation**). In cases of sickness and emergency, private baptism is permitted. The liturgy of the Reformed Church in France provides a separate rite for this, and others contain special prayers. Here it might be worth making into a universal practice the decision of the Perth Assembly (1618):

> That the minister shall the next Lord's day after such private baptism declare in the church that the infant was so baptized, and therefore ought to be received as one of the true flock of Christ's fold.

The early Reformed liturgies and the Westminster *Directory* make no provision for the baptism of adult believers. The first such rite was prepared by the Dutch Reformed Church in 1604. The first in English is in the third edition of *Euchologion* (1874). The latter casts the rite as baptism-confirmation, for the baptism is followed by prayer 'with imposition of hands'. This theological position remains basic in all the rites, and the changes taking place are parallel to those in the rites for the children of believers.

(*e*) *Theology.* Baptism is a gift of God to men through his church, in which he 'presents' and 'seals' Christ to them, admitting them to the fellowship of the church and demanding from them the response of faith and a life of godliness through the power of the Holy Spirit. All these rites do set forth clearly the Reformed doctrine of 'the grace

of baptism'. At the same time, two questions require to be raised: (1) If in a sacrament God, through the 'visible sign', 'presents and seals Christ', should the prayer before the act of baptism not always include a petition that the 'visible sign' may fulfil God's purpose? (2) Does the eschatological significance of baptism always receive adequate expression?

JOHN M. BARKLEY

15. *Seventh-day Adventist.* Seventh-day Adventists believe that baptism is the ceremony of initiation into the Christian church, and is therefore a solemn ordinance, the proper form of which is to be administered by immersion. Baptism is the antitype of the Genesis flood, which prefigured the freely accepted 'reduced flood'. It 'typifies the death, burial, and resurrection of Christ, and openly expresses faith in His saving grace' (*Church Manual*, 1967, p. 58). As such it is a condition of entrance into church membership. In addition to the etymological argument stemming from the basic meaning of the Greek word *baptizo* ('to dip', 'to plunge', 'to overwhelm'), Seventh-day Adventists hold that the soundest argument for baptism by immersion is the theological one derived from Paul's symbolism (Rom. 6.1-11) of baptism as representing death, burial and resurrection. Baptism signifies death to sin, moral resurrection in this life and corporal resurrection in the life to come. The practice of another mode of baptism by the apostolic church would have rendered meaningless the significance of the symbolic character Paul gave to the baptismal ceremony.

In harmony with other followers of the Baptist tradition, Seventh-day Adventists reject infant baptism, believing that there is no biblical support for this custom. Accordingly they practice believer's baptism, administering it only to those who have reached accountability and meet the prerequisite of active faith.

Baptism is not just a momentary act, but should be a continuous sign witnessing to the believer's acceptance of Jesus Christ as his personal Saviour. Persons joining the SDAC, who have already been baptized by immersion, are not rebaptized, except when they desire rebaptism. Seventh-day Adventists who have apostatized and have publicly violated the faith and principles of the SDAC, thus nullifying the sign and witness of baptism, are in the case of reconversion asked to enter the church as in the beginning, namely by baptism (*Church Manual*, 1967, p. 72).

Adventists do not view baptism as a ritual washing with some kind of supernatural power or magical cleansing of sin *per se* without true repentance. In common with their Protestant heritage, they therefore reject the sacramentalist view of baptism as imparting grace *ex opere operato*, that is, as an act or sign that, in and of itself, imparts grace and effects salvation. Though baptism does not automatically convey grace, it is intended to be a public sign of grace that comes through incorporation into the family of God.

Baptismal candidates are thoroughly instructed in the Christian faith, and prior to baptism an examination takes place either before the church board or at the baptismal service itself, when they are asked to affirm publicly their assent to the teachings of the SDAC. Baptism is usually administered by an ordained minister, but 'in his absence the local church elder may officiate' (*Manual for Ministers*, 1954, p. 84) after making proper arrangements with the conference or mission president.

A typical baptismal service is preceded by a hymn, prayer and short discourse on the meaning of baptism. As each candidate is immersed, the congregation often sings a stanza of some appropriate hymn. Where the local church does not have a baptistery, a stream, lake or other aquatic facility is used.

Before the candidate is immersed, the minister performing the baptism raises his right hand and pronounces the following formula (or a very similar one): 'My brother, upon the profession of your faith in Jesus Christ as your personal Saviour, I now baptize you into the name of the Father, and of the Son, and of the Holy Spirit. Amen' (*Manual for Ministers*, 1954, p. 88).

B. B. BEACH

Baptism and Confirmation, Prayer Book Studies I, 1952; *Baptism and Confirmation*, Report of the Church of England Liturgical Commission, 1959; *Baptism and Confirmation Today*, Report of the Joint Committees on Baptism, Confirmation and the Holy Communion of the Convocations of Canterbury and York, 1955; J. Baillie, *Baptism and Conversion*, 1964; *Le Baptême dans l'Église Réformée par un groupe de pasteurs*, 1954; J. M. Barkley, *Worship of the Reformed Church*, 1966; G. W. Bromiley, *Baptism and the Anglican Reformers*, 1953; J. D. Benoit, *Initiation à la liturgie de l'Église Réformée de France*, 1956; R. L. Child, *A Conversation about Baptism*, 1963; Church of Scotland, *Biblical Doctrine of Baptism*, 1958; N. Cryer, *By What Rite?* 1969; J. G. Davies, *The Spirit, the Church, and the Sacraments*, 1954; W. Elert, *The Structure of Lutheranism*, 1962; J. D. C. Fisher, *Christians Initiations – the Reformation Period*, 1970; W. Jetter, *Die Taufe beim jungen Luther*, 1954; R. Josefson, *Luthers tära omdepet*, 1944; U. Kury, *Die altkatholische Kirche* (Die Kirchen der Welt II), 1966, pp. 185-187 (Old Catholic); G. W. H. Lampe, *The Seal of the Spirit*, 1967; G. W. H. Lampe and D. M. Paton, eds., *One Lord, One Baptism*, Studies in Ministry and Worship 17, 1960; M. Luther, *The Holy and Blessed Sacrament of Baptism* (*Works*, American ed., vol. 35), 1960; *Manual for Ministers*, 1965 (Seventh-day Adventist); A. J. Mason, *The Relation of Confirmation to Baptism*. 1893; B. S. Moss, ed., *Crisis for Baptism*, 1965; K. F. Müller and W. Blankenburg, eds., *Liturgia. Handbuch des evangelischen Gottesdienstes*, 5. Taufe, Konfirmation, 1952; Don F. Neufeld, *Seventh-day Adventist Encyclopedia*, 1966, pp. 102ff.; C. E. Pocknee, *The Rites of Christian Initiation*, 1962; A. Segond, *Le Baptême Chrétien*, 1954; *Seventh-day Adventist Church Manual*, 1967; G. Wainwright, *Christian Initiation*, Ecumenical Studies in History, No. 10, 1969; J. Warns, *Baptism*, ET, 1957; E. C. Whitaker, *Documents of the Baptismal Liturgy*, 1960.

Baptist Worship

Baptist worship can only be understood from the Baptist understanding of the church. For Baptists, the chief manifestation of the visible church is the gathered congregation. The gathered or local congregation which is faithful has within it, according to Baptist ecclesiology, the fullness of the church visible. It is made up of persons who have committed themselves to Jesus Christ and his church and upon profession of faith have been baptized and received into church membership. Such a congregation 'gathers' for worship. Worship is celebration of the gospel, i.e. the good news in Jesus Christ. Thus worship for Baptists is primarily a time of praise and thanksgiving, but it is also marked by private and corporate confession, by petition and intercession. The worshipper seeks a living presence of Christ and that spiritual renewal which will enable him to live as a Christian in the world. Congregational worship can take place where two or three are gathered together in the name of the Lord, and he is in the midst of them. Robert Browning's recollection of his Christmas visit to a nonconformist chapel describes well Baptist worship at its heart:

> I remember, he did say
> Doubtless that, to this world's end,
> Two or three should meet and pray,
> He would be in the midst, their friend;
> Certainly he was there with them!
> (Robert Browning, *Christmas Eve and Easter Day*)

The modern Baptist movement had its beginnings in the early years of the seventeenth century as a part of English separatism. It manifested itself first in a congregation of separatists which had fled persecution in England and settled in Holland. Under the leadership of John Smyth this group in the first decade of the seventeenth century separated from the parent congregation over the question of believer's baptism. Smyth's group felt that a local congregation (church) should be made up of those who were baptized after they had made their personal professions of faith. Such 'gathered' congregations met regularly for worship, yet little is known of the form and content of their worship. No manuals of worship have come down to us, for they did not exist. For these early Baptists, such books would have been hindrances to spiritual worship. Smyth himself left a few directions which doubtless reflect the way in which the Baptist congregation of Amsterdam worshipped. He wrote:

1. We hold that the worship of the New Testament properly so called is spiritual proceeding originally from the heart: and that reading out of a book (though it is a lawful ecclesiastical action) is no part of spiritual worship, but rather the invention of the man of sin, it being substituted for a part of spiritual worship.
2. We hold that seeing prophesying is a part of spiritual worship: therefore in time of prophesying it is unlawful to have the book (i.e. the Bible) as a help before the eye.
3. We hold that seeing singing a psalm is a

part of spiritual worship: therefore it is unlawful to have the book before the eye in time of singing a psalm (John Smyth, *The Differences of the Churches of the Separation: Contayning a Description of the Leitourgie and Ministerie of the Visible Church*, 1609, in W. T. Whitley, *The Works of John Smyth*, 1915, p, 273).

According to a contemporary description, the Sunday service in Smyth's church would begin at 8 a.m. with a reading from the Bible. The book would then be set aside. Sermons up to five in number, as time would permit, would be preached on the text. These would be interspersed with prayers (from the heart); psalms from memory would be sung. At 12 noon the service would be concluded with prayer. Another service following the same pattern would begin at 2 p.m. and go on until 5 or 6 o'clock.

Smyth's worship pointed to the centrality of the remembered and experienced word and the freedom of the Spirit in worship. In these points he made a permanent contribution to Baptist liturgy. When the refugee congregations returned in part to England and the Baptist movement began to grow, the main stream of Baptist church life that developed took on the worship patterns of its Presbyterian and Congregational counterparts. The typical worship of these churches consisted of the reading and proclamation of the word preceded and followed by scripture sentences, prayers and the singing of psalms, particularly at communion services. Later, hymns came into general usage.

With the Congregationalists and others, Baptists became a part of the Free Church Movement. While the term 'free', when used in relation to the church, has a variety of meanings, such as freedom from clerical control, freedom from the state, freedom to organize and maintain churches, freedom of worship, etc., in relation to worship it means primarily freedom from prescribed liturgical forms. Thus the Baptists, as other Free Churches, have no one required form of worship such as the divine liturgy of the Orthodox churches, the Roman mass, or the forms of worship of the Anglican *BCP*.

To say that Baptists have no required orders for public worship does not mean that Baptists believe that worship should be disordered. Worship that is careless and undisciplined is an offence to God and may be the means of destroying rather than of building the faith of a congregation. Baptists frequently quote Paul's well-known words on spiritual gifts. He urged that 'all things should be done decently and in order' (I Cor. 14.40). He further directed the Corinthian congregation: 'When you come together, each one has a hymn, a lesson, a revelation, a tongue, or an interpretation. Let all things be done for edification . . . For you can all prophesy one by one, so that all may learn and all may be encouraged . . . For God is not a God of confusion but of peace' (I Cor. 14.26, 31, 33). Baptists believe in ordered worship but not required ordered worship. For them, as for others, word and table are the two basic points for the ordering of Christian worship, for here the primary foci of God's revelation are presented. The believer responds to this revelation by acts of adoration, repentance, thanksgiving, petition, dedication, and intercession. His response comes in the forms of prayers, litanies, doxologies, *Glorias*, sung psalms and hymns, the spoken word, and the breaking of bread and drinking of wine.

In a Baptist church, the responsibility for public worship lies with the congregation. No hierarchy hands down forms and materials for worship. This means that great variety characterizes Baptist worship. Some Baptist churches, particularly those that have been influenced by the movement for liturgical renewal, have formal services. They use set prayers which are read from printed orders distributed to the congregation beforehand. Choirs and clergy are robed, and church buildings are often neo-Gothic in architecture. In such churches one can find present lamps, candles and crosses, often set upon altars backed by a reredos and decked out in seasonal liturgical colours. On the other hand, Baptist worship may be completely informal and spontaneous. Such informality and spontaneity would characterize most Black church worship in America. While Black church worship does have a structure or pattern, the structure is not allowed to interfere with the free flow of the spirit. The congregation gathers to find joy in the Lord and it feels that such joy can only be hindered by set forms. In between the highly formalized and the completely informal, most Baptists worship according to a pattern generally developed over a period of time by the congregation and yet sufficiently free to allow for considerable spontaneity.

Baptist worship has been largely conditioned by the culture in which it has found itself. Reference was made above to the informality and spontaneity of Black church worship. This spirit goes back to the days when the Black man was a slave and the church was the only place where he could express his human freedom. Thus in the church he turned himself loose and lived, at least during the time of worship, as a man free in the sight of God. On the American frontier the characteristic Baptist service was the revival meeting. Here lively singing, testimonies as to the freedom and forgiveness which has come in Christ, and spontaneous prayer characterized the first part of the revival service. These 'preliminaries' prepared the congregation for the reading and the preaching of the word and the call to repentance, followed by the response of the sinner or 'backslider'. When these revival services resulted in churches, the people who formed them had become used to the style of the revival meeting and the services of worship tended to be planned as a repetition of the revival service. In Germany and the Scandinavian countries where Baptists arose out of the pietistic ferment of past centuries, worship still has strong overtones of pietistic devotional life. Bible reading and meditation, spontaneous prayer and introspective hymns tend to characterize such services. In England as well as New England, Baptist worship has been strongly influenced by the plain and decorous character of the chapel service.

Historically, Baptists have been strong exponents of the Reformation doctrine of *sola scriptura*. Nothing is to be done that is unscriptural and everything that is done is to be done in accordance with the scriptures. Reading and proclamation of the word have occupied a central place in Baptist worship. The Baptist stress upon the importance of preaching has produced a striking number of 'great' preachers. From John Bunyan to Charles Haddon Spurgeon, Harry Emerson Fosdick and Billy Graham, Baptist preachers have gained hearings far beyond their own churches and denomination. So central is preaching to worship for Baptists that most Baptists when asked to evaluate worship will immediately turn to the sermon, and the success or failure of a given worship service will stand upon the fact as to whether or not the sermon is good or bad. In some areas Baptists tend to distinguish or to separate worship and preaching. The morning service is called a service of 'worship *and* preaching'. Or the worship segments are characterized as 'preliminaries'. The *pièce de resistance* is invariably the sermon. In most Baptist worship it occupies the concluding and climactic point of the service. It is often followed by a hymn of invitation in which an opportunity is offered for non-believers to give themselves to Christ and for believers to rededicate themselves to the Christian life. This self-offering is doubtless related to what has been called the offertory in the traditional liturgy.

While the Lord's Supper is regarded highly by Baptists, it is not frequently practised. Relatively few churches observe weekly communion. Most churches will hold communion on a monthly or a quarterly basis. Formerly communion was often separated from the preaching service. At the conclusion of the preaching service the congregation would be dismissed and only those who were members of the local congregation would remain for the Lord's Supper. For those who were included, communion was indeed a high and holy time in which the congregation remembered in deep solemnity the life and passion of their Lord, and renewed their hope in his return in power and glory. Today the services of word and table are generally one service.

Baptists differ on the issue of open and closed communion. Many churches invite all who believe in Jesus Christ to participate. Others seek to restrict communion to Baptists and in some places reserve communion to those who are members of the local congregation. The pastor of the congregation generally presides at the communion service, but if no pastor is available, a layman can be designated by the congregation to officiate. Baptism, as well as other elements of worship, can be performed by a layman if no ordained minister is available or present. Such lay leadership is done by licensing. The congregation votes to designate one or more of its members to serve its needs.

The communion service is primarily a memorial meal. Any 'real presence' comes as the individual believer renews his faith and fellowship in Jesus Christ. In most Baptist churches today, the elements of bread and wine are distributed by the deacons to the congregation as they sit in their places. They eat the bread simultaneously as the leader repeats the words of Jesus, 'Take, eat. This is my body which is broken for you. Do this in remembrance of me.' Then, as the minister says, 'Drink of it, all of you; for this is my blood of the covenant, which is poured out for many for the forgiveness of sins,' the congregation drinks the wine (*see* **Communion**).

The structure of the Sunday morning preaching service in a Baptist church is relatively simple. The service generally begins with a scripture sentence followed by a prayer of invocation and a hymn of praise. A responsive reading, usually from the psalms, is read, followed by the singing of the *Gloria.* Then comes the pastoral prayer which covers such elements as adoration, confession, thanksgiving, and intercession. Following the prayer, church announcements are made and the offering is received with the singing of the doxology. A hymn may then be sung followed by the reading of the scripture and the sermon. After the sermon a hymn of dedication and invitation is sung and the benediction is pronounced. If a choir is present, suitable anthems come at various places in the service and responses, introits, etc. provide introductions and conclusions to the spoken parts of the service.

Baptists have no official manuals of worship or books of common prayer. In Britain Ernest A. Payne and Stephen F. Winward compiled *Orders and Prayers for Church Worship*, and in the USA John E. Skoglund published a *Manual of Worship*. While books like these have no official endorsement, they have received denominational encouragement. The orders which are included in the books are not in any way required of the congregations, but are intended to provide guide lines for worship done 'decently and in order'.

Baptists have not been at the centre of the movement for liturgical renewal. Individuals have participated in liturgical conferences and have written on the issues of worship, but for the most part church life has not been greatly influenced. The freedom allowed in worship in Baptist congregations has afforded opportunities for a number of experiments. Baptist worship can be readily adapted to such informal gatherings as housechurches, to services with high lay participation, and to other experimental forms. In this Baptists may make in the future a significant contribution to liturgical renewal.

Winthrop S. Hudson and Norman H. Maring, *A Baptist Manual of Polity and Practice*, 1963; Ernest A. Payne, *The Fellowship of Believers*, 1952; Ernest A. Payne and Stephen F. Winward, *Orders and Prayers for Church Worship*, 1960; John E. Skoglund, *A Manual of Worship*, 1968; John E. Skoglund, *Worship in the Free Churches*, 1965; Stephen F. Winward, *The Reformation of Our Worship*, 1965.

JOHN E. SKOGLUND

Baptistery

Baptism does not of itself require any particular building type or indeed any building at all, any more than does any other form of Christian worship (*see* **Architectural Setting**). Nevertheless to study Christian initiation upon a textual basis alone is to indulge in something of an abstraction, for the rites need to be considered in their setting, which was both architectural and iconographical. In such a context the documents assume a deeper and more real meaning, and conversely the conjunction of text and monument illuminates the latter, which tends to be no more than an empty shell if there is ignorance of what took place within it.

The story of the baptistery does not begin until the opening decades of the third century. Baptisteries may have existed before then, but of these no literary evidence survives and no archaeological traces have been discovered. In the apostolic age and during the second century, baptism was administered in rivers and pools, while the gatherings for eucharistic worship were held in private houses. When at length special architectural provision was made for the latter, we may assume that it would embrace the former, so that as accommodation was created for the liturgical assembly of the church, it was also set aside for the sacrament of initiation into the church.

The earliest baptisteries of the third and fourth centuries were square or rectangular with or without an apse at one end. This type persisted in such areas as Greece, Palestine and North Africa until the seventh century. In other parts of the empire, notably France and Italy, the quadrilateral was superseded from the middle of the fifth century by round or octagonal designs. In many provinces these baptisteries were either detached from or loosely attached to the main building for worship, but in Greece they frequently formed part of the church, being an adjoining room opening off the narthex (q.v.).

The adoption of the quadrilateral in the first instance was the outcome of three factors. First, when baptism ceased to be administered out of doors and a baptistery was arranged in the house-church, it naturally had the shape of an ordinary room, i.e. it was quadrilateral, and as such is to be found at Dura Europos. Second, since the baptismal rite had affinities with bathing, the *frigidarium* of the Roman baths, often a square or rectangle, had its influence. Third, from NT times baptism was understood in terms of a death and resurrection with Christ; the baptistery was therefore a kind of tomb, and since many pagan funerary monuments were domed quadrilaterals it was natural to reproduce this design. Its persistence in certain areas is explicable because it was in precisely the same provinces that the square tomb was and continued to be the norm.

This last factor provides the clue to the reason for the adoption of other shapes in Italy and in those countries under her direct influence. Here there was a transition from the square to the circle and also to the hexagon and octagon. The circular plan with ambulatory was the plan of many tombs and this funerary association was also expressed through the six- and eight-sided design. The symbolism of the hexagon refers to the sixth day of the week, i.e. Friday, upon which Christ was crucified and buried, so it declared the baptismal co-death with the redeemer. The octagon represented the day of Christ's resurrection, i.e. the first day of the new week, and so it served to emphasize co-resurrection with Christ in baptism and the dawn of the Age to Come.

Other less widespread forms derived from the same association of ideas. Thus trefoil and quatrefoil baptisteries reproduced the designs of tombs and martyria (q.v.), and the few cruciform examples relate directly to the manner of Christ's death. The iconographical scheme of baptisteries is further evidence of the close connection in belief between baptism and death, for the mosaics which decorated many of them reproduced the same themes as sepulchral art, e.g. the Good Shepherd who lays down his life for the sheep, the star-studded domes which represent heaven and eternal life.

Baptism (q.v.) itself was gradually elaborated into a complex rite which included the disrobing of candidates, their affirmation of faith, their entry into the water, their anointing, their clothing in white robes and their procession to the main building for the eucharist. In planning their baptisteries, Christians could have produced a series of rooms, each corresponding to one element in the rite as a whole. Indeed this is what took place, and although, probably due to lack of material resources, some were no more than a single room, others had two or more adjoining the one in which the font (q.v.) was placed. As an example we may take the complex opening out of the north end of the narthex of Basilica A at Philippi (*see* Fig. 13).

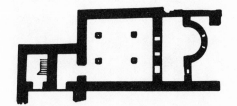

Fig. 13   Basilica A, Philippi, Macedonia

There are three rooms: the first cannot be anything other than vestibule; the second is the baptismal area with font, and beyond that is a third with an apse in one of its walls. There is every reason to suppose that the apse was constructed with a specific purpose in view, namely to enshrine the episcopal throne. This permits the identification of the room as a *chrismarion*, i.e. the place where the bishop administered the chrism which completed the rite of initiation. Sometimes, in default of other rooms, 'confirmation' (q.v.) could take place in the area of the font, and where there is an apse (q.v.), such as the one at Tropaeum Traiani, this was almost certainly to provide a space for the *cathedra* (q.v.).

Whether simple or complex, baptisteries were at first erected only in episcopal cities, since it was the bishop's office to confirm and since baptism and confirmation were for centuries united. The occasional baptisteries in non-episcopal centres existed to spare candidates too long a journey. In the East, where priests were eventually allowed to confirm in place of the bishop, using for the

Fig. 14   Baptistery, Florence, Italy

purpose oil that had been episcopally blessed, baptisteries became more numerous, and were therefore not confined to episcopal centres. In parts of Syria in the sixth century, each town had its baptistery, not infrequently two and sometimes three. In the West, on the other hand, where the bishop did not delegate this authority, it was not until baptism and confirmation were finally separated that each parish came to possess its own.

From the seventh to the fourteenth centuries, detached baptisteries (*see* Plate 17), after the model of the early Christian ones and with the same plan and ideological content, continued to be erected, of which the ones at Florence (*see* Fig. 14) and Pisa are perhaps the most well known. But the later Middle Ages witnessed a complete transformation of the architectural setting of baptism in so far as the detached type ceased to be built and the font was placed within the church itself. The factors that contributed to this result were all different aspects of the situation that obtained when the whole population of a country had become nominally Christian. The virtual cessation of adult initiation and the corresponding preponderance of infant baptism meant that provision for undressing and privacy for the nude were no longer required. The public nature of baptism, with all present accepting the Christian faith, meant that a separate building was no longer necessary. Hence there was no reason why a simple font should not be introduced into the nave, usually by the main door to indicate that baptism is the means of entrance into the church. The result of this movement was that baptism ceased to have an architectural setting properly so called. However, in a number of churches a

Plate 17 Detached baptistery, Parma, Italy

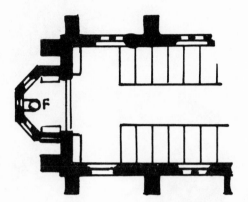

Fig. 15   Dodford Church, England

baldachin or ciborium (qq.v.) was erected over the font and occasionally a low wooden railing surrounded it, thus defining a space and dignifying the celebration of the first gospel sacrament.

Within the Roman Catholic Church this practice was fostered by Charles Borromeo who issued directions for his diocese of Milan in 1559. In legislating for parish churches, Borromeo ordained that 'an oratory or chapel should be built, inside close to the chief doorway and on the gospel side, and it should be alike to the other lateral chapels erected to contain altars'. So he advocated the creation of a defined space which was to be enclosed by iron or wooden railings, with the font sunk in the centre to the depth of several steps. Being of a practical turn of mind, he had to acknowledge that there were some buildings in which even this would not be feasible, and so he was prepared to allow the font to stand alone at the rear of the church in the medieval fashion, but this was clearly not his ideal, and this ideal, formulated in great detail, has continued to have its effect upon the architectural setting of baptism within Roman Catholic churches right down to the present.

Within Protestant churches the baptistery proper ceased to exist. Anglicans were content with a font by the church door, following the medieval practice. Calvinists used shallow basins placed either on the holy table or in brackets fixed to the pulpit. The Lutherans eventually adopted the *Prinzipalstück* (*see* **Architectural Setting**) and located the font close to the table and pulpit at the east end.

With the Gothic Revival the medieval precedent continued to be observed, but about the middle of the nineteenth century influences were at work to produce exceptions to this norm and ultimately to issue in a new approach to the architectural setting of baptism and indeed in the restoration of the baptistery. The first of these influences was a growing awareness of the detached baptisteries still standing in Italy. As more and more architects made the grand tour, ignorance of the baptistery proper was no longer possible. The second influence was the contemporary Roman Catholic practice. Pugin argued forcibly that the font should be given prominence by an enclosing chancel and in several of the churches he designed he did create a baptistery at the west end. Architects working for Anglican patrons began to adopt the same concept and they were further affected by the gradual re-use of the many chapels and chantries in the English cathedrals for weekday services; this suggested that one of them could house the font, so creating a baptistery. In existing buildings, where the font had been an isolated object, baptisteries were introduced by defining the space with rails. In some new churches western apses were deliberately planned as baptisteries (*see* Fig. 15).

In the twentieth century this movement has continued. Architects and their clients began to think no longer in terms simply of a font but in spatial categories. It was thought that the rite required not only certain necessary items of furniture but a defined space suitable

Plate 18   Macgregor Chapel, Afikpo Teacher Training College, Eastern Nigeria

to its importance and meaning. Consequently the practice increased of creating baptisteries within existing churches and making provision for them within those that were rebuilt after damage or destruction during the Second World War.

In the majority of modern Roman Catholic churches the idea of a separate baptistery, apart from the main assembly hall for worship, has predominated. The baptistery may project from the western facade; it may be located to one side of the church, usually the north; it may be contained within the entrance hall or narthex. Other denominations represent a greater variety, with no one concept entirely to the fore. In some modern Anglican churches the medieval disposition continues; in others the baptistery is combined with the porch, while in others again the idea of the *Prinzipalstück* is being reproduced with the font inside or close to the sanctuary (*see* Plate 18). This last arrangement, which was for centuries the Lutheran norm, has now commended itself to many Calvinists and is frequent in Holland, but in some recent Lutheran designs the font is

actually at the rear of the congregation in medieval style and occasionally within its own baptistery (*see* Plate 19 and Fig. 16). Within the Free Churches the *Prinzipalstück* has been widely accepted, while the Baptists necessarily give prominence to the font, to which they apply the term baptistery, by placing it at the sanctuary end, although since it is for submersion and so below floor level, it is covered and so lost to sight except when actually in use.

As we look to the future, it may be said that past history and the understanding of the nature of baptism suggests three principles to be observed. These are (1) the need to make provision for congregational participation; (2) the need to give the setting a visual importance that accords with the celebration of the first gospel sacrament; (3) the need to devise a shape and décor that conveys some of the meaning of the rite. Clearly these can be applied in a variety of ways and no one can say that there is any single correct solution.

J. G. Davies, *The Architectural Setting of Baptism*, 1962; A. Khatchatrian, *Les baptistères paléochrétiens*, 1962.   EDITOR

Plate 19
St Andrew, Malmö, Sweden

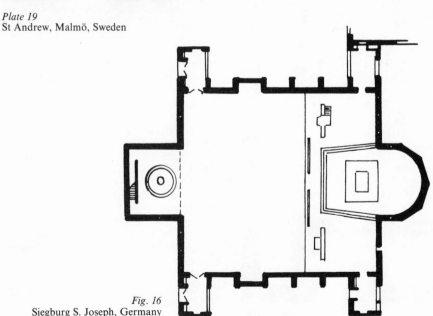

Fig. 16
Siegburg S. Joseph, Germany

Basilica

The basilica is an early form of church building derived from pagan prototypes (*see* **Architectural Setting**). Although initially there were many varieties, from the late fourth century four main types may be distinguished.

1. *Roman or Latin*. Its main characteristics were: (*a*) a projecting apse (q.v.); (*b*) an architrave or continuous beam supported on the abacus of each column; (*c*) a covered porch; (*d*) an atrium; (*e*) a transept (q.v.) – although this is also found in the second type.

2. *Hellenistic*. Its main characteristics were: (*a*) the apse was polygonal on the outside or was flanked by side chambers which, especially in Syria, were contained within one wall to preserve the rectangular shape; (*b*) archivolts, i.e. arches linking the columns; (*c*) galleries over the aisles for the women; (*d*) there was often but not invariably an atrium; (*e*) transepts were included in Greece and the adjoining lands, but in North Africa no examples are known and only one in Palestine and one in Syria; (*f*) a narthex (q.v.) was attached (*see* Fig. 17).

3. *Oriental*, also known as the barn or hall church (*Hallenkirche*), originating in Mesopotamia and found in Anatolia, Armenia, Crete, Cyprus and Greece. In plan, it is indistinguishable from the previous one (*see* Fig. 17), but it differed in elevation, in that the walls of the nave were not carried up above the roofs of the aisles to form a clerestory. Hence its characteristics are: (*a*) a blind nave; (*b*) windows in the apse and aisles; (*c*) no atrium; (*d*) a narthex; (*e*) it was usually vaulted.

4. *Transverse*. This is a primitive Mesopotamian form found in Armenia, Cappadocia, the Hauran and the Tur Abdin. It consisted of a single nave at right angles to the line connecting the entrance door with the apse.

Under the impact of the modern Liturgical Movement (q.v.) in its somewhat archaeological phase, a number of churches were built in the twentieth century which reproduce the basilica plan.

EDITOR

Basilican Position
see Postures (1*c*)

Bells

Gregory of Tours (*c*. 585) is the first person to mention their considerable use in Christian worship with any certainty. The story that they were first introduced into Christian worship by Paulinus of Nola, Campania, is doubtful. But it has given us two Latin words for a bell, *campana* and *nola*. It may be that the story was invented to account for the origin of the words. Bells were much used in the British Isles from the sixth century. From the eighth century they came into widespread use and were blessed by a bishop with holy water and chrism and they were 'named' and bore inscriptions. They were not only used to summon people to worship but also a bell was rung at the death of a parishioner. Small bells were used at the altar and in some instances a special small bell in the belfry at the elevation of the host. Bells are used in the Eastern Orthodox rite not only to summon people to worship but also during the liturgy and offices to mark certain points in the services.

H. B. Walters, *The Church Bells of England*, 1913 (with extensive bibliography).

C. E. POCKNEE

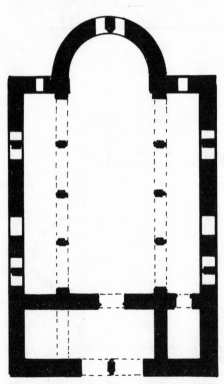

Fig. 17   Church no. 4, Bin Bir Kilisse, Turkey

Benediction

The word has a wider and a narrower use in liturgy. For the wider use *see* **Blessing**. In the narrower use, Benediction is a rite which springs from two distinct sources, Marian and eucharistic.

A litany or hymn to the Blessed Virgin, which often follows the rosary (q.v.), is derived from evening canticles, originating in Italy under the name of *laude*, in the thirteenth century. The custom spread throughout Europe. Later, it became the practice to expose the sacrament in a monstrance (q.v.) during these canticles and, finally, to give a blessing with the sacrament before the congregation dispersed.

Marian devotion and eucharistic devotion were thus joined for an afternoon or evening service, which in England goes by the name of Benediction. It was very popular from the seventeenth century until the recent introduction of evening mass, but it was seldom, if ever, seen in the British Isles until Catholic emancipation in 1829, except, possibly, in the chapels of the foreign embassies. The rite is begun, normally, by placing the monstrance (q.v.) on a throne elevated above the altar. After the devotions, which are optional, the hymn *Tantum ergo* ('Therefore we, before him bending' *Hymns Ancient and Modern, Revised*, 1950, no. 383, part 2) is sung and the sacrament is censed. Then, after a prayer, the priest takes the monstrance from the throne and, at the altar, makes a cross with it over the kneeling congregation. A bishop or an abbot makes a threefold sign of the cross (q.v.).

Benediction can also be given with the host enclosed in a ciborium (q.v.), but for the use of a monstrance the express permission of the bishop is necessary.

The rite expresses for Roman Catholics a lively and practical sentiment of the real and perpetual presence of Christ in the holy eucharist.

A. A. King and C. E. Pocknee, *Eucharistic Reservation in the Western Church*, 1965.

A. A. KING

Benedictus
see Anaphora, Canticles

Bible Services

In the Roman Catholic Church these services are the fruit of the Liturgical Movement (q.v.) and the biblical revival of more recent years and they received official recognition in the *Constitution on the Liturgy* (35,[4]) of Vatican II.

They remain a free form of service, may be conducted by a lay person, though where, for want of an ordained minister they replace the mass, it is recommended that they follow the order of the ministry of the word in the new *Ordo Missae*.

They consist of three main elements, the reading of God's word, homily or homilies on it, the response of the people by word, song or silence and intercessions or other forms of prayer.

The Council saw them as a useful means of giving the people a deeper appreciation of holy scripture and strongly urged that the clergy should organize such services especially during the great seasons of the year, such as Lent and Advent, and as vigils of preparation before the greater feasts.

These services are much used in informal groups of laity, and in those parts of the church where there is a lack of ordained ministers they are used (and must be used) as a preparation before communion from the reserved sacrament.

Constitution on the Liturgy (as above); *Instruction for Implementing the Liturgical Constitution* (37-39); commentary 'Bible Services' by Edmund Jones, OSB, in *The Liturgy and the Future*, ed. J. D. Crichton, 1966.

J. D. CRICHTON

Bible, Use of in Worship

The Bible of the early church was the OT in its Septuagint or Greek version. Passages from it were read out in the course of Christian worship, following the practice in the synagogues, and indeed this, with the sermon, formed part of the first half of the eucharist, known variously as the ministry of the word, the synaxis and the mass of the catechumens (qq.v.). To lections from the Jewish sacred book were soon added others from documents believed to be of apostolic authorship, so that by the middle of the second century, according to Justin Martyr, 'the memoirs of the apostles or the writings of the prophets are read as long as time permits' (*Apol.* 1.67). The portions of scripture assigned for worship were eventually collected in several books, the gospels in the *evangelarium*, the epistles in the *epistolarium*, the psalms in the *psalterium* and the OT lections in the *lectionarium*. Even after the production, in the sixth century, of pandects, i.e. manuscript copies of the entire Bible, the separate volumes were in use for convenience.

This practice was not greatly altered by the invention of printing and the publication of more manageable complete Bibles, so that to the present day the Orthodox Churches still have several volumes, while the Roman Church has grouped the mass lections in the missal and the office readings in the breviary. Similarly the churches of the Anglican Communion print the epistle and gospel in full but provide only tables of lessons for morning and evening prayer. Other churches give tables for all lections, so that the complete Bible is regularly in use, e.g. by the Church of Scotland, the Church of South India, the Methodists and the Presbyterian Churches of England and Wales.

In the Church of England the Bible remains permanently on the lectern or is placed there immediately before a service, although in the seventeenth and eighteenth centuries it was common for copies of the Bible and the *BCP* to stand upright at the back of the altar. In the French Reformed Church it lies open continually on the holy table. In the Church of Scotland it is carried in at the beginning of a service. As a liturgical object, the Bible is also used in the gospel procession, the little entrance (q.v.) and in ordination (q.v.), it being the almost universal practice to present a NT or complete Bible to the candidates.

EDITOR

Bidding Prayer

The element of intercession (q.v.) in the eucharistic rites of the Western church has been variable. The Good Friday *orationes solemnes* of the Roman rite survive as the only example of the earliest known form of the prayers of the faithful at the beginning of the mass of the faithful. In the sixth century their place was taken by a litany (q.v.) of Eastern origin, found among the introductory material in the rite, and the *kyries* survive as a relic of this litany. When the litany fell out of use after about a century, the element of intercession virtually disappeared from the Western liturgy, apart for the brief prayers for the living and the dead in the canon of the mass, until the bidding of the bedes appeared in the unofficial vernacular element in the Latin rite known as the prone. The prone is an example of a measure of pastoral concern in the Middle Ages, and was a vernacular passage in the course of the mass consisting of a sermon, which was preceded or followed by the bidding of the bedes, notices, and instruction in the Decalogue, the Lord's Prayer, and similar formularies. The word 'bid' in Anglo-Saxon means 'pray', and the 'bidding of the bedes' means the 'praying of the prayers': *cf.* 'Ye shulle stonde up and bydde your bedys . . .' in a fourteenth-century example of the bidding prayer which was used at Worcester. In its earlier and better examples the prayer covered the full range of matters for intercession, the church, the state, the departed, and all men in their various callings: it was flexible and gave scope to the initiative of the celebrant. With the passage of time it became formalized, and at the time of the Reformation, when such freedom was not acceptable, precise forms were laid down, as appears in Canon 55 of 1604. The canon lays down that the bidding prayer shall be said before sermons, although so far as the sermon at the eucharist is concerned this seems pointless, since the prayer book since 1549 has restored the provision for intercession which the old rite lacked. Canon B 19 of 1967 leaves the bidding prayer optional. The association between the sermon and the intercessions which is found in the liturgical forms of some of the Reformed churches is probably derived from their association in the prone.

F. E. Brightman, *The English Rite*, 1921; H. O. C(oxe), *Forms of Bidding Prayer*, 1840.

E. C. WHITAKER

Bishop

The highest order in the traditional pattern of the ministry, though there was a medieval view that bishops are not to be reckoned as an order entirely separate and distinct from the priesthood but are merely priests with additional powers and functions. This view arose from contemporary eucharistic theology which stressed the importance of the sacrament as a sacrifice and made it difficult to imagine an order of ministry higher than the priesthood. NT evidence is not entirely clear, but there are passages which suggest that originally the terms 'bishop' (*episcopos*, overseer) and presbyter (q.v.) were interchangeable (Acts 20.17-28). It has been widely assumed that the early Christian communities were governed by colleges of elders, as Jewish synagogues were, and that in the course of time a monarchial episcopate developed. Disagreement about when and how this happened is notorious. It is possible that the need to have a liturgical president (like the ruler of the synagogue) may have contributed to the process. By the time of Ignatius of Antioch it was possible to claim that the presence of the bishop or his authorized representative was essential for the eucharist, and in Cyprian's writings the same argument is further developed. But by this later date the process of delegation had had to be taken further. In earlier days the presbyters had been associated with the bishop in his liturgical as well as his governmental function. They had a place if not a separate liturgical activity and were gathered round the bishop as he celebrated. But by the middle of the third century it was evidently no longer possible for the Christian community in the larger centres to assemble in a single congregation. Presbyters were given authority to take charge of separate districts and there to preside over celebrations of the eucharist. There is evidence for this in Rome and Carthage and in rural areas. But the bishop remained in theory the chief minister in all sacramental acts. Ordination and confirmation (qq.v.) remained in some sense the bishop's special prerogative, though not in quite the absolute sense that has sometimes been suggested. There is some evidence that persons not in episcopal orders have on rare and extraordinary occasions been authorized by the papacy to ordain. And in the East confirmation is administered by the priest at the same time as baptism, using chrism that has been blessed by the bishop.

At the Reformation the office of bishop was retained by Anglicans and some Lutherans. In some cases it was the intention to retain the historic succession (e.g. in England and Sweden), in other cases it was deliberately not so (e.g. in Denmark). The *Unitas Fratrum* (Moravians) also preserved the episcopal order and claim an unbroken succession through the Bohemian Brethren, but they have not always regarded the laying on of the bishop's hands as necessary for ordination. In some parts of the Methodist Church the title is used, particularly in America where Thomas Coke introduced it, having been set apart by John Wesley as superintendent of Methodist work there. Methodist bishops have the power of appointing ministers and exercise a pastoral and disciplinary oversight over them. They also perform all ordinations but not confirmations. In the third decade of the twentieth century German Lutherans adopted the title for the majority of those ministers who had been called superintendents up to that date. In the Church of South India bishops have been part of the ministry since that church came into existence by the reunion of separate Christian denominations in 1947. All ordinations are performed by them, though confirmation is not necessarily an episcopal act. The schemes proposed for united Churches of North India, of Pakistan and of Ceylon also make provision for an episcopal ministry as do most other reunion proposals.

K. M. Carey, ed., *The Historic Episcopate*, 1954; R. P. Johnson, *The Bishop in the Church*, 1966; K. E. Kirk, *The Apostolic Ministry*, 1946; G. Simon, *Bishops*, 1961; W. Telfer, *The Office of a Bishop*, 1962.

P. HINCHLIFF

Blessing

1. A blessing is an authoritative declaration of divine favour addressed to persons. It is used liturgically: (*a*) Immediately before the act of communion. Although not primitive, this was customary in all eucharistic rites by the end of the fourth century, being an encouragement and preparation for those about to communicate. It assumed elaborate forms in the Gallican rite and survives in the ritual of the Church of Lyons. It was omitted from the Roman rite *c.*500, and no post-Reformation order has retained it. (*b*) At the end of the eucharist. Although not prescribed in the missals, this became customary in the late Middle Ages, and probably derived from the blessing by the bishop of his flock as he went out. This medieval feature has been perpetuated in most reformed rites (except the Zwinglian), with the Aaronic form (Num. 6.24-26) appearing in the Lutheran, Calvinist and derived orders, and Phil. 4.7, with the medieval episcopal blessing as the second half, in the Anglican and most British churches. (*c*) During the eucharist and other services, e.g. the blessing of the deacon who is to sing the gospel and of the penitent about to make confession. (*d*)

Frequently at the end of other services, e.g. the Sunday services of the Free Churches, confirmation in the *BCP*, etc.

2. A blessing can also be a verbal formula for the sanctification of objects, which include the water at baptism, oil for exorcism or for the anointing of the sick (*see* **Unction**), the Paschal Candle (q.v.), etc.

EDITOR

Books, Liturgical

Liturgical books are those used in the performance of church services. Both in manuscript and printed form they are an essential source of information for the worshipping practice of any group of believers.

1. *The Early Church*. Since liturgical prayer was largely extempore until the early third century, the only books required were rolls of the scriptures. In time, however, there were produced the church orders, a series of documents, claiming apostolic authority, which contained both liturgical prescriptions and also rules for the life of the congregation. The earliest extant example is the *Didache* or *Teaching of the Twelve Apostles*, probably a product of the second century. There followed the *Apostolic Tradition* of Hippolytus, c.217, the *Didascalia*, c.250, the *Apostolic Church Order*, c.250, the *Apostolic Constitutions*, c.375, and the *Testament of Our Lord*, c.400.

In addition to these general handbooks, individual bishops made their own compilations, e.g. the prayer book of Serapion of Thmuis, c.350, containing prayers for the eucharist, baptism, ordination (qq.v.), the blessing of oils and a commendation of the dead. With the elaboration of the liturgy and the acceptance of stereotyped forms, numerous service-books eventually became necessary.

EDITOR

2. *Orthodox*. (More properly, Byzantine.) The service books at present in use in the Byzantine rite are as follows:
(*a*) *The Euchologion* (Greek, 'book of prayers') contains those parts of the sacraments and other services, together with many occasional offices and blessings, which are required by the officiating ministers (bishop, priest and deacon). It exists in two forms, in addition to which excerpts from it are often printed separately, individually or in com-

bination.

The Great Euchologion (Greek, *euchologion to mega*) normally contains:

(i) The fixed parts, or ordinary, of vespers, mattins, the eucharistic liturgy, and the liturgy of the presanctified (q.v.), the priest's part being given in full, and those of deacon, reader and singers usually in an abbreviated form.

(ii) The six remaining sacraments, namely: baptism, with a number of related offices; chrismation or confirmation (which forms an integral part of the baptismal rites); ordination; confession; marriage; and the anointing of the sick. A more complete text of these is provided in most editions, the deacon's, reader's and singers' parts not being so readily available elsewhere as those of the services in the preceding group.

(iii) Other occasional offices, some of them what in the West would be called sacramentals (although the Byzantine books do not distinguish liturgically between sacraments and sacramentals so rigidly as do those of the West), such as the various services connected with monastic profession, the consecration of a church, the greater and lesser blessings of holy water, and so forth; and others such as the various rites connected with the burial of the dead.

(iv) A large number of offices for the particular blessing of persons and things.

The Small Euchologion (Greek, *mikron euchologion*, or *agiasmatarion*, 'book of blessings') omits the whole of the first group of services listed above, and also those rites, such as ordination and the consecration of a church, which appertain specifically to the bishop; it contains the five remaining sacraments, the funeral offices, and those occasional offices and blessings most commonly required. Some editions do add the priest's part of the major daily offices and the liturgy.

The Liturgikon (Greek, 'book of the liturgy') or *Hieratikon* or *Hierotelestikon* (Greek, 'book for the priest') is an altar book, containing the priest's, and in some editions also the deacon's, part at vespers, mattins and the liturgy, together with related supplementary matter, the extent and arrangement of which differ from one edition to another.

The Archieratikon (Greek, 'book for the bishop') corresponds to the Western pontifical, and contains services and blessings either reserved to or most commonly performed by the bishop. Some editions use *Hieratikon* as the title of this book and not of that considered in the preceding note.

The next group of books, seven in number, is concerned principally, although not exclusively, with the divine office.

(*b*) *The Horologion* (Greek, 'book of hours') is a book for the use of readers and singers, just as the *Euchologion* is for the use of priest and deacon. Its fuller form, the *Great Horologion* (Greek, *horologion to mega*) includes:

(i) The ordinary, or fixed part, of the daily offices, namely, nocturns, mattins, the lesser hours (prime, terce, sext, none), vespers and compline (qq.v.), together with graces before and after meals. The reader's and singers' parts are given in full; most of the priest's and deacon's parts is omitted.

(ii) A list of feasts and saints' days throughout the year, for each of which a short account of the feast or the life of the saint is given, together with certain of the principal anthems appointed for the day.

(iii) A similar section, covering Sundays and movable feasts, within the periods of the *Triodion* and *Pentekostarion* (see below).

(iv) The common principal anthems for the days of the week.

(v) A miscellany of other services related to the divine office and in frequent use.

All the lesser hours can be recited in full from the *Great Horologion*. But a number of other books are required for vespers and mattins, books containing the proper texts which change from day to day. These volumes contain the material of the three cycles which together constitute the Byzantine liturgical year: (i) the weekly cycle, contained in the *Oktoechos*; (ii) the annual cycle of movable feasts, contained in the *Triodion* and *Pentekostarion*; (iii) the annual cycle of fixed feasts, contained in the *Menaia*.

(*c*) *The Oktoechos* (Greek, 'book of the eight tones'), also known as the *Parakletike* (Greek, 'book of supplication'), contains the variable parts of the daily offices through the week. Eight series of offices are provided, one for each of the eight tones of Byzantine chant, and each series comprises seven sets of services, one for each day of the week. The eight tones are used in sequence, week by week, through the year, beginning with the first tone on the Sunday after Easter. The texts contained in the *Oktoechos* are combined, when appropriate, with those for fixed feasts contained in the *Menaia*. The *Oktoechos* is used in Lent only on Saturdays and Sundays, and it is not used at all from the Saturday preceding Palm Sunday until the Sunday after Pentecost, any material from it which is used during these seasons being repeated in full in the proper seasonal books. An edition of the *Oktoechos* for Sundays only also exists.

(*d*) *The Triodion* (Greek, 'book of the three odes', from the circumstance that for most days it provides only three proper odes or canticles for mattins) contains the propers for Lent.

(*e*) *The Pentekostarion* (Greek, 'book of the fifty days') contains the services proper to Eastertide and Pentecost.

(*f*) *The Menaia* (Greek, 'books of the months') contain the propers of fixed feasts throughout the year; most editions are divided into twelve volumes, one for each month. Various combinations of excerpts from the *Menaia* are also published.

(*g*) *The Eirmologion* (Greek, 'book of the *eirmoi*') contains the texts of the anthems known as *eirmoi* which are sung at the beginnings of the odes or canticles of mattins. The major books listed above commonly give only the opening words of these, assuming, apparently, that the reader will know them by heart; hence the need for the *Eirmologion*.

The next group of books comprises three volumes, the *Evangelion*, the *Apostolos*, and the *Psalterion*.

(*h*) *The Evangelion* (Greek, 'book of the gospels') contains the text of the four gospels; in some editions the text is printed continuously, the lessons to be read on particular days being noted in the margins, or in some similar way, while in others the text is arranged in the order required for liturgical use, the latter being the more common arrangement. The *evangelion* is treated with great reverence: it is usually bound in a cover decorated with silver or gold, often indeed actually made of silver or gold; when not in use it is usually kept on the altar; it is carried in procession and venerated by the congregation when there is a gospel lesson at mattins, and on certain other occasions.

(*i*) *The Apostolos* (Greek, 'book of the apostle') contains the lessons from the Acts of the Apostles and the epistles, together with the *prokeimena* or graduals (q.v.) which are sung before the epistle at the liturgy, and the alleluias which are sung after it.

(*j*) *The Psalterion* (Greek, 'book of psalms') contains the psalms, arranged according to their normal liturgical use, together with the necessary canticles from the OT and NT.

The lessons from the OT are normally included in the appropriate choir book for the day in question – *Triodion, Pentekostarion*, or *Menaion*; some editions, however, do include a separate book containing them.

(*k*) *The Synaxarion* (Greek, 'book of the assembly') or *Menologion* (Greek, 'book of remembrance') contains brief lives of the saints, and brief accounts of the mysteries of redemption celebrated on particular days, and is an exact counterpart of the Western martyrology (*see* 3[2] below).

(*l*) *The Typikon* (Greek, 'book of the ordinances') corresponds to the Western *ordo* (in the older sense of a permanent book, not the more recent one of an annual one), and contains the rules and rubrics governing the celebration of services throughout the year. The history of the *Typikon* is extremely involved: that now in use represents a crystallization of liturgical practice in the high Middle Ages, and includes elements of two originally very distinct liturgical traditions within the Byzantine rite, the 'monastic' and the 'cathedral' (*see* **Cathedral Office**), which were fused during that period; the Greek-speaking churches now follow a redaction of this *Typikon* dating from no earlier than 1888, and many aspects of modern Russian usage do not antedate the seventeenth century.

From the preceding remarks on the *Typikon* the reader will realise that the Byzantine rite liturgical books described here embody an order of service which is essentially medieval, although many of its parts are very much older. It will also have been noticed, however, that whereas in the West the whole division and arrangement of the service-books was changed in the medieval period, in the Byzantine East the old division and arrangement of the books was retained, notwithstanding the considerable changes of content. There is unfortunately no book in English which deals in detail with either the pre-medieval or the post-medieval books.

W. JARDINE GRISBROOKE

3. *Medieval and Roman Catholic*. (1) *Medieval*. This section is concerned with the books used in liturgical worship during the Middle Ages, a period running roughly from the sixth to the thirteenth centuries. Today, the books used for worship in the Roman rite may be numbered as seven: the missal, the breviary, the gradual, the antiphonal, the pontifical, the ritual and the martyrology. In medieval times this was not so. The books used in worship were many and complex. C. Vogel has counted as many as a hundred. The reasons for this number and diversity are to be sought in the facts of history. The Middle Ages knew no principles of uniformity in matters liturgical, despite the attempts of pope and emperor. Each ecclesiastical province, each diocese, each monastery had its own liturgical books and rites. Before the thirteenth century, and even as late as the *incunabula* of the fifteenth century, this diversity was widespread. A further reason for this is to be found in the fact that each minister or celebrant had his own book, and often enough a special book for each rite or ceremony. In the following pages we can treat only the main liturgical books of the period. This may be done under two headings: the mass and the divine office.

(*a*) *The mass*
(i) *The sacramentary*. This was the celebrant's book. It contained all the texts needed for the celebration of the eucharist, the administration of the sacraments, the formularies of blessing, the rites of ordination. Its history is obscure, but it would seem that from the sixth century onwards the compilation of a sacramentary was part and parcel of a bishop's charge. Already in the times of Augustine collections of euchological formularies were being drawn up in Africa and authorized for official use by the local bishop's synod. This was a countermeasure to the many such productions emanating from heretical sects. The sacramentary was preceded by small collections of euchological texts, to which the name *libelli missarum* has been given. The earliest collection of such books would seem to have been gathered together to form the well known sacramentary preserved in the chapter

library of Verona, the *Sacramentarium Vero-nense*. Other official sacramentaries have come down to us under the names of Gelasius and Gregory the Great. By the thirteenth century each see, each church, each monastery had its own collection of sacramentaries, until the process ended with the production of the missal.

(ii) *The antiphonale missarum*. In origin this book developed from the antiphonal. This latter was a book containing all the sung portions of both the office and the mass. In time the collection became voluminous and the portions were divided into two distinct parts. The material to be used in celebrating the eucharist was called the *antiphonale missarum* or the *graduale*. Ehrensberger divides the book used at mass into *gradualia*, *troparia* and *rotuli paschales*. Bannister added a further division into *kyrialia* and *sequentiaria*. Historically such divisions are justified. Manuscripts of these books are rare, and their contents are found in the graduals.

(iii) *The lectionary*. This book contained the epistles and gospels read at mass. It is found in several forms during its history. Its most perfect form is the *lectionarium missae* containing in full the liturgical pericopes read at mass throughout the liturgical year. In origin this book consisted of a list of references to the Bible. Each reference began with the first and last words of the passage to be read. Such lists were known by different names: *capitulare epistolarum* or *evangeliorum*; *comes* or *liber comitis* or *comicus*. Over the past sixty years the Roman lectionary system has been studied by such scholars as Beissel, Godu, Frere, Herbert, Klauser, Wilmart, Chavasse, and Gamber.

(iv) *The missal*. This is a book which resulted from the fusion of the above three distinct volumes into one. This fusion, however, was gradual. Its history is not clear, but the book itself appears in MSS from the end of the tenth to the middle of the thirteenth centuries. The evolution seems to have begun with small collections of complete mass formularies within the compass of one volume. This type of book seems to have been a link between the sacramentary and the later *missale plenum*. The Vatican library contains some forty interesting examples.

(b) *The divine office*
(i) *The psalter*. At the origins of Christian

worship the Bible itself was sufficient for the essential prayer of the church. Once the period of improvisation was over, and the liturgy was celebrated within the bounds of set forms, various books for use in the celebration of the divine office came into being. One of the earliest books to be formed was the psalter. This was a distribution of the psalms for liturgical use over the period of a week or according to feasts. Little by little these psalters attracted additions. From the twelfth century onwards, antiphons and versicles are found written in the margins or between the lines of the psalms. Later other elements of the office were added: invitatories, responds, the opening words of hymns, etc. By the fourteenth century it became the practice to group certain psalms according to the offices celebrated during the day or the week. Thus evolved the liturgical psalter described by V. Leroquais and P. Salmon.

(ii) *The antiphonal*. This book contained the antiphons and responds of the divine office. There are two types, a monastic type, easily recognized by the number of responds for the celebration of mattins (twelve), and the Roman type, containing only nine responds. Normally this book contains the chant for the antiphons and responds, but there are exceptions.

(iii) *The hymnal*. The collection of hymns, used at the celebration of the office, was often combined with the psalter, but there are many MSS which contain the hymns alone.

(iv) *The breviary*. Like the missal, the breviary is the result of the fusion into one volume of the above elements. Like the missal also it was the product of an evolution. Towards the eighth/ninth centuries, the collects used at the office became separated from the sacramentaries, and formed a book of their own, called a *collectarium*. From the eleventh century onwards other elements of the office were added to this book: the calendar, the antiphons, responds, hymns. Later still a description of the office and its celebration was added under the title *Breviarium sive ordo officiorum per totam anni decursionem*. It was only a step to the formation of the breviary. The result of this evolution, and the fusion of four or five distinct books into one volume, was a shortening of the elements of the office, hence the name *breviarium*. The biblical and patristic lessons were no longer read from the Bible or the great tomes of the patristic authors. This was one of the results of the reform begun during the eleventh and twelfth centuries, and ended with that of the office of the Curia under Innocent III. The composition of these breviaries, especially those of the eleventh to twelfth centuries, is highly diverse, and often run into several volumes.

HENRY ASHWORTH OSB

(2) *Roman Catholic.* By the end of the Middle Ages both liturgical observance and the liturgical books were in a state of disarray. Reform had become necessary; the Council of Trent decreed it and committed the task to the papacy. A small commission, of whose work little is known, produced the liturgical books that were in use until recently. The *Missale Romanium,* 1570, was substantially the same as the first printed missal of 1474, containing the Roman rite as celebrated in the papal chapel in the thirteenth century and as propagated throughout Europe by the Franciscans. Like the *missalia plenaria* of the earlier Middle Ages, it contained the order of mass, the propers (q.v.) and the lessons to be read at the eucharist. It was prefaced by a long document, *Ritus Servandus,* giving minute directions about the celebration of the mass.

The *Breviarium Romanum,* 1568, giving the offices of the night and day (mattins, lauds, prime, terce, sext, none, vespers, and compline [qq.v.]), represented a conservative reform. The offices were long and the form monastic.

To these must be added the *Pontificale Romanum,* 1596, giving the rites celebrated only by a bishop, and the *Rituale Romanum,* 1614, for the administration of baptism, marriage and a great variety of other rites.

Apart from the breviary, which received a newly arranged psalter in 1911, these books remained substantially the same throughout the centuries. New feasts required new propers and there were one or two revisions, notably that of the liturgy of Holy Week in 1955.

The reform of the liturgy decreed by the Second Vatican Council (1963-1965) necessitated a complete revision of all the liturgical books. At the time of writing they are:

Missale Romanum, 1970, containing the order of mass with the four eucharistic prayers, the prefaces (82) and the collects with their corresponding prayers over the offerings and after communion and the entrance and communion verses.

Lectionarium, 1969, containing the course of scripture readings for Sundays (three-year cycle) and weekdays with the responsorial psalms and other texts used in the ministry of the word.

The *Breviary,* now called *The Liturgy of the Hours,* 1971, is a radical revision of the divine office and is intended for use both by the pastoral clergy and the people.

The *Pontificale Romanum* underwent partial revision in 1961 and a further revision (the rites of ordination) in 1968 and 1971.

Parts of the new *Rituale Romanum,* the Orders of Baptism (Infants, 1969), Marriage (1969), Confirmation (1971), have appeared and the revision of the other rites is proceeding.

Other book used in the Roman Rite are the *Martyrology* (last edition, 1956), a list with brief biographies, of the saints recognized by the Roman Catholic Church; the *Graduale Romanum* (1907), giving the plain-chant propers for the eucharist for the year, and the *Antiphonale* giving the plain-chant texts for the day hours of the divine office. The *Caeremoniale Episcoporum* (1600) gives the rubrical directives for episcopal ceremonies and like the foregoing books is in need of revision.

J. D. CRICHTON

4. *Anglican.* The book with the best claim to be called the first Anglican service-book is the *Litany* of 1544, which was published under the auspices of 'the King's Majesty and his clergy'. It was followed by *The King's Primer* (1545), *The Book of Homilies* (1547), and *The Order of the Communion* (1548). Each of these, however, presupposed the continuance of the traditional Latin services, and the first book to provide a complete range of reformed services in English was the *BCP* of 1549. This was a translation and abridgement of the Sarum rite with a strong admixture of Reformed ideas, owing much to the services of the continental Reformers, notably Luther and Bucer. It covers the ground formerly occupied by the breviary, the missal, the manual, and the processional, and was supplemented in 1550 by a set of ordination services, replacing the pontifical. The saying of the daily office requires in addition the use of a Bible, as the psalms and lessons are not printed in full. The other services are self-contained. A music edition

by John Merbecke appeared in 1550, and a French translation for use in the Channel Islands and a very inaccurate translation into Latin.

A revised version was issued in 1552, of a much more definitely Reformed character, though the main outlines of 1549 are retained. Zwingli is now the influential figure. It was followed by a similarly reformed *Primer*, but the two books had a life of only a few months before the Roman allegiance was restored under Mary.

On Elizabeth I's accession the book of 1552 was reissued with minor alterations designed to make it slightly less Protestant. The Edwardine *Primer* reappeared, together with three new books of devotion which attempted to reintroduce traditional forms (*Primer*, 1559; *Orarium*, 1560; *Preces Privatae*, 1564). A new Latin translation of the *BCP* appeared in 1560, followed by a more accurate rendering in 1571; and a Welsh translation was issued in 1567. A second *Book of Homilies* followed in 1563. From 1578 onwards unofficial editions appeared, conforming the book to Puritan ideas.

The accession of James I resulted in further minor changes, this time with an eye to the Puritans. This version appeared in Irish in 1608. Charles I commissioned a book of devotions for the ladies of the court from John Cosin, who took the *Orarium* of 1560 as his model. In 1637 a prayer book was printed for use in Scotland, which reintroduced many of the ideas of 1549 that had been discarded in 1552. Not surprisingly, the book proved completely unacceptable. In 1645 the *BCP* was banned and was only restored with the return of Charles II in 1660. Despite vigorous demands for revision from both wings of the church, Laudian and Puritan, the book eventually annexed to the Act of Uniformity of 1662 was substantially the book of 1552 with minor ceremonial additions. There were, however, numerous small improvements in the text, and some additional services.

It will be convenient at this point to list the contents of the book, which remained almost unchanged for 300 years. After three prefaces, tables of psalms and lessons, and much calendrical matter, the services included are:

Morning and evening prayer
The litany, prayers, and thanksgivings
Collects, epistles and gospels
Holy communion
Baptism (public, private, and for those of riper years)
Catechism and confirmation
Matrimony
Visitation and communion of the sick
Burial of the dead
Churching of women
Commination
The psalms
Ordination services (deacons, priests and bishops)
Forms of prayer for use at sea
State services

The Psalter, either in the translation of the Great Bible (Coverdale) or in metrical form (Sternhold and Hopkins), had often been bound up with the *BCP*, but now became an integral part of it; and the same is true of the ordinal. The state services added in 1662 were withdrawn in 1859; an accession service was a normal part of the book from Queen Anne onwards. The Thirty-Nine Articles, though customarily printed at the end of the book, have never formed part of it. There has never been an official music edition; pointed psalters, chant-books and hymnals have been left to private enterprise, though the metrical psalter of Tate and Brady (1696) was so widely used in the eighteenth century that it acquired a virtually official status.

The 1662 *BCP* was translated into French (1662), Greek and Welsh (both 1665), and Latin (1670). With the spread of missionary enterprise in the nineteenth century, the number of languages in which the *BCP* was available had reached a total of 140 by 1970. Editions of the book for use in Ireland from 1666 onwards contained supplementary services such as consecration of churches and visitation of prisoners. The disestablished Episcopalians in Scotland produced a series of 'wee bookies' containing a communion service based on primitive liturgies, which reached its definitive form in the communion office of 1764. This was taken as a model by the infant Protestant Episcopal Church of the USA, which produced an entire prayer book in 1790. During the eighteenth century various bodies in the process of secession from the Church of England made their own revisions of the prayer book, notably the Non-jurors, the Unitarians, and the Methodists. The disestablishment of the Irish Church in 1871 led to the issue of a conservative revision in

1877, while the Americans revised their own book in 1892.

From the beginning of the twentieth century revision took different forms. In England it was unhappily seen as a means of enforcing uniformity, especially upon Anglo-Catholics. Others, especially overseas, saw it as an opportunity for 'enrichment', usually from medieval sources. A considerable encouragement was given to the process of revision by the Lambeth Conference in 1908. This was soon reflected by draft proposals in Scotland, Canada, and South Africa, and later in the USA and Ireland. Each of these drafts is closely related to the others and to the English book of 1928, the product of twenty years' drafting. The latter book, intended as an alternative to 1662, was rejected by Parliament, though it subsequently came into wide, if unofficial, use. It departed sufficiently from the doctrinal standards of the Thirty-Nine Articles to alarm the Evangelicals, but without appealing to many Anglo-Catholics. In other parts of the world there was no need for parliamentary sanction, and the revisions duly appeared in their final forms as follows: 1922, Canada; 1926, Ireland; 1928, America; 1929, Scotland and South Africa. Of these, the first two are Evangelical in churchmanship, the others Anglo-Catholic. The South African is perhaps the most thorough and satisfactory.

In 1947 the archbishops of Canterbury and York issued an abridged version of the prayer book incorporating the more popular proposals of 1928. These were reintroduced in 1966 in a modified form entitled *Alternative Services: First Series.* Interest in liturgy had become much keener since the Second World War, and in 1955 the archbishops set up a Liturgical Commission to prepare new alternative services. At the time of going to press it had produced services of morning and evening prayer (1966, revised 1970), holy communion (1967), and baptism and confirmation (1958, revised 1967-8); other services were in preparation.

The pace continued to quicken: 1959 saw the adoption of new revisions in Canada, Japan, and the West Indies, and 1960 in the Church of India, Pakistan, Burma, and Ceylon. In the 1960s Scotland, Ireland and America resumed the work of revision; Wales, Australia and New Zealand entered the field for the first time. Experimentation was also proceeding in East Africa, Nigeria,

Brazil, Chile, Iran and Hong Kong. The last twelve countries were concerned with individual services rather than service-books; and it seems that the 'omnibus' volume containing all the occasional offices as well as the normal Sunday services, to say nothing of psalms, epistles, and gospels, is obsolescent, if not already obsolete. Future service-books will probably consist only of the eucharist and the daily office, the other services being printed in booklets or on cards. *The Revised Psalter Pointed* (1966) is a semi-official psalter, but there is no sign of an official hymn-book.

G. J. CUMING

5, *Baptist.* The use of liturgical books was regarded by John Smyth, the founder of the General Baptists, as 'the invention of the man of sin'. It was incompatible with the spiritual worship of the NT proceeding from the heart. The Separatists rejected not only prescribed liturgies but also the use of books of any kind in worship. As books were excluded prayers could not be said or praises sung by all together. During the course of the seventeenth century, the singing of metrical psalms, paraphrases, and hymns was introduced, and by the eighteenth century congregational singing had become general among Baptists. Many collections of praise material were made by individuals, the most notable of which, after revision by a committee of ministers, was published in 1858 under the title *Psalms and Hymns.* The publication of *The Baptist Church Hymnal* (1900, revised 1933) was a landmark, for in addition to hymns and metrical psalms, it contained the traditional canticles, a selection of prose psalms for chanting, and anthems. *The Baptist Hymn Book* (1962) is now widely used throughout Britain and by English speaking Baptists overseas. It contains hymns, canticles, prose psalms, a few prayers, and passages of scripture for alternate reading. Responsive readings are also a feature of American hymnals. It should be understood that the hymnal is *the* liturgical book of the Baptists, in comparison with which all other service-books are of secondary importance. Concerning the latter, there are three facts to be emphasized. First, since each Baptist church is autonomous there is no prescribed liturgy, and a service-book may be used much, occasionally, little, or not at all. Secondly, the service-books have been prepared for the pulpit, not the pew; they are manuals for ministers, not congregational prayer books. Thirdly, they have been compiled by individual initiative, not by representatives commissioned by the denomination. In Britain, a small book of services for special occasions was compiled by Dr M. E. Aubrey, General Secretary of the Baptist Union (*A Minister's Manual*, 1927). The current service-book, in widespread use throughout Britain, is a comprehensive book of common order (Ernest A. Payne and Stephen F. Winward, *Orders and Prayers for Church Worship*, 1960, revised 1965, adapted for use in the USA by James W. Cox under the title *Minister's Worship Manual*, 1969). A second comprehensive service-book has been produced in the USA (John Skoglund, *A Manual of Worship*, 1968). While these, together with the service-books of other communions, are now used by many ministers and lay preachers, the hymnal is the only liturgical book used by the congregation in all Baptist churches.

S. WINWARD

6. *Christian Church*. In its century and a half of history the Christian Church (Disciples of Christ) has made the congregation, with its minister and elders, responsible for ordering worship. One result of this policy has been to avoid the publication of official liturgical books. Not until 1953, with the publication of *Christian Worship: A Service Book*, did the denomination produce an authorized book, and this was for voluntary use only. This volume was largely the work of Professor G. Edwin Osborn (1897-1965), who for a third of a century was the denomination's acknowledged authority in liturgics. Educated at the University of Edinburgh, Osborn was an advocate of a psychological basis for worship. He represented a liberal attitude, holding that a service should be planned by the minister around a theme that he had chosen.

The book included recommended liturgies for the several rites of the church, a lectionary and some 400 pages of biblical materials and prayers for use by ministers and congregations. Although the book enjoyed only modest sales, it remained in print for some two decades and greatly influenced Disciple liturgical practice. Prior to the publication of this volume there were other books of lesser quality developed by pastors and

published for wider use.

Throughout their history Disciples have published hymnals. A hymnal first published by Alexander Campbell in 1834 was in widespread use throughout the several decades that followed. Other hymnals were developed under unauthorized auspices, including *Hymns of the United Church* co-edited by C. C. Morrison, editor of *The Christian Century*, and published in 1924.

In 1941 a new hymnal was published by the denomination's publishing house in cooperation with publishers for the American Baptist Convention. In 1970 a successor was published in similar fashion. Each one is representative of mainstream Protestant hymnals. The 1941 book, while superior to many other hymnals also in use among Disciples, was less highly regarded by musicians than were other leading hymnals, such as the *Hymnal 1940* of the Episcopal Church. The 1970 volume was superior to the earlier hymnal in two ways: it contained fewer of the sentimental revival songs of the late nineteenth century and it included a sizeable collection of modern hymns.

KEITH WATKINS

7. *Congregationalist*. Since the first Congregationalists believed in free prayers, not in a liturgy, there are no early Congregational prayer books. There is, however, an influential manual for ministers in the Westminster *Directory for Public Worship* (1644), which was the joint work of Presbyterians and Congregationalists. This became the standard for English-speaking Calvinist churches (Congregational, Baptist, and Presbyterian) for 250 years.

In the nineteenth century and after, some influential Congregational ministers compiled their own service-books. The two most famous were John Hunter's *Devotional Services for Public Worship* (1882) and W. E. Orchard's *Divine Service* (1919), the former being a liturgical expression of the social gospel, the latter being more traditional and Catholic in character.

The twentieth century sees the publication of denominational service-books. In England the first was *The Book of Congregational Worship* (1920), strongly imitative of the *BCP*. No attempt was made to return to the biblical or Reformation sources of worship. The same is even more decidedly true of its successor, *A Manual for Ministers* (1936).

An important but unofficial service-book which did return to the scriptures and original Calvinism was *A Book of Public Worship Compiled for the Use of Congregationalists* (1948) by John Huxtable, John Marsh, Romilly Micklem, and James Todd. A companion volume was the latter's *Prayers and Services for Christian Festivals* (1951). 1959 saw the publication of another official English Congregational manual of worship, *A Book of Services and Prayers*, the chairman of the compilers being W. Gordon Robinson. The eucharistic theology shows a notable advance from the book of 1920 by the following of the traditional structure of the Western prayer of consecration, with the addition of an epiclesis.

On the American side two important denominational service-books have appeared. *A Book of Worship for Free Churches* (1948) was prepared under the direction of the General Council of the Congregational Christian Churches, Boynton Merrill being the chairman of the compilers. It has many alternative orders, uses ecumenical resources, and stresses the importance of symbolism.

The United Church of Christ, which came into being with the union of the Congregational Christian Churches and the Evangelical and Reformed Church in 1950, necessitated the provision of new orders of worship. The new commission on worship, under the leadership of Louis H. Gunnemann, produced as its first fruits *The Lord's Day Service* (1964). Two years later the commission published *Services of Word and Sacrament*, and the two orders have exactly the same structure stressing the unity of word and sacrament, but the first uses traditional and the second contemporary language. Recognizing the transitional character of modern liturgical productions, the commission has committed its successive works to paperback publication, thus combining realism with modesty and tentativeness.

Modern Congregational liturgical books seem to be based upon five liturgical principles: (1) the reaffirmation of the biblical basis and content of Christian worship; (2) the importance of claiming our ecumenical inheritance; (3) the combination of a firm order of liturgy with a place for free prayers and silent prayer; (4) the provision of many alternatives to provide variety and flexibility within order; and (5) the inclusion of both classical and contemporary prayers.

There are three current hymn-books in use. The English Congregational hymnal is *Congregational Praise* (*see* E. R. Routley and K. L. Parry, *Companion to Congregational Praise,* 1953). The United Church of Christ in the USA is in the process of compiling a new hymnal, but the pre-union hymnals are still being used. The ex-Congregationalists use *The Pilgrim Hymnal,* while former members of the Evangelical and Reformed Church use *The Hymnal Containing Complete Orders of Worship* (1941).

HORTON DAVIES

8. *Jehovah's Witnesses.* The society of Jehovah's Witnesses is Bible-orientated, and the Bible is the one book consistently to the foreground in all meetings.

Until the 1950s the translation generally used was the Authorized Version, supplemented by the American Standard Version, Weymouth's, Moffatt's and others. In 1950 the Watch Tower Bible and Tract Society published the first volume of the *New World Translation of the Christian Greek Scriptures* (i.e. NT). By 1960 the entire Bible had been translated and published and by 1970 was available in English, Spanish, Portuguese, Dutch, Italian, and (Matthew to Revelation only) French and German.

The translation has played an important part in the meetings of Jehovah's Witnesses; not so much in development of basic theology, where its effect has been peripheral – Witnesses had established a framework of Bible teaching long before 1960 – as in that analytical Bible study which is the groundwork of all Kingdom Hall meetings.

The translation's aim is to be as literal as possible, 'where a literal rendition does not for any clumsiness hide the thought' (Foreword). Each major word is assigned one meaning 'as far as the context permits', the object being to make for good cross-reference work and 'a more reliable comparison of related texts or verses'. This method restricts diction but is helpful in research. The result is an intelligible and highly practical work for the Bible analyst.

One stage further, 1969 saw published in English *The Kingdom Interlinear Translation of the Greek Scriptures*, a word-for-word translation beneath Westcott and Hort's Greek text, with the above modern-English translation in a right-hand column. A feature of the interlinear is its analysis of the Greek's particles and compound words, the aim being to help the reader determine what the '*koine* Greek basically or literally says'. Its use is now a feature of Witness meetings.

Other set books for use in congregation worship include: a song-book (latest edition 1966; all the [anonymous] songs written and composed by Witnesses); '*Your Word Is a Lamp to My Foot*', a Bible-based guide to the Society's structure; *Qualified to Be Ministers*, a textbook for the public ministry; and *The Watchtower*, the Society's official semi-monthly magazine (monthly circulation, 15,250,000 in January 1972).

The place of *The Watchtower* in congregational instruction is important. Through it scriptural exegesis is presented. '*The Watchtower* is no inspired prophet, but it follows and explains a Book of prophecy the predictions in which have proved to be unerring and unfailing till now' (title-page). Much is said about family life, promotion of the public Christian ministry, moral cleanness, and adoption of missionary service by Witness youths.

Where new congregations of Witnesses are formed, the first meeting arranged is the weekly *Watchtower* Bible study. The Bible, in whatever translation, is central to the worship of Jehovah's Witnesses; *The Watchtower* encourages and promotes its study.

                                                          A. HELEY

9. *Lutheran*

(1) *European*. Lutheran liturgical books have their starting point in two orders of service outlined by Luther, the *Formula Missae* of 1523 and the *Deutsche Messe* (German mass) of 1526. These in turn followed the pattern of the Roman mass, which was altered to follow the perspectives of the Reformation.

(*a*) *Germany*. Because of the territorial divisions of Lutheranism, there was no single service book used by all the German-speaking Lutheran churches in common, as was the case with Luther's translation of the Bible, his catechism and his hymns. Indeed, appeals to article VII of the Augsburg Confession even prevented energetic efforts at such a book. Nevertheless, a series of common liturgical features are to be found within the various 'church orders' that appeared. The North German orders, in which Luther's friend Johannes Bugenhagen played a substantial part, come close to the type of the

Deutsche Messe. Their freedom in shaping the eucharist is striking. Similar influence was exercised by the Brandenburg-Nürnberg church order of 1533, which continued the conservative line prefigured in the *Formula Missae*. In South-West German Lutheranism, a liturgy going back to the medieval Dominican pattern was used.

The Reformation orders of service were preserved down to the period of pietism, when the traditional liturgical forms rapidly began to break up. Their place was taken by private forms of service, newly-constructed artificial orders in the spirit of rationalism. A restoration counter-movement began in the nineteenth century. In Prussia, where in 1817 a union had been brought about between the Lutherans (numerically, by far in the majority) and the Reformed, a 'church order' (with fundamentally a Lutheran structure) worked out by king Friedrich Wilhelm III was introduced. The great Lutheran churches of Bavaria, Hanover, Mecklenburg and Saxony similarly took upon themselves regulative orders, which were based on the sixteenth-century forms of service. They also set the pattern for the smaller district churches. The formation of the United Evangelical Lutheran Church of Germany (VELKD) in 1948 led to the creation of a great four-volume work which for the first time in the history of German Lutheranism provided a common basis for liturgical action. The main liturgy has the structure of the 'evangelical mass', from which the sacramental part can be excluded. Lutheran churches which belong to the United Evangelical Church also have the possibility, after the new service book of 1959, of using the main Lutheran liturgy as well as the preaching service and the eucharist following the Reformed pattern. So far, the separation of the organizations of the Lutheran churches in East and West Germany has not led to any sacrifice of liturgical uniformity.

In many places, the demand for new, contemporary forms of service alongside those forms of service shaped by traditional patterns has led to modern attempts at liturgies. Such experiments are not, however, given fixed forms in service books. Suggestions and models are published in 'work books', which do not have any official standing. The tendency to avoid the constricting pressures of a service book is at present stronger than ever.

(b) *Northern Europe*. The *Swedish* service books similarly begin from Luther's reform of the mass. However, from 1560 onwards, a predilection for richer liturgical forms is perceptible, though intensive efforts to restore the liturgy of the ancient church (Liturgy of king Johann III) were rejected as being too 'catholic'. With the service book of 1693, the particularism of the episcopal sees was broken and a national church uniformity was introduced throughout Sweden, with the full support of Lutheran orthodoxy. Orders of service maintained a much purer form than in Germany through the period of the Enlightenment. The church books of the nineteenth century, stamped with the spirit of the age, were replaced by the new service book of 1942. This is characterized by a far-reaching reform of the lectionary of the ancient church.

Until the separation of Finland from the Swedish communion of churches in 1809, the *Finnish* liturgy was closely connected with developments in Sweden. After two service books of 1886 and 1913, a new liturgy was adopted in 1969.

Bugenhagen was also an influence on the *Danish* mass of 1539. Even now, the 'Church Ritual' of 1685 is the basis of the Danish liturgy. An 'Experimental Book of Ritual' which appeared in 1963 is intended once again to make greater room for sung liturgical prose.

The most recent order of the *Norwegian* church, which received its church ritual in 1683, is the Norwegian mass of 1920. Since 1969, a new experimental service book has been introduced, which seeks to pioneer new liturgical music.

(c) *The rest of Europe*. The minority Lutheran churches have mostly adopted new service books since the Second World War, following the line laid down in the great book of the VELKD (e.g. France 1953, Czechoslovakia 1954, Poland 1955).

F. KALB

(2) *United States*. Lutheran settlers in the USA brought with them their own vernacular liturgies and it was not until 1748 that the foundation was laid for an American liturgy, when H. M. Mühlenberg devised an order in German which was adopted by the Ministerium of Pennsylvania; the same body adopted an English liturgy in 1860 and eight years later the General Council approved a revision. The General Synod and the United Synod of the South then joined with the Council to produce the *Common Service* of 1888, and a complete book, the *Common Service Book*, was published in 1917 to coincide with the foundation of the United Lutheran Church of America. In 1957 there was issued a *Service Book and Hymnal* which contains forms for the eucharist, mattins, vespers, baptism, confirmation, confession, burial and matrimony (qq.v.).

EDITOR

10. *Methodist*. The first Methodist liturgical book, as distinct from collections of prayers and hymns, was *The Sunday Service of the Methodists in America, With Other Occasional Services*, 1784, an abridgement, with some amendments, mostly of a Puritan character, of the *BCP*, 1662, of the Church of England. There were many subsequent editions, two at least for Methodists in the USA, one for Methodists in His Majesty's Dominions, and the rest simply for Methodists. The Americans did not view it with much favour and soon discarded it, but they incorporated some parts of it in their *Discipline* under the title 'Sacramental Services, etc.'; the title was subsequently changed to 'The Ritual'. There were extensive revisions in 1864, 1916 and 1932 in the Methodist Episcopal Church and from 1854 to 1870 and in 1910 in the Methodist Episcopal Church South. The *Methodist Hymnal*, 1935, incorporated some orders of service for optional use which were not part of 'The Ritual' but had come to be printed with 'The Ritual' in the *Discipline*. The *Book of Worship for Church and Home*, 1944, was an innovation, and contained 'The Ritual' and much else, though many people in the pew used only the material in the *Methodist Hymnal*. All these books were revised in 1964 and *The Book of Worship for Church and Home*, 1964, included orders and offices for the official rites of the church and all the other liturgical material, except hymns, which were needed in this church. It has now united under the title of the United Methodist Church with the Evangelical United Brethren, whose *Book of Ritual*, 1959, is recognized together with the books previously mentioned.

In England *The Sunday Service* went through many editions until 1910. Between 1839 and 1881 a shorter version, containing only certain services, *Order of Administration of the Sacraments*, also went through many editions. There were revisions in 1846 and 1864. The Wesleyan conference of 1882 produced a modified version of it known as *The Book of Public Prayers and Services*, which was intended to safeguard the principles of evangelical Protestantism; at several points, however, it restored portions of the *BCP* which Wesley had omitted. It is curious that this also had a shorter version with the same title as its predecessor, *Order of Administration of the Sacraments*, and that *The Sunday Service* continued to be published for many years after it had been officially superseded. The non-Wesleyan branches of Methodism also produced service-books, which were very much simpler and less Anglican than the Wesleyan books and also were probably much less used.

After the union of the Wesleyan Methodists, the Primitive Methodists and the United Methodists in Britain in 1932, the conference in 1936 published *The Book of Offices*, being the orders of service authorized for use in the Methodist Church, together with *The Order for Morning Prayer*. This book, though it had the characteristically liberal Protestant tone of that period, is still recognizably indebted to the *BCP*. It is still the official book, though various supplementary services are published, to some extent under the control of the Conference.

Liturgical books do not have the same binding authority in Methodism which they have in some other churches. The services in them are authorized and generally followed (at ordinations invariably); but other forms are not prohibited. As the order for morning prayer is not widely used, the preaching service can and usually does proceed in Britain without any reference to the book. A book, *Divine Worship*, 1935, intended for such services, is not widely used.

It has often been said that the true liturgy of Methodism is to be found in its hymns, and this is reflected by the fact that its hymn-books are authorized by its Conferences. The Wesleys published many hymn-books; the definitive edition was that of 1780. British Methodism currently uses *The Methodist Hymn-Book*, 1933, together with a recent supplement *Hymns and Songs*, 1969.

The lectionary is also an official publication of the Conference. This has frequently been changed in recent years. The British Conference of 1969 authorized a new lectionary incorporated in *Collects, Lessons and Psalms* based on *The Calendar and Lectionary*, 1967, of the Joint Liturgical Group. Parts of *Collects, Lessons and Psalms* are authorized for experimental use, but the lectionary itself is authorized fully.

The British Conference has undertaken the revision of *The Book of Offices*, and certain portions of it have been authorized for experimental use, notably *The Sunday Service*, 1968. These services represent a considerable revision, adopting many of the insights of the Liturgical Movement and thus showing considerable resemblance to the liturgies of the churches which have been similarly influenced. When the work of revision is complete, the main services are likely to be gathered in a volume probably to be called 'Services and Sacraments'; the other services will have the same authority, but will probably be published as separate pamphlets.

There are many Methodist churches in other parts of the world, but they all stem originally from either British or American Methodism, and their service-books are usually adaptations, sometimes indeed abbreviations, of the English or American books, often translated into other languages.

A. RAYMOND GEORGE

11. *Old Catholic*. Each of the Old Catholic churches belonging to the Utrecht Union has its own liturgical books. The *jus liturgicum* (i.e. the right of ordering the liturgy in the church) belongs to the bishops of each church; they also have the duty of supervising the versions of the liturgical books.

The basis of the liturgical books of the Old Catholic churches is the books of the Roman Catholic rite. As the liturgy has long been celebrated in the vernacular, these books have had to be translated into various languages. Sometimes they are almost literal translations; sometimes they are free revisions. Corresponding to the geographical spread of the Old Catholic church, there are liturgical books in the following languages: German for Germany, Austria and the German-speaking parts of Switzerland; French for the French-speaking part of Switzerland and France; Italian, Croatian, Dutch, Polish (and also English for the Polish National Church in the USA and Canada), and Czech.

The following is a list of the more important liturgical books of the Old Catholic churches as far as they are known to the authors of this article.

(*a*) *Altar books and mass books for the congregation*: Germany has the *Altarbuch für die Feier der heiligen Eucharistie im Katholischen Bistum der Alt-Katholiken in Deutschland*, Bonn 1959; Austria has the *Altkatholisches Altar-Buch*, Vienna 1933. For the ordinary of the mass it has now been replaced by the *Ordnung des Heiligen Amtes der Gemeinde*; the proper is still to come. The volume *Das heilige Amt für die Gemeinde, II Ordnung*, provides alternative texts for the eucharistic prayer as experimental forms.

Switzerland has the *Messliturgie der Christkatholischen Kirche der Schweiz*, Bern [2]1905. The French edition (1910 is its most recent date) is at present out of print. In 1971 a completely revised text of the ordinary of the mass has been published (*Nouvel Ordinaire de la Messe*); a new proper will follow. Italy has the *Messalino e piccolo Catechismo, Chiesa Cattolica Antica*, no date.

Holland has the *Misbook ten dienste van de Oud-Katholieke Kerk van Nederland*, 1909. The edition in a small format for the congregation last appeared in 1960 in a fourth edition (with some alterations); in addition an experimental *Tweede Misorde* (second order) appeared in 1968. The order of mass for the Polish National Catholic Church is to be found in *A Book of Devotions and Prayers according to the use of the Polish National Church in Polish and English*, Scranton, Pa, 1951.

(*b*) *Books of ritual*, containing the rites for the celebration of the sacraments, burials, blessings, etc., are as follows: *Katholisches Rituale der alt-katholischen Kirche des Deutschen Reiches*, Bonn 1876, abbreviated edition 1933. A thorough revision is planned. *Das österreichische Rituale* of 1929 is out of print; a new edition is being prepared. There was a completely revised second edition of the *Rituale der Christkatholischen Kirche der Schweiz*, Bern 1940. For the Netherlands, *Gebed en Sacrament* has gone through a number of editions since 1935; it also contains private devotions and the order of the mass. *Rytual Kosciola Polskokatolickiego* for the Polish Catholic Church appeared in Warsaw in 1961. It also contains the Holy Week liturgy and a number of benedictions, liturgies and hymns.

(*c*) *Prayer books* for congregational use corresponding approximately to the English *BCP* usually contain the order of the mass, morning and evening prayer and the sacraments, as well as private prayers, especially for the sick; some also have a hymn-book. One is the *Katholisches Gebet- und Gesangbuch für die Alt-Katholiken in Deutschland*, Bonn [2]1965. It also contains the special liturgies for Good Friday and Easter Even. *Unser Beten* is the prayer book for the Old Catholic Church of Austria, Vienna [2]1962. The *Gebetbuch der Christkatholischen Kirche der Schweiz*, Allschwil [11]1968, is bound up with a hymn-book (*see* [*d*] below); it also contains all the propers of the mass. *Prières liturgiques en usage dans l'Eglise Catholique-Chrétienne de la Suisse* (the last full edition, Soleure 1910) is about to appear in a considerably altered new impression (1971). For Holland *see* (*b*) above, *Gebed en Sacrament*. For the Polish National Catholic Church *see* (*a*) above, *A Book of Devotions* . . . and (*b*) *Rytual* . . .

(*d*) *Hymn-books*. These contain truly liturgical hymns and above all the congregational hymns which are much loved in Old Catholic churches.

For Germany, *see* (*c*) above. The *Gesangbuch der Christkatholischen Kirche der Schweiz* is combined with the prayer book (*see* [*c*] above). A new and enlarged edition of the French hymn-book, now out of print, is in preparation (1971). There are three hymn-books for the church of the Netherlands: *Misgezangen* (mass hymns), new edition, 1949; *Vesperboek*, several editions since 1909; *Gesangboek ten dienste van de Oud-Katholieke Kerk*, enlarged edition, 1942.

(*e*) *The rites for the consecration of priests* (major and minor orders) were produced in German at the request of the Conference of Old Catholic Bishops in a free rendering that followed the *Pontificale Romanum*, Bern 1899. This was translated into Dutch in 1900 and Polish (in *Rytual* . . .), *see* (*b*) above. In addition there are formulae for the consecration of a bishop and for the consecration of churches, altars and bells.

New editions of most of the Old Catholic liturgical books are being produced in the course of the movement for liturgical renewal.

KURT PURSCH
A. E. RÜTHY
C. TOL

12. *Pentecostal*. E. Leonard called attention

to the oral, non-literary character of classical Pentecostalism (*L'illuminisme dans un protestantisme de constitution récente*, 1953, p. 99). Since classical Pentecostalism (*see* **Pentecostal Worship**) represents a pre-literary culture whose tools of socialization are the story, the parable, a witness, a prophecy, a song, and face-to-face encounter, since the Pentecostal ethos is experience-oriented and leader-dominated, since their liturgical presuppositions are the actuality and immediacy of God's presence ('He is real; the really real'), and since all is under the guidance and prompting of the Holy Spirit, there are many classical Pentecostals who look upon a written liturgy and liturgical paraphernalia as a quenching of the Spirit. However, in South Africa the Apostolic Jerusalem Church in Sabbath has taken over the office of bishop together with copes, capes, mitres, acolytes or deacons (qq.v.). In Chile certain denominations have developed a ritual of entrance for the pastor. 'Like the bishop who enters only after the ceremony has begun, he (the pastor) comes with hat on head and a cape on his shoulders, three councillors following him, one carrying a Bible. When they reach the platform, an elder takes the hat, one the cape, and the third hands the Bible to the bishop, who then takes his seat' (C. Lalive d'Epinay, *Haven of the Masses*, 1969, p. 52). Though such rituals might never be reduced to print – indeed to do so might in some cases be a scandal – yet rubrical observance might be as rigorous as in any of the high liturgical churches.

Some of the tendencies towards ritual are motivated by desire for social respectability. In South America norms of social acceptability are determined by the mores of Catholic practice. To disassociate their churches from the image of the culturally disinherited, Pentecostal churches conform to the socio-cultural patterns of the more respectable churches, i.e. the liturgical practices of Catholicism.

Those churches which have lost some of their prophetic character and become more or less centralized and bureaucratized also tend to move away from the oral and non-literary culture of classical Pentecostalism. These groups have published manuals with ceremonies for the reception of members, Lord's Supper, baptism, marriage, burial, dedication of churches and children (*Discipline of Pentecostal Holiness Church*, 1961;

Ministers' Manual, 1965). When these manuals are used it is as a servant rather than a master. An Assemblies of God pastor wrote: 'I believe that the Holy Spirit should be able to break in at any time he chooses. When we lose this – we've lost everything' (F. Masserano, *A Study of Worship Forms in the Assemblies of God Denomination*, Master's Thesis, Princeton, 1966, p. 70).

Classical Pentecostals are not at their best when composing liturgical texts, even in those churches which have moved beyond an oral, pre-literary culture to a literary culture. Their liturgical experience is, even in these cases, determined by their pre-literary origins. This can be deceptive. A classical Pentecostal eucharistic service the author attended in Minneapolis, Minnesota, was a liturgical success; but if it were reduced to the printed page it would look impoverished. Also, the rite is not understandable apart from spirituality of which it is an expression.

Neo-Pentecostals tend to follow the liturgical books of their own churches but with a freedom which allows for the exercise of charismatic gifts. In some Lutheran neo-Pentecostal groups (e.g. Arnold Bittlinger, Schloss Craheim, Germany; Larry Christenson, Trinity Lutheran Church, San Pedro, California), the charismatic element has been integrated into the total Lutheran approach. Instead of an aggressive self-conscious Pentecostal message, there is the quiet availability of the Pentecostal dimension within the Lutheran framework. Roman Catholic Pentecostals follow the liturgical order with greater fidelity than the underground churches, but with moments within the eucharistic action for community participation through the exercise of the gifts.

The weaknesses of the classical Pentecostal liturgical practice (e.g. excessive subjectivism, restricted theological horizon, ritualization of impoverished patterns, want of theological penetration) indicate that for the liturgical churches to abandon their tradition of printed texts would be an ill-advised move. But the strengths of the Pentecostal tradition would indicate that to concentrate on a purely literary tradition is to ignore those elements of the non-rational, pre-literary in the theological and liturgical traditions of the early church (O. Cullmann, *Early Christian Worship*, 1953, p. 20; E. Schweizer, *Church Order in the New Testament*, 1961, p. 221) and also to ignore the experience orientation of much of contemporary culture with its sensitivity sessions, T-groups, drug addiction, hippy movement, and participatory theatre. The classical Pentecostals have been especially productive and successful in creating new worship forms. A negro preacher from the Dominican Republic sang his worship service to a Chilean congregation. It was a free rhythmed spontaneous composition of high musical quality (film *Gloria a Dios, Pfingstkirchen in Chile*, Zweites Deutsche Fernsehen, directed by Fritz Puhl). From the Pentecostals the historic churches can learn how to maintain a more immediate contact between cultural patterns and liturgical forms, a contact which is established in an oral, pre-literary mode. What Ernst Troeltsch wrote of the social ethics of the churches is in a measure also true in the area of liturgical renewal:

It is the lower classes which do the really creative work, forming communities on a genuinely religious basis. They alone unite imagination and simplicity of feeling with a non-reflective habit of mind, a primitive energy, and an urgent sense of need. On such a foundation alone is it possible to build up an unconditional authoritative faith in a divine revelation with simplicity of surrender and unshaken certainty. (*The Social Teaching of the Christian Churches*, ET, 1931, I, p.44).

Though classical Pentecostalism can no longer be identified without qualification with the lower strata, it is from this level that its liturgical creativity still comes. (For bibliography *see under* **Pentecostal Worship**.)

KILIAN MCDONNELL

13. *Plymouth Brethren.* The Brethren have no liturgical books in the ordinary sense. Traditionally they interpret the freedom of the Spirit as ruling out such 'aids' to public worship. If this interpretation were pressed to its logical conclusion, it would rule out the use of hymn-books, but in fact liberal use is made of hymn-books in their worship. The selection of appropriate hymns for various services, and especially for the successive stages of the communion service, will sometimes be regarded as a mark of spiritual intelligence.

Among the Exclusive Brethren the standard hymn-book since 1856 has been *Hymns for the Little Flock*, compiled in that year by G. V. Wigram, revised in 1881 by J. N. Darby and subsequently issued in several further revisions for the use of the various Exclusive bodies. In the body led by the late James Taylor, Jr, successive revisions (by T. H. Reynolds in 1903, James Taylor, Sr, in 1932 and A. E. Myles in 1951) have increasingly made this collection a handbook to the liturgy (*see* **Liturgies** 13: Plymouth Brethren). It accurately reflects some notable features of this body's doctrine and practice, as in the avoidance of any reference to the eternity of Christ's relation as Son to the Father and in the absence of any note of confession of sin (which is not, however, a sign of antinomianism).

Among the Open Brethren a variety of hymn-books is in use. The most widely used in Great Britain and Ireland are *The Believer's Hymn Book* (1884; enlarged with a supplement, 1959), *Hymns of Light and Love* (1900) and *Hymns for Christian Worship and Service* (1909). Some of their churches prefer to use interdenominational collections, such as *Christian Praise* (1957) or *Hymns of Faith* (1964). To the latter of these the Brethren at Mitchley Hill Chapel, Sanderstead, Surrey, have provided an excellent supplement of hymns specially suitable for use at the communion service.

Apart from its use as the basis for expository ministry, the Bible serves in some degree as a liturgical book. At the communion service in particular, one or another of the worshippers may read (with or without brief comment) a scripture bearing on the purpose of the meeting – for example, a suitable passage from the NT or a 'messianic' psalm or prophecy from the OT calculated to promote the spirit of worship and anamnesis. As with the selection of suitable hymns, use and wont have established a feeling for what scripture lessons are appropriate for this purpose, so that the reading of passages that are deemed inappropriate may be put down to lack of spiritual intelligence. Departure from the accepted though unwritten liturgical pattern may be the result of inexperience or of mature and deliberate breaking with tradition.

F. F. BRUCE

14. *Reformed.* The Protestant Reformation brought changes in service books for use in worship as in other things. The replacement of Latin by the vernacular was a far-reaching change adopted by all the reformers, which

enabled the worshipper to understand the service. But on other points the reformers adopted differing policies. In the *Book of Common Prayer* (*BCP*) the text had to be strictly adhered to. But in other books there were specific points where variation was permitted. Thus in Calvin's *Forme des prieres* (1542) one rubric says, 'on use de cette action de graces ou semblable', and in the Scottish *Book of Common Order* (*BCO*) 1564, at a few places the rubrics permit the minister to pray 'either in these words following or the like in effect'. Another change was that the books were used by all the worshippers. Indeed in the case of *BCO* an Act of Assembly of 26 December 1564 ordered 'every minister, exhorter and reader to possess a copy' and use it, and an Act of Parliament of 1579 decreed that every person of a certain rank and class had to have copy. Possession of a copy by the worshipper was required because it contained metrical psalms for singing. Calvin's *La Forme* of 1542 contained thirty-five psalms with music and others were added in later editions. *BCO* of 1564 for the first time provided metrical versions of all the psalms. How widely used the various editions of *BCO* were is shown by the condition of most surviving copies, the beginning and the end being usually defective, leaves missing or heavily finger-marked and dirty.

Out of the many Reformed liturgical books that have been produced, the following deserve special mention. The story begins with Zwingli, who produced two forms, both for the Lord's Supper. The first in 1523, *De Canone Missae Epicheiresis,* was an attack on the Canon of the Mass and indicated his ideas for the service. The second, two years later, entitled *Action oder Bruch des Nachtmals*, was more radical, but it became the guiding rule for Zwinglian worship. Next to be noted is Farel's *La manyere et fasson qu'on tient es lieux que Dieu de sa grace a visites,* dated 1533, prepared for the use in Strasbourg of the Zwinglian Reformed congregation. This was Zwinglian in tone and had little influence on other rites, though Calvin adopted the marriage rite almost as it stood.

Strasbourg had already seen the important first reformed German Mass, arranged by Diebold Schwartz in 1524, and frequently revised, more and more under the influence of Bucer. When John Calvin came to Strasbourg in 1538 he made a Latin version of the Schwartz form; this was later translated into French as *La manyere de faire prieres aux eglises francoyses* and used by the Strasbourg French congregation. A later edition was printed in Geneva in 1542. This contained thirty-five psalms with melody, the creed, the Lord's Prayer, and an order of service for Sunday morning with the addition necessary when the eucharist was celebrated, the marriage service, and a section for the visitation of the sick. Some revisions of this were issued in succeeding years. A Latin translation was issued in Geneva in 1552, and one in English, by William Huycke, in London in 1550. Other editions continued to appear, a very important one being that printed in Geneva in 1556, under the title, *The forme of Prayers and ministration of the sacraments as used in the English Congregation at Geneva.*

This was John Knox's *Genevan Service Book*. There was also a Latin translation, *Ratio et Forma*. An edition similar to that of 1556, but containing additional prayers and the Genevan Confession of Faith, was issued in Geneva in 1561. The next edition takes us to Scotland where in 1562 Robert Lekprewick printed *The Forme of Prayers and Ministration of the Sacraments* at the order of the General Assembly, which gave him a grant towards his expenses. This was adopted for use in the Church of Scotland under the title *The Book of Common Order.*

La Forme des prieres continued to exert great influence both in Switzerland and in France. Many of the Swiss Cantons, such as Geneva, Vaud and Neuchâtel produced their own books, based on the great original though with many local accents. A notable attempt at revision was that of Jean-Frédéric Osterwald, who published a liturgy in 1713 which showed the influence of *BCP*, but had little influence on further Swiss books, except that of Vaud in 1725, but, translated and revised, it became the book of the Huguenot congregation in Charleston, South Carolina, 1853. Recent Swiss revisions include those of Vaud (1945) and Geneva (1946).

In France liturgical books were issued from time to time, and there were many attempts to revise and enrich the content. One important attempt was that of Eugène Bersier who in 1876 issued a *Projet de revision* and in 1888 a liturgy. Here was evidenced a moving towards a new spirit of worship. Its influence is seen in the recent *Liturgie de l'Église Réformée de France* of 1963, the result of the prolonged work of a Commission de liturgie.

The German and Dutch Reformed Churches gave much attention to the problems of the liturgy, and issued various service-books. The majority of the German Reformed churches joined with Lutheran churches in 1817. But in the Dutch Reformed Church there was a liturgical revival with the foundation in 1920 of the *Liturgische Kring* and in 1938 of the *Kring Eeredienst* which published its *Kanselboek* in 1944.

Now we return to consider the liturgical books of the churches which came to be known as Presbyterian. The original of these was *BCO*, popularly known as the Psalm-book. From 1564 to 1644 fully seventy editions appeared. The contents of these editions varied very considerably, but usually included the calendar; the psalter with music; scripture songs or hymns, i.e., metrical versions of the Ten Commandments, the Lord's Prayer and the Veni Creator, etc.; the catechism (Calvin's up to 1611, the Palatinate or Heidelberg in 1615); the order of baptism, the Lord's supper, marriage, visitation of the sick, the order of burial. Much other material appeared in some editions. This book was widely used, though not without some criticism at times, but its use ceased in 1645, when the General Assembly adopted the *West-minster Directory*.

The *Directory* was not a liturgical book. It did not provide prayers or forms of prayer, but detailed subjects for prayer. It completely superseded *BCO*, but itself soon came to be much neglected, and worship reached a low level. But by the end of the eighteenth century many ministers grew tired of the baldness and poverty of the services, and not a few published orders especially for holy communion. The Church Service Society of the Church of Scotland was formed in 1865 and its influence, especially through the issue of *Euchologion*, gradually led to much improvement. Other Societies, with the same intention, were formed in the United Presbyterian and Free Churches in Scotland, and they also published service-books. The United Free Church after 1900 followed the same course, leading to the issue in 1928 of the *Book of Common Order, 1928*. Similar movements were taking place within the Church of Scotland, an influential book, *Prayers for Divine Service*, appearing in 1923, revised in 1929. The reunited Church produced the *Book of Common Order, 1940*, which was revised in 1952, and is now under

detailed revision. This book has greatly influenced the books of other Presbyterian churches throughout the world. These churches, in England, Canada, Australia, New Zealand and South Africa, have all issued service-books and have all revised them. In the USA three Presbyterian churches produced their own books, but have recently joined in the publication of a new book for all – *The Worship-Book* (Philadelphia 1970). In spite of many differences in detail, these all show some evidence of their derivation from Calvinist sources. Yet in many services, especially in the eucharist, many of the ancient forms, such as *Sursum Corda* and *Agnus Dei*, have been adopted, thus enriching them and adding to their value.

JOHN A. LAMB

15. *Seventh-day Adventist.* The Seventh-day Adventist Church, in the tradition of Evangelical Protestantism, does not use special liturgical books for its worship services. Various publications are drawn upon for guidance in worship, but they are not authorized or used as service-books.

The early leaders of the Seventh-day Adventist Church emphasized the blessedness of genuine worship, as opposed to what they called the evil of formal worship. Adventists still generally keep to the relative informality of early years and do not worship according to a prescribed ritual with fixed words and formalized prayers. In recent years form consciousness in the regular services for worship has become more pronounced. *The Seventh-day Adventist Church Manual* (1967 ed.) states: 'We do not prescribe a set form or order for public worship' (p. 109). Nevertheless, the *Manual* does suggest a longer and shorter order of worship and offers considerable guidance regarding the Sabbath worship service.

The Church Hymnal (USA, Australia, etc.) and the *New Advent Hymnal* (Britain, some West African countries) are the two most widely used hymn-books in English-speaking Adventist churches. *The Church Hymnal* also contains a selection of responsive scriptural readings. A series of special devotional readings is prepared annually for use in all Seventh-day Adventist churches around the world during the yearly Week of Prayer in November.

The Manual for Ministers contains suggested services and prescribes certain ritual forms for special occasions, such as ordinations, burials, church dedications and marriage ceremonies. In addition, various Seventh-day Adventist publishing houses issue every year quite a number of new books and inspirational readings for private and corporate devotions.

B. B. BEACH

J. S. Andrews, 'Brethren Hymnology', *Evangelical Quarterly* 28, 1956, pp. 208-29; J. C. Bowmer, *The Sacrament of the Lord's Supper in Early Methodism*, 1951; F. E. Brightman, *The English Rite*, 1915, 2 vols., esp. pp. xlix-ccxxx (Anglican); C. O. Buchanan, *Modern Anglican Liturgies, 1958-1968*, 1968; Horton Davies, *The Worship of the English Puritans* 1948; Horton Davies, *Worship and Theology in England, 1900-1965*, 1965, ch.x; Jean Deshusses. *Le Sacramentaire Gregorien. Ses principales formes d'après les plus anciens manuscrits*, 1971; K. Gamber, *Codices Liturgici Latini Antiquiores*, 1963; A. R. George, 'The People called Methodist – 4. The Means of Grace' in *A History of the Methodist Church in Great Britain*, ed. S. R. Davies and G. Rupp, 1965, pp.259-73; N. B. Harmon, Jr, *The Rites and Ritual of Episcopal Methodism*, 1926; W. K. Lowther Clarke, ed., *Liturgy and Worship*, 1932; A. G. Matthews, 'Puritan Worship' in *Christian Worship*, ed. N. Micklem, 1935, reissued 1955; Pierre Salmon, *Les Manuscrits liturgiques latins de la Bibliotheque Vaticane*, Vols. I, II, 1968, 1969; Cyrille Vogel, *Introduction aux Sources de l'Histoire du Culte Chrétien au Moyen Age*, 1965; B. J. Wigan, *The Liturgy in English*, 1964 (Anglican).

Bowing *see* Postures (2*a*)

Buddhist Worship

Buddhist worship is a peculiarly delicate topic, in a religion or ethic which has been called atheistic and appears to emphasize meditation rather than prayer. Buddhism began as a reform movement within Hinduism; and its religious objects may be compared with those which feature in Hindu worship (q.v.). Some of the Hindu gods remain in Buddhism, so that it is not atheistic but perhaps 'transtheistic', since the gods Indra and Brahmā which figure in Buddhist texts are subordinate to the Buddha. To this day many, perhaps all, Buddhist temples in Ceylon have images of at least two Hindu gods, usually Vishnu and Indra (Sakka), though they are often behind curtains. But Kataragama (or Skanda), second son of the great Hindu deity Shiva, is the most popular god of the Hindus of Ceylon and his temples are visited by Buddhists to pay reverence and make vows.

In Buddhism it is the Buddha or Buddhas who are pre-eminent, even in the conservative Theravāda Buddhism of South-east Asia. The gods exist, as part of the world of beings, above most men except monks, but the Buddha is supreme, 'the teacher of gods and men' and the 'god above the gods', as the texts call him. Although in monkish theory the Buddha was a man, who is now dead, and only one in a series of Buddhas, yet in practice from olden times till now he is the supreme object of worship. It was the first lay convert, therefore about 500-400 BC, who is said to have invoked the Threefold Refuge, or the Three Jewels, which are still the daily expression of Theravāda Buddhist devotion: 'I go to the Buddha for refuge, I go to the Doctrine (*dharma*) for refuge, I go to the Order (*sangha*) for refuge.'

The earliest centres of Buddhist devotion were probably small *stūpas*, relic-holders, containing some fragment of the Buddha's body or an object associated with him or his disciples. Already at the cremation of Gautama the Buddha, eight cities are said to have shared his relics. Buddhism was established in Ceylon by the arrival of the collar-bone and begging-bowl of the Buddha, and a shoot of the Bo-tree under which he had been enlightened. Relics not only show the teacher to have been historical, but even more convey his power. All great temples claim some outstanding relic, and one was brought to England in 1964 by the Prime Minister of Ceylon to hallow a new Buddhist temple in Chiswick. In Ceylon the relic-holders have developed into dome-shaped buildings, *dāgobas*, which are called pagodas in Burma and beyond. Some great *dāgobas* are over a hundred feet high and made of brick. The relic is enshrined in the depths, but unseen by most visitors who lay their gifts of flowers, incense and money in small shrine rooms full of images. Burmese pagodas and Thai wats have spires above the images and wide courtyards for worshippers.

Images are of the Buddha in various postures, meditating, teaching or passing into ultimate Nirvāna. In making the images, great care is devoted to painting in the eyes, a dangerous operation which reveals the power of the being represented. In front of these images, monks and laymen meditate and repeat sacred texts from the extensive Buddhist scriptures. But prayers are also offered. One widely known prayer in Ceylon, in the Pāli liturgical language, is used daily at the Temple of the Tooth, the greatest relic in the town of Kandy: 'Forgive me my transgression committed through carelessness by body, word or thought, O Tathāgata (Buddha) of great wisdom' (R. F. Gombrich, *Precept and Practice*, 1971, p. 140). The significance of such a prayer is that it not only reveals religious worship, but contains an appeal to cancel sin which in theory might be held to depend on the individual's own efforts in conquering Karma.

Although there have been and will be other Buddhas, yet Theravāda texts say that there can only be one Buddha in this present long world-eon, and in practice he holds the centre of worship in monotheistic fashion. In Northern Mahāyāna Buddhism, however, in Tibet, China, Japan, Korea and Vietnam, there are countless Buddhas and Bodhisattvas, 'beings of enlightenment', to whom men pray for help and salvation. Amitābha or Amida, Buddha of 'infinite light', rules in the Buddha-fields or Western Paradise to which he guides the faithful over the sea of sorrows. Avalokita, who 'looks down', becomes Kwanyin and Kwannon in China and Japan, not a goddess but a gracious Bodhisattva who 'hears the cry' and gives children. Maitreya, the Buddha to come, is the fat jolly figure depicted with money-bags and giving fortune.

Tibet has been noted for its prayer and praising wheels, prayer flags, prayer walls, and common invocation: *Om mani padme hum*, 'Hail to the jewel in the lotus', the doctrine in the scripture. In China and Japan, the Pure Land schools repeat the names of Amida endlessly on great rosaries and their prayer is adoration rather than petition. In Japan also, great Buddhist temples were built for regular congregational worship comparable to that of Western religions.

Much Buddhist worship is individual and occasional, with invocations at home and visits to pagodas when time permits. But great festivals are held on anniversaries of events in the lives of the Buddha or Buddhas, and at ancient national ceremonies such as the famous Perahera festival in Ceylon in August, where processions of four gods join up with that of the sacred Tooth. There are also important feasts for the dead, to ensure their rest and blessing, since although Nirvāna is the goal, it is far distant. In China, where many temples have been destroyed or turned into museums, ceremonies for the departed remain and Buddhist texts are used.

The Sangha, the church and monastic order, is not a priesthood, though monks have been teachers and leaders of the religion in Theravāda lands. In Mahāyāna countries there are Buddhist priests, often married, who officiate in temples, while monks may also participate or meditate and teach in monasteries. But for monks and laity Buddhism is not merely an ethic but a religion of devotion and salvation.

S. Dutt, *Buddhist Monks and Monasteries of India*, 1962; C. Eliot, *Hinduism and Buddhism*, 1921; R. F. Gombrich, *Precept and Practice*, 1971; K. W. Morgan, ed., *The Path of the Buddha*, 1956; E. G. Parrinder, ed., *Man and His Gods*, 1971; E. G. Parrinder, *Worship in the World's Religions*, 1961; K. L. Reichelt, *Meditation and Piety in the Far East*, 1953; M. E. Spiro, *Buddhism and Society*, 1971.

GEOFFREY PARRINDER

Burial

The solemn interment of the dead is a practice found in almost all the great religions. Christian funeral rites express the church's care for the departed, its belief in the resurrection and its reverence for the body as sharing in redemption.

1. *The Early Church*. Funeral rites consisted of five main items, of which certain were in pointed contrast to contemporary pagan customs. (*a*) Prayer in the house – the corpse was washed and anointed and swathed in white linen to the accompaniment of prayers. (*b*) Procession – whereas the Romans chose night for interment because of a belief that a funeral was of evil omen, the Christians chose the daytime, and, wearing white garments, sang psalms of hope and alleluias of victory. Palm leaves were carried, together with lights, and incense was burned – all expressing the idea of triumph over death. (*c*) Office – a short service of praise and thanksgiving, around the body, including Bible readings and psalms. (*d*) Eucharist – the celebration

expressed the belief in the communion that still exists between the living and the dead. The kiss of peace (q.v.) was given to the corpse. (*e*) Interment – the corpse was placed in the grave with feet towards the east as a sign of hope in the coming of the Sun of Righteousness (*see* **Orientation**).

An agape (q.v.) often followed, and on the third, ninth and fortieth days afterwards friends and relatives met to join in psalms, hymns and prayers. The procedure was not immediately stereotyped and differences are to be noted depending upon whether the procession went to the church or directly from the house to the cemetery. The whole was characterized by the note of peace and hope, confidence in the felicity of the departed and the certainty that death had erected no real barrier.

EDITOR

2. *Orthodox*. 'Death is swallowed up in victory' (I Cor. 15.54). Christ is risen! (Orthodox Christians exchange this greeting with one another for the entire forty days between Easter and Ascension Day.) This fact, the central point of the Christian 'Good News' (*see* in particular Acts 2-4, or I Cor. 15.3-7, the resurrection of Christ was the central point of the apostolic proclamation after Pentecost), is the cardinal preoccupation of the worship of the Orthodox Church. All of Orthodox liturgy is permeated by the celebration of the resurrection of Christ from the dead. 'If Christ has not been raised, then our preaching is in vain and your faith is in vain' (I Cor. 15.14). Around this inner pattern, the whole liturgical life of the Orthodox Church unfolds.

In this scheme of things the Orthodox rite of burial is no exception. While the burial service imparts the whole of the Orthodox view concerning anthropology, i.e. paradise and man's original beauty and calling before God, the fall and its destructive effect on man, the full reality of death, the incarnation, the power of Christ's own death and resurrection, and the eschaton, all is reduced to the basic questions of death or life. Is there ultimately tragedy or victory, death or resurrection? During the course of the Orthodox rite of burial these questions are both posed and answered.

The character of death is exposed in all its realism. The Orthodox burial rite does not avoid the fact of death, brush it casually aside

in the 'joy' of the resurrection, or poetically explain it away. It is the final enemy and the greatest tragedy to confront man. Not forgotten in the inner reasoning of the service are the moments when Christ himself, the 'Resurrection and the Life' (John 11.25), wept before the tomb of his dead friend, Lazarus (John 11.35), and later prayed in Gethsemane that the cup of his own passion and death might be removed (Luke 22.39-44). John Damascene unflinchingly describes the reality of death in one of the hymns which he composed for the burial service: 'I weep and I lament, when I contemplate death, and see our beauty, fashioned after the image of God, lying in the tomb disfigured, dishonoured, bereft of form' ('The Order for the Burial of the Dead' in I. F. Hapgood, *Service Book of the Holy Orthodox-Catholic Apostolic Church*, [3]1956).

During the burial service the deceased lies in the centre of the church facing the altar. The coffin is generally open so that the body is in full view. The 'disfigured, dishonoured, bereft' form spoken of in the above anthem, however, is not just man's body (this is especially true in view of the funeral practices which really beautify the corpse). 'It is the whole of man. Here the ultimate tragedy of death is revealed. Death destroys man, not just man's body. Man is the unity of soul and body. Death separates the two and ontologically mutilates man. It makes man's body a corpse and his soul a ghost. In effecting this breakdown of man as man created by God, death is the greatest sign of man's separation from God' (Georges Florovsky). Such are the sober and realistic categories in which the Orthodox burial service reveals the character of death.

The open evaluation of death leads to the true appreciation of Christ's resurrection. The great tragedy is overcome by an even greater victory. Christ shatters death by entering into its very depth, by 'trampling down death by death' (*Troparion*, or main hymn, of the Easter liturgical cycle). He who rises is he who was within the tomb. Thus, during the rite of the burial of the dead the light of the resurrection begins to shine forth. The order of the service is that of mattins, the same resurrectional type used on Sundays (Sunday is the weekly day of commemorating the resurrection in the liturgical cycle of the Orthodox Church) throughout the year as well as on Great and Holy Saturday, when

Christ reposed in the tomb. The clergy wear light-coloured vestments (q.v.). Liturgical expressions typically used by the Orthodox Church as signs of the victorious presence of the risen Christ, e.g. an abundance of lights, burning candles and incense, dominate the external actions of the service. The body of the deceased in particular is repeatedly censed as a sign that in it, 'the redemption of our bodies' (Rom. 8.23) has already begun. The deceased is a baptized, chrismated and communing member of the body of Christ. Sacramentally, his whole substance is permeated by him who, having risen, is 'the first fruits of all those who have fallen asleep' (I Cor. 15.20).

A large portion of the text of the service is occupied by Ps. 119, the praise of the law of God. The love of this law is the love and obedience to him in whom it is fulfilled – Christ. As the gospel section (John 5.24-30) read at the service says: 'He who hears my word and believes in him who sent me has eternal life' (John 5.24).

The epistle section (I Thess. 4.13-17) strongly emphasizes the hope engendered through Christ's resurrection: '. . . that you may not grieve as others do who have no hope' (I Thess. 4.13). The 'funeral dirge' of the service is the singing of 'alleluia', that ecstatic Hebrew word used in this case to glorify the presence of Christ – even in death ('The Order for the Burial of the Dead' in Hapgood, p. 383).

In the same experiential way that the Orthodox Church understands Christ's resurrection, i.e. as the gradual yet shattering overcoming of death from within death, the Orthodox burial service reveals the destiny of each member of the church. He comes to death in all its reality, but already has the token of his deliverance through his sacramental unity with the abundance of life, Christ himself. The inner pattern for the whole of Orthodox liturgy remains the hymn of Easter:

Christ is risen from the dead,
trampling down death by death
and upon those in the tombs bestowing life.

(The rite described in this essay is that used for the burial of laymen. The Orthodox Church also has special rites to be used for the burial of clergy and children, along with variations to be applied during Easter Week.)

PAUL LAZOR

3. *Medieval and Roman Catholic.* This topic requires a threefold division: the Middle Ages, the *Rituale Romanum* of 1614 and the 1969 *Ordo Exequiarum.*

(*a*) *The Middle Ages.* In the early Middle Ages the funeral liturgy consisted essentially of the preparation of the body for burial, accompanied by psalms and prayers, the procession with the body from home to church, a period of prayer for the dead person which might include the eucharist, and finally the procession from the church to the grave and the interment. By this time the ancient custom of continuous psalmody for the dead person had become ritualized in the form of the office of the dead, consisting of vespers, mattins and lauds (qq.v.) This office was sung daily in addition to the normal office of the day. The word *Dirige,* beginning the first antiphon of mattins, gives us the English 'dirge'.

Later the preparation of the body for burial is accomplished in private, without liturgical accompaniment, and the eucharist becomes a normal part of the funeral liturgy. It is followed by responsories, prayers of absolution and the incensation and aspersion of the corpse. These rites indicate an increased stress on need for forgiveness and fear of judgment, and also the value attached to the priest's prayer of absolution, an extension of his power to absolve the living.

These developments find excellent expression in the *Dies irae* chant, composed in the twelfth or thirteenth century, and they modify somewhat the atmosphere of joy and hope so characteristic of the ancient funeral liturgy, which looked forward to the resurrection of the body and entrance into God's kingdom. The medieval liturgy is conscious rather of sin and death, purgatory and judgment, thinking of the soul's destiny rather than the body's.

(*b*) *The Rituale Romanum of 1614.* Our sources for the medieval burial rites are mainly monastic, but the Roman ritual's burial rite is a simplified version of the medieval one, designed for use in parishes. While permitting local adaptation it remains the first official and universal funeral rite.

It begins with the processional transfer of the body from home to church, accompanied with psalmody. After the reception of the body into church the office of the dead follows, in whole or in part, though it is acknowledged that circumstances may prevent this. Mass is followed by a single absolution, after which the body is taken out to burial, the traditional antiphons *In paradisum* and *Chorus angelorum* being sung. Interment is preceded by the canticle (q.v.) *Benedictus*, versicles and a prayer. The rite retains some of the best of the ancient burial chants and prayers which stress welcome into paradise and bodily resurrection, yet the medieval emphasis on the need for forgiveness and fear of judgment remains.

(*c*) *The Ordo Exequiarum of 1969*. The Second Vatican Council's Liturgy Constitution called for the revision of funeral rites to express the Paschal character of Christian death, while taking account of local customs. Accordingly, the new funeral rite envisages three types of service, the traditional one with prayers at home, in church and at the graveside, a second form in the cemetery chapel and at the graveside, more in line with German custom, and a third form taking place entirely in the home, in accordance with conditions in Africa and elsewhere. The rite is extremely flexible, with great scope for local variations.

Provision is made for funeral vigil in the home, and it is no longer presumed that the eucharist will always be celebrated as part of the burial rite. The absolution after mass is transformed into a final farewell to the deceased. There is a wide choice of readings, prayers and chants, prayers for the mourners are included, and the whole rite expresses Christian hope in our share in Christ's resurrection and enjoyment of God's presence in his kingdom.

It may be noted that cremation has been permitted for Roman Catholics since 1963.

BRIAN NEWNS

4. *Anglican.* In medieval England, burial rites had two distinguishing features, their complicated and drawn-out structure and their purgatorial theology. Thus when Cranmer put the service into English in 1549 he simplified its structure and assimilated material from the previous vespers and mattins into the 'office'. The rite began with the churchyard procession, and this 'office' in church might come before or after the committal. Finally came proper introit, collect, epistle and gospel for the (presumably optional) eucharist. In doctrine, cautious petitions for the departed were retained, but with the excision of mass-sacrifice (let alone the earlier confiscation of chantries) votive masses for

the dead ceased. The atmosphere now reflected a new emphasis on rest in Christ and resurrection to life. The service was generally directed to giving hope to the living, rather than indicating the deliverance from sufferings of the departed.

1552 worked out the logic of 1549 more exactly. The service was further truncated, and was performed wholly at the graveside. The procession to the grave led almost immediately to the committal, and to an 'office' consisting solely of the reading from I Cor. 15, lesser litany, Lord's Prayer and two other prayers, one of which was the 1549 eucharistic collect (there was now no eucharist). Petitions for the departed disappeared. For the living there was prayer that they should be joined with the departed in the general resurrection to life. (The 1552 communion service dropped all mention of the departed.) Petitions for the departed (though perhaps theoretically a possible private practice) were now contrary to the policy of the Church of England for public worship. They escaped condemnation in the 1571 Articles, but the Homily on Prayer discountenanced them as lacking commandment in scripture, and as devoid of rationale once purgatory is rejected.

The 1552 rite, revived in 1559, remained unchanged till 1645 (though the 1637 Scottish eucharist reintroduced remembrance of the departed). Then the Puritan Westminster *Directory of Public Worship* forbade all burial services, and bodies were to be interred without ceremony, prayer, scripture or preaching.

At the 1661 Savoy Conference the Puritans objected that the 1552 rite was too assured about the state of the departed. They gained the addition of a 'the' to the committal – thus giving to the living hope not specifically of the deceased person's resurrection to life, but more objectively in *the* (general) resurrection of all at the last day. A new rubric disallowed use of the rite over the unbaptized, the excommunicate and suicides.

Other additions were made. The service could now be read in church and psalmody preceded the reading of I Cor. 15 straight after the procession. The committal followed, and the 1552 'office' (except the reading, but including 'The Grace . . . etc.') completed the service.

The hundred years since 1870 have seen great changes in the ecclesiastical and social context within which burials are conducted, and the following in particular have inevitably affected the liturgical evolution not only in England, but also in the Anglican Communion around the world.

First, the gulf between church and society has broadened visibly and continues to do so. Yet the great bulk of society still expects a Christian burial, and this has set up a tension for the church (and particularly for the Church of England).

Secondly, the church building has been slowly but surely set aside from the majority of funerals in England. Until the second part of the last century parish churches generally had their own churchyards attached, and the committal would take place under the walls of the church building. Then, as churchyards filled and were closed under the pressures of fast-increasing population, corporation cemeteries, divorced from the churches and boasting their own chapels, slowly took their place. In recent decades these in turn have given way to crematoria, and cremation appears to be the almost invariable future practice. Curiously, in a crematorium chapel, the 1662 sequence can once again be followed, as the 'committal' can come naturally before the prayers, which is difficult when a service is split between church and graveside. However, the practice of cremation calls in question the suitability of a committal 'to the ground' and 'earth to earth'. The wording has to be amended.

Thirdly, the practice of the last century has seen a growing flexibility introduced. Clergy who have treated the requirements of the Act of Uniformity fairly loosely in their Sunday services are hardly likely to take it very seriously in the cemetery or crematorium chapel on a weekday. The pastoral situation has often cried out for more relevant liturgical material (e.g. at the funeral of a child). And liturgical revision has inevitably followed what was already being done without controversy. Thus the 1928 rite (now authorized as the Church of England's *First Series* rite) provided other psalms, alternative readings, prayers for the bereaved and other occasional material. Overseas revisions have gone the same way, and there is often renewed provision for communion services at funerals.

Fourthly, there has been a reintroduction of petitions for the departed. Partly this arose through the doctrinal convictions of the 'Catholic Revivalists' of the last century,

partly through a growing national sentiment (e.g. in the First World War) that wished to say *something* about the departed, while being hesitant to state they were undoubtedly in bliss. The petitions have usually had a rationale which excluded belief in purgatory, and with that exclusion have some show of primitive, and possibly even Anglican, precedent. In Scotland, America and other 'Catholic' provinces the reintroduction has usually gone unchallenged. But Evangelicals have always contested the move. Thus the Church of England's *First Series* rite only just secured the requisite two-thirds majority in the House of Laity in 1966, and the Liturgical Commission's *Second Series* rite (which also raised the problem of petitions for the *un*faithful departed) was never put to the final vote in the same House in 1968. The dialogue necessitated by such controversies led to a more satisfactory 'remembrance' of the departed in *Second Series* communion. In January 1971 the Archbishops' Commission on Christian Doctrine published their Report *Prayer and the Departed*. The intention of the recommendation here was to produce cautious and unitive proposals in which the whole Church of England could agree. The Liturgical Commission's *Third Series* burial rite has been drawn in accordance with these proposals at the doctrinally sensitive points.

C. O. BUCHANAN

5. *Baptist.* No common practice prevails in Baptist memorial, including burial, services. Local custom usually dictates the time, place and form. Also, Baptist services tend to be similar to those in the other free churches.

Generally the service is in two parts: the first in the church or funeral chapel and the second at the graveside or crematorium. An ordained minister generally conducts the service, but if no ordained minister is available a lay minister, designated by the congregation, may conduct the service.

The service at the church or funeral chapel begins with the minister saying a number of suitable scriptural texts, followed by a hymn, choral or solo musical number. After a prayer the scripture lessons are read. These may be followed with the *Gloria Patri*, a doxology or a hymn of affirmation. The minister then usually interprets a scripture passage dealing with Christ's victory over death. He follows this with a prayer and a blessing. Occasionally a eulogy will be included.

The service of committal at the grave or crematorium begins after the people have assembled with several scripture sentences followed by the words of committal, a prayer and a benediction.

Increasingly Baptists along with others are moving away from the 'funeral' service with the body present to memorial services in which family and friends gather to remember with thanksgiving the life of the one who has departed. For such a service the setting may be a home with an informal service of readings, prayers and words of remembrance. Or a more formal service is held as part of the regular Lord's Day service and incorporated as an act of thanksgiving and remembrance for 'the saint (or saints) who from their labours rest'. When such a service is held, then a family memorial usually takes place at the time of death.

Present-day Baptists generally have no special places of burial such as 'Baptist cemeteries'. They generally use the common grounds provided by the community or a burial association.

JOHN E. SKOGLUND

6. *Congregationalist.* In their earliest days the Independents had deep doubts about the propriety of burial services, partly because they led to superstition and partly because they were the occasion of hypocritical eulogies.

In modern days these dangers are overcome by services that avoid elaborate eulogies, or, in many cases, have no eulogy at all, and by keeping strictly to the biblical promises. The emphasis in 'burial' services (English) or 'funeral' services (American) is on scriptural readings and prayers that reiterate the promises of the risen Christ, the enduring covenant love of the divine Father, and the comfort of Christian friends in the hope of the gospel, with a solemn reminder of the transitoriness and accountability of human life.

According to the most recent English Congregational service-book, *A Book of Services and Prayers* (1959), provision is made for three separate but related burial services. There is first a short, simple, and intimate family service in the home. This consists of the reading of declarations of notable divine promises and affirmations of faith from the scriptures, including Ps. 23, and

of prayers for faith and hope and comfort, concluding with the Lord's Prayer. The minister usually offers one or more extempore prayers.

The second service, no longer restricted to family and close friends, but now including former associates in many walks of life, takes place either at the church or cemetery chapel. It may well include a hymn (frequently the favourite hymn of the deceased), and a short address, especially if the deceased were a pillar of the church and community. It will include scripture lessons and prayers which will normally include thanksgiving for our hope and assurance of eternal life through the gospel; a prayer of grateful memories; supplication for the mourners; and a petition for grace to live the life of faith (*ibid.*, p.78).

The third service is held either at the graveside or in the crematorium. The form of committal is that of the *BCP* 'For as much as it hath pleased Almighty God of his great mercy to take unto himself the soul of our dear *brother* here departed, we therefore commit *his* body to the ground: earth to earth, ashes to ashes, dust to dust; in sure and certain hope of resurrection to everlasting life through our Lord Jesus Christ . . .' At a cremation the wording of the committal is changed to read, 'we therefore commit *his* body to the elements . . .'

The same service-book also provides two very moving alternatives for use on special occasions. The one is for the burial of a child. The other is 'A Service for use in Circumstances of Deep Distress', including the burial of a suicide. Each is as compassionate as is appropriate.

HORTON DAVIES

7. *Jehovah's Witnesses.* Burial services by Witnesses are simple and restrained. They are designed to give comfort to the bereaved and explain the Bible's hope for the dead.

Since the congregation has no separate clergy, any suitable male speaker may be invited to take the service. In March 1888, *Zion's Watch Tower* carried the article 'How Shall We Bury Our Dead?' (pp.7,8) with suggestions for a funeral discourse. Nowadays a printed outline is provided. The most recent (January 1966) has five sub-headings: God's purpose in creating man; why man dies; condition of the dead; hope for the dead; and, Kingdom will accomplish God's purpose towards man. The speaker, of course, varies the outline as he chooses. The discourse does not exceed thirty minutes in length.

Witnesses do not believe the Bible teaches inherent immortality of the soul (Ezek. 18.4; I Cor. 15.6; etc.). They have hope in a resurrection for the unconscious dead (Acts 24.15). Those dead whom God holds in his memory will be restored to life. They are in 'memorial tombs' (mnemeion, e.g. John 5.28; cogn. mimnesko, mneia, remind, remembrance, etc.). It is scripturally proper to speak of a 'dead soul' (e.g. Num. 19.13 [Heb.]; Rev. 16.3 [Gk]). Mourners look to the dead soul's resurrection.

The restraint mentioned above extends to clothing worn and to mourning. In the spirit of Matt. 6.16-18 mourners do not normally wear black. Of extended mourning, The Watchtower (15 September 1958, p. 575) said: 'It would seem, therefore, that a Christian who has advanced to a mature appreciation of these things [Christ's resurrection, his enthronement, and the resurrection hope] would not feel called upon to carry on mourning along with the wearing of special types of clothing as an outward show . . . [However,] it is his own personal conscience that must guide the course he takes (I Thess. 4.13, 14).'

Cremation is left to the individual conscience. 'As to how the dead body shall be disposed of is a matter of no consequence to the dead, but the proper disposal of the remains of our departed friends is a mark of our respect and affection' (Zion's Watch Tower, March 1888). And more recently, 'So whether a body returns to the elements by decaying in the ground or is burned to ashes does not in any way affect God's ability to resurrect the person . . . it remains a matter for personal decision' (The Watchtower, 1 July 1965, p. 416).

No special burial grounds are used. 'The Christian will not be as concerned about the place of burial as he is about the prospect of a resurrection' (Awake!, 22 September 1965, p. 7).

Rather than elaborate ritual, the death of a Witness is followed by practical consideration for the deceased's family, who are much comforted in the hope of the resurrection.

A. HELEY

8. *Lutheran*. Luther and the Reformers had more criticisms to make of the Roman Catholic rite of burial than of any of the other traditional offices of the church. As early as the writing 'To the Christian Nobility of the German Nation' (1520; *Martin Luthers Werke*, Weimar, 1883 ff. = WA 6,444 f.), Luther vigorously attacked masses for the dead and vigils. In a late writing, a collection of Christian hymns for funerals, he regards vigils, requiems, funeral pomp and purgatory as 'papistical abominations' which must be completely rejected because they contradict scripture, especially in the fact that their help is enlisted to influence the fate of the dead (1542; WA 35,478; cf. *Apolog. der Conf. Aug.* 24, 89 ff.). On the Reformed side this radical rejection of traditional rites meant that for a long time burial was left to the personal initiative of the members of the family, the guilds or the authorities; the church did not co-operate. The same tendency can also be found, to begin with, in Lutheran areas. But very soon a criticism of this attitude makes itself felt: having laid aside 'superstitious pomp of the dead', people treat them 'quite bestially' (Strasbourg 1533). However, for some decades there is no liturgical formulary to lay down the details of a funeral. Luther produced manuals for baptism and marriage, but no order for funeral services; he was content – as has been said – to publish a few German and Latin chorales for this purpose. The lack of an order of service authorized by Luther is presumably the reason why there is a confusing number and variety of forms and orders for burial in individual Lutheran churches and areas. This position has only been changed in the last few decades.

Nevertheless, some common principles and even some basic structures for funerals can be found in the sixteenth century. According to Luther, a funeral should serve to 'strengthen our faith and encourage the people to true devotion. For it is right and fitting that a funeral should be performed honourably, to the praise and honour of the joyful article of our faith, the resurrection of the dead' (WA 35, 479). Accordingly, from now on (a) the focal point is no longer to be the dead body but faith in the resurrection, which is to be expressed in hymn, prayer and sermon. In addition, (b) even in early times, burial was regarded as an act of love by the congregation towards the dead man and his family. 'For the dead are still our brothers, and have not fallen from our community by death; we still remain members of a single body'; therefore it is one of the duties of 'civic neighbourliness' to accompany the dead to the grave (Church order of Schwäbisch Hall 1526; Richter I, 47). Finally, (c) burial is to remind us of our own deaths and to cause us to lead an appropriate way of life (for these three points see Württemberg 1536; Richter I, 273).

Traditional features retained are the ringing of the church bells, either at the moment of death or at the burial, and the walk to the grave. The church ordinances of the sixteenth century prohibit 'secret burials'. Pastor, verger, teacher, school children and as far as possible one person from each house in the community are to join the family in accompanying the body to the grave, usually in a strictly prescribed order. On the way to and at the grave, hymns are to be sung by the congregation or at least by the children, 'not mourning hymns nor sorrowful, but comforting hymns about the forgiveness of sins, rest, sleep, the life and resurrection of departed Christians' (Luther, WA 35, 478 f.). It seems that at the beginning people were content simply to sing hymns at the burial. This expressed the fact that it was the congregation that bore the body to the grave and confessed its faith in the resurrection. Prayers and a sermon were added relatively soon; there is not always explicit mention of either, but in the course of time they will have become the rule, though with exceptions.

According to Schulz, some forty-five funeral prayers have been preserved from the sixteenth century; they have a christological basis and express faith in the resurrection, ask for a strengthening of faith in earthly life and give thanks for the life of the departed. At first there are only hints of a prayer for the departed at the burial itself (e.g. Württemberg 1536, Richter I, 273); they occur occasionally later (e.g. Hessen 1566 and 1574; Sehling 8, 336 and 450). The coffin or body is at first lowered into the grave to the singing of a hymn. Only later are affirmations made, e.g. 'Earth thou art . . .' (following Gen. 3.19; Dessau 1532, Sehling 1.2, 541), Rev. 14.13 (Pfalz-Neuburg 1543, Sehling 13, 90) or, as earth is thrown three times: 'Of dust thou art made and to dust must thou return. May the Lord Jesus Christ raise thy body and soul (!) that thou mayest rise again with the righteous on the Last Day. Amen' (Waldeck 1556; Richter II, 171).

To begin with, a sermon was only preached in the case of people of standing (princes and other notables), usually not at the burial itself but as a memorial sermon some time afterwards. Generally speaking, if there was a sermon at all, short admonitions were thought to be sufficient, often in connection with the readings I Thess. 4.13-18 and John 11.21-27. In the course of time the sermon became an essential part of the funeral; thus the *Kursächsische Kirchenordnung* of 1580 contains four funeral sermons, two each for adults and young people, which are to be read in the church after the burial (Sehling I, 1, 371 ff.). At this particular point, however, ominous differences arise at an early stage. According to the *Wittenberger Kirchenordnung* of 1533, 'common men' are to be buried without bells, 'citizens of middle degree' with the singing of school children, and 'honourable people' with a procession and the sound of the great bells (Sehling I, 1, 195). As early as 1540 it is mentioned on many occasions that differing fees are exacted for the different forms of funeral. This is related above all to the sermon: 'funeral sermons' or 'eulogies' are delivered only on the payment of an appropriate fee; otherwise, people have to be content with a brief 'dismissal' or a mere 'blessing'. This shameful classification of funerals lasted right down to the beginning of our century; it involved not only the sermon, but the whole form of the funeral.

Leaving aside new hymns and prayers for funerals, the structure of the funeral service hardly altered over the next two centuries, down to the time of the Enlightenment. This was not, however, the case with funeral sermons, where they were required and given. In the sixteenth century the preaching was predominantly biblical and christological, but in the seventeenth century a strong personal element was added, among other things by the inclusion of a *curriculum vitae*; at the same time, funeral sermons took on a learned tone, used allegory and often occupied an intolerable amount of time. A eulogy of the dead person took precedence over what were originally the main themes of funeral sermons (the proclamation of the last things, preparation for a happy death) (E. Winkler). At the time of the Enlightenment the biblical orientation of the funeral sermon disappeared still more; at its centre stood the life of the dead person and the parting from him, both presented in the baroque and sentimental style of the time.

In many places there was no funeral sermon at all. This was connected with an extremely strange development. Silent 'interments', once provided for suicides, notorious sinners, etc. took the place of public funerals. It became the custom to inter the dead at a late hour of the evening or at midnight, by torchlight, with only family and friends present, and usually without any participation by the pastor. The place of the funeral sermon was taken by the 'eulogy' of a friend at the graveside. The funeral service of the congregation in many cases, particularly in towns, became a family gathering. In addition, under the influence of the numerous private forms of service published and used, the hymns, prayers and words of committal were adapted to the language of the time. For example, one committal takes the following form: 'Take this body, mother earth, into thy protection under the oversight of almighty God! The day will surely come again when death must return even this its prey' (1802, according to P. Graff, II, 275).

Contradictory intentions arise with the movement for liturgical reform in the middle of the nineteenth century. Using portions of church orders from the sixteenth century, W. Löhe and others propose complete funeral services for the first time; their characteristics are that a number of passages are proposed as readings, and a large number of collects and prayers, especially the committal from King Edward VI's prayer book of 1552 (with a few alterations), are suggested. Most local churches in Germany shaped their funeral services along these lines about 1900. Usually the funeral begins – often after a biblical sentence – with Ps. 130 or another psalm; one or two lessons, for which a number of passages are suggested, are followed by the sermon (which has become a permanent feature) and a prayer, for which a few models are provided. At the graveside, the coffin is lowered with the committal from the prayer book, occasionally (as in Prussia, 1895) with the additional words: 'From the earth thou art taken, to the earth thou shalt return. Jesus Christ, our Redeemer, will raise you on the Last Day.' Here, too, a lesson and prayers are provided for. The service can begin at the grave and be continued in the church (or cemetery chapel) or vice versa. There is singing by the congregation or a choir at appropriate places.

Some private forms of service have had an influence on the further shaping of the funeral by providing different psalms, scripture readings (sometimes made up of isolated verses from the Bible) and prayers depending on the life, status, age and sex of the dead person. Newer official forms, which have appeared since 1960, take up this suggestion; they offer a considerable number of introit psalms, readings, prayers, hymns and committal prayers to suit individual cases. The prayers aim at a modern form of expression, without always being successful. One leading funeral service is that in the *Agende für Evangelisch-Lutherische Kirchen und Gemeinden* (vol. III, 1964, pp. 155-222). First of all it has the ordinary forms for different places: (*a*) house of mourning or undertaker's chapel (greeting, collect, hymn, invitation to proceed to the cemetery); (*b*) cemetery chapel or church (introit hymn, biblical sentence, Ps. 130 or another, scriptural reading, hymn, sermon, possibly with *curriculum vitae*, hymn, prayer, invitation to proceed to the grave with Ps. 121.8); (*c*) at the grave (hymn, greeting, biblical sentence, committal ['Since it has pleased almighty God to call from this life our brother N., we lay his body in God's earth, that he may become again the earth from which he is taken: earth to earth, ashes to ashes, dust to dust. We commend our brother N. into God's hand. Jesus Christ will raise him on the last day. May he be gracious to him in judgment and assist him to his everlasting kingdom'], scripture reading I Cor. 15.42-44, 55-57; I Thess. 4.13-18; Rom. 14.7-9 or Rev. 21.1-5a, possibly an anthem, Lord's Prayer, a collect, possible Apostles' Creed, hymn and trinitarian blessing); the forms also contain suggestions for cremation and the committal of ashes. This is followed by a proper of about ten psalms, thirty readings (all from the New Testament) and about the same number of prayers, mostly with indications of individual usage.

The new forms produced by the Pfalz (1963), the Union Church (1964), Hessen and Nassau (1967), Baden (outline 1967) and Kurhessen-Waldeck (1970) are similar; some have alterations and a different and larger selection of psalms, readings and prayers. However, criticisms are already being voiced, especially of the antiquated language of the prayers and the committal sentences. Kurhessen-Waldeck form B (1970) presents a modern, very brief proposal, but it is not always adequate theologically. As always, the funeral sermon remains a problem; it has as many dangers as possibilities. (For full references to the authors cited above *see* the bibliography below.)

ALFRED NIEBERGALL

9. *Methodist.* John Wesley, in the Preface attached to some copies of *The Sunday Service of the Methodists*, 1784, said that he had omitted some sentences in the office for the burial of the dead. He had in fact omitted Ps. 39, the committal, and the prayer 'Almighty God, with whom we live, etc.'. These changes were largely in harmony with Puritan objections. In other respects Wesley followed almost exactly the *BCP*, 1662, of the Church of England. Methodist funerals were marked by a strong note of joy, as was shown by the use of such hymns as:

Rejoice for a brother deceased,
Our loss is his infinite gain.

In the following century these omitted passages were for the most part restored, often with some alterations, in the service books, both in America and in Britain. In England, Methodists in country districts are often buried in the Anglican parish churchyard, and the service was thus the Anglican service performed by an Anglican clergyman until a change in the law in 1880 made it permissible for burials to take place in such churchyards without the Church of England service and thus by a non-conformist minister.

In the present century there have been further changes. The current form for the United Methodist Church in America is in *The Book of Worship*, 1964; the British form is in *The Book of Offices*, 1936, but we describe rather the form authorized for experimental use in 1968. Both the American and the British forms have sentences, prayers (an addition to Anglican use), psalm(s), lesson(s) (parts of Ps. 90 and of I Cor. 15 being retained among a wider selection), optional sermon, prayers to conclude the service in church (an addition; the old custom was that the service had prayers only at the graveside). The British service has a further new feature designed to make the service in church more complete, namely a commendation of the deceased to God's mercy and wisdom. This was suggested by a similar Anglican proposal.

Both services have the optional use of the Apostles' Creed, but at different points. At the grave or in the crematorium, both services have sentences, committal (both services have variant forms to provide for different circumstances), Rev. 14.13, prayers. Both services have unambiguous prayers for the dead; they are, however, optional. Both services make special provision for the burial of a child. Funerals are much influenced by local customs. In practice the whole of the first part of the service is sometimes said in the home rather than the church.

A. RAYMOND GEORGE

10. *Old Catholic.* Rites for the burial of the dead differ in detail in the Old Catholic churches, and in addition, liturgical practice is influenced by regional and local customs. Nevertheless, some common features can be established. These, in essentials, are: blessing of the corpse and the grave, the recitation of appropriate psalms, intercessions for the dead and the bereaved, thanksgiving for God's grace towards the dead and through them to us. A eucharist often accompanies the funeral. All Souls' Day (q.v.) (2 November) is celebrated as a day of remembrance for all the departed.

As an example, we give a brief description of the form of funeral to be found in the Old Catholic Church of Germany.

The service opens with a prayer for blessing on the departed, after which the priest says an appropriate psalm. Then he delivers an address to the congregation. The Lord's Prayer, said together, follows the *Kyries*, and finally comes another prayer. At that point the coffin is sprinkled with holy water. The congregation then moves to the graveside, which is first blessed. The coffin is lowered, and the priest says Ps. 130, followed by the promise of the resurrection, 'I am the resurrection and the life' (John 11.25f.). Then follows the Lord's Prayer and another prayer. The priest sprinkles the grave with holy water, and in some places also censes it. Then he throws the first handful of earth into the grave. Once again he makes the sign of the cross over it, and then says a prayer for all the departed who lie in the cemetery and for the one whom God will next call home.

There are some alterations to this rite when the ceremony takes place in a crematorium, and at the burial of children. For a long time it has not been possible, in cities, to let the dead lie at home or to take them into church. Funerals are therefore usually held in the cemetery chapel.

In the Old Catholic Church in the Netherlands, it is in some places the custom to have a prayer-meeting with scripture reading, prayers and hymns selected by the officiating clergyman, on the eve of the burial. The official rite is made up of the requiem mass and burial prayers. The requiem mass is an almost literal translation from the Roman missal. As it was forbidden in the Netherlands to practise the Old Catholic faith openly between the beginning of the Reformation and 1800, and as it was only possible to do so secretly and in hidden churches, the different elements of the funeral are still gathered up into one continuous whole: bringing the body to the church, prayers in connection with the absolution after the mass and the ritual in the burial ground. This is usually said in the church building after the requiem mass (in former times, more often in the home of the dead person). After a month and after a year (and, if required, monthly and annually), the departed is remembered during the mass.

KURT PURSCH
A. E. RÜTHY
C. TOL

11. *Plymouth Brethren.* There is no distinctive order for the burial of the dead among the Brethren. Frequently, when a member of the fellowship dies, a service is held at his home or at the meeting-place which he attended, before the departure of the funeral procession for the ceremony, and a short committal service is held at the graveside. These services may be conducted by elders of his church or by friends of himself or of his family who are able to say what is appropriate for such an occasion. At these services emphasis is customarily laid on the faith in which the departed lived and died, and reference will be made to features of his Christian life, service and witness which can be commended as an example to others. It will be made clear that their friends' assurance of their eternal bliss is based not on their record or merit but on the faithfulness of God, in whom they had put their trust. Sometimes one or two suitable hymns of confidence and hope will be sung. Scriptures read will probably make mention of the immediate and present well-being of departed believers

as being 'absent from the body and at home with the Lord' (II Cor. 5.8) and of the coming day of resurrection and reunion at the Second Advent. Prayers for the dead are never heard, for it is not doubted that the dead in Christ do rest in peace; interesting situations arise, however, when an informal service is conducted jointly by (say) the vicar of the parish and a member of the Brethren; it is not unknown for the former to pray for the soul of the departed and the latter (presumably for the sake of Christian unity) to add a loud Amen.

Where the deceased has lived to a good age, or has been released from long illness and pain, this atmosphere of confidence and hope can make a burial service a remarkably joyful occasion. The confidence and hope will still be present, but the feeling and language will be different, at the burial of a child or young person, or of someone whose life has been tragically or suddenly cut short; yet the comfort of the scriptures will send the mourners away greatly strengthened in heart. Where the departed person is a known unbeliever, the character of the service will be perceptibly modified, but it will be emphasized that the only hope for eternal life lies in the Saviour who died and rose again.

In some areas (e.g. in the north of Scotland) it is taken for granted that a funeral service will be the occasion for a full-blown proclamation of the gospel, but this is not confined to one denomination.

Cremation is chosen only exceptionally, though probably in a larger proportion of instances over the years.

F. F. BRUCE

12. *Reformed.* In the early Reformed Church the procedure at burial was influenced by the medieval background and reaction against it so that in some places no service was held at the grave. This appears to have been the practice at Strasbourg to, at least, 1533, when at the first Synod of Strasbourg the Kirchenpfleger protested against the custom for its irreverence, citing the OT patriarchs and early Christian usage (*Arch. S. Thos*, 45.1, fol. 87). It was ordered that a pastor should be present at burial, but no order for burial was drawn up until 1537. It consisted of scripture reading, exhortation, silent or free prayer, collect and almsgiving (Hubert, *Die stras. lit. Ordnungen*, pp. 128-130).

This would have been Bucer's practice, and he makes similar provision in the *Con-*

sultatio he prepared for Cologne in 1543 (*Con.* fol. ccxliv). Calvin would have known it, but no such provision is made in either his Strasbourg or Genevan liturgies (*Op.* vi, 172-208). The Genevan *Ordonnances ecclesiastiques* (1541) simply says:

> The dead are to be buried decently in the place appointed. The attendance and company are left to each man's discretion. It will be good that the carriers be warned by us to discourage all superstitions contrary to the Word of God . . .

Calvin approved an 'appropriate sermon' being given 'in the churchyard' (*Letter to Farel*, 1543), and considered 'the Spirit no less attentive to the burial rites . . . than to the chief mysteries of the Faith' (*Inst.* III. xxv. 8), so his practice may not have been so severe as in the *Ordonannces* but have approximated to Pullain's *Liturgia Sacra*:

> The corpse shall be carried by trusty men from the city to the cemetery. The whole church shall follow with great modesty, the pastor or other minister leading. When it is come to the place where the body is to be placed in the ground, a brief address concerning death and the resurrection of the dead is given, with commendation of the deceased, if he has any virtues from which to edify the church. Prayer shall be made for the church that as God gives us this transient life so we may pass through death into his Kingdom, and that he will raise all through Christ at the last day to immortality. The people shall be dismissed with an admonition that they give an offering for the relief of the poor.

The *Form of Prayers* (1556) of the English congregation in Geneva ordered:

> The corpse is reverently brought to the grave, accompanied with the congregation, without any further ceremonies, which being buried, the minister goeth to the church, if it be not far off, and maketh some comfortable exhortation to the people, touching death and resurrection.

This was incorporated into the Scottish *Book of Common Order* (*BCO*, 1564), adding after 'minister' the words 'if he be present and required'. This leaves the question of a service open, as had the first *Book of Discipline* in 1560, although the General Assembly in 1562 had enacted:

> That one uniform order shall be taken or kept in ministration of the Sacraments, and solemnization of the Marriages and Burial of the Dead, according to the Kirk of Geneva.

Funeral services were not uncommon in Scotland, although in some places there were none, until with the growth of Brownism the Glasgow Assembly in 1638 decided 'to discharge funeral sermons, as savouring of superstition'. In England, the *BCP* contained a burial office, but among the Puritans there is evidence for 'sermon' only or 'singing of a psalm' only, and no service at all.

The debate on burial in the Westminster Assembly show the Scots to be opposed to 'sermons', but that the opinion of the divines was that there should be liberty concerning whether 'something might be said at the very interment of the body' and that the clause 'without any ceremony' did not prevent a minister 'at putting the body in the ground' saying, 'We commit the body to the ground, etc.' (Lightfoot, *Works*, xiii, p. 340). The text of the Westminster *Directory of Public Worship* adopts the extreme Puritan position, but tries to keep open the door for the 'positive' approach demanded by Palmer, Whitaker and Marshall:

> When any person departeth this life, let the dead body, upon the day of burial, be decently attended from the house to the place appointed for public burial, and there immediately interred, without any ceremony. . . .
>
> For that, praying, reading both in going to, and at the grave, have been grossly abused, are no way beneficial to the dead, and have proved many ways hurtful to the living, therefore let all such things be laid aside.
>
> Howbeit, we judge it very convenient, that the Christian friends, which accompany the dead body to the place appointed for public burial, do apply themselves to meditations and conferences suitable to the occasion; and that the minister, as upon other occasions, so at this time, if he be present, may put them in remembrance of their duty.

This, together with the triumph of Independency during the Commonwealth, resulted in a position where it was possible to write in 1867 of Scotland (equally true of

Ireland and England):

> In many, if not most, parts of the country, the religious observance at present consists of prayer alone . . . the solemn reading of the pure Word of God, without which no Protestant Service is true to its character, or complete – is generally omitted . . . The religious Service at funerals . . . is, as a general rule, confined to the house of mourning, except on the occasion of the death of ministers, and of others who have filled positions of special prominence, when sometimes a Service is held at the Church or the place of interment.

In the renewal of English rites the main influence was the Church Service Society, who in the first edition of *Euchologion* (1867) included a 'Manual for the Burial of the Dead' based on the American 'Manual of Devotional Services' and the Dutch and German Reformed rites.

American Presbyterianism followed the 1788 revision of the Westminster *Directory of Public Worship*, and, if anything, this was even more deficient than the original. Indeed, the deficiency of this aspect of the church's ministry to people was one of the factors leading to liturgical renewal, which resulted in the formation of a Church Society, on the Scottish model, in 1897, and eventually to the *Book of Common Worship (BCW)* in 1906, which was revised in 1932 and 1946. In the last and the *BCW: Proposed Services* (1966), the influence of the Scottish *BCO* (1940) is evident.

Modern Rites

English. An examination of modern Reformed burial rites in Scotland, England, Ireland, Wales, Canada, Australia and South Africa reveals a common structure and content, and that they have all been much influenced by the *Euchologion* and *BCP*. All provide for two services, one in church or home, and the other at the graveside. While there are variations in details, the general order of the former is scripture sentences, invocation, psalm, scripture readings, address, prayers of adoration, confession, thanksgiving, supplication, intercession and commemoration of saints, hymn and benediction. At the graveside the order is scripture sentences, committal, prayers and benediction. The prayers are drawn from the Reformers, *BCP*, *Euchologion*, Dutch, German,

Scottish, English and American sources.

American. The rite used in the United Presbyterian Church in the USA and the Presbyterian Church in the US (Southern) provides for two services – one for use in the church, and one for the committal service. No provision is made for worship in the home. Each is entitled 'Witness to the Resurrection'. The church service consists of scripture sentences, prayer, OT and NT lections with a prayer, hymn, sermon (optional), Apostles' Creed, prayer of thanksgiving and intercession, hymn and benediction. The committal service is brief, consisting of scripture sentences, committal, prayer, Lord's Prayer and benediction.

French. Taking the liturgies of France, Geneva and Vaud as representative of French rites, the *Liturgie de L'Église de Genève* and *Liturgie de L'Église Nationale Évangélique Réformée du Canton de Vaud* provide for two services as in the English rites and are similar to them in content. The church or home service is invocation and introduction, scripture texts and psalm, prayer before Bible reading, scripture reading, address, prayer after address and benediction. At the graveside the order is invocation and committal, scripture reading, prayer, conclusion (scripture sentences of exhortation) and benediction.

On the other hand, the *Liturgie de L'Église Réformée de France* provides for three services – home (*levée de corps*), church (*service principal*) and cemetery. The first consists of invocation, declaration (*accueil*), Apostles' Creed, prayer, psalm, scripture reading, address or meditation, chant, prayer, Lord's Prayer and benediction. The third is introduction, prayer, scripture sentences of exhortation and benediction.

German. These rites retain many of the exhortations of the Reformation era against 'abuses' and emphasize the necessity for 'absolute simplicity and common decency'. Structurally they do not differ greatly from the English and French rites, but lay a greater stress on the necessity for 'sermon'. Basic to them all is à Lasco's *Forma ac Ratio*, the Palatinate order for the preaching of the word of God at burial, and the Zurich order for burial (1529).

The prayers in the French and German rites are drawn from Strasbourg (1537), Calvin, *BCP* (1549, 1552), à Lasco, Micronius, Pullain, Cassell (1657) and St Gallen

(1699), adding in the case of the German rites Zurich (1529, 1626) and Pfalz (1563), and of the French Neuchâtel (1713).

Others. As Reformed rites belong to the one family, they contain many common features. The Dutch rites remain closely related to à Lasco and Pullain. The Hungarian and Czechoslovak rites are akin to the German, as are the Waldensian and Belgian to the French. The Portuguese and Brazilian rites (through American influence) and the Spanish (through Irish) have much in common with the English.

Theology
In all these rites the centrality of the life, death and resurrection of Christ is basic. The Strasbourg order (1537) declared: 'It is our task at burial to comfort each other in the Lord and to encourage to Christian endeavour.' All give adequate expression to this. On the other hand, one point appears to receive inadequate expression. With Paul and the Fathers, Calvin could write 'baptism is the seal of our future resurrection (Col. 2.12); no less does the sacred Supper invite us to confidence in it' (*Inst.* III.xxv. 8). Few, if any, of the rites include a specific reference to this.

In all these rites a large selection of lections is provided, some of them numbering over seventy. While recognition must be given to the fullness of scriptural teaching, surely for liturgical purposes this could be reduced considerably.

JOHN M. BARKLEY

13. *Seventh-day Adventist.* The burial service of the Seventh-day Adventist Church does not differ a great deal in its forms from that of most Protestant churches. Since interment customs vary from country to country, there are naturally also some variations in Adventist burial rites in different parts of the world; there are, however, also many constants. It is the generally accepted practice for SDA ministers to charge no fee for conducting funerals. They co-operate closely with the funeral director and endeavour to meet the wishes of the sorrowing family in making arrangements for the funeral service at the home, the funeral parlour or the church.

The doctrinal basis for the SDA funeral service is conditionalism, that is, the belief that immortality or everlasting life is the gift of God through faith in Christ. As condi-

tionalists, Adventists believe that the Bible teaches that man rests in the grave until the resurrection and they therefore consider as unscriptural the doctrine of immortal-soulism, according to which man was created with a soul that has a separate, indefeasibly immortal existence, apart from the body.

A typical church funeral service is opened by a hymn followed by a brief prayer. Then a suitable collection of scriptural passages may be read, taking into consideration the age, life and experience of the deceased. As a rule, the reading includes such Bible passages as Ps. 90.1-4, 10, 12; Job 14.1, 2, 14, 15; I Cor. 15.51, 57. Then a short obituary sketch presenting the life of the deceased is read. There follows a brief homily, not a long doctrinal sermon on the state of the dead, pointing the bereaved to the glorious hope of the resurrection and underlining the power of Christ to deliver from sin and conquer death by bestowing immortality upon the righteous at his second coming – the blessed hope of all ages.

After the homily or address a prayer follows, making thanksgiving for all that God's goodness has done for the departed, for the assurance of the resurrection's restoration, praying for the finishing of the gospel work on earth, and remembering the dear ones left to mourn. Another song may be sung at this point in the service, which closes with the benediction.

At the graveside a quartet or some other group may sing, and as the casket rests above the grave, or is being lowered into the earth, the minister reads appropriate scriptural passages, such as John 11.25; Rev. 1.17, 18; 14.13; 21.3-5; I Thess. 4.13-18.

In some countries the minister or funeral director drops a little earth or flower petals on the casket as the minister repeats the liturgical committal. If a hymn is sung at the graveside it is usually sung at this point. A closing prayer follows together with the benediction.

B. B. BEACH

S. Benko, *The Meaning of Sanctorum Communio*, 1964; B. Bürkli, *Im Herrn entschlafen. Eine historisch-pastoral theologische Studie zur Liturgie des Sterbens und des Begräbnisses*, 1969; G. Cope, ed., *Dying, Death and Disposal*, 1970 (a treatment of pastoral, architectural and theological problems arising in connection with funerary practice today); O. Cullmann, *Immortality of the Soul or Resurrection of the Dead?*, 1958; J. Dowdall, 'The Liturgy of the Dead' in *Studies in Pastoral Liturgy*, I, ed. P. Murray, 1964; L. E. Froom, *The Conditionalist Faith of our Father*, 1966 (Seventh-day Adventist); P. Graff, *Geschichte der Auflösung der alten gottesdienstlichen Formen in der evangelischen Kirche Deutschlands*, ²1937, I, pp. 345-372; II, 272–279; M. Gy, OP, 'La Mort du Chrétien' in *L'Église en Prière*, ed. A. G. Martimort, 1965; B. Jordahn, *Das kirchliche Begräbnis. Grundlegung und Gestaltung*, 1949; T. Kliefoth, *Liturgische Abhandlungen*, I and II, 1869; M. Luther, *Werke*, Weimar 1883 ff.; *La Maison Dieu*, 101; *Manual for Ministers*, 1965 (Seventh-day Adventist); H. Maser, *Die Bestattung*, 1964; R. Mehl, *Notre vie et notre mort*, 1953; K. F. Müller and W. Blankenburg, eds., *Leiturgia. Handbuch des evangelischen Gottesdienstes* (6: Begräbnis, etc.), 1952; *The Prayer Book of Edward VI* (Everyman or other editions; there exists no collection of later Anglican funerary rites); A. L. Richter, *Die evangelischen Kirchenordnungen des 16. Jahrhunderts*, 2 vols, 1846; G. Rietschel-P. Graff, *Lehrbuch der Liturgik*, ²1951, pp. 764-788; M. Righetti, *Storia Liturgica*, II, ²1955; F. Schulz, 'Die Begräbnisgebete des 16. und 17. Jahrhunderts', in *Jahrbuch für Liturgie und Hymnologie*, XI, 1966, pp. 1-44; E. Sehling, *Die evangelischen Kirchenordnungen des XVI Jahrhunderts*, 14 vols, 1962 ff.; *Services Funebres*, 1963 (Reformed); John E. Skoglund, *A Manual of Worship*, 1968 (Baptist); E. Winkler, *Die Leichenpredigt im deutschen Luthertum bis Spener*, 1967.

Calendar

The list of commemorations observed throughout the Christian year. It represents a fusion of a series of christological festivals, such as Christmas, Easter, etc. (qq.v.), together with Mariological feasts (q.v.), e.g. the Purification, and saints' and holy days (q.v.).

EDITOR

Camp Meeting

The origin of the camp meeting lies in the American frontier around 1800. People travelled several miles to reach the place where the preaching took place. They could not leave early enough to return home the same night. Therefore they brought their equipment for camping on the spot. The preaching was soul-searching. People were faced with a choice between God and the devil. Terrible was the description of hell, when a sinner was 'sinking into the liquid, boiling waves of hell, and accursed sinners of Tyre and Sidon, and Sodom and Gomorrah sprang to the right and left and made way for him to pass them and fall lower down even to the deepest cavern in the flaming abyss. Here his consciousness like a never-dying worm stings him and forever gnaws his soul ... Now through the blazing flames of hell he sees that heaven he has lost ... In those pure regions he sees his father, or mother, his sisters or brothers, or those persons who sat under the same means of grace with him, and whom he derided as fools, fanatics, and hypocrites' (J. C. Brauer, *Protestantism in America*, 1965, p. 107). Such preaching led to highly emotional results. Men and women began to cry for mercy. Turning and twisting, wringing their hands, beating their breasts, they struggled to be released from sin and to experience the new birth in Christ.

The camp meeting matched the needs of the frontier: an un- or even anti-intellectual preaching, a personal decision on things which were controllable (sinners were swearing, drinking and dancing; saints abstained from such things; there was no middle way), the possibility of leaving the isolation of every-day life and enjoying fellowship with a crowd.

In the middle of the last century the mainline churches abandoned the camp meeting. Some Christians, longing for revival, gathered together and revived the old customs, which eventually gave birth to the Holiness denominations, with their tangible experience of sanctification, including 'holy laughter', 'holy barking' and 'holy jerks'. At the beginning of the twentieth century the Holiness denominations became more fashionable. The camp meeting tradition was then taken up by the Pentecostal movement.

Today the camp meeting has lost its cruder sides. It is a place where one lives as the forefathers did, assembles around a fire, sleeps in country houses or tents, far away from the jungles of modern cities.

The future of the camp meeting can be just this (or – what is not excluded – a re-awakening of the former emotionalism). But it could also be an exercise in using leisure time intelligently, rediscovering those parts of the person which are suppressed in today's society, through relationship with other persons and nature, through a growing awareness of intuition, through means of art and meditation.

J. C. Brauer, *Protestantism in America*, 1965; W. J. Hollenweger, *Handbuch der Pfingst-bewegung* (02a.02.001), 1965/1967; W. L. Sperry, *Religion in America*, 1948.

W. J. HOLLENWEGER

Candlemas *see* Mariological Feasts

Candles, Lamps and Lights

The use of the term 'lights' in Christian worship refers to the use of candles and lamps not only for the purpose of illumination but also for liturgical observance. The history of the use of such lights is complicated and somewhat obscure. There is some difference of opinion as to how far Christian usage was influenced by the use of such lights in the worship of the Jewish Temple and synagogue.

The reference to the 'many lights' in Acts 20.8 at the celebration of the eucharist at Troas probably implies no precise liturgical use, since this observance was at midnight. The reference to the seven lamps of fire in Rev. 4.5 probably reflects an apocalyptic vision of the heavenly temple rather than current Christian practice. Also the argument that such lights are derived from their use in Christian worship in the catacombs during the early centuries is no longer regarded as valid, and the use of the catacombs for public worship in times of persecution was not normal; they were too confined and too well-known to the Roman authorities.

Tertullian (*c.* AD 200) inveighs against 'the useless lighting of lamps at noonday' (*Apol.* 46); but he is probably referring to their use in pagan worship if we consider his words in their context.

It is most likely that the lighting of candles and lamps in Christian worship is bound up with the vigil service that was held on the Saturday night-Sunday morning, and to which the reference in Acts 20.8 may be early evidence, if it preceded the mass held at dawn. The kindling of light at this service, although probably originally entirely functional, became a liturgical celebration of which the

lighting of the Paschal candle (q.v.) is a traditional continuance.

By the fourth century, both lamps and candles were in normal use in Christian worship. The Spanish Christian poet, Prudentius (*c.* 348), in his hymn *Inventor rutili*, says: 'The lamps hang by flexible cords and shine over the ceilings to which they are fixed, and the flame, fed by floating wicks, casts its light through clear glass. You would believe that the heavens were adorned with the twin constellation of the Wain' (*Cath.* V.141). A similar kind of testimony comes to us from Italy in the poems of Paulinus of Nola about the same date. The *Liber Pontificalis* tells of lamps of gold given by Constantine the Great to burn before the altars of the Roman basilicas erected by him. Lamps burnt before the shrine of St Peter, a custom which has continued to the present day not only at Rome but before the shrine of St Francis at Assisi. In the fourth and fifth centuries, the *Liber Pontificalis* records the gifts of bronze and silver candlesticks as well as crowns and candelabra given by popes Damasus, Innocent I and Celestine. While some of these were utilitarian, the suspension of lamps in the form of dolphins from the corners and under the canopy of the altar (*see* **Altar**) must clearly have had a votive and honorific significance.

For over a thousand years it was not the normal custom to stand candlesticks on the altar. Indeed, there is little explicit evidence for this arrangement until the twelfth century. The evidence of Pope Innocent III (*c.* 1198) in his *De Sacro Mysterio* is the most important. In the earlier usage it was the custom to carry lights and incense before the bishop and his assistants at the entry for the mass; and some commentators have derived this from secular custom in which the emperor and other persons of note had such ceremonies accorded them. The bishop came to be regarded as a civil dignitary from the fourth century. *Ordo Romanus Primus*, an eighth-century document, but which reflects the customs of the papal mass in the time of Pope Gregory the Great (d. 604), shows that the papal cortege was preceded by seven acolytes with candlesticks which were set down round the altar and not on it during the mass.

As we have indicated, it is not until the second part of the Middle Ages that the placing of candlesticks on the altar commences; but there was no invariable rule about this matter, and medieval paintings and illuminated MSS of the fourteenth and fifteenth centuries often depict the mass in progress with no candlesticks on the altar. What was regarded as of importance from the thirteenth century was the holding of a lighted torch or candle by the parish clerk or one of the assistant ministers at the elevation (q.v.) of the host.

Until the sixteenth century there was considerable latitude and freedom of action in the Latin West as to how candles were employed in the Mass and in the choir offices, and there were variations as to the number of candlesticks placed on the altar in the later Middle Ages. The custom of the Roman Catholic Church is now to require six lights on the altar at high mass and seven when a bishop sings such a mass. This, however, is a requirement first laid down in the *Caerimonale Episcoporum* of 1600 and there is no explicit evidence for this arrangement before its mention by Burchard and the writers of the Counter-Reformation. In France until the nineteenth century, modern Roman Catholic ceremonial both in regard to lights and other customs was widely disregarded. A point that should be noted is that candlesticks were not left on the altar as a permanent form of decoration but were only placed there at the time of liturgy.

In the Church of England in the nineteenth century there was considerable litigation and dispute as to the legality of the use of lights at the eucharist. But since the Restoration under Charles II there is continuous evidence for their use and some of our cathedrals and greater churches possess altar candlesticks belonging to the seventeenth century. Upholders of Anglican tradition point to the injunction of Edward VI in 1547 referring to the retention of 'two lights upon the high altar, before the sacrament, which for the signification that Christ is the very true light of the world, they shall suffer to remain still'. There is also evidence that during the reign of Elizabeth I not only were candlesticks in use in the Queen's Chapel but 'in many cathedral churches, besides the chapels of divers noblemen' according to Bishop Cosin in his *Notes on the Book of Common Prayer* (*c.* 1640).

A matter that has also been disputed is the question of a continuous light burning before an aumbry (q.v.) or tabernacle containing the reserved sacrament. While reservation (q.v.) can claim a very high antiquity, the custom of a perpetual light can only be found in the later Middle Ages. In 1240, Walter de Cantilupe, bishop of Worcester, ordered that 'a lamp must burn day and night before the eucharist'. There is little evidence earlier than this time.

In the Eastern Orthodox Church it is customary to have a seven-branched candlestick standing on the altar; and the bishop blesses the people during the liturgy holding the *dikiri* and the *trikiri* (a two branched and three-branched candlestick) in either hand.

D. R. Dendy, *The Use of Lights in Christian Worship*, 1959; L. Hertling and E. Kirschbaum, *The Roman Catacombs and their Martyrs*, 1960; A. A. King and C. E. Pocknee, *Eucharistic Reservation in the Western Church*, 1965; V. Staley, ed., *Hierurgia Anglicana*, pt. I, 1902.

C. E. POCKNEE

Canon

The Greek word *kanon* means a rule or measuring rod; it came to be applied to the consecration prayer in the eucharistic rite of the West. In some early sacramentary manuscripts the word appears in the heading above the *Sursum Corda – incipit canon actionis* – indicating that the text from this point was fixed. The word then came to be used for the whole prayer. As early as Justin Martyr (*c.* AD 150) this prayer was not regarded as fixed, for at this point the president prayed 'as he was able'. By the time of Hippolytus of Rome (*c.* AD 210) it would appear that a text existed, but was still not regarded as definitive: it was simply a model to be used as required. The precise origins of the Western canon remain obscure: but the basic elements must have existed by the late fourth century, for Ambrose in *De Sacramentis* (*c.* AD 378) quoted portions of a eucharistic canon which is found in its entirety in manuscripts of the sixth century. The texts of the canon as they appear in the Gelasian and Gregorian sacramentaries of the seventh century have remained basically the same until the twentieth century.

A noteworthy characteristic of the Roman canon is its small amount of variation throughout the church's year. In this respect it resembles the eucharistic prayer or anaphora (q.v.) of the Eastern liturgies rather than the canon of the non-Roman Western or Gallican rites, which was simply a collection of constantly changing elements. The Roman canon is a combination of short prayers lacking any real cohesion; its pattern would suggest that at an early stage in its history the text suffered some dislocation. Its elements are as follows:

Introductory dialogue – *Sursum Corda*
Preface, culminating in *Sanctus* and *Benedictus*
A plea for the acceptance of the offerings
Prayer for the living and departed
Prayer of offering
Narrative of the institution
Anamnesis – oblation
Prayer for acceptance and fruitful reception
Prayer for the living and departed
Two doxologies

At the Reformation the abolition of the canon was almost an article of faith with the Reformers except for Cranmer. In nearly all Reformed rites it was normally reduced to the narrative of the institution with the possible addition of a prayer for worthy reception. But in the 1549 Anglican prayer book Cranmer retained the main elements of the Roman canon. In 1552, however, these were divided into three distinct prayers at different points in the rite – the prayer for the church militant, the severely truncated prayer of consecration ending with the narrative of the institution, and the prayer of oblation following communion and the Lord's Prayer. Today there is a general movement among both Catholic and Reformed Churches to recover a primitive Trinitarian pattern of canon, in which God is blessed or thanked for his mighty acts of creation, redemption and sanctification, the total redemptive activity of Christ is 'remembered' and proclaimed, and the Holy Spirit is invoked to unite and strengthen the communicants.

J. M. Barkley, *The Worship of the Reformed Church*, 1966; B. Botte, *Le Canon de la Messe*, 1935; F. E. Brightman, *The English Rite*, 1915; W. S. Porter, *The Gallican Rite*, 1958; L. D. Reed, *The Lutheran Liturgy*, 1947; C. Vagaggini, *The Canon of the Mass and Liturgical Reform*, 1967.

R. C. D. JASPER

Canonical Hours

The *canonicae horae* are the times of daily prayer laid down in the Roman Catholic breviary, or the comparable hours of the Eastern Churches and, hence, the services appointed to be recited at these times. The seven hours officially appointed in the Western Church are mattins and lauds (reckoned as one hour), prime, terce, sext, none, vespers and compline. This rota of prayer was already complete in the West probably by the end of the fifth century, but the structure and content of the hours were modified by later reforms of the breviary, notably by the Council of Trent, which led to the issue of the *Breviarium Romanum* in Rome in 1568 under Pius V, by Benedict XIV and by Pius X (1911).

In his Tract No. 75 'On the Roman Breviary', published in 1835-36, J. H. Newman asserted that 'the Jewish observance of the third, sixth, and ninth hours for prayer, was continued by the inspired founders of the Christian Church' (*Tracts for the Times*, III, ²1837, Tract 75, p.3). He proceeded: 'Such was the Apostolic worship as far as Scripture happens to have preserved it . . . in subsequent times the Hours of prayer were gradually developed from the three, or (with midnight) the four seasons, above enumerated, to seven, viz. by the addition of Prime (the first hour), Vespers (the evening), and Compline (bed-time); according to the words of the Psalm, "Seven times a day do I praise thee . . ."' (*ibid.*, p.4).

The origin of the canonical hours, however, is not so simple as Newman supposed. Newman relied on Scripture to prove that the Jews observed the third, sixth and ninth hours for prayer. He cited Daniel who prayed three times a day (Dan. 6.10); at the third hour the Holy Spirit descended at Pentecost (Acts 2.15), at the sixth hour Peter 'went up upon the housetop to pray' (Acts 10.9), and at the ninth hour 'Peter and John went up together into the temple' being 'the hour of prayer' (Acts 3.1). Tertullian had already noted these biblical references, but wisely contented himself with the remark, 'these facts are simply stated without any command about the practice' (*De Orat.* xxv).

A more modern approach to the subject is reflected by Mgr Pierre Salmon who, while recognizing the NT teaching, reiterated by Tertullian, Cyprian and Clement of Alexandria, that the whole Christian life should be one of prayer, sees the origin of the canonical hours in the Roman division of the day into four 'hours' (*prima, tertia, sexta* and *nona*) and the night into four 'watches' – the first in the evening, the second at midnight, the third at cock-crow and the fourth at dawn (P. Salmon, 'La prière des heures' in *L'Église en Prière: Introduction à la Liturgie*, ed. A. G. Martimort, [3]1965, p. 814). The present writer had already drawn attention in 1944 to the fact that Tertullian called the third, sixth and ninth hours 'these common hours, which mark the intervals of the day' (*De Orat.* xxv; *cf. De Jejun.* x); that they were publicly announced (Varro, *De Ling. Lat.* vi. 89); and that it would be natural for Christians to adopt them as hours of prayer, hallowed as they were for them by the events connected with the crucifixion (C. W. Dugmore, *The Influence of the Synagogue upon the Divine Office*, 1944, pp. 66f., repr. Alcuin Club Collections, XLV, 1964). The *Apostolic Tradition* of Hippolytus of Rome (*c.* AD 215), indeed, was already urging prayer at home or 'if thou art elsewhere' at these hours for this specific reason (*Ap. Trad.* xxxvi. 2-6, ed. Gregory Dix, reissued with corrections and preface by H. Chadwick, 1968, pp. 62-64). Lechner rightly regarded the prayers at terce, sext and none in the second century as 'private daily practice', but, like Salmon, he thought the night office and the prayer at dawn were also private-prayer hours (Ludwig Eisenhofer-Joseph Lechner, *The Liturgy of the Roman Rite*, ET edited by H. E. Winstone, 1961, pp. 438f.). Salmon noted that Tertullian described the (older) morning and evening prayers as *legitimae orationes* (Salmon, *op.cit.*, p. 815; *cf.* C. W. Dugmore, *op.cit.*, pp. 47, 60) but failed to give the context or to point out that the prayers at dawn and at dusk (*ingressu lucis et noctis*) derive, through the hours of prayer in the Synagogue, from the hours of sacrifice in the Jerusalem Temple. Tertullian was supporting the new rota of private prayer at the third, sixth and ninth hours, introduced by the ascetics in North Africa – but these must, he said, be in addition to the regular hours of public prayer, on Sundays and weekdays, *quae sine admonitione debentur ingressu lucis et noctis* (*De Orat.* xxv; *cf.* Cyprian, *De Orat. Domin.* xxxv). The morning prayers, consisting of the four elements of synagogue worship (namely prayer, psalmody, scripture lections, and a sermon expounding the lections), formed the first part of the Sabbath and Sunday service of the eucharist. The evening prayers were probably conducted on the same plan, without the sermon, as in the synagogue. We have the evidence of Hippolytus that the *missa catechumenorum* (as this part of the service was later called) was used on weekdays (*Ap. Trad.* xxxi. 2; xxxv. 2), but nothing is said about public assembly in the evening: the *lucernarium* of the Ethiopic version and the *Testamentum Domini* (Dix-Chadwick, *op. cit.*, pp. 49-52) clearly belongs to a service preceding the agapé (q.v.) or eucharist, and was therefore, originally not a daily service.

Among the canonical hours, lauds (or mattins) and vespers are the ancient prayers of the church, said at dawn and at sunset. Terce, sext and none have no basis in Jewish usage, except that none (3 p.m.) was the hour at which the 'evening sacrifice' was offered in the Herodian Temple (*cf.* Acts 3.1). There is no evidence of Jewish worship, either in temple or synagogue, at noon (the sixth hour) and the prescription that Christians should say the Lord's Prayer thrice daily (*Didache* viii. 3) makes no mention of the time of prayer. The hours of terce, sext and none were first observed as times of private prayer by the specially devout (the ascetics) and later were incorporated with the older lauds/mattins and vespers into the cycle of daily prayer developed by the monks. Jerome wrote in the fourth century, in a letter to the virgin Eustochium: 'Prayers, as everyone knows, ought to be said at the third, sixth and ninth hours, at dawn and at evening' (*Ep.* xxii. 37). Cassian tells us that it was at Bethlehem (where Jerome ruled the men's monastery from *c.* 386) that prime was introduced, at the first hour, to put an end to the laxity of the monks *c.* 382 (Cassian, *De Coenob. Instit.* iii. 4). Compline, consisting of Ps. 90, is mentioned by Basil, but was probably not introduced to the West as part of the regular cycle of daily prayer before Benedict (P. Batiffol, *History of the Roman Breviary*, ET by A.M.Y. Baylay, p. 28). Thus the 'seven times a day do I praise thee' referred to by Newman were complete.

It has been noted above that the earliest Christian daily public prayer was at dawn and at sunset (*ingressu lucis et noctis*, to use Tertullian's phrase), and that these times of prayer were basic to the canonical hours observed by the ascetics and the later monks. There is no problem concerning the evening prayer (vespers), but the relationship between mattins and the nocturnal offices has been the subject of much discussion among liturgical scholars. Mgr Salmon has remarked that 'it is difficult to know what were the night offices' (*op. cit.*, p. 816). Anton Baumstark, the author of a famous study entitled *Comparative Liturgy* (revised by B. Botte, ET by F. L. Cross, 1958) maintained in his *Nocturna Laus* (ed. Odilo Heiming, 1957) that the Christian nocturnal hours of prayer were modelled on those of the Graeco-Roman world – the Dionysian rites (*Nyktelia, Nyktophylaxia*), the *Bacchanalia*, known at Rome about 168 BC, the *Pannychis* of the cult of Aphrodite, and so forth. In his view the Christians imitated, or took over, non-Christian custom, and the origin of the nocturnal hours is to be found in the early Christian night-time vigils. But there is no evidence of any nightly vigil, except the Easter Vigil, before the time of Tertullian and Cyprian. Baumstark was apparently not acquainted with the work of J. M. Hanssen (*Nature et Genèse de l'Office des Matines*, Analecta Gregoriana, LVII [Series Facultatis Theologicae, Sect. A No. 7], Rome 1952), who rightly saw that the dawn office is the oldest (though he did not trace its origin to Temple and synagogue) and rejected the hypothesis of an origin derived from pagan nocturnal acts of worship. Hanssen argued critically, with reference to the various liturgical texts, the case for the three possible hypotheses concerning the origin of mattins. He utterly rejected, first, the theory that it was partly a nocturnal and partly a dawn office, on the grounds that the 'midnight office' was purely a later monastic invention (despite Paul and Silas, Acts 16.25); secondly, the theory that mattins resulted from the juxtaposition of two offices (nocturns and lauds), previously recited separately, the one in the night and the other at dawn. He concluded that mattins as it was later known was the result of the amplification of the primitive mattins, or lauds, augmented by the addition of a pre-mattins, or prime. The use of the psalms is the key. The recitation of one or more chosen psalms and the recitation of the psalter itself are two totally different modes of psalmody: the first characterizes a well-defined office to be celebrated at a precise hour, the second provides the means of occupying piously a more or less long space of time, such as was the vigil. The office of mattins consisted of specified psalms, hymns and prayers. The earliest documents mention Pss. 50; 66; 117; and especially Pss. 148-150, called *laudes*.

The first text which describes in any detail a regular cycle of prayer comparable to the later canonical hours is to be found in the journal of a woman pilgrim, named Egeria (or Etheria), who visited Jerusalem about 385-88. In the *Peregrinatio Egeriae* there is a description of a service at the tenth hour ('called here [Jerusalem] *licinicon*, which we [in the West] call *lucernare*') and another at dawn. The services of the hours are obviously of a monastic nature, attended by ascetics and nuns, but at the evening and morning services (*vespers* and *mattins*) the laity were also present in the church of the Anastasis.

But it was in the monasteries that the hours found their natural home. Some Eastern features were introduced at Milan by Ambrose and in Gaul by John Cassian, who had spent the early years of his life in a monastery at Bethlehem and had studied the monastic systems of Egypt. But the greatest influence on the development of monasticism in the West was Benedict of Nursia, who was probably the first to give a permanent place in the hours to compline (*completorium*), as a last office in the evening before retiring to rest. According to Professor David Knowles, at Monte Cassino in St Benedict's day the following would seem to have been the skeleton time-table.

In winter, on 1 November

2.00 a.m.	rise for nocturns (the modern mattins)
2.10-3.30	nocturns
3.30-5.00	reading
5.00-5.45	lauds
5.45-8.15	reading, including prime (20 mins.)
8.15-2.30	work, broken by terce, sext and none (10 mins. each)
2.30-3.15	dinner
3.15-4.15	reading
4.15-4.45	vespers, collation (reading), compline
5.15	in bed

In summer, say 30 June

1.00-2.00 a.m.	nocturns
2.15-3.00	lauds
3.00-4.30	reading
4.30-9.15	prime and work
9.30-11.30	reading
11.45-12.30	dinner
12.30-2.00	siesta
2.00-6.30	work
6.30-7.00	vespers

7.00-7.30   supper and collation
7.30-8.00   compline and bed

The most remarkable thing, to us in the twentieth century, about this daily programme is the early rising and early end of the day, but in central Italy darkness fell about 5 p.m. at the winter solstice and about 7.45 p.m. at midsummer. (The author wishes to thank Prof. Knowles for permission to reproduce these tables and facts from his *Christian Monasticism* [World Christian Library], 1969, pp. 213f.) Candles (q.v.) or olive oil lamps would suffice for reciting the hours at the beginning of the day and for reading, but work could only be done in daylight, and if the day began at 1 or 2 a.m. it was reasonable to retire at nightfall. In more northern climes the hours of daylight were different and five centuries after St Benedict the *horarium* of the English monastery of Christ Church, Canterbury, began in winter at 2.30 a.m. and ended at 6.30 p.m., but the scheme drawn up by Lanfranc differed greatly from that of St Benedict. 'Of the time, roughly fourteen hours, available after the hours of sleep, meals and toilet have been deducted, no less than eight are occupied in religious services in church, while reading has less than three hours and work three at most . . . What, we may ask, had made the change? Above all, two weighty additions. The first was the two masses daily attended by the whole community – perhaps three, if the priest's private mass was taken out of reading or work time. The second was the large quantity of psalms, prayers, litanies and minor offices. Besides these, both office and mass had been lengthened by the chant [q.v.], which was now far more elaborate than in St Benedict's day' (*ibid.*, pp. 218-20).

In the later Middle Ages the divine office became so elaborate that reform of it was almost continuous from the time of Gregory VII to the Council of Trent. The Gregorian Reform and the twelfth-century Renaissance did not immediately produce changes in the *Ordo Romanus* of the office, which Gregory VII confirmed against those who wished to reduce the psalmody of mattins to three psalms. Indeed, he extended to all Christendom the obligation of observing the festivals of martyr popes and, while he ordered that on Easter Day and the six week-days following, as on Pentecost and the six days following, the nocturnal office should have only

three psalms, three lessons and three responds, for the rest of the year, the nocturnal office for festivals was to have nine psalms, nine lessons and nine responds; the ferial office twelve, three and three; and the Sunday office eighteen, nine and nine. Gregory VII suppressed the Mozarabic rites in favour of the *Ordo Romanus* – an illustration of the Holy See's new interest in the canonical hours, which was part of the progressive assertion of the Roman primacy in the field of liturgy, as elsewhere. Attempts by the clergy, through laziness, to reduce the office to one nocturn of three psalms and three lessons were thwarted by Gregory VII. But the offices were too long for the changed circumstances of the twelfth century, when travel became more frequent, many beneficed clerks frequented the universities and non-residence increased. Thus the *modernum officium*, used by the pope and the curia in the papal chapel, came into use during the twelfth century. This modified the calendar, abbreviated the lectionary and adopted the monastic hymnal (which had been gradually making its way into the monastic hours, despite Roman disapproval, since the time of Ambrose). It also added the *Quincunque vult*, the daily office of the Blessed Virgin Mary (a brief office in honour of the Virgin modelled on the divine office [q.v.] and containing the usual canonical hours) and the office of the dead (*see* **Burial** 3) as supplements to the canonical office, together with commemorations (*Memoriae*) of the saints, always comprising an antiphon, versicle and response, appended to lauds and vespers.

The *modernum officium* was shorter than the old *Ordo Romanus* and it was adopted by the Franciscans in 1223, but they needed an office still shorter; thus, their general, Haymo of Faversham, undertook a revision of the *Breviarium Romanae Curiae* which was approved by Gregory IX in 1241. Already in 1227 a Council of Trier obliged all priests to possess a breviary which would permit them to recite the hours when travelling. The Franciscans, because of their itinerant and apostolic way of life, could not always recite the solemn office in choir: they often had to recite it privately. Thus, in the thirteenth century a profound change occurred, not so much in the structure of the canonical hours as in the manner of their observance. The scripture lessons were further reduced, the number of festivals was increased; the Franciscans did not celebrate the double office still maintained in the Roman basilicas, but recited only the office of the festival, omitting that of the day. Thus the recitation of the breviary office became a succession of festival observances, and the old office of the day or season fell largely into disuse. This, in turn, resulted in the introduction of lessons from mythical and spurious 'lives' of the saints. By the fifteenth century the structure of the earlier canonical hours, based on regular recital of the psalms and scripture lections, had become so overlaid by later accretions that council after council vied with one another 'in deploring the coldness with which the clergy perform their duty of reciting the canonical office, even in choir' (P. Batiffol, *History of the Roman Breviary*, ET 1912, p. 173). The offices were now almost entirely the concern of the clergy and there was little attendance by the laity, except at mattins sung before mass and vespers on Sundays and festivals. It is interesting to observe here the continuity of tradition, despite all the medieval changes, with the observance of the hours of morning and evening (originally sunrise and sunset) by the laity in the early church. We noted above that these hours of prayer, taken over by the church from the synagogue, were observed in the period before Tertullian in North Africa and Hippolytus in Rome, as well as in Jerusalem in the late fourth century. They were destined to survive the sixteenth century Reformation.

By the sixteenth century the *modernum officium*, with its complicated service due to the multiplication of festivals, the frequent recitation of the office of the Blessed Virgin Mary and of that of the dead, and of the gradual and penitential psalms, was felt to be burdensome, unedifying and far removed from the canonical hours of the early church as they had been enshrined in the old *Ordo Romanus*. Two attempts to remedy the situation were made under Clement VII (1523-34). He first approved the plan of Carafa, General of the Theatine Order and later Pope Paul IV, to revise the office and also the missal for the use of his order. Nothing came of this. More important, in 1529 Clement issued a commission to Cardinal Francisco de Quiñones, General of the Franciscans, to prepare a new breviary which would simplify the divine office by a return to the practice of the fathers of the church and so attract the

clergy to discharge their canonical duty of reciting it (as laid down by Innocent III in 1215). Quiñones's *Breviarium Romanum nuper reformatum* was published in 1535 (modern ed. by J. Wickham Legg, 1888). 'The reform was drastic: antiphons, responds, chapters and preces are abolished. The Psalter is redistributed, three Psalms being assigned to each office throughout the week, except in so far that the *Venite* is added at Mattins, and the Old Testament canticle of each day serves as the third Psalm in Lauds' (F. E. Brightman, *The English Rite*, 1915, I, xxvi, where further details of the reform may be found). In July 1535 the Sorbonne condemned these innovations and Cardinal Quiñones produced a further revision in July 1536 (*The Second Recension of the Quignon Breviary*, 1908). This restored the antiphons to the psalms in all the offices, and some other features which had become traditional, but it was abandoned by the Council of Trent and suppressed by Paul IV in 1558. Eventually a new reformed breviary was issued by Pius V by the bull *Quod a nobis* of 15 July 1568, which abolished that of Quiñones and all other Roman breviaries of less than 200 years' standing.

Meanwhile, reform of the canonical hours which comprised the breviary had been urged by Hermann von Wied, archbishop-elector of Cologne, in 1536. By 1543 he had become a Lutheran; he invited Martin Bucer from Strasbourg, Philip Melanchthon from Wittenberg and others to help in carrying through his reform. The resulting Church Order, in which Bucer was mainly responsible for the liturgical parts, was issued in a Latin version, known as the *Simplex ac pia deliberatio* in 1545 (ET entitled *A Simple and Religious Consultation* published in 1547 and 1548). This made use of several Lutheran German Church Orders, but chiefly Osiander's Brandenburg-Nürnberg order of 1533.

Since Thomas Cranmer was certainly in Nuremberg in 1532, where he married Margaret, niece of Osiander's wife, it is inconceivable that he was unaware of the existence and content of the last-named Church Order. It does not follow from his contacts with Lutherans that he himself became a Lutheran, either now or later. The important point in the present context is that he was acquainted with the Lutheran revisions of the canonical hours to form two vernacular services of morning and evening prayer. Within the year he became Archbishop of Canterbury (30 March 1533).

There is in the British Museum a manuscript (MS Royal, 7.B.iv) which contains two draft schemes for the reform of the Latin daily office (best edition in J. Wickham Legg, *Cranmer's Liturgical Projects*, I, 1915). 'The handwriting of a part of the manuscript is that of Cranmer's secretary, Ralph Morice. The additions and corrections are in Cranmer's own hand. The manuscript undoubtedly once belonged to Cranmer. We need not hesitate in attributing the authorship of these schemes to him' (E. C. Ratcliff, 'The Liturgical Work of Archbishop Cranmer' in *Journal of Ecclesiastical History*, 7 [1956], p. 190). As Ratcliff pointed out (*ibid.*, p. 194), Cranmer had the choice of two methods of revision. Either he could follow Quiñones and preserve the traditional cycle of eight canonical hours of the breviary, or he could follow the Lutheran church orders and reduce the daily services to two. In the British Museum MS, Scheme I is Lutheran in type: Scheme II is Quiñonian. Since the later *BCP* is closer to Scheme I, in the matter of two daily services (mattins and evensong), the monthly recitation of the psalms and the system of lessons, Gasquet and Bishop concluded that this Scheme was nearer in date to the *BCP* and that Scheme II was earlier. This theory was accepted by Frere and Brightman, but C. H. Smyth and E. C. Ratcliff have concluded that the reverse is the truth. In Ratcliff's words: 'Scheme I, therefore, may be assigned to 1538, the year in which Thomas Cromwell was conducting Henry VIII's last and abortive negotiations with the Lutherans . . . Scheme II, on the other hand, belongs to the period between 1543 and 1546 when, more conservative ideas having regained ascendancy, Cranmer was obliged to conform his liturgical projects with the prevailing mood' (*ibid.*). Both Schemes were in Latin and, therefore, could only concern the clergy. In the next reign, when a vernacular *BCP* became possible, an English translation of Scheme I provided the basis for mattins and evensong.

The prayer book of 1549 and the services of mattins and evensong which it contained were, nevertheless, no mere English reproduction of a Lutheran liturgical book or rite. The Preface to the *BCP* was modelled on that of Quiñones's *Breviarium Romanum nuper*

reformatum (1535), but the order for mattins and evensong was derived directly from the Sarum breviary. Cranmer's innate conservatism, as also his creative skill, may be seen in the fact that, while the Lutheran church order of Calenberg-Göttingen (1542) provided an ingenious fusion of the old services of mattins and lauds for use on Sundays and festivals, Cranmer drew upon mattins, lauds and prime for his English mattins, and where the Lutheran order depended on vespers alone, Cranmer no less ingeniously fused vespers and compline to form his English evensong. Thus the two offices retained by the English church represented in their contents five out of the eight medieval offices. The result was as follows:

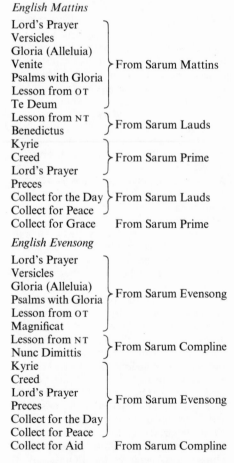

English Mattins

Lord's Prayer	
Versicles	
Gloria (Alleluia)	
Venite	From Sarum Mattins
Psalms with Gloria	
Lesson from OT	
Te Deum	
Lesson from NT	From Sarum Lauds
Benedictus	
Kyrie	
Creed	From Sarum Prime
Lord's Prayer	
Preces	
Collect for the Day	From Sarum Lauds
Collect for Peace	
Collect for Grace	From Sarum Prime

English Evensong

Lord's Prayer	
Versicles	
Gloria (Alleluia)	From Sarum Evensong
Psalms with Gloria	
Lesson from OT	
Magnificat	
Lesson from NT	From Sarum Compline
Nunc Dimittis	
Kyrie	
Creed	
Lord's Prayer	From Sarum Evensong
Preces	
Collect for the Day	
Collect for Peace	
Collect for Aid	From Sarum Compline

The sixteenth-century Englishman was not entirely unfamiliar with regular liturgical prayer. For a hundred years the educated layman had been accustomed to use the psalms, prayers and litanies (q.v.) of the Prymer, and the early years of the sixteenth century saw the publication of various Prymers in English. Now the Tudor Englishman had a more truly catholic as well as more scriptural form of liturgical service for use on Sundays and week-days. For the clergy there was provided a less complicated and more easily discharged form of daily devotion, much more suited to the needs of the parish priest now that monastic communities had ceased to exist. Moreover, the congregational services held in the early church at dawn and at dusk were restored to the laity as mattins and evensong, while the terce, sext and none of the ascetics, together with the night offices of the later monks, ceased with their demise. Quite naturally, they were revived in the Anglican Communion with the re-establishment of religious orders in the nineteenth and twentieth centuries. But for four centuries the mattins and evensong of the 1549 *BCP* (with small additions in the revisions of 1552 and 1662) remained the chief services on Sundays and festivals in the English-speaking world, since weekly communion was almost unknown before the Evangelical and Tractarian revivals of the nineteenth century.

Attempts at further reform of the prayer book in the eighteenth and nineteenth centuries concentrated mainly on the communion office, and although they bore fruit outside the Church of England they had little impact within it (*see* A. Elliott Peaston, *The Prayer Book Reform Movement in the XVIIIth Century*, 1940; R. C. D. Jasper, *Prayer Book Revision in England 1800-1900*, 1954). The proposed prayer book of 1928 which was rejected by Parliament made only minor alterations in mattins and evensong, apart from a revised lectionary and calendar (qq.v.) (for details *see* W. K. Lowther Clarke, *The Prayer Book of 1928 Reconsidered*, 1943). Between 1929 and 1965 the climate of opinion in Parliament and in the country underwent a change and the Prayer Book (Alternative and Other Services) Measure 1965 was passed by Parliament, received the Royal Assent in March 1965, and came into force on 1 May 1966. Under the provisions of this Measure, morning and evening prayer in *Alternative Services: First Series* were authorized for permissive use in the Church of England for seven years from 10 June 1966.

These were basically 1662 with the amendments and additions proposed in 1928, together with a new 'Table of Psalms' for Sundays and certain other days and ordering the holy scriptures to be read either in accordance with the lectionary of 1871, or that of 1922 (as revised in 1928), or that revised by the Convocations of Canterbury and York and authorized by them in May 1961. *Alternative Services: Second Series*, which began 'The Order for Morning Prayer, commonly called Mattins' – similarly 'Evensong' – at 'O Lord, open thou our lips', making the introductory scriptural sentences and penitential introduction voluntary, even on Sundays, was authorized for experimental use for three years from 16 February 1968. The *Second Series (Revised)* 'Morning and Evening Prayer' was laid before the new General Synod of the Church of England in November 1970 and was approved in February 1971 for experimental use for four years from 28 November 1971. This departs still further from the *BCP*, both in the penitential introduction by providing alternative forms, and in the services themselves, by introducing as alternative canticles at mattins, a shortened form of *Benedicite*, *Salvator Mundi*, and *Gloria in Excelsis*, and at evensong Psalm 134, 'Hail, gladdening Light', 'Great and wonderful' (Rev. 15.3b-4) and 'Worthy art thou' (Rev. 4.11; etc.). Provision is thus made both for Sunday and weekday use of the daily offices, and an alternative lectionary is provided for weekdays.

The canonical hours in the Orthodox Church are virtually the same as in the Latin rite of the old *Ordo Romanus*. There are eight hours, beginning with vespers, since the day starts at sundown as among the Jews (Gen. 1.5; Lev. 23.5; *cf.* II Cor. 11.25). They are vespers (*esperinos*), compline (*mikron apodeipnon*), mattins (*mesonuktikon*), lauds (*orthros*), together with the minor hours (*mikrai horai*) of prime, terce, sext, and none. During certain periods of fasting each of the hours is followed by an intermediate office, or inter-hour (*mesorion*). The offices consist principally of liturgical compositions – hymns and chanted prayers – but the whole Psalter is read each week, divided into twenty parts (*kathismata*), each comprising seven or eight psalms. These services are to be found in the *Horologion*, which corresponds to the *Breviarium* of the Western (Latin) Church.

The discussions in the Second Vatican

Council reflected a widespread desire for the reform of the Roman breviary. The breviary had its roots in the monastic choral office and the Council had no intention of rejecting this tradition. At the same time it was desired to make it easier to pray at least some of the canonical hours with a congregation in church. Thus, since 1965, over eighty experts from various parts of the world, divided into twelve study groups, have been working on the revision of the Latin Roman breviary. When the *editio typica* appears, English, French, German, etc. official translations will be authorized for use by the pope and the hierarchy in each country. In the meantime, an 'Interim Version of the New Roman Breviary', entitled *The Prayer of the Church* was issued in London and Dublin in 1970, authorized for interim optional use in England and Wales by the Bishops' Conference of 9 April 1970 and confirmed by the Sacred Congregation for Divine Worship (in Rome) on 15 April 1970. Experimental use of the new office is proceeding in the houses of the various religious orders, but the introduction to *The Prayer of the Church* (Geoffrey Chapman, 1970) asserts that 'one of the main aims of the new Breviary is that its riches should not be reserved to priests and religious, but that it should also be a prayer book which many of the faithful could use whether in church or on their own. This holds especially for the Morning and Evensong Prayers' (p. xviii). The general structure of the new office presents us with 'two major hours: Morning Prayer (Lauds) and Evening Prayer (Vespers); an Office of Readings (Mattins) which may be said at whatever time of the day is found most suitable, or as a Vigil; a Midday Prayer (Little Hour); a Night Prayer (Compline)' (p. xix). A French version of *The Prayer of the Church* was published in Paris in 1969. In the words of the Constitution on the Liturgy (art. 89a): 'Lauds as morning prayer and Vespers as evening prayer are the two hinges on which the daily Office turns: hence they are to be considered as the chief hours and are to be celebrated as such.' As we have seen, this return to the usage of the early church, together with the participation of the laity, was achieved by Cranmer for the Church of England in 1549. The present series of interim (or experimental) rites in the Roman Church is paralleled in the Anglican Church, and *The Prayer of the Church* provides a revised lectionary over a period of two

years similar to, but not identical with, the Anglican two-year cycle of lections. As in the morning and evening prayers of the Anglican *Alternative Services: Second Series*, in the new arrangement of the breviary the day begins with 'O Lord open my lips': in the evening prayer, the office starts with the second suffrage of the Anglican office – 'O God, come to my assistance. Lord, make haste to help me.' This is followed in the morning by Ps. 94 and then a hymn, which is always found at the beginning of the other hours. Among the other principal changes are the redistribution of the psalms over a four-week period; the psalter includes fourteen new biblical canticles for the morning office and seven from the NT (Paul or the Apocalypse) for the evening office; the short lections of each hour are much more varied than in the past; the intercessory aspect of prayer, restored to morning and evening prayer, permits the expression of the needs of the church and of the world in the chief prayers of the daily office. Times of silence are indicated in the actual structure of the hours. In the interim rite 'different texts for Terce, Sext and None are not given, but only a *Midday Prayer*. In the *editio typica* provision will be made for those who want to say only one Hour and for those who want to say all three of the Little Hours' (*The Prayer of the Church*, p. xxi). The common offices and prayer for the dead conclude the main book, but there are supplements containing the propers (q.v.) of the seasonal cycles and those of saints' days. All this suggests that eventually there will be a revised breviary for the monks, whose chief duty is to sing the full office in choir, and a shortened version based on the present interim rite for the use of parish priests and the devout laity.

C. W. DUGMORE

Canticles

From the Latin *canticulum*, a little song. Canticles are songs from the Bible other than from the book of Psalms. The four canticles most used in Christian worship are the *Benedictus* (Luke 1.68-79) (not to be confused with the *Benedictus qui venit*, which in most eucharistic liturgies follows the *Sanctus* [q.v.]), the *Benedicite* (vv. 35-66a of the Song of the Three Holy Children in the Apocrypha), the *Nunc Dimittis* (Luke 2.29-32) and the *Magnificat* (Luke 1.46-55). The title is also applied to the *Te Deum* and, in the Roman Breviary, to several songs derived from the OT, namely, two songs of Moses (Ex. 15.1-18; Deut. 32.1-43); the song of Hannah (I Sam. 2.1-10); of Isaiah (Isa. 12); of Hezekiah (Isa. 38.10-20); and of Habbakuk (Hab. 3.2-19).

EDITOR

Cantor

The person, clerical or lay, who sets the pitch and leads the singing – especially unaccompanied singing. In synagogue worship the cantor is a minister of considerable importance and the office existed early in both Eastern and Western Christendom. With the elaboration of psalmody and its accompanying antiphons in the monastic and cathedral services of the medieval West, the cantor became essential for the proper performance of the liturgy and offices. Elaborate rules were laid down to govern the number of cantors proper to the various feasts and seasons. The titles of precentor and succentor borne by clergymen in cathedral and collegiate churches are derived from the term, as is the custom of describing the northern side of the choir as 'cantoris'.

P. HINCHLIFF

Carol

In common use, the name given to a type of simple, traditional, essentially rhythmic song, particularly one whose words concern the Nativity. Obscure in origin, the term has been conclusively traced only so far as the Old French form *carole*; but ultimate derivations have been claimed from the Latin *corolla*, Greek *choros*, and even *kyrie eleison*. Continental equivalents of the Christmas carol are the French *Noël* and German *Wiegenlied*.

In England, from their first appearance in the fourteenth century, carols were marked by a characteristic *refrain* or *burden* intended for dancing. The opening words of one of the earliest surviving burdens (*c.* 1350) describe the singers joining hands in a ring-dance: 'Honnd by honnd we schulle us take . . .' Early use (1470) of the term carol for 'a ring of standing stones' (OED) reflects this implicit meaning. There is thus a clear distinction between a carol and a Christmas hymn.

During the fifteenth century, the carol developed as an art-form, both words and music being produced at the hands of learned ecclesiastics, not semi-literate minstrels. Pre-

served in manuscript form rather than by popular tradition, the 'art-carol' of the fifteenth century differed from the 'folk-carol' in a number of respects. First, its text had a highly organized fixed form closely related to the stanza-pattern of the French *virelai* and the Italian *ballata*. Secondly, it was not necessarily composed in the vernacular; many surviving examples are in Latin while others are *macaronic* – having alternate lines in English and Latin throughout. Thirdly, unlike the folk-carol sung by a soloist or a chorus in unison, the art-carol was set for a group of singers in two or three contrapuntal parts. However, such sophisticated examples retained the pronouncedly rhythmic character of the popular carol – though their association with physical movement was likely to have been limited to processional use. In recent years a full study of the fifteenth-century art-carol has been made (*see* bibliography); but the most familiar ancient carols in modern use are folk-carols, handed down by oral tradition until their collection and publication after 1820.

The medieval carol may be seen as the result of a desire to introduce a more jovial element into particular acts of worship – both in and out of church – than the sober traditional melodies of plainchant could afford. The Christmas crib introduced by St Francis of Assisi, and the miracle and mystery plays of the thirteenth century, forecast that desire, doubtless later providing some of the first occasions for carol-singing.

The great age of the English carol was the fifteenth century – the age of humanism and the emergence of the ballad. Subjects treated include many beside the Nativity. Some are purely secular – the *Agincourt Song* is an example. Others are intended to celebrate particular seasons of the year, particularly from Advent to Candlemas. A third type retells in many-versed form a Christian legend (*The Cherry Tree*) or propounds a homily (*Remember, O thou man*). Akin, though hardly to be considered a true carol, is the *Wassail Song* – pagan in origin, but made respectable by its commendation of the virtue of hospitality.

The impact of the Reformation and the consequent growth of Puritanism in this country changed the nature of the English carol, without causing its disappearance. After the ban imposed upon Christmas festivity during the Commonwealth was lifted, the singing of folk-carols was revived, to last in dwindling popularity throughout the eighteenth century.

In 1822, two amateurs independently remarked the imminent disappearance of the carol; and each attempted to 'rescue from oblivion some carol melodies which in a few years will be heard no more'. William Hone's article *Christmas Carols* and Davies Gilbert's *Some Ancient Christmas Carols* were the first printed collections of modern times. Their appearance heralded the rebirth of carol-singing. Other more important collections were to follow: W. Sandys, *Christmas Carols, Ancient & Modern* (1833); E. F. Rimbault, *Little Book of Carols* (1846); Neale and Helmore, *Carols for Christmastide* (1853) and *Carols for Easter-tide* (1854); and Edmund Sedding, *Ancient Christmas Carols* (1864) marked the first stage. Stainer and Bramley, *Christmas Carols New and Old* (1871), brought the carol into every pew.

During the last quarter of the nineteenth century a flood of so-called carols issued from the pens of an army of would-be composers, some of whose effusions are still unfortunately current. A first attempt at redress came with G. R. Woodward's *Cowley Carol Book* (1901); and in 1928 the appearance of the *Oxford Book of Carols*, edited by Percy Dearmer, R. Vaughan Williams and Martin Shaw, presented a model carol collection of authentic character. Since that book became available, popular standards of taste and awareness have been strengthened, and carols have recovered something of the health and vitality which was theirs during the fifteenth century. Modern composers have shown that they are able to present the simplicity, strength and honesty requisite in a true carol; but the modern commercialization of Christmas has also encouraged the production of a repertoire of spurious carols of a type as sickly, sentimental and inappropriate as anything produced during the decadence of a century ago.

P. Dearmer, Preface to *The Oxford Book of Carols*, 1928; R. L. Greene, *Early English Carols*, 1953; E. Routley, *The English Carol*, 1958; J. Stevens, *Medieval Carols: Musica Britannica*, Vol. IV, 1952.

BERNARR RAINBOW

Cassock

see Vestments (2*b*)

Catechumen, Catechumenate

An organized preparation for baptism (q.v.) came into being in the second century. Under the heading of the Two Ways the *Didache*, a Syrian document, included moral teaching to be given to catechumens. Justin Martyr in Rome briefly alluded to a moral and doctrinal preparation, which included also prayers and fasting. Tertullian in Carthage mentioned frequent praying, fasts and all night vigils before baptism. Much fuller information is given in Hippolytus' *Apostolic Tradition*, where the catechumenate is divided into two parts, the long-term preparation or catechumenate proper, lasting up to three years, when the candidates were trained in Christian doctrine and morals, and the final intensive preparation, when those accepted for baptism were exorcised daily, fasted on the two days before Easter, kept an all-night vigil consisting in the reading of scripture and instruction, and were finally baptized on Easter morning. A very thorough preparation such as this was possible during the age of persecution when inquirers were comparatively few.

After the peace of the church, however, converts were so numerous that this long and meticulous preparation could not be maintained. Much valuable information concerning the catechumenate in this period is found scattered among the writings of Augustine, in the sermons of Ambrose on the sacraments, in John the Deacon's letter to Senarius, the Pilgrimage of Etheria and the catechetical lectures of Cyril of Jerusalem. Those catechumens who wished for baptism and were approved by the church were enrolled at the beginning of Lent, during which they met frequently for prayer, exorcism (q.v.) and instruction, being taught the creed (q.v.) (*traditio symboli*), and repeating it from memory (*redditio symboli*) shortly before their baptism at Easter. Catechumens who were taken ill could be baptized in haste. Although they attended the first part of the eucharist, they were dismissed before the eucharist proper began, never being allowed to see the communion of the faithful until they were themselves eligible by baptism to communicate.

As infant baptism prevailed the long term preparation necessarily disappeared. All the time that infants were reserved for baptism at Easter or Pentecost they were enrolled as catechumens half way through Lent and were brought to a number of scrutinies which consisted in prayer and exorcism, instruction being now out of the question. But when in the late Middle Ages it was deemed necessary to baptize all infants within a week of birth for fear that they might die unbaptized and consequently be deprived of salvation, the ceremonies of the catechumenate became compressed into a rite, based on the old order for the making of a catechumen, which took place at the church door immediately before baptism. In England this practice is seen in the Latin Sarum manual and in the first English prayer book of 1549. In response to Bucer's criticism, this rite at the church door was abolished in 1552, everything henceforward taking place around the font. So ended the last trace of a catechumenate before baptism.

J. D. C. Fisher, *Christian Initiation: Baptism in the Medieval West*, 1965; E. C. Whitaker, *Documents of the Baptismal Liturgy*, 1960.

J. D. C. FISHER

Cathedra

From Greek, meaning 'a thing sat upon', with particular reference to the official seat or throne of the bishop. Hence the church in which this seat is placed is known as the cathedral church. This is undoubtedly the oldest insignia of a bishop's authority, and many centuries before bishops assumed the wearing of mitres, rings or even the carrying of pastoral staves and croziers, they were enseated in their throne or *cathedra* on the day of their consecration to the episcopate as the sign that they were invested with authority to preside over the church in their diocese. Thus the writer of the fourth-century *Apostolic Constitutions* (8.5) says: 'And early in the morning let him be placed in this throne in a place set apart for him among the bishops, they all giving him the kiss in the Lord.'

In the earlier centuries the bishop's throne was normally placed in the centre of the apse (q.v.) behind the altar; on either side there were lesser seats for his presbyters. It was from this seat that the bishop presided at the eucharist and also preached the sermon.

In the later Middle Ages the consecration of a bishop tended to take place in the church of the archbishop or metropolitan, and thus the enseatment of the new bishop in his own cathedral took place in a separate ceremony on another day. The lawyers discovered that

by this means they could ask for two fees in connection with the consecration and enthronement of a new bishop.

In northern Europe in the later Middle Ages the east ends of cathedral churches were developed into a series of chapels and so the bishop's *cathedra* had to be brought round to one side of the sanctuary (q.v.) before the high altar, but the idea that this throne was always on the north side is not correct. In Norwich Cathedral we can see the restored bishop's throne today behind the altar (*see* Plate 20).

In East Syria an entirely different arrangement prevailed, where the bishop's throne was placed half-way down the nave inside a horseshoe-shaped chancel facing east. Thus the bishop sat in his *cathedra* with his back to the congregation and his presbyters on

Plate 20 The restored bishop's cathedra or throne behind the high altar, Norwich Cathedral, England

either side. This arrangement was the apsidal arrangement in reverse. In the first part of the East Syrian liturgy the bishop sat facing east; but at the offertory (q.v.) he advanced to the altar with his assistants and stood facing east as the altar was right against the east wall.

F. Cabrol-H. Leclercq, *Dictionnaire d'archéologie chrétienne et de liturgie,* 1907 ff., Tome 3, 19-75 and Tome 15, 1866-1884.

C. E. POCKNEE

Cathedral

A church in which the bishop's *cathedra* (q.v.) is located. All other churches, from the fourth century onwards, were in a sense pro-cathedrals, in that the presbyters who presided and taught there did so as the delegates of the bishop; these buildings were so many extensions of the cathedral necessitated by the growth in the number of Christians and by the fact that the bishop could not be in more than one place at once.

Functionally these buildings were not just centres of worship alone, and it is historically incorrect to visualize them as large liturgical halls with baptisteries attached and with no other accommodation whatsoever. On the contrary, the space for worship was only one of a number of interrelated rooms which made the bishop's church a real service-centre for the Christian community. Living quarters for the clergy, libraries, guest chambers and even bath installations were common. The main hall itself was not exclusively reserved for worship and could be, and was, used for a host of secular activities, among which were included living and sleeping, eating and drinking, dancing, the storage and sale of goods, meetings of all kinds and legal proceedings.

Architecturally, cathedrals began to diverge from parish churches under the influence of four factors. (1) The monastic movement. In the Middle Ages many cathedrals, especially in England, were under the direction of monks, and for the saying of their offices an almost self-contained sanctuary and choir (qq.v.) were fitted into the building. (2) The cult of the saints led to the increase of side altars, containing relics of the saints, and these were also required for votive masses and for the daily celebration of mass by each and every priest. (3) The elaboration of ceremonial. The increase in

processions etc. required provision of circulation space, which was also needed for (4) pilgrimages.

The function of the cathedral has been differently conceived throughout the ages. Initially it was the church of the bishop and a centre of mission. In the Middle Ages each one existed mainly to provide intercessions for deceased benefactors. After the Reformation, cathedrals were regarded as providing for (1) worship; (2) theological education; (3) the care of the poor and aged; (4) the upkeep of the surrounding area. In the nineteenth century their role was much discussed but little new thinking emerged. At the present day a whole host of possible fresh uses is under consideration.

G. Cope, ed., *Cathedral and Mission,* 1969.

EDITOR

Cathedral Office

Liturgical scholars are becoming increasingly interested in an important aspect of liturgical history in the late patristic and early medieval periods: the disappearance, more or less complete over a large part of Christendom, and everywhere to some extent, of what is for convenience called the 'cathedral office', the regular public services of the church, other than the eucharist itself, in their original form, and the forms which developed from it, and their replacement by other forms which originated in the private worship of monastic communities in the fourth century.

The original public worship of the church, apart from the eucharist, comprised only two regular gatherings, evening and morning – vespers and mattins; on the eves of Sundays and great feasts a third, a vigil or night office, was added. But the same fourth century which saw the definitive establishment of this pattern – derived ultimately from the synagogue, and in respect of the vigil from the Paschal vigil (q.v.) of the early church – saw also the growth of the movement which was destined to overthrow it, organized cenobitic monasticism. In a very short time monastic ideals and spirituality were dominant, and it was inevitable that the consequent monasticizing of the church's life should extend to its worship. From the beginning the monastic movement had developed a way of worship of its own, which was naturally very different from the public worship of 'secular' churches. In some places, where monastic establishments were attached at an early stage to the public churches, a liturgical compromise grew up between the old way – the 'cathedral office' – and the new way of the monks. The latter was marked, first, by an increase in the number of daily services from two or three to seven or eight (*see* **Canonical Hours**), and second, the structuring of these services round the continuous reading of the scriptures in a given period, and the continuous recitation of the psalter in another given period (in most places, a week), together with the virtual elimination of most other elements of public prayer. Ultimately the monastic round and structure of the office conquered nearly everywhere. In some places the cathedral office disappeared almost completely: at Rome, for example, where monastic clergy were early placed in charge of the great basilicas, the disappearance was so fast and so complete that so far it has proved impossible to reconstruct the Roman cathedral office at all. The Roman breviary offices are purely monastic in structure, and the differences between the 'secular' and 'monastic' breviaries are no more than minor variants within one essentially monastic rite. Elsewhere in the West, elements of the cathedral office survived, and continue to survive, at Milan, and to a much greater extent in the books, although less in actual use, at Toledo. In the East the Chaldean rite preserves more of the structure and content of its original cathedral office than does any other rite in Christendom; the Byzantine rite has preserved far more elements of its cathedral rite than has its Roman counterpart – the persistence of these side by side with the monastic elements is the principal cause of the often excessive length of Byzantine services. (An essentially cathedral office survived at Constantinople, although with some monastic additions, down to the Latin conquest in 1204.)

The principle of *lectio continua* (continuous reading of the scriptures and recitation of the psalter, with little reference to the church's year), which makes the divine office less an act of liturgical worship in the strict sense than a ,corporate occasion of individual meditation, has dominated attempts at reform or renewal of the office in the West from the early Middle Ages to the present day. In England, Cranmer may have reduced the number of daily services to two in the *BCP*, but the structure and content of those two

services are based on a purely monastic *concept* of the office; and this is true, to a large extent, of the recent *Daily Office* published by the inter-denominational Joint Liturgical Group. It does not seem to have occurred to the authors of this and similar attempts at producing a divine office suitable for modern use that the fundamental principle on which their work is based is itself highly questionable both theologically and pastorally, and is itself part and parcel of a spirituality which, whatever its virtues (and they are many), no longer provides a viable foundation for public devotion. Such a foundation can only be found in a return to the principles of the cathedral office, and an imaginative application of them to the contemporary situation, by which a form of divine office may be produced which is truly integrated with the eucharist, with the church's year, and with the pattern of everyday life.

At the time of writing it is impossible to suggest further reading, as the little that has so far been written on the subject is of a highly technical character, and for the most part hidden in the pages of learned journals in languages other than English.

W. JARDINE GRISBROOKE

Celebrant

The principal minister at the eucharist. Originally Christian worship, like its synagogue equivalent, was probably directed by a liturgical president and there is some evidence to suggest that in the early church the celebrant was actually called 'the president'. When the office of bishop (q.v.) was fully developed, he was the normal celebrant at the eucharist for so long as it was possible for the greater part of the Christian community in each city to worship as a single congregation. Presbyters (q.v.) later became the normal celebrant at the eucharist. By an ironical twist in the meaning of the terms, the bishop when present was said to 'preside' but not to 'celebrate', i.e. the bishop sat in his throne and performed certain actions such as blessings, but a priest at the altar actually celebrated. For various reasons it became the custom, in the medieval West, for the number of celebrations to be multiplied and for the celebrant to recite almost the whole of the service himself. In the East this has never happened and there are certain parts of the rite that can only be recited by another minister, e.g. a deacon (q.v.). The Liturgical Movement (q.v.) has tended to revive the practice of participation by several ministers (ordained or lay) in the taking of the service, and there is a new interest in 'concelebration' (q.v.) (several clergymen sharing together as joint celebrants). The position of the celebrant (whether he should face east, west or south) has also attracted a good deal of attention (*see* **Postures**). In most churches the celebrant is required to be an ordained person, but the Congregational tradition maintains the rights of laymen to preside at the eucharist and in the Methodist Church it is possible for a layman to be specially authorized to celebrate the sacraments.

G. Dix, *The Shape of the Liturgy*, 1945; A. A. King, *Concelebration in the Christian Church*, 1966; B. Minchin, *Every Man in his Ministry*, 1960.

P. HINCHLIFF

Centralized Building

By the central type of architecture no one uniform plan is indicated but the general principle of eurhythmic disposition around a central vertical axis. The buildings for liturgical use to which this classification applies did not develop from the basilica (q.v.) but existed side by side and independently from the beginnings of Christian architecture. Centralized buildings are of three types: (1) *martyria* (q.v.); (2) baptisteries (q.v.); (3) congregational churches (*see* **Architectural Setting**).

EDITOR

Ceremonial

According to strict ecclesiastical usage, ceremonial refers to the prescribed and formal actions that constitute worship. It is therefore to be distinguished from ritual (q.v.), which refers to the prescribed form of words. Hence the use of incense falls within the category of ceremonial, while the canon is within that of ritual. However, the two terms are often used interchangeably and this may lead to some confusion. The Royal Commission, which was established in 1867 to inquire into the differences of ceremonial practice in the Church of England, was known as the Ritual Commission and within its purview it included vestments, incense and lights (qq.v.). In fact, vestments are neither an essential part

of ceremonial nor of ritual but are rather to be classified as ornaments, while lights may be no more than a necessary source of illumination. Lights only come under ceremonial when their use is an integral part of the service, as, for example, at Tenebrae (q.v.).

If this strict sense of ceremonial is adhered to, it includes such actions as the kiss of peace, the fraction, elevation (qq.v.), the pouring of water in baptism, the laying on of hands in ordination (q.v.), etc.

EDITOR

Chairman of District

In the Methodist Church circuits, which are under a superintendent (q.v.), are grouped in districts under a chairman who presides over the district synod and may exercise certain pastoral and disciplinary functions in relation to other ministers. No special liturgical position is reserved to him though, in practice, he may officiate at ordinations. In America the corresponding office is that of the superintendent of the district under the bishop.

P. HINCHLIFF

Chaldean Church *see* East Syrian Worship

Chalice and Paten

The term 'chalice' is an anglicized form of the Latin *calix*, meaning cup. The vessel used by Jesus for the wine at the institution of the eucharist may reasonably be supposed to have been one of the ordinary two handled cups of that period. The cathedral at Valencia, Spain, has in its treasury what has been claimed to be this identical cup. It is a circular cup nearly four inches in diameter, hollowed out from a single hair-brown sardonyx, with a plain stone moulding round the lip. Its style shows it to be of antique Roman origin. While it is not actually impossible that this vessel was used at the Last Supper, modern archaeologists feel that the evidence does not satisfy all the requirements of historical criticism.

In tracing the history of the use of the chalice in Western Christendom and its evolution, two historical facts need to be borne in mind: (1) the recognition of Christianity by the emperor Constantine the Great in the early fourth century; (2) the gradual withdrawal of the chalice from the laity, begun in the twelfth century, which was officially confirmed by the Council of Constance in 1415.

Chalices of precious metal were not unknown in the early days of the church, nor were cups made from large jewels that had been hollowed out. But cups of glass and base metal such as pewter or lead were also used. The official recognition of Christianity gave a considerable impetus to the use of chalices of gold and silver decorated with precious stones. But Boniface, the English missionary to Germany, was not unfamiliar with wooden chalices in the eighth century. Among religious communities there were ascetic objections to the use of any appearance of luxury in worship which chalices of precious metal encouraged.

Prior to the withdrawal of the cup from the laity in the West, two kinds of chalices were in common use at the eucharist, the chalice used by the celebrant on the altar for the consecration, and the ministerial chalice used for the communion of the congregation, known as the *scyphus*. The latter was furnished with two handles for convenience when carrying (*see* Plate 21). The ministerial chalice was filled with wine at the time of the offertory and held by one of the deacons or acolytes. In *Ordo Romanus Primus* we are told, 'when . . . the lay folk are to be communicated, the archdeacon pours a little of the consecrated chalice into the ministerial chalice, the contents of which are supplied by the offering of the faithful'. It was the teaching of the church in the earlier centuries that the addition of a small quantity of the consecrated species to another chalice was enough to extend the virtue of consecration to the whole contents of the second chalice. The consecration chalice was usually smaller than the ministerial chalice. In the larger churches several ministerial chalices were used at one eucharist.

The communicants imbibed the consecrated wine through a gold or silver tube or reed known by a variety of names such as *fistula*, *pipa* or *calamus*, rather like the modern lemonade straw in form. As late as 1269 an inventory of St Paul's Cathedral mentions 'two calami'. The pope at Rome still receives the chalice in this manner. The reception of both sacred species by the congregation was made standing and not kneeling. After the twelfth century with the withdrawal of the cup from the laity the chalice became smaller, since only the celebrant communicated from it; and it assumed the form with which we are now familiar, being composed of three distinct parts or members, the bowl, the knop, and the foot (*see* Plate 22).

The Reformation brought about the restoration of the chalice to the laity in the Church of England. The late medieval form of chalice was then found to be too small and was replaced by the 'fayre', 'decent' or 'comely' communion cup, a vessel of German form, but lacking the grace of the pre-Reformation chalice. In some instances the foot and knop of a pre-Reformation vessel were brazed to a new and larger bowl. But in the seventeenth and eighteenth centuries some magnificent cups of silver-gilt were produced in England. Under Archbishop

Plate 21   The Gourdon Chalice and Paten,
gold and enamel, c. 527, France

Plate 22   A modern chalice and paten

Laud in the middle of the seventeenth century a number of chalices based on a modified form of the pre-Reformation chalice were brought into use.

Since the Oxford Movement in the nineteenth century, there has been the tendency, as in other matters, to revert to pre-Reformation forms of the chalice.

In the Roman Catholic Church in the seventeenth and eighteenth centuries the design of the chalice was considerably affected by the liberal art of the Renaissance. The chalice tended to assume a greater height and the bowl passed from a conical to a bell-shaped form and the decoration assumed secularized motifs.

In Eastern Christendom, where the chalice has never been withdrawn from the laity, it has remained larger in form. In the Eastern Orthodox rite communicants are given both species together, the bishop or priest dipping the consecrated bread into the chalice and then conveying the bread thus intincted on a spoon into the mouth of the communicant.

The Paten. According to tradition, the church of St Lorenzo, Genoa, possesses the dish used by Jesus at the Last Supper for the consecrated bread. It is a shallow glass bowl, hexagonal in form, with two small handles, deep green in colour and was at one time thought to be an emerald. As with the chalice, it is much more likely that Jesus used an ordinary domestic vessel of the time.

Furthermore, as with the chalice it is likely that the paten may have had more than one form and use for many centuries: (1) the dish or paten used by the celebrant at the altar; (2) the ministerial paten for use in distributing the consecrated species. It should be understood that throughout the whole of Christendom for the first millennium the use of leavened bread was more usual. Only in the Latin West did wafer-bread gradually replace leavened bread from the end of the ninth century onwards. Consequently the ministerial paten, used probably for collecting the offerings of bread from the people, and subsequently used also for the administration of the consecrated loaves, was more like the modern tea-tray in form, being made of gold or silver and decorated round its borders with precious stones and filigree design.

The consecrating paten was circular in form and this remained in use after the introduction of wafer-bread in the West. The later medieval forms usually fitted into the top of the chalice bowl by having a 'well' sunk in them.

In the post-Reformation era in England, when leavened bread was reintroduced the cover of the communion cup often served as a paten when reversed. It was usually surmounted by a disc on which the date was frequently engraved. Towards the end of the eighteenth century the paten took the form of a circular dish of considerable size known as a 'tazza' standing on a raised foot. The Eastern Orthodox rite employs a paten of this type. With a revived use of wafer-bread, under the second phase of the Oxford Movement and the Catholic Revival in the nineteenth century, the late medieval form of paten has also been reintroduced.

J. Gilchrist, *Anglican Church Plate*, 1967; J. A. Jungmann, *The Mass of the Roman Rite*, 2 vols., 1951, 1955; E. Mercenier, *La Prière des Églises de Rite Byzantin*, I, 1947; C. Oman, *English Medieval Base Metal Church Plate*, 1964; W. W. Watts, *A Catalogue of Chalices*, 1922.

C. E. POCKNEE

Chancel

The term chancel is derived from the Latin *cancellus* or balustrade and originally referred to that part of a church which was reserved for the officiating clergy and was divided from the rest of the building by low screens. In this sense it was synonymous with the first meaning of the word sanctuary (q.v.).

In the medieval two-room plan (*see* **Architectural Setting**), chancel continued to be used of the whole space east of the nave, demarcated by the chancel screen, but now it was understood to comprise two sections: the sanctuary, in its second sense, i.e. the limited area immediately around the altar, and the space between it and the screen (q.v.).

In popular parlance, the intervening area from the chancel steps up to but not including the sanctuary is often called the chancel, and therefore corresponds to the restricted sense of choir (q.v.). As with the term sanctuary, this dual usage can lead to ambiguity, since the same word refers both to the whole of an area and to a subdivision of the same area.

EDITOR

Chants

For the purpose of this article chanting may

be defined as the recitation of prose – as opposed to verse – to a melodic formula. Thus, the rhythm of chanting reflects the irregular stresses of speech rather than the regular rhythmic flow of simple melody. The prose psalms provide the main occasion for congregational chanting today, but different systems have been employed for chanting the psalms over the centuries.

Throughout the Middle Ages the psalms were chanted in unison to a series of short plainsong melodies known as tones (*see* **Psalm Tones**).

As their technical competence increased, composers began to 'harmonize' the psalm tones by adding parts for higher and lower voices above and below the original plainsong. These ornamental versions, known as *faux-bourdons*, were sung alternately verse by verse with the unison tones.

From these faux-bourdon settings emerged the Anglican chant. One of the earliest surviving examples of the Anglican chant is given below. Dating from the sixteenth century and sometimes attributed to Adrian Batten, its tenor part comprises the first Psalm tone:

Several other early examples to be found in most modern chant books similarly include one of the tones in their tenor parts.

During the Commonwealth, psalm-chanting was suppressed in England and thus tradition was broken. Efforts to revive the choral service at the Restoration (1660) encouraged the writing of new Anglican chants, both 'single' and 'double', in which the melodic interest of the treble part – rather than the presence of a psalm tone in the tenor – became the main feature. Because of their own independent rhythmic character, such chants lent themselves less readily to the prose of the psalms; and it has frequently been remarked that such 'tuneful' chants, with melodies designed for boys' voices, tend to discourage congregational participation. These characteristics were to be responsible for later attempts to supplant the Anglican chant.

Until the nineteenth century, the psalms were customarily chanted *extempore* from the Prayer Book – the length of the recitation in each half-verse being decided according to the 'Rule of Three and Five', whereby the third and fifth syllable from the end of each half-verse were made to correspond with a change of note in the chant. The standard of chanting, even in cathedrals, was therefore extremely haphazard. Pointed psalters were prepared in an attempt to achieve unanimity, the first example to appear being that of Robert Janes, organist of Ely cathedral, published in 1837. It was followed by those of Stimpson (1840), S. S. Wesley (1843), and Hullah (1844); but the age of congregational chanting of the prose psalms cannot be said to have begun until the publication of Mercer's *Church Psalter and Hymn Book* (1854).

Dissatisfaction with the 'jaunty' character of the Anglican chant led to various attempts to re-introduce the use of Gregorian tones to the Anglican service. The first plainsong psalter with English text was *Laudes Diurnae*, produced by a leading Tractarian, Frederick Oakeley, and his organist Richard Redhead, in 1843. In spite of its faulty pointing the book enjoyed considerable use among Tractarians, until the appearance of Thomas Helmore's more practical *Psalter Noted* in 1849. Thereafter, the use of 'Gregorians' for the psalms tended to be regarded as the prerogative of High Anglicans.

More recently, continuing dissatisfaction with the Anglican chant has encouraged the use of 'Gelineau' psalms in many churches. Originally produced for Roman Catholic use in France in 1953 by Joseph Gelineau, SJ, new translations from the Hebrew gave to the words a regular pattern of stress designed to be readily reconcilable with the simple rhythmic tunes provided. These new versions of the psalms have since been prepared in English translations and adopted for occasional use in many churches – without, however, achieving universal acceptance.

Chanting of the prose psalms and canticles necessarily presents much greater technical challenge than the singing of hymns; and most congregations find themselves at a disadvantage in these parts of the service. The metrical psalms (q.v.) introduced by Calvin in the sixteenth century were an attempt to overcome the problem. Yet the beauty of the prose psalms in English is such that few churchmen would be prepared to dispense with their use. In recent times, many attempts have been made to provide pointed psalters edited to enable the psalms to be sung with the 'speech-rhythm' which they require. Perhaps the most widely adopted of these has been Nicholson's *Parish Psalter*, which the Royal School of Church Music has made familiar throughout the English-speaking world.

P. le Huray, *Music and the Reformation in England*, 1967; C. H. Phillips, *The Singing Chruch*, rev. ed. 1968.

BERNARR RAINBOW

The Chants of the Proper of the Mass

The texts of the proper (q.v.) determine the forms of the music set to them. The introit, offertory and communion are processional texts consisting of an antiphon and as many verses of the particular psalm as may be necessary for the procession of the celebrant and his retinue to reach the altar at the introit, to accompany the offering of the bread and wine, and the procession of the faithful to receive Holy Communion. The gradual has a responsorial text in which the congregation, as described by Augustine, originally responded to the verses of the psalm with a brief interjection, such as alleluia, or a verse of the psalm itself. The usual form of the alleluia is threefold – alleluia, verse of a psalm or other text, repeat of alleluia – but in Paschal time two alleluias are sung, the first one supplanting the gradual responsory and having the same form as above, the second having no repeat after the verse. The tract and sequence are *sui generis*, and will be explained in the notes on these various pieces below.

Introit. Only one verse of the psalm is found in the Roman gradual and the antiphon is repeated only after the *Gloria Patri*. This may well have been the practice long before in ordinary parish churches, which did not employ elaborate ceremonial. The descriptions of ritual found in the *Ordines Romani* or the *Ceremoniale Episcoporum* always refer to a high mass celebrated by pope or prelates.

Gradual. This became a virtuoso piece, in the literal sense, and tempted the deacons who sang it to exercise their skill for their own glory. In a decree of 5 July 595, Gregory forbade them to sing it for the good of their souls! Both gradual and alleluia are sung when no action takes place in the sanctuary and all attention is fixed on the choir. The verse is customarily sung by one or two cantors or by treble voices only.

Alleluia. An interesting feature of this piece is the repetition of the *jubilus*, that is, the vocalized final vowel of the alleluia, at the end of the verse and so before the formal repeat of the whole of the opening section. It is quite wrong to regard the alleluia as part of the gradual. They are two separate chants.

Tract. This penitential chant is sung between Septuagesima and Easter when the alleluia is silenced. Its melodies are extremely old and venerable monuments of the chant of the Latin church and were sung by a solo voice. The texts consisted of either a part of or, more rarely, a whole psalm.

Sequence. One result of the new creative impulse to add to existing Gregorian chant that arose in the eighth century was the sequence. It was an addition to the alleluia, either of melody or text, or both, and came about because of the difficulty in memorizing the florid vocalizations of the alleluia. It owes much to Notker Babulus, a monk of St Gall, whose master instructed him to set every note of the *jubilus* to a separate syllable; this shows that Notker did not invent the form. A very large number of sequences was composed, all but four of which were discarded by the Council of Trent. The remaining ones, of which *Dies irae, dies illa* is the best known, are very beautiful, but many others might well be revived, at least by choral groups who almost alone in the present situation can keep plainsong alive.

Offertory. The complete form of this chant dates from Gregory. It consisted at the start of psalms sung between the two sides of the choir. This responsorial treatment ceased when the antiphon alone remained without any psalm verses and so it then became an antiphonal chant, psalm verses only finding a place now in the requiem mass. These chants of the offertory are alone in having repetition of the words. The plainsong of the discarded verses was published by Carlus Ott in 1935. These form superb motets.

Communion. The musical form of this chant was the same as that of the introit, but the major proportion of the words of the antiphon were taken from other parts of the Bible than the psalter, those of the verses being taken from the latter source. It is, as in the case of the offertory, the antiphon that survives in the gradual.

ALEC ROBERTSON

Chapel

From the *cappella* or cloak of St Martin, the term was applied to the sanctuary in which it was preserved and ultimately to any building for worship not being a church. It is now used of: (1) public places of worship in many Christian traditions; (2) a private place of worship, as in a college or school, or belonging to an individual, in which case it is known as a proprietary chapel; (3) part of a large church or cathedral with its own separate altar.

EDITOR

Chasuble *see* Vestments (1*f*)

Choir (Architectural)

Originally that part of the church which contained the clergy, i.e. it referred to the chancel (q.v.) or the sanctuary (q.v.) as a whole, situated at the east end of the building. A church therefore had two interrelated parts, the choir and the nave (q.v.).

In the medieval plan these two were separated to form two rooms (*see* **Architectural Setting**) and the choir itself was further subdivided into the sanctuary, containing the altar, and the place of the clergy, the term choir now being restricted to the latter. So what was once a designation of the whole came to be applied to a part of the whole. The size of the choir, in the narrower sense, was much increased and often equalled in length a half or two-thirds of the nave. This enlargement was to provide space, particularly in monastic establishments, for the staff of clerics. So a tripartite division was created, consisting of: (1) the nave, which constituted one room; (2) the choir, with (3) the altar precincts together forming the second room.

An exception to this separation of the laity from the altar, common to most European countries, is to be noted in Spain. There the short eastern apse containing the altar was retained, and the choir or *coro*, enclosed on the north, west and south sides, was placed at the west end of the nave. The laity therefore had their place between the sanctuary and the choir and were not separated from the former by the latter.

After the Reformation the choir was used in England for the celebration of the eucharist, the communicants coming from the nave to gather round the altar (q.v.), which was brought forward from the east wall. By the nineteenth century this practice had tended to lapse and the choir was pressed into use for the singers. Two men in particular were responsible for this innovation, J. Jebb and W. F. Hook, who adopted the expedient in the newly built parish church of Leeds immediately after its consecration in 1841. They placed the musical choir, robed in surplices, in the architectural choir, and this practice has become widespread in all denominations. As a tradition it has not had a very long history, and at the present day many question the rightness of this separation of the congregation from the altar.

G. W. O. Addleshaw and F. Etchells, *The Architectural Setting of Anglican Worship*, 1948.

EDITOR

Choir (Musical)

The presence of a white-robed assembly of the sons of Kohath 'cunning in song' is the subject of frequent reference in Old Testament accounts of worship both before and after the dedication of Solomon's Temple. Under Asaph, Heman and Jeduthun the Temple choir was divided into sections which undertook their ministry 'by course'. The tradition was preserved until the destruction of the Temple in AD 70, at which time Rabbi Joshua ben Hananiah, a member of the Temple Levitical choir, recorded that the Temple choristers were accustomed to sing as a body both in the Temple itself and in the synagogue. Thus may be traced the pre-Christian ancestry of those choirs which formed a constant element in Christian worship once the days of active persecution were over. A concrete link between the two traditions is provided by the psalms and by the antiphonal mode of singing which they suggest. Another is found in the insistence, both in Judaism and the early Christian church, that skill and training were requisite in those to whom was entrusted the ministry of song. The Council of Laodicea (c. 360) even forbade all others to sing in church beside the canonical singers. That inflexibility was not, happily, to survive; but the need to ensure the worthiness of the music offered in worship which it emphasized is noteworthy.

With the evolution of the Gregorian repertory, by the year 600 clear principles had emerged governing the respective contributions of choir and people in the music of the liturgy. The congregation was given simple melodies and refrains within their competence to perform; the choir was allotted more elaborate melodies, some of which called for skilled solo cantors. The same principle was to govern the situation as the art of musical composition developed to make available the splendid polyphony of the fifteenth and sixteenth centuries as an accessory to heighten worship – so long as trained singers competent to perform such music were available.

It is a fallacy that at the Reformation choirs were abolished, so as to allow the people themselves to sing. This was by no means the case. Luther certainly introduced the chorale with the intention of encouraging the congregation to take an active musical part in the service; but his musical understanding prevented him from robbing the Reformed service of those devotional elements which a trained choir could provide. Calvin, too, introduced the metrical psalm (q.v.) as the people's song; but though his fear of a possible abuse of music's emotional power made him destroy the organs at Geneva, Calvin yet preserved, even developed, the choir as an agent to lead corporate singing. We thus find that, after the Reformation, Protestant choirs assumed a new role. In addition to their former function as performers of music beyond the capacity of the general congregation, they were now required to lead the voices of the people. That situation still exists today – the relative importance attached to one or other aspect varying according to the liturgical ideal observed.

In English cathedrals the choirs are endowed. Thus, apart from an interruption during the Commonwealth (1649–1660), choral services of some elaboration and competence have been performed there daily since their foundation. In English parochial churches, during the seventeenth and eighteenth centuries, the custom arose of introducing 'cock and hen' choirs of men and women into west-gallery singing pews. In urban churches at this time a choir was often provided by Charity Children – pupils from the local charity school. The result was seldom devotional; and in neither case was it usual to find congregational singing stimulated by the development. As a result, with the growth of the Oxford Movement, consistent attempts were made from 1839 onward to introduce surpliced choirs of men and boys into Anglican churches. The avowed intention was to encourage the people to take up again their responsibility as a *singing* congregation; to provide a choir which should lead the people in singing the psalms and chanting their responses, and where possible to add the singing of a simple anthem as a stimulus to devotion. The eventual success of this movement to develop surpliced parochial choirs provided the Anglican church with a feature unique in Christendom.

Like any other institution, the parochial choir proved capable of misuse. And before the end of the nineteenth century, many instances occurred where, perhaps through the use of unworthy music, or because the choir was allowed to monopolize the service, the original role of the parochial choir was forgotten. Under the leadership of the Royal School of Church Music, the situation has been considerably improved during the present century. Certain principles govern choral worship: (1) The music should be subservient to the words. (2) The music should be good, as music. (3) The music should be in keeping with the spirit of the liturgy. (4) The music should contribute to a corporate act of worship, not be addressed to the congregation. (5) The performers should sublimate their own personalities. Current trends in church music frequently fall short of these ideals, and reversal of ancient practice does not necessarily constitute progress or enhance worship. Writers as diverse as St Chrysostom, Calvin and Robert Bridges have emphasized the necessity to distinguish between secular and sacred musical styles. A present trend toward equating them risks reducing the dignity of worship and introduces hazards otherwise easily avoided.

L. Dakers, *Church Music at the Crossroads*, 1969; S. Nicholson, *Quires and Places where they Sing*, 1942; C. H. Phillips, *The Singing Church*, rev. ed. 1968; B. Rainbow, *The Choral Revival in the Anglican Church*, 1970; E. A. Wienandt, *Choral Music of the Church*, 1965.

BERNARR RAINBOW

Chrismatory

A metal receptacle or casket of precious metal, such as silver, but more frequently of latten or brass, designed to hold the three sacramental oils that have been in use since at least the second century: (1) the oil of the catechumens (q.v.), for the pre-baptismal rites; (2) the oil for the sick used in the anointing of the infirm. Both of these were composed of olive oil. But the chrismatory gets its name from (3) the third oil, chrism, which was rather a cream or ointment composed of olive oil and balm, and used in the rite of confirmation (q.v.) and in the anointing of sovereigns at their coronation. All three oils were blessed by the bishop on Maundy Thursday. (*See* **Unction**.)

J. Gilchrist, *Anglican Church Plate*, 1967.

C. E. POCKNEE

Christian Church (Disciples of Christ) Worship

The Christian Church (Disciples of Christ) began in the USA in the early nineteenth century when a loose alliance of independent congregations was drawn together by the leadership of Barton W. Stone (1772-1844), Thomas Campbell (1763-1854), his son Alexander Campbell (1788-1866), and other frontier preachers. This movement now includes three American denominations – Christian Church (Disciples of Christ), the Churches of Christ (using only vocal music), and the Christian Churches (affiliated with the North American Christian Convention) – and denominations in other countries. Worship in all of these denominations is characterized by these practices: (1) the regular act of congregational worship, celebrated each Sunday, is a service that includes preaching and the Lord's Supper; (2) their liturgical practice is in the family of Reformed-type worship, as distinguished from the modified-mass type or the Spirit-filled type; (3) they have entrusted the care of congregations and administration of the sacraments to local elders who ordinarily have not studied theology nor receive salary for their ecclesiastical work; (4) baptism is by complete immersion or submersion and limited to those old enough to answer for themselves; (5) the normal practice has been to use extempore prayer even for the eucharistic prayers.

This liturgical practice emerged in one of the most interesting periods of American intellectual life. Beginning in New England in the early eighteenth century, and spreading through the populated eastern seaboard, a powerful surge of religious revival transformed the American spirit, effectively severing its ties with Europe and the scholasticism of the Middle Ages. Under the most eminent of its theologians, Jonathan Edwards, this Great Awakening re-established a passionate Calvinist theology and created a new social striving for the creation of the Kingdom of God in North America. The American Revolution and Jeffersonian republicanism both resulted.

One last episode in the Great Awakening was the Kentucky Revival of 1800-01. The celebration of the Lord's Supper proved to be one of the chief stimulants of glossolalia and related phenomena. One reporter stated: 'The greatest work was on sacramental occasions.' With the dying of revivalism, the new frontier churches – notably Baptist and Methodist – came to depend more upon preaching services than upon the Lord's Supper as the focus for Sunday worship.

In contrast, the newly emerging Disciples of Christ built their congregational life around the Lord's Supper as the major act of worship. Furthermore, they avoided the emotionalism that had been associated with the revival. Indeed, their approach to things increasingly emphasized reason in religion. In this way they were very much like the anti-revival party during the eighteenth-century awakening, a party made up mostly of 'old side' Presbyterians and Episcopalians. Yet their liturgical practice differed from others of the enlightenment, especially Episcopalians. Like most other Protestants on the frontier, Disciples rejected the use of imposed liturgies. Instead, following the lead of Alexander Campbell, they sought to find a basis for their worship, and everything else in church life, in the 'clear' teaching of the NT. This principle had two implications: everything should be discarded from faith and practice which 'is not found written in the New Testament of the Lord and Saviour', and 'whatever is there enjoined' is to be believed and practised. In order to further the study of scripture by the people, Alexander Campbell prepared a modern speech translation of the NT, first published in 1826 under the title *The Living Oracles*. Probably the best English version then available, it was used widely by Disciple preachers through much of the nineteenth century and was in many congregations the one translation generally read and studied.

Their examination of the scriptures led them to conclude that the Lord's Supper is the significant act of Christian public worship. Their restorationist approach to the Bible led to a tendency towards legalism, that is towards the tendency to minister communion because Christ commanded it. Yet, their understanding of the meaning of 'the breaking of bread' suggests a more profound grasp of this sacrament. When each disciple receives the bread and cup, Campbell wrote, Christ says to him, 'For *you* my body was wounded; for *you* my life was taken.' When he receives these elements, the disciple says, 'Lord I believe it. My life sprung from thy suffering; my joy from thy sorrows; and my hope of glory everlasting from thy humiliation and abasement even to death.'

Interpretation of the meaning of the Lord's Supper has moved in two directions since that time. Formal theological discourse has tended towards commemoration, with very little effort to explain that term. Under the influence of liberal theology, especially in the first third of the twentieth century, this interpretation was drained of the content suggested by related terms in NT Greek. Despite this academic thinning out of meaning, a second trend persisted, the insistence that 'Christ is the unseen host at this table'. Consequently, the piety of church people and the devotional homilies at the table have maintained a seriousness of tone that is felt rather than defined. A theology of the eucharist based on these sources would be closer to Calvin than to Zwingli.

In the mid-twentieth century two reform movements have affected the shape and sense of Disciple worship. The first revolved around G. Edwin Osborn (1897-1965), for long a Professor of Worship at Phillips University in Oklahoma. His doctoral dissertation granted by the University of Edinburgh in 1935 dealt with the psychology of Christian public worship. His work culminated in *Christian Worship: A Service Book*, published in 1953, where he presented a rationale and materials for worship that are biblically rich and ecumenical.

During this same period the Disciples shared with most branches of American Protestantism the trend towards aestheticism in worship. One evidence was the erection of Romanesque and Gothic churches, with the largest number built after 1925, especially under the influence of A. F. Wickes (1880-1958), for a long time architectural consultant to the denomination.

The second influence began when William Robinson (1888-1963), British Disciple theologian, came to teach at Christian Theological Seminary in Indianapolis. He helped a new generation of students discover what had become obscured during the previous decades – that the Lord's Supper is the very principle of Sunday worship rather than something added on. He opened the doorway to serious theological engagement with classical Christian theology, especially as represented by P. T. Forsyth. Similar lessons have been learned by the Disciples in their extensive activities in ecumenical and union negotiations, most notably the Consultation on Church Union.

At this time, one major question continues: will the Disciples remain 'rigidly Protestant', as one interpreter terms their former stance, or will they move fully into the new ecumenical scheme? There is reason to believe that the latter will be the case and that the one Protestant denomination experienced in the practice of extempore prayer in a service of preaching and the Lord's Supper held every Sunday will bring this experience into the fuller service of Christ's church.

Alexander Campbell, *The Christian System*, 1843; W. E. Garrison and A. T. DeGroot, *The Disciples of Christ: A History*, 1948; G. Edwin Osborn, *The Glory of Christian Worship*, 1959; Keith Watkins, *The Breaking of Bread*, 1966.

KEITH WATKINS

Christmas

In Egypt in 1996 BC the calendar recorded the winter solstice as being on 6 January, but by the time Alexandria was founded in 331 BC the inaccuracy of the calendar meant that the solstice was on 25 December. The dates of the Christian festivals of Christmas and Epiphany (q.v.) are *both* linked with the winter solstice, transmuting celebrations of the pagan world. It is at Rome in the early fourth century that we find the first evidence for Christmas. In the year 274, the emperor Aurelian introduced in the imperial capital the festival of the Invincible Sun, *Natalis Solis Invicti*, on 25 December. At some point before

336 the church must have established on this date the commemoration of the incarnation, the birth of the Sun of Righteousness.

The evidence is contained in a martyrology written by Philocalus in 354 containing two lists of anniversaries, the one detailing the burial days of Roman bishops and the other those of martyrs. Both lists are set out in the order of the months, and it is highly significant that the opening date in the first is 27 December, and in the second 25 December, where the entry makes reference to the Nativity. The evidence of both lists is that by 354 Christmas was in existence at Rome, and was the beginning of the liturgical year.

But an analysis of the first list makes it possible to carry the evidence further back. If the last two insertions are omitted, the list begins on 27 December and ends on 8 December, thus running within the limits of a liturgical year which started at Christmas. The historical period covered is from 255 to 335, from Lucius to Silvester. The two names appended to this series are those of Marcus, who died on 7 October 336, and Julius, who died in 352. Philocalus evidently made use of an earlier list, completing it with the names of the two bishops who had died between 335 and 354. The initial list must therefore have been compiled after the death of Silvester on 31 December 335, but before that of Marcus on 7 October 336. It may be concluded that by 336 the Christian year at Rome began with Christmas, and it would be reasonable to affirm that Christmas originated in Rome in the early part of the fourth century.

___

B. Botte, *Les Origines de la Noël et de l'Épiphanie*, 1932; O. Cullmann, *Weihnachten in der alten Kirche*, 1947; A. A. McArthur, *The Evolution of the Christian Year*, 1953.

A. A. MCARTHUR

Church of South India Worship

The Church of South India (CSI) is a union of Anglicans, Presbyterians, Congregationalists and Methodists which was inaugurated in 1947. Initially it was assumed that its congregations would continue to use the service-books to which they were accustomed before union, with occasional united worship as directed by Synod. The rite of ordination (q.v.), prepared before union and inspired mainly by Anglican models in its first edition, was alone obligatory on the whole church.

At an early date, however, the need was felt for new forms to be used when the heirs of the different heritages met together for worship. Priority was given to orders for the Lord's Supper and confirmation (q.v.). The ready acceptance of these prompted the production of others covering all the normal requirements of worship. These were each revised after a period of experimental use before being brought together in *The Book of Common Worship Supplement* (1967). Though the old service-books, not least Anglican *BCP*, are still in use, it is increasingly regarded as old-fashioned to adhere to these pre-union traditions.

The Synod Liturgy Committee, though indebted in its compilations to the rites of the uniting churches, has eschewed any mere amalgam of them. Its intention has been threefold: (1) to return in some measure to the classical heritage of liturgy; here it has been guided by studies emanating from the Liturgical Movement (q.v.); (2) to give value to the insights of the Reformation which were the common heritage of the uniting churches; (3) to take account of South India's own cultural *milieu* and to produce forms of worship which, while treasuring the church's universal legacy of worship, would nevertheless be expressive of India's own religious genius and relevant to the needs of her people.

This third intention may not always be apparent in English, the *lingua franca* which had to be used for the original compositions. In fact the Indian ethos of CSI worship can only be fully appreciated where hymns composed by Indian poets in Tamil, Telugu, Malayalam or Canarese are sung to Carnatic *ragas*, and psalms, canticles, the *Gloria in excelsis*, *Sanctus*, etc. are rendered poetically and sung in the same way. Such Indian musical settings are still in an experimental stage, but are becoming increasingly popular.

Points of particular interest in the several orders are:

1. *The Lord's Supper or Holy Eucharist*. This is on the classical pattern with a preparatory section of adoration and confession, a liturgy of the word and a liturgy of the sacrament. Variability of collects, lections and prefaces, derived from the ancient Western and the Anglican traditions, has been retained. The greeting of peace in its Kerala Syrian form of handclasp (*see* **Gestures 4**) may be passed throughout the congregation at

the point before the offertory (q.v.). Responses derived from the Eastern liturgies are said or sung after the narrative of institution and the anamnesis. The offertory sentences and the epiclesis (which is of a Hippolytean rather than later Eastern type) both stress the theme of congregational corporateness and Christian unity. As in all CSI worship, value is given to congregational participation.

2. *Morning and Evening Worship.* Three alternative orders are specified: (*a*) Antecommunion (q.v.) with adaptations for non-eucharistic worship. (*b*) An order modelled on Anglican mattins and evensong. In this the *Trisagion*, or *Kauma*, to give it its Syrian name, may be said or sung as an initial adoration of the Trinity. The *Benedictus* comes between OT and NT lections as belonging between the Testaments, and the *Te Deum* after the NT lection as expressive of the faith of the church which has heard the gospel. The canticles (q.v.) traditionally linked with mattins and evensong respectively may be sung at either of them. More elasticity than in the Anglican tradition is permitted in the concluding prayers. (*c*) A simpler and 'freer' order with 'responsive readings' of scriptural verses and permission to sing either hymns, psalms or canticles between the lections, but with some encouragement to use at the discretion of the minister liturgical pericopae from the other orders.

3. *Baptism and Confirmation.* Appropriately in a church which is in a 'missionary situation', priority in the printed text is given to baptism of believers, with infant baptism taking second place. Baptism by immersion is encouraged, though not obligatory. The fiction of adult promises made 'in the name of the child' in infant baptism has been abandoned in favour of promises made by parents (and godparents if any) to bring up the child in the Christian way. The proleptic character of baptism (q.v.) and of the Christian life as 'becoming what we are' appears in the post-baptismal prayers. Some thought has been given to the relation between baptism and confirmation (q.v.) There is stress in confirmation on the fulfilment of baptism in repentance, profession of faith and self-dedication on the part of the candidates. One petition in the confirmation prayer (which closely follows the Roman/Anglican model)

sums up the meaning of confirmation: 'Establish them in faith . . . by the Holy Spirit . . .', that is, the Spirit is already present and operative in the life of the baptized; but confirmation, which is the occasion for public commitment to the Christian faith and life, is a prayer for and effective sign of the operation of the Spirit in a new way. In baptism there is a brief reception by the congregation of the newly baptized. In confirmation the act of reception is highlighted, and the greeting of peace is given to the newly confirmed for the first time. There is provision in the rubrics for baptism, confirmation and first communion to be linked closely together if desired, as in the ancient tradition of Christian initiation.

4. *The Ordinal.* The radical revision of 1957 was much indebted to the ordinal of the Church of Scotland. At the same time it was warmly commended at its publication by the Anglican liturgist, E. C. Ratcliff, as a model for future revision of ordination services. Some significant amendments were made in it in the ordinal produced in 1965 for the proposed united church in Nigeria. The churches of North India and Pakistan, where union was inaugurated in 1970, have for an experimental period adopted the CSI rites of eucharist and ordination.

5. *The Lectionary and Calendar* have, both in Daily Bible Readings and Propers for Sundays and Special Days, implemented a simplification of the structure of the Christian year, as suggested by A. A. McArthur in *The Evolution of the Christian Year* (1953). Collects and lections have been chosen with a theme for the day in mind.

An alternative Sunday lectionary is in preparation and is expected to be authorized by Synod in 1972. At the same time, synodal authorization is expected for a shorter and simpler order for the Lord's Supper in contemporary English as a prelude to a full-scale revision in this direction of *The Book of Common Worship*, both in its English original and Indian translations.

The Church of South India Book of Common Worship, 1963; *BCW Supplement*, 1967; T. S. Garrett, *Worship in the Church of South India*, ²1965; E. C. Ratcliff, 'The Ordinal of the Church of South India', *Theology*, January 1960. A commentary by several authors on the CSI orders of worship, edited by

E. C. John (title as yet unspecified), is expected to be published in India in 1972.

T. S. GARRETT

Churches of Christ see Christian Church (Disciples of Christ) Worship

Churching of Women

The title of the Sarum 'order for the purification of a woman after childbirth before the door of the church' sufficiently indicates the purpose of the rite. Its scriptural authority is to be found in Lev. 12, according to which a woman who has given birth is unclean, and must not 'come into the sanctuary' until she has made a burnt offering and a sin offering, which she brings to the door of the tent of meeting. Luke 2.22 provides an example of compliance with these regulations by the parents of Jesus. The Sarum service was brief, consisting of the lesser litany and Lord's Prayer, Pss. 121 and 128, the *preces* also used in marriage, and a collect; the priest then sprinkled the woman with holy water and led her into church, and the mass followed. The collect gives thanks for deliverance from the dangers of childbirth, and prays that the woman may finish her temporal course faithfully and attain eternal life. A rubric defines the purpose of purification as enabling the woman to enter the church to give thanks. According to ancient custom the woman wore a veil.

The 1549 'Order of the Purification of Women' follows the medieval service quite closely. It is to be held 'nigh unto the quire door' (i.e. the chancel screen). There is no suggestion of ritual impurity barring the woman from entering the church. The priest's opening address states that baptism of the child has already taken place, and puts the emphasis on thanksgiving for safe delivery. Psalm 128 is omitted and the collect is freely paraphrased. The woman is bidden to offer the chrysom (the white robe given to the baby at baptism) and 'other accustomed offerings'. If the holy communion is to follow, it is fitting that she should communicate.

The 1552 *BCP* reflects the change of emphasis by a change of title to 'The Thanksgiving of Women after Childbirth, commonly called the Churching of Women'. The service is now to be held 'nigh unto the place where the table standeth'. The only other alteration is the removal of the reference to the chrysom, which was no longer given in baptism.

During the seventeenth century, the custom of wearing a veil came under heavy fire from the Puritans, and in many churches special churching-pews were provided in the nave. Laudian bishops in their visitation articles insisted on the retention of the veil and also on the service being said at the altar rail. A rubric proposed in the 'Durham Book' directed that the woman should come 'a month after her delivery . . . decently veiled', but in the 1662 *BCP* this was toned down to 'at the usual time after her delivery . . . decently apparelled', while the place was to be 'as hath been accustomed, or as the Ordinary shall direct'. Psalm 116 with vv. 14-17 omitted was substituted at the suggestion of Robert Sanderson, with Ps. 127 as an alternative.

In the proposed book of 1928 the presence of the woman's husband was encouraged; and a blessing and two optional prayers were added, one dealing with the child's upbringing, the other for use when the child had died. An entirely new service put forward by the Church of England Liturgical Commission in 1965 was rejected by Convocation.

In the current Roman rite, now in process of revision, the old symbolism of kneeling at the church door and admission into church is retained, but the psalm is now 24. The Methodist *Book of Offices* (1936) includes a form for 'The Thanksgiving of Mothers' which is partly derived from the *BCP*.

G. W. O. Addleshaw and F. Etchells, *Architectural Setting of Anglican Worship*, 1948, pp. 84-6; F. E. Brightman, *The English Rite*, 1915, I, pp. cxxviii, clxiv, ccxxii; II, pp. 880-5; A. J. Collins, *Manuale Sarum*, 1960, pp. 43 f.; William Maskell, *Monumenta Ritualia Ecclesiae Anglicanae*, I, 1846, pp. 37 f.

G. J. CUMING

Church Modes

In the eighth or ninth century the Gregorian melodies were classified under one or another of the church modes, a system which postdated the bulk of them, just as did the major-minor diatonic and chromatic system that replaced them from the seventeenth century onwards in modern European music. The pattern of the latter system is invariable: whether you start in the major key on a white or a black note, there will be a series of five whole tones and two semitones always on the same degrees of this scale, and the same is true of the forms of the minor scales.

The modal system is both more complex and more subtle. Each mode has its special melodic flavour: here the tones and semitones occur in each mode on different degrees and there is a complete absence of the characteristic cadence made up of the leading-note rising by a semitone to the key note: e.g. in C major, the semitone B/C. The eight modes can be reduced from eight to four, as each pair shares a portion of the same complete mode.

This explanation can be made clear in the simple diagram below which will avoid the misleading, if picturesque, Greek names, such as Dorian, Lydian, Phyrgian, given them in the textbooks and in use for many years.

		Final (or key note)	Range	Dominant
1	1	d	d – d'	a
	2	d	a – a'	f
2	3	e	e – e'	c
	4	e	b – b'	a
3	5	f	f – f'	c'
	6	f	c – c'	a
4	7	g	g – g'	d
	8	g	d – d'	c'

The even-numbered modes start a fourth below the odd ones. Their dominants are a third below those of the odd modes, but it will be seen that the dominant of the third mode is not the normal fifth note (as in the modern scale), but in no. 3 it is C, not B; in the fourth it is A, not B; in the eighth it is C, not B. The reason for these changes is because the theorists wished to avoid putting the dominant on B so as to avoid the interval F-B, the so-called *diabolus in musica* or, in modern terms, the augmented fourth, consisting of three whole tones. Thus there is an artificiality about the system. Furthermore, the only permitted accidental was B flat, which was another avoidance of the same difficulty. Contemporary scholarship, however, is inclined to be more favourable towards the *diabolus in musica* and in earlier days the avoidance of B was not general.

The beauty of the chant is enhanced by the modal structure of the melodies. Modal writing was not extinguished by the appearance of the modern scale system, but lived on to give welcome variety and contrast to diatonic melody and harmony. It is used in such great works as Bach's B minor and Beethoven's D major masses, and in a large number of church and secular works from the eighteeenth to the twentieth century.

ALEC ROBERTSON

Ciborium

This term is thought to be derived from the Greek *kiborion*, which originally meant the hollow seed-case of the Egyptian water-lily, and the term came to be applied to a drinking-cup because of its resemblance to the seed-case. The use of the word ciborium now applies to two distinct objects in ecclesiastical usage: (1) a canopy of stone, wood or metal supported on four columns over an altar (q.v.); (2) a chalice-like vessel with a cover for holding a large number of wafer-breads. The latter must have developed from a pyx (q.v.) with a stem and foot and this could only have happened when wafer-breads finally replaced the use of leavened bread in the West after the twelfth century. The term was also applied to a little canopy on four columns standing on the altar under which the metal pyx or ciborium containing the reserved sacrament stood. In England some splendid examples of a flat chalice-like vessel with a cover all in silver-gilt and known as the bread cup appeared during the time of the Caroline divines in the middle of the seventeenth century. While the metal ciborium has usually been of silver or silver-gilt, examples of such vessels completely decorated with coloured enamels are known, such as the thirteenth-century Kennet ciborium.

J. Gilchrist, *Anglican Church Plate*, 1967; A. A. King and C. E. Pocknee, *Eucharistic Reservation in the Western Church*, 1965; C. E. Pocknee, *The Christian Altar*, 1963.

C. E. POCKNEE

Class Leader

The class leader is a layman given special pastoral responsibility within the Methodist societies established by John Wesley. One of Wesley's problems was the provision of proper continuing care and discipline for his converts. Part of his solution was to group them in 'classes' under a leader who was responsible for instructing them, developing their devotional life and seeing that they maintained the high moral standards required of all members of the societies. Members of the classes also contributed one penny a week to the funds of the society. At one time the office of class leader was generally regarded as one of great importance and influence. It is still a real ministry in some parts of Methodism, though in others the class system seems to have become vestigial.

P. HINCHLIFF

Collect

(1) A prayer of a distinctive stereotyped form, peculiar to the Western liturgies, although with certain parallels in the Eastern rites, with which the president closes a unit of liturgical worship, or some part of such a unit; (2) one such prayer in particular, namely, that referring to the mystery or person commemorated on a given day, which closes the entrance rite in the eucharistic liturgy; (3) derivatively, any other prayer written in the same form.

In the Roman rite the prayer cited in definition (2) above is called simply *oratio* – 'the prayer'. In some ancient Western liturgical books, however, it is called *collectio*, *collecta*, or *ad collectam*, whence the English name is derived. The meaning of the Latin is not certain: it means literally 'assembly', but it may refer either to a prayer in which preceding devotional themes are assembled, or to a prayer – such as that in definition (2) – which is spoken when the congregation is assembled. These interpretations, however, are complementary, for both throw light on the function of the prayer. In the historic Western liturgies collects are normally preceded, directly or indirectly, by a mutual greeting of president and people and a bidding to prayer, to emphasize the nature of the collect as a solemn summary by the president of the corporate prayer of the assembly.

Ancient examples of the collect after the entrance, of which many survive to this day in the Roman rite, exhibit an all but unvarying structure: (1) an address to God the Father; (2) a reference to some divine attribute or act as a ground for prayer; (3) the prayer proper, short, simple and definite; (4) a concluding doxology, offering the prayer to the Father through the Son and in the Holy Spirit. They also follow a distinctive literary pattern, following the rules of late classical Latin artistic prose. The collects of the Hispano-Gallican rites exhibit much more variation, and are often both theologically and stylistically excessively complicated. Other prayers of the collect type in the historic Western rites, such as those

which close the offertory (in the Roman rite called *secreta* or *super oblata*, q.v.) and the communion (in the Roman rite called *post-communio*), exhibit a theological and literary pattern similar, although with differences according to their function, to those of the collects proper.

The translation of a prayer of this type from Latin into the vernacular presents a considerable problem; the most successful solution of it so far, in its own day, was that of Cranmer in the collects of the *BCP*. The attempts of modern liturgical revisers to translate or compose collects in a more informal style, supposedly more appropriate and intelligible today, have so far been markedly less successful than those of their sixteenth-century predecessors, and it must be queried whether it is in fact possible to produce prayers of this kind without obeying the conventional rules for their formulation.

J. A. Jungmann, *The Mass of the Roman Rite*, I, 1951, pp. 359-90.

W. JARDINE GRISBROOKE

Colours, Liturgical

The association of particular colours with seasonal worship and personal commemoration has developed for several reasons – some psychological and some historical. It seems 'natural', for instance, to associate red with blood, yellow with energy, white with purity, gold with festivity, purple with dignity, green with growth, light blue with hope, dark blue, violet and black with despair and mourning, and drab earth colours with burial.

The use of colours in connection with Christian worship has had a varied history. For the first millennium the colour of vestments (q.v.) and hangings was without liturgical significance and, save for a preference for white robes, did not differ from what was customary among the Roman middle and upper classes of the empire and of its Byzantine continuation.

Although liturgical vesture remained the same in form as civilian dress, the indications are that the clergy reserved special 'suits' of alb and chasuble for use in church, and also that increasingly these vestments were of white material only. Jerome, in argument with Pelagius (*c.*415), asks what objection could be made if bishop, priest, deacon and the rest of the clergy appeared at the administration of the sacrifice in white array (*candida veste processerit*). Pseudo-Alcuin in the tenth or eleventh century writes only of white vestments and mentions red stripes on those of the deacons.

Not until the twelfth century is there evidence of correlation between significant colours and the seasonal feasts and fasts of the church's year and the various classes of saints, etc., in the calendar. The Augustinian canons at Jerusalem prepared the first known sequence of liturgical colours and, somewhat surprisingly, this proposed the use of black for Christmas and for festivals of the Blessed Virgin Mary, and blue for Epiphany and Ascension. Presumably the growing wealth of the church had permitted the use of a wider variety and richness of textiles for vestments, hangings and accessories and, understandably, their colours came to be associated with the developed medieval system of annual liturgical observances. At first such sequences were local and informal: they were unavoidably restricted to wealthy cathedrals and abbeys and to rich collegiate and parish churches. A common practice was to wear the newest or most magnificent vestments – virtually irrespective of colour – on the great festivals and to use the older ones on other occasions. Gradually, however, a generally accepted pattern of colour association emerged in the medieval West: Innocent III (1198-1216) outlined the Roman rule based on white for feasts, red for martyrs, black for penitential seasons and green at other times.

A general rule was not formally defined in rubric until 1570 in the reformed missal under Pius V: in brief, the type of sequence which eventually emerged was as follows:

Advent to	
Christmas Eve	Violet / Blue / Black
Christmas to Epiphany	White / Gold
Sundays after Epiphany	Green
Septuagesima to Ash	
Wednesday	Violet / Blue / Black
Throughout Lent	Veiling of colours
Passion Sunday to	
Easter Eve	Red / Rose
Easter	White / Gold
Pentecost	Red
Trinity	White / Gold
Sundays after Trinity	Green
Ordinary weekdays	Green
Blessed Virgin Mary	White / Red
Apostles, evangelists,	
martyrs	Red
Saints other than	
martyrs	White / Yellow
Baptisms / confirmation	White / Red
Ordination / marriage	White
Funeral	Violet / Blue / Black
Dedication of a church	White

As the above list indicates, there was latitude in the choice of liturgical colours, especially in the 'mourning' range of violet, dark blue and black: further, distinctions were made in the various shades of red, and in pre-Reformation England, green and yellow were regarded as interchangeable. Regional variation persisted and other colours altogether were sometimes employed, e.g. the brick-red of Sarum for the Sundays after Epiphany. Latin names in medieval inventories include *albus* and *candidus* for white, *rubeus, sub-rubeus* and *coccineus* for various shades of red (including rose), *purpureus* for red-purple and *violaceus* for blue-purple, *viridis* for green and *croceus* for yellow.

The Eastern Orthodox churches use coloured materials in great variety and Eastern churches in communion with the Roman Catholic Church broadly follow the Western customs; they do not, however, regard themselves as bound so strictly to adhere to a colour sequence as did the Roman Catholic Church in the period preceding Vatican II.

The liturgical colours were primarily to be seen in the material of the chasubles and copes and that of altar cloths and textile hangings. The colours were also used in the embellishment of the vestments – orphreys and apparels – and in the material or decoration of the stole and maniple. In this connection it may be noted that the colour of the stole and maniple generally accorded with that of the orphreys and apparels and contrasted with the predominant colour of the chasuble. This custom has been contradicted by the recent practice which is concerned to make everything 'match'.

It is interesting to note that the English Lenten vestments were for the most part *white* (often with a limited amount of red decoration), and that those of passiontide, including Palm Sunday and Good Friday, were *red*.

Many of the Lenten entries include veils (q.v.) and other hangings which were used to cover all pictures and images, and on fast days to curtain off the high altar. The purpose of these hangings was to some extent contradicted when themselves they came to be 'steyned', i.e. painted, with symbols and scenes of the passion. Modern practice is to shroud the coloured adornments of a church with a Lenten array of buff-coloured material sparsely embroidered with red emblems.

In the sixteenth century the Reformed Churches generally rejected colour as an adjunct to worship. Where the Calvinist or the Puritan spirit prevailed, all vestments and coloured textiles were abrogated and the ministers were content merely with a black preaching gown worn over dark civilian clothes. Among other Protestants (especially Lutherans and Anglicans), in sectors where it has been customary to retain or to re-introduce some or all of the traditional vestments and hangings, it has also been usual to observe the 1570 Roman Catholic colour sequence so far as this was possible.

A rubric in the 1549 *BCP* of the Church of England ordered that the parish priest should wear 'a white albe plain, with a vestement or cope', and Canon XXIV (1603-4), based also on the *Advertisements* (1566), curiously ordered that the principal minister at the eucharist in cathedrals and collegiate churches should wear a coloured cope over a plain alb. This perverse practice became quite widespread in the seventeenth century among the so-called Laudian school and, in the early eighteenth century, the high churchmen among the Non-jurors restored the eucharistic vestments in the contemporary Roman Catholic style and sometimes took the liberty of interpreting 'cope' as 'chasuble'. Only in this tenuous way was regard for liturgical colour maintained in the Established Church, for the majority of the clergy obeyed Canon LVIII which prescribed surplice and academic hood or black scarf for the eucharist; there were, however, some clergy who continued to wear a black gown for the celebration as well as for preaching and singing the choir offices until the end of the seventeenth century.

The Catholic sacramental revivalism of the Oxford Movement and the romantic Gothic revivalism of the Cambridge Ecclesiologists converged in the middle of the nineteenth century to focus attention upon Anglican ceremonial, and hence to advocacy of the eucharistic vestments and the liturgical colours for renewed use in the Church of England.

The result of this stimulus was twofold.

On the one hand, Evangelicals denounced the neo-medievalism as 'popery' and refused to wear liturgical vestments other than those prescribed by Canon LVIII, namely surplice and academic hood or black scarf. On the other hand, to meet the growing demand of the high-churchmen of the Church of England and of the clergy of the Roman Catholic Church, Victorian commercial interests were mobilized to supply full sets of vestments and hangings in the 'correct' liturgical colours. It is stated by several writers on the subject that complete standardization of the colours in the Roman Catholic Church was not attempted until the nineteenth century, and this, presumably, is an allusion to the persistence of local uses in France until this time, and to the growing commercial pressures for mass-produced correctness.

Eventually, all but the most extreme of the low-church Evangelicals adopted the strange compromise of wearing a seasonally coloured stole over a surplice for the eucharist, while a different compromise (though with some historical justification) in the form of a complete set of all-white linen vestments was accepted by moderate churchmen.

As a result of the influence of the Liturgical Movement (q.v.), radical changes are taking place in the design and decoration of vestments and the liturgical use of colours. In general it is recognized that there is historical and psychological virtue in the traditional seasonal colours – provided that they are interpreted in terms of mood rather than in conformity to a rigid system of rules. Thus, it is reasonable in penitential periods to use drab materials in the violet-brown-grey range (though avoiding black), to use red-purples and gold to express majesty and high-priesthood, challenging reds for leaders and martyrs, green and yellow to signify renewal, and to employ white and gold (with the whole palette, if desired) for festivals.

In the Roman Catholic Church the post-Vatican II *Ordo Missae* (1969) generally reaffirmed current practice, *white* for Easter, Christmas, feasts of Christ (other than the Passion), of Mary, of angels and of saints (not martyrs), All Saints, John Baptist, John Evangelist, Chair of Peter and Conversion of Paul; *red* for Passion and Palm Sundays, Good Friday, Pentecost, feasts of the Passion of Christ and of martyrs; *violet* for Advent and Lent and possibly for funeral masses in place of *black*; *rose* for Gaudete Sunday

(Advent III) and Laetare Sunday (Lent IV); *green* at other times. It is also recommended that on special occasions more solemn vestments may be used, even if not of the colour of the day.

The combination of a whole range of new materials and colours, together with a fresh understanding of the emotional effect of colours, their optical relationships and their design possibilities, permits a renewed approach to all aspects of their use in worship. For example, especially in new churches, it is possible to integrate all the coloured items – vestments, hangings, carpets, glass, furnishings, timber and other structural materials and finishes – into a total liturgical environment: even in existing churches much can be done to create a meaningful sense of seasonal colour and to refrain from a sterile following of what commercial church furnishers may insist is correct.

J. Braun, *Die liturgische Gewandung im Occident und Orient nach Ursprung und Entwicklung, Verwendung und Symbolik*, 1907; P. Dearmer, *The Ornaments of the Ministers*, 1908/1920; W. H. St J. Hope and E. G. C. F. Atchley, *English Liturgical Colours*, 1918; J. W. Legg, *Notes on the History of Liturgical Colours*, 1882; C. E. Pocknee, *Liturgical Vesture*, 1960.

GILBERT COPE

Commination

In pre-Reformation times after Sext on Ash Wednesday, a sermon was preached, and the imposition of ashes followed. The rite consisted of the seven penitential psalms (6, 32, 38, 51, 102, 130 and 143), *preces*, seven collects for penitence and forgiveness, and a solemn absolution; the blessing of the ashes was accompanied by two more collects, and the ashes were applied to the foreheads of the penitents with the words 'Remember, O man, that thou art ashes, and unto ashes shalt thou return'; further antiphons and collects then led into mass.

This ceremony (and by implication the rite accompanying it) was abolished by the Council in January 1548, and there is no reference to ashes in the *BCP* of 1549. Indeed, the name 'Ash Wednesday' is eliminated from the *BCP* of 1552. The occasion is put to a rather different purpose. After mattins, the people are summoned by the ringing of a bell, and the litany is said, in accordance with the injunctions of 1547, 'in the midst of the church . . . before High Mass'. A completely new section follows, which gives the service its name 'commination' (*Oxford English Dictionary*: 'a threatening of punishment'). The priest goes into the pulpit and reads 'a declaration of scripture' consisting chiefly of 'the general sentences of God's cursing against impenitent sinners' (Deut. 27.15-25). This is meant to take the place of the primitive discipline of open penance, and was probably suggested by the medieval rite called the greater excommunication, a denunciation of sinners read three or four times a year. It is followed by a long catena of scriptural texts on judgment and repentance woven together into a continuous sermon.

The priest then returns to the midst of the church, and the rest of the service (described in the title as 'certain prayers') is an abridgment of the Sarum rite, shorn of course of its ceremony. The *BCP* retains only one of the penitential psalms (Ps. 51), the *preces*, the first collect, a collect made up of phrases from four of the Sarum prayers, and one of the antiphons, which leads into the introit psalm (Ps. 6) of holy communion.

The title 'A Commination against Sinners' dates from 1552, and in 1662 Bishop Wren added to it the explanatory phrase 'or Denouncing of God's Anger and Judgments'. The connection with Ash Wednesday, severed in the 1552 *BCP*, was maintained in practice throughout the sixteenth century, and was restored in 1662, with provision for use 'at other times, as the Ordinary shall appoint'. By then the service seems to have become separated from the holy communion, and a blessing was added at the end.

Modern revisions have tried various expedients to keep the service in use. England 1928 substitutes censures based on the Decalogue and abbreviates the catena; Scotland 1929 has the Decalogue itself and the Lucan Beatitudes (6.20-26), while omitting the catena altogether. America 1928 omits the whole of the first part; England 1966, First Series, the whole of the second. Only in India, where penitential discipline is still in force, does Deut. 27 survive; and even here the catena is shortened.

F. E. Brightman, *The English Rite*, 1915, I, pp. cxxix, clxiv, ccxxii; II, pp. 886-901; A. J. Collins, *Manuale Sarum*, 1960, pp. 9-12.

G. J. CUMING

Commixture

The commixture is the placing of a particle of the consecrated host in the chalice (q.v.) after the fraction (q.v.) at the eucharist (q.v.). The origins of this ceremonial act are complex. It appears to have derived from the *fermentum*. This was a fragment of bread consecrated at an episcopal celebration and taken to a church where a presbyter was presiding, it being added to the chalice after the fraction as a symbol of unity. This custom died out in the East, probably in the fourth century, but continued in Rome until the eighth or ninth. At that period there was also current the practice of sanctifying extra chalices by adding a piece of the already consecrated host. It would appear that the *fermentum* was transformed into the commixture under this influence. The commixture was further affected by a Syrian symbolic interpretation, to the effect that the words of consecration represent the death of Christ and so the separation of his body and blood, while the bringing together of these two through the commixture shows forth his resurrection. Hence in the Liturgy of St James it is called the *henosis*, i.e. union, while in that of St Chrysostom it is accompanied by the words: 'The fullness of the Holy Spirit' – the Spirit being regarded as the agent of the resurrection.

J. A. Jungmann, *The Mass of the Roman Rite*, rev. ed., 1959, pp.475-9.

EDITOR

Communion

1. The partaking of the consecrated elements at the eucharist (q.v.), whereby there is a communion or participation (*koinonia*) in Christ and in him with all the members of the congregation. Methods of partaking and of distribution as well as posture have varied throughout the ages and from church to church.

In the patristic period the worshippers received the bread in their hands but do not appear to have touched the chalice. Cyril, or John, of Jerusalem describes the fourth-century practice when he says: 'As you approach then, come not with your wrists extended or your fingers open, but make of your left hand a kind of throne by placing it under your right which is about to receive the King, and in the hollow of your hand receive the body of Christ, replying Amen.

Carefully hallow your eyes with the touch of the holy body, and then partake of it, seeing to it that you lose no particle . . . Then, after the communion of Christ's body, approach also the cup of his blood, not stretching forth your hands, but bending forward in an attitude of adoration and reverence, and saying Amen, be hallowed as well by the reception of the blood of Christ. And while the moisture thereof is still on your lips, touch it with your hands and hallow both your eyes and brow and other senses' (*Catech.* 5.21 f.).

Before the end of the sixth century women were forbidden to receive the bread on the naked hand and the *Ordo Romanus VI* (? *c.* 900) only allows this for bishops, priests and deacons, apparently from a desire to protect that which is holy from profane or superstitious uses. This practice was also required by the 1549 *BCP* but was thereafter omitted. By the thirteenth century communicating under the species of wine had almost universally disappeared in the West, probably to avoid the risk of spilling. Objections to this were raised by the Hussites in Bohemia, and the Reformers insisted that communion in both kinds alone had scriptural warrant. In the Roman Church communion in one kind persists, although since Vatican II there is a move to 'restore the cup to the laity'.

Another method of partaking is by intinction, i.e. the bread is dipped in the wine so that the two kinds can be administered conjointly. This became popular in the seventh century but was condemned in the West in the thirteenth. In Orthodox churches it is the almost universal practice to partake from a spoon containing the bread sprinkled with a few drops of wine. Today this method is sometimes used in the USA for hygienic reasons. Similar motives have also led to the use in many non-episcopal churches of small individual cups.

Distribution of communion has also varied. In the early church the worshippers came up to a balustrade demarcating the sanctuary (q.v.) and this has continued to be the practice in many churches, e.g. Anglican, Orthodox and Roman. An alternative method is to bring the elements to the communicants. This change was instituted by the English Puritans who then influenced Congregationalists, Methodists and Presbyterians. Some Presbyterians, however, particularly in Holland and Westphalia, leave their seats and sit around a table in the nave or sanctuary.

This last statement indicates that for these Christians the posture for communion is sitting. However, in the early church it was usual to stand, and this is still the norm in many Reformed congregations in Alsace, France and Switzerland. Reception kneeling only gained ascendance gradually in the Roman Church between the eleventh and the sixteenth century and remains usual as well as among Anglicans.

2. Communion can also be a translation of the Latin word *communio* which denotes a psalm sung during communion. According to Cyril, Ps. 34 was sung at Jerusalem in the fourth century, and both the *Apostolic Constitutions* and Augustine refer to the practice. The psalm is sometimes replaced by a communion hymn at the present day.

EDITOR

Communion Table

This term has been preferred by those churches that have sprung out of the Protestant Reformation in the sixteenth century rather than the term altar (q.v.), which in the later Middle Ages in the West had become associated with the idea that in the mass Christ was somehow immolated afresh. The Reformers were concerned to rebut such an idea and to assert the unique character of Christ's atoning work on the cross, which could in no sense be repeated. Perhaps those who have taken this position mistakenly supposed that the term 'altar' could only be applied to a structure of stone, while the term 'table' was applied exclusively to a structure of wood.

In the *BCP* the usual term is 'the Lord's table'; but in common parlance in the Church of England the term 'altar' is in frequent use. Moreover, in the official rite for the coronation of the sovereigns of England the term altar is always used and retained.

We may say that the term 'communion table' underlines an aspect of the eucharist which had become obscured in the later Middle Ages when eucharistic devotion had tended to become too pietistic and highly individualistic. Hence by underlining the corporate aspect of fellowship at the Lord's table this aspect was redressed. Much of the present-day liturgical revival is connected with the idea of the fellowship of the people of God at the holy table.   C. E. POCKNEE

Compline *see* Canonical Hours

Concelebration

Concelebration in the full meaning of the word is a specific rite in which several priests say mass together, consecrating the same bread and wine.

In the first centuries of the church the president alone recited the eucharistic prayer, since there was no fixed formula throughout the Christian communities. The priests, who stood on either side of the bishop, extended their hands over the oblation and prayed, but without saying aloud the consecratory words. This was the rite described in the *Apostolic Tradition* of Hippolytus (*c.*225), for long considered of Roman origin, but now thought by some liturgists to have an Alexandrine provenance. The 'crowns of priests', who in the eighteenth century surrounded the bishop at the altar in the cathedrals of France, seldom said the eucharistic prayer aloud, except on Holy Thursday. The concelebrants in the Greek Orthodox Church are also silent in the prayer, but in the Russian part of the church they recite the prayer with the president.

It is disputed whether a silent concelebration is fully sacramental or merely ceremonial. Pope Pius XII stated in 1956 that if the concelebrants did not say the 'essential words' aloud it was a ceremonial concelebration, but a lack of evidence leaves the question unanswered.

The custom of a verbal concelebration developed in Rome in the seventh century. The concelebrants recited the words of the canon, with the words of the consecration, aloud with the pope: a function which was later confined to certain days in the year. The primary purpose of the rite was a manifestation of unity. Visiting priests were invited to concelebrate out of hospitality and as a sign of communion.

The rite was introduced into other countries by the spread of the Roman service books. There is no evidence for concelebration in England, unless the title of 'cardinal' for two of the clergy of St Paul's Cathedral, London, originated in this way. It would, however, be rash to infer a universal practice of concelebration. By the thirteenth century the traditional rite had ceased in the Western Church, but the practice was defended by Thomas Aquinas (d. 1274).

Some time between the eighth century and the twelfth, concelebration in the ordination of priests and the consecration of bishops was introduced. It is not known with certainty why another form of concelebration appeared at this time. There is, however, a possible explanation. The Germano-Roman pontifical of the tenth century had adopted the practice of handing a chalice and paten to the candidate at his ordination. This 'porrection of the instruments', as it is called, assumed a very disproportionate importance and was regarded by some as the authentic matter of the sacrament. It is possible that concelebration at an ordination was motivated by the desire that the new priests, who had been appointed to offer sacrifice by the reception of the sacred vessels, should immediately exercise this right. The first known witness to this innovation seems to have been Thomas Aquinas, who spoke of 'the custom of some churches for priests newly ordained to co-celebrate with the bishop ordaining them'. Concelebration at the consecration of a bishop was already attested in the pontifical of Apamea (Syria), taken from a Roman model at the end of the twelfth century. The concelebration of priests was not exact as, although the canon including the words of consecration, and the other prayers after the offertory of the mass were said aloud with the bishop, the priests received the sacrament kneeling and in only one kind.

The Codex of Canon Law, issued for the Roman Catholic Church in 1918, affirmed that concelebration in ordinations was the sole form permissible in the Western Church.

The second Vatican Council (1962-3) discussed a revival of traditional concelebration, in which were emphasized some of the important theological and liturgical truths which centuries of individualism had greatly obscured. The debates were lively and hotly contested, but the final voting gave a very substantial majority in favour of the revival. This meant that the hierarchical nature of the church, the unity of the sacrifice of the mass and the collegiate character of the priesthood were once again put into their rightful perspective.

A commission was set up for the implementing of the liturgical decisions, in which an official text for the rite of concelebration was formulated.

The concelebrants may read the lessons in the liturgy of the word, as the first part of the mass is called, but it is not essential. Full concelebration begins at the liturgy of the eucharist. The concelebrants, at the offertory, stand on either side of the president at the altar.

Sacramental concelebration is effected in the eucharistic prayer or canon (q.v.), with the full co-operation of all the priests. The prayer is recited in a distinct and loud voice, with one of the concelebrants saying the memento of the living, *Communicantes* ('In union with the whole church we honour the memory of the saints') and the memento of the dead. The words of consecration are said by all the priests. The president performs the actions and the concelebrants extend their right hands, first towards the bread and then towards the wine.

Changes have been made in the ordination rites to make them authentic concelebrations.

A concelebrated liturgy is, to the whole people of God, a sign of their unity and a sign that helps them to be more aware that 'they are the body of Christ, not many bodies, but one body', as John Chrysostom affirms.

Concelebration is normal in the Orthodox churches of the Byzantine rite. The Syrians have a 'synchronized' form and the Maronites, about the end of the seventeenth century, adopted a rite under the influence of Catholic doctrine.

The rite is not very general in the Anglican Church, but it was started in St Stephen's House at Oxford in 1955. The concelebrants recite the prayers *sotto voce* and unite with the president in the prayer for the church, preface and eucharistic prayer.

Concelebration has also been practised from time to time in recent years in an attempt to overcome the problem of intercommunion. Where two churches are not in communion with each other, a eucharist has been held with, e.g., an Anglican and a Methodist concelebrating. It is difficult to determine how far this is a valid way forward and how far it is a masking of the issues.

A. A. King, *Concelebration in the Christian Church*, 1966.

A. A. KING

Confession *see* Prayer (2)

Confirmation

The earliest attestation of the ceremony which ultimately came to be called 'confirmation'

(Lat. *confirmatio*, Gk, *bebaiōsis*) is to be found in the baptismal rites of Hippolytus' *Apostolic Tradition* (AD 215) and Tertullian's treatise *De Baptismo* (AD 198). Both works attest a ceremony after baptism (q.v.) consisting of a prayer said by the bishop with his hands extended over the candidates, the anointing of the candidates on the forehead, the imposition of the hand on the head of each, and the sign of the cross (q.v.) on the forehead. The precise manner and order in which these elements were combined varied in the subsequent development and they did not always appear in their entirety. Thus according to the *Ordo Romanus XI* of the late sixth century 'the pontiff makes a prayer over them . . . and when the prayer has been said he makes the sign of the cross with his thumb in chrism on the forehead of each one, saying, "In the name of the Father and the Son and the Holy Spirit. Peace be to thee".' On the eve of the Reformation, the Sarum Manual and the Roman Pontifical differed from this only in so far as the formula which accompanied the anointing had grown longer and the Roman rite specifically preserves a mention of the extension of the bishop's hands over the candidates as he prays for the seven-fold gifts of the Spirit. The *BCP* has abandoned the anointing and the sign of the cross but preserves the imposition of the hand, in the belief that this accords better with the example of the apostles, and has provided a new formula, 'Defend O Lord . . .', to accompany it. The *BCP* order retains also the prayer for the sevenfold gifts of the Spirit from the Sarum rite, but does not provide any more than the Sarum rite for the extension of the bishop's hands over the candidates while it is said. This prayer is broadly the same as that which appears in the early sixth-century Gelasian Sacramentary and has formed a constant feature of the Roman rite ever since that date. It is believed to be first attested by Ambrose in his treatise *De Sacramentis*, and is almost certainly quoted by some of his Roman contemporaries.

Originally no distinction was made between infants and adults in the use of this post-baptismal ceremony. When infants were baptized they were also anointed and hands were laid on them. But the requirement of the Roman and African churches that the anointing and imposition of the hand must be reserved to the bishop came to result in their

separation from baptism, for infants and adults alike. In cases of emergency baptism, administered by a priest, or when bishops were no longer able to preside over all baptisms, the post-baptismal ceremony was inevitably delayed until the candidates could appear before a bishop. This separation between baptism and confirmation, which was originally imposed on the church by practical necessity, came ultimately to be regarded as the normal practice, and led to a situation in which baptism was thought to be appropriate to infancy and confirmation to later years.

Although in the Roman rite this ceremony was associated with the gift of the Holy Spirit, it is not clear that this was the case with the other rites of the Latin West. These provide for a simple post-baptismal anointing of the forehead, which in Gaul and Spain was performed by the priest who baptized, with oil which had been consecrated by the bishop. But in rites which were unaffected by Roman influence there is nothing to indicate that the bestowal of the Spirit was understood to be the purpose of the anointing.

In the early Syrian church no post-baptismal ceremony corresponding to the Western anointing and imposition of the hand intervened between the baptismal washing and the holy communion. Although some scholars have claimed that the pre-baptismal anointing in this rite must therefore have been for the bestowal of the Spirit, it seems more probable that this anointing served the same apotropaic purpose as it did in the West and that the Syrian church recognized no sign other than water by which the Spirit was imparted in Christian initiation. If this is correct, it carries with it the important implication that a second sign other than water in Christian initiation was not a matter of universal observance in the early church.

The earliest Syrian attestations of a post-baptismal anointing are to be found in the *Apostolic Constitutions* (c. AD 375) and the *Catecheses* of Cyril of Jerusalem, and these most probably represent an importation from the churches of the West. By degrees this anointing after baptism was adopted throughout the churches of the East, where it is now accepted as a sacrament, although the Nestorian rite to this day has no such anointing. The rite consists of a chrismation made in the sign of the cross to the forehead and other parts of the body, but not the imposition of the hand. The formula varies, but the formula of the ancient Byzantine rite is still used in the Orthodox Church, 'The seal of the gift of the Holy Spirit'. This chrismation is performed by the priest who baptizes and has therefore retained its original connection with baptism and is administered to infants.

1. *Origins.* The significance and origin of this post-baptismal ceremony is a matter of controversy. According to the Council of Trent, confirmation is one of seven sacraments instituted by Christ. Roman Catholic theologians define the matter of the sacrament variously as chrism, the imposition of the hand, or the combination of both. The form used throughout the Roman Catholic Church is as follows: '*I sign thee with the sign of the cross, and I confirm thee with the chrism of salvation, in the name of the Father and of the Son and of the Holy Spirit. Amen.*' A distinction is commonly made between the grace of baptism and that of confirmation: in baptism the Holy Spirit is given for pardon and new birth, in confirmation for strength to preach the gospel and to live the adult Christian life. Such a distinction does not seem tenable in the context of infant confirmation, and appears to have originated in the Middle Ages as a rationalization of the situation when baptism was administered in infancy and confirmation in later years.

A. J. Mason, followed by Dom. G. Dix and Fr L. S. Thornton, has argued that baptism and confirmation make up one sacrament consisting of two signs, each one conveying its own distinctive grace. In baptism the Holy Spirit operates from the outside to convey pardon and new birth; in confirmation the gift of the indwelling Spirit is bestowed.

The *BCP* states that '*It is certain by God's word, that children which are baptized, dying before they commit actual sin, are undoubtedly saved*, and this appears to imply the view that confirmation is not necessary to salvation. Consistently with this, the Thirty-Nine Articles distinguish confirmation and other ceremonies 'commonly called sacraments' from baptism and holy communion, which are 'sacraments of the gospel'. Since confirmation is not regarded as a sacrament in the strict sense by the Church of England, its form and matter are not defined: but the laying on of hands with prayer are commonly regarded as its necessary features. While the Church of England has retained inflexibly the ancient rule that only bishops may confirm, the Church of Rome permits bishops to delegate this function on appropriate occasions: and as we have seen, the priest is the normal minister of the sacrament in the Eastern churches.

In the Middle Ages the origin of confirmation was variously traced to the action of our Lord laying his hands on children (Mark 10.16), or in breathing on the apostles (John 20.22) or to his teaching after the resurrection of 'the things pertaining to the kingdom of God' (Acts 1.3). An alternative to these speculations was the view that confirmation was exemplified, if not instituted, by the apostles when they laid hands on the baptized and the Spirit came upon them (Acts 8.15; 19.6). These passages in Acts had been cited by Irenaeus and Tertullian and others of the fathers to show that the apostles regularly laid hands on their converts for the bestowal of the Spirit. But this interpretation has been contested by leaders of the continental Reformation and at the present day notably by G. W. H. Lampe, who claim that the events recounted in the Acts are not to be understood as normative: and the evidence of the Syrian rite to which we have referred above suggests that in fact it was not normative.

The ablutionary customs of the ancient world called for the use of oil as well as water in bathing, and it has therefore been suggested that confirmation may have originated in the oil which would commonly have been used after the baptismal bath. Passages in the NT which have been thought to refer to the use of oil or chrism in initiation include II Cor. 1.21 and I John 2.20, 27; but the anointing to which these texts refer may be nothing more than a metaphor for the gift of the Holy Spirit in baptism.

Another explanation for the origin of confirmation has been sought in the complexity of the Gnostic and mystery religions in which candidates proceeded from one stage in initiation to higher and more advanced stages.

While some of these accounts of the origins of confirmation may seem more probable than others, their variety indicates that there is no certainty on the point, which remains a matter for speculation.

2. *The Age of Confirmation.* The practice of

infant confirmation did not entirely disappear until the end of the Middle Ages, so that it was still possible in 1533 for the Princess Elizabeth to be baptized and confirmed at the age of three days. Nevertheless, over the previous centuries a number of circumstances led to the situation in which confirmation came to be reserved to the 'years of discretion'. First, the difficulty of obtaining confirmation and the sense that baptism itself conveyed the grace of the Holy Spirit and all that was necessary for salvation (which few medieval theologians denied) led to a general neglect of confirmation and a disposition to delay it indefinitely. This neglect was then countered by the teaching that confirmation was necessary in order to become fully Christian, and by the regulation which in England originated with Archbishop Peckham in the thirteenth century, which laid down that no one should be admitted to holy communion until he had been confirmed. Although a number of continental and English councils laid down that children must be confirmed by the age of two, three, or seven, the result of the process was that the age of seven or more became established as the normal age for confirmation. At the same time a theology of baptism and confirmation had been developing to match the facts of the changed situation, teaching that baptism restores innocence and gives new birth and that confirmation gives the strength to live the Christian life and to preach to others. It was in the light of this that the Catechism of Trent laid down seven to twelve years old as the appropriate age for confirmation, and preferred the latter. Since then pastoral considerations have led the Roman Catholic Church to admit children to holy communion some years before their confirmation: but if confirmation is a sacrament of initiation, this seems hard to justify.

In the Church of England today the most suitable age for confirmation is a matter of debate. To some it is determined by the fact that the laying on of hands is associated with the re-affirmation of baptismal vows, which suggests that confirmation should be deferred to an age when candidates can speak from personal conviction. On the other hand, those who regard confirmation as a source of sacramental grace argue for an earlier age. The school-leaving age and modern insights into child psychology are other factors in the debate.

The Reformers regard confirmation as an 'idle ceremony'. In their experience it was administered with oil (which they sometimes chose to call 'grease'), and thus appeared to have no foundation in scripture. Moreover, as we have noted above, many of the Reformers did not accept that the imposition of the apostles' hands described in the Acts was to be taken as an example which the church must necessarily follow. In their view the NT gives no indication that confirmation can be traced to the institution of Christ, nor indeed says anything at all about confirmation. They regarded baptism as the one sacrament of initiation and resented the teaching that before confirmation a man was only half a Christian. At the same time, they perceived the value of an occasion when the child baptized in infancy might make a public profession of his baptismal faith in later years. This matched their convictions about the importance of individual faith and the need to answer the Anabaptists who criticized the practice of infant baptism; and it was supported by their mistaken belief that Christians in the primitive church commonly made such a declaration when they reached maturity. From these premisses there developed in the Reformed churches a rite of 'confirmation' of which the principal element was an examination of the candidates and a declaration of their Christian commitment: and this was followed by the imposition of the pastor's hands, which was understood as a blessing. In the late Middle Ages it had already been required that parents and godparents should teach their children such elements of the faith as the *Paternoster*, *Ave Maria*, and *Credo*, and from this the Reformers quickly developed the system of preparation for confirmation in classes and by catechisms.

Although Calvin would have been content to see the 'restoration' of the laying on of hands when children made a personal confession of faith, on condition that it was understood as a blessing, he did not provide or practise such a rite himself. The churches of the Reformed tradition have varied, some observing a confirmation of this kind and others not Today, in response to pastoral needs, many churches which formerly had no rite of confirmation have now adopted one, which is often associated with admission to holy communion. Thus the Methodist Church has provided a service of 'Public

Reception into Full Membership, or Confirmation'. Services of this kind provide a form of commitment to the Christian faith and life, followed by the laying on of hands in blessing performed by the local minister, and often include a prayer for the strengthening of the Holy Spirit. Sometimes they also provide that the minister or some other member of the church shall extend 'the right hand of fellowship' to the new member.

In many parts of the Anglican Communion the restoration of anointing to accompany the imposition of the hands is under discussion, and has already been adopted in some countries.

3. *The word 'Confirmation'.* To many people today the word connotes the fact that candidates confirm their baptismal vows at confirmation. This interpretation of the word dates only from the Reformation and takes no account of such prayer-book expressions as 'to be confirmed by the bishop', which go back to a higher antiquity. The words *confirmatio, confirmare,* began to be used of the post-baptismal anointing or hand-laying in the early fifth century in the sense that the bishop then ratified or completed what had been begun in baptism. At a later stage, when the church had accepted the doctrine that this rite supplied strength for the adult Christian life, it was natural that the word *confirmation* came to be understood as 'strengthening'.

For confirmation in the Orthodox rite *see* **Baptism** 2.

―――――

A. D'Ales, *De Baptismo et Confirmatione,* 1927; J. D. C. Fisher, *Christian Initiation. Baptism in the Medieval West,* 1965; J. D. C. Fisher, *Christian Initiation. The Reformation Period,* 1970; P. J. Jagger, *Christian Initiation, 1552-1969,* 1970; G. W. H. Lampe, *The Seal of the Spirit,* 1951; A. J. Mason, *The Relation of Confirmation to Baptism,* 1893; L. L. Mitchell, *Baptismal Anointing,* 1966; S. L. Ollard, ed., *Confirmation or the Laying on of Hands,* 1926; E. C. Whitaker, *Documents of the Baptismal Liturgy,* [2]1970; J. Ysebaert, *Greek Baptismal Terminology,* 1962.

E. C. WHITAKER

Congregationalist Worship

The earliest worship of the English Congregationalists had affinities with Presbyterianism and with the Society of Friends. It was both biblical in seeking precedents for all its ordinances and for their content and also charismatic in stressing the role of the Holy Spirit in worship. Had it been biblically-based alone, it would have been indistinguishable from the liturgies of the Presbyterian churches, as in Calvin's *La Forme des Prières* or in John Knox's *Genevan Service Book.* Had it been simply Spirit-led, without a consistently biblical basis, it could easily have led to the silent worship of the Quakers. Like Presbyterian worship, early Congregationalist worship insisted upon six ordinances: prayer; praise; preaching; baptism and the Lord's Supper; catechizing; and the exercise of discipline. Its single important difference from the Presbyterians was in the demand that public prayer, following Rom. 8.26,27, should be 'not in any *prescribed* form of prayer, or *studied* liturgie, but in such manner as the Spirit of grace and of prayer who teacheth all the people of God, what and how to pray . . . helpeth our infirmities, we having respect therein to the necessities of the people, the estate of the times, and the work of Christ in our hands' (John Cotton, *The Way of the Churches of Christ in New England,* 1645, p. 65).

This distinctive emphasis on free prayer was supported by six arguments. The reliance upon liturgy would deprive minister and people of the capacity to pray in their own thoughts and words. It was also argued that set forms could not meet the varied needs of differing congregations and occasions. Further, the implication that God could only be worshipped properly in a set liturgy was idolatry, in that it equated the liturgy with the Bible and infringed Christian liberty. Yet again, the constant use of set prayers would lead to the familiarity that breeds contempt or heedlessness. John Owen, the Puritan Vice-Chancellor of Oxford, accused the imposers of liturgies of bringing persecution into the church – 'Fire and faggot into the Christian religion'. Finally, and most compellingly, the point was made that read prayers utterly contradicted the appropriate approach to a heavenly Father by his children, especially as he had promised to help the infirmities of his children by the Holy Spirit. Liturgies or set forms must be abandoned like crutches that God's people may walk in the power of faith. So persuasively were these arguments presented by the small number of independent ministers (the earlier name for Congregationalists) at the Westminster Assembly of Divines called to provide a national settlement of religion in the Cromwellian era that they compelled the Presbyterians to drop their demand for a more biblically-based Genevan type liturgy and instead provided a manual or *Directory for the Public Worship of God Throughout the Three Kingdoms* (1644).

The importance of this manual of worship, prescribing the order of the items in public worship, but not the words which are to be used, is that it has provided the standard shape of worship for the Calvinistic churches (Presbyterian and Congregational, as well as that of the Particular Baptists) in the English-speaking world for approximately two hundred and fifty years.

The other pioneering contribution made to worship by Congregationalism came from the pen of Isaac Watts; the Baptist Benjamin Keach had preceded him in time, but not in quality. Watts, in *The Psalms of David imitated in the Language of the New Testament*, made the transition from the old covenant to the new, teaching 'my author to speak like a Christian'. It was then only a short step to the hymn of Christian experience; Watts took this in *Hymns and Spiritual Songs*. His most famous paraphrase is of Ps. 90: 'Our God, our help in ages past' and his most famous hymn is 'When I survey the wondrous cross'.

The strength of the Congregationalist and Puritan tradition in worship was fourfold. (1) Its biblical and revelational emphasis gave it an august objectivity, unchallenged until the arrival of the eighteenth-century Deists and the nineteenth-century historical critics of the Bible. (2) Its second quality was its relevance to life, for this worship held in simple scrubbed meeting-houses was the incentive to, never the substitute for, civic duty, and the exercise of ecclesiastical discipline guarded against unworthy recipients of the Lord's Supper. Also, special days of thanksgiving and humiliation, and the keeping of spiritual diaries as moral ledger books, as well as the practice of family and private prayer daily, all kept morality rooted in devotion. (3) This worship also had the merit of flexibility, spontaneity and warmth. (4) Finally, on the positive side, any tendency to eccentricity or subjectivity due to the absence of a set liturgy was corrected by

the biblical authority of the worship, the unity of Calvinistic theology which controlled it, and the standard shape of worship provided by the Westminster *Directory*.

It did, as its later history was to prove, have serious weaknesses. These included the absence of creeds for which covenants were not wholly a satisfactory substitute; the disuse of the red-letter days of the Christian year; the infrequent celebration of the Lord's Supper; the excessive didacticism of the pastoral prayers and prolix sermons; and the depreciation of symbolism and colour in art and architecture, and of ceremony in worship.

In time the Puritan and classical heritage was dissolved through rationalism, moralism, and pietism, and activism replaced adoration, while the warm-hearted fellowship replaced the theocratic community. There ensued a serious revaluation of the tradition in the late nineteenth and early twentieth centuries. The trend was away from spontaneous to pre-composed prayers, and from the combination of forms of prayer and free prayer to the adoption of liturgies. What individual congregations or their ministers of a 'high church' outlook did in the nineteenth century became a permissive option for all congregations in the twentieth century. By 1920 the Congregational Union of England and Wales had published its own denominational service-book, *The Book of Congregational Worship*, the work of a committee that included the theologian P. T. Forsyth. It was a portent of the future. In the USA the Congregational churches produced in 1948 an important book, *A Book of Worship for Free Churches*. The wheel had come full circle. A denomination that had originated in North America because of the dissatisfaction of the Puritans with a nationally-imposed liturgy (*BCP*) was now seeking to unify its people in a liturgy that expressed the ecumenical insights of the century.

Horton Davies, *The Worship of the English Puritans*, 1948; Horton Davies, *Worship and Theology in England, 1900-1965*, 1965, ch.X; A. G. Matthews, 'Puritan Worship' in Nathaniel Micklem, ed., *Christian Worship*, 1935.

HORTON DAVIES

Consecration of Churches

The consecration of churches is the act of solemnly dedicating them to God for the purposes of worship.

Solomon's dedication of the Temple (I Kings 8.63) provided the model for the consecration of churches by Christians, but no special rite was at first devised. The dedication of the cathedral of Tyre in 314, described by Eusebius, simply involved the celebration of the eucharist. As late as the sixth century the saying of mass was still regarded as the essential element and so the Leonine Sacramentary (c. 540) has only a proper collect, *oratio super oblata*, preface (qq.v.) and postcommunion. The first special feature to be introduced was the deposition of relics which were brought into the new building and enclosed in the altar (q.v.) immediately before the mass. A second feature, which was adopted in the eighth century, consisted of lustrations. This practice of sprinkling buildings with holy water had been used in relation to pagan temples converted for use as churches and thence became an element in the rite of consecration of a new building. So by the eighth and ninth centuries the Roman form of consecration consisted of the following: (1) the carrying of the relics in procession; (2) the entrance of the bishop and his party to prepare the mortar for sealing the altar stone and to wash the altar with exorcized water; (3) the temporary withdrawal of the clergy; (4) a second entrance, followed by the anointing of the altar and the deposition of the relics; (5) the blessing of the entire building; (6) the mass. The model of this rite is that of a funeral, the central idea being that the tomb-altar of the saint, represented by his relics, is prepared and he is conveyed to it and buried within it.

The Gallican model was based upon a different rationale, that of baptism and confirmation (qq.v.), the church being washed and anointed. The main elements of this form are to be found in the Angoulême Sacramentary (c. 800), the material probably dating from the eighth century. They are: (1) arrival of the clergy; (2) blessing of a mixture of wine and water; (3) aspersion of the whole church and then of the altar; (4) the anointing of the altar and then of the whole building; (5) the blessing of the altar linen and vessels; (6) withdrawal to fetch the relics; (7) return and placing of the relics in the altar; (8) the mass. *Ordo* XLI (775-800) adds a further feature to this sequence, the alphabet ceremony which took place immediately upon the first entrance of the clergy.

This consists of inscribing the alphabet twice along the lines of a St Andrew's cross traced on the pavement in ashes or sand. In this way the building was claimed for Christ, represented by the initial of *Christus* in Greek.

The medieval Western rite was the result of the fusion, in the tenth century, of these Roman and Gallican forms. The prominence given by the former to the deposition was retained, but the washing and anointing and alphabet ceremony were preserved from the latter. This rite, with some minor modifications such as the inclusion of the seven penitential psalms (i.e. Pss. 6, 32, 38, 51, 102, 130 and 143), has persisted within Roman Catholicism up to the present day, since the revision of 1961 was largely an abbreviation and simplification by the removal of doublets, leaving the elaborate fundamental structure untouched. The form is therefore: (1) the bishop is met by the clergy and a procession goes to fetch the relics; (2) the procession makes a threefold circuit of the exterior while the bishop sprinkles the walls; (3) the procession enters, after the bishop has knocked on the door, and the alphabet ceremony follows; (4) lustrations and anointings; (5) the relics are placed in the altar, which is censed and anointed; (6) the mass begins.

Although the deposition of relics is a common feature in Eastern Orthodox rites, e.g. in the Byzantine and Syrian, it is not considered to be an essential element. Rather, the focal point is the solemn consecration of the altar, which is washed and anointed and draped with the *antimension* – a square of linen or silk with relics inserted in one corner. Even the aspersion of the walls and their anointing with oil are to be understood as an extension of what is done to the altar. A circuit of the exterior, a series of litanies, the blessing and censing of the iconostasis (q.v.) and finally the celebration of the eucharist bring the rite to its conclusion and reveal certain parallels with Gallican customs.

Consecration rites were not an immediate concern of the Reformers. The number of churches existing in England in the sixteenth century was ample, and so the question of a form of dedication scarcely arose. Similarly in Germany, it was not until after the Thirty Years' War that new Lutheran churches were built in any quantity. The Puritans rejected all idea of consecrating buildings, partly because they would not countenance the continuation of any medieval practice and partly because they could find no reference to consecrated buildings in the NT. It was not until 1620 that the first Anglican rite was produced by Bishop Andrews and this consisted of a perambulation with appropriate prayers at each stopping place – baptistery, pulpit, lectern, etc. – followed by morning prayer and the eucharist, the general concept being that consecration is effected by use. In 1662 and 1663 the convocations discussed the provision of an official form, but none was ever promulgated with authority, and to the present day, in England, there are only diocesan uses, often based on rites by Bishop Wordsworth of 1887 and 1898. Other provinces of the Anglican Communion, however, have authorized forms, frequently included in their prayer books. In 1666 an Irish rite was promulgated; in 1799 one was approved in the USA, and there exist similar orders for South Africa, Canada and Scotland.

The orders in use in Lutheran churches are noticeable for their simplicity. One example will suffice as an illustration. The rite published by the United Evangelical Church in Germany in 1952 consists of four parts: (1) the bishop, clergy, elders, confirmation candidates, builders, etc. all gather in the building that has been in use for worship prior to the erection of the new church. A short service takes place, with address and prayers; (2) procession to the new building to the singing of hymns and blowing of trumpets. One of the confirmation candidates carries the key, while the clergy bear Bible, vessels, etc. A hymn is sung before the door, which is eventually opened; (3) after an introit psalm or hymn, there is prayer and short address, the Lord's Prayer and consecration formula. The vessels, etc. have prayers said over them; (4) the main Sunday service follows, frequently with communion.

Reformed practice is not markedly different. So the consecration service of the French Reformed Church (1955) opens with a procession in which are carried a Bible, the baptismal bowl, the paten and chalice. During the ensuing prayers and lessons, the Bible is placed on the lectern, the bowl on the table, etc. and the whole culminates in a celebration of the eucharist.

Other churches, which have no authorized service-books, have a number of models suggested. *The Call to Worship* (1956) includes a possible dedication rite for the Baptists. The service begins at the church door which is ceremonially opened. The minister proceeds to the pulpit and leads the congregation in an act of dedication of the church and people to God. A prayer for the dedication of the baptistery is also included, and there is provision for a lesson, hymn and sermon. According to a Congregational form (*Services and Prayers*, 1959), the presiding minister knocks on the door and, to the accompaniment of verses from the psalms and followed by the choir and congregation, takes his place. Lessons from OT and NT follow and then the act of dedication which is concluded with a blessing. In the Methodist book for optional use (*Divine Worship*, 1935) there is a form for the dedication of churches which may be adapted for use on anniversaries – it consists of prayers, lections, hymns, sermon and an act of dedication.

At the present day it is particularly the rationale of consecration that needs further exploration and analysis rather than the exact forms it may take. In the past there have been three ways in which consecration has been understood to be effected. First, by the provision of relics (the Roman form) – but this cannot be regarded as a *sine qua non* of Christian worship, since this was celebrated for decades before any relics existed and is performed to this day in houses, in the open air, etc., apart from any relics of a saint. Second, by being baptized and confirmed – but to treat a building as a human being is hardly more than a pious fiction. Thirdly, by use – but if this were correct the regular celebration of the eucharist in places other than churches would consecrate these too.

Basically consecration is thanksgiving. The rendering of thanks to God upon the opening of a new church is natural and right: this is its consecration. The result is that its God-relatedness is acknowledged, its function is declared and it is dedicated as an instrument of the mission of God.

J. G. Davies, *The Secular Use of Church Buildings*, 1968; R. W. Muncey, *A History of the Consecration of Churches and Churchyards*, 1930; G. G. Willis, *Further Essays in Early Roman Liturgy*, 1968.

EDITOR

Consecration Prayer

One of the many names of the eucharistic prayer or anaphora (q.v.); its currency in

English-speaking countries is due to the use
of 'Prayer of Consecration' as the title of this
prayer in the English *BCP* of 1662, following
the Scottish *Book of Common Prayer* of 1637.

W. JARDINE GRISBROOKE

Cope *see* Vestments (2*a*)

Coptic Worship

The official liturgical language of the Coptic
Church is the Bohairic (North Egyptian)
dialect of Coptic, although some use of Greek
continued for several centuries after the
definite separation of the Copts and the
Chalcedonians or Greek Orthodox of
Alexandria in the sixth century. *Kyrie eleison*
and other acclamations are still in that
language. The service-books were printed at
Rome by Coptic Catholics in 1736 and following; since the mid-nineteenth century, bi-
lingual Coptic-Arabic editions have been
produced in Egypt. Arabic was then introduced for a second reading of the lessons, and
is now commonly used for the audible parts
of the service.

A distinctive feature of the eucharistic
liturgy is the series of four lessons, all from
the NT. Those from the Pauline and Catholic
epistles and Acts precede the gospel, which
is commonly read by the senior cleric present.
Three eucharistic prayers are in use, though
there are traces of others used formerly.
The Anaphora (q.v.) of St Cyril represents the
ancient Alexandrian liturgy in a somewhat
purer form than the Greek St Mark; it is,
however, only used occasionally in Lent.
The normal Anaphora 'of St Basil' is a shorter
form of the Syro-Byzantine type represented
by the Greek Basil and Chrysostom. It
probably came into Egypt through the influence of Constantinople as the metropolis of
the empire in the sixth century. The third
Anaphora 'of St Gregory', used at the midnight liturgies of Christmas, Epiphany and
Easter, has the unusual feature of being
addressed to the Son. In the intercessions
there are prayers for blessing on the land in
varying forms for the ancient Egyptian
seasons of inundation, sowing, and harvest.
Other interesting features are the Three
Great Prayers – for peace (of the church and
the world), for the patriarch and clergy, and
for the congregations, which derive from
ancient Alexandrian forms – and the priest's
moving profession of faith before his communion – 'this is in truth the body and blood

of Emmanuel our God . . .' The eucharistic
bread is in small leavened loaves, stamped
with a design including the *trisagion* in Greek.
Several are presented to the celebrant at the
beginning of the liturgy, of which he selects
one. The wine is commonly made from the
fermented juice of raisins.

Baptismal and other sacramental rites
resemble those of the Greek Orthodox.
Baptism begins with exorcisms (qq.v.) which
assume that the candidates are converts
from idolatry, and anointing. Four lessons
follow, as in the liturgy, further anointings,
and the actual baptism, for which the positive
form 'I baptize thee . . .' is used, as in the West;
and finally christmation for the gift of the
Spirit with the chrism consecrated by the
patriarch. Unction of the sick calls for the
lighting of seven lamps by seven priests if
available. It is often administered as a public
healing service on the Friday before Palm
Sunday. Funeral offices, varying for adults,
children, clergy, and monastics, each consist
of a psalm, epistle, gospel, and prayers. Holy
Week is marked by long readings from the OT
and NT terminating with the Apocalypse and
Gospel of John on Easter Eve. An impressive
ceremony is the procession of the entombment on Good Friday afternoon. Water is
blessed at the Epiphany, and there are foot-
washing ceremonies on Maundy Thursday
and the feast of St Peter and St Paul. The
temporale is arranged by the ancient Egyptian
calendar, with twelve thirty-day months
beginning on 29 August and five or six extra
days at the end.

There are seven daily offices (q.v.) – midnight, dawn, third, sixth, and ninth hours,
vespers and compline, with a final prayer of
the curtain for monks. Following ancient
monastic practice they provide for daily
recitation of the entire psalter, but even in
monasteries selections are now used in the
morning and evening. A special feature is the
morning and evening offering of incense
(q.v.) with hymns and prayers, perhaps
derived from the customs of ancient Egyptian
temples. It precedes the morning and follows
the evening offices, and on certain occasions
replaces parts of them.

A traditional (medieval) Coptic church has
a solid sanctuary screen (q.v.), with a central
door flanked by windows and side doors, and
lighter screens to mark off the choir and the
men's and women's sections of the nave
(q.v.). But the latter divisions are now omitted

in modern churches, and often removed from old ones. Music has been preserved by oral tradition, but is now also studied formally. The blind are often trained as church singers and ordained as deacons.

O.H.E. Burmester, *The Egyptian or Coptic Church, A Detailed Description of her Liturgical Services*, 1967.

E. R. HARDY

Corporal

A square of linen measuring about twenty inches square which is spread in the middle of the altar-top before or at the time of the offertory (q.v.) (Latin *corpus*, body, referring to the sacramental context). The correct material is linen of good quality, rather than lawn trimmed with lace. The *BCP* in the rubric (q.v.) after the administration of holy communion expects that there will be a

Plate 23   Two corporals, one beneath and one covering the chalice

second corporal to be used to cover the chalice and paten (qq.v.) if they still contain the remains of the consecrated elements of bread and wine. These two corporals are derived from the one very large cloth, known as the *palla corporalis*, which in the earlier centuries was used as a corporal and drawn up over the chalice. Our present custom of having this cloth divided into two parts belongs to the Gothic or late medieval period. When the corporals are not in use they are kept in a case known as the *burse*. *See* Plate 23.

P. Dearmer, *The Linen Ornaments of the Church*, 1929; C. E. Pocknee, ed., *The Parson's Handbook*, rev. ed., 1965.

C. E. POCKNEE

Corpus Christi

This observance on the Thursday after Trinity Sunday is associated with eucharistic devotion. It was established by Rome in the thirteenth century following the advocacy of Juliana of Liège. It is still celebrated in many countries by a procession of the eucharistic host in a monstrance (q.v.).

A. A. MCARTHUR

Covenant Service

The covenant service is, at present, a special Methodist service, usually held on the first Sunday of the year, at which church members rededicate themselves to God.

1. *Beginnings of the Custom.* John Wesley held the first formal covenant service in London on 11 August 1755. He knew the idea of covenanting with God from OT literature (*see* II Kings 23), Anglican devotional writing on baptism, confirmation and communion, and the devotional writings of Puritans and later Free Churchmen (notably Philip Doddridge). He transformed a custom of private devotion into a corporate renewal of dedication.

2. *Development of the Custom.* Introduced by Wesley at main centres of his work (London, Dublin, Bristol, Newcastle), the service spread throughout early Methodism. It was held in London during Wesley's annual visitation around the New Year. Many other societies imitated this, and the covenant service thus came to seem almost essentially a New Year observance. Apparently, Wesley usually linked the service with the communion. This his unordained helpers could not do, but the combination of covenant and communion service became general when the Methodists, after Wesley's death, came to hold their own communions regularly.

The service was most widely observed by Wesleyan Methodists, less regularly in the smaller Methodist denominations (Methodist New Connexion, Primitive Methodism, Bible Christians, United Methodist Free Churches, United Methodism). It is now almost universal in British and related Methodist churches and districts. It is known, but apparently little used, in American and cognate branches of Methodism. Charles Wesley wrote a hymn for the covenant service, 'Come, let us use the grace divine', now incorporated into the official liturgy. Participation, originally limited to Methodists in good standing, is now (in Britain) open to all Christians, as is communion.

Other traditions have shown interest in the covenant service. It has been adapted for use in the Church of South India, and for special occasions in the Church of England. It is frequently used for ecumenical services, especially where occasional intercommunion is possible.

3. *Content and Form of the Service.* Wesley's own service (published 1780) consisted of a long exhortation to make an explicit covenant with God (derived from *Vindiciae Pietatis*, 1663, by the Puritan Richard Alleine), followed by a lengthy prayer of self-dedication composed by Joseph Alleine. The communion apparently went on from the prayer of humble access. Wesleyan Methodism used this service, with only two major revisions (1879, 1897) until Methodist union (1932). Private individuals made unofficial revisions: J. A. MacDonald, 1883; anonymous Minister in Eccles, 1884; G. B. Robson, *c.* 1922. The smaller Methodist denominations each produced one or more forms of the service. After Methodist union, a form based on that of G. B. Robson was prepared for the *Book of Offices* (1936). The service begins with Charles Wesley's hymn, the *BCP* collect for purity and *Our Father*. The lesson is John 15.1-8. The first exhortation describes the Christian situation as God's promise (covenant) made to us in Jesus Christ, and our commitment (covenant) to live for God. This commitment is now to be renewed. Three acts of devotion now follow: adoration of the gracious Trinity; thanksgiving for God's faithful generosity to us; and confession of our unfaithfulness, with absolution. The second exhortation describes the difficulty of the Christian life, in self-abandonment to divine providence and readiness for total self-denial. This leads into the covenant prayer, the former part said by the celebrant, the second by the whole congregation: 'I am no longer my own, but thine. Put me to what thou wilt, rank me with whom thou wilt; put me to doing, put me to suffering; let me be employed for thee or laid aside for thee,

exalted for thee or brought low for thee . . .' The communion goes on with 'Lift up your hearts'.

A slight revision of this service was authorized by the Methodist Conference (1969) for experimental use, in preparation for the new service-book of British Methodism.

4. *Ecumenical Interest of the ·Covenant Service.* The interest lies in the unusually distinct emphasis on Christian self-dedication, congregationally expressed. No other act of worship regularly observed in any tradition does this in the same way (the nearest equivalent is the renewal of baptismal vows, in the Roman rite of Easter Eve). The pursuit of complete dedication to God in the strength of Christ's incarnation and passion and in the power of the Holy Spirit is a concept shared by the great confessions, and sufficiently central to the faith to serve as a major theme of common devotion.

5. *Some Questions of Principle on the Covenant Service.* The reluctance of some Methodists to take part in the service has raised the questions whether its delineation of the Christian life is too intense for regular repetition, or too demanding for most Christians, and therefore whether or not it should be a principal act of worship for the whole church. Various occasions for it have been suggested: the New Year (to consecrate a natural unit of human life), early September (to hallow a new Methodist church year), or Easter (to show our common dependence on the Risen Christ). The existing forms of the service have been accused of being wrongly introspective and man-centred, of paying inadequate attention to the resurrection and the Holy Spirit, and of saying too little of the maturity and liberty promised to the children of God. The custom of renewing the covenant has in itself been deprecated as tending to overshadow sacramental Christian initiation and to usurp the function of the eucharist in the constant renewal of the Christian life, and as being inconsistent with the uniqueness of Christ's mediation of the New Covenant. These serious issues, still under discussion, will doubtless affect the future development of the covenant service.

D. H. Tripp, *The Renewal of the Covenant in the Methodist Tradition*, 1969.

DAVID TRIPP

Creed, Creeds

In the earliest Christian church, candidates for baptism were required to confess their personal belief ('I believe') in the presence of the congregation. The earliest confessions of belief were short and simple: e.g. 'Jesus is Lord' (I Cor. 12.3) or 'I believe that Jesus Christ is the Son of God' (Acts 8.37, RV margin only). Eventually such simple baptismal creeds developed into the confession which we know as the Apostles' Creed. Later, another kind of creed, the Conciliar Creed ('We believe') was promulgated with the authority of a council; its purpose was to define the true faith as over against the teaching of heretics. The Nicene Creed (now usually regarded as a product of the Council of Constantinople in 381, but expressing the faith of the preceding Council of Nicea in 325) is the most important and best known of the conciliar creeds of the patristic age. Its use at the eucharist appears to have been introduced by Peter the Fuller at Antioch in 473 to emphasize the adherence of the Monophysites to Nicea as opposed, by them, to Chalcedon. In the early sixth century its use spread to Constantinople and it was adopted in Spain by the third Council of Toledo in 589 as a test for Arians, being recited before the fraction (q.v.); in the Mozarabic rite it still retains this unusual position. It was later favoured by Charlemagne but was not accepted in Rome until 1014 by Benedict VIII under the influence of the emperor Henry II.

But besides these two credal types there was a third form of confessional utterance, viz. the credal hymn. Examples are, in the opinion of the majority of NT scholars, to be found in the NT, and at least some of these date from the apostolic period. The best known is Phil. 2.6-11, in which the pre-existence of Christ with God, his taking the form of man (and a slave at that), his death on the cross and his exaltation and universal lordship, are quoted by Paul as if from a liturgical setting which would be well known to the recipients of his letter. Other examples might be I Tim. 3.16; Eph. 4.4-10; and the doxologies in the Apocalypse. O. Cullmann writes: 'The need to confess one's faith according to a fixed text manifested itself in every gathering of the community. The believer wants to confess with the brethren before God what unites them before him. It was so already in the worship of the Syna-gogue, where in pronouncing the Shema, one confessed with all Israel that Yahweh is One. The confession of faith is pronounced within the liturgy at every divine service of the primitive Christian community.' Even more cogently Cullmann might have pointed to the recital of the *Heilsgeschichte* in the liturgy of the Temple (e.g. Pss. 105, 106 and many others).

This credal recital of God's saving acts is indeed an on-going characteristic of biblical-Christian liturgical worship. It arises naturally from the character of the faith as *historical*; it is a spontaneous thanksgiving for the salvation which God has wrought. Thus, many of the hymns which are most popular among Christian congregations to-day are those which embody the great themes of the proclamation of God's action in Christ 'for us men and for our salvation'. For example, 'At the name of Jesus' is a hymnal paraphrase and exposition of Phil. 2.6-11, and there are countless other examples in the hymn-books of all the churches. And, of course, in the main tradition of Christendom the recitation of the ancient creeds, whether said or sung, is a normal ingredient of liturgical worship. The choral singing of the Nicene Creed, set to the music of Merbecke in the sixteenth century and by many other composers right down to Beaumont in our own times, bears witness to the continuing 'need to confess one's faith according to a fixed text' in liturgical worship.

O. Cullmann, *The Earliest Christian Confessions*, ET, 1949; R.P. Martin, *Carmen Christi: Philippians ii. 5-11 in Recent Interpretation and in the Setting of Early Christian Worship*, 1967; J. T. Sanders, *The New Testament Christological Hymns: their Historical Religious Background*, 1971, which takes the view, not universally accepted, that the NT hymns are modelled on pre-Christian Gnostic forms.

ALAN RICHARDSON

Cross

The history of the use and development of this emblem in Christian worship is a long and complicated one. There was considerable reluctance to depict the crucifixion of Christ in the earlier centuries as that event was regarded by the early Christians from the side of Easter Day rather than Good Friday (qq.v.).

The complete absence of the depiction of the crucifixion in the paintings of the Roman catacombs, and even as late as the fifth century mosaics at Ravenna, should be noted. The cross was certainly used as a decorative symbol of triumph, as we can see in the mosaic in the saucer of the apse of St Apollinare in Classe, Ravenna. The earliest depictions of the cross with a figure are far from realistic and Christ is frequently shown with a diadem on his head and vested in the kingly *colobium*. His eyes are open and his arms outstretched (*see* Plate 24).

It is not until we come to the twelfth and thirteenth centuries under the impetus of the Franciscans, when the cultus of the passion was greatly developed, that realistic crucifixes (i.e. a cross bearing a figure of the crucified Christ) begin to appear, but this development does not reach its zenith until the fifteenth century in such works as those of Matthias Grünewald (d. 1528). (*See* Plate 25).

Processional crosses can be found as early as the fourth century, but the altar cross was introduced much later. In the Middle Ages altars in England seldom had a cross standing upon them since the Crucified was depicted in the middle of the reredos (q.v.). In the case of free-standing altars the processional cross was sometimes placed in a socket behind the altar. But towering crucifixes standing on a shelf behind the altar are a product of the Counter-Reformation in the Roman Catholic Church.

F. Cabrol-H. Leclerq, *Dictionnaire d'Archéologie Chrétienne et de Liturgie*, 1907ff., Tome 3, cols. 3045-3131; C. E. Pocknee, *Cross and Crucifix*, 1962.

C. E. POCKNEE

Plate 25   Grünewald crucifixion, Isenheim altar, Colmar, France

Plate 24   Thirteenth-century crucifix with
crowned and vested figure

Cross, Sign of *see* Gestures (1)

Crucifer

The person who carries the processional cross
on liturgical or ceremonial occasions.

P. HINCHLIFF

Crucifix

A cross (q.v.) bearing the figure of the crucified Christ.

EDITOR

Cruet

Derived from the medieval French *cruette*,
means 'little jug'. A pair of such vessels is
used to contain the wine and water for the
eucharist; while they are now usually made of
glass, sometimes with a lip or mounting of
precious metal, they were anciently made of
base metal such as pewter, or else of silver or
silver-gilt. Some very handsome examples of

silver-gilt 'flagons' for holding the wine and
water were made during the seventeenth and
eighteenth centuries for the churches in the
City of London and elsewhere.

J. Gilchrist, *Anglican Church Plate*, 1967.

C. E. POCKNEE

Culture and Worship

'Culture' is derived from the Latin 'colo', i.e.
'I devote, or apply, myself to'. It is concerned
with man's attempt to understand himself in
relation to his environment, personal and
impersonal. Through this confrontation,
patterns of culture emerge: language, ritual,
forms of art, buildings, structures of time.

Language is a primary activity of interpersonal communication. It also interprets
and implies action. Language cannot be
divorced from action. Yet, as a medium of
rational analysis, with its tendency to separate
reason and exalt it above the other human
faculties, language can inhibit or prevent
fully integrated action. Ritual (q.v.), by
stylizing and objectifying basic actions, events
and relationships, serves to give them continuity, validity and authority: so with the
cosmic myths enacted in ritual drama; the
theatre; ritual connected with such basic
functions as sex, eating and washing; and
worship. But ritual can also become an end in
itself, a means of escape. Art makes present,
and apprehensible, aspects of reality which
may not otherwise be apparent, or cannot be
conveyed adequately through other media.
Hence the great part played by art in the
religious life. Art can also merely imitate,
photograph-like, confirming perhaps a traditional pattern or approach to a thing, yet
giving no deeper insight into its reality.
Buildings may arise from purposeful action
by which people are drawn into deeper
community: so, ideally, with buildings for
worship. But they may, by enclosing people
within separate fields of space, inhibit or
prevent communication. Time can be the
sphere of creative action, and so of freedom
and of hope. Yet, as a pre-existing continuum
of space into which our activity must be
fitted, it can be a restrictive and anxiety-
producing phenomenon: the past conditions
and limits, the future threatens.

Man makes various judgments as to the
value of his environment and the patterns
through which he confronts it. First, that the
environment as it now stands is the only

given frame of reference within which man must discover his position: reality does not extend beyond this. Secondly, that such an environment proves inadequate, deceptive and imprisoning: man must be freed from this, stand outside it, if he is to reach a more genuine apprehension of reality. Thirdly, that this environment does provide the framework within which man must live. But it has definite limitations. The need for ecstasy (standing outside) and revolution is recognized, and this has to happen through cultural patterns within the environment.

Patterns of culture, therefore, can be either creative, or divisive and limiting. They are for the development of understanding and communication. They provide necessary safeguards and frameworks within which man may grow in relationship and knowledge. They help man to position himself in relation to his environment and so reach some idea of his identity, some sense of security. As such they are creative. But these patterns can also limit or prevent understanding and communication. They can divide men through lack of creative interchange between them: undoubtedly this is reinforced by the analytical, compartmentalizing tendency of classical, Western culture, with its stress on the rational. They can become negative safeguards, shields behind which man hides to avoid the pain of exposure to other viewpoints and apprehensions of reality, and the discovery of his own weaknesses. Man comes to find security and identity in the patterns of culture, rather than in the growth towards deeper understanding and communication for which they provide the framework. As such they are divisive and limiting.

Culture essentially is for the formation of man in relationship, primarily with persons, but beyond this with his total environment, so that he may reach authentic knowledge of reality and of his position within this reality. For this to happen two things must be realized. First, that reality is many-levelled, and that, within this, patterns of culture are complementary. Secondly, that whenever such patterns become divisive and limiting there is the need for revolution.

Christian worship is man's expression of the worth of God and of his environment within the dimension of God's action. It is concerned with understanding and communication in the context of the divine. Worship involves the patterns of culture –

language, ritual, art, buildings, time. It is a ritual action for the projection and objectifying of one's position in relation to environment within the divine context. The degree of structure in worship varies between different traditions, according to views as to how far the direction and content of worship must be controlled by definite structure. But the fact that worship is an objective ritual action, leading towards deeper understanding and communication, argues strongly for the importance of regular acts of worship.

Worship has three fundamental dimensions. First, the work of God in Christ towards man and creation, revealed finally and most completely in the ministry, death and resurrection of Jesus Christ: this is an action of total self-giving, reaching out in relationship towards man and creation. Secondly, the life of the church as embodying within itself God's action. Thirdly, the life of the church as representative of the world, where God is active in creation and redemption, and as pointing to this action.

The central act of Christian worship is the eucharist (q.v.). This is the sacrament of eating and drinking in community: it interprets and makes present the self-giving action of God in Christ through the cross and resurrection. In this sacrament the church, by its response, is drawn into God's action: and through the church, all creation. How is this so? In the ministry of the word God communicates his purpose to man and challenges him to respond. Here it is basically through language that man attempts to understand, make present, and respond to the communication of God. In the ministry of the sacrament this divine activity of self-giving communication, and man's response, is confirmed and fully realized. The bread and wine represent Christ's life offered completely for man and, through his self-giving on the cross, transformed into the new life of the resurrection: the bread and wine become the resurrection body and blood of Christ. But they also represent man's life – his work, his culture – and the life of creation: he offers this in self-giving to God, for himself and all creation – but only through Christ. By sharing in Christ's body and blood, that is, his life, we and all that we offer are drawn into this life and so into deeper understanding and communication with one another. We become what we eat and drink.

There are in the eucharist two levels of action. On the one hand it is a thanksgiving for, and celebration of, God's finished work in creation and redemption. The offering of bread and wine affirms and celebrates man's community, his culture and his environment in so far as they realize God's self-giving love. But it is also a penitential action in which man confesses his brokenness and division and that of the world for which he offers. Through the eucharistic action, the fullness of God's work, which is far from being realized in the church's life or that of the rest of the world, is made present: this stands over against man's failure to realize self-giving love, not least in the patterns of culture which divide him and prevent understanding and communication.

Thus the eucharist action is ecstatic and revolutionary, breaking through all the attitudes, the patterns, and images of ourselves, other persons, and environment which divide and limit us. If culture, therefore, is for the formation of man, Christian worship, summed up in the eucharist, is for the transformation of man – the deepening of understanding and communication in relationship through union with Christ. This involves not only the celebration and preservation of existing community and culture, but also the creation of community and even of revolutionary cultural patterns.

There is naturally a strong formation element in worship, since it involves cultural patterns within which man's response to God, and so a transforming encounter between God and man, can take place. Hence the need for a regular, structured pattern of worship, as well as acts of worship more tied to particular situations and cultural patterns. The most pressing problem with regard to such regular, public worship is to determine a recognizable common culture to provide adequate patterns for response, understanding and communication in worship.

Worship is the activity of man in relationship with God. But the eucharist is primarily the action of God, though made present through man's responsive action. This places a big question mark over man's concern as to how he does worship, and what cultural patterns are most adequate and relevant for contemporary worship. All liturgical revision must be seen in the context of the God-man relationship, in which man responds to and realizes the action of God.

This action is outside time, though made present within time. Therefore worship can never become a mere cultural activity within time, conditioned by this or any other cultural patterns.

Worship, because it is both ecstatic and revolutionary, and also celebratory, is open to two dangers. First, it can become an ecstatic activity of the church, divorced from the life and concerns of the world. The church before the fourth century suffered from this. Admittedly it was in an underground situation. But also, to judge from its penitential discipline, it seems in great part to have viewed itself as the redeemed community which has nothing more to do with the world. Secondly, through its effort to meet, work through and transform the life of the world, the church can become accommodated to this life and conditioned by cultural patterns so that it loses the ecstatic and revolutionary dimension inherent in the divine action. The church of the fourth century and following, after Christianity had become the recognized religion of the state, by no means avoided this danger. To keep the necessary balance in its worship, both affirming and yet standing over against culture, is a task which the church has always been hard put to realize.

What of culture and worship today? There are at present two basic trends in culture to be noted. The first is a dissatisfaction with traditional patterns, an exploration into new possibilities, a disintegration of previously settled and monochrome cultures. Together with this there is a meeting of different cultural traditions, and an awareness of the relativity and complementarity of cultural patterns. The second is a deep concern for honest and genuine personal relationship in the face of the challenge from electro-technology, which while on one level it facilitates communication and awareness of concerns and needs on a worldwide scale, also keeps people apart and prevents face-to-face relationships. The church, in meeting and expressing the contemporary situation in its worship, must start primarily, not from any particular cultural tradition, but from the essential fullness of Christian belief and practice. There is much that is positive in the present exploratory climate and the search for meaningful experience outside the given, traditional patterns of culture and structures of society. Here is a search for understanding and communication, which can never rest content in any set of patterns held up as ultimate, but must always be open to new possibilities. The church and its worship has much to learn from this. On the other hand, in being open to the world, the church in its worship cannot afford to become so conditioned by the world that it jeopardizes its ecstatic and revolutionary dimension. The balance is one which is crucially difficult to maintain, and yet it is fundamental to Christian worship.

L. Bouyer, *Rite and Man*, 1963; R. Haughton, *The Transformation of Man,* 1967; M. McLuhan, *Understanding Media*, 1966; B. Wicker, *Culture and Liturgy*, 1963.

P. V. FISHER

Daily Offices *see* Canonical Hours

Dalmatic *see* Vestments (1*g*)

Deacon

The office of deacon is frequently mentioned in the NT though there is no evidence at all to support the tradition that the seven, whose appointment is described in Acts 6, were deacons. The tradition was strong enough, however, to persist over many centuries and to create the feeling that seven was the proper number of deacons, and in Rome the order was for a long time restricted to that number. In the NT the deacon was a minister associated with the presbyter/bishops (q.v.) in the ministry of the local church. They appear in much the same sort of position in the writings of the apostolic fathers. A little later there seems to have been some tension and jealousy between the orders of presbyters and deacons. Deacons are always formally reckoned as the third order and below the presbyters. On the other hand, they were a full-time and professional ministry, with clear liturgical and administrative functions at a time when the presbyters were hardly more than an advisory board. In Rome, especially, the deacons were of considerable importance and were often chosen to occupy the episcopal throne. Evidence for the importance of the deacon is to be found in the leading part played by Felicissimus in the opposition to Cyprian at Carthage, and the schism of Hippolytus may have been partly a result of presbyteral jealousy of the deacon's growing

importance. As presbyters gained a new position as the normal minister in charge of particular districts and congregations, the balance began to swing the other way. In the Middle Ages the parish priest became the local embodiment of the church's life, while the diaconate lost most of its real functions. In the early church the deacon had often exercised real power as the officer responsible for poor relief and, therefore, for administering the church's property. He had also possessed a prominent liturgical role, reading the lessons and especially the gospel, distributing the elements at the eucharist, directing the prayers of the congregation, generally maintaining order in the services, and assisting at baptism. By the end of the medieval period in the West the office of archdeacon, representing the deacon's administrative function, was almost invariably occupied by a priest. The vestigial liturgical functions, chiefly reading the gospel, were also normally performed by a priest. In the modern Anglican and Roman Catholic Churches the diaconate has become a grade through which a candidate for priest's orders passes for a brief period before being ordained to the higher grade. In the Eastern Churches the deacons have remained a quite distinct order with a liturgical function proper to them alone.

John Calvin included the office of deacon (together with pastors, doctors, and elders) in the fourfold ministry which he believed to be most consonant with the pattern of the apostolic church. In the Reformed tradition the deacon remains the officer charged with the care of the sick and the poor. It is a pastoral, charitable and administrative, rather than a liturgical, office. Baptist and Congregational Churches also use the title but the deacon in these traditions has a role in the celebration of the eucharist and distributes the elements.

H. W. Beyer, in *TDNT*, II, pp. 88-93; L. Vischer, ed., *The Ministry of Deacons*, 1965.

P. HINCHLIFF

Deaconess

In the fourth century the general and informal ministry and service of women in the Christian community seems to have been formalized in the office of deaconess. Before that there are many references to the service and devotion of widows and virgins and other Christian women without necessarily implying that they comprised a special order of ministry. By the fourth century, however, the deaconess's duties and functions were clearly defined. She performed many of the duties of a deacon (q.v.) in relation to the care of the sick and the poor, the maintenance of order in church and, particularly, assisting at the baptism (q.v.) of adult women. The office disappeared by the Middle Ages, but has been revived since about the middle of the nineteenth century in the German Lutheran, Anglican, Methodist and Presbyterian Churches. Her duties are usually to act as a general pastoral assistant in the parish or congregation. How far the deaconess is a 'minister' in any technical sense is usually far from clear and in the Anglican Church, for instance, there is considerable disagreement about whether a deaconess can properly be described as part of the 'ordained ministry' or not. Methodist deaconesses are sometimes in pastoral charge of congregations and are authorized to administer the sacraments.

P. HINCHLIFF

Dedication

Dedication is the act of formally making over something or somebody to another, and in Christian usage the other is God. Dedication is related to five liturgical acts.

1. The term has been used interchangeably with consecration, and so to describe the dedication of a church is to outline the rite of consecration (q.v.). A distinction is, however, made in modern English law between the two, dedication being a simple blessing while consecration is regarded as separating the building for ever from unhallowed uses. This differentiation has little or no basis in Christian usage or theological thought.

2. The dedication of a church also refers to the name given to a particular building, e.g. St Paul's or St Mary's. Strictly speaking the church is dedicated to God in honour of a saint or a divine mystery.

3. A dedication festival is the annual commemoration of the day of a church's consecration and is therefore to be distinguished from the patronal festival which is in honour of the patron saint. The first observance of such a feast is recorded by the fourth-century pilgrim Egeria, who describes the practice at Jerusalem in connection with the Church of the Resurrection and the Martyrion. According to her this takes place

on the same day as the dedication of the Jerusalem Temple by Solomon and it would appear to have been observed on 23 September.

The dedication festivals of the four main Roman basilicas were included in the general ecclesiastical calendar: the Lateran (9 November), St Peter and St Paul (18 November), Santa Maria Maggiore (5 August). Gregory the Great ordered the conversion of heathen festivals connected with temples in England into dedication festivals.

In 1536 the English Convocation fixed the first Sunday in October as the universal date. The Scottish and American prayer books provide for the festival, and the 1928 book does also, with the directive that, if the day of consecration is not known, the feast may be observed on the first Sunday in October.

4. Dedication is also used of the blessing or offering of liturgical objects to God. So the Church of Scotland has a series of forms for the dedication of an altar, the font (qq.v.), etc.

5. In churches which do not practise infant baptism, a service of dedication of the child is sometimes held at which the child receives a Christian name.

EDITOR

Dedication Festival
see Dedication (3)

Devotions *see* Benediction; Exposition; Forty Hours' Devotion; Reservation; Rosary; Sacred Heart; Stations of the Cross; Veneration of the Cross

Diptychs

The name diptych is derived from a hinged board, on the two wings of which were anciently written the names of persons, both living and departed, for whom the prayers of the church were specifically desired in the offering of the eucharistic sacrifice.

The diptychs (*see* **Anaphora** 9) appear to go back to the reading by a deacon (q.v.) of the names of those who had brought an offering of bread for the eucharist. Once the custom of making an offering as an act of prayer or thanksgiving on behalf of other individuals was established (which had certainly occurred by the middle of the third century), their names also, by a natural development, were read together with, and in the same way as, those of the offerers themselves. Originally, such vicarious offerings appear to have been made only, or at least normally, on behalf of the departed; hence there was added to the existing list of the names of the (living) offerers a second list containing the names of the (departed) beneficiaries of the offerings. It was not long before a further development took place – that of making offerings for other people still living: early examples of this include the provision of the ancient Roman rite that godparents should offer for their godchildren while the latter are still catechumens (q.v.). Except in cases of this kind, however, for which special provision was made, the names of the living beneficiaries of the offerings appear not to have been read separately, but to have been added to the list of the offerers. Another slightly later development was the addition of yet another list, containing the names – sometimes only the classes – of martyrs (and then other saints as well) for whom it was desired to give thanks, separately from the rest of the departed. The diptychs, then, may be defined for practical purposes as 'intercessions for, or commemorations of, specified persons, living and departed, by name, offered in close and intimate connection with the offering of the eucharist itself'; the name 'diptychs' should not be interpreted too literally, as there are often sub-divisions within the basic divisions of living and departed – the Roman diptychs in the early Middle Ages, for example, may on certain occasions have comprised up to seven lists of names. The actual place in the eucharist at which the diptychs are read in the historic liturgies varies: this variation, indeed, is one of the principal structural distinctions between the eucharistic prayers of different traditions. In the Eastern liturgies of the Antiochene family (including the Byzantine, commonly called 'the Orthodox liturgy') they are placed in the second part of the prayer, after the consecration; in those of the Alexandrine family they are placed in the first part of the prayer, before the consecration; in the West, the historic Roman canon divides the diptychs – the diptych of the living occurs in the former part of the prayer, and that of the dead in the latter part; the ancient Hispano-Gallican liturgies of the West placed the diptychs before the eucharistic prayer, after the offertory (q.v.). Some scholars have said that this was their original position in the Roman rite as well, but the

evidence which is cited in favour of this assertion does not, when closely examined, support it.

In the East the diptychs very early came to be expanded into a more general intercession; in the West, except for certain isolated instances, they retained their original character more closely. In East and West alike the practice, dating from the early Middle Ages, of reciting the greater part of the eucharistic prayer in secret (q.v.) inevitably diminished the pastoral effectiveness of diptychs recited in the course of it, and other provision was made to supplement them, e.g. in the Byzantine East in the prothesis (q.v.) and at the great entrance (q.v.), and in the West during the Middle Ages, in the bidding (q.v.) of the bedes. The theological rationale of the diptychs, and any other intercession, in the eucharistic prayer is briefly discussed in connection with the anaphora (q.v.).

W. Jardine Grisbrooke, 'Intercession at the Eucharist', in *Studia Liturgica*, V, 1, 1966, pp. 20-44; *ibid.*, V. 2, 1966, pp. 87-103. For a detailed study of the Roman diptychs, *see* J. A. Jungmann, *The Mass of the Roman Rite*, II, 1955, pp. 152-87, 237-59.

W. JARDINE GRISBROOKE

Disciples of Christ *see* Christian Church (Disciples of Christ) Worship

Dismissal

The act of sending forth the worshippers at the end of a service. In the early church, the catchumens (q.v.) were dismissed after the ministry of the word. By the third century, a prayer for those being dismissed was inserted at the beginning of the community prayer. Then in the next century, they were allowed to stay until the completion of that part of the prayer of the church which was on their behalf. With the disappearance of the catechumenate, the need for these dismissals ceased, but they still survive in the Byzantine rite.

At the conclusion of the whole service, there was a further act of dismissal of the faithful. The Roman form was terse, namely *Ite missa est*, to which was added an introduction and a response: *Dominus vobiscum – Deo gratias*. The Gallican formula, however, seems to have *Benedicamus Domino*. From the eleventh century both were used, the

Roman when there was a *Gloria* and the Gallican on other occasions. At the present day several new formulae are in use to emphasize that the Christians' duty is in the world and that worship is not an isolated incident.

J. A. Jungmann, *The Mass of the Roman Rite,* rev. ed., 1959, pp. 301-4, 535-58.

EDITOR

Disposal of Eucharistic Remains

During the patristic period there was universal agreement that the consecrated elements at the eucharist should be treated with reverence. As early as Tertullian we read: 'We feel pained should any wine or bread, even though our own, be cast upon the ground' (*de Cor.* 3). What was left after communion was carried into the sacristy (q.v.) at the conclusion of the service. There the remains were kept for at least one day following a precept of the Mosaic law in relation to the disposal of certain sacrifices (Lev. 7.16). They were then consumed by the priests or, in certain areas, burned, again following Jewish practice (Lev. 7.17), or given, in Evagrius' phrase, to 'uncorrupted boys' (*Hist. eccl.* 4.36). The practice of having the ablutions (q.v.) immediately after communion meant that in the West the consumption of the remains eventually took place in the church itself before the end of the mass.

In the Eastern Orthodox churches the early practice has continued, i.e. consumption in the sacristy after the service. The Anglican custom is similar to the medieval and modern Roman practice, i.e. what is left is eaten and drunk immediately after all have communicated. In the Lutheran churches the elements remaining are often stored with those that are to serve for future celebrations, but sometimes they are thrown away. The Reformed practice is not uniform, but the bread is sometimes burned. Among Methodists the wine is returned to the bottle and the bread put out for birds or otherwise thrown away.

W. Lockton, *The Treatment of the Remains at the Eucharist after Holy Communion and the Time of the Ablutions,* 1920.

EDITOR

The Divine Office

It is generally only at Christmas, Holy Week and Pentecost, that the average Catholic hears any part of the divine office – to which Benedict in his Rule declared 'nothing should be preferred' by the monks. On these days mattins and lauds are sung, but this is otherwise rare except in monasteries or convents of strict observance, and even there the vernacular said office is becoming the 'in' thing. A revival of participation in the lovely hours of vespers and compline (qq.v.) would be most welcome and in particular would give opportunity for the many fine polyphonic settings of *Magnificat* or *Nunc Dimittis* to be heard where adquate choirs exist. *Tenebrae* (q.v.) ('Darkness'), in structure a variant of mattins, takes its title from the responsory '*Tenebrae factae sunt*' ('There was darkness when they crucified Jesus'). The *Tenebrae* is sung on the three great days of Holy Week, Maundy Thursday, Good Friday and Holy Saturday. The service is divided into three nocturns, each containing three psalms with their antiphons and three 'lessons', each followed by long responsories. Victoria's settings of the latter are to be found in his masterpiece *Officium Hebdomadae Sanctae* (Office of Holy Week). The texts ('lessons') of the first nocturns are taken from the *Lamentations of the Prophet Jeremiah*, of which Palestrina composed four sets. The plainsong settings of all this material are among the finest in the whole *corpus* of the chant.

ALEC ROBERTSON

Doxology

An ascription of praise (Greek *doxologia*, lit. 'words of glory'), usually trinitarian in form, and often beginning with, or including, the word 'glory'.

The 'lesser doxology' (*see* **Anaphora** 10) is composed of the two verses commonly added, in most Christian liturgies, to the end of psalms and canticles: 'Glory be to the Father, and to the Son, and to the Holy Spirit; as it was in the beginning, is now, and ever shall be, world without end. Amen.' In the Eastern liturgies the second verse usually runs: 'both now, and for ever, and world without end. Amen.'

The 'greater doxology' is the hymn *Glory be to God on High*, which exists in a number of versions, and dates from at latest the third quarter of the fourth century. In the fifth-century Codex Alexandrinus it is entitled 'morning hymn', and it features as such in the divine office of a number of the historic liturgies, notably the Byzantine rite, in which it is the climax of the morning office of *orthros* or mattins (q.v.).

The use of this hymn at the eucharist is peculiar to the West. By the beginning of the sixth century it had already an established place in the mass at Rome, although only when a bishop was the president; not till the eleventh century was the present rule finally settled, by which it is used at all masses on Sundays and feasts, although this had already been the custom in many places for some centuries. In the Roman rite, and in other historic Western rites when it has been used at the mass, as well as in the Lutheran liturgy, the *Gloria* has always been sung after the entrance and before the collect (q.v.) of the day, as a preparatory hymn of praise and prayer, for which use it is particularly well suited; its transference to a position after the communion is a peculiarity of the *BCP* and liturgies derived from it.

J. A. Jungmann, *The Mass of the Roman Rite*, I, 1951, pp. 346-59.

                                                            W. JARDINE GRISBROOKE

Dry mass *see* Ante-communion

East Syrian Worship

1. *Historical.* The East Syrian Church (known to many as the Nestorian or Chaldean church) is the Syrian Church of Antioch as it developed east of the frontiers of the Roman-Byzantine empire. Its centre was Nisibis, but its distinctiveness as a tradition could be dated from the Synod of Beth Lapat in AD 484, when this church recognized Theodore of Mopsuestia as its official teacher, i.e. his teachings were to be the standard by which the faith of other churches was to be tested. During the seventh and later centuries this church spread to Turkestan (now in the Central Asian republics of the USSR) with bishops in Samarkent, Tashkent, Karakoram and also in Tibet as well as in China and India. Today this church, apart from a part now in the Roman Catholic communion, is limited to small pockets in USA, Iraq, Iran and India. The patriarch, Mar Shem'un, lives in America.

2. *Liturgical books.* The main eucharistic liturgies are three, which go by the names of (1) Addai and Mari, (2) Theodore of Mopsuestia and (3) Nestorius. In addition to various lectionaries (one for the gospels, a second for the apostle Paul and the *qaryana* which contains the first two lessons for the liturgical office, from the OT and the Acts), they have the *turgame*, which are homilies on the lessons in the form of hymns to be chanted with the aid of the psalter (*Dawida*), consecration of an altar (without chrism), prayers for ferial days, rites of marriage, the ordination manual, etc. The offices are chanted with the aid of the psalter (*Dawida*), the *hudra*, which contains the propers of the office, antiphons, hymns and prayers, the *gazza*, which contains the offices for the feasts of our Lord and the saints (except those that fall on Sundays), and other books for the choirs.

3. *The eucharistic liturgy.* What has astonished many liturgists about the liturgy of Addai and Mari is the absence of the words of institution; this is not unusual in the West Syrian tradition either. (The two other Chaldean anaphorae (q.v.) do have the words of institution.) This is shocking only to those who believe that the recital of the words of institution effect the consecration. There is a form of the Liturgy of the Presanctified (q.v.) for use on Good Friday.

The Liturgy of the Catechumens begins with the *Trisagion*, which is followed by the lections: one from the OT, and a second from either the OT or the Acts of the Apostles. These are supposed to be read from the *bema*, the raised platform in the centre of the church. After the first two lections, as the priest leaves the *bema* to ascend the altar, the *turgama* or the homiletic hymn for the day is sung, interpreting the main point of the lection from the Pauline epistles which follows it. The *turgama* of the gospel comes next, followed by the gospel itself.

The Liturgy of the Faithful begins with a litany of intercession much as in the Byzantine liturgy. The diptychs (q.v.) after the creed and the *lavabo* (q.v.) are also in the form of litanies. Mary is commemorated thus: 'For the memorial of Lady Mary the holy virgin who bare Christ our Lord and our Saviour.' The 318 fathers of Nicea are commemorated, and among the other fathers are mentioned both Theodore and Diodore as well as Nestorius, Flavian, Ambrose and Meletius. Emperor Constantine, his mother Helena, and later Byzantine emperors like Constans and Theodosius are also commemorated.

Even when the words of institution are missing, the epiclesis of the Holy Spirit upon the offering is given in full.

There is a second *lavabo* before the fraction and consignation. The priest censes his hands after the *lavabo* before proceeding to the fraction. The Lord's Prayer precedes the elevation and communion. The deacon who read the apostle is to administer the body from the paten and the deacon who gave the peace to administer the blood from the chalice.

The eucharist is called the *kudasha* or sanctification; the liturgical language is Eastern Syriac, though the vernacular is used in most churches today. Leavened bread is used and communion is generally now in both kinds by intinction.

4. *Offices.* The canonical offices are mainly three: *lelya* (nocturns), *sapra* (mattins) and *ramsha* (vespers) (*see* **Canonical Hours**).

5. *Other liturgies.* The baptismal liturgy is modelled on the eucharistic liturgy, with a pre-anaphora and anaphora for the consecration of the water with the chrism. Confirmation does not exist as a separate rite. Neither penance nor the sacrament of confession is used in this tradition. The anointing of the sick was also unknown until it was borrowed from the West in the sixteenth century. The marriage liturgy includes crowning and common drinking of wine from the same cup, but it is doubtful whether the East Syrians regarded marriage as a sacrament. The ordination practices are similar to those of other Eastern churches.

The text of Addai and Mari is given in ET in F. E. Brightman and C. E. Hammond, *Liturgies Eastern and Western*, vol. I, 1896, pp.247-305; G. P. Badger, *The Nestorians and Their Rituals*, 2 vols., 1852; H. W. Codrington, *Studies of the Syrian Liturgies*, 1952.

PAUL VERGHESE

East, Turning *see* Postures (1*a*)

Easter

The Pascha, the Christian Passover, the transformation of the Jewish Passover, was the great festival of redemption, and was a unitive commemoration of the cross and the resurrection. In the fourth century there was

a process of evolution, and with the development of Good Friday as we know it, the Pascha became limited to the theme of the resurrection. So Easter emerged in our understanding of the term.

The gospel narrative makes it abundantly clear that there was no coincidence in the fact that the passion and victory of the Lord took place at the season of the Passover. He chose the place and time of crisis, and with this in his heart he went up to the Holy City. The secrecy of the arrangements for the Last Supper indicate his intense desire to hold this meal with his disciples. The synoptic narrative in its various forms plainly states that the meal was the Passover. Therefore the Jewish day which began at sunset on Thursday was 15 Nisan. It began with the Passover, and before that day had ended at sunset on Friday the Messiah was dead. The Passover commemorated with joyfulness and thanksgiving the central event of the old covenant, the deliverance from Egypt. But in his cross and resurrection, the central events of the new covenant, the Lord Jesus Christ was to accomplish a new and supreme deliverance for all mankind, the redemption from sin and death. The cross and resurrection, seen as a unity, constituted the new exodus.

The Lord had foretold his passion and triumph and, within the context of these events, the Last Supper was of immense significance. The Pascha which was the interpretation of the exodus became on this most sacred night the interpretation of what was now at hand – the entering of the Lord into his kingdom through the gate of suffering and death. This Pascha therefore stands as the decisive frontier between, on the one side, the Jewish Passover of the old covenant and, on the other, both the annual Christian Pascha and the weekly celebration of the Christian eucharist. It is essential to remember that the annual and weekly Christian commemorations were related in the closest possible way. It was a perfectly natural development that the Christian 'Passover' should be an all-night festival, and that it should be divorced from the Jewish liturgical year, that is, from 15 Nisan. Rather, it was linked with the weekly liturgical day of the church, the Sunday, the day of the resurrection. The Christian Pascha began on the Saturday evening, that is, at the commencement of the primitive Sunday, and it culminated at the resurrection dawn with the sacraments of baptism and the eucharist. For it was in the light of the victory of the Lord's Day that the church looked upon the cross. The weekly Lord's Day (*see* **Sunday**) was very like the annual Pascha, for the eucharist was a memorial, not of the death alone, but of the death and the triumph.

The evidence of the third century enables us to see in the baptism at cockcrow, followed at once by the holy communion, the culmination of the Pascha, that is, the rejoicing in the resurrection. So also in the preliminary fast of the Pascha, which normally extended over the Friday as well as the Saturday, although early in the second century it would have been restricted to the Saturday, the dominant note must have been the passion. But the vigil contained the hope of the resurrection, and there would be no rigid distinction. The unity of the passion and victory was what the whole celebration of the Pascha conveyed. The great redeeming action into the benefits of which the candidates were baptized at dawn was the action of the cross and the resurrection. Baptism took place at the point where the sternness of the fast and vigil yielded to the rejoicing of that hour in which, according to tradition, the Lord rose triumphant over death, and into the joy of which the sorrow of the cross was merged. The sacrament of baptism led at once to the first communion of the newly-baptized. It is to be remembered that the sacrament of the Lord's Supper was essentially a recalling before God of the redeeming work of the Lord in his death and resurrection. This fundamental unity of conception must be grasped so that we may understand the full significance both of the primitive Sunday eucharist and the primitive Pascha.

If we wish to appreciate the evidence for the Paschal controversy of the late second century it is necessary to clear away the obstacle produced by the assumption that the Friday before the Pascha in the Christian world outside Asia had the character of the later Good Friday. Nor is there any warrant for assuming that the Pascha of the Asian Christians was different in nature from the Pascha elsewhere, that, in fact, it commemorated only the Passion. In the evidence of Eusebius, 14 Nisan is set over against the Lord's Day as the occasion of the Paschal festival. The identification of these days in terms of contrast and comparison includes the statement that 14 Nisan in Asia and the Lord's Day elsewhere were the days on which to complete the fast. But the ending of the fast meant the joy of the resurrection. There is no justification for the idea that at this time the Pascha of the church as a whole excluded the passion, nor that the festival of the Asian Christians excluded the resurrection.

The churches in general obviously felt that the festival of the cross and the resurrection, culminating as it did at cockcrow with the conclusion of the fast and the real beginning of the rejoicing in Christ's victory, must coincide with the weekly commemoration of the resurrection, the Lord's Day, and ought therefore to fall on the Sunday after the Passover. On the other hand, the minority group, the Asian churches, must have been impressed by the apparent appropriateness of celebrating the festival of the cross and the resurrection on the ancient day of 14 Nisan, the day when the Paschal lambs were sacrificed, the day of the crucifixion in the Fourth Gospel. Since this liturgical date was determined by a lunar, not a solar, calendar, the Pascha might fall on any day of the week, and the joy of the great annual commemoration of the resurrection would not usually coincide with the Lord's Day. This is strange to our minds, and it was not acceptable to Christians generally in the second century. Asia took a different starting-point from the church as a whole, and it may be said, simply as a statement of fact, that Asia began from the passion whereas the other churches began from the resurrection. But it cannot be said that the different starting-points controlled the whole nature of the festival. Rather, the evidence suggests that everywhere the Pascha, a unitive commemoration, moved through the austerity of the vigil and the memorial of the cross to the end of the fast and the glory of the triumph. The difference consisted, not in the nature of the liturgical celebration, but in the mode of the liturgical calculation.

If the Asian custom had involved the celebration of the Christian festival on 15 Nisan, the date of the Jewish Passover, it could be claimed that in that province there was not the decisive breach with the Jewish liturgical tradition which resulted elsewhere in the alignment of the Christian Pascha with the Lord's Day, the day of the resurrection. In that case it could be said that the Asian Christians were in this matter very conservative and were holding to the old Jewish ways. But the evidence indicates that the Asian festival was not kept on 15 Nisan, the day of the Jewish Pascha. The reference is specifically and plainly to 14 Nisan. It may well be that the Sunday Pascha and the Asian custom were not independent developments from the same source, but that the latter was a secondary form of growth dependent on the Last Supper of the Fourth Gospel, the meal described by the synoptists as the Passover, but which in terms of the Johannine account took place on 14 Nisan. The peculiar features of the Asian Pascha lead to the conclusion that it did not antedate the Fourth Gospel, and that it may be set aside as we look to the first century and the origin of the Pascha. Significantly, the Pascha has always been dependent on a lunar calendar. But during the first century the lunar yielded to a solar calendar except among the Jews and in the Greek cities. Towards the end of the first century the Jewish influence in the church was weakening. The institution of the Pascha must derive from a time when that influence was effective. It may be that the absence of details referring specifically to Passover customs in the Marcan story of the Last Supper indicates that when the narrative was shaped the annual Sunday Pascha and the weekly Sunday eucharist were already part of the established tradition of Christian worship. Certainly it is to the earliest days that we must look for the origin of these transformations of the natal Jewish environment.

G. Dix, *The Shape of the Liturgy*, [2]1945; G. Dix, *The Treatise on the Apostolic Tradition of St Hippolytus of Rome*, I, 1937; A. A. McArthur, *The Evolution of the Christian Year*, 1953.

A. A. MCARTHUR

Easter Garden or Sepulchre

The Easter garden is a model of the holy sepulchre used in the Holy Week (q.v.) services. Its origins are uncertain; it may have arisen, as did the Christmas crib, as a more or less spontaneous act of devotion during the early part of the Middle Ages. It took the form of a simple walled recess, a tomb, a vaulted enclosure, a chapel or a temporary structure. On Good Friday (q.v.), after vespers, it was the practice to place a cross in the sepulchre to represent the burial

of Christ and a candle was lit in front of the shrine. In the thirteenth century, in England and Normandy alone, one of three hosts consecrated at the mass on Maundy Thursday (q.v.) was also placed in the sepulchre. On Easter Day the cross and/or host was removed to represent the resurrection.

EDITOR

Eastward Position
see Postures (1*b*)

Elder

Etymologically the word is simply the Anglo-Saxon equivalent of 'presbyter', though for some curious reason the two terms are thought of as being quite different. 'Presbyter' almost always means an ordained minister: 'elder' refers to an office in the Reformed tradition which is usually described as 'lay' (though there has at times been considerable controversy over whether an elder is ordained or lay). Calvin distinguished between the minister of word and sacrament and the kind of elder who had no such responsibility but was associated with others in the government of the church. This distinction between presbyter/minister and elder has been retained in almost all churches of the Calvinist, Reformed or Presbyterian tradition. The elders belong to the board or session which governs the local congregation. They may have a certain pastoral responsibility for a part of the community and may sit or stand round the minister when he performs his liturgical functions. Representative elders will also be chosen to participate in the higher courts of the church.

J. H. S. Burleigh, *A Church History of Scotland*, 1960; J. Calvin, *Institutes of the Christian Religion*, bk. IV, ch. iii; G. Donaldson, *The Scottish Reformation*, 1960.

P. HINCHLIFF

Elevation *see* Gestures (2)

Ember Days

These are the Wednesday, Friday and Saturday of three (or four) weeks of the year. Probably there were once only three such weeks, with a fourth added later. In any case, the first Ember week of the year is in fact indistinguishable from the Lenten observance.

Ember weeks, like Lent, were times of spiritual renewal – times of prayer, fasting and almsdeeds. Pope Leo the Great used to remind the people of the purpose of Ember-tide and repeatedly ended his homilies with the words: 'On Wednesday and Friday let us fast; and on Saturday let us all keep vigil at St Peter's.' The Ember vigil was very like the Easter one in having, at different times, either six or twelve lessons – the only days with this arrangement in the old missal.

The Roman Christians chose the times of the agricultural festivals for the Ember weeks – sowing time, the corn harvest and vintage time. The old Ember formularies clearly show this harvest connection.

The ordination of new ministers calls for the united prayer of the whole community and presupposes its spiritual renewal. Lent was such a season of prayer and renewal, and its concluding service, the Easter vigil, was the oldest ordination service. Ember weeks were small-scale Lents and so, at least since Gelasius I (AD 494), the Ember Saturdays have been ordination days. The modern practice of candidates for ordination pre-paring themselves by prayer and retreat comes from the older custom of the whole community preparing themselves for the ordinations by the Lenten or Ember observ-ances.

J. CONNELLY

Enarxis

The name commonly given to the prepara-tory office of prayer and praise which pre-cedes the liturgy of the word and the euchar-ist in the Byzantine rite (Greek 'opening' or 'beginning'). It comprises an opening blessing of the Trinity, three litanies (q.v.) (the first a general intercession, the second and third very brief) each concluding with a collect-like prayer, and three anthems (q.v.) (one after each litany) which vary somewhat according to the day, and are usually psalms or based on psalms, with additional material proper to the feast or season. The regulations concerning the use of these anthems vary somewhat from one Orthodox national church to another; the concluding prayers of the litanies have since the later Middle Ages, and probably since a much earlier date, been said secretly, except for their concluding doxologies (q.v.), a practice which deprives the two lesser litanies of their rationale, their function being simply to act

as an introduction to the prayer.

It is difficult to determine the date of the introduction of the enarxis. There appears to be no evidence for it in the sixth century; it was certainly in use by the end of the eighth century, but for a considerable period after this there were many days on which it was omitted, and there are still a few – those when the liturgy is (in theory) celebrated in the evening, and is therefore combined with vespers (q.v.). Nor is it easy to determine exactly how it was originally used, although there are indications that it may well have been a processional rite, and it was certainly not sung, as it is today, with the celebrant in the sanctuary, a practice which makes nonsense of the entrance rite which follows it. *See also* **Liturgies** 2.

H. Holloway, *A Study of the Byzantine Liturgy*, 1933, ch. 11.

W. JARDINE GRISBROOKE

Entrance, Great

The name now given to the procession of the ministers bringing the gifts of bread and wine to the altar at the beginning of the eucharist proper in the Byzantine rite, together with the rites and ceremonies before and after it. The celebrant and deacon go to the pro-thesis (q.v.) on the north of the sanctuary, take up the paten and chalice, and preceded by acolytes (q.v.) bearing tapers (and, accord-ing to the customs of some, of the Orthodox national churches, cross and censer also), leave through the north door of the screen, proceed down the north aisle and up the nave (but in most Slav churches this longer procession is omitted) and, after certain intercessory commemorations before the holy doors (the central doors of the screen), re-enter the sanctuary through these doors, and place the gifts on the altar. For further details, *see* **Liturgies** 2.

H. Holloway, *A Study of the Byzantine Liturgy*, 1933, pp. 76-79; A. Schmemann, *The World as Sacrament*, 1966, pp. 39-42.

W. JARDINE GRISBROOKE

Entrance, Little

The name now given to the entrance of the ministers with the book of the gospels at the beginning of the synaxis (q.v.) or liturgy of the word in the Byzantine rite. Originally the beginning of the service, and therefore a real entrance of the ministers through the church and into the sanctuary, the prefixing to it of the enarxis (q.v.), has reduced it to a purely decorative ceremony: the celebrant, already in the sanctuary, together with the deacon, who takes up the book of the gospels, already on the altar, and the acolytes bearing tapers, leaves the sanctuary through the north door of the screen, and re-enters it almost immediately through the central doors, the deacon carrying the book of the gospels before him, and replacing it on the altar.

Inevitably, the ceremony having lost its purpose, far-fetched 'symbolic' meanings have been invented to explain it, despite the fact that they in no way correspond either to the action itself, or to the texts which accompany and follow it. *See also* **Liturgies** 2.

H. Holloway, *A Study of the Byzantine Liturgy*, 1933, pp. 56-59; A Schmemann, *The World as Sacrament*, 1966, pp. 35-37.

W. JARDINE GRISBROOKE

Epiclesis *see* Anaphora 8

Epiphany

In order to understand Epiphany on 6 January and the complicated problem of its relation to Christmas (q.v.) we must free ourselves from the Western tradition which understands the festival in terms of the coming of the Magi. Its significance as 'Epiphany' or 'Manifestation' conveys, primarily and normatively, not the manifestation of Christ to the Gentiles as such, but rather the manifestation, the revelation of God to the world in Jesus Christ.

Nor can the problem be summarized by saying that Christmas on 25 December was the festival of the incarnation in the Western empire while Epiphany on 6 January was its counterpart in the East, and that in the course of the fourth century when, after the cessation of persecution, there was easy communication among the churches of the Mediterranean, there took place an interchange of festivals with some modifications in meaning. This does not explain why, in the West, Epiphany became a kind of doublet of Christmas, whereas in the East it had for its eventual content the baptism of Jesus. A true solution depends on an awareness of the fact that, before Christmas came into existence in the fourth century, there was already, at least in the Eastern empire, an ancient

festival commemorating in unitive fashion the manifestation of God both in the birth and baptism of Jesus Christ. The result of the spread of the festival of 25 December, which fulfilled the function of a reagent, was that in the East the dual significance of the Epiphany resolved itself into its distinct elements. The commemoration of the incarnation was established on 25 December, and that of the baptism alone retained on 6 January. The Western development was somewhat complex in comparison with this logical process of evolution.

It is from Egypt that we obtain unmistakable evidence concerning the unitive nature of the original Epiphany. John Cassian, who was probably a Western, received a monastic training in Bethlehem. But he and his friend Germanus were anxious to go to Egypt, where monasticism had first developed. Between the years 380 and 400 they paid two visits, and they spent a long time in the country. In the *Conferences* Cassian notes that in Egypt the Epiphany was a unitive festival, commemorating both the incarnation and the baptism.

It was during the last quarter of the fourth century that Christmas acted as a reagent on the original Epiphany in the geographical area of Constantinople, Asia Minor and Antioch. Sermons by Gregory of Nazianzus when he was in Constantinople make it clear that by 380 Christmas was being celebrated there, and that it was called the Theophany or the Birthday. The theme was the incarnation, including, of course, the adoration of the Magi. The festival on 6 January was named the Holy Day of the Lights, or the Day of the Holy Lights, and it commemorated the baptism of Jesus. Thus it seems obvious that, before Christmas was introduced, the Church of Constantinople must have had a festival on 6 January commemorating both the birth and the baptism, and called the Theophany, 'Manifestation of God', clearly a synonym for Epiphany. When the primary theme, the incarnation, was transferred to 25 December, the title also was taken. Evidence from Asia Minor is to be found in an Epiphany sermon by Gregory of Nyssa where the situation is obviously the same as in Constantinople. The evidence from Antioch confirms the outline and completes the picture. In a sermon preached on Whitsunday in the year 386, John Chrysostom makes reference to

Epiphany as the first of the Christian festivals, commemorating the appearance of God on earth. But by the end of that year the situation had changed and, manifestly, Christmas was being celebrated for the first time. It is described as the festival upon which all the others depend. Only within the preceding decade had the tradition of Christmas, derived from the West, become known in Antioch. As in Constantinople, the commemoration of the incarnation included the adoration of the Magi. Unlike Gregory of Nazianzus in the metropolis of the East, Chrysostom retains the term 'Theophany' as a synonym for 'Epiphany' and does not apply it to Christmas. There can be no doubt that in Antioch, towards the close of 386 and the beginning of 387, 25 December now signified the birthday and 6 January the baptism.

The *Apostolic Constitutions* show that in the region of Antioch, at some point towards the end of the fourth century, the process of change revealed by the sermons of Chrysostom was complete. The ordered and coherent nature of these developments during the last quarter of the fourth century in the region Constantinople–Asia Minor–Antioch compels us to regard this as the standard process of evolution of Christmas and Epiphany. The simple and brilliant pattern characteristic of the region where the church was most strongly established did not repeat itself in the whole Christian world, and there were elements of confusion. It is possible that fourth-century Jerusalem commemorated in the Epiphany the incarnation alone. At Rome in the middle of the fifth century the Magi formed the only theme of Epiphany, and with the ascendancy in later centuries of the Roman use the Magi-Epiphany became general in the West. The lectionary of Luxeuil has an Epiphany commemorating the baptism, showing us that far in the West, towards the end of the seventh or the beginning of the eighth century, there was preserved the standard process of evolution.

The last two chapters of the *Epistle to Diognetus* constitute a fragment, the end of a sermon by a different writer, to be dated early in the third or late in the second century. It may be suggested, on the basis of the scriptural references, that the fragment was part of a sermon for Epiphany, the manifestation, the appearance of God in Christ, both in the incarnation and in the baptism.

At the beginning of the third century Clement of Alexandria refers in the *Stromata* or *Miscellanies* to the Gnostic heretic Basilides who had taught at Alexandria in the second quarter of the second century. Apparently his followers celebrated a festival of the baptism, and one date to which reference is made is 6 January. If the Epiphany existed in Egypt towards the end of the second century as a unitive commemoration, it is conceivable that the attitude of the Gnostics would be similar to their reaction to the faith. They could not tolerate the doctrine of the incarnation but they could accept the baptism, although, inevitably, they would misrepresent the true understanding of that event. Another point of considerable significance is that the pagan background of 6 January was the festival of the birth of a god. On this date the church may well have established its festival of the manifestation in the incarnation and the baptism. It does not seem at all likely that the Gnostics would initiate a commemoration of the baptism on this date, for the factor of *birth*, which must form the link between the pagan context of 6 January and the heretical worship on that day, is missing. It could be from the unitive festival of the church that the heretics derived their partial commemoration.

B. Botte, *Les Origines de la Noël et de l'Épiphanie*, 1932; O. Cullmann, *Weihnachten in der alten Kirche*, 1947; A. A. McArthur, *The Evolution of the Christian Year*, 1953.

A. A. MCARTHUR

Epistle

The term epistle in its strict sense refers to the liturgical reading in the eucharistic celebration of a pericope from any of the NT epistles. The term is, however, commonly applied to the first reading of the eucharistic celebration where only two readings (the other being the gospel) are proclaimed. In such a case it may in fact be from any scriptural source other than the gospels.

The traditional Roman lectionary draws on the Pauline epistles for the Sundays from Pentecost to Easter, and the Sundays of the year still show traces of the ancient system of continuous reading, from Romans onwards, though this is far from apparent and as a rule the choice of epistle seems purely haphazard and without any connection with the gospel. During Paschaltide the Sunday epistles are chosen from I John, I Peter and James.

The Lenten Sunday epistles are specially chosen, as are those for the feasts and commons of saints, and for votive masses. The OT first readings used on Lenten ferias are specially chosen and accord with the accompanying gospels.

The new Roman *Ordo Lectionum Missae* (1969) has three readings on Sundays and major feasts, the epistle being the second. On Sundays the epistle is unrelated to the other readings, pursuing the continuous reading of the Pauline epistles, with James and Hebrews, in a three-year cycle. I Peter, I John and the Apocalypse are read during Paschaltide. On weekdays the first reading alternates every few weeks between OT and NT books, in a two-year cycle.

BCP; J. A. Jungmann, *The Mass of the Roman Rite*, new rev. ed., 1959; *Missale Romanum; Ordo Lectionum Missae; M.* Righetti, *Storia Liturgica*, III, ³1966.

                                        BRIAN NEWNS

Ethiopian Worship

1. *Historical*. The Orthodox Church in Ethiopia was organized by Frumentius in the decade immediately following the council of Nicea (AD 325). According to Rufinus' narrative, Frumentius was from Syrian Tyre, and must have had his early education in the Syrian Church. He was consecrated Bishop by Athanasius of Alexandria (c. AD 340), and brought the Alexandrian or Coptic tradition of faith and worship to Ethiopia.

On the foundation of this fully formed Nicene tradition as interpreted by the Church of Alexandria, the nine Syrian monks who came to Ethiopia at the end of the fifth century built a liturgical structure derived from the Coptic and Syrian Orthodox traditions which had rejected the council of Chalcedon (451). During the sixth century the monastic movement spread throughout the country and propagated the faith of the 'Nine Saints'.

A great revival of the Ethiopian Church took place in the fifteenth century under king Zara Yaeqob (1434-68). Many liturgical and theological books were translated from Coptic or Arabic. The sixteenth century Portuguese missions and later Protestant missions have made the Ethiopian Church somewhat hostile towards Western churches.

In 1959, as a result of the efforts of Emperor Haile Selassie, the Ethiopian Church became autocephalous under Patriarch Baselius, after being for some sixteen centuries an integral part of the see of St Mark in Alexandria. The emperor has introduced the use of the vernacular (q.v.) (Amharic) in a few churches, but most parishes still worship in the ancient classical language (*ge'ez*).

2. *Liturgical books*. The main sources for Ethiopic worship are *Sunodos* (Apostolic Canons), *Mets'hafe – Kidan* (The Testament of our Lord), *Didaskalia, Feteha Negest* (Nomocanon), *Ser'at-we-tezaz* (Ordinances and Instructions), *Mets'hafe Bahr'i* (The Book of Nature), *Te'aqebe Mestir* (Stewardship of the Mystery). The seventeenth-century liturgical revision resulted in four major liturgical books: *Mets'hafe Qeddase* (Missal), *Mets'hafe Nuzaze* (Manual of Penitence), *Mets'hafe Taklil* (Matrimony) and *Mets'hafe Qandil* (Manual of Unction of the Sick). The missal has two parts, one containing sixteen to twenty anaphorae (*Qeddase*) and another with the psalmody for the eucharist (*Zemmare*), often chanted by choirs specially trained.

In addition there are four books for the canonical daily offices: (1) *Deggwa*, or the antiphonal chants for the whole liturgical year except Lent; (2) *Tsomedeggwa*, containing chants for Lent, but not for Holy Week; (3) *Mawase'et*, an alternate form, less frequently used, of the daily offices; (4) *Me'eraf*, the common order for the daily office.

One could also mention paraliturgical works produced in the monasteries like *Wuddase Mariam* (Praises of Mary) and *Anqetse-Berhan* (Gate of Light).

3. *Eucharistic anaphorae* (q.v.). Twenty different anaphorae are known, under the names: (1) The Apostles; (2) Our Lord Jesus Christ; (3) Our Lady Mary (by Cyriacus or Qirqos); (4) St Dioscurus; (5) St John Chrysostom; (6) St John the Evangelist; (7) St James the Brother of our Lord; (8) The Hosanna – Liturgy of St Gregory; (9) The Christmas Liturgy of St Gregory; (10) The Anaphora of our Lady Mary by St Gregory; (11) Another Anaphora of our Lady by St Gregory; (12) The 318 Orthodox Fathers of

Nicea; (13) St Basil; (14) St Athanasius; (15) St Epiphanius; (16) The longer St Cyril; (17) The shorter St Cyril; (18) St James of Sarug; (19) St Mark; and (20) Yet another Anaphora of our Lady Mary. Marcos Daoud, the Egyptian layman who was the first director of the Theological School in Addis Ababa, published in 1954 an English version of the pre-anaphora and fourteen anaphorae (Apostles; Our Lord; St John the Evangelist; St Mary; The 318 Fathers; St Athanasius; St Basil; St Gregory; St Epiphanius; St John Chrysostom; St Cyril; St James of Sarug; St Dioscurus and St Gregory II). The Ethiopic and Amharic texts of these also have been published. Many of the anaphorae indicate a Syrian origin, possibly in the Syrian monastery of the Skete in Egypt. The Liturgy of St Mark is not widely used in Ethiopia; only three of the Ethiopic anaphorae are found in the Coptic Church of Egypt (Cyril, Gregory and Basil). There is no reason to believe therefore that the Ethiopian Church simply copied the Egyptian liturgical practice. Elements of Coptic, Syrian and Byzantine liturgical practices are seen in the Ethiopian tradition, but the latter has a personality of its own.

4. *Structure of eucharistic liturgy.* The Ethiopic liturgy has two main parts: (1) the pre-anaphora, common to all the anaphorae, (2) the anaphora proper. The pre-anaphora, which is unusually long, consists of six psalms (Pss. 25; 61; 102; 103; 130; 131), prayers for the cleansing of the celebrants and the vessels, prayers of vesting, the prothesis of the elements (ending with Ps. 117), the enarxis (the prayers of the oblation, the prayers of the 'wrappings', the prayers for absolution and a long litany of intercession), and then the liturgy of the catechumens (censing of the elements, prayers of intercession for the living and the departed, censing of the priests and people, the three lections from Pauline epistles, Catholic epistles and Acts, the *Trisagion* addressed to Christ and embellished with incarnational epithets; prayers of the gospel, the chanting of an antiphon from the psalms, the blessing of the four quarters of the world, the censing of the gospel, and then the reading of the gospel and a sermon). The pre-anaphora concludes with a long litany of intercession for the church, the catechumens and the people, especially the poor, the dismissal of the catechumens, a creed or confession of faith in the mystery of the Holy Trinity, in the full deity and humanity of Christ, in the goodness of all that is created, about the undefiled nature of marriage and childbirth, a repudiation of circumcision, etc., followed by the *lavabo*, the prayer of salutation and the kiss of peace.

The Ethiopic anaphorae vary considerably in structure. The basic structure is: (1) eucharistic thanksgiving, parallel to the Western canon (q.v.) up to the words of institution; (2) prayers of intercession and conclusion of the thanksgiving prayer; (3) *Sanctus* (which is missing in one or two anaphorae); (4) institution narrative (replaced by a prayer in James of Sarug); (5) anamnesis, epiclesis; (6) fraction and commixture; (7) Our Father and continuation prayer; (8) inclination of the head and prayer of penitence before communion; (9) elevation of the body and blood for adoration; (10) the communion, during which Ps. 150 is chanted; (11) post-communion thanksgiving and a special prayer called the 'Pilot of the Soul' and (12) the benediction and dismissal with the imposition of the hands of the priest.

5. *Hymnody and music.* Syro-Byzantine and Coptic musical elements must have come to Ethiopia as early as the fifth century. But it was Yared, a disciple of the nine Syrian saints who came in the sixth century, who is the father of the distinctive Ethiopian hymnody and musicology. He is regarded by Ethiopian tradition as the author of all the divine offices, and of the system of Ethiopian chant called *zema*, with its three different chants: *ge'ez*, *'ezl* and *araraye*. Yared is also credited with being the author of the Ethiopian musical notation system, which uses letters of the alphabet written above syllables to indicate the note.

6. *Liturgical year.* The Ethiopian Church follows the Julian calendar. The year is divided into thirteen months – twelve of thirty days each and one of five or six days. The year commences on 1 Maskaam which corresponds to 11 or 12 September in the Gregorian calendar. The year is seven or eight years behind the Western year (AD 1972 would be 1964 or 65 in the Ethiopian calendar). The major feasts are (1) the nine feasts of our Lord – incarnation, passion, resurrection, appearance to Thomas, ascension,

Pentecost, transfiguration, epiphany-baptism, and the miracle of Cana; (2) six secondary feasts – exaltation of the cross, circumcision of the Lord, feeding of five thousand, presentation in the Temple, invention of the cross, and sojourn of Jesus in Egypt; (3) the thirty-two Marian feasts established in the fifteenth century by king Zara Yaeqob; (4) the fifty main feasts of the saints, of the OT and NT, universal and national, including the archangels Michael, Gabriel, and Raphael.

There is also the special peculiarity of the Ethiopian Church – the liturgical *month*, with its eighteen monthly commemorations, four for our Lord, six for Mary and eight for other saints.

7. *Fasting*. The following fasts are observed very strictly in Ethiopia: The great Lent fast (fifty-five days preceding Easter); Advent fast (forty days); the fast of the apostles (from the day after Pentecost till the feast of the Apostles); the fast of Mary; the fast of Nineveh; and Wednesday and Friday each week.

8. *Daily offices*. Forms of the daily offices (q.v.), of Ethiopian origin, follow the traditional structure used in all ancient churches. There are forms of vigil (*Wazema*); offices for Sunday (*Mawaddes*); offices for special feasts of saints (*Kestat'aryam*); offices for Lent (*Za-atswam*); daily mattins (*Sebhate-nage za-zawoter*) and mattins for principal feasts (*Sebhate-nage za-ba'alat 'abiyan*). Each office consists of: (1) scriptural praises – the 150 psalms and 15 biblical hymns of the OT and NT; (2) special prayers for the feasts or for seasons; (3) poetic or hymnic elements (*qene*); (4) readings from the scriptures; (5) prayers and invocations.

The main manual for the daily offices is the *Me'eraf*, which has been studied in detail by Bernard Velat in the *Patrologia Orientalis*, XXXIII (1966).

Marcos Daoud, *The Liturgy of the Ethiopian Church* (text of pre-anaphora and fourteen anaphorae in English), 1954; E. Hammer-schmidt, *Studies in the Ethiopic Anaphoras*, 1961; S. Mercer, *The Ethiopic Liturgy*, 1915; Bernard Velat, *Études sur le Me'eraf, Commun de l'office divin Ethiopien, Patrologia Orientalis* XXXIII, 1966.

PAUL VERGHESE

Eucharist

Since the beginning of the second century and possibly in the NT itself (*cf.* I Cor. 14.16), the term 'eucharist', which derives from a Greek word meaning 'thanksgiving', has been used as a title for the service of holy communion. Its appropriateness rests upon the giving of thanks by Jesus at the Last Supper and upon the character of the rite itself which is the supreme act of Christian thanksgiving. In the gospels the verb *eucharistein* is used interchangeably with *eulogein*, meaning 'to bless', since the Jewish *berakah* was in fact a blessing of God by rendering thanks to him for a particular act. So, e.g., the Jewish blessing of bread took the form: 'Blessed art thou, O Lord our God, King of the universe, who bringest forth bread from the earth' – words that almost certainly were used by Jesus at the Last Supper.

This Jewish understanding underlies all primitive liturgies, so, e.g., the consecration prayer in the *Apostolic Tradition* of Hippolytus is essentially one of thanksgiving.

At the present day this term is widely used, not only because it directs attention to one important aspect of the rite as a whole but also because it is free from the doctrinal undertones of other titles.

A full discussion of the eucharistic prayer will be found under **Anaphora**. *See also* **Communion, Liturgies.**

G. A. Michell, *Eucharistic Consecration in the Primitive Church*, 1948.

EDITOR

Eucharistic prayer *see* Anaphora

Evensong *see* Canonical Hours

Exorcism

The practice of exorcism depends on the belief that persons and things may be subject to evil or diabolic power, and that this power may be driven out through the words and actions of the exorcism rite. The ancient Assyrians, Babylonians and Egyptians practised exorcism, and it is also found in late Judaism, *cf.* Tobit 6.8; 8.2; Mark 9.38; Luke 11.19; Acts 19.13. The gospels mention Jesus exorcizing on numerous occasions; he gave his disciples power to exorcize, *cf.* Matt. 10.1, and we find Paul exorcizing in Christ's name in Acts 16.18.

In the Christian church the power to

exorcize was initially seen as a charismatic gift. This view survived in the East until the end of the fourth century at least, but in Rome in the middle of the third century the exorcistate is listed as one of the minor orders. This was the case until recently in the Roman Catholic Church, whose clerics received the order of exorcist on their way to the priesthood, without, however, exercising this order.

Exorcism played an important part in the preparation of catechumens for baptism (qq.v.), besides being used to assist those thought to be possessed by the devil. The water, salt and oil used in the rites of exorcism came to be exorcized themselves, before they were blessed. The rites of exorcism vary greatly in length and content. They usually involve prayers, commands to the devil to leave the afflicted person, and the imposition of the exorcist's hands on the person. Signs of the cross and anointing with oil are also sometimes used, as is aspersion with blessed water, and the imposition of the exorcist's stole.

The Roman Catholic Church retains exorcisms in its rite for adult baptism, but in its new rite for infant baptism (1969) the exorcism is replaced by a prayer for deliverance from original sin, or from the power of darkness. The pre-baptismal anointing with oil remains, but may be omitted in some cases. Exorcisms precede the blessings of oil, salt and water. *Titulus XII* of the *Rituale Romanum* gives the norms and rites for exorcizing those troubled by the devil. Only priests may exorcize, the bishop's permission is required and priests are warned against confusing diabolic possession with psychological ailments. Nowadays this rite is rarely used.

The Orthodox Church uses exorcism in preparation for baptism and where diabolic possession is suspected. In the Church of England's baptismal rite the pre-baptismal exorcism, retained in the first *BCP* of 1549, was omitted in the 1552 *BCP* in response to Bucer's criticism that it implied all unbaptized persons were demoniacs. No other exorcisms were included in the *BCP*, yet the practice survived, for in 1604 Canon 72 forbade Anglican clergy to exorcize without episcopal permission. Exorcism is uncommon in the Church of England today.

Science reveals that many cases once treated by exorcism can now be helped by medical treatment. This development will not disconcert the Christian, who believes that all evil is of malign origin and that all healing comes from God.

1. Texts: L. C. Mohlberg, ed., *Liber Sacramentorum Romanae Ecclesiae* (Gelasian Sacramentary), 1960; *Rituale Romanum*, 1st ed., 1614, Titulus XII; C. Vogel, ed., *Le Pontifical Romano-Germanique du dixième siècle*, II, 1963.

2. Studies: J. Forcet, 'Exorcisme', *DTC*, ed., A. Vacant, V, 1913, cols. 1762-80; C. Harris, 'Visitation of the Sick' in *Liturgy and Worship*, ed. W. K. Lowther Clarke, 1932; A. G. Martimort, ed., *Introduction to the Liturgy*, 1968; F. Procter and W. H. Frere, *The History of the Book of Common Prayer*, 1901; M. Righetti, *Storia Liturgica*, IV, [2]1959.

BRIAN NEWNS

Experimental forms of Worship

I recall once when I was at Green Lake, Wisconsin, for a conference, and we had a folk singing in the lobby. Christians were gathering together singing for joy. We sang 'We Shall Overcome', a song that expresses the hope which is part of God's *shalom*. Then we sang about God's drowning the Egyptians, 'Pharaoh's Army Got Drowned', and 'He's Got the Whole World in His Hands'. These songs were very good theology. Then someone said, 'Oh-oh! Time for the worship service.' We all filed out over to the vesper circle, the organ came in with its tremolo, and we sang some songs about our own souls. That was supposed to be 'worship'. But it wasn't!

That is how the Baptist theologian Harvey Cox describes in his *God's Revolution and Man's Responsibility* (1969, p.84) an experience which most Christians have had. There are everyday experiences which have a dimension of worship, and formal worship services which appear to us very ordinary and boring. Yet it is not true that worship is out of favour. What is out is our present way of conducting worship. Worship has ceased to be *une expérience*, as the French understand the word, i.e. an experience which includes the risk of an experiment. That is what is meant by experimental forms of worship. But this is in fact a pleonasm. Worship is either experimental (in the sense of being a real experience and in the sense that in this experiment one never knows what is coming next) or it is not worship at all. The reason for this is that in worship one expects God himself to act. And who would pretend that we can prejudge his actions?

That worship is not rejected can be seen from the fact that even today secular forms of celebration are continually being invented (*see* **Secularization and Worship**). In an enquiry which was made in the autumn of 1968 among the personnel of the Ecumenical Centre in Geneva it became evident that in principle even the critical observers still expect something from the weekly worship service. 'I keep hoping for something better', said one. And another one was 'sad and sometimes irritated because of the verbal impotence'. People asked for fellowship. They wanted to learn to pray, 'but then scarcely anyone knows how to pray in this day and age, and the clergy are as weak in this as anyone'. We have forgotten how to pray! Responsive prayers are 'almost never true reflections of our lives', particularly if they must be read at breath-taking speed. So the prayers on paper prevent the prayers of heart and body, in which one could find and articulate one's own job, sorrows, joys and faith (or the faith of one's church). So the questions remain: How can we pray together without trying to teach each other theology? How can there be an intensive silence full of content from which well up intercession, praise, celebration and mutual care?

People ask – according to this enquiry – for intelligible interpretative information. They are looking for mutual help and tolerance. No question of secularism breaking into the Ecumenical Centre, of the rejection of the gospel, although many of the staff do not attend worship.

Many other enquiries give similar results. Section V of the w c c's Assembly at Uppsala had the task of dealing with worship in a secular age, but it camouflaged the problem by the alliteration: 'Worship, for a Christian, is not a problem but a privilege' (*Drafts for Sections*, p.97). The hiatus between secular and sacred liturgies – it proposed – should be overcome by education. People should be adapted, conditioned and shaped for the liturgy of the church, so that the church does not need to change. The document adopted at Uppsala is no better than the draft, except that it proposed a Faith and Order Consultation on 'Worship in a Secular Age'. The *status quaestionis* was formulated by Lukas

Vischer as follows:

The main questions were how to worship and how to worship together. The present generation, however, is less concerned with modes and ways. It rather raises the more radical question as to whether it is possible at all. How can we, as men, speak of God and, even more difficult, speak to God? How can we meaningfully pray? All forms of worship are equally challenged by these questions and in the face of these new challenges it is clear that the differences between the various traditions cannot claim more than secondary importance. (W. Vos, ed., *Worship and Secularization*, p. 1.)

Indeed, one can go a step further, saying that in worship the difference between those who are commonly called believers and those who are commonly called unbelievers becomes secondary. This lesson I learnt from a group of agnostic nuclear researchers. They wanted to organize a worship service with me. The topics which I proposed to them (Faith and Technology, Art and Technology, etc.) did not interest them. They concentrated on one question, saying: 'We do not believe in God. But we want you to teach us to pray.' These are the people who pray, even when they believe they do not believe.

At the Faith and Order consultation mentioned above the Indian theologian Raymond Panikkar stated: 'Only worship can prevent secularization from becoming inhuman, and only secularization can save worship from being meaningless.' 'Probably one of the reasons (effect or cause, I leave it open) of the crisis of the United Nations organization is that it could not or did not know how to develop a really common and thus universal and meaningful liturgy, cult, worship' (W. Vos, ed., *op.cit.,* pp.28, 53). And the German theologian Will Adam, in describing Jesus' practice of worship, came to the conclusion that he not only broke the social and political taboos of his time, but violated – in order to do the will of God – what at that time people considered to be the will of God. In celebrating communion with people who were excluded from communion, he defined what he considered to be worship. That is experimental worship in the truest sense! Adam even thinks that worship was the most efficient instrument for mission, because it celebrated the overcoming of segregation (between slaves and free people, rich and poor, men and women), which in their society was considered impossible, immoral or both. Nobody can measure the power worship could regain, if we were to take up once more this original experimental dimension, which at the moment we have frozen with memories of past experiences (called agenda).

The literature on experimental forms of worship – particularly in German – is extensive. New forms of worship do not need to justify themselves any more. They are not the hobby of liturgical playboys. But if they relate mainly to jazz attractions as the worm on the church extension hook to draw the fish into the empty ecclesiastical aquarium, then they are just brushed-up varieties of worship, which are wrongly understood as Christian duty or religious matinees, instead of being the worship 'which the world needs as badly as its daily bread' (Adam), 'the reasonable worship' (Paul).

The question is not to change instruments and words, although this is in many cases necessary and overdue. The question is, how to celebrate communion in the face of the real segregations of this world, how to celebrate hope amid despair, instead of creating artificial barriers by confessional frontiers and then trying to overcome them by so-called intercommunion.

The celebration we have in mind cannot happen unless liturgy becomes an event of the whole people of God and even of those who believe they do not believe. The methods and tools for this 'liturgical alphabetization' of the people of God cannot be described in detail here. They can probably be transmitted by literature only very incompletely, just as one cannot learn to make a film, or to produce a play by reading a book on film-making or play-producing. Learning by doing, with the help of people who have some experience in the field, seems to be the most appropriate method (almost a definition of practical theology!).

Instead of theoretical theses on experimental worship, I mention here an example, which in spite of some liturgical weaknesses, articulated and celebrated hope among the real segregations of our time.

As is the custom on a Swiss Thanksgiving Day, the parishioners wore black at the Sunday morning service. But what a strange smell in the church? Surely, it was the smell of freshly-brewed coffee. And there were present Italian and Spanish waiters, greeting every one as they came into the church and offering them a cup of hot coffee.

During the prelude, the *Kyrie* from the *Misa Criolla*, Italian and Spanish waiters, some Swiss participants and a pastor processed through the church. They were carrying bread and wine for the Lord's Supper, but also a big bag of coffee beans, which was emptied on the altar. Then the foreigners led the service in Italian and Spanish, sometimes with a translation for the Swiss congregation.

First came the *coffee*. Every person received a little bag of coffee. The Spanish layman explained to the congregation how much the Brazilian coffee worker was earning for his work; only enough to feed himself and his family during eight months, even if the harvest is good. For the rest of the year he must suffer from hunger. He only survives by begging and by taking odd jobs.

The bread: an Italian read the famous story by Ignazio Silone of the picture of the Lord's Supper. The Christ in the picture of the eucharist in the church at Fontamara has a piece of wheat-bread in his hand, not maize-bread such as the poor farmers of Southern Italy have to eat. Maize-bread is for the farmers, for the pig and goats. But Christ has a real piece of bread and says: this – the wheat-bread – this is my body. The one who has wheat-bread has me, he has God. The one who does not eat it, is like the pigs and the goats. And the Italian finished: how could we help thinking of wheat-bread, when we work day and night to produce the wheat-bread of the rich but never eat it?

A Spanish worker told the story of the Roman Catholic bishop of Cuernavaca in Mexico. He had removed all the images of saints from the church, except one of Mary, pointing to the Crucified. Even the tabernacle was removed. In its place a table was brought into the church for the actual celebration of the eucharist, as in Zwingli's liturgy. The body of the Lord is present in Cuernavaca, when the people of God celebrate the Lord's Supper, when the believers are *sola gratia* transformed into the body of the Lord.

The Bishop of Cuernavaca trains the workers and Indians, so that they can understand the revolutionary undertones of the Lord's Supper. That is why they go to their directors and landowners and talk with them about the Lord's Supper: 'How is it that we are equal partners at the Lord's table, but not at the conference table?'

'*The cup* is the new covenant' (Luke 22.20), the new covenant which the Father has created through his Son between himself and men and between men of all classes and nations. The Swiss parishioner who introduced the cup, mentioned the eucharistic hymn by J. C. Lavater which the congregation had just sung. J. C. Lavater knew what he was doing, when he made the new covenant the topic of his eucharistic hymn. He was pastor at St Peter's in Zürich during the French occupation of Switzerland. Lavater had the courage to live the new covenant, because he believed in it. He had to pay for his belief with his own life. He tried to protect a fellow citizen who was persecuted by a French soldier. The bullet which should have hit his fellow-citizen killed him.

Sermon. The pastor preached for five minutes (in a Reformed service!) in French (which was the common language) on Levi. But not many words were necessary after the congregation had introduced themselves and their foreign fellow human beings into the right context. Levi was an outsider in his society. But when Jesus came to him, he organized a feast for his friends and neighbours with Jesus at the centre. The text does not say that Jesus preached at this feast, but he was the occasion for the feast. Such a feast, the pastor said, we are going to celebrate now.

During the distribution of the Lord's Supper the congregation received cards. They were invited to answer the question: what can we do so that the Brazilians may receive more money for their coffee, so that the people from Southern Italy can eat enough bread, so that the outsiders in our society (both Swiss and foreigners) are not put aside? What are the things in our world which the Lord's Supper changes? The comments of the congregation (published later in the church bulletin) were resumed in the final prayer, a real 'collect' and not the usual pre-written prayer which goes by the name of collect. About half of the people did not react to the question given them, but expressed their thoughts on this form of the Lord's Supper. One woman wrote: 'During the whole week we have to hear these foreign languages. Why should they bother us again in church?' Others confessed that for the first time in their life they had experienced the real presence of the Lord. A Spaniard wrote in impossible

Spanish orthography: 'I thank the Lord for the privilege of celebrating the Lord's Supper with my Swiss brethren.'

Harvey Cox, *The Feast of Fools: A Theological Essay on Festivity and Fantasy*, 1969; J. G. Davies, *Worship and Mission*, 1966; Wiebe Vos, ed., *Worship and Secularization*, 1970; WCC, Monthly Letter on Evangelism (Geneva).

W. J. HOLLENWEGER

Exposition

The showing and adoration of the host became a devotion of the church when, in the Middle Ages, the doctrine of the real presence of Christ in the eucharist had been developed by theologians and councils.

The first instance of this 'showing' would seem to have been the practice of the elevation (q.v.) of the host, 'so that it can be seen by all', after the consecration in the mass. The elevation was instituted by the bishop of Paris, Eudes de Sully (1196-1208).

In the centuries which immediately followed, communion was rarely received except at Easter, and this 'visual communion' unfortunately resulted in superstition. Some people would only come to church just in time to see the elevation and leave directly afterwards, while at Eton College the boys were encouraged to leave their games or studies for the elevation.

Religion became more real and spiritual as a result of the Tridentine reform, with more frequent communion and better religious education.

The elevation at mass had an effect on the more prolonged form of exposition, which was introduced at the end of the fourteenth century, for which the feast of Corpus Christi (q.v.), with its procession of the sacrament, was largely responsible.

The host was placed in a vessel known as a monstrance (q.v.), with the sacrament visible. The monstrance would then be placed on or above the altar (q.v.) for the adoration and prayers of the faithful to Christ hidden under the sacred species.

Exposition became too frequent, especially in north Germany, to have a spiritual benefit, and provincial councils and synods gave repeated warnings against excess. Many of the sacrament houses were constructed with a grille, in order that the monstrance with the host might be seen at all times.

Strict regulations concerning exposition of the sacrament were embodied in canon law, requiring the express permission of the bishop of the diocese.

Exposition occurs today preceding Benediction (q.v.) in an afternoon or evening service, and in October during the recitation of the rosary (q.v.). On specified occasions, such as the Feast of Christ the King, exposition is permitted for some hours, with at least two of the faithful present.

In this way, the church encourages silent prayer and worship to Christ present in the sacrament.

A. A. King and C. E. Pocknee, *Eucharistic Reservation in the Western Church*, 1965.

A. A. KING

Extempore Prayer

Spontaneous prayer composed at the time of utterance, though possibly with some preparation. The NT implies (e.g. I Cor. 14) that the ability thus to pray is a gift of God. In the early church the eucharistic prayer was often thus composed by those competent to do so, but according to a fixed pattern. The clearest example is in the *Apostolic Tradition* of Hippolytus, X: 'Let each one pray according to his own ability.' But in course of time the formulae became fixed, and the invention of printing favoured uniformity. In traditional liturgies only a few parts survived where some spontaneity was permitted, e.g. the insertion of names into intercessions.

After the Reformation in England, whereas all Puritans disapproved of the imposition of conformity to the *BCP*, some favoured the production of Puritan liturgies, but others were opposed to all set forms, and conducted a considerable polemic against them. Some even argued that the Lord's Prayer was given only as a model, and was not intended for actual repetition. The objection to read prayers was based on Rom. 8.26; the promised help of the Holy Spirit was to be obtained at the moment of utterance. It was also thought that set prayers could not meet the varying needs of congregations, that they quenched a gift of God, and that their use was hypocritical and insincere. In reply it was pointed out that not all ministers have the gift of extempore prayer, that it is not always easy for a congregation to follow extempore prayer, and that many extempore prayers are florid and ostentatious. This controversy,

which incidentally has somewhat distorted the meaning of the word 'liturgical', often taken to mean 'fixed, stereotyped', has never been entirely resolved in the English Free Churches and in the Church of Scotland. Apart from the Society of Friends, they have now not merely directories, but liturgical books, whether official, as among Presbyterians and Methodists, or unofficial, as among Congregationalists and Baptists; yet these books are guides, not rigidly binding. Many ministers judiciously alternate both methods. It is also possible to combine the two methods as by writing a prayer suitable to a particular occasion, or by composing as one utters it a prayer which nevertheless follows a fixed pattern as in the early church. Probably on the whole extempore prayer is declining in the English Free Churches.

Meanwhile the churches with more traditional liturgies are rapidly adopting more flexible methods, especially in the intercessions of the eucharist. The English Anglican *BCP* of 1928 had a rubric: 'Note: that subject to any direction which the Bishop may give, the Minister may, at his discretion, after the conclusion of Morning or Evening Prayer, or of any Service contained in this Book, offer prayer in his own words.' New Roman Catholic services often have many permitted alternatives and often the rubrics attached to homilies contain the phrase 'or in like words'. These are similar tendencies and may encourage extempore prayer. *See also* **Prayer Meeting.**

A. RAYMOND GEORGE

Fan

The use of liturgical fans was at one time very widespread. In a rubric found before the eucharistic prayer in the eighth book of *The Apostolic Constitutions* (fifth century), their use is ordered thus: 'Let two deacons on either side of the altar hold a fan of thin tissues, or of peacock's feathers, and let them gently ward off the small flying creatures, so that they may not approach the cups.'

In the Latin West fans were undoubtedly employed for a similar purpose, as we can see from the rubrics in the liturgical rites of the Dominicans and the Cluniacs. In the present Eastern Orthodox liturgy, fans are waved over the elements during the recitation of the

Nicene Creed and at the commencement of the anaphora (q.v.) or eucharistic prayer. These fans now have a symbolic meaning, since they have a six-winged cherub depicted on them, whence the name hexapterigon (six-winged). They are carried in processions by deacons, acolytes (qq.v.) and choir-boys on either side of the book of the gospels or at the great entrance (q.v.) of the offerings of bread and wine.

F. E. Brightman, *Liturgies Eastern and Western, I: Eastern Liturgies,* 1896; S. Salaville, *An Introduction to the Study of Eastern Liturgies,* 1938.

C. E. POCKNEE

Fast Days

Fasting is recommended by the scriptures and practised by the church as a means of atoning for sin and commending ourselves and our prayers to God. Hence the fast days of the Christian calendar and their connection with times of prayer, such as Lent and Ember weeks (qq.v.) and the eves of great feasts. *See also* **Ethiopian Worship** 7.

J. CONNELLY

Ferial

Christians, like the Jews, designated the days of the week by numbers, not by names. A day was called a *feria* (without the meaning of a day of rest or a feast). Sunday was the first day, *feria prima*, but from earliest times it was called the 'day of the Lord', *dies dominica* (*cf.* Rev. 1.7). Saturday, the seventh day, was called the Sabbath, *Sabbatum.*

In Christian usage, ferial is opposed to dominical. A *feria* or a ferial day is a weekday to which no solemnity or feast is assigned. Some ferial days have a special place in the calendar, namely the weekdays of Lent, 17 to 24 December, the Ember and rogation days (qq.v.); but most ferial days are an extension of the preceding Sunday. As Sunday is the weekly commemoration of the resurrection, the ferial days make the week a reflection of the Easter Octave. 'Ferial', therefore, is not essentially a synonym for penitential or sorrowful.

J. CONNELLY

Font

A receptacle to hold water for the administration of baptism (q.v.), the term deriving from the Latin *fons* meaning 'a spring of water'.

A sufficient number of datable fonts, from the beginning of the third century onwards, is now known to allow the determination of the historical sequence of their shapes. The most primitive form was the quadrilateral; this was succeeded by the hexagon, octagon and the cruciform. Round or oval fonts were next adopted and finally, in the sixth century, the quatrefoil. Apart from the hexagon and octagon in Italy and France, no one shape seems to have been preferred in any one area, although it is possible to affirm that the cruciform and quatrefoil (*see* Plate 26) were Eastern creations and were thence introduced into North Africa.

Each and every one of these shapes had its own ideological content, the form being a symbol to convey some aspect of the meaning of baptism. The initial adoption of the quadrilateral, which is the design of the first extant font from Dura Europos, is explicable on the grounds that it is similar to a sarcophagus; i.e., since in baptism the believer is buried with Christ, the font was made to look like a coffin. So Ambrose refers to 'the font, whose appearance is somewhat like that of a tomb in shape'. Numerology provides the clue to the meaning of hexagon and octagon: six refers to the death of Christ on the sixth day of the week and eight to his resurrection (*cf.* Rom. 6.4). So fonts were shaped in the same way and with the same intention as the baptistery (q.v.), and various combinations were possible. As the candidate entered an octagonal building, he was buoyed with hope in the resurrection of Christ; as he entered the hexagonal font, he knew he was to die with Christ, but as he left the font and stood once more in the eight-sided room he also knew he was to walk in newness of life. Alternatively, as he entered an hexagonal building, he knew that the baptismal death awaited him, but as he entered the octagonal font he knew that this was the means of rising again.

The round font, as the circular baptistery, introduces a different aspect of baptism, namely that of rebirth (*cf.* John 3.3ff.), and so this type of font was regarded as a womb whereby the children of God are regenerated and have the church as their mother. The cruciform font, on the other hand, together with the quatrefoil which is no more than a variant, connects once more with the idea of death. So according to John Chrysostom: 'Baptism is a cross. What the cross was to Christ and what his burial was, that baptism was to us.'

One further feature of the arrangement of the font has bearing upon the meaning of the rite and that is the steps with which many were provided, anything from one to four. Their main purpose was not to allow easy access but to emphasize the fact of descent. So Cyril of Jerusalem, or his successor John, comments: 'You descended three times into the water, and ascended again; here also covertly pointing by a figure to the three days' burial of Christ.'

All these fonts were more frequently placed in a decorative setting, with mosaics on the dome, walls and floors, than they were decorated themselves. Some of them, however, were ornamented, either with simple geometrical patterns, as the one at Timgad, or with a multitude of symbols, as the one at Kélibia. The latter depicts an ark, stressing salvation in the church, fish, based on the *ichthus* symbol of Christ (the initials of the Greek word stand for Jesus Christ, Son of God, Saviour), and a cross, affirming that by baptism we share in the victorious death of Christ.

The fonts themselves not only provide evidence of the early Christian understanding of baptism; they also give a clue to the actual method used. Strictly speaking, there are four principal methods of baptizing: (1) submersion, when the candidate goes completely below the surface of the water; (2) immersion, when the head is dipped, with or without the candidate standing in the water; (3) affusion, when water is poured over the head; (4) aspersion, when water is sprinkled on the head. However, method (2) is now rarely used, and the term immersion normally denotes (1). If the dimensions of all the early Christian fonts known are examined, it is evident that the great majority of them were not capable of being used for submersion; in only a few would this have been possible. Hence if baptismal practice were uniform, then it must have been either by immersion or affusion; even in this case the parallelism with burial would not have been lost, since the essential feature of this was the casting of a handful of earth upon the corpse, and affusion does no more than reproduce this action.

From the medieval period a vast number of fonts have survived, and they are so plentiful and diverse that an exact typology is not easy. However, it is possible to make certain general statements which may be taken as usually valid despite exceptions. In the eleventh and twelfth centuries the tub-font was prevalent and this consisted of an unmounted bowl resting on the ground. Over-

Plate 26   'Quatrefoil font', Stobi, Yugoslavia

lapping this in the twelfth century and continuing through the thirteenth, a mounted type came into use and was polypod in form, i.e. the bowl was supported on four or more legs. This was superseded in the fourteenth century by a monopod, i.e. the receptacle was held up on a single central shaft. This last type was tripartite and consisted of bowl, pedestal and base (*see* Plate 27) but there had existed previously a bipartite form which derived from the tub-font. Many examples of the tub have a band or cable-moulding around the middle; a tightening of this girdle contracts the tub in the centre and both elongates it and makes it assume the appearance of a cup – hence the appearance of the bipartite chalice.

Plate 27   Font, Stottesdon, England

This evolution is explicable in the light of two factors. First, the universal practice of infant baptism required the raising of the font so that the celebrant could handle the children with greater ease. Second, submersion had now become the norm and so the bowls had to be fairly large and, if they were to be at a convenient level, supports were required. Nevertheless submersion did not continue in all countries, being eventually replaced by affusion. In France affusion appears to have been widespread by the fourteenth century, in Italy by the fifteenth, but in England it was not adopted until after the Reformation. Where this was the practice, a second receptacle was required to catch the drops of

consecrated water that dripped from the children's heads; hence the presence of secondary bowls by the side of a number of medieval fonts. Hence also the appearance of font covers to prevent the consecrated water from being stolen for the purposes of magic and witchcraft. The earliest covers were simply flat lids, but their decorative possibilities were soon appreciated and the result, from the fourteenth century, was the towering tabernacles of open-tracery work.

Medieval fonts were covered with sculptural ornament and the subjects chosen naturally refer to baptism. Scenes from the life of Christ were not infrequent, in particular his nativity, baptism, crucifixion and resurrection, each therefore affirming either baptismal rebirth or co-death and co-resurrection. But one of the most dominant themes of the early medieval iconography of baptism was not so much death as the struggle against and destruction of the devil and his minions, hence the host of bas-reliefs depicting the powers of evil as toads, serpents, dragons or griffins. In the fifteenth and sixteenth centuries there was a decline in the artistic merit of these decorations, at the same time as the cult of the saints was reaching its zenith. The result of this was the representation of the saints and/or of scenes from their lives, they being regarded as protectors and intercessors, their names given in baptism to the children, whose patrons and models they thereby became.

From the Reformation to the eighteenth century, the history of the font is relatively uninteresting. There were two main types, either those designed on traditional lines and perpetuating the general features of the fifteenth-century examples, or those of Renaissance pattern, which were usually like vases on slender pillars, the diminutive bowl marking the final discontinuance of submersion (*see* Plate 28). The chief decoration was realistic cherubic heads, disposed around the rim; only rarely were any of the subjects of the medieval iconography reproduced. Among the Calvinists, basins were general, while among Roman Catholics a divided font bowl came into use, one part holding the consecrated water and the other collecting the drops from the children's heads. With the Gothic Revival, octagonal fonts of the decorated period were introduced into church after church, often dispossessing the ancient ones *in situ*.

Plate 29   Font, Audincourt, France

ing of baptism. Perhaps the time has come
when the refined austerity that characterizes
so many of them should give way to a little
more boldness in experiment and symbolic
representation, in the light of what has
previously been achieved.

S. Bedard, *The Symbolism of the Baptismal
Font in Early Christian Thought*, 1951;
F. Bond, *Fonts and Font Covers*, 1908; J. G.
Davies, *The Architectural Setting of Baptism*,
1962.

EDITOR

Forty Hours Devotion

The name probably originated in the prayers
said before the 'sepulchre', in the Middle
Ages from Good Friday until Easter morning
(*Triduum Sacrum*), symbolical of the time
when our Lord's body rested in the tomb.

The present devotion to the blessed sacrament exposed began in Milan in the Church
of the Holy Sepulchre (San Sepolcro), which
may be relevant, but any connection there
may have been soon faded into the background, and Pius IV in 1560, when granting
permission for the devotion, pointed to
Christ fasting forty days in the wilderness.

A missioner by the name of John Antony
Bellotti in 1527 instituted the Forty Hours
Devotion four times in the year, as it was a
time of war. Two years later, it was prescribed
in the cathedral church of Milan, to pray for
rain, and from thence to other churches in the
city.

Plate 28   Font, Ruabon, Wales

The twentieth century has witnessed the
production of a large number of fonts (*see*
Plate 29), some of which are no more than
bizarre, but the majority are sufficiently
similar to those of the medieval period to
allow them to be classified in the same way.
So there are unmounted fonts, consisting of
either tanks or different forms of the tub-
font standing on the ground. There are also
mounted ones, both monopods and polypods,
but their decorative treatment is almost nil.
The result is that few really convey the mean-

The year 1534 has been assigned to the beginnings of a universal Forty Hours Devotion, through Antony Maria Zaccaria and others of the Clerks Regular of St Paul (Barnabites). It received papal sanction from Paul III in 1539, and about 1550 Philip Neri brought the devotion to Rome. By this time, when exposition was finished in one church it passed to another and Clement VIII in a constitution of 1592 spoke of it as an 'uninterrupted chain of prayer'. From Italy, the devotion spread throughout Latin Christendom and became very popular in the Baroque centuries. It came to England as a regular diocesan devotion after the restoration of the hierarchy in 1850, as a means of stimulating the faithful in prayer and adoration to Christ present in the sacrament.

The present form of the devotion was regulated by Clement XII in 1731 in what has been called the 'Clementine Instruction'. The full time, however, is forty-eight hours, but where the night watch, at which there are only men, is impracticable, the sacrament is replaced in the tabernacle until the following morning.

The devotion begins with a mass of exposition (q.v.) and procession; then on the following day there is a mass for peace, but not at the altar of exposition. The final ceremony is the mass of deposition with a procession and Benediction (q.v.).

During the exposition, the church or chapel may never be left without at least two persons in prayer before the sacrament.

A. A. KING

Fraction

The ceremonial breaking of the eucharistic bread for distribution. It derives from Christ's own action at the Last Supper (Matt. 26.26) and was a sufficiently striking element to make 'the breaking of bread' (Acts 2.42) a title for the eucharist.

In all non-Byzantine Eastern rites and in all non-Roman Western rites, the fraction takes place before the Lord's Prayer. In the Roman mass, since Gregory the Great, it is performed after the Lord's Prayer, as in the Byzantine rite. The rubric in the Roman mass requires the host to be broken into three, and one particle is then placed in the chalice at the commixture (q.v.). The Mozarabic rite prescribes an elaborate ceremonial, the host being broken into nine, and seven of these pieces being arranged in the shape of a cross.

The 1662 *BCP*, in order to emphasize that the fraction is in imitation of Jesus' action at the Last Supper, requires it to take place during the consecration prayer at the words 'he brake', and this is also the practice in the Coptic and Abyssinian rites.

Originally the fraction was entirely utilitarian and so Augustine refers to the bread being 'broken small for distribution' (*Ep.* 149.16). It soon attracted a symbolic interpretation, Paul paving the way with his argument for unity on the grounds that the communicants have all partaken of the fragments broken from a single loaf (I Cor. 10.17) – so it was a sign of the gathering into one of the children of God (*cf. Didache*, 9.4). Later it was thought to symbolize the death of Christ, although this is in contradiction to John 19.36. The Stowe missal accompanies it with a quotation from Luke 24.35 to the effect that the Lord is known in the breaking of the bread.

EDITOR

Frontal

In the earlier centuries the altar was enveloped in a silk cloth on all sides (*see* **Altar Hangings**). But in the second part of the Middle Ages, when altars came to be placed against screens or walls, this cloth had to be adapted to meet this changed setting of the altar. Thus only that side of the altar which was visible to the congregation came to have a flat silk or brocade cloth hung in front of it; this is what is termed the 'frontal' and in the Latin *antependium*. The frontal is suspended on legs that project from the altar. Over the top of the altar there is hung another strip of silk attached to a coarse linen cloth and this has a fringe running along its length and is termed the *frontlet*, sometimes miscalled the 'super-frontal'. Frontals are often made in various colours to agree with the liturgical colour of the season of the church's year. Where an altar is free standing and visible on both sides two 'frontals' are necessary if the throw-over type of cloth is not adopted. *See* Plate 2 (p. 7 above).

Examples of precious metal frontals were not unknown in the Middle Ages; and we may see an outstanding example still in use at the Church of St Ambrose in Milan by a ninth-century goldsmith.

The present cult of naked and unvested altars so that the structure of the table is visible is not only contrary to the new canons of the Church of England but also to the official rules of the Roman Catholic and Eastern Orthodox Churches.

The practical details for the making of altar frontals and other hangings are given in: C. E. Pocknee, *The Parson's Handbook*, rev. ed., 1965, and The Warham Guild, *The Warham Guild Handbook*, rev. ed., 1963

C. E. POCKNEE

Furnishings *see* Altar Hangings; Corporal; Frontal; Pall; Purificator; Veil

Furniture *see* Altar; Altar Rail; Ambo; Baldachin; Cathedra; Communion Table; Cross; Crucifix; Font; Iconostasis; Lectern; Piscina; Pew; Pulpit; Reredos; Rostrum; Screen

Gallery

A gallery is a platform or balcony projecting from the interior wall of a building. Such galleries were not uncommon over the side aisles in pagan basilicas and were included in the fourth-century Christian basilica (q.v.) as well as in the centralized architecture (q.v.) of the East. They served a twofold purpose: (1) They provided space for the worshippers where the nave was largely occupied by the clergy for the performance of the liturgy and (2) they enabled the women, in the East, to be segregated from the men.

In the large churches of the Middle Ages, particularly cathedrals, the gallery persisted as the triforium, which allowed for circulation and for extra accommodation at the great festivals.

In post-Reformation churches galleries were often erected at the west end for the singers. In auditory churches, galleries, occupying three sides, enabled large numbers of worshippers to have places as close as possible to the minister. So-called Free Church architecture has made great use of this feature. It has one drawback, however, and that is its tendency to divide the congregation to such an extent that its unity and sense of corporateness is impaired.

EDITOR

Genuflexion *see* Postures (2*b*)

Gestures

Liturgical gestures and postures (q.v.) are stylized forms of natural movements of the limbs, especially the hands, in the context of corporate worship. These movements are basically instinctive in character and constitute an important non-verbal mode of communication. The invention of written language eventually made possible the separation of words and gesture and, thus, in religious terms, the differentiation between rites and ceremonies, i.e. the written text of the liturgy and the accompanying gestures and movements.

Protestant rejection of liturgical gesture is based on the association of the gestures with doctrines which are held to be objectionable, e.g. the elevation of the eucharistic elements associated with the theory of transubstantiation and with the eastward position (q.v.).

The significance of liturgical gestures and postures is to be understood mainly in terms of the conversion of personal relationships into directional movements. Thus upward and downward movements can express feelings and beliefs about the man-God relationship, while horizontal movements – towards-self and away-from-self – can be employed to communicate social man-man relationships. Significantly, the Eastern Orthodox name for the central part of the eucharist is anaphora (q.v.) – the Greek word for 'lifting up' or 'offering' (Heb. 7.27). Correspondingly, the kiss of peace is a ritual gesture in which the emphasis is upon the human personal relationships within a Christian community.

1. *Cross, Sign of.* One of the earliest references to signing with the cross is found at the end of the second century in some words of Tertullian: 'at every forward step and movement, at every going in and out, when we put on our clothes and shoes . . . in all the ordinary actions of everyday life, we trace the sign [of the cross]' (*de Cor. Mil.* 3). It is impossible to know whether such continuous domestic self-crossing was ever generally observed, but as a liturgical gesture it certainly became customary and eventually was prescribed as a regular ceremonial gesture at many points in the whole cultus.

A sacramental interpretation is clearly expressed by Augustine (354-430): 'Unless the sign of the cross is made on the foreheads of the faithful, as on the water itself wherewith they are regenerated, or on the oil with which they are anointed with chrism, or on the sacrifice with which they are nourished, none of these things is duly performed' (*Tract.* cxviii *in Joan.* xix 24). Augustine's view of the need for the sign of the cross in the 'due performance' of sacramental acts prevailed in the medieval church, and by the eighth century it was customary to incise crosses on altars and churches at the places where they had been manually anointed with the sign of the cross in the course of their consecration (q.v.).

Thus, signing with the cross became an integral part of the *ex opere operato* sacramental theory of the medieval church and, as such, was rejected by Protestant reformers.

Signing with the cross is still extensively used in this sense in the Roman Catholic Church, but in the Anglican *BCP* it is ordered only in baptism and there merely as a custom which 'is no part of the substance of the sacrament' but which may be accounted 'a lawful outward ceremony and honourable badge, whereby the person who has been baptized is dedicated to the service of him that dies upon the Cross' (Canon XXX, 1603).

The *First Prayer Book* of Edward VI (1549) included two signings in the great eucharistic prayer, but these were omitted in 1552 and the sign of the cross has never been reintroduced into any other authorized *BCP* of the Church of England.

It should be noted that the sign of the cross may be made on or over both persons and things, that it may be single or multiple, and that it may be self-administered or directed towards others. Further, this gesture may take several different forms: originally it seems to have been restricted to the forehead and made with the thumb of the right hand. Subsequently (probably at the time of the Arian controversy), the signing became associated with the Trinitarian formula and the crossing was extended from forehead to heart and across the upper chest – now from left to right in the West and from right to left in the East. Alternatively, a number of small thumb-crossings may be made at various parts of the body, customarily as acts of anointing in the course of rites of initiation or sickness. Self-crossing is common in association with the reading of the gospel, and also at the words 'resurrection of the body' in the creed with the implication 'this, my body'.

2. *Elevation.* This gesture is made in the Roman Catholic Church when the 'celebrant' of the mass raises the host so high that all present may look upon it. The origin and significance of this important act are complex matters and, perhaps more than any other liturgical gesture, it serves to focus attention upon a syndrome of essential differences between Catholics and Protestants, in the matter of sacramental theology.

The elevation itself was first formally recognized in 1210 when the bishop of Paris ordered that before the 'consecration' the bread should not be held more than breast-high, and only after the words 'This is my body' should the host be raised high enough for everyone to see.

The theological arguments of the previous centuries had largely turned upon eucharistic change, and involved the concept of a 'consecration-moment' when the offered bread and wine were so transformed through the words of the priest that the real presence of Christ was an event to be recognized. The faithful had been taught that not only was the 'substance' of the bread and wine changed into the 'substance' of the body and blood of Christ, but that the whole Christ, *totus Christus,* was present on the altar – concealed under the appearance of the bread and wine. The sacrament came to be regarded as so holy that it might not readily be received in hands or mouth, so that, correspondingly, for the faithful, it was all-important to *see* the host. The popular impatience to see led to premature reverence when the priest took the bread and cup into his hands *prior* to the 'consecration', and for this reason it was ordered that the elevation should be a distinct gesture indicating to all the achievement of the real presence and the moment for appropriate reverence.

The eucharistic participation of the congregation consisted in observing with adoration the 'realization' of Christ in their midst and, therefore, it became more important to 'see' *him* in the transubstantiated bread and wine than to eat and drink *them* at the communion.

Other factors in the mainstream emphasis on elevation were the proto-Reformation challenges to the feudal structure and ostentatious wealth of the church from the Albigenses, who virtually denied the hierarchy and the sacraments, and the Cathari, who advocated a church of primitive poverty in which the eucharistic body was accepted as pure bread, *purum panem*. Thus, by emphasizing the real presence of Christ in the cultus, the hierarchy defended its own status and, at the same time, defended a particular theory of eucharistic change against what was judged to be heresy. Essentially the same challenges and reaction reached a climax three centuries later at the Reformation and led to the rejection of any elevation in the Protestant churches. Even the 1549 *BCP* directs that the words of the Last Supper are to be said 'without any elevation, or shewing the sacrament to the people'.

The elevation itself is an extension of a modest 'raising' (*anaphora*) of the sacramental elements as the eucharistic president takes the bread and the cup into his hands when he repeats the corresponding words of the institution narrative. Whether or not it is justifiable to develop this ancient custom into a distinct theological gesture is clearly dependent upon particular theories of how 'consecration' is achieved and how the eucharistic presence of Christ is envisaged.

Prior to the eleventh century the church had not concerned itself with speculation about a precise moment when 'consecration' took place, but, during the thirteenth century, the elevation having been established, a natural ceremonial consequence was that reverence should be expressed by bowing or kneeling and subsequently by prostration and genuflexion, by censings, and by ringing of bells. However, the desire to see waned and it became customary to kneel with bowed head at the elevation. A temporary revival of looking occurred after 1907 when Pius X granted an indulgence to all who said 'My Lord and my God' while contemplating the host, but this practice was officially renounced in 1925.

Current celebration of the mass in the vernacular (q.v.) from the basilican position (q.v.) itself tends to reduce the original significance of the elevation and to reproduce the situation of the first millennium of eucharistic worship when such a gesture and the accompanying reverences were entirely unknown.

3. *Elevation, Little*. The so-called little (minor or lesser) elevation is a gesture of raising both host and chalice (q.v.) at the end of the canon (q.v.), after the words *per quem haec omnia, Domine, semper bona creas, sanctificas, vivificas, benedicis et praestas nobis* (through whom, O Lord, all these gifts are ever created as good, sanctified, vivified, blessed and bestowed upon us). Having said this, the priest then uncovers the chalice and takes it into his left hand and makes a threefold sign of the cross over it with the host held in his right hand, saying 'through him +, with him +, and in him +', and continuing with two more signings between the chalice and his breast 'is to thee God the Father + Almighty, in the unity of the Holy + Spirit', and at this point elevating host and chalice, and concluding 'all honour and glory, world without end'.

The paragraph appears to be a twofold doxology (q.v.), the former part referring to divine creativity mediated through Christ as Logos, while the latter is a declaration of praise being offered through Christ 'present' in the bread and wine. The words '*all* these gifts . . .' are really a vestige of a much earlier prayer associated with the custom of 'eucharistizing' other produce (water, milk, honey, oil, cheese, fruits, seeds, wine and bread) at this point in the mass.

The close association of other 'good gifts' with this elevation of the bread and cup has a certain symbolic value, but in the new *Ordo Missae* (1969) it has been minimized and would generally pass unnoticed in the recitation of the words: 'We hope to enjoy for ever the vision of your glory through Christ our Lord, from whom all good things come. Through him, with him, in him, in the unity of the Holy Spirit [*little elevation*], all honour is yours, almighty Father, for ever and ever.'

The little elevation in the Roman Catholic rite corresponds to a similar ceremony in the Eastern liturgies: the priest within the sanctuary says a secret prayer recognizing the invisible presence of Christ and, as he reaches for the holy bread, the deacon (outside the sanctuary doors) says 'Let us give heed', and then the priest elevates the host and says 'Holy things to holy people'.

4. *Kiss of Peace and the Pax*. As a liturgical gesure, the kiss (actual or token) is a mutual salutation of participants in the Western eucharist: it is now initiated by the president shortly before the communion and, in one form or another, the greeting is exchanged by some or all of those present as a sign of

fellowship.

In the NT there are a number of references to a kiss of greeting, e.g. a 'holy kiss' (Rom. 16.16, etc.), and the linking of the gesture with 'peace' occurs thus: 'Greet one another with a kiss of love. Peace to you all who belong to Christ (I Peter 5.14). Liturgically, the gesture accompanies the pax: *Priest*: The peace of the Lord be always with you; *People*: And with thy spirit. According to Hippolytus a liturgical kiss was given at the conclusion of the initiation rite (thus signifying membership in Christ), and also to a newly consecrated bishop.

It seems probable that the eucharistic kiss originally concluded the synaxis (q.v.) and then, in the light of the command of Jesus to make peace before bringing a gift to the altar (Matt. 5.23f.), became more closely associated with the offertory (q.v.). In the second century, Justin Martyr writes in the *Apology*: 'At the conclusion of the prayers we greet one another with a kiss. Then bread and a chalice containing wine mixed with water are presented to the one presiding over the brethren.' In all Eastern Orthodox rites the kiss remains in this position, but in the Latin rite by the beginning of the fifth century it had been moved to the end of the canon, and was subsequently moved into the midst of the communion ritual.

In the first English liturgy, 1549, the pax remained in a comparable position but without rubrics concerning the kiss: the pax disappeared in the 1552 prayer book but has since been re-inserted in several revisions in English. In the 1967 Series II holy communion of the Church of England, the pax appears as an optional salutation at the end of what is called 'The Preparation of the People' and immediately before the placing of the bread and wine on the table: thus, although no rubrics are provided concerning a ceremonial kiss, the opportunity is provided at the original place in the liturgy, namely the offertory (even though this word is not used). In the 1971 Series III, the pax is made mandatory in the same position, namely, at the beginning of 'The Communion' and immediately before 'The taking of the Bread and Wine': again no suggestion is made concerning any gesture which might accompany the salutation. Similar provision is made in other recent rites, and in some there is a rubric indicating how the gesture may be made; e.g. immediately before the offertory

of bread, wine and alms the Church of South India has: 'The "Peace" may be given here. The giver places his right palm against the right palm of the receiver, and each closes his left hand over the other's right hand . . . The Presbyter gives the Peace to those ministering with him, and these in turn give it to the congregation . . .'.

With few exceptions the liturgical kiss has ceased to be a literal touching with the lips of one person by another, and the gesture may be a light embrace, a hand-clasp or a bow. Again the kiss may be restricted to the sanctuary, or it may be general throughout the congregation. In the latter case, the eucharistic president may initiate a kiss which passes in hierarchical order down through the clergy to the laity or, alternatively, each member of the congregation may simultaneously salute his immediate neighbour. The form of the salutation depends much on what kind of greeting is customary on civil occasions in any community: thus, among East Syrians each person clasps the hand of his neighbour and kisses him, while Armenians merely bow. In the Roman Catholic Church the kiss is limited to a formal 'continental' embrace between the clergy and only at high mass: it is not given on Maundy Thursday, Good Friday or Holy Saturday nor in masses for the dead.

5. *Imposition of Hands.* The gesture of laying hands upon (or over) a person or a thing has the multiple significance of blessing, setting apart, consecrating, commissioning, absolving, healing, confirming, declaring, ordaining, and other associated ideas. Underlying the liturgical act is the notion of the transmission of power, *mana*, authority, spiritual grace, etc., from one specially endowed or recognized person in a community of others. Such channelling of unseen 'charisma' is thought of as being achieved through the physical action of touching with the hands – a visible gesture which can also serve to establish the concept of continuity of role in a sequence of persons, e.g. the apostolic succession.

There are descriptions of laying on of hands in a number of biblical passages – both in the sense of blessing, ordaining or healing and in the sense of setting apart for sacrifice – and these form the basis of the liturgical practices of imposition which developed in the church (e.g. Gen. 48; Acts

8.19; 13.3; I Tim. 4.14; Mark 6.5; 16.18; etc.).

Laying on of hands is often closely associated with anointing with oil and, in this way, the spiritual purposes of ordination, consecration and unction (qq.v.) receive additional visible expression. In the Christian cultus, oil has become a symbol of the gifts of the Holy Spirit – the 'Giver of Life' – and is so used in some rites of baptism, confirmation and ordination (qq.v.) along with the imposition of hands. Such ceremonies still form part of the liturgical practice of the Roman Catholic and Eastern Orthodox Churches, but Protestants generally have discontinued the use of unction, while laying on of hands survives only in those Reformed churches where episcopal ordination is the rule.

In the rites of initiation in the early church, water baptism was always accompanied by anointing and invocation of the Holy Spirit and, through this sacramental gesture, the candidate was incorporated into the 'royal priesthood' (I Peter 2.9; cf. Rev. 5.10) and proceeded to participate in the eucharist. These ceremonies are kept together in the Eastern Orthodox rite of infant baptism without any specific laying on of hands by the priest. In the West, however, the imposition of hands (with anointing) developed as the rite of confirmation (q.v.) and, since the late Middle Ages, in the Roman Catholic Church the sacrament is administered by a bishop anointing the forehead, signing with a cross and extending his hands over the candidate's head. In the Church of England the bishop lays his hands on the head of each candidate but there is no anointing.

Laying on of hands is also an essential ceremony in the rites of episcopal ordination. In the Anglican Church, for example, in the 'making' of a deacon the bishop lays his hands on the head of the kneeling ordinand; in the ordering of priests, not only the bishop but other priests present collectively lay their hands on the head of the deacon; at the consecration of a bishop, the archbishop and other bishops lay their hands on the head of the elected priest. Similar ceremonies accompany the rites of other episcopally ordered communions.

E. Beresford-Cooke, *The Sign of the Cross in Western Liturgies*, 1907; F. Cabrol, *Liturgical Prayer*, 1922; *Dictionnaire d'archéo-*logie chrétienne et de liturgie, 1907/1953; G. Dix, *Shape of the Liturgy*, [2]1945; A. Fortescue and J. B. O'Connell, *The Ceremonies of the Roman Rite*, 1917/1937; J. A. Jungmann, *The Mass of the Roman Rite*, rev. ed. 1959; J. A. Jungmann, *Public Worship*, 1957; C. E. Pocknee, *Cross and Crucifix*, 1962.

GILBERT COPE

Girdle *see* Vestments (1*c*)

Good Friday

In the course of the second century we find the development of the religious observance of fasting on certain days of the week. These 'stations' were half-fasts, lasting until 3 p.m. – the word was a military term conveying the idea of the soldiers of Christ on guard. The observance was clearly an application to the Christian life of the Pharisaic custom of fasting on Monday and Thursday, a change being made, however, to Wednesday and Friday, the days of the Lord's betrayal and crucifixion. Although the stations were accepted by the church, they were regarded as matters private and individual. There was a definite feeling that they were innovations, and that the only real time for general Christian fasting was in the period immediately preceding the great annual festival of the Pascha, commemorating the death and resurrection of the Lord. It seems reasonable to affirm that the existence of the weekly Friday station led naturally to the station on the Friday before the Pascha being transformed from a half-fast into a full fast and being integrally linked with the Saturday of the Paschal fast. This may be regarded as the root of the Good Friday of the late fourth century. Early in the third century the Paschal fast normally extended over the Friday and the Saturday, but in cases of necessity the former could be omitted. At this stage there is not the slightest indication of anything in the nature of Good Friday and, indeed, the Friday is less important than the Saturday. Towards the end of the previous century the custom of fasting on Friday as well as Saturday was not by any means universal, although it was obviously not a recent innovation. It may be affirmed that in the early part of the second century the Friday had no place at all in the fast, which must have been limited to the Saturday. The absence of Friday in the earliest period underlines the truth that there was nothing in the primitive Pascha of what we regard as historical realism.

At Jerusalem late in the fourth century it was beginning to be light on Good Friday when, following services throughout Thursday night, the procession from Gethsemane reached the city. At the Sanctuary of the Cross the entire narrative of the trial before Pilate was read and soon after, still before sunrise, all went to pray at the column where Jesus was scourged. After the people had rested in their homes they returned to the Sanctuary of the Cross. A casket containing a relic which was believed to be wood from the cross was placed on a linen-covered table in front of the bishop. The people filed past, bowing, touching the cross and the title with their foreheads and their eyes, and kissing the wood. At noon they assembled in the open courtyard of the Sanctuary, and from that hour until three o'clock the time was entirely occupied with lessons about the passion, from the psalms and the prophets, the epistles or Acts and the gospels, prayers suitable to the day being said between the lessons. At three o'clock the passage from St John's gospel about the death of the Lord on Calvary was read, and soon after the service ended. In the evening the story of the burial was read in the Anastasis, the Sanctuary of the Resurrection, and a vigil was maintained there throughout the night by all who were able to sustain it. A great crowd took part, although some did not begin their watch until midnight.

It was the development of Holy Week (q.v.) at Jerusalem in the late fourth century which transformed the Friday of the Paschal fast into Good Friday as we understand it. The full growth of Good Friday meant that the commemoration of the passion was detached from the unitive Pascha which eventually came to be designate the resurrection alone. But time was required for the evolution of Good Friday and Easter to become the clear pattern for Christendom.

G. Dix, *The Shape of the Liturgy*, [2]1945; G. Dix, *The Treatise on the Apostolic Tradition of St Hippolytus of Rome*, I, 1937; A. A. McArthur, *The Evolution of the Christian Year*, 1953.

A. A. MCARTHUR

Gospel

The reading of a passage from one of the four canonical gospels concludes and forms the climax of the liturgy of the word which precedes the eucharist proper. The gospel-reading is surrounded with much greater ceremony than the other readings; since the fourth century it has been reserved to the deacon (q.v.). It is customary for all to stand while the gospel is read. The gospel book itself is venerated as a symbol of Christ; before the reading of the gospel the book is carried in procession to the lectern (q.v.), accompanied by lights and incense.

As with the other readings, there are basically two systems for determining the choice of texts to be read. Either a gospel is read more or less continuously, or else pericopes particularly appropriate to the occasion are chosen. Examples of the second system abound in the traditional Roman lectionary as contained in the Roman missal, but the remains of an ancient system of continuous reading can also be discerned. Almost all the gospels of the second half of Lent and of Paschaltide are taken from John's gospel.

The new Roman lectionary (*Ordo Lectionum Missae*, 1969), with its three-year Sunday cycle, devotes a year to the continuous reading of each of the synoptic gospels, John's gospel occupying its traditional place in Lent and Paschaltide annually. The weekday lectionary covers all four gospels every year; in addition a wide choice of gospels is provided for votive masses and the commons of saints, though a number of feasts and saints' days retain proper gospels.

BCP; J. A. Jungmann, *The Mass of the Roman Rite*, new rev. ed., 1959; *Missale Romanum*, 1970; *Ordo Lectionum Missae*; M. Righetti, *Storia Liturgica*, III, [3]1966.

BRIAN NEWNS

Gradual *see* Chants of the Proper of the Mass

Gregorian Chant

From the chronological point of view the chant, which is the traditional music of the Roman Church, is inaccurately described as (1) *Cantus Romanus* (Roman chant); (2) *Cantus planus* (plainchant or plainsong); (3) *Cantus Gregorianus* (Gregorian chant). The term *Cantus planus* was first used in the thirteenth century to distinguish the traditional chant from the various kinds of measured polyphonic music that had come

into being. Pope Gregory (590-604) may
have had some part in the codification of the
chants of the mass *Antiphonale Missarum*
that bears his name and perhaps in the
organization of a *Schola cantorum*, but there
is no certain knowledge about the extent of
his activities, and his writings rarely mention
music. In any case, the early sources of the
so-called Gregorian chant lay not only in
Rome but in Western Europe, in such
centres of liturgical activity as St Gall, Metz,
Einsiedeln, Chartres, Laon, etc. This chant,
moreover, arose also in the Franco-German
empire, and the Frankish clergy stubbornly
resisted the efforts of King Pepin and pre-
eminently those of his son Charlemagne to
establish the Roman liturgy in their lands and
did their best to hold fast to their traditional Gallican rites. The result was that in
the tenth century the Roman liturgy began
to return in force from Franco-Germanic
lands to Italy and to Rome, but it was a
liturgy which meanwhile had undergone
radical changes and a great development.
This importation entailed supplanting the
local form of the Roman liturgy by its
Gallicanized version, even at the very centre
of Christendom.

This is, in fact, substantially the liturgy
which has been in use up to the radical
reforms arising out of the Liturgy Constitution of Pope Paul VI. The two main choir
books before this, were (1) the *Graduale*,
which contains the proper, or variable parts
of the mass, together with the *Kyriale*, containing the ordinary, or invariable part of the
mass; (2) the *Antiphonale*, which contains
the chants of the divine office with the
exception of those used at mattins. These
books contain the largest assemblage of
monophonic music in existence, totalling
about 3000 melodies for cantors, choirs, and
congregations and 'recitatives' for priests,
and cover every phase of the church's
worship from baptism to the blessing of
aircraft. Gregorian chant – to use the now
generally accepted term – is spiritually,
aesthetically, and practically the ideal kind
of church music – truly sung-prayer and
prayer-song.

W. Apel, *Gregorian Chant*, 1958; G. Reese,
Music in the Middle Ages, 1941; A. Robert-
son, *The Interpretation of Plainchant*, 1937;
A. Robertson, 'Plainchant' in *The Pelican
History of Music*, ed. A. Robertson and D.
Stevens, Vol. I, 1960.

A L E C   R O B E R T S O N

Harvest Thanksgiving

Although the OT prescribes a feast to celebrate
the first fruits of the harvest (Pentecost), and
another to celebrate the ingathering of the
threshing floor and the winepress (Tabernacles: Ex. 23.16; Deut. 16.9, 13), the church
does not appear to have observed any such
festivals until relatively recent times. The
Ember (q.v.) seasons of June, September, and
December were agricultural in origin and
very probably related to the pagan observances of Rome at the time of sowing and the
harvests of corn and wine; but in Christian
liturgy these have always been observed as
fasts. However, Lammas (loaf mass: August
1) has been observed in England from Saxon
times and throughout the Middle Ages with
the blessing of bread made from the first ripe
corn.

The harvest home was a secular, weekday,
observance, but it is to be noted that since the
Reformation, in a period when people made
their communion only a few times in the
year, 'afore and after harvest' was one of the
occasions prescribed by George Herbert and
others for the purpose. In 1843 when the
Rev. R. S. Hawker, Vicar of Morwenstow in
Cornwall, revived the Lammas custom (on
the first Sunday of October) and used bread
made from the first ripe corn for the bread of
the sacrament, it was partly his purpose to
redeem the secular character of the harvest
home.

A special prayer of thanksgiving for an
abundant harvest was first officially provided,
for use after the General Thanksgiving, in
1796. Similar provision was made at intervals
for the next fifty years, whenever the abun-
ance of the harvest seemed to justify it. This
led to the belief that such an observance
should be made regularly. It was about this
period that most of the popular harvest
thanksgiving hymns were written, and in 1862
Convocation made official provision for the
occasion with proper psalms, lessons, and
prayers. With the exception of the *BCP*, all
prayer books of the Anglican Communion
today make similar provision for the harvest
thanksgiving, and the American prayer book
has done so since 1790 and the Irish since

1877.

G. Harford and M. Stevenson, eds., *The Prayer Book Dictionary*, 1912. For Ember days (q.v.), *see* G. G. Willis, *Essays in Early Roman Liturgy*, 1964.

E. C. WHITAKER

Hindu Worship

Hinduism is a complex term invented by the West to indicate the majority religion of the Indian sub-continent, but this is a vast area of great religious diversity in which many kinds of worship are practised. There are ancient models, with elaborate scriptural directions, but restricted today to comparatively small circles, and great popular festivals and pilgrimages which attract millions.

The most revered texts are the Vedas ('knowledge'), which were compiled from about 3000 years ago but not written down for many centuries. The most important is the Rig Veda ('praise'), composed of 1028 hymns to the gods of the Aryan tribes of North India. The three other Vedas are the *Sāma* ('chant'), *Yajur* ('sacrifice') and *Atharva*, named after a priest. The Vedas are followed by a series of Brāhmanas, which explain the hymns and their ritual for Brahmin priests, and by philosophical deductions in the Upanishads, which are the 'Veda's end', Ved-ānta.

Vedic religion was priestly and public and it concerned the worship of the gods (*devas*, related to Latin *deus*). These are chiefly ritual and sky gods and nearly all male. Agni (like Latin *ignis*), the god of fire and messenger to the gods, has nearly a quarter of the hymns. Soma, a fermented drink for libations, also has many hymns in the Rig Veda and much of the Sāma Veda. A third most prominent god was Indra, who combined the functions of storm and national warrior deity. There were countless lesser divinities addressed in hymns and sacrifices, but many of these are long forgotten or survive in little-understood texts since the Vedic form of the Sanskrit language has long been obsolete.

The Rig Veda names eight kinds of priest, and in later times double this number might be required. Sacrifices were performed in the open on a brick altar but not in a temple. They centred upon the sacred fire and libation, and other materials were offered, of butter, milk, wine and animal flesh. Priests recited Vedic formulae and these verses were regarded as having sacred and magical power, so that on the one hand Brahmin priests were masters of magic utterance, and on the other the sacred word or power was developed in philosophy to the supreme power of the universe, the cosmic soul or Absolute. There were also great communal sacrifices, royal consecrations and a Horse Sacrifice (*Ashvamedha*) by which kings strengthened and extended their territory.

The chief survivals of Vedic religion today, among high caste Hindus only, are found in marriage and ancestral ceremonies. When a household is established at a wedding the sacred fire is kindled, which is not used for domestic purposes and should never go out, and here three times a day Five Great Sacrifices should be offered. These are to the gods or Supreme Being, the ancestors, living beings including animals, the poor, and wise men through hearing the Vedas. The most elaborate offerings are those made to the ancestors, who receive food and water every day, and gifts of rice-balls (*pinda*) in an open place at each new moon in a Shrāddha ('faithful') ceremony. This begins after the cremation of the dead, and is held to nourish the departed so that they can bless their descendants. This domestic religion is performed by the householder, who has been initiated previously by the conferment of the sacred thread in adolescence which makes him 'twice born'. He also received at that time the sacred verse (*mantra*) which all high caste Hindus recite daily in all rituals: 'Let us meditate on the glorious light of the Sun, may he inspire our minds.'

Most Indians are not high caste males, and even among the latter, many of the Vedic rites have disappeared and popular gods have replaced Aryan deities. Vishnu, Shiva and the Goddess, with hosts of lesser divinities, are the modern objects of worship. Vishnu is for millions the only god, but his transcendental beneficence is coloured by his Avatars (*avatāra*, descent, 'incarnation') who are glamorous personifications. The two most popular Avatars are Krishna, the herdsman and lover, and Rāma, the noble epic king. Shiva is also regarded as the supreme and only real god by his millions of devotees, and many scriptures sing of him in monotheistic terms. His mixed character makes him at once the Lord of the Dance and the Great Ascetic and Yogi, a god of death and destruction and also a gracious teacher who appears in visions to his worshippers. Shiva is the Great God (*Mahā-deva*) whose spouse is the Great Goddess (*Mahā-devī*), known to her followers by various names: Shakti, Durgā, Kālī. In the latter form she is the destroyer-goddess who at Calcutta (*Kālī-ghat*, 'Kālī's steps') and in the region still receives animal sacrifices, practices which most Hindus now find abhorrent. Other very popular gods are the elephant-headed Ganesha, son of Shiva and the Goddess, who brings good luck, and Lakshmi the wife of Vishnu, who is celebrated every New Year. To all of these deities offerings and prayers are made at home and in public.

India is noted for its countless temples, many of them in the south of great beauty and covered with lavish stone sculpture which surpasses even that of Gothic cathedrals. Many northern temples were destroyed by Muslim iconoclasts. Temples are not built for regular congregational services but contain a central sanctuary, usually small, surrounded by courtyards and walls which contain great decorated gateways and pillars, and there are large water tanks for ritual washing. Temple worship is the concern of priests whose rites are not normally observed by the laity. Images and symbols are bathed and anointed, to the accompaniment of repeated texts. In home worship also, images of Krishna and other gods are similarly dressed and washed, and receive food, flowers and incense. Laymen crowd to the temple for special occasions, and notably the annual festivals when temple images are taken to a river and bathed, being drawn in temple cars like the Juggernaut (*Jagan-nātha*, 'world-lord', a title of Krishna).

Other annual festivals mark ancient rites: Holi in the spring as a fertility ritual, Dashara in the autumn celebrating both Kālī and Rāma where carnival processions provide entertainment, and Dīvālī for Lakshmi at the New Year. Many temples are famous places of pilgrimage connected with stories of the gods, and Benares (Varanasi, or Kashi) is the holiest city of all, with rather dilapidated shrines but of antique sanctity, where cremations take place and many holy men come to die. There are also occasional pilgrimage festivals, especially Kumbha Mela ('pitcher fair'), held every twelve years or so, at which millions of people and many holy men attend.

J. N. Banerjea, *Development of Hindu Icono-*graphy, 1946; A. L. Basham, *The Wonder that was India*, 1954; A. Daniélou, *Hindu Polytheism*, 1964; E. G. Parrinder, *Worship in the World's Religions*, 1961; B. Rowland, *The Art and Architecture of India*, 1955; M. Singer, ed., *Krishna, Myths, Rites and Attitudes*, 1966; P. Thomas, *Hindu Religion, Customs and Manners*, 1956; H. Zimmer, *Myths and Symbols in Indian Art and Civilization*, 1953.

GEOFFREY PARRINDER

Holy Saturday

In the primitive church the great festival of the Pascha began on Saturday evening and continued through the night, the fast lasting until midnight or dawn. Although the unity of the cross and the resurrection would be more important than differences of emphasis, the cross would be the great motif of the vigil and the resurrection of the vigil's end, with the sacrament of baptism, followed by holy communion, celebrated at the point where the one yielded to the other. It was inevitable that the evolution of the Pascha into Good Friday and Easter day (qq.v.) should modify in due course the relationship to the latter of Saturday in Holy Week.

A. A. MCARTHUR

Holy Week

When Etheria made her pilgrimage to Palestine towards the end of the fourth century, the complex structure of Holy Week services at Jerusalem was clearly something new in the church's worship. There is no evidence elsewhere at the time for anything of this nature. The week before the Pascha had held a unique position in the Christian year since the middle of the previous century, but there is nothing to suggest that observances on the lines of this rich development existed before the latter part of the fourth century. Now for the first time we find Palm Sunday and Good Friday (qq.v.). The essential feature was the attempt to link the culminating events of the ministry with the days of their occurrence and the places where they happened. Jerusalem was the one locale where the process of change could go forward quite naturally. The essential conservatism of Christian worship makes it most unlikely that important transformations will originate in a region or period which, in respect of the particular matter, is a liturgical vacuum. In Constantinople or Carthage or Rome a development of this nature would not have been evolution but revolution. It was otherwise in Jerusalem. In and around the city were the sacred sites themselves. With the ending of persecution and the erection of sanctuaries on the holy places, pilgrims were arriving from every quarter of the Christian world and ascetics were coming to stay in Jerusalem. Thus, for the enrichment of its worship, the church of Jerusalem doubtless evolved the structure of these services in the third quarter of the fourth century.

Holy Week at Jerusalem was intimately and topographically related to the sanctuaries of the holy places. It was entirely natural in the environment. Etheria described the customs in detail because they were novel. The original contribution of the Jerusalem church involved also the introduction of order and cohesion and the sense of advancing movement from Epiphany to Pentecost. The fundamental aim of this whole development, providentially inspired by the environment, was to make the life of Christ more real and contemporary for the worshipper. So the liturgical year led the Christian realistically from place to place in the sacred narrative, from Bethlehem and the Lord's birth to the Mount of Olives and the ascension, and to the coming of the Holy Spirit upon the disciples in the upper room on Zion. No later complexities could obscure this structure. As for Holy Week itself, there was necessarily some modification in the details of the celebrations as they spread beyond Jerusalem, for complete realism was possible only in the Holy City. It must be emphasized how powerfully the dynamism of this profound innovation surged throughout the Christian world. The pulsation of that movement has never ceased to throb with energy through all the Christian centuries. For it is this idea of liturgical realism, this idea that the life of Christ is manifested to the worshipper in the liturgical year, which has not only transformed Holy Week but has also been the motive power behind the mature growth of the Christian year as a whole.

F. Cabrol, *Les Origines Liturgiques*, 1906; J. G. Davies, *Holy Week: A Short History*, 1963; G. Dix, *The Shape of the Liturgy*, [2]1945; A. A. McArthur, *The Evolution of the Christian Year*, 1953; J. W. Tyrer, *Historical Survey of Holy Week*, 1932.

A. A. MCARTHUR

Hood *see* Vestments (2*d*)

Hour Services
see Canonical Hours

Hymns
1. *Latin*
In his commentary on Ps. 148.14, Augustine described a hymn as 'the praise of God in song', adding that praise to God that is not sung is not a hymn. Ambrose (d. 397) is named as the real father of Latin hymnody, and gave his people hymns in iambic rhythm (short-long) that were easy to understand, to remember, and to sing. *Aeterne rerum conditor* (Eternal creator of the world), sung at the Sunday office of lauds and the most beautiful of the Ambrosian hymns, is unfortunately rarely heard now outside monasteries of strict observance – it has thirty verses! – but a number of hymns of later date such as *Veni creator spiritus* (Whitsunday), *Pange lingua gloriosi corporis mysterium* (Corpus Christi) and *Te Deum* are well known and loved.

About 230 hymn texts occur in the various hours of the divine office (q.v.), but the melodies to which they are set that can be read in the manuscripts date from about the twelfth century. The psalms were regarded as hymns and tradition links the great Hallel group (113-118), which was recited or sung at the principal Jewish festivals and so at the Passover, with the hymn sung at the Last Supper by Jesus and his disciples.

Benedict (*c.*480-*c.*550) made provision in his Rule for hymns to be included in all the hours of the divine office, but the Roman Church did not admit them into the secular office until the twelfth century on account of prejudice against importing other than biblical words into the liturgy, and even more because the form was used by heretics for propaganda purposes.

Polyphonic settings of the hymns began in the thirteenth century and were contributed by such great church composers as Dunstable, Dufay, Josquin des Pres, Tallis and Byrd. Palestrina published a fine collection of forty-five, mostly for vespers, founded on the plainsong melodies.

ALEC ROBERTSON

2. *Vernacular*
Perhaps the first appearance of vernacular hymns came with the Italian *Laudi Spirituali*,

introduced as part of the revivalist apparatus of the Franciscan movement in the thirteenth century, to grow in number and popularity over the next four centuries. Hymn-singing in the vernacular also formed a feature of the worship of the Bohemian Brethren led by John Huss early in the fifteenth century. With the Lutheran and Calvinist reforms of a century later, and the translation of the liturgy itself, new types of vernacular song were introduced – to exert lasting influence upon congregational music. The Lutheran *chorale*, epitomized in *Ein' Feste Burg* and the *Passion Chorale*, provided a melodic line of great strength familiar today in four-square Bach-type harmonized form. Once evolved, the Lutheran chorale-book was to to be preserved in its integrity – no new tunes being added. Succeeding generations of Lutherans thus inherited an unvarying repertoire of congregational song. In Geneva, Calvin introduced the metrical psalm (q.v.), which was a verse translation by Marot and Béze of the prose psalter. Sung in unison to subtly rhythmic melodies largely composed by Goudimel and Bourgeois, the Genevan model was to be adopted in Dutch, Scottish and English churches.

Metrical psalmody thus became for two centuries the staple of congregational music in England – at first in the *Whole Book of Psalms* of Sternhold and Hopkins (1562) and subsequently in the *New Version* of Tate and Brady (1696). Both collections included a few supplementary hymns; and the appearance of Wither's *Hymnes and Songs of the Church* (1623) and Bishop Ken's *Morning, Evening and Midnight Hymns* (1674) indicates that hymn-singing was not dead in England at this time. The signal for its revival was the publication of John and Charles Wesley's *Hymns and Sacred Poems* (1739). Thereafter, Wesleyan congregations soon became noted for the fervour of their hymn-singing; while Anglican bishops remonstrated with their clergy upon the neglected and apathetic state of parochial psalmody.

Under the influence of the Oxford Movement, efforts were made after 1833 to restore to the Anglican service something of its lost dignity; and although the hymn was at first regarded by Tractarians as too reminiscent of Nonconformity to receive approval, under J. M. Neale's leadership that view changed with the appearance of the *Hymnal Noted* (1851), a collection of Latin hymns in translation associated with their plainsong tunes. Less 'advanced' churchmen adopted other collections – such as Havergal's *Old Church Psalmody* (1847) and Gauntlett's *Hymn and Tune Book* (1852) – while Maurice's *Choral Harmony* (1854) introduced the German chorale to English congregations.

All these trends were to merge with the appearance of *Hymns, Ancient and Modern* in 1861. Remarkable for its eclecticism, the new book assembled examples of plainsong, psalm-tune, chorale and old church-tune, adding to that traditional element some new tunes of a distinctive type by Dykes, Ouseley and Monk. During the remainder of the nineteenth century *Hymns, A & M* in successive editions was almost to attain the status of an official Anglican hymnal. Later reaction against the quality of some of the words and music in that book, however, was to produce the *English Hymnal* (1906) and *Songs of Praise* (1926), both of which sought to provide a less emotional tone.

The first authorized modern hymnal for Roman Catholic use in England was the *Westminster Hymnal* (1912). Important collections issued for Nonconformist use include *Wesley's Hymns* (1877), the *Congregational Church Hymnal* (1887) and the *Baptist Church Hymnal* (1900). Perhaps the most challenging hymnal to appear in recent years, the *Cambridge Hymnal* (1967), was designed 'to produce a fitting expression of Christian thought and feeling in the twentieth century'. The words which it contains have been chosen to bear study in their own right, while the tunes have been selected for their excellence and include several commissioned from contemporary composers. The ideals lying behind its compilation are no more exalted than the church is entitled to expect.

P. Dearmer, *Songs of Praise Discussed*, 1952; W. H. Frere, Preface to *Hymns, A & M, Historical Edition*, 1909; J. Julian, *Dictionary of Hymnology*, 1892; K. L. Parry and E. Routley, *Companion to Congregational Praise*, 1953; E. Routley, *Hymns and Human Life*, 1959.

BERNARR RAINBOW

Iconostasis

The term is Greek in origin, and means, literally, 'picture-stand'; it refers to the screen (q.v.) separating the altar in Eastern Orthodox churches from the nave where the main body of the worshippers are assembled. The history of the development of this type of screen has, until recently, been misunderstood by writers in Western Christendom; it has been mistakenly assumed that this kind of screen, entirely covered with icons or pictures and made of wood, has always been a prominent feature of the Eastern Orthodox rite. But this is a telescoping of the historical development of the screen in the Orthodox or Byzantine liturgy.

In the earlier centuries the screen in the Orthodox rite was made of stone or marble (*see* Plate 30) and it differed little from the type of screen still to be found in some of the older Roman basilicas, e.g. Santa Maria in Cosmedin. At first, at Constantinople, pictures were hung on the altar screen on festivals and these were rather like large medallions and made of mosaic or painted with a brush; but they were comparatively small. But as time went on these began to multiply and they tended to become a more permanent feature of the screen in the Byzantine rite.

The solid wooden screen or iconostasis proper, with gates and completely covered with large pictures or icons, appears to be a development in Russia in the late fourteenth and early fifteenth centuries under Theophanes the Greek and the Russian Andrei Rublëv; under them the Byzantine screen was raised in height so that it completely hid the altar from the congregation. With this action, the icons themselves were increased in size from half-length to full-length figures. The fact that these later screens are of wood rather than stone indicates that they are Russian in origin, since that country is a land of vast forests, whereas the stone screen with carved panels and columns was a feature of Byzantium and the eastern Mediterranean area.

The usual explanation of the solid iconostasis is that it veils heaven from earth, the altar being heaven and the saints who are depicted on the screen the mediators between the church on earth and the church in heaven. When the celebrant speaks from the altar obscured by the screen it is as the voice of God speaking to his people on earth. When

Plate 30   Sixth-century Byzantine screen and altar, Archaeological Museum, Athens

the gates are opened and the ministers come forth from the altar to the people at the reading of the gospel and the giving of holy communion, it is like the incarnation when Christ came forth from heaven to earth for the salvation of the human race.

In lesser Eastern churches, such as the Armenian and the Coptic, the iconostasis is not employed, but at certain points in the liturgy a veil or curtain may be drawn across the sanctuary.

V. Lasareff, *Russian Icons*, 1962; C. E. Pocknee, *The Christian Altar*, 1963.

C. E. POCKNEE

Immaculate Conception
see Mariological Feasts

Imposition of Hands
see Gestures (5)

Incense

The term incense is used of a number of

woods and resins which, when heated or burned, give off a fragrant smell; 'frank' or pure incense, otherwise known as *olibanum*, is the solidified resin of trees belonging to certain species of *Boswellia*.

The use of incense in divine worship appears to be of great antiquity and is exceedingly widespread. In the pre-Christian cultures of the Middle East and the Mediterranean, seven religious uses of it may be distinguished: (1) as a sacrifice to the god or gods; (2) as a sacrifice to the shades of a deceased human being or beings; (3) as a symbol of honour to a living person or persons; (4) as a demonifuge, to drive away evil spirits, whether from the living or from the departed; (5) as a means of purification or healing (a use not always to be distinguished from the preceding); (6) as a festive accompaniment for processions and similar ceremonies; (7) simply to create a worshipful atmosphere. It was also used on non-cultic as well as cultic occasions for practical purposes; but there is no evidence for, and considerable evidence against, the theory that this is the origin of its religious use.

During the first three centuries of the Christian era there was no ceremonial use of incense in the church's worship, and many writers of this period refer to it, as to most other practices of other religions, in terms of disapprobation. It is not difficult to account for this attitude; on the one hand incense was inevitably associated in the Christian mind with its use in the emperor-worship test; it was also used in the ceremonies of what the Christians regarded as false religions.

Christian writers of the fourth and fifth centuries modify this disapprobation; they condemn only the sacrificial use of incense. And, indeed, from the middle of the fourth century the honorific use of it spread rapidly in the Christian church. By the sixth century there are clear cases of the use of incense as a sacrificial offering, in the sense of an act of adoration in return for which divine blessings are asked, a use which persists to this day in most of the Eastern liturgies. In the West this sacrificial interpretation has almost completely disappeared since the early Middle Ages, being replaced by the offering of incense not in itself, but simply as a symbol of prayer. The use of incense in one way or another has been common to all the historic liturgies since the beginning of the sixth century at the latest, and in most places it is probably at least a century older.

1. *Incense at the eucharist*. The earliest use of incense at the eucharist was honorific: it was borne before the celebrant at the entrance, and before the book of the gospels before the reading of the gospel. The use of incense in the entrance procession gave rise in the medieval West to a censing of the altar on arrival, a sacrificial or devotional censing, to which was commonly added an honorific censing of the celebrant, and sometimes of others as well. A censing of the altar, or of the book of the gospels on it, came commonly to be prefixed to the bearing of incense in the gospel procession, and in many places a censing of the ministers and the choir was added after the reading of the gospel. From the tenth century a sacrificial or devotional censing was added after the offertory, often with a censing of ministers, choir and people as well. From the thirteenth century, in many places, with the introduction of elevations of host and chalice at the consecration, censing came to be added at this point, as an act of adoration. The detailed arrangements of the censing at any of these points in the service varied widely. According to the revised Roman missal of 1970, incense, when it is used at all, is used in the entrance procession, to cense the altar after the entrance in the gospel procession and during the reading of the gospel; after the offertory, to cense the offerings, the altar, the ministers and the people; and at the elevation of the host and chalice at the consecration.

In the Byzantine as in most other Eastern rites, the eucharist is never celebrated without incense. According to current Byzantine usage, the celebrant or the deacon censes the altar, the offerings on the prothesis (q.v.), the icons, and the people, before the commencement of the service; further censing, the extent and detailed arrangement of which varies from place to place, takes place before the gospel; before, during and after the offertory or great entrance (q.v.); after the consecration; and after the communion.

2. *Incense at the divine office*. Incense is used at the major offices in all the historic rites (in the Roman rite only on Sundays and festivals, in the Eastern rites normally daily). The most characteristic use is a devotional – in origin, and still in some rites, sacrificial – one which is probably a conscious imitation of Jewish Temple practice, at the principal

morning and evening offices (in the Roman rite at the *Te Deum* at mattins, the *Benedictus* at lauds, and the *Magnificat* at vespers; but at the time of writing the Roman office is in the process of considerable re-arrangement). The origin of this use is almost certainly to be traced to the reference to incense in the classic evening psalm, 140 (141).

3. *Incense at other services.* The use of incense in the Eastern rites is extensive, being prescribed in most of them for all major, and many minor, services. Its use in the West is more restricted: its use at funerals (with what original significance is not easy precisely to determine) appears to have been the origin of its use at the consecration of an altar (having been used in the procession of relics to be sealed in the altar), and its use on this occasion is possible itself the origin of other censings of the altar; its use in other processions may also derive from its funeral use, but may be of independent origin; its use, with holy water, at many blessings may originally have been demonifugal.

4. *Incense outside the historic rites.* The non-ceremonial – and occasionally ceremonial – use of incense was common in the Church of England during the seventeenth century; it disappeared in the eighteenth century, to be revived in the later nineteenth century, together with so many other traditional practices, under the influence of the Tractarian movement, in a considerable number of churches. Those Anglican churches which use incense today usually follow the Roman use of it. Incense is also used in a very small number of churches of other Reformed traditions.

E. G. C. F. Atchley, *A History of the Use of Incense in Divine Worship*, 1909.

W. JARDINE GRISBROOKE

Indigenization

The dictionary meaning of the word 'indigene' is 'native'; that of its adjective, 'indigenous', is 'native, belonging naturally (to soil, etc.)'. Indigenization thus presupposes the making, or becoming, indigenous of that which originally is not so. With particular reference to the church, it means that the church in every land should *belong* in its locality in such a way that it will not be seen as a foreign body, an absurd intrusion, or an

engine of a certain ulterior purpose which will be no longer necessary in a free, independent country, or in a society which is claiming to have come of age. It means further, and more significantly, that the church has to be of an intimate, meaningful, and creatively operative relevance by meeting the spiritual and moral needs of the people and thus serving to inform and give guidance to national activities and aspirations.

Placide Tempels writes with perception when he observes, 'It has repeatedly been said that evangelization and catechetical work should be adapted ... Adapted to what? We can build churches in native architecture, introduce African melodies into the liturgy, use styles of vestments borrowed from Mandarins or Bedouins, but real adaptation consists in the adaptation of our spirits to the spirits of these people' (*Bantu Philosophy*, 1959 p. 18). This statement, made out of sincere, deep concern, raises a few issues which show how delicate is the subject of indigenization. First, the word 'adaptation' must be carefully evaluated with regard to meaning and connotation. It signifies that something is being made to fit into a place or situation where it does not belong naturally or originally. It may involve a deliberate, purposive action, something planned and executed towards a definite end; implied in it is a sense of borrowing and fixing or appropriation. Now, there may be a case for 'adaptation' in this sense as far as the externals of things are concerned; but with the delicate, inner, spiritual aspect, it will more than likely fall short of the proper end: for there will always be those deep things of the body which will not accept a foreign element which has been improperly introduced. Secondly, although Tempels sees clearly that a change of heart is necessary on the part of those who evangelize (or go out to civilize!), he appears not to have seen clearly that God's instruments in evangelism have only a transmissive function. 'Adapting our spirits to the spirits of these people', as he recommends, may lead the agent of evangelism to assume that what is essentially the work of the Spirit is his own work. Here, in fact, is the most delicate point in the process of indigenization. The word itself suggests too much the activity of man with regard to the inauguration and development of the church. And this constant, attending danger has always translated itself into a hybridization or a syncretism, or a structural formalism, which leaves the heart practically untouched.

The basic principle of evangelism which will result in a true living church in every area of the world is contained in our Lord's enunciation: 'Truly, truly, I say to you, unless a grain of wheat falls into the earth and dies, it remains alone; but if it dies, it bears much fruit' (John 12.24). The evangelist, be he a foreigner or a national, is a person who, by implication, is always working to liquidate himself. He works to make people see more and more of the Lord of the church and less and less of himself until people are led to know the Lord as the only Saviour, and are endued with the indwelling Spirit who will constantly inform the heart about what is of God (John 16.14,15). John the Baptist was true to this principle when he said, 'he must increase, but I must decrease' (John 3.30).

The theology of the church is a factor of vital importance with regard to indigenization. The root of the predicament and bewilderment of the church today is its lack of bold, clear-cut theology; and that means that it has neglected the cultivation of the presence of God, meditation and prayer. Theology here does not mean anything abstract, merely 'correct', and deliberately and conformingly systematic. It means the saving knowledge of God in the Lord Jesus Christ, which is boldly taught without quibbling and communicated under the guidance of the Holy Spirit to congregations everywhere; the means by which God speaks to the communities of believers and to individual persons in answer to spiritual and moral needs and the ordering of the total life; something, therefore, which brings people into a dynamic, creative, covenant relationship and living communion with the living Head of the Body.

We are beginning to see clearly that this lack of theology is the major handicap in the areas of the world which used to be known as 'mission fields'. We can afford to ignore, for the moment, the fact of the mixed motives of missions and look with unbiased eyes at the honest, genuinely concerned men and women who went out into the 'fields' to preach the gospel and as a result of whose ministry congregations came into being. It is the fact that, almost without exception, these were well-meaning but theologically ill-guided persons. As 'practical' men and women they set out with their major assets which were their Christian convictions, their lives of devotion, and a consequent *practical* Christianity: these were used by God to bring about genuine conversions. But, however good the intentions that they brought to the task, they were little more than evangelistic cobblers who more often than not ended as unintentional founders of a Christianity which is heavily diluted with Westernism, and as advocates of a superior culture and new legalism, to all of which they somehow attach more importance than to the inward reality of conversion. Not only is this so, but their concern to preserve and perpetuate what they have planted is such that they feel called upon to be dispensers of paternalism and to act frequently with such a naive kindheartedness as that of the man who saw a butterfly struggling to free itself from its cocoon, took pity on it, and tried to help it by prizing the cocoon open, with the result that he only succeeded in killing the butterfly!

When Naaman (II Kings 5) decided impulsively, out of gratitude, no doubt, 'that there is no God in all the earth but in Israel', he ordered 'two mules' burden of earth' from the place where he thought that God resided exclusively. 'Two mules' burden of earth' has been the concomitant bane of evangelism all along. It is either the missionaries who decide that it is a *sine qua non* to the local churches in the 'missionary fields', or it is the young congregations who clamour for it. Whichever way its ordering is initiated, plentiful supply of it has never been wanting. And thus, churches throughout most of the world are living, moving, and having their beings, in prefabricated structures, predetermined doctrines and values, and made-in-Europe liturgies – all of which they hardly understand, but which they regard as acceptable because of their foreign 'trade marks which, to them, are of a vital prestige value.

Experience is now showing that, by and large, this method of work is building with hay and stubble. Africa and Asia afford unmistakable illustrations of the predicament of the church in consequence of the shakiness of its position, the questioning of its motives, the indictment of it as a body existing unnecessarily and irrelevantly, and its spiritual and moral paralysis in face of rampant injustice and wrongs.

With the preachers of the early church, the case was different. To the Corinthians, Paul declared his theological position: 'I decided to know nothing among you except Jesus Christ and him crucified . . . that your faith might not rest in the wisdom of men but in the power of God' (I Cor. 2.1-5). He was a herald, with the one aim of presenting Jesus Christ, so that by knowing him the believers might appropriate for themselves and within their own natural contexts the reality of his saviourhood and lordship. Just as education, properly defined and properly conducted, is not a matter of stuffing the mind with ideas, but of 'leading out' or 'bringing out' the best that is in men so that, through discipline and intellectual exercise, the inner man may be liberated to express itself to the fulfilment of personality, so it is with evangelism that is to have real success: it should end in leading congregations of believers to see and discover for themselves that Jesus Christ is the Saviour and the Lord indeed. This is exemplified in John 4. First, as a result of the testimony of the woman, the initial step was taken: 'Many Samaritans from that city believed in him because of the woman's testimony . . .' This may be enough to bring about an organization of people into some form of congregation, but it is not sufficient to achieve a *koinonia*. For that the second step was also necessary: 'They said to the woman, "It is no longer because of your words that we believe, for we have heard for ourselves, and we know that this is indeed the Saviour of the world." '

This brings us to the heart of the matter. The church has to get its Christology right if indigenization is to be realized. A proper understanding of the implications of the incarnation is vital to the life of the church in every age and every context. For the church to have a real sense of *belonging* and direction, each congregation must appreciate the full meaning of 'And the Word became flesh and dwelt among us, full of grace and truth; we beheld his glory, glory as of the only Son of the Father' (John 1.14).

'The Word became flesh and dwelt among us' signifies the relevance and reality of the living Christ to every age and every culture; that is, Christ as the embodiment of the creative, redeeming love of God who in each national or racial situation continues to fulfil the sympathetic, spiritual nurturing of love: 'A bruised reed he will not break, and a dimly burning wick he will not quench; he will faithfully bring forth justice' (Isa. 42.3;

Matt. 12.20). And this is supported by the divine declaration, 'Think not that I come to abolish the law and the prophets; I have come not to abolish them, but to fulfil them' (Matt. 5.17). Thus, the question of what Jesus Christ means to every people in their own home, in their own particular cultural, political, spiritual and moral situations, during their own passages and crises of life, in the celebrations of their joys, in their peculiar weaknesses and temptations, as they 'labour and are heavy-laden', and in the very depths of personal being – what he means in all these must be *personally settled by the people themselves*. And there is no way to bring this about while the 'Jesus' that is being preached and presented is tethered to the confines of the imported 'two mules' burden of earth', wearing a foreign complexion and lacking in the understanding of the day-to-day joys and sorrows and problems of the people. Such a 'Jesus' has always proved inadequate, and those who accept him have always made him only a fashionable addition to the divinity of the traditional culture, which situation has always resulted inevitably in an ambivalent spiritual life.

What we are saying here should be clear. 'Neither theology nor evangelism can be defined in terms of what *we* think *we* want to teach and say to people. They are properly defined as what God is saying through the church to every people in their own native context and in their own circumstances. Theology and evangelism are not directions as to what *we* think that people should be or what *we* want them to be: they are declarations of God and his sovereign will to every race and every nation' (E. Bolaji Idowu, in the Foreword to Kwesi Dickson [ed.], *Biblical Revelation and African Beliefs*, 1969).

This brings us to a still more crucial point – that of the concept of God. In an access of particularity, Paul describes certain people as 'having no hope and without God in the world' (Eph. 2.12). Surely, this should not be taken seriously today? A Jew with a false particularity can say that because he has travelled a long way in his spiritual pilgrimage, forgotten the process by which God in history has led him so far, and is not reckoning with the streams of revelatory knowledge which have merged into the confluence of his current 'developed' concept of God; a modern European can say it of other nations if he is in ignorance of the blend of cultures and beliefs which are upholding his own current culture, or if he will not accept the existence of any other cultures and values apart from his own; but only a brainwashed or imbecile African or Asian will accept it categorically of his own race.

The point here is a serious one indeed; for it is this false particularity, wittingly or unwittingly adopted, which has all along bedevilled all efforts to realize the selfhood of the church in most of the world. It is the major sin which has consistently interfered with the course of the gospel. A wrong conception of God inevitably results in false Christology. The consequent situation, then, is not of God – the living God, 'The Lord . . . the everlasting God, the Creator of the ends of the earth' (Isa. 40.28) sending forth his Son 'when the time has fully come' (Gal. 4.4), but of the strange but good Marcionite Supreme God sending his Son who is caught in a conflict with a Marcionite divinity of evil dispositions. Perhaps there would have been no problem if the thoughts of the missionaries had been the thoughts of the people to whom they present the strange God. As the contrary is the case, a stage has always been set for two Gods in the minds of the congregations of converts – 'the indigenous God', ever alive and active in the intimate places of the passages and crises of life, and 'the imported God', useful only in his own sphere of external, fashionable, and sophisticated activities.

We see, then, that indigenization is first and foremost a thing of the heart. It should come out of the response of the whole being to the authentic and *bona fide* knowledge of the Lord of the church. To be genuine, it must be bound up with true conversion and come as an evolution from within before it expresses itself in outward forms. 'Therefore, if any one is in Christ, he is a new creation, the old has passed away, behold the new has come' (II Cor. 5.17). The antinomous law of discontinuity and continuity applies to individual converts as it does to the corporate personality of a church which forms an organic presence of *the Body* in a nation. The essential person and personal gifts are not destroyed by conversion: on the contrary, the personality is charged with a new life and a new vitality, given a new orientation and purposive direction by the living Head of the Body. For God's purpose to be fully effective

in life, he does not use a person deprived of all sense of initiative; he does not employ a cultural imbecile. The individual or corporate personality whom God uses to fulfil his purpose must be addressable and responsible. 'Such was the appearance of the likeness of the glory of the Lord. And when I saw it, I fell upon my face, and I heard the voice of one speaking. And he said to me, "Son of man, stand upon your feet, and I will speak with you." And when he spoke to me, the Spirit entered into me and set me upon my feet; and I heard him speaking to me' (Ezek. 1.28b-2.2). This is significant. And with it goes the new covenant as prophesied by Jeremiah: true worship and service of God consist in a state of intimate covenant relationship whereby God speaks directly to his people and actuates them in their expression and fulfilment of his will and purpose – God will put his 'law within them, and . . . will write it upon their hearts', then 'they shall all know' him, 'from the least of them to the greatest' (Jer. 31. 31-34).

Indigenization is thus not a mere rearrangement, by borrowing or by imposition or by modification, of external things. Essentially, it is not, and cannot be, man-made. It is essentially of God, in consequence of the deep understanding of the basic facts of Christianity both by spiritual discernment and intellectual grasp on the part of man. This does not by any means signify a suspension of judgment; rather it calls for the conscious pressing on 'to make it my own, because Christ Jesus has made me his own' (Phil. 3.12).

We may now illustrate specifically. Indigenization of the church in Africa, for example, will signify a church that has attained, or is in the definite process of attaining, selfhood. It means that Christian Africans have come to the saving knowledge of God and of his Christ in the way that we have outlined above; and that in everything that has to do with the ordering of the life of the church, they can always say consciously and decisively, 'It has seemed good to the Holy Spirit and to us . . .' The point of this is that in the 'indigenous' church, God is worshipped and served 'in spirit and truth' and not in the way prescribed by some ecclesiastical power-that-be who lives somewhere else. The voice that is heard and obeyed will be the voice of God, and the authority that is the rule of the church's life will be that of the living Head of the church, directly and immediately communicated to it. As I have observed elsewhere (*Towards an Indigenous Church*, 1965, p.13), with particular reference to Nigeria, so it is with the whole of Africa: the absolute lordship of the church and total, undivided allegiance to him is hardly the characteristic of the church. And consequently, he is not as *real* to Christian Africans as he should be if the church were truly indigenous. 'The result is the detrimental fact that it is these over-lords (overseas authorities), and not the Lord of the church, who are "pre-eminent" over the church ... The authority which must be obeyed is largely that of some "oracle" enshrined in the Vatican, in Canterbury, in Scotland, or elsewhere in the United Kingdom or Europe, or of some "Providence" dispensing dollars from America.' A church still shackled with foreign authorities or with foreign conventions cannot be truly *the* church.

The nature of a truly indigenous church I have also discussed amply (*Towards an Indigenous Church*, pp. 11 ff.). It will constitute, in its own locality, a true presence of the one, holy catholic and apostolic church. 'As an organic cell belonging to the whole Body, it naturally partakes of certain characteristics which belong to that Body and shares in various forms as common heritage with other organic cells. Thus, she maintains not only the "faith once for all delivered to the saints", but also certain inevitable elements which have become in various forms integral marks of the life of the church. We may compare the church to a powerful, living stream which flows into and through the nations, giving of itself to enrich the people and transforming the land, bringing from and depositing in each place something of the chemical wealth of the soils which it encounters on its way, at the same time adapting itself to the shape and features of each locality, taking its colouring from the native soil, while in spite of all these structural adaptations and diversifications its *esse* and its *differentia* are not imperilled but maintained in consequence of the living, ever-replenishing, ever-revitalizing spring which is its source. Thus, the local church everywhere has to live up to a distinctive character and keep up a cherished heritage which runs down the ages.'

In connection with this, we must give a warning about the relational attitude of churches to one another, especially with reference to the attitude of the older to the younger churches. It is an elementary theological fact that no ecclesiastical authority or church anywhere who *really* understands the nature of the church and God's purpose in the world has any right to disqualify, or refuse to accept, another *bona fide* church as such, simply because it expresses Christianity in its own cultural spirit under the direct authority of Christ and the immediate guidance of the Holy Spirit. And the younger churches have to be aware of their own position as the redeemed of the Lord and ignore anyone who is threatening to excommunicate them or to stop sending in dollars for no other reasons than that they are 'casting out the demons in your name' and they do 'not follow with us'. The attitude of the churches to one another should be such as is exemplified by Paul: 'To the church of God which is at Corinth, to those sanctified in Christ Jesus, called to be saints *together* with all those who in every place call on the name of our Lord Jesus Christ, both their Lord and ours' (I Cor. 1.2). And here is a message for each local church as well as for all churches in general: 'Therefore, holy brethren, who share in a heavenly call, consider Jesus, the apostle and high priest of our confession ... Let no one disqualify you, insisting on self-abasement and worship of angels . . . and not holding fast to the Head, from whom the whole body, nourished and knit together ... grows with a growth that is from God' (Heb. 3.1; Col. 2. 18-19).

What is indicated with regard to the 'younger churches' is that the real help which they need with regard to their growth towards selfhood is training in theological leadership. Wherever leaders who are theologically equipped are missing in the church, where the leaders themselves do not understand the nature of the church or the metaphysics of their offices, it will always be the case of the blind leading the blind. The matter of training of the right kind is an urgent necessity. Theologians who are equipped to interpret Christianity, for example, in Africa to Africans, or in Asia to Asians, in their own home and cultural setting, are the only ones qualified to help in this delicate task. The need is, in fact, for Pauls who are at home with regard to the knowledge of their own people and are at the same time adequately equipped with firsthand knowledge of God in Christ as well as of the Christian heritage down the ages. Thus will the indigenous church be able to have a guiding theology and a sense of stewardship which today is detrimentally lacking in the lives of the 'younger churches', and which makes of them grovelling beggars who are left with no other choice than to sing the tune dictated by those whose bread they eat.

With regard to 'vestures and gestures', liturgy in general, hymnody, Bible translations, eradication of the denominationalism concomitant of missionary efforts, the unity of the church, and Christian literature, all these are things that will come naturally, though not without discipline, as things to be added unto the churches when they seek *first* the kingdom of God and his righteousness.

One final word: indigenization is a requirement of all churches everywhere, anywhere, in the world, if they are to be adequate for their witness in contemporary situations. It is a mistake for the older churches to live in the notion that their *oldness* as a status symbol is what gives them the right and authority to be called 'orthodox' churches. Every church needs constant renewal, the periodic 'Pentecost' by which the Holy Spirit gives it the utterance meet for the need of the moment in a world which is constantly changing.

———

E. A. Ayandele. *Holy Johnson*; C. G. Baeta, ed., *Christianity in Tropical Africa*, 1968; T. A. Beetham, *Christianity and the New Africa*, 1967; Ernest E. Best, *Christian Faith and Cultural Crisis : The Japanese Case*, 1966; Kwesi Dickson, ed., *Biblical Revelations and African Beliefs*; H. H. Farmer, *Revelation and Religion*, 1954; Adrian Hastings, *Church and Mission in Modern Africa*, 1967; E. Bolaji Idowu. *Towards an Indigenous Church*, 1965; H. A. Johnson, *Global Odyssey*, 1963; Stuart Louden, *The True Face of the Kirk*, 1963; C. Michalson, *Japanese Contributions to Christian Theology*, 1960; H. W. Mobley; *The Ghanaian's Image of the Missionary*; Stephen Neill, *Creative Tension*, 1959; J. Akinele Omoyajowo. *Cherubim and Seraphim Church in Nigeria* (Thesis accepted for the degree of Doctor of Philosophy in the University of Ibadan, 1971); W. Stanley Rycroft, *Religion and Faith in Latin America*, 1958; B. G. M. Sundkler, *Bantu Prophets in South Africa*, 1961; John Taylor, *The Growth of the Church in Buganda*, 1958; Harry Thomas, *The New Religions of Japan*; Charles Williams, *The Descent of the Dove*, 1950; S. G. Williamson, *Akan Religion and the Christian Faith*, 1965.

E. BOLAJI IDOWU

Institution Narrative
see Anaphora (6) and Canon

Insufflation

Having the precedent in John 20.22, the church used insufflation to signify the conferring of the Holy Spirit, and also the expulsion of the evil spirit. This ceremony, however, is found not in the rites of ordination but in those of baptism (qq.v.), where it occurs among the preliminaries in Hippolytus' *Apostolic Tradition*, when the bishop exorcized the candidates, breathed on their faces and sealed them with the sign of the cross, in symbolic fashion expelling the evil spirits and barring the door against their return. Cyril of Jerusalem too said that exorcisms (q.v.), infusing fear by a divine breath, made the evil spirit flee. Infants, said Augustine, are exorcized and breathed upon to show that they are delivered from the power of darkness and transferred to the kingdom of Christ. Quodvultdeus explained that it was not the person created by God that was breathed upon but he who holds in his power all who are born in sin.

According to Gennadius of Marseilles, exorcism with insufflation was an ecclesiastical custom universally observed. Other authorities who mentioned it are John the Deacon of Rome (but not the Gelasian Sacramentary or *Ordo Romanus XI*), Isidore of Seville, Hildephonsus of Toledo, the Mozarabic *Liber Ordinum*, the Gallican Bobbio Missal, and in Germany Alcuin, *Ordo Romanus L* and the Sacramentary of Fulda.

The Latin rite of baptism known to the Reformers began with a breathing on the child's face, together with the words, 'Depart from him, unclean spirit, and make room for the Holy Spirit, the Comforter.' In his first *Taufbüchlein*, Luther retained the ceremony while translating the formula into German; three years later he abolished the ceremony but kept the formula. The first services of baptism in the vernacular used in Strasbourg and Zurich included the insufflation; but

Bucer and Zwingli subsequently abolished it. There was no insufflation in Calvin's Genevan or Knox's Scottish rite. In England the prayer book of 1549 ordered the priest to look upon, as opposed to breathe upon, the child, as he said a prayer of exorcism. Thus among the Reformed churches Luther's view prevailed that insufflation was an unnecessary outward ceremony. It has, however, survived in the Roman Catholic Church to the present day.

Insufflation for the purpose of exorcism accompanied the renunciation of Satan in the Byzantine and Coptic rites and the *Effeta* (*see* **Baptism** 11) in the Ambrosian Manual.

In the Gregorian Sacramentary, Sarum Manual, the medieval rites of Gaul, Spain and Germany, and in the Jacobite and Maronite rites, the officiant breathed on the water in the font while reciting the prayer for its consecration. This symbolized the entry of the Holy Spirit into the water, as a result of which the ensuing baptism was a regeneration by water and the Spirit and not a merely physical washing. Timothy of Alexandria and the Coptic rite supply evidence of a breathing on the candidates at the anointing with chrism which concluded the rite of baptism, and which had the purpose of imparting the Holy Spirit to them.

H. Denzinger, *Ritus Orientalium*, 1863; J. D. C. Fisher, *Christian Initiation: The Reformation Period*, 1969; E. C. Whitaker, *Documents of the Baptismal Liturgy*, 1960.

J. D. C. FISHER

Intercession

Intercessory prayer has from the very beginning been given a prominent place in Christian worship. Its earliest formal embodiment in the liturgy appears to have been in the common prayers which concluded the synaxis (q.v.), to which reference is made in the first detailed outline of the eucharistic liturgy, that in the *First Apology* of Justin Martyr; the forms which these prayers have taken in the principal historic rites are briefly considered in the article just cited.

Intercessions in the eucharist proper appear to have been a slightly later development, although it is not possible to assert this categorically; while no conclusion can be drawn from a possibly ambiguous phrase in Justin Martyr, and there are certainly no intercessions in the eucharistic prayer contained in the *Apostolic Tradition* of Hippolytus of Rome, the earliest text of such a prayer which is known to survive, all other ancient liturgies, and those of the historic rites following them, include an intercessory element either in the eucharistic prayer itself (the most common place) or in close connection with it. Assuming that these intercessions are no original part of the prayer, in its earliest forms, it is most likely that they originate in the diptychs (q.v.), especially as in some eucharistic prayers, most notably the historic Roman canon, they retain a marked diptychal formulation. The theological rationale of intercessions in the eucharistic prayer is briefly considered in the article anaphora (q.v.).

From the last quarter of the fourth century at the latest, intercessory prayers have been included in the divine office (q.v.), their form and content, as well as their prominence, varying considerably from one historic rite to another. A similar considerable variation is to be found in the treatment of the intercessions in the liturgies compiled during and after the Reformation and their later revisions, both in eucharistic and in non-eucharistic services.

Contemporary liturgical revision displays a marked trend towards restoring the intercession of the synaxis (q.v.) where this has been dropped over the centuries, and with it, in some circles, to the suppression of any intercessory element in the eucharist proper; the latter tendency appears to owe more to liturgical archaeologizing than to serious theological consideration. A further contemporary trend is towards a more free and flexible form of intercession than has been customary for at least sixteen centuries, a change admirable in theory, but often productive of considerable problems in practice.

W. Jardine Grisbrooke, 'Intercession at the Eucharist' in *Studia Liturgica*, IV, 1965, pp. 129-55; *ibid.*, V, 1966, pp. 20-44, 87-103, and works therein cited.

W. JARDINE GRISBROOKE

Introit *see* Chants of the Proper of the Mass

Invocation

A calling upon God or the saints in prayer or attestation. So the epiclesis (q.v.) is an invocation of God to send down the Holy

Spirit. Prayers before sermons, calling on
God to assist the preacher in declaring his
word, are similarly invocations.

EDITOR

Islamic Worship

The Muslim's concept of worship is *'ibādat*
or 'service' rendered to God by man, the
'abd or 'servant' of God. *'Ibādat* is traditionally coupled with *mu'āmalāt* or 'works',
in order to stress the Islamic view that
spiritual and secular duties, duties to God and
duties to one's fellow men, belong together.

The duties of worship are summed up in
the 'five pillars of the faith': (1) confession
of the unity of God and prophethood of
Muḥammad (*shahādat*); (2) ritual prayer
(*ṣalāt*); (3) almsgiving (*zakāt*); (4) fasting
(*ṣawn*); (5) pilgrimage (*hajj*. These are all
obligatory (*wājib*) on the capable adult believer, and all have a communal dimension.
There are also many additional duties recommended (*sunnat* or *mandūb*) for the
believer; these may have a more individualistic flavour, such as intercessory or supplica-
tory prayer (*du'ā'*) or free-will almsgiving
(*ṣadaqāt*).

The central act of Muslims' worship is the
ritual prayer. This is offered five times per
day by the orthodox Muslim: between dawn
and sunrise; after noon; before sunset;
after sunset; when night has fallen. These
prayers may be offered anywhere, although it
is recommended for men that they should be
offered in the mosque (women are permitted,
though not recommended, to use the
mosque). On Friday the midday prayers
should be congregational prayers in the
mosque, with a sermon preached in addition.
The basic furniture of the mosque is simply a
niche (*miḥrāb*), directed towards Mecca (the
direction [*qiblah*] of all Islamic prayer), and a
pulpit or ladder (*minbar*) from which the
sermon is preached; small mosques may have
nothing more than an indication of the *qiblah*.

The words used in the call-to-prayer
(*adhān*), given by the muezzin (*mu'adhdhin*)
from the minaret, if there is one, or from the
entrance to the mosque, include, with various
repetitions: 'God is most great . . . I bear
witness that there is no god but God . . . I
bear witness that Muḥammad is the prophet
of God . . . Come to prayer! . . . Come to
the good! . . . (in the early morning) Prayer is
better than sleep! . . .' Only in Turkey have
there ever been reforms attempted to use a

vernacular for these formulae; otherwise
Arabic, the language of Qur'ānic revelation, is
used all over the Muslim world for the call-
to-prayer and for the liturgical service of
ṣalāt which follows. After ritual ablution
(*wuḍū'*) of the face, hands and feet (assuming
that the body and clothes of the worshipper
are already clean), the worshippers line up
behind the *imām* who is chosen to lead the
prayers by virtue of his learning or seniority;
every one joins in the prayers both physically
and verbally. They stand and recite the prayer
of intention (*niyah*) that they may be sincere.
With their open palms by their ears and held
facing forwards they say, 'God is most great'
(this prayer is called the *takbīr*). Standing
with downcast eyes and hands folded, they
pray a prayer of praise called the *subḥān*, and
then the first *sūrah* of the Qur'ān followed by
at least one long or two short verses from
elsewhere in the Qur'ān. Bowing from the
waist, with hands on the knees, the *takbīr* is
repeated with another prayer of praise
(*tasbīḥ*). Everyone then stands erect, with
arms at the side, and after the *imām* has said,
'God hears him who praises him', they reply
'Lord, thou art praised' (if one is alone one
recites both sentences). With knees, nose and
forehead touching the ground in full prostration the *takbīr* and *tasbīḥ* are repeated;
sitting back on the heels with hands on the
thighs the *takbīr* is again offered before
renewed prostration and *tasbīḥ*. After repeating this rite (from the Qur'ān recitation
to the prostration) one or more times (depending on the time of day), the liturgy
concludes with the worshipper kneeling and
offering prayers of blessing upon the prophet
and upon God's righteous servants. Finally
the 'peace' (*salām*) is said first to the right and
then to the left.

With the completion of this rite of *ṣalāt* the
worshipper may go on to offer further more
intimate prayers of 'secret whisperings' or
'supplication' (*munajāt* or *du'ā'*); these are
offered in a kneeling position with the open
palms held together facing the neck. There is
a very rich devotional literature in Islam containing such prayers selected from the Qur'ān,
the biography of the prophet and the traditional *Ḥadīth* literature of the prophet and
the early community of Muslims. To this has
been added a wealth of prayers and poetry
attributed to famous mystics of Islam, many
of whom asserted their influence over their
followers by prescribing particular forms of

supererogatory prayer. An excellent analysis of their prayer manuals is Constance Padwick, *Muslim Devotions*, 1961.

A famous treatise on the external and the internal aspects of *ṣalāt* and *du'ā'* is the book on worship in the *Iḥyā'* of al Ghazalī, translated as *Worship in Islam* by E. E. Calverley, 1925.

Special acts of worship are associated with annual feast days (since the lunar year is followed dates must be calculated from tables such as those in G.S.P. Freeman-Grenville, *The Muslim and Christian Calendars*, 1963). The chief festivals are *'Id al-Fiṭr* at the end of the month of fasting and *'Id al-Aḍḥā* during the month of pilgrimage. Descriptions of these occasions could be found in T. P. Hughes, *A Dictionary of Islam*, 1885, and further details of the pilgrimage to Mecca are given in A. Kamal, *The Sacred Journey*, 1961.

The discipline and the rhythm of Islamic worship has been a unifying and appealing factor in Islamic history. Without any dependence upon a 'clergy' (which does not properly exist in Islam), the individual, the group or the whole 'people' have demonstrated a pattern of response to God and communion with God which has commended itself to increasing numbers, especially in Asia and Africa. While other aspects of Islamic jurisprudence have undergone modernization, the 'five pillars' remain intact in theory and also in the practice of many Muslims. Few Muslim parents would neglect to instruct their children in matters of worship.

J. TAYLOR

For bibliography see above.

Jacobite Church
see West Syrian Worship

Jehovah's Witnesses' Worship

Jehovah's Christian Witnesses are a body of ministers 'announcing Jehovah's kingdom' and anticipating an early end to the present system of things.

'Jehovah's witnesses are not a sect but are an association of men and women who put God's service first' (*The Watchtower*, 15 April 1970, p. 249). That is to say, they do not follow any man as founder or leader. Abel was 'the first true witness of God' (*ibid.*). 'You are my witnesses,' Jehovah said to Israel, 'and I am God' (Isa. 43.10-12). Jesus is God's 'faithful witness' (Rev. 1.5). Today's Christian Witnesses believe they continue this ancient line.

A belief that we are in this order's last generation necessarily affects one's worship. Witness meetings reflect this in a sense of urgency and earnestness. All congregations have five weekly meetings, each an hour long, designed (1) to give Bible instruction and (2) to equip the hearers for public ministry.

Foremost is the *Watchtower* Bible study, a question-and-answer discussion of some twenty-five to thirty paragraphs of *The Watchtower*. Subjects reviewed in 1969 included 'Look to the Bible as Our Guide in Life' (on conduct), ''Sounding Down'' the Truth into Minds and Hearts of Learners' (*katecheo*, Gal. 6.6). 'Why Almighty God Laughs at the Nations' (Ps. 2.4), and '"Between-the-Lines" Translations of the Bible' (introducing a new interlinear Bible translation).

Generally held mid-week, the Theocratic Ministry School provides training in public speaking and teaching. Men and women, old and young, are encouraged to enrol. A qualified minister gives commendation and offers counsel to the students in turn as they deliver six-minute talks and demonstrations.

The Congregation Book Study, held in private homes, enables a small group to scrutinize Bible topics. The subject might be a year-and-a-half's study on Christian doctrine and practice, or a verse-by-verse analysis of Revelation, two courses which were featured from 1967-1970.

Remaining are the Sunday Public Talk, on general scriptural exposition, and the Service Meeting, where suggestions for the public ministry are offered, particularly how to conduct home Bible studies with interested persons.

A newcomer to the Kingdom Hall would notice the audience participation and variety of presentation. There is little 'preaching' at the audience. Use may be made of a blackboard, charts, diagrams, platform discussion, short demonstrations, and other teaching aids. In time, everyone in the congregation has some share. Witnesses address one another as 'brother' or 'sister'. The presiding minister and his assistants are termed 'servants': congregation servant, *Watchtower* study servant, ministry school servant, etc.

Modern Witness congregations began in

the 1870s when Charles Taze Russell began a Bible-study class with friends in Pittsburgh, USA. An early book, *Three Worlds* (1877), pointed forward to the year 1914 as the time for God's kingdom to be fully established in heaven. Since 1914 the prophecies of Matt. 24, II Tim. 3, Rev. 6, etc. have seen fulfilment. The generation alive in 1914 will see this system end. Then follows the 'restoration of all things' (Luke 21.29-32; Acts 3.20, 21).

Not unrelated to this, Witnesses are conscientiously honest and law-abiding, and cheerful. They acknowledge governments as 'superior authorities' by God's permission (John 19.9-11; Rom. 13) but adopt a course of 'neutrality', political non-involvement, and are conscientious objectors in war-time (John 18.36). As a consequence, totalitarian governments have found them hard to tolerate – Hitler put some ten thousand into concentration camps, and countries like Portugal, Spain and the communist bloc have a history of maltreatment. Thousands were arrested in the democracies from the thirties to the fifties on the non-combatant issue and for public preaching, followed by vigorous litigation by the Witnesses in the highest courts of the lands. (On Rom. 13 and neutrality, *see Life Everlasting – In Freedom of the Sons of God*, chs. 7 and 11.)

From 71,509 ministers in 1939 they had grown to 317,877 by 1949; to 871,737 by 1959; and by 1969 to 1,345,111 in 200 countries. A weekly average of 1,097,237 free home Bible studies were conducted worldwide with non-Witnesses in 1969. To aid in this 'final witness' the New York printing plant alone produced 502,739,345 Bibles, books, magazines and other items of literature in 1969.

Aid to Bible Understanding, 1969; *Jehovah's Witnesses in the Divine Purpose*, 1959; *Make Sure of All Things*, 1965 (all published by the Watchtower Bible and Tract Society).

A. HELEY

Jewish Worship

Prayers are regarded as the service of the heart (*avoda*), which has the same meaning as the Greek word 'liturgy', connoting duty and service. The custom of saying fixed prayers was established long before the Temple of Jerusalem was destroyed in AD 70. In synagogues (assembly-halls) the local communities met for instruction, communal prayers and recitals of biblical texts. Three quotations from the Pentateuch (Deut. 6.4-9; 11.11-21; Num. 15.37-41) form even today the central part of the morning and evening prayers. They declare God's unity (*Sh'ma Israel* – 'Hear, Israel, the Lord our God, the Lord is one') and the duty to love him and to follow his commandments. Before and after these recitals God is praised as the Master of the Universe 'who creates the light' (morning prayer); 'who lets the night follow the day' (evening prayer); who gave his Law to Israel and who is the Redeemer of his people in past and future.

Many more prayers and petitions were added in the course of time, above all the 'Eighteen Prayers' (*sh'mone esre*) which are said three times a day and contain petitions for the granting of knowledge, forgiveness, health and material well-being, as well as the fulfilment of messianic hopes, referring to the rebuilding of Jerusalem, the coming of the Messiah, the restoration of the temple-service in its old place and a prayer for peace. To create the right devotional atmosphere, many psalms and prayers of great teachers, adopted by their disciples, were added. Though the temple-service with its regular sacrifices came to an end with the destruction of the Temple in Jerusalem, the order of the service left its mark on the liturgy of later times. Not only does the Jew say prayers turning in the direction of Jerusalem, the prayer-times were fixed to correspond with the former daily morning and afternoon-sacrifices. Prayers are said at morning, afternoon and evening. On Sabbath, New Moon and Festivals, when extra sacrifices used to be offered, an additional prayer (*mussaf*) is said in the synagogue.

Readings from the Torah ('Five Books of Moses') and the Prophets are an essential part of the service on Sabbath-days and festivals. Two thousand years ago the Hebrew texts were also translated into a language which the ordinary people could understand, Aramaic (Targum) or Greek. The reading of the Torah is divided into weekly portions throughout the year. The religious leaders, the 'Rabbis', added their own interpretations in homiletical sermons.

After the dispersal of the Jews over many countries and their ensuing separation from their homeland, many poets described the religious message of the festivals and other special days of the Jewish calendar in lyrical form (piyutim). Some of them, like the verses by Eleazar Kalir (eighth century), were universally acclaimed and became part of the prayer-book. Further contributions were made by the great Spanish poets Solomon Ibn Gabirol, Yehuda Halevy, Abraham Ibn Ezra and others, who combined mastery of language and beauty of verse-form with deep spiritual thought. They also wrote prayers of supplication (s'lihot) to be recited on days of penitence and fasting, particularly during the weeks before and after the Jewish New Year and the Day of Atonement.

The great multitude of prayers caused many communities to make their choice from the abundant literature available. This led to different collections of prayers. Though prayers were not written down in earliest times, the continuing spread of Jewish communities in the Diaspora made it necessary to give guidance on the form and contents of the prayers. The first known prayer books were compiled by the heads of the Babylonian Academies in the ninth and tenth centuries. Other prayer books were written in different European countries, the best known in the twelfth century, the Mahzor Vitry. The prayer books not only contain the daily prayers, but are a compendium for the devotions for all days of the year and for all occasions like birth, wedding and mourning.

In spite of the fact that the Jews who lived for centuries in Mediterranean countries (Sephardim) differed in their customs from the Jews of Central and Northern Europe (Ashkenazim), the main prayers and the essential mode of worship remained fundamentally the same. Only the additional prayers (piyutim) show a variation according to the place of origin. A great unifying force for Jewish worship is the calendar, common to Jews throughout the world.

Prayers in the synagogue are led by a reader (hazzan) and the other worshippers respond by saying amen. The reader is no priest, and anyone with the necessary knowledge of the order of service and its content may act in this capacity.

There are no sacramental features in Jewish worship; even weddings and burial ceremonies are no exceptions. The spiritual head of the community is the Rabbi, which means 'teacher'. His contribution to Jewish worship in modern times is the sermon, which nowadays is an important part of the synagogue service and mostly based on the text

provided through the weekly readings from the Torah.

A new element in the order of service came with the spread of mysticism among wider circles of the Jewish population in Europe (seventeenth and eighteenth centuries), above all through the Hassidic movement. Many meditations, the origin of which are to be found in cabbalistic works, were introduced into the prayer book, a number of them containing references to heavenly beings, whose intercession is invoked. The desire to modernize the synagogue service was felt strongly in the nineteenth century, at the time when the medieval isolation of the Jews had finally come to an end. In many communities the knowledge of Hebrew had declined and translations of the texts have found their way into the prayer books. The traditional prayers were revised and cleared of obscurities and grammatical errors (Heidenheim). To enhance the beauty of the service, greater care was taken with the vocal part, in particular the recitations by the reader who is now often supported by a choir. In Orthodox synagogues the use of musical instruments is not permitted, as a sign of mourning for the destruction of the Temple, but in Reform synagogues the organ and other instruments are used and many great musicians have contributed compositions for synagogue services. In Reform and Liberal synagogues the overall length of the service has been reduced; also, contrary to traditional usage, women sit with the men, and take an active part in the conduct of the service. Jewish worship is not confined to the synagogue. It is the duty of the individual to say prayers even when he cannot join in corporate worship. Many prayers have their setting in the home, e.g. kiddush and havdallah, to be recited at the beginning and the conclusion of the Sabbath and festivals. Grace before and after meals and the well-known Passover-service, the Seder, are also acts of worship performed in the home.

On all occasions when prayers are to be recited, heads remain covered.

Ismar Elbogen, Der jüdische Gottesdienst in seiner geschichtlichen Entwicklung, 3rd ed., 1931; N. H. Glatzer, Language of Faith, 1967 (a selection of Jewish prayers of all times); J. H. Hertz, The Authorised Daily Prayer Book, rev. ed. with commentary, 1947; A. Z. Idelsohn, Jewish Liturgy and its Development,

1967; L. Zunz, *Gottesdienstliche Vorträge der Juden*, 2nd rev. ed., 1892; L. Zunz, *Literaturgeschichte der Synagogalen Poesie*, 1865.

JACOB POSEN

Kiss of Peace *see* Gestures (4)

Kneeling *see* Postures (2*c*)

Kyrie

The invocation *Kyrie eleison* (Greek, 'Lord have mercy') is found in nearly all the historic liturgies, in many of them in the original Greek, whatever the language of the rest of the service, and appears to have been derived both from Jewish and from pagan liturgical formularies. The first definite evidence of its use as the response to the petitions of a litany (q.v.) comes from fourth-century Jerusalem and Antioch, whence both the litany form itself and this response rapidly spread to all parts of the Christian world.

At Rome an intercessory litany of this type was inserted after the introit of the mass in the fifth century, probably during the pontificate of Gelasius (492-6), who was responsible for considerable changes in the Roman liturgy; texts of this and related litanies survive. At the time of Gregory the Great (590-604), and probably at his instance, the petitions of this litany were omitted on ordinary days, the responses being sung alone, as precatory acclamations. By the end of the eighth century the litany had disappeared altogether, and the acclamations were arranged in a way which remained fixed for over eleven hundred years – *Kyrie eleison* three times, the variant *Christe eleison* three times, and finally *Kyrie eleison* again three times. In the revised *Ordo Missae* of 1969, the same order is retained, on those occasions when the *Kyrie* is ordered to be used, but the threefold form has been replaced by a responsorial twofold one. The *Kyrie-Christe-Kyrie* alternation has often been explained in a trinitarian way, the prayer being said to be addressed first to the Father, then to the Son, then to the Holy Spirit. This is historically incorrect: there is no question that the whole prayer was originally addressed to the Son.

Kyrie eleison is still the most common response to litanies in the Eastern rites, although the acclamation alone, in variously numbered groups, is found in them also; the ninefold and sixfold Roman forms, with other variants, are found also in many reformed liturgies in the West.

———

J. A. Jungmann, *The Mass of the Roman Rite*, I, 1951, pp. 333-46.

W. JARDINE GRISBROOKE

Lammas *see* Harvest Thanksgiving

Lamps *see* Candles

Last Gospel

The reading of the Johannine prologue (John 1.1-14) at the end of mass only became general with the *Missale Romanum* of Pius V, published in 1570. It was suppressed in 1964 as part of the reform of the rite of mass for which Vatican II legislated. In the Middle Ages this gospel was considered to have miraculous efficacy when read; it was used as a blessing for fine weather and was read over the sick. The 1614 *Rituale Romanum* concludes the rite for the visitation of the sick with the reading of this gospel.

It is first found as the conclusion of the mass in the Dominican Mass Ordinary of 1256. It was said in the sacristy (q.v.) by the priest as he took off his vestments (q.v.), or later. From the Dominicans the custom passed to the Armenians, who retained it even after the schism of 1380. At the end of the Middle Ages the last gospel was read, like the gospel of the mass, at the north end of the altar, and the people often joined in its recitation.

Originally it seems likely that the Johannine prologue was read as a blessing; it came of course immediately after the blessing at the end of mass. As time went on, however, the content of this pericope came to be emphasized for its own sake. This trend clearly predominated once it became customary to read as the last gospel the gospel of a second mass formulary merely commemorated in the mass of the day, a practice found from the fifteenth century which originated in the 'dry' mass (q.v.).

———

J. A. Jungmann, *The Mass of the Roman Rite*, new rev. ed., 1959; A. G. Martimort, ed., *Introduction to the Liturgy*, 1968; M. Righetti, *Storia Liturgica*, III, ³1966.

BRIAN NEWNS

Last Rites *see* Unction

Lauds *see* Canonical Hours

Lavabo

Lavabo is the first word of Ps. 26.6: 'I will wash my hands in innocency' – the verse which is recited at the ceremonial washing of the hands in the eucharist. From the patristic period this washing usually accompanied the offertory (q.v.). Cyril of Jerusalem is the first witness, although it was probably practised long before his day. According to him, it is essentially symbolic: 'We do not set out for church with defiled bodies' (*Mystag.* 5.2). In the *Apostolic Constitutions* (8.11f.) the sequence is pax, handwashing, offertory and *Sursum corda*. So the action was not a cleansing of the hands after the reception of the gifts.

In the Ethiopic rite, the priest does not dry his fingers but sprinkles the remaining drops towards the people with a warning that only the pure should approach. The emphasis therefore is not upon hygiene but upon purity symbolized by the ceremonial cleansing.

In the Middle Ages in the Roman rite the symbolism was subordinated to the cleansing – an unusual reversal, since the general rule was for utilitarian actions to be given a symbolic meaning – and the *lavabo* was transferred to a position after the reception of the gifts and the censing. The ancient position is retained only in the Carthusian rite.

Since Carolingian times a preliminary washing of the hands has accompanied the vesting and a similar practice is found in some manuscripts of the Liturgy of St Chrysostom, but it would be incorrect to apply the term *lavabo* to this.

J. A. Jungmann, *The Mass of the Roman Rite*, new ver. ed., 1959, pp. 349-52.

EDITOR

Lay Preacher

This is often a term used simply to describe a lay person who takes services and preaches when there is no minister. In some Baptist, Congregational and Presbyterian churches, however, lay preachers are formally recognized and authorized, after receiving the necessary training, and are often responsible for maintaining services in small congrega-tions who could not support a full-time minister.

P. HINCHLIFF

Laying on of Hands
see Gestures (5)

Lectern

Lectern, as its name implies, means a structure from which lessons are read in public worship. Sometimes the desk for holding the liturgical book or Bible is attached to a pulpit-like structure, known as an ambo (q.v.). But in other instances the lectern is a desk supported on a post or column of wood or metal with feet at the base. Lecterns of this kind were made of wood, bronze and latten

Plate 31 Modern lectern designed by Colin Shewring

in the Middle Ages. Examples of the desk being supported by an eagle or pelican with wings outspread were much in evidence. But other examples of lecterns made of wood and carved in great detail, and sometimes with a double-desk that revolves on the column, came into use in the late Middle Ages, e.g. the one in Shipdam, Norfolk, England. *See* Plate 31.

C. E. POCKNEE

Lectionary

The term is employed in both a wider and a narrower sense. In the wider sense it denotes an ordered system of selected readings ('pericopes') appointed for liturgical use on specific occasions in the church year, thus presupposing a calendar, while in the narrower sense it is used to designate a MS (especially in Greek) with the pericopes thus used written out in full. Lectionaries in this latter sense provide important evidence for the history of the NT text.

The concept of the lectionary in the wider sense evidently goes back to the synagogue, which also had fixed readings from the OT appointed· for the Jewish feasts, with pericopes chosen on the principle of *lectio continua* (*l.c.*) for ordinary Sabbaths. But the extent to which the church took over the synagogue system for its OT lessons is unclear, except for Ex. 12,. which was used at the Jewish Passover and also for the Christian 'Pascha' (better: 'Passa', so J. Jeremias), as evidenced both in Rome *c.* 200 and among the Quartodecimans (Melito, *c.* 180). The church added gospels and apostolic writings to the OT readings (Justin Martyr, *I Apol.* 67). It has been suggested that the gospel materials were designed for lectionary use in their pre-literary stage, and that the evangelists arranged the pericopes in the order in which they were already used liturgically in the course of the year (P. Carrington), but this theory has found little acceptance. The notes in early manuscripts, $\alpha\rho\chi$ and $\tau\epsilon\lambda$, denoting the beginning and end of the pericopes, and the assignations of these pericopes to particular days in the church year in marginal notes are indicative only of the later liturgical use of the written gospels, not of their pre-literary use. Specially selected lessons were appointed at first only for Passa and Pentecost, then for other feasts and fasts of the Easter and Christmas cycles and Ember days (qq.v.) and martyrs' days as the calendar

grew. For ordinary Sundays the principle of *l.c.* was used, a book being selected apparently at local discretion and read in successive pericopes until it was finished. Thus in pre-Nicene times there was a more or less fixed lectionary only for major feast days.

During this period there were several lessons, both OT and NT, interspersed with psalms (*see below*). Later, the use of three lessons (OT, epistle or other apostolic writing, gospel) was widely standardized (Armenian, Mozarabic, Milanese, Gallican), but at Constantinople (fifth century) and Rome (from sixth century) the lessons were increasingly reduced to two, which eventually became the norm in both East and West. Usually the two lessons were an epistle and gospel, but sometimes it is the OT lesson rather than the apostolic lesson that survived (e.g. especially in Lent in *Missale Romanum. Missale Romanum* has occasionally preserved a multiplicity of OT and NT lessons (e.g. in Lenten Embertide).

In the West, Alcuin standardized the mass lectionary from existing local provisions (Roman for the gospels, Gallican for the epistles), though the provisions were never quite complete (last Sundays in Epiphany and Pentecost), the combinations of lessons were largely fortuitous, and only the debris of the earlier *l.c.* survived (as can often be seen in the epistles of the Pentecost season). Sarum, the Lutheran orders, *BCP* and *Missale Romanum* represent variations and successive modifications of Alcuin's standardization.

Modern dissatisfaction with the traditional eucharistic lectionary arises from: (1) the minimal use of the OT; (2) the haphazard selections for ferial Sundays; (3) the non-use of many significant parts of scripture; (4) lack of inter-connection between the pericopes on any given occasion.

To meet these deficiencies new lectionaries have been compiled on the following principles: (1) A two- or three-yearly cycle, (the former: German Lutheran 1896, British-Ecumenical 1968; the latter: Roman Catholic 1968 ff., Protestant Episcopal Church of USA [PECUSA], now [1971] in trial use); (2) OT lesson additional to or alternative to the epistle; (3) more *l.c.* in ferial seasons; (4) the designation of one lesson, usually the gospel, as the controlling lesson for the day, the other lessons being selected to go with it.

In the breviary of the West, *l.c.* was

featured in one office only, namely nocturns or mattins, the scripture readings of the day hours being only a short text (*capitulum*). At nocturns lessons were read in threes or groups of three (*cf.* the tenuous survival in the popular Christmas service of nine lessons and carols). Non-canonical ecclesiastical writings were used. As the preface to *BCP* complains, this system had broken down completely in the later Middle Ages. Following Quiñones, Cranmer sought to restore the ancient *l.c.*, with an OT and NT lesson at his two daily offices (q.v.), and based his lectionary on the civil calendar. The traditional reading of Isaiah in Advent was preserved by beginning that book on 28 November. Recent Anglican revisions of Cranmer have reverted to the church year as the basis, shortened the lessons (especially PECUSA) and restored other traditional features, e.g. the beginning of the Pentateuch in pre-Lent.

Psalmody. At mass, the standardized Western lectionary provided psalms for the introit, gradual, offertory and communion (qq.v.), the gradual being the most ancient. In the Middle Ages the psalms were drastically reduced in length as the music became more elaborate. At the Reformation the Lutheran orders retained the traditional introits and graduals, but dropped the offertories and communions. Cranmer provided a new introit for each mass (1549), comprising a whole psalm. His principle of selection, except for major feasts, is obscure, but was seemingly governed by considerations of length. The introits were dropped in 1552. Psalmody at the eucharist is being recovered in some current Anglican revisions of the eucharistic lectionary, e.g. Canada (1959) and the PECUSA proposals (introit and gradual), the attempt being made to fit the psalmody to the season, to the lessons, or to both.

For his two offices Cranmer provided (1549) a monthly course of continuous recitation of the psalter, following the civil calendar. In 1552 this system was interrupted by the provision of proper psalms (as also lessons) for 'diverse feasts and fasts'. Cranmer's system has been widely replaced in Anglican revisions by a selection of special psalms for each Sunday and major feast, and in some cases (PECUSA 1944 and British-Ecumenical 1968) by a complete system of daily selections based on the church calendar. In Lutheranism the daily offices have never been widely used, although the American Lutheran *Service Book and Hymnal* (1958) provides a lectionary of psalms and lessons.

R. C. D. Jasper, ed., *The Calendar and the Lectionary*, 1967; Standing Liturgical Commission of PECUSA, *The Liturgical Lectionary*, 1950; *ibid., The Church Year*, 1970. *See also* bibliography under **Sermon**.

R. H. FULLER

Lector

The second of the traditional minor orders after the acolyte (q.v.), his function was originally to read liturgical portions of scripture at the eucharist, especially the OT lesson, but also the epistle and in some cases even the gospel. The order of lector continues to exist in both the Roman Catholic and the Eastern Churches, but has tended to be absorbed by the major orders. *See also* **Reader**.

P. HINCHLIFF

Lent

The English word 'Lent' means 'spring', but this does not express the significance of the six-week period of spiritual discipline before Easter as conveyed by the 'forty days' of the Greek *tessaracoste* or the Latin *quadragesima*. For an understanding of the external structure of the season, the essential requirement is the knowledge that, when Lent was developed, Good Friday as a distinct commemoration of the Passion did not exist. Lent was a preparation for the primitive Pascha, the Christian Passover, the nocturnal festival of Saturday-Sunday, the unitive commemoration of the passion and the resurrection. As for the internal character of the season, Lent had a particular reference to the instruction of the candidates for baptism at the great festival of redemption.

Late in the second century Irenaeus said that some people fasted for one day before the Pascha, while others fasted for two days and others again held to a longer period. In addition he mentions that some counted their day as 'forty hours', but this has the appearance of being a special method of calculating a continuous fast extending over the Friday and the Saturday. Early in the third century the custom was to fast for two days. It is not until we reach a point towards the middle of the third century that we encounter unmistakable evidence of a fast extending throughout six days. It is of fundamental importance to note that a distinction is drawn between the additional period from Monday to Thursday and the long-established fast of Friday and Saturday, the latter retaining a special place within the context of development of a six-day Paschal fast.

There is a gap of about three-quarters of a century between this evidence and the earliest information concerning Lent, to which reference is made by the Council of Nicea in 325. We receive the impression that Lent was not a recent innovation but was something familiar. It is in the *Festal Letters* of Athanasius, towards the middle of the fourth century, that we first obtain the detailed evidence which enables us to understand the external structure of the season. Athanasius appears to make a distinction between the 'forty days' and the final week, but this simply means that the Holy Week (q.v.) fast formed a specially important part of the inclusive *tessaracoste*, understood as embracing the entire six weeks preceding the Pascha. In the third century the old two-day fast was not quite absorbed in the six days but retained a real independence and a compelling obligation. Similarly, we gain the impression from the *Festal Letters* that, although the one week had been extended to six weeks, yet for Athanasius the first five were not on the same level as the sixth. The innate conservatism of the liturgical tradition ensured that the concluding week kept a distinctive position within the inclusive *tessaracoste*. It is important to note that the rich development of 'Holy Week' as we understand it had not yet been made, and it was not this particular significance – that only in the latter part of the century attached itself to the successive days – which prevented the complete absorption of the sixth week within the 'forty days' in the time of Athanasius.

It is precisely when we bear in mind the natural process of formation whereby an additional period of five weeks was added to an older six-day fast that we can understand why Lent was called the 'forty days'. The fast of the Paschal Week is invariably calculated in the *Festal Letters* as beginning on the Monday. It lasted until the Saturday, the eve of the Pascha, that is, for six days. Although the week began on the Lord's day, there was no question of this being included in the period, since fasting was forbidden on

Sunday. When we consider the extension of the period to six weeks, we are to think of the five weeks as forming a distinct element in the total calculation. Once again the fast is calculated as beginning on a Monday, the Monday of the first week of Lent. There is no reason, however, to think that *within* the five weeks the days of fasting only would be included in the computation. That would be in accordance with the artificial manner of a later period. The whole season was doubtless regarded generally as one of discipline and purification. Reference is made to the first five weeks as a time of continued fasting although the fast was actually suspended on Saturdays and Sundays. If therefore the first five weeks are considered as a group added to the Paschal Week, and if it is remembered that the Monday of the first week is always considered in the *Festal Letters* to be the starting-point of the fast, this period of thirty-four days being added to the six days of the older fast gives the result of exactly forty days. It is to be observed that Athanasius consistently refers to the new beginning of the fast on the Monday of Holy Week and so, within the compassing circle of the *tessaracoste*, sets an inner fence around the Paschal Week. The Sunday of this week was the line which separated the old six-day fast from the additional five weeks. It is the frontier of this Sunday which makes it possible for us to envisage the formation of the *tessaracoste* as the superimposition of five weeks on an older six-day fast, both periods starting on a Monday and combining to make forty days.

The internal character of the season of preparation before the Pascha was governed by the fact that it was the time of training of the candidates for baptism. This may well be the reason for the origin of Lent, the instruction being spread over a period of six weeks and the old six-day fast extended to cover the 'forty days' on the model of our Lord's fast in the wilderness. The object of this arrangement would be to ensure, so far as possible, that only those of real sincerity in their Christian profession were received into the church at the paschal baptism. It is reasonable to suppose that the Lenten fast was meant to apply not only to the candidates but to the church as a whole. But it is in the nature of things unlikely that such a radical change was immediately accepted everywhere in its entirety. It is quite possible that in practice only the candidates, who were under discipline, and also the more devoted members of the church, or at least those most strongly attracted by ascetic practices, observed the whole period of fasting. Others may have fasted for a restricted period. Time was necessary so that the custom could root itself in the devotion of the church generally, and it was important that church members should be encouraged to exercise themselves in the spiritual discipline of the extended season of fasting. Doubtless there were many who regarded the *tessaracoste* as an innovation. The contrast in the *Festal Letters* between the general assumption that Lent is an established season and the occasional exhortations regarding its due observance disappears at once if we understand that the *tessaracoste* was organized primarily as a form of discipline for baptismal candidates, but that church members were also expected to observe it. It is perfectly comprehensible that the secondary purpose could not be realized immediately. Lent was associated with fasting and study, prayer and humility, and it is manifest that the church member was expected to approach the Pascha each year in the way he had done when he himself was solemnly preparing for his baptism.

G. Dix, *The Shape of the Liturgy*, [2]1945; A. A. McArthur, *The Evolution of the Christian Year*, 1953.

A. A. MCARTHUR

Lesson

This term refers generally to liturgical readings from the scriptures or elsewhere. Apart from the occasional reading from the *Acta* of the martyrs in Africa, Gaul and Milan in patristic times, readings at the eucharist have always been scriptural. In the divine office at mattins (qq.v.) there are, however, patristic and hagiographic readings. Here we are concerned only with OT readings in the eucharist and with scriptural readings in the office.

1. *The Eucharist.* The church inherited the OT readings from the synagogue service (*see* **Jewish Worship**), supplementing them with NT ones. The East Syrian (q.v.) liturgy accordingly still has lessons from the law and the prophets preceding the epistle and gospel. In the Roman liturgy, the OT readings survived only on Lenten ferias, vigils and in the commons of saints.

The new Roman Lectionary (1969) restores the OT lesson on Sundays as the first reading, except in Paschaltide when Acts is read. On Sundays *per annum* the lesson is chosen to accord with the gospel; during Advent Isaiah is prominent, while in Lent passages covering the main stages of the history of salvation are read. The lessons are spread over a three-year cycle, include the principal passages of the OT and in relation with the gospels manifest the harmony between the two Testaments.

On the weekdays of Advent and Lent an OT reading precedes the gospel; during the rest of the year, apart from Paschaltide, the OT lessons alternate every few weeks with NT epistles, over a two-year cycle. The Church of England's *Alternative Services: First Series* (1965) includes a table of OT lessons for Sundays and certain feasts to supplement the epistles and gospels of the *BCP*.

2. *The Divine Office.* The Roman office is monastic rather than popular in form, hence its lessons are found only in the night hour of mattins, other hours having only a *capitulum* (*see* **Canonical Hours**). The present system of lessons (1970) goes back to the seventh or eighth century and once covered most of the Bible, but the gradual abbreviation of the lessons means that much is now omitted.

Cardinal Quiñones' reformed breviary (1535), eventually rejected by Rome, influenced Cranmer, whose office lectionary has OT lessons morning and evening, with readings from the gospels and Acts in the morning and from the other NT books in the evening. Unlike the Roman system which began at Septuagesima, Cranmer's lectionary followed the civil year, covering the OT once and the NT three times annually. Cranmer's lectionary has been greatly revised since, and Sundays and feasts now have their own readings.

The new post-conciliar Roman Breviary provides longer scriptural readings for mattins, which will henceforth be known as the *Officium Lectionis*, and much more of the Bible will be covered than at present. The Joint Liturgical Group, made up of representatives of the Church of England and the Free Churches, includes a new lectionary as part of its proposals for morning and evening services.

Alternative Services, First Series, 1967; *BCP*; *Breviarium Romanum*; W. K. Lowther Clarke, 'The Lectionary' in *Liturgy and Worship*, 1932, pp. 296-301; *The First and Second Prayer Books of King Edward VI*; R. C. D. Jasper, ed., *The Daily Office*, 1969; J. A. Jungmann, *The Mass of the Roman Rite*, new rev. ed., 1959; *Missale Romanum; Ordo Lectionum Missae*; F. Proctor and W. H. Frere, *The Book of Common Prayer*, rev. ed., 1901; M. Righetti, *Storia Liturgica*, IV, ²1956; S. P. Salmon, *The Breviary through the centuries*, 1962.

BRIAN NEWNS

Lights *see* Candles

Litany

'A litany is a form of prayer in which fixed responses are made by the people to short biddings or petitions said or sung by deacon, priest, or cantors' (E. C. Ratcliff). Most litanies are precatory, although litanies of adoration or thanksgiving are not unknown; most precatory litanies are either in whole or in part intercessory.

Some early forms of the litany in Christian worship are reminiscent of pagan formularies: 'We need not, therefore, conclude with some scholars that the Christian Litany is borrowed from pagan usage; but it is nevertheless reasonable to think it an adaptation to a new purpose of a form which was traditionally associated with prayer and devotion, and which in the directness and simplicity of its address was intrinsically appropriate to that purpose' (Ratcliff).

The first definite evidence of the use of litanies in Christian worship suggests that the litany originated at Antioch in the second half of the fourth century; by the end of the century a litanic form of intercession was in use at Jerusalem; from Syria the litany travelled to Constantinople, and thence (apparently) it spread rapidly throughout the East. Whether the importation of the litany to the West was originally directly from Syria, or whether it was from Constantinople, is a question which cannot be definitively answered.

Constantinople certainly took to the litany more thoroughly and more enthusiastically than any other of the great liturgical centres, and to this day it is prominent and frequent in the services of the Byzantine rite. The *lesser litany*, a short form of general content, is the normal introduction to any formal prayer by the celebrant, corresponding in function to the mutual greeting and bidding to prayer in the Western rites; the *greater litany*, a more extended form, containing a number of intercessory biddings, occurs, with variations, in a number of services, commonly near the beginning, in what was originally a 'preparatory' or sometimes a 'processional' context. These litanies are mainly composed of biddings; other litanies of the same type are the *morning litany* at mattins and the *evening litany* at vespers, and the litanies preceding the prayer over the offerings and the Lord's Prayer at the eucharistic liturgy. The *litany of fervent prayer*, so called because the response to each petition (and in this case most are direct petitions, not biddings) is tripled, is the main intercessory litany of the Byzantine rite, coming at the end of the liturgy of the word before the eucharist, and as the intercession at mattins and vespers (qq.v.). Other litanies are those for the catechumens after the liturgy of the word, the proper litanies of the baptismal and marriage liturgies, the greater and lesser litanies for the departed, and the processional festal litany which in addition to intercessions includes a lengthy commemoration of the saints.

The earliest surviving text of a Western litany is that of the *Deprecatio Gelasii*, a Roman litany of the late fifth century, which bears a close relationship both in form and in content to the Byzantine litanies, and was almost certainly inserted between the entrance chant and the collect of the day in the Roman mass by Pope Gelasius (492-6), whose name it bears, replacing the older intercessory biddings and prayers after the readings and sermon. Related texts are found in non-Roman Western rites; one of them is still used at Milan on Sundays in Lent, at the same point in the mass.

At Rome this litany was already beginning to fall into disuse in the late sixth century (*see* **Kyrie**), and later litanies in the Roman rite and its variants differ considerably from it both in form and in use. The latter difference is marked by the change of name: Gelasius' litany was called a *deprecatio*, that is, an intercession without further qualification; *litania*, from which 'litany' is derived, and which is the name used for its successors, signifies either a penitential observance, or a procession, or, ultimately, a penitential procession, and is clearly connected with a particular use of this type of litany on the three days preceding Ascension Day, known as the rogations (q.v.), from which use the combination of penitence and intercession found in the later Roman litany originates.

This rogation litany, commonly called, from one of its parts, the litany of the saints, may be divided into six sections: (1) the introductory *kyrie* and invocations of the Persons of the Trinity; (2) the invocations of the saints; (3) the deprecations, or supplications for deliverance; (4) the obsecrations, or appeals for deliverance by virtue of events in Christ's redemptive life; (5) the intercessions; (6) a concluding invocation of Christ as the Lamb of God; a number of other prayers, of Gallican origin, with the Lord's Prayer and a concluding collect or collects, the set differing somewhat from time to time and place to place, are added to these six sections of the litany proper. Different though this form of the litany is from the type to which the Byzantine litanies and the *Deprecatio Gelasii* belong, it appears nevertheless to have originated, as they did, in Antiochene Syria, and to have been imported to the West in the seventh century, probably during the pontificate of Sergius I (687-701), who was himself of Antiochene descent (*see* **Agnus Dei**).

In medieval England the litany was sung on the rogation days (q.v.), and also daily in Lent and in many places in procession every Sunday before the parish mass. It is hardly a coincidence that Cranmer provided in the *BCP* what is probably the best-known, and certainly the finest, litany to be found in any of the liturgies of the Reformation, the structure of it based on that of the Roman litany, but the contents showing the influence of Luther's litany of 1529, as well as of the Byzantine greater litany, while from 1549 onward all invocations of the saints were omitted. Cranmer's one departure from the Roman structure is in his treatment of the deprecations and obsecrations, where he combines several of the original petitions in each one of his.

A considerable number of litanies have been produced in the course of liturgical revision during the last few years, which lack of space, unfortunately, precludes us from considering further. Of all forms of public prayer, the litany is perhaps the most flexible and the most conducive, when used competently, to effective congregational partici-pation in the liturgy.

W. Jardine Grisbrooke, 'Intercession at the Eucharist', in *Studia Liturgica*, IV, 3, 1965, pp. 129-55; J. A. Jungmann, *The Mass of the Roman Rite*, I, 1955, pp. 333-46; E. C. Ratcliff, 'The Choir Offices: The Litany', in *Liturgy and Worship*, ed. W. K. Lowther Clarke, 1932, pp. 282-7.

W. JARDINE GRISBROOKE

Liturgical Movement, The

This present century has seen an extraordinary recovery and renewal by the Christian church of its worship and the understanding of that worship as central to its life and work. The name usually given to the means by which this recovery and renewal has been brought about is the Liturgical Movement. Its origins are to be found in the Roman Catholic Church in France during the nineteenth century. In the year 1832, Dom Prosper Guéranger refounded the Benedictine Abbey of Solesmes as a monastery dedicated especially to the study and recovery of the authentic Gregorian Chant (q.v.) and the church's liturgical heritage generally. Solesmes became a centre of liturgical worship and life, and its publication *L'Année Liturgique*, the first issue of which appeared in 1841, had a wide influence. The work of Guéranger and the Solesmes monks awakened a new interest in the liturgy. It was a springboard for a revival by the Benedictines of their traditional concern for the liturgy which eventually placed the monks among the pioneers of the Liturgical Movement, and it spurred an investigation into the origins and history of the liturgy in which such scholars as Cabrol and Batiffol provided the foundation for present-day liturgiological study. Guéranger's work has been adversely criticized as being too narrowly medieval, too limited in pastoral concern, and too archaeological. While this criticism may be right from our present point of view, Guéranger's work must be seen in the setting of the church of his day in order to be evaluated justly. Guéranger and the monks of Solesmes were not alone in their medievalism. Their contemporaries were discovering the Middle Ages, and to many these times were the ideal ages, in which had been all that was right and good. This was the time of the Gothic revival, of romanticism in art and literature. To men of the church, the

Middle Ages appeared to be the epitome of Christian life, to be indeed the Christian Ages. In them was to be found an ideal of worship and church life which must be recovered in order to release the church of their own time from its lassitude and sterility. Guéranger was able to recall men in the church of his time to an interest and concern for the liturgy as something to be prayed and lived, and it is interesting to note that most of the major points which the Liturgical Movement has made in recent times were in some way anticipated by Guéranger. He must justly be called the precursor of the Liturgical Movement.

However, the Liturgical Movement itself began to get under way in the opening years of the present century. In 1903, Pope Pius X issued a *Motu Proprio* on church music. He saw in the active participation of the faithful in the liturgy the source of the renewal of the Christian spirit, and called for more active participation in the worship of the church. A few years later the same pope called for a more frequent reception of holy communion. In 1909, a Catholic conference was held in Malines in Belgium; it is this conference which was probably the real inauguration of the Liturgical Movement. The conference saw the liturgy as the fundamental means of the instruction of the people in the Christian faith and life. An active participation by the people in the liturgy was the best means of nourishing and deepening the spiritual life. The conference called for a translation of the Roman missal into the vernacular (q.v.) so that it could more readily serve as the main manual of devotion for the church. It called for a centring of the Christian life in the liturgy of the church, the restoration of Gregorian Chant as a means of helping participation, and it asked for retreats for church people to be held in centres of liturgical worship and life. The outstanding leader in the conference was Dom Lambert Beauduin, of Mont César in Louvain. His book, *La Piété de l'Église*, published in 1914, contained ideas which became fundamental principles in the Liturgical Movement, and is still necessary reading if the purpose of the movement is to be understood. Beauduin saw that a better understanding of the incarnation and its meaning would lead to a deeper understanding and appreciation of the dignity of human life and all life. He pointed out that an understanding of the nature of the church as the body of Christ would enable the development of a deeper sense of community in both worship and life, and he emphasized that an understanding of the sacrifice of Christ would result in the living out of the eucharistic sacrifice by the people of God and the offering of their lives along with the offering of Christ. Worship, Beauduin stressed, was the common action of the people of the church, an action which involved them all in a sharing in the saving work of Christ in and for the world. The orientation of the Liturgical Movement during these early years was deeply pastoral. While it was not anti-traditionalist and aimed at renewal rather than revolution, it was concerned with the present situation in the church and how that situation might be changed to bring about a better future. It thus sought to reach the ordinary church people rather than the theologian and the intellectual. It sought to recall the members of the church to an active involvement in the liturgy of the church. That liturgy was not to be a resuscitation of the past, nor something to be merely seen and heard, but a living worship in which the whole church should take part actively and with understanding, and the wellspring of a renewal of Christian life and mission. In these years the principal organ of the movement was *Les Questions Liturgiques*, later entitled *Les Questions Liturgiques et Paroissiales*. It was particularly the eucharist which the leaders of the movement saw as the central act of Christian worship, and it was an active participation in this on the part of the 'people in the pews' which the first stage of the Liturgical Movement sought in every way to encourage. The movement sometimes ran counter to the established ideas and practices of the church of the time; hence it aroused considerable opposition. Despite this, the movement began to spread and to become more and more an influence in the thinking and acting of the Roman Catholic Church, especially at the parish level.

In the years between the two world wars, the focus of leadership in the movement shifted from Belgium to Germany, and the second phase in its development got under way. The ideas of worship which the Liturgical Movement actively propagated had come under criticism as being too radical, too much a departure from the tradition of the church. Some felt that the movement was too modernist, and lacked a sound basis in the theology of the Roman Catholic Church, indeed was contrary to it. There was some justification for the criticisms, given the official patterns of worship and the Ultramontane theology in the early decades of this century; further, the earlier phase of the movement had been more concerned with the immediate pastoral needs of the church than with the production of an apologetic for its position. In the second phase of the development of the Liturgical Movement the emphasis was reversed. The work of building a sound theology of worship was spearheaded by the Rhineland Abbey of Maria Laach. The Abbot Ildefons Herwegen and Dom Odo Casel pioneered in this work, and the publication *Ecclesia Orans*, begun in 1918, enjoyed wide circulation and was an important means of dissemination of the new theology. Soon other theologians and church historians were turning their attention to the study of the liturgy. The result has been the production over the past half-century of a huge literature on Christian worship which has not only provided a deep knowledge and understanding of the origins and development of the liturgy, but has also opened up liturgical theology as an important field of theological studies. The list of contributors to this development is too long to give in full; we mention Josef Jungmann, Jean Daniélou, and Louis Bouyer as outstanding. Neither the historical nor the theological investigation shows signs of flagging at the present time; rather, both will doubtless increase in scope as the liturgy is seen in relationship to modern social sciences, psychology, and the like. While Maria Laach spoke primarily to the expert, the Canons of Klausterneuberg, and especially Pius Parsch, gave the same ideas a more popular expression. Klausterneuberg also turned to a study of the biblical basis of the liturgy, and inaugurated a biblical movement which has spread widely in the Roman Catholic Church, made important contributions to biblical theology and hermeneutics, and has served as a link between Roman Catholics and the Ecumenical Movement. In the period immediately before the Second World War and during the early war years the Liturgical Movement was spreading widely outside Europe. By the late twenties, St John's Abbey in Collegeville, Minnesota, was becoming, under the leadership of Dom Virgil

Michel, a major centre of the movement in the USA. The Abbey's periodical *Orate Fratres* (later renamed *Worship*) was addressed especially to the parish clergy and the laity, and became one of the most important means of spreading the movement in America. The Abbey also published a large selection of tracts and service leaflets which have found their way into churches and homes throughout the USA. Liturgical conferences began to be held and were well attended by clergy and laity. A Liturgical Arts Society was organized to find ways of improving the standards and craftsmanship of church art and architecture and for encouraging contemporary expression in liturgical art. Its journal *Liturgical Arts Quarterly* has become one of the finest reviews of the building and decorative arts. By 1940 a series of annual Liturgical Weeks was begun, and these have trained many for the liturgical apostolate and have taken on ecumenical significance. The Liturgical Movement in the USA has always tended to be less strongly intellectual in its appeal than it was in Europe. It took the form of a more grass-roots movement in the Roman Catholic Church. Liturgical theology was by no means neglected, but in the USA especially the Liturgical Movement and the rediscovery of the ministry of the laity were strongly inter-linked.

By the end of the Second World War, the movement had spread widely in the Low Countries, Germany and France. The Centre de Pastorale Liturgique had been founded in Paris in 1940, and its principal publication *La Maison-Dieu* combined the emphases of Maria Laach and Klausterneuberg and went beyond them. In North America generally the movement was affecting deeply the patterns of worship, and bringing about many changes in them. The church in Asia and Africa in the post-war years was faced with the challenge of nascent nationalisms and the resurgent indigenous religions. The Liturgical Movement was beginning to assist the church in searching for expressions of worship and art drawn from the local cultures, and it was in these lands that the missionary implications of a liturgical renewal were being explored. The movement was less widespread in Southern Europe and in the British Isles, and its influence had hardly begun to be felt in large parts of South America and in some parts of Southeast

Asia. But the Liturgical Movement had become a force to be reckoned with in the Roman Catholic Church. It could not be overlooked or disregarded as something passing and unimportant. It was producing a growing revival of worship, and was a major source of the growing ferment within the Roman Catholic Church which resulted eventually in the summoning of Vatican II. The official framework of the liturgy was proving too restrictive and out-dated to meet the needs of the church in the post-war secular society. Demands for reforms in the liturgy were being made from all parts in the Roman Catholic Church and were constantly becoming more insistent. The attempt to carry out in practice the principles which the Liturgical Movement had widely disseminated led to experimentation and to a search for new expressions of worship which would have more meaning for people in the present day. These often began to outrun the official liturgical rules of the church. Some members of the hierarchy, as in the Low Countries, sought to give leadership and encouraged the experimentation; others adopted a negative and restrictive posture and attempted to restrain or forbid it. The situation in respect to the liturgy was tending to became chaotic, and considerable controversy was being aroused by well-meant, but misguided, efforts at liturgical reform.

Concrete evidence that Rome was now at last prepared to give official recognition to the liturgical renewal and to implement at least some of its demands, while placing a guiding and restraining hand on the more radical tendencies, came in the promulgation by Pius XII in the year 1947 of the encyclical *Mediator Dei et Hominum*. This document has been regarded by some as the charter of the Liturgical Movement, and as endorsement of it. The pope praised the liturgy and emphasized that its celebration should be the work of the whole church. He expressed the desire that the faithful should be able to participate fully in the liturgy with understanding, and that they should take an active part in the services. He recalled the church to the need to live the liturgical life which was renewed and strengthened by the liturgy. This encyclical was the first papal encyclical to be devoted wholly to a discussion of the church's liturgy. Positive steps were taken to implement the encyclical in 1951 by the restoration of the Paschal Vigil

(q.v.), and four years later by the decree *Maxima Redemptionis* followed by the *Instructio* reforming and restoring the whole Holy Week celebration. The intention was a recovery of an important part of the tradition which had been lost. As the Paschal mystery was the centre of the liturgical life of the church, so the annual celebration of that mystery should be the centre of the liturgical year. At the same time, the restoration was intensely pastoral in outlook. The restoration of the major rites to evening hours made possible an attendance on the part of working people, and the provision of an up-dated and reformed liturgy for the rites made a more active participation in them possible. Other reforms followed. The pope sought to meet the need of people living in the industrial-urban complex by relaxing the rigour of the eucharistic fast and by permitting evening celebrations of mass. The rubrics (q.v.) governing the conduct of the services were simplified, and a new codification of them undertaken. Pius XII issued another encyclical, *De musica sacra*, in 1955, which laid down guidelines and rules for increased participation of the faithful in the rites of the church. Further indications of reforms to come were given in the pope's address to a congress meeting in Assisi in 1956. Some of the reforms which were undertaken during the pontificate of Pius XII were completed and promulgated by his successor John XXIII, including the new rubrics and the revision of a part of the Roman Pontifical.

But it was in Vatican II that the work of the Liturgical Movement bore fruit, and the extent to which it had aroused the church became fully apparent. There was no doubt from the beginning of the Council that the assembled council fathers had every intention of making the liturgy more responsive to the needs of the contemporary church. A schema had been prepared after some discussion by a representative group, and this was submitted to the Council. Between 22 October and 13 November 1962, the Council devoted fifteen sessions to debate on the proposed constitution, and its text was approved in principle. But the discussion continued and many amendments and additions were proposed. Finally the Constitution *De sacra liturgia* was passed by an overwhelming majority in 1963. It was promulgated by Paul VI on 4 December 1963, the first Constitution to be published by Vatican II. The Constitution on the Sacred Liturgy contains what is probably one of the best and clearest statements of the theology of the liturgy, its meaning and its function in the life of the church which has as yet been made, a statement which is in its approach thoroughly biblical, patristic, and eirenical. At the same time it is a statement which exhibits an intense pastoral awareness of and concern for the needs of the church and its mission in the present-day world. The Constitution unleashes the liturgy, so to speak, and allows it to become the living service of the Christian community in a way which has not been possible since the beginning of the Middle Ages. Of special significance for the Roman Catholic Church was the opening of the gate for the use of the vernacular tongues in the rites of the church. The Constitution might also be said to be the best and most concise statement of the principles and objectives of the Liturgical Movement. Entirely ecumenical in its scope and significance, the Constitution on the Liturgy must be given thorough study by anyone who wishes to understand the liturgy and the importance of the liturgical renewal of the whole Christian Church. Immediate steps were taken to implement the Constitution. Large parts of the Roman rite, and especially that for the celebration of the eucharist, have now been issued in the vernaculars of the different peoples of the church, and have been received with enthusiasm. The rites themselves have been thoroughly revised and updated. The result of all this is that the worship of the Roman Catholic Church is changing and developing in a truly thrilling manner. It is too soon to judge objectively the full impact of Vatican II upon the liturgical life of the Roman Catholic Church. At the present time that life is being revolutionized. The reforms in the liturgy made as a result of Vatican II have been so sweeping and so many that it will take a number of years for them to be assimilated and their significance realized. The work of the Liturgical Movement by no means ended with the publication of the Constitution on the Liturgy; rather, Vatican II opened the door to new opportunities. The movement in the Roman Communion today is part of the vanguard of the ferment in that church which has not been allayed; if anything, it is increasing. We may predict that in the immediate future the

activities of the Liturgical Movement will be chiefly along two lines: (1) leadership and encouragement in still more spontaneity and freedom in worship and in finding new and contemporary ways of expressing that worship; (2) leadership in the re-thinking and renewal of mission and Christian action as necessary parts of liturgical renewal, as part of the service which the church offers to God.

But the Liturgical Movement has not been confined to the Roman Communion. Although it first got under way in that church, it has spread particularly during the past thirty years or so to almost every part of the church, and has made an impact upon the worship of most of the Christian communions. At the present time the Liturgical Movement may fairly be said to be part of the Ecumenical Movement, and it is proving more and more instrumental in drawing together the different Christian traditions of worship. In Anglicanism, the preliminary work carried out by Guéranger was in many ways paralleled by the activities of the ritualist wing of the Tractarian Movement. There was much common ground between the French Catholics of the persuasion of Guéranger and the tractarian Anglicans. Both emphasized the centrality of the eucharistic worship in the life of the church, and both were inspired by that worship to self-sacrificing service to the people of God. The Anglicans, like Guéranger and his associates, were unable to get behind the medieval church and accepted it as their ideal. But they did succeed in provoking interest in the liturgy and discussion of it, even if some of it was of a controversial nature. There was evidence on all sides of a growing dissatisfaction with the limitations of the normative Anglican patterns of worship and with the restrictions and limitations of the 1662 *BCP*. This dissatisfaction was not limited to England. Anglican liturgical scholars of the stature of W. H. Frere, Bishop Parsons, and Howard Baldwin St George both prepared the way for the spate of *BCP* revision which swept the Anglican Communion in the late twenties of the present century and made permanent contributions to the rediscovery of the liturgical tradition. But these revisions proved to be a kind of watershed. It was after them that the Liturgical Movement began to influence Anglicanism more and more widely. If there is any one thing to which we might point as the real beginning of the Liturgical

Movement in the Anglican Communion, it is to the publication in 1935 of the book *Liturgy and Society* by Father Gabriel Hebert of the Kelham Fathers. A movement to restore the parish eucharist as the common central act of parish worship got under way, and its effects are to be seen in the ever-increasing number of Anglican parishes where this has taken place. In the USA, the *Associated Parishes* came into being in 1946 to further the movements objectives and to implement them in parish worship. A few years later in England the *Parish and People* movement began its work with the same objectives. The Anglican Liturgical Movement has also produced a large literature, which has influenced the thinking of leaders in the movement in the Roman Communion, just as the works of Roman Catholic scholars greatly influenced Anglican thinking. We can mention here but a few of the most outstanding Anglican contributors to liturgical knowledge: Dom Gregory Dix, E. C. Ratcliff, Massey E. Shepherd, H. B. Porter, and J. G. Davies. The extent to which the Liturgical Movement has become grounded in Anglicanism and is bringing about a deep liturgical renewal in the Anglican churches may be gauged by a comparison of the proposals for revision of the *BCP* which are at present before most of the Anglican churches for evaluation and decision with the revisions of 1927-30. There is a ferment in Anglicanism which in many ways is very like that in the Roman Communion, and which is arousing the churches of the Anglican Communion to the realization that the *BCP* is not the final expression of liturgical worship and does need to be revised and changed, and which is deeply concerned with renewal of worship in the ordinary parishes as part of the much-needed renewal of Christian life and mission.

Among Christians of the Reformed and other traditions also the Liturgical Movement has come of age. The Reformed churches have also had their liturgical pioneers. In the latter part of the past century Eugène Bersier of Paris emphasized the centrality of the worship of the church in Christian life and the need for the Reformed churches to recover liturgical worship. In the liturgy which he produced may be seen the understanding of the worship of the church as a fully corporate action, and a balance between the word and sacraments which was uncharacteristic of Protestant worship in his time. In Scotland, we may point to the work of the Church Service Society and its *Euchologion*, which was certainly one of the major influences behind the present liturgical renewal in the Scottish church and that church's excellent liturgies, which in so many respects incorporate the insights of the Liturgical Movement. But probably the extent to which the Liturgical Movement has gained ground in the Protestant traditions may be seen in the liturgy of the Church of South India, in which a number of these traditions, including the Anglican, have been brought together and submitted to the normative tradition of the scriptures and the early church which underlies them all. Yet the liturgy of the Church of South India is not an essay in liturgical archaeology; it is a restatement of the essential Christian tradition of worship in a liturgy which is immediately relevant to the life of Christians in South India. The work of the Church of South India has influenced practically all liturgical revision in the Protestant churches, and it is recognized also as an influence upon Vatican II. Or again, we may point to the thrilling work of the Taizé Community, with its emphasis upon the living of a common liturgical life of worship and mission, its deep ecumenical understanding and outreach, and the contributions of such writers as Max Thurian. The Taizé liturgy is undoubtedly among the very finest expressions of the principles of the Liturgical Movement. Yet it is fully ecumenical, and is an excellent illustration of a liturgy which can at one and the same time stand squarely in both the Reformed and Catholic traditions. The same awakening and ferment as that within Romanism and Anglicanism is today evident in Protestantism, and is bringing all parts of the church to a new willingness to submit to self and mutual criticism and to learn from each other. For the churches of the Protestant tradition as well as those of the Catholic, this is meaning a deep renewal of worship and rediscovery of the liturgy. Of special significance for the future is the growing tendency to search for liturgical expressions which will transcend and draw together the different Christian traditions. In this connection we may mention the new proposed ecumenical texts for the creeds, Lord's Prayer, and other common parts of the liturgy, which will undoubtedly serve to make our worship more truly common, the proposals of the Conference on Christian Union in the USA, the work of the Joint Liturgical Group in Great Britain, the establishment of such societies as the Societas Liturgica, and centres for the study of the liturgy on an ecumenical basis. The church as a whole is finding in the Liturgical Movement a new frontier on which, in the words of H. G. Hageman (*Studia Liturgica*, II, 4), 'all the churches, regardless of the rigidity of their liturgical traditions, now find themselves. In the common exploration of what is for all of us, in one way or another, new material, we are bound to reach easier ecumenical conversation. I do not know where these new agreements may take us; I would be suspicious of any attempt to overplay their importance. But the fact remains that the liturgy is the most fruitful area for ecumenical exploration. If that fact is recognised, and, in the best sense of the word, exploited, we shall know what the next step may be.'

The Liturgical Movement is part of the reawakening of the church. It seeks a recovery of those norms of liturgical worship of the Bible and the early church which lie behind Reformation divisions and medieval distortions, and which are fundamental to Christian liturgy in every time and place. It aims, however, not at an attempt to resuscitate the liturgy of the early church in the twentieth century, but at the restatement of the fundamentals in forms and expressions which can enable the liturgy to be the living prayer and work of the church today.

J.-J. von Allmen, *Worship, its Theology and Practice*, 1965; W. Bardin, 'Phases of the Liturgical Movement', in *Studies in Pastoral Liturgy*, II, 1961; L. Beauduin, *Liturgy the Life of the Church*, [2]1929; L. Bouyer, *Liturgical Piety*, 1950 (also published as *Liturgy and Life*, 1958); L. Bouyer, *Rite and Man*, 1963; O. Casel, *The Mystery of Christian Worship and Other Writings*, 1962; I. H. Dalmais, *Introduction to the Liturgy*, 1961; J. G. Davies, *Worship and Mission*, 1966; J. Jungmann, *Pastoral Liturgy*, 1962; A. G. Martimort, ed., *The Church at Prayer*, ET, 1966; J.A.T. Robinson, *Liturgy Coming to Life*, 1963; A. Shands, *The Liturgical Movement and the Local Church*, 1965; M. H. Shepherd, *Liturgy and Education*, 1965; B. Wicker, *Culture and Liturgy*, 1963. Periodicals and Series: *Ecumenical Studies in Worship*, London, Lutterworth Press; *Studies in Pastoral Liturgy*, Maynooth, Eire, The Farrow Trust; *Studia Liturgica*.

H. ELLSWORTH CHANDLEE

Liturgies

In the singular the word 'liturgy' denotes an act of worship, more specifically the eucharist. Derived from the Greek *leitourgia*, it was used in Hellenistic Greek of an act of public service. In the NT it is employed of an act of service or ministry (e.g. Phil. 2.30). In time it was confined in Christian usage to the idea of service to God and finally, since worship was regarded as the supreme service to God, it was applied to the eucharist. Consequently to study liturgies is to examine the forms which the eucharistic rite has taken throughout the centuries.

1. *Patristic*. The New Testament does not provide a detailed description of the worship of the early church. Because worship was a regular element in the lives of the first Christians, a great deal was taken for granted. Our knowledge of this period is therefore restricted. It is clear, however, that the eucharist was of great importance, in virtue of Jesus' institution at the Last Supper. His followers continued to partake of bread and wine 'in remembrance of him'. Whether the Last Supper was actually the passover meal or not, it was associated with passover ideas, and it must also be seen in connection with the other references to meals in the gospels – particularly the feeding of the five thousand, to which John attached eucharistic teaching. These NT passages would appear to have been influenced by current liturgical practice in the areas in which they were written; and books such as Hebrews and Revelation clearly indicate a knowledge of the eucharist. The tendency to read liturgy into every page of the NT must be treated with reserve, however.

The early Christian eucharist followed the pattern of the Last Supper. Bread was taken, blessed, broken and distributed before a meal; and wine was taken, blessed and distributed after it. For the Jew, thanksgiving and blessing were synonymous, and bread and wine were blessed when God was thanked over them for his mighty acts of creation and redemption. When Paul wrote his first letter to the Corinthians the eucharist and the meal aere apparently still together; but at some early date, precisely when is unknown, the meal disappeared and the rites over bread and wine were brought together and became a single entity.

Forms of thanksgiving used over bread and wine which date from the late first or early second century appear in the *Didache*. Scholars differ as to whether they all apply to the eucharist, but as forms of thanksgiving they may well indicate the kind of prayer which was used at the eucharist. The first writer to give a detailed account of the liturgy is Justin Martyr in his *Apology* to the Emperor Antoninus Pius, written in Rome *c.* AD 150; this is supplemented by further information in his *Dialogue* with the Jew Trypho. The eucharist was celebrated every Sunday. It began with a synagogue type of service – scripture reading, a sermon by the president, and intercessions concluded by the kiss of peace. Bread and a cup of wine and water were then brought to the president, who said a prayer of thanksgiving over them; the congregation said Amen (q.v.). After the administration, there was a collection for the needy and the deacons took the sacrament to those who were absent. The prayer of thanksgiving was Trinitarian in form and extempore: it referred to God's activities of creation and redemption, the bread and wine was described as a memorial of the passion, and there was an odd passage on 'the prayer of the word which is from him', which might apply to Jesus at the Last Supper or to the Logos. Like the *Didache*, Justin also referred to the eucharist as a sacrifice, quoting Malachi 1.11.

Some sixty years later Rome also provided the first eucharistic text to be discovered. The presbyter, Hippolytus, wrote the *Apostolic Tradition* as a guide to church life in the early third century; in describing the consecration of a bishop, he set out the text of the eucharistic prayer. It was neat and compact, and followed the lines described by Justin. The original Greek text has never been found, and we have to rely on an early fifth-century Latin version, together with Coptic, Arabic and Ethiopian translations: and many scholars argued that the text has suffered changes in the process of transmission. But basically it was a prayer of thanksgiving for creation and redemption, an offering of the bread and cup in memory of Christ's death and resurrection, and a prayer for the gift of the Spirit on the communicants – a primitive form of epiclesis (q.v.). Clearly this was not

the Roman rite of the time, but simply a pattern which could be followed; later its influence was felt, not in Rome and the West, but in Egypt and Syria in the East, and not least in the Ethiopic liturgies.

Much of the liturgical material from the East during the second and third centuries is unreliable, for it derives from Gnostic sects. With strange beliefs about creation, the incarnation and the atonement, their prayers do not follow the lines of Justin and Hippolytus: but one interesting feature was a primitive form of invocation, which became an important element in eucharistic prayers of the East by the middle of the fourth century.

Two centres which were influential in the East were Egypt and Antioch. From Egypt in the fourth century comes the prayer book of Bishop Sarapion of Thmuis (*c.* AD 350) a private and untidy collection containing all the main elements of the eucharistic rite. Noteworthy features in its eucharistic prayer were the absence of the phrase 'Do this in remembrance of me' and the presence of two invocations – one before and one after the institution narrative. The second more explicit invocation invoked the Logos and not the Spirit, and it was characteristically Eastern in that it prayed for the consecration of the elements. The prayer ended with intercessions, which probably came during the third or fourth century in both East and West. Sarapion was the precursor of the Alexandrine Greek Liturgy of St Mark, from which in its turn came the Coptic Liturgy of St Mark or St Cyril.

From Antioch in the later fourth century came the so-called Clementine Liturgy in the eighth book of the *Apostolic Constitutions*. It agreed with the descriptions of the rite given in Chrysostom, and textually it owed much to Hippolytus. Its preface was very long; the institution narrative was introduced by the eastern form 'in the night in which he was delivered up'; the anamnesis (q.v.) included the second coming; the epiclesis was of the developed Eastern type; and it was followed by intercessions. From this rite developed the Liturgy of St James and the West Syrian family of rites, and ultimately the orthodox rites of St Basil and St John Chrysostom.

One further Eastern rite to be mentioned is that of SS Addai and Mari from Edessa in East Syria. It was written in Syriac and it lay outside the main influences of Greek-speaking Christendom. The extant text is very late and corrupt, but it may well point to the existence of an independent liturgical tradition as ancient as the third century. The main part of the eucharistic prayer is addressed to Christ, and it contains no institution narrative (q.v.); the epiclesis is of the Hippolytean type. Its users finally became Nestorians, and the rite came to be known as the Nestorian Liturgy.

Just as there were families of rites in the East, so there were families in the West. There was, for example, a North African family. Unfortunately no liturgical texts or treatises survive from this area: and the only evidence is references in the writings of Tertullian, Cyprian, Augustine and Optatus. It would seem, however, that there was borrowing from both East and West. So some churches used an epiclesis and some did not. On the other hand the kiss of peace (q.v.) was in the Roman position before communion, not before the anaphora (q.v.). At some stage freedom of experiment must have been excessive, for the Council of Carthage (397) and the First Council of Milevis (402) forbade uncontrolled freedom and insisted that all prayers should be officially approved.

In Rome the development of the rite was obscure. After Hippolytus there was a gap of some 150 years about which we know almost nothing. The first solid piece of evidence comes from the end of the fourth century with *De Sacramentis*, the lectures of Ambrose of Milan to the newly baptized. Here he made numerous quotations from a eucharistic text which later appeared in its entirety in the Gelasian Sacramentary. Its original form is unknown, but the disjointed text in the Sacramentary makes it clear that it has undergone revision. Ambrose also wrote of the eucharist in another treatise, *De Mysteriis*, and it would appear that in his time Milan used a rite which was fundamentally Roman. It followed the familiar pattern, but with significant features: intercessions came before the institution narrative, which was introduced in the characteristic Western manner – *Qui pridie*; consecration was effected, not by an epiclesis but by Jesus' own words in the institution narrative; and the Lord's Prayer had now found a place in the rite after the canon.

Other parts of the church in the West would also appear to have enjoyed an independent liturgical life in the early centuries, and the later evidence for what are known as the Gallican family of rites would suggest this; but of their origins virtually nothing is known.

It remains to note a few general developments, particularly in the East. First there was in the fourth century a growing attitude of awe towards the sacrament. Cyril of Jerusalem spoke of the 'holy and most dread sacrifice'; and Chrysostom and Theodore of Mopsuestia used similar language. Furthermore, with the imperial toleration and then the imperial establishment of Christianity, worship became more public and formal. So there developed a growing separation between clergy and laity: the corporate aspect of the eucharist faded; non-communicating attendance by the laity grew; the priest celebrated on behalf of the laity; and the most significant parts of the rite were withdrawn from their sight and hearing. In the West, however, changes were less serious. Gradually the canon came to be recited silently, and non-communicating attendance grew: but the priest remained in sight of the people, and no significant changes in dress or ceremonial occurred until after Gregory the Great.

R. C. D. JASPER

2. *Orthodox*. More correctly, Byzantine: what is commonly called the Orthodox liturgy, because by the historical and geographical accidents of subsequent Christian divisions it has come to be that in practice, is the liturgy of the Byzantine rite; that is, the liturgy of those churches which follow the order of service of the patriarchal see of Constantinople or Byzantium. The word 'liturgy' is normally used in the Byzantine rite only of the eucharistic liturgy, and not of the whole of formal public worship as it is in the West.

In the Eastern Orthodox Church today (as in those churches of the Byzantine rite in communion with Rome) the holy eucharist is celebrated according to three liturgies. The *Liturgy of St James the Brother of the Lord* is now used only on the feast of that saint in certain places. The historic liturgy of the Church of Jerusalem, and in its essentials the oldest of the three, it differs considerably from the other two, although its main parts, such as the eucharistic prayer or anaphora (q.v.), follow the same structure. The *Liturgy of St Basil the Great*, the anaphora of which, at least, was written by the father whose name it bears (on the basis of an older form which has in recent years been distinguished), is used on the eves of Christmas and the Epiphany, on the feast of St Basil (1 January), on the Sundays of Lent (except Palm Sunday), and on the Thursday and Saturday of Holy Week (qq.v.). The *Liturgy of St John Chrysostom* (which has little or nothing to do with St John Chrysostom, the ascription to him not being found until at least three hundred years after his death) is now the normal form: it is celebrated on all other days except those on which Byzantine liturgical law forbids the celebration of the eucharist altogether (*see* **Presanctified Mass**). The liturgies of St Basil and St John Chrysostom are identical in their order; they differ only in the texts of the principal prayers, those of the Liturgy of St Basil being much longer and fuller. They may therefore be considered together; further consideration of the Liturgy of St James must perforce be omitted.

Four principal divisions of the liturgy may be distinguished: (1) the preparation of the bread and wine, or prothesis (q.v.), which is performed privately before the service; (2) the introductory office of prayer and praise, or enarxis (q.v.); (3) the synaxis (q.v.), or liturgy of the word, or liturgy of the catechumens; (4) the eucharist proper, or liturgy of the faithful. A full account of the prothesis, and of its history, is given in a separate article.

The enarxis is also considered in a separate article, but a summary of its order and contents here may be useful: (1) opening blessing of the Trinity, by the celebrant; (2) the first (or greater) litany (q.v.) by the deacon, with responses by the people (in most churches in practice these and other responses are sung by the choir), and a concluding prayer (now said, as are most such prayers, silently, apart from its doxology) by the celebrant; (3) the first anthem (variable, usually a psalm, or based on a psalm); (4) the second (short) litany, with its concluding prayer; (5) the second anthem; (6) the third (short) litany, with its concluding prayer. The enarxis is now sung with the celebrant standing in the sanctuary before the holy doors: originally it was certainly sung with all the ministers outside the sanctuary, and possibly in the narthex (q.v.), or in

procession; the present usage removes all meaning from the beginning of the synaxis.

The synaxis comprises three parts: (1) the entrance rite; (2) the readings from the scriptures; (3) the common prayers of the church.

The entrance rite commences with the entrance with the book of the gospels, commonly called the little entrance (q.v.); further details will be found in the article devoted to it. It is followed by censing, during which anthems proper to the day (*troparia*) are sung: the original entrance chant has been shortened to a single verse sung between the last anthem of the enarxis and these *troparia*. The latter are followed by the hymn called the *Trisagion* (q.v.), corresponding here to the the *Gloria in excelsis* (*see* **Doxology**) in the Roman rite, and a lengthy prayer by the celebrant taking up the theme of this hymn (corresponding in function to the collect [q.v.] of the Roman rite), which is now said silently, and often before the hymn itself during the *troparia*.

The readings from the scriptures comprise: (1) the *prokeimenon*, part of a psalm, corresponding to the Roman gradual or responsorial psalm (the OT lesson, to which it was originally a response, has long since disappeared); (2) the epistle; (3) the alleluia (a verse or verses from the psalms, with the response 'Alleluia'); (4) the gospel. The sermon, if there be one, should follow the gospel, but is often postponed to a later point – in Greek churches before the communion (a practice comparable to the Italian *fervorino*), and in Russian churches to the end of the whole service.

The common prayers of the church comprise three litanies: (1) the litany of fervent prayer, so called from its tripled response, and essentially a litany for the living, although a petition for the departed has been added to it; (2) the litany for the departed (often sung only when there are particular departed persons to be prayed for); (3) the litany for the catechumens (q.v.). They end with the dismissal of the catechumens. In Russian churches all these litanies, together with the dismissal, are used, even when there are no catechumens; in Greek churches, on the other hand, they are commonly all omitted. The prayers which conclude each of the litanies are in most churches said silently, apart from their doxologies.

The eucharist proper commences after the

dismissal of the catechumens, and comprises seven parts: (1) the first part of the preparation of the offerers, or 'prayers of the faithful'; (2) the great entrance (q.v.) or entrance with the offerings; (3) the second part of the preparation of the offerers (the kiss of peace and the creed); (4) the eucharistic prayer or anaphora; (5) the breaking of the bread; (6) the communion; (7) the conclusion.

The 'prayers of the faithful' (which should not be confused, in the Byzantine or any other historic liturgy, with the common prayers of the church closing the synaxis) consist of two litanies introducing prayers (now said silently) of preparation for the offering of the eucharist.

The great entrance comprises five acts, the first four of which are covered by the singing of the almost invariable offertory chant, the 'hymn of the cherubim' (*cherubikon*): (1) a long secret private preparatory prayer of the priest, a typical 'apologetic' interpolation of the early Middle Ages; (2) censing of the altar, prothesis, and the whole church and congregation; (3) the actual 'entrance' itself, in the midst of which the *cherubikon* is interrupted for certain intercessory commemorations related to the diptychs (q.v.); (4) censing of the offerings now placed on the altar; (5) a litany leading to a prayer over the offerings, the latter exactly parallel to the Roman *super oblata* (q.v.), but now, confusingly, said secretly under cover of the litany.

The second part of the preparation of the offerers consists of the kiss of peace (which is no longer passed throughout the congregation, and is therefore omitted in practice unless several priests are present), the Niceno-Constantinopolitan Creed, and a brief exhortation by the deacon to reverence and awe in the offering of the eucharistic sacrifice which is about to take place.

The eucharistic prayer or anaphora is of the Antiochene pattern; it is difficult for anyone not well acquainted with the Byzantine liturgy to follow it in a contemporary celebration, due to the long standing custom, still all but universal, by which the celebrant says the greater part of it secretly (*see* **Silent Prayer**), while the congregational or choral responses are extended to cover his praying. Its order is:

(1) Introductory dialogue, of the universal pattern with certain minor elaborations.

(2) Preface, or first part of the thanksgiving, basically a brief and simple thanksgiving for creation and redemption in general terms, expanded at some time in the Middle Ages by Trinitarian interpolations which confuse the theme. Each of the two liturgies has its own form, as it has for every part of the prayer, but apart from this the preface, like the rest, is invariable. The preface is now said secretly, while the choir sings the last response of the introductory dialogue; the last clause is sung aloud, to provide a cue for the *Sanctus*.

(3) *Sanctus* and *Benedictus*, sung by the choir; the text is identical with that of the Roman rite, except that it reads 'Lord of Hosts' instead of 'Lord God of Hosts'.

(4) *Post-sanctus*, being a continuation of the thanksgiving, said secretly while the choir sings the *Sanctus*. In the Liturgy of St John Chrysostom a brief thanksgiving for the first coming of Christ, introducing the narrative of the institution; in the Liturgy of St Basil an extended and detailed thanksgiving for the whole history of creation and redemption, one of the finest examples of theological writing in the whole corpus of Christian liturgical literature, concluding with the introduction to the institution narrative.

(5) Narrative of the institution. The actual words of institution are sung, each of the two sentences being followed by the response 'Amen' by the choir.

(6) Anamnesis, normal in structure and content (*see* **Anaphora**); said secretly under cover of the prolonged closing 'Amen' of the institution narrative, apart from the penultimate clause, which serves as the cue for a choral response which now covers the epiclesis.

(7) Epiclesis, of a normal descendant type in both structure and content.

(8) Diptychs: commemoration of the saints, said secretly apart from one clause, which introduces an anthem, in honour of the Mother of God, which now covers the secret recitation of the next two sections.

(9) Diptychs: commemoration of the departed.

(10) Diptychs: commemoration of the living (one clause, that for the bishop, sung aloud).

(11) Doxology and final Amen (aloud).

The breaking of the bread comprises (1) a blessing of the people by the priest (many Western rites once had a corresponding blessing, which is in origin a preparation for communion); (2) a litany, similar to that after the great entrance, leading to the Lord's Prayer; (3) the breaking of the bread, with various secondary ceremonies, such as an elevation and a commixture, preceded by the original invitation to communion and its response, now purely formal, and covered by the communion hymn of the day, now thus used as a fraction hymn.

The communion comprises (1) the communion of the ministers; (2) the invitation to communion, to which the choir respond with Ps. 117 (118).26-27; (3) preparatory prayers, said aloud, a medieval interpolation; (4) the communion of the people, during which the choir sing appointed anthems; (5) the blessing after communion; (6) the first post-communion anthem. Communion is given in both kinds, administered together with a spoon, the bread having been placed in the chalice after the communion of the ministers; in the accompanying formula the communicant is referred to by name.

The conclusion comprises (1) the second-post-communion anthem; (2) a brief litany of thanksgiving, leading to the post-communion prayer (the latter said secretly); (3) the prayer over the people, or prayer outside the chancel, the original form of blessing; (4) the dismissal anthem, properly Ps. 33 (34) but now usually abbreviated; (5) the blessing and dismissal, with various responses, all of medieval origin.

The Byzantine eucharistic liturgy is unsurpassed in Christendom for clarity and coherence both of liturgical structure and of theological content – virtues which, unfortunately, are almost entirely obliterated by the combination of medieval interpolations and alterations and the current manner of celebration; there is no rite which would benefit more from a comparatively small measure of informed and intelligent reform.

W. JARDINE GRISBROOKE

3. *Medieval and Roman Catholic*

(a) *Medieval liturgies*. The Celtic liturgy, of which little is known before it had received Roman interpolations, was by the time of the Norman Conquest (1066) confined to Scotland and Ireland. It was probably of Gallican origin, and the lingering Celtic practices were suppressed in Scotland by St Margaret in 1069 and in Ireland in the twelfth century.

The Roman rite was introduced into England by the missionaries of St Augustine (d. 605) and the main structure continued throughout the Middle Ages.

After the Conquest, the building of churches, cathedrals and abbeys on a grand scale involved the compilation of a series of liturgical books of what came to be called different uses or even rites, although all were of the Roman rite.

There were extensive borrowings from the books in the Duchy of Normandy, and the process was completed by the thirteenth century. It is impossible to identify any specific 'ancestors' for the English uses, except, probably, Rouen for that of Hereford.

The structure was the same in each of them, but the prayers often differed, especially the preparatory prayers and those at the offertory and before communion.

By the time of the Reformation only three of the uses remained, since those of Bangor and Lincoln were virtually Sarum: Sarum, York and Hereford. All the others had adopted the Sarum liturgy, which became a model for the greater part of England and also for Scotland and Ireland. York had resolutely refused to give up its local use, but over the centuries many Sarum interpolations were accepted by Hereford.

The elaborate ceremonial of the 'Illustrious Church of Sarum' contrasted vividly with the comparative simplicity of liturgical worship in Rome.

The compiler of this English use could not have been St Osmund (d. 1099), although he may have laid a simple foundation. It is much too elaborate for his period. It was in all probability Richard Poore, dean and bishop (1217-28) of Salisbury, in whose time the cathedral was moved from Old Sarum into the city.

The last Sarum missal was printed in 1557 in the reign of Queen Mary.

In all the countries of Europe, diocesan missals appeared in the course of the Middle Ages, but, like the English service-books, they were variants of the Roman rite, with a choice of prayers.

(b) *Liturgy of Trent*. The fathers of the Council of Trent (1545-63) requested the pope to reform the liturgy, as it varied in almost every diocese. The new missal was completed under Pius V in 1570 to be an exemplar for all churches, and the mass was to be followed for all time. It was not until 1964 that it was superseded and then again in 1970. An exception had been made for those churches and religious orders which could show a distinctive use for at least two hundred years. All of them, however, were variants of the Roman rite, with the exception of the Mozarabic in a few churches in Toledo and that of Milan (Ambrosian), if a Gallican origin is maintained.

A few Marian priests in hiding continued their Sarum, York or Hereford mass, but the 'missioners' who came to England in the time of Elizabeth I followed the new Tridentine missal. Ancient sources had been studied in its production, but it preserved without change or verification the elements added in the Franco-German period to the original form of the Roman mass. The number of the feasts of saints was diminished and only four sequences were admitted. Unnecessary accretions were eliminated, such as the added words (tropes) in the *Kyrie* (q.v.) and the Marial fencing in the *Gloria in excelsis*. The time was unpropitious to reintroduce communion under both kinds. In order to answer difficulties in the celebration of mass, Sixtus V in 1588 founded the Congregation of Rites, but it could not change existing rubrics (q.v.) or the text of the prayers. An epoch of stability followed.

It is a mistake to think that this was a virtually silent mass. The rubrics ordered three voices: heard by the faithful, heard by those near to the celebrant, and silent, as in the canon. Above all, the epistle and gospel, the word of God, were for the benefit of the people and were to be read or sung in a clear and distinct voice. There was no justification for the subdeacon to chant the epistle in the sanctuary with his back to the congregation. True, the gospel was read in the vernacular (q.v.) in the pulpit before the sermon, but this was extra-liturgical, not part of the mass.

There were four revisions of the Tridentine liturgy, but the changes brought little modification of the text. The reform of Pius X (1911) affected the calendar: so that 'the very ancient Masses of Sundays throughout the year and of the week days, especially in Lent, might be restored to their proper place'. Clement XI (1721-24) had decreed that the preface of the Holy Trinity should be said on Sundays and Leo XIII (1878-1903) added the prayers after Low Mass. In 1953, the Liturgical Congress of Lugano discussed revolutionary changes in the mass, with the intention of simplifying the rite, removing what was redundant and giving the faithful a

more active part in the liturgy. At that time, some alterations appeared possible, but not the abandonment of the rite which had served the Western Church since the sixteenth century and the substitution of the vernacular for the Latin. A new Easter vigil appeared under Pius XII in 1951, with a change in all the offices of Holy Week in 1956.

The result of the debate on the liturgy in the Second Vatican Council (1962), which had been called by John XXIII, left no doubt that the changes would exceed mere alterations in the Tridentine mass.

(*c*) *Post-conciliar liturgies.* The aim of the post-conciliar commission was to produce a liturgy which should make the mass more alive and meaningful. Life was very different from 1570.

The priest should lead the community in worship, but the congregation must take a more intelligent and active part. 'Participation' is the key-note of the new liturgy, and, in order to effect this, the mass is said in the vernacular, although Latin is not altogether suppressed.

An 'interim' liturgy was ordered as from Advent Sunday 1964, with the people reciting the *Gloria in excelsis* and the creed, as well as responses and the variable 'chants' of the mass. Instructions were given as to when the faithful should stand, sit or kneel. The psalm 'Judge me, O God' in the preparatory prayers and the last gospel at the end of the mass were suppressed. The prayers of the faithful, general petitions linking the world with the eucharist, were introduced after the creed. The prayer after the offertory (q.v.), known hitherto as the 'secret', was said aloud and rightly renamed the prayer over the offerings (gifts). The Roman canon (q.v.) or eucharistic prayer, unaltered since the sixth century, remained the same, although said aloud and with the final doxology in a more solemn form, with the people responding amen. Three new eucharistic prayers, bringing fresh expression of the role of the Holy Spirit, were introduced in 1969. After the consecration, at the words 'mystery of faith', a choice of four acclamations by the faithful was introduced. Before the communion of the priest, 'Lord, I am not worthy' was said by all. The communicant replied 'Amen' after the words of administration: The body of Christ. Finally, the dismissal was transferred until after the blessing.

The ceremonial (q.v.) of the mass had been

greatly reduced, as had the signs of the cross and genuflections. The commission regulated also the rite of concelebration and, for certain occasions, the administration of communion under both kinds. The number of communicants in large churches would make the giving of the chalice at all times very difficult.

The final and normative order of the mass was first said in France, Italy and Spain on Advent Sunday 1969 and in Great Britain on the first Sunday in Lent 1970. Rome had conceded that its use was not compulsory for two years, but it was largely adopted. The various changes in the 'interim' rite have been retained in the new liturgy.

Incense may be used whether the mass is sung or said. The mass begins with an entrance song, which may be either the old introit or a hymn. Then, after a greeting of the people, there is a penitential act with a shortened confession in which the faithful join with the priest. 'Lord have mercy' and 'Glory be to God on high' are followed by the first of the presidential prayers, the collect, of which there is never more than one.

The liturgy of the word, since the council, has a more vital role. The pope has said that 'the treasury of the written word of God should be more generously distributed'. A third lesson, from the OT, is provided for Sundays and feasts, and a new lectionary has been compiled. The four sequences or hymns before the gospel have been retained, but only those of Easter and Pentecost are obligatory. The creed and the prayers of the faithful follow.

The offertory procession, at the beginning of the eucharistic liturgy, linking the gifts of bread and wine with the giving of money, is encouraged where possible. The prayers at the offertory are shorter and have been modelled on the prayer spoken by the father of the family at the beginning of a formal Jewish meal.

Eight new prefaces have been added, making twenty-two in all. The Roman canon, as an alternative to the three eucharistic prayers, has been retained, with a few minor alterations. The list of saints before and after the consecration may be considerably shortened, and what may be called the three false conclusions in the canon suppressed. An acclamation by the faithful has been introduced after the words 'mystery of faith', as in the other prayers. This acclamation highlights Paul in his First Letter to the Christians of Corinth.

The central and vital part of the canon, including the words of consecration, may be sung, as well as the final doxology. The prayer following the Our Father has been simplified and changed at the end, with an acclamation of faith in the glorified Christ.

The 'sign of peace and mutual love', adopted in some countries for the kiss of peace (q.v.), is not normally in use in Britain. The consecrated bread is broken at the threefold *Agnus dei*. After communion, a silence for thanksgiving is prescribed. Notices are given before the blessing. The ablutions may be taken after mass.

The calendar has been simplified. The titles of the three Sundays before Lent have been suppressed. There are fewer feasts of saints, and very many of the commemorations are optional. John the Deacon (872) in his assessment of the work of St Gregory could be writing of the new mass: 'leaving out much, changing little, adding something for the exposition of the lessons of the Gospel'.

J. D. CRICHTON

4. *Anglican.* The roots of Anglican eucharistic liturgy lie in the reforming work of Cranmer in the reign of Edward VI (1547-53). By 1547 he had already come to strong convictions about the *desiderata*, and when Edward, a minor, inherited the throne, Cranmer's Protestantism in theology was reflected in the Council of which he was a member, and the opportunity came to reform the liturgy.

Cranmer's main aims were: a wholly vernacular (q.v.) liturgy, a simplification of ceremonies, participation by the people (including receiving communion regularly and in both kinds), and elimination of transubstantiation, mass-sacrifice, and other unreformed doctrines. His purpose was far more to write a liturgy embodying receptionism than to revive patristic usage. It was not that he lacked scholarship or materials – rather he was not interested in copying patristic use for its own sake anyway. Certainly his developed liturgy was *sui generis* and unlike any earlier production.

Reform came by stages – a method advertised in advance in the Royal Proclamation prefixed to *The Order of the Communion* of 1548. In 1547 the epistle and gospel had been read in English. Now this brief inset into the mass came as the first new eucharistic work in Cranmer's planned programme. Written in English, it implemented reception in both kinds by being inserted after the priest's communion in the mass. It contained a long exhortation to worthy reception, a short exhortation, confession, absolution, 'comfortable words', and the famous 'prayer of humble access' leading into communion in both kinds. A blessing followed, and if the wine were insufficient more was to be consecrated.

In the 1549 *BCP* the whole service was in English. The mass-plus-*Order* shape was followed closely, but the contents were subtly changed. The ante-communion (q.v.) merely lost the priest's preparation and the gradual chant. It gained a sermon or homily after the creed, and the 1548 long exhortation followed that. The offertory (q.v.) – consisting of a collecting of money – concluded the ante-communion. The worshippers left their places to put their alms in a box near the screen, and intending communicants proceeded on to the choir or chancel.

The elements were then made ready and the cunningly altered canon ensued. The Roman intercessions remained, but only prayers, not oblations (q.v.), were offered. The saints were honoured, but not expected to help. Prayer was made for the departed, now grouped with the living. The intercessions broke off, and the sacramental theme began abruptly. God was invoked as having given his Son to make on the cross 'a full, perfect, and sufficient sacrifice, oblation and satisfaction' for sins – words serving devotional, didactic, and polemical purposes. The *quam oblationem* petition then asked God to bless and sanctify the gifts by his 'Holy Spirit and word'. This is sometimes called an epiclesis (q.v.), but occupied the Western position and owed little or nothing to Eastern models. The institution narrative (q.v.) had two manual acts but no other ceremonial. But the anamnesis was the key to Cranmer's step by step reform. The old canon (q.v.) responded to the command 'Do this in remembrance' with 'we offer a pure victim'. Cranmer removed this oblationary terminology, but left the response unexplained. It read 'we . . . celebrate and make . . . the memorial which thy Son hath willed us to make'. In brief, whatever he meant, we mean! The canon continued with self-oblation, petition for fruitful reception, some wisps of the old canon and a doxology. After it came the Lord's Prayer, the peace, and the whole 1548 *Order* from the short exhortation to communion (including the priest's). After a brief post-communion, rubrics ordered 'something more larger and thicker' wafers, to be divided during distribution. Further consecration was lacking.

Reactions to this service merely paved the way for the next round, which may have been already in preparation. Implementation came in 1552. Now the shape was altered, slightly in the ante-communion, drastically around the anamnesis (q.v.). To the question, 'What do we do in response to our Lord's command?' the 1552 *Order* answered, 'We eat bread and drink wine'. This was incorporated after the institution narrative not by mere verbal assertion, but by *actual eating and drinking*. New words of administration reflected not new doctrine but the new 'anamnesis' role of communion – 'Take and eat this in remembrance . . .'. The 1552 *Order* left no break between reading the Lord's command and obeying it, the table was in the midst and the distribution was immediate.

Further consequences followed. Sacramentally speaking, nothing preceded reception. There was no trace of consecration, whether name or thing. The elements were not mentioned rubrically till distribution, and the minister took the remains home. The *quam oblationem* petition located consecration in reception, and this is the logic of the whole rite. Further consecration was thus impossible.

The promoted administration squeezed considerable 1549 material out of its place. The end of the 1549 canon became an alternative post-communion 'prayer of oblation' (still, oddly, asking for fruitful reception). The Lord's Prayer opened the post-communion. The peace was lost, and the 1548 *Order* began the sacramental half of the service. Cranmer hit on the happy transition from the fourth 'comfortable word' to 'lift up your hearts', but this excluded 'humble access' from the sequence. It, however, replaced the 1549 intercessions after the *Sanctus*. As these had lost their connection with the 'oblations' they no longer belonged in the canon, and went more naturally (and perhaps primitively) at the end of the ante-communion. Thus they were read each week, even when there was no communion. The saints and the departed disappeared and the intercessions were explicitly labelled for the 'church militant here in earth'. Inserting 'humble access' after the *Sanctus* (q.v.) has been thought to break up the canon, but to Cranmer there was a gaping hole there, and a subjective approach to the table suited the progress of the service, to a single climax in reception, far better than the 1549 intercessions could do. Thus the 1552 'canon' was merely the 'one oblation' paragraph, the receptionist *quam oblationem*, and the institution narrative ending in the administration. The post-communion included *Gloria in excelsis*, and the rubrics ordered bread 'usual to be eaten'.

Mary brought back the mass, but Elizabeth in 1559 revived the 1552 *Order*, though she clumsily prefixed 1549 words of administration to the 1552 ones. Jewel's controversy with Harding made it policy to assert that the dominical words in the narrative of institution consecrated the elements, and a Puritan, Robert Johnson, was imprisoned in 1574 for omitting a 'further consecration'. The 1604 canons underlined this new policy.

The ill-fated 1637 Scottish rite was a half-reversion to 1549. After the *Sanctus* 'humble access' fell out, and the 'one oblation' paragraph followed immediately. The 1549 *quam oblationem* returned, manual acts were reintroduced, the 1549 anamnesis dislodged the administration, and the 1552 'prayer of oblation' followed as in 1549. The Lord's Prayer and 'humble access' intervened before communion, but the rest of the 1549 *Order* held its 1552 position. The canon was now called 'the prayer of consecration', and rubrics ordered both further consecration and consumption of consecrated remains.

The 1662 Restoration liturgy kept the 1552 text and structure, but firmly clamped the 1637 'consecration' rubrics upon it. Cranmer's words were to enact Jewel's theology! A discreet (non-petitionary) mention of the departed came into the intercessions, and an amen concluded the 'prayer of consecration'. As, under Laud's influence, tables had already returned to the east wall of the chancel, a break between the institution narrative and distribution had arisen. Thus the amen merely regularized a *de facto* departure from the continuity which Cranmer had planned.

The 1662 *Order* still remains today the official service of the Church of England and of many other Anglican provinces. However, some provinces have superseded it, and most have at least some alternative. Its use is now more deeply entrenched in vernacular languages (in, say, Africa) than it is in English-speaking communities. These latter show impatience at its antique (but majestic) language, its unique shape, and (sometimes) its Cranmerian theology.

Early variants occurred in eighteenth-century Scotland. A scholarly theory that the *Apostolic Constitutions* were really apostolic led to changes from 1637 to 1764. The 1637 *quam oblationem* was moved to the Eastern position and made into a full-blown epiclesis. The 1549/1637 anamnesis had an explicit oblation of the elements attached. The intercessions were moved to the end of the canon. Finally, the whole 1548 *Order* returned to its 1549 position. The current Scottish rite descends from 1764. The same text was taken to America by Samuel Seabury in 1784, was crossed with the 1662 rite over there, and a hybrid rite emerged in 1790. The 1790 rite lies behind current American and Brazilian use.

In the early twentieth century the Universities' Mission to Central Africa and Korean mission fields went over to near-Roman rites (usually only available then in vernacular tongues). An Eastern-type epiclesis also had its advocates again, and was not only retained in the Scottish and American rites when they were revised, but was also introduced in South Africa (1924), England (1927-8), and in the 1930s in Ceylon, China, Madagascar and elsewhere. Anglo-Catholics led all these revisions, seeking a more primitive pattern for the canon, petitions for the departed, and some form of Godward 'memorial' in the anamnesis. They were divided, however, about the propriety, wording and position of the epiclesis. In England the 1927-8 rite created grave suspicions among Protestants for these very reasons, but it was finally defeated over the (non-liturgical) question of reservation.

In the late 1940s India experimented with a 1928-type rite, and Japan and the West Indies followed in the 1950 on a more 1549-cum-Roman basis. The 1959 Canadian rite stood between 1662 and the Indian rite.

The 1960s brought a new era. Experimental revision started all round the Anglican Communion. G. Dix's *The Shape of the Liturgy* (1945) had focused attention on the *action* and less on the *words*. The first result of this had been the ecumenical South India liturgy of 1950; its principles, embodied in the 1958 Lambeth Report, were worked out for Anglicans in *A Liturgy for Africa* (1964). Offspring of this family includes ecumenical liturgies in East Africa (1966) and Nigeria (1966). They all have a fuller ministry of the word, including the OT. The creed follows the sermon, and the intercessions are litanical. Penitence has moved to the beginning of the rite, so the sacramental section is a simple placing of the elements on the table, a thanksgiving, a breaking of bread, and a sharing of the elements. The thanksgiving 'consecrates', but not by this brief set of words, but by the totality of the action. The thanksgiving includes emphasis on the cross, but makes mention of the other mighty works of God. There are congregational acclamations at intervals in it.

The Church of England's 1967 *Second Series* experimental rite is similar but not dependent. Penitence remains in the 1552 position, special emphasis on the cross has almost disappeared (for there is no link in salvation-history between the *Sanctus* and the institution narrative), and the anamnesis is a tentative, half-done job, with echoes of 1549. A more modern English form of it occurs in *Modern Liturgical Texts* (1968), and an adaptation of it (suggesting another new family of rites has started) issued from the South African Liturgical Committee in 1969. The next stage on from *Second Series* in England itself is the *Third Series* rite published in September 1971. Here the language has been thoroughly modernized, and the whole service worked over. A richer style of biblical and other imagery returns, and the anamnesis is a far clearer doctrinal statement than before. Congregational acclamations are added in the thanksgiving, a fuller provision is made for the high seasons of the church's year, and a new Sunday eucharistic lectionary is included. At the time of writing *Second Series* will be extended beyond July 1972, and *Third Series* will be amended and should be authorized from a similar date.

C. O. BUCHANAN

5. *Baptists.* While most Baptists would affirm their worship as 'eucharistic' in the sense that it is a time of thanksgiving, they would not use the term 'eucharist' to describe it. Likewise, they generally do not use terms like 'sacrament' or 'holy communion'. They rather prefer the 'Lord's Supper', or the 'breaking of bread' or the 'memorial meal' to designate the central act of Christian worship.

The Lord's Supper is understood as anamnesis (q.v.). The Lord's death is remembered and re-enacted as a memorial 'until he comes'. The bread and wine are symbols of the body and blood of Jesus Christ. The presence of the Lord is a spiritual presence.

Baptists, though having a high regard for the Lord's Supper, do not observe it with great frequency. Daily communion is not practised by Baptists. Weekly communion is only rarely observed, and then usually by congregations which have had some contact with the contemporary movement for liturgical renewal. The general practice among Baptist churches is monthly communion, usually on the first Sunday of the month. Baptist churches in some places observe only four communion Sundays a year.

The administrator of the communion is generally an ordained minister, but if no ordained person is available the congregation may designate a layman as the administrator. He will also be assisted by deacons (q.v.). They serve the elements, pass the peace, and assist in the prayers. The service is generally conducted from behind the table, the minister facing the congregation.

Communion is in two kinds. Formerly a common loaf was broken and distributed to each communicant and a common cup was passed among the congregation. Today communion wafers or small bits of bread and individual cups are in general use, although in some places the common loaf and cup are being reintroduced. Communion is generally received in the pews. The bread is eaten at the same time by the minister and congregation as the minister says: 'Jesus said, "Take eat; this is my body which is broken for you. Do this in remembrance of me."' The cup is drunk simultaneously as the minister says: 'Jesus said, "Drink of it, all of you; for this is my blood of the covenant, which is poured out from many for the forgiveness of sins."'

Communion among the early Baptists was generally reserved for those who were members in good standing of the local congregation or who were members of sister congregations in good standing. That meant that only those who had been baptized 'on profession of faith' as believers were to be communicants. In many places the practice was to hold two services on a communion Sunday. The first, including the sermon, would be for all who came; the second was only for those who were entitled to receive communion. In recent decades this practice has been greatly modified. While some churches still practise 'closed communion', most Baptist churches issue a general invitation to 'all who believe in Christ and who are in love and fellowship with the brethren' to partake in the service. The service of word and table is one, and all, including those who do not communicate, remain.

Each congregation determines the structure of its worship. Thus no one service would be considered typical, but with modifications the following would find acceptance in most Baptist churches.

THE SERVICE FOR THE LORD'S DAY
(with the Lord's Supper)

Affirmation of purpose and entry of scriptures
Adoration
  Scripture sentences
  Hymn
  Prayer
  Ascription
Confession
  Call
  Prayer
  Assurance of forgiveness
  Praise: *Gloria patri, Gloria in excelsis*, or hymn

Ministry of the Word

Scripture lessons
Prayer of illumination
Sermon
Affirmation of faith or church covenant

Ministry of the Table

Offertory: gifts, bread and wine, and self
Prayer of dedication
Invitation to communion
Affirmation of unity and peace
  Scripture sentence
  Right hand of fellowship (the peace)
Words of institution
Prayer of thanksgiving
Prayer for the presence of the Holy Spirit
Lord's Prayer
Breaking and distribution of the bread
Eating of the bread
Pouring and distribution of the wine
Drinking the wine
Agnus Dei
Prayers of petition and intercession

Dismissal

Hymn
Benediction

The service generally includes several hymns, an anthem and service music. A choir is used to assist in the service and to offer the special music.

JOHN E. SKOGLUND

6. *Christian Church (Disciples of Christ)*. From its earliest days, in the early nineteenth century, the Christian Church (Disciples of Christ) has combined two principles bearing upon the order of worship. First, the regular service of worship has included preaching and the 'breaking of bread'. Second, this church has entrusted decisions about the order and words of the liturgy to each congregation. Although there has been considerable similarity among congregations, it must be said that the practice is neither common order nor common prayer.

The first exposition of this practice was developed by Alexander Campbell (1788-1866) in his writings during the third and fourth decades of the century. After observing that the NT, in contrast to the OT, gives no formal requirements for worship, Campbell concluded that Christians have reached the 'manhood of the religious world', and are therefore 'permitted to exercise their reason, and to act from the principles infused into their minds from the development of the divine philanthropy'. He affirmed that the weekly observance of the Lord's Supper on the Lord's Day is commanded but that the rules are not. Accounts of that period indicate that a typical service began with readings from scripture interspersed with hymns. There followed brief extempore prayers over bread and wine with the distribution of each. Impromptu exhortations or preaching, spiritual songs, and a collection concluded the service.

During the period from 1880 to 1920 this combination of elements was gradually formalized in general practice: opening praise, scripture lessons, pastoral prayer, communion, offering and sermon. The position of the sermon is a vestige of earlier practice when the congregation always ministered the Lord's Supper whether there was a preacher or not. Communion was ordinarily conducted with these sub-sections: a brief homily on the meaning of the act, an extempore prayer over the loaf by one elder, a second prayer over the cup by a second elder, and distribution of both to the congregation. An invitation to confess faith in Christ was regularly extended following the sermon. A number of private service-books was published during this time giving suggestions for pastors for the construction of their services.

Not until after the Second World War did Disciple congregations in large numbers develop an order of worship more closely parallel to that followed in other denominations. By transposing communion and sermon, they overcame their one major disparate practice. By 'enriching' the service with devotional elements previously not used they developed a tone to their services increasingly like that of other denominations.

The use of extempore prayer at the communion table has continued with little change, illustrating positive and negative values in such a practice. Ordinarily these prayers have referred specifically to the bread and the cup and have given thanks for Jesus who gave himself for our sins. Frequently there have been requests for the Holy Spirit to come and for our sins to be forgiven. A common element has been a vow that we will give our lives now to greater service to God. The use of extempore prayers at the table makes possible a directness and immediacy that rarely is present in the language of prescribed eucharistic prayers. At the same time, this practice opens the way for unevenness and irregularity.

Disciples, despite a long-time tendency towards legalism, have never raised questions about the validity of the Lord's Supper, about the 'form' and 'matter' of the eucharist. Consequently, the varied theological content of the eucharistic prayer has not raised for them the problems that would arise in other portions of the church. Adequacy of the rite has been gauged by different criteria: Is the table spread in remembrance of Christ? Has the conducting of the service been according to the congregation's unwritten standards or expectations? Does the combination of music, word, and act communicate a sense of divine presence? On every Sunday the entire congregation present communicates and in this way affirms the integrity of the rite.

KEITH WATKINS

7. *Congregationalist.* As is explained under **Congregationalist Worship**, there is no single official Congregational liturgy. None the less the structure, order, and content of Congregational services of word and sacrament do not differ greatly between Britain and the USA (for the sources of these services *see* **Books, Liturgical** 7: Congregationalist).

The nearest approach to an archetypal Congregational liturgy, and one which unites the largest number of Congregationalists in the world, is the first recommended service in *Services of Word and Sacrament,* first published in 1966 by the United Church of Christ. It is archetypal yet not monopolistic, since alternatives are provided. It is a firm guide to worship with a coherent theology and careful order, but welcomes the supplementary use of free prayer, silent prayer, and bidding prayers, as long as they do not break the basic order and progression of the service.

The service has two parts, which correspond to the origin of Christian worship in the synagogue and the upper room. The first part is essentially a service of the word; the second part is essentially the service of the Holy Supper or eucharist. The first part consists of praise, prayers, the reading and exposition of scripture, an affirmation of faith, and the response of the people in the offertory – the climax of the service of the word and the beginning of the service of the Lord's Supper.

The second part of the service recalls not only in words, but also in symbolic and prophetic acts, the four actions of the Lord who *took* the bread and wine, *blessed* them by prayer, *broke* or poured them, and *gave* them to his disciples, as the anticipation of his sacrifice on the cross and of his messianic banquet in eternity.

The aims of the entire service are: to stress the unity of word and sacrament; to offset an overly introspective and penitential character in historic Western worship by accenting the elements of adoration and joyful gratitude and the presence of the risen Christ; to make the central eucharistic actions plain; and, finally, to emphasize that the true consecrator is the Holy Spirit. These are not, of course, uniquely Congregational or even Reformed contributions to liturgical theology – they are the common gains of the liturgical and ecumenical movements of our days.

In two respects only has this liturgy made a distinctive contribution, and these are worthy of elaboration. The peril of the exclusively retrospective gaze and of a theological memorialism are minimized by beginning the eucharistic part of the service with Luke's account of the risen Saviour breaking bread with his disciples. Since the Pauline account of the Holy Supper in I Corinthians is by far the commoner usage as a warrant in our tradition, this feature is genuinely innovative.

The second innovation, for which the Church of South India provides a partial precedent, was to provide some new responses for the people in the great prayer of consecration. The most significant response, after the anamnesis and epiclesis (qq.v.), affirms the priesthood of all God's people, in the following words of oblation: 'Here we offer ourselves in obedience to Thee, through the perfect offering of thy Son Jesus Christ, giving Thee thanks that Thou has called us to be a royal priesthood, a holy nation, thine own people . . .' The distinctive Congregational witness has not been lost, but rather recovered in this rich rite which won the approval of the late E. C. Ratcliff as having recovered 'the spirit and emphasis of the Early Church'.

There have been two significant changes incorporated in the more recent Congregational communion services in both Britain and the USA. One has been the increasing appropriation of the historic structure and wording of the consecration prayer of the Western tradition, including the salutation, the *Sursum corda*, the *Sanctus*, the anamnesis, and the oblation.

A second change has been towards a deeper sense of the real presence in the sacrament as evidenced by the requirement of an epiclesis, in contrast to earlier eucharistic theologies which were virtualist at best and memorialist at worst. The evidence for this claim can be found in the most recent servicebooks of the Congregational Church of England and Wales and the United Church of Christ in the USA.

The theology of the first and second communion orders of *A Manual for Ministers* (1936) is clearly memorialist. Four of the five communion orders in *A Book of Public Worship Compiled for the Use of Congregationalists* (1948) have an explicit epiclesis, and a fourth has an implicit doctrine of the real presence. Both communion orders in *A Book of Services and Prayers* (1959) have an explicit epiclesis.

In the American Congregational publication, *A Book of Worship for Free Churches* (1948), two communion orders include an ambiguous epiclesis in the words: 'We humbly beseech thee to grant thy Holy Spirit and to sanctify this bread and wine, which now we offer unto thee; that they may become unto us symbols of the body that was broken and of the blood that was shed for us . . .' (pp. 108, 115-6). On the other hand, the two communion orders of the United Church of Christ published in *Services of Word and Sacrament* (1966) include the following epiclesis: 'Bless and sanctify by thy Holy Spirit both us and these thy gifts of bread and wine that in this holy communion of the body and blood of Christ we may be made one with him and he with us . . .'

HORTON DAVIES

8. *Jehovah's Witnesses.* Once yearly Jehovah's Witnesses keep the Lord's evening meal, 'the memorial'. The date is 14 Nisan in the ancient Jewish calendar. Christ instituted the celebration on Passover day (Mark 14.12-26). In the Christian calendar the evening meal replaced the Jewish Passover. It is a yearly reminder of the sacrifice of the Lamb of God, held the same day his death occurred.

For similar historical reasons, it is observed after sundown. The Jewish day commenced at sundown: that was when the fourteenth of the month began. Jesus held it after sundown. It is a 'supper', and 'evening' meal (Mark 14.17; I Cor. 11.20, 21).

Jesus passed both unleavened bread and wine to his eleven faithful disciples (Judas apparently having been dismissed before the memorial meal began; compare John 13.26, 27, 30 with Matt. 26.23-25, 26). The wine would have fermented by the time of the spring festival.

Jesus said the meal was to be kept 'in remembrance of me'. He also connected it with two covenants. Those celebrating would be in the 'new covenant' (Luke 22.20). The old (law) covenant was for a 'kingdom of priests' (Ex. 19.6). Likewise, the new covenant is for a kingdom of priests (I Peter 2.9; Rev. 1.6). The other covenant Jesus mentioned was a covenant 'for a kingdom, that you may eat and drink at my table in my kingdom, and sit on thrones to judge the twelve tribes of Israel' (Luke 22.29, 30).

Interestingly, both these covenants had to do with a kingdom. Those entitled to partake of the emblems of bread and wine were those who would 'eat and drink at my table in my kingdom'. This could not include everyone; for these heavenly kings 'sit on thrones to judge' others. This kingdom of priests who 'rule as kings with the Christ for a thousand years' is limited in Rev. 14.1-3 to 144,000 persons. With Christ in his heavenly kingdom, they rule the rest of creation, including obedient mankind (Rev. 20.4-6; 21.2-4).

Thus, although 2,719,860 worldwide gathered with Jehovah's Witnesses on 14 Nisan 1969 at the Lord's evening meal, only 10,368 who felt they had the witness of the spirit that they would be joint heirs with Christ in his kingdom partook of the bread and wine passed to all. The remainder were respectful observers, remembering too that their everlasting life depended on Christ's ransom sacrifice, yet looking forward to being earthly subjects of the kingdom rather than heavenly kings and priests (Heb. 2.5).

The memorial takes the form of an explanatory discourse followed by passing the emblems to all present, with the invitation to those convinced of a heavenly hope to partake. The meeting lasts about one hour.

A. HELEY

9. *Lutheran.* At the time of the Reformation (1517-), liturgical reform among Lutherans had a twofold motivation: theological and didactic. There was no attempt to break the mould of Western Catholic tradition nor to return to liturgical practices of the primitive church. The inherited rites were judged theologically by the Reformation norm: justification by grace through faith. Neither the Roman canon nor offertory prayers were acceptable because their emphasis on sacrifice suggested that the mass is primarily man's service of God. Lutherans insisted on the opposite, that the mass is primarily God's work among men. The need to release people from medieval superstition and expose them to the teaching of the gospel was met by a strong emphasis on preaching and by the use of the vernacular in the liturgy. Preaching was accorded sacramental status as the living voice of the gospel: Christ present and active.

Martin Luther turned his hand to liturgical reform reluctantly, being forced by what he considered ill-advised attempts of others. Because of his prestige, his two major reforms of the mass were widely imitated. The first, *Formula missae et communionis (FM,* 1523), was a Latin rite which provided for vernacular hymns and sermon. Only minor changes were made in the *missa catechumenorum.* The

sermon might come either before the introit or following the creed. The excision of offertory and canon resulted in the following order for the *missa fidelium*: preface, words of institution (sung), *Sanctus* (with elevation), Our Father (omitting doxology), pax (interpreted as a public absolution), communion in both kinds (with *Agnus Dei*), collect, *Benedicamus* (replacing *Ite missa est*), Aaronic blessing (qq.v.). Compared with other Reformation rites the *FM* is conservative, but Luther cut out the heart of the medieval mass, i.e. the offertory and canon (q.v.).

Though he realized its inevitability, Luther took the step towards the vernacular with reservations. The Latin rite was imbedded in his piety and he loved its music dearly. He insisted that a German rite must be supplied with 'German music'; he viewed with horror attempts to fit the heavy accents of modern languages to the fluid grace of plainsong. But the pastoral need triumphed and the *Deutsche Messe (DM)* was published in 1526. (English versions of *FM* and *DM* are in *Luther's Works,* vol. 53, American edition, 1965. Original texts are in the Weimar edition: *FM*, vol. 12; *DM*, vol. 19.) It was designed especially for village churches and the unlettered majority. It was not intended to supplant the Latin mass in city churches or schools. (Portions of the Latin rite survived in parts of Germany into the eighteenth century.)

The basic structure of the *DM* is traditional though greatly simplified. The prose texts of the Ordinary were put in metrical paraphrase and assigned to the congregation. The popularity of this practice estranged large portions of Continental Lutheranism from the ancient mass texts. Again the *missa fidelium* is most altered: paraphrased Our Father, exhortation to communicants, words of institution and communion. There was an abortive attempt to divide the words of institution and distribute each element after its appropriate blessing. But the *DM* provided the people with a rite admirably suited to their needs and ability. The post-communion collect is one of Luther's finest prayers.

The Lutheran Reformation in Germany was scattered geographically. Since there was no unified church structure, there could be no liturgical equivalent of the *BCP*. Instead there was a proliferation of local *Kirchenordnungen,* most of whose liturgies were modelled after Luther. These church orders fall into two major groups: the Brandenburg-

Nürnberg type (*FM* as model) and the Bugenhagen type (*DM* as model) (original texts in E. Sehling, ed., *Die Evangelischen Kirchenordnungen des XVI. Jahrhunderts*, vols. 1-11). Johann Bugenhagen was one of Luther's emissaries to churches accepting the Reformation stance, and was responsible for the rites of many churches in Northern Germany and the Church of Denmark (1537). Liturgical development in Norway was tied to that in Denmark.

The Swedish liturgical tradition begins with the vernacular rite (1531) of Olavus Petri which follows the *FM* structure. The *Church Order* (1571) of Laurentius Petri was a revision which restored Latin texts in certain parts. After several abortive attempts at both left and right wing reform, the *Prayer Book* of 1614 was authorized. It followed the 1531 rite and established the *FM* tradition for the following three centuries.

By the eighteenth century, Lutherans were firmly established on the eastern seaboard of North America. Their worship reflected the languages and traditions of their various motherlands. But Henry Melchior Muhlenberg, patriarch of American Lutheranism, dreamed of the day when these groups could be united and have a common rite. Towards that end he produced a communion liturgy based upon several German models which was remarkable for its Reformation fullness. This German rite, together with English orders for baptism and marriage (from the *BCP*), constituted the first American liturgy. The first Lutheran communion service in English was not published until the mid-nineteenth century.

Generally, however, the eighteenth century was a time of liturgical decline affecting Lutheran churches everywhere. Pietism, with its anti-liturgical bias, and rationalism, which had little place for cultic action, took their toll. Liturgies were rationalized (employing deistic expressions), then psychologized as a passion for relevance set in. But by the mid-nineteenth century a neo-orthodox movement brought with it the glimmer of liturgical renewal. Wilhelm Löhe, a leader in establishing a female diaconate in the Bavarian church, joined other voices calling for a churchly and sacramental revival which would return the church to its own rich tradition. Because of his connection with mission pastors on the American frontier for whom he prepared a liturgy, Löhe's work was more directly influential there than in Germany.

The ecumenical Liturgical Movement (q.v.) of the late nineteenth and early twentieth centuries resulted in various 'high church movements' throughout Lutheranism. But its enduring contribution was to stimulate a recovery of pre-eighteenth-century fullness. The various national and provincial churches on the Continent produced service-books which re-established contact with their own Reformation traditions. Several groups in the USA began work on a Common Service which would exemplify the consensus of the 'best liturgies of the sixteenth century'. This service appeared in 1888 and with musical setting formed the nucleus of the complete *Common Service Book* (with hymnal) of 1917. Subsequently the Common Service was incorporated into other North American service-books and became the common rite for a majority of English-speaking Lutherans.

As a result of earlier development and the impetus of the Second World War, the postwar years were marked by greater Lutheran unification and inter-Lutheran co-operation. *The Liturgy of the Church of Sweden* had already appeared in 1942. 1955 saw the publication of *Agenda I* for the Lutheran Churches of Germany. *The Service Book and Hymnal* for about two-thirds of the Lutherans in North America appeared in 1958. Australian Lutherans brought out their *Orders of Service* in 1966, and in 1970 the *High Mass* for the Church of Norway was published. These books mark the culmination of a long period of recovery of the Reformation tradition. They also symbolize the high degree of uniformity within major geographical areas and among them.

Without its having been imposed by ecclesiastical authority, and allowing for different linguistic traditions, world Lutheranism has achieved a remarkable liturgical unity. It is, of course, only part of a larger unity observable throughout Western Christianity. The newer Swedish, German, American and Norwegian rites all include eucharistic prayers, thus showing an openness to Western Catholic tradition antedating the Reformation.

Lutheran participation in the various ecumenical agencies has opened lines of communication with liturgical commissions of other bodies. The increased ecumenical co-operation in liturgical revision growing out of Vatican II has caused the Liturgical Movement to round a corner. Rapid cultural change has opened a wide gap between church and society and dramatized the need for new approaches.

Having reclaimed their liturgical identity, Lutherans are now prepared to step forward creatively beyond their own tradition. A provisional order for holy communion published by the Inter-Lutheran Commission on Worship (North America) in 1970 is one of the first official products of the new mood. In its relocation of corporate confession, abbreviated entrance rite, fuller offertory section, and expanded eucharistic prayer, it departs from the tradition of the sixteenth-century church orders and exhibits similarities to work being done by other Christian churches. This is shown not only in its structure but also in its use of common texts prepared by the International Consultation on English Texts.

EUGENE BRAND

10. *Methodist.* Methodist communion liturgies are based on John Wesley's revision of the 1662 *BCP* rite as published in his *Sunday Service of the Methodists in North America* in 1784. As Wesley said, it was 'a liturgy little differing from that of the church of England'. Wesley is correct in saying that he made 'little alteration' in the book as a whole and especially with regard to the communion service. Most of the holy days were omitted, the word 'priest' was translated as 'elder' throughout, and the pronouns of the prayer of absolution changed from 'you' to 'us'. Service music was not expected and it was indicated that the *Gloria in excelsis* and the *Sanctus* were to be recited. Wesley expected that hymns would be sung and he and his brother, Charles, wrote 165 eucharistic hymns. A few changes were made in the rubrics, while the Nicene Creed, exhortations, and second post-communion prayer were dropped. One collect for the king was eliminated and the other changed to pray for 'the Supreme Rulers of these United States'. Only one word was omitted in the prayer of consecration, a redundant 'one'. Before the final blessing a significant new rubric appeared: 'Then the Elder, if he see it expedient, may put up an Extempore Prayer'.

Wesley, it soon proved, was a poor judge of the 'poor sheep in the wilderness' to whom the *Sunday Service* was directed. The year after his death in 1791 his book was drastically abbreviated to thirty-seven pages of 'Sacramental Services, &c.' in the 1792 *Discipline*. The men of the frontier had little learning and less love of what seemed to them overly formal types of worship. 'The Order for the Administration of the Lord's Supper' was drastically abbreviated, the whole synaxis disappeared along with the prayer for the church, the comfortable words, the *Sursum corda*, and all proper prefaces. The collect for purity took the place formerly held by the *Sursum corda*. It was even provided that 'if the elder be straitened for time, he may omit any part of the service except the prayer of Consecration'. Actually, the Lord's Supper usually followed a preaching service hence a service of the word could be presumed. And few words in the eucharistic portion had been changed, perhaps none of theological significance.

Only small changes were made in the next half century. In 1844 the Methodist Episcopal Church underwent a major split on the question of slavery, the Methodist Episcopal Church, South, and the Methodist Episcopal Church emerging. An earlier split had produced the Methodist Protestant Church in 1830 which published a communion service in 1831, a curiously scrambled version of the 1792 service. Changes in the communion service appeared in the *Discipline*, published every four years by each of the three main branches of Methodism.

The most important of these changes are mentioned here. The Southern Church remained the most conservative and made minor changes, none of great theological consequence, from what was left of the 1662 *BCP* rite. The Methodist Episcopal Church was less reluctant to change. Many minor changes appeared, especially in 1864 and 1916. The invention of pasteurized grape juice and the temperance movement became apparent in 1876 when 'unfermented juice of the grape' was first recommended in the rubrics (wine had always been used previously). The most important changes occurred in 1932 when a synaxis was recovered. The liberal theology of the time made some radical changes in the prayer of consecration and the prayer of humble access. With the reunion of Methodism in 1939 both the then current Northern and Southern services appeared in *The Methodist Hymnal*, though liturgically and theologically they had become distinct; the Northern service was more traditional liturgically and the Southern more traditional theologically. Both services were in the first (1944) *Book of Worship.*

A major revision occurred in the 1964 *Book of Worship,* currently in use by the United Methodist Church. It is essentially a revision within the Anglican-Methodist tradition. In a sense it returns to the 1549 *BCP* rite, removing some of the quirks of 1552 by eliminating the Decalogue, restoring the *Gloria in excelsis* to a position at the beginning of the rite, and recovering the *Agnus Dei.* Some of the other changes move in the direction of making the service of the word similar to that used in many Methodist churches when the sacrament is not celebrated. Hence the intercessions precede the lections, the Lord's Prayer comes at the beginning of the service, and the creed precedes the sermon. Compromises have been made in the theological language with regard to the presence of Christ in the sacrament. For better or for worse, the service was completed and published just before the new emphasis on contemporary language came to the fore and so sixteenth-century words and phrases dominate. The outline of the service is: prelude, hymn, scripture sentences, salutation, collect for purity, Lord's Prayer, *Gloria in excelsis,* invitation, general confession, prayer for pardon, comfortable words, prayer for the church, epistle, anthem or hymn, gospel, creed and sermon. After the sermon come notices, hymn, offertory, prayer of dedication, *Sursum corda,* preface, *Sanctus,* prayer of consecration, prayer of humble access, *Agnus Dei,* communion of clergy, communion of people, peace, post-communion prayer, hymn, blessing and postlude.

In 1972 the Commission on Worship published an alternative text, 'The Sacrament of the Lord's Supper'. It is in contemporary language and is not simply a revision of Cranmer but an attempt to follow classical and universal patterns.

The communion rites of the black churches have been among the more conservative. The African Methodist Episcopal Church and the Christian Methodist Episcopal Church have retained essentially the 1792 service. Both also contain rubrics for the benefit of those who have scruples about kneeling, similar to those the two large white churches introduced during the nineteenth century but later removed.

In Britain, Wesley's *Sunday Service* went through various editions till the twentieth century. Other service-books appeared as well. The *Book of Offices* of 1936 contains collects, epistles, and gospels for the church year and two orders of service 'For the Administration of the Lord's Supper; or, The Holy Communion'. The first of these is very similar to the 1662 *BCP* rite minus a few rubrics, exhortations, and collects. The second is shorter and has some of the same material rearranged, placing the words of institution after the prayer of humble access.

More recently (1969) a new *Sunday Service* has been published which makes provision for morning worship with or without the sacrament. It represents some major improvements over preceding liturgies, envisioning a wider horizon of revision than simply the Anglican-Methodist pattern. The location of the Nicene Creed between the peace and the offertory is distinctive. The eucharistic prayer contains new items such as a greatly expanded common preface, *Benedictus qui venit,* epiclesis, a distinct oblation, and acclamations of the people. It is followed by a fraction, and after the communion are a new and brief post-communion prayer and a dismissal. In many ways the service is a major step to more ancient and ecumenical forms, a most appropriate move in the present age. Both 'thee' and 'you' forms are published for portions of the service. How long it will be necessary to hop thus on both legs remains to be seen.

JAMES F. WHITE

11. *Old Catholic.* In the Old Catholic churches of the Utrecht Union, the celebration of the eucharist stands at the centre of liturgical life. Alongside that, however, the greatest emphasis is also placed on the proclamation of the word of God in the reading of scripture and in preaching. The celebration of the mass must therefore be supported by the two pillars of the service of the word of God and the liturgy of the sacrament.

In the Old Catholic churches, the whole service has for a long time (in some cases for almost a hundred years) been celebrated in the vernacular. Some of these churches have been content with an accurate translation of the Latin text with very few deviations; this has been the case in the Netherlands and in the Polish National Catholic Church in the USA and in Poland. Elsewhere, however, the Roman model has been treated with rather more freedom, and this has led to some theologically significant alterations; this has been the case above all in Switzerland, but the same thing has also happened in Germany and Austria. Nevertheless, even here the structure of the Roman mass remains clearly recognizable. It should be noted that the basis for the Old Catholic forms of mass is the *Missale Romanum* in its old form, as laid down by Pius V in 1570, and not the liturgy as revised after Vatican II. It can be seen, however, that some alterations were made to Old Catholic liturgies at an early stage which have only been introduced in the Roman Catholic church in the last few years (for the texts and books used today for celebrating mass in the Old Catholic churches *see* **Books, Liturgical** 11 : Old Catholic).

New ways of structuring the liturgy are still being investigated in the Old Catholic churches today. The Old Catholics of Germany received a new missal in 1959. In Austria and Switzerland, attempts are being made with new formulae, especially for the canon of the mass. Even in the Church of the Netherlands, which until recently has been very conservative in liturgical matters, an experiment is now under way with a new 'second order of the mass'.

It is impossible here to indicate all the differences and peculiarities of the Old Catholic liturgies. The following are the most important points:

Service of the Word of God. In the German and Swiss liturgies the selection of biblical readings has been considerably increased. In Switzerland there are now three readings (OT, epistle and gospel) for each mass in a three-year cycle; in Germany there are two (OT or epistle and gospel) in a four-year cycle.

Creed. The Western addition *filioque* is omitted, with particular concern for the close relationships with the Orthodox church.

Prayer of the Faithful. As in the revised Roman liturgy, the general intercessions, which had vanished from the Roman mass on every day except Good Friday, have been restored before the offertory.

Offertory. The prayers of the old Roman missal imply an anticipation of the epiclesis (q.v.) and consecration, elements which only belong in the canon. Even the notion of an offering of the as yet unconsecrated gifts ('*Suscipe . . . hanc immaculatam hostiam, quam . . . offero tibi*') is rejected. The offertory prayers are therefore rightly limited, in one

part of the Old Catholic liturgies, to the notions of the preparation of the gifts and thanksgiving.

Prefaces. The number of variable prefaces (q.v.) has been considerably increased in Old Catholic missals. The Altar Book of the Old Catholic Church of Germany (1959) contains 19 prefaces (Netherland 15, Austria 14).

Canon. The link between the *Sanctus* and the canon in Austria (second order) and in the Swiss outline of 1971 is made by a *Vere Sanctus* prayer on the Gallican pattern, as in the second and third formulations of the eucharistic prayer in the Roman *Ordo Missae* of 1969.

It is in the Swiss liturgy that the canon has undergone the most significant transformation. Whereas in the Roman canon the account of the institution occupies the central place, here it is brought quite close to the beginning. The words of institution are followed by the anamnesis (q.v.) and the 'sacrificial prayer' (*Unde et memores*) which closes with a petition for a blessed communion (*Supplices te rogamus*). The 'remembrance of the saints' (*Communicantes*), the prayer for the dead (*Memento etiam*) and for the living (*Memento, Domine*) are brought together into a group.

In the Swiss canon, all expressions are avoided which might suggest that the eucharistic sacrifice was a repetition of the sacrifice of the cross or an offering by the priest. On the other hand, the position of Christ as the one high priest is strongly stressed (*see* Bishop Herzog in *IKZ*, 1911, pp. 340ff. and Küry, *Die altkatholische Kirche*, pp. 190-200).

Epiclesis. The Swiss liturgy has an explicit invocation of the Holy Spirit, *before* the institution, as in some of the oldest Egyptian liturgies and in the new texts of the Roman canon. This has partially been taken over into the German liturgy (first order) and the Austrian missal of 1933. On the other hand, in the second Austrian order and the second experimental Swiss order of 1971, the epiclesis follows the account of the institution as in present-day Eastern liturgies. This is also the case in the 'second order' of the Church of the Netherlands, which closely follows the eucharistic prayer of Hippolytus.

Lord's Prayer. In missals in German and French, the Lord's Prayer now appears in the agreed ecumenical text, which also contains the doxology as in the Anglican order of the holy communion.

Breaking of the Bread. According to the German rite of 1959 (second order), this takes place during the singing of the *Agnus Dei*. Instead of the usual sequence of Lord's Prayer, breaking of the bread, kiss of peace, *Agnus Dei*, we have here *Agnus Dei* with breaking of the bread, kiss of peace, Lord's Prayer.

Communion. Whereas earlier the faithful only received communion on a few days in the year, it is now usually given at every mass and indeed in both forms, sometimes also by intinction.

KURT PURSCH
A. E. RÜTHY
C. TOL

12. *Pentecostal.* In open-air meetings, in worship and evangelistic services, classical Pentecostalism follows the pattern of different Protestant traditions (for Neo-Pentecostalism *see* **Pentecostal Worship**). In certain North American Pentecostal denominations, written liturgies have been developed along Protestant lines. Yet the most interesting liturgies in Pentecostalism are those of the eucharistic service, which is celebrated in British Pentecostal churches usually once a week, and in most of the other Pentecostal churches once a month. The eucharistic service has created some difficult problems for Pentecostals. Donald Gee (1891-1966), a British Pentecostal leader, warns against those Pentecostals who want the eucharist to be wholly unstructured. The result of this, he says, 'is to produce meetings so stereotyped that, for all their boasted freedom, they become more barren than the very liturgical services they deprecate – and with less aesthetic appeal' (*Study Hour* 5/2, 15 February 1946, p.2).

How is the problem solved? On the one hand a minority of Pentecostal churches use written liturgies as indicated above. In the majority of Pentecostal churches, on the other hand, an 'oral liturgy' is followed which consists of the classical liturgical elements: invocation, *Kyrie*, confession, *Gloria in excelsis*, eucharistic canon and blessing (qq.v.). Yet these parts are never so named and for most observers not recognizable as such, since the elements which structure the different parts of the service are the so-called choruses, i.e. short spontaneous songs, known by heart by the whole

congregation. Some of the key choruses indicate the transition from one part of the service to the next. They are intoned either by the minister (*see* **Ordination** 14: Pentecostalist) or by members of the congregation. Key choruses vary from one congregation to another, yet everyone in the congregation understands them as signals. During the time of participation of the whole congregation, if someone sings a song of praise in the *Kyrie* part, or gives a prophecy in the invocation part, he will be corrected either by the pastor, or by an elder, or if he persists, by the immediate and spontaneous singing of the whole congregation. Most Pentecostals are not aware of the liturgical function of these choruses, yet they are clearly observable. The Pentecostals thus demonstrate that the alternative to a written liturgy is not chaos, but a flexible oral tradition, which allows for variation within the framework of the whole liturgical structure, similar to the possibilities of variation in a jam session of jazz musicians (*see* **Spirituals**). For bibliography *see under* **Pentecostal Worship**.

W. J. HOLLENWEGER

13. *Plymouth Brethren.* The Brethren's most distinctive meeting is the communion service normally held every Sunday morning. The communion table is frequently placed in the centre, with the congregation seated in rows round three or four sides of it; where it is not convenient to rearrange the seating, the table will be left in front.

The first part of the service is devoted to suitable hymns, prayers of thanksgiving and scripture readings, introduced or carried through by various members. Then the thanksgiving for the bread is followed by its distribution from hand to hand, each communicant breaking off a small piece and eating it. (The bread is usually an entire loaf, which may be broken in two before distribution.) The thanksgiving for the cup is followed by the passing of the common cup from hand to hand, each communicant drinking a little from it. The wine may be fermented or unfermented according to local preference. It is normally senior members of the church who give thanks for the bread and the cup. In the Exclusive tradition the same brother will give thanks for both elements on any one occasion, breaking the bread in two and pouring the wine into the cup before distribution. The practice of Open Brethren is more variable. Open Brethren customarily welcome all Christians present to communicate, in accordance with the Brethren's original policy.

The communion is followed either immediately or after some further exercises by the offering. Those who regard the offering as an integral part of the worship take it up in close proximity to the eucharist.

In many places the eucharist is followed by a short period of expository ministry; elsewhere this may be given in a separate service preceding the communion service.

Among Exclusive Brethren of the late James Taylor's connection the liturgy is much more uniform. R. C. Walls, writing in *Theology* 60 (1957), pp.265f.: 'A Visit to the Brethren – A Lesson in Liturgy', indicates the Trinitarian sequence which would have been followed at that time in almost any of their assemblies throughout the world on any Sunday morning. An introductory hymn to the Holy Spirit was followed by a prayer of thanksgiving addressed to him and a lesson from Ephesians. The Son then became the focus of devotion in the eucharist, which was accompanied by a long anamnesis (q.v.) or thanksgiving for his person and work from his incarnation through his passion, triumph and present high-priestly ministry and abiding presence to his parousia. This part of the service was concluded with a hymn of praise to the Son and a reading from the gospels. Then the worshippers claimed access to the Father, to whom a hymn of praise was sung, and after further devotions and silent intervals the service ended with a hymn to the Trinity. (A more recent development has moved the eucharist right to the beginning of the service.)   F. F. BRUCE

14. *Reformed*. Although the Reformed churches have been accused of neglecting the eucharist, their liturgies all stress its importance. The Reformers were unanimous in their aim to provide liturgies suitable to the new views on religion. Thus Zwingli produced two books entitled *De Canone Missae Epicheiresis* (1523) and *Action oder Bruch des Nachtmals* (1525). These were derived from the mass, but with all accretions removed. He provided separate orders for the ordinary preaching service without communion, and for the eucharist, which he regarded as another form of preaching. The order of the eucharist is simple – exhortation and fencing of the table, Lord's prayer,

prayer of humble access, the words of institution, fraction, communion first of the ministers and then of the people, a psalm (said, not sung), post-communion prayer and dismissal. There is no consecration prayer and no intercession. Celebration was only four times in the year. This rite had little influence on later developments.

Another rite with little influence was Farel's *La manyere et fasson* (Neuchâtel, 1533), the first liturgy of the Reformed churches. The eucharist contains a long exhortation, Lord's Prayer, Apostles' Creed, institution narrative, the communion of all, post-communion prayer and dismissal.

The rite of John Calvin, *La forme des prières* (1542), was of much greater importance. It was derived from the Strasbourg Reformed German rite of Diebold Schwartz, which was derived from the mass. It was greatly simplified through the influence of Bucer. For Calvin the correct procedure was a preaching service followed by the eucharist. The full order was as follows: scripture sentence, confession of sins, metrical psalm (sung), prayer for illumination, lesson, sermon; intercessions, Lord's Prayer (an uninspiring paraphrase), preparation of elements, Apostles' Creed, words of institution, exhortation, consecration prayer, fraction and delivery (during communion, psalm sung or read or scripture lesson), read post-communion prayer, Aaronic blessing.

This form was somewhat bare, but Calvin was prevented from carrying out all his desires. Thus he regarded weekly communion as scriptural, and therefore essential, but the Genevan magistrates allowed it only quarterly. However, the form has had great influence on all succeeding Reformed liturgies. Of these there were many varieties in the Reformed Churches in Switzerland, France, Holland and elsewhere. From time to time suggestions for revision were made, and of these two may be noticed.

In 1713, Jean-Frédéric Osterwald published a liturgy. He had already expressed an aversion from Calvinism and his good opinion of Anglicanism, but his proposals, influenced by these feelings, were too radical for general acceptance. The revision proposals of Eugène Bersier (1874) had more influence. He desired to give the eucharist 'the central place which is its due in Christian worship' and thus to 'return to the true primitive teaching of our Reformed Church'.

The eucharist was to follow (as if not an essential part of) the morning service. The minister, after dismissing those who were not to communicate, descends from the pulpit and, standing before the table, addresses the people who group themselves as near the table as possible. Then he goes behind the table, uncovers the bread and wine, and prays. *Sursum corda* and the consecration prayer follow. 'It is verily right, just and salutary . . .' The prayer includes *Sanctus* and *Hosanna* and words suited to the season of the Christian year. There is an epiclesis, followed by the words of institution, fraction, Lord's prayer, the distribution, thanksgiving and dismissal. Much of this has been found acceptable in France, and the liturgy of 1958 follows many points of this form. The consecration prayer includes thanksgiving, *Sanctus*, epiclesis, Lord's Prayer, Apostles' Creed, words of institution, followed by communion, thanksgiving and blessing. A revision of 1963 has a new eucharistic prayer, which shows some dependence on the liturgy of the church of South India.

The Reformed rites of some other countries have been of interest. Several of the Swiss cantons, such as Vaud (1940), Geneva (1946) and Bern (1955), have issued revised liturgies, influenced both by the earlier Reformed rites and by the classic forms. In Germany and Holland there has been much liturgical work. The two Dutch groups, *Liturgische Kring* and *Kring Eeredienst*, have been specially active, and the *Kanselboek* (1949) and *Dienstboek* (1955) express concern for congregational participation in responses and allow many alternatives.

The Genevan rite of 1556, known as *John Knox's Genevan Service Book*, was the first Reformed rite in English. It was adopted, with only slight changes, by the Church of Scotland in 1562 under the title, *The Forme of Prayers and Ministration of the Sacrament*. In 1564 it became *The Form of Prayers or Book of Common Order*, but with some additions, especially in the completion of the metrical psalter. The full eucharistic order here was as follows: confession of sins and prayer for pardon, metrical psalm, prayer for illumination, lesson, sermon, thanksgiving and intercession, Lord's Prayer, Apostles' Creed, offertory, words of institution (i.e., the warrant), exhortation, consecration prayer (including adoration, thanksgiving for creation and redemption, anamnesis and dox-ology), fraction and delivery (minister's communion followed by the people's), post-communion thanksgiving, Ps. 103, Aaronic or apostolic blessing. This form lacks an epiclesis, but contemporary evidence shows that one was included in the consecration and was regarded by many as essential. This form remained generally in Scottish use from 1564, many editions being published. Some editions were printed in England or on the Continent for the use of English Puritans. *The Book of Common Order* was superseded by the Westminster *Directory* in 1645.

The *Directory*, as a compromise between the Independents and the Scottish and English Presbyterians, was rather unsatisfactory, but it remained and indeed still remains an authority for public worship. There are no prayers, but only lists of subjects for prayer. The eucharistic order is little changed, but an epiclesis is now prescribed. During the eighteenth century the standard of worship in Scotland, as elsewhere, fell very low, with the loss of the creed, Lord's prayer, *Gloria Patri*, and the people's amen.

By the opening of the nineteenth century some clergy had begun to publish books of their own. In 1867 the Church Service Society was formed, and before long produced a service book with the title *Euchologion*, many editions of which appeared. The eucharist here followed the preaching rite for the morning service, the order of which was influenced by *BCP* mattins, with an exhortation (following the prayer after the sermon), the institution warrant, an address on the significance of the sacrament, Nicene Creed, *Agnus Dei*, prayer of the veil, *Sursum corda*, the consecration prayer including thanksgiving for the divine gifts, anamnesis, *Sanctus*, epiclesis, Lord's prayer, fraction, distribution, pax, exhortation, prayer of thanksgiving and self-dedication, intercession for the church, thanksgiving for the church triumphant, hymn, benediction.

Prayers for Divine Service (1923), issued by the Church of Scotland, largely followed *Euchologion*, but a second edition (1929) supplied two eucharistic forms, the additional one being a shortened form with the intercessions in the post-communion prayer. The United Free Church of Scotland issued *The Book of Common Order*, 1928, which was rather less liturgical but of a high standard. Both of these were influential on the next to be noted.

The Book of Common Order (1940), the authorized book of the reunited Church of Scotland, as revised in 1952, contains five orders for the eucharist. The first is regarded as the regular form; the second is slightly shortened; the third is for use at a second table where communicants receive elements previously consecrated; the fourth is an alternative with slightly different order and less liturgical in tone; the fifth is a short order for use in communicating the sick or where a very short order is desirable. These mostly follow the pattern of *Prayers for Divine Service*. The intercessions are in the 'Liturgy of the Word', with which, however, the 'Liturgy of the Faithful' is continuous. This has the offertory, invitation with comfortable words, psalm (while the elements are brought forward), Nicene Creed, unveiling of elements, the offertory prayer, warrant, salutation and *Sursum corda*, prayer of consecration (including preface and prayer for the season, *Sanctus* with *Benedictus qui venit* and *Hosanna*, thanksgiving for redemption, anamnesis, epiclesis, oblation, brief intercession and doxology), Lord's Prayer, words of institution with fraction, *Agnus Dei*, celebrant's communion, people's communion, pax, post-communion thanksgiving and commemoration of the departed, psalm (usually 103.1-5) or hymn, benediction. This service is now being revised and will probably allow for the words of institution to be included in the consecration prayer and the omission of the warrant, and the addition of *Gloria in Excelsis*.

This book has had wide influence on other Presbyterian service-books, as those of England, Wales, Ireland, Canada, Australia and elsewhere. Most of these books have been revised, in some cases more than once.

In the USA there has been much liturgical activity of late. The recent *Worship-book* (Philadelphia, 1970), prepared by a joint committee of three Presbyterian churches, employs 'the straightforward use of words and language in current contemporary use', and therefore the words of some new translations have been employed for scriptural quotations. The book opens with the only form for the eucharist. The 'Liturgy of the Word' includes confession of sin and declaration of pardon, prayer for illumination, lessons, sermon with ascription, Nicene Creed (using 'we'). The 'Liturgy of the Faithful' includes intercessions, pax, the offering, invitation to the table, thanksgiving (with *Sursum corda*, the seasonal preface, *Tersanctus*, Lord's Prayer), fraction, distribution, post-communion prayer, hymn, benediction.

All Presbyterian books are for voluntary use, and even where used there are many variations due to the ideas of individual ministers. In many places books are not used at all, but there is in general a growing sense of the importance of the eucharistic liturgy. This is evidenced by, among other things, the appointment by many Reformed churches of committees with instructions to prepare forms for specific purposes for submission to the assemblies or other governing bodies. Some churches have standing committees, charged with the study of forms of worship and at times with the preparations of specific forms, eucharistic or otherwise. This is becoming so widespread in the churches that on many points ecumenical discussion is required, often with excellent results.

J. A. LAMB

15. *Seventh-day Adventist (Communion Service)*. In the Seventh-day Adventist Church the communion service includes the ordinance of foot-washing or humility and the Lord's Supper. Adventists believe that in washing his disciples' feet Christ instituted a consecrated ordinance, a religious service with a promise of blessedness (John 13.14-17). It is a memorial of Christ's act of self-abasement and a symbol or type of higher cleansing. Like early church fathers such as Origen, pioneer Adventists considered foot-washing a spiritual experience and a symbol of humility. It was sometimes referred to as Christ's 'least commandment' (*Day-Star*, 7.8, 18 August 1845). While baptism is a symbol of justification once and for all, the daily experience of sanctification is represented by foot-washing. 'This ordinance is Christ's appointed preparation for the sacramental service' (E. G. White, *The Desire of Ages*, p.650). For this reason Adventists often call this ordinance the 'preparatory service'. It is a time for self-examination, confession of sin and reconciling of differences. Two emblems are used: water, symbol of cleansing, and towel, symbol of service. Some regard the ordinance of humility as a 'miniature baptism' (*see* John 13.10).

Adventist churches have a communion table, not an altar (qq.v.). The Lord's Supper is not a mystery but a memorial, not a sacrifice but a sacred service. Its theme is salvation through the sacrifice of Christ on Calvary. It is a memorial of the deliverance from the power of sin and as such is a continual reminder of the atonement. It also has an eschatological orientation pointing forward to the parousia and is designed to keep this hope vivid (Matt. 26.29; I Cor. 11.26).

Adventists believe in the real spiritual presence of Christ at the supper, but not in the elements as such. 'As faith contemplates our Lord's great sacrifice, the soul assimilates the spiritual life of Christ . . . The Service forms a living connection by which the believer is bound up with Christ' (White, *op.cit.*, p. 661).

In most Adventist churches the communion service is held once a quarter. In early Adventist history the Lord's Supper was a regular part of the 'quarterly meeting'. While other aspects of this meeting have largely faded away, communion is still sometimes called in Adventist parlance the 'quarterly service'.

The opening service may be as usual for divine worship, but the sermon is limited to 10-15 minutes and deals with some aspect of the communion service. The congregation then separates for the ordinance of humility, the men in one place and the women in another. Hymns may occasionally be sung during its progress.

After the foot-washing, the congregation reassembles for the Lord's Supper. The minister and elder (or elders) take their places by the table on which the deaconesses have previously placed the unleavened bread and unfermented wine, covered by a white linen cloth (*see* I Cor. 5.7,8). After a hymn the minister (in some churches the deaconesses) removes and folds the linen covering. Then he reads I Cor. 11.23,24 or a parallel passage from the gospels, after which the blessing of God is asked on the emblem of the bread, representing the body of Christ, while the whole congregation kneels (in some churches only the officiating minister and elders kneel, while the congregation remains seated with bowed heads). Following the breaking of the bread by the officiating minister, the deacons serve the congregation and, after returning, the minister serves them; then in turn one of the deacons, taking the plate, serves the minister. All are seated and silent prayer is offered while they partake of the bread together.

The minister then reads I Cor. 11.25,26 or a similar passage from the gospels. The blessing is asked on the emblem of the wine, representing the shed blood of Christ, and the deacons serve the congregation following a similar procedure as with the bread. For health reasons the recommended and prevailing practice in Seventh-day Adventist churches is to use small, individual communion cups.

The remaining emblems are recovered and after the service the deaconesses clear the table and the deacons dispose of any bread or wine left over, by burning the bread and pouring out the wine.

In the Seventh-day Adventist Church only ordained ministers or ordained local church elders may conduct the communion service. Adventists practise 'open communion', believing that Christ's own example forbids exclusiveness at his table (*see* Matt. 26.21-25).

B. B. BEACH

K. Amon, 'Das eucharistische Hochgebet in den altkatholischen Kirchen des deutschen Sprachgebiets', *Liturgisches Jahrbuch* 18, 1968; A Baumstark, *Comparative Liturgy*, 1958; F. E. Brightman, *Liturgies Eastern and Western*, 1896; Yngve Brilioth, *Eucharistic Faith and Practice*, 1930; R. Bruinsma, 'Christ's Commandment of Humility', *The Ministry*, July 1966, pp. 24-6 (Seventh-day Adventist); C. O. Buchanan, ed., *Modern Anglican Liturgies 1958-68*, 1968 (a successor to *Liturgy in English* containing texts subsequent to 1960); R. H. Connolly, *The Liturgical Homilies of Narsai*, 1909; A. C. Couratin, *The Service of Holy Communion 1549-1662*, 1963 (a brief but penetrating review of the controlling motives in each successive revision); J. D. Crichton, *The Church's Worship*. Considerations on the Liturgical Constitution of the Second Vatican Council, 1964; G. J. Cuming, *A History of Anglican Liturgy*, 1969 (a definitive and authoritative history from 1500 to 1966); G. Dix, *The Shape of the Liturgy*, ²1945; Paul Graff, *Geschichte des Auflösung der alten gottesdienstlichen Formen in der Evangelischen Kirche Deutschlands*, 2 vols. 1921, 1939; A. Hänggi and I. Pahl, *Prex Eucharistica*, 1968; J. Jungmann, *The Mass of the Roman Rite*, 2 vols., 1951-55; T. Klauser, *A Short History of the Western Liturgy*, 1969; U. Küry, *Die altkatholische Kirche* (Kirchen der Welt, Band III), 1966; M. Luther, 'Liturgy and Hymns', *Works*, American ed., vol. 53, 1965; *Manual for Ministers* (Seventh-day Adventist), 1965; G. A. Michell, *Landmarks in Liturgy*, 1961 (a liturgical and theological analysis of each part of the rite in turn, tracing its development from Apostolic times to 1662); C. F. D. Moule, *The Worship of the New Testament*, 1961; Don. F. Neufeld, ed., 'Lord's Supper', 'Foot Washing', *Seventh-day Adventist Encyclopedia*, 1966, pp. 414-6, 720-2; Ernest A. Payne and Stephen F. Winward, *Orders and Prayers for Church Worship*, 1960 (Baptist); N. F. Pease, *And Worship Him*, 1967, pp. 76-8 (Seventh-day Adventist); K. Pursch, 'Das Opfermahl und die Neuordnung seiner Gestalt', *IKZ* 46, 1956; K. Pursch, 'Die Probleme des Offertoriums und Versuche zu ihrer Lösung', *IKZ* 46, 1956; Luther D. Reed, *The Lutheran Liturgy*, rev. ed., 1959; A. E. Rüthy, 'Bemerkingen und Erwägungen zu den altkatholischen Liturgien', a series of articles in *IKZ* 47-60, 1957-70; S. Salaville, *Introduction to the Study of Eastern Liturgies*, 1938; Emil Sehling, ed., *Die Evangelischen Kirchenordnungen des 16. Jahrhunderts*, vols. 1-5, 1902-1913; vols. 6 and 11, 1955-1961; *Seventh-day Adventist Church Manual*, 1967, pp. 115-21; L. Sheppard, ed., *True Worship*, 1963; John E. Skoglund, *A Manual of Worship*, 1968 (Baptist); J. H. Srawley, *The Early History of the Liturgy*, 1947; E. G. White, *The Desire of Ages*, 1946, pp. 642-61 (Seventh-day Adventist); B. J. Wigan, ed., *Liturgy in English*, 1964 (this contains virtually all Anglican eucharistic texts from 1549 to 1960); L. Winterswyl, 'Das eucharistische Hochgebet der altkatholischen Liturgien', *IKZ* 24, 1934.

F. F. BRUCE

Local Preacher

An office (open to both men and women in the Methodist Church) instituted by John Wesley to provide, as the name implies, a local ministry to supplement that of the few itinerant ordained clergymen who joined his movement initially. The ministry is a 'part-time' one, being exercised normally by a layman with a secular job. A local preacher regularly conducts Sunday worship and appears on the preaching plan. He does not normally celebrate the eucharist, though there are cases where a layman may be specially authorized by Conference to do so if a congregation might otherwise be almost totally deprived of the sacrament. Baptism may also be administered by a local preacher or other layman in very exceptional circumstances.

P. HINCHLIFF

Lord's Prayer

Not surprisingly, the Lord's Prayer has come to be used universally and frequently in liturgical worship. It was not always so, however; its use at the eucharist, for example, does not antedate the middle of the fourth century at the earliest, being first clearly attested in the *Mystagogical Catecheses* of Cyril of Jerusalem. From John Chrysostom onwards, liturgical commentators in the East witness to its use after the eucharistic prayer as a preparation for communion; Augustine and Ambrose presuppose its use at the same place and for the same purpose in the West at about the same time. Since about 400 it has been so used in all the historic liturgies, and in many others as well; it is only in some of the post-Reformation Protestant rites that it has been removed from this position and function, and placed elsewhere. Early commentators stress its suitability for this purpose, laying emphasis on the petitions for the forgiveness of sins and, above all, for daily – or, rather, arguing from the alternative reading, heavenly – bread: Ambrose advocates frequent communion on the ground of the relationship between the two texts.

In most of the historic rites the Lord's Prayer is placed after the breaking of the bread which follows the eucharistic prayer; in the two most widespread of them, however, the Roman and the Byzantine, it precedes the breaking of the bread, the Roman usage in this respect being probably a Byzantine importation.

The use of the Lord's Prayer in a quasi-liturgical context outside the eucharistic liturgy probably antedates its use in the latter; certain early writers prescribe it as the essential prayer to be used by the faithful at set hours of prayer. Its use in the divine office, which is universal in the historic rites as well as in most of the post-Reformation liturgies, presumably originates in this prescription.

J. A. Jungmann, *The Mass of the Roman Rite*, II, 1955, pp. 277-93.

W. JARDINE GRISBROOKE

Lord's Supper

1. This title was used in the patristic period of the Last Supper, e.g. by Hippolytus.

2. It was also employed by Paul (I Cor. 11.20) of the central act of Christian worship, which when he was writing would appear to have consisted of a repetition of the Last

Supper in its entirety, i.e. blessing, breaking and distribution of bread, followed by a meal and concluded with the blessing and distribution of wine.

3. In the fourth century, it was the practice on Maundy Thursday (q.v.), in commemoration of the institution of the sacrament on that day, to combine the agape or love feast (q.v.) with the eucharist, and this, too, was known as the Lord's Supper.

4. The separation of eucharist and agape and the discontinuance of the latter led to the title Lord's Supper being applied to the sacrament alone. This use was widespread in the Middle Ages and the Catechism of Trent endorsed it. The Reformers favoured the title because of its scriptural basis and so, e.g. in the 1549 *BCP*, the service is headed: 'The Supper of the Lorde and the Holy Communion, commonly called the Masse'.

EDITOR

Love Feast

There is little doubt that a common meal with at least semi-liturgical features was regularly held by Christians shortly after the death of Jesus, or that it combined observances which were later separated to become on the one hand the agape or love feast, and on the other the eucharist or holy communion. Such meals were a common feature both of pagan and of Jewish circles, and regulations for that observed by the Qumran sect are found in their *Manual of Discipline*. Dom Gregory Dix, in *The Shape of the Liturgy*, makes a strong case for the Christian meal being a variant of a typical *chaburah* or formal fellowship meal of pious Jewish friends. The early Christians seem to have met for this purpose weekly on the evening of 'the Lord's Day'. The term 'Lord's Supper' may well have been applied both to the occasion as a whole and also to its major components, the meal itself and the liturgical commemoration of the Lord's living presence which accompanied it. Both agape and embryonic eucharist emphasized the fact that his followers constituted a community in spiritual fellowship both with each other and with their risen Lord. Associated with the meal was the distribution of food to the needy, especially widows. The technical term eventually reserved for the meal among the Greek-speaking Christians was *agape*, literally 'a love'. In other words it was an occasion for the display and growth of God-centred

Christian love as opposed to merely human *eros* or *philia*. Among the Latin-speaking Christians this became *caritas*, 'charity', a word whose meaning degenerated (as did the love feast itself) from an expression of the purest of emotions to the social activities which normally demonstrated that emotion, but which could too easily be divorced from it and be regarded as self-sufficient.

Unambiguous evidence about the love feast in the NT is scanty. It is quite clear, however, that throughout his ministry Jesus stressed the importance both of meals in general, especially the evening meal, or supper, and the banquet with invited guests – a favourite symbol of his messiahship. He taught his disciples to pray for food. He was even chided for his emphasis upon eating and drinking (Matt. 11.18f.; *cf.* 9.10-15). Not only the apostles but two anonymous followers who met the risen Lord on the road to Emmaus were apparently familiar with some idiosyncrasy in his prayer and breaking of bread at such meals (Luke 24.30f.). At one of his last recorded appearances he presided over a meal with seven disciples by the Sea of Galilee, a meal climaxed by a threefold emphasis alike upon *agape* and upon the pastoral feeding of the Christian flock (John 21.1-17). The 'breaking of bread' was linked with the sharing of goods and temple worship as a distinctive feature of the earliest church (Acts 2.41-47).

In Paul's classic description of the eucharist in I Cor. 11.17-34, a common meal either precedes or is inseparably linked with a more liturgical celebration. Paul's words show, however, that already abuses were creeping in, the table-fellowship occasionally being marred by examples of gluttony and drunkenness. The same was true a generation or two later when Jude wrote – the only undoubted use of the term *agape* (in the plural) in the NT: 'These men are a blot on your love feasts, where they eat and drink without reverence' (v. 12, NEB). Without a familiar background of Jewish piety in the *chaburah* such meals could easily become assimilated to the less restrained pagan banquets, and joy in the fellowship of the risen Lord and his followers could deteriorate into unbridled joy in food and wine, with an emphasis upon variety and luxury such as encouraged gluttony, pride and selfishness. It is sadly clear that this indeed happened, even during the apostolic age, and apparently formed the chief reason for separating the liturgical celebration of a commemorative token meal (the eucharist) from a genuine meal (the agape). Overlapping and some mutual influence continued, however. The need was constantly felt to urge moderation even in the separated agape, which gradually developed its own distinctive rituals, differing from area to area.

The *Didache* preserves the prayers associated with the Eastern agape early in the second century, probably in Syria. It contains groups of prayers to be used by the presiding minister before and after the meal, together with congregational responses, which rang the changes on the theme of 'To thee be glory for ever', the final petition being the Aramaic *Maranatha*, 'Our Lord, come!' Tertullian's *Apology* (c. AD 197) reveals the rite as it was practised in Carthage and probably in Rome – a genuine meal, to which the poor were invited, begun and ended with prayer. The meal was followed with scripture reading, spiritual discourse, the singing of hymns, and apparently an opportunity for individual testimonies of some kind. The *Apostolic Tradition* of Hippolytus shows that in Rome by the third century the agape was celebrated in private homes, guests being invited by the host, though a minister was always present to 'say grace' and to offer a spiritual exhortation. The guests were urged to 'eat sufficiently, but so that there may remain something over that your host may send it to whomsoever he wills, as the superfluity of the saints, and he [to whom it is sent] may rejoice with what is left over' (Dix, *op. cit.*, p. 82). The guests were also urged to pray for their host. Strong evidence exists that the agape gradually came to be assimilated with pagan funeral banquets, which were thus transformed both into occasions for feeding the poor and into symbolic representations of the messianic banquet, a foretaste of the joys of heaven. Conciliar rulings show that from the fourth century onwards the possibility and actuality of abuse, combining with a more formal approach to church life, had steadily undermined the ancient fellowship meal, at least as an official element in Western worship. In the Eastern Church the agape lingered on for two or three centuries more.

By the eighth century the agape seems to have been almost universally defunct apart from vestigial remains whose origins were forgotten and occasional survivals in out-of-the-way sects. Vestiges are probably to be seen in the offertory for the poor at holy communion, in the distributions to the poor on Maundy Thursday, and (in Eastern Churches only) in the distribution of pieces of unconsecrated bread after the eucharist. One example of what appears to be a genuine survival (albeit indirect) is to be found among the Christians of St Thomas in Southern India. Another was probably among the Paulicians of Armenia, who may in turn have sown some of the seed which eventually led to the revival of the love feast among the Moravians.

Along with the Protestant Reformation went a somewhat self-conscious attempt among several pietistic sects to reproduce the actual customs as well as the spirit of the primitive church. Although the details and the dimensions of this process are difficult to recover, it appears that this imitation of the early church combined with the vestigial remains of the agape to foster the modern love feast in some western European communities such as the Mennonites, the German Baptist Brethren (or 'Dunkers'), and the Moravians (q.v.), frequently allied with the kiss of peace (q.v.) and the ceremonial washing of feet. Encouraged by Pietism, the love feast flourished especially during the eighteenth century in Germany and the Netherlands, and was imported to America by the more zealous (and therefore the more persecuted) members of those bodies.

Although the ancient agape thus survived or was revived during modern times in various small sects, the mainstream denominations were hardly affected until John Wesley introduced it to his societies. In his own search for spiritual renewal by means of imitating primitive Christianity, Wesley was greatly impressed by the Moravian love feast as he experienced it both as a missionary in Georgia and as a pilgrim to Herrnhut in Germany. In 1738 he transplanted it to British soil. Convinced as he was of the stabilizing and stimulating power of Christian fellowship, he moulded the love feast into a climactic concentration of the more subdued fellowship of the band meeting and (later) the class meeting. The love feast became the occasion par excellence when after the symbolic sharing of a token family meal the assembled members of several classes and possibly of several societies would take turns in testifying to their Christian experience as they were so moved by the

Holy Spirit. New converts especially were encouraged to speak of the change wrought in them, and their testimonies frequently led to further conversions. Charles Wesley put his genius to work in composing special hymns for these occasions, though strangely enough there was never a distinct love feast collection. At first Methodist love feasts were held monthly, but after a time this gave place to a quarterly, and later still to an annual, celebration, which thus tended to become the more momentous. Enthusiastic Methodists assembling from a wide area rarely failed to experience a spiritual blessing, and the love feast became one of the more exciting events in the Methodist year, to which the general public sought entry, out of curiosity if not always from spiritual expectancy. The fact that these were private gatherings, to which admittance was secured by the possession of a current class ticket or a special note from the itinerant preacher, encouraged scurrilous rumours about immoral practices, though these were readily refuted as without foundation.

When Methodists emigrated they took with them (among other practices) their love feast, so that the Methodist variant became familiar in many parts of the British Commonwealth, as in America. The British offshoots of Wesley's Methodism also adapted the observance. During the nineteenth century, however, with the growing church-consciousness of the Methodist societies, and a consequent lessening of the emphasis upon the conversion experience, as also upon the class meeting and the prayer meeting, the spiritual testimonies at the love feasts lost much of their colourful spontaneity, while the more liturgical element was not by itself sufficient to retain popular adherence. Throughout World Methodism the love feast died out except for a few local survivals and an annual observance in some Methodist Conferences.

During the middle years of the twentieth century there has been a revival of interest in and practice of the love feast, both aspects linked closely with the ecumenical movement. The eucharist has proved the chief symbol both of Christian unity and of Christian disunity. Many Christians have therefore favoured experiments in interdenominational fellowship at a meal which like the eucharist had its origin in the Last Supper, yet which because of a different theological focus and comparative disuse had not become so hedged around with inhibitions and prohibitions.

In *Christian Worship* (1961), T. S. Garrett speaks of modern revivals of the love feast such as 'the parish breakfast following the parish communion', including a Cambridge college occasion when the breaking of pieces from a loaf was accompanied by the recital of a passage from the *Didache*. He also tells of Christian festivals in Tamil villages historically linked with non-Christian festivities yet in fact called 'love feasts' and having genuine spiritual links with the primitive agape (p. 43). There is a sense in which the 'faith tea' of British churches and the 'covered-dish supper' or 'home-coming' meal of American churches may similarly be regarded as modern forms of the love feast.

Much more self-conscious revivals have taken place during recent years, however, with an avowedly ecumenical intention. After lengthy preparations the two denominations represented in the parish of Hilgay, Norfolk, England – Anglicans and Methodists – came together on Maundy Thursday, 1949, and again on Wednesday in Holy Week, 1951, to celebrate a love feast deliberately representing the church both Eastern and Western, both primitive and modern.

The issue was taken up by the Friends of Reunion and discussed in successive issues of their *Bulletin*, arousing correspondence from many parts of the world. The instigator, the Rev. Ian Thomson, claimed that this was 'a serious attempt to break a deadlock that has long existed between separated churches'. The Ecumenical Institute organized at the Château de Bossey in Switzerland by the World Council of Churches has for years treated the last meal of its course there as an agape, when the participants are urged 'to express, by a symbolical act, the reality of our unity'. In more recent years a revival of the agape in Holland has linked Catholics and Protestants in a joint search for unity. From the initial gathering attended by 800 people of all ages and denominations in The Hague on the Friday evening before Pentecost in 1961 the movement has spread to other places, and has been received with such enthusiasm as a 'pre-eucharistic' meal emphasizing the desire and need for fuller Christian unity around the Lord's table that in 1965 the bishops of Holland issued directives about such 'agape celebrations'.

Granted that an undue emphasis upon a revival of the ancient agape in order to bypass the problems presented by joint communions may be fraught with spiritual peril, any such revival should surely be encouraged if it falls within the terms of the Dutch bishops' directive: 'The conscious intention of the agape celebration is to act in the service of that unity of which the eucharist is the decisive sign and the highest sacramental expression.'

Frank Baker, *Methodism and the Love-Feast*, 1957; R. Lee Cole, *Love-Feasts*, 1916; Dom Gregory Dix, *The Shape of the Liturgy*, [2]1945; J. F. Keating, *The Agape and the Eucharist in the Early Church*, 1911; G. I. F. Thomson, *An Experiment in Worship*, 1951; *One in Christ*, II, 1 (1966).

FRANK BAKER

Low Sunday

The English designation for the Sunday after Easter may denote its relationship to the great festival of the resurrection.

A. A. MCARTHUR

Lutheran Worship

The Augsburg Confession (1530) sets the tone for the Lutheran Reformation and clearly indicates that the protest is theological. Structures and tradition of the church are valued though they are attacked where authoritarianism has perverted them. The Augsburg Confession purports to be the authentic voice of Western Catholicism, repeatedly citing the church fathers to register its point. Lutheran reformers harboured no romantic notion of re-establishing the primitive church and were, therefore, conservative in liturgical reform.

> Our churches are falsely accused of abolishing the Mass. Actually, the Mass is retained among us and is celebrated with the greatest reverence. Almost all the customary ceremonies are also retained . . . the Mass among us is supported by the example of the church as seen from the Scriptures and the Fathers . . . (*Augsburg Confession*, 24).

When the protest did not register and Rome severed ecclesial ties, liturgical reform became a necessity. Because of its prestige, Luther's own work was widely imitated. He purged the inherited rites ruthlessly where in his view they reflected an anti-biblical theology, but was remarkably conservative in matters of ceremony. Biblical preaching was restored to the mass and also included in mattins and vespers (qq.v.). The fundamental emphasis on preaching grew out of both polemical and didactic concerns: it would free the people from ecclesiastical bondage and teach them the basis of the faith. The same pastoral concerns led to vernacular services.

Lutheran churches share this common liturgical orientation, but have developed three families of rites: Germanic, Scandinavian, North American. (Lutherans in eastern Europe and South America are Germanic in orientation; Australian Lutheranism combines Germanic and North American influences; Lutheran churches of Africa and Asia combine all three influences.)

All the sixteenth-century German *Kirchenordnungen* show their affinity to 'justification by grace through faith', the synoptic theology of the Lutheran protest. The Roman canon and offertory (qq.v.) were cut out and, unfortunately, nothing replaced them. Thus the words of institution, stripped of their context of prayer, gained unprecedented prominence which was intended to enhance their proclamatory function. Instead, 'consecration piety' was reinforced and Lutheranism was kept tied to the medieval ethos of the awesome and dread presence. Disputes with the Swiss reformers made such piety even more tenacious.

In spite of heroic efforts to restore frequent communion among the people and thus balance sermon and sacrament, old habits prevailed. Awe of the presence and the need for solemn self-preparation, the individualism resulting from an almost exclusive emphasis on the forgiveness of sins as chief fruit of the sacrament and the strong stress on the importance of preaching all contributed to infrequent celebrations. This did not result, as it did in England, in the ascendency of mattins. Lutherans used ante-communion (*missa catechumenorum*) as their preaching service with the result that, in spite of the infrequency of the eucharist, their devotion remained oriented to the mass.

Dominance of proclamation produced glorious results in church music. Such giants as Heinrich Schütz and J. S. Bach used music in the exposition of the scriptures. Though their music is not liturgical in the usual sense, neither is it autonomous as masses of Mozart and Beethoven tend to be. It was related to lessons and sermon rather than the Ordinary. From the beginning Lutherans fostered the use of vernacular hymns (q.v.), giving impetus to the chorale tradition. These hymns, in turn, generated a superb body of organ literature based on their melodies. Music is one key to the liturgical ethos of the Lutheran churches.

Scandinavian Lutheranism parallels the German development to a great degree. Denmark, especially, has a similar tradition. Norway, long under Danish rule, was late in developing its own style of life. But Norwegian worship bears the imprint of an intense pietism and tends, accordingly, to be individualistic in mood.

The Church of Sweden made the Reformation transition structurally intact. Because Roman influence virtually disappeared and Calvinistic influence was never significant, the Swedish Church has been comparatively free of theological strife. Structurally, Swedish liturgies resemble the German. But in such matters as ceremony and vestments there has been more continuity with Western Catholic tradition. Even so, the Swedish Reformation could not restore frequent communion, and it also became a preaching church.

North American Lutheranism became the heir to the various European traditions. Since their arrival, the numerous immigrant groups have been engaged in the process of merging into one Lutheran tradition which is at home in the new world. This has required learning a new, common language, confronting a Protestantism of Anglo-Saxon origins with its different theological mentality, and adjusting to being a minority among Christians.

American Lutheran liturgies have followed the Reformation models in matters of structure, but have adopted the verbal habits of the *BCP*. Their musical practice has absorbed the Anglo-American tradition of hymnody and other conventions typical of American Protestantism. Ceremony and vestments have increasingly reflected the influence of the Episcopal Church, the Swedish heritage, and the catholicizing tendencies of the Liturgical Movement (q.v.).

The Liturgical Movement has influenced all branches of Lutheranism. Primarily it resulted in a recovery of the fullness of the sixteenth-century heritage after 150 years of decline. New service-books in the decade after the Second World War demonstrate this. Since then a more ecumenical mood has developed as the result of increased knowledge of the pre-medieval church and the conviction that liturgical renewal cannot take place in isolation.

Most recently, Lutherans have been challenged by Vatican II Roman Catholicism. A reformed Roman Church forces Lutherans to ask whether their protest has registered at last and, if so, whether the time for reconciliation has come. The spirit of rapprochement is strongest, at least on a practical level, in North America. The new American Lutheran rite (1970) for holy communion bears striking parallels to the new Roman mass (1969) and also the eucharist of the (pan-Protestant) Consultation on Church Union (1968).

Liturgical renewal among Lutherans shares goals similar to those of other communions: restoration of significant practices of mainstream Western Catholicism, expressing the interrelation of worship and mission, recovering the spirit of joy and celebration in the eucharist, grasping the mystery that God's work and man's work are indistinguishable. But in all this there is a sustained commitment to proclamation as the living voice of God among his people and a pardonable pride in a rich musical heritage to be shared with others.

Peter Brunner, *Worship in the Name of Jesus*, 1968; F. Kalb, *The Theology of Worship in 17th-Century Lutheranism,* 1965; Vilmos Vajta, *Luther on Worship*, 1958.

EUGENE BRAND

Maniple *see* Vestments (1e)

Mar Thoma Church Worship

The Mar Thoma Church is unique in the sense that it is at once Eastern and Reformed. This church still maintains aspects of its Eastern Orthodox heritage, but has undergone a thorough reformation along the lines of the English and Continental Reformations.

The church claims historical continuity with the ancient church supposed to have been established by the apostle Thomas in the first century. The Reformation of the nineteenth century, which originated this church as an independent unit, distinct from the Syrian Orthodox Church of which it formed part before that time, was ostensibly an effort to restore the purity of faith and practice of the original apostolic church which had been corrupted by the Syrian Orthodox.

The liturgical tradition of the Mar Thoma Church thus follows very much the patterns set by the Syrian Orthodox tradition. There have been several revisions of the prayers, especially in the eucharistic liturgy, to eliminate certain supposedly wrong teachings, e.g. (1) to take out all intercessions to the saints or the Blessed Virgin Mary since Christ is the only mediator; (2) to take out all prayers for the departed, since there is no biblical teaching that tells us that the dead will be benefited by our prayers; (3) to take out elements in the liturgical prayers which over-emphasize the sacrificial element in the eucharist; (4) to revise prayers which may seem to imply a doctrine of transubstantiation of the bread and wine into the body and blood of our Lord; (5) to revise texts which over-emphasize the powers of the priesthood.

In these reforms the Mar Thoma Church was guided especially by the pattern of the English Reformation as the Church Missionary Society had interpreted it. As in the English *BCP*, sometimes two alternate versions are given of prayers, one of which has a 'high' theology of the sacrament, whereas the second may reflect a 'low' view. In the revisions, the basic allusions of the Orthodox text have been maintained wherever possible. For example, the opening words of the public celebration of the eucharistic liturgy in the Orthodox and Mar Thoma texts are: *Orthodox* – 'Mary who brought Thee forth and John who baptized Thee – these are intercessors on our behalf before Thee – Have mercy upon us.' *Mar Thoma* – 'Our Lord Jesus Christ who took flesh from Holy Mary and received Baptism from John, pour forth Thy blessing upon us.'

The introduction by Metropolitan Yuhanon Mar Thoma, Head of the Mar Thoma Church, to the finally revised (1954) text of the eucharistic liturgy, gives these basic principles of the revision: (1) removal of all prayers addressed to the saints; (2) removal of all prayers for the departed; (3) removal of the prayer (at the time of communion): 'Thee I hold, who holdest the bounds of the world, Thee I grasp, who orderest the depths; Thee, O God, do I place in my mouth . . .'; (4) change of the prayer 'we offer thee this bloodless sacrifice for thy Holy Church throughout the world . . .' to read 'We offer this prayer . . . for the Church'; (5) change of the prayer 'we offer this living sacrifice' to read 'we offer this sacrifice of grace, peace and praise'; (6) removal of the statement 'this eucharist is . . . sacrifice and praise'; (7) removal of the declaration that the Holy Spirit sanctifies the censer; (8) omission of the rubric about blessing the censer; (9) alteration of the epiclesis, giving freedom to say '(may the Holy Spirit sanctify it) to be the body of Christ' or 'to be the fellowship of the Body of Christ'; (10) insistence on communion in both kinds separately; (11) abolition of auricular confession to the priest; (12) prohibition of the celebration of the eucharist when there is no one beside the priest to communicate.

Changes along similar lines were made in all the forms of prayer and administration of sacraments. Since the revision has not yet been carried out in a thorough manner, elements of the Orthodox tradition now co-exist with definite Reformation features.

In the canonical offices, the use of incense has been largely discontinued. The prayers for the offering of incense are retained, however, the word 'incense' being replaced by the word 'service' or 'prayers'. The typical Syrian Orthodox pattern of *proemion* (introductory doxology) followed by a *sedra* (long meditative prayer) is retained, but the invariable reference to the departed at the conclusion of the *sedra* is either omitted or replaced by reference to 'all believing members of the church'.

The Mar Thoma Church remains Eastern in not adding the *fiilioque* to the Nicene Creed, in insisting on the celibacy of bishops, in vestments and church utensils, in full congregational participation in worship, in the use of the mother-tongue in worship, in adding 'O Christ, who was crucified for us, have mercy upon us' in the *Trisagion* and in many other respects.

At the same time there has been a liberal acceptance of and accommodation to Western Protestant or Evangelical forms of worship. The prayer meeting finds a place in the constitution, and each parish is divided into regional groups which meet together for informal group prayer. The eucharistic service is not obligatory on all Sundays, and quite often the priest or presbyter presides over a meeting around the preached word and prayer alone.

Hymns from the Anglican, Presbyterian, Lutheran, Methodist, Baptist and other books are found in the manuals of worship and are frequently used, either in English or in Malayalam. Several litanies and collects have also been similarly adopted.

The traditional seven canonical offices have been reduced to two (morning and evening), following the Reformers at this point. A form for compline has, however, been retained. There are special offices for Sundays and certain feast days, but different forms for the different days of the week are no longer in use.

A special feast called 'Community Day' (*Samudayadinam*) has been added, and a special form of service provided for the day, which coincides with the feast of St Thomas. A special offering is taken on this day for the central treasury of the church.

PAUL VERGHESE

Mariological Feasts

The Christian church has always held Mary the Virgin in special honour. The church's calendar shows clearly the place Mary has in the liturgy, while private devotions as well as the work of artists and poets show the place she has in the minds and thoughts of individuals.

From early times Mary was honoured with the title 'Mother of God', which emphasized the status she enjoyed by virtue of her Son. In addition, however, the continuing devotion of the church to her person over the centuries led to her being given such titles as 'sinless' and 'immaculate'. Consequently two elements may be traced in the feasts in her honour, the vocational and the personal. The Immaculate Conception, for instance, may well be called a personal feast, while the Annunciation is rather to be regarded as a vocational one. These vocational, mother-and-son, feasts are, in a way, twofold celebrations and they become feasts of the mother or the son according to where the emphasis is put. Thus the Annunciation, Lady Day in England, is renamed in the new Roman calendar 'The Annunciation of the Lord' (by the angel to the mother). The octave day of Christmas has for centuries been called the Feast of the Circumcision, but originally it was a day in honour of the mother of God and in the new calendar it is now called 'The Solemnity of Holy Mary, Mother of God'.

The oldest feasts of our Lady have a local connection with the church at Jerusalem. They also came into being largely because of the Christological controversies of the early church. As the true humanity of our Lord (as well as his divinity) came to be stated in clearer and more emphatic terms, the reality of the status of the Mother of God came to be better appreciated and underlined by feasts in its honour.

The feasts of the Purification, the Annunciation, the Birth and Assumption seem to be the oldest Marian feasts and to have been of Byzantine origin. They are recorded in the Gelasian Sacramentary, and so must have been known at Rome in the seventh or eighth century. To these very many other feasts, especially of local usage, have been added over the centuries. Only a brief mention of the principal feasts is here possible.

The dogma of the *Immaculate Conception* was not defined until 1854, but the feast is very old. A feast was certainly observed in the East in the seventh century, and spread from there to Naples, Ireland, England and so to the continent. It gained a measure of universal observance through the breviary of Pius V, and became a feast of the highest rank for the whole Roman Catholic Church after 1854. Its date is 8 December.

The *Birthday* of our Lady, 8 September, is a very old feast – in origin as much a feast of her parents, Joachim and Anne, as of Mary. No reason can be given for the choice of date.

The *Annunciation* celebrates the incident related in Luke 1.26-38. It is recalled, in the framework of the Advent liturgy, in the Ember Wednesday mass. But from quite early times it was given a special day of its own – 25 March in the Western calendar. The hymn *Ave maris stella* is said to have been first used as a hymn for this feast.

The *Visitation* (Luke 1.39-55) is recalled in the Advent liturgy on Ember Friday. There is an old Eastern feast on 2 July. The Western feast is probably not connected with the Eastern one and dates from the Middle Ages. The new Roman calendar has transferred it from 2 July to 31 May.

The *Purification* of our Lady, as it has long been called by the Western church, is observed in the East as a feast of the Saviour. In the new calendar it is called the 'Presentation of the Lord'. Both names are derived from Luke 2.22. The real significance of the feast is the meeting (*hypapante*) of the old dispensation and the new, of Simeon and Jesus. The day is also known as *Candlemas*, for candles are blessed for liturgical use and also distributed to the faithful on this day. It also marks the end of the Christmas cycle and, through the candles, emphasizes the 'light' motif of the Christmas feasts: 'a light for revelation to the Gentiles, and for glory to thy people Israel'.

The *Assumption* of our Lady, 15 August, commemorates her death. It also celebrates her entrance into heaven. The dogma was not defined until 1950, but the feast is one of the earliest Marian ones.

Other feasts of our Lady have a local origin or are a development, often devotional and subjective, of one of the earlier feasts. The feasts listed above are Christocentric and celebrate Mary's unique honour of being the mother of God and mother of man's Redeemer.

J. CONNELLY

Martyrium

A building enshrining the tomb and/or relics of a martyr. The forms adopted by the church were those already in use for pagan tombs. Almost invariably roofed with a dome to symbolize heaven, they could be, depending upon local customs and prototypes, cuboid, circular, cruciform, octagonal or triconch, or they could combine more than one of these plans, e.g. Church No. 8, Bin Bir Kilisse, which unites the cross with the eight-sided figure (*see* Fig. 18).

<hr />

A. Grabar, *Martyrium. Recherches sur le culte des reliques religieux et l'art chrétien antique*, 2 vols., 1946.

EDITOR

Mass, High

The term 'high' translates the Latin *sollemnis* and *Missa sollemnis* (or even *sacra sollemnia*) meant a sung mass at which the deacon and subdeacon (qq.v.) assisted the celebrant and performed certain duties that belonged to them alone. Thus it was the deacon who sang the gospel, the subdeacon who sang the epistle, as well as other lessons if there was no lector. In addition, the deacon was the immediate minister of the priest, pouring the wine into the chalice at the offertory (q.v.) and covering and uncovering the chalice during the canon (q.v.). The subdeacon poured the water with which the wine is mingled. The subdeacon held the paten in a humeral veil (q.v.) from the offertory until the end of the Lord's Prayer. This observance, which had its origin in the papal liturgy when the bread was brought to the altar on large platters at the offertory, which were then held by the subdeacons until just before communion, has now been abolished. At the end of mass the deacon sang the dismissal (*Ite, missa est*) before the celebrant gave the blessing.

The ceremonial of high mass was somewhat complicated not only in the sanctuary, where the deacon and subdeacon had to make their movements in concert with acolytes, thurifer and master of ceremonies, but also in the total organization of the rite. Thus the choir sang the introit, the gradual, the Alleluia and its verse (in Lent replaced by the tract), the offertory verse and the communion verse, and the people were supposed to sing the *Kyries*, the *Gloria in excelsis*, the *Sanctus*, the *Benedictus* (until recently sung *after* the consecration) and the *Agnus Dei*. In fact in most places the choir sang all these too. Before a high mass on Sundays there was the rite of the *asperges* (q.v.), although celebrant, ministers, servers and, where there was a

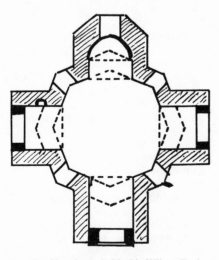

Fig. 18   Church no. 8, Bin Bir Kilisse, Turkey

surpliced choir, the choir had already made their solemn entry. In addition, the celebrant was required to say the prayers of preparation with the ministers in a low voice and to read everything that was sung by anyone else. In cathedrals and parish churches where the gospel was read out in English after its singing in Latin, the gospel was thus recited three times in one mass.

Incense (q.v.) was used (and might only be used at sung masses); the altar was censed after the prayers of preparation and at the offertory, the gospel book before the singing of the gospel and the celebrant on all three occasions. In addition, the ministers and servers were censed at the offertory and the people on the latter occasion only. The blessed sacrament was censed at the two elevations (q.v.) of the consecrated bread and wine.

The whole of this ceremonial was controlled by a rigid corpus of rubrics, elaborated by the ceremonialists whose practical regulations sometimes acquired the force of law.

Its origins are to be found in the Gregorian tradition (the 'Gregorian' sacramentary and the *Ordo Romanus Primus*) of the seventh century, with the elaborations and adaptations of the *Ordines* and pontificals of the following centuries. The 'Gregorian' sacramentary and the *Ordo Romanus Primus* give the ceremonial of the mass when the pope celebrated. North of the Alps this had to be adapted to the conditions of an episcopal celebration and it was the episcopal high mass which, in spite of accretions, gave the best picture of the Roman mass of the seventh century. Then, with the multiplication of churches within a city and outside it, with the spread of monasticism, it was necessary to arrange the rite for celebration by the simple priest. It was shorn of certain ceremonies proper to a bishop (thus the priest did not use a throne but a seat at the side of the sanctuary), and so we get by the thirteenth century the rite known in English-speaking lands as 'high mass'. In spite of the ever increasing prevalence of low mass (q.v.), at least the ceremonialists regarded high mass as the typical rite of the Roman Catholic Church. It had the advantage of indicating that the mass is celebrated not by one man, the priest, but by a community, even if by the eighth century this community had become almost entirely clericalized. The Carolingian reform of the ninth century made attempts to

keep a community spirit alive by enjoining on the people the duty of singing the *Kyries*, the *Gloria*, etc., but apparently without great success. The ceremonial of high mass, as it was known until recently, was finally fixed and imposed as of obligation on the whole church of the Roman rite by the corpus of rubrics called *Ritus servandus* which was inserted into the missal of Pope Pius V in 1570.

The term 'high mass' and much of its ceremonial is now obsolescent or obsolete. The *Ordo Missae* of 1969 has brought a great flexibility to the celebration of the mass. Singing may and should take place at every kind of mass, incense may or may not be used at will, the ceremonial is much simplified, a subdeacon is no longer necessary, but above all, the emphasis is put on the worshipping community and their part in the celebration is considerable. The people are required to sing or say those parts of the rite that properly belong to them, the celebrant never says anything read, said or sung by anyone else, and lay-readers for the first and second lessons are allowed and recommended. The celebration of mass in its simplest or more elaborate form is now once more a paradigm of the Christian community, the church.

J. D. CRICHTON

Mass, Low

The low mass (also called in some languages and places the 'said mass' or the 'read mass' or even 'private mass') is, ceremonially speaking, one that is celebrated by a priest with single server. In practice, for a variety of reasons, it was for hundreds of years the form of mass with which the laymen were most familiar. It was celebrated without song, with a minimum of ceremonial, and the celebrant faced eastwards. The rubrics of the Pius V missal (1570) assumed that the people would be on their knees throughout, occupied with their own devotions and hearing only occasional phrases from the celebrant. On Sundays in parish churches, its rigours were somewhat reduced by the reading of the epistle and gospel in the people's tongue after they had been read in Latin and (usually) by the sermon. In some places vernacular hymns were allowed to form an accompaniment of the rite, notably in Germany. From the eighteenth century, a style of mass that came to be called the *Betsingmesse* (prayer-and-song-mass) was introduced. Here the sung texts were paraphrases (more or less close) of the mass texts and were sung while the Latin text was being read by the celebrant. It was a way of securing some popular participation and became common in the church after the Second World War until the liturgical reform of Vatican II.

The rite of low mass, which the rubrics of the Pius V missal seem to have regarded as typical is the result of a long development. The classical Roman mass of the seventh century (*see* **Mass, High**) was a community celebration. But with the spread of monasticism, the custom of private masses in chapels for special 'intentions' began to come in, and as Christianity spread into the rural parts of Europe, it became impossible to celebrate the mass in country churches with all the ceremonial of the papal-episcopal rite. The sung parts of the mass (introits, etc.) seem to have been omitted, but the priest himself said all the rest, the collect, the epistle, the gospel, etc., and the single minister or server responded for the people. With the changing habits and organization of the papal curia which gave employment to a considerable number of clerics, mostly priests, and with the rise of the new religious orders like the Dominicans and Franciscans who were clerks (in holy orders), the custom of low masses became ever more prevalent. Concelebration, apart from ordinations, was unknown. When in the thirteenth century the Franciscans adopted the papal-curial liturgy and penetrated into every corner of Europe, the Roman rite of low mass became very common. They took over from the Roman books certain prayers provided for the devotion of the priest at the offertory and before communion, and a selection of these prayers was included in the missal of Pius V and were made a matter of obligation.

For this kind of celebration a single book was needed, for it was manifestly impossible for a man to take around with him a small library consisting of sacramentary, collectary, epistle and gospel book and gradual. This the monks had provided by the eleventh century with the so-called *Missale Plenarium*, which contained *all* the texts of the mass whether sung by others or said by the priest. It was this book, reformed in the sixteenth century, that became the *Missale Romanum* and that was the official mass book of the Roman Church until 1969.

Like the term 'high mass' (q.v.), the term 'low mass' is now practically obsolete. The thinking of the *Ordo Missae* of 1969 moves in a quite different direction. It emphasizes the community participation of the people and admits singing at any and every kind of celebration. It does indeed envisage the 'private' mass (a term now frowned on) and provides an order for a priest who has to celebrate in the absence of people. The ritual is slightly adapted, though he is still required to say the entrance text and the communion verse. The server has to make the responses of the people.

J. D. CRICHTON

Matrimony

Matrimony is the rite or action of marriage. Since, according to Western Christian thought, but not according to Eastern Orthodox thinking (*see below*), the actual ministers of the marriage are the bride and groom who marry each other, the liturgical act is not of the essence of marriage and is rather a blessing additional to the primary entering into a contract in front of witnesses.

1. *The Early Church.* A clear distinction was drawn between the betrothal or engagement and the nuptials or marriage ceremony proper, although the former was considered to be as binding as the latter. There remains no full description of the primitive rite, but from scattered allusions it may in part be reconstructed and it can be seen to consist of practices current in paganism.

(*a*) *Betrothal.* According to Ignatius, this must take place with the bishop's cognizance (*ad Poly. 5*). It involved the giving of *arrhae* or earnest money as a pledge that the marriage would eventually take place. Next a ring was given, used for the sealing of household effects, to indicate that the future wife would be in charge of the home. A dowry was then promised and the woman was veiled – the veil being part of the engaged or married woman's normal dress. The couple's hands were joined and a kiss was exchanged (Tertullian, *Apol.*6; *de Virg.Vel.*11). In the course of time some of these elements were transferred to the marriage ceremony itself.

(*b*) *Nuptials.* According to Tertullian this included the celebration of the eucharist and a blessing (*ad Ux.*2.6). From later writers we learn that the man was given a crown, according to Chrysostom 'as a symbol of victory, indicating that he approaches the marriage bed unconquered by pleasure' (*Hom.in I Tim*.9). An agape or love-feast (q.v.) usually followed.

EDITOR

2. *The Orthodox Church*. The Orthodox Church understands marriage as the sacrament whereby two members of the body of Christ become one. Ephesians 5.31, 32 form the root of this understanding:

> For this reason a man shall leave his father and mother and be joined to his wife, and the two shall become one. This is a great mystery, and I take it to mean Christ and the church.

The Orthodox Church sees several fundamental inferences inseparably bound up with this concept:

(*a*) It is Christ who unites the couple in the sacrament of marriage. He is sacramentally present in this great act taking place within his body.

(*b*) The unity accomplished in the sacrament of marriage, just as the unity between Christ and his church, is truly unique and is given the full potential to be total and eternal in character. Therefore, the priest acts as the actual minister of the sacrament.

(*c*) Through the sacrament of marriage the husband and wife are crowned as the king and queen of a family: a small image of the Kingdom of God and a concrete witness to that Kingdom in the world.

The present Orthodox rite of holy matrimony uses symbolic actions and movements to convey these basic, above-mentioned realities concerning marriage to the couple being united as well as to the faithful gathered to witness the event. (The Orthodox rite of holy matrimony has a long history of evolution. A text of its present form may be found in: Father John Meyendorff, *The Sacrament of Holy Matrimony*. A review of the historical evolution of the rite can be found in: Alvian Smirensky, 'The Evolution of the Present Rite of Matrimony and Parallel Canonical Developments' in *St Vladimir's Seminary Quarterly* 8.1 [1964], pp. 38-47.)

The ceremony begins in the vestibule, that part of the church building which represents the world outside the church. In the vestibule marriage, as the world has known it since pagan antiquity, takes place: the promise is made and the rings are exchanged. For a member of the church, however, such a marriage is not sufficient. All the events of his life must be integrated into the saving life of Christ. His birth in Christ is baptism, his food in Christ is the holy eucharist; the inspiring content of his life is the Holy Spirit. His desire for love, companionship and family must likewise be made new, i.e. permeated throughout by the transforming presence of Christ. The marriage of this world must be brought to the church and, through the great mystery of the sacrament, made into the image of the unity existing between Christ and the church.

This movement from the world to the church, from the fallen to the transformed, is symbolized by the first great liturgical action of the marriage rite, the *procession*. The priest leads the couple in procession from the vestibule to the centre of the church building, where the group stops in front of a small lectern or table on which are located the gospel book and cross. The couple hold lighted candles as the sign of their common faith in Christ, the Light of the world. The priest announces the purpose of the gathering by intoning:

> Blessed is the Kingdom, of the Father and of the Son, and of the Holy Spirit, now and ever, and unto ages of ages.

The marital union of the couple is to be integrated into the transformed and eternal life of the Kingdom of God.

The priest then reads three long prayers filled with a multitude of scriptural references. The references point out the interaction between God and man throughout biblical history. They illustrate the way in which God has blessed and fulfilled promises to couples starting from the time of Adam and Eve. The prayers ask that the same blessing be showered upon the couple present.

The *crowning* is the high point of the ceremony. Literally, the priest places crowns or wreaths upon the heads of the couple. The bride and groom are shown to be the king and queen of a little image of the Kingdom of God; they are to increase and multiply, and see their children's children. The crowns also signify the crowns of martyrs and indicate that the newly-joined couple is to be a living witness to Christ in the world. The crowning is concluded by the *prokeimenon*, based on a verse from Ps. 21, which says:

Thou hast set upon their heads crowns of precious stones; they asked life of thee and thou gavest it them.

The epistle section, Eph. 5. 20-33, read following the *prokeimenon*, contains verses used as the basis for this article. The gospel reading, John 2.1-11, tells of the performing by Christ of his first sign – at the marriage feast in Cana of Galilee. At Cana he changed the water into wine, the old into the new. In the sacrament of marriage he changes a union of this world into an eternal unity in his Kingdom.

After the gospel reading and further prayers, the priest presents a *common cup* of wine to the couple. In drinking from the common cup, the couple again realize the nature of their unity in Christ: they drink from one cup, they share one life; they proclaim one source for that life – Christ.

As a conclusion to the service the bride and groom join hands and are led by the priest, who carries a cross indicating the way in which all Christians must walk, in a *triple circling* around the centre table. The circle thus formed is symbolic of the nature of marriage as accomplished in Christ: it has its beginning now in the sacrament, but it has no end.

This is a great mystery, and I take it to mean Christ and the church. (Eph. 5.32).

PAUL LAZOR

3. *Medieval and Roman Catholic.* The marriage liturgy to be found in the early sacramentaries (*Veron., Gelas.* and *Greg.*) was never obligatory and it was not until the social order had broken down (seventh to eighth century) that the church felt it necessary to take cognisance of the matrimonial consent and the conditions attaching to it. This was necessary to protect freedom of consent and to prevent clandestinity. Hence the rite of marriage *in facie ecclesiae*, which meant, literally, at the doors of the church. This is first recorded in Normandy in the early twelfth century. The minister addressed the couple and inquired about the consent. The bride was 'given away', the scrip of the dowry was read, the ring was blessed and put on the right hand of the bride, the bridegroom gave some pieces of gold or silver (according to his wealth) and the priest concluded the rite with a blessing. If there was to be a wedding mass, the spouses (with their party) entered

the church, carrying candles. They made an offering at the offertory, there was the recital of the nuptial blessing (the text being that of the sacramentaries), and at this date and until much later, while the prayer was said, the veil was laid on the head of the bride and on the shoulders of the bridegroom. Thus was preserved the ancient rite of *velatio* which, according to some modern authorities, derives not from the ancient Roman *flammeum* but from the Christian rite of the *velatio virginis*. No formula is supplied in the Norman books, but in other medieval French rituals formulae very much like those of the Sarum rite are to be found.

It is there, however, that the origins of the Sarum rite of marriage are to be found, a rite that was retained by the Roman Catholic Church in England after the Reformation and with a few modifications (e.g. the omission of the blessing of the ring) by the Church of England. In medieval England it is worth noting that the text of the wedding mass was not used; it was replaced with that of the Holy Trinity, often used in England for joyful occasions.

The rite of the Roman Ritual of 1614 derives from the medieval one described above but, as its rubrics remark, since there are many local customs in the celebration of marriage, those countries and regions which have local rites may continue to use them. This is the explanation of the brevity and sheer starkness of the Roman rite of that time. In fact, in Europe there has always been a variety of marriage rites though in the nineteenth century there was a tendency to uniformity.

In recent years, with a developing theology of marriage, it was felt that a more adequate rite was needed. This appeared in 1969. It assumes (but does not order) that marriage is to take place at mass and appoints that it should take place after the ministry of the word where now other sacramental rites like confirmation and ordination are administered. The celebrant greets the couple who are seated in the sanctuary. After the homily he questions them about their willingness to undertake the obligations of marriage and their freedom. It is noteworthy that the English civil form declaring freedom and the matrimonial consent that follows has been incorporated into the rite for use in England. The form of consent has retained most of the phrases of the Sarum rite and these have now become part of the official Roman rite of marriage. After the blessing of the ring (or rings) the bride's is put on her finger with a new formula expressing love and fidelity (the one for the giving of gold and silver has been omitted as being archaic and obscure). In *all* weddings the nuptial blessing is given in one of the three forms that are provided. Bride and bridegroom may receive communion in both kinds if they so wish. The mass (or service) ends with blessings for the bride and bridegroom and for all present.

If there is no mass, the marriage service must be celebrated with a ministry of the word (lessons from the lectionary), including a homily, which may never be omitted. In the case of marriages between Catholics and non-Christians certain adaptations (given in the official texts) are to be made.

Three mass formulae for weddings are provided in the *Missale Romanum* of 1970 with a rich collection of prayers, prefaces and insertions (*Hanc igitur*) into the Roman canon (q.v.).

J. D. CRICHTON

4. *Anglican.* The marriage service is probably closer to its medieval predecessor, and has changed less in the ensuing four hundred years, than any other in *BCP*. The obvious example of this is the vernacular form of vows, which is found in the Sarum and York manuals in almost exactly the same words that are used today. Cranmer keeps the traditional division into two parts (*sponsalia* and *nuptiae*), but allows the espousals to take place in the body of the church, marking the beginning of the second part by the customary procession to the altar.

The service begins with a long address, expanded from the medieval 'banns' with material that was evidently traditional, since Chaucer uses it in *The Parson's Tale* (1387), and much of it is found in the Cologne *Encheiridion* (1538). Marriage was instituted by God in paradise, adorned and beautified by Christ at Cana, and commended by Paul in the Epistle to the Hebrews; it must not be entered upon for the wrong reasons; the right reasons are the procreation of children, continence, and 'mutual society, help and comfort'. The third 'cause' is stressed throughout the service: the medieval promise to love, honour, hold, and keep becomes love, *comfort*, honour, and keep; and the vows now include the duty 'to love and to cherish'.

The introduction of Matt. 19.6 ('those whom God hath joined . . .') and the subsequent declaration of marriage are German customs derived from Luther. The possibility that the woman may be past childbirth is covered by the suggestion of Ps. 67 as an alternative to the traditional Ps. 128 and a rubric before the collect for fruitfulness. This latter reveals a change of emphasis in the second part of the service, which was originally the blessing of the bride. Now there are prayers that 'they may *both* be fruitful' (instead of 'that she may be . . .'), and that 'this man may love his wife' (compare the interpretation of the ring as a token of the '*covenant* betwixt them made'). The attributes of Christian married life include 'quietness, sobriety, and peace' and 'holy love'.

In 1552 the only change of importance was the omission of the 'tokens of spousage' (gold and silver, often bracelets), whose place was taken by the priest's and clerk's fees. The tokens, however, continued to be brought in the North of England well into the seventeenth century. Surprisingly enough, the ring is retained. This became one of the major grievances of the Puritans, on a par with the surplice, the sign of the cross in baptism, and kneeling at the communion. They also objected to the phrase 'with my body I thee worship', but neither objection was successful in 1662.

In 1928 the phrasing of 'the causes for which matrimony was ordained' was modified to suit a more refined taste. The bride was no longer required to promise to obey her husband; and instead of endowing her with all his worldly goods, he was to share them with her. The Puritan criticism of 'worship' was at last met by substituting 'honour'. The prayers in the second part were shortened, chiefly by leaving out allusions to OT figures. No blessing of the ring was provided, though this was done in most other contemporary revisions. The omission was made good in *Alternative Services, First Series* (1966). A eucharistic proper was appointed in which divine love was the chief theme ('Love one another as I have loved you'). The American revision of 1929 omits the second part of the service altogether; the Scottish and South African books provide a form for blessing a civil marriage.

G. J. CUMING

5. *Baptist.* Baptists are found in many parts

of the world, but in no country do they have a prescribed marriage service. These two facts taken together account for a wide diversity of practice. Marriage may be solemnized in a home, or in a church, in a civic hall, or in a registry office. In Britain, since the marriage act of 1863, after the civil preliminaries, it is customary for the ceremony to take place in a Baptist place of worship registered for marriages. The practice of blessing in church a marriage already contracted in a civil registry office, while much less frequent, is on the increase. Civil marriage is obligatory in many countries, but in the USA, where Baptists are most numerous, the church marriage ceremony is recognized by the state. Two convictions are common to Baptists – marriage is not a sacrament of the church, but a divine institution for mankind; believers should enter the marriage covenant in the presence of God and with prayer for his blessing. The persistent opposition of the early Baptists to marriages outside their own communion has disappeared, but unions between believers and unbelievers are still discouraged. A marriage service in church usually includes the singing of hymns, the reading of scriptures, a message, and extemporary or free prayer. The three main parts of the service are the introduction, the covenant, and the word. The ministry of the word sometimes precedes, but more usually follows the marriage covenant. The introduction commonly includes a hymn, a statement of the purposes of marriage, a declaration by the couple that they know of no legal impediment, and a prayer. The marriage covenant is made by the exchange of promises, the joining of hands, and the giving and receiving of a ring or rings. In Baptist manuals, the actual wording of the promises has been profoundly influenced by the service-books of other communions, especially by the BCP. The ceremony concludes with the declaration that the couple are now husband and wife, and a blessing. Then the scriptures are read, there is usually a short sermon or address, and prayer(s) for the divine blessing on the marriage contracted. The service ends with a hymn and the benediction. Marriages are solemnized usually on week-days, occasionally on Sundays in the context of the congregation at worship, rarely at the Lord's Supper.

S. WINWARD

6. *Congregationalist*. Traditionally there have been two reasons for Christian marriage. The first is for the avoidance of concupiscence (or, in Pauline words, the choice is 'to marry or burn'). The second is for the procreation and upbringing of children. The third emphasis was added by the Puritan predecessors of the modern Congregationalists: for companionship through life. This also has biblical authority for God is said to have created Eve for Adam 'because it is not good for man to be alone'. This is the dominant emphasis in modern Congregational marriage services, often called 'solemnizations of marriage' because they are regarded as ecclesiastical blessings of civil covenants, and in no sense as sacraments. In common with other Christians, Congregationalists recall that Jesus hallowed marriage by his presence at the marriage at Cana in Galilee, and that Paul used marriage as an analogy of the intimate relationship of Christ to his church.

Though there is no single, exclusive and official form of marriage service for Congregationalists, the many services from which a minister can select have a common lineage and common characteristics. If the English Free Churches have borrowed any single ordinance from the Church of England, it is surely the service of holy matrimony. The ceremonies of the giving away of the bride by her father and the giving and receiving of rings, as well as the very words of the solemn promises which bride and groom make to each other in plighting their troth, are all borrowed from the BCP. (The exact words are used in *A Book of Public Worship for the Use of Congregationalists*, 1948, p.174, and there is a revised version in *A Book of Services and Prayers*, 1959, p.67.)

The essentials of a Congregational marriage service comprise: reminders of the purposes of Christian marriage in an opening exhortation and in NT lessons; the charge that any impediments to the marriage be openly declared; the affirmations of mutual loyalty made by groom and bride; the mutual pledging of their troth and the exchange of rings; the minister's pronouncement in the triune name of God that bride and groom are married; and prayers and hymns for the keeping of the promises made and for the building of a Christian home, with the divine assistance, concluding with the Lord's Prayer and the blessing. Occasionally the service includes a celebration of holy communion in which the bride and groom are the sole communicants, but this is very infrequent.

HORTON DAVIES

7. *Jehovah's Witnesses.* Biblically, wedlock to be valid must have (*a*) recognition by the state, and (*b*) recognition by God.

In the temporal sphere, common-law marriage is not accepted by the congregation. 'Those living together in common-law marriage should have a legal marriage ceremony performed' and 'this should be definitely registered in the registry of the civil government', since common-law marriage 'has such an uncertain position because it is not universally recognized' (for source of quotations, *see below*.) A consentient arrangement is fornication, forbidden by scripture (Heb. 13.4), and deprives the participants of legal protection, contrary to Matt. 22.21.

In the spiritual sphere, the two must be scripturally free to marry: that is, neither of them must be married, legally or scripturally, to another person. It appears that the only scriptural ground for divorce is adultery (Matt. 5.32). Thus a person merely separated from a marriage mate or being in a state of legal divorce on a ground other than adultery would not scripturally be free to remarry. Death severs the marriage bond (Rom. 7.2).

Polygamy is scripturally improper for Christians (Matt. 19.5, 6). In lands where it is practised, the polygamist wishing to become one of Jehovah's Christian Witnesses must first put away all wives except the first, making suitable provision for the secondary wives and his children by them.

Witness children are discouraged from early marriages and are counselled to marry 'only in the Lord', that is, to fellow-believers, with spiritual and practical advantages (I Cor. 7.36, 39).

For 'those who have the gift' (Matt. 19.11) and can cultivate it, singleness is a fine course. It affords greater freedom to serve the Lord, and many young Witnesses postpone marriage for some time while they enjoy full-time ministry or missionary service; others remain single permanently. However, singleness has its price ('because of prevalence of fornication, let each man have his own wife'), celibacy is imposed upon no one (I Tim. 4.3), and the choice should be 'that which is becoming and that which means constant attendance upon the Lord without distrac-

tion' (I Cor. 7.2, 35).

The wedding ceremony itself, like most other Witness meetings, is opened and closed with song and prayer. A discourse specially directed to the couple and offering admonition and advice usually includes reference to the Genesis account and the prior creation of man, but also his duty to exercise his headship with understanding and love, while the bride is reminded of her relative subjection to her husband (relative, that is, to the absolute subjection due to God) (Eph. 5.21-33). After about thirty minutes the vows are taken. The wording recommended, with variations where necessary in accordance with the law of the land, is: 'I take you to be my wedded wife [husband], to love and to cherish [the bride adds: 'and deeply respect'] in accordance with the divine law as set forth in the holy scriptures for Christian husbands [wives], for as long as we both shall live together on earth according to God's marital arrangement.' A wedding meal is generally provided after the ceremony, very often paid for and prepared by the local congregation. Frequently considerable numbers will join in the festivities, a wedding reception being one of the very few occasions for large informal gatherings of Witnesses.

Divorce on grounds other than adultery, and separation, are strongly discouraged: a man should 'stick to his wife'; 'Jehovah has hated a divorcing' (Matt. 19.5; Mal. 2.16; I Cor. 7.10, 16). There are, of course, innumerable variations on these problems associated with marriage. Basic principles relating to such matters as the wedding ceremony, paying marriage dues, rearing children, engagement, and singleness have been discussed at length in such issues of *The Watchtower* as 15 September 1956, 15 November 1960, 1 May 1962 and 15 September 1965.

Both Jehovah God (Isa. 54.5, 6) and Christ Jesus (Rev. 19.7) are symbolically represented as 'married', and this in itself elevates the privilege of marriage to the highest level.

A. HELEY

8. *Lutheran.* On the eve of the Reformation, and indeed throughout the sixteenth century, marriage law and forms of marriage were still developing. At this time we find the precepts or customs of Roman, Germanic, canon and imperial law, according to which the mutual agreement of the nuptial pair is the foundation of their marriage (*consensus facit*

nuptias); certain degrees of relationship are given as hindrances to marriage, and to a limited extent it is presupposed that the marriage will be held in public. The involvement of the church authorities in the ceremony (namely, the publication of banns, the wedding itself as the questioning of the nuptial pair before the congregation, and the nuptial mass) will also have been a widespread custom. At the beginning of the sixteenth century, there can be no question of rules which embraced every detail. Responsible authorities, and later both the Roman Catholic and Protestant churches, fought passionately against *clandestina sponsalia* or *matrimonia*, 'secret marriages' or 'hedge marriages', but they were still permissible under the systems of law mentioned above, as they rested on the principle of *consensus facit nuptias*. Despite prohibitions by the church, lay marriage continued for a very long time. There is no mistaking a certain emancipation movement, which not only grants the female partner in the marriage a greater degree of independence but represents a move towards a greater freedom in the formation of individual modes of living. At the same time, the sources continually lament the detrimental effect this has on the sphere of sexual morality; official ordinances seek to rectify this situation even before the Reformation, and still more after it.

In view of this situation, during the sixteenth century, marriage in church becomes increasingly important on both the Roman Catholic and the Protestant side; towards the end of the century it acquires an unprecedented significance on the Roman Catholic side in canon law as a result of the Tridentine *tametsi* and a growing place in civil law on the Protestant side with the rise of regional churches.

Over against Roman Catholic tradition, all Reformed churches are agreed that the conception of marriage as a sacrament and obligatory celibacy are not in accordance either with scripture or with the original Christian tradition. Consequently the association of marriage with the eucharist in the nuptial mass is rejected, and permission for priests, monks and nuns to marry is passionately required. Virginity is no longer regarded as a merit; marriage is seen as a state or calling in which everyone should and must prove himself as a Christian. This fundamentally different conception, reached from

the testimony of scripture, did not exclude the adoption of features of Roman Catholic marriage where they did not conflict with the Reformers' norm of the word of God; instead of marriage being linked with the mass, scriptural statements about marriage were given a greater place in the service.

The history of Lutheran marriage ordinances is further complicated because in the centres of the Lutheran Reformation (Wittenberg, Strasbourg, Nürnberg, etc.) marriage formulae from the liturgies of the respective Roman Catholic dioceses (Brandenburg, Magdeburg, Mainz, etc.) were often taken over. There were also certain differences in the legal conceptions of marriage in the different areas – at any rate, different terms were used.

There is a report of a first 'priest's marriage' from Augsburg in 1523; as the priest concerned was refused entry into church, he had his betrothal, or marriage, confirmed by an already married priest in the presence of 32 witnesses at a marriage feast in an inn. He and his bride made a mutual declaration that they took each other in marriage (E. Sehling, *Die evangelischen Kirchenordnungen des XVI Jahrhunderts*, XII, pp. 33 f.). The first Reformed marriage formula comes from the year 1524; in its original version it is most probably from the city pastor of Wittenberg, Johannes Bugenhagen. After a brief address, based essentially on the relevant statements of Gen. 1-3, the nuptial pair are asked: 'N., will you take N. to be your wedded wife (wedded husband) according to God's ordinance?' etc. After the exchange of rings ('a sign of betrothal'), the pastor says: 'So I give you both in wedlock before the face of God and our Lord Jesus Christ and before this congregation in the name of the Father . . . God our Father and our Lord Jesus Christ be with you. Be fruitful and increase the world.' Principal additions to other versions of this formula are the declaration in Matt. 19.6 and NT readings. The formula spread very rapidly, especially in South Germany. However, in Strasbourg, in the same year 1524, another form of marriage arose (printed in 1525) which largely followed the diocesan liturgy of 1513. It was more extensive than the Wittenberg formula and regarded the 'blessing of the marriage' as 'confirmation'. The Strasbourg order also had a significant influence on the marriage formulae of South German Lutheranism.

It is Luther's *Traubüchlein* (Little Wedding Book) of 1529, however, that had the greatest significance. Here Luther principally follows the order already existing in Wittenberg, but in some places he also takes up Roman Catholic formulae and the tradition of the early church. The service consists of three parts, public announcement, betrothal and blessing. The proclamation of the marriage, which is also a public summons to prayer for the couple, is first followed by the 'betrothal' (*copulatio*) in front of the church door ('bridal door'). The questions run: 'Hans, will you have Grete as your wedded wife? Grete, will you have Hans as your wedded husband?' After the exchange of rings, joining of right hands and the pronunciation of Matt. 19.6b (in the present tense), the pastor says: 'Seeing that Hans N. and Grete N. seek each other in marriage and acknowledge the same publicly before God and the world, and have given each other hands and rings of betrothal, I join them together in marriage in the name of the Father, the Son and the Holy Spirit, Amen.' The 'confirmation' in the church itself, presumably only on the day after the betrothal, essentially consists of scripture reading and prayer. The first lesson, Gen. 2.18, 21-24, is a kind of word of institution. The following three lessons are addressed directly to the bridal pair: 'Because you have both entered into the state of marriage in God's name, hear . . .' The lessons themselves present a systematic approach: Eph. 5.25, 29, 22-24 (God's commandment), Gen. 3.16-19 (the cross) and Gen. 1.27, 28-31 (consolation), together with Prov. 18.22. At the end there follows a prayer taken over from earlier examples, which the pastor is to say over the bridal pair with hands raised: 'Lord God, who has created man and woman and hast ordained the state of marriage, who hast blessed them with the fruit of the body and hast designated therein the sacrament of thy Son Jesus Christ and the church, his bride . . . We pray that thou wilt not allow thy creation (foundation), ordinance and blessing to go astray or to perish in us, but wilt graciously preserve it in us . . .'

In the 'Preface', Luther describes the purpose and conception of the marriage order that he proposes. In other respects no friend of ceremonies and ordinances, he feels it necessary to compose the *Traubüchlein* because of widespread uncertainty and con-

fusion, and in order to educate the people. In Luther's view, marriage is a matter which falls within the competence of the authorities, especially as 'weddings and the state of marriage are a worldly concern', though at the same time marriage is a 'divine state' as well. Luther does not hold that the order he proposes is in any way obligatory; it is there in case a pastor is asked for it – a further indication that final regulations are still to come and that Luther neither wants to stand in the way of the tradition where it does not conflict with the word of God, nor seeks to create new law. Nevertheless, his order of marriage does have a legal character; anyone who submits to it has (after the preceding betrothal in the family circle) fulfilled all the necessary legal conditions for a valid marriage. That Luther felt it necessary to compose the *Traubüchlein* for pastoral reasons also is clear from the writing 'Marriage Matters' (1530, *Martin Luthers Werke* (WA) 30, III, pp. 205 f.) and countless other statements on the questions of marriage, betrothal and divorce.

Luther's *Traubüchlein* has influenced almost all forms or church ordinances and liturgies in North and Central Germany. There are, however, numerous alterations, expansions and re-arrangements. To the scripture readings provided by Luther with which the ceremony now usually begins are sometimes added Matt. 19.3-9; John 2.1-11, etc. The questions are expanded, partly following the Strasbourg order of 1530: 'N., do you acknowledge before this Christian congregation that you have taken (and take) N. as your wedded wife (husband) and promise to love her (him) as your spouse in the Lord and with the help of God never to leave her (him)?' As in the Brandenburg-Nürnberg order of 1533, a declaration by the nuptial pair can also take the place of a question: 'I N. take thee N. as my wedded spouse and plight thee my troth.' The question can be omitted altogether, as in the Augsburg order of 1527 and the Hessen order of 1539. As far as the betrothal formula is concerned, in North Germany Luther's vow is almost always used which 'pronounces' or 'makes' the nuptial pair man and wife. Instead of this, the Strasbourg and Brandenburg-Nürnberg orders have: 'The obligation of marriage, which you have commended to each other before God and his congregation, I confirm at the behest of the Christian con-

gregation in the name of the Father etc.'
There is a controversy as to whether there is a
material difference between 'pronounce' (con-
stitutive) and 'confirm' (declaratory); towards the end of the sixteenth and in the
seventeenth century, there was a clear tendency to see church marriage as the con-
stitutive act, whereas earlier betrothal had
had this function. Matthew 19.6, in the
present or the perfect, is almost always
used in connection with the act of marriage
proper. The usual benediction is that of
Luther, occasionally in conjunction with a
prayer from Hessen dated 1539. A wedding
sermon, whether free or with a liturgical
formulation, found its way into the service
(first at Strasbourg, as did choir and congregational singing (Pss. 128, 127, Te Deum, etc.)
or organ music and more elaborate forms. In
some places the service was spread over two
successive days, first of all the wedding
ceremony with questions and 'saying together' or 'confirming'; the following day
the entry into the church with sermon and
blessing, in some places still called the
'nuptial mass' or 'nuptial office'. With increasing frequency the ceremony was concluded with the Aaronic blessing.

In the sixteenth century, church weddings
were still voluntary acts almost everywhere;
as before, there were lay weddings. However,
there was an increasing recognition that
marriage 'is very useful for the improvement
of the church' (Württemberg 1553), that the
state of marriage is hallowed not only by
faith and trust in the word but also by a
ceremony which needs particular conditions
and has particular consequences. Among the
conditions are often to be found a catechetical
examination of the nuptial pair, fulfilment of
the requirements of the 'marriage ordinances'
that arose everywhere, the strict prohibition
of secret betrothals and pre-marital inter-
course and the introduction of ecclesiastical
and civil penalties for 'fallen couples' ('church
discipline'). The ceremony, at first a proclamation and act of blessing, acquired increasing legal significance. Towards the end
of the sixteenth century official certificates
were required, and the authorities stated that
no one was legally married without a ceremony in church. The betrothal questions
become more imperative: the nuptial pair
promise ('swear', Hamburg 1726) love, faithfulness, support to each other in good and
bad times, 'until death do you part'; the

formula of marriage becomes weightier:
'. . . in God's stead . . ., as an ordained servant
of the church of Jesus Christ . . .'

The strong influence of the ecclesiastical
lawyer J. H. Boehmer (d. 1749) led to the view
that the marriage ceremony, or more
accurately the affirmative answers to the
marriage questions as a public declaration of
the *consensus matrimonialis* and their public
confirmation by the pastor, represented the
legitimate conclusion of a marriage. Church
marriage thus becomes a legal act which the
church performs for the state: 'A fully valid
marriage is brought about by the marriage
ceremony of the church' (*Allgemeines Preus-
siches Landrecht*, 1794). While in this way the
marriage ceremony acquired a clear legal
significance, during the Enlightenment it
increasingly lost its ecclesiastical character.
The service became a family celebration. In
many places the tradition was given up in
favour of a sentimental, verbose loquacious-
ness; the address to the bridal couple stood in
the foreground. Proposals to this effect are to
be found in the private liturgies which now
appear, but they also occur in official liturgies
as well. The traditional formula is expanded
at Württenberg 1809 as follows: 'God's
peace be with you. May your hearts and lives
be dedicated to him. May your home be a
dwelling of contentment, love and blessing.
May each of your days until you go down to
the grave be a new testimony to the grace of
the eternal Father, who rules over you.'

It is a mark of the nineteenth century that
in the West an obligatory civil marriage was
introduced, in 1848 by the Civil Code in
many districts, and in 1875 by national law.
The churches at first fought bitterly before
accepting the new situation ('Throne and
altar'), without of course fundamentally
altering the marriage formulae and without
being able to solve the problem of the 'double'
marriage, the official act and the church
ceremony. The local liturgies which arose
about 1900 provide either the scriptural
readings from Luther's *Traubüchlein* or a
formulated address in the form of a biblical
paraphrase; the questions are presented in
the traditional, verbose form, and the traditional expression 'pronounce' is used in the
formula of betrothal. Some private liturgies
are freer. Some of them understand marriage
as 'ordination to the priesthood of the home'
(J. Smend).

It is only the marriage forms that have been

produced in the last decade, above all the *Agende für Evangelisch-Lutherische Kirchen und Gemeinden* (1964, III, pp. 139-154), that draw the consequences from the introduction of obligatory civil marriage. Now the marriage ceremony is regarded as being the concern of the congregation. Accordingly, on the analogy of a congregational service it is introduced with a biblical vow, prayer or psalm, and then followed by the wedding sermon. The scripture readings provided are those from Luther's *Traubüchlein*. The questions now run: 'N., will you love and honour this N., born N., whom God entrusts to you, as your wife, and live a married life with her according to God's command and promise, in good and in bad days, until death parts you? Your answer should be, "Yes, with God's help."' The question to the wife takes the same form. There follow the exchange of rings, the joining of right hands, Matt. 19.6b and the Lord's Prayer. A new principle is that the marriage formula is to be understood as a consequence of the preceding prayer of intercession for the nuptial pair, as recently also in confirmation and ordination. The first formula runs: 'God the Father, Son and Holy Spirit bless your marriage. May he enlighten you by his word and fill you with his grace, so that you may remain in his community and reach everlasting life.' The second formula comes from pre-Reformation times: 'The blessing of the triune God be upon you and remain with you now and always.' A general prayer brings the ceremony to an end. Some other district churches have adopted the same principle of understanding the wedding as a liturgical ceremony directed towards the congregation and developing the marriage formula as a word of encouragement from the intercession for the bridal pair, though they have occasionally used other formulae (e.g. Evangelische Kirche der Union, 1963/64; outline form, Baden 1967; outline form, Kurhessen-Waldeck 1969). Most recently there have been attempts to provide more scriptural readings, to replace the questions by a 'form of assent' and to formulate the marriage formula as a personal wish, following a meditative prayer.

ALFRED NIEBERGALL

9. *Methodist*. The basis for Methodist marriage services is in John Wesley's edition of the 1662 *BCP* which appeared in 1784 as *The Sunday Service of the Methodists in North America*. Wesley's editing of the wedding service was relatively minor. For unexplained reasons he dropped the giving away of the bride. He also changed the phrase 'plight thee my troth' to 'plight thee my Faith', omitted the rubrics on impediments and receiving communion, removed any reference to the giving of the ring (perhaps in deference to Puritan practice), and dropped out the psalms and exhortation (probably for sake of brevity). In 1792 American Methodists abbreviated the service further, deleting the list of the ends of marriage and omitting the versicles and the prayer for childbearing.

The subsequent development of the service, both in Britain and in America, shows remarkable conservatism, though this may be natural in a service which is rooted in the structures of society itself. In America, the banns were dropped by the Methodist Episcopal Church South (MECS) in 1854 and in the Methodist Episcopal Church (MEC) in 1864, but the giving away of the woman was restored in MEC in 1916. The promise on the woman's part to obey was dropped as early as 1864 in the northern church and in 1910 in the second vows of the southern church. In 1864 MEC and in 1866 MECS restored the giving of the ring. Eventually all but one of the concluding prayers were omitted except for the Lord's Prayer.

Changes in the twentieth century have not been drastic and reflect the conservatism perhaps natural to rites of passage. Some indication of changed theological currents is reflected in the omission of such phrases as 'the dreadful day of judgment'. A prayer over the rings appeared in the 1944 *Book of Worship*, but the words of giving the rings did not recover the mention of one's body and worldly goods. Nor have the rest of the concluding prayers been restored. A rubric in the 1964 *Book of Worship* states that the sacrament of the Lord's Supper should be provided (if requested) at another time. Nevertheless, this sacrament seems increasingly to follow the wedding service.

In general the Black Methodist churches have preserved conservative versions of the 1792 service, especially the African Methodist Episcopal Church which retained the banns and concluding prayers. The Christian Methodist Episcopal Church was more prone to brevity and dropped the second vows though adding an optional ring ceremony.

The Book of Offices of the Methodist Church in Britain (1936) has been likewise conservative. Though the banns have disappeared, the basic shape is still that of the 1662 *BCP*. A new opening collect and the Lord's Prayer begin the service, followed by alternative charges. The concerns of civil laws are represented by inquiries as to legal impediments. Psalm 67 has been restored and I Cor. 13.4-8, 13 added, as has been one concluding prayer and another one rewritten. The giving of the rings has reappeared as has the phrase, 'I give thee my troth', a curious linguistic regression.

JAMES F. WHITE

10. *Old Catholic.* In the period after the Council of Trent, the view became widespread in the doctrine and practice of the Roman Catholic Church that it is the bridal couple themselves who mutually celebrate the sacrament of marriage. This view is also held to some degree in the Old Catholic Church. Alongside, however, and with even greater emphasis, the church teaches that according to an earlier and more correct view, the sacrament is bestowed by the priest through blessing and the laying on of hands; this is the case above all in the Netherlands, but also in the Polish National Catholic Church, in whose catechism it is said, 'The *priest* is the minister of the sacrament of matrimony' (Scranton, Pa. 1962, Question 410).

The Old Catholic churches in common recognize the civil betrothal as a legitimate contract of marriage. This is expressed by the fact that when the bridal couple answer 'Yes', there is always a reference to the marriage vows made earlier before the civil authorities. Thus according to the rite of the Old Catholic Church of Germany, the priest says, 'And now repeat before me, as the servant of the Christian church, and before these witnesses, the declaration of your marriage bond which you made before the representatives of the civil law, and receive the blessing of the church.'

The rite takes different forms in individual churches. Everywhere, however, it is composed of the same elements: address, repetition of the word 'Yes', blessing and giving of the rings, mutual joining of hands, blessing of the bridal couple, the Lord's Prayer and other prayers. The ceremony often, though not always, takes place within the framework of a nuptial mass.

In the Old Catholic Church of the Netherlands, there are two different forms of marriage:

(*a*) The sacrament of the blessing of the church. This sacrament is administered when two Old Catholics, or an Old Catholic and a Roman Catholic, get married. Since 1968 this has also been the case if the partner who is not an Old Catholic is a baptized and communicant member of a Protestant church and accepts this sacramental form of blessing. The formulary is taken from the *Rituale Romanum*, but is fairly freely revised.

(*b*) A non-sacramental form of blessing. Here there is no question of a lesser blessing – this is up to God alone – but this rite seeks to meet with the conviction of the partner who is not an Old Catholic if the latter is not a communicant member of any denomination, yet wants to place his marriage under God's blessing. It is a fairly simple form, consisting of readings (Ps. 121 and Eph. 5.22-33), some prayers, and a concluding blessing.

KURT PURSCH
A. E RÜTHY
C. TOL

11. *Plymouth Brethren.* The marriage service among the Open Brethren closely resembles the order followed in other Free Churches. Some variations arise, as in other denominations, because of differences in national law. In England, where a church building must be registered for the solemnization of matrimony, the person who conducts the marriage ceremony does not need to be specially licensed; what is important is the presence of a member of the local registrar's staff or of a member of the church recognized by the Registrar-General as custodian of the church's marriage register. In Scotland, where the place of the ceremony need not be registered, the person conducting the ceremony must be registered for that purpose by the Registrar-General for Scotland. Normally one responsible member of each Open Brethren congregation is so registered. It is his responsibility to see that the marriage certificate is duly completed by the bridal couple and the witnesses, signed by himself and delivered to the local registrar. As a matter of convenience, an office in Glasgow serves as a clearing-house for communication

between the local churches throughout Scotland and the Registrar-General.

The service takes the usual form: introductory words setting forth the divine institution and purpose of marriage and its indissoluble bond, so that the bridal couple and the congregation may understand clearly what Christian marriage involves by way of blessing and responsibility; then the mutual plighting of troth (for which national law may stipulate a minimum form of words), made while the couple clasp each other by the right hand and followed by the giving of the wedding ring. After pronouncing the couple to be husband and wife, the person conducting the ceremony prays for God's blessing on their marriage, and either he or someone else gives a short address appropriate to the occasion. Two or three suitable hymns are usually sung in the course of the service.

Among the Exclusive Brethren it has been customary for the legal part of the marriage to be performed in the registrar's office. This is followed by a service of prayer, thanksgiving and exhortation in the meeting room or other suitable place, which may well be combined with the wedding breakfast. In their way of life there is no line of demarcation between religious and social activities, just as there was none in the early church.

There is no uniform ruling among Brethren on the admission of divorced (more especially, of divorced and remarried) persons to church fellowship. The importance of maintaining Christian standards is recognized by all, but charity is recognized as one of those standards, so that in some places a less rigorist and in others a more rigorist attitude is taken up on this issue. A common attitude would admit them to church fellowship but not to public ministry in the church.

F. F. BRUCE

12. *Reformed*. All Reformed communions rejected the medieval idea that marriage is a sacrament, yet held high views of its importance. According to them the essence of marriage lies in the mutual declaration and promise of fidelity before witnesses, the consequence being that the 'pronouncing-together' by the minister was only a confirmation of the marriage. Yet marriage services appeared in all the service-books. Many changes have taken place from time to time, though there is a clear ancestral line through them all, since they were derived ultimately from the form of Farel.

Farel's *La manière et fasson*, first printed in 1533, was adopted by Calvin in his *La forme des prières* (1542) and in the *Forme of Prayer and Ministration of the Sacraments* (1558, 1561), followed by Knox's *Genevan Service-Book* (1556). *The Form of Prayers and Ministration of the Sacraments* (1562) came from the Genevan *Forme of Prayer* with only few changes. This was followed by the *Forme of Prayers* of 1564/5, printed in Edinburgh, which came to be known as *The Book of Common Order (BCO)*, of which fully seventy editions appeared before 1645. Throughout these the marriage service remained practically the same. The Westminster *Directory* (1644/5) made little change in the order though no prayers were printed. These books have greatly influenced the many service-books issued by English-speaking Presbyterians throughout the world.

Similarly the French and Swiss (Vaud, Geneva, Neuchâtel, etc.) Reformed service-books were derived from Farel through Calvin. We now indicate the form of the marriage service in Calvin and note some of the variations found in later service-books.

The first requirement is the proclamation of banns of marriage, though this was a pre-Reformation custom (as in Sarum). Banns were to be read on 'three several days'; in practice these would normally be Sundays or preaching days during the week, the point being that intimation should be made when the largest proportion of the parishioners would be present in church. The marriage was normally to take place in church before the sermon on Sunday. But later, at least in Scotland, Sunday marriages were prohibited to prevent 'riotous profanation' of the day, (cf. Westminster *Directory*). Modern service-books do not usually specify any particular day.

The service opens with an exhortation based on scripture, preceded in continental books and in modern English forms by the words, 'Our help is in the name of the Lord . . .'. The exhortation is long in early books (*BCO* has some 600 words), but much shorter in modern books. The couple are then challenged to confess any impediment, and the same challenge is made to the congregation. If none is alleged, the minister says, 'Forasmuch as no man speaketh against this thing, you, N., shall protest here before God and his holy congregation, that you have taken and are now content to have N. here present for your lawful wife, promising to keep her . . .' The answer is, 'Even so I take her before God and in the presence of this holy congregation.' The woman is addressed similarly and gives the same reply. (In some forms the two parties say the words of promise, either by repeating them after the minister, or by memory, or by reading them from a book or card.) The minister then addresses the people on the duties of marriage, reading from Matt. 19. The service ends with the blessing. In the early forms there is no declaration that the parties are married. The ring is not mentioned in early forms. But its use was widely customary, though the Westminster *Directory* says the two parties join the right hands during the vows, 'with no further ceremony'. This has been regarded as prohibition of the ring.

Two other points must be made. First, in some modern continental forms (e.g. Geneva, 1946 and Paris, 1963) there are two alternative addresses after the vows, the first being the more instructive, and the second the more intimate in nature. Secondly, some modern books (e.g. *BCO*, 1940) contain not only the marriage service itself but also a form for 'Blessing of a Civil Marriage' (*cf.* the title in some French books for the marriage service, 'Bénédiction du mariage', due to the French law which insists on a civil marriage).

J. A. LAMB

13. *Seventh-day Adventist.* While attributing no sacramental value to the marriage relationship, Seventh-day Adventists believe that marriage, a divine institution established by God himself prior to the fall of man, is the foundation of human society and was designed to be a blessing to mankind. True affection between man and woman is thus ordained by God. 'Central to God's holy plan was the creation of beings made in His image who would multiply and replenish the earth, and live together in purity, harmony, and happiness' (*Seventh-day Adventist Church Manual*, 1967, p. 251). Thus marriage and the family relationship should be the means for ennobling both partners and facilitating the development of mature, unselfish characters in the home. The marriage relationship is highly exalted in scripture, by using it to represent God's relationship to his people, to symbolize the union between Christ and his church, and thus typify the union of humanity

with divinity.

Monogamy (e.g. Gen. 2.21-24; Matt. 19.5) has ever been God's ideal plan, and any existing polygamous situations were simply tolerated. In the light of God's plan that man should have only one living wife, today when the gospel message in certain countries reaches a man living in a state of polygamy, he is upon conversion required to put away all his wives save one before he is eligible for baptism and membership in the SDA Church. In such cases proper provision is required to be made for the future support of the wives put away and of their children, and for their protection from disgrace (*see* General Conference *Working Policy*, 1968, pp. 48, 49).

In harmony with Christ's statement in Matt. 19.3-6, Seventh-day Adventists believe that the marriage relationship is to be indissoluble. The only scriptural ground for divorce is unfaithfulness to the marriage vow, and this rule is to be followed by the church, whether or not the state or prevailing custom allow larger liberty. In the case of adultery and in the event that reconciliation is not effected, 'the innocent spouse has the Biblical right to secure a divorce, and also to remarry. A spouse found guilty of adultery by the church shall be subject to church discipline . . . [He] has not the moral right to marry another while the innocent spouse still lives and remains unmarried and chaste, should he (or she) do so, he (or she), if a member, shall be disfellowshipped' (*Church Manual*, 1967, pp. 253, 254).

In the SDA Church only ordained ministers (*see* **Ordination** 14: Seventh-day Adventist) are authorized to perform the marriage ceremony. Since laws regarding marriage vary a great deal from country to country, the role played by the minister also takes on different forms. In countries where marriage is legally regarded as a state responsibility and purely civil contract, the SDA minister conducts a marriage service that takes the form of a nuptial blessing. Being a world-wide church, the SDA Church has 'no prescribed nuptial liturgy that must be followed' (*Manual for Ministers*, 1954, p. 100). Though customs vary in different countries, there are some well-defined principles adhered to by Adventists. The marriage of believers with unbelievers is expressly contrary to the teachings of the church. Relative simplicity and dignity in decorations and arrangements are recommended and ostentatious display in dress and ceremony should be avoided.

A typical Adventist marriage ceremony would include the wedding march, sermonette, musical item, charge, vows, prayer, and benediction. The SDA *Manual for Ministers* contains suggestions for sermonettes, charges and vows, providing for variation and allowing the minister to choose the form best suited for the occasion. In all cases, however, the ceremony must be kept strictly within the legal requirements.

B. B. BEACH

F. E. Brightman, *The English Rite*, 1915, I, pp. cxxiv, cxxv, clxiii, clxiv, ccxx; II, pp. 800-17; A. J. Collins, *Manuale Sarum*, 1960, pp. 44-59; *Constitution, Bylaws and Working Policy of the General Conference of Seventh-day Adventists*, 1968; H. A. Dombois and F. K. Schumann, *Familienrechtsreform. Dokumente und Abhandlungen*, 1955; H. A. Dombois and F. K. Schumann, *Weltliche und kirchliche Eheschliessung. Beiträge zur Frage des Eheschliessungsrechtes*, 1953; P. Graff, *Geschichte der Auflösung der alten gottesdienstlichen Formen in der evangelischen Kirche Deutschlands*, [2]1937, I, pp. 331-54; II, pp. 260-72; Clifford Howell, SJ, *Companion to the New Order of Marriage*, 1970; P. Jounel, in *L'Eglise en Prière*, 1961, pp. 594-605; T. Kliefoth, *Liturgische Abhandlungen*, 1896, I, p. 1; U. Küry, *Die altkatholische Kirche* (Die Kirchen der Welt, III), 1966, pp. 212-14; M. Luther, *Werke*, Weimar ed. 1883 ff. (WA), 30, III; C. Mahrenholz, *Die Neuordnung der Trauung*, 1959; William Maskell, *Monumenta Ritualia Ecclesiae Anglicanae*, 1846, I, pp. 42-64; A. Niebergall, 'Geschichte der evangelischen Trauung in Hessen, Teil I', in *Jahrbuch der hessischen kirchengeschichtlichen Vereinigung*, Vol. 21, 1970; A. L. Richter, *Die evangelischen Kirchenordnungen des 16. Jahrhunderts*, 2 vols., 1846; G. Rietschel-P. Graff, *Lehrbuch der Liturgik*, [2]1951, pp. 701-56; M. Righetti, *La Storia Liturgica*, 1959, IV, pp. 455-72; A. Rinkel, 'Ehe und Sakrament', *Internationale Kirchliche Zeitschrift*, 31, 1941, pp. 1-28; E. Schillebeeckx, *Marriage, Secular Reality and Saving Mystery*, 1965; E. Sehling, *Die evangelischen Kirchenordnungen des XVI Jahrhunderts*, 14 vols., 1902 ff.

Mattins *see* **Canonical Hours**

Maundy Thursday

The title for Thursday in Holy Week (q.v.) derives through Old French *mandé* from the Latin *mandatum novum*, 'a new commandment' (John 13.34), associated with the ceremonial of washing of feet, which is still continued in some token form in Rome. The English distribution of Maundy money by the sovereign is a vestigial trace of this

A. A. MCARTHUR

Methodist Worship

1. *Britain*. John Wesley, a presbyter of the Church of England, intended his preachers and his people to follow his own example by attending 'the Church Service', i.e. the services of the parish churches of the Church of England; they were to be supplemented, not superseded, by simple Methodist preaching services at 5 a.m. and 5 p.m. The Methodists were increasingly reluctant to attend the parish churches where indeed they were not always welcomed and, though the custom of attending the parish churches lingered for a long time in country districts, they increasingly established in their chapels a complete pattern of their own Sunday services, which after the Plan of Pacification in 1795 included in nearly all places the Lord's Supper. From this pattern the preaching service at 5 a.m. eventually disappeared, as did evensong in the afternoon; but evening services, usually at 6 p.m. or 6.30 p.m. became very popular. The morning service, usually at 10.30 a.m. or 11 a.m. replaced attendance at the parish church for morning prayer, litany, and ante-communion (qq.v.). In a few chapels in England and a larger number overseas this morning service still consists of morning prayer, either from the *BCP* or from Wesley's version of it in *The Sunday Service*, together with hymns and sermon. But in most churches the service was a simpler preaching service, though not quite as simple as the supplementary 5 a.m. preaching service had been. It consisted of hymns, lessons, extempore prayers and sermon, though occasionally with traces of morning prayer such as a psalm before the OT lesson. The evening service almost always took this simpler form.

The holy communion was usually observed monthly in towns, quarterly in villages, after the morning or evening preaching service. For that service a liturgical book was generally used, at least in the Wesleyan chapels, as also for occasional offices. In the preaching services, liturgical books (q.v.)

were little used except where the custom was retained of saying morning prayer, often called 'the liturgical service'.

These services were enriched, as Methodist worship still is, by the use of hymns, especially those of Charles Wesley, which are in some sense the 'liturgy' of Methodism.

To these services were added not only such 'instituted' means of grace as scripture reading, prayer (private, family, public) and fasting, but also 'prudential' means such as the love feast (q.v.), the watch-night, the covenant service (qq.v.), and the distinctive Methodist forms of fellowship meeting; society meeting, class meeting (q.v.), band meeting. Some of these survive, and they have given a distinctive tone of fellowship to all Methodist worship. There was also open-air preaching. The pattern of Sunday during most of Methodist history also included morning and afternoon sessions of the Sunday school, which in various ways involved many people.

The main pattern still remains, but in recent decades fresh tendencies have appeared. The afternoon session of the Sunday school is tending to disappear, and the morning session is combined with the morning service under such titles as junior church. The children attend the earlier part of the service, and then depart to their own session. The morning service has acquired a greater prominence; the evening service has a declining attendance, and will probably take more experimental forms.

The British Methodist Conference of 1968 authorized for experimental use *The Sunday Service*, a revival of Wesley's title. This seeks to establish, primarily at morning services, a flexible structure, combining fixed and free elements, which may be used whether or not the service culminates in the Lord's Supper. The structure of the preaching service is as follows, optional elements being in brackets: (hymn or psalm), invocation or prayer of adoration, (commandments), confession, (text declaring forgiveness), (*Gloria in excelsis* or other hymn), collect of the day or other prayers, OT lesson or epistle or both, (hymn or psalm), gospel, (dismissal of children), sermon, (hymn), (announcements), (baptism or other ordinances of the church), intercessions, Lord's Prayer, (hymn), (grace). When there is no communion, a prayer of thanksgiving for creation and redemption and of dedication is to be said before or after the intercessions. Other forms may be substituted for all the prayers except the Lord's Prayer.

The structure of the Lord's Supper, which immediately follows the preaching service or some simpler form of ministry of the word, is as follows: (peace), (Nicene Creed), offertory, (with hymn), the thanksgiving, the breaking of the bread, (prayer of humble access), communion, final prayer, (hymn), dismissal, (blessing). The thanksgiving includes the dialogue, long preface with recital of the mighty acts of God, *Sanctus*, *Benedictus qui venit*, words of institution, acclamation, anamnesis, modified forms of oblation and epiclesis, prayers for benefits of communion, doxology (qq.v.).

A. RAYMOND GEORGE

2. *USA*. The forms of worship used in American Methodism reflect in many ways the social and cultural situations of American Methodists. These forms of worship often have had more in common with those of other American denominations than with English precedents.

John Wesley remained a priest of the Church of England throughout his lifetime, highly esteeming and utilizing the *BCP* even while supplementing it with other forms. In 1784 he sent his followers in the newly independent USA a book of over three hundred pages, entitled *The Sunday Service of the Methodists in North America with Other Occasional Services*. It was his revision and abridgement of the 1662 *BCP*, not too different from that adopted a few years later by the new Protestant Episcopal Church. Perhaps even more significant, Wesley sent over at the same time a hymn-book.

Wesley was, it turned out, a poor judge of the American situation. Though the *Sunday Service* was reprinted in 1786 and 1790, it hardly survived Wesley as far as American usage was concerned. One year after Wesley's death, the *Sunday Service* was replaced by thirty-seven pages of 'Sacramental Services, &c.' in the 1792 *Discipline*. Gone were morning and evening prayer, the psalms, litany, and the collects, epistles, and gospels for the Lord's Supper. Orders remained for both sacraments, weddings, funerals, and the forms for the ordination of deacons, elders, and bishops. These services appeared thenceforth in the *Disciplines*. After the split of 1844 the Methodist Episcopal Church renamed this section of the *Discipline* 'The Ritual' (1848). The Methodist Episcopal Church, South, dropped the term 'Sacramental Services, &c.' in 1854 in favour of no title and adopted the term 'The Ritual' in 1870. Both churches eventually added services for the reception of new members and various dedications.

'The Ritual', however, was only used on those occasions when the sacraments or occasional offices were celebrated. Methodist worship tended to centre around preaching services. This is especially the case in the evangelization of the west, a process largely contributing to the rapid growth of Methodism from a small sect to the largest Protestant church in America during the nineteenth century. Bishop Francis Asbury (the American John Wesley) and many of his preachers were men of the frontier, preaching and organizing societies wherever they could gather a few individuals. In such frontier situations, worship usually consisted of fervent preaching and hymn-singing. Since many of the frontiersmen were illiterate, a type of hymn involving considerable repetition evolved. These so-called 'gospel songs' were often testimonials to the worshipper's conversion experience.

At yearly intervals, camp meetings (q.v.) were held in which crowds assembled from considerable distances to hear evangelistic preaching. At times the services developed highly emotional reactions. After several days, the camp meeting ended with separate communion services conducted by the various denominations sponsoring the session. In the second third of the nineteenth century, the revival system spread similar techniques to the churches on the more sedate eastern coast, utilizing such practices as preaching for conversions, the sawdust trail, the mourner's bench, and protracted meetings. Much of the historic content and forms of Christian worship were bypassed in favour of a pragmatic spirit that pointed to results calculated in the number of converts.

The period from 1920 to 1970, on the other hand, has been the era of middle-class respectability due to the upward social mobility of most Methodists. A second Gothic revival occurred in Methodism prompted by denominational executives. Choral music, sometimes of high quality, came to be a normal part of worship, often while congregation singing declined. Orders of worship began to appear in *The Methodist Hymnal* in 1905. In 1944 the Methodist Church published its first *Book of Worship* and another one followed twenty years later.

Beginning about 1966, another tendency appeared in the growth of experimentation with the forms of worship and a refusal to believe that recovery of past forms was the answer to making worship authentic and relevant. Many innovators have looked to new communications media as indicating directions that worship might move, especially in adding non-verbal forms of worship.

In general, the black Methodist churches have been less attracted by the forms of respectability. Their worship has often retained the spontaneity, rhythmic music, and high degree of participation characteristic of the revival system.

In all these changes Methodist worship has reflected profound changes in the people who worship. Perhaps without deliberation, they have often adopted those forms which seemed most natural to them.

JAMES F. WHITE

The Book of Worship, 1964; William F. Dunkle, Jr and Joseph D. Quillian, Jr, eds., *Companion to the Book of Worship*, 1970; H. Grady Hardin, Joseph D. Quillian, Jr, James F. White, *The Celebration of the Gospel*, 1964; *The Methodist Hymnal*, 1964.

Metrical Psalms

The ancestor of the modern hymnal was the metrical psalter, comprising versifications of the psalms with simple strophic tunes designed to fit the metres employed. Perhaps the most familiar example of a metrical psalm is the version of the hundredth psalm in which the original prose, 'O be joyful in the Lord, all ye lands', has become 'All people that on earth do dwell'. Included in almost every modern hymnal, and hence usually thought of as a hymn, those words first appeared in *Fourscore and Seven Psalms of David* published in Geneva in 1561. The tune always associated with them is from the still earlier *Genevan Psalter* of 1551. Thus, both words and music take us back to the same source – the English Protestant exiles who fled to Geneva in 1553 to escape persecution under Queen Mary at home.

First given a formal place in Protestant worship by Calvin, the metrical psalm owed its origin, not to him, but to Clement Marot, a poet at the court of Francis I who had begun to translate the psalms into French verse in 1533. Marot's versions soon began to enjoy great popularity at the Catholic court; but they were quickly taken up in Protestant circles, first by the Huguenots and later by Calvin for use among his 'little flock'.

By coincidence, shortly after Marot had begun to produce his versified psalms, Thomas Sternhold started upon a similar task at the court of Edward VI; and some time before his death in 1549 nineteen of his metrical psalms were published under the title *Certaine Psalmes . . drawen into Englishe metre*. To that nucleus, John Hopkins added several versifications in 1551, certain of the English exiles in Geneva completing the translation of the Psalter between 1556 and 1562. The complete version of the metrical psalter thus produced was first published in the latter year – four years after the accession of Elizabeth I – under the title *The Whole Booke of Psalmes, collected into Englysh metre by T. Starnhold, I. Hopkins and others . . .* The book contained, in addition, a few hymns, metrical versions of the canticles, and a selection of tunes, some of which were drawn from the *Genevan Psalter*. Under the Royal Injunctions of 1559, a hymn was allowed to be sung 'in the beginning or at the end of Common Prayer'; thus legally sanctioned, *The Whole Book of Psalms* became recognized as the chief song book for Anglican worship. Commonly bound up with the Bible and the *BCP*, the collection begun by Sternhold and Hopkins (and invariably referred to by those names) held that authorized position until a *New Version* was published in 1696.

The work of Nahum Tate, the Poet Laureate, and Dr Nicholas Brady, the *New Version* was designed to supplant the 'scandalous doggerel' of Sternhold and Hopkins. It was to become the source of many of the hymns in current use, including 'As pants the hart' – the metrical version of Ps. 42. Authorized for use in churches by an Order in Council of William III, 'Tate and Brady' yet never superseded 'Sternhold and Hopkins', the two collections serving side by side until the advent of the hymn-book ousted them both during the nineteenth century. The best of the contents of both Old and New Versions were then incorporated into the new hymnals where they still serve, together with the fine old tunes originally associated with them.

M. Frost, *English and Scottish Psalm and Hymn Tunes*, 1953; J. Julian, Preface to *Hymns Ancient and Modern, Historical Edition*, 1909; R. R. Terry, *Calvin's First Psalter*, 1932.

BERNARR RAINBOW

Mission and Worship

The contemporary development of the doctrine of mission (*see* **Mission**, *DCT*), has inevitably raised the question of its relationship to worship. This relationship may be examined in three complementary ways: (1) The precise nature of the relationship may be considered. (2) Specific acts of worship, e.g. the eucharist, may be interpreted in terms of mission. (3) Particular elements in the cultus, e.g. prayer, may be given a missionary dimension. An examination of worship and mission under each of these three heads will illustrate the scope of this subject.

1. A contrast has to be noted between the OT understanding of Israel's vocation and the role that worship has to play within that vocation, and the NT understanding of the vocation of the church and the role that worship has to play within that vocation. Briefly put, Israel's vocation is to be a holy people (Lev. 19.2), i.e. a people whose life is patterned after the very being of its holy God. In so far as this is achieved, Israel then becomes a 'light to the Gentiles'; it is a witness before the nations to Yahweh in order that the nations themselves may come to acknowledge his universal lordship. The function of worship in relation to this vocation is to enable Israel to be holy; it is a means of sanctification for the Chosen People, who are set apart for the worship of Yahweh (Ex. 19.6). The Temple cultus is both the guarantee of the purity of Yahwism and the centre to which the nations are to· come (Isa. 2.2f.). It will be noticed that Israel's vocation is interpreted centripetally; Israel is not sent to the nations; instead they are to come to it, attracted by its life and worship. In exact conformity with this, Israelite worship is understood centripetally; it has its true centre in a single place, namely the Jerusalem Temple, and it is to this that all the nations are to come.

The NT presents the antithesis to this view,

in that this centripetal attitude is replaced by a centrifugal one. The church's vocation is to go out; it is to participate in the divine mission (Matt. 28.19; John 20.21; Acts 1.8). It is to join in God's action in the world as he continues his movement of humanization, assisting man towards that maturity or fullness that is embodied in Christ. The function of worship in relation to this vocation is to celebrate God's action in the world and 'so to proclaim the Lord's death until he come' (I Cor. 11.26), this being involved in the eating of the bread and the drinking of the wine at the eucharist (q.v.). Thus, as the church's vocation is interpreted centrifugally, so is its worship; it does not have a centre in a single place; anywhere is the place of encounter with God in the context of everyday life, and in so far as any temple continues to exist, this is not a building of stone but a community living in the world (II Cor. 6.16). Hence the OT is consistent in understanding both the vocation and the worship of Israel centripetally, while the NT is equally consistent but understands both the vocation and worship of the church centrifugally.

To these concepts must be added a third, namely the contrast between the general understanding of Christians today of their vocation and worship and that which we have just examined in the NT. As a consequence of the great missionary awakening of the eighteenth and nineteenth centuries, many Christians now understand the vocation of the church centrifugally, but they still persist in viewing their cultic acts centripetally. They thus give up the logical consistency that is to be found in both the OT and NT, and attempt to combine the NT centrifugal concept of vocation with the OT centripetal concept of worship in terms of ingathering. Hence the relationship of worship and mission has for decades been defined in terms of gathering and sending. The idea of gathering and sending was prominent in German missiological thought at the end of the last century and it is often re-presented at the present day. According to this, worship is an occasion for the gathering together of the Christian community in order that its members may be strengthened to engage in mission. So cultic acts and missionary activity can be compared to breathing in and breathing out, which are both necessary for life, and hence both worship and mission – gathering and sending – are

essential for the church. The analogy is a plausible one, but is it accurate? In effect it merely associates centripetalism – breathing in – with centrifugalism – breathing out – and therefore fails to resolve the basic tension between them. Moreover, it involves the idea that cultic acts are interruptions in the church's participation in mission. When the church ceases its centrifugal action in mission, for however brief the periods may be, in order to engage in centripetal actions or worship, it is no longer being missionary during those cultic acts – in terms of the analogy, one is breathing either in or out; one cannot do the two at once. Whereas if mission and worship are to be truly united, the cultic assembly must be understood within the context of mission; the coming together takes place in mission and it is not preparatory to mission. The church is the church when it is participating in the mission of God; if it is to fulfil its role constantly, it cannot disengage itself from mission in cultic activity. The church services then must not be conceived as halting places on the way nor as iron rations; they are an essential part of being on the way. So while the gathering and sending analogy does point to a relationship, it is not a relationship of unity, and this is precisely what has to be rediscovered if we are to be true to the NT. Worship then is not a means to mission; nor is it a preparation for mission, since we worship in mission. The inadequacy of the analogy should become more apparent, as we examine what worship means from a centrifugal or missionary perspective.

Worship, as presented in the NT, is the joyful celebration of life in the world; it is the response of man to what God has done and is doing in history. Two examples will serve to illustrate this.

In Luke 17, Jesus is met by ten lepers who ask him to have mercy on them. He accedes to their request and they are made whole. One of them, a Samaritan, recognizes in this the act of God and accordingly he worships – 'praising God with a loud voice, he fell on his face at Jesus' feet, giving him thanks' (17.16). The man does not draw apart from the world in order to worship; the basis of his act of worship is his response to God's action in the world – his restoration to wholeness by Christ – and this takes the form of expressing thanks and giving praise. The Lord's Supper (q.v.) itself, throughout the apostolic age, was also essentially a secular act, since it was an everyday meal, although one which, while not ceasing to be a source of physical nourishment, was at the same time a vehicle of worship. So it can be said that in the NT worship was not defined in terms of what happened at a certain time when and at a certain place where Christians assembled. What happened on those occasions was understood within the context of response to God in their total existence.

Here we have worship interpreted from a centrifugal position. Just as the world is the sphere of mission, so it is of worship which is to be offered in terms of the Christians' total existence. The church of the apostolic age does not withdraw from mission to engage in cultic acts which prepare it for mission; it never ceases to be in mission in the secular world whether it is preaching, serving or worshipping. There can therefore be no great single centre of worship corresponding to the Jerusalem Temple.

2. The two chief Christian liturgical acts, baptism (q.v.) and the eucharist, can themselves be understood in terms of mission. It is possible to indicate this by a series of theses which, in a full treatment, would require considerable expansion:

(*a*) Baptism is ordination to the royal priesthood and acceptance into the covenant, both priesthood and covenant being understood in terms of mission. The eucharist renews both the ordination and the covenant.

(*b*) Baptism, with its pattern of life and death, initiates us into mission. The eucharist re-establishes us in this pattern.

(*c*) Baptism includes us in the obedience of Christ and so in his mission. The eucharist renews our commitment to God and so to mission.

(*d*) Baptism is an eschatological sacrament and so is the eucharist; both are intimately related in this sense to mission.

3. Of the many specific elements that make up an act of worship, two may be selected to demonstrate their necessary missionary dimension, namely prayer and the dismissal (q.v.).

According to Karl Barth, Christ's 'earthly mission was accepted through his prayers as well as by his preaching and his mighty works'. This means that prayer is a part of mission. Prayer is not something separate

from mission nor is it the cause of mission. When the church prays, as when Christ prayed in Galilee, it is engaged in mission; it participates in the divine action for the world. So in Eph. 6.18, prayer is referred to in the context of the weapons of warfare against the alien powers that threaten to dominate men and from which they are to be liberated through mission. Prayer is therefore one aspect of the total missionary outreach.

Next, the dismissal. Although it is now customary to conclude every service with a blessing (q.v.), in the early church the dismissal did not take this form and was very brief. Indeed it is or should be an echo of the missionary command in Matt. 28. Any and every service is most fittingly brought to an end by a dismissal which expresses this outgoing to the world at large. It is therefore not a cosy rounding-off of a cultic act but part of the sending of God's servants in mission.

Within the NT there is a continual emphasis upon the unity of worship and mission. Not only does Paul describe mission in cultic terms and cultic acts in terms of mission (*cf.* Rom. 12.1; II Cor. 2.15; Phil. 2.17), but the life and work of Jesus are similarly spoken of in terms both of mission and of worship (John 6.51, 57; 12.49; Heb. 3.1). It is this relationship of unity that is gradually being rediscovered at the present day.

J. G. Davies, *Worship and Mission*, 1966; J. Rossell, *Mission in a Dynamic Society*, 1968.

EDITOR

Mitre *see* Vestments (2*j*)

Mixed Chalice

The reference is to the mingling of water and wine in the cup at the eucharist. This was the invariable practice of the early church (*cf.* Justin, *Apol.* I, 65, 67; Cyprian, *Ep.* 63.13) and was probably what Jesus himself did at the Last Supper, since it was usual for the Jews to mix water with their wine. All the ancient liturgies either contain a direction for the mixing or refer to it in the prayers, e.g. in the *Apostolic Constitutions* (8.12), reading the words of institution, the priest says: 'Likewise also mixing the cup of wine and water and blessing it, he gave it to them.'

Various symbolic meanings have been attached to this. Some have seen it as a sign of the union of the people with Christ, others of the issue of water and blood from his side on the cross, and others again of the union of the two natures in Christ. This latter interpretation has led the Armenians to reject the practice because it conflicts with their monophysitism, i.e. belief in the one nature of Christ.

It was rejected, too, at the Reformation by Luther, who regarded it as symbolizing an impossible participation of the human with the pure work of God. Churches in the Calvinist tradition, e.g. the Church of Scotland and the Reformed Church of France, do not practice it. The 1549 *BCP* ordered it, but the rubric was omitted in 1552. It is customary in the Episcopal Church of Scotland, but was expressly forbidden by canon 37 of the Church of Ireland. It is widespread, but not universal, in the Anglican Communion, having been declared legal in a judgment in the case of the bishop of Lincoln (1891).

In the Liturgy of St Chrysostom *hot* water is added to the chalice at the commixture (q.v.). The origins of this are unknown, but it appears to have been established from at least the sixth century. This *zeon* or living water, as it is called, is said to symbolize the fervency of faith and the descent of the Holy Spirit.

EDITOR

Monstrance

A vessel designed for the purpose of showing the consecrated host to the people came into use from the thirteenth century in the Latin West as a result of the increased cultus of the reserved sacrament that arose in the later Middle Ages. No such cultus has ever existed in the Eastern Orthodox Church or the lesser Eastern Churches. The earliest forms of the monstrance were pyxes (q.v.) standing upon a stem and foot with openings or fenestrations on the sides of the pyx as in the thirteenth-century example preserved in the Church of St Quentin, Hasselt, Limburg. The next stage was to replace the metal sides with a cylinder of glass (*see* Plate 32); then finally it assumed the form of a circular window surrounded by a silver or gold frame with rays. The ceremonies associated with the use of the monstrance arose in the Low Countries and Germany, first in connection with the Feast of Corpus Christi (q.v.), but in the Counter-Reformation era

Plate 32 The Belem Monstrance,
Lisbon, Portugal

the exposition of the host became very much more frequent (*see* **Benediction, Exposition**).

The monstrance and its associated ceremonies have come into use in the Church of England since the Catholic revival, but liturgical reforms now taking place in the Roman Catholic Church are tending to discourage this type of devotion to the blessed sacrament.

A. A. King and C. E. Pocknee, *Eucharistic Reservation in the Western Church*, 1965.

C. E. POCKNEE

Moravian Worship

Moravian worship cannot properly be understood or evaluated without some introduction, however brief, to the history of the church itself.

The Moravian Church came into being in the kingdom of Bohemia (now part of Czechoslovakia) in the year 1457. It consisted at first of a small group of men and women who lived in brotherly fellowship according to the principles of the Sermon on the Mount. They called themselves 'The Unity of Brethren', or in Latin, *Unitas Fratrum*, which is the official name of the Moravian Church. In 1467 they established their own ministry with episcopal orders and withdrew from the Church of Rome.

In 1620 Protestantism was overthrown in Bohemia and the *Unitas Fratrum* ceased to exist as an organized body. But about a century later some survivors from the old *Unitas* fled into Saxony and were allowed to settle on the estates of a Lutheran nobleman, Count Nicolaus Ludwig von Zinzendorf. Other religious refugees joined them and together they founded a new community called Herrnhut. This diverse and often disunited group experienced a 'second Pentecost' at a celebration of the Lord's Supper on 13 August 1727, which marks the birth of the renewed Moravian Church.

One direct result of this renewal was a burning desire to carry the gospel wherever Christ should call, and it was in fulfilment of this task that the renewed church became established in the eighteenth and nineteenth centuries in England, North, Central and South America, the Caribbean, Africa and India.

Moravian worship as it is practised today contains active elements from these three periods of the Church's history – the ancient church, the renewed church and the missionary church.

In the ancient *Unitas Fratrum*, in sharp contrast to the Roman Church, worship was Bible centred and congregation orientated. To provide for this, the first hymn-book of the *Unitas Fratrum* was published in 1501 and was followed a few years later by a translation of the Bible into the Czech language, the Kralitz Bible. The services in this early period were extremely simple and consisted of the singing of a hymn or hymns, a threefold reading of psalm, gospel and epistle, and a sermon. 'Free' prayer was linked with the Bible reading and the sermon, but from about 1566 onwards Luther's 'German litany' was introduced into the Moravian hymn-book. A liturgy retaining elements from these early sources is still used in parts of the Moravian Church.

In the renewed church some of the forms of worship from the ancient *Unitas* were taken over and adapted, but other distinctive services developed to meet particular needs. Of these the following are of special interest in that they are still in use:

1. The love feast (q.v.). The 'agape' of apostolic times was part of the common meal which ended with the Lord's Supper. The spontaneous revival of this custom in the renewed Moravian Church at Herrnhut followed the rich experiences of unity and fellowship in the historic communion service on 13 August 1727. At the close of this service many members were loath to leave the church but continued in prayer, in religious conversation and hymn singing. Hearing of this Count Zinzendorf sent food to the church – 'in order for them to stay undisturbed together'. From this the love feast grew into a recognized service expressing in a special way the fellowship of each member with his brethren and sisters. The Moravian love feast today consists of the singing of hymns and an informal discourse by the minister on the life and work of the church, during which a simple meal is served and partaken of together.

2. The use in public and private worship of the Moravian 'Daily Texts' or 'Watchwords'. Soon after the renewal of the church, the Herrnhut elders went each morning from house to house giving a scriptural 'watchword' for the day as a guide to meditation and conduct. Count Zinzendorf selected these texts and later added to them a few lines from hymns in current use. In 1730 a collection of these 'watchwords' was printed in advance for the year 1731. Moravian family worship usually consists of the reading of the texts for the day followed by Bible reading and prayer. The 'text book' is printed in twenty-six languages with a circulation of over a million copies. It is frequently used in public worship especially in the love feast, which closes with a short homily on the NT text for that particular day.

In the missionary period, with the granting to the provinces and mission fields of the Moravian Church of a greater measure of autonomy, coupled with a diminution in the control and influence formerly exercised by Herrnhut, each province has tended to develop worship forms and usages to suit its own needs. But in the Moravian Church throughout the world there is still a recognizable basic pattern of worship which owes something to the two earlier periods of the ancient and the renewed church. The chief characteristics of this basic pattern are:

1. The use in public worship of liturgical forms of service, and of 'free' services comprising hymns, 'free' prayer, scripture reading(s) and a sermon.

2. Regular observance of the Lord's Supper in which common features are the distribution of the elements to the congregation during the singing of hymns, partaking of the elements together, and the conclusion of the service with a so-called 'covenant hymn' during which the members of the congregation exchange the right hand of fellowship with each other in token of the renewal of their 'covenant' of love and service with Christ and with one another.

3. The use of the love feast as a preparation for the Lord's Supper, or to mark some special church gathering, festival or anniversary.

Congregational singing has always had a major part in Moravian worship. It is therefore not surprising that the Moravian Church has produced down the centuries many famous hymn writers, including Michael Weisse, Count Zinzendorf, John Cennick and James Montgomery, whose works are to be found in most Protestant hymn-books.

J. T. and K. G. Hamilton, *History of the Moravian Church*, 1967; J. E. Hutton, *A History of the Moravian Church*, 1909; A. J. Lewis, *Zinzendorf, The Ecumenical Pioneer*, 1962.

J. H. FOY

Motet

The motet, a part song for two or more voices, usually unaccompanied, derives its name from the French *mot* (word) on account of the upper part in the early medieval motet having a text and music of its own, instead of being a *vocalise* as in twelfth-century *organum* (*see* **Polyphony**).

The medieval motet and its allied forms cover a huge quantity of music, little of which in modern times is sung in church but which can be fairly frequently heard in the concert hall, on the radio and gramophone records, performed by specialist vocal groups. The characteristic features of the thirteenth-century motet were that the text in the upper part (*duplum*) was a paraphrase of the plainsong text in the *tenor* or lower part, and another paraphrase would be added when a third voice (*triplum*) was included. This plan is well shown in the example below:

1. *In. saeculum saeculi, Artifex saeculi,* etc.
2. *In saeculum saeculi, supra mulieres,* etc.
3. *IN SAECULUM* (plainsong *cantus firmus*).

Each part was independent, so that if, in fact, one of the two upper parts was omitted or was sung alone, the music still made sense, but the fragmented plainsong, deprived of its flowing phrase and rhythm, by itself would not.

Polytextuality enabled the clerical poet-musicians to make a kind of musical mosaic in this way but, as prayer, one that could only be appreciated fully by the singers. This inherently attractive scheme became corrupted by the use of polylingual texts, sometimes of purely secular origin; thus a French *chanson* might be in the top part with the liturgical Latin texts below. Among the many developments in succeeding centuries the most important was, at the start of the fifteenth century, free invention replacing the use of plainsong and a contrapuntal treatment in which the parts were equally dependent on one another, often imitating one another's phrases and none being *primus inter pares*. About 1530 the Renaissance-style motet spread throughout Europe, inspiring some of the finest church music in existence, contributed by such great masters as the Flemish Josquin, de Monte, and Lassus, the Roman Palestrina and the Venetian Gabrielis, the Spanish Morales and Victoria, the English William Byrd and Peter Philips.

The motet was always an extra-liturgical piece, that is, it had no necessary place in mass or vespers (qq.v.); the liturgy, strictly speaking, required that if a motet used the text (or a part) of the offertory, the latter had still to be sung in plainsong in its usual place in the mass before the motet was introduced.

Settings of the proper of the mass have been called motets, for example, those in Byrd's *Gradualia*, his greatest work, but in this case they should properly bear their liturgical titles. Palestrina, for example, set the offertory texts for the whole of the church's year and they are published under that title.

ALEC ROBERTSON

Music *see* **Anthem, Antiphon, Canticles, Carol, Chants, Chants of the Proper of the Mass, Choir (Musical), Church Modes, Divine Office, Gregorian Chant, Hymns, Metrical Psalms, Motet, Music (Modern), Music in the Mass of the Roman Rite, Notation and Rhythm, Office Hymn, Organ, Polyphony, Psalmody, Psalm Tones, Responsorial Psalms and Responsories, Roman Missal, Spirituals, Tract**

Music, Modern

A vague term used to denote the music of the present century or its antecedents in the romantic movement. In the later nineteenth century the Austro-German tradition, and its means of structuring music through tonality or key relationships, was extended by composers within it and challenged by those from outside. Particularly crucial was the work of Arnold Schoenberg and his pupils Anton Webern and Alban Berg, sometimes referred to as the Second Viennese School – a misleading title, as the tradition was continuous, even though Schoenberg's development of twelve-note technique appeared revolutionary at the time. Claude Debussy (France), Bela Bartok (Hungary), Igor Stravinsky (Russia), and Charles Ives (USA) must also be included among the major innovators of the first half of this century.

After the Second World War there emerged a generation less radical than some of their elders and often showing humanitarian or specifically religious commitment: Olivier Messiaen (France), Luigi Dallapiccola (Italy), Michael Tippett and Benjamin Britten (England), Hans Werner Henze (Germany). There is a breadth of popular appeal in much of the work of Aaron Copland (USA) and Dmitri Shostakovitch (Russia). John Cage (USA) is the pioneer of the musical avantgarde where some of the recent work of Karlheinz Stockhausen (Germany) also belongs.

The twentieth century is the age of jazz, which has grown rapidly from Negro folk music into a performing art of great virtuosity and international acclaim. The 1960s have seen a flowering of pop, or rock, and the importance of groups such as The Beatles is recognized by critics and historians as well as fans. The range of musical experience is now greater than ever, thanks to recordings and broadcasting, and electronic resources are increasingly used for musical composition of all kinds.

These developments have resulted in a fragmentation of musical society where separate groups of listeners specialize in jazz, orchestral or avant-garde. There is no longer a common musical language, although there are signs that these categories can interact. A recent example is the *Sinfonia* by Luciano Berio (Italy), which uses the Swingle Singers and quotes from Mahler in the context of Berio's own idiom.

The use of contemporary music in church presents problems which reflect wider debates. On the purely musical level, church choirs find the rhythms and harmonies of a Stravinsky difficult to master and congregations do not always respond to Messiaen's visionary organ music. Stockhausen's electronic *Gesang der Jünglinge* was written in 1956 for a large cathedral but is not often heard in such places. There is a split between the most vital music and the opportunities the church affords. Some composers have specialized in writing music for their liturgy, and some churches have commissioned works from living composers. Some are undistinguished, but there have been many inspiring concert works to sacred texts, such as Stravinsky's *Symphony of Psalms, Canticum Sacrum* and *Threni*; Britten's *War Requiem*; the *St Luke Passion* of Penderecki (Poland), which brings together monody, choral polyphony and avant-garde effects.

Some composers, like Britten, have written church music in an existing tradition which respects the formalities of public worship. But in the search for a means of communication, the church has turned enviously to the success of folk groups and there are now many masses and hymns in popular style. The situation can only be regarded as transitional, a challenge to the future, where a questing and experimental attitude is healthier than the formulae of the past.

William W. Austin, W. W. Norton and J. M. Dent, *Music in the Twentieth Century*, 1966; Wilfred Mellers, *Music in a New Found Land*, 1964; E. Routley, *The Church and Music*,

1967; Eric Salzman, *Twentieth-Century Music
– An Introduction*, 1967; H. H. Stucken-
schmidt, *Twentieth-Century Music,* 1969.

P. DICKINSON

Music in the Mass of the Roman Rite

The Tridentine *Missale Romanum* of 1570 is
frequently spoken of as if it were a creation
of the Council of Trent as a result of proceedings concerning it in the session presided
over by Pope Pius V. In fact, as Dom David
Knowles has pointed out, it was in all
essentials a replica of the Roman missal of
1474, and that, in its turn, followed the
practice of the church in the reign of Innocent
II which itself derived from the usage of the
epoch of Gregory the Great and his successors in the seventh century. The 1570 missal
was, therefore, essentially traditional, more
so, some scholars think, than the reformed
missal published in 1971.

It is important to realize that when the
present Latin mass is celebrated today (replacing the Tridentine mass) 'the treasury of
sacred music', as Pope Paul VI called it,
dating from Gregorian chant (q.v.) to the first
decade of the seventeenth century when the
greatest era of liturgical music came to a
close, is available to choirs competent to do
justice to it.

The new Roman missal is now imposed on
the whole Roman Church and normally only
retired priests are allowed to use the Tridentine mass. An English translation of the new
missal has not yet been published.

ALEC ROBERTSON

Narthex

The porch or vestibule in the Hellenistic
basilica (q.v.), closed to the exterior but
opening into the nave. It was the place
where people waited before services, and
from which the Great Entrance (q.v.), in its
original form, began.

EDITOR

Nave

The body of a church, usually separated
from the aisles or wings by pillars. The term
derives from the Latin *navis* meaning a 'ship'.
This comparison of a church building to a
ship was made at an early date, so the

Apostolic Constitution (*c.*375) says: 'When
thou callest an assembly of the church as
one that is the commander of a great ship,
appoint the assemblies to be made with all
possible skill, charging the deacons as mariners to prepare places for the brethren as
for passengers, with all due care and decency.
And first, let the building be long, with its
head to the east, with its vestries on both
sides at the east end, and so it will be like a
ship. In the middle let the bishop's throne be
placed, and on each side of him let the presbytery sit down; and let the deacons stand
near at hand, in close and small girt garments,
for they are like the mariners and managers
of a ship: with regard to these, let the laity
sit on the other side, with all quietness and
good order. And let the women sit by themselves, they also keeping silence. In the
middle let the reader stand upon some high
place' (2.57).

In certain areas during the patristic period
the nave was kept free from the laity who
were confined to the aisles, either because the
altar was placed there, as in North Africa,
or because, as in Syria, it was occupied by a
large semi-circular construction containing
the bishop's throne and seats for the presbyters.

In the Middle Ages, churches were widely
used for secular activities, the nave in
particular being the scene of dancing, eating,
drinking, plays, etc.

EDITOR

Nestorian Church *see* East Syrian Worship

New Fire

The lighting and blessing of the 'new fire'
takes place at the opening of the Paschal
Vigil (q.v.).

Fire, a most important element to primitive peoples as the source of warmth and
light, was added to the rite of the Paschal
Vigil most probably under the influence of the
Irish monks in Gaul in the eighth century,
though its use was known in Spain, too.
From Gaul it came eventually (not before
the twelfth century) to the Roman liturgy.
Roman usage was quite different. Light from
the church lamps was preserved from Good
Friday (later from Maundy Thursday) until
the beginning of the Vigil on Saturday evening. The lamps were brought back into the
church, and from them all the other lamps

and candles were lighted. The Roman use probably recalls the Jewish custom of the blessing of God for the gift of light on the Sabbath, a custom that was christianized and is witnessed to by Hippolytus in the *Apostolic Tradition* (XXV. 18-27), *c.* 215. This in turn gave rise to the ceremony known as the *Lucernarium*, still preserved in the Ambrosian rite and of which there are echoes in Roman vespers.

Even in the Gallican tradition the significance of the new fire is to be found rather in light than heat. But to understand its use at all, it is necessary to give the background of the whole liturgy of Good Friday and Holy Saturday. The church celebrates the Passover of the Lord in which he suffers, dies and rises again. In the phrase of Tertullian, Good Friday is the day *ubi ablatus est sponsus*: the bride (the church) is bereft of her bridegroom. The church as it were dies and has to be brought back to life again. This is done in symbol through fire and light, and the lighting of the new fire at the beginning of the Paschal Vigil is the first sign that the church is returning to life. The new fire thus had to be kindled from a virgin flame, struck from a kindling stone and steel. Or, as one of the prayers of blessing had it in the rite before 1951 when it was suppressed, Christ is the corner stone which, struck by the rod of the cross, sends forth the light of the Holy Spirit.

However, as the order of the service indicates to this day, the new fire is in fact lighted before the service proper begins and in some places is a great bonfire. It is on account of this that the rite has to take place outside the church; since there are practical difficulties in city and town churches, the procedure may be considerably modified. Once the fire is lit, the celebrant with ministers and servers comes to the place of the fire and after a short address giving the sense of the whole Vigil, blesses the fire with a single prayer. Then, from the fire, light is taken for the lighting of the Paschal Candle. This now becomes the centre of interest, for it is the candle that is the symbol of the Risen Christ. The fire having served its purpose is left to die out.

In many parts of Europe in former ages and perhaps even now, not only were all the lights in church extinguished, but the all-important hearth-fire was allowed to die. From the new fire or the candle people took light with which to re-kindle their fires at home. It is an interesting example of how the liturgy could influence social customs outside the church and in the life of the people.

J. D. CRICHTON

Nocturns *see* Canonical Hours

None *see* Canonical Hours

Notation and Rhythm

Saint Isidore (*c.* 560-636), Archbishop of Seville, says in one of his writings that in his day music was taught and handed down orally, for there was no way of setting down audible sounds on paper. In fact, the Vedic hymns of Southern India had a system of writing down the syllables of the spoken language in which each symbol represented a group of notes; a similar – but very complicated – system was in use in the early Byzantine church. The Greeks used a system derived from the letters of the alphabet and Boethius (d. 524) adapted the Latino-Greek alphabet to the musical scale. The introduction of stave lines by Giulio d'Arezzo (born *c.* 995) was a most important step in fixing accurately the step interval from one note to another. He determined the pitch by the use of coloured lines, yellow for C, red for F, and there prefigured our modern treble and bass clefs.

Neumatic notation will be familiar to those who look even casually at the manuscripts, often beautifully illuminated, of plainsong on show in museums; it is also known in its final stage to choirs who sing plainsong in square notation, from the modern Roman *Graduale* and *Antiphonale*.

The term neumatic is derived from the Greek word *pneuma*, a breath. These signs were developed from grammatical accent-signs said to have been invented by Aristophanes of Byzantium (*c.* 180 BC): they were basically called the *virga*, the acute accent, and the *punctum*, the grave accent. They combined with other 'signs' to form symbols representing melismas, that is, groups of notes sung to one syllable, which were often of considerable length. The earliest surviving manuscripts with neumatic notation probably date from the middle of the eighth century, but the system may well have been in use earlier than this. Before staff lines were invented, the neumes were written in what musicologists call *campo aperto*, 'in the open field', and so showed only a rise or fall of uncertain pitch between one neum and another. As the chant repertoire had to be learned by heart, these signs would have served at least as an *aide-mémoire* to the cantors gathered – as we see them in illuminated manuscripts and later in pictures – round a large choir book on the lectern. In the eleventh century there appeared 'heighted' neums in some Italian manuscripts, in which staff lines had been either imagined or are actually shown. These can be read, unlike the earlier manuscripts. Finally, in the thirteenth century came the quadratic or square notation familiar in the modern chant books today.

In origin the grammatic accents were purely melodic in character and carried no notion of duration or stress. Raising and lowering of pitch could be shown as time went on but, as has been said above, not the actual intervals between notes. When these intervals came to be shown, there remained the question of rhythm, a matter on which the singers must have been agreed. The proof lies in the presence in the earliest 'rhythmic' manuscripts of the tenth century of a whole set of valuable markings which do not appear in the later documents. The researches of the monks of the Abbey of St Pierre, Solesmes – pioneers in the restoration of Gregorian chant – showed that here was to be found the clue to the rhythmic tradition followed. The principal markings, or letters, placed above the notes are 'c.' (*cito* – lightly, quickly) and 't' (*trahere* – holding back, slowing down). There is still a considerable area of disagreement as to the correct interpretation of the rhythm of the chant.

ALEC ROBERTSON

Oblation

A synonym for 'offering', derived from the Latin *oblatio*, and like the latter may refer either to an act of offering, or to the thing offered. Four different Christian uses of the term may be distinguished: (1) the self-offering of Christ in the Last Supper and on the cross for the redemption of the world; (2) the celebration of the eucharist as an anamnesis (q.v.) of this self-offering; (3) its application to the material elements of bread and wine with which this anamnesis is made, according to Christ's command; (4) its application to the dispositions of the worshippers which are externalized by (2) and (3).

Other uses, such as the application of the term to monetary offerings in general, would seem to fall outside the legitimate Christian usage of the term. In the Christian dispensation the only offering or oblation which may strictly be so described without qualification is that of Christ himself, the only oblation which is intrinsically acceptable. Its application to the eucharist, which is ancient, and universal until the period of the Reformation, depends upon the doctrine that what the church does in the eucharist is, in virtue of the divine command, and by divine grace, identified with the self-oblation of Christ; its application to the eucharistic elements is further dependent upon that identification, which was anciently and universally held to be effected by the identification of the bread and wine with Christ's body and blood; its application to the dispositions of the worshippers is equally dependent upon it, in that they can only offer themselves *in Christ*, into whose self-offering they are assimilated by participation in the celebration of the eucharist.

The Protestant Reformers denied the legitimacy of describing the eucharist, and *a fortiori* the eucharistic elements, as an oblation, on the ground that to do so denigrated from the uniqueness of Christ's offering, an objection based on a misunderstanding of the doctrine involved, as well as on *a priori* grounds derived from their novel doctrine of justification and grace. Some of them, however, were still prepared to apply it, with qualification, to the dispositions of the worshippers – an application which, outside the context of its application to the celebration of the eucharist itself, would seem to merit their condemnation of the latter.

No other individual issue has so divided Western Christendom since the sixteenth century as the oblatory concept of the eucharist. In recent years, however, there has been a considerable softening of attitudes and drawing together on this subject; at the same time, there has been an increase of emphasis on the offering of the material elements of bread and wine as symbols on the one hand of the natural order, and on the other of the lives and labours of the worshippers, in a way which, valuable as these concepts are in themselves, has tended towards an implicit doctrine of the possibility of oblation other than, or in addition to, that of Christ. Only the doctrine of the identification of the oblation of the church, and of the individual member of it, with the oblation of Christ in the celebration of the eucharist as the divinely-appointed anamnesis of the latter is able to safeguard the uniqueness of Christ's oblation on the one hand, and provide for man's desire and need to offer all that he is and has to God on the other.

W. Jardine Grisbrooke, 'Oblation at the Eucharist' in *Studia Liturgica* III, 4, 1964, pp. 227-39; *ibid.*, IV, 1, 1965, pp. 37-55, and the works therein cited.

W. JARDINE GRISBROOKE

Octave

This reference to the continued commemoration of a festival denotes the *eighth* day, that is, one week later since the calculation is inclusive, or the *eight* days, that is, the week itself.

A. A. MCARTHUR

Offertory

The name given to the oblation rites which come at the beginning of the liturgy of the eucharist (as distinguished from the liturgy of the word). The motif of oblation (q.v.) runs throughout the eucharist, but the offertory is specifically concerned with oblation. The theme of the offertory is that the church must provide the elements for the sacrificial meal. The elements of bread and wine are presented, prepared and formally offered by the presiding priest, who then prays over them. These elements are to be transformed into the one gift that pleases God during the eucharistic prayer which follows the offertory, though their transformation is curiously anticipated, particularly in the Roman offertory. Still, Roman Catholic theologians hold that the offertory is not essential to the sacrifice. However, though the offertory may not be theologically essential, some presentation, preparation and perhaps formal offering of the elements, no matter how simple, seems practically indispensable. It is this presentation, preparation and formal offering of the elements which might be called the function of the offertory and which offers us insight as to the nature of the offertory. The offertory is that part of the mass which is concerned with the fitting oblation of the elements to God for their consecration.

The theme of offering gifts is as old as religion, and the ancient cults and folk practices were a providential preparation for the Christian offering of gifts for the eucharistic sacrifice and the service of the poor and the otherwise needy. There is reason to believe that the early church had an understanding of the eucharist as a corporate action, with each rank having its special task in relationship to the offering of the gifts. Writing as early as the autumn of AD 96, Clement of Rome reminds the church at Corinth that Christ is the 'high priest of our oblations' (*I Cor.* 36.1) and that he 'commanded us to celebrate oblations and liturgies' (*I Cor.* 40.2). Clement continues: 'Unto the high priest (bishop) his special liturgies have been appointed, and to the priests their special place assigned, and on the levites (deacons) their special ministry; the layman is bound by the ordinances for the laity. Let each of you, brethren, make eucharist to God according to his own order, keeping a good conscience and not transgressing the appointed rule of his own liturgy' (*I Cor.* 40.5-41.1). That Clement was talking about the oblational aspects of liturgy is indicated further on in the letter where he says that it is the bishop's office to 'offer the gifts' (*I Cor.* 44.4). We might conclude from this that every rank in the church had its role to play in the offering of the gifts. This implies that the layman, too, has a role, though his role is in no way spelled out by Clement.

Justin Martyr, in the early years of the second century, is the first to give explicit evidence about the offertory. In the first and fuller reference in his *Apology* (ch. 65), he gives the following order of service: the prayers are concluded; the kiss of peace (q.v.) is given; bread and wine are presented to the one who presides over the assembly; he takes them and over them he pronounces the thanksgiving. Justin, in his *Dialogue with Trypho* (9-13), also seems to reject all oblation of things which might be used for sustenance. But this is in reality a rejection of the material sacrifices of creatures as practised by Jews and pagans. His ideal is the *oblatio rationabilis*, the spiritual sacrifice, which the Greek philosophers declared to be the only veneration worthy of God. He sees that there is no longer any room for bloody sacrifices since the Logos himself, Jesus Christ, is the victim of the spiritual sacrifice which is the eucharist. But emphasis on the spiritual sacrifice gives way to a re-statement of the importance of the material and material sacrifices in the face of Gnosticism in the latter part of the second century. Irenaeus leads the battle against those who would spiritualize the Christian sacrifice out of existence.

The *Apostolic Tradition* of Hippolytus (AD 215-217) offers two descriptions of the eucharistic order of service. In the first account we find one item to add to Justin's description, namely, the deacons (q.v.) are expressly mentioned as offering the oblation. The second account, which is an account of the eucharist in conjunction with baptism, does add something further. On this occasion, milk, honey and water are added to the usual oblations of bread and wine, and these are received by the newly baptized at communion before the consecrated wine. Interestingly, the catechumen (q.v.) is earlier told to bring some offering for the eucharist which will follow his baptism. Hippolytus' accounts therefore give some confirmation to what is much earlier suggested by Clement as to the participation of deacons and laymen in the offertory rite. In North Africa in the same century we have the witness of both Tertullian and Cyprian to lay participation in offering the elements, though the precise time when these elements were presented (before the mass began or at the offertory) is not indicated.

In the fourth and fifth centuries, after peace had come to the church, there was a great growth of the liturgy. In the East during the fourth century, the laity provided the elements for the sacrifice, though, except in the Egyptian rite, the exact time of their offering is not known. It is also generally agreed that during this century whatever presentation of the gifts at the offertory there had ever been in the East died out, and with the beginning of the fifth century we have the evidence of Theodore of Mopsuestia (in his *Catechesis*) that the offertory was moving in the direction of a 'processional' rite as opposed to the Roman 'oblational' rite. The East now substitutes the great entrance (q.v.) for the simpler presentation, preparation and offering of the elements, and the participation of the laity and even the meaning of oblation is more and more obscured in the representational rite of the Byzantine liturgy. The evidence from the West during this two-century middle period is sparse indeed. Except for passing references in Spain and Milan which indicate that the laity in those cities provided the oblations according to a certain ritual, the only important Western evidence we have is from North Africa where Augustine reports that the laity actually offered the elements at the offertory.

If there was ever a real offertory procession of the laity, it occurred during the following centuries at the papal stational liturgy in the city of Rome. *Ordo Romanus Primus* describes in detail the action, but instead of the laity coming up to the altar to hand in their offerings, the pope and his assistants go down to the laity to take up those gifts to be used for the sacrifice and for the needs of the church and those who were in the care of the church. It is the opinion of this author that the formalization of the people's offertory in the Roman stational liturgy dealt the death blow to a sense of liturgical role which until that time the laity had understood themselves as having. During this same period the Gallican rite developed an approach to the offertory which was in spirit closer to the later Eastern practice. Duchesne, describing the Gallican rite in *Christian Worship*, [6]1931, p. 204, states categorically that 'the offering by the people at this point in the mass (i.e. the offertory) is a ceremony of Roman origin, and is incompatible with that of the *processio oblationis*, a custom common to the Gallican and Oriental rite'. Before passing on to the post-developmental period, it is important to note that the secret prayers which we find in the Roman sacramentaries of this period, particularly the Leonine and the Gregorian, reflect a highly developed theology of the offerings as oblations (*see* **Silent Prayer**). One can learn a great deal about the theology of the offertory by a study of these prayers, many of which are still to be found in the Roman missal.

By the year AD 800, the eucharistic liturgy of the Western church, like that of the East, had become more or less uniform and established. Substantially the liturgies of both East and West manifested no important change after this date, though the actual offertory rite was considerably modified in the West, particularly by the addition of prayers full of Gallican symbolism and piety to accompany the simple actions. All of this was made uniform and unchangeable in the West with the publication of the Roman missal in its first edition in 1474. So it remained until the recent missal of Pope Paul VI. In this missal the prayers are considerably simplified or omitted. The offertory is once again restored to a relatively simple, straightforward rite. The gifts are brought up. Bread is offered to the accompaniment of a modified OT blessing. Wine with a little water is taken and similarly offered to the accompaniment of a similar blessing. After hand-washing and an invitation to the gathering to pray that the sacrifice may be acceptable to God, an invitation which evokes a proper corporate response, the ancient secret prayer, re-named the 'prayer over the gifts' (see **Super Oblata**), is spoken by the presiding priest. And so ends the present offertory of the Roman mass.

One might argue that even greater simplification would make the offertory rite more effective. More importantly, there is still a great need to find a way to re-awaken in the laity a sense of their having a proper liturgy – probably in connection with the offertory and the heightened sense of the social needs of less fortunate brethren.

A. Clark, 'The Function of the Offertory Rite in the Mass', *Ephem. Liturg.* 64 (1950), pp. 309-344; G. Dix, *The Shape of the Liturgy*, [2]1945; A Hamman, *Vie Liturgique et Vie Sociale*, 1968; J. A. Jungmann, *The Mass of the Roman Rite,* rev. ed., 1959.

THOMAS PHELAN

Office Hymn

A hymn appointed for use at the hour services (q.v.). They were omitted from the *BCP* for lack of English versions, but many have now been translated and find their place in Anglican hymnals. A custom had arisen in some churches of singing such a hymn after the first lesson and before the *Magnificat* at evensong.

EDITOR

Old Catholic Worship

Of the Old Catholic churches, linked together in 1889 in the Union of Utrecht, the church in the Netherlands is by far the oldest. This church was a continuation of the church for which Willibrord was consecrated first archbishop of Utrecht in Rome, in 695, and after the period of the Reformation, which was extremely difficult, it was involved in an increasingly sharp conflict with Rome

in the seventeenth century. In 1703, the archbishop Peter Codde was suspended by Pope Clement XI. From that time onward the episcopal succession was continued in the church as the 'Roman Catholic Church of the old episcopal clergy'. As this was a split for reasons of canon law and not because of dogmatic differences, there was a continual hope that the difficulties might be resolved. During the early period of the split, the old Roman post-Tridentine liturgy was adhered to almost completely.

There was an important turn of the tide after 1870. Vatican I and the development of Old Catholic movements outside the Netherlands not only caused the 'Old Episcopal' clergy to call themselves increasingly 'Old Catholics'; it also induced them to be more closely connected in theological thinking as well. This led to the Union of Utrecht in 1889. The influence of the German and Swiss sister churches was also felt in the liturgy through the spread of the idea of community, the introduction of the vernacular, the rejection of private masses and the renewal of the liturgy. Thus several new liturgical books came out, especially in the period between 1900 and 1910, taking the place of the old Roman formularies (*cf.* **Books, Liturgical** 11: Old Catholic).

Compared to the Old Catholic reforms abroad, those in the Netherlands were on the whole less radical. For instance, in the translation of the liturgy of the mass and especially of the canon dating from 1909, there were very few departures from the Roman missal. The cycle of saints' days was far less restricted than elsewhere. After the Second World War, the voices clamouring for a renewal of the liturgy grew louder and louder. In 1960 a revised liturgy of the mass did in fact come out, but as research had not yet been completed, the alterations were still fairly limited. Under the influence of very lively liturgical renewal movements in the Netherlands, both among Roman Catholics and among Protestants, the desire for radical changes has grown very strongly since. What is specifically aimed at is directness, greater transparency and ecumenical openness. This desire for radically revised formularies has by no means been fulfilled yet. In 1968 there appeared an alternative 'Second Order of the Mass', and here and there new formularies for the administration of the sacraments have been tried out. It looks as if, within a couple of years, tangible results in the shape of official formularies may be expected.

In the Old Catholic churches which separated from Rome because of their rejection of the Vatican dogmas of 1870 (above all in Germany, Austria and Switzerland), powerful reform movements soon became evident, in contrast to the situation in the Netherlands. As a result of their separation from Rome, these churches gained the freedom to carry out reforms which had long been desired in progressive Catholic circles. In those parts of Switzerland and South Germany which had belonged to the See of Constance until 1814 or 1821, the ground for liturgical reform had been prepared by the activity of the Vicar General (later vicegerent of the See), I. H. von Wessenberg. His German ritual served as a model for Old Catholic rituals, and the tradition of German vespers still lives on in the Old Catholic congregations in Switzerland. In Austria, the church reforms of Emperor Joseph II (1741-1790) had a wide influence.

Soon after 1870 the liturgical books were produced in German and French editions. The editors were not, however, content with a translation of the Latin books, as in the Netherlands, but worked over them more freely. Of course, all Old Catholic liturgies are descended from the Roman liturgy, like those of the Anglican and Lutheran churches, though like them they differ to a greater or lesser degree from their ancestor.

A considerable part in the reform of the liturgy was played by Eduard Herzog (1841-1924), the first bishop of the Christian Catholic (Old Catholic) Church of Switzerland, and Adolf Thürlings (1844-1915), Professor of Liturgy in the Christian Catholic theological faculty in Bern (Switzerland), who was also a distinguished musicologist. In the Polish Old Catholic Church in the USA and Canada (founded in 1897), as in Poland itself, the liturgy was translated into Polish, but the translation strictly followed the Roman rite. In America, English has been used to an increasing extent alongside Polish.

In the Old Catholic churches, some of the manifestations of so-called vulgar Catholicism have been rejected, e.g. pilgrimages, reverencing of images, indulgences, the Cult of the Sacred Heart, and so on. The liturgy is meant to be celebrated in a clear and pure form, bringing the Christological element, in particular, to the fore. Thus the Old Catholic churches play a lively part in the liturgical renewal that is taking place in both Roman Catholic and Protestant churches.

For Old Catholicism with particular reference to worship, *see*: K. Algermissen, *Konfessionkunde*, [8]1969; P. Fox, *The Polish National Catholic Church*; U. Kunz, *Viele Glieder – ein Leib*, 1953 (and especially P. Pfister, 'Die altkatholische Kirche'); U. Küry, *Die altkatholische Kirche* (in: *Die Kirchen der Welt*, III), 1966; C. B. Moss, *The Old Catholic Movement*, [2]1964; A. E. Rüthy, 'The Place of the Old Catholic Church in the Liturgical Scene', *Studia Liturgica* II, 1963, pp. 66f.; F. Siegmund-Schultze, ed., *Ekklesia*, III: *Die altkatholische Kirche*, 1935.

KURT PURSCH
A. E. RÜTHY
C. TOL

Open-Air Meeting

The tradition of the open-air meeting was common in Europe among the persecuted minorities of the Middle Ages (Hussites, Waldensians). It was also used by popular preachers like Bernard of Clairvaux and Francis of Assisi. Later the French Protestants held their meetings in woods and fields (*L'église du désert*). In another form this tradition was taken up by Fox, Wesley, the Salvation Army, the Pentecostals in Latin America and many African churches (*see* **Liturgies** 12: Pentecostal). The latter three added to the oral methodology of communication the tradition of folk music. So, the Salvation Army used the folk music of the turn of the century (brass-band!). By now this has become traditional in the Salvation Army, although some attempts are made to use today's folk music.

Of the greatest importance are the open-air meetings of the OT prophets. They did not preach from a pulpit, nor did they usually interpret a written text, though they related themselves critically *and* positively to the tradition of their listeners. They had to formulate their message in short, easily memorized sentences and parables, not unlike the modern commercial spots on television, but very different from today's sermons. The same method was used by Jesus and the apostles. This form of concentrated communication was forgotten in the main-line churches for many centuries. It was replaced by the sermon, which has no precedent in

Ordinary

biblical tradition, but has its roots in the cultural background of the early church and the Reformation.

Roughly speaking there are two types of open-air meetings today:

1. *The public religious mass meeting.* With the invention of high-powered loud-speaker systems, it has become possible to address thousands of people in the open air. Billy Graham and the German Kirchentag, Martin Luther King and ecumenical youth gatherings at Taizé, Roman Catholic congresses and ecumenical festivals are public demonstrations which seek to strengthen certain (evangelical, catholic, ecumenical, or pentecostal) beliefs among their followers and friends. In the case of the German Kirchentag this public propaganda is corrected and deepened by controversial public debates and small discussion groups.

2. *The open-air meeting as an encounter with the world* is in certain cultures one of the best schools for the humanization of man. Every one – and not only the pastor – who has the courage and the gift can speak. The speakers realize themselves as persons who have something worthwhile to contribute, a tremendous process of experiencing the value of the human person. One must have seen these people, reduced to silence by political and religious powers through centuries, suddenly discovering that they have something to say, although they do not have much formal education. For this process it is not of the first importance for them to use the ready-made language of their tradition. The main thing is that they discover the possibility of standing up and speaking. In a more sophisticated stage the open-air meeting could offer the chance to rediscover the proclamation of the gospel in the world's agenda, i.e. a proclamation which does not protect itself from any criticism by basing itself on a biblical text; by confining itself to biblical thought patterns and to a religious public which agrees with the preacher's basic assumptions; and by shutting itself in a church building, where counter-arguments are rarely allowed and never expected. Thus, this preaching could be more biblical than the usual sermon, not by basing itself *expressis verbis* on a biblical text, but by risking the biblical method of proclamation, which begins with the listener's questions, with his concrete situation, and accepts his interruptions as a vital means of communicating the gospel.

W. J. HOLLENWEGER

Ordinary

A term of the Roman rite which has had three different, although related, meanings: (1) the unvarying parts of the mass; (2) those unvarying parts of the mass which are rendered chorally, and which compose the 'mass' as a musical work, namely, the *Kyrie, Gloria in excelsis, Credo, Sanctus* and *Benedictus*, and *Agnus Dei*; (3) the unvarying parts of the mass up to the secret prayer or *super oblata* (q.v.), a usage followed in the page headings of the Roman missal of 1570, but abandoned in the *Ordo Missae* of 1969.

W. JARDINE GRISBROOKE

Ordination

Ordination is the act of conferring holy orders and so admitting a candidate into the ministry of the church. Strictly speaking only presbyters or priests undergo ordination, and it is customary to refer to the consecration of bishops, to the making of deacons, and to the admitting of readers, etc., to the minor orders. The central element in ordination is the laying on of hands with prayer, and various NT passages are regarded as the basis for this practice (Acts 6.1-6; 13.1-3; 20.28; I Tim. 4.14; 5.22; II Tim. 1.6).

1. *The Early Church*

(*a*) *Bishops.* They were elected by the people and consecrated by a fellow bishop laying his hands upon them and uttering prayers in the presence of other bishops and the local Christian community. After being saluted with the kiss of peace (q.v.), the new bishop presided at the eucharist, occupying the *cathedra* (q.v.), so consecration can be described as 'being placed in the *cathedra*'. Consecration rites were not greatly elaborated, but by the fourth century deacons held a gospel book over the candidate's head (*Apost. Const.* 8.4) and one of the other bishops present is instructed to 'elevate the sacrifice upon the hands of him that is consecrated' – possibly in imitation of the consecration of the Jewish high priest (Lev. 8.27).

(*b*) *Presbyters.* They were ordained by the laying on of hands with prayer, of both the local bishop and other presbyters.

(*c*) *Deacons.* The bishop alone laid his hands upon them with prayer.

EDITOR

2. *Orthodox*. In Orthodox ecclesiology the sacrament of holy orders is essentially bound with the realization of the church as the body of Christ (I Cor. 12.27; 10.17).The directly implied ecclesial structure of this body is hierarchical, having head and members. The hierarchical order, however, is not to be confused with a power structure. The ministries of the church are those of love and service, not power and domination. All ecclesiastical functions are performed precisely *within* the church – not over and above it. The Holy Spirit, the one source behind all ministerial gifts, resides in the whole church (I Cor. 12.4-11). It does not reside in one member to the exclusion of others. The church taken together is the realization of the body of Christ.

The priestly function is no exception to this rule of corporateness. It is a function ascribed to the whole membership of the church: '. . . you are a chosen race, a royal priesthood, a holy nation . . .' (I Peter 2.9). All church members are called upon to '. . . offer spiritual sacrifices acceptable to God through Jesus Christ' (I Peter 2.5). Orthodox baptismal rites support this view of the priestly function. They are full of liturgical acts and words which point to the ordination of each church member to the royal priesthood. Some signs of this priestly consecration which appear in the present Orthodox liturgy of baptism (q.v.) and chrismation are: the laying on of hands, anointing with oil, the tonsure and the vesting in a white robe. The NT speaks of the *whole church* as the clergy: the lot which God has chosen and separated from the fallen world (Acts 26.18; Eph. 1.11). This wholeness lies at the root of the Orthodox understanding of the specifically ordained functions of bishop, priest and deacon.

The bishop is the 'overseer', which is the meaning of the word from the Greek of the NT. He is specifically consecrated to oversee the total life of the local church. He is the head of the body. He presides at the eucharistic assemblies and literally oversees the entire community of priests, the holy nation, as it makes its offering to God in Christ. The bishop is the archpriest, the first among the whole community of priests, and through his presence the church as an hierarchical organism, the body of Christ, is realized. He is the guardian and first teacher of the apostolic faith and tradition. In this sense, and not in some magical understanding of the continuity in the laying on of hands, he is consecrated in the apostolic succession. He in turn ordains priests and deacons to their respective ministries and continues to check them in the manner in which they discharge their duties. He is the mouth of the local church before God and the church as a whole; he is the image of God and the link with the church as a whole within the local church. Ignatius of Antioch offers an excellent summary of the function of the bishop in his letter to Smyrnaeans:

> Nobody must do anything that has to do with the church without the bishop's approval . . . Where the bishop is present, there let the congregation gather, just as where Jesus Christ is, there is the Catholic Church (*Smyrn*. 8.1 f.).

The ordained priest has a role in the church subordinate to that of the bishop. In the early church each individual community had its own bishop, and the priests, or presbyters as they are called in the NT, served as a council of advisers and assistants around him. The growth of the church expanded the role of the priest. The bishops began to send priests from their councils to lead the life of the new parishes. At an earlier time Ignatius had already commented that a valid eucharist can be celebrated by someone duly authorized by the bishop (*Smyrn*. 8.1). The local church in Orthodoxy has thus come to be a diocese: a specifically defined territory led by a bishop, with the parishes therein attended by duly authorized priests. The role of the parish priest or presbyter is that of an 'elder', the one who leads his parish in the name of the bishop. The essential link between parish, parish priest and bishop is continuously emphasized by the presence of a cloth called an *antimension* on each Orthodox altar table. This cloth is unfolded at each celebration of the holy eucharist and the holy gifts are placed thereon. It bears the signature of the bishop and demonstrates that the realization of the church is dependent upon communion with him.

The function of the diaconate has followed a curve opposite to that of the ordained priest. In the early church the deacon was more active than the priest, but today, practically speaking, he is less active. Properly, he is to perform the 'ministry of Jesus Christ' (Ignatius, *Magnes*. 6.1). He is to 'serve tables' at the eucharistic assemblies by bringing forth and helping to distribute the holy gifts (Acts 6.2-6). In general he acts as the 'right hand' in the assistance he renders to the bishop or priest during the celebration of all liturgical services.

The ordinations of deacons, priests and bishops take place at varying times during the celebration of the holy eucharist. As one who is consecrated to 'serve tables', the deacon is ordained after the consecration of the holy gifts. He is then prepared to perform the high point of his function: the carrying of the eucharistic chalice to the faithful.

The priest is to lead the congregation in the celebration of the eucharist. He is therefore ordained prior to the consecration of the holy gifts.

The manner of ordaining both priests and deacons is very similar. The candidate for ordination in both cases is brought before the bishop, who is seated at the front-left corner of the altar table. He is then led in a triple circling around the altar table and brought to a halt, on his knees, at the front-right corner of the altar table. The bishop rises and, placing his hands upon the head of the candidate, says the prayers appropriate for the ordination. At the conclusion of the prayers the newly-ordained rises, and the bishop gives him the vestments (q.v.) proper to his ministry. All present sing: '*Axios* (worthy)!'

A new bishop is consecrated by a minimum of two other bishops. The corporate character of the consecration is a sign of the full communion which must exist between the respective local churches. As the prime teacher and preserver of the apostolic faith and tradition within the community, the bishop is consecrated just prior to the didactic portion of the eucharistic liturgy. The candidate to be consecrated is brought on his knees before the altar table. The consecrating bishops place an open gospel book, with the writing downward, upon the head of the candidate. They then lay their right hands upon the head of the candidate and, through the saying of the proper prayers by the presiding bishop, complete the consecration. The new bishop is given his vestments and all present sing: '*Axios!*'

In conclusion, the sacrament of holy orders is the vehicle through which the church is provided with its essential, hierarchical order and assured of an objective, sacramental basis for an inner life of unity and harmony.

Hence, I urge you to do everything in godly agreement. Let the bishop preside in God's place, and the presbyters take the place of the apostolic council, and let the deacons . . . be entrusted with the ministry of Jesus Christ who was with the Father from eternity and appeared at the end of the world (Ignatius, *Magnes.* 6.1).

PAUL LAZOR

3. *Medieval and Roman Catholic.* The sober rites of the Roman tradition underwent a considerable change in the ninth and tenth centuries when certain observances, deriving from Gallican and German sources, were added to them to give a rather different picture to holy orders. These observances are found in the Roman-German pontifical (tenth century) which made its way to Rome in the eleventh century and became part of the tradition. By way of the pontifical of Durandus of Mende (d. 1298), who made further additions, they came to form the rite of the Roman pontifical of 1485 which in turn was substantially the pontifical of 1596. These new rites consisted principally of anointings (of the head for a bishop, of the hands for a priest) and of the *porrectio instrumentorum*, the handing over of the symbols of office. The intention was to explicate the meaning of the various orders, but in the process the emphasis was somewhat changed. For instance, the handing of chalice and paten to the priest heavily emphasized that his chief duty was to offer sacrifice. On the other hand, the delivery of the gospel book to the deacon underlined that he was a minister of the word. What was more important is that the *porrectio* overshadowed the ancient rite of the laying on of hands (which always remained) and was generally thought to be necessary for validity. This was corrected by Pius XII, who in the Apostolic Constitution *Sacramentum Ordinis* of 1948 laid down that the laying-on of hands for the three orders of episcopate, the presbyterate and the diaconate, with certain formulae in the ordination prayers, was all that was necessary for validity.

The minor orders of doorkeeper, reader, exorcist and acolyte with the ceremony of tonsure before them and the subdiaconate (until 1207 ranking as a minor order) also underwent development. These officers were from the third century appointed by a simple blessing with the delivery of the symbols of office. Now the formulae were elaborated and the rites expanded. There was an address, the delivery of the symbol of office with a formula and two prayers of blessing.

Modern. That part of the *Pontificale Romanum* containing the liturgy of ordination to the episcopate, the presbyterate and the diaconate was revised in 1968 and the liturgy of tonsure, the four minor orders and the subdiaconate in 1972 when it appeared that the subdiaconate had been suppressed and the minor orders reduced to two.

The pattern of the services for all three major orders is the same: they are conferred within the eucharist, after the gospel and homily; there follow the questions, prayer (litany of saints), the laying-on of hands (in silence), the prayer of ordination and the delivery of the symbols of office.

For the ordination of a presbyter the bishop lays hands on the candidate first and then all the presbyters present do likewise; the anointing of the hands has been retained with a different formula, charging the presbyter to serve God's people and to offer the eucharist. The paten and chalice and the bread and wine to be used at the eucharist are then delivered to him with a new formula indicating that they are the offerings of the people to be used in the mass.

The texts of the prayers of ordination for diaconate and presbyterate remain those of the (early) Roman tradition, that for the presbyterate being slightly shortened. Noteworthy in the rite for the 'Ordination' (*sic*) of a bishop are that the consecrator and then the assistant consecrators lay hands on him, the book of the gospels is placed on his head and held over it during the consecration prayer by two deacons and the principal part of the prayer is said by all the consecrators together. It is a true con-celebration. The anointing of the head remains as well as the delivery of the gospel book (now in first place), the ring and the staff or crozier. The consecrator puts the mitre on the candidate without formula. The whole service has been much simplified. The prayer of ordination (or consecration) is that found in the (Latin) Verona fragment of the *Apostolic Tradition* of Hippolytus, very slightly revised.

Like the major orders, the minor orders are conferred after the gospel and the homily (or during a service of the word). There is an invitatory, a prayer and the delivery of the symbol of office. Tonsure is replaced by a service of 'Admission to the Clerical State'. The candidates are questioned, admitted by the bishop to the clergy, there are prayers of intercession and the final prayer of the bishop.

J. D. CRICHTON

4. *Anglican.* Services of ordination did not appear in the 1549 *BCP* but were published independently in March 1550. In 1552 they were revised and annexed to the second *BCP*. A third edition appeared in 1559, again as a separate document, and finally a fourth edition was annexed to the *BCP* of 1662.

In the Preface to the 1550 Ordinal, Cranmer and the Reformers stated their intention of continuing the threefold order of bishops, priests and deacons which had existed since apostolic times; they made no provision for the subdiaconate and other minor orders. In an attempt to simplify the obscurities of the medieval Roman rite they retained the eucharist as the frame for ordination and emphasized the essential elements as expressed in the NT and by the early church, namely prayer and the imposition of hands. Thus the basic pattern of the rites in the Roman Pontifical was followed, but a number of individual features were changed, and the influence of Bucer's tract *De Ordinatione* was recognizable. The anointing of bishops and priests and the formal vesting of all three orders was abolished. The delivery of the instruments (*porrectio instrumentorum*) was retained in the case of priests, but the staff was the sole insignia delivered to the bishop. A Bible instead of the gospels was laid on the bishop's neck, a Bible was delivered to priests, and the NT instead of the gospels was delivered to deacons. While it was undoubtedly right for the Reformers to avoid the traditional multiplied and diffused acts of ordination and to concentrate on the central imposition of hands with prayer, it would seem that they were misled over the relation between the form and the matter. Not only did the traditional eucharistic pattern of prayer introduced by the *Sursum corda* disappear, but the ordination prayers which were used were separated from the imposition of hands, and the latter were accompanied by imperative formulae addressed to the candidates and authorizing them to execute the functions of the order which they were receiving.

In 1552 further medieval elements in the rites disappeared. Bishops were no longer invested with the pastoral staff, and the Bible was not laid on their necks but handed to them, although the formulae which had accompanied these two ceremonies in 1550 were retained. The delivery of the instruments was also modified for priests: they too received only the Bible, the delivery of the chalice and the bread being omitted. In 1559 and 1662 no further basic changes were made, but in 1662 an addition was inserted in the formulae accompanying the imposition of hands in the case of bishops and priests. A specific reference was made to the order being conferred, 'for the office and work of a bishop' and 'for the office and work of a priest', thereby meeting the Puritan argument that from the similarity of the earlier formulae there had been no clear distinction between the episcopate and the priesthood.

Throughout the Anglican Communion the 1662 rites have continued with little change until the twentieth century. One improvement was made in the Scottish prayer book of 1929 and in the proposed English prayer book of 1928. A eucharistic type of ordination prayer introduced by the *Sursum corda* was inserted before the imposition of hands in the rite for deacons, while the existing prayers for bishops and priests were remodelled to conform to the same pattern. But the most thorough revision appeared in the Ordinal of the Church of South India in 1958. Here the rites for all three orders followed the same pattern within the framework of the eucharist. Candidates were first presented to the congregation, and the latter was required to express approval or disapproval. Then the ordination followed the ministry of the Word: the examination, the prayer for the Holy Spirit, then the solemn ordination prayer itself during which the imposition of hands occurred. Thus form and matter once again were closely related. This Ordinal has met with widespread approval; and it has provided a model for recent revisions – West Africa 1965-6, Anglican-Methodist in England 1968, and America 1970.

R. C. D. JASPER

5. *Baptist*. Baptist ordination is primarily for ministry in a local congregation; therefore, the service of ordination is an affair of a local congregation, generally the one to which the ordinand will minister. When a congregation determines that one of its members should be 'set apart for the gospel ministry' (be ordained) it sends out a call to its sister congregations, usually the area association, asking that a council meet to examine the candidate's qualifications for the ministry. While such a council is not required by strict Baptist polity, it represents symbolically the unity of the Baptist churches as well as the fact that ordination is mutually recognized by other churches than the one actually doing the ordaining. The council reviews the candidate's educational qualification, hears his statement on his Christian commitment and call to the ministry and examines him on his doctrinal views. If the candidate proves satisfactory on these points the council recommends to the congregation that it proceed with the ordination.

The service of ordination is generally held at a time when representatives of the other churches of the association can attend. It is set within a full service of worship which generally includes the Lord's Supper. The act of ordination takes place as part of the offertory, at which time the ordinand offers himself to be set apart for the gospel ministry (for the outline of the Lord's Day service *see* **Liturgies** 5: Baptist). As the gifts and the bread and wine are brought to the table by the deacons, the chairman of the deacons escorts the ordinand to the table. After a prayer of dedication the chairman of the deacons presents the ordinand to the congregation along with the recommendation of the Council that the church proceed with the ordination of the candidate. After receiving vows from the ordinand, the presiding minister declares that he has responded faithfully to the call of the gospel and is fit through preparation to be ordained at this time. After a blessing upon the ordinand, clergymen, and in many cases representative laymen, are invited to lay hands on the ordinand for the ordination prayer. Following the prayer a charge is given to the candidate, after which a charge is given to the church to which he is to minister. In many ordinations a Bible is given to the newly ordained minister, symbolizing his role as a minister of the word. After the presentation of the Bible the newly ordained minister is led to the communion table by the presiding minister and welcomed into the pastoral ministry of the church of Jesus Christ. He then is invited to begin his ministry among his people by presiding over the Lord's Supper. The new minister takes his place at the table and leads the congregation in the observance of the Lord's Supper according to the manner of the local congregation.

Most Baptists view ordination as an act of recognition on the part of a congregation of a person's call and fitness to ministry. It is not the conferring of some special grace, but rather the recognition of graces already received. He still remains a layman in essence; he is set apart to function in special ways within the congregation. Yet nothing that he does as a minister cannot be done by a layman providing the congregation so designates. This process is generally called licensing and is used when no ordained minister is available or when there is need for the extension of the ministry to other areas.

JOHN E. SKOGLUND

6. *Christian Church (Disciples of Christ).* The Christian Church (Disciples of Christ) is like other churches in that it sets people apart for the office of ministry by an act of prayer and laying on of hands. Where it has differed from many has been in its understanding of the persons who should receive this rite of the church. From their studies of the NT, Disciple leaders in the early nineteenth century derived three ministerial offices. Evangelists were itinerant proclaimers of the gospel whose chief work was to found and organize churches. Elders were mature men, resident in the community, who would be elected by members of the local church and ordained by them for the overseeing of the church's life. Although they held secular employment, they were to preach – if possessing the necessary skill – and administer baptism and the Lord's Supper, the latter every week. Deacons were also local men and their service was limited to matters more temporal than preaching and praying.

During the course of the last third of the nineteenth century and the first half of the twentieth, Disciples developed an educated, salaried ministry. Until the 1960s such ministers would ordinarily preside over the Sunday service and would preach. Always a part of that service, however, was the Lord's Supper and invariably elders (as described in the above paragraph) would preside over that portion of the service. They offered the eucharistic prayer while the minister sat at his place near the pulpit. In recent years the minister came to share in this service at the table – delivering a homily before the prayer and reciting the words of institution after the prayer.

It is normal practice for such a minister to be ordained. Elders from several congregations, and a small group of other ministers, lay their hands on his head while a prayer of dedication and invocation is offered by one of them. There is divided opinion among Disciples concerning the ordination of the elders. Before the rise of the office of minister, the elders in a congregation were ordained because they were understood to be fulfilling the ministerial functions of teaching and overseeing. In some congregations this practice of ordaining elders continues unabated. In others, however, the service of prayer and laying on of hands has been replaced by installation into a functional office.

It is not yet clear what will happen to the Disciple elder in the coming decades. The current trend seems to be in the direction of continued diminution of his office with the result that ordination would be increasingly inappropriate. This trend continues even though there is growing interest in some quarters of the church for a ministry that is not dependent upon the church for livelihood.

At the present time there is no official definition of ordination. There would be widespread agreement to the definition that ordination is a corporate act by the church in which it appoints certain persons to the work of public ministry. Ministers, as distinguished from elders, are ordained, usually after graduation from seminary.

KEITH WATKINS

7. *Congregationalist.* The classical Congregational theory and practice of ordination is described in *The Savoy Declaration* of 1658:

> The way appointed by Christ for the calling of any person, fitted and gifted by the Holy Ghost, unto the Office of Pastor, Teacher, or Elder in a Church, is that he be chosen there unto by the common suffrage of the Church itself, and solemnly set apart by fasting and prayer, with Imposition of Hands of the Eldership of that Church . . .

If exception was taken to the laying on of hands, it could be omitted.

Congregational ordination today is not materially different, except that it is more liable to be preceded by feasting than fasting, and that the moderator of a province (in Britain) or a conference minister (in America) will represent the wider fellowship of Congregational churches. Essentially though, the service is still the solemn recognition that the ordinand has been called by God to the ministry and that he (or she) has the necessary gifts and grace, and is now by the invocation of the Holy Spirit and the laying on of hands set apart for this ministry and invited to be pastor of this local fellowship and congregation of Christ.

The order of service for the ordination of a minister in *A Book of Services and Prayers* (1959) is the most recently authorized form for the use of English Congregationalists and will be taken as the model.

After an introduction of sentences of scripture and an invocatory prayer, followed by the reading of appropriate lessons from both Testaments, the presiding minister summarizes the foundation and duties of the church and ministry. Then he calls upon the secretary of the local church to record the steps that have led the congregation to the issuing of the invitation to the ordinand to be their minister. The ordinand is then called upon to make a statement expounding 'his Christian experience; his assurance of his call by God to the holy ministry; (and) his Christian belief' (*ibid.*, p. 93). Thereupon the ordinand is required to confess his belief in the Holy Trinity, the lordship of Christ, in the scriptures as containing 'all doctrine required for eternal salvation through faith in Jesus Christ', and to give assurance he is truly called to the ministry, and to promise that he will fulfil the pastoral office with all fidelity. The presiding minister then asks the members of the local church to stand in silent prayer in token that they receive the ordinand as their minister.

After the singing of a hymn of the Holy Spirit or the *Veni Creator*, the ordination prayer follows. During the saying of this prayer ministers and church representatives lay their hands upon the head of the ordinand, while the presiding minister prays for the continuance of the gifts of the Holy Spirit, and for the welfare of pastor and flock, ending with the Lord's Prayer said by all. The presiding minister then says in the name of Christ and of the churches of the Congregational faith and order, 'We declare you to be ordained to this ministry of the gospel in the church of Christ, and to be appointed pastor of this church and congregation.' The minister is then given a Bible as token of his privilege and duty to preach God's word, and he receives the right hand of fellowship from representatives of the local and wider churches.

It is then customary for two invited ministers to preach, one of them reminding the congregation of its privileges and duties, and the other reminding the minister of his. Sometimes a single address covers both aspects. The newly-ordained minister gives the final blessing to the congregation.

HORTON DAVIES

8. *Jehovah's Witnesses*. Jehovah's Witnesses hold to the principle of the general priesthood; that is, to 'the Biblical teaching that every spirit-begotten Christian is a priest' (*The Watchtower*, 1 March 1963, pp. 137f.; 1 July 1963, pp. 415f.). I Peter 2.5-10 says of the entire Christian congregation: 'You are . . . a royal *priesthood*, a holy *nation* . . . that you should declare abroad the excellencies of the one that called you.' Here priesthood and nation are identical. There is no division into 'priesthood' and 'people' within that nation. Every member of that nation is a priest.

The word 'priest' is drawn from the Greek *presbyteros*, but *presbyteros* does not mean in itself a sacrificing priest who serves at an altar: it means simply an elder, an older man, whether in physical age or in spiritual growth. It refers, not to an office, but to a state. The presbyters of I Peter 5.1 were spiritually older members of the Christian nation of royal priests of 2.9.

To be ordained means to be invested with ministerial functions, or to be appointed authoritatively. Since the early Christian congregation was a working organization, it was necessary to appoint (ordain) some of the members to special service. To be appointed to such a position of service, one had to be a mature, older man (*presbyteros*). From among the older men, congregation overseers (*episkopoi*) and their assistants or ministerial servants (*diakonoi*) were selected. These were not a special priesthood in contradiction of Peter's statement: they were simply the servants of their Christian brothers (Acts 6.1-7; Matt. 20.25-28).

Offices in Witness congregations are thus scripturally limited to two: overseers and ministerial servants. These terms translate *episkopoi* and *diakonoi*, rather than transliterate them as bishop and deacon (I Tim. 3.1, 2, 8, 12). Such ordinations or appointments are made through men by the Christian governing body (*The Watchtower*, 1 November 1955, pp. 666 ff.). These special appointments correspond to the laying on of hands in the early church.

However, if all are priests or participate in the principle of the general priesthood, all must be ordained. To all the words apply: 'but with the mouth one makes public declaration for salvation' (Rom. 10.10). This Christian ministry is not limited to a few but is for all. The ordination to such ministry comes from God through his word (II Cor. 3.5, 6; Isa. 61.1, 2).

Jehovah's Witnesses understand, therefore, that following from the principle of the general priesthood, ordinations are made both to an internal and to an external ministry. All Christians are ordained by God to preach the good news in a ministry external to the congregation (Matt. 24.14); and for some among the spiritually older men there is an ordination to special office in the internal ministry of the congregation.

A. HELEY

9. *Lutheran.* The Reformation led to a complete change in the understanding of the ordained ministry. Luther denied the traditional view of the priestly office as having a sacrificial and mediatorial character. He turned against the idea of the clerics as a separate order from that of the laity and the idea of the transfer from the ordinator to the ordinand of a *character indelebilis* which was supposed to give him a sacramental character and enable him to perform the right sacrifice when celebrating the eucharist (*Werke*, Weimar, 1883 ff., = WA 6,562, 567; 12,172,190).

As a support for this view of the ordained ministry, he referred to the biblical office, which he considered instituted by Christ when he chose his apostles and sent them out to preach. The apostles in turn sent others thus continuing the office. He could find no support for the idea that the apostles had transferred the office to an order of bishops (q.v.) separated from the elders (q.v.) (*presbyteroi*) (WA 40, 59; cf. 16, 33). So since a special office of bishop did not exist in NT times, there can be no fundamental division between bishops and priests, and hence a non-

episcopal church cannot be considered less apostolic than one which has the office of bishop. The arrangement may serve the church for practical reasons. According to the Lutheran Confessions, therefore, no other authority was vested in the bishop except to ordain, and this authority was not by virtue of any inherent power in the bishop, but was entrusted to him by the church (WA 6,407). The authority to proclaim the word, administer the sacraments and the power of the keys belongs to everyone ordained, as a trust given for reasons of order by the church. Ordination provides for orderliness but does not constitute an 'order'. This development was dictated by the 'enthusiasts' who claimed only an inner and immediate call from the Holy Spirit (WA 30,519,524; 31,211; 32,483).

Basically every Christian is in baptism ordained priest (priesthood of all believers) with the duty to proclaim the word to those around him. (WA 8,423; 11,413). According to Lutheran teaching the main emphasis lies on *ministerium verbi divini*, in which the office is subordinate to the word. 'The ministry of the word makes ministers, not ministers the ministry' (WA 6,566; 8,422).

Ordination bestows the office of a public servant of God in his church (WA 38,228; 15,721). The office belongs to the church and ordination to it is to be administered by regularly constituted authorities of the church. It is a function, not a rank of the church.

Necessary to ordination are:

1. The assertion of an inner conviction that God has called a person to the ministry of the Gospel.

2. A public confession of evangelical faith with a pledge of loyalty to the revealed truth and the confession of the church.

3. A specific and regular call received and accepted (WA 11,40 ff.; 12, 169 ff.).

4. A readiness to give unconditional devotion to the work of the Lord.

The rite. In view of the doctrine outlined above the first change in the Lutheran ordination ritual was the exclusion of anointing considered to be an expression of the new character in traditional teaching. In 1535 Luther produced a Rite for Ordination which has been the base for the rites of most Lutheran churches. It is found in toto in *Kirkeordinansen* of 1539 for Denmark and Norway and in its major features in *Kyrkoord-*

ningen 1571 for Sweden and Finland.

To the one ordained is given both authority and assurance as the instrument of the Holy Spirit in the performance of his duties. The laying on of hands, not instituted by Christ but from the old dispensation, is not decreed as necessary. It is however considered symbolically valuable as an expression of the church's interest and intercession. (*See* **Imposition of Hands**.)

Elements included in the rite of ordination:

1. Confirm the call to a specific task in the church's ministry.

2. Commit to the ordinand the office of public ministry of word and sacrament.

3. Pledge the ordinand to faithful service.

4. Invoke the Holy Spirit on the ordinand.

5. Mark the apostolicity of the office by the laying on of hands.

The order for ordination includes distinctive propers (q.v.), the formal presentation of candidate, reciting the approving actions of the church, a series of pertinent questions calling for answers by the ordinand to bind the ordinand to the confession of the church and a life consonant therewith, the laying on of hands, and the commissioning followed by appropriate prayers. An admonition to the congregation assembled is also included.

The fact that ordination is a responsibility of the church at large is seen in the liturgy by the fact that:

1. It is performed by the appointed head of the church or his appointee.

2. Ordained ministers representing the church at large participate especially in the laying on of hands.

3. It takes place in the context of the main service of the church.

4. Candidates are presented as approved by the regularly constituted council of the church.

In Europe ordination takes place in the diocesan cathedral, while in North America some churches ordain in connection with synodical conventions while others ordain in the congregation where the ordained is to serve. In Germany the Lutheran churches have since 1951 had a common liturgy based on Luther's Ordination Liturgy (WA 38, 401 ff.) The Scandinavian countries vary slightly in their forms, while the American churches have had a common one since 1958.

E. J. R. H. S. VON SICARD

10. *Methodist.* John Wesley in *The Sunday Service*, 1784, in general copied the ordinal of the *BCP*, 1662, of the Church of England, but used the names superintendants (sic), elders, and deacons. There were, however, several changes, of which the most important were the omissions both of John 20.23 in the formula for ordaining an elder and of the gospel containing it in the form for ordaining a superintendant. Coke, a presbyter of the Church of England whom Wesley had set apart as a superintendant, took this book to America, and it passed into the Ritual in the American *Discipline*, where it underwent various changes. The current form of it is in the *Book of Worship*, 1964. 'The Form of Ordaining of a Superintendant' has become 'The Order for the Consecration of Bishops'. The word 'bishop' goes back to 1792. There has been much discussion about the difference between ordination and consecration, but it is difficult to attach much significance to it. The phrase 'Receive the Holy Ghost' is replaced by 'The Lord pour upon thee the Holy Spirit', a change which was effected (except for the change of 'Ghost') in 1792 for elders, though not till later for bishops. The terms 'epistle' and 'gospel' are retained, but there is no mention of the rest of the communion service.

In British Methodism the services of 1784 continued to be printed in the subsequent editions of *The Sunday Service*, very curiously because the British ministry is not divided into superintendants (though the word is used), elders and deacons, and ordination services with the imposition of hands were not often held until the Wesleyan Conference adopted the practice in 1836. But in the edition of 1846 and subsequent editions the three ordinations were replaced by the 'Form for Ordaining Candidates for the Ministry in the Wesleyan-Methodist Connexion', which contained features from all three. This was not greatly altered in the revision of 1882, nor indeed in that of 1936 after the union, though the services of the non-Wesleyan churches had been very much simpler. At this service, which is in current use, the President of the Conference or his representative presides, assisted by other ordained ministers. 'Receive the Holy Ghost' has become 'Mayest thou receive the Holy Spirit'. The link with the first part of the communion service has been lost, but after the ordination there follows the administration of the Lord's Supper, beginning with the prayer of humble access. The charge to the newly ordained ministers comes after the communion.

In 1968 the Anglican-Methodist Unity Commission produced new services for the ordination of deacons, presbyters also called priests, and bishops, with a preface on the doctrine, with important changes from both traditions. Whether or not the unity scheme is adopted, this is likely to influence the next revision.

There are also services for the conse-cration (America) or ordination (Britain) of deaconesses, and American services for licensing persons to preach, and for admission of ministerial candidates to membership in an annual conference.

A. RAYMOND GEORGE

11. *Old Catholic.* The Old Catholic churches of the Utrecht Union have always attached the utmost importance to maintaining the apostolic succession. This holds even for the earliest of them, the Old Catholic Church of the Netherlands, which, despite its separation from Rome since the beginning of the eighteenth century, has succeeded in main-taining canonically valid episcopal orders. As a result, the Old Catholic churches which arose in protest against the papal dogmas of 1870 were able to carry on the apostolic succession. The validity of Old Catholic episcopal orders has always been recognized, even by Rome.

Because they possess the apostolic succes-sion, the Old Catholic churches have a validly ordained clergy at all stages: the lower orders, the diaconate, priesthood and episco-pate. Although the traditional system of lower orders (door-keepers, lectors, exor-cists, acolytes) has been felt to be prob-lematical for some time, so far it has been kept on in the Old Catholic churches, with an eye to the mother church of Rome. But now that the problem of these lower orders has been recognized in the Roman church within the framework of liturgical renewal, and a new church order has been sought, the question is being re-examined.

The rites of consecration valid in 1971 have been taken from the *Pontificale Romanum*, and in 1899 were produced in German by order of the Old Catholic Bishops' Conference, and then translated into other languages (*cf.* **Books, Liturgical** 11: Old Catholic). All ordinations take place within the mass, but at different points. 'Clothing in the spiritual state' comes first for the lower orders. Candidates are dressed in a white surplice. There is no tonsure. The lower orders are bestowed in accordance with the traditional rites. The office of exorcist, which is no longer held actively, is now interpreted as the entrusting of the duty of pastoral care. It is still an open question whether the subdiaconate is to be included among the lower or the higher orders.

The most important elements of the rites of consecration are: presentation of the ordinands, address by the bishop (instruction on the meaning and the duties of the order to be bestowed), handing over the *instru-menta* (i.e. the vessels and books necessary for exercising the office in question), the prayer of consecration, and dressing in the garments proper to each order. From the consecration of subdeacons upwards, the litany is added, and from the diaconate upwards the invocation of the Holy Spirit; with priests, the hands are anointed and with bishops, the head. At the consecration of priests, hands are laid on the candidate by the bishop and the other priests present, the Apostles' Creed is recited and a promise of obedience is made to the bishop; at the con-secration of bishops there is an examination of faith and the handing over of insignia (cross, staff, ring and mitre). The new presbyters and the newly-consecrated bishop concelebrate with the bishop who con-secrated them. Two other bishops, at least, should assist at the consecration of the bishop, and should lay hands on the bishop with the bishop who consecrates him.

The forms of address and prayers are not translated from the Latin completely literally, but have been reshaped in a form that has strongly biblical colouring. The rite as it has been described will presumably soon be replaced by a new and simplified form.

KURT PURSCH
A. E. RÜTHY
C. TOL

12. *Pentecostal.* In younger Pentecostal churches ordination is not the initiation into the ministry but its acknowledgment by the church. A young Pentecostal, therefore, be-gins (with or without Bible school education) to preach, to lead services, to pray with the sick *before* his ordination. If the church recognizes in him the gifts of a preacher he

will *then* be ordained. This pattern is particularly common in Africa, Latin America and Indonesia, but it was also the rule in USA and Europe thirty years ago. With the establishment of Bible schools this pattern begins to be changed towards a system which approaches that of the main-line Protestant churches. The liturgical formulae for ordination vary. In Santiago I witnessed the ordination of pastors and of a deaconess by the bishop and the superintendents of the Iglesia Metodista Pentecostal according to the Methodist ordination liturgy, including laying on of hands. The only difference from a Methodist ordination service was the highly intense participation of the whole congregation by loud Hallelujahs, shoutings and singing. After the ordination there was the 'kiss of peace' among all the pastors, from which the deaconess was not excepted!

The special gifts for which the congregation tests the candidate for the ministry are not in the first place those of intellect and education – although formal Bible school or theological education are beginning to play a greater part in European and North American Pentecostal denominations. Rather they search to learn whether the future minister is able to lead the Pentecostal liturgy by his sensitivity and his musical ability to intone a chorus (*see* **Liturgies** 12: Pentecostal), so that chaos *and* cold stiffness are alike avoided, and further whether he is a man who is able to articulate what his people feel, what they fear and what they rejoice about. (For bibliography *see* **Pentecostal Worship**.)

W. J. HOLLENWEGER

13. *Reformed.* The Reformed Church holds itself to be part of the one, holy, catholic and apostolic church. It is, says Knox:

a part of that holy Kirk universal, which is grounded upon the doctrine of the prophets and apostles, having the same antiquity that the Kirk of the Apostles has as concerning doctrine, prayers, administration of sacraments and all things requisite to a particular Kirk (Knox, *Works*, VI, p.492).

On the basis of the NT (Acts 20.17-35; I Tim 4.14; Titus 1.5-7; I Peter 5.1-4; etc.) and also of the *communior sententia*, found in Aquinas and the scholastics, that the highest order of the Christian ministry is the presbyterate and that the bishop is only

a presbyter who has been given the episcopal office (Barkley in *The Newman*, IV, 3, pp. 115-31), the Reformed Church accepts the original identity of presbyter and bishop. Presbyterianism means government by presbyters (not presbyteries), just as episcopacy means government by bishops. Ordination is an act of God through presbyters, constitutionally associated, within the people of God. In the words of the Provincial Assembly of London, who carried on the work of the Westminster Assembly,

The power of ordination of ministers exercised for these many hundred years by bishops did belong to them as presbyters and not as bishops (*Jus Divinum Ministerii Evangelici*, II, 20, 33).

The procedure for ordination in the Genevan *Ecclesiastical Ordinances* (1541) was:

It will be good in this connection to follow the order of the ancient Church, for it is the only practice which is shown us in Scripture. The order is that ministers first elect such as ought to hold office; afterwards that he be presented to the Council; and if he is found worthy the Council receive and accept him, giving him certification to produce finally to the people when he preaches, in order that he be received by the common consent of the company of the faithful. . . . As to the manner of introducing him, it is good to use the imposition of hands, which ceremony was observed by the apostles and then in the ancient Church, providing that it take place without superstition and without offence. But because there has been much superstition in the past and scandal might result, it is better to abstain from it because of the infirmity of the times (*Corpus Reformatorum*, X, 15).

These regulations cover (i) the election and examination, and (ii) the act of ordination. The former varied in different places. For example, in the English congregation in Geneva, the congregation nominated several candidates to the ministers and elders, who examined them as to their life and education. The one approved was made known to the congregation, and time provided for them to enquire as to his fitness and character. If nothing was charged against him, a day was appointed for his ordination. The same procedure, in broad outline, was followed in

France and Scotland.

One of the essential elements in ordination is the 'call'. As the Genevan *Ordinances* put it, 'No one ought to intrude himself into this office without a call'. This emphasis is found in Zwingli (*CR*, IV, 425), Calvin (*Inst.* IV, iii, 10), the second *Helvetic* (18) and *Gallican* (31) *Confessions*, as well as in Holland (G. Brandt, *The Reformation in the Low Countries*, 1720, I, p. 318). In Scotland however they preferred to speak of a double call: 'called of God and duly elected by men'. The 'call' of the people was seen as confirming the inward 'call' of God. The Holy Spirit works not only in the aspirant, but also in the electors.

With regard to the ordination, it was by prayer with the laying on of hands in Zurich (H. A. Daniel, *Codex Liturgicus*, III, 1851, 234). This is also true of the first and second *Helvetic Confessions* (H. A. Niemeyer, *Collectio Confessionum*, 1840, pp. 110, 119, 507), of Calvin in Strasbourg, John a'Lasco in Frankfurt (*Forma ac Ratio*, 1556), Valerand Pullain (*Liturgia sacra*, 1551) and in France (J. Quick, *Synodicon*, 1692, I, 3, 62). On the other hand, in Geneva and Holland (Brandt, I, p. 319) the laying on of hands would appear to be an open question. The Scottish first *Book of Discipline* (Knox, *Works*, II, 193) contains wording similar to that in the Genevan *Ordinances*, but this may only refer to those who had formerly been priests in the medieval church. In 1566, the Scottish assembly approved the second *Helvetic Confession*, and in 1581 adopted the second *Book of Discipline* (III, 6), both of which prescribe the laying on of hands. It also was the practice of the English Puritans, as the 1586, 1587, and 1602 editions of the *Form of Prayers* show. In all these rites the essence of ordination is prayer (cf. L. Duchesne, *Christian Worship*, [6]1931, p. 377).

Calvin's ordination service is based on the practice of the early church rather than the medieval ordinals, but the liturgical sections do not appear to go farther back than himself or perhaps Bucer.

In the Scottish *Book of Common Order* (1564) the service is headed *The Form and Order of the Election of the Superintendent which may serve in election of all the Ministers*. It is really the form, drawn up by John Knox in 1560, largely based upon a'Lasco, for the admission of John Spottiswood as Superintendent for the Lothians (*BCO*, ed. Sprott, pp. 20-7).

After a sermon, which, as with Calvin, dealt with the office and nature of the ministry, the people were asked if they accepted the minister and would 'obey him as Christ's Minister'. Then a series of questions was put to the minister-elect, and after satisfactory answers had been given the people were again asked whether they would receive him. A short exhortation 'to the nobility' followed, and then came the ordination-prayer ending with the Lord's Prayer. After this the ministers and elders gave the right hand of fellowship. A benediction followed, and then an exhortation to the minister, the final direction being 'Sing the 23rd Psalm'.

Spottiswood was in Anglican Orders, so there is no reference to the laying on of hands. The same applied to priests of the medieval church. They were admitted, not ordained.

> Our reformers did not set up a new Church but did reform the old apostatized Church, so that there needed no new ordination (J. Menzeis, *Roma Mendax*, 1675, pp. 350, 379; *Jus Divinum*, II, 28).

Ordination was a catholic rite, not merely an admission to the ministry of a particular church. The people were given a place in the choice of the ordinand, but he was ordained by those already holding the office. His commission was not from the people, but from God through presbyters, lawfully associated, within the people of God.

In 1570 and 1620 further ordinals were produced in Scotland, and both make prayer and laying on of hands the main portions of the ceremony (*Miscellany of the Wodrow Society*, 1844, pp. 597ff.). In 1645, the Westminster *Form of Presbyterial Church Government* was adopted, and it remains the basic document to the present day in English-speaking Presbyterianism. It states:

> No man ought to take upon him the office of a minister of the word without a lawful calling. . . .
>
> Every minister of the word is to be ordained by imposition of hands and prayer, with fasting, by those preaching presbyters to whom it doth belong. . . .
>
> He that is to be ordained minister, must be duly qualified, both for life and mini-

sterial abilities. . . .

He is to be examined and approved by those by whom he is to be ordained.

No man is to be ordained a minister for a particular congregation, if they of that congregation can shew just cause of exception against him.

Preaching presbyters orderly associated . . . are those to whom the imposition of hands doth appertain, for those congregations within their bounds . . . (XVIII 1, 4, 7, 8, 9, 10).

It then sets out *The Directory for the Ordination of Ministers*. The structure of the service is:

Sermon 'concerning the office and duty of ministers of Christ'.

Questions to ordinand concerning his faith in Christ, the truth of reformed religion . . . his sincere intentions, his diligence in praying, reading, meditation, preaching, administration of the sacraments, his willingness to submit to the discipline of the church.

Questions to people 'concerning their willingness to receive and acknowledge him as the minister of Christ' . . . 'to obey him . . .', 'and to maintain, encourage, and assist him in all the parts of his office'.

Prayer of ordination with laying on of hands. Following thanksgiving for the incarnation, atonement and ascension of Christ, the gift of the Holy Spirit, and the Christian ministry comes an epiclesis (q.v.) asking God 'to fit him with his Holy Spirit, to give him (who in his name we thus set apart to this holy service) to fulfil the work of his ministry in all things . . .'.

Charge to minister and people.

Prayer 'commending both him and his flock to the grace of God'.

Psalm.

Dismissal with a blessing (XIX 5-9).

These works contain the basic principles which govern all modern rites.

Following the Westminster Assembly, owing to the rise of Independency and Brownism there was a period of liturgical decadence. Renewal came with the founding of the Church Service Society in 1865. It published the second edition of its *Euchologion* in 1869. This included an introductory article (pp. 294-303) on the ordination service, a table of scripture lessons 'proper for the Service preceding the Ordination of Ministers and their Induction to Office' and 'portions of psalms proper to be sung' (p. 317), as well as a text for the rite (pp. 303-316). Its structure may be seen from the rubrics:

Divine Service shall be celebrated according to the usual order, or to such special order as the Presbytery may judge proper. . . .

After the Sermon, the presiding Minister shall read . . . a Narrative . . . of the proceedings of the Presbytery . . . concluding with these words: All having accordingly been so far done in this matter as is required by the law and usage of the Church, the Presbytery will now proceed to ordain the said A.B. to the Holy Ministry. . . .

Then the Candidate . . . shall answer the questions appointed by the Church to be put to those who are to be ordained. . . .

The presiding Presbyter . . . shall pray as follows . . . It is a prayer of thanksgiving, and at the epiclesis the presiding Presbyter and the other Presbyters standing near lay hands upon the head of the candidate.

The presiding Presbyter . . . shall take him by the right hand, saying, We give you the right hand of fellowship, to take part with us in this ministry.

Thereafter the presiding Presbyter shall give a solemn charge to the new Minister, and . . . to the people present, setting forth their respective duties from the Word of God.

Then shall be offered the following prayer. . . . The Service shall conclude with singing, and the following Benediction: Now the God of Peace. . . .

The liturgical sources for the prayers in this rite are Calvin, Knox, the Westminster *Directory*, and the *Provisional Liturgy* of the German Reformed Church in America, 1850 (*Euchologion*, ed. Sprott, p. 431).

In the *Euchologion*, ordination is treated as an ordinance following the liturgy of the word, and this is still the practice in some places. On the other hand, Scotland, Ireland, England-Wales, Canada, Geneva and Vaud see the rite as a unity and set out the service as consisting of both the liturgy of the word and ordination. All include the order for ordination in their service-book, except the Church of Scotland, the United Church of Canada, and America, where it is published in a separate ordinal. As a result of the *Euchologion* in Scotland, Osterwald in Switzerland, van Dyke in America, Bersier in France, van der Leeuw in Holland, and Albertz in Germany, all modern rites show traces of a more careful handling of the theological implications of ordination. As the various rites, whether in English, French, or German, follow a common pattern it is unnecessary to deal with them in detail. The rite of the Church of Scotland is representative:

Psalm
Scripture sentences
Prayer: confession, pardon, and illumination
Old Testament lection
Psalm
New Testament lections
Apostles' Creed
Prayer: intercession, commemoration of faithful departed
Hymn
Sermon on the holy ministry
Declaration of intention
Prescribed questions to ordinand
Prayer of ordination with laying on of hands and Lord's Prayer
Declaration with right hand of fellowship
Vow of people
Charge to minister and people
Prayer
Psalm or hymn
Benediction, The peace of God . . .

Only a few comments are necessary:
(*a*) The lections set forth the biblical basis for the ministry. The following are those most commonly used:

Old Testament
Exodus 3.1-6   Ireland
     4.11-12   Geneva
     18.18b-20   France
Isaiah 6.1-8   Ireland, Germany, England
     61.1-6   Scotland, England
Jeremiah 1.4-9   France
Ezekiel 1.26-2.5   Canada
     34.11-16   England

Epistle
Acts 1.7-9   Canada

     20.17-35   Ireland
Romans 10.13-17   Geneva, Germany
I Corinthians 12.27-13.13   England, Germany
II Corinthians 4.1-13   England
     5.17-21   France
Ephesians 4.4-8, 11-16   Ireland, France
I Timothy 3.1-3   Vaud, Geneva, England
     6.3-12   England
II Timothy 2.4-6   Geneva, Vaud
     4.1-5   Geneva, Vaud, Canada
Titus 1.1-7   England
I Peter 5.1-4   Scotland, Ireland, England, Germany, Vaud, France, Geneva, Canada, America

Gospel
Matthew 5.1-16   England
     28.17-20   Vaud, Geneva, Germany Ireland, England
Mark 10.42-45   France, Vaud, Geneva
Luke 12.35-38   England
John 10.1-11   Canada, England
     10.11-16   France, England
     20.19-23   France
     21.15-17   Scotland, Ireland, Canada, England, France, Germany

(*b*) In the Presbyterian church in Canada a Statement on the Ministry may be read instead of the sermon.

(*c*) The prescribed questions differ in each church because they are drawn up by the various assemblies. They always cover: 'call of God', belief in the fundamental doctrines of the Christian faith, acceptance of scripture, obedience 'in the Lord' to the church, and fidelity as a minister of Jesus Christ.

(*d*) Some rites, for example, the Scottish, have the *Sursum corda* before the ordination prayer. Basically all are thanksgivings with an epiclesis and the laying on of hands. Though the words vary they are all identical in substance.

The following may be taken as representative:

France
We pray thee, Father Almighty, to send thy Holy Spirit upon our brother, N . . ., whom we consecrate to thy service and ordain a pastor in thy holy Church to the ministry of the Word and Sacraments.

Lausanne
In the name of the Father, of the Son, and

of the Holy Spirit, we consecrate to the service of Christ our brother by the laying on of hands to the ministry of the Gospel in his Church.

Scotland

Send down thy Holy Spirit upon this thy servant, whom we, in thy name, and in obedience to thy most blessed will, do now, by the laying on of our hands, ordain and appoint to the Office of the Holy Ministry in thy holy Catholic Church, committing unto him authority to minister thy Word and Sacraments, and to bear rule in thy flock.

Canada

Send now the Holy Spirit in power upon thy servant here kneeling, whom we in thy name do by the laying-on of our hands, receive and ordain to the Ministry of thy Word and Sacraments in the Holy Catholic Church. . . .

America

Send down thy Holy Spirit upon this thy servant, whom we, in thy name and in obedience to thy holy will, do now by the laying on of our hands ordain and appoint to the office of the holy ministry in thy Church, committing unto him authority to preach the Word, administer the Sacraments, and to bear rule in thy Church.

Germany

We ordain and ratify you with prayer and the laying on of hands as an ordained minister of the Church and teacher of the Gospel in the name of the Father, and of the Son, and of the Holy Spirit.

(*e*) Some churches, for example, Scotland, provide a Charge which may be read.

In conclusion, in the Reformed Church, the rite of ordination is an ordinance of the Word and always takes place within the setting of public worship, thus placing the holy ministry within the context of the sovereign grace of the Lord Jesus Christ, sole King and Head of the church. All ministry is ultimately his ministry within the life of his body. The holy ministry is of divine institution and derivation, renewed in every age by Jesus Christ through the creative power of the Holy Spirit, acting through his church when it is faithful to its apostolic institution, practice and doctrine.

JOHN M. BARKLEY

14. *Seventh-Day Adventist*. In the Seventh-day Adventist Church ordination is the liturgical act by which a member of the church is set apart by prayer and the laying on of hands for a special function of service in the church and is authorized to perform this function.

In the very early days of the SDAC there appears to have been little need for ordaining new ministers, because congregations were small and most of the ministers had already been ordained in the churches of their former membership. However, as the need for some clear form of church organization arose, and in order to avoid any tendency towards want of method or lack of co-operation by self-appointed preachers, the leaders of the movement began to practise ordination in the early 1850s. It was not instituted to build up a religious hierarchy or to exalt a clergy to a place of special privilege, but rather to provide for proper church order as the ordained individual receives new responsibilities and consecrates his life to God, the special service of the church, and to the world.

The SDAC ordains three categories of church workers: (*a*) ministers, (*b*) local church elders and (*c*) deacons.

Ordained ministers are full-time, salaried workers of the church, who have completed the requisite academic and theological studies prescribed by the church. Candidates for ministerial ordination have for the most part served as licensed ministers for a minimum of four years (including a two-year ministerial internship). Customarily they are married men; however, marriage is not a prerequisite for ordination. Though the church has taken no stand against the ordination of women, in practice only men have been ordained so far. The General Conference *Working Policy* outlines a careful procedure for authorizing ordination. The usual process is for local conference (or mission) and Union committees to suggest ordinands to the committee on credentials and licences at the triennial conference (or mission) session, on whose favourable report the session delegates make the final decision. Before ordination is carried out, a careful interview of the candidate is held, usually in the presence of his wife. It is conducted by ordained ministers only. There must be evidence of the person's divine call before the church sets him apart by ordination. Seventh-day Adventists reject as without biblical foundation the concept of 'apostolic succession', seeing little guarantee in the physical act of imposition itself. The laying on of hands *per se* adds no new grace or virtual qualification. By this act the church sets its seal upon the work of God.

The ordination service is one of the most solemn of all services of the church. It usually takes place on a Sabbath (Saturday) afternoon and is conducted with a view to exalting the office of the ministry in the eyes of the people and solemnizing the call in the heart of the candidate. For this service all ordained ministers present, if feasible, are invited on to the rostrum. Three ministers are chosen to take the three leading parts in the service: *ordination prayer*, the *charge*, the *welcome*.

After a brief sermon on the high calling and responsibility of the ministry, followed by the presentation of the candidate, the ministers, with the candidate in the centre of the group, kneel for the ordination prayer, while the congregation remains seated with bowed heads. When in the prayer mention is made of the laying on of hands, those kneeling near the candidate place a hand upon his head, continuing thus until the close of the prayer.

Rising from prayer, all the ministers stand while the charge is given. It is largely in the language of scripture, including such passages as Ezek. 33.7-9, 11; Acts 20.28; I Tim. 4.12-16; II Tim. 2.3, 4, 24; 4.1-5; I Peter 5.2-4. Following the charge, words of welcome are spoken, usually by the conference president.

Local church elders and deacons are laymen elected by the local church they serve, in contrast to the ordained minister who serves the world-wide church. Local elders and deacons are usually ordained in a simple ceremony during the divine service on Sabbath, with an ordained minister in charge. After reading a few appropriate passages of scripture (e.g., I Tim. 3.1-7 for elders, and I Tim. 3.8-13 for deacons), the candidate and minister kneel for the consecration prayer and the laying on of hands. After the prayer, the minister clasps the candidate's hand with a word of blessing. A local elder need not be reordained again upon re-election by the same congregation or another local church, or if subsequently elected as a deacon. Likewise a deacon is not reordained; however, if he is elected as an elder, he must be ordained as an elder, since this is an office of a higher degree.

In ordaining ministers, elders and deacons,

Seventh-day Adventists believe they are operating in harmony with the NT custom of having apostles and evangelists (itinerant ministry) to look after the general interests of the church as a whole, elders ('presbyters' or 'bishops') looking after the spiritual welfare, and deacons after the more temporal interests, of their local congregation.

B. B. BEACH

P. Bradshaw, *The Anglican Ordinal: Its History and Development*, 1971; F. E. Brightman, *The English Rite*, 2 vols., 1915; W. Brunnotte, *Das geistliche Sint bei Luther*, 1959; Church of South India, *The Book of Common Worship*, 1963; *Constitution, Bylaws and Working Policy of the General Conference of Seventh-day Adventists*, 1968; P. Edwall, E. Hayman and W. D. Maxwell, eds., *Ways of Worship*: Report of a theological commission of Faith and Order, 1951; W. K. Firminger, 'The Ordinal', in *Liturgy and Worship*, eds. W. K. Lowther Clarke and C. Harris, 1932; T. F. Gulixson, 'The Ministry' in *What Lutherans are Thinking*, ed. E. C. Fendt, 1947; Winthrop S. Hudson and Norman H. Maring, *A Baptist Manual of Polity and Practice,* 1963; B. A. van Kleef, *Geschiedenis van de Oud-Katholieke Kerk van Nederland,* 2nd ed., 1953; U. Küry, *Die altkatholische Kirche (Die Kirchen der Welt)*, 1966; N. Lindroth, *En bok om Kyrkans ämbete*, 1951; M. Luther, *Ordinationsformular*, WA 38, 401 ff.; *Manual for Ministers*, 1965 (Seventhday Adventist); Don F. Neufeld, ed., *Seventh-day Adventist Encyclopedia*, 1966, pp. 925 ff.; A. Nygren, *This is the Church*, 1952; F. Proctor and W. H. Frere, *A New History of the Book of Common Prayer*, 1949; F. C. Ratcliff, 'The Ordinal of the Church of South India' in *Theology*, 63, January, 1960; *Report on Anglican-Methodist Unity: The Ordinal*, 1968; *The Standing Liturgical Committee of Protestant Episcopal Church in USA (Prayer Book Studies No. 20)*, 1970; V. Vajta, *Luther on Worship: An Interpretation*, 1958.

Organ

A keyboard instrument, which can be traced back to the ancient Greeks, in which wind is blown through pipes by mechanical action or, in modern imitations, tone is produced electronically. Pipe organs vary in size from the medieval portative, which can be carried

Plate 33   Organ, The Lyons Concert Hall,
York University, England

about, to modern giants with four, or more, manuals (keyboards) and pedals. The tone of the instrument is varied by the use of different ranks of pipes brought into action by the player through controls called stops. A medium-sized church organ is likely to have three manuals: swell, great and choir. The first of these gets its name through the practice of enclosing its pipes in a box with shutters, so that the swell pedal controls crescendo and diminuendo. Alternative, or further, manuals to be found are: positive, solo and echo. The pedal keyboard is a separate division of the instrument requiring a foot technique only otherwise found in the pedal harpsichord, now obsolete.

The compass of an organ manual is normally five octaves (sixty-one notes), or slightly less, and of the pedals two and a half octaves (thirty-two notes) or a few less. Some organ pipes play at unison, or piano pitch, whereas others sound an octave lower or one, two, or more octaves higher, with various fractions of an octave also available. As a result the instrument has a wider compass

than a piano, or even the whole orchestra. The characteristic tone of the organ comes from diapason or principal stops, but flutes and string-toned stops are common, as well as a variety of reeds based on wind and brass instruments. High-pitched stops, called mixtures, reinforce the upper frequencies to create a brilliant sound of high definition.

The glory of the organ is its association with Bach in the Baroque era. The magnificence of his organ music, and that of some of his contemporaries, has caused twentieth-century organ builders to re-create the finest features of the Baroque organ, which had been a lost art. Many composers before Bach made contributions to the literature of the instrument: outstanding among these is Buxtehude, and later on Handel wrote his concertos. The changing ideals of romantic composers are reflected in the works of Mendelssohn, Schumann and Liszt. Cesar Franck and Max Reger wrote extensively for the organ, and many twentieth-century composers have written for the instrument at a time of transition. The only major modern composer to specialize in the organ has been Olivier Messiaen, whose innovations have revealed new possibilities to later generations. Avant-garde examples include György Ligeti's *Volumina* and Mauricio Kagel's *Fantasia for Organ with Obbligati*, which requires an electronic tape. The portative organ and the harmonium have been revived by modern composers, and the electronic organ has a life of its own in certain works of Stockhausen quite apart from extensive use in jazz and pop (rock) music.

Organs and church choirs have long been adjuncts to Christian worship, although the Puritans in England and America distrusted music in church and organs were even destroyed during the English civil war. This was a temporary setback following the golden age of Elizabethan music and succeeded by the Restoration era of Purcell and Blow, both of whom were organists at Westminster Abbey. From the sixteenth to eighteenth centuries much concerted music was written for church use (e.g. Bach's cantatas) with an essential part for the organ. Throughout this period and up to the present day the English cathedral tradition has concerned choir and organ, and most British (and some American) composers have written for these resources. Apart from recital music, such as the Preludes and Fugues of Bach, or the Symphonies of Vierne, there is a quantity of organ music from all periods designed for liturgical use, often based on hymn-tunes, the mass, or passages of scripture.

In times of economic stringency churches find organs an expensive luxury, as a large instrument requires skilled and continuous maintenance, not to mention periodic rebuilding. As a result, small churches have had recourse to cheap electronic organs which, although they have been improving in quality, rarely give satisfaction to musicians. A parallel development among organ builders has been the revival of the chamber organ, a small instrument of almost domestic size consisting of four or five ranks of pipes only, with one or two manuals and pedals. The modern trend in organ building is to retain all features of the historic instrument so that the music of all periods can be performed, and the varying demands of church use be met. After a century of attempting to imitate the orchestra the organ has rediscovered its heritage. *See* Plate 33.

William Leslie Sumner, *The Organ, Its Evolution, Principles of Construction and Use,* [2]1955.

P. DICKINSON

Orientation

The siting of a building so that its sanctuary (q.v.) points to the east (Lat. *oriens*) ultimately derives from the early Christian practice of facing the east for prayer. In Judaism, prayer was offered towards the Temple at Jerusalem as the place of the presence of God; the Christian eastward direction could well have begun in conscious contrast to the Jewish custom, but it would also have been influenced by the general pagan understanding of the time that the east is the direction in which the good divine powers are to be found, a view originally connected with sun worship. Moreover, the NT itself suggests that the *parousia* of Christ will be from the east (Matt. 24.27), and since the ascension is a type of the second coming – he 'shall so come in like manner as you beheld him going into heaven' (Acts 1.11) – this, too, was envisaged as taking place in an eastward direction. As primitive Christian prayer was directed towards Christ and particularly towards the coming Christ, it was quite natural for orientation to be adopted.

Patristic teaching on the subject also referred to Jesus as 'the dayspring from on high' (Luke 1.78; *cf.* Clement of Alexandria, *Strom* 7.7) and suggested that in praying to the east the soul is hoping for restoration to its ancient home in Paradise through Christ the Second Adam (Basil, *de Spir. Sanct.* 27).

The Constantinian buildings, however, had their sanctuary at the west end. It is difficult to decide which of three possible explanations of this is correct. It may have been that the direction reflected Constantine's continued devotion to the Unconquered Sun. Again, since the president at the eucharist, adopting the basilican position, faced the congregation across the altar, to have the sanctuary at the west end meant that he and his assistant clergy did in fact look towards the east. Finally, it could be that Constantine and his architects understood their buildings as types of the Jerusalem Temple, of which the holy of holies was itself at the west end (I Kings 6).

From the middle of the fourth century the practice of locating the sanctuary at the east end was adopted and became all but universal, but without complete accuracy in every case; so in Rome St Maria Maggiore is north-west, but both St Sabina and St Agnese are south-east. Throughout the centuries since there has been a basic preference for the east-west orientation, and we find Durandus of Mende (1285-96) listing eight reasons for this: (1) 'The east is the image of Christ who, like the rising sun, lighteth every man that cometh into the world.' (2) 'Our souls be thereby taught to turn themselves to the things that are most desirable.' (3) 'Because those who praise God ought not to turn their backs on him.' (4) 'To show that we seek our country.' (5) 'Christ is the true east.' (6) 'Christians look towards Paradise from whence man has been excluded.' (7) 'Christ on the cross looked towards the east, he ascended thither and will come again from that direction.' (8) 'Daniel prayed towards the temple when he was in captivity' (*Rat. div. off.* 5.2.57).

Nevertheless, despite this array of allegory and symbolism, orientation has never been considered absolutely essential and many churches have been built regardless of it to accommodate them to the site available. Certainly in the twentieth century many modern churches neglect it entirely, the primary consideration having been how best to arrange the building in a given confined area.

EDITOR

Orthodox Worship

(More properly, Orthodox worship of the Byzantine rite.)

> The normal Orthodox lay worshipper, through familiarity from earlier childhood, is entirely at home in church, thoroughly conversant with the audible parts of the Holy Liturgy, and takes part with unconscious and unstudied ease in the action of the rite, to an extent only shared in by the hyper-devout and ecclesiastically-minded in the West (A. Oakley, *The Orthodox Liturgy*, 1958, p. 12).

Orthodox worship is indeed marked by this character of natural corporate participation. But in what does its character consist? In current practice, practice of very long standing, it is certainly not the product of those constituents which are commonly held to be necessary to it in modern Western theology of the liturgical reform school.

Some of these constituents are, of course, present. The worship of the Byzantine rite, in contrast to that of the Roman rite in the West, has never suffered from celebration in a language 'not understood of the people'; at every stage of its expansion, from the conversion of the Slavs in the ninth and tenth centuries to Russian missionary activity in central and eastern Asia in the nineteenth, it has been taken for granted that one of the first prerequisites is the translation of the scriptures and the service-books into the appropriate language. And today, while Byzantine Greek and Old Slavonic are very different from modern Greek and Russian, in neither case is the language so far removed from its modern counterpart as to be unintelligible to the regular worshipper. Consequently, the clericalization of worship which occurred in the West during the Middle Ages has little counterpart in the Byzantine East: in particular, laymen (readers and cantors) play a far greater part in the conduct of services than they have done in the West until very recent years. Nor is there any Orthodox parallel to the overshadowing of the liturgy by popular devotions, embodying a very different spirituality, such as the Roman Catholic Church has suffered from for some centuries: there is no

absence of popular devotions, but they have always been cast in a liturgical mould, and integrated into the liturgy itself, and the latter has in any case always remained *the* popular devotion, the staple diet of the ordinary worshipper.

On the other hand, congregational participation in the sense in which the phrase is usually understood today in the West is in most churches markedly absent. Practically the whole of Byzantine public worship, apart from those prayers recited *secreto* by the celebrant, is sung, and commonly only the choir sing. (This is especially true of Russian churches, in which elaborate harmonized music is used.) The sanctuary is separated from the nave by a solid screen, through the central doorway of which the altar is usually visible only from part of the church. The reception of holy communion by the adult laity is infrequent.

But by far the most important aspect of Orthodox worship is its general ethos, which is succinctly summed up in the words of an eighth-century patriarch of Constantinople, Germanos: 'The church is the earthly heaven in which the heavenly God dwells and moves.' The oneness of the worship of the church on earth with that of the church in heaven, and the consequent participation of the former in the latter, is the fundamental sacramental concept on which Orthodox worship is based. The incarnate Christ himself, in whom divine and human, heavenly and earthly, are joined together, is *the* sacrament; because the church is his body on earth, the extension of the incarnation, the church itself is a sacrament; therefore the church's worship is sacramental – all of it, not only those rites specifically called the sacraments. It was not until the seventeenth century that Orthodox dogmatic theology, under the pressures of Reformation and Counter-Reformation, came definitely to reckon seven sacraments, and to this day the service-books do not normally distinguish between sacraments and what in the West are called sacramentals (*see* **Books, Liturgical,** 2).

Nor is this sacramentality confined to sacraments and sacramentals; it is to be found also in the daily offices and the special observances of the church's year. The extent to which the latter involve the ordinary worshipper is well summed up by an Anglican writer:

Nobody who has lived and worshipped amongst Greek Christians for any length of time but has sensed in some measure the extraordinary hold which the recurring cycle of the Church's liturgy has upon the piety of the common people. Nobody who has kept the Great Lent with the Greek Church, who has shared in the fast which lies heavy upon the whole nation for forty days; who has stood for long hours, one of an innumerable multitude who crowd the tiny Byzantine churches of Athens and overflow into the streets, while the familiar pattern of God's saving economy towards man is re-presented in psalm and prophecy, in lections from the Gospel, and the matchless poetry of the canons; who has known the desolation of the holy and great Friday, when every bell in Greece tolls its lament and the body of the Saviour lies shrouded in flowers in all the village churches throughout the land; who has been present at the kindling of the new fire and tasted of the joy of a world released from the bondage of sin and death – none can have lived through all this and not have realized that for the Greek Christian the Gospel is inseparably linked with the liturgy that is unfolded week by week in his parish church. Not among the Greeks only, but throughout Orthodox Christendom the liturgy has remained at the very heart of the Church's life (P. Hammond, *The Waters of Marah*, 1956, pp. 51-52).

It should not, however, be supposed that the Byzantine rite is not in need of liturgical reform. It has passed through phases of development and decadence parallel to those through which the Roman rite in the West has passed; much of it, in its present form, does not antedate the Middle Ages, and much of its current presentation, especially in the Slav churches, does not antedate a much later period still. So far little has been done, except here and there, to cope with the liturgical needs of the very changed situation of the Orthodox Church in the twentieth century, especially in the churches of the emigration: in particular the problem of language has become acute – for the first time in Orthodox history there are many churches in which the congregation does not understand the language in which the church's worship is celebrated. Whether, in the absence of appropriate measures of reform and renewal, it will continue to play the part in the lives of future generations which it has played in those of their forebears is a question to which it would be dangerously complacent to return an affirmative answer. Yet, while reform and renewal are necessary, it is equally necessary that they take place within the church's authentic liturgical tradition, and that their value should not be compromised by the kind of distortions which in recent years have come increasingly to compromise it in the West.

W. JARDINE GRISBROOKE

Pall

1. The term is applied to any cloth or covering that envelops or covers some object. The cloth of silk which in the earlier centuries completely enveloped the altar, and which was revived in the Church of England in the seventeenth century, was sometimes termed 'altar-pall' (*see* **Altar Hangings**).

2. It is also used for the cloth of velvet or damask that envelops a coffin when it stands in church at a funeral service. This should reach almost to the ground and cover the bier or trestles as well as the coffin. Most parish churches had such a pall until the middle of the last century and it covered the coffin of all parishioners, rich and poor alike, without distinction.

3. The term is also sometimes applied to the cloth that is hung from the desk of the pulpit (q.v.). At the Reformation period, only persons who had a doctor's degree were permitted to have such a cloth displayed when they preached, and preachers who were merely masters or bachelors of arts had no such cloth.

C. E. Pocknee, ed., *The Parson's Handbook*, 1965; The Warham Guild, *The Warham Guild Handbook*, rev. ed., 1963.

C. E. POCKNEE

Palm Sunday

The origin of Palm Sunday is to be found at Jerusalem in the latter part of the fourth century. On the Sunday with which the Great Week, i.e., Holy Week (q.v.), began, the people went to the Mount of Olives in the early afternoon. About five o'clock the gospel passage telling of the triumphal entry was read, and there was a procession by foot from the summit of the Mount of Olives into the city, children also sharing in the celebration and all carrying branches of palm or olive. In the course of time the observance spread from Jerusalem, but at Rome in the middle of the following century there is no hint that the Sunday bore the special characteristics of Palm Sunday, nor do we hear of Good Friday.

Palm Sunday is still regularly marked in Roman Catholic and Anglican churches by the distribution of palms, which are blessed and often carried in procession.

A. A. MCARTHUR

Papal Rites

The title which is borne by the head of the Catholic Church is that of *pontifex maximus*, which conveys the idea of a great high priest. The solemn performance of the sacerdotal functions of the pope first became practicable after the Emperor Constantine the Great had given peace to the church at the beginning of the fourth century. We can get some idea of what the papal liturgy was like up till the Middle Ages from the ancient sacramentaries and the *Ordines Romani*. The popes officiated in the various basilicas and other churches of Rome, chiefly of course in the Lateran basilica, *mater et caput omnium ecclesiarum urbis et orbis*, beside which they dwelt till their exile in Avignon at the beginning of the fourteenth century. When there, they worshipped in the palace chapel. After they returned to Rome in 1376, they went to live in the Vatican and there they continued the custom, begun in Avignon, of celebrating divine worship in their domestic chapels. For this reason Sixtus IV erected the magnificent Sistine Chapel in 1473, and Paul V the Pauline Chapel in the Quirinal palace in 1616. The Sistine Chapel had its daily divine office and high mass till 1788.

The dynamic Sixtus V (1585-90) made a grand effort to restore the pontifical ceremonies in the Roman basilicas and stational churches, but after his death they ceased again. Nevertheless, a good number of the papal 'chapels' continued to be held both in the Vatican and in the churches of the city. Gaetano Moroni (*Le Cappelle Pontificie*, 1841) enumerates ten days in the year on which the pope assisted at vespers and

thirty-five when he assisted at mass. But after the occupation of Rome by the Italian army in 1870, these solemn liturgical functions were considered to be incompatible with the state of mourning adopted by the holy see. The pope never left the Vatican palace till the Concordat was signed with the Kingdom of Italy in 1929. In the Sistine Chapel were celebrated only the anniversaries of the pope's election and coronation, the anniversary of the death of the late pope and a requiem mass in November for the cardinals deceased during the preceding year. Pius XI also celebrated the rites of Maundy Thursday and Good Friday each year. The late Pope John XXIII pontificated several times in St Peter's. He also assisted at the ceremonies of Palm Sunday, Maundy Thursday and Good Friday in the other papal basilicas. His present Holiness Paul VI also takes part in the Easter Vigil in St Peter's and in the Ash Wednesday rite.

High mass celebrated by the pope. The solemn celebration of the papal high mass (q.v.) is in our day a rare event. Before 1870 the pope used to sing high mass regularly three times a year in St Peter's: on Christmas day, on Easter day, and on the Feast of St Peter and St Paul. But after this date the papal high mass was only celebrated on some extraordinary occasions such as canonizations, certain centenaries and papal coronations. In the early medieval ages, on the contrary, it would seem that the sovereign pontiff sang mass on nearly all the Station days, on various feasts and perhaps on Sundays, but of course the rite was much simpler than it became later on, when it took something like four hours to carry it out. Even so, Gregory the Great complained in a letter to the patriarch of Alexandria that he suffered so much from gout when he had to spend three hours in the celebration of mass on feast days.

The best description of the papal mass in the eighth century is to be found in the *Ordo Romanus I*, of which an English version was published by E. G. C. F. Atchley in 1905. For a later period we have *Le Cérémonial Apostolique avant Innocent VIII* by Joaquim Nabuco, published in Rome in 1966. There is no official book regulating the ceremonies of the papal mass today. In 1516 Christopher Marcellus, archbishop of Corfù, wrote the *Rituun ecclesiasticorum sive sacrarum caeremoniarum sanctae Romanae Ec-*

clesiae libri tres, which ran through several editions till the one edited by Joseph Catalani in 1750. Domenico Giorgi had previously, in 1730, published a treatise *De liturgia Romani Pontificis in celebratione solemni missarum*. Francesco Girolamo Cancellieri, in 1788 and in 1814, published editions of his *Descrizione de' tre pontificali, che si celebrano per le feste di Natale, di Pasqua e di S. Pietro*. In 1841 Gaetano Moroni published an extract on the *Cappelle pontificie* from his *Dizionario di erudizione ecclesiastica*. More recent is the *Caeremoniale missae, quae a Summo Pontifice Ecclesiae universalis ritu solemni celebratur*, by Peter Joseph Rinaldi-Bucci.

But, like the general reorganization and democratization of the church's liturgy, which is proceding today, all the papal rites are under review and a special *Coetus* was erected in the *Concilium ad exsequendam Constitutionem de Sacra Liturgia*, concerned particularly *De Ritibus Cappellae Papalis*.

It is at least certain that the papal mass will never again be celebrated in all its solemnity. The pope celebrates frequently in public, but his masses are more or less like the former 'low masses' (q.v.), sometimes with a certain amount of singing. For a canonization he sings a solemn mass at the high altar of St Peter's, but without the throne formerly erected in the apse (q.v.) of the basilica. A smaller throne was erected on the south side for the singing of terce after the imposing entrance of clergy and dignitaries with the pontiff carried shoulder high on the *sedia gestatoria*. In the hall of benedictions above the portico a band of silver trumpets played the march of Longhi. As well as the usual vestments (q.v.) the pope wore a voluminous white skirt called the *falda* and a mantle or large-sized cope. For the mass itself he wore the *succinctorium*, a girdle from which hung a sort of wide maniple with the *Agnus Dei* embroidered on it, also the fanon, a double cape of silk with stripes of gold, white and amarinth. The pope does not use a crozier, instead of it he carries a ferula, a tall staff surmounted by a cross.

The mass followed the ordinary rules of a pontifical mass with the following special rites. After incensing the altar the pope gave the kiss of peace (q.v.) to the three cardinal deacons at the altar. After the singing of the epistle in Latin it was sung again in Greek by the Greek subdeacon, recalling the time when Greek was commonly used in the liturgy in Rome. At the singing of the Latin gospel the seven acolytes with their candles were in attendance, and at its conclusion the Greek deacon sang the same gospel in Greek. Then the pope read his homily seated on his throne. After the verse *Et incarnatus est* in the creed the deacon and the subdeacon spread over the altar a linen cloth adorned with gold braid and called the *Incarnatus*. For the pregustation the deacon chose two out of three hosts and gave them to the sacrist to consume. On Easter day the two junior cardinals came and stood at either corner of the altar to represent the angels at Christ's tomb. During the elevation (q.v.) the pope turned with the host and the chalice first to the right and then to the left, while the silver trumpets sounded Silveri's harmony from the dome. After the kiss of peace the pope returned to the throne. The paten with the host, covered with the 'asterisk' to keep it in place, and the chalice were carried to the throne. The pope, in former times seated, consumed part of the host and part of the precious blood through a fistula, and then communicated the deacon and the subdeacon and kissed them on the cheek. The ceremony ended with the solemn blessing. The pope then mounted on the *sedia gestatoria* and the tiara was placed on his head. The cardinal archpriest approached and presented him with a purse containing twenty-five 'jules', the stipend for a mass 'well sung'.

Several ceremonies are, or were, peculiar to the papal liturgy, such as the blessing of the wax medallions stamped with the figure of the *Agnus Dei*, of the golden rose, destined to honour some sovereign or some community, of the ducal sword and cape to be sent to a Catholic prince and of the palliums worn by the occupants of metropolitan sees.

The creation of cardinals was always a simple ceremony, but now it has been still more simplified, and even the famous red hat has disappeared from the scene. The canonization of saints is still performed as occasion demands, but with reduced rites. The summoning of and the presiding over an ecumenical council is still a possibility, as we have seen in our own day; so too the opening of the holy door for the year of jubilee and the closing of it at the end of the period.

When the pope died, the Cardinal Camerlengo recognized the body and ordered that the Fisherman's Ring be broken. Presently the body, dressed in red vestments, was carried into St Peter's and exposed for a few days and the Novemdiales began, a series of nine requiem masses sung daily. The traditional place of burial of the popes is the Vatican basilica, *juxta corpus beati Petri*. In fact one hundred and thirty-six popes have been buried there. Pius IX was buried, at his own wish, at St Lorenzo Fuori le Mura, among the poor people of Rome, who lie in the great cemetery of the Camp Verano. Leo XIII has his tomb in St John Lateran, which he did so much to restore. Pope John XXIII also expressed in his will an alternative wish to be buried in his Lateran cathedral, but the commission of cardinals decided to keep his remains in the crypt of St Peter's.

On the fifteenth day after the death of the pope the Sacred College of Cardinals attended a solemn mass of the Holy Ghost, sung by the Dean of St Peter's and a sermon *Pro eligendo Pontifice*, then in the afternoon they entered the conclave. The scrutinies of the votings took place in the Sistine Chapel. Against the walls were seats and tables for the electors. They were surmounted by movable baldachins (q.v.), which after the election were all dropped except that over the new pope, who had to obtain two thirds plus one of the votes. When this was achieved, the Dean approached the elected cardinal and asked him 'Dost thou accept thine election canonically made to the sovereign pontificate?', and if the answer was affirmative, the new pope was asked what name he would take and then in an adjoining cabinet he was dressed in the papal garments. He went to a seat before the altar and received the adoration of the cardinals, while the first cardinal deacon from the balcony over the porch of St Peter's proclaimed the election to the people. Soon afterwards he himself gave his first blessing from the same place. A few days later he was solemnly crowned with the *triregnum* or tiara by the senior deacon saying: 'Receive this tiara adorned with three crowns and know that thou art the father of princes and kings, the ruler of the world, the vicar upon earth of our Saviour Jesus Christ, to whom is honour and glory, world without end. Amen.'

(This item is partly abridged from a series of articles which were published in the Westminster Cathedral Chronicle, whose editor I thank for permission to make use of them.)

RONALD PILKINGTON

Paschal Candle

The lighting of a large and special candle on its own stand or candlestick forms one of the ceremonies in the vigil service on the eve of Easter, all candles and lamps having been extinguished on Maundy Thursday. The rekindling of fire and light, including the lighting of the Paschal candle, symbolize the triumph of the resurrection over darkness and sin. The lighting of the Paschal candle was accompanied by the singing of a special chant known as the *Praeconium* or *Exultet* sung by the deacon from the ambon by the side of which stood the Paschal candlestick. In the words of the *Exultet* there were allusions to the Passover and the crossing of the Red Sea which were types foreshadowing the new Passover effected by Christ's cross and resurrection. It is not possible to say with certainty when and where these ceremonies originated. Jerome in the fourth century complained about the deacon's hyperbole of language as he chanted the *Praeconium*. Also the hymn *Inventor rutili*, composed by Prudentius in the same century, was sung during the Easter vigil service; its allusions leave little doubt about the rekindling of fire and light. In the older Roman and Italian basilicas the Paschal candlestick was of marble or porphyry decorated with tessellated inlay and it stood as a permanent feature either on one side of the chancel (q.v.) or even part-way down the nave (q.v.). The idea that this candlestick could only stand immediately on the north side of the altar (q.v.) is a late medieval innovation.

The Paschal candle is now in use from the eve of Easter until Ascension Day (q.v.); but in earlier days its lighting continued in some rites until Whitsunday (q.v.). In some examples the candle was on a pan or dish suspended by chains instead of on a stand. In the late English medieval rites this candle assumed enormous proportions, that at Salisbury Cathedral being thirty-six feet (eleven metres) high, while that at Westminster Abbey weighed three hundredweight (740 kilograms).

At one time it was customary to insert five grains of incense in this candle signifying the five wounds of Jesus; this has now been discontinued by those who note that it is based on a misreading of the meaning of the term *incensum* in the Latin of the *Exultet*. Prior to its being placed on its stand the candle is used in connection with the blessing of the font, and the date of the year is inscribed on its length.

D. R. Dendy, *The Use of Lights in Christian Worship*, 1959; H. J. Feasey, *Ancient English Holy Week Ceremonial*, 1897; J. W. Tyrer, *Historical Survey of Holy Week*, 1932.

C. E. POCKNEE

Paschal Vigil

The celebration of the *Pascha*, the passion, death and resurrection of the Lord, on the Saturday night and Sunday morning of Easter (q.v.), is the church's oldest liturgical observance with the sole exception of the week-end vigil that was celebrated in NT times and from which the Paschal vigil itself is derived.

The church was conscious that it owed its existence to the saving events of the cross and the resurrection, and there was a vivid sense of the presence of the Lord who was with his people in and through the celebration of these events and who would come again in glory to complete the work of his redemption. The Paschal celebration therefore was not a mere recalling of the past events; it made the power of those events present to the worshippers, who could thus make a renewed encounter with their Lord. The first-century vigil centred upon the eucharist, the passover meal of the Lord, but by the second century, baptism, by which new members were added to the church, was celebrated as part of the Paschal vigil. Possibly the Jewish observance of the lighting of the lamps on the eve of the sabbath influenced the Christian liturgy and so we get the third element, light. In the Johannine tradition, Christ is the light of the world, and out of these two elements, Jewish and Christian, the church gradually evolved the symbolism of the candle which in the fourth century became the centre of interest of the first part of the rite. But the Christian vigil had always included the celebration of God's saving deeds in the word of the scriptures, and with the development of the catechumenate (q.v.), the word-service came to be regarded as the last instruction of the candidates before their baptism. Thus by the end of the fourth century all the elements of the vigil celebration had been assembled, and light, word, water and the bread and wine of the eucharist all became efficacious symbols conveying the power of the redeeming Christ to the gathered assembly.

The Paschal vigil was the total and unitive celebration of the redeeming work of Christ, and until the end of the third century, Good Friday (except in Asia, where Christians kept the vigil on 14 Nisan instead of the Saturday/Sunday, hence their name Quartodecimans) was observed only by a solemn fast, and Maundy Thursday became a separate celebration only when the historicization of the liturgy was well under way in the fifth century. Yet, the sense of a unitive celebration of Christ's redeeming work was retained for centuries, and it was not until in the seventh century, when the hour of the vigil began to be anticipated, that a tendency set in to break up the pattern. All during the early Middle Ages the vigil was celebrated earlier, until by the late Middle Ages it was celebrated in the morning of Holy Saturday. This was the position consecrated by the missal of Pius V (1570) which *ordered* that the service (hardly any longer to be called a vigil) was not to be celebrated *after* mid-day on Saturday. Yet, with astonishing fidelity, the church retained all the ancient rites and texts (though with some strange accretions) and still sang of the 'holy night' when Christ liberated man from sin. With the gathering momentum of the Liturgical Movement, this anomaly became increasingly obvious and intolerable. In response to requests, Pius XII in 1951 restored the proper hour of the vigil celebration and partly revised the rites and texts. This restoration was at first experimental only, and the definitive reform of the whole of the Holy Week liturgy came in 1955. Since then there has been a further revision in the direction of simplicity, and it is this revision that will be described now.

The church is in darkness and the new fire (q.v.) is lighted. From this light is taken to the Paschal candle. This may be simply lighted and then carried into and through the church by a deacon who sings three times 'Christ our light', the third time in the sanctuary (q.v.). Meanwhile the people's candles are lighted from the Paschal candle. There follows the Easter proclamation (*Exultet*) in which the saving events of the OT and NT are recalled. The word-service now begins, and there are readings from the OT (five, to be used at choice, are provided) and the NT (the epistle). Before the epistle, the *Gloria* is intoned and the bells rung, heralding the arrival of Easter. The gospel and the homily follow, and after these the blessing of the baptismal water and baptism itself if there are candidates. If there are no baptisms, the formula of blessing is shorter. There follows the renewal of baptismal promises and the sprinkling of the people with the newly blessed water. The mass then continues as usual.

Two special observances may be noted. (1) The Paschal candle may be marked by the Alpha and Omega, the sign of the cross and the year of salvation, thus indicating that Christ the redeemer is present among his people. Five incense grains may be inserted into the candle with a formula which interprets the gesture: 'May Christ by his glorious wounds preserve and guard us.' (2) After the epistle the *Alleluia* (q.v.), suppressed at the beginning of Lent, is now solemnly intoned. The vestigial lauds which was attached to the rite in 1955 is now suppressed.

J. D. CRICHTON

Paten *see* Chalice and Paten

Pax *see* Gestures (4)

Pentecost

The day of Pentecost, commonly called Whitsunday, was a unitive festival commemorating both the ascension of Jesus and the descent of the Holy Spirit. In the course of the fourth century it was resolved into two commemorations corresponding to the distinct parts of the primitive celebration, the institution of Ascension Day in the latter part of the century resulting in the limitation of Pentecost to the second theme.

The Greek word 'Pentecost' refers to the *fiftieth* day, defining the time after the season of the Pascha when Pentecost, one of the pilgrim festivals of the old covenant, celebrated the wheat-harvest. In the OT itself this agricultural festival is not identified with the law-giving on Mount Sinai. If the identification had been made in Judaism by the time of the gospel, it would be profoundly significant that on the day of Pentecost the disciples experienced the dynamic power of the Holy Spirit. In that case the event, in the particular sense of the occasion as well as in the general sense of the revelation given, would be the action of the divine purpose. As the old covenant, ratified in the Exodus which the Passover commemorated, was completed on Mount Sinai, so the new covenant, ratified in the events which the Christian Pascha commemorated, the cross and the resurrection, was completed on the festival of Pentecost when the power of the Holy Spirit came upon the disciples. Pentecost was the birthday of the church as the New Israel of God. The link between the law-giving and the descent of the Holy Spirit was appreciated by Augustine and Leo the Great. When Paul made his contrast between the law and the Spirit he may have written in the context of a liturgical connection between the Pentecost of the old covenant and that of the new. It is possible that he regarded the law-giving as such, the consecration of the Old Israel, as the work of the Spirit within the time of the old covenant. His emphatic rejection of the legalism of rabbinic Judaism from which he had been delivered by the gospel does not invalidate the comparison which gives point and relevance to the contrast.

At the beginning of the third century Tertullian refers to the day of Pentecost in terms which are consistent with a unitive commemoration, but the evidence does not permit a precise statement. Eusebius, describing the death of the Emperor Constantine in 337, makes specific reference to the festival as the occasion of the ascension of Jesus and the descent of the Holy Spirit. It is unmistakably clear that Ascension Day was not in existence at this time. On the contrary, the liturgical commemoration of the ascension on the day of Pentecost must have been so familiar to Eusebius that he forgets the book of Acts and identifies the event historically with that day. In view of the direct evidence, it cannot be doubted that early in the fourth century the day of Pentecost was a unitive festival, commemorating both the ascension of Jesus and the descent of the Holy Spirit.

Towards the end of the fourth century at Jerusalem, according to Etheria's description, there was a procession on the fiftieth day after Easter to the traditional site of the event of Pentecost, the Church on Mount Zion, where, at 9 a.m., a service was held in the course of which the passage was read concerning the descent of the Holy Spirit. This was a commemoration in the Jerusalem fashion at the proper place and time. Just after midday the people gathered at the sanctuary on the traditional site of the ascension, and the passages about the ascension from the gospel and Acts were read. A great candlelight procession came to the city in the darkness, and it was eventually about midnight when the people returned to their homes. This is the early unitive Pentecost, commemorated, in the way worship was now celebrated in the Holy City, with careful attention to the symbolism of the sacred sites.

In the early period of the church the term 'Pentecost' does not simply indicate the fiftieth day as such, but frequently refers to the entire period of fifty days which would begin with the day of the Pascha. This season, our Eastertide, was regarded as a time of joy and triumph. As every Lord's Day was a commemoration of the glory of the divine kingdom in the resurrection of Christ, so the fifty days of Pentecost echoed to the same trumpet note of victory. Kneeling in prayer and fasting were forbidden on Sundays, and this privilege applied also to the great fifty days.

A. A. McArthur, *The Evolution of the Christian Year*, 1953.

A. A. MCARTHUR

Pentecostal Worship

Following the terminology of K. McDonnell ('Catholic Pentecostalism', *Dialog*, Winter 1969/70, pp. 35-54), we must distinguish between Pentecostals within *traditional* churches – Roman Catholic, Anglican, Lutheran, Presbyterian, Methodist, Congregational and Baptist – (called *Neo-Pentecostalism* below) and the different Pentecostal denominations (*classical Pentecostalism*). Clearly the worship of the Neo-Pentecostals either forms part of their traditional worship or is celebrated in prayer-groups within the traditional parishes. One finds interesting combinations, therefore, between a Roman Catholic mass and Pentecostal speaking in tongues, or between an Anglican service and prayer for the sick through laying on of hands. Neo-Pentecostals also celebrate separate 'charismatic services' with all the elements of classical Pentecostalism, yet in a different social and cultural environment, since Neo-Pentecostals belong mostly to the upper middle-class. This phenomenon has shattered the 'economic deprivation theory' which held that spontaneous Pentecostal worship was only to be expected in the so-called 'underprivileged' classes. Yet Neo-Pentecostal prayer-groups –

this applies more to the Roman Catholic than to the Protestant section of Neo-Pentecostalism – are not frequented by the uncritical, but by the critical exegetes, not by the unlearned, but by the intellectuals, not by frustrated Puritans, but by normal Christians. In their prayer meetings they not only sing, but create new hymns, they not only speak in tongues, but discuss theological and political problems, they not only pray, but eat, drink and smoke.

In this context, speaking in tongues plays a great role, because it allows prayer in a non-rational meditative language. This is an important prayer experience for the rationally unskilled as well as for the intellectually overburdened academician, an experience which made the apostle Paul say: 'He who speaks in a tongue edifies himself' (I Cor. 14.4).

The worship of *classical Pentecostalism*, on the other hand, follows the lines of the Protestant Free Church tradition with hymns, prayers (often with spontaneous participation of the congregation through prayers, and sometimes speaking in tongues and interpretation) and preaching (which in the younger Pentecostal churches is open to everyone, but in the older churches is the duty and privilege of an emergent clergy, (*see* **Ordination** 12; Pentecostal).

The indigenous African churches, of which many belong historically and phenomenologically to the Pentecostal family, have adopted many interesting sacramental or quasi-sacramental rites, such as ritual washings, pilgrimages to places which played a great role in the history of the church (e.g. the Kimbanguists in the Congo). Their ministers, sometimes called prophets, bishops, the spiritual head, priests, apostles, etc., wear colourful garments or stoles and carry staffs.

The following example from personal experience in Chile is not, of course, representative of all Pentecostal churches, but may serve as an introduction to Pentecostal worship. The writer was asked to sit in front of the congregation in the red plush seat reserved for honoured guests. An ocean of faces floated before my eyes, 2000 to 3000 faithful, some with car-tyres on their feet instead of shoes. But as soon as the trumpet blew the first melody, those faces creased with the signs of age-long oppression came to life. They danced slowly in a circle the dances of their Indian ancestors. Those who did not dance stood reverently and clapped their hands slowly. A woman prophesied in a deep, soul-searching voice. All of a sudden there was silence! The whole congregation fell down on their knees in order to thank God for the dance he had given them. Above in the gallery at the left side sat fifty to one hundred *cyclistas* in grey blouses. These are the bicycle-evangelists who cycle into the surrounding villages in order to preach, sing, and heal the sick every Sunday. In the evening they come back and the congregation will greet them with a loud '*Gloria a Dios*'. They will draw behind them a queue of curious people, who will be converted tonight. 'Do you also dance? they ask me. This was the test-question. They wanted to know whether I despised them or not. 'I would like to,' I answered sincerely, 'but I do not know your dances.' They were satisfied with this answer. Their own preachers do not dance either; their duty is not to dance, but to interpret the dances.

The most important element of Pentecostal worship is the active participation of every member of the congregation, even if this amounts to several thousand people (M. de Melo, *Monthly Letter about Evangelism*, February/March 1969, Geneva, wcc), in dancing, singing, pilgrimages, praying individually and collectively (called 'prayer in concert'), playing all kinds of instruments from the hand-harmonica to triangle and drum, from the saxophone to the violin, evaluating and judging the sermon by inspiring shouts or critical remarks and questions.

Yet if one considers the future of Pentecostal worship, there are several possibilities open. *Classical Pentecostalism* can adapt itself to the mainline churches, adopting a fundamentalist theology and a written liturgy. This process is in full swing for most of the European and North American Pentecostal churches. The other possibility is to develop a really post-literary liturgy with all the means of that culture, where the main medium of communication is not the written word but the proverb, not the newspaper but the parable, not the statement but the story, not the Gregorian hymn but the chorus. This liturgy, too, can be adapted to non-proletarian cultures, but its main mission would be in the third world and among the subculture of the younger generation.

Neo-Pentecostalism has also two options. In emphasizing the personal aspect of Christianity it can develop into a spiritual revival movement for higher social classes, which would lead to worship services, refreshing and equipping the individual, but would be relatively unaware of collective sins and evils. The other possibility is that Neo-Pentecostalism might develop its charismatic worship in such a way that – following the Pauline rather than the Lucan pneumatology (*cf.* E. Schweizer, 'Spirit of God', *TDNT*, VI, pp. 389-455) – it would include among the charismata not just those common to classical Pentecostalism, but also charismata in the social, political and artistic field – as the Pentecostal leader D. J. Du Plessis has put it – the charismata of those people who are not generally considered to be Christians. This would be a healthy ecumenical complement to the classical Pentecostal understanding of worship.

N. Bloch-Hoell, *The Pentecostal Movement*, 1964; C. Lalive d' Epinay, *A Study of the Pentecostal Movement in Chile*, 1969; W. J. Hollenweger, *The Pentecostals*, 1972; Research Review by W. J. Hollenweger, *Die Pfingstkirchen*, 1970; J. T. Nichol, *Pentecostalism*, 1966.

W. J. HOLLENWEGER

Petition *see* Prayer (3)

Pew

Seating in the naves of churches was unknown in any degree for many centuries, as the worshippers normally stood during the liturgy. In some instances there were stone ledges round the wall of a church, hence (it is said) there arose the expression, 'the weakest goes to the wall' as the infirm sat on these ledges. In the Eastern churches today seating is still unusual.

In the West, and particularly in northern Europe, seating was gradually introduced in the naves of churches from the thirteeenth century. At first such seats were simply backless benches. But most of the medieval examples in England belong to the fifteenth and sixteenth centuries, when the wood carver's craft reached its climax in skill, as we can see in the remarkable examples in East Anglia and the West Country. These late medieval benches or pews are always constructed in 'islands' of seating and they never crowd right up to the chancel or choke up the west end; there is always room for ordered movement.

After the Reformation, pews tended to increase both in number and in their size and proportion, so that almost the whole nave was crowded with 'box-pews' which screened the occupants from their neighbours. In the nineteenth century many of these high pews were done away; but they were sometimes replaced with benches of poor design with the seats being too narrow. The planning and arranging of seating in churches is an important matter both from the point of the comfort of the worshippers and also in regard to the proportions of the building and the setting of the liturgy.

The Warham Guild, *The Warham Guild Handbook*, rev. ed. 1963.

C. E. POCKNEE

Piscina

A Latin word, meaning literally 'fish-pond' or 'fish-tank'. The term was probably transferred to the baptismal font (q.v.), since the fish was one of the symbols of Christ in primitive Christianity. Tertullian, writing at the end of the second century in his treatise *De Baptismo* (ch. 1), says, 'We, being little fishes, as Jesus Christ is our great Fish, begin our life in the water, and only while we abide in the water are we safe and sound.' Examples are known of the fish being depicted inside the basin of the primitive font, e.g. the one in Kélibia, North Africa.

But the term piscina came to assume another meaning in the Middle Ages, and it was applied to a shallow saucer-like basin in a niche in the wall of the south side of an altar. This basin has a drain attached to it leading into the earth. This arrangement was also termed *lavacrum* and *sacrarium*. The purpose of this type of piscina has been disputed. But as early as the ninth century Pope Leo IV ordered that a receptacle was to be provided near the altar for the disposal of the water that had been used in the ablutions of the hands and the chalice. Until the fourteenth century there was a single drain and piscina attached to any altar; then we get examples of the double piscina, e.g. in Exeter Cathedral, England. It is supposed that one drain was used for the ablutions from the chalice and the other for that of the hands. In the fifteenth century there was a reversion to the single piscina.

F. Bond, *The Chancel of English Churches*, 1916; J. G. Davies, *The Architectural Setting of Baptism*, 1962.

C. E. POCKNEE

Plymouth Brethren Worship

The Plymouth Brethren are so called by others – not by themselves – from the fact that their first congregation in England was established at Plymouth, about 1831. They called one another 'brethren', and when they moved into neighbouring areas they were referred to as 'the brethren from Plymouth' or Plymouth Brethren. Their movement began in Dublin some years earlier, when a few young men came together to take the Lord's Supper informally in an attempt to surmount the denominational barriers which otherwise would have prevented their intercommunion and in the hope that they might thus recapture the simplicity of apostolic times. When they were joined by John Nelson Darby (1800-82), a priest of the Church of Ireland, he quickly dominated the group by his powerful personality and forceful ecclesiology, which aimed at reconstituting the faithful remnant of the end-time. During a visit to Francis William Newman at Oxford in 1830, Darby influenced some other young men there, especially Benjamin Wills Newton (1807-99), Fellow of Exeter College, who returned to his native Plymouth the following year and founded the Brethren congregation in that city. Darby then carried his teaching to the Continent, especially to French Switzerland, where his followers are known to this day as *Darbistes*. On his return to the British Isles his imperious pressing of an exclusive church doctrine and polity occasioned a cleavage (1848), those who followed his lead being thereafter referred to as Exclusive Brethren and the others, by contrast, Open Brethren.

The Open Brethren, because of their evangelistic energy, were profoundly influenced by the Revival of 1858-60. In some parts of the UK (e.g north-east Scotland) there were formed, as a result of that revival, independent congregations which were soon attracted into the Brethren orbit; elsewhere their ethos was recognizably modified by the revival. One symptom of this was the widespread use of the term 'Gospel Hall' to denote their meeting-places (nowadays 'Evangelical Church' is becoming increasingly popular). Among Exclusive Brethren places of worship were more commonly and modestly called 'The Room' or 'The Meeting Room'. The initiated can usually tell from the phraseology on the notice-board which group of Brethren worships in the building.

The Exclusive principle of church fellowship has been summed up in the title of one of J. N. Darby's treatises: 'Separation from evil God's principle of unity' – the separation in question being understood in terms of the Darbyite exegesis of II Tim. 2.19-21, in which the 'great house' is the sum-total of Christendom. By contrast, Open Brethren have generally preferred, with Anthony Norris Groves (1795-1853), to accept 'recognition of Christ alone in my brother, as the Alpha and Omega of terms of communion'. Groves, who has been called the archetypal Open Brother, declared in a letter to Darby in 1836, regarding certain Christians who seemed to him in some respects to be following the wrong path: 'I would infinitely rather bear with all their evils, than separate from their good.' Groves was also the Brethren's first foreign missionary; he led a pioneer band to Baghdad in 1829 and spent the last twenty years of his life in India. The missionary work which he initiated is carried on today by over 1000 missionaries in all five continents, especially in India, Central Africa and South America; this enterprise is commonly designated 'Christian Mission in Many Lands' and its records are published in the monthly periodicals *Echoes of Service*, Bath, England and *The Fields*, New York. Other pioneer Brethren missionaries were the two Scots, Frederick Stanley Arnot (1858-1914), the first European to explore Katanga, and Dan Crawford (1870-1926), who opened up to Western knowledge other uncharted areas of Central Africa.

Groves's brother-in-law, George Müller (1805-98), was the Prussian-born founder of the Bristol orphanage which bears his name. Along with Henry Craik (1805-66), a St Andrews graduate and Hebrew scholar, he was joint-pastor of Bethesda Chapel, Bristol, which took a foremost part in resisting the authoritarian demands of J. N. Darby in 1848 and thus became, among Darby's followers, a by-word for all that is ecclesiastically reprehensible. The Exclusive adoption of separation as the principle of unity, when pressed to its logical conclusion, has led to a diversity of Exclusive divisions, the most 'exclusive' of which is that led until his recent death by James Taylor, Jr, of New York. Some Exclusive groups, however, are 'exclusive' only in name, in the sense that they stem from the Darbyite side of the 1848 cleavage, but in practice they are as evangelically co-operative as the Open Brethren.

The Brethren accept the doctrines of the historic creeds, except that the Taylorite Exclusives have manifested an Apollinarian tendency and, since about 1929, have denied the eternity of Christ's relation as Son to the Father – this relation, they hold, started with the incarnation, although they believe in his eternal pre-existence. The Brethren are evangelical in doctrine and practice, leaning for the most part towards Calvinism rather than Arminianism. Their most distinctive feature is that (like the Friends) they reject all differentiation between clergy and laity. While several of their members are set apart for an evangelistic, teaching or pastoral ministry, this gives them no special status. They do (unlike the Friends) administer the sacraments of baptism and the Lord's Supper (*see* **Baptism** 13: Plymouth Brethren, **Liturgies** 13: Plymouth Brethren). In polity the Open Brethren are uncompromisingly congregational, their churches being administered by elders; the Exclusive Brethren have centralized control, most stringent of all in the late James Taylor's connection.

The Open Brethren participate freely in interdenominational evangelical activity, e.g. in the Evangelical Alliance, the Inter-Varsity Christian Fellowship, etc. Their closest affinities in England are with evangelical Anglicans. In Great Britain and Ireland the Brethren's numbers are estimated at about 100,000 of whom perhaps two-thirds are Open Brethren.

F. R. Coad, *A History of the Brethren Movement*, 1968; H. H. Rowdon, *The Origins of the Brethren*, 1967; B. R. Wilson, ed., *Patterns of Sectarianism*, 1967.

F. F. BRUCE

Polyphony

Polyphony is the musical term for two or more voices singing individual parts simultaneously, as opposed to monophony, where one part only is sung by one or more voices. Homophony is where the voices in polyphonic music sing the same words at the same time to a succession of chords, the upper voice having the melody, the rest supplying the harmonies below it. It provides an effective contrast to polyphony. In settings of the mass, particularly in the sixteenth century, *Et incarnatus est* is often set homophonically to emphasize the solemnity of the incarnation, and at other times, as so often in the masses of Palestrina, homophony is used for massive effects.

There are many theories as to how polyphony came to be used, about the ninth century, in church music. It existed in a primitive form in secular music; it might have been suggested by chants that lay too high for basses at times and too low for tenors at other times. The medieval polyphony did not involve the invention of melodies. The procedure, at first, was to select a piece of plainchant, called the *cantus firmus*, or 'fixed-song', which was exactly reproduced a fifth lower, or later, with the chant doubled an octave below and above. This simple start soon gave place to various kinds of innovations such as the transference of the *cantus firmus* from the top to the lowest part, where it was known as the *tenor* or holding part, above which one or more voices indulged in the long florid phrases called melismas. The chosen chant, put into long notes, lost its character altogether. The increasing complexity, rhythmically and melodically, of these developments gave composers and singers much enjoyment, no doubt, but cannot have nourished the spirit of corporate prayer; Gregorian chant (q.v.), though still a liturgical necessity, no longer held undisputed pride of place. The notating of exact time values to enable several voices to sing together in a disciplined way, led to measured rhythm and, again, put the free rhythm of the chant in chains.

Gregorian chant found its architectural counterpart in the churches of the Romanesque period, the measured music in the cathedrals of the Gothic period, those mounting prayers in stone and glass that from about 1180 to 1250 were offered by the fervour of Germany, England, Spain and pre-eminently France with Notre-Dame Cathedral, Paris, and Notre Dame at Chartres as prime musical centres.

Leoninus and Perotinus – possibly his pupil – were the two great masters of the developed polyphony (*organum*) of the Notre-Dame school. Perotinus was perhaps the first composer to write for three and four voices in a truly contrapuntal style. Some of his works

were sung by the choir of the Vienna Hofburg in 1927, during the Beethoven centenary, and were described as 'a revelation, a flash of beauty, like the windows of Chartres or of Bourges suddenly illuminated by the sun'.

From the little-known achievements of this period church music moves forward to others in the succeeding centuries, ever enriching the treasury of sacred music, but subject to abuses rebuked by various popes and councils. This greatest epoch of liturgical church music came to an end with the first decade of the seventeenth century.

ALEC ROBERTSON

Postures

1. *Orientation.* The attribution of religious symbolism to direction is basically concerned with sunrise and sunset: eastwards is the direction of light, hope and rebirth and, correspondingly, westwards is the direction of darkness, evil and death. Very early in the belief and custom of the church there developed the notion that the parousia of Christ would be 'like lightning from the east, flashing as far as the west' (Matt. 24.27): this imagery is in accord with a few other biblical expressions, e.g. 'sun of righteousness' (Mal. 4.2), 'dayspring from on high' (Luke 1.78), and 'the morning star' (Rev. 22.16). On this basis some importance came to be attached to turning or facing eastwards in the ceremonies of the church. (*See* **Orientation**.)

(*a*) *Eastward turning.* From the second century it became customary to turn eastwards when praying because, according to Clement of Alexandria: 'the East is an image of the day of birth', while other writers suggest that the rebirth of the soul through the Second Adam will be associated with Paradise 'eastward in Eden'. Such interpretations of orientated prayer are linked with the custom at the beginning of the initiation ceremonies (q.v.) for the candidate to turn first westwards to renounce Satan and then eastwards to profess Christ. A similar symbolic movement was adopted in the Church of England in the seventeenth century, and since then eastward turning has been common for every liturgical recitation of a creed. In the medieval West it was customary for the whole congregation to turn eastwards (i.e. altar-wards) at the *Gloria Patri* and the *Gloria in excelsis*. As with most liturgical gestures, this posture also has been discontinued by many Protestants, especially when, in non-orientated buildings, ministers and elders face the rest of the congregation throughout corporate worship.

(*b*) *Eastward position*. This term is used to describe the posture of the eucharistic president when he stands before the altar with his back to the people: in church buildings which are literally 'orientated' so that the altar is at the eastern end, the priest also is literally eastward-facing, but the term is generally used irrespective of compass direction.

(*c*) *Westward position*. This term (identical with basilican position) is used when the liturgical president faces the people across the communion table or altar, no account being taken of actual direction. The first churches to be built under Constantine were in the form of a modified basilica (q.v.) with the apse at the western end, thus enabling the bishop and presbyters to face eastwards over the altar. In the middle of the fourth century the orientation was reversed so that the altar in the apse was at the eastern end, with the consequence that the people faced eastwards and the clergy westwards. In order that they too might face the east (and for other reasons), the clergy in the West eventually abandoned the basilican position in most church buildings and assumed places to the west of the altar. Thus, the eastward position was the norm in the Middle Ages and remained so in the Roman Catholic Church until the second half of the twentieth century. In the medieval period when altars came to be placed very close to the east wall and to be furnished with hangings, pictures or more permanent structures, it became impossible to take the basilican position which (with very few exceptions) had been the norm in the early church.

The Reformed Churches generally reverted to the original disposition of ministers facing the people across the holy table at the eucharist, but deliberately ignored questions of solar orientation in the building. When existing medieval churches continued to be used, the Calvinists usually set up a wooden table in the nave on a north-south axis, whereas Lutherans and Anglicans retained the traditional orientation. Characteristically the English church proceeded by way of compromise: at first the 1549 *BCP* ordered the priest to stand 'afore the middle of the Altar' i.e. in the middle of the long side of the wooden table which replaced the fixed stone altar; then, when this was set up 'table-wise'

in the chancel or the nave, the minister faced south in accordance with the rubric of the 1552/1662 *BCP* 'The Priest standing to the north side of the Table . . .'. When, subsequently, in the seventeenth century, the table was returned to its former position 'altar-wise' along the east wall, this rubric was interpreted by some as requiring the minister to stand at the north *end* (or short side) of the table in order to avoid the eastward position, while others faced east but stood at the northern end of the west side. The inherent ambiguity of the rubric was recognized in the 1637 Scottish prayer book and the presbyter was ordered to stand 'at the north side or end' of the table. The option was tacitly accepted in the Church of England, though the 'north end' eventually became a token of evangelicalism while the middle eastward position (Roman Catholic) came to be favoured by the Oxford Movement. Anglican concern was really that superstition should be avoided and that the manual acts of the priest should not be concealed from the people, hence the 1552/1662 rubric before the consecration prayer which reads: 'When the Priest standing before the Table hath so ordered the Bread and Wine before the people that he may with the more readiness and decency break the Bread before the people and take the Cup in his hands . . .'

All these ambiguities and awkwardnesses are obviated when, as under the influence of the Liturgical Movement (q.v.), a return is made to the westward position: and, since this basilican position is acceptable to virtually all sectors of the church, the ecumenical advantage also is considerable.

2. *Reverence*. Various types and degrees of 'respect' for a person (or an object which is symbolic of a person) can be expressed and communicated by bodily posture. In the animal world, bodily attitudes are powerful means of communicating dominance or submission, the 'pecking order', and in the spectrum of human relationships 'respect' (or lack of it) is easily expressed by postural change, e.g. standing for the magistrate, saluting the flag. Comparable attitudes are naturally to be found in religious observance, from a slight bow of the head to complete prostration, and conventions develop concerning the meaning of each and every posture. However, such liturgical postures cannot be wholly rationalized and personal

or group emotions do, from time to time, break through the most stylized forms in movements of revivalism.

In the Christian religion the duality of belief and faith concerning Jesus – human and divine, servant and lord – may result in a corresponding ambivalence of posture according to whether his liturgical 'presence' is being reverenced in terms of historical person or the second person of the Trinity. In some situations the worshipper may stand to greet one who 'did not prize his equality with God, but made himself nothing . . .' (Phil. 2.6f.), while in other circumstances the same worshipper may feel impelled to kneel before one whom God raised 'to the heights and bestowed upon him the name above all names, that at the name of Jesus every knee should bow . . .' (Phil. 2.9f.).

With this complexity of personality at the heart of devotion it is not surprising that temperamental and cultural differences have produced every possible variation of liturgical posture in the history of the church.

(*a*) *Bowing.* Bowing the head, as a natural gesture of recognition and respect, developed liturgically as a reverence to the bishop (esp. on his throne behind the altar), to the altar (as the 'throne' of Christ, or even as a symbol of Christ), to icons of Christ and the divine persons (esp. the crucifix), and more generally as a mutual salutation between participants in the liturgical action. For more than a thousand years, a simple bow was the only reverence given in the course of the Latin mass: in the medieval period it was customary to bow at the *Gloria Patri*, at the mention of the Holy Spirit in the Nicene Creed, and at the *Sanctus*.

A distinction is sometimes made between a simple reverence, i.e. an inclination of the head and shoulders, and a profound reverence, i.e. a bending forward from the hips. The latter tended to be replaced by genuflexion when the clergy came to have their backs to the people, but in the basilican position the bow is more seemly.

(*b*) *Genuflexion.* This posture consists of a brief kneeling on the right knee with body erect. It is usually associated with the *incarnatus* of the Nicene Creed (from the eleventh century) and with reverence for the blessed sacrament (from fourteenth century). It derives from civil recognition of imperial officials in antiquity and previously had no place in the ceremonial of the Christian eucharist. In the Roman Catholic church it is also commonly used as a reverence towards prelates and to crucifixes.

(*c*) *Kneeling.* In the early church there was for a time a class of penitents who were permitted to be present only for the synaxis (q.v.): they knelt at the west end of the nave and were known as *genuflectentes*. Originally, then, kneeling was not a common posture for prayer of all kinds as it has become in the Roman Catholic and Anglican churches. The primitive posture for prayer was standing (often with arms outstretched – as in the catacomb paintings), and this is still the custom in the Eastern Orthodox churches: in contrast, in most Protestant churches sitting is the preferred posture.

The change from standing to kneeling in the West came about through the omission of a command to rise after a short period appointed for silent kneeling prayer. It became customary in many liturgies after the *Gloria in excelsis* to call the people to prayer with the word *Oremus* and then to summon them to kneel with the words *Flectamus genua* for private devotions; this was then followed by the invitation to stand, *Levate*, for the succeeding collective prayers. By the twelfth century the period for silent prayer had been eliminated and, as the command to stand was no longer given, the people were left kneeling for the collects. From this beginning the penitential posture spread to other parts of the service – at first in the Latin rite and thence into the English rites. Thus in 1662 *BCP* the faithful are ordered to kneel from the opening Lord's Prayer and collect, through the ten commandments, collects and epistle, and to stand only for the gospel and the creed; it is also common for the people to kneel from the offertory onwards through the communion to the blessing since there is no rubric ordering them to stand – not even for the *Gloria in excelsis*!

However, in order to guard against a mistaken inference from the requirement to kneel to receive the sacrament, there was inserted in 1552 *BCP* a Declaration on Kneeling. This statement, which was printed without the authority of Parliament, was to the effect that kneeling did not imply the 'real and essential' presence of Christ, and that no adoration was intended but, rather, that kneeling signified the humility and worthy reception of 'the benefits of Christ'. The 'rubric' was omitted in the 1559 edition, but was re-inserted in the 1662 *BCP* with the alteration of 'real and essential' to 'corporal' in order to avoid gross superstition and yet to maintain the reality of the *sacramental* presence. In the nineteenth century it was customary to print rubrics (q.v.) in red and, in order to indicate that this 'declaration' was not technically a 'rubric', it was printed in black: perversely it became known as the *Black Rubric*.

Under the influence of the Liturgical Movement (q.v.) it is now customary in the Roman Catholic Church in England to stand to receive the sacrament, while the currently authorized experimental Anglican *Second* and *Third Series* give no direction concerning posture at this point in the liturgy.

There is much to be said, in principle, for kneeling only for penitential prayer and for either standing or sitting at other points in the liturgical action – standing for praise in fellowship and sitting to listen to readings, sermons, notices, lengthy musical renderings and for meditation. It is to be remembered, first, that for more than a millennium in Christian churches there were seats only for the officiating ministers and for the aged and the disabled ('the weak must go to the wall', i.e. to the seats by the wall), secondly, that 'Let us pray' is not the same as 'Let us kneel', and thirdly, that crouching between seats is not kneeling.

(*d*) *Sitting*. Liturgical sitting was originally the prerogative of the bishop (or his deputy) who at the eucharist was the enthroned president ('one who sits before'), and of the senior members of the congregation – the presbyters – who had their seats alongside him around the apse. No other seats were provided in churches, except for the elderly and infirm, until monastic choir stalls with misericord seats made their appearance. In the medieval period, in line with increased seating on secular public occasions, some additional seating was provided in church buildings in the form of backless benches (from the twelfth century onwards). But not until the period of the Reformation (with long sermons) and the Counter-Reformation (with long musical settings) did extensive lay seating become general. Eventually, what was once only a convenience came to be regarded as a necessity and, correspondingly, there occurred the curious liturgical inversion which gave the clergy little opportunity to sit down and the laity no occasion to stand up –

except for the singing of popular hymns.

Sitting, like standing or kneeling, should really be reappraised as a positive liturgical posture. The clergy, who have usurped much of the liturgy of the laity, need to sit down more frequently or for longer periods in the course of the action, and so enable the latter to rise to their own liturgical occasions: in this way the people will be less inclined to remain seated in order to 'hear mass' or to 'listen to the Word' in a negative manner but will sit down for definite liturgical reasons.

Finally, it may be noted that there is no virtue in postural uniformity *per se*, and that in corporate worship the guidance of the Spirit is not to be resisted in the matter of standing, sitting or kneeling.

GILBERT COPE

Praise *see* Prayer (4)

Prayer

Prayer is the generic term for all aspects of man's conscious relationship to God, as in 'the life of prayer'. As such it has been held to include liturgical worship, meditation and individual prayer, as well as such other religious duties as fasting and almsgiving. In a more specific sense, it denotes that part of man's relationship which consists of mental and verbal fellowship with God. The word can also refer, in the plural or with the indefinite article, to forms of words addressed to God.

Current writing about prayer is generally concerned to direct attention more to the second sense than to the third, and most of all to the first sense given. There is a widespread quest for forms of contemplation and meditation which attach less importance to the recitation of forms of words. Of late there has also been a growing quest for forms of the spiritual life which do not seem to involve emphasis on withdrawal from secular concerns so much as the discovery of the presence of God within the concerns of daily living. Those who are concerned with specific acts of prayer and times of prayer have therefore to discover a way in which these can form a framework for the constant practice of the presence of God.

The traditional divisions of prayer into adoration or praise, thanksgiving, confession and petition or supplication are relevant to all kinds of spirituality whether they involve specific acts of prayer or not, because they describe essential components of man's relationship to God. This is due to the fact that forms of prayer have been considerably moulded by theological considerations; since prayer is the expression of man's relationship to God, the content of it is closely linked with the nature of that relationship as man has discovered it, and the present discussion of prayer results directly from theological questionings. Forms of prayer which have traditionally been valued now raise very serious questions about how God is conceived and how, if at all, he is thought of as intervening in the life of the world.

1. *Adoration.* This aspect of prayer consists in the contemplation and worship of God as he is in himself. It is the word that most accurately describes the prayers of the mystics, and consists in focusing on and celebrating the qualities of the Godhead as they have been revealed to and experienced by the believer. The forms under which such prayer has occurred are many and various; the vision of heaven recorded in Isa. 6 appears to include an intense visual experience of God, and many of those who have been best known for their constant adoration of God, and who are classified as mystics, have experienced visions of God which have given rise to intense adoration. Much adoration has also included intense emotional expression, with extensive use of erotic imagery as the believer has contemplated with joy the deeply intimate relationship between God and the soul.

Others have been led to adoration by the contemplation of the world around them. The word adoration connotes a 'resting' in the presence of God, and of the forms of prayer described here is the least tied to verbal forms of expression. As such it has a strong contemporary appeal to those who are disillusioned with institutional religion and seek a spirituality which would involve the contemplation of the timeless qualities of God, such as truth, beauty, love and faithfulness. The parallels between the adoration of the mystics and the experiences of many who have used the techniques of Eastern religions or hallucinogenic drugs are easy to draw.

The church's attitude to adoration, especially as practised by the mystics, has been characterized by a certain ambivalence.

On the one hand it has been said that God is to be adored, and indeed the traditional picture of heaven includes the constant adoration of God by the angels and the saints. On the other hand it has been suspected, by some because of the quality of freedom from restraint which characterizes much mystical adoration, and by others for a certain 'other-worldly' sense which pervades adoration. On the whole the tendency has been to commend for most believers the practice of a much more disciplined variety which is tied to more verbal forms of expression and is in fact a combination of praise and thanksgiving related both to the biblical account of God and to the specific experiences of the believer. Adoration remains, however, that which is thought by many to be the highest form of prayer, and the canons of most eucharistic liturgies begin with the *Trisagion* (Holy, holy, holy), the song of heaven recorded in Isaiah's vision.

2. *Confession.* The acknowledgment by the believer of his sin. This occurs under three chief forms, general, personal and sacramental.

General confessions are characteristic of most liturgies. They occur extensively in the Bible (e.g. Ps. 51) and consist of the acknowledgment by the believing community of its unrighteousness before God and of its need of his forgiveness. The forms of such confessions vary greatly, but generally include an expression of sorrow for past transgression, a petition for God's forgiveness and, in some cases, the expression of resolve to amend. Under the influence of the Reformation many of the expressions of sorrow were highly elaborate, and there is a tendency at the present time to modify both the tone and the length of such general confessions.

Personal confession after self-examination has always been a feature of Christian private prayer, and in the past some elaborate lists have been provided of questions with which the believer is asked to face himself at the end of the day or at least as part of his preparation for receiving of holy communion. With the questioning of ethical theories which relied heavily on rules there has also come a questioning of this kind of approach to self-examination. Once again, the extensive discussion about God is raising questions that have implications for self-examination; the issue is whether the shortcomings we need to confess actually consist in the breaking of a series of small rules.

Sacramental confession, or confession before a priest, is a practice enjoined on Orthodox and Roman Catholics, but optional in the Anglican churches and some Protestant denominations. In some cases this form of confession is undertaken at regular intervals as a discipline, and in others as a means of quieting a conscience which is burdened with guilt for some specific offence, though Roman Catholics hold that mortal sin can only be forgiven by this means.

3. *Petition.* This aspect of prayer, known also as supplication or, when it is on behalf of others, intercession, has always been part of prayer, and indeed may be the most common and instinctual prayer which men offer. It is the asking of God for something which is desired. There are records of people of all religions and civilizations asking their gods for rain, for success in war, for the healing of the sick, for the blessing of a new ruler and indeed for the satisfaction of just about every conceivable need. It is in some way or other an almost invariable part of liturgical worship, and some liturgical acts are devoted almost entirely to petitionary prayer, e.g. the litany (q.v.).

There has been a tendency among teachers of the devotional life to regard petitionary prayer as the 'lowest' form of prayer, as something which ought not to occupy too large a place in the life of prayer. This is largely because it is seen as that part of prayer which gives the most opportunity for selfish asking in one's own interest. It remains true, however, that this most basic form of prayer occupies a large place in the life of praying people. It early occurs in the psalms, and formed a part of Jesus' prayers recorded in the gospels, as well as seeming to be a feature of some of the healing miracles. He prayed on behalf of the disciples and, in the Garden of Gethsemane, is recorded as asking that the cup of suffering might pass from him.

Petitionary prayer, probably more than any other form of prayer, has been affected by secular patterns of thinking, and the question of whether and how God answers prayer presents an inescapable dilemma. On the one hand, the abandonment of petitionary prayer altogether would seem to deny a basic part of prayer and also to deny to God the power to change and overrule events. On the other hand a '*deus ex machina*' God, who in response to individual requests does things which would not otherwise happen, becomes less credible as more and more of the life of the world is brought under control or at any rate explained. Various solutions to this dilemma are offered: it is suggested that prayer has its primary effect in attuning the mind of the one who prays to the will of God, increasing and focusing concern in a way which could be effective, without the need of miraculous divine interventions. Jesus' prayer in Gethsemane is cited as an example of the way in which all petitionary prayer has to be modified by the petition 'Thy will be done', and thus negative 'answers' have to be expected.

What does need to be pointed out, however, is that prayer in the biblical tradition has always been presented as an activity which did not limit the freedom of God, that is to say it was not a mechanical, magical procedure which was designed to produce automatic effects; rather it appears to be thought of as communication between the believer and God which accepts the liberty and integrity of both. There can be no doubt that petitionary prayer more than any other depends upon the view of God which undergirds it.

4. *Praise.* The outward expression of the believer's worship and adoration of God, in words, music and ceremonial. The focus of praise is not only upon God himself, as in adoration, but above all on his mighty acts in nature and history. Hymns and acts of praise are a common feature of all liturgy, and frequently the distinction between it and adoration on the one hand and thanksgiving on the other is not clear-cut.

A feature of praise in the Christian tradition, but going back to pre-Christian times, is the recital of the great deeds of God in the past. The reading of the gospel in the liturgy is, for example, answered with the response 'Praise (or thanks) be to thee, O Christ', and the ancient hymn of praise *Te Deum Laudamus* (fifth century) begins with the adoration of God but includes the recollection of the work of Christ as the basis of the praise that is being offered ('When thou tookest upon thee to deliver man, thou didst not abhor the virgin's womb; When thou hadst overcome the sharpness of death, thou didst open the kingdom of heaven to all believers').

In being invited to share in the offering of praise, the believer is asked to share in the life of the whole community of believers through the ages and to join in the praise they gave for their deliverance. He is responding to his own prayer in the Lord's Prayer, 'Hallowed be thy name', by participating in the hallowing of God for that which he has done for the world and for mankind.

5. *Thanksgiving*. A feature of prayer both public and private is that the believers are invited to offer thanks to God for their personal experiences of his goodness. It is natural that it should be closely linked to praise, as in the General Thanksgiving in the *BCP*, where thanks for God's 'loving-kindness to us and to all men' passes on to a recollection of 'his inestimable love in the redemption of the world by our Lord Jesus Christ'. The specific need for thanksgiving, however, is part of what is involved in the believer's relating what he knows of God to his experience in daily living. Once again there are problems about the listing of his experiences at the hand of God, and difficulties about the extent to which, in a secular age, it is appropriate to thank God for things which can be otherwise explained. The possibility of thanksgiving, however, is available if the model of a personal relationship with God can be rediscovered in a contemporary form. (For liturgical prayers, *see* **Agnus Dei**, **Collect**, **Consecration Prayer**, **Doxology**, **Intercession**, **Kyries**, **Litany**, **Lord's Prayer**, **Ordinary**, **Preface**, **Proper**, *Sanctus,* **Silent Prayer**, **Suffrages**, *Super Oblata, Trisagion*.)

PETER SELBY

Prayer Meeting

An informal meeting, usually additional to the regular worship of the church, at which those who are present offer spontaneous vocal prayers. Scriptural warrant for such meetings may be found in such passages as Acts 4.24ff.; I Cor. 14; they have sometimes been described as 'the liturgy of the Holy Ghost'.

The English Puritans, in addition to the use of extempore prayer by the minister in the regular services, sometimes held meetings, usually on weekdays, at which members, often without a minister, themselves prayed aloud; and some element of spontaneous prayer often formed a part of the church meeting of the Independents. The Sunday 'meetings for worship' of the Society of Friends still contain this element, interwoven with silence and exhortation.

Pietism and the evangelical revival gave a fresh impetus to spontaneous prayer, and this no doubt formed a large ingredient in the various kinds of fellowship meeting in early Methodism. In some places, meetings for prayer with appointed leaders were planned as carefully as preaching services. The actual term 'prayer meeting' came into use in evangelical circles in the early part of the nineteenth century. A fresh impetus came from the camp meetings (q.v.) which the Primitive Methodists adopted from America, for, while some preached, they were supported by others in praying bands. In some parts of England the custom became widespread, especially in Methodism, whereby almost every Sunday evening, except when the Lord's Supper was observed, the more devout members of the congregation stayed to a prayer meeting after the service. At such an 'after-meeting', as it was sometimes called, fresh converts were made welcome, and the young could listen to the prayers of others and make their own first efforts at praying aloud spontaneously. Individuals would also strike up well-known hymns and choruses in which the others would join. Sometimes the prayers would have an ecstatic, affectionate quality usually more characteristic of mental than of vocal prayer.

Such meetings, whether on Sunday or on weekdays, were indeed prominent in all the Free Churches. They were also widespread in Evangelical Anglicanism, though naturally not in such close connection with the services of the church. They were also held in undenominational gatherings and conferences of evangelical societies, and were often called for special purposes, as to support evangelistic campaigns.

In recent years prayer meetings, especially those closely linked with the services of the church, have tended to die out. One reason is that intense fervour was difficult to maintain, and some members of congregations, lacking fresh inspiration, tended, perhaps unconsciously, to repeat the prayers which they had uttered on previous occasions, so that the meetings lost their spontaneity. The practice has recently grown in some churches of inviting members of the congregation to suggest topics at the time of the intercession, and this could develop into a kind of prayer meeting. This is perhaps the most suitable form for such congregational participation in close association with the regular worship of the church, but prayer meetings of the older pattern are still held where religious fervour continues or revives in evangelical circles.

A. RAYMOND GEORGE

Preface

A name, originally proper to the Roman rite, for the thanksgiving which opens the eucharistic prayer or anaphora (q.v.). The Latin *praefatio* in this context does not mean a preliminary, but a proclamation. In the ancient Gallican liturgy the word *praefatio* was used differently, of a descriptive invitation or bidding to prayer.

—————

J. A. Jungmann, *The Mass of the Roman Rite*, II, 1955, pp. 115-28.

W. JARDINE GRISBROOKE

Presanctified Mass

Mass or liturgy of the presanctified (i.e. 'of the previously consecrated') is a form of service prescribed in the historic rites for use on certain days when the eucharist is not celebrated, but when it is at the same time necessary or desirable to make provision for communion.

In the early church the eucharist was held to be a festive act, by definition, and it was therefore not celebrated, even when it came generally to be celebrated on weekdays as well as Sundays, on days of penitence. From a very early period, however, daily communion was common, being normally made at home from the reserved sacrament taken from church by the worshippers on the previous Sunday; and when more frequent celebration of the eucharist became widespread after the peace of the church in the fourth century, the desire to provide a public opportunity for the reception of communion on the days when it was, for liturgical reasons, not celebrated, became increasingly felt, even with the decline in frequency of communion which set in at this time. This was the origin of the mass or liturgy of the presanctified. For reasons of space consideration of the service today must be restricted to the provision for it in the two most widespread of the historic rites, the Byzantine and the Roman.

In the Byzantine rite the eucharist is not celebrated on any day in Lent other than Sundays and Saturdays (which like Sundays are not fast days) and the feast of the Annunciation if it falls in the season. On other days the liturgy of the presanctified is used; today there is no communion at all on Good Friday, but this is a medieval innovation, the liturgy of the presanctified having originally been used on that day like all other Lenten weekdays. As in theory it is not permitted on fast days to take any food until after vespers, the office for communion from the reserved sacrament is attached to that office, which exhibits certain variants from its normal order, and this combination forms the liturgy of the presanctified. Today it is celebrated in most churches only on Wednesdays and Fridays, and except in the increasing but still small number of churches to which liturgical reform is beginning to penetrate, it is celebrated by anticipation in the morning, which makes nonsense of a large part of the service.

The reserved sacrament is prepared for communion during the recitation of the psalms of the day in vespers; it is taken from the tabernacle on the altar to the prothesis (q.v.) table, where wine and water are also poured into a chalice. Vespers is cut short at the lessons, after which the altar, and then the whole church and congregation, are solemnly censed, to the singing of Ps. 140 (141). The second part of the service is composed almost entirely of extracts from the eucharistic liturgy: (1) the litanies which close the synaxis (q.v.) and open the eucharist proper, with special closing collects; (2) the great entrance (q.v.), in an especially solemn form, with a proper anthem, as it is a procession with the consecrated, instead of the unconsecrated, gifts; (3) the Lord's Prayer, with the litany which usually introduces it, slightly modified; (4) the elevation of the gifts, the fraction, and the placing of the particles of the broken bread in the (unconsecrated) chalice, the contents of which were anciently regarded, in East and West alike, as consecrated by this commixture (q.v.); (5) communion; (6) the normal concluding rites, although with certain proper texts. For further details of these parts of the normal liturgy, *see* **Liturgies** 2: Orthodox.

In the Roman rite, the mass of the presanctified (no longer called by that name since 1955) is celebrated on only one day in the year – Good Friday. For this reason the service exhibits a number of striking features peculiar to that day, such as the veneration of the cross, but in essence, like the Byzantine service, it is simply part of a normal service followed by communion from the reserved sacrament – the first part of the Roman service being not vespers as in the Byzantine rite, but the pre-eucharistic synaxis, in an unusually primitive and simple form, and concluding after the readings with the full ancient Roman synaxis intercession, somewhat adapted to modern use. (The veneration of the cross is interpolated between the intercession and the communion.) The communion rite is extremely simple: the sacrament reserved overnight from the mass of the Last Supper on Maundy Thursday is brought in by the deacon while three short anthems are sung; the Lord's Prayer, with certain other normal prayers of preparation for communion, is recited; the communion follows, and the service is concluded with three post-communion collects. (There may be minor changes in this service in the new edition of the Roman missal in preparation at the time of writing.)

Since 1955 the Roman mass of the pre-sanctified, which like its Byzantine counterpart was for many centuries anticipated in the morning, has again been celebrated at its proper hour – in this case, three o'clock in the afternoon. It has undergone a number of minor changes since its first introduction, which appears to have been not later than the sixth century (the opinion of some writers that it is of later date is based on a misreading of the evidence; the communion is absent from the Good Friday service in the earliest *papal* books of the urban Roman rite because the papal service was held in the morning, while the *parochial* books include it, the parochial services being held in the afternoon, and many people no doubt going to both).

W. JARDINE GRISBROOKE

Presbyter

The term is derived from the Greek word meaning elder (q.v.), and appears to be used in the NT as interchangeable with the word *episcopos*, from which 'bishop' (q.v.) is derived. It is notorious that there are widely differing views of the way in which the early ministry of the church developed. One view, held by a good many authorities, is that in each Christian centre there was a college of presbyter-bishops from among whom the monarchical bishop emerged in due course. Whatever may be the truth of the matter, it is clear that by the second century the presbyters formed an advisory body associated with the bishop in the pastoral and administrative work of his office and also associated with him (by their physical presence round him) in his liturgical functions. In the third century the presbyter began to be the person to whom the bishop delegated the responsibility for the pastoral oversight of an area and the duty of presiding at celebrations of the eucharist. In due course the medieval concept of the parish priest developed, the man who was almost the personification of the church in the local community, who baptized and said mass and performed all other Christian rites except confirmation and ordination. The English word 'priest', like its equivalents in most Germanic languages, is derived from 'presbyter' and not from the Greek or Latin terms for priesthood. (The Greek and Latin terms are hardly ever used for the Christian ministry in the early church, and then of bishops rather than of presbyters. Thus Cyprian uses *sacerdos* to mean bishop, not presbyter.) After the Reformation, Anglican and some Lutheran churches retained 'priest' for the second order of the ministry, though it became more usual for churches of the Reformation to use the term 'presbyter' or the vaguer term 'minister' to describe the person normally responsible for the preaching of the word and the administration of the sacraments. In most modern schemes for a reunion of the churches, 'presbyter' rather than 'priest' is used for the order next below that of bishop.

G. B. Henderson, *Presbyterianism*, 1954; D. N. Power, *Ministers of Christ and his Church*, 1969; B. H. Streeter, *The Primitive Church*, 1929; A. Prolante, P. Siffrin and E. Josi, in *Enciclopedia Cattolica*, IX, cols, 1961-4.

P. HINCHLIFF

Presbyterian Worship
see Reformed Worship

Prime *see* Canonical Hours

Procession

A planned movement of a group of people from one place to another for some specific religious purpose. It may be a self-contained, independent act, e.g. a Rogationtide procession around the fields, or an act within a service, e.g. an offertory (q.v.) procession at the eucharist. Early evidence for processions is found in the *Pilgrimage of Egeria* (late fourth century) which describes the pilgrimages to the sacred sites in Jerusalem during the rites of Holy Week. A valuable Western source is *Ordo Romanus Primus*, which describes the seventh century pontifical stational masses of Rome. In the later Middle Ages material for various occasions was collected from such books as the *Missal*, the *Ritual* and the *Pontifical* to form the *Processional*.

A procession could be held for various reasons. It could be an act of Christian witness, an act of penitence or praise, or an act of supplication. Some processions served more than one purpose. The St Mark's Day procession, instituted in Rome in the sixth century, was an act of Christian witness on the same day as the old pagan festival of the Robigalia, when the gods were asked to preserve the crops from mildew; but it was also used as an act of supplication similar to the Rogationtide (q.v.) procession, at which litanies (q.v.) were sung, praying for God's blessing on the crops. Again, the Corpus Christi (q.v.) procession, instituted in the thirteenth century in honour of the blessed sacrament, was combined in Germany with a supplication for God's protection on the countryside. Other processions were held in connection with pilgrimage to shrines, or the transference of relics to a new home, or the dedication of a new church. On such occasions full use was made of external aids to excite devotion – incense, lights (qq.v.), banners, relics and rich vestments (q.v.).

Other processions were integral to particular rites: the procession to the font at baptism; the procession of the bridal party to the altar at matrimony; the procession to the grave at burial; the procession before the eucharist; or the gospel and offertory processions (the lesser and greater entrance, qq.v.). The Reformers in general protested against abuses connected with processions and abandoned, not only the processions themselves, but also – with the exception of Luther and Cranmer – the litanies associated with them. Cranmer and Henry VIII apparently contemplated a new English *Processional*, but the project came to nothing. By a royal injunction of 1545 Cranmer's litany of 1544 became the sole procession in England; and by the royal injunctions of 1547, even the litany could only be used kneeling in church. After a temporary reprieve under Queen Mary, processions were again suppressed under Elizabeth in 1559 except those of Rogationtide. The 1662 BCP, however, sanctioned processions occurring within rites – namely in baptism, matrimony and burial. These, with the gospel and offertory processions at the eucharist, are found in whole or in part in the Roman, Orthodox, Anglican and in some Reformed Churches: and their use is still spreading. The public procession as an act of Christian witness or as a pilgrimage has also revived, and, on occasions such as Good Friday, often has great ecumenical value.

M. Andrieu, *Les Ordines Romani du Haut Moyen Age*, 5 vols., 1931-61; F. E. Brightman, *The English Rite*, 1915; C. Dunlop, *Processions*, 1932; W. H. Frere, *The Principles of Religious Ceremonial*, 1906; W. G. Henderson, *Processionale ad usum Sarum*, 1882; *La Maison Dieu*, no. 43, 1955.

R. C. D. JASPER

Prone *see* Bidding Prayer

Proper

A term of the Roman mass (although applicable to other rites also), having two different but related meanings: (1) those parts of the service which vary according to the day or season; (2) those variable parts of the service which are rendered chorally, principally composed of psalmody, and comprising the introit or entrance chant, the gradual or responsorial psalm (formerly sung after the epistle, but since 1969 before it and after the OT reading), the alleluia (sung between the epistle and the gospel), the offertory chant, and the communion chant. Derivatively, the term may be used of those parts of any service which vary according to the day or season.

W. JARDINE GRISBROOKE

Prothesis

The name prothesis (Greek 'preparation') is used in the Byzantine rite (commonly miscalled the Orthodox liturgy) to designate three different but related things: (1) the rite of preparation before the divine liturgy or eucharist; (2) the chamber to the north of the sanctuary in which the greater part of this rite takes place; (3) the table in that chamber on which the elements, usually referred to in the Byzantine rite as the gifts, are prepared.

The rite of preparation currently in use is elaborate, and falls into two principal parts, the preparation of the ministers and the preparation of the gifts. The former comprises three acts: (1) introductory prayers which are recited by the celebrant and deacon together outside the gates of the sanctuary, with the veneration of the principal images on the iconostasis (q.v.) or sanctuary screen; (2) the vesting of the ministers, the putting on of each garment being accompanied by the recitation of a supposedly appropriate verse from the psalms or some other part of the OT; (3) a washing of their hands by the ministers, with the recitation of Ps. 25 (26).6-12. The second and third of these properly take place in the chamber called the *diakonikon* (Greek lit. 'deaconry', commonly translated 'vestry') on the south of the sanctuary, corresponding to the prothesis on the north, but not every church today has such a chamber, and where it is absent the vesting and washing often take place in the sanctuary itself.

The preparation of the gifts opens with the recitation of an anthem about the passion, after which it falls into four distinguishable parts: (1) the preparation of the bread, (2) the preparation of the chalice, (3) commemorative and intercessory prayers, a kind of anticipated diptychs (q.v.), and (4) veiling and censing of the prepared gifts. The preparation of the bread, which varies somewhat in detail from one Orthodox national church to another, consists principally in the cutting out of a square from a pure wheaten leavened loaf (the square being called the 'lamb', an exact counterpart of the Western 'host'), and placing it on the paten, to the accompaniment of a number of scriptural formulae which relate the cutting of the loaf in a highly literal way to the wounding of our Lord in the passion. The preparation of the chalice is much simpler: it consists simply of blessing wine and water, and pouring them into the chalice. There follows a lengthy and involved commemoration of the saints, and of the living and departed for whom the prayers of the church at the eucharist are particularly desired; a small particle of bread is taken from the loaf or loaves at the mention of each name or group of names, and placed

upon the paten beside the 'lamb', theoretically in an intricately specified order. The commemorations completed, the celebrant blesses incense, covers the vessels with their veils, censing each veil as he does so, and saying appointed formulae, including Ps. 92 (93). He then censes the gifts thus prepared and covered, and says a concluding general prayer, after which he or the deacon censes the altar, the sanctuary, and finally the whole church and congregation.

This rite of preparation has undergone a long development, and the greater part of it dates from a comparatively late period. The preparation of the ministers is entirely absent from the earliest surviving texts, and does not arrive at something like its present form until the thirteenth century; the earliest evidence for the washing of the ministers' hands at this point is in a printed edition of 1526. As for the preparation of the gifts, until the ninth century it was done with the utmost simplicity, with a single prayer; as late as the middle of the eleventh century there are still texts in which it has developed no further; not until the late twelfth century is there definitive evidence for more intricate ceremonial at it, and even then this was performed in silence, with a single prayer before and after; something resembling the present form is found in a text of 1225. The pseudodiptychs first appear in the twelfth century, and become longer and more elaborate during the course of the later Middle Ages, finally achieving their present form (apart from a few minor details) in 1600. The whole rite, in its present form, is an outstanding example of the medieval tendency to confuse the essentials of liturgical action by superimposing on them a mass of secondary, and often theologically inappropriate, detail.

On the other hand, the prothesis still makes provision for the ancient custom of individual offering of the bread and wine for the eucharist, lost for centuries in the West, a provision still largely made use of by the faithful, and unless and until the restoration of the diptychs in the anaphora (q.v.) to their pristine integrity is accomplished, the lengthy intercessory commemorations in the prothesis are necessary in this connection.

H. Holloway, *A Study of the Byzantine Liturgy*, 1933, ch. I.

W. JARDINE GRISBROOKE

Psalmody

From the earliest times the Christian community sang the psalms following the practice of the synagogue, in antiphonal or responsorial forms (qq.v.), and the psalter became basic to the liturgy of mass and office. We learn from the fathers of the church how psalmody spread over the Christian world. Eusebius (260-340), Bishop of Caesarea, paints a vivid picture of the result: 'The command to sing psalms in the name of the Lord was obeyed by everyone in every place: for the command to sing is in force in all churches which exist among the nations, not only the Greeks but also the barbarians throughout the whole world, and in towns, villages and in the fields.' Tertullian speaks of the use of psalms at household prayer and exhorts married Christians to emulate one another in psalm singing.

It is certain that all the people took part in psalm singing in the fourth century when Christians were free of persecution. Certain of the fathers forbade women to take part and others, in the next century, gave grudging permission, since if the women were not allowed to sing they would talk during the service. The fathers exhorted monks and clergy to learn the psalms by heart – a practice which was to last for many centuries, until service-books were available to all. Jerome told the nuns of the Convent of St Paul at Jerusalem 'no sister may remain if she does not know the psalms'. Enthusiasm for the psalms followed from the realization that the psalter – as still to-day – was, in the words of Athanasius (296-373), 'a book that includes the whole life of man, all conditions of the mind and all movements of thought'.

As regards the laity, the number of psalms and canticles they knew by heart cannot have been large, hence the simplicity of the refrains which they contributed to the responsorial psalms (q.v.).

ALEC ROBERTSON

Psalm Tones

The eight tones, or melodic formulae, used in the singing of the psalms, have an obvious relation to the eight church modes of the Roman chant. Each tone begins with an intonation used only at the start of the psalm or canticle, but on major feasts in every verse of the canticles (*Benedictus*, *Magnificat*, *Nunc Dimittis*), so as to give greater solemnity. The intonation leads to the reciting note, on the dominant of the tone, and at the end of the half-verse to a cadence known as the mediant. In medieval times the pause after the half-way cadence was accommodated to the time it took to say 'Ave Maria'. The reciting note is then resumed and leads to the termination.

A ninth tone, the beautiful *Tonus peregrinus* ('stranger tone') has two reciting tones, the second, after the mediant cadence, lying a second lower than the first. It is traditionally associated with Ps. 113 (114), '*In exitu Israel*' ('When Israel went out of Egypt'). Bach uses this tone, in its Lutheran form, at a high pitch on the oboes in the sixth verse of his Latin setting of *Magnificat*. The other tones are most effectively used, with some variations such as the introduction of chromatic notes, in all but one of the five psalms of Monteverdi's *Vespers* of 1610. They exert a stabilizing influence, especially in the decorative florid passages in one part or another. Mozart makes effective quotation of the first tone on the oboes, in his fine *Masonic Funeral March* (K 477) for small orchestra.

During the fifteenth and sixteenth centuries it was a favourite practice of church composers to set the odd verses of the canticles of lauds, vespers, and compline (qq.v.) polyphonically, leaving the even ones to be sung directly to one or another of the eight psalm tones.

The codification of the psalm tones as they appear in the *Antiphonale* today dates from about the eleventh century. The notable resemblance between the first psalm tone and the *Tonus peregrinus* and Jewish psalmody discloses a link with the practice of the synagogue, as do the recitatives, or chanting tones, of the priest.

ALEC ROBERTSON

Pulpit

Although in the fifth century BC it is recorded that 'Ezra the scribe stood upon a wooden pulpit which they had made for that purpose' (Neh. 8.4), and though in the early Christian centuries the apostles and fathers of the church delivered sermons, there is little evidence that such sermons were given from a pulpit in the nave or body of the church building. It is thought that such sermons were given by the bishop from his throne or *cathedra* (q.v.) from behind the altar. The pulpit-like structure still found in Roman and other basilicas known as the ambo (q.v.) was mainly employed for the reading of the gospel at the eucharist and not for preaching.

In England, pulpits do not seem to have come into use in parish churches until the twelfth and thirteenth centuries. They were usually placed against the first pier on the north side of the nave west of the chancel step. Most of the medieval pulpits belong to the fifteenth century when the wood carver's craft reached its apogee in East Anglia and the West Country.

The Reformation brought about an increased demand for more adequate teaching and preaching, and many fine wooden pulpits were erected in the seventeenth and eighteenth centuries, often with a sounding-board or tester over them. The necessity of providing a pulpit as part of the furniture of a church was underlined by Canon 83 of 1604, 'a comely and decent pulpit to be seemly kept for the preaching of God's Word'. In the eighteenth century, examples of the three-tier arrangement came into use, known as the 'three-decker' pulpit. In this the parish clerk was in the lowest stage, the officiant read the service from the middle tier, while the pulpit-proper was reserved for the sermon.

In the planning of modern churches two pulpits are sometimes provided which can be used for the reading of the liturgical lessons at the eucharist as well as for preaching.

G. W. O. Addleshaw and F. Etchells, *The Architectural Setting of Anglican Worship*, 1948; F. E. Howard and F. H. Crossley, *English Church Woodwork*, [2]1927.

C. E. POCKNEE

Purification
see Mariological Feasts

Purificator

A towel or napkin that is used to dry the chalice and other vessels after the consumption of the remains of the consecrated elements at the eucharist when the ablutions are taken. Another towel is also used for drying the hands of the celebrant and this is termed the *lavabo* cloth. This cloth is somewhat larger than the purificator.

P. Dearmer, *The Linen Ornaments of the Church*, [2]1950; C. E. Pocknee, ed., *The Parson's Handbook*, 1965; The Warham

Guild, *The Warham Guild Handbook*, rev. ed., 1963.

C. E. POCKNEE

Pyx

Also spelt pix. A receptacle used chiefly for housing the consecrated elements of bread, and sometimes wine, when reserved outside the time of the celebration of the liturgy. The custom is of very high antiquity, being mentioned by Justin Martyr (*Apol.* I. 65.) about AD 150. This reservation (q.v.) was chiefly for the sick and those prevented from attending the Sunday eucharist. Also, it was the custom during the first three centuries to permit the faithful to take away from the Sunday eucharist portions of the consecrated bread in order to communicate themselves at home during the week. For this purpose, little boxes of wood, ivory or metal with a cord that could be suspended round the neck were in use. These were known as *arcae* or *arculae*; examples have been found on the breasts of the deceased buried in the Vatican catacombs during the second and third centuries. This custom led to the abuse of the *arcae* and their contents as a charm or talisman, so it was discontinued.

From the fourth century the reserved sacrament was kept in the church or its sacristy (q.v.). But not until the ninth century were precise regulations issued regarding the kind of receptacle to be used for this purpose. Pyxes or containers of ivory and precious metal as well as latten and brass were in use; not infrequently the metal ones were decorated with coloured enamels.

In the second part of the Middle Ages in the Latin West, with the development of the cultus of devotions to the reserved sacrament, pyxes displaying the skill of the silversmith and craftsman came into use. Such pyxes were mounted on a stem and foot (*see* Plate 34). A particular form of pyx that has excited antiquarian interest since the last century is that which came into use in England and France in the later Middle Ages, when the blessed sacrament was reserved in a vessel suspended by a chain over the high altar. Sometimes this pyx was contained in a steeple-like tower; in other instances it was suspended under a trumpet-shaped canopy of silk or fabric. A modern revival of this custom is to be seen in Gloucester and Ely Cathedrals. This whole arrangement including the canopy is frequently referred to as a

Plate 34 Fourteenth-century Italian standing pyx, silver-gilt and enamel, Victoria and Albert Museum, London

'hanging pyx'. A particular form of metal pyx associated with this method of reservation was that made like a dove into which the consecrated hosts were placed by lifting a lid on the back of the 'dove'.

Since the revival of continuous reservation in the Church of England and the churches of the Anglican Communion in the nineteenth century, the use of a pyx has been revived. When a priest takes the holy communion reserved to a sick person it is usually in a circular silver pyx suspended round his neck by a cord. Another form of this receptacle is the so-called 'double-pyx' containing

two sections, one for the element of bread, and the other for the consecrated wine.

W. H. Freestone, *The Sacrament Reserved*, 1917; A. A. King and C. E. Pocknee, *Eucharistic Reservation in the Western Church*, 1965; C. E. Pocknee, *The Christian Altar*, 1963.

C. E. POCKNEE

Quadragesima *see* Lent

Quaker Worship

Ecumenical discussion recognizes the existence of three broad types of worship, often referred to as 'altar-centred', 'pulpit-centred' and 'waiting upon the Spirit'. Traditional Quaker worship, with its abandonment of prearranged form, ordained ministry, and sacraments, is then seen as the extreme example of this third type. Its true character is positively determined, however, by the full seriousness with which it witnesses to the reality behind the words 'Where two or three are gathered together in my name, there am I in the midst'. It is thus the central activity of a fellowship committed to the discerning and 'answering' of him who, as 'the light that enlightens every man, coming into the world', is hiddenly present in every situation and relationship. Such a group seeks to *offer*, in attentive and expectant waiting, its present experiences, needs, confessions, thanksgivings and intercessions. It *awaits* a word, expressed either 'inwardly' or in such spoken words as the Spirit may prompt in any person present. Such words may include prayer, exhortation, reflection upon experience, exposition of a biblical passage or theme. The keynote of Quaker worship is, therefore, not the quest for mystical absorption, nor preoccupation with individual meditation and private devotions. It is, rather, the profoundly simple intention, by a gathered group, of opening itself to the presence of Christ, to the implications of the discovery that Christ's presence in the Spirit requires no other mediation and is that by which isolation is overcome and communion is experienced.

Inseparable from this conception of worship is a no less profoundly simple conception of ministry. Worship is both nourished by ministry and issues in ministry. The form this ministry takes, whether in word or in action, will depend for each individual upon personal gifts, responsibilities and opportunities. But ministry is seen as a function, not a profession; for Quakers the difference between cleric and layman is irrelevant. All Christ's followers, men and women equally, are 'ordained' and, in the Spirit, have access to gifts and graces sufficient for their several needs.

This richly varied and fully shared ministry is directed towards the needs of the world, either indirectly, by the building up of the life of the worshipping community, or directly, through the rendering of service by the community corporately or by any member of it. As the members become sensitized in this corporate life, through worship and faithful caring for one another, they become painfully aware of areas of darkness and oppression, both in and among themselves and also in the world around them. These are seen as areas in which the strivings of the Spirit of God in human life are being ignored or withstood. In relation to them, individuals or groups may find themselves 'under concern' to bear witness and to accept obligations, so that liberation and true community may be more truly known and more widely shared.

The early Quaker attitude to the sacraments expressed the conviction that no external rite could effect spiritual change and that clerical celebration was a limitation upon the 'priesthood of all believers'. Quakers regarded 'water baptism' as merely diverting attention from the reality of 'baptism in the Spirit'. They understood themselves to be obeying Christ's command 'Do this in remembrance of me' whenever, in everyday life, they took food and drink. They supported their convictions regarding worship and sacraments biblically and theologically by reference (1) to the 'New Covenant' whereby, with the coming of Christ, all ceremonial and 'typical' forms of worship were abrogated, and (2) to the 'offices of Christ' as prophet, priest and king, exercised in the gathered, worshipping group in such wise that silent, attentive and expectant waiting was the sole appropriate response. Their eucharist was inward: 'Behold, I stand at the door and knock; if any man open the door, I will come in and sup with him.'

The mode of worship so far described has continued, from the seventeenth century, to be practised in Britain, in overseas areas where Quaker groups have close links with Britain (e.g. Australia and New Zealand), on the continent of Europe, in Canada and in parts of the USA. In other parts of the USA, and in areas of Asia, Africa and Latin America influenced by Quaker evangelical missionary activity, a form of worship is practised similar to that of most Protestant 'Free Churches', and pastoral leadership is generally accepted. Rather less than half the total membership of the Society of Friends now worships in the traditional manner described in this article. The four World Conferences of Friends held since 1920 have made possible a growth of understanding among Friends of the psychological, theological and historical grounds of their diversities, and have encouraged mutual openness and appreciation as well as a desire to rediscover, in appropriate contemporary forms, the experience which gave birth, in seventeenth-century England, to the mode of worship here delineated.

Both for the Society of Friends and for the Christian church as a whole, this mode of worship today raises far-reaching questions. If it is not, as early Friends claimed, the *only* form of worship appropriate to the new covenant dispensation, what is it? Is it simply a mode which appeals to certain temperaments? Or is it an emphasis – even an exaggeration – justified so long as it is balanced or off-set by other emphases? Or is it possible that it represents an essential ingredient or dimension of worship which, historically, found separate expression in conscious opposition to others? To express the matter otherwise, is it possible to think that, with other forms, it points beyond itself and them towards an understanding of the fullness of worship appropriate to today?

The Reports on Worship adopted by the World Faith and Order Conference (Montreal) 1963 and the British Faith and Order Conference (Nottingham) 1964, and the Fourth Assembly of the World Council of Churches (Uppsala) 1968, emphasized the need to go beyond all our inherited and traditional patterns of worship. They also recognized the obstacles posed for many of our contemporaries by the prescribed forms of ecclesiastical ritual, embodying traditional formulations of doctrine. They also deplored the gulf which appears to many to separate worship from responsible life in the world. Is it inconceivable that a mode of worship which minimizes ritual, requires no doctrinal affirmations but, instead, strongly requires the full and equal responsible participation of every worshipper, issuing directly in his service in and to the world, may have a contribution to make far greater than might be inferred from the fewness of those who, for more than three centuries, have practised it?

Robert Barclay, *An Apology for the True Christian Divinity . . .*, 1675, Propositions xi, xii, xiii; H. Brinton, *Creative Worship*, 1931; *Christian Faith and Practice in the Experience of the Society of Friends*, 1960, chs. 3, 4, 5, 7; George Fox, 'Concerning Silent Meetings', *Gospel Truth Demonstrated*, 1657, p. 103; T. F. Green, *Preparation for Worship*, 1952; T. Edmund Harvey, *Silence and Worship: A Study in Quaker Experience*, 1923; L. V. Hodgkin, *Silent Worship, the Way of Wonder*, 1919; George Keith, *The Benefit, Advantage and Glory of Silent Meetings*, 1670; James Nayler, 'Concerning Worship', *Collected Works*, 1656, pp. 272 ff.; Isaac Penington, 'Concerning the Worship of the Living God', *Works*, 1681, Part I, pp. 350 ff.; 'A Brief Account of the Ground of Our Worship', *Works*, Part II pp. 258 ff.; 'A Few Words concerning the Worship which our God Hath Taught Us', *Works*, Part II, pp. 374 ff.; 'A Brief Account concerning Silent Meetings, the Nature, Use, Intent and Benefit of them', *Works*, Part II, pp. 256 ff.; D. V. Steere, *Where Words Come from*, 1955; John Woolman, *Journal and Essays* (1772), ed. A. M. Gummere, 1922, pp. 508 ff.; John Woolman, 'On Silent Worship', *Works*, [2]1775.

M. A. CREASEY

Quinquagesima

The name denotes the Sunday preceding Lent, being *fifty* days before Easter, but there is less obvious relevance in Sexagesima, 'sixtieth', and Septuagesima, 'seventieth', the terms applied to the two preceding Sundays. Lent (q.v.) was a preparation for the Pascha; to prepare for Quadragesima was a development which may be regarded as a tendency towards unnecessary elaboration.

Before the fourth century had ended there were places where the period before the Pascha was longer than six weeks. With the growth of monasticism the discipline of fasting rooted itself more and more firmly in the course of the century. The increasing emphasis on fasting would lead in time to a gratuitously meticulous calculation of the forty days. Sundays, and in some regions Saturdays also, would be excluded from the computation. Manifestly, there were factors which were liable to affect the integrity of the original six-week period. There is evidence of a seven-week Lent and an eight-week Lent at various centres in the eastern Mediterranean during the latter part of the fourth century. But it appears that in the East generally the period of preparation came to be seven weeks.

The situation was different in the West where Lent retained its character of six weeks. But between the middle of the fifth century and the end of the sixth Quinquagesima, Sexagesima and Septuagesima emerged to form a preparatory cycle. Western practice outside Rome during the period of the sixth to the eighth centuries varied between two Sundays and one Sunday before Lent, although two predominated. On the other hand, there were no preparatory Sundays in the lectionary of Luxeuil or the Bobbio Missal. Septuagesima, Sexagesima and Quinquagesima were established at Rome before the end of the sixth century, and the spread of the Roman rite ensured their eventual acceptance throughout the West.

A. A. MCARTHUR

Reader

Etymologically, reader is simply the English translation of 'lector' (q.v.), one of the minor orders of the ministry. In the Church of Scotland after the Reformation readers acted as assistants to parish ministers and in a number of cases were given full pastoral responsibility for a parish. They were authorized to *read* the prayers, the lessons from scripture and a homily and, after 1572, to perform baptisms and marriages. In the Church of Scotland at the present time readers are nominated by presbyteries and authorized to conduct services when there is no minister. In the Anglican Church, laymen (and, more recently, women) have been licensed as 'lay readers' since 1866. They may take services and preach (except at the eucharist) and may be authorized to administer the chalice.

P. HINCHLIFF

Reformed Worship

The origins of Reformed worship in the strictly Calvinistic sense are to be found in Strasbourg, where in St John's chapel below the high altar of the cathedral the first German mass, translated and modified by the ex-Dominican Diebold Schwarz, was celebrated in 1524. It was simply the Latin eucharist translated into plain homely German designed to express the new spirit, while retaining as far as possible the old familiar things. The ceremonial, e.g., was not appreciably altered – that is to say the action itself looked much the same as before. The words also were not much changed, except unobtrusively to remove from the canon (the consecration prayer) phrases which seemed to confirm the Roman doctrine of the sacrifice of the mass as a repetition of what took place on Calvary. The really far-reaching change, however, was to say the whole service in a clear audible voice and in the vernacular tongue. Low mass had been the popular form of service for a considerable period before the Reformation, and this meant that the old service had been said in Latin and also inaudibly. Now, for the first time, the people both heard the words and understood them, while at one stroke the old secret prayers disappeared and the central rite stood clear of its medieval accretions. It was in fact very similar to the new liturgical revolution which has taken place in the Roman Church during the last few years, even in some respects perhaps less radical.

During the next five years the reforms were carried farther (and independently) in Strasbourg. German metrical psalms and hymns were introduced to enable the people to take an active part in the worship, and more than one observer remarked that the church was full of the people's song. The Apostles' Creed, as simpler, is offered as an alternative to the Nicene; the lectionaries are abandoned, and the epistle and gospel read in course and at greater length; sermons are preached at every service; and the ceremonial is much reduced. The ancient basilican posture of the celebrant, when he stood behind the holy table facing the people, replaces the eastward position (q.v.), and the holy table itself, now no longer called the altar (q.v.) is moved forward in the sanctuary to be nearer to the people.

From 1530 onwards Bucer's influence became dominant and the reforms more radical. Choices were offered in the prayers, necessitating departure from the old text; each successive variant was more verbose and didactic. The responses long ago of course had disappeared from the people's usage, but now they were excised from the text. Sermons were very long, an hour or so in length, and the abandonment of the old lectionary which could have been profitably revised was a loss, as in fact reading the scriptures in course is unworkable for weekly worship. The eucharistic vestments (q.v.) now gave way to cassock and bands, black gown and scarf (or tippet), formerly the outdoor and preaching garments of the clergy. The *Orate fratres*, a bidding to prayer where no prayer then existed, was expanded into a long didactic exhortation and fencing of the table; and such exhortations became a feature – in truth, a somewhat tedious feature – of every subsequent Reformed liturgy. A central and important reform was the restoration of weekly communion, to replace the yearly communion of the medieval church. This became a primary principle of nearly all the Reformers (Zwingli, e.g., was an exception), though it was not always successfully given effect to. In Strasbourg there were weekly celebrations in the cathedral and monthly celebrations in the parish churches. When holy communion was not celebrated, all except that immediately pertaining to communion was retained, the eucharist thus remained the norm of worship, and in the *BCP* later issued it was described as ante-communion. Communion was received standing. It will be seen that to give effect to such reforms as we have mentioned, service-books became necessary for the people's use, and these were prepared and issued. Such books were unknown in the medieval church (there were rare exceptions); thus the people's prayer-books were an invention of the Reformers, and were in use thereafter in every Reformed church, though abandoned by some in the seventeenth century.

This was the situation when Calvin came to Strasbourg late in 1538, exiled from Geneva because of differences with the magistracy. Bucer and the other Reformers there welcomed him (after a while Bucer even found this somewhat reserved young man a charming wife) and gave him charge of the small congregation of French exiles in the city. The condition was that the same form of worship as used in the German churches be adopted and holy communion be celebrated once a month. This was very congenial to Calvin, and as he did not speak German he had prepared a Latin translation of the German service-book, then cast it into French. He made minor changes, such as substituting a metrical decalogue (divided into two tables by a collect) for the *Kyries* and the *Gloria in excelsis*.

Persuaded upon urgent invitation of the magistrates to return to Geneva in 1541 he took this book with him for use there. By this time it included an order for holy baptism, directions for the ordination of ministers, and other occasional offices, and metrical psalms were gradually added to it as they became available. Entitled *La Forme de Prières*, it became the standard of Reformed worship among Calvinists everywhere. During Mary's reign it was translated into English, slightly revised, and used in the Congregation of Marian exiles in Geneva, of which such men as John Knox and Whittinghouse were ministers. Thus after Mary's death it was taken back to Britain to be used in Scotland and among many Puritans in England. In 1560 it became the official service-book of the Church of Scotland, passing through over sixty editions between 1564 and 1638, variously known as the *Forme of Prayers*, the *Book of Common Order* and the *Psalm Book*, and later nicknamed Knox's Liturgy. In England it was generally known as the *Forme of Prayers*, 'the Waldgrave Liturgy', the 'Middleburg Liturgy', the 'Genevan Form', etc. The last editions known were printed in London in 1641, 1642 and 1644 for submission to Parliament and the Westminster Divines.

None, I think, would now hold the liturgical quality of this book or advocate it for present-day use. But it presented certain principles of enduring value, many of which have been forgotten by subsequent generations including our own. For example, it presupposed the Lord's Supper as the normative worship of the church, desired frequent communion, weekly to be preferred. Calvin declared infrequent communion to be 'an invention of the devil' and held that 'once a

week at the very least the Lord's Supper should be celebrated in the Christian Congregation'. This he made clear upon his first visit to Geneva, fought for it all his life, and declared that 'our practice is defection' because his purpose was not achieved, 'owing to ignorance' and other conservative opposition. The Sunday worship, even if there was no communion, was always based upon the eucharist.

One may summarize the Calvinistic rite as follows. It contained no order for daily prayer, though daily services took place, chiefly of a didactic nature with prayers added; and family prayers were also encouraged in the homes at a later period. The Sunday service consisted of (in this order): scripture sentence, Ps. 124.8; confession of sins, with scriptural words of pardon or absolution; the commandments sung in metre with Greek *Kyries* (q.v.) after each, the two tables divided by a collect for grace to keep God's law; a collect for illumination; scripture reading, and sermon; collection of alms; intercessions and Lord's Prayer (sometimes in a long paraphrase); Apostles' Creed in metre; metrical psalm; Aaronic blessing. In addition, as we learn from contemporary descriptions, one or two other metrical psalms were inserted at what were considered to be appropriate points. When holy communion was celebrated, the Lord's Prayer and blessing were omitted from the above and the prayer of consecration followed the creed and was completed by the Lord's Prayer. Then followed the words of institution, the fraction, the celebrant's communion, and the delivery to the people who came forward to the holy table standing to receive in both kinds during which a psalm was sung or the scriptures read. The service concluded with a brief post-communion thanksgiving, the *Nunc dimittis* in metre and the Aaronic blessing. Originally, Calvin's service was conducted from the communion table, with readings and sermon from the pulpit. Later, the whole service gravitated to the pulpit as any understanding of liturgical appropriateness disappeared, as it did also for a time in Anglican practice. The Christian year was followed widely in its main feasts, but not in detail. *See also* **Baptism** 15; **Books, Liturgical,** 15; **Liturgies** 15.

Strasbourg liturgies; F. Hubert, *Die Strassburger liturgischen Ordnungen im Zeitalter der Reformation*, 1920; for genealogy of *Form of Prayers* and text in use in Scotland, *see* W. D. Maxwell, *Genevan Service Book*, 1931, reprinted 1965, and for English translations of two Strasbourgian liturgies, *see* W. D. Maxwell, *An Outline of Christian Worship*, 1936 (both of these books contain extensive additional bibliography); Calvin's liturgy will be found in Calvin's *Opera*; William Cowan has given in the papers of the Edinburgh Bibliographical Society (vol. X, 1913) a *Bibliography of the Book of Common Order*, and a large number of Puritan liturgies of the period have been collected in Hall, *Reliquiae Liturgicae*, 1847, and *Fragmenta Liturgiae*, 1848. *See also* W. D. Maxwell, *The Book of Common Prayer and the Worship of the Non-Anglican Churches* (Dr Williams' Lecture, 1949).

WILLIAM D. MAXWELL

Reredos

In the English parish church of the later Middle Ages there was usually a large east window, or a series of lancet windows, the sill of which came down to within three or four feet of the altar-table. The intervening space on the wall between window and altar was filled in with a structure of wood or stone which extended the length of the altar, and this is the reredos. It was sometimes made of alabaster, but it was seldom, whether wood or stone, left without gilt and colour. In the middle was a crucifix and on either side there were carved or painted figures of the saints. The whole structure was encased in a frame. In some instances a fabric hanging of embroidery was preferred (*see* **Altar Hangings**.

In cathedrals and larger churches where there was a solid screen behind the high altar, e.g. Winchester Cathedral, England, the panel immediately above the altar was treated like the reredos in a parish church with more detailed and refined carving (*see* **Screen**).

In the Baroque era in France, Italy and Spain there was a great development of the reredos into a vast altar-piece with dramatic and theatrical details, e.g. in the Church of St Ignatius, Rome. But in England the altar-pieces designed by Wren and Hawksmoor seldom attained such proportions, although rising well behind the altar, since they usually had panels on which the Lord's Prayer and the ten commandments were inscribed.

J. W. Franklin, *The Cathedrals of Italy*, 1958; J. Harvey, *The Cathedrals of Spain*, 1957; C. E. Pocknee, *The Christian Altar*, 1963.

C. E. POCKNEE

Reservation

Reservation of the sacrament for the sick and dying has been customary in the church from the earliest times. Justin Martyr (*c.* 155) said that it was taken 'to those who were absent'. The faithful in the time of persecution were permitted to take the eucharist into their own homes, in order to give themselves holy communion. The clergy would keep the sacrament, for a sick call, in their houses, and after the Peace of the Church (313) often in the sacristy (q.v.). About the end of the ninth century, some churches issued regulations for reservation within the church itself, in close proximity to the altar.

The sacrament must have been reserved in both kinds, at least in some places, especially in northern countries, as it was often the custom to give the sick man the species of bread dipped in the chalice (intinction). By the twelfth century it became the normal practice to reserve the consecrated bread only.

The first official regulation for reservation in the Western Church comes from the Fourth Lateran Council of 1215, when it was already the custom to reserve the sacrament in cathedrals, parish churches and chapels of the religious orders on or, more usually, about the altar. The Council did no more than direct that the reserved sacrament should be kept with strict care under lock and key.

The mode of reservation in the Middle Ages differed in the various countries of Europe. A hanging pyx (q.v.) above the altar was usual in England and France (often in the form of a dove). Germany and the Low Countries developed the sacrament house, an elaborate structure, isolated from the altar. A niche in the wall of the sanctuary was customary in parts of Italy, Portugal, Sweden, Scotland and elsewhere. (*See* **Aumbry**.)

The Tridentine reform, which encouraged a more frequent reception of holy communion, prescribed, without formally forbidding other usages, a tabernacle (q.v.) fixed to the centre of the altar. In the brief reign of Queen Mary, when an effort was made to restore reservation, Cardinal Pole, archbishop of Canterbury, issued regulations for a tabernacle, but the bishop of London, Edmund Bonner, who was not so influenced by the Continent, envisaged a restoration of the hanging pyx. Since Trent, the tabernacle has become the usual mode of reservation in all Roman Catholic churches, although there are exceptions in Germany and Belgium, where the old sacrament houses are permitted to be used (*see* Plate 35).

Communion from the tabernacle is the norm on Sundays and feasts, as it is impossible to estimate the number of communicants. The liturgical commission, following up the findings of Vatican II, has again raised the question of the mode of reservation. The old altar against the east wall has been abandoned for a simple table in the middle of the sanctuary, with the celebrant facing the people. In such circumstances, a tabernacle is out of the question. If the old altar has been suffered to remain with its tabernacle, the celebrant can conveniently get the blessed sacrament to give communion to the people, but if, as in some places, the altar has been removed, an awkward pause would result while the celebrant went to a side chapel. The solution would seem to be an aumbry or sacrament house in close proximity to the present altar. This has been done in the cathedral churches of Cologne and Aachen. A hanging pyx would not solve the difficulty, as it would not hold sufficient hosts for communion.

In the latter part of the eleventh century, with the growth of a realization of the real presence of Christ in the eucharist, outward honour was paid to the reserved sacrament, which was increased over the years by theologians and councils. Prayers were offered to Christ present in the church under the species of bread. A feast was introduced for the express purpose of worshipping the sacrament: Corpus Christi, on the Thursday after Trinity Sunday. A form of devotion to the reserved sacrament is given in the 'Ancren Riwle', written for anchoresses in the thirteenth century. The Carmelite Sibert de Beka, who revised the ordinal of the order in the early years of the fourteenth century, added the words 'for the devotion of the choir' to 'for the use of the sick', as the purpose of reservation. Centuries later, St Alphonsus Liguori (d. 1787) encouraged the faithful to 'pay a visit' and pray before the tabernacle.

In the Middle Ages, the sacrament was reserved in what was known as the 'Easter

Plate 35 Sacrament house, St Pierre, Louvain, Belgium

sepulchre' (q.v.) from Good Friday until the morning of Easter. There were elaborate ceremonies for the 'burial' (*depositio*), when the host was taken there and for the 'resurrection' (*elevatio*), when it was taken out and restored to the normal place of reservation. A watch was kept during the time that our Lord lay in the 'tomb', and there are contemporary accounts extant recording the number of pence given to the watchers for refreshments. The old ceremonies of the 'sepulchre' have been preserved in the rite of Braga, unless the recent liturgical changes have destroyed the distinctive Portuguese usages. The sacrament on Good Friday was taken in a bier to a side chapel, where it remained, without watchers, until the morning of Easter. Then, before the high mass, it was carried in a monstrance in a solemn procession to another chapel, where benediction was given.

Throughout Latin Christendom, the term 'sepulchre' has, since the Baroque period, been applied to the 'altar of repose', where the sacrament has been kept from Maundy Thursday until the Liturgy of Good Friday, surrounded by flowers and lights, with the faithful praying before the reserved sacrament. Since the recent Council, this has been simplified, with watchers only until midnight.

Extra-liturgical devotions to the sacrament belong exclusively to the Western or Latin Church and there is no trace of them in the Eastern Churches, except in those united to Rome.

Regulations for the renewal of the sacred species have varied over the years, but today the normal practice is once a week.

The custom of having a continual light burning before the reserved sacrament grew up in the Middle Ages.

The Eastern Churches, with the exception of Egypt and Ethiopia, reserve the sacrament, but without any exterior honour.

The Orthodox renew the consecrated bread annually on Maundy Thursday, when the bread is intincted from the chalice and dried by fire. It is moistened with a few drops of wine in giving communion to the sick.

The Copts equate the sacrament with the 'manna', which, they say, was supplied daily and not kept until the next day. A canon of the Ethiopian Church forbids the sacrament to be reserved.

In the Anglican Church, there were many instances of the sacrament being taken to the house of a sick person, but perpetual reserva-tion began in a few churches in the nineteenth century. The bishops at first bitterly opposed the practice, especially in a tabernacle in the open church. The custom, however, continued, but more often in an aumbry, where there was less likelihood of extra-liturgical devotions. Parliament rejected the proposed prayer books of 1927 and 1928, largely because of the rubrics permitting reservation.

Reservation is now generally accepted and is found in several of the cathedral churches.

Official recognition of reservation exists in the rubrics of the Scottish prayer book of 1929 and in the South African rite of the same year.

A. A King and C. E. Pocknee, *Eucharistic Reservation in the Western Church*, 1965.

A. A. KING

Responsorial Psalmody and Responsories

These two terms signify two different modes of performance. In responsorial psalmody the chant was sung by a soloist in alternation with the congregation as opposed to the antiphonal psalmody (q.v.) of a later date, and was adopted from the Jewish liturgy. The congregation responded after each verse with a refrain such as 'Alleluia' or 'Amen'. A familiar example is Ps. 136 in which each verse ends with the refrain 'For his mercy endureth for ever'.

Responsories have a structure corresponding to rondo-form. The short ones come in prime (now discarded in the reformed office), the little hours of terce, sext and none, and at compline (*see* **Canonical Hours**). In the longer responsories, which come after each lesson in the nocturns of mattins, the procedure is more elaborate (*see* **Divine Office**).

ALEC ROBERTSON

Rite

A rite is a formal act constituting a religious observance; hence one refers to the sacrificial rites of the OT or to the eucharistic rite.

Rites are a universal phenomenon to be found in all the major religions. In origin they are based upon human actions, e.g. washing underlies baptism, and eating and drinking the Lord's Supper. Hence rites have a natural meaning which has been amplified and enriched by religious associations, without the new and additional meaning being forced arbitrarily upon the original. In other words, rites are not artificial constructions but rest in the natural order and in the sphere of human activities, and unless this connection is preserved they can easily degenerate into magic or intellectualism.

According to Cazeneuve, rites may belong to any one of three types: (1) Those whose object is to establish an intimate contact between man and the holy in order that man may control the divine power. These belong to the sphere of magic. (2) Those whose object is to isolate man from the holy which is regarded as dangerous. These are negative rites, relating to impurity, and are often connected with the idea of taboo. (3) Those whose object is to facilitate man's contact with the holy in such a way that man may be preserved and at the same time enter into a relationship with the source of his being.

The corollary of the last type, which is predominant within Christianity, is that rites are frequently regarded as being the work of the gods themselves, i.e. they are considered to have been instituted by the deity and their real agents are the god or gods working in and through them. So within Christianity, the eucharist is held to rest upon a command of Christ and he is the celebrant.

At the basis of religious rites are four further concepts: (1) That of *symbolism*. All have a symbolic character whereby the natural object or action symbolizes the divine, e.g. the bread of the eucharist symbolizes Christ who is the bread of life. (2) That of *consecration*. Their main function is to enable the human situation, in its entirety or in certain aspects, to share in a principle which goes beyond it and is its basis. (3) That of *repetition*. The divine power is thereby represented as being brought into the present. Rites are therefore representative actions, not in Schleiermacher's sense of the symbolic representation of the content of faith but in the sense of a representation of the original sacred action. So in the eucharist it is believed that the sacrifice of Christ on the cross is made present through its effects. (4) That of *remembrance*. They are the media for preserving and transmitting the founded tradition of the community and at the same time for sharing experience. This shared experience through the rites sustains the common faith and framework of understanding whereby the community is perpetuated and renewed.

L. Bouyer, *Rite and Man*, ET, 1963; J. Cazeneuve, *Les rites et la condition humaine*, 1958.

EDITOR

Ritual

Ritual refers to the prescribed form of words which constitute an act of worship. It is therefore not identical with ceremonial (q.v.) which relates to the actions. Nevertheless in common usage the two are treated as synonymous. Strictly speaking, however, ritual does not include such actions as processions nor the sign of the cross (qq.v.) and instead refers to the collect, the Lord's Prayer, the preface, etc.

EDITOR

Rogation Days

These days of intercession or prayer were much more frequent in earlier days, some occurring annually and others being arranged to suit local needs. But only four such days have been universally kept for many centuries – April 25 and the three days preceding Ascension Day.

April 25 was chosen to replace with a Christian procession the pagan Robigalia processions of that date. As this always occurred in the Easter season, it was not a fast day and the procession was festal, like the Easter week processions.

The other three days have their origin in France. In the fifth century, Mamertus introduced three days of fasting and prayer when disaster threatened Vienne and its neighbourhood. This practice spread to other places, but Rome did not adopt it for some while, since it thought fasting incompatible with Paschal joy. When it did adopt these rogation days, the fasting obligation was removed.

The feature of rogation days is the singing of the litanies (q.v.) of the saints in procession. April 25 is known as the greater litanies and the other three days as the lesser. Conflicting reasons have been given to explain 'greater' and 'lesser'. The litanies used are the same on all four days.

In the recent revision of the Roman liturgy, Ember and rogation days have been removed from the general calendar and their observance is now a matter of local arrangement.

The practice of processing round the parish

before Ascension Day is still retained in some Anglican churches.

J. CONNELLY

Roman Catholic Worship

In the Catholic tradition, both of the East and the West, worship from the earliest days was sacramental, communal and always associated with the proclamation of God's word. It was sacramental in the sense that it was held that the liturgy mediated to the worshipping community the saving power of Christ's redeeming work effected in his passion, death and resurrection. This view implied that the church was 'sacrament' manifesting and making Christ present in the here and now, and in the older Roman tradition (*Gelasian Sacramentary*, 432, ed. Mohlberg) the church is called the 'wonderful sacrament'. Worship was communal in the sense that its celebrants were the gathered people who, together with the clergy, celebrated the great events of salvation. The word was proclaimed by the reading of the scriptures, by preaching, but also by the very liturgical texts which unfolded the meaning of the sacramental celebration.

The liturgy, based on those foundations, remained in its main lines, even though from the fifth century onwards ceremonial became more elaborate. But as the sociological composition of the Christian people changed and with the entry of the northern races into the church, especially from the eighth century onwards, an increasing emphasis was laid on the sacramental *action*. Latin was not understood by the new races, and to compensate for the unintelligibility of the word, there was a further elaboration of ceremonial. At the same time, there is observable a tendency to the clericalization of the liturgy which became the preserve of a professional class. For reasons, it is true, of practical rather than theological significance, the cup was withdrawn from the laity (to avoid profanation) and the bread used became unleavened. The gap between the liturgy and the people was not closed by the proliferation of usages and observances of the later Middle Ages, though they did something to mitigate the rigours of a liturgy that had become remote. By the end of the Middle Ages liturgical 'pluralism' had become chaos and reform was necessary.

The reform initiated by the Council of Trent and carried out by the papacy aimed at uniformity, desired by many humanists and made possible by the printing press. The answer to the irreverence and chaos of the last phase of the Middle Ages was a corpus of rubrics that dictated every movement and word of the celebrant. Little enough attention was given to the people who were assumed to be devout onlookers and offerers in their secret hearts of the eucharistic sacrifice. Yet Catholic worship remained warm and devout, much assisted by the art and music of the Baroque era, and the murmured Latin mass with its periods of silence fitted the need of the devout whose spirituality had now become intensely individualistic. Moreover, what was lacking in liturgical worship was made up for by a great variety of popular devotions, expositions of the blessed sacrament, the rosary, processions, the stations of the cross (qq.v.) and others. By the end of the nineteenth century, when most of the laity attended only a low mass (q.v.), Catholic worship had become inward-looking, almost cosy, a devotional exercise.

The way of reform has been long, slow and painful. But with the coming of the Second Vatican Council (1962-65) a reform was initiated which, it is interesting to observe, takes sacramentality, communal celebration and the proclamation of God's word as the foundations of its theology of the liturgy as laid out principally in the *Constitution on the Liturgy* of 1963. Here we find that the liturgy 'is the action of Christ the priest and of his body, the church' which is made manifest in a worship made up of 'signs that are perceptible to the senses'. This sacramental liturgy mediates to the worshipping community, and beyond it to the world, the saving power of the mystery of Christ which consists of his passion, death, resurrection and ascension. Through the celebration of the liturgy the church looks on to the *eschaton* and up to heaven and sees the earthly liturgy as the counterpart of the heavenly. The whole Christian people, by virtue of their participation in Christ's priesthood, celebrate the liturgy, 'all liturgical services are celebrations of the church', both people and clergy, and from it they derive as from its source the true Christian spirit. For the liturgy is the summit of the church's activity and the source of all its power, and through its celebration the Christian people are able to make their own the saving mystery of Jesus Christ.

But Christ is known by the word and the liturgy itself, which must be within the people's grasp, must be self-explanatory. Hence liturgical reform must make it possible for the people to share fully in liturgical services; they must always hear God's word for which better provision must be made. If this was to be achieved, it was necessary that the language of the liturgy should be changed from Latin to modern vernaculars (q.v.).

These principles have been applied to the whole range of Catholic worship, including not only the eucharist but all the other sacraments, the divine office and the organization of the liturgical year. The reformed liturgy has also affected the style of celebration – the eucharist is normally celebrated facing the people – and necessitated the reordering of old churches and the designing of new ones. In particular, the emphasis on the importance of the word is striking, so much so that one can say 'No celebration without proclamation'.

In addition, new liturgical forms are emerging and the uniformity that was characteristic of post-Tridentine worship is no longer insisted on (*Constitution*, 39, 40). Adaptation is built into the new services.

Popular devotions continue alongside the official liturgy and it is recommended that they should do so but, as the *Constitution* observes (13), they are to be harmonized with the liturgy. Already new forms have emerged (*see* **Bible Services**) and if Catholic worship retains much of the warmth of the past, it has already become markedly biblical. It has been observed that the *Constitution on the Liturgy* does not emphasize mission very strongly, but it must be taken with the other documents of Vatican II, notably with the *Constitution on the Church in the Modern World*, which decisively turned Catholic Christians away from an exclusive concern with their own affairs to their mission in the world.

J. D. CRICHTON

Rosary

The rosary is a method of prayer. It combines repetition of familiar prayers with meditation on the mysteries of the faith. The prayers used are fifteen decades (i.e. groups of ten) of the 'Hail Mary', with each decade preceded by the 'Our Father' and followed by 'Glory be to the Father'. The mysteries are fifteen events in the life of Jesus or of his mother.

Normally, one third of the complete rosary is said at a time. It is divided into three groups of five: the joyful mysteries are the annuncia-

tion, visitation, nativity, presentation in the Temple and finding in the Temple; the sorrowful mysteries are the agony in the garden, scourging, crown of thorns, carrying of the cross, and crucifixion; the glorious mysteries are the resurrection, ascension, descent of the Holy Spirit, assumption of the Virgin and coronation of the Virgin. They are rightly termed 'mysteries', as they contain depths of spiritual meaning beyond anything the eye can see or the imagination describe. They have a relevance to daily Christian living and are not concerned only with a distant past or indefinite future. The introduction of these meditations, as the very essence of the rosary devotion, have been ascribed to a Carthusian two hundred years after the time of St Dominic.

The saying of repetitive prayers on a rosary is common to Buddhism and Islam, and a sculpture of ancient Nineveh depicts two females with rosaries in their hands.

Until the middle of the twelfth century, when the first part of the 'Hail Mary' came into Christian devotion, the 'rosary' consisted of the 'Our Father'. The lay brothers of Cluny in the tenth century counted them on knots made on a string. Such prayers became common in every part of Europe, aided by pebbles, berries or threaded discs of bone. They finally gave their name to beads (*see* **Bidding Prayer**). The devotion was called 'Pater Nosters' and in London the members of the craft who made these devices congregated in Paternoster Row.

Nowhere do we find the rosary associated with St Dominic (d. 1221) until the latter part of the fifteenth century, when a Dominican, Alan de Rupe (*c.* 1470-5) not only promulgated the devotion, which became very popular, but stated that the Saint had either instituted or revived it. Since that time, the rosary has been a universal devotion in Latin Christendom.

A. A. KING

Rostrum

Rostrum means literally the beak of a bird, and by transference it came to mean the beak-like prow of a ship. Then it was applied to the speaker's platform or tribune in the Roman forum because it was ornamented with the prows of ships taken from the people of Antium (the modern Anzio), in 338 BC. Hence the word has come to mean any platform from which public addresses or lectures are given.

C. E. POCKNEE

Rubrics

Rubrics are ceremonial (q.v) directions for the conduct of a service, and are so-called because in medieval books they were written in red (Lat. *ruber*) to distinguish them from the text of the services.

In the earliest liturgical books, few or no directions were given, simply the words to be used being provided. In time a special book, known as the *Ordinale*, was produced, being a directory for the arrangement of the altar service. Known also as the *Directorium* or *Pie*, this ·corresponded to the later rubrics which were included with the texts themselves.

Although at the present day rubrics are frequently not printed in red, the term is still used of the ceremonial directions.

On the so-called 'Black Rubric' *see* **Postures**, 2(*c*).

EDITOR

Sacred Heart

The devotion expresses our Saviour's love for us and our loving gratitude to him. It is based upon the symbolism of the heart as the emblem of love and self-sacrifice: 'The heart that has so loved men.' Devotion to the Sacred Heart is to the person of Jesus. The singling out of the heart as a symbol has grown out of private devotion, with a return of love and a desire to make reparation for the sins of men. Sinners are encouraged to find a sure refuge and a promise of pardon in the heart of Jesus. The devotion has sometimes been over-sentimentalized, but it has not ceased to be true and firmly rooted in Christian tradition. The development of the thought underlying the Easter-motif in the mystery of redemption led to a more subjective and psychological way of regarding the redeeming love of Christ, especially as revealed in the passion.

The first unmistakable devotion to the Sacred Heart developed in the German convent of Helfta, with St Mechtilde (d. 1298) and St Gertrude (d. 1304), as a private devotion of the mystical order. It became an objective devotion to the Five Wounds under the influence of the Franciscans, but it remained individual.

A church was dedicated to the Sacred Heart at Cuarapary in Brazil in 1585, but it was not until the seventeenth century that a public devotion was established. Its first expression, outside religious communities, was during the plague in Marseilles in 1720.

Several countries received permission to observe a feast of the Sacred Heart, and it was admitted into the Universal Calendar of the Roman rite in 1856, the second Friday after Corpus Christi.

A. A. KING

Sacristy

The room or repository in a church in which are kept the vestments, vessels, etc. Sacristies were introduced first in Syria, *c.* 400, as side chambers to the apse (q.v.). In the Middle Ages they were often placed on either side of, or behind, the high altar and were sometimes used for reservation (q.v.). In current usage, the term is virtually synonymous with vestry (q.v.).

EDITOR

Saints' Days

'By celebrating the passage of the saints from earth to heaven the Church proclaims the Paschal mystery achieved in those who have suffered and been glorified with Christ; she proposes them to the faithful as examples drawing all to the Father through Christ, and through their merits she pleads for God's favours' (*Liturgical Constitution of Vatican II*, para. 104). In this paragraph the Council sums up the church's reasons for honouring the saints.

The early Christians, like their pagan neighbours, kept the anniversaries of their dead, especially of the martyrs; for the martyrs had conquered in and for Christ and were now with Christ. At these anniversary services the eucharist was celebrated as the completion of the vigil service.

Lists of the earliest martyrs are practically non-existent, but later generations were exhorted to keep records of the date of the death of the martyrs, the *dies natalis*, and the place of their burial, *depositio*, for the anniversary celebrations depended on these facts. Such celebrations were naturally local at first, for they were held at the martyr's tomb, but some eventually became feast days for the whole church.

Some Christians acknowledged, *confessed*, Christ before men (*cf.* Matt. 10.32) not by death, but by imprisonment or exile. These were called confessors, *confessores* – a title which was eventually extended to men whose way of life was a confession of Christ and a proclamation of the Paschal mystery. The early confessors came to be honoured alongside the martyrs. Pope Sylvester, Anthony the Hermit and Martin of Tours seem to have been the first to be so honoured in the West.

Beside the feasts of martyrs and confessors, the Christian calendar contains feasts of those intimately connected with the work of salvation – John the Baptist, Mary, Joseph and the apostles.

J. CONNELLY

Saints' and Holy Days *see* All Saints, All Souls, Ember Days, Fast Days, Ferial, Rogation Days, Saints' Days

Salvation Army

In common with other churches the public worship of the Salvation Army always includes praise, prayer, a reading of scripture, together with an exposition of a selected Bible verse or portion. But, in addition, a recognized place is given to Christian testimony and there, at the conclusion of a meeting, there is usually an invitation to Christian decision or dedication at what is known as the Mercy Seat or penitent-form.

Two further features should not be overlooked. One is that women take equal place with men in public worship, whether as leaders or as participants. The other is that the Salvation Army has no fixed liturgy, if by that is meant an order of service from which no deviation may be made. On the contrary, worship may commence with praise, or with prayer, or with a reading of scripture, nor is there any pre-determined place for the biblical exhortation. The leader of the meeting is at liberty to alter the order of that meeting in any way which may be for the greater spiritual good of the congregation.

This freedom, however, is not the fortuitous by-product of any casual approach to public worship, but the expression of a considered endeavour to act upon the principle that 'God is Spirit, and those who worship him must worship him in spirit and in truth' (John 4.24, NEB). The fact that there is no set liturgy upon which to lean requires everyone in the congregation to make a personal effort to contribute to the worship of the whole. Yet this, far from giving rise to spiritual tenseness and overstrain, results in frequently that joy which is one of the first fruits of the Spirit and that liberty wherewith the children of God are set free.

Were this not made clear, it might be supposed that the absence of a set structure of worship might lead to a formless informality which, at its worst, could degenerate into a chaos which would defeat the very purpose of worship. But this is averted because, in the first place, Salvationists recognize – in the memorable phrase of van Unnik, quoted by C. F. D. Moule – that worship must always be 'within the magnetic field of the Holy Spirit'. As the Spirit's office is to glorify Christ, the worship which he guides will exalt that Christ as Saviour and Lord of men. Thus no contribution, whether of testimony or of prayer, becomes a private exercise in egoism, and the desire of the preacher is ever to speak 'in demonstration of the Spirit'.

In the second place, the congregation is not passive but active, and this seems to be in harmony with NT practice (I Cor. 14.26). In Salvationist parlance, one will have a prayer to offer, another a word of witness to give, another a 'Hallelujah' or an 'Amen' to utter – yet all will contribute to the edifying of the church. For the reality of Christian worship depends not on the use, or the refusal to use, a formal liturgy, but on the presence of the Holy Spirit.

Music and song play an integral part in the worship of the Salvationist. Here again his approach is truly catholic, for his song-book draws upon verses which have come down from the medieval church as well as the classic hymns of the Reformation, is undergirded by the two Wesleys, Watts and Doddridge, and does not pass by the Tractarians Faber and Newman. In addition, there is a substantial amount of original Salvationist material, some of which could well find a place in other hymn-books.

In like manner, the Salvation Army band can draw upon a Bach chorale, or a composition by one of the many gifted Salvationist musicians, to deepen the spirit of worship in a meeting. For such a contribution is not regarded as a programme item which might be applauded if decorum or convention allowed. But, as Walford Davies and Harvey Grace used to insist, there are moments when musical utterance becomes the highest expression of public worship.

Finally, it must be added that while worship, directed to the glory of God, is a worthy end in itself, that end is nullified if public worship does not strengthen the worshipper's public witness. Divine service does not end when the benediction is pronounced; it has only begun. The uniform worn by the Salvationist at his meetings – both in and out of doors – is his way of identifying himself as a soldier of Jesus Christ. He seeks the holy place on Sundays so that, by the renewal of grace, he may be a more effective Christian soldier on weekdays.

In the thought and practice of the Salvationist, worship and witness can never be divided – save to the impoverishment of both. As has been well said: 'What we become in the presence of God, that we can be all day long.'

The Handbook of Doctrine, 1969; *The Year Book of the Salvation Army.*

F. COUTTS

Sanctuary

In relation to religious architecture, the term sanctuary may be applied in three different ways: (1) Originally it designated that part of a church which was reserved for the clergy, which was often fenced off by chancels (q.v.) or balustrades. (2) It may also be used of the limited area immediately around an altar, often demarcated by an altar-rail (q.v.). These two different uses can lead to confusion, because while according to the first the term describes the whole of an area, according to the second it refers to a subdivision of the whole. (3) Occasionally it is employed of the church building as a whole.

EDITOR

Sanctus

An anthem which in most eucharistic liturgies forms part of the thanksgiving with which the eucharistic prayer or anaphora (q.v.) commences.

W. JARDINE GRISBROOKE

Screen

This article deals only with screens in Western Christendom. For the screen in the Eastern Orthodox Church, *see* **Iconostasis**.

1. There were screens in the Roman and other basilicas, which separated the altar from the nave (qq.v.). These screens were constructed of stone and had carved or decorated panels rising from the floor about four feet in height. Above this were columns of marble or porphyry which supported an architrave or beam from which votive lamps were sometimes suspended. Thus the altar was visible through the columns of the screen. On the nave-side immediately outside the screen were the singers or the *schola cantorum*. Many of these screens were pulled down in the baroque era.

2. The chancel screen in the English parish church developed in the Middle Ages from the narrow opening in the wall that separated the nave and the altar. By the fifteenth century, the English parish church had developed in style, and in the large parish churches there was frequently a wooden screen both carved and decorated with colour of great beauty. This screen extended not only across the main chancel but also across the aisles, thus forming chapels for lesser altars, e.g. the one in Southwold, Suffolk. Where this was the case there were lesser *Parclose* screens, separating the side chapels from the high altar as we can see at Southwold.

Above the chancel screen there was a loft with parapets and above this a beam, the rood beam, upon which were tenoned the crucifix with the figures of the Blessed Virgin Mary and St John. Hence the old term for this screen was rood screen. Unlike the Roman basilica, such churches usually accommodated the choir inside the screen in proximity to the altar.

3. In cathedral and the larger conventual churches there was a solid stone screen known as the *pulpitum* with an opening in the centre, which filled one bay of the arcade west of the choir. On the nave-side there were usually lesser altars on either side of the opening. The loft on the top of the pulpitum usually supported the pipe organ, as we can still see at the cathedral church at Norwich, while on occasions singers used the loft. Also on festivals the gospel was sung from this loft.

4. In the larger churches where there was the body of a notable saint, e.g. St Albans Cathedral, England, from the end of the fourteenth century, the increasing number of pilgrims coming to pray at the shrine of the saint necessitated separating the shrine by a solid screen from the high altar as we can still see at Westminster Abbey and Winchester Cathedral. On the west side the screen rose above the high altar and this side was usually decorated with tabernacle-work with the

statues of the saints. A canopy was projected out from the screen over the altar and a hanging pyx was suspended from this containing the reserved sacrament. *See also* **Reredos**.

F. E. Howard and F. H. Crossley, *English Church Woodwork*, [2]1927; A. A. King and C. E. Pocknee, *Eucharistic Reservation in the Western Church*, 1965; C. E. Pocknee, *The Christian Altar*, 1963; A. Vallance, *English Church Screens*, 1936.

C. E. POCKNEE

Secret *see Super Oblata,* Silent Prayer

Secularization and Worship

Secularization is an imprecise term, since it can be used with a variety of meanings. It may refer, for example, to a process of social differentiation, involving the division of labour and the separation of home and work as well as a continuing specialization of social groups and institutions. Again, it can be applied to a shift of responsibility from ecclesiastical authority to worldly authority; so the secularization of the monasteries at the Reformation involved the transfer of property from church ownership to private tenure. For the purposes of this entry, however, the term is employed to refer to the process of change from a sacral to a secular universe.

A sacral universe is one in which the functioning of nature and society is explained in terms of the divine. In the sacral universe, man is at the mercy of nature; not only is he dependent upon it, but he finds himself largely unable to control it. Nature appears to be superior and sovereign, while man is weak and helpless. Nature is the central factor in his life, but in a pre-technical age, he is powerless to impose his will upon it. Unable to master nature, man then has to seek divine assistance, in order even to live. Nature appears to have almost divine features; it is an epiphany of God himself and the workings of nature are understood as the workings of God.

Within this sacral universe religion has a dual function. It acts as a preserver of society and it provides rituals to protect man against a world which he dominates neither intellectually nor materially. Worship is then a *cultus publicus*, securing the public

well-being and fulfilling the supreme end of the state. It safeguards man from the uncontrollable forces of nature and channels the divine assistance in his direction.

With secularization man enters a secular universe. This is one in which the functioning of nature and society is explained in terms of themselves. No longer is recourse had to the divine in order to understand either the material world or man. The natural sciences seek out the 'laws' of nature, their interrelationships and their workings; sociology analyses society, while man himself is investigated in terms of biology, psychology, etc. In the secular universe man is no longer at the mercy of nature, rather he is its master. Through the development of technology, man can control his environment; to a large extent he is therefore liberated from nature, in the sense that he has ceased to be dependent upon its changes and chances. This newly-won domination, precarious though it may be in the face of pollution and the need for conservation, results in a reversal of roles. Whereas previously man was in submission to natural forces, now he can bend them to his will. This change in the relationship of man and nature leads to a new concept of man in the universe. Man and his power become fundamental values which direct his efforts towards research into development and progress. So man fast becomes the lord of nature, dominating it by scientific and technological means. So far from being static and rigid, society now enters into a process of change – change that is constant and never ending. Society becomes also pluriform with different cultures and subcultures existing side by side. The mobility which technology brings breaks open the uniformity of society.

The result is that within the secular universe, religion loses the functions it exercised previously in the sacral universe. When change is the keynote, religion can no longer perform the role of preserver of society; if it tries to do so, it will be regarded as a bulwark against progress and a supporter of social stagnation. Moreover, when society is pluriform, there can be no *cultus publicus*. All religions tend to become *cultus privati*, with the abandonment of the public sector of life and with concentration upon forms of individual piety. When man dominates the universe, he no longer needs rituals to protect himself. If in former days it seemed reasonable to sprinkle water on an ox that was ill, today few would think of doing this to a tractor that has broken down.

Consequently the association of the words secularization and worship points, in the first instance, to a crisis of worship, because the passage from the sacral to the secular universe (secularization) renders those liturgical forms created within and for the sacral universe void of meaning and relevance within the new context of existence in the modern world. This crisis is intensified by another factor comprehended under secularization as social differentiation. Today, with the progress of urbanization, social life is very different from what it was in medieval Christendom. This latter was integrated with a civilization based largely upon agriculture and village units. The village was a social unity; it was a territorial area of restricted dimensions within which everyone knew everyone else. Its population found its residence, its work and its play all within its boundaries. There was an unavoidable interchange which promoted interest in other people, over and above any utilitarian project in which they may have been engaged. Worship, in this situation, was the occasion when those who knew one another gathered together and strengthened the ties that bound their already existing community, i.e. it was an assembly of a pre-existing community. The Sunday service was an important occasion for going out of the house and encountering one's fellow villagers; hence the importance, too, of conversation and inter-personal contacts, before, during and after the service. This pattern of life and worship favoured stability, respect for tradition and for nature and it allowed for the development of primary relations.

In the modern urban situation, however, specialization and diversification lead to the dispersal of man's social functions over a very wide area indeed. The husband goes to work in one quarter, the wife may shop in another, the children may go to school in a third, while the family as a whole will seek entertainment elsewhere. The consequence is that in a residential area personal relations may be non-existent and without this direct contact and sharing of interests, ideas and news, there exists no local community within which anyone can be integrated. The result of this transformation is that relations between fellow citizens become less and less primary, i.e. face-to-face, and more and more func-

tional. What is the effect of the demise of the village and the neighbourhood-based community upon worship? Clearly worship in this new context can no longer be understood in terms of the gathering of a pre-existing village type community. So worship loses its communal dimension and its necessary basis in inter-personal relations.

It now has to be affirmed that the association of the words secularization and worship points, in the second instance, to the need for a reformulation of the meaning and function of the latter in the light of the former. The inherited forms of worship are rooted in the view that it is an activity whereby we retire for a time from the secular world and, leaving all that is common behind, penetrate into another, sacred, world, where we enter the presence of the all-holy God and sing his praises in company with the heavenly choir of angels, archangels and saints. So worship is a special, religious activity, performed in special holy buildings; it may strengthen us to fulfil the divine purpose within our daily lives but it is, in itself, something separate from our daily lives in the world. In contrast to this, if worship today is to have any meaning in the face of secularization, it has to be redefined as an activity which springs out of life in the world; it is a celebration of that life. Instead of involving a divorce from the secular, it takes the secular or common as its basis, and so the cultic action is a means whereby we express the unity of the sacred and the secular. It does not need for its performance holy shrines, and while it is essentially a coming to awareness of and a response to God, this is achieved through that which is human and secular.

'Secular' worship, then, has a festive character in that it is a highlight in everyday existence and is based upon world involvement and not upon world rejection. It is an encounter with the divine and expresses and makes explicit the unity of the sacred and the secular by showing how the holy is a dimension of the whole of life. It is a sensitizing process, shaping our perception of the divine so as to open the secular to the holy and assist us to find the holy in everyday life. In a world in rapid change, it must also be a vehicle of social criticism and so a celebration of hope, bringing the hoped-for future into contact with the present and providing a stimulus for re-shaping the world. It points to the service of others; it expresses the love of neighbour and it comprises commitment and acceptance of responsibility for one another.

Since worship must have a communal basis, it has to be celebrated primarily in small groups, involving face-to-face encounters, social interaction, participation, mutuality, reciprocity and corporateness. It then fosters inter-personal relations and functions in terms of personalization and community identity. It is a shared activity, which is both intelligible to all and is related to past and future.

The norm of the worshipping community then becomes the primary group and the large liturgical assembly has to be redefined as a gathering of groups. The small group is a key factor in promoting participation in the large one; an occasional coming together allows for integration in the greater whole.

The meaning and function of worship as thus redefined in the light of secularization corresponds closely with that to be found in the NT, which, after all, belongs to the period before the emergence of Christendom. The disintegration of the latter, although producing a crisis, allows for a more radical interpretation of worship, in the sense that it compels theologians to reassess their roots. Clearly this understanding has to be embodied in new forms, but that is a subject to be considered elsewhere (*see* **Experimental Forms of Worship**).

J. G. Davies, *Every Day God*, 1973; W. Vos, ed., *Worship and Secularization* (Studia Liturgica 7, 2/3), 1970; J. F. White, *The Worldliness of Worship*, 1967; *Worship in the City of Man* (Liturgical Conference, Washington D.C.), 1966.

EDITOR

Sentences

Short passages of scripture read out during services. They have two separate purposes. First, they may serve as an introduction to or commentary upon the next stage in the act of worship. So the sentences in the 1552 *BCP* for use at the beginning of morning and evening prayer preface the confession and absolution with scriptural thoughts of penitence and of the assurance of forgiveness. Similarly the sentences used in association with the funeral procession declare the nature of death and the hope of resurrection. The sentences that accompany the offertory (q.v.) frequently stress the necessity of almsgiving.

The second purpose for which sentences may be used is to relate a particular act of worship with seasons, festivals, saints' days and other special occasions.

EDITOR

Septuagesima *see* Quinquagesima

Sepulchre *see* Easter Garden

Sequence
see Chants of the Proper of the Mass

Sermon

The preaching of a sermon in the liturgy is rooted in the synagogue practice (*cf.* Luke 4.16 ff.; Acts 13.14 ff.) of following the readings of scripture by exposition. Paul is related to have discoursed at Troas before breaking the bread (Acts 20.7 ff.) and, although not specified, the prior reading of scripture is probably to be presumed. Preaching by prophets or by tongue-speakers was a feature of the assemblies at Corinth (I Cor. 14). The fourth gospel says that the Paraclete 'will take of mine and declare it to you' (John 16.14f.), suggesting that in the Christian assemblies the Jesus tradition, as well as the OT scriptures, became preaching material. The evident intention of Paul that his letters should be read in the assembly (I Cor. 16.22-24; *cf.* Col. 4.16) led to the reading and exposition of 'apostolic' writings also.

In the pre-Nicene church the bishop succeeded the prophet as the preacher of the sermon after the reading of the lections, as he also recited the great eucharist prayer (*cf.* *Mart. Pol.* 16 where the bishop is called a 'prophetic teacher'). (For a second-century bishop's understanding of his preaching *see* Irenaeus, *Adv. Haer.* I, x, 2.) An example of such liturgical preaching has survived in Melito of Sardis' homily *On the Passion*.

After Nicea the sermon continued to be a normal part of the liturgy. Thus, for Egypt, Serapion (*c.* 340) instructs the bishop to pray for the Holy Spirit to assist him in proclaiming the message of the scriptures to the congregation.

During the dark ages a number of factors (mass conversions, the multiplication of presbyteral masses, the decay in educational standards, the Western development of low mass) contributed to the decay of preaching, so that the sermon ceased to be a normal part of the liturgy.

Medieval revivals of preaching (e.g., the friars) occurred largely outside the context of the liturgy, and it was devotional and moralistic rather than expository. The conservative Reformers sought to re-establish a liturgical sermon (*cf.* Luther's 'postils' and the rubric of the *BCP* requiring a sermon), but although there was much expository preaching in the Reformation churches, its integral relation to the liturgy was obscured in Protestant orthodoxy, pietism and rationalism. In reaction, the nineteenth-century liturgical revival in Anglicanism was often accompanied by a depreciation of preaching. Only with the twentieth-century Liturgical Movement (q.v.) has the sermon come to be understood once more as an integral part of the liturgy in which the word of God read in the lections is proclaimed for the present and becomes the material of the thanksgiving (*cf.* Vatican II, *Constitution on the Sacred Liturgy*, IV.35).

Y. Brilioth, *Landmarks in the History of Preaching*, 1950; G. Dix, *The Shape of the Liturgy*, [2]1945; B. S. Easton and H. C. Robbins, *The Eternal Word in the Modern World*, 1937; D. Ritschl, *A Theology of Proclamation*, 1960.

R. H. FULLER

Server

Though not ordained, the server performs many of the functions which originally belonged to the office of acolyte (q.v.). He prepares the altar and sanctuary before the eucharist, makes or leads the responses, brings the bread and wine to the celebrant at the offertory, etc. In the Roman Catholic Church only male persons are permitted to act as servers, and most Anglicans follow the same custom. In the Church of England the term is loosely used to describe any lay person who assists the officiant at any service and in practice the modern server has inherited many of the functions of the parish clerk.

P. HINCHLIFF

Seventh-day Adventist Worship

According to Seventh-day Adventist belief and practice, public worship is the corporate assembly of the community of faith for the adoration and praise of God, for thanksgiving, sacrifice and communion. 'The duty

to worship God is based upon the fact that He is the Creator' (E. G. White, *The Great Controversy between Christ and Satan*, [1900], p. 436). Worship is the wholeheated response of the creature to his Creator and Redeemer, otherwise the coming together of worshippers is of no avail (*see* Matt. 15.8, 9). Worship involves an attitude of mind and heart which enables man to love God with all his being. Adventists recall that Christ said this was the fulfilment of the first great commandment. True worship is the fruit of the working of the Holy Spirit and is tied to conduct based on willing obedience to all God's requirements, for 'without obedience to his commandments, no worship can be pleasing to God' (White, *loc cit; see* Matt. 15.3-9; I John 5.3 and Prov. 28.9). The experience of worship must merge into a worshipping life.

In contrast to most other Christians, Seventh-day Adventists assemble for the weekly divine worship service on Sabbath, the seventh day of the week. They believe that the biblical Sabbath is a weekly memorial of God's creative act as recorded in the OT and of Christ's redemptive or re-creative act in the NT. The importance of the Sabbath as a day of rest and worship is that it keeps ever present the true reason why worship is due to God – because he is the Creator and Redeemer. The Sabbath, therefore, in Adventist theology, lies at the very foundation of Christian worship and continues to have heterocentric significance for modern man. The historical process which brought about a change in the *day* of worship also modified the *way* of worship (*see* N. F. Pease, *And Worship Him*, pp. 25-35). While Adventists have no quarrel with the dictum *lex adorandi est lex credendi*, they further believe that the worship of the church never rises higher than its theology, for worship is also a reflection of theology.

Because Adventist worship is 'free', charismatic, rather than liturgical, the emphasis is on extempore prayer, circumstantial, spontaneous inspiration, rather than on a formal liturgy and set prayers. However, the *Seventh-day Adventist Church Manual* does provide three suggested orders of worship and guidelines. On certain occasions, such as marriage, burial and ordination services and the Lord's Supper, the service is more formal.

Ceremonial is usually quite limited. Vestments are not used, except on occasion academic gowns and choir and baptismal robes. In some churches there is a choir procession. When the platform party (consisting customarily of the minister and one or more lay elders) steps up to the pulpit they kneel in silent prayer, while the congregation stands or remains seated (in some churches the congregation kneels). Adventists believe that usually the most appropriate and reverential attitude in prayer is shown in the bending of the knee. In public worship both ministers and congregation kneel for prayer facing the pulpit, whence go forth messages from God's holy word.

After an organ prelude, the service may begin with a scriptural or musical call to worship or a hymn. Invocation, hymns, one scripture lesson (either from the OT or the NT), pastoral prayer, offering, special music and sermon follow in one order or another. After the benediction is pronounced there may be an organ postlude. While the pastoral prayer represents perhaps the 'holiest exercise of the whole service' (*Seventh-day Adventist Church Manual*, p.113), the reading and expounding of the scriptures constitute the central act of Adventist divine worship. For this reason the pulpit is normally in the centre of the rostrum, with the communion table in front.

The Seventh-day Adventist Church generally pays less attention than do more liturgical churches in worship services to the 'church year'. However, for over half a century it has had its own yearly calendar, with considerable emphasis on evangelistic outreach. Approximately forty special days, weeks and offerings are included.

The ethos of Seventh-day Adventist worship is best conveyed in the idea of a closely knit *koinonia of believers*, meeting for adoration, consecration and communion and desiring in unity to pattern their lives in closer harmony with the will of God and increase the church's evangelistic witness in preparation for the Second Advent of Christ. The intention of the service is to make the power of saving grace a joint reality in the life of the congregation.

W. R. Beach, *Dimensions in Salvation*, 1963, pp.183-192; Harold B. Hannum, *Music and Worship*, 1969; 'Highways of Worship', *Sabbath School Lesson Quarterly*, Adult Division, No.307, First quarter, 1972; *Manual for Ministers*, 1965; N. F. Pease, *And Worship Him*, 1967; *Seventh-day Adventist Church Manual*, 1967; E. G. White, *The Desire of Ages*, 1946, pp.157-189; E. G. White, *Testimonies for the Church*, V, 1948, pp.491-500.

B. B. BEACH

Sexagesima see Quinquagesima

Sext see Canonical Hours

Shinto Worship

Shinto, the traditional national religion of Japan, is of particular importance in the comparative study of worship in that of all the world's 'greater' religions it is the one nearest to a 'natural' religion; in the sense in which a Westerner understands the terms, it has no founder, no canonical scriptures, no creeds, and no developed dogmatic theology. The word *shinto* itself means 'the way of the gods', but the word *kami*, translated as 'god' or 'gods', has a much wider connotation than the translation normally bears in Western languages; in the words of a distinguished Shinto scholar, 'the term is an honorific for noble, sacred spirits which implies a sense of adoration for their virtues and authority. All beings have such spirits, so in a sense all beings can be called *kami*.' Shinto worship, then, is the worship of divinity perceived in and through the whole of creation; in Western terms it is both pantheistic and polytheistic. The whole of life, properly lived, is regarded as an act of worship; its worshipful character is ensured by specific ceremonial acts of worship at particular times and in particular places, notably by the daily devotions which a devout Shintoist performs before the domestic shrine (*kami-dana*, literally 'god-shelf') in his home, and his participation in the services celebrated on the many festivals in public temples or shrines, as well as by more informal devotional visits to the latter on other occasions.

There are about 100,000 Shinto shrines in Japan. While there is no linguistic ground for the common practice of translating *jinja* as 'shrine' rather than as 'temple', it does perhaps make clearer the essential nature of these sanctuaries, which are regarded primarily as divine dwelling-places, and only consequently as places of meeting for worship. The original shrines appear to have been 'natural' holy places – sacred mountains, sacred forests and so forth – without added buildings; the persistence of the *himorogi*, or small enclosure containing a sacred tree, appears to witness to the next stage in the development of the shrine. The great majority of shrines today, however, take the form of an enclosure containing a complex, simple or elaborate, of buildings; where possible, surroundings of natural beauty and impressiveness are chosen, and even in the great modern conurbations the attempt is made to provide a shrine with an attractive garden enclosure.

The centre of the shrine is the symbol of the *kami* to whom it is dedicated (which may take any of a number of forms, but is usually not a representative image), in which the spirit or power of the *kami* is believed to dwell in a particular manner for the benefit of the worshippers, and which is enshrined in the *honden* or sanctuary. The other principal buildings common to most shrines are the *heiden* or hall of offerings, and the *haiden* or hall of prayer. Other buildings of various kinds are also found in the enclosure; a structure which is universal is the *torii* or sacred gateway which marks each of the public entrances to the enclosure.

Shinto worship comprises a great and rich variety of observances, ranging from the extremely simple to the extremely elaborate. The regular forms of worship, however, whether simple or elaborate, always include four essential elements – purification, offering, prayer, and a sacred meal. They are seen at their simplest in the daily private devotions at home: the worshipper washes his hands and rinses his mouth, places a fresh food offering before the symbol of the *kami*, stands or sits before the shrine, and prays briefly as he will, bowing before and after; the food offering is removed and served at a later meal. When he wishes to pay his devotions at a shrine, the worshipper washes with particular care, puts on clean linen, on arrival at the shrine removes his outdoor clothes, and purifies his mouth and hands with holy water, proceeds to the hall of prayer, places an offering (today usually money) in the box provided, and prays, as at home, as he will; he may also request the celebration of a votive office by one of the priests, for which he makes a small offering. Offices of this kind are frequently requested, on all kinds of occasions, both by individuals and by groups. The regular shrine services, which commonly centre round morning and evening offerings of food, follow approximately the same

pattern as the domestic devotions of the faithful, although each of their constituent parts is, of course, more formal and more elaborate. Most elaborate of all are the observances of festivals, of which there are a great number, and which, as many of them are of a local character, vary greatly from place to place in accordance with the traditions of different shrines. Those taking part, especially the officiating priests, prepare themselves by rituals of purification, and by a period of abstinence and recollection which can vary from half an hour to a week or more; the offerings of food are numerous and complicated, and presented with solemn ceremony accompanied by the playing of sacred music; and often sacred dances are performed. Processions, either within the shrine enclosure or through the streets, are a prominent feature of many festivals, as are also traditional entertainments of various kinds, which are regarded both as an offering to the *kami* and as a carnival for the worshippers.

Lack of space precludes even the mention of many important and interesting features of Shinto worship, but two basic characteristics of the whole of its rich variety of liturgical observance stand out. The first is the essential simplicity and 'naturalness' of Shinto rites, even of the most elaborate; the second is their high aesthetic quality – beauty, as both a manifestation of divinity and a tribute to it, is sought for, and commonly achieved, in order to express both the transcendence and immanence of the divine, and the power of the divine to transfigure the whole of life.

J. Herbert, *Shinto*, 1967.

W. JARDINE GRISBROOKE

Sick, Visitation of the

The Sarum 'order for visiting a sick man' begins with nine prayers for the sick man's recovery, for which scriptural precedents are freely invoked; it is nowhere suggested that his illness is due to sin. At first there is no hint that recovery is unlikely, but before long he is told that he is 'about to go the way of all flesh' (hence the name *viaticum*). So when he has professed his faith, he is exhorted to have hope and charity, and to make a full confession, since soon he will not be able to do so. No penance is given: instead, he is to give alms. Two absolutions and two more collects for renewal and restoration to the church end the service, which may be followed immediately by extreme unction (q.v.). After this, the priest administers communion; if the sick man is too ill to receive in a seemly way, the priest assures him, 'only believe, and you have eaten'.

Popular opinion in the Middle Ages regarded unction as a sign of terminal illness rather than as a means to health, and attached gross superstitions to it. But the service was certainly intended for chronic illness also, and one bishop suggested that weekly communion and yearly unction was sufficient.

As usual, Cranmer greatly abbreviated the medieval rite, keeping, for instance, only two of the nine collects. These are followed by an exhortation to acceptance of suffering, based on Heb. 12.6-10, which is also the proper gospel. This introduces a new view of illness, that it is God's will for purposes of discipline. The sick man's faith is tested by putting the creed to him in interrogatory form, as in baptism; after which the minister is to exhort him to forgive others, make reparation, make his will, and discharge all his debts. All this is included in being 'in charity with all the world', but no mention of hope is kept. The sick man is then to 'make a special confession, if he feel his conscience troubled with any weighty matter': as in the communion service, it is not regarded as normal and mandatory. The absolution still speaks of Christ's 'authority committed to me'. Unction (of forehead or breast only) is accompanied by a collect assembled from four separate Sarum prayers, on the themes of recovery, forgiveness, and grace to withstand temptations.

Two methods are suggested for the communion of the sick: the priest should either reserve sufficient 'at the open communion', or say the whole service in the house in the short form appointed for weekdays. In the latter case there is a proper psalm, collect, epistle, and gospel. Rubrics lay down that there must always be 'some of his own house, or else of his neighbours' to communicate with the sick man. If he is unable to receive, he must be instructed that 'if he do truly repent . . . and stedfastly believe that Jesus Christ hath suffered . . . for him . . . he doth eat and drink spiritually . . .'.

Bucer regarded the service as 'agreeing sufficiently with holy scripture', and commended the practice of communicating the sick directly from the Lord's table, rather than from the reserved sacrament. Peter Martyr, on the other hand, would only approve the use of the complete service in the house. His view prevailed, and the first method is omitted in the 1552 *BCP*. Unction, being too closely bound up with superstitious ideas, also disappears completely. Curiously enough, the absolution remains untouched.

The service seems never to have become generally acceptable, and Canon 67 of 1604 says that the minister shall instruct and comfort the sick 'in their distress according to the Order of the Communion Book, if he be no preacher; or if he be a preacher, then as he shall think most needful and convenient'. Individual services have survived by Lancelot Andrewes, John Cosin, Jeremy Taylor, and Denis Granville, which shows that the liberty offered by the canon was readily accepted, and there is abundant evidence of confession *in articulo mortis* throughout the seventeenth century.

In 1662, in response to Puritan criticisms, the minister is directed to *move* the sick man to make his confession, and absolution is only to be given 'if he humbly and heartily desire it'. The second collect was enlarged to stress the need for faith and repentance, and the third to include prayer for the presence of the Spirit. Most important of all, four new prayers by Robert Sanderson were added. In these there is no suggestion that illness is God's will, and the titles imply that the service may be used in cases of chronic illness as well as terminal.

Even these changes proved insufficient, and demands for an improved office continued to be made. In recent times organizations such as the Guild of St Raphael have put out their own unofficial forms. In the 1928 *BCP* the service was printed in five sections, as suggested by W. H. Frere. The first exhortation is replaced by a list of subjects upon which the minister may make an exhortation of his own. New material includes a form of confession, a litany, two prayers from Sarum, and 'Go forth upon thy journey, Christian soul'. An appendix suggests twenty-five collects, sixteen psalms, and forty passages of scripture as especially useful. Provision was made for reservation (q.v.). In this form the service is enormously improved, and was adopted by other revisions; but, as has been pointed out, the result really belongs to a manual for parish priests rather than to a *BCP*. This may well be true of any attempt to provide for a private occasion of this character.

,The Roman rite, now in process of revision, has a form for communion of the sick who are in danger of death, and another for extreme unction (q.v.). The service of visitation consists of Pss. 6, 16, 20, 86, 91, between which is read a healing miracle from each of the four gospels in turn, followed by a collect. The penitential psalms and the litany of the saints are also appointed for use in the sickroom.

F. E. Brightman, *The English Rite*, 1915, I, pp. cxxv, cxxvi, clxiv, ccxx, ccxxi; II, pp. 818-847; A. J. Collins, *Manuale Sarum,* 1960, pp. 97-114; William Maskell, *Monumenta Ritualia Ecclesiae Anglicanae*, 1846, I, pp. 66-95.

G. J. CUMING

Silent Prayer

Silent prayer within the liturgy falls into three categories: (1) periods of silent prayer which are integral to the structure of the service; (2) the silent, or nearly silent (technically 'secret'), recitation of certain prescribed prayers of private devotion by one or other of the ministers; (3) the similar recitation of prayers which should properly be recited aloud, or at least were originally so recited.

The second of these categories calls for little comment: such prayers are to be found in most of the historic liturgies, in which they were inserted in the Middle Ages. The most outstanding example of the third category is the eucharistic prayer itself, large parts of which are recited secretly in many of the historic liturgies.

This custom appears to have arisen from the desire to express and evoke an attitude towards the eucharistic mystery of awe and fear, the use of the secret voice being psychologically effective to this end. Such an attitude certainly existed to some extent from the very beginnings of Christian worship, as is clear from I Cor. 11.26-33, but it was in fourth- and fifth-century Syria that it came to dominate the approach to the eucharist, and it is in a Syrian document of the end of the fifth century, *The Liturgical Homilies of Narsai*, that we have the first definite evidence for the silent recitation of the anaphora

(q.v.). By the second half of the sixth century the practice had become widespread, although it was as yet by no means universal: in 565 the Emperor Justinian found it necessary to legislate against it. His legislation produced no lasting effect, and by the end of the eighth century the practice had become the established usage in the Byzantine rite. The first definite evidence of it in the West is found in the second Roman *Ordo* of almost exactly the same date. It became and remained the normal usage in the Roman rite until 1966, when the recitation of the canon aloud was again prescribed.

The silent recitation of the eucharistic prayer is undoubtedly a corrupt practice, but however undesirable it may be liturgically, the spread and persistence of the practice bear witness to an evident devotional need for silence and for its psychological fruits in worship. This need should, however, be provided for in other ways.

Among the possibilities are the provision of a space for silent prayer between any bidding to prayer and the formal prayer following it, of a space for silent meditation after readings from scriptures and after communion, and of a space for silent recollection between major sections of any service. Some of these provisions have been included in several recent liturgical reforms, and it is to be hoped that they will become more thorough and more widespread, for in an age of far too little silence they could be of great devotional and psychological value.

W. JARDINE GRISBROOKE

Sitting *see* Postures (2*d*)

South India Church
see Church of South India Worship

Spirituals

The spiritual was born in the American Negro Christian community. Opinions vary regarding its origin and function. It is considered as a misinterpreted hymn of the white Christians (G. P. Jackson), as a 'confession of faith' of the Negro church (S. Läuchli, T. Lehmann and many others), as the 'clearest exponent of the Negro's real self' (H. W. Odum), as a reminiscence of historical events in the history of the American Negro (M. M. Fisher), as a protest against social injustice (J. Lovell), as an adaptation of African songs (H. E. Krehbiel, W. E. Burghardt Du Bois), as originating in the camp meetings (q.v.) of the white revival movement (B. T. Washington), as the products of Negro bards like 'singing Johnson' and 'Ma White' (J. W. Johnson), and a blending of American and European melodies with African rhythm (E. M. v. Hornbostel, B. Nettl). Whatever the history of the spiritual, it is the origin of at least four musical trends today. (1) The different styles of jazz, including the blues. (2) It has been taken up, greatly changed and adapted to the white ear in the Pentecostal churches, particularly in USA, where Pentecostalism originated in a Negro church in Los Angeles and where some of the earliest Pentecostal hymn writers were Negroes. (3) It is further cultivated in a manner faithful to the original tradition in the American Negro Pentecostal churches and in some Negro Baptist churches. (4) Attempts have been made to adapt it to European and American traditional church music (example: Michael Tippett, *A Child of Our Time*, 1944). There is great controversy whether the Negro spiritual has a place in a non-Negro church service, a controversy which becomes even sharper if the spirituals are translated into French or German, or if they are sung in English in a non-English congregation.

Recently church musicians recognized that it was useless to introduce the songs of a contemporary, yet foreign sub-culture. Some of them therefore discovered a popular (not a pop-) musical language in the sub-culture of their own language groups and created new masses, ballads and community hymns (e.g. in Czechoslovakia, East and West Germany, Scandinavia). Some of these songs were created not by church musicians, but by folksingers and chansonniers who took up biblical topics in their chansons (Latin America, France).

T. Lehmann, *Negro Spirituals, Geschichte und Theologie*, 1965; J. Lowens, in *Musik in Geschichte und Gegenwart*, XII, 1965, pp. 1050-4; R. M. Stevenson, in *New Catholic Encyclopaedia*, XIII, 1966, pp. 609-10.

W. J. HOLLENWEGER

Stations of the Cross

Since the Peace of the Church under Constantine (313), many Christians have wished to walk where Christ walked in the week of his passion. Crowds of pilgrims have achieved this over the centuries, but for the majority it was an unrealizable dream.

Some churches in the Middle Ages had chapels to commemorate an event in the passion of Jesus and, from these, the Franciscans, since the fifteenth century, have developed the devotion that has come to be called the Stations of the Cross. The word 'station' (*statio*) implies either 'standing still' or 'gathering at a place'.

It was not until the seventeenth century that stations came to be erected in churches, ranged at intervals around the walls. They took the form of wooden crosses, with a representation of an event in the passion underneath to fix the incident in mind. They are now almost universal in Roman Catholic churches of the Latin rite and also in many Anglican churches.

At first, the number of stations varied considerably, and at Birnau on Lake Constance there are eight superb examples of the rococo period (1724). In 1731, the number was finally fixed by Clement XII at fourteen: nine commemorating events related in the gospels and five from early tradition.

The devotion can be either public or private. Prayers are said at each station, with a short meditation on the scene from the passion. When it is public and taking the form of a church service, a verse from the hymn *Stabat Mater* is sung between each of the stations. An English version of this hymn, 'At the Cross her station keeping', can be found in *Hymns Ancient and Modern Revised* (1950), no. 118.

Every Friday in the year a Franciscan makes the stations along the authentic Way of the Cross in Jerusalem, although the ground has risen considerably since the time of our Lord. Since 1773, it is possible for invalids, prisoners and those at sea to make the devotion on a crucifix blessed for the purpose.

A. A. KING

Stole *see* Vestments (1*d*)

Stoup

A vessel for holding holy water placed near the entrance of churches, into which the faithful who enter dip the fingers of the right hand, blessing themselves with the sign of the cross. Holy water stoups (also called stocks) are probably derived from the fountains in the atrium of the older basilicas (e.g. old St

Peter's, Rome) in which those who were entering the church washed their hands and faces. They seem to have come into more general use from the ninth century, when the custom of sprinkling the people with holy water known as the *Asperges* (q.v.) before the Sunday mass became widespread. The blessing of the water into which salt was thrown crosswise with an invocation took place before this ceremony, and the stoups at the entrance to the church were replenished. The significance of the ceremony of holy water was to remind the worshipper of the promises made at his baptism and that the water had cleansed not only his body but also his soul for which Christ shed his blood.

In English medieval churches the stoup is usually found in a niche inside the porch in the form of a stone basin. But in France and Italy stoups are found inside the church itself, often standing on a stem or pillar. Holy-water stoups are in use in the Roman Catholic Church and in the churches of the Anglican Communion there has been a revival of their use.

F. Bond, *The Chancel of English Churches*, 1916.

C. E. POCKNEE

Subdeacon

The office seems to have originated in Western Christendom in the middle of the third century and its function seems to have been chiefly to provide assistance to the deacon. The principal liturgical duties of the subdeacon were to read the epistle and to prepare the elements and vessels for the offertory. The office was regarded as one of the minor orders in the West until the thirteenth century and still is so regarded in the East. In the Roman Catholic Church the subdiaconate is now the lowest of the major orders, and those admitted to it are normally bound to celibacy. It is usually no more than a stage through which candidates for the priesthood pass, and the vestigial ceremonial duties of the subdeacon at a high mass are performed by a priest, a deacon or even a layman. The office has recently been revived in some parts of the Anglican Communion where it is the equivalent of that of a lay reader (q.v.) with additional authority to administer the chalice, a curious device, since the administration of the elements does not seem to have been a traditional part of the subdeacon's duties.

P. HINCHLIFF

Suffrages

Suffrages (Lat. *suffragia*, prayers seeking favour or support) are found in the divine office in the historic Western rites, and in some rites derived from them, e.g. in morning and evening prayer in the *BCP*. They are always petitionary, sometimes intercessory; they are usually couched in general, but sometimes in particular terms; they are normally in the form of versicles and responses, commonly include the Lord's Prayer, and usually conclude with a collect or collects.

Suffrages were no part of the original Roman offices; they were added to them when the latter were adopted in the Frankish lands, where they were probably part of the Gallican offices, and were then accepted at Rome. Their use has been all but completely suppressed in the latest reform of the Roman breviary.

The suffrages in the morning and evening offices of the *BCP*, comprising the material from the creed to the third collect, are typical; they are largely derived from those found in the Sarum books.

W. JARDINE GRISBROOKE

Sunday

The Lord's Day is the foundation of the entire structure of the Christian year. In the Jewish system, the days of the week were known simply as the first day, the second day, and so on. The last day of the week had a title, the Sabbath, and, dependent on this, Friday was called the preparation. The Sabbath set the pattern of a weekly day of worship, but in Christianity it was 'the first day of the week' (Acts 20.7) which took this position. By the end of the first century that designation had given place to one which more adequately conveyed the day's significance – the Lord's Day. The use of the name Sunday dates from about the middle of the second century. In 321 the official recognition by the Roman state of Sunday as the day of Christian worship and as a day of public rest meant that the Sabbath had now been incorporated into and transformed by the Christian tradition.

As the Sabbath provided the model of a weekly day of worship, so its general influence is demonstrated by the fact that for a considerable period the Christian Sunday began about 6 p.m. on the Saturday evening, the hour at which the Sabbath began on the Friday evening. Centuries passed before the old Semitic reckoning from sunset yielded completely to the Roman conception of the day as beginning at midnight. About the middle of the fourth century the *Testament of our Lord* refers to the evening as the beginning of the day. The 'eves' of the great festivals represent the survival of the beginning of the Semitic day, the 'eve' being part of the festival itself. It was natural enough that when this reckoning had disappeared from common use, it should remain in connection with the outstanding days of the Christian year.

The relationship between the Lord's Day and the Sabbath of the old covenant serves as the context within which to emphasize the immense difference between these liturgical days. The gospel narrative of the resurrection furnishes the true normative use of the designation 'the first day of the week' as a proper name for the Christian day of worship. When we remember that primitive worship took place at an early hour of the morning, the binding link between Sunday and the resurrection becomes more obvious. Late in the fourth century at Jerusalem the central service of Christendom, consisting of the reading and preaching of the word and the celebration of the sacrament, was held at daybreak. Thus the true note of the Lord's Day must always be joy, thanksgiving, victory. It is surely from the lordship of Jesus Christ, made manifest in the resurrection on 'the first day of the week' (Mark 16.2), that the title 'the Lord's Day' is ultimately derived. The early church never lost this conception of Sunday as the sign of the inbreaking of the eternal order of God, and it remained a day of praise and triumph. Fasting and the penitential observance of kneeling in prayer were strictly forbidden.

The profound revolution which substituted the Christian Sunday for the Jewish Sabbath took place within the first generation of the church's life. Certainly by the middle of the sixth decade when Paul, writing to Corinth, refers to 'the first day of every week' (I Cor. 16.2), the Lord's Day must long have been supreme. In the second century there was a group of Jewish Christians who celebrated the Sabbath as well as Sunday. But the church in general would tolerate no compromise and delivered itself from the impoverishment of Judaizing Christianity. Early in the third century there is the hint of a tendency to make the Sabbath a liturgical day, but it is in the fourth century that the whole question moves into the foreground. The liturgical commemoration of the Sabbath brought with it the holy communion on that day. It can scarcely be doubted that, although the celebrations on the station days (*see* **Good Friday**) have a longer history, those on Saturdays and other days are the result of developments in the fourth century. It is when we appreciate the eucharistic unity of the passion and victory of Christ Jesus that we understand the uniqueness of Sunday. To set weekdays as such beside Sunday as days for celebrating the holy communion served to obscure the uniqueness of Sunday and may have affected the understanding of the sacrament, for it weakened the connection between the resurrection, the Lord's Day and the eucharist.

A. A. McArthur, *The Evolution of the Christian Year*, 1953; H. B. Porter, *The Day of Light. The Biblical and Liturgical Meaning of Sunday*, 1960; W. Rordorf, *Sunday*, 1968.

A. A. MCARTHUR

Super Oblata

Since the mid-fifth century, the offertory ceremony in the Roman rite has been concluded with a prayer called originally, and again since 1969, the *oratio super oblata* ('prayer over the offerings'), but for many centuries called the *secreta* ('secret'). As the latter name first appears in France and Germany, where the custom of saying the prayer in a low voice (*secreto*) originated, it probably refers to this custom, although other meanings are possible. At Rome it was anciently sung, and the singing or saying aloud of it has been restored in the new *Ordo Missae* of 1969.

The prayer, which varies according to the day, is in form a variant of the collect type; its basic content is always a prayer for the divine acceptance of the gifts just placed on the altar within the context of the eucharistic mystery about to be accomplished. A prayer parallel to the *oratio super oblata* in function and content is found in a corresponding place in most of the historic liturgies.

J. A. Jungmann, *The Mass of the Roman Rite*,

II, 1955, pp. 90-97.
W. JARDINE GRISBROOKE

Superintendent

The Greek term *episcopos*, from which 'bishop' is derived, means 'overseer'. In the Reformation period, when a term was wanted which would express the element of oversight while avoiding the hierarchical and prelatical overtones of 'bishop' (q.v.), the title 'superintendent' seemed an obvious choice. Many of the churches of the Reformation used the term. In German Lutheranism there were superintendents until the 1920s, when the title of bishop was revived. In the Church of Scotland, five superintendents were appointed in 1561 and they, with three bishops who threw in their lot with the Reformation, exercised oversight over other clergy. The superintendent was required to minister in a congregation of his own besides overseeing the work of other men. The office was subsequently discontinued, and there has been a good deal of controversy about whether it was intended as a reformed and permanent, if limited, episcopate or whether it was a temporary expedient made necessary as ministers could not be found for every parish. In the Methodist Church the superintendent minister is the minister in charge of a circuit.

P. HINCHLIFF

Surplice *see* Vestments (2c)

Synaxis

The name *synaxis* (Greek 'meeting' or 'assembly'), anciently used in the Christian church of any meeting for public worship, is today normally used only of that service which is the most ancient and archetypal of them all, the office of readings and prayers which precedes the celebration of the eucharist, and which has indeed, from a very early date, come to be reckoned as a part of the eucharistic liturgy.

The close relationship of *synaxis* to *synagogue* (Greek 'gathering' and hence 'gathering place'), although it is intrinsically no more than a grammatical one, serves to underline the essential character of the first part of the eucharistic liturgy, as an inheritance from, and development of, the worship of the synagogue. The earliest Christians, as we learn from the Acts of the Apostles, continued to worship in the synagogue, while celebrating the eucharist in their own houses; when they were expelled from the synagogue they prefixed the essential elements of the synagogue service to the eucharist, and made one service of the two (except on certain occasions when the eucharist was preceded by some other function, e.g. the baptismal vigil at Easter).

The synagogue service was composed basically of three elements – reading from the scriptures, psalmody, and prayer, and these three are from the beginning the constant basic elements of the Christian synaxis, which is characterized by Jungmann as essentially a biblical instruction. It appears originally to have opened abruptly with the readings, preceded by no more than the exchange of a mutual greeting between the president (bishop or presbyter) and the assembly. Neither the number nor the order of the readings can be definitely gathered from the earliest evidence, but it seems likely, from a comparison with the synagogue, and from the evidently archaic arrangements of the synaxis which survive in some of the Eastern rites, as well as on certain days in the Roman and Byzantine rites, that there were originally at least four readings in a normal synaxis – from the law, the prophets, the epistles, and the gospels. From earliest times the readings appear to have been followed by a sermon expounding them. From the fourth century onwards there was a universal and rapid tendency towards disuse of the readings from the OT, and nearly everywhere in Christendom the ordinary synaxis came to include only two readings, the epistle and the gospel. During the Middle Ages the sermon also came to be a less frequent feature of the synaxis than in earlier times.

The earliest form of psalmody at the synaxis of which we have any evidence is the singing of selected psalms in a responsorial manner (i.e. the psalm sung by a soloist, and an unvarying refrain sung after each verse by the congregation) between the readings. This survives in all the historic rites, although commonly in a very reduced form (e.g. the gradual – since 1969 replaced by a return to a more extended responsorial psalm – and alleluia of the Roman rite, and the prokeimenon and alleluia of the Byzantine rite) (*see* **Liturgies** 2).

The element of prayer in the early synaxis took the form of more or less extended intercessions which followed the readings and sermon. The oldest formal arrangement of these is probably that still found in the Roman rite on Good Friday – a series of biddings by the deacon, each followed by a period of silent prayer by the congregation and a collect by the president or a concelebrant presbyter; a parallel form still exists in the Alexandrine rite. From the late fourth century onwards a litany (q.v.) became a more common form in most parts of the Christian world; in the Roman rite the older form was replaced by a litany (elsewhere in the service) late in the fifth century, and by the seventh century this also had fallen out of use, with the result that with the spread of the Roman rite in the former Gallican lands the common prayers of the synaxis disappeared for many centuries over the greater part of Western Christendom.

While between the fourth and eighth centuries there was an almost universal tendency to reduce the quantity of readings and psalmody, there was a simultaneous universal tendency to add secondary matter to the synaxis: notably, parallel introductory rites developed everywhere during this period. The order and contents of these vary considerably, but there are constant features, such as the introit or entrance psalm, an introductory hymn of prayer and praise – e.g. the *Gloria in excelsis* or great doxology (q.v.) in the Roman rite and the *Trisagion* (q.v.) in the Byzantine rite – and an introductory prayer by the president – e.g. the collect of the day in all the Western rites and the prayer which accompanies the *Trisagion* in the Byzantine rite. During the Middle Ages a further parallel development led to the widespread prefixing of preparatory rites of various kinds to the introductory rite itself – e.g. the enarxis (q.v.) of the Byzantine rite, and the preparatory prayers and confession of the Roman rite.

Modern revisions of the synaxis, whether in the great historic rites themselves or in the post-Reformation liturgies (in most of which the principal features of the synaxis, so far as they had been preserved during the Middle Ages, survived in a recognizable form), tend to concentrate on the restoration of the integrity of its primary elements – readings, psalmody and common prayers – and the rationalization (and in part elimination) of the secondary and tertiary growths of introductory and preparatory matter. In particular there is an all but universal move to-

wards the recovery of the OT material – reading and psalmody – which had come over the centuries to be greatly abbreviated or even, in some post-Reformation liturgies, completely eliminated.

The original relationship between the synaxis and the divine office is an obscure and complex problem, but there seems little doubt that the morning and evening services of the early centuries (corresponding to the mattins and lauds and the vespers of the later office) bore considerably more resemblance to their common synagogal origins with the synaxis than do their later forms: a brief consideration of this question will be found under the heading **Cathedral Office**.

Further information on the synaxis and its component parts will be found in most books dealing with Christian worship in general, and especially in those dealing with the eucharistic liturgies of the several rites.

W. JARDINE GRISBROOKE

Tabernacle

This term has been employed to describe a number of disparate objects.

1. It has been used to describe the silk 'tent' or canopy which covered the pyx (q.v.) suspended over the altar in medieval England and France.

2. The term is applied to niches with a carved canopy which housed the statue of a saint.

3. The term was also used in the Middle Ages for a type of altar-piece with carved niches and having hinged wings.

4. Its more usual application now is to the safe or cupboard which stands in a central position at the back of the altar or immediately over it for the reservation (q.v.) of the blessed sacrament. This is the normal method of reservation in the Roman Catholic Church today; the tabernacle has to be circular in design, so that the whole structure of metal is completely enveloped by a silk or fabric veil of white or the appropriate liturgical colour. The term 'tabernacle' to denote this kind of receptacle fixed to the altar for the reserved sacrament was introduced by the reforming bishop of Verona, Matthew Giberti, about 1525; his ideas were later endorsed by the Council of Trent.

A. A. King and C. E. Pocknee, *Eucharistic Reservation in the Western Church*, 1965.

C. E. POCKNEE

Table Prayers
see Ante-Communion

Tenebrae

A quasi-popular term, found in the Roman books not before the twelfth century, for mattins and lauds of the last three days of Holy Week (q.v.). The reason was that to allow the easier participation of the people, these offices were anticipated to the evening before the day to which they referred (thus *tenebrae* of Maundy Thursday was sung on the evening of Wednesday). The term came into use most probably because the lights (candles) were gradually extinguished in the course of the office and all departed in darkness (*tenebrae*) and silence.

Mattins and lauds of these days were originally simply the ordinary offices sung by monastic or quasi-monastic communities serving the Roman basilicas and other collegiate churches throughout Europe (*see* **Canonical Hours**). In their form they reveal certain primitive features of the Roman (cathedral) office. Thus, there were no hymns, no invitatory, no introductory versicles and responses and the *Gloria Patri* at the end of each psalm was suppressed. Mattins consist of nine psalms and nine readings (Lamentations, patristic readings and NT), the old Roman pattern. The Lamentations were sung to a chant of peculiar poignancy and all the readings were divided by responsories of great musical beauty. They almost certainly derive from the Roman *schola cantorum* of the seventh, eighth and ninth centuries.

These offices are a prolonged meditation on the events of salvation running from the Last Supper to the entombment. The note of betrayal is sounded in Thursday *tenebrae*, the judgment, crucifixion and death of Christ on Friday and his burial and the expectation of his resurrection on Saturday.

A unique feature of the offices of these days was the triangular candlestick which stood in the choir and on which fifteen candles of natural, dark-coloured wax were placed. They were extinguished one by one after each psalm (nine for mattins and five for lauds) until one only remained. During the *Benedictus* this was hidden either behind the altar or elsewhere in the church and when the signal for departure (*strepitus*) was given it was replaced on the top of the candlestick. This has been understood as an anticipated sign of the resurrection, but probably was no more than a way of providing light for the congregation to depart.

The eventual appearance of the part of the breviary giving the Holy Week offices may modify this inevitably provisional statement.

J. D. CRICHTON

Terce *see* Canonical Hours

Thanksgiving *see* Prayer (5)

Three-hours Service

In fourth-century Jerusalem the custom originated by which the events of redemption were celebrated each year on what were believed to be their original sites, and in their original chronological sequence. Accordingly the three hours of Jesus' passion were observed by a service from the sixth to the ninth hour on the day now called Good Friday (q.v.). The bishop presided and the service included readings from all passages of scripture which relate to the passion interspersed with prayers and ending with the passion story from St John's gospel. Although many features of the Jerusalem observances, e.g. Palm Sunday, were adopted throughout Christendom, this particular observance was not, probably because it intruded on the liturgical activities which had already developed in the West, notably the preparation of catechumens (q.v.) for baptism. The three-hours service as it is known today originated in Peru as an extra-liturgical devotion as recently as the late seventeenth century and has since been adopted in many Roman Catholic and Anglican churches. In Peru it consisted in essence of addresses on the seven words from the cross, and this remains the common basis of the service today. But it interferes with the proper observance of the traditional liturgy, and in the Church of England the attempt is sometimes made to observe the three hours with a complete use of the official liturgy, mattins, litany, and ante-communion, and to end with evensong (qq.v.). Changing social patterns, however, make it very uncertain whether it is any longer desirable to adhere to the hours in question, which are commonly understood to be twelve noon to three o'clock, as a means of presenting the Lord's passion either to the church or to the world.

___

J. G. Davies, *Holy Week*, 1963; J. W. Tyrer, *Historical Survey of Holy Week*, 1932.

E. C. WHITAKER

Thurible

More commonly termed in English *censer*. A metal pan designed to hold heated charcoal upon which powdered or granulated perfumed gums, the most common being *olibanum*, are sprinkled. The most usual form of the censer is now a pan having a cover which is pierced with a number of apertures so that the fumes of the incense may be exuded as the censer is swung to and fro on the chains to which it is attached. The use of incense (q.v.) in pagan religions as well as in OT rites and also its association with the deification of the Roman emperors probably accounts for its rejection by Christians in the first three centuries. It is unlikely, therefore, that the reference to a censer in Rev. 8.5 reflects the custom of Christian worship at the end of the apostolic era. About AD 200, Tertullian in North Africa rejects the use of incense because of its association with emperor worship (*Apol.* 30).

The first definite evidence for the use of incense in Christian worship is at the end of the fourth century in *The Pilgrimage of Etheria*, describing the services in Holy Week and Easter at the Church of the Holy Sepulchre, Jerusalem. Also the Pseudo-Dionysius refers to the act of censing about AD 500. The earliest use of the censer was in processions when it was carried before the bishop at the entrance of the ministers, and also in the procession which preceded the reading of the gospel at the mass. In both these instances its use was probably honorific. This custom may have been derived from imperial usage, since it was customary for torches and incense to be carried before the emperor, and when the bishop acquired a status as a court dignitary in the fourth century this custom may have applied to him. As time went on, the use of the censer was elaborated to include the censing of the ministers and congregation as well as the elements of bread and wine as they were carried in and offered at the altar. After the thirteenth century, with the introduction of the new ceremony of the elevation of the host, the consecrated element was censed as it was lifted up by the celebrant. The censer was also used at the offices of lauds and vespers on festivals.

The use of censers did not entirely cease after the Reformation in England, as the records from the reign of Elizabeth I clearly show, and the use of a censer was maintained at Ely cathedral until 1752. Also a pan with a handle for the use of incense was part of the ceremonies in the coronation processions of all the Stuart kings including James II.

In the Eastern Orthodox Church the censer is used with considerable elaboration not only in the celebration of the eucharistic liturgy, but also in the rites associated with baptisms, marriages and funerals.

Another form of the censer is to be seen in the cathedral at Lyons, France, where at the pontifical high mass a large urn is in use on either side of the altar and these are replenished with incense at certain stages of the progress of the liturgy. The grains of incense are usually kept in a metal container known as a 'boat' on account of its shape.

___

M. Andrieu, *Les Ordines Romani du haut moyen age,* 5 vols., 1931-61; E. G. C. Atchley, *History of the Use of Incense*, 1909; J. Wickham Legg, *Church Ornaments and their Civil Antecedents*, 1917.

C. E. POCKNEE

Thurifer

The person who, in processions or on liturgical occasions, carries the thurible (q.v.) or censer (a metal brazier hanging from chains and fitted with a lid) in which incense (q.v.) is burnt.

P. HINCHLIFF

Tower

The most familiar use of this term is a stone, brick or wooden structure attached to a church building often containing one or more bells. The term has also been applied to a tower-like vessel used at the eucharist in the Gallican rites. There is some difference of opinion among ecclesiologists as to whether this tower housed the reserved sacrament or whether the bread it contained was for consecration at the eucharist. In our opinion the poem written by Venantius Fortunatus (*Carm.* XX) indicates that the tower given by Felix, Bishop of Bourges, *c.*573, was for the purpose of reservation (q.v.).

C. E. POCKNEE

Tract

The name given to the psalm sung after the epistle and gradual instead of the alleluia during Lent and other penitential seasons and at masses for the dead in the Roman church. English versions are printed in the *English Hymnal* under 'Introits and Other Anthems'.

EDITOR

Transept

The transept is the transverse part of a church at right angles to the nave and usually inserted between it and the chancel (q.v.).

Transepts originally filled two functions and can therefore be classified as (1) a *transept-martyrium*, which provided a large space around the tomb of a saint; (2) a *transept-prothesis*, which provided an area for the tables on which the congregation placed the gifts at the offertory (q.v.).

A second classification, by form instead of function, allows transepts to be divided into six groups (*see* Figs. 19-23): (1) *Continuous transept*. The transverse space is undivided, the colonnades being cut short to leave an open rectangle, e.g. St Peter's, Rome. (2) *Cross transept*. The colonnades

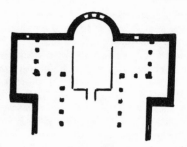

Fig. 21   Basilica A, Philippi, Macedonia

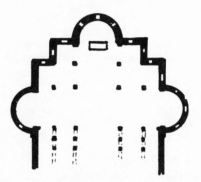

Fig. 22   Church of the Nativity, Bethlehem, Israel

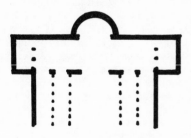

Fig. 19   St Peter's, Rome, Italy

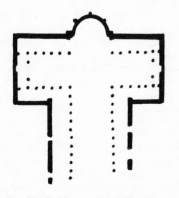

Fig. 20   St Menas, Abu Mina, Egypt

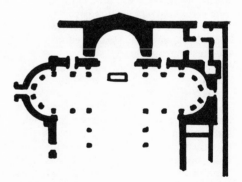

Fig. 23   Hermopolis (Ashmunein), Egypt

are turned at right angles into the wings and then envelop them on three sides, e.g. St Menas, Abu Mina. In a reduced cross transept, the colonnades are bent at right angles and then turn through another to join the east wall, e.g. Basilica A, Philippi. (3) *Trefoil transept*. The two extremities of the transept are provided with apses, and these, with the sanctuary, produce an integrated design with three semi-circles, e.g. the Church of the

Nativity, Bethlehem. (4) *Triconch transept.* This is similar to the former, but nothing intervenes between the sanctuary and the transept apses, so that the plan is like that of a three-leaved clover, e.g. the cathedral of Hermopolis (Ashmunein). (5) *Dwarf transept.* This form is not discernible from the plan, since it relates to the elevation and designates a transverse space whose wings are lower in height than the nave. (6) *Tripartite transept.* This, too, refers to the elevation, when the wings are shut off by arcades from the central area.

EDITOR

Transfiguration

This commemoration on 6 August, deriving from the Eastern Church, became general in the west in the fifteenth century. It is not related to the structure of the liturgical year formed by the festivals of Christmas, Epiphany, Good Friday, Easter, Ascension and Pentecost (qq.v.).

A. A. MCARTHUR

Trinity Sunday

This festival is different in character from those which commemorate the historical events of salvation. It is also remote in time, originating in the West in the tenth century. Late in the following century Pope Alexander II was not persuaded that the festival was a valid development, but Rome adopted it in the fourteenth century.

A. A. MCARTHUR

Trisagion

The name (Greek, lit. 'the thrice-holy') of a hymn in the Byzantine rite which is sung after the little entrance (q.v.) at the pre-eucharistic synaxis (q.v.), its place and purpose corresponding to the *Gloria in excelsis* (*see* **Doxology**) in the Roman rite. Also used at many other points in the services of the Byzantine rite, it consists of the invocation 'Holy God, Holy and Mighty, Holy and Immortal, have mercy upon us' three times, followed by the lesser doxology (q.v.) and in some contexts a final repetition of the invocation.

The Byzantine form of the *Trisagion* is occasionally met with in the historic Western rites also, notably in the Roman rite on Good Friday at the veneration of the cross. Another form of the *Trisagion*, of a more festal character, appears to have been in use in the ancient Hispano-Gallican liturgy, as an acclamation before the singing of the gospel.

The *Trisagion* should *not* be confused with the *Sanctus* (q.v.); the use of the Latin name of the *Trisagion* – *Tersanctus* – as a title for the latter by some writers is a misleading error.

———

H. Holloway, *A Study of the Byzantine Liturgy*, 1933, pp. 59-62.

W. JARDINE GRISBROOKE

Tunicle *see* Vestments (1*g*)

Unction

The anointing of persons and things is ancient and widely used in a great many religions, not merely in those of the Mediterranean basin. Various substances (oil, fat, blood, water, saliva) were used at different times and in different places with various significance. Of these, consecration or the making of a person or thing sacred seems to have been the dominant one.

This was so in OT. Things, Jacob's stone (Gen. 28.18), the ark and tabernacle furniture were consecrated with oil (Ex. 310.25ff.). Kings were the special object of unction (I Sam. 10.1ff.; 16.13; etc.) as also were priests (Lev. 8.12, high priest; Lev. 8.30, other priests). There is a possible reference to the anointing of prophets (Ps. 105.15), though the injunction to anoint Elisha (I Kings 19.16) seems never to have been carried out. None the less, the consecration with oil with which 'priests, kings and prophets' were anointed by God was destined to have a long history in the Christian liturgy.

In the NT there is a reference to the apostles' healing with oil (Mark 6.13) and what in the Catholic tradition is regarded as a ritual use of oil for healing in James 5.14-15. However, the key-factor in the use of unction in the liturgy seems to have been the figure of Jesus, the Messiah ('Anointed', *Christos*), who was 'anointed' at his incarnation (Heb. 1.9), for his messianic ministry at baptism (Mark 1.9-11 and par.), and who was conscious of the presence of the Spirit with him in his saving work (Luke 4.16-22). After his death and resurrection he becomes the source of the Spirit (Acts 2.33) whom he sends upon his church. This coming of the

Spirit to the individual Christian is symbolized in the liturgy both by the laying-on of hands and in a great variety of ways by unction. The precise purpose (whether gift, grace or ministry) intended by unction has to be discerned both from the circumstances in which it is given and the words that accompany it. However, the overriding significance of anointing is that it conveys the Spirit of Christ who is at once the source of the Spirit and the exemplar of the life of the Christian.

The relationship between the anointing and the Spirit-filled Christ can be seen in a very striking manner in the post-baptismal unction, usually called chrismation. Apart from the Syrian Church which most probably has never had it (E. C. Whitaker, *Documents of the Baptismal Liturgy*, ²1970, Introduction), all liturgies with remarkable unanimity have had this rite. The oil used is *chrisma* (from the same verb *chrio* as *Christos*) and it signifies the positive side of baptism, the conformation of the Christian to Christ, his participation in the priestly, royal and prophetic quality of Christ and the giving of the Spirit (*cf.* the prayer of consecration, Roman pontifical, liturgy of the chrism mass). But as in OT unction signified richness and abundance of life, the chrism acquired a very rich symbolism. This is particularly noteworthy in the Eastern Church where from the fourth century onwards chrism was called *myron* (Cyril of Jerusalem, *Cat. Myst.*, III, 2, 3, 7) on account of the many aromatic ingredients that went to its composition. It was accordingly interpreted as 'the good odour of Christ' (*cf.* II Cor. 2.15) which should perfume the life of the Christian who has died and risen with Christ and who henceforth should live with him (*Apostolic Constitutions*, VII, 44). To this the Council of Laodicea adds that it makes the candidate a sharer in the kingdom of God (can. 48). To this the anointing with chrism in confirmation, when it came to be combined with the imposition of hands, adds the significance of completion and the giving of the fullness of the Spirit (*Ap. Trad.*, 22. 1, 2).

The pre-baptismal anointing is more closely related to the culture of the Greco-Roman world where the anointing of athletes before the *agon* was well known. This rite, which is found in every baptismal liturgy until the sixteenth century, signifies the strengthening of the candidate for the struggle

with the powers of darkness he will meet in the waters into which he will be plunged. Originally, he was anointed all over as were the ancient wrestlers so that the opponent could not get a firm grip on him – a symbolism that was known to St Gregory the Great. This anointing was really an exorcism and this fact gave its name to the oil which in more recent centuries has been called the 'oil of catechumens'.

In spite of James 5.14-15, the use of unction for the healing of the sick is not attested until the first decades of the third century (*Ap. Trad.* V). The oil is blessed after the eucharistic prayer and is very clearly intended for healing. The prayer envisages the sick persons as not only being anointed with it but also as drinking it. This is found also in the *Sacramentary* of Serapion (*c.*350, ed. Funk, 17[1905], pp. 178-181) where the terms are strongly medical (the oil is a healing *medicine* but there is also an element of exorcism in the prayer. This is not surprising since both in OT and in the Graeco-Roman world physical illness was connected with sin and evil. The emphasis on healing in the liturgical tradition is marked, and the main elements of the prayer of the Apostolic Tradition have remained in the Roman Pontifical to this day. The modern version of the prayer has omitted the mention of people touching and drinking the oil but this was a very common practice. They used to bring their phials of oil to church (not only on Maundy Thursday) and when ill anoint themselves or get others to do so for them. Several ecclesiastical writers recommend them to do so, no doubt to eliminate superstitious practices.

At first there was no particular order of anointings and some texts suggest that the oil should be applied where the pain was greatest. It was only when the anointing of the sick became entangled with current penitential practice in the tenth century that the anointing of the separate senses to remove sin committed through them became customary.

In the Roman Catholic church sick persons in danger of death are still anointed, usually in conjunction with confession, absolution and communion where these are possible (Last Rites).

The use of unction in the ordination (q.v.) of bishops and priests undoubtedly came in under the influence of the Carolingian practice of anointing kings. Behind this is the influence of OT, which was dominant in all the liturgy of that time. It was easy to make the transference from the anointing of kings in OT (and one or two texts in the consecration of the oils suggested it) to the anointing of Gallic monarchs. Once this transference was made, it was felt that bishops and priests, too, must be anointed. The rites are first found in the Romano-German pontifical of the end of the tenth century. The bishop was anointed on the head but the text suggests that his whole body was regarded as being anointed. He became a sacred, even a sacrosanct, person. The hands of the priest were anointed and made sacred for the celebration of the eucharist and the handling of the sacred elements.

Unction was and is used in rites that are not strictly sacramental, in consecrating chalices and bells and above all in the dedication of a church (q.v.). This ritual, very elaborate until recently and still undergoing revision, saw the physical church as a symbol of the Christian people and the anointings with chrism were parallel to the initiation rites of baptism and confirmation. But all these later anointings had for their overriding purpose the consecration of persons and things, setting them apart from the 'profane' world so that they might accomplish their ministry or the purpose for which they were made.

———

L'Eglise en Prière, ed. A. G. Martimort, 1961, Part 3 on the sacraments, where the meaning of unction in connection with various sacraments is given; *cf.* pp. 169-183 for dedications of church, etc.; Bruno Kleinheyer, *Die Priesterweihe im Römischen Ritus*, 1961 (for priesthood only); L. L. Mitchell, *Baptismal Anointing*, 1966; Mario Righetti, *Storia Liturgica*, ²1959, IV (on the sacraments, dedication of churches, etc.); *Dictionnaire d'Archéologie Chrétienne et de Liturgie* VI, cc. 2777-2791 (Cabrol) s.v. 'Huiles'; *ibid.* XII, cc. 2116-2130 (Leclercq) s.v. 'Onction'; *ibid.* XII, cc. 2130-2147 (Leclercq) s.v. 'Onction dans l'Ordination'.

J. D. CRICHTON

Unitarian Worship

Manchester College, Oxford, which is affiliated to the General Assembly of Unitarian and Free Christian Churches, is dedicated to Truth, to Liberty and to Religion. This is a principle dear to Unitarians the world over. Guided by reason and conscience, but not unmindful of continuing revelation and tradition, the Unitarians seek to serve the Lord in sincerity and truth.

Unitarianism, at its worthiest, is a rational mysticism, and tolerance a genuine article of faith. This goes far to explain variations of church government and modes of worship. Unitarians see no inconsistency in having a General Assembly in Britain and a succession of bishops in Transylvania in continuous line from the Reformation. A revised *BCP* is still found in use at King's Chapel, Boston, Massachusetts, where English governors once worshipped. But at Dr Preston Bradley's famous 'People's Church' in Chicago emphasis is laid on the sermon. Not infrequently in America the sermon is followed by discussion.

The 'free services' of Nonconformity and a vigorous liturgical tradition have coexisted in England for two centuries. Traces of Calvinist worship, notably the Great Prayer, long survived among the 'English Presbyterians' from whom the Unitarians are in the main derived. But in the eighteenth century these 'Rational Dissenters' began to bring forth prayer books of their own. Even Joseph Priestley produced *Forms of Prayer for the use of Unitarian Societies* (1783). Nor did theological change stem the flow. From 1741 to our own day over a hundred liturgies have been forthcoming. For the purpose of this article it is the liturgies that are examined. They illustrate the development of doctrine common to all congregations, the majority always preferring conceived prayer. The Rational Dissenters were profoundly influenced by Locke's common-sense psychology and Newton's mathematical cosmology. Their service-books were scriptural in language, and often incorporated many responses for minister and people. They were dignified and devout and, what appealed to the spirit of the Age, entirely devoid of 'enthusiasm'.

Anglican worship entered these churches with the advent of Theophilus Lindsey who much admired the great Semi-Arian Samuel Clarke. Lindsey resigned his living to establish a Reformed Church of England with a revised *BCP*. In fact he established the first avowedly Unitarian church in the country in 1774. At Essex Street, London, he used *The Book of Common Prayer reformed according to the Plan of the Late Dr Samuel Clarke*. This soon attained an enormous popularity among the English Presbyterians now venturing into Biblical Unitarianism. The services amended were usually mattins and evensong. Lindsey followed Clarke in addressing all prayers to the Father. The virgin birth was rejected as unhistorical. Satan was expelled from the litany!

In 1862 Sadler and Martineau published *Common Prayer for Christian Worship*; it is the finest of the Unitarian liturgies. The last two services by Martineau are historic. For the first time Nonconformity had produced a liturgical editor of rare genius. The haunting beauty of the prayers, the timely responses, and the scripturally inspired canticles attain poetic felicity and prophetic piety.

But Martineau was troubled in conscience. He sang the song of the Lamb, but like Lindsey before him he objected to the perpetual termination of every prayer '*per Jesu Christum, Dominum nostrum*'. He did not rest until these words were deleted. *Ten Services of Public Prayer*, a revised edition published in 1879, repudiates the redemptive and intercessory functions of Christ.

No noteworthy change is to be found in *Orders of Worship* published in 1932. Nor is there any approach to a eucharistic norm. But the many fine prayers have been adopted by non-liturgical congregations to their spiritual enrichment.

Infant baptism is common among Unitarians although they reject the doctrine of original sin. The triune formula is to be found in many of the older liturgies. But *A Book of Occasional Services* (1932) and *In Life and Death* (1968) suggest 'I baptize thee in the name of God our Father, and in the spirit of his Son, Jesus Christ'. Holy communion is for Unitarians memorialism. The rite often varies as there is no rigidly prescribed form, still less a eucharistic doctrine. But the ancient Christian piety makes this service sacred and sanctifying. There is always a celebration at the General Assembly in Great Britain.

Dr Rowe's *Book of Occasional Services* and a similar compilation by the Rev. Kenneth Twinn, *In Life and Death*, are useful aids to ministers. Both, rather surprisingly, include 'Thanksgiving after Childbirth'. Mr Twinn's book contains a remarkable number of very appropriate extra-biblical readings.

Especially is this true of his funeral service.

Unitarians seem always to have encouraged the people of God to take an active part in worship. Litanies and responses are part of their heritage. An admirable modern example is the American *Hymns for the Celebration of Life* (1964). This book includes litanies and responses derived from many sources. The themes are most comprehensive and include science, the countryside, and the democratic way of life.

A quest for more meaningful worship among the younger English Unitarians has given rise to some experimentation. The impulse undoubtedly comes from contact with some of the Unitarian-Universalists in America. The Americans are making greater use of music and of periods of silence. In America and England alike there is a tendency in some quarters to depart from the preacher-hearer tradition and to develop a dialectic. But it is dangerous to generalize about Unitarians anywhere!

Unitarians have been accused of being 'cold' in their worship. This has never been true but the older piety was perhaps too unobtrusive and almost shy. The secret of their piety is disclosed in their own fine hymns. Such names as Sarah F. Adams and Oliver Wendell Holmes come to mind.

Unitarian sermons tend to be thoughtful meditations; for the English have remained Rational Dissenters, and the Americans have not forgotten their roots in Boston and Harvard. Alike they remember an abiding aspiration for the Beauty of Holiness.

A. E. PEASTON

Utensils *see* Aumbry, Alms-dish, Bells, Candles, Chalice and Paten, Chrismatory, Ciborium, Cruet, Fan, Monstrance, Paschal Candle, Pyx, Stoup, Tabernacle, Thurible, Tower

Veil

1. A veil or curtain was drawn before the altar at certain points in the liturgy from the fourth century onwards; and some of the Greek fathers liken this veil to that which hung before the holy of holies in the temple at Jerusalem. This custom has continued until today in the lesser Eastern churches such as the Armenian and the Coptic. But the need

Plate 36
Lenten array and
veiling, Southwark
cathedral, London

for this veil has been obviated in the Eastern Orthodox rite with the development of the solid iconostasis (q.v.).

2. In the West this veiling has not developed to the same extent as in the East. But during the season of Lent in the Middle Ages in England and elsewhere, the altar was shrouded from the congregation by the Lenten veil drawn across the sanctuary, which was only drawn aside at the reading of the gospel at the parish mass on Sundays. This veil is not to be confused with another veil which hung before the crucifix on the rood beam during Lent. Both these veils were made of unbleached linen or holland; they formed part of the general shrouding with this material which took place in all churches at the beginning of Lent and continued until the eve of Easter Day. This shrouding is known as the *Lenten Array* (*see* Plate 36). It covered every crucifix, statue, and reredos (q.v.), including the three figures on the rood beam. The veils often had emblems of red, black or blue stencilled on them; and the emblem frequently gave a hint of the object that it veiled. The Lenten Array has been revived in a number of the cathedrals and parish churches in Britain.

In the modern Roman rite it is customary to veil all crucifixes, statues and pictures with purple-toned veiling from the eve of the fifth Sunday in Lent, commonly called Passion Sunday, until the eve of Easter Day.

A. A. King, *The Rites of Eastern Christendom*, 2 vols., 1947; C. E. Pocknee, *The Christian Altar*, 1963; C. E. Pocknee, *Cross and Crucifix*, 1962; H. B. Walters, *London Churches at the Reformation*, 1939.

C. E. POCKNEE

Veneration of the Cross

The Veneration of the Cross, which forms a part of the liturgy for Good Friday, originated in Jerusalem after the finding of the cross by St Helena (325). At the end of the fourth century, a relic of the cross was venerated in silence, as witnessed by the bishop, Cyril, and the pilgrim Etheria. Relics were sent to other churches; to Rome in the seventh century, probably from Greece. Here, at first, the same austere ceremony took place as in Jerusalem, but at the end of the eighth century a service-book records the singing of 'Behold the wood of the cross' and Ps. 118. Churches in the West, which were without a relic, substituted a plain wooden cross, which later was changed for a crucifix.

The ceremony was more dramatized in the churches of Spain and Gaul, and all the elements of the present rite are found in the Roman-German pontifical of Mainz about the year 950.

By the eleventh century, the Roman liturgy had introduced this more solemn form of the Veneration of the Cross. It included the showing and kissing of the cross, a dialogued chant of the 'reproaches' ('My people, what have I done to you?'), the Byzantine *Trisagion* ('Holy God, Holy and strong'), an antiphon ('Lord, we worship thy cross') and the hymn, 'Sing, my tongue, the glorious battle' (*Hymns Ancient and Modern*

Revised, 1950, 97). The chants are mainly Eastern in origin, and are sung as the ministers and people come up and kiss the cross.

In the Middle Ages, the ceremony was called 'Creeping to the Cross'. In 1955, the 'Restored Order of Holy Week' added to the solemnity of the rite, which in future is to take place in the afternoon and not in the morning, as has been the case for many centuries.

The veiled crucifix, taken from the sacristy (q.v.) to the altar between two taper bearers, is unveiled in three stages, at each of which 'Behold the wood of the cross' is sung, with the response 'Come, let us worship'. The crucifix is held upright, flanked by two candles, and the feet of the Crucified are kissed first by the ministers and then by the people, while the chants and hymn are sung.

The veneration and kissing of the cross on Good Friday are an act of worship to Christ the Redeemer of the world, and a wooden cross is merely an aid to this devotion.

                                                A. A. KING

Vernacular

Liturgy is of its nature social worship, and therefore must involve the use of audible communication between members of the worshipping community. *A priori* one would expect that the speech used would be in a language intelligible to all present, i.e. a vernacular. This is the natural, sensible and practical means of intercommunication.

History shows that all liturgies did, in fact, come into being in vernacular forms. No religious body using a liturgy has ever deliberately chosen to start with a liturgy in an unintelligible language. (Glossolaly constitutes no exception since it never hardened into liturgical forms.) Yet history shows also another fact which seems surprising: nearly all religions have come to, or passed through, a stage where they employed, either wholly or in part, a liturgy which worshippers understood with difficulty or not at all. The language was antiquated, dead or even foreign. There has been a contradiction between what would seem the natural thing and what actually happened.

No single cause suffices to explain this phenomenon; but some of the factors which produced it are these: (1) Mankind is innately conservative in matters of religion. For religious things are holy things; they are

thought to partake in some way of the unchangeableness of the divinity in whose honour they are said or done; it is felt to be improper to change them. Once a liturgy has settled down into a definite form, this form tends to persist from generation to generation as a precious heritage. Yet it is an inescapable fact that living languages change. Therefore if the language of a liturgy remains unchanged it becomes archaic; in time it becomes a dead language. (2) An antiquated or dead language, precisely because it is not a vernacular, comes to be considered as a sacred language. Its exclusive use in liturgy is rationalized in terms of the reverence due to the divinity who, it is felt, ought not to be addressed in the language used for fellow men (equals) but only in a very special and sacred style or language. Any attempt to change this sacral language is denounced as impious desecration. (3) A dead language is totally unintelligible. Its use in liturgy produces in the popular mind a mystification which, when allied to its 'sacredness', results in a 'sense of mystery' (more correctly described as a 'sense of the numinous'). As this is a very important element in any religion the fact that an unknown tongue fosters it militates against change. (4) It has often happened that some nation has been evangelized by foreign missionaries who already possess a traditional liturgy; this they have imposed, without any change in language, upon their converts. Thus, even if the language is living or merely archaic for the missionaries, it starts off among the converts as something unintelligible and foreign.

For these and other reasons there exists in all liturgies a tension between the need for intelligibility and the tendency to become stabilized, sacralized and mysterious. It is only when this tendency has become excessive that a reaction may set in and cause a demand for the use of the vernacular.

The Christian religion was faced with a choice at its very beginning, for it originated among the Jews. But they, in their temple liturgy and in their scriptures, employed the Hebrew language, a tongue that was archaic and hardly understood except by the learned. But in their synagogues Jewish worship, though partly in Hebrew, was largely in Aramaic, the then vernacular which was closely allied to Hebrew. Throughout the diaspora the Aramaic was replaced by Greek, then the common language outside Palestine. Faced with a choice of a dead or a living language, the Christian church unhesitatingly chose the latter. In Palestine the early Christian liturgy took shape in Aramaic; outside Palestine in Greek. But, though Greek was widely spoken in urban areas, it had never completely driven out native languages which were the vernaculars of country people. So when the Gentiles began to be converted they worshipped in their own tongues – Syriac, Armenian, Coptic and many others.

The early church had no inhibitions whatever about changing its liturgical language or translating scriptures into vernaculars. The classic instance of this flexibility is Rome itself where the liturgy started in Greek. This was because the first converts were the poor and humble, almost all from the Greek-speaking slave class. By the third century, however, many Christians were speaking Latin; during the next hundred years Greek died out in Rome. So the Greek liturgy was gradually replaced by Latin until Latin was the sole language for worship. However, in the seventh century many Greek merchants and craftsmen immigrated into Rome and formed quite a large colony there. This resulted in a partial return to Greek in public worship; the scriptures at mass and at vigils were read in Greek as well as in Latin; baptism and other sacraments were administered in either language. This practice continued as long as there was any need for both vernaculars. When Greek died out again only Latin (the remaining vernacular) sufficed. The original policy of the church was undoubtedly to use vernacular languages in worship, and this policy has remained unchanged in the East.

But in the West conditions were different, and a different policy ultimately prevailed. The East was fairly well civilized and its languages were developed; even though Greek became spoken almost everywhere, the other languages survived. But when the Romans conquered the West, its peoples were still uncivilized, and there were no developed languages. By the time Christianity began to spread into the West nearly all the inhabitants of the Roman empire spoke Latin, even if only vulgar Latin. For Latin had now become the vernacular; it had driven out all the undeveloped native languages which hardly survived anywhere.

Different liturgical rites, such as the Roman, the Gallican, the Celtic did indeed arise, but they were all in Latin from their very beginning. No other possibility existed.

This complete hegemony of Latin explains why the West has differed from the East in its policy about liturgical language. Latin was kept even when it ceased in later centuries to be the vernacular. As living languages always do, it gradually changed in different parts of the empire; there arose dialects which, after centuries of development, have ended up as Italian, French, Spanish and Portuguese. But Latin was retained as the language of the liturgy because it, too, had matured and given rise to Christian literature. All educated persons in the West remained able to speak and write Latin fluently until at least the fifteenth century. It was the language of culture, of government, of theology and even of commerce. But it was not the language of the common people who now could not understand the liturgy.

From time to time the need for the people to understand their worship was perceived and voiced, but the demands for a vernacular liturgy were usually small, localized and without result. A notable exception, however, was the missionary activity of St Cyril and St Methodius who, in the ninth century, evangelized the Slavonic peoples of Moravia. The whole story is immensely complicated, involving political intrigues, the Photian schism, forged documents and contradictory rulings by successive popes; but it all ended up with the establishment of a vernacular liturgy in the Slavonic tongue. In time permission was granted for the use of Dalmatian, Croatian, Slovenian and Czech (all of them Slavic languages). These are genuine vernaculars even today, though the tongue used by Cyril and Methodius, called Staro-Slav, is now archaic and thus but partially intelligible.

In the fourteenth century the Dominicans who had a house in Constantinople were allowed to celebrate their own (Latin) rite in the local Greek; others, working among the Armenians in Cilicia, translated the Dominican liturgy into Armenian. Missionaries in Georgia were likewise permitted to translate their Latin rite into the local vernacular.

In the sixteenth century came the great upheaval of the Reformation. Almost all Protestant Reformers demanded the use of the vernacular in the liturgy, but their reasons for this always involved dogmatic contentions judged by the Council of Trent to be heretical. The question was very thoroughly discussed at the Council; many of the bishops saw clearly that the replacement of Latin by vernacular languages (at least in parts of the liturgy) was in itself desirable. That is why the Council was careful not to condemn the vernacular as such; it decreed that its introduction was not at that time expedient. Because the language question was, in those days, so inextricably bound up with dogmatic positions, the Council could hardly have decided otherwise. Hence, for the next four centuries, Latin continued to be the official liturgical language of the western patriarchate of the Roman Catholic Church.

The Protestants, of course, took to the vernacular very quickly for some (usually for all) of their worship. Some of the churches dating from that era have vernacular liturgies of which the prayer-texts are 400 years old. As a result these texts have reached the stage of being archaic, and many voices are being raised in favour of modernization. There are new versions of prayers, new translations of holy scripture being used in public worship with or without authorization; there is a process of liturgical reform going on in nearly all the churches, and this usually entails a reform of rites and of texts now expressed in twentieth-century language, that is, in the current vernacular. These churches are acting before the original languages of their liturgies have become dead languages.

In the Roman Catholic Church the liturgical language had certainly reached the stage of being a dead language; its liturgical movement, which began with an aesthetic and archaeological phase about a century ago, became pastoral early in the present century. By the time of Pius XII it had become a reforming movement and its leaders were urging (against much powerful opposition) that the Latin liturgy should not only be reformed but also put, wholly or in part, into the vernacular. Partial concessions were granted to several countries and missionary dioceses; the movement grew in intensity and influence till the whole question was examined at the Second Vatican Council convened by Pope John XXIII. The upshot has been a radical reform which has included an almost complete adoption of the vernacular wherever this is feasible.

CLIFFORD HOWELL, SJ

Vespers *see* Canonical Hours

Vestments

There are four basic types of ecclesiastical vesture. First, the garments which are worn for the cultus, i.e. at the eucharist and at other sacramental ceremonies – these are vestments in a strict sense. Secondly, there is vesture which may be worn on other liturgical occasions. Thirdly, there are various items of clothing which indicate rank or specific role – including those of religious orders. Fourthly, there are garments which are, or have been, customary clerical dress on non-liturgical occasions – the civilian dress of the clergy.

A cross-division of these types also has to be made between the vesture of different sectors of the whole church – Eastern Orthodox Churches, Roman Catholic Church and various Reformed Western Churches. Further, it is necessary to consider in outline the historical succession of comparable garments and to trace derivation and development when this has occurred.

In addition to a purely descriptive account of vestments, it is also desirable to consider their significance as a means of communication – both liturgical and theological, and even political and personal.

The organization of such a mass of material creates many problems in the matter of presentation, and some framework of reference is necessary. At the risk of oversimplification, it is possible to state that ecclesiastical vesture can be studied from the proposition that there are two main garments and many accessories. The basic garments are: 1. an *indoor tunic*; 2. an *outdoor cloak*. The classical Christian form of the tunic is the white *alb*, while the cloak exists as both the *chasuble* and the *cope*. Derivatives and variations of the tunic include the following garments: tunicle, dalmatic, rochet, surplice and cotta. Obviously, in clement weather, indoor clothing may also be worn outside without an overgarment, just as, conversely, for ceremonial reasons, outdoor robes may be worn indoors. It should also be remembered that, though worn under a chasuble or cope, the tunic is an outer-garment rather than an under-garment.

The ecclesiastical accessories correspond generally to the accessories of convenience which are normally found in association with civilian dress at any period (e.g. handkerchief and napkin), and also with the rank insignia of the ceremonial dress of the officers of any institution or society. Ecclesiastical accessories, like the garments themselves, are conveniently considered under the following headings:

1. Liturgical (*a*) eucharistic or generally sacramental; (*b*) 'choir' or generally for other services of worship.

2. Non-liturgical (*a*) ceremonial; (*b*) civilian.

Since any classification is being imposed upon a range of costume which has developed 'organically' under a variety of influences, there are likely to be some items of dress which are difficult to classify or include in any general scheme. This qualification applies to those which are characteristic of a particular locality or period, and which belong mainly to the non-liturgical dress of dignitaries (e.g. Anglican apron and gaiters): for this reason, apart from pontificalia, they need not be discussed in this context. Several further considerations may be noted before a systematic description and discussion of the liturgical garments. First, the Christian vestments are derived primarily from the civilian dress of the late Roman empire and owe nothing directly to the vesture of the Jewish priesthood: the original differentiation and development from lay attire took place from the fourth to the ninth centuries. Secondly, they have undergone some changes corresponding to differences in the actual mode of conducting the rites and to the addition or omission of particular ceremonies. Thirdly, they have been subject to fashion, and to the availability of various types of material used for their manufacture and embellishment. In this connection the influence of the commercial church furnishers and haberdashers is not without significance. Fourthly, the changes in style reflect to some extent various ecclesiological and sacramental doctrines concerning the status and role of the ministers of the church and the nature of worship in general. Fifthly, like most ceremonial garments, some of their features have lost their original usefulness and survive as vestigial appendages which are no more than visual reminders of the continuity of Christian worship and

which, ultimately, may be abandoned (e.g. the maniple). Sixthly, vestments (in common with other 'church furnishings') have undergone periods of rejection and revival in the Western church and, at times, have become objects of controversy and symbols of party: their use may also be subject to law – both internal ecclesiastical regulations and external national enactments.

Each item of vesture will now be considered within the following scheme:

1. *Vestments of the Cultus*: alb, amice, girdle, stole, maniple, chasuble, dalmatic and tunicle.

2. *Other Liturgical and Clerical Garments*: cope, cassock, surplice, tippet and hood, almuce, mozetta, pallium, chimere, rochet and mitre.

3. *Eastern Orthodox Vesture*.

1. *Vestments of the Cultus*

(*a*) *Alb*. The ecclesiastical alb is directly derived from the *tunica alba* of classical times. It is now usually a long white tunic reaching to the feet, made of linen, and belted with a girdle or cincture at the waist: it has close-fitting sleeves and is collarless.

In antiquity such a garment existed in two forms – short and long. The knee-length Greek *chiton* was more like a modern shirt and was sometimes sleeveless. The long type, *chiton poderes* or *tunica talaris*, has either narrow sleeves (corresponding to the alb) or wide sleeves (corresponding to both the dalmatic and the surplice). If made of linen, the garment might be called *tunica linea*. On occasion two tunics might be worn – one as an undergarment and the other as an outer garment.

In the NT the word *chiton* is used in the saying: 'If a man wants to sue you for your shirt (*chiton*), let him have your coat (*himation*) as well' (Matt. 5.40). It is also used of the seamless tunic worn by Jesus (John 19.23) in contrast to his other garments (*himatia*) which were shared by the soldiers, and *chiton* is also implied in the description of the visionary personage of Revelation as being 'robed to his feet' (*chiton poderes*) (1.13).

The long white tunic was sometimes decorated with *clavi*, i.e. full length thin strips of purple or russet material – either a single stripe down the middle (front and back) *latus clavus*, or one such stripe over each shoulder. This elementary decoration probably served to cover and strengthen joins in the material, and was discontinued if the alb was to be worn under a dalmatic. Tunics so embellished were generally worn without a girdle and thus their character of verticality was emphasized. In addition, some early tunics carry similar decoration around the hem near the ground and thus suggest a basis for the medieval application of apparels.

The long white tunic which was worn generally by professional people did not really begin to become a specifically Christian vestment until the beginning of the fifth century. For example, in a transitional stage, Jerome (341-420) distinguishes between everyday clothing and a special 'suit of clean clothes' for wear in church. The mosaics at Ravenna show that by the sixth century it had become customary for bishops to wear not only the *paenula* (or chasuble) but also a wide-sleeved *tunica* (or dalmatic) over a narrow-sleeved alb (*see* Fig. 24). In S. Vitale, this is quite clear in the case of Archbishop Maximianus – the narrow sleeve of the under-tunic shows at his wrist; moreover, the edges of the wide surplice-like sleeves of his 'dalmatic' (like those of his two clerical attendants) are embellished with double

Fig. 24   Sixth-century vestments, Ravenna

purple stripes which correspond with the two full-length clavi. (It is not clear whether or not the assistants are wearing albs under their dalmatics.) Similarly, in S. Apollinare in Classe the narrow sleeves of the bishop's alb are plainly seen to emerge from the broader sleeves of his dalmatic.

Incidentally, the sleeves of the alb (or, more correctly in the East, the *sticherion*) are also decorated with double bands of what appears to be golden embroidery, corresponding to the later Eastern *epimanika* (detachable cuffs) and, more remotely, to wrist apparels of the alb in the West. This vestment, which is common to all the clergy in the Ravenna mosaics, is remarkably like the long medieval surplice in shape, but because of its context and its decoration is best understood as the forerunner of the later tunicle and dalmatic.

All ranks of the clergy wore the plain alb until the eleventh century, but at about this period two changes occurred in the West. First, a wide-sleeved and somewhat shorter version of the alb, namely the *surplice*, began to replace it as the clerical vestment for non-eucharistic worship, and also for wear by clergy and monks in choir. Secondly, there grew up a custom of applying apparels (*paramenta*), i.e. oblong pieces of richer material or embroidery attached to the cuffs, and also front and back in the middle near the ground: these *alba parata* were, perhaps, being forbidden by implication in the *First English Prayer Book* which orders 'a white Albe plain' to be worn by the priest.

The alb, plain or with apparels, and with only minor changes in fashion (e.g. amplitude of cut, use of lace or other decoration), has continued to be worn until the present day and, in a sense, is to be thought of as the archetypal 'white robe' of Christianity.

(*b*) *Amice.* The amice is a rectangular piece of linen which originated as a neckerchief used to protect other vestments from sweat. The Latin name *amictus* is derived from *amicio* which means 'to wrap around'. The Ravenna and other mosaics show that such a neck-cloth was not worn before the sixth century, and in the Eastern Orthodox churches it has never become an official vestment.

In the West, the amice slowly became adopted as an essential mass vestment from the eighth century onwards. The *Ordo Romanus Primus* refers to the amice (*ana-*

golagium) as being part of the pope's vesture, but *Ordo IV* (*c.*800) indicates that sub-deacons wore amices only when the pontiff was vested in a dalmatic. Other names used of the amice are *humerale* (shawl), *super-humerale* and *anaboladium*.

Originally, as was natural, the amice was not assumed until the alb had been put on. This earlier mode survives in the liturgies of Lyons and Milan, but generally the amice is now the first vestment to be donned. The latter custom derives from the tenth century when a longer hair style was fashionable and, in order to protect the other garments during vesting, the amice was first put on like a helmet and kept there until all the other vestments were in place. Thus the amice is provided with long tapes which are tied around the waist in order to keep it over the hair until vesting is complete. This procedure is further facilitated if a long narrow apparel is attached to the front of the amice so that when the 'helmet' is pushed back from the head the apparel forms a kind of collar. Medieval apparels accorded in colour with the stole and maniple and contrasted with that of the chasuble or dalmatic.

In spite of the medieval development of the amice into a hood, its origin as a protective neckerchief is attested by the admonition at the ordination of a sub-deacon that he receives the amice as the *castigatio vocis*.

(*c*) *Girdle*. It was normal to wear a girdle of some sort with the classical *tunica* simply for the sake of convenience in moving about. Thus, when the long *tunica alba* emerged as a Christian vestment it was accompanied by the customary *cingulum* and was recognized as such in the eighth century. Worn with a very full alb, the girdle is not visible and may be referred to as the *subcingulum* – especially in connection with the attachment to it of a deacon's napkin. In the Eastern Orthodox churches the deacon wears an ungirdled *sticharion*, and the corresponding belt, *zone*, is worn only by priests and bishops.

In the past, the girdle has taken the form of a broad belt or cincture of white or coloured material. Today it is usually a long white rope with tasselled ends. It is put on immediately after the alb and the ends of the stole are customarily tucked under or through it.

(*d*) *Stole*. The stole is a strip of material about four inches (ten centimetres) wide and up to twenty-six feet (eight metres) long. It may be made of white or coloured textiles and may be plain or embroidered. It is worn over one or both shoulders in distinctive ways by bishops, priests and deacons. It is normally worn immediately over the alb and under any other outer vestment, though there are some exceptions.

The remote origin of the stole is obscure: it may have been some sort of napkin or kerchief or, alternatively, it is more likely to have been a ceremonial garland worn in honour at a festival. However, there can be no doubt that its Christian use derives directly from a scarf worn by Roman officials as an ensign of rank, and there is much to be said for the view that the stole and the *pallium* (*see below*) have a common origin as a status symbol.

Under the civil law in the Theodosian Codex (AD 395) senators and consuls were ordered to wear a coloured scarf or pall over alb and paenula as a badge of office (cf. a mayor's chain). There seems little doubt that by this time the dignitaries of the church had adopted a similar ensign: bishops wore a *pallium* (*see* Plate 37) (equivalent to the Eastern *omophorion*) over the chasuble, while priests and deacons wore a corresponding scarf known as the *orarium*. This *orarium* was forbidden to sub-deacons by the Council of Laodicea (*c.*372), and is certainly the same vesture which, in the ninth century, is referred to as the *stola* received by deacons at ordination.

In the East the corresponding vestment of the deacon is still called the *orarion* and is a long narrow strip hanging down, back and front, from the left shoulder, while that of the priest is joined together in front and slipped over the neck – hence the name *epitrachelion*.

Much confusion has been caused by the fact that in the classical period, the Latin *stola* was the name of a long outer garment and, further, that this name corresponds to the NT use of *stole* for a similar flowing or festal raiment (e.g. Mark 16.5; Luke 15.22; Rev. 6.11). In a very remote way it is possible that the Roman scarf (or pallium) itself is derived from an earlier toga-like garment (also called pallium) which came to be closely folded length-wise and worn as a sign of rank, but even this possible derivation in no way connects the ecclesiastical stole with the classical *stola* or biblical *stole*. It is not known why the name was changed from the tra-

Plate 37 Pallium worn by Bishop Apollinare. The originally mid-sixth century apse mosaic in Ravenna, S. Apollinare in Classe, depicts the founder bishop vested in two albs – a tight-sleeved under-tunic decorated on the forearms with coloured bands and over this a wide-sleeved alb with vertical *clavi*. Over these he wears a chasuble, or phelonion, surmounted by the episcopal pallium. The saintly bishop stands in the *orans* posture of prayer with arms outstretched and hands upraised.

ditional *orarium* to *stola* from the ninth century onwards and, regrettable though it may be, there is now no alternative but to continue to use the word which was universally accepted by the thirteenth century.

Historically there have been many different ways of wearing the stole, but today the general Western practice is as follows: a deacon wears a stole as a sash over the left shoulder, fastening or looping it below the right arm; a priest wears the stole round the back of his neck and, when worn over an alb, crosses it on the breast, while, over a surplice, the ends are allowed to hang down vertically; a bishop always wears a stole in the latter manner.

The current Western custom that the bishop should wear a stole hanging straight down from both shoulders is not supported by the Byzantine mosaics at Ravenna where, with one exception, the bishops there depicted all wear a pallium over a chasuble instead of a stole beneath it: the exception is Archbishop Ecclesius (in the apse of S.

Vitale) who appears to be wearing both. (The validity of this evidence has been doubted, and it has been suggested that the mosaic in question was inaccurately re-made in the twelfth century.)

Apart from being worn at the eucharist, the stole is commonly worn in the Roman Catholic Church when administering the other sacraments, when preaching, and when hearing confessions.

In the course of time its form has been modified and its decoration varied. It remained long and narrow until the late Middle Ages, when it was shortened and the ends were made wider to accommodate more extensive decoration. From about the tenth century it became customary to embellish stoles with embroidery – usually with simple geometric patterns: sometimes fringes were attached to the ends. In the baroque period stoles became very short indeed and very heavily decorated. Stoles also came to be made of coloured material – originally, like orphreys and apparels, in contrast to the colour of the chasuble or other vestment, but in the post-Reformation period when the sequence of liturgical colours (q.v.) was stabilized, stoles were worn in the same colour as the chasuble or dalmatic.

During the Gothic revival stoles were again lengthened and commonly decorated with three crosses – one in the middle and one at each end. In the Evangelical sector of the Anglican Church, the stole is the only item of the early suit of liturgical vestments which is generally found acceptable.

(e) *Maniple*. The maniple of today is a strip of material some two to four inches wide (6-10 cms.), varying in length up to three feet (1 metre) or thereabouts: it is looped over the left wrist with some sort of fastening beneath. The maniple normally matches the stole both in material and decoration; its use is now discouraged in the Roman Catholic Church and it is not even mentioned in the new missal.

There is no doubt that this vestment derives directly from the rank ornament of a consul, the *mappa*, which he held in his right hand and waved as a signal for the games to begin: correspondingly, in the seventh century, the maniple of the pope was used as a signal for the beginning of a stational mass.

The *mappa* itself originated as a folded handkerchief or napkin which, since pockets were not a feature of classical clothing, was normally carried in the hand. Thus, a purely practical rectangle of linen developed into an ensign of rank and authority in the empire and in the church, and in the course of this development was known variously as *manipulus, mappula, sudarium, mantile, fano, manuale* and *sestace*.

For a long time the maniple continued to be carried in the hand (e.g. Archbishop Stigand in the Bayeux Tapestry) and, so far as deacons and sub-deacons were concerned, may well have served practical purposes well into the medieval period. However, it eventually became solely an ornament worn on the wrist, and other cloths were used to wipe the sacramental vessels and the hands and faces of the ministers.

Further, in the Middle Ages the maniple was commonly worn by all clerics, but it was subsequently restricted to those of at least the rank of sub-deacon.

(f) *Chasuble*. Chasuble and cope (*see below*) alike are derived from an outer cloak, *byrrhus, paenula*, or *lacerna*, generally worn in the Graeco-Roman world by all classes and both sexes. Made from a semi-circle (or more usually two quadrants) of about twelve feet (four metres) in diameter of woollen material, the two edges could be either sewn together to form a conical or tent-shaped cloak (a hole being left for the head), or joined together by a clasp to form an enveloping cape – in either case the garment would fall to cover the hands. The former type became known as a *casula*, or 'little house', from which the name chasuble is derived, while the latter type is the forerunner of the cope, or *cappa*, signifying 'topmost' garment. The 'overcoat' left by Paul at Troas is called *phelones* (II Tim. 4.13), and related words are used in the Eastern Orthodox churches for the vestment which corresponds to the chasuble – *phelonicon, felon, phenolion*, and *phainoles* – various equivalents of the Latin *paenula*.

The *paenula*-type chasuble has undergone many changes in the course of its ecclesiastical history (*see* Fig. 25) – mainly by way of reduction in size and increase in decoration, but also through being (so to speak) turned through a right-angle. The two quadrants of material which comprised the original chasuble were joined by two seams which appeared vertically in the middle of the front and back of the garment when worn: these seams were strengthened and hidden by narrow strips of braid which, since they often were woven with gold thread, came to be known as *orphreys* (*auriphrygia* or *Phrygian* gold). Subsequently the conical chasuble was cut away at the sides to give greater freedom to the arms, and eventually it was found to be more convenient to make this reduced chasuble by joining two shield-shaped pieces of material in such a way that the seams came along the shoulders and down the sides. The seams of such chasubles are not usually decorated, but non-functional vertical orphreys are often applied and provided with 'arms' to form a kind of cross – back and front.

Starting from a semi-circular design, it is obvious that this shape is easily modified, e.g. by increasing or reducing the extent of the notional circle by making the semi-circle a semi-oval, or by making the front smaller than the back.

Illustrations of various kinds from the sixth century onwards (by which time the chasuble had become a specifically ecclesi-

Plate 38   Full Gothic chasuble,
fourteenth-century Germany.

astical vestment) show that such modifications were made, but that, in general, the full
conical chasuble with its characteristic cres-
cent-shaped folds persisted until the thirteenth century. One variation was that there
was at times a tendency to make the bottom
of the front more pointed (e.g. the *phelonion*
of S. Apollinare in the apse mosaic at
Classis), and in the eleventh century there
appears to have been a temporary fashion
for cutting away a considerable part of the
front – not unlike the subsequent development of the *phelonion* in the Eastern Orthodox
churches.

From the tenth and eleventh centuries in
the West chasubles began to be made of much
richer materials, when the church became
wealthier and as silks became less expensive.
Until this time they had been made principally of fine wool and had been worn
generally by the clergy. The eighth-century
Ordo Romanus Primus documents the gradual

emergence of the chasuble as the distinctive
outer garment of the presiding celebrant
at the eucharist: at the stational mass only
the pontiff retained his *paenula* for the whole
of the mass. And in the ninth century
Amalarius of Metz reports that at the mass in
Rome the deacon removed his *paenula* before
the gospel and thenceforth rolled it in such a
way that he could wear it with his stole over
the left shoulder and under his right arm –
the so-called 'broad stole'.

By the thirteenth century, then, the
chasuble was established a rich 'high-priestly'
ornament (*see* Plate 38), but one which had
not lost the essential character of the original
garment. At this time, however, the ceremonial of the elevation of the host (q.v.) was
introduced into the eucharist. This meant
that the president had to raise his hands high
above his head in order that the congregation
might see the eucharistic bread since, by this
time, he no longer faced the worshippers but

Fig. 25 HISTORY OF THE CHASUBLE

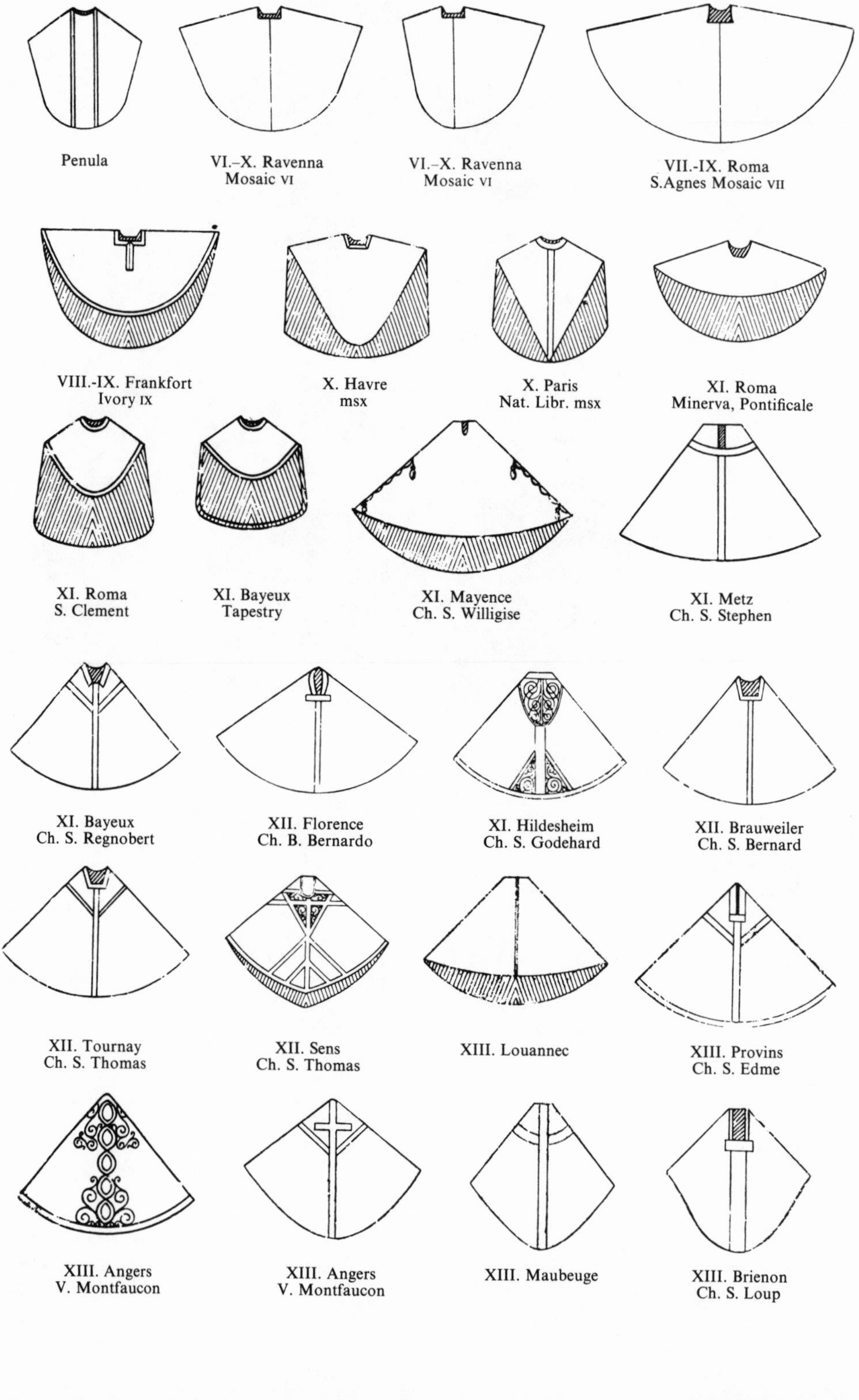

Penula

VI.–X. Ravenna
Mosaic VI

VI.–X. Ravenna
Mosaic VI

VII.-IX. Roma
S.Agnes Mosaic VII

VIII.-IX. Frankfort
Ivory IX

X. Havre
msx

X. Paris
Nat. Libr. msx

XI. Roma
Minerva, Pontificale

XI. Roma
S. Clement

XI. Bayeux
Tapestry

XI. Mayence
Ch. S. Willigise

XI. Metz
Ch. S. Stephen

XI. Bayeux
Ch. S. Regnobert

XII. Florence
Ch. B. Bernardo

XI. Hildesheim
Ch. S. Godehard

XII. Brauweiler
Ch. S. Bernard

XII. Tournay
Ch. S. Thomas

XII. Sens
Ch. S. Thomas

XIII. Louannec

XIII. Provins
Ch. S. Edme

XIII. Angers
V. Montfaucon

XIII. Angers
V. Montfaucon

XIII. Maubeuge

XIII. Brienon
Ch. S. Loup

BY THE MONUMENTS

XIII. Reims

XIII. Reims
Ch. for Deacon

XIII. Brunswick
mus.

XIII. Dreux
v. Montfaucon

XIII. Brussels
v. Bollandists

XIV. Aix la Chapelle

XIV. Roma
S. M. Transtav. tomb

XIV. Brussels
v. Bollandists

XIV. Cologn
Dominican Church

XIV. Vatican
Pontifical

XV. Roma
S. Peter a Vinc. tomb

XV. V. Baluze

XV. Coire

XV Dantzig
N. Dame

XV. Binche
Ch. S. Ursmer

XVI. Bern
Museum

XVI. Roma
Pict. Titian

XVI. Roma
Pict. Tintoretto

XVI. Florence
Cathedral

XVI. Brussels
Museum

XVI. Brussels
Museum

XVII. Roma
Pict Sacchi

XVII. Roma   XVII. Brussels   XVIII. Brussels
Pantheon   Museum   Museum

XVIII. Rheims
Cathedral

Roman Shape

Roman Shape
Cross at the back

French

Belgian

Austrian

Spanish

Brazilian

Polish

Austrian

Gothic

Large Gothic

Plate 39 Elevation in the eastward position at a medieval mass. Priest vested in a very full alb (girdle covered) with apparels on skirt and cuffs and on amice; stole not visible but maniple worn on left wrist. Chasuble thrown back for the elevation. Characteristic medieval altar with front and reredos. (*The Mass of St Giles*. Flemish diptych *c*. 1495. National Gallery, London.)

Plate 40 The Clare chasuble. Originally a full Gothic chasuble made and embroidered at the end of the thirteenth century – a splendid example of the *Opus Anglicanum*. Cut down to a baroque shape in the seventeenth or eighteenth century. (Victoria and Albert Museum, London.)

had his back to them. Therefore, either the front of the chasuble had to be thrown back over the shoulders, or the vestment had to be re-designed with cut-away sides giving greater freedom to the arms (*see* Plate 39). The latter practice prevailed and was carried a stage further still in the baroque style of the Counter-Reformation (*see* Plate 40).

From the late medieval period, the embellishment of the vestment with embroidery was vastly extended and this, together with an increased regard for liturgical colours (q.v.), endangered the very character of the vesture. The front of the chasuble was cut away even more and the way was prepared for the baroque 'ornament' which, by the seventeenth century, had really ceased to be a garment and had become merely a vehicle for the display of the highly developed art of embroidery with rich silks, velvets, metallic threads, pearls and jewels.

Such vestments continue in use, but the nineteenth-century Romantic Movement includes much ecclesiastical harking back to the fashions of the medieval period – real or supposed. This neo-medievalism of the Cambridge Ecclesiologists and of the Ritualists led to the advocacy of the so-called Gothic chasuble together with matching stole and maniple, and their mass-production by commercial interests in a period of rapidly expanding population and religious revival. These 'reproduction antiques' have been accepted as the only alternative to the baroque style up to the middle of the twentieth century, but recently further research and new designs have begun to replace them.

(*g*) *Dalmatic and Tunicle.* The dalmatic, like the tunicle, is essentially a variant form of the *tunica alba* or alb: the name *tunica dalmatica* would seem to indicate an origin in the region of Dalmatia. As a wide-sleeved over-tunic it was a popular garment in second century Rome and, in a somewhat shortened version, appears to be the garment worn by some praying figures in catacomb frescoes.

By the fourth century the dalmatic was commonly worn over an alb as part of the distinctive 'uniform' of both bishops and deacons, as may be clearly seen in the mosaic of Maximianus and his attendants in S. Vitale. The dalmatic did not, however, become a vestment until the ninth century or thereabouts. At this time it was formally accepted in the West that over the alb at the eucharist the priest wore a chasuble, the deacon a dalmatic, and the subdeacon a tunicle. In the Latin rite the dalmatic is bestowed upon the deacon at his ordination and, correspondingly, a simpler version of it, the tunicle, belongs to the subdeacon. The bishop continued to wear the dalmatic under the chasuble and, in the ninth century, some bishops adopted the practice of wearing a tunicle under the dalmatic on solemn occasions.

Originally, the dalmatic was made of white linen or wool, and, like the alb (*see above*), was decorated with two coloured strips, *clavi*, running from front to back over the shoulders: the original tunicle lacked such *clavi*. Later, the dalmatic was shortened to knee-length, the sleeves were cut broader still and slits were introduced at the sides. From the tenth century onwards the dalmatic, and to a somewhat lesser extent the tunicle, came to be made of richer materials and to be more elaborately decorated with apparels, orphreys, fringes and tassels. Thus, like the chasuble, dalmatic and tunicle tended to become ornaments rather than garments. They have, indeed, been regarded as festal vestments not to be worn in penitential seasons.

In Eastern Orthodox churches, a dalmatic-like vestment, the *sakkos* (*see below*), is worn only by bishops and, since the sixteenth century, has replaced the chasuble (*phelonion*) as the liturgical outer garment of Greek metropolitans and all Russian bishops.

(It may also be noted that during the coronation ceremony, the English sovereign is vested in a dalmatic.)

2. *Other Liturgical Garments*

(a) *Cope*. The cope, like the chasuble (*see above*), is a ceremonial version of an outdoor cloak commonly worn in the Roman empire. Basically it is a semi-circular piece of cloth worn around the shoulders and held together at the front by a clasp (morse). Apart from a curious deviation in the Church of England (*see below*), the cope is worn at non-eucharistic ceremonies (e.g. baptism, marriage, procession) in place of the chasuble: it may also replace the dalmatic or tunicle since its use is not restricted to bishops and priests.

The forerunner of the ecclesiastical cope was known by the name *cappa* (signifying 'topmost' garment) by the end of the sixth century, and other names by which it was known include *pluviale* (rain-coat'), *planeta* (possibly from the Greek word meaning 'to wander' or travel around) and *amphibalus* (a Gallican term).

The original *paenula* or *cappa* was often fitted with a hood, and as a functional garment made of thick black material (*cappa nigra*) continued to be worn in choir as a protection against cold throughout the Middle Ages. As increasingly the *cappa* became a ceremonial garment (probably from the sixth century onwards), so the hood ceased to be functional and eventually was reduced to a triangular or shield-shaped decoration on the back.

The employment of silks and other expensive materials, together with the use of embroidery and other means of embellishment of the cope, has run parallel to that of the chasuble. A certain variation in style has occurred, but apart from the reduction of the hood to a vestigial flap, there has been no substantial change in its form. In the West the cope is a general ecclesiastical robe of splendour and has never been a distinctive clerical vestment. There is no liturgical equivalent to the cope in the Eastern Orthodox churches, though cope-like mantles are worn on occasion by some bishops.

At the time of the Reformation in England, the *BCP* of 1549 ordered the parish priest at the eucharist to wear 'a vestment (i.e. chasuble, stole and maniple) or cope': this rubric was withdrawn in 1552, but in Canon XXIV (1604) it was ruled that the principal minister at the communion in cathedrals and collegiate churches should wear a coloured cope over a plain alb. This custom is still observed in some cathedrals and ex-collegiate churches in spite of the fact that a cope is an extremely inconvenient garment in which to perform the eucharistic actions and gestures.

Oddly enough, in the S. Vitale mosaic of Melchizedek offering bread, the priest-king appears to be attired in a 'cut-away' cope: this is probably an imagined Jewish vestment, though it may reflect some aspects of sixth-century Christian ceremonial clothing.

Also in S. Vitale the emperor Justinian is shown wearing a hoodless ceremonial *paenula* fastened with a clasp on his right shoulder, thus leaving his right arm free. Some modern copes may be worn in this way as well as in the more customary manner.

(*b*) *Cassock*. The cassock is now an ankle-length tunic with long narrow sleeves; it is usually girt at the waist with a belt or cincture, but may be buttoned from neck to foot; it may be of any colour (*see* **Colours, Liturgical**). Its form and use demonstrate the difficulty of classifying the garments worn by the clergy: thus, it is universally worn under the eucharistic vestments and all other liturgical garments, but it is not itself a vestment. Again, although it is an under-garment, as the Latin name *subtanea* (soutaine) indicates, it is also worn as an over-garment for wear indoors and outdoors. Further, the cassock is not an exclusively clerical garment and may be worn by servers, choristers, vergers and other ecclesiastical persons.

The word in English is derived from Italian *cassaca*, or French *casaque*, possibly themselves derived from the name of a barbarian tunic known in the second century as *caracalla*. A long tunic, *vestis talaris*, was part of normal civilian dress in the late Roman empire, but when under barbarian influence (*c.* sixth century) lay fashions became shorter and more military, the clergy retained the ankle-length coat. Its use was ordered by the Council of Braga (572) and, in one form or another, it has subsequently been an important element in the distinctive attire of the clergy. Thus, the Anglican Canon LXXIV (1604) forbade beneficed clergy to go out in public 'in their doublet and hose without coats or cassocks' and, together with gown, hood, scarf and square cap, this comprised the outdoor dress of the clergy until the beginning of the nineteenth century. (Correspondingly, Roman Catholic clergy were forbidden by law to wear cassocks in public in England.) Cassocks have from time to time been fitted with hoods or capes and, unless worn with an academic hood, are often still so designed. In the medieval period in cold regions cassocks were lined with fur or sheepskin (*pellicia*), hence the wide-sleeved full alb worn over the bulky lined cassock acquired the name 'surplice'. Very full cassocks with a train were fashionable for prelates in the fifteenth and sixteenth centuries but are no longer favoured. In contrast, in the eighteenth century the cassock was shortened to form an 'apron' for horse-riding bishops, deans and archdeacons and, together with corresponding gaiters, forms an outfit still affected by some dignitaries. The ministers of the Reformed churches (apart from some Methodists) do not normally cover their civilian clothes with a cassock, but prefer simply to wear a version of the medieval gown (known as 'Geneva' gown) with or without an academic hood, for liturgical or other ceremonial occasions. Gowns and hoods are not, of course, exclusively items of ministerial attire and are worn as ceremonial dress not only by churchmen but by academics and lawyers: it is often the case that two linen strips called 'bands' are worn in place of a tie or stock when a cassock or gown is worn. The decline in the practice of wearing a cassock as distinctive outdoor dress by clergy of the Church of England coincided with the separation of the neckerchief into collar and tie shortly before the middle of the nineteenth century. At about this time the back-fastening so-called Roman collar was devised to be worn with a black stock and without a tie. Until recently it was universally worn as a 'label' by ministers of virtually all denominations, sects and faiths, and the cut of the neck of cassocks was adjusted to accommodate it. Since about 1965 increasing numbers of clergy have abandoned the clerical collar and in their outdoor everyday attire are as indistinguishable from their fellows as were their predecessors in the first five centuries or so in the life of the church.

(*c*) *Surplice*. The surplice is a wide-sleeved ample version of the linen alb which was adopted in northern countries in the twelfth century for wear over fur-lined cassocks, hence the name: *superpelliceum* = over a fur garment. The actual shape of the surplice (as distinct from the name) is much earlier, as may be seen in the sixth-century mosaics of the bishops in S. Apollinare in Classe; apart from the decorative *clavi*, their albs are identical in form with the medieval surplice.

From the twelfth century onwards the surplice became the distinctive dress of the lower clergy and was worn by priests outside the mass: today it is commonly worn over the cassock by both clerics and laymen in choir or otherwise assisting in the conduct of worship.

Originally ankle-length, the surplice was progressively shortened and by the eighteenth century on the Continent barely reached the waist and had short sleeves: in this form it is known as the *cotta*. In the Roman Catholic Church it has also been trimmed with lace from the sixteenth century onwards. The surplice now exists in many different styles and, from time to time, attempts are made to restore its original simplicity and amplitude.

In the Church of England it has been a prescribed eucharistic vestment since Elizabethan times (*see below*).

(*d*) *Tippet and hood.* The long black scarf worn by Anglican clergy over the surplice. The exact origin of this ecclesiastical accessory is as obscure as its Latin name *liripipium* (liripipe or typet), though it is probable that it derives from an appendage of the medieval hood – either the 'poke' which hung down at the back or extensions of the cape which hung down at the front. In either case, hood and scarf would appear to be separated parts of the same garment – just as collar and tie are derived from the single neckerchief. In the fifteenth century the hood was commonly worn over the surplice and then, having been adopted by the universities as a token of graduation and given distinctive colours and linings, was further accepted in its academic form in the emergent Anglican Church as part of the choir habit of the clergy. The 1549 *BCP* recommends the hood as 'seemly' for preachers and the 1604 Canons (XXV and LVIII) order it for all graduate ministers. Correspondingly, non-graduates are ordered to wear a tippet instead of a hood in church. For outdoor wear Canon LXXIV orders all clergy to wear the tippet over a gown (*see below*).

(*e*) *Almuce.* This garment originated as a protection for the head and shoulders against the winter cold of medieval churches and, in the course of time, became a mark of rank or distinction. Originally either a lined hood or a fur scarf worn over the surplice, it emerged as a fur-lined hood with two ends hanging down in front and was regarded as part of the choir habit. The colour and the type of fur of the almuce came to have hierarchical significance – grey squirrel being the highest ranking and reserved for bishops and cathedral canons. Its used was discontinued in the Established Church under Elizabeth I when it became customary to wear a black tippet or scarf.

A transitional stage may be noted at St Paul's Cathedral when in 1549 it is recorded that minor canons wore 'tippets like other priests' instead of their almuces.

The name almuce (Latin *almutia*) sometimes appears as 'amess' or even 'amice', and confusion with the eucharistic amice must be avoided.

(*f*) *Mozetta.* A short hooded cape of coloured silk or fur worn over a cope by pope, cardinals, abbots, bishops and other dignitaries of the Roman Catholic Church. Probably derived from the almuce (*see above*) which it has largely replaced.

(*g*) *Pallium.* A narrow band of white woollen material, marked with six dark crosses, and worn in one way or another around the neck and over the shoulders by patriarchs, archbishops and some other bishops. In the Roman Catholic Church it is now usually in the form of a circular band with two hanging strips back and front, but in the Ravenna mosaics the bishops all wear a straight band looped over the shoulders with the ends hanging down back and front from the left shoulder: it is still so worn in the Eastern Orthodox Churches and is called the *omophorion*.

In the Codex of Theodosius (395), a scarf or pall of several colours is ordered to be worn over the *paenula* by senators as an ensign of their rank; shortly afterwards this civil ornament became a distinctive badge of episcopal status. In the West the custom grew of reserving the pallium to archbishops who received it directly from the pope as a sign of their jurisdiction: the pope also acquired discretion to confer it on other bishops.

(It is a matter of dispute whether or not the 'scarf-pallium' is derived from the classical 'wrap-round' toga-like *pallium*: some writers believe that the latter was folded to form a narrow bundle and then reduced to the size of an ornament.)

(*h*) *Chimere.* A silk or satin sleeveless gown, black or scarlet, now worn by Anglican bishops and doctors of divinity. The name may be derived from the Spanish *zamarra*, and by the twelfth century the chimere was a short cloak worn by bishops when riding horseback. In a longer version it soon became part of the customary attire of bishops on both liturgical and civil occasions.

(*i*) *Rochet.* A variant form of the alb with

narrow sleeves, or without sleeves, which was in general use by clerics, sacristans, servers, etc., up to the thirteenth century. Later it became the prerogative of bishops, cardinals and canons regular.

Contrary to its origin as a convenient sleeveless 'dust-coat', the rochet of Anglican bishops (as worn under the chimere) acquired full lawn sleeves gathered at the wrist: in the eighteenth century the sleeves became so voluminous that they were commonly sewn to the chimere.

(*j*) *Mitre*. The origin of the mitre is obscure, but by the eleventh century it has emerged as the distinctive liturgical hat of bishops. Its shape has undergone many changes, starting from a simple conical cap of white linen with two lappets (or fanons) hanging down at the back. Subsequently, in the twelfth century, there was a front-to-back dent in this cap, but a century later the dented cap was being worn the other way round and the present form of a tall divided hat began to develop. In the thirteenth century three types of mitre are recognized in Roman ceremonial corresponding with different degrees of ceremony – *mitra pretiosa* (jewelled), *mitra aurifrigiata* (decorated without jewels) and *mitra simplex*.

The wearing of a mitre is not entirely restricted to bishops in the West, and some abbots and cardinals have been granted the privilege.

The Eastern Orthodox form of the mitre (*mitra*) resembles the Byzantine imperial crown and is sometimes worn by archpriests.

3. *Eastern Orthodox Vesture*. Deriving from the same source, the vestments and ornaments of the Eastern Orthodox churches are basically similar to those of the West. The differences arise either from the 'fixing' of a particular form or style in the East in contrast to Gothic and subsequent developments in the West, or to minor additions or variations following the Great Schism which have no parallel in the West. Broadly speaking, the vestments in use in the Eastern Orthodox churches are all 'eucharistic', and with only minor modifications are worn at all services; i.e., such garments as cope, surplice, tippet, hood, etc., have never come into existence.

Most of the corresponding Eastern vestments have been mentioned in the above account and the same order will be followed in this summary:

(*a*) *Corresponding vestments*
Sticharion or Stikir. The liturgical tunic, equivalent to the alb, but usually of coloured material.

Zone. Equivalent of the girdle but usually fitted with a clasp.

Epitrachelion. Corresponding to the stole, but a broad band with the ends joined together from the chest downwards to leave an opening for the head. Usually made of silk or brocade and ornamented with metal and jewels. Worn by bishops and priests.

Orarion. A narrow band of silk, also corresponding to the stole, but worn by deacons over the left shoulder with ends either hanging straight down back and front or arranged otherwise.

Phelonion. Equivalent to the Western chasuble and worn by all bishops and priests. From the eleventh century the white phelonion of a patriarch began to be embroidered all over with crosses (*polystaurion*), and from the fourteenth century this decoration was used for the vestments of all bishops. In the Russian church the phelonion (or *felon*) is cut away at the front from the breast downwards while at the back it falls to the feet and covers the arms at the sides. Since the fall of Constantinople in 1453 the phelonion has been replaced by the *sakkos* (*see below*) in the Byzantine rite by all bishops.

(*b*) *Western vesture without equivalent in Eastern Orthodox churches*
Amice.

Maniple (but see *Epimanikia*).

Cope (a modern form of phelonion in the Armenian and Syrian churches is open at the front like a cope).

Dalmatic (but see *Sakkos*).

(*c*) *Eastern vesture without equivalent in the West*
Epimanikia. Cuffs of embroidered silk worn over the sleeves of the sticharion of bishops and priests and known from the eleventh century. They take the place of the Western maniple but are not really its equivalent.

Epigonation. A lozenge-shaped ornament suspended from the *zone* on the right side in the Greek and Armenian churches (*see* Fig. 26) (*cf*. the decoration worn by Emperor Justinian and his courtiers in the mosaic in Ravenna, S. Vitale). It probably originated as a functional handkerchief and, in this sense, would correspond to the Western maniple.

Fig.26 Epigonation

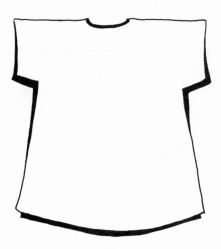

Fig. 27 Sakkos

Sakkos. An ample tunic with short wide sleeves and slit at the sides (*see* Fig. 27). Such a garment was one of the ceremonial vestments of the Byzantine emperors and it may well have a common origin with the Western dalmatic. As a liturgical vestment it appears at first to have been a mark of imperial favour for selected patriarchs, but by the thirteenth century it was worn by all

patriarchs and metropolitans at Christmas, Easter and Whitsun. After the fall of Constantinople it gradually came to be worn generally by all bishops.

The outdoor dress of Eastern Orthodox clerics is basically cassock, gown and hat: priest-monks and bishops wear a veil on the hat. There is considerable variety from one country to another in the type of hat. Black is most usual colour, but some patriarchs wear white and other hierarchs wear Roman purple belts.

4. *The Role of Vestments.* Liturgical vestments comprise a special case of ceremonial clothing and are, therefore, part of a complex pattern of communication. They serve both to express the nature of the occasion when they are worn and to distinguish the respective role and rank of each participant. Until the church began to be 'imperialized' under Constantine, the ministers (bishops, presbyters and deacons) wore their everyday civilian clothing in the acts of worship of the community: at the Reformation, and again recently, attempts have been made to revert to the principle that contemporary lay clothes should be worn by all at the eucharist and other services. Thus, characteristically clothing becomes an item in a movement of protest – in these cases against alleged distortions of both sacramental doctrine and hierarchial authoritarianism. And in this way, vestments (themselves derived from ordinary clothing) become badges of party in ecclesiastical conflicts.

This 'political' significance of vestments is, of course, in addition to the allegorical meanings which have been attributed to them and to their more profoundly religious significance associated with concepts of transcendence, incarnation, majesty, priesthood, mystery, revelation, sacrifice and communion. However, on all sides, it is recognized that whatever particular meanings vestments may have acquired, there must, from time to time, be an appraisal of the symbolism of vesture and its relevance and effectiveness in the total communication pattern of worship. Psychologically, it seems that people who engage in the corporate performance of ritual desire that some, if not all, of the participants should wear special clothing. The question then tends to resolve itself into: What type of special clothing? In the church the emphasis has tended to be upon the expression of historical continuity

and, hence, each succeeding style has been a
modification or a revival of a previous one.
Thus, any sector of the church is faced with
the further question: To what point in the
historical development of vesture shall we
seek to return? Roman Catholics, some
Anglicans and some Lutherans favour
modern versions of Gothic, Gothic-revival
and even Baroque styles, while Protestants
generally are content with the everyday gown
as worn by Renaissance Puritans.

There are, then, three basic choices: first, to
dispense with ceremonial clothing; secondly
to modernize or modify a particular historic
style; thirdly, to attempt to design vestments
which express a renewed understanding of
Christian liturgical celebrations (*see* Plate 41).

Plate 41   Roman Catholic priest in lay dress for
liturgy. At this experimental mass in a Jesuit high
school chapel in Amsterdam the priest wore lay
clothes for the synaxis but put on a grey gown for
the eucharist itself.

The first choice perhaps needs to be made
from time to time in order to highlight the
underlying problems, but only a minority of
worshippers is ever likely to accept the
absence of all special clothing as a permanent
solution.

The second choice finds clear expression in
the most recent Roman Catholic regulations:
the *Ordo Missae* (1969) states unequivocally
that 'the vestment common to all ministers is
the alb' and that, if necessary, it should be
tied at the waist with a cincture. Also
optional is the amice, and the maniple is not
mentioned at all. A surplice may replace the
alb: a stole may be worn with it, but not a
chasuble, dalmatic or tunicle. A cope may be
worn in processions and some other services.
Vestments may be made of either traditional
materials or natural regional fabrics; artificial fabrics may be used for vestments provided they are 'in keeping with the dignity
of the sacred action and the person wearing
them'. The 'instruction' assumes that the
traditional vestments (except the maniple)
will be worn for the celebration of the mass
and that they will constitute an external
demonstration of the diversity of function of
members of the body of Christ in worship:
the possibility that the ministers should wear
ordinary lay clothes is not considered.

This attitude, welcome though it is, does
not really go far enough at a time when there
is a confluence of the Liturgical Movement
(q.v.) and the Ecumenical Movement, creating a situation in which all 'sides' may be
willing to accept similar well-designed simple
robes. Increasingly, Roman Catholics realize
that most of their customary vestments now
have little meaning, while some Protestants
recognize the fact that quasi-academic gowns
are not entirely appropriate for the *celebration*
of sacraments. The restoration of greater lay
participation in the ceremonies provides an
opportunity for a fresh appraisal of the
functional character of vestments in a purely
practical sense of convenience for movement,
posture and gesture as well as in the symbolic
senses of cultic hierarchy and historical
continuity.

Outstanding in the field of re-designed
vestments is the work of Sr Flüeler (*see* Plate
42): she has designed and made a new form of
wide-sleeved *tunika* which may be worn
directly over the civilian clothing of the
minister. In a single off-white garment – at
once dignified and practical – the functions
of both alb and cassock are combined: as a
free-falling tunic it is essentially an outer
garment and, therefore, does not require a
chasuble to be worn over it because it already
has the 'enshrouding' quality of sacred
vesture, though, obviously, either a chasuble
or a cope may be worn over it, if desired (*see*
Plate 43). A long stole has been designed to

Plate 42   Basilican mass in modern vestments. The vestment worn by all the sacred ministers is the wide-sleeved *tunika* designed by Sr Flüeler at Stans, Switzerland. The celebration is in the modern college chapel at Sarnen.

Plate 43   Modern alb, stole and chasuble. The wide-sleeved alb functions as both cassock and alb and may be worn directly over everyday clothes: the *tunika* is made from commercially produced material but the stole is hand-woven. The chasuble is optional and the vestments appear 'complete' without it; alternatively, a cope may be worn with the fastening either at the centre or on the right shoulder. Vestments designed by Sr Flüeler at Stans.

wear with the *tunika* in such a way that a pleasing draped effect can be obtained and, further, a number of variations of the basic garment have been designed to make possible a distinction between the various ranks of ministers. It is easy to imagine that such new garments would be perfectly acceptable to most Protestants and, thus, it would be possible to use a vestment as an aid to Christian unity and not as a badge of division. This is already happening in an Anglican-Methodist shared church in Birmingham where the vesture of the ministers is identical, namely, an inexpensive version of the off-white combined cassock-alb now commercially available in England.

Archbishop's Commission, *The Canon Law of the Church of England*, 1947; G. R. Balleine, *A History of the Evangelical Party*, 1908/51; J. Braun, *Die Liturgische Gewandung im Occident und Orient nach Ursprung und Entwicklung, Verwandung und Symbolik*, 1907; O. Chadwick, *The Victorian Church*, 1966; H. J. Clayton, *The Ornaments of the Ministers as shown on Monumental Brasses*, 1919; H. J. Clayton, *Cassock and Gown*, 1929; Convocation of Canterbury, *The Ornaments of the Church and its Ministers: Upper House Report 416*, 1908; P. Dearmer, *The Ornaments of the Ministers*, 1908/20; P. Dearmer, *The Linen Ornaments of the Church*, 1929; A. Flüeler, *Das Sakrale Gewand*, 1964; A. K. Fortescue, *The Vestments of the Roman Rite*, 1912; A. K. Fortescue and J. B. O'Connell, *The Ceremonies of the Roman Rite*, 1917; H. Gee, *The Elizabethan Prayer Book and Ornaments*, 1902; J. A. Jungmann, *The Mass of the Roman Rite*, rev. ed., 1959; J. W. Legg, *Church Ornaments and their Civil Antecedents*, 1917; J. T. Micklethwaite, *The Ornaments of the Rubric*, 1897; H. Norris, *Church Vestments*, 1949; *Ordo Missae* 1969; C. E. Pocknee, *Liturgical Vesture*, 1960; C. E. Pocknee, *The Christian Altar*, 1963; F. Procter and W. H. Frere, *The Book of Common Prayer*, new rev. ed. 1961.

GILBERT COPE

Vestry

A side room in a church where the clergy and/or choir may vest or dress. The term is virtually synonymous with sacristy (q.v.).

EDITOR

Visitation *see* Mariological Feasts

Watch-Night

Watch-night is the British Methodist form of vigil-service, now generally confined to the New Year's Eve.

The watch-night began in spontaneous meetings held by enthusiastic Methodists in Kingswood (a mining area near Bristol), who often spent 'the greater part of the night in prayer, and praise, and thanksgiving'. Discovering these unofficial gatherings, probably in the early spring of 1742, John Wesley adopted and regularized the idea (*see* **Covenant Services**).

Within a few months the watch-night had become a regular event at the main Methodist centres (Bristol, London, Newcastle), held from about 8.30 p.m. to about 12.30 a.m. on the Friday nearest the full moon, so that members walked safely home through moonlit streets. It was also held on public and Methodist fast-days, and especially on New Year's Eve. (This may have been suggested by folk-customs of 'seeing in' the New Year; where such folk-customs are still lively, the watch-night remains popular.) Through the nineteenth century, the watch-night came to be restricted to the New Year, possibly because such a service, to be psychologically effective, needs some defined moment to aim at (namely, the 'seeing in' of the year). In some areas, Anglican and Free Churches adopted this New Year watch-night. At present, services of a 'vigil'-type for great festivals (Christmas midnight communion) and nights of intercession for world need appear to be winning favour in Methodism, while the New Year's Eve service is losing it.

The first watch-nights were preaching-services designed to deepen the spiritual life. Later themes are light and darkness, newness of Christian life, shortness of human life and imminence of judgment, or 'solemn praise to God for continuing his great work in our land' (John Wesley, *Journal*, 31 December 1777).

L. F. Church, *More about the Early Methodist People*, 1949; Charles Wesley, *Hymns for the Watch-Night*, 1744; Charles Wesley, *Hymns for New Year's Day*, 1750, 1766; John Wesley, *Journal*, ed, N. Curnock, 8 vols., 1909-16; John Wesley, *Plain Account of the People called Methodists*, 1749.

DAVID TRIPP

West Syrian Worship

1. *Introduction.* The West Syrian Church, known to many as 'Jacobite' (after Jacob Baradeus, the sixth-century reorganizer of the West Syrian Church) and as Monophysite (after the erroneous idea prevailing in Byzantium and the Latin West that the West Syrians believed only in the divine nature of Christ), historically inherited the Semitic, Palestinian tradition of Christianity, though not uninfluenced by the Hellenistic milieu in which they lived.

The Syrian tradition broke up soon into four families – the East Syrian (Edessa), the West Syrian (Antioch), the Melchite (Greek), and the Maronite (Lebanon).

2. *Liturgical rites.* The West Syrian Church has probably the richest and most diverse heritage in respect of eucharistic anaphorae and canonical offices (qq.v.). In addition to these there are the rites of baptism and chrismation of which three different forms are known. Ordination rites also vary substantially; the whole liturgical corpus also includes rites of matrimony (separate rites for first and second marriages), burial (different for clergy, laymen, women and children), anointing of the sick (not extreme unction – again different for clergy and laity), profession of monks, consecration of churches and altars, translation of relics, etc.

3. *The eucharistic liturgy.* The liturgy is nowadays celebrated mostly in the vernacular – Arabic in the Middle East, English in America, Malayalam in India and so on – though certain portions may still be said by the priest in Syriac. The officiating priest and the people alternate in practically all the prayers, and the deacon plays an important part, admonishing and directing the people to stand with fear, pray and understand the nature of the event that is going on in the liturgy. Choirs have not been allowed to usurp the place of the congregation as in certain other Eastern liturgies.

Some scholars have spoken of a hundred different West Syrian anaphorae, though only about seventy can be traced by the present writer. Some of these, especially the principal Anaphora of St James, go back in their basic structure to the Jerusalem church of apostolic times. Other anaphorae come from the second (Ignatius of Antioch) to the fourteenth centuries, if we take the names of

the anaphorae at face value. New liturgies continued to be created in every century up to the fourteenth, though production was most prolific from the fourth to the seventh. The twelfth century produced at least six new anaphorae and about the same number was produced in the thirteenth. With the thirteenth century the development reached its peak in Gregory Bar-Hebreus and has remained more or less static ever since.

Two peculiarities of the West Syrian rite are (1) the liturgy of incense between the liturgy of the word and the liturgy of the eucharist proper; (2) the prayer of adieu to the altar at the end of the liturgy. The liturgy of incense, which recalls the offering of incense in the Temple (Ex. 30.1-10), seems to have replaced the dismissal of the catechumens, and comprises a general absolution of the priest and people before the offering of the eucharistic sacrifice. It also represents a sort of offertory; incense (q.v.) symbolizes the good works and prayers which are well-pleasing to God. It symbolizes also the prayers of the departed saints which mix with those of the congregation, as a true spiritual offering of praise and adoration.

The epiclesis occurs in all the seventy known liturgies, though the form of the epiclesis varies verbally from anaphora to anaphora, as also does the verbal content of the 'words of institution'.

Not all the seventy anaphorae are in common use. The ones most commonly used in India are St James (on all principal feasts, for the first eucharist offered by a priest, or offered at a new altar), Dionysius Bar Salibhi, St John Chrysostom and St John the Evangelist.

The canonical offices for ordinary days are called the *Shimo*, and have recently been translated into English by the Benedictine Fr Griffiths. The more elaborate office, the *Fenqith*, has not yet been translated into English or Malayalam and is rarely used even in the Syriac. The Syriac text of the Fenqith is available in an Indian edition as well as in a Mosul edition (1886-1896).

One major feature of the eucharistic liturgy and the daily offices is the *Sedro*, a long meditative-homiletical prayer, preceded by a proemion which seems to be an elaborated form of the *Gloria*. These prayers are rich in theological content, and play a considerable role in the religious education of the faithful, especially in the absence of biblical preaching.

An introduction and critical text of the Syriac anaphorae with Latin translation have been published by the Pontifical Oriental Institute in Rome (*Anaphorae Syriacae*, 1953). The ninth-century commentary of Moses Bar Kepha on the Syrian liturgies was published with an English translation by R. H. Connolly and H. W. Codrington (*Two Commentaries on the Jacobite Liturgy*.).

The people communicate rather rarely, the legal minimum of once per year being observed by most, usually on Holy Thursday. Communion is in both kinds, usually by intinction for the laity. The priest usually administers, though the deacon is allowed to serve communion to the laity.

Reservation of the sacrament for adoration is forbidden; it may be reserved in case of need for the sick, and for those who fast till the evening.

Confession before communion is often demanded, though this is not necessary for those who communicate frequently. Fasting from the previous midnight is required.

The lections during the liturgy of the word are three, one from the Acts or catholic epistles (representing the twelve), then from the Pauline epistles, and then finally the gospel, which is read with great ceremony by the officiating priest. Sermons had gone out of use, but are coming back more recently as priests become better trained.

The creed recited is the Niceno-Constantinopolitan, introduced into the liturgy by Peter the Fuller in the fifth century as an anti-Chalcedonian measure.

Two of the West Syrian anaphorae, those of Matthew the Shepherd and Sixtus of Rome, lack the actual words of institution. The latter says: 'He, when he was prepared for his saving passion, by the bread which by him was blessed, broken and divided among his holy Apostles, gave us his propitiatory body for life eternal; in a like manner, also by the cup . . .'.

The canon of the mass, with words of institution, anamnesis and epiclesis (qq.v.) is said aloud by the priest, with responses from the people.

A. Fortescue, *The Lesser Eastern Churches*, 1913; W. de Vries, *Sakramententheologie bei den Syrischen Monophysiten*, 1940; I. Ziade, 'Syrienne' (église), *DTC*, XIV, cols. 3017-88.

PAUL VERGHESE

Westward Position
see Postures (1*c*)

Whitsunday
The English title for Pentecost (q.v.), so-called from its association with the white robes of baptism.

Words of Administration
The words of administration are those that accompany the giving of the sacramental bread and wine to the communicants at the eucharist. The earliest recorded formula is that preserved by Hippolytus (*Ap.Trad.* 23.5) concerning the bread: 'The bread of heaven in Christ Jesus', to which the recipient responds with 'Amen'. The same answer is made to the words of the priest in the Ambrosian rite – 'The Body of Christ' – and in the *Apostolic Constitutions*, where the formulae are: 'The Body of Christ . . . The Blood of Christ, the Cup of Life.' In the Byzantine liturgy the formula reads: 'The servant of God N. partakes of the precious and holy Body and Blood of our Lord and Saviour Jesus Christ for forgiveness of his sins and life eternal.' The form in the Roman mass is that of a blessing, adopted in the eighth century: 'The Body of our Lord Jesus Christ preserve thy soul unto everlasting life.' Indeed, the words in all orders are variations and expansions of those current in the patristic period; so, for example, those in the rite of the Church of South India are: 'The Body of our Lord Jesus Christ, the Bread of Life . . . the Blood of our Lord Jesus Christ, the True Vine.' Within the Church of England, there was a fusion in 1559 of the 1549 words, which were close to the old formulae, and those of 1552, which were substituted in accordance with the views of the European Reformers and avoided calling the elements the body and the blood of Christ.

EDITOR

MIND⇔BODY DECEPTIONS

The Psychosomatics of Everyday Life

MIND ⇔ BODY DECEPTIONS

The Psychosomatics of Everyday Life

STEVEN L. DUBOVSKY, M.D.

W. W. NORTON & COMPANY, INC.

NEW YORK / LONDON

Library of Congress Cataloging-in-Publication Data

Dubovsky, Steven L.
  Mind-body deceptions : the psychosomatics of everyday life /
Steven L. Dubovsky.
        p.   cm.
  Includes bibliographical references and index.
  ISBN 0-393-02943-3
  1. Medicine, Psychosomatic.   2. Mind and body.   I. Title.
  RC49D74   1997
  616'.0019—DC20   90-23027   CIP

W. W. Norton & Company, Inc., 500 Fifth Avenue, New York, N.Y. 10110
http://www.wwnorton.com
W. W. Norton & Company, Ltd., 10 Coptic Street, London WC1A 1PU

1 2 3 4 5 6 7 8 9 0

To Jack Wasinger, D.D.S., M.A., Ph.D.,
a model of the psychosomatic approach to treatment,
and Anne Dubovsky,
a model of the psychosomatic approach to
overcoming disease.

Contents

Acknowledgments

Don Fusting and Anne Dubovsky developed the idea for this book, and Anne came up with the title. Susan Barrows Munro reorganized the original draft completely and mobilized the resources to turn it into a real book. This is Susan's project as much as anyone's. Susan also located Christi Albouy, a master typist who was able to convert indecipherable notes into an integrated unit.

Without Margaret Ryan's invaluable editing, this book would have been uninterpretable by anyone but me. Margaret had the remarkable good grace to tolerate my anxiety as she magically turned convoluted collections of unrelated concepts into actual prose.

Finally, I would like to acknowledge the inspiration provided by my wife, Anne, as she has worked to overcome cancer. Conventional wisdom has called cancer patients "survivors," but Anne has shown that people don't just passively live through cancer; they actively engage and conquer it. In this book, I hope to demonstrate how people can be victorious over all illnesses of the mind and body.

Denver, Colorado
August 1996

Introduction

Jean Murphy, a sixty-year-old woman, developed headaches and memory loss after her mother died of Alzheimer's disease. Worried that she was developing the same illness, Jean consulted her family physician, who reassured her that there was no evidence of Alzheimer's on his examination. Unconvinced, she consulted a neurologist, who performed additional tests, which were also normal. Despite the reassurance, Jean's memory problems increased. When she began having trouble sleeping, her physician prescribed a sleeping pill. That night, Jean took the entire prescription, along with a bottle of vodka, and died.

Jean's husband of thirty-five years, Gerald, had mild narrowing of the blood vessels supplying his heart, but he felt well. Three weeks after his wife's death, he learned that shortly before her death she had given away a priceless heirloom left to her by his mother. He did not see how he could be angry at someone he loved, but he could not understand why she would make such an important decision without consulting him. He had some fleeting chest pain, which he dismissed as being due to anxiety about his situation. That night, when he was in a state of intense conflict, Gerald's heart suddenly stopped beating and he, too, died.

Both Jean and Gerald were deceived—Jean into developing a hidden mental problem that masqueraded as a physical one, and Gerald into developing a hidden medical problem that seemed less important than the mental one. In both cases, the deception proved fatal. This book will describe these and other deceptions ranging from the bothersome to the disastrous. We will see how they develop, how they can be recognized, and how they can be cured.

Everyone knows by now that mind and body hurt or help each other—or do they? Even though the media, not to mention the scientific literature, have been full of stories about ways in which the mind can hurt the body, many physicians pay no attention to the state of their patients' minds, even while they spare no effort to apply the latest technology of the body. Despite phenomenal advances in knowledge about mind-body interactions, the pressure that medical cost containment has placed on physicians to spend less time with more patients is making it almost impossible to figure out the mental side of the mind-body equation in the doctor's office. Even psychiatrists, who deal with mental syndromes, spend so much time writing prescriptions these days that they barely have time to talk to their patients. Many of the rest of us, whether we are clinicians, patients, or both, either idealize technology so much that we think that all of human experience can be reduced to a series of chemical equations or an X-ray printout, or idealize the mind so much that we believe that willpower can do anything—even cure cancer. In this book, we will see how to avoid being deceived by these all-or-nothing ideas about mind and body and to distinguish fact from theory, clinical reality from opinion, and data from fantasy.

To understand how mind and body really help and interfere with each other, we will consider four deceptions. The first, which is discussed in Part I, is the deception that the study of the mind is fundamentally different from the study of the body. This belief has a proud history that goes back to the time of Plato, who separated the immortal essence of humanity, which he called the soul and which we have come to call the mind, from the mortal and mechanical body. Since the soul, and by extension the mind, was made in God's image, it was relegated to the realm of spirituality and was not considered a legitimate topic of scientific study. Meanwhile the body, which was just a vessel that housed the soul, could be dissected and its secrets learned. As a branch of philosophy, psychology had nothing to do with the principles that governed the functioning of bodily organs and the microscope, the X-ray, and the laboratory had nothing to do with the study of the mind.

In the 1990s, biomedical technology has caught up with the mental health field. The test tube, the CT scanner, and other measures of biology now *are* applicable to the mental realm, and it has become clear that mind and body follow the same basic laws. However, even though research on the influence of mind and body on each other has been almost as widely publicized as new and highly effective treatments for mental disorders, deceptive dichotomization of mind and body continues to be the rule in our society.

For example, politicians in the United States have been unable to agree on any aspect of health-care reform except that it would be too expensive to provide the same coverage for psychiatric illness as for medical illness. The one point on which legislators agree is the only point on which they are clearly deceived, since there is ample evidence of the cost effectiveness of psychiatric treatment, as well as years of research showing that addressing mental problems reduces the cost of medical care.

In the first of three clinical deceptions we will consider, a mind that has not developed beyond the stage at which all "feelings" are purely physical and distress is communicated in behavior conceals itself within a barrage of physical actions and dysfunctions. The bewildering array of pseudo-physical problems that are exaggerated, imagined, and, in their most dramatic form, actually created by active destruction of the body described in Part II are the products of a mind that feels deprived and hateful, that desperately wants love, that is afraid of normal human needs, that worships strength but is too weak to be aware of its own feelings, that clings to those it needs at the same time that it undermines them. In the face of a demand for medical therapies that never work, the only treatment with any chance of success is an intervention of the mind.

In contrast to deceptions in which the illness seems to be in the body but is really in the mind, the deceptions described in Part III—depression and related conditions—are obviously mental. The sufferer's entire personality is organized around unhappiness and negative thinking, but the mind has been deceived by the body out of a healthy engagement with life's challenges. The body's misdirection of the mind may be inborn, or experience may program it into every cell in the body. In either case, a treatment aimed at the body can reverse symptoms in the mind, even if the mental component is not directly addressed.

The last deception veers off in yet another direction. Part IV shows how feelings of being trapped, abandoned, or hopeless deceive the body out of its health by setting into motion physical events that contribute to potentially lethal illnesses like heart disease and cancer. The mind is able to injure the body by virtue of connections between the brain and a network of nerves and hormones that connect to the heart and affect immune defenses against cancer in every nook and cranny of physiology. By the same token, resolving grief, overcoming fear, and developing a fighting attitude toward the illness can increase the effectiveness of treatment for cancer and heart disease.

All of these mind-body deceptions begin with a sense of incompetence in the face of a situation that feels dangerous. There is nothing wrong with danger; all of us face it every day. Most of the time, our minds are mobilized to find a solution to the problem, and our bodies are activated to help us to attack or run away. As we begin to take action, the physiology of bodily activation abates and our minds relax. But when we are unable to come up with an effective strategy, either because past experience has conditioned us to feel helpless or because we sense that a defective stress response system is not up to the task, even everyday stress can feel overwhelming. When either mind or body is overwhelmed, the extensive overlap of the two dimensions allows the other to suffer the same fate by mechanisms that will be described throughout this book.

The ability to cope with stress is the end result of a complex interplay between inborn response styles, experiences with stress, and relationships with other people. The distinction between genetically programmed traits and individual psychology is not as distinct as one might think, since genetics can determine our attitudes, our behavior, and even our preference for television, while experience, and even strong feelings, can alter the expression of our genes. This interplay between experience and heredity determines our readiness to interpret a situation as dangerous and to react to the danger when it is perceived.

When the perception of danger reaches the brain, alertness centers are "turned on" and our senses are directed toward finding the threat. Nerves and hormones controlled by the brain make the heart beat faster, direct blood flow to action organs, prepare muscles to contract, increase the production of energy, and suppress immunity. This state of mobilization is balanced by dampening of all stress response systems, slowing the heart, lowering metabolism, and inhibiting behavior. Everyone can recognize the physiology of the stress response: feeling tense and alert for any sign of danger; feeling light-headed as the rate of breathing increases to infuse more oxygen into the blood; not being able to get to sleep; perhaps skipping a heartbeat or two. With protracted stress, there are often headaches, backaches, and sore joints from prolonged muscle contraction, insomnia and difficulty concentrating from continued arousal, and fatigue and low energy as energy runs out and the stress response starts to turn itself off. People who are more aware of their bodies than their minds may be captivated by such physical signs of the stress response while remaining oblivious to the thoughts and emotions behind them.

An important reaction that is driven by the stress response is the drive to be near other people, which provides protection from the dangers that exist in the environment and a direct calming effect on the physiology of arousal. The drive to be near other people when we are under stress is as natural as the drive to eat when we are hungry. By the same token, losing someone to whom we are attached is the worst of disasters for mind and body. For people who fear closeness for reasons that are explained in Part II, the scariest aspect of a loss or other stress is the prospect of needing someone else's help to cope with it. Infirmity under these circumstances can provide distraction from overwhelming emotions, as well as a secret way to find the caring, affection, and security that they have missed out on in life.

Just as vulnerability in the personality can channel a stress response run amok into pseudo-problems of the body, other kinds of vulnerabilities can lead to different mind-body deceptions. For example, when brain systems that regulate arousal, emotion, and readiness to interact with the environment are vulnerable to being destabilized, certain stresses, especially a loss, bring out profound disturbances of mood that are called mania and depression. If the immune response is susceptible to suppression, efficiency at destroying cancer cells may be reduced, and if the rhythm of the heart is subject to destabilization, emotional stress may stop the heart. We will encounter each of these syndromes of mind and body being deceived out of their normal function in "pure culture" in order to better understand them, but because mind and body share the same basic mechanisms of regulation, physical *and* psychological deceptions are much more common than one *or* the other.

Knowledge is power. As we separate the wheat from the chaff of research into mind-body interactions, you will be able to evaluate the information that has accumulated so far and avoid being deceived by premature and incomplete information in the future. Understanding the manifestations and mechanisms of clinical mind-body deceptions enables us to prevent them or at least figure out how to cope better with them when they do creep up on us. Even if some of the material you read here is eventually replaced by updated information, you will know how to interpret whatever new information comes along and how to apply it in your daily life.

A WORD ABOUT PATIENTS AND TREATMENTS

In order to bring the concepts discussed in this book to life, I have made liberal use of examples from actual clinical practice. All patients have been so thoroughly disguised that they probably would not recognize themselves, but the descriptions of what happened are factual. If you recognize some of these cases, it will serve as a reminder of the universality of mind-body deceptions.

I have discussed a number of treatments throughout the book, some of them medications. These descriptions were up-to-date at the time the book was written, but anyone contemplating using them should check with a reliable clinician to be certain that indications and uses have not changed significantly and that better alternatives have not been developed.

PART I

MIND-BODY DECEPTIONS AND MODERN SCIENCE

Let no one persuade you to cure the headache until he has first given you his soul to be cured. For this is the great error of our day in the treatment of the human body, that physicians separate the soul from the body.

—HIPPOCRATES

When you have a physical disease—that's a mental illness.

—A MODERN-DAY PATIENT

1
—

How the Body Lost Its Mind:
The Early Days of Medicine

MY NEW PATIENT entered the office, carrying a newspaper article that quoted me. "I read that you have a laboratory that studies depression," he said, "and I'd like to be tested."

"Do you feel depressed?" I asked.

"Of course I feel depressed. I've been treated for depression before, and it's coming back."

"If you know that you're depressed," I wondered, "why do you need a lab test?"

"Everyone knows that depression is caused by a biochemical deficiency. I want the latest test to find out if that's what I've got and to pick the right treatment."

"No lab test has yet outperformed a doctor's clinical evaluation in diagnosing and treating depression," I informed him. "If I can confirm the diagnosis and review the therapeutic options with you, what will we gain by spending money on tests that are really research tools for looking into one or another specific component of depression?"

"You sound old-fashioned to me," the patient replied grumpily. "I want the latest and the best. The latest shows that depression is nothing more than a disease of the brain, and these new tests will prove that."

Despite being well-informed about the latest advances in scientific research, my patient was more old-fashioned than he thought I was! In considering depression to be a brain disorder that does not involve the mind, the patient was unwittingly following a tradition of separating mind and body that goes back in Western society at least to the time of the classical Greeks. In the human organism, the brain and the rest of the body are inseparable from those less tangible qualities that have been called *mind* or *soul*. However, in their quest for understanding (not to mention their drive for intellectual territoriality), philosophers, clerics, physicians, researchers, and psychologists—from antiquity to the present—have placed wedges between the mind and body, sometimes emphasizing one, sometimes the other. Their disputes over which side of the mind-body duality is more valid or more important than the other have led to many intriguing deceptions—deceptions that are not merely theoretical but reflect battles between mind and body that are played out every day on the field of mental and physical health and disease.

PLATO'S PART IN THE SCHEME OF THINGS

Where did the idea come from that mind and body are separate phenomena, one more important or amenable to study than the other? In the days of the Greek philosophers, it was thought that because breath ceased with death, the soul—and by extension the mind—was not dependent on the body. Plato, who was the first to describe the soul as something that survived beyond the body, codified this division when he separated diseases of the mind from those of the body, calling mental illnesses "divine madnesses" that came in four varieties: prophetic, religious, poetic, and erotic. Because divine madness was bestowed by the gods, it could never be understood by studying the human body. It was Plato who developed a formal philosophy of the soul separate from the body. In the *Phaedo* he opined:

> Is [death] not the separation of soul and body? . . . [W]hen the soul exists in herself, and is released from the body and the body is released from the soul, what is this but death? . . . And does the soul admit of death? No. Then the soul is immortal? Yes.

CHRISTIAN "CONTRIBUTIONS"

In the Bible, the word *soul* is literally translated as *living person*. However, as Christian theology evolved, the concept of soul eventually acquired Plato's views of it as an immaterial and immortal agency separate from the earthly body. This redefinition was introduced in the fifth century by St. Augustine and was codified during the Middle Ages by Thomas Aquinas.

The notion of an immaterial soul had such universal appeal that twelfth-century rabbi Judah Halevi assured his community that "Judaism is the religion which insures the immortality of the soul after the demise of the body." The influence of the Church, which had begun to pervade society with the conversion of the Roman Empire, was extended to much of the Western world by medieval Popes Gregory VII and Innocent II and had an even more profound impact on popular thinking.

With the ascent of Christianity as the major Western social and political force during the Middle Ages, the Church's Platonic view of a soul that transcended the body became society's view. This official dichotomization of body and soul ultimately laid the foundation for modern biological science. Christian dogma had held that because the human body was made in God's image, it would be a spiritual defilement to study the body, even after death. However, if the soul were truly the spiritual essence, then a nonsacriligeous way might be found to study the earthly vessel that housed it.

Once religious leaders extricated the soul from the body, it became possible to portray the body in mechanical terms in popular thought, as nothing more than a fancy collection of nuts and bolts. The Church was still intimately involved in worldly politics, but its domain of philosophical study was drawn away from a body that would wither and die and centered on a soul that would last forever. The mechanical body could then be relegated to worldly scientific investigation, separate from the spiritual and intangible soul. Included in the concept of soul were all those intangibles that are now equated with the *mind*—will, the impulse to act, passion, conscience, pleasure, agony. Like closeness to God, goodness, and the meaning of life, subjective experience—and the thoughts and feelings that comprise it—were relegated to the mythical rather than material realm, to be understood only by those who knew the spirit.

BIRTH OF THE SCIENCE OF THE BODY

No longer prohibited from studying the body, scientific medicine acquired more knowledge over the next 300 years than it had in the previous millennium. During the same time, the study of the mind remained the province of religion and, as time went on, of philosophy. When psychology emerged as a formal discipline in the early eighteenth century, it was a branch of philosophy, not of medicine, concerned with the subjective, the mystical, the non-material.

To study bodily afflictions, the science of the body had to move a world away from the religion and philosophy of the mind. Only then was it politically feasible to investigate possible treatments for bodily afflictions, but these had to remain clearly distinct from treatments for mental disorders. Under the best of circumstances, the mentally ill were relegated to asylums, where they were separated geographically as well as philosophically from those in hospitals receiving treatments for maladies of the body.

The study of the body could not be separated from the study of the mind without separating the *methods* of these two domains. As a result, when new technologies were developed to measure biological processes, there was little thought of applying them to mental phenomena. While the activities of the mind remained invisible, bodily phenomena became increasingly accessible to observation. And observable meant *real*. The unobservable was either spiritual or imaginary. The philosophical wall between the body and the mind came to parallel an ever-widening barrier between the *observed as real* and the *experiential as unreal*.

THE LIMITATIONS OF SPECIALIZATION

The exclusive focus of early medicine on purely physical observations did prove useful in defining areas of knowledge that could be studied by using the technology of the day to test speculations instead of just accepting or rejecting them as articles of faith. It was just as well to ignore those amorphous, complex, and confusing interactions with the mind, for which there were no techniques of study anyway. Using the example of cardiovascular physiology, psychoanalyst Arnold Cooper recounts the accelerating rate at which this method made it possible to replace myth with facts:

> In 1628 William Harvey, after at least a dozen years of thought and experimentation, published *De Mortu Cordis,* setting forth the evidence he had accumulated, and the arguments in support of, the concept of the circulation of the blood. This greatest of all physiological discoveries encountered violent opposition and resulted in the falling off of Harvey's personal practice.
>
> After Harvey's discovery, it took almost 150 years to the next great discovery by Priestley and Lavoisier that the purpose of the circulation was to distribute oxygen to the tissues. It took almost 300 years for the development of practical methods for measuring blood pressure, and the great advances in clinical cardiology—anticoagulants, diuretics, antihypertensives, cardiac surgery, and now the artificial heart—have all occurred in the last half-century, and at an increasingly rapid pace.
>
> This truncated account of 350 years of circulatory physiology illustrates commonalities of scientific development: the great discovery, often initially resisted, followed by slow, steady accumulation of basic knowledge, punctuated by epochal discoveries, and an enormous quickening of the pace of both knowledge acquisition and application as a field matures.

Advances in the technology of observing and measuring the body began to produce so much information that it could not be contained within a single body of knowledge. The microscope, for example, created the need for a specialist who understood how the equipment worked and how to interpret what it revealed. As technical innovations made it possible to obtain more and more information from each isolated area of study, it became necessary to subdivide the body into specialized—and then *sub*specialized—fields. Anatomy of the organs became anatomy of the cell and the subcellular environment; physiology of the body became physiology of the glands, of the nervous system, of the heart, and, finally, of molecules. The study of pathological processes of all these body parts also had to be created. With diseases of *organ systems* supplanting diseases of the organism (the person), more divisions arose as physicians sought to keep pace with research advances by developing specialized therapies for specific organ diseases.

Subspecialization made it possible to expand knowledge about diagnosis and treatment in manageable amounts. However, the subdivision of the body contained the seeds of the deception that if the topic were sufficiently narrow, it would be possible to know everything there is to know about it.

Bacteriology, the study of the cause of disease by bacteria, is an example of how a rapidly advancing field can produce subspecialized knowledge that is mistaken for total knowledge. In 1850, scientists showed that anthrax, a fatal disease of farm animals, could be transmitted to healthy sheep by the blood of ill sheep. By 1863 the conclusion had been reached that, since anthrax was always associated with the presence of microscopic rod-shaped forms, these forms must be the cause of the disease. However, the nature of the tiny critters was not known. Enter German scientist Heinrich Hermann Robert Koch, who became the "father" of the field of bacteriology, winning the Nobel Prize in 1905 for discovering the cause of tuberculosis. Koch figured out how to grow these forms—really, microorganisms—in cultures and showed how they could remain dormant in the soil for years. This was the first time that a specific bacterium was described and definitively shown to be the cause of a specific disease. Koch was able to use techniques he devised for culturing bacteria and viewing them under a microscope to discover the bacterial causes of tuberculosis and cholera. Over the next fifty years Koch's students went on to develop a scientific discipline that discovered and identified numerous bacteria, viruses, and other infectious agents.

Being able to identify microbial causes of disease has made it possible to control diseases that ravaged earlier generations, but it is not the entire story of infectious disease. After all, not everyone who is exposed to a bug gets sick, and not everyone who becomes infected has the same illness. Some people get a touch of pneumonia, while others become deathly ill. Some people get a mild case of the flu, while others with the same virus cannot get out of bed for a week—and some even die. What is the source of so much variation? The "dose" of the microbe, the state of the infected person's immune system, compliance with treatment, and the person's state of mind all play a role in whether infection occurs and how serious it becomes. It does little good to synthesize new antibiotics if people do not take them, or if they take them so frequently that the microbes become resistant to them. The subspecialization of biological knowledge made it possible to advance knowledge phenomenally, but not as completely as was believed at the time.

SECULAR PURSUITS OF THE MIND

Just as the shifting tides of religious authority opened the body to objective study, the shifting tides of economic authority set processes in motion that opened the mind to its own investigators.

The Industrial Revolution in the eighteenth century created a class of self-made industrialists who gradually consolidated their power at the expense of the Church. As society became more secularized, according more respect to money than religious indulgence, the Church's monopoly on non-physical realms of knowledge began to diminish and formal study of the mind could be extended to other disciplines. At this point, students of the mind might have been expected to compare notes with students of the body, who were rapidly increasing their databases. However, new disciplines that studied psychopathology—problems of the mind—remained on parallel rather than convergent paths with disciplines that studied pathobiology—problems of the body. As we will see in Chapter 2, the emergence early in the nineteenth century of the field of psychiatry, a medical specialty of the mind, illustrates the continued separation of the domains of mind and body in medicine.

2

How the Mind Lost Its Body: A Brief History of Psychiatry

HOW HAD DISEASES of the mind been conceptualized before they became a legitimate topic for scientific study in the eighteenth century? In the absence of anything resembling an objective understanding of the mind, the most reasonable cause of malfunctions of this earthly representation of the soul seemed to be demonic possession. Mental illness was regarded as alien—which is why those who first treated the mentally ill were called "alienists." Mentally ill people were sequestered in asylums, where they could not contaminate society.

All this began to change at the end of the eighteenth century. In 1792 Phillippe Pinel, a French physician and mathematics professor, became chief physician at Bicêtre, an asylum for men. When Pinel arrived at Bicêtre, he found inmates chained to the walls—some had been thus confined for as long as thirty or forty years. Casting aside this traditional "treatment," Pinel unchained the men; two years later he unchained the inmates of an asylum for women at Salpêtrière.

Pinel also began to free the mentally ill from the chains of demonology. Insisting that mental disease was the result of observable social, psychological, physiologic, and genetic forces, he developed one of the first objective classifications of psychoses. Taking an objective approach to diagnosing mental disorders, Pinel also cast aside the standard therapies of bleeding, purging, and blistering. Instead he talked to his patients about their problems—and thus became the unheralded founder of modern psychotherapy.

The word *psychiatry* (which means "mind healing" in Greek) was coined in 1808 by anatomist Johann Reil. Unlike psychology, which was still a branch of philosophy, psychiatry was seen as an offshoot of neurology. Neurologists studied alterations in motor and sensory function that were thought to be caused by specific lesions in the nervous system. Psychiatrists, who at that point were concerned mainly with what today we would call the major psychoses, believed that these disorders would ultimately be linked to specific anomalies in the brain. During the twentieth century, many of these disorders were found to be caused by treatable illnesses affecting the central nervous system, such as neurosyphilis, epilepsy, and hypothyroidism.

Neurology and psychiatry walked hand-in-hand down the same path until technological advances forced them onto separate paths. Advances in gross and microscopic neuroanatomy made it possible to identify the causes of discrete neurological syndromes, such as aphasia, epilepsy, and hemiplegia, but these advances could not uncover causes for schizophrenia, mania, depression, or dementia.

In order to maintain its connection to the observable world of medical science, neurology abandoned mental syndromes (like schizophrenia and mania) for which there seemed little chance of discovering demonstrable pathology. By default, everything distinctly mental was relegated to psychiatry, which became the specialty of the unknown! Within this newly boundaried domain of psychiatry, a split developed between the empiricists and the non-empiricists, parallel to the one that distinguished neurology from psychiatry. The empirically-oriented psychiatrists continued to believe that objective—that is, physiological—causes of mental disorders existed and had only to be discovered; they studied severe mental illnesses that seemed likely to reveal underlying physiological causes. These psychiatrists created the conceptual foundation for the soon-to-emerge subdivision known as *descriptive psychiatry.*

The other group, though initially espousing biological underpinnings, eventually moved away from the objective parameters of science and toward the purely subjective, non-observable realm of "intrapsychic" processes. This group, lead by Sigmund Freud, created *psychoanalytic psychiatry.* Within the study of mental disorders, a clear division between the objective and the subjective emerged that would persist through most of this century.

DESCRIPTIVE PSYCHIATRY: WHAT YOU *SEE* IS WHAT YOU GET

The most influential founder of the descriptive branch of the new psychiatry was Emil Kraepelin (1856–1926). Kraepelin, who was trained in neurology as well as psychiatry, had two important mentors. One was Wilhelm Wundt, a physiologist and psychologist who had helped to move psychology away from philosophy and toward becoming an experimental science. The other was Wilhelm Griesenger, an early nineteenth-century psychiatrist who contended that "psychological diseases are brain diseases." As late as the 1940s, Griesenger's view was still commonly held, supported by the fact that psychoses caused by neurological and medical diseases (such as syphilis and hypothyroidism) accounted for more than forty percent of psychiatric hospital admissions.

Kraepelin and psychiatrist Eugen Bleuler devoted most of their professional lives to describing the major mental illnesses in a systematic way. Lacking any effective treatments, they had to content themselves with meticulous observations of a vast array of abnormal behaviors, which led to an organized classification of discrete syndromes for which they hoped causes and cures might eventually be found. Many of their descriptions have remained central to modern-day psychiatric diagnosis.

The classification of mental disease by the descriptive psychiatrists was most detailed for the psychoses ("insanity"). Kraepelin acknowledged that, even for these severe conditions, it was impossible "to form anything like a reliable idea of the *causes* of the morbid phenomena, and still more seldom can we give an account of the way in which those causes work." Nevertheless, he continued to believe that persistent application of the scientific method would eventually uncover the neurological basis of all psychiatric illness, resulting in specific, organic remedies. Once psychiatrists had succeeded in demonstrating that "their" diseases were no less physical than those of the neurologists, they would be able to take their rightful place in the community of scientific physicians.

Although Kraepelin's hope that his major categories of psychoses would be shown to have tangible, medical causes was fulfilled in many cases, psychiatry did not reunite with other medical specialties. Instead, each condition for which a physical cause was found was simply relocated—outside the domain of psychiatry! In all, about half of the conditions considered psychiatric in Kraepelin's day have been shifted to other branches of medicine. How the *physical* was continually redefined as being *not mental* is well illustrated by the story of syphilis.

Syphilis: General Paresis of the Insane

Syphilis was first reported toward the end of the fifteenth century, when an epidemic devastated Europe and Asia. Because of its secondary-stage skin lesions, the epidemic was initially called the "Great Pox" to distinguish it from smallpox. In the nineteenth century, as dissection became permissible and physicians began to study the interior of the body, they realized that syphilis progresses from the skin to the internal organs and then to the nervous system. The final stage of syphilis is dramatic. Damage to the central nervous system causes a general paresis (partial paralysis) a full twenty to thirty years after the infection began. The most obvious manifestations of this condition are mental in nature: memory loss, impaired judgment, and confused thinking, along with extreme emotional fluctuations ranging from manic to apathetic. Also common are illusions (the false perception of something that has objective existence), hallucinations (sensory perceptions of something that is not there), delusions (fixed, false beliefs out of keeping with cultural and religious background), and disorganized, assaultive behavior. Untreated general paresis progresses to dementia (deterioration of intellectual functioning), paralysis, and death within three to four years.

Because of the marked changes in emotion and behavior that accompany the final state of syphilis, patients were housed in mental hospitals and their illness was considered psychiatric. Since they never recovered, they simply remained on the psychiatric ward, eventually constituting a large percentage of the population, as other patients with more episodic conditions came and went. Psychiatrists studied this condition at great length, convinced that its symptoms must be due to some physical agent, even if no one had any idea what it might be. If only that agent could be identified, the door might be opened for finding the causes—and maybe even the cures—of the other major mental syndromes.

Imagine, then, the excitement generated by the discovery in 1905 that syphilis is caused by a spiral-shaped microorganism called *Treponema pallidum*. Just five years later bacteriologist Paul Ehrlich discovered the first effective therapy for halting the progression of the infection: a "magic bullet" injection—a derivative of arsenic known as "arsphenamine" or "salvarsan." As psychoanalysts Franz Alexander and Thomas French noted, this first biological treatment in psychiatry was hailed as proof that . . .

> Now the psychiatrist could raise his head: He, too, was a physician who could approach his patient with laboratory methods of diagnosis and treatment. . . . Whatever therapy existed before was either based on magic, as in exorcism of evil spirits of the prescientific era, or was thoroughly ineffective. . . . Ehrlich's chemotherapy of postsyphilitic conditions . . . contributed more than anything else to the prestige of psychiatry. . . . Under the influence of this method, hopes ran high that soon the whole field of psychiatry would be conquered by the usual methods of medical research and therapy.

Alas, psychiatry's jubilation was short-lived; syphilis was not considered a model psychiatric illness for long. In fact, as soon as a biological cause was identified, it became *not psychological.* It was removed from psychiatry and hastily relocated to neurology and infectious disease specialties. "Cretinism" and "myxedema madness" (both forms of hypothyroidism) fell to the endocrinologist; "imbecility" (mental retardation) became a pediatric disorder; and "epileptic insanity" (confusional state due to seizures) was handed over to neurologists. Throughout the first half of the twentieth century, the fate of syphilis was repeated many times. Instead of enriching their understanding of how changes in the structure of the nervous system affected the functioning of the mind, mental specialists lost all contact with problems for which a physical source was found. The only reason psychiatry did not disappear altogether was that it was impossible to demonstrate any changes in the nervous system—or anywhere else in the body for that matter—in most mental illnesses. In short, these conditions remained psychiatric only because they could not be proven to be physical.

PSYCHOANALYTIC PSYCHIATRY: WHAT YOU *FEEL* IS WHAT YOU GET

While the descriptive psychiatrists continued the search for biological underpinnings of mental disorders, another group of psychiatrists believed that, even if there were a physical basis for most diseases of the mind, it would not be found by the limited biomedical technology of the day. Why not rely on techniques that made use of abilities inherent in the mind, such as insight, intuition, and logic? After all, unlimited "data" could be gathered with this method, and since treatments of the body were removed from psychiatry when they worked, why not develop therapies that began and ended in the *mental* sphere?

The new subspecialty that evolved from this strategy—named *psychoanalysis* by its founder, Sigmund Freud—emphasized the role of anxiety and unconscious conflicts in psychic distress, not of lesions and bacteria. The principal investigative tool was not the microscope or petri dish but a relationship between analyst and patient, through which important personality dynamics could be enacted. Psychoanalysis thus tossed its weight to the *mental* side of the mind-body split, approaching mental and emotional states as if they had nothing to do with the body.

Like descriptive psychiatry, the roots of psychoanalysis can be found in the soil of neurology. Jean-Martin Charcot, who had opened the most important neurological clinic in Europe in 1882 at the Salpêtrière Hospital (where Pinel had practiced a century earlier), accepted Sigmund Freud as a student in 1885. Charcot suspected that some dramatic neurological symptoms—such as paralysis, deafness, blindness, and sensory loss that occurred in the absence of any demonstrable physical pathology—were actually *somatic* expressions of *emotional* conflicts. His theory was proven correct when purely psychological techniques—first hypnosis and suggestion, then Freud's "talking cure"—abolished the physical symptoms, in some cases, in the proverbial wink of an eye. Since early practitioners of psychoanalysis were all physicians, psychoanalysis seemed destined to become one of the first medical subspecialties of the mind.

Having begun his career as a neurologist, Freud never stopped believing that "mental phenomena are to a large extent dependent upon physiologic ones." In 1895 he attempted to develop an ambitious theory of the biology of the mind in his "Project for a Scientific Psychology." This attempt proved futile; no direct correlations could be drawn between how the mind functioned and how neurons were believed to function. In frustration, Freud ordered the Project destroyed, commenting to his close friend Wilhelm Fleiss, "I no longer understand the state of mind in which I concocted it." Freud remained convinced, however,

> ... that mental activity is bound up with the function of the brain as with no other organ. . . . But every attempt to deduce . . . a localization of mental processes, every endeavor to think of ideas as stored up in nerve cells and of excitations as passing along nerve fibers, has completely miscarried.

Realizing that it was impossible to draw direct correlations between the way the *brain* worked and the way the *mind* worked, Freud made a tactical decision about how, at that moment in history, psychoanalytic thinking should proceed:

> I have no desire at all to leave psychology hanging in the air with no organic basis. But . . . I have nothing, either theoretical or therapeutic, to work on, and so I must behave as if I were confronted by psychological factors only.

By restricting himself to a purely psychological frame of reference, Freud was able to maximize the information he could obtain from the psychoanalytic method. Just as biologically-oriented researchers were able to gather data more efficiently by ignoring the psychological, Freud proceeded unencumbered by neurological principles that did not amplify his work. However, in severing his intellectual ties with neurology and its methodology of observation, he also drew away from descriptive psychiatry, which had remained on the somatic side of the mind-body dichotomy. As the theoretical moorings of psychoanalysis in biology were severed, so were its clinical moorings in medicine.

Descriptive psychiatry retained the scientific method by abandoning the subjective non-observable realms; psychoanalysis retained the vast tapestry of human experience by abandoning the objectivity of the scientific method. Once psychoanalysis abandoned the biological for the emotional, however, its practitioners entered a realm that was particularly vulnerable to the distortion of passions and prejudices. Had it been possible to retain an attitude of objectivity while still utilizing intuition and introspection, the analytic strategy might have penetrated the psyche with a precision comparable to biological methods. But such was not the case. The politics of medicine, the very human motivations and needs of psychoanalysts, and the power of the unconscious as it emerged in the analyst-patient relationship—all these factors made this hope of "objective subjectivity" as much an illusion as was the hope that a purely biological approach could explain the totality of the mind.

Circling the Wagons

Freud's theories, especially those of infantile sexuality and the Oedipus complex, were greeted by the mainstream scientific community with incredulity and shock, if not outright revulsion. Even the most open-minded physicians rejected his ideas, often before they knew what they were! For example, Freud's *The Interpretation of Dreams* received a scathing review from a well-known doctor who, never having read the book, was nonetheless certain that he did not like it. The fact that Freud was a Jew in a gentile and largely anti-Semitic Austrian medical establishment did not make his reception any warmer.

In such an inhospitable climate, it was only natural that Freud and his followers circled their wagons. Finding open communication with the scientific community increasingly difficult, they became more concerned with banding together with like-minded professionals to ensure the emotional survival of their discipline. In analytic societies, discussion groups, and journals, it became more important to protect the field from attacks from without, provide mutual support, refine theories in which the members already believed, and indoctrinate recruits than to open their theories to rigorous outside scrutiny and debate.

As the psychoanalytic community insulated itself from hostility from without, its ranks became increasingly inbred and less tolerant of dissent from within. To disagree with Freud became either a personality flaw or a betrayal. Freud described the defection of "the two heretics"—C. G. Jung and Alfred Adler—as "secessionist movements." Refusing to "alloy" what Freud called "the pure gold of analysis" with the "copper" of other techniques, psychoanalysis degenerated from "a science of the mind" to what Arnold Cooper called "the doctrine of a founder."

Loyalty to the "father figure" of the field rather than to the scientific method isolated psychoanalysts from advances in parallel fields of study of the mind. For example, Eugen Bleuler was greatly interested in psychoanalytic observations, which he felt contained a depth that descriptive psychiatry lacked. Because Bleuler was one of the most influential figures in the field of psychiatry, Freud wanted him not only to believe in his analytic model but to fight wholeheartedly for a worldwide psychoanalytic movement. Bleuler's position was one of moderation. In a letter to Freud, Bleuler spoke bluntly:

> For me, the theory is only one new truth among other truths. I stand up for it, for psychoanalysis, because I consider it valid and because I feel that I am able to judge it, since I am working in a related field. But for me it is not a major issue, whether the validity of these views will be recognized a few years sooner or later. I am therefore less tempted than you [Freud] to sacrifice my whole personality for the advancement of the cause of psychoanalysis.

Freud attributed Bleuler's lack of total commitment to unanalyzed resistance and stopped cultivating the collaboration, thereby losing contact with the other major direction in psychiatric thinking.

The emotional and personality differences between descriptive psychiatrists and psychoanalysts as *individuals* led to intellectual and theoretical differences between descriptive psychiatry and psychoanalysis as *disciplines.* Freud decided that because psychiatry "looks for the somatic determinants of mental disorders and treats them like other causes of illness," it had nothing to do with psychoanalysis, which was interested in the "purely mental." It was not a great leap from this stance to the position that, unlike psychiatry,

> . . . psychoanalysis is not a specialized branch of medicine . . . [but] a part of psychology. . . . The medical degree does not give to doctors a historical claim to the monopoly of analysis. . . . In fact . . . a non-physician who has been suitably trained can, with occasional reference to a physician, carry out the analytic treatment . . . of neurotics.

Demonstrating the courage of his convictions, Freud taught psychoanalysis to his daughter, Anna, who became the first analyst who had no medical training.*

---

*Making essentially the same points that Freud had made at the beginning of the century, in the 1980s non-medical therapists successfully sued the American Psychoanalytic Association for the right to train for the same certification in psychoanalysis that is awarded to physicians.

Center Stage

After psychoanalysis was introduced to the United States in the 1940s, it became not just one of a number of views of the mind, as Bleuler had suggested, but *the* theory of the mind. The reasons for this primacy are not difficult to understand. Biological investigations had failed to turn up much that could compete with the power of psychoanalytic theory to explain virtually any kind of psychological or social deviancy. Support for almost any psychoanalytic explanation could be found in the complexity of human experience, if the therapist searched hard enough. Even though the majority of psychiatrists were not formally trained as psychoanalysts, many relied heavily on analytic techniques and concepts.

An even more compelling reason for the profound influence of psychoanalysis on American psychiatry was the fact that more than half of the psychoanalytic patients in the United States were themselves mental health practitioners and their relatives. Many of the foremost psychiatric educators of this era had been analytically trained, and they passed on this psychoanalytic tradition to each new class of psychiatrists. Psychoanalysts were among the most influential chairmen of psychiatry departments, where they shaped the intellectual development of a generation of specialists.

"Shell Shock" Prestige

Confidence in psychoanalytic theory was based on more than the feeling that it seemed to have a certain universal truth. Analytically-oriented psychiatrists gained enormous prestige when they created a psychological means of returning 60 percent of soldiers suffering "shell shock" or "battle fatigue" (now called "posttraumatic stress disorder") to the World War II battlefield within two to five days. During the First World War, such soldiers had remained permanently disabled from shell shock. In recognition of the contribution of psychiatry to the health of the soldiers under its care, a psychiatrist was promoted, for the first time, to the rank of general.

Within the military, many psychiatrists were convinced by their experience with battle fatigue that psychologically significant events could indeed produce disorders that could be cured by psychological interventions. When they left the service, their battlefield successes encouraged them to move psychiatry out of the asylum. They hoped that, early treatment of milder syndromes in their consulting rooms would prevent progression to the more severe psychoses that were encountered in the hospitals. Whereas two-thirds of the members of the American Psychiatric Association worked in psychiatric hospitals prior to World War II, by 1956 the percentage had dropped to seventeen.

In the decade following World War II, as psychoanalysis moved the mind away from the body—and the office away from the hospital—mainstream psychiatry moved with it. The impact of this move was profound, for it meant that the most important psychiatric treatment available was psychological. To this day there are still psychiatrists who do not "believe in" medications and who view physical interventions of any kind as a sign of failing to understand the patient or of "giving up" on the patient psychologically. Classification of syndromes became less important than understanding individual psychology, and some psychiatrists completely rejected the concept of formal diagnosis. Everyone is different, they argued; pigeonholing people with labels is an injustice to the uniqueness of each person's illness.

In working with patients for whom immediate results were not as essential as exploring their own motivations, psychiatrists paid more attention to the open-ended process of the therapy than to diagnosable symptoms and structured interventions. This therapeutic strategy—which ignored the biological aspects of problems—moved psychiatry further away from other medical specialties and closer to the non-medical mental health fields. As the boundaries between clinical professions of the mind became blurred, so did the boundaries between professional versus popular wisdom. Freud foresaw the pitfall that, sooner or later, everyone would feel like an expert on the human condition:

> If you raise a question in physics or chemistry, anyone who knows he possesses no "technical knowledge" will hold his tongue. But if you venture upon a psychological assertion, you must be prepared to meet judgments and contradictions from every quarter. In this field, apparently, there is no "technical knowledge." Everyone has a mental life, so everyone regards himself as a psychologist. . . . The story is told of how someone who applied for a post as a children's nurse was asked if she knew how to look after babies. "Of course," she replied, "why, after all, I was once a baby myself."

Psychiatrists who continued to be interested in the physical roots of mental dysfunction were not part of the new mainstream. Like the psychoanalysts earlier in the century, this group banded together for intellectual and emotional support, forming their own inbred and isolated clique. In opposition to the exclusively mentalist focus of the psychoanalysts, the "biological psychiatrists" dismissed anything resembling a psychological component. A preposterous comment by a noted psychopharmacologist illustrates this new form of tunnel vision. When asked whether the expectation of a magical cure expressed by patients in his waiting room might explain why these patients began to feel better before they even saw him, the renowned physician replied with a scoff that any such expectation was a *symptom* of the patients' illnesses, a symptom that would be duly eradicated by the right drug.

ABANDONING SCIENCE

The perspective that emerged from looking at just one side of the mind-body unity had its advantages when psychoanalysis began to study the mind, but it could not endure as an organizing principle of psychiatry. The problem went beyond the fact that psychoanalysts (and psychoanalytically-oriented therapists) had abandoned empiricism as a standard of research and treatment—and with it, the empirical tools of microscopes, brain scans, and diagnoses. They had also abandoned the scientific *ethic* as a guiding influence, and this loss ultimately undermined the credibility of the Freudian-based therapies of the mind. Even if psychotherapists did not always do so, they were at least expected to *try* to approach the clinic with the same rigor as the laboratory, generating hypotheses that could be confirmed or rejected by further data.

Lacking an empirical foundation may sound like "no big deal," but when it occurs in the therapeutic setting, very concrete—and unwanted—consequences can occur. Here is what happened to a twenty-five-year-old man who was treated by a therapist who believed that the empirical approach is irrelevant to problems of the mind.

The man entered psychotherapy because he "felt anxious." Because the therapist believed that anxiety is a signal of unconscious conflict, usually related to childhood trauma, she encouraged the patient to look for unresolved feelings from his past that might be coming to the surface and making him anxious. The patient, who had always been eager to please, complied with the implicit suggestion and began talking about his father, a successful businessman who had always seemed to expect too much. No matter how hard the patient had tried to please him, he never felt that he succeeded. He had been an A-student in college and had sailed through a prestigious MBA program, but it seemed to him that it wasn't enough. Dutifully joining the family business, he had introduced a number of innovations that saved the company millions, but even this accomplishment didn't seem to elicit the kind of affection for which he had always longed.

Observing that this patient acted very deferentially toward her, the psychiatrist wondered aloud if his feelings for her were similar to his feelings for his father, since patients often transfer feelings they have had about their parents (and other caretakers) onto the therapist. Impressed by the therapist's capacity to bring his past feelings alive in a present relationship, the patient became progressively preoccupied with his feelings in the present for *her*. He had dreams in which he was involved in sexual bondage with her—which she interpreted as evidence that he must have been sexually abused as a child, since his feelings about her as a parent figure had become sexualized. The patient could not remember any abuse, but he worked hard to try to recall it and soon was having dreams in which a masked figure tied him up and teased him.

Both patient and therapist were delighted with the progress he was making. The frequency of therapy was increased from once to twice and then three times a week (as vice-president of his company, he could afford it). There was only one catch: he was still anxious. Indeed, he was more anxious than ever. Because the dreams kept him awake at night, he was too tired during the day to function effectively and his performance began to slip. This made him even more convinced that his father, who remained the president of the company, disapproved of him, and his anxiety increased further.

The therapist used this experience, as well as the patient's growing feeling that she, too, disapproved of him, to learn even more about the feelings of disappointment and anger he had toward his father, feelings he could not express because the as-yet unremembered abuse made him fearful of standing up to his father. The relentless increase in symptomatology over two years of therapy was interpreted as proof that it was working; if patient and therapist were not onto something important, why would he be so upset?

At this point, the therapist was offered an attractive job, and she decided to move to another city. Her patient spent the three months prior to her departure working on his feelings of loss, which—lo and behold—seemed similar to the feelings of loss he had always felt in relation to his father. In his intensifying dreams about the therapist, he had married her and she took care of him in a way his father never had.

On the day that she moved, the patient consulted the colleague to whom she had referred him. Upon hearing the patient's theory about the nature of his problem, the new therapist was impressed that, not only had this theory of treatment (early experiences are the root of all current feelings) failed to cure the symptoms, but it seemed to have worsened them! Meanwhile, the patient thought that his new therapist was disappointed in him, just as his father always was. He couldn't stop thinking about how this new therapist might feel about him. When the therapist wondered why the patient had such strong feelings about someone he had just met, he said that he had learned that, to be successful, therapy had to focus on his fantasies about the therapist. "That may be true," the new therapist allowed, "but let's see if there are any alternative hypotheses about the cause of your problem and its treatment. For instance, before you started therapy, you must have had some problem other than preoccupation with your therapist."

Patient: "Well, I had conflicts about my father."

Therapist: "Do you mean that you went into therapy because of conflicts about your father?"

Patient: "No, I made the appointment because I was anxious."

Therapist: "If you weren't aware of being anxious about your father, what were you aware of?"

Patient: "It was so trivial, it couldn't have been the whole problem."

Therapist: "What was it, then?"

Patient: "Just that I don't like my executive assistant."

Therapist: "Why not?"

Patient: "He's too slow at getting things done, and sometimes he's sloppy in his work. It can take days to do something that should be accomplished in an hour."

Therapist: "Why don't you fire him?"

Patient: "Can I do that?"

Therapist: "I don't know, can you?"

Patient: "Well, I *am* the vice-president. But I'm afraid of hurting his feelings. Usually, I get my assistant to do this kind of thing."

Therapist: "Perhaps you need to learn how to set better limits with your employees."

Patient and therapist had two more sessions. In the first, they figured out that the patient's father would find it easy to fire the troublesome employee and would look down on his son for asking for help. At this point the patient began to reiterate all the times his father had expected him to need help in handling things. The therapist asked him what evidence he had that his perception of his father was accurate. As it turned out, the only real proof he had was the way he *felt*. The only statement that could be made with certainty was that his father was not usually very open about his feelings.

"If he's really so bad, what have you got to lose by asking his advice?" the therapist suggested. "The worst that could happen would be that he would confirm your fears." The patient finally agreed. The next day he spoke to his father.

To the patient's amazement, his father was very interested in his son's quandary. In fact, he had always been interested in—and proud of—his son. The main reason that the patient had not been aware of his father's opinion was that he had never asked for it and his father had never been one to volunteer his opinions. With some coaching from his father, the patient developed a list of written expectations for his assistant who, upon seeing these, acknowledged that he would not be able to meet them and quit. His father now readily volunteered his opinion that the patient had handled the situation well.

After reporting these results at the second session, the patient wondered if the therapist approved of what he had done or if she was disappointed in him for not being able to solve the problem on his own. He wanted to tell her about the fantasies he had had about her before coming to therapy that day.

Therapist: "I'm sure that this could be interesting to discuss, but why are you bringing it up at this particular moment?"

Patient: "Don't therapists like to talk about how their patients feel about them?"

Therapist: "They may, but does this mean that there's nothing else that might be of interest to you?"

Patient: "Don't I need to say more about my father and how you remind me of him?"

Therapist: "Why?"

Patient: "It's my main problem."

Therapist: "I thought your main problem was anxiety."

Patient: "But I'm not anxious anymore."

Therapist: "When did this happen?"

Patient: "As soon as I resolved things with my assistant."

Therapist: "Perhaps you feel that your problem has been resolved."

Patient: "But if that's true, I might not need any more therapy."

Therapist: "And what would be wrong with that?"

Patient: "I'd disappoint you if I didn't want to see you anymore."

Therapist: "You seem to feel that I, like your father, have unrealistic expectations that make you feel that it is more important to gratify my wants than your own needs. However, your impression of your father turned out to be a fantasy, and the same could be true of me."

Patient: "How *do* you feel, then?"

Therapist: "I feel that if your only reason to be in therapy is to talk about *me,* you might want to consider other ways to spend your time. If you need help with your relationship with your father, I'm certainly available."

Patient: "You wouldn't be angry if I thought I no longer needed help?"

Therapist: "You become so preoccupied with how others might experience your actions that you don't think about yourself. How do *you* feel about not needing help?"

Patient: "Now that you mention it, I feel fine. Can I call you if I have more problems in the future?"

Therapist: "Certainly."

Three years later the therapist did get a call from the patient, but it was not to make an appointment. He simply wanted to tell her that his father had retired and had asked him to become president of the company. The patient had handled a number of difficult personnel issues without any anxiety. He and his father had become close friends.

Some therapists believe that as long as the patient consents to it, there is nothing wrong with continuing psychotherapy indefinitely. After all, the patient is a customer, a client, a purchaser of services, free to consent to whatever seems to make sense.

These points are valid only if psychotherapy is regarded as a form of entertainment. But if the goal is to improve functioning or relieve distress, the question must be asked: does the therapist have a responsibility to measure the usefulness of the treatment as well as its enjoyability? In the first episode of treatment described above, a patient who was anxious to please anyone in a parental role was convinced to relive his relationship with his father—or what he imagined that to be—with his therapist. Three years later, he was as anxious as ever, he was still dissatisfied with his employee, and he had never questioned his basic assumptions about his father. Although it is certainly true that early experiences influence current feelings, the first therapist did not frame her interpretation of the cause of the patient's problem as *one possible* explanation—which might or might not prove to be true. Rather, she presented it as a fact, implying that it would be supported in time.

The second therapist was more interested in gathering information about the actual usefulness of the treatment to the patient. She viewed her impressions as speculations rather than facts, and her goal was to determine whether or not these speculations were correct. The assumption that the patient's feelings about his father were accurate turned out to be incorrect. The assumption that past feelings had to be worked through in order to solve a problem in the present also turned out to be incorrect; indeed, solving the present problem mobilized the patient to change the more longstanding interaction with his father.

Efforts to control the unending use of psychotherapy without meaningful results were initiated in the 1980s, when a group of experts in the field began to question the common assumption that it is impossible to apply the scientific method in evaluating psychological treatment approaches. The first step in overturning this assumption was to develop a means of quantifying the goals of treatment. One universal goal of therapy is clearly to reduce symptoms—to help patients feel less depressed or less anxious. A number of checklists, which can be filled out by both patient and therapist, have been developed that reliably measure symptoms of depression, anxiety, schizophrenia, and many other disorders. Do these checklists reduce a person's experience to a series of meaningless numbers? Not at all. They merely make it possible to track whether specific symptoms reported by the person in the beginning of treatment are getting better or worse.

Another common treatment goal—that of improving overall functioning—proved a little more challenging to track. However, a number of rating scales were developed that could be used, not only by patients and therapists but by family members and other caretakers, thus providing a more complete view of how a person is functioning in several arenas.

Objectively measuring patients' satisfaction with therapy, on the other hand, is quite easy to do. An extensive technology has been developed for this purpose that is used quite successfully by businesses, television networks, and political parties by asking people to fill out rating scales. A battery of rating scales was created that provided independent assessment of treatment outcomes by someone not directly involved in the therapy. This approach avoids the obvious bias of the therapist, whose desire for the treatment to work precludes truly objective assessment by just that individual.

The question of whether it is intrusive for third parties to demand evidence that a particular form of treatment is effective must be balanced against the question of whether patients have a right to get what they are paying for. Many of these third parties now maintain that if psychotherapy is to be a growth experience or a form of education, there is no more need to study it than to study meditation or Outward Bound—and no more reason to pay for it as a form of health care.

Even if outcome measurements are developed that reliably evaluate different therapeutic approaches, how can they be meaningful when every patient—and every treatment—is so different? The study of mental disorders suggests that while each person is unique, each illness is not. People with depression, generalized anxiety, or panic disorder certainly have different personalities, different reactions to their conditions, and different kinds of family problems. But their symptoms, levels of functioning, and outcomes tend to be similar *or they would not qualify for the same diagnoses.* Effective treatments for these disorders also have something in common or they would not be effective. Therefore, it should be possible to objectify the study of psychotherapies in the same way that observing certain symptoms leads to certain diagnoses. Over the past two decades, psychotherapies have been developed that last a specified period of time and use standardized interventions. With the consent of patients interested in contributing to knowledge in the field, an entire course of psychotherapy can be videotaped and scored by unbiased observers, who assess whether the therapist actually follows the theory of a particular psychotherapy and whether the intervention produces the desired result. Does this dehumanize psychotherapy? Or does it make it possible to tell whether psychotherapy does what its proponents claim it does?

During the 1990s, the methodology of "managed care" has become the dominant form of health-care review in the United States. Managed care is based on the concept that health-care providers, like the therapist discussed earlier, are not objective enough to keep treatment on course. Instead, "case managers" review each patient's treatment to ensure that it is the best approach. If treatment seems to be taking too long achieving its goals, no further payments are authorized.

Managed care has been applied with great gusto to the field of psychotherapy, which was viewed as a "black hole" by third-party payers. Despite their claims of objectivity, however, managed-care companies have not been any more scientific in their evaluation than the therapists they review. Instead, they have applied their own understanding of the direction treatment should take. The main outcome measurement used by these companies has been whether a particular form of therapy lowers the cost of care. This goal is easy to achieve if the reviewers simply do not pay for more than a few psychotherapy sessions, regardless of the appropriateness of extended treatment. However, now that bids for contracts to manage psychotherapy have reached such a low level that it is becoming impossible to bring the cost down further without seriously jeopardizing patient welfare, managed-care companies are attempting to assess quality as well as cost. This is a setting rife for deceptive use of pseudoscientific methodology for the purpose of marketing.

As one group of mental health practitioners discarded the scientific method, they recapitulated Freud's split from specialists of the mind who were committed to the research ethic of biology. Some of these specialists—the descendants of Kraepelin and Bleuler—developed modern psychiatric diagnoses and medications described later in this section. Others founded the specialty of *psychosomatic medicine,* which, in the 1950s and 1960s, presaged the eventual integration of mind and body in clinical psychiatry.

3

—

The Psychosomatic Movement

EVEN DURING THE heyday of psychoanalysis in the 1950s and 1960s, some psychiatrists remained grounded in biomedicine. These psychiatrists, who were involved in the care of the medically ill, knew that some of the dramatic physical symptoms they encountered were produced by mental stress. Yet the mechanism remained a mystery. It was obvious, for example, that the mind was to blame when a soldier with no eye disease suddenly went blind after a ferocious battle in which his best friend was killed—and recovered his sight just as abruptly after one psychotherapy session in which he talked about not wanting to see any more battles. The blindness appeared to be the result of some kind of "conversion" process, whereby the wish to see no more death is converted into denial of visual input; the patient thereby experienced blindness even though all visual pathways were intact. It is still not known exactly how the mind fools the body into blindness; some of what *is* known is discussed in this chapter.

The mind also seemed to be the instigator when patients developed peptic ulcers when they were under stress. However, the development of an ulcer appeared to involve an actual change in the structure of the body, not just in the function (as occurred in conversion). This kind of disorder was called a "psychosomatic illness": the mind (psyche) directly changed some part of the body (soma).

The term *psychosomatic* was coined in 1818 by German physiologist Johann Heinroth when he proposed that insomnia was a mental as well as a physical condition. However, he had no idea how mind and body interacted. The concept fell into disuse until the 1920s, when American psychoanalyst Felix Deutsch described seven illnesses (peptic ulcer, thyrotoxicosis, rheumatoid arthritis, asthma, hypertension, neurodermatitis, and ulcerative colitis) that seemed to be strongly influenced, if not caused, by psychological factors. In the absence of any technology to study mind-body interactions in medical illness, the psychosomatic concept languished again until it was popularized by another psychoanalyst, Flanders Dunbar. An organized effort to study psychosomatic disorders was announced in the inaugural issue of the *Journal of Psychosomatic Medicine* (now called simply *Psychosomatic Medicine*), which sought to show how "psychic and somatic phenomena take place in the same biological system and are probably two aspects of the same process."

As a formal movement, psychosomatic medicine, whose purview was the diseased body, was distinct from psychiatry—which treated the diseased mind—and from classical medicine—which was more interested in the physical than in the mental aspects of medical disease. Psychoanalysts Franz Alexander and Thomas French hailed the psychosomatic view as introducing "a new era in medicine . . . [that] includes the study of the participation of the total personality in the disease process."

Analytically trained psychiatrists and internists first learned about the personalities of psychosomatic patients in the course of treating them with psychoanalysis. The analysts discovered that certain emotional conflicts seemed to recur in case after case. Because the patients were able to trace their conflicts to a time prior to their illnesses, it was assumed that mental factors must have played a causative role. (Were it the other way around, the emotional problems would have begun *after* the illness.)

MIND INTO MATTER

A basic principle of psychosomatic theory is that painful experiences early in life result in feelings of shame, guilt, or fear. Natural human emotions and needs, such as anger, anxiety, grief, love, sexual longings, and dependency, become forbidden, unbearable feelings. For its own protection, the conscious mind quickly relegates these forbidden responses to the shadowy world of the unconscious. This is a costly kind of protection that requires continuous vigilance to prevent an accidental breakthrough of the unacceptable and encapsulates an important segment of psychic life. It is also a flawed kind of protection for the simple reason that repressing emotions does not make them go away; it just conceals their influence. This influence may take the form of unconsciously determined psychological symptoms, such as phobias, depression, and anxiety, which indirectly reflect the pressure toward expression of the hidden emotions. If the person is unable to process emotions on a psychological level, the conflict may be transferred to the body.

In the mid-1940s Dunbar pointed out that people with certain personality types are more prone than others to physical disaster—"People hurt themselves much more often than they are hurt by others or by fate or by the impersonal failure of machines"—and often the way in which they hurt themselves is to get sick. Dunbar observed that people who are susceptible to psychosomatic illness "will talk with gusto and a wealth of gruesome detail about their operations and their fevers [but] will shrink from confiding to anyone a hint that they might be a little sick mentally or emotionally." Their conscious belief is "that mental and emotional upsets are trivial outbreaks, largely imaginary and relatively harmless, or else rather shameful and hopeless exhibitions of complete collapse." According to Dunbar the *real* reason they keep their problems out of sight is that they are incapable of dealing with them.

In her clinical work with patients, Dunbar found that emotional conflict may turn into bodily dysfunction when people do not have the psychological resources to deal with their problems more directly. In such instances, getting sick can be an unconscious means of expiating guilt, humiliating oneself, punishing and manipulating others, obtaining caretaking and attention, to cite but a few possible hidden agendas. People who have learned that it is "wrong" or threatening to express their feelings, needs, or emotions directly (through language) must rely on their bodies to communicate psychological states indirectly (through physical symptoms).

Self-Induced Injuries

The most direct psychosomatic translation from the mental to the somatic level occurs when people intentionally injure their own bodies. Part II discusses people who, with full conscious awareness of their *actions* but without conscious awareness of their *motivations,* inflict pain on themselves for a variety of reasons. There are also individuals who, without any conscious intention, repeatedly but accidentally hurt themselves. Dunbar observed that many of these accident-prone individuals deceive themselves about the causes of their injuries:

> There are a good many incorrigibly inept individuals who cannot hammer a nail in straight but do not smash their fingers, who trip over their own feet but break no bones. They tumble down stairs, fall off docks, bump into stone walls, slip on the ice, and scrape the fenders of their cars with-

out damage to themselves or anyone else, although their friends sometimes wonder how they remain in one piece. The fact is that for all their clumsiness they do not have the accident habit. On the other hand, some deft, seemingly well-balanced men and women turn up repeatedly in the accident wards of our hospitals. They think they are the victims of pure bad luck or divine punishment. In reality they have been struck down by their own emotional conflicts.

Dunbar pointed out that self-destructive behavior is one way to transfer intolerable mental conflict about others into the bodily realm. Accidents tended to occur, she observed, when the person felt angry or rebellious, especially in relation to authority figures who were both needed and resented. As subtle but vicious attacks on the self, "accidentitis" seemed to Dunbar to be a way that people, who could not tolerate feeling anger toward someone they depended on, were able to express hostility in the only direction in which it could be controlled—at the self.

Conversion Symptoms

Freud's answer to the mind–into–matter riddle was that repressed needs, pushing to the surface of awareness, are converted into symptoms that covertly gratify the needs while keeping them safely out of conscious awareness. In Freud's day, the most common psychosomatic symptom was a sensory or motor dysfunction—blindness, deafness, paralysis—which he called a "conversion symptom": an unconscious mental state was converted into bodily disability or pain in the absence of underlying physical pathology. The conversion symptom retains its connection to the repressed conflict, idea, or need it is symbolizing. For example, chest pain might be substituted for a broken heart, blindness might be a way of not seeing something painful, paralysis might express the need to lie down and let others do the work, or an excruciating headache might express, and at the same time conceal, the memory of a parent who had a stroke. Although dramatic conversion symptoms, such as the blindness and paralysis treated by Freud and by military psychiatrists during World War II, are less common today, they still can occur, as will be shown in Part II.

An example of a more mundane case of conversion pain is that of "Eric." Eric's mother, who was chronically ill, did not have the energy to meet his normal childhood needs for caretaking and attention; indeed, he often had to take care of her. His father was always at work, trying to pay the family's medical bills. In response to his parents' emotional unavailability, Eric convinced himself that he had no needs—that way, he would not experience any of the pain, desperation, and rage that would be normal for a child who was consistently deprived. Eric reinforced this deception that he had no needs himself by becoming the kind of person on whom others always depended. This allowed him to do for others what he secretly wished others would do for him, even as he maintained a conscious image of himself as someone who was needed *but does not need*. The stronger Eric's underlying needs pushed for expression, the greater effort he expended in affirming the deception of self-sufficiency.

Eric began working to help support his family when he was fourteen, and he did not miss a day of work until he was well into his thirties. One day at work he received an e-mail message informing him that, in response to economic pressures, he would have to take on additional duties; at the same time, the performance bonuses that had been promised would have to be cancelled. Receiving such a message, it would be natural for Eric to feel betrayed by his superiors and to yearn for someone to relieve the escalating burden he was experiencing. For Eric, however, feeling helpless and needy would be an intolerable threat to the super-independent self-image on which his security and self-esteem depended. In the midst of this conflict, Eric developed acute abdominal pain, which he ignored for a few days until it became so overpowering that he had to stay home from work. The next day he tried to return to his job, but the pain was clearly incapacitating and within a week he was hospitalized for a medical evaluation. His tests revealed no pathology.

Eric's unacceptable need for caretaking was converted into stomach pain that symbolized his wish to be taken care of and, at the same time, left him too sick to take care of himself. The pain had the additional benefit of allowing him to feel closer to the only person who had ever been available to him—his grandfather, who had died of stomach cancer!

Conversion symptoms are one example of a mental process called "somatization," which fools the body into perceiving a malfunction that does not exist in physical terms. This kind of mind-body deception, which is the subject of Part II, solves an emotional problem that is intolerable to the mind: the problem is relocated to the realm of the body, where symptoms seem more deserving of sympathy and care, and where interventions feel less threatening to the person's self-esteem. Even though a conversion symptom is experienced in the province of the body, its pathology remains strictly the province of the mind because it does not lead to any actual alteration of anatomy or physiology.

Psychosomatic Illness

Conversion symptoms change the person's perception of the body, and accidental or purposeful self-injury changes the structure of the body. The kinds of psychosomatic illnesses initially described by Deutsch and further studied by Alexander and French involve changes in the perception *as well as* in the structure and function of the body. Because the brain, which is the organ of the mind, is connected to virtually every organ of the body through nerves and hormones, it is possible for the mind to cross over the line between ailments like conversion pain that feel as if they reside in the body, and those that actually reside in the body, such as peptic ulcers. This line is most likely crossed when the brain, aroused by strong emotions, mobilizes changes throughout the body in order to respond appropriately to the emotions.

When an emotion is expressed openly, the resulting mental and/or physical activity leads to resolution of the physiologic changes it has evoked. For example, anger stimulates blood flow to muscles, acceleration of heart rate, and elevation of blood pressure to prepare for action—say, punching (or preferably yelling at) the source of the anger. Once action is taken, muscles that no longer need to be so active can relax, and the heart and blood vessels reset themselves to their baseline level of activity.

If feelings are repressed or denied, however, then they cannot be dissipated through action. As a result, the body continues to respond to the emotion, even though the mind refuses to acknowledge it. Rapid heart beat (tachycardia), elevated blood pressure, muscle tension, headache, an upset stomach will continue for as long as the emotion remains unresolved.

If the body is basically healthy, the chronic physical stimulation of unresolved emotional conflict might be uncomfortable but not necessarily dangerous. However, a body that is susceptible to continued bombardment may begin to break down. For example, a chronically angry person whose heart is vulnerable to overstimulation might experience rapid, uncontrollable cardiac rhythms; someone else with the same emotional problem but a normal heart will experience nothing more than a few skipped beats from time to time; still another person with hyperactive blood vessels may develop high blood pressure. The psychosomatic illness, provoked by emotions that cannot be resolved by the mind, might make the sufferer feel weak, helpless, dependent, anxious, guilty, ashamed, or angry—and it might provide such "secondary gains" as attention or relief from responsibilities—*but the bodily symptoms do not directly symbolize the original conflict.*

Initially, the physical effects of unresolved emotions can be reversed once the emotion is dealt with in a satisfying way. However, a vulnerable organ subjected to ongoing stress may be permanently changed. Once the heart adjusts to beating at an excessive rate, or the blood vessels remain in spasm long enough, *the affected system may reset itself to a pathological level of functioning that is independent of the emotional state that originally mobilized it.* At this point, resolving the problems that first set off the psychosomatic chain of events will not necessarily return the body to normal.

According to psychosomatic theory, emotional and physical states influence each other: there is a complex two-way relationship between *psychological vulnerabilities to emotional conflicts* and *physical vulnerabilities to the*

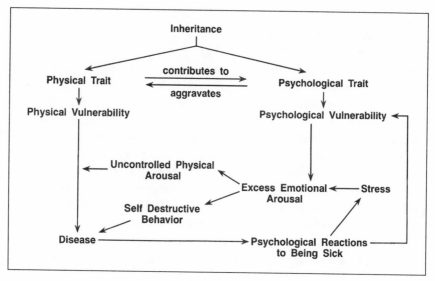

Figure 3-1.
The psychosomatic model

accompanying biological states of stress. The same inborn factors that create weak blood vessels may also create tendencies to excessive responses of fear and anger that overstimulate those blood vessels. Figure 3-1 illustrates the dynamic two-way interactions between mind and body that can create psychosomatic disorders.

People who hurt themselves through direct action, those whose bodies feel ill but remain well, and those whose bodies break down from within all have one trait in common: *They rely on the body to express problems that the mind cannot handle.* These are people who would rather be sick than needy, who become tense rather than anxious, who get an upset stomach instead of an uneasy mind. Beneath a facade of strength and independence, they are so fragile in the face of conflict that they unconsciously translate emotional distress into concrete symptoms of the body. If the body has inherent vulnerabilities, it may break down under the physical pressure of hidden emotions. At the same time, physical predispositions may affect the mind to create the very vulnerabilities that later subject the body to attack.

THE SPECIFICITY THEORY OF PEPTIC ULCER

We can gain a better understanding of the two-way interaction between psychology and biology proposed by psychosomatic theory by examining a common malady of modern life—the peptic ulcer. Psychosomatic researchers became interested in peptic ulcer, which is characterized by ulcerations, or erosions, of the duodenum (the first portion of the small intestine) due to digestion of intestinal tissue, because it appeared that certain kinds of stress caused it. Their experience in psychoanalyzing ulcer patients led them to hypothesize that an *inherent biological factor* interacted with a specific *psychological factor*, which in turn was intensified by a specific kind of *stress*. Developed by Franz Alexander and his colleagues, this was called the "specificity theory" of psychosomatic illness. Let us look at how this hypothesis was tested experimentally and expanded over the years.

Psychosomatic theorists thought that the biological factor underlying peptic ulcer was congenitally high levels of a hormone called *pepsinogen*. Pepsinogen is secreted by the stomach and is converted into pepsin, which in normal concentrations helps to break down food in the duodenum. The presence of excessive amounts of this digestive hormone from infancy onward would overstimulate the duodenum, resulting in chronic intestinal distress that is relieved only by food—in other words, there is a constant sensation of hunger. How would the baby's insatiable need for relief of gastric distress create a bodily change that would lead to more caretaking? Let's take a closer look at how this pattern might unfold.

The Making of an Ulcer

During early development, eating occurs at the same time that a child is being held, comforted, and made to feel secure. Some mothers* can adapt themselves to the neediness of an overly sensitive or reactive baby; as the baby is calmed by the additional efforts of the mother, physical distress diminishes. However, if the mother cannot respond comfortably to the excessive demands of a chronically uncomfortable baby, who does not relax after what should have been a normal feeding, she might respond with frustration and withdrawal. Without the physical comfort of continued food in the stomach and the emotional support of the mother's closeness, the baby's first and most important dependent relationship becomes unrewarding instead of soothing. Unless someone else steps in for the mother, who cannot respond appropriately to her baby's powerful needs, the child never learns to feel completely calm and secure.

Throughout development and into adulthood, any threat of loss will be reacted to by the most vulnerable part of the body—in this case, causing excess pepsinogen secretion in the duodenum. Eventually, damage accumulates in the form of peptic ulcer. The ulcer then produces physical symptoms that create new opportunities either to express dependent needs or to struggle against them. (See Figure 3-2.)

*For simplicity, the primary caretaker is referred to here as the mother.

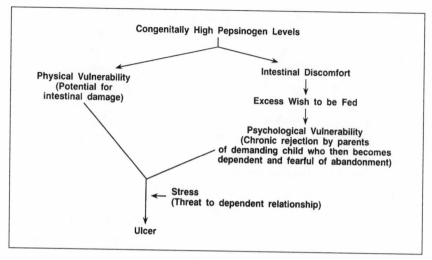

Figure 3-2.
Specificity theory applied to peptic ulcer

Testing Specificity

As modern psychiatry was flexing its muscles after World War II, the first formal psychosomatic studies of the specificity theory were carried out by gastroenterologist I. Arthur Mirsky and his psychoanalyst colleagues. Mirsky's group identified two factors common to ulcer patients, one physiological and the other psychological. Physiologically, virtually everyone who developed peptic ulcer was found to secrete large amounts of pepsinogen, even after the ulcer had healed. Psychologically, ulcer patients tended to have strong dependency needs that made it difficult for them to assert themselves in any way that might threaten a relationship on which they relied.

Since there are many people who have either high levels of pepsinogen or excessive dependency needs but who do not get ulcers, Mirsky argued that it must take both somatic and psychological components to set the stage for ulcer disease. Even then, an ulcer might never develop unless a specific stressor—involving the loss of an important relationship—upset the delicate balance between unmet dependency needs and defenses against feeling needy. But how to prove all this?

Mirsky had the kind of resources that later psychosomatic researchers could only envy. He convinced the U.S. Army to allow him to study 2,073 recently drafted eighteen- and nineteen-year-old men. It was assumed that, for most of these physically healthy inductees, living away from the security of home for the first time would be a threat to dependency needs, but it was also assumed that this initial sense of threat would become a problem only for those who had unresolved conflicts about these needs. Mirsky proposed that soldiers who had these unresolved conflicts *and* high pepsinogen levels would be less likely to handle the challenge in the realm of the mind and more likely to produce an ulcer.

Mirsky administered a psychological test to identify individuals with the kinds of dependency traits he thought would act as predisposing factors to ulcer disease (immaturity, a need to please others, difficulty dealing with hostility). Next, he assessed the new recruits' physical vulnerability by measuring pepsinogen levels upon arrival at basic training and again eight to sixteen weeks later. Lastly, the presence or absence of a peptic ulcer was determined via gastrointestinal series (barium X-rays of the stomach and small intestine). Sixty-three of the inductees had high pepsinogen levels; three of these men had begun their service with healed peptic ulcers, and one had an active ulcer. At the completion of basic training, new ulcers had developed in five more men, all of whom also had high pepsinogen levels. The ulcers were not causing symptoms, but they could be seen clearly on X-ray. None of the fifty-seven men with low pepsinogen levels developed an ulcer.

What differentiated the nine men who developed ulcers prior to, or by the end of, basic training from the 2,064 who did not? All the ulcer subjects were in the high pepsinogen group, but there must have been some additional factor, since fifty-four of the sixty-three men with high pepsinogen levels remained healthy. A review of the psychological tests provided an answer.

The initial psychological test results had suggested that only ten soldiers had the kind of intense dependency conflicts that were predicted to be associated with ulcers. Of these ten individuals—all of whom also had high pepsinogen levels—seven developed ulcers. The other two ulcer patients did not have the characteristic dependency conflicts, although they were in the high pepsinogen group. Thus ten of 2,073 people undergoing the same stress of basic training had a combination of high pepsinogen *and* strong dependency conflicts, and seven had, or developed, an ulcer. The interconnection of the physical and psychological variables was further supported by the fact that eighty-five percent of high pepsinogen secretors could be identified, without even looking at the blood levels, by their dependency traits on the psychological tests.

Psychiatry's Reaction to the Mirsky Study

In most scientific disciplines, Mirsky's results would be considered provocative findings that also contained important limitations that had to be addressed. Replications of his study to address these limitations were not conducted, however, and the opportunity was lost to settle some of the questions that his work had raised.

One obvious problem with Mirsky's study was the small number of affected individuals; if there had been just a few more ulcer patients who did not have strong dependency conflicts, the results would have been interpreted entirely differently. This might well have happened if the study had been extended beyond a mere two months. Ten percent of the general population develop ulcers at some time in their lives, but only less than half of one percent of Mirsky's sample had this problem. Perhaps the additional 9.5 percent who were likely to develop ulcers six months, a year, or fifteen years later had different conflicts—or no conflicts at all. Some of these subjects may even have had ulcers at the time of induction, which did not show up in imperfect X-rays of that time. For those soldiers whose ulcers could be seen when the study began, the process of erosion of the duodenum may have begun long before they were exposed to the stress of being drafted.

These are just some of the methodological problems that challenge Mirsky's conclusion that dependency conflicts are a causal factor in the emergence of peptic ulcer. But even if the psychological vulnerability and the physical outcome were legitimately associated, it would not necessarily mean that the conflict *caused* the ulcer. The dependency problem could be a reaction to a conscious or unconscious perception of being ill; it could be a psychological response to the effect of high pepsinogen levels on the brain, or it could be linked to an unknown third factor that had nothing to do with gastric distress in response to the threat of separation. One such factor is infection with an organism called *Helicobacter*, which contributes to 80 percent of cases of peptic ulcer and which may be linked to dependency in an unknown manner.

NONSPECIFICITY TAKES THE STAND

Because of these limitations, researchers developed new ways of testing psychosomatic theories that go beyond the concept of a single specific psychological factor resulting in a specific physical illness. Recognizing that mental and emotional states have the potential to set the stage for more than one specific illness, researchers turned toward a theory of psychosomatic illness in which stress was viewed as subjecting the body *as a whole* to generalized physiologic arousal. Whether or not the body sustained injury from the stress reaction would depend on which bodily systems, if any, were most vulnerable to the effects of arousal.

Numerous studies have tended to refute the idea that there are *specific* psychological traits and emotions that set the stage for *specific* diseases. Instead, it appears that certain *global emotional states* (such as anxiety, hopelessness, and grief) lead to *global alterations in bodily functioning,* which in turn interact with propensities to illness transmitted by heredity or early experience. However, personality vulnerabilities to *specific* kinds of stressors do appear to play a significant role in the development of physical disease. Thus, early life experiences, compounded by constitutional predispositions, leave some people more vulnerable to relationship losses, some to any kind of loss, some to the expression of anger, some to anxiety, others to giving up in response to a challenge. Only when stress overwhelms the mind's capacity to cope with it is the body subjected to excessive pressures that result in mental or physical breakdown.

The Stress of Grief

A dramatic and unfortunately common example of the ways in which a single stressor can have a variety of mental or physical consequences is loss. Grief, the inevitable response to loss, is a universal activator of the stress response. Grieving people are sad, anxious, and angry, often at the same time, and these strong feelings evoke physiological changes, such as rapid heart rate, muscle tension, and suppression of immune function. For most people, the process of mourning is inevitably agonizing, but the emotional and physiological arousal abates as feelings about the lost person are worked through. However, someone who is vulnerable to loss may be prone to excessively strong or prolonged emotions and continued activation of the stress response during times of loss.

According to the nonspecificity theory of psychosomatic illness, pathological outcomes of grief depend on each person's area—or areas—of vulnerability. People whose only vulnerability is in the psychological capacity to tolerate grief might develop a kind of emotional paralysis, without any physical consequences beyond the discomfort of a rapid heartbeat, fatigue, or insomnia. Individuals predisposed to severe depression, anxiety, schizophrenia, or other major mental illnesses (by virtue of inherited or acquired abnormalities in the structure or function of the brain) might develop one of these disorders following the trauma of a loss. In those whose heart or blood vessels are vulnerable, the continued pressure of excessive arousal may lead to heart disease or hypertension. People whose immune systems are subject to excessive suppression by the stress response may become less able to fight infection or cancer. (These interactions between the stress of loss, psychology, and inherent physical vulnerabilities are discussed in greater detail in Part IV.)

The concept of psychosomatic medicine has grown from the "one stress, one disease" model of specificity theory tested by Mirsky to a model in which the only specificity is each person's unique psychological vulnerability. The specific mental or physical disease that emerges in a psychologically vulnerable person depends on where specific weaknesses exist in the brain and/or the body. *All illnesses, medical and psychiatric, can now be considered psychosomatic in nature.* The same forces can unleash both kinds of illnesses, and the same physiology can be present, whether the major manifestation of an illness is mental or physical.

FAMILY AND SOCIAL CONTEXTS OF PSYCHOSOMATIC DISEASE

Ironically, the psychosomatic viewpoint was broad enough to consider the effect of the mind on the body yet too narrow to recognize the effect of *significant people* on the mind and the body of the individual. Psychosomatic treatment approaches were directed toward the individual's reaction to an impersonal factor referred to as *stress,* as though the stress were not created *in relation to other people.* However, the full reality is that a host of non-inherited psychological and physical factors that aggravate or ameliorate disease arise, and can only be treated, within the family. Just as people can use their bodies to deflect the full impact of emotions that feel too powerful to handle in any other way, so too can they use their bodies as an unconscious means of coping with *other people's psyches.*

In studying family interactions with physically ill children, renowned family therapist Salvador Minuchin added another dimension to psychosomatic medicine. He expanded the nonspecificity theory by proposing that, at least in the case of children who become ill, the psychological precipitant for the chain of physical events that results in psychosomatic disease in the child is a crisis within a family that lacks the capacity to solve conflict directly. Asthma has been studied thoroughly in this regard, but Minuchin finds the same factors operating in anorexia nervosa, which is traditionally considered a psychological disease but has roots in the body, and diabetes mellitus, which most people think of as a medical illness but has strong psychological input.

Because children's defenses are not as well developed as adults', they rely on their parents to buffer the effects of intense emotions and to supply the resiliency they do not yet possess to cope with a stressful world. "Psychosomatic families," who combine inability to solve everyday problems with pathological dependence on each other to meet needs and bolster weak egos, may add to, rather than moderate, the impact of whatever stress comes along. Minuchin observed that such families never learn problem-solving skills because they spend too much time encouraging each other's weaknesses as a means of turning their attention away from their own interpersonal deficiencies and feeling that there is something outside of themselves they can control. They ignore potentially manageable problems they feel incompetent to address, while overreacting to minor stresses. Because movement of one member toward independence threatens the enmeshed relationships of all members, growth is subtly discouraged, while dependency and weakness are fostered. Independence of any family member presents a severe threat to a pathological balance that depends on everyone having something wrong that requires the attention of everyone else. Actual departure from the family seems unthinkable.

While many families are mobilized by an illness to do everything possible to restore the afflicted family member to normal functioning, the psychosomatic family described by Minuchin does everything possible to covertly maintain the malfunction. While the illness may appear on the surface to be a threat, it is really a blessing in disguise because it allows everyone to focus on the illness rather than on meaningful issues in the family. By responding solicitously whenever the sick family member displays any symptoms and withdrawing when that person seems to feel better, the family subtly encourages the sick member to remain in the sick role.

In turn, the "identified patient" learns to use the illness as a means of getting certain needs met and expressing unacceptable emotions through the language of the body at the expense of learning more mature ways of communicating. The sick role is continually reinforced as the disease process itself is aggravated by escalating family dynamics, which family members are increasingly unable to resolve because they do not know how to express feelings directly; they can only respond to signs of illness. The pathogenic contribution of the family to the maintenance of medical illnesses is illustrated in Figure 3-3.

During the 1970s, internist and psychoanalyst George Engel expanded the psychosomatic concept beyond the family when he introduced the term "biopsychosocial" to convey the convergence of three different sets of factors: *biological vulnerability,* such as susceptibility to an abnormal heartbeat; *psychological vulnerability,* especially proneness to feelings of helplessness and hopelessness; and *social pressures,* such as an important loss along with absence of social supports to buffer the loss. Certain mental illnesses were already recognized as culturally dependent—for example, the delusion that one has been turned into a flesh-eating monster (*wendigo*) is specific to some Native Canadian tribes. Likewise, cultural factors were recognized as altering the experience of physical disease—as when patients of Mediterranean descent complain of pain in a far more dramatic fashion than those of Nordic extraction. However, Engel added the concept that social pressures could interact with other psychosomatic forces to influence the actual development of physical and mental illnesses and even death.

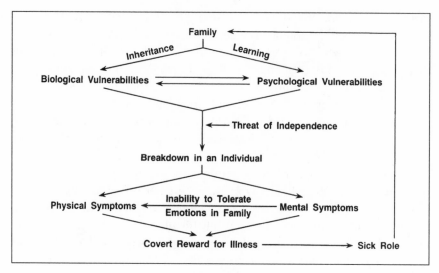

Figure 3-3.
The role of the family in psychosomatic illness

As scientific understanding of the breadth and complexity of mind-body in-teractions continued to expand, the chasm between these two parallel do-mains of human experience began to lessen at last. The next chapter explores the tentative steps taken toward the reunification of mind and body, as the *study of mind* and the *study of the body* began to converge.

4

—

The Rumblings of a Mind-Body Reunion

IN SPITE OF the exile of the mind from the intricacies of bodily subspe-cializations, psychosomatic medicine remained a gadfly pestering psychiatry and biomedicine for a reunion. Eventually, the compelling impetus to take notice of the psychosomatic viewpoint came from pragmatic realizations. During the 1980s, studies began to emerge showing that, no matter how medically inconsequential the mind might appear to the specialist of the body, the social and economic realities of mental syndromes were far from inconsequential. Statistics now took the stand. This research, which involved household surveys (first reported in 1984 by psychiatric epidemiologist Lee Robins), has shown that:

- Between 15 and 23 percent of the entire population of the United States has a diagnosable mental disorder.
- Between 28 and 38 percent will develop a mental disorder at some time in their lives.
- Between 12 and 18 percent of the population will become alcoholics.
- An estimated 6 percent will abuse drugs.
- Between 10 and 20 percent will become depressed.
- Between 10 and 25 percent will develop unmanageable anxiety.
- Between 5 and 10 percent will display severe personality disorders.
- At least 30,000 people will commit suicide each year, with an estimated

3,000–15,000 additional deaths that are attributed to accidents or "heart attacks" that may be suicides.

Since the greatest risk for the development of mental problems occurs during a person's most productive years—between the ages of twenty-five and forty-four—the United States loses more than $185 billion annually in productivity to mental conditions. The annual cost of mental health treatment is $20–50 billion, which is 15 percent of all expenditures for health care. Yet federal support for research into these disorders amounts to *less than* a quarter of 1 percent of what they cost us.

Physicians who believe that people with mental disorders are going to see psychiatrists are deceiving themselves. No matter how much the medical system limits itself to the purely physical, about 30 percent of patients in primary-care practice, and up to 10 percent of medical inpatients, have diagnosable psychiatric illnesses that contribute to or masquerade as physical complaints. Whether they are aware of it or not, primary-care physicians provide 60 percent of the mental health care in the United States. Some of this care is transacted in the form of prescriptions for antidepressant and antianxiety drugs, and some in the form of recommendations for psychotherapy. However, non-psychiatric physicians treat or refer only a minority of their patients with mental disorders; the rest of these patients get medicines for physical complaints that never go away because the mental distress that causes them is not directly addressed.

For their part, psychiatrists have found that no matter how strongly they believe that the body has nothing to do with the mind, the body does not cooperate in supporting their belief. Recent research shows that 39–60 percent of psychiatric patients have medical illnesses that cause or contribute to their mental symptoms. Nevertheless, researcher E.K. Koryani showed that in 50 percent of cases, psychiatrists, primary-care physicians, and even the patients themselves are unaware that there is anything medically wrong.

This pervasive oblivion to the biological component of psychological distress is a direct result of the tendency to dichotomize the mental and physical areas: the assumption is made that if there is a mental problem, there cannot be a physical one, too. No examination is performed—and nothing is found! The following examples from Koryani's experience demonstrate how blatantly it is possible to be deceived:

A submissive, anhedonic boy of nineteen years of age with conversion hysteria, headaches, withdrawal, and postural abnormality . . . of the head was referred by the family physician. His vocal mother accompanied him, blaming herself for having interfered with the boy's first love affair, "resulting in his symptoms." Final diagnosis was medulloblastoma [brain tumor]. . . .

A "quarreling couple" were treated with marital therapy. Both have a few drinks before dinner and routinely quarrel at bedtime. A five-hour glucose tolerance test showed a hypoglycemia [low blood sugar] at three hours in both [spouses]. . . .

A postmenopausal woman with rheumatic heart disease receiving digitalis for many years with no previous psychiatric illness was referred by her cardiologist for depression and diarrhea. Recently, quinidine was added to her medication [can increase blood levels of digitalis]. The final diagnosis was digitalis poisoning. . . .

In each of these cases the assumption was made that a psychological disorder was the cause of the problem because the symptom was psychological. The result: treatment was misdirected and potentially dangerous. When the possibility was finally recognized that the psychological symptoms were responses to changes in the body, the actual problems—neurological and medical illnesses and toxicity from a medication—were easy to identify.

DIAGNOSING THE INTANGIBLE

One of my colleagues, who had completed his psychiatric residency in the early 1930s, recalled a (now) humorous experience from his training days. While on rounds one day, he had disagreed with the chief resident about the diagnosis of a severely disturbed patient. "Put up your dukes," the chief resident had said, "we'll see who's right!" The chief resident's approach to diagnosis was probably as reliable as any other at that time; diagnosis was based more on guesswork, suppositions, etiquette, and politics than observable data.

For example, psychotic patients brought to hospitals and emergency rooms were likely to be diagnosed as *schizophrenic* in the United States but as *manic* in Great Britain. The difference did not reflect differences in the incidence of the two disorders but *differences in diagnostic habits*. During the 1960s, it was common for American psychiatrists to assign a diagnosis of "hysteria" or "hysterical personality" when a patient was histrionic, self-destructive, and generally difficult to treat. However, as the theories of psychoanalysts Otto Kernberg and Heinz Kohut on borderline and narcissistic personality disorders became popular, therapists of all persuasions began to give these diagnoses to the former "hysterics"—even though the pioneers in the field disagreed about what particular set of symptoms indicated the presence of the "new" disorders. More recently, some diagnosticians have concluded that many patients who used to have diagnoses of hysterical, borderline, or narcissistic personality disorder really have mood disorders—again without formal diagnostic studies that would allow other clinicians to confirm their impressions formally.

During the 1970s, enormous strides were taken in measuring states of mind. Objective rating scales for subjective mental states were devised that made it possible for observers from different theoretical orientations to agree, at least, on what symptoms a patient seemed to be experiencing. Identifying and labeling clusters of symptoms made it possible to study the course of mental disturbances and the impact of various treatments on them. As we saw when we discussed attempts to evaluate psychotherapy in a scientific manner, the movement to objectify psychiatric diagnosis was an important step toward applying the scientific method to concepts previously considered too intangible to observe and too ephemeral to be evaluated by anything besides intuition.

This technology of measurement has been codified in the *Diagnostic and Statistical Manual of Mental Disorders,* first published in 1952 and now in its fourth edition (*DSM-IV*). This manual now relies on *descriptive* rather than *causal* terms. Whereas in *DSM-I* depressive neurosis was defined by terms that denoted its supposed causes, such as "loss of a love object" and "internal conflict," a major depressive episode is defined in *DSM-IV* by the presence of at least five of nine symptoms that could be rated objectively, such as loss of pleasure, weight change, altered sleep, difficulty concentrating, and thoughts of death. Psychiatric diagnoses in *DSM-II* were called "reactions" (e.g., schizophrenic reaction) on the grounds that each diagnosis represented a reaction to an external or psychological stressor, even though it is clear that many psychiatric symptoms arise spontaneously. In *DSM-IV,* psychiatric diagnoses are called "disorders," indicating that they are identified by measurable manifestations and not by inferred dynamics that no one has ever proven.

The *DSM-III/DSM-IV* approach has been most reliable when it is applied to major psychiatric disorders such as depression, mania, panic disorder, or schizophrenia. However, none of the personality disorders listed in *DSM-IV,* except for antisocial personality disorder, has much research supporting its identity as a unique condition with symptoms, a course, and a treatment response that distinguishes it from the other personality disorders. This fact was illustrated in an interesting study by researcher J. Christopher Perry, who showed that trained evaluators could have a very high level of agreement about whether the pathological traits listed as criteria for personality disorders were present, but their agreement was no better than chance about whether those traits signified a personality *disorder,* and if so, which disorder it might be. While *DSM-IV* has gone a long way toward developing a consensus about what the experts mean when they diagnose disorders like depression, it still has some distance to go when it comes to objectifying more subtle twists and turns of the personality.

INHERITING THE INTANGIBLE

At about the same time that psychiatric diagnoses were being objectified, a technology for measuring the complex biology of heredity was developed. This exciting breakthrough led to studies investigating whether mental attributes were inherited in the same way as physical traits.

Adoption Studies

Studying the impact of heredity on psychological and emotional development involves more than just seeing whether a trait or disorder runs in families. After all, money and political affiliations run in families, but they are not genetic. One way of distinguishing the acquired from the genetic is to determine whether people who are adopted at birth end up resembling their adoptive or their biological families more when they grow up. Using this method, S. Scarr and R.A. Weinberg at the University of Minnesota were the first to report the important role of heredity in personality development, when they found that young adults who were adopted as infants were not like their adoptive siblings psychologically "in anything." This remarkable finding was expanded by a 1990 research report by Robert Plomin and his colleagues, stating that the best predictor of the amount of time an adopted child would spend watching television was the time the *biological parents— not* the adoptive parents the child lived with—spent watching TV. Adoption studies of psychiatric diagnoses have revealed the equally dramatic findings that, for example, having a blood relative with depression, panic reactions, alcoholism, or antisocial personality disorder is a more important determinant of whether an individual develops the same condition than being raised in nonbiological families with that disorder!

Twin Studies

An additional window into the role of inheritance is provided by comparisons of identical and fraternal twins. Both kinds of twins share approximately the same prenatal environment (although identical twins may or may not share the same attachment to the placenta, which can influence the development of the fetus). Identical twins come from the same egg (monozygotic) and therefore have exactly the same genes, while fraternal twins come from different eggs (dizygotic) and have only the same degree of genetic similarity as any other siblings. When any condition (say, alcoholism) occurs more frequently in identical than in fraternal twins, this suggests that a genetic factor plays an important role in its etiology. Since identical twins often are treated more similarly by their families than are fraternal twins, researchers have compared twins raised in different households to eliminate environmental influences from assessments of genetic factors in psychological development.

Like the adoption studies, twin studies have consistently suggested a genetic contribution to some psychiatric disorders, especially bipolar disorder (manic depression) and certain personality traits. University of Minnesota psychologists Thomas J. Bouchard, Jr. and David T. Lykken studied 100 sets of identical and fraternal twins and triplets who were reunited as adults after having been raised from infancy in different households. These researchers evaluated a number of psychological traits that were measured during a total of fifty hours of testing that extended over ten years. One finding, not too surprising, was that identical twins' electroencephalograms (brain waves) resembled each other, regardless of their upbringing. A more hotly debated finding was the discovery that about 70 percent of the variability in IQ between individuals in the study could be attributed to genetic factors.

The most startling conclusion of the Minnesota study was that average scores on measures of eleven personality traits and twenty-three personal-interest variables were as similar in identical twins *who were reared separately* as they were in identical twins *who grew up in the same household.* In other words, being raised in the same environment did not alter the influence of the genes in these complex psychological areas. The traits measured included tendencies toward sociability, criminality, introversion, extraversion, traditionalism, religiosity, altruism, aggression, as well as vocational interests and political attitudes. The genetic influence was further confirmed by the finding that fraternal twins, who have *half the genetic similarity* of identical twins, were about *half as likely to share the same traits.* These results led the researchers to conclude that ". . . most parents are less effective in imprinting their distinctive stamp on the children developing within their spheres of influence—or are less inclined to do so—than has been supposed."

Although it would be ridiculous to say that personality is simply inherited, it is true that heredity has a more powerful influence on personality than was once thought. Twin and adoption studies suggest that 30–60 percent of factors contributing to major personality traits are genetically based. The shared experience of a common upbringing is typically filtered through inherited temperamental differences, resulting in siblings who have drastically different personalities. Genetic endowment may make the difference between children who are easy to raise and children who continually rub their parents the wrong way. Some children raised in grossly abusive or neglectful homes have the inborn resiliency to use what little the environment offers as a positive foundation from which they shape a cohesive and adaptable personality, while others, exposed to similarly traumatic experiences, are unable to muster the psychological resources to survive intact. Genes therefore set the broad limits within which experience can direct the development of personality.

UNCOVERING THE GENETIC MYSTERIES

Family, adoption, and twin studies provide indirect evidence of genetic influences. New biomedical technologies have made it possible to identify the actual genetic counterparts of mental conditions. About 5,000 human genes have been catalogued, and the "addresses" or locations on specific chromosomes of 1,900 of these genes have been identified. It has even been possible to clone 600 genes, revealing *exactly* what they do.

Genetic information is stored in desoxyribonucleic acid (DNA), which is composed of strings of small molecules, called *nucleotides.* There are five different kinds of nucleotides, depending on their chemical composition. In DNA, two strings of nucleotides are connected to each other, ladder-like, by links between them.

The "words" of the genetic language are formed by varying sequences ("letters") of three nucleotides. These words or *codons* instruct the body to make one of twenty amino acids, groups of which are then assembled into proteins. It takes about 1,000 nucleotides to create a code for the average protein. Genes, which are DNA segments ("paragraphs") that carry the codes for cellular structures, contain up to two *million* nucleotides! The DNA needed to "make" a human being, which includes about 100,000 genes in forty-eight chromosomes, contains three *billion* nucleotide pairs. When stretched out, the human DNA strand is about one meter long, but it contains enough information to fill thirteen sets of the Encyclopedia Britannica!

Genetic linkage studies attempt to identify chromosomal segments that distinguish people with psychiatric disorders from those who do not have these disorders. It is now possible to draw pictures of multiple sequences that make up segments of a chromosome of varying length, and to identify variations in these sequences from individual to individual.

Of the 4,000 known genetic diseases in humans, more than 100 have been linked to readily identifiable chromosome sequences. Examples include Huntington's disease (chromosome 4), cystic fibrosis (chromosome 7), sickle-cell anemia (chromosome 11), premature coronary artery disease (chromosome 11), a familial form of Alzheimer's disease (chromosome 21), and Duchenne's muscular dystrophy (X chromosome). It has also been possible to identify the actual *gene* for about twelve diseases, including Huntington's disease, cystic fibrosis, and one of the Alzheimer's disease genes. Many more specific genes will probably be identified in the next few years. Locating the actual gene makes it possible to clone the gene and allow it to make its abnormal protein, placing the scientist within striking distance of a treatment to *compensate* for the altered protein or even to change the action of the gene. Steps in this direction have recently been taken for cystic fibrosis.

Linkage studies are most likely to be successful when patterns of inheritance suggest that an alteration in one copy of a *single gene* is responsible. In psychiatry, this criterion is best fulfilled by bipolar (manic-depressive) illness. However, research described in Part III raises the possibility that different subtypes of this condition may be linked to different chromosomes, suggesting that genes on *different chromosomes* can convey susceptibility to the *same syndrome*. Vulnerability to schizophrenia, which in some populations is associated with specific nucleotide sequences on chromosome 6 and in other populations is not, seems to interact with physical factors occurring during or after birth to produce different kinds of schizophrenic conditions in different people.

GENES AND DISEASE: A COMPLEX RELATIONSHIP

As will be demonstrated in Parts III and IV, abnormal genes that affect complex biological processes may be *inherited,* they may result from *errors in gene copying processes,* from spontaneous changes (*mutations*) in structure, from the presence of *physical toxins* during gestation, or their function may be modified by *early experience.* In all of these instances, the untoward occurrence of one or more physical events directed by a gene, or the failure of an altered gene to prevent a biochemical event, can set the stage for mental aberrations as certainly as it can lead to the development of physical abnormalities.

One common misconception among non–geneticists is that abnormal genes *cause* disease. In fact, situations in which an illness is inevitable (for example, Huntington's Chorea) are rare. Actual illness usually depends on the outcome of an *interaction* between genes and environmental influences. Even then, the outcome may not necessarily be fixed. For example, the effects of a disease like phenylketonuria (PKU), which is a form of inherited mental retardation caused by abnormal metabolism of the amino acid phenylalanine, can be prevented by identifying the metabolic defect at birth and administering a phenylalanine-free diet.

In the case of more complex psychiatric illnesses, such as bipolar disorder or schizophrenia, genes do not directly cause the disease like they directly cause neurological illnesses such as Huntington's. Identical twins of schizophrenic parents have an increased risk of developing schizophrenia themselves, but the increase is moderate and most will not develop the disorder. In a study of schizophrenic adults with identical twins, psychiatrist Richard Suddath found that twins who became schizophrenic had enlarged cerebral ventricles (fluid-filled spaces in the brain), a finding frequently noted in schizophrenia. However, twins who were not schizophrenic did not have the enlarged ventricles, even when their identical twin was schizophrenic.

Since they have exactly the same genes, identical twins of schizophrenics should have the same genetic risk for schizophrenia. However, the development of the illness itself may depend on the interaction of the genetic risk with some kind of environmental insult, either before birth or while the brain continues to develop in childhood, to cause the specific change in brain structure found in schizophrenia. (It might appear that identical twins would share identical prenatal environment, but as we have already seen, these twins may have different attachments to the placenta that can make the circulation of toxins or other substances from the mother's system different for each twin.) The finding that Swedish adults who had been in their second trimester of fetal development during a 1957 influenza epidemic were more likely to develop schizophrenia than people of approximately the same age whose mothers were not pregnant during the epidemic suggests one possibility: that the insult may be a virus. However, as we saw in our discussion of peptic ulcer, the interaction between heredity and environment is complex enough that other—mostly unknown—factors determine whether the interaction actually leads to disease.

In early 1996, a series of studies appeared in the journal *Nature Genetics* that illustrated how advances in objectifying mental states could be coordinated with advances in studies of genetic linkage to identify a DNA sequence—and an actual gene—associated with complex psychological traits. The first of these studies, by Stella Hu of the National Cancer Institute, showed that about 66 percent of homosexual men whose brothers were also homosexual shared a particular sequence of nucleotides (on the far end of the long arm of the X chromosome), while only 22 percent of heterosexual brothers of homosexual men had the same sequence. The association held not only with overall sexual orientation but with such subcategories of sexual orientation as exclusive attraction to males, fantasy about males, and actual sexual activity. No other genetic marker on the X chromosome was associated with male homosexuality. The investigators decided to study the X chromosome, which comes from the mother in males (the father contributes a Y chromosome), because earlier research had shown that gay males have more homosexual relatives on their mother's than on their father's side of the family. The findings that lesbian sisters of homosexual women did not share the X-chromosome marker, that the majority of sisters of homosexual men were heterosexual, and that female homosexuals have more sisters who are lesbians than they do brothers who are gay, suggested that the genetic component of male homosexuality differs from that of female homo-sexuality. As with every other psychological element we have considered, even identical twins of male or female homosexuals have no more than a 70 percent chance of being homosexual themselves, indicating that genetics is an important but not sole component of sexual orientation.

Two additional studies, one by Richard Ebstein of the Herzog Memor-ial Hospital in Jerusalem and the other by Jonathan Benjamin of the Na-tional Institute of Mental Health, have demonstrated linkage between one particular gene and a psychological trait called novelty-seeking. People with high scores on novelty-seeking scales are characterized as impulsive, ex-ploratory, fickle, excitable, quick-tempered, and extravagant. Those with low scores are said to be reflective, rigid, loyal, stoic, slow-tempered, and fru-gal.

Studying Israeli subjects of various ethnic backgrounds, the Ebstein group found that individuals who had significantly higher novelty-seeking scores also had a gene that coded for a slightly larger receptor for a neurotransmit-ter called dopamine than subjects who did not have this version of the dopamine receptor gene. Other personality traits (e.g., persistence, reward dependence, and harm avoidance) were not associated with the specific dopamine receptor subtype.

Using a different kind of instrument that measured the same trait in an ethnically diverse American population, the Benjamin group found the same association between novelty-seeking and the dopamine receptor gene iden-tified by the Ebstein group. This gene variation was also associated with sev-eral related traits, such as warmth, excitement-seeking, lack of deliberation, extravagance, and disorderliness.

These studies used different methodologies to find exactly the same thing—and in an average group of people rather than a clinical population: that the tendency to seek stimulation and excitement is greater in people who have a dopamine receptor gene that seems to code for a somewhat big-ger receptor. In both studies, the linkage held regardless of age, sex, ethnic-ity, country of origin, and sexual orientation. Why the dopamine receptor? Dopamine is involved in the regulation of such aspects of human experi-ence as reward, motivation, and action-oriented behavior. A larger receptor for dopamine could accentuate the action of dopamine in promoting activ-ity and interest in a stimulating environment.

However, it seems unlikely that a single gene could contribute to such a complex personality trait as novelty-seeking, and the data bear this out. Twin studies suggest that heredity contributes about 40 percent to novelty-seeking behavior, and that the dopamine gene variation identified in the above studies accounts for only 10 percent of the genetic influence on this trait. It appears that there may be as many as ten genes that together form the hereditable component of novelty-seeking. These pioneering studies show that it may be possible in the foreseeable future to clarify exactly which genes are involved in personality development, and to what extent.

It is as inaccurate to say that mental states are inherited as to contend that they are not. The interaction of a host of genetic influences may determine the general direction of development but not necessarily the ultimate outcome. Experience may compensate for, aggravate, or even mimic inherited disruptions of physiology that produce mental instability. The next section provides one illustration of how experience altered the functioning of an organism's genetically determined "hard wiring."

WHAT ROLE DOES EXPERIENCE PLAY?

Technological advances have made it possible to study the ways in which inherited "hard wiring" can be modified by experience. Two of the pioneers in this area of research are Daniel Alkon of the National Institute of Neurological, Communicative Diseases, and Stroke at Woods Hole, Massachusetts and Eric Kandel at Columbia University in New York City. Both investigators study species of sea snails, organisms that are so simple that it is possible to construct a complete diagram of their nervous systems and observe changes in neurons that mediate behavioral responses to signals in the environment. The marine snail is born with all the connections between neurons it will ever have, but some of these connections are not active until they are "turned on" by experience. In other words, the nervous system's *hardware* is fully developed at birth, but the *software* that instructs the hardware to carry out its broadest repertoire is acquired through experience. Although the sea snail's nervous system does not grow further once it is fully formed, it does have the capacity to reprogram its functioning in response to a changing environment.

One of the prewired connections in the marine snail *Hermissenda crassicornis* (let's call it "Hermi" for short) studied by Alkon occurs between a sensory cell located in a balance organ called a "statocyst" which detects movement, and a motor cell located in the animal's foot muscle, which makes its single foot contract. An intervening neuron ("interneuron") connects the statocyst neuron to the foot muscle neuron. Rotating the animal activates the statocyst and produces contraction of the foot. The purpose of this automatic connection between rotation and foot contraction is to anchor Hermi to the ocean floor when seas are turbulent, so that its fragile appendages are not damaged.

Hermi has another pre-wired connection between a neuron in the eye (a photoreceptor) called an "A-cell," which is activated by light, and a motor cell that makes the foot extend (lengthen) rather than contract. This connection allows Hermi to push itself off the ocean floor and toward the light of the surface, where its food lives. Slow but steady pulsatile movements gradually bring Hermi to its dinner.

In the laboratory, Hermi can be taught to modify the inborn association between light and foot extension by the application of simple classical conditioning. This is the paradigm of learning that Ivan Pavlov and his dogs introduced at the turn of the century. Remember that Pavlov's experiment involved pairing food—the *unconditioned stimulus* (UCS)—which triggers an automatic salivation response in anticipation of eating—the *unconditioned response* (UCR)—with a neutral stimulus, such as a bell—the *conditioned stimulus* (CS)—which ordinarily produces no particular response. If the food is repeatedly presented at about the same time as the conditioned stimulus, the bell eventually elicits the same degree of salivation—now called the *conditioned response* (CR) because it has been conditioned to the sound of the bell. Every high-school student knows that conditioning changes the way organisms from snails to dogs to people respond to common events, but until recently no one has known how this kind of learning occurs.

In classical conditioning experiments with Hermi (diagrammed in Figure 4-1), the unconditioned stimulus is rotation, which produces the unconditioned response of foot contraction. If Hermi is exposed to light (the conditioned stimulus) one-half to one second before the rotation, the response to light changes from foot extension to foot contraction, which has become a conditioned response. Pairing light with rotation reverses the normal effect of light on the foot muscle, and light may continue to elicit foot contraction instead of extension for weeks when it is presented without rotation.

How does Hermi learn to change the way its foot responds to light? It turns out that, as illustrated in Figure 4-2, the photoreceptor contains not only an A-cell that makes the foot extend but a B-cell that inhibits the A-cell and connects to the interneuron that causes foot contraction. Ordinarily, the B-cell is relatively inactive and the effect of the A-cell predominates. However, pairing of light with rotation increases the activity of the B-cell, replacing the innate response of foot extension to light with the conditioned response of foot contraction—in other words, a shift from inborn predominance of the A-cell to conditioned predominance of the B-cell. What good is the capacity to shift to B-cell predominance? It allows light to trigger the contraction response that anchors Hermi to the ocean floor instead of extending to the surface when seas are stormy and the search for food is dangerous.

The shift in connections between Hermi's eye and its foot is like a train that is rerouted from its main line to a previously unused spur that, though built at the same time as the main track the train has been following, has not

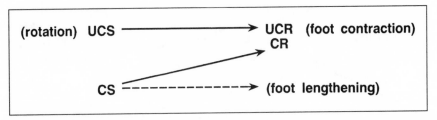

Figure 4-1.
Classical conditioning in Hermissenda

yet been used. The "switch" that turns the neuronal train onto the unused track—prolonged B-cell activity—is the result of a change in the way the B-cell regulates its activity, a complex process described in more detail in Chapter 11. Briefly, the statocyst signals the B-cell through a neurotransmitter called norepinephrine. When norepinephrine reaches the B-cell at around the same time that the B-cell has been turned on by light, a change occurs in the internal dynamics of the B-cell that makes it so much more excitable than the A-cell that its influence predominates. This change in the basic level of B-cell excitability comes from an alteration in the way in which its genes tell it to act. Neurons are not static structures like a brick or a piece of wood but living, dynamic entities that are continually broken down and rebuilt under the direction of the genetic messages from DNA. Although DNA does not change, neurotransmitters can alter the message DNA sends to the neuron (called messenger ribonucleic acid or messenger RNA) that tells it exactly which proteins to construct. In Hermi's case, norepinephrine presented at the right time changes the messenger-RNA signal to construct a hyperactive B-cell. This is a microscopic example of the profound influence of experience on the structure as well as the function of the nervous system.

Human beings, of course, are much more complex than snails, but the same principles of learning apply: inherited neuronal connections determine the range of things it will be possible to learn, and changes in the basic activity of key neurons in response to life experience can shift the balance between intricate networks of neurons to make certain mental and physical events more or less prominent. The number of connections between neurons is more extensive in humans than in snails, and the range of events that can occur when one system of neurons is emphasized over another is almost infinitely greater. And because the human nervous system continues to grow for as long as ten years after birth, early experience can influence not only which existing connections between neurons it will be possible to establish, but the actual number and range of connections that can be activated by later experience. Our genetic equipment therefore is modified by experience throughout the life span.

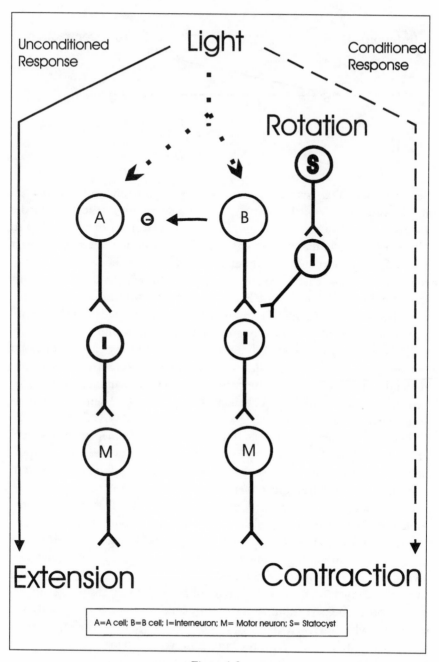

Figure 4-2.
The neuronal basis of conditioning

RISKS OF THE SCIENCE OF THE MIND

As exciting as they are, studies of the genetics of mental disorders and the neurobiology of learning can be deceiving if they are interpreted as suggesting that the biology of the mind *is* the mind. For example, we will see in Chapter 11 that a gene for mania does not *cause* mania; it is only one factor whose contribution to the actual development of illness may be either enhanced or reduced by experience. Even if we could explain fully how learning occurs in terms of the shifting predominance in systems of neurons, we could still not explain why people learn one thing and not another or why they benefit from one thing they learn and not another.

It is now clear that psychological events have biological components. What we do not know is whether the biological side of the equation is the cause of the mental side, the result, or a basic but unrelated event. We need more views of the equation in order to be able to move from guessing about the relationship between mind and body to fully understanding it. One way to gain additional perspectives on the interaction of mind and body is to examine the treatment of medical illnesses with psychological therapies and the treatment of psychological illnesses with medical therapies, which we will do in the next two chapters.

5

—

Biological Treatments of
Psychological Illnesses

ONCE MENTAL MALFUNCTIONS are shown to have physical correlations, and once medical illnesses are shown to be influenced by mental factors, it would seem impossible to maintain the belief in a dichotomy between mind and body. For psychiatrists and therapists, however, reuniting mind and body remained academic until biology had something concrete to offer in the treatment of mental disorders. This became possible when physical therapies (medications, electroconvulsive therapy, etc.) were introduced for schizophrenic, manic, and depressed patients. As one therapy after another was proven helpful for people with less drastic problems, more and more clinicians began to appreciate the relevance of the new methods. Seeing their patients' *minds* get better with treatments of the *body* (not to mention listening to the demands of patients who had heard about the new advances) nudged all but the most recalcitrant mental health practitioners into considering the value of combining treatments of the body with those of the mind.

ELECTROCONVULSIVE THERAPY

Convulsive therapy, the first modern bodily approach to treating the psyche, was introduced for schizophrenia in 1933 by Laslo Von Meduna, a Hungarian psychiatrist.Von Meduna observed that psychotic patients who were also epileptic were less psychotic following a spontaneous seizure; it also seemed that schizophrenia and epilepsy did not occur together. He therefore reasoned that if schizophrenic patients could be made to have an epileptic seizure, it would improve their condition.Von Meduna used camphor as a convulsant, unaware that camphor-induced convulsions had been reported to improve mania as early as the sixteenth century.

Electricity, a means of seizure induction that was to prove more reliable than the chemical means, was first used in 1938 by two Italian psychiatrists, Ugo Cerletti and Lucio Bini, and became the standard approach—hence the name: electroconvulsive therapy (ECT). The first person to receive ECT, a patient found wandering around a street in an incoherent state, was able to speak lucidly for the first time after one treatment. The first words he uttered were, "Not another—it will kill me!" Fortunately, he turned out to be wrong: after a few more treatments, he recovered completely. Cerletti and Bini were awarded the Nobel Prize in medicine for their ground-breaking treatment of schizophrenia.

Like many treatments in medicine, the original theory about ECT proved to have little to do with its eventual applications. Not only do schizophrenia and epilepsy not antagonize each other, but Cerletti and Bini's first patient, as well as many of their later patients, would meet modern criteria for catatonia, a condition associated with mania and neurological disease much more frequently than schizophrenia. Only 15 percent of schizophrenic patients diagnosed according to current criteria benefit from this treatment. On the other hand, ECT has proven to be the safest and most reliable treatment for both depression and mania. The overlap of all bodily treatments is illustrated by the usefulness of ECT for a number of non-psychiatric disorders, especially intractable Parkinson's disease. Even though confusion is the most common side effect of ECT, it rapidly reverses delirium, an acute confusional state caused by a host of medical, neurological, and toxic factors. Another paradox is that ECT, which works by producing an electrical seizure in the brain (but not a convulsion in the body), can also be used as a treatment for epilepsy, because artificially induced seizures make it more difficult to have spontaneous seizures.

THE DEBUT OF PSYCHIATRIC MEDICATIONS

The first medication to be developed for a psychiatric disorder was lithium, which was introduced in 1949 by Australian psychiatrist John Cade. Cade suspected that manic behavior was caused by excess levels of uric acid, a product of the metabolism of purines, which are essential components of many bodily substances, including DNA. He attempted to prove his hypothesis by injecting lithium urate, a chemical combination of uric acid and lithium, into guinea pigs, expecting the urate portion to produce manic behavior. Instead, the injection had the opposite effect: it was *tranquilizing.* Since Cade believed that the urate should cause mania (it does not, although elevated uric levels do cause gout), he concluded that the lithium must have an anti-manic effect. When this possibility was tested by giving lithium to a small group of manic patients, they all improved.

It took many years for other psychiatrists to accept the anti-manic efficacy of lithium. In part, Cade attributed this resistance to the fact that the original work on the drug was performed by "an unknown psychiatrist, working alone in a small chronic hospital with no research training, primitive techniques and negligible equipment." Today, lithium is recognized as one of the most effective treatments for the "mental" conditions of mania and recurrent depression as well as for some "physical" conditions like cluster headaches and low white blood cell count.

A year after Cade published his initial work, chlorpromazine (Thorazine) was synthesized in an attempt to find another antihistamine. In 1952, when it was noted that chlorpromazine induced a state of "artificial hibernation," it was given to acutely ill schizophrenic patients and found to control psychosis and agitation. The decision to introduce chlorpromazine and related antipsychotic drugs—such as haloperidol (Haldol), synthesized in 1957—into the psychiatric hospital had profound implications for psychiatrists. Even though psychodynamic psychiatry had demonstrated no success in ameliorating psychosis, many psychiatrists continued to believe that better psychological techniques would, one day, prove as effective in psychotic disorders as they were with the neuroses. If treatment in the bodily realm proved successful, it might represent a failure of the psychotherapist's art. As is true of all of the advances in medicine we have reviewed, this theoretical concern was eventually turned aside by actual experience with the benefits of the new treatment modalities, the impact of which was captured by psychiatrist Frank Ayd Jr., himself a pioneer in the emerging field of psychopharmacology:

> In January 1955, Henry Brill . . . was Assistant Commissioner of Mental Hygiene in New York State. At that time, only courageous, dedicated psychiatrists with great foresight were advocating the use of psychotropic drugs, despite much opposition from adherents to psychodynamics, psychotherapy, and psychoanalysis. At considerable risk to his own career, and with much bureaucratic opposition, Brill initiated the general use of chlorpromazine [Thorazine] and reserpine [Serpasil, a medication now used to treat high blood pressure] in New York public hospitals, the first state in the nation to do this.

Ayd goes on to point out that the following year, the number of chronically ill patients residing in New York's public mental hospitals began to decline, and research indicated that the "major identifiable influence in producing a population reduction" over the next few years, especially of schizophrenic patients, was "the large-scale use of psychotropic drugs within New York public hospitals." Some patients even began to communicate for the first time "after five to ten years of mute withdrawal."

Chlorpromazine and the other first-generation antipsychotic drugs do not cure psychosis, and some of their side effects can be irreversible or even fatal. But without question, these drugs make the difference between incapacitation and functioning in a substantial number of people afflicted with schizophrenia, severe mood disorders, personality disorders, and acute medical illnesses that cause uncontrollable agitation. In 1957 imipramine (Tofranil), which chemically resembles chlorpromazine, was synthesized in an attempt to find an antipsychotic drug with fewer side effects. Imipramine actually worsened psychosis but turned out to be the first of a family of medications for depression. Like the antipsychotic drugs, the antidepressants seemed miraculous in their ability to relieve severe depressive states that had been impervious to psychological interventions. The excitement of extending biological treatments of the mind to milder conditions encountered outside the psychiatric wards of hospitals was conveyed in the first scientific report of imipramine's effectiveness by one of its developers, as reported by Ayd:

> . . . The effect begins to be apparent after a few days or weeks. . . . The patients show a more upright bearing, are more lively in their gestures, again take part in a more active social life. . . . Subjectively the tiredness, heaviness, and despondency disappear, a general sluggishness and inhibition is relieved, and weeping stops. . . . The ability to be happy, and interest in the family and in work are restored, positive ideas and a capacity to make decisions again become evident.

Each new psychiatric medication has followed the same course of development. A drug is investigated for a particular purpose because of a supposition—often later found to be mistaken—that it should be helpful, or because it resembles other effective drugs. There is an initial period of enthusiasm, during which the drug is applied to almost every disorder, followed by a more sober appraisal of its real uses. Next, medications that have similar biochemical actions but fewer side effects are synthesized, and applications for the drug are discovered that were never considered when it was first developed. A tremendous amount of information accumulates about biochemical actions of the drug, but most of the time it remains unclear what these actions have to do with the therapeutic effect: it is possible to say *that* the drug works but not *how.* Of course, for a patient who is relieved of suffering, that the drug works is enough.

Once the study of the physical correlations of the mind began to produce practical results, it was possible for science and society to begin to renegotiate the centuries-old agreement that had removed the mind from the purview of biological investigations. Science had so permeated popular culture by this time that even the Roman Catholic Church could acknowledge the legitimacy of the mind as an object of scientific study, the result of which could contribute to, rather than compete with, spiritual health. This profound change was noted in a 1958 address by Pope Pius XII to an international meeting on neuropsychopharmacology that Frank Ayd attended and recorded for posterity:

> We have, gentlemen, the most sincere esteem for your work, for the aims of your labor, and for the results already shown. In examining the articles and works published on the subjects which interest you, it is easy to see that you render valuable service to science and to humanity. You have already been able to come to the assistance of many sufferers for whom, previously, medical science admitted it had no help. You are now able to bring back mental health to sick people who were formerly considered lost and we sincerely share the joy that this knowledge brings you.
>
> In the present state of scientific research, rapid progress can be obtained only by means of wide cooperation on an international scale. . . . It is to be hoped that it will extend not only to all specialists in psychopharmacology, but also to psychologists, psychiatrists, and psychotherapists—to all those, in short, who have anything to do with mental sickness.

PSYCHOTHERAPY AND MEDICATIONS

Not everyone in the mental health professions had as much foresight as Pope Pius XII. Many continued to adhere to the erroneous belief that treatments of the body have nothing to do with treatments of the mind. Even after almost four decades of experience with the fruits of psychopharmacological research, some psychotherapists continue to believe that relieving symptoms with medications will rob patients of the motivation to continue psychotherapy. Far from undermining the motivation needed for psychotherapy, however, medications reduce the overwhelming distress and paralyzing despair that make it impossible to confront life issues psychologically.

A more sophisticated version of this incorrect reasoning is that patients will attribute improvement to the drug and feel less responsible for the problems that remain. Some therapists who do not want to cross what they perceive as the mind-body barrier worry that patients who receive medications will feel that their doctors do not value them enough to use psychotherapy. An argument that sounds persuasive but is not supported by research is that any change resulting from medication is temporary at best, while psychotherapy gets at the "real cause" of the disorder and fixes it permanently.

A scientific approach to the development of new medications has not prevented practitioners in the psychopharmacology camp from adhering to equally unsupported assumptions. Some view mental disorders purely from the biological viewpoint, believing that *any* undesirable mental condition has an underlying biological as opposed to psychological cause and can be treated only with medications. Others worry that "needlessly" stirring up emotions in psychotherapy will counteract the beneficial effects of medication. A few ignore evidence of the effectiveness of psychotherapy and continue to view it as harmless but useless. However, even schizophrenia, a condition that has visible roots in malfunctions of the brain, can be positively affected by individual and family psychotherapy.

To some extent, the mind-body gap is being bridged by evidence that physical therapies of the mind can be highly beneficial—evidence that is so compelling that even the most psychologically oriented therapist now sees the use for medications. Some non-medical therapists are even beginning to demand the training and licensing that would allow them to prescribe medication. However, more often than not, this latest trend is the result not of bridging the mind-body gap but of oversimplifying the bodily side of the mind-body equation, allowing therapists to believe that anyone can and should prescribe psychiatric medications and making psychiatrists feel that medications are all they need to know about. Managed-care companies, most of which now pay psychiatrists only for brief sessions to prescribe and follow up on medications and insist that psychotherapy be relegated to non-medical therapists, have given this trend a big push. The managed-care companies believe that it is cheaper to split medications and psychotherapy between two kinds of providers than it is to have the same clinician provide both kinds of treatment—despite the fact that there is no scientific evidence to support this contention. Only when these kinds of cherished but incorrect beliefs are overcome by dispassionate examination will mind and body truly be united. In the next chapter, an evaluation of the data will show us that, just as bodily treatments can affect the mind, psychological therapies can benefit the body.

6

Psychological Treatments of Physical Diseases

JANICE STONE HAS just been told that the breast biopsy performed last week is positive for cancer. Her physician has reviewed the latest research on treatments with her; now she is trying to choose between lumpectomy (removal of a small portion of tissue) and mastectomy (removal of the entire breast). The doctor also has told her about a support group for women with cancer that has been shown to improve survival rates. Should she give the group a try?

If biological approaches to mental problems can produce positive results, does it follow that psychological methods of treatment can help heal actual physical disease? In 1923 Freud noted that "the analytic treatment of gross organic disease is not unpromising, since a mental factor not infrequently contributes to the origin and continuance of such illnesses." Research during the modern psychosomatic era supported this hoped-for possibility by confirming that therapies of the mind could contribute to the restoration of the body.

INDIVIDUAL AND GROUP PSYCHOTHERAPY

Ulcers

The first step in developing a psychotherapeutic approach to medical illnesses was taken when psychoanalysts, who had followed the Mirsky study described in Chapter 3, made the logical assumption that treating the dependency conflicts believed to be associated with ulcers might help heal the ulcer itself. But to their dismay, their ulcer patients got *worse* in analytic psychotherapy. Still, analysts reasoned that this result confirmed the hypothesis that emotions contribute to disease: therapy brought more conflict to the surface than the patient could handle, which added to, rather than resolved, the psychophysiology of ulcers.

Would an approach that *strengthened* a patient's defenses, rather than analyzing and challenging them, improve things? In one study, by Sjodin, thirty-two ulcer patients spent six weeks attending daily group lectures that explained the relationship between emotions and the stomach and offered hints about how to think more flexibly. Three years later, thirty of these patients were either in excellent health or had only minor symptoms. During the same time period twenty comparable ulcer patients, who received the same dietary and medical regimen as the experimental patients but no group experience, had suffered serious recurrences of the disease.

A more recent experiment found that ulcer patients who participated in weekly supportive psychotherapy for three months in addition to their medical treatment reported much less abdominal pain fifteen months later than the half who had received only routine medical care. (Since medical tests were not performed, it is not known if the actual physical pathology was ameliorated by the psychotherapy.)

Colitis

There have been a few studies suggesting that ulcerative colitis, another of the "classical" psychosomatic illnesses described by Franz Alexander's group, can be improved by psychotherapy. One study by Kellner showed that psychotherapy, consisting of advice and help with coping skills, led to greater than expected improvement of physical pathology as seen on a proctoscope. However, the medical benefit was limited to those who were "temperamentally" suited to the psychotherapy—which implies that the conditions of patients whose personalities did not match the therapeutic approach might not have benefited or might even have worsened. Reports still surface of patients with ulcerative colitis who developed life-threatening gastrointestinal bleeding that responded poorly to medical therapy while undergoing psychoanalysis for their condition.

Asthma

Minuchin found that vigorous family therapy, without any notable change in medical treatment, led to significant improvement in children with conditions of intractable asthma, severe diabetes, or anorexia nervosa. This finding could mean that harmful physiological overload, caused by unresolved family stress, was reduced. It could also mean that as children and their families learned better ways of communicating, they no longer needed the language of disease and were freer to work toward curing or controlling the illness. In either case, it is apparent that it impossible to treat the sick individual without taking into account the interpersonal context in which the illness occurs.

In 1989 an Italian group of researchers led by Onnis confirmed this finding. These investigators randomly assigned twenty asthmatic patients, aged six to thirteen, to receive medical therapy alone, and twenty to receive medical therapy plus family therapy. Compared with families and patients who received medical treatment only, families in group therapy showed improvement in psychological overprotectiveness, conflict avoidance, and rigidity, which was correlated with a fewer asthma attacks, fewer hospitalizations, and less overall disability.

The importance of reducing tension to improve asthma was also confirmed by Andhra, a researcher in India, who found that thirty-four adult asthmatic patients who learned to practice yoga had better lung function than the remaining fourteen patients who did not.

Heart Attacks

As we will see in Chapter 20, psychological approaches have also been shown to improve survival in patients with heart disease. In one study by Rahe, forty-four patients who had recently suffered myocardial infarctions (heart attacks) were divided into two groups: one group received only medical management; the other, medical management plus six ninety-minute group psychotherapy sessions in which patients discussed their adjustment to the illness. Patients attending the group sessions resumed normal physical activity so much faster than those not in the group that the researcher created a second group of sixteen heart patients to address strategies for rehabilitation. Three years after these limited psychological interventions, fewer patients in both psychotherapy groups had died or had had recurrent heart attacks than matched controls without group psychotherapy.

Why this improvement occurred is no mystery: group therapy patients were helped to feel more comfortable and knowledgeable about their disease and were better able to modify diet, exercise, and other risk factors. Feeling less frightened by the heart attack, they would also have been less subject to the physical effects of chronic anxiety on an already damaged heart.

Warts

A remarkable application of the experimental method to investigate nonphysical treatments of physical disease can be found in several studies in which hypnosis was used as a treatment for warts. One study found no effect; however, two other reports found the opposite. In one experiment, seventy patients with multiple warts received the hypnotic suggestion that they would improve, while another seventy patients received no suggestion (the control group). Warts, which have a natural tendency to resolve anyway, went away much faster in the hypnosis group.

In another fascinating study by Surman and colleagues, fourteen patients with warts on both sides of their bodies were told under hypnosis that the warts would disappear on one side only. Six patients responded exactly as suggested. In another patient, warts disappeared on the suggested side, followed by the warts on the side where resolution had not been suggested. Six additional patients had either partial but significant remission on the suggested side only or improvement on both sides. Only one patient did not respond at all to the hypnosis.

THE HIGH COST OF LESS PSYCHOTHERAPY

Politicians looking for ways to save money in health care should be interested in the finding that people who receive *any* type of psychological treatment visit their primary-care physicians one-third less frequently than they did prior to the psychotherapy. Of course, people probably receive at least as much encouragement, advice, and the opportunity to ventilate in the doctor's office as they do medical treatment. It is a well-known fact that family physicians spend more time treating anxiety and depression than hypertension, heart disease, and diabetes. It is possible that when other avenues of emotional support are available, there is less need to lean on the primary-care doctor.

However, one large study by psychologist Herbert Schlesinger, sociologist Emily Mumford, and their colleagues disproved the idea that the decreased need for medical visits that characterized people in psychotherapy could be explained in terms of a simple transfer of office time from the physician to the psychotherapist. Examining the insurance records of thousands of patients with chronic lung disease, diabetes, angina, or hypertension, this group found that patients who received *any* mental health care at all spent less time in the hospital than patients with equally severe physical illnesses who did not receive such care. More impressively, the benefit was proportional to the amount of psychological treatment: the more psychotherapy the patients received, the less time they spent in the hospital.

This significant correlation might have been due to the direct effects of improved psychological well-being on the body or to a decreased need, as patients became more stable emotionally, to exploit their illnesses for psychological or interpersonal purposes. In other words, they may have attended to their illnesses before they became severe enough to require hospitalization. If a healthy mind does not necessarily create a healthy body, a healthy mind at least takes better care of its body!

The same study debunked the popular myth that psychological therapy takes forever. Seventy-five percent of the mental health treatment received by the 222,000 people whose records were reviewed required an average of only twenty-two visits (even though insurance covered at least fifty-two visits per year). Only 10 percent of all people receiving outpatient psychiatric treatment visited the therapist twenty-five times or more. Since these figures were collected, elaborate strategies (known as "managed care") for controlling utilization of psychotherapy have been introduced, *but no one has bothered to study whether the cost of medical treatment has risen as a result.*

CARING FOR THE CARETAKER

Psychological interventions can help not only the ill person but his or her caregivers as well. Therapies aimed at offering support to those around the patient can have a dramatic impact on a person's physical recovery.

Two decades ago I headed a project at the University of Colorado Health Sciences Center that demonstrated that it was possible to help sick patients by providing psychological assistance to those taking care of them. A psychiatrist met regularly with the nurses on a coronary care unit (CCU) that housed critically ill cardiac patients. The purpose of the meetings was to discuss how to manage problem patients and resolve interpersonal conflicts among the nurses. Information in the following areas was gathered before the group began, and then every two weeks for the next year and a half: patient mortality, nursing efficiency, and nurses' attitudes toward their patients, each other, and the ward.

The same kinds of data were also obtained from another coronary care unit at the same medical center. Like the first unit, this CCU had a psychiatrist who was available for consultation with any physician or nurse about problem patients, but there were no regular psychiatric meetings with the nurses. Nurses on both units did not know what kind of study was going on, and the experimenter who gathered the data bimonthly did not know which unit hosted the nurses' group.

The results revealed dramatic differences between the two units. After a year and a half, the mortality rate had dropped by a third on the CCU that held the regular group meetings with the psychiatrist, and the nurses were significantly more efficient at recognizing and charting changes in their patients' physical status. In contrast, the other CCU showed no change in death rate and no change in nursing efficiency. Amazingly, when the results of this study were presented to hospital administrators, they expressed no interest in continuing regular group meetings of CCU nurses with their psychiatrist. The findings were convincing, they acknowledged, but helping nurses recognize changes in patient behavior and mood that required rapid medical intervention did not fit into any insurance code—and no one would pay for the service. Despite the lip service given nearly two decades later to the ideal of reorganizing health-care funding to support innovations that improve overall efficiency, instead of paying only for expensive technologies for individual patients, third-party payers still view treatments for the people who comprise the system as luxurious administrative costs that only reduce the profit margin.

This was not the first Colorado study investigating the benefits of psychiatric consultation in the medical hospital, nor the first time the results did not lead to a change in hospital policy. In 1941 psychiatrist Edward Billings, the director of one of the first programs in America to establish regular liaisons between psychiatry and hospital medical and surgical services, reported on changes that had occurred in length and cost of inpatient medical treatment during the five years (1934–1939) after regular psychiatric consultation was made available to the physicians of Colorado General Hospital. Before the psychiatrists' arrival, the average length of stay for patients was fifteen days. Billings estimated that about one in seven of these patients had psychiatric problems, such as hypochondriasis, depression, anxiety, and organic mental syndromes (now called "psychiatric disorders due to general medical conditions"). Patients with psychiatric as well as medical symptoms remained in the hospital twenty-eight days—nearly twice the average length of stay for all patients. The economic consequences of the difference in hospital stays between patients with and without concurrent psychiatric problems were not trivial by the standards of the day. The average cost of a hospital stay before the psychiatric consultants arrived on the scene was $52. General hospital patients who also had psychiatric disorders were costing $45 more than that, or almost twice as much as the other patients, because they stayed in the hospital longer and received more tests.

During the first five years of psychiatric consultation, the price of an average medical stay went up to $71—about a fifty percent increase—probably due to innovations in medical technology. The average length of stay for all general hospital patients did not change much, but patients who also had psychiatric problems remained on the wards for progressively less time, until by the end of the five-year study their stay was no longer than everyone else's, and their cost of care was only two dollars more.

With the addition of psychiatric consultation to hospital procedures, patients with mixed psychiatric-medical problems still received diagnostic work-ups, but many inappropriate tests were eliminated. For example, it had been common practice to X-ray *everything* in patients who had multiple aches and pains, but this practice ceased once physicians understood that no matter how thoroughly they searched, nothing definite would ever be found in the bones when the problem was depression. Billings concluded that teaching non-psychiatric physicians to "consider the patient and his complaint in terms of psychobiology as well as physics, chemistry, anatomy and physiology" made it possible for these physicians to identify and treat problems of the psyche that masquerade as problems of the body more efficiently instead of "relying on X-rays, various special consultations and test tubian tactics to 'rule out' something or other."

In 1981 Columbia University psychiatrists Stephan Levitan and Donald Kornfeld published a report of research they had conducted over a six-month period. Levitan was the regular psychiatric consultant to an orthopedic ward specializing in surgical repair of fractured femurs in elderly women (a difficult problem to treat because of the frailty of the patients and the frequency of complications). He followed every patient who survived and was able to talk to him (a total of twenty-four) throughout their hospital stay, consulting about their care with physicians, nurses, physiotherapists, social service agencies, and families. These patients' outcomes were compared with those of twenty-six patients with the same problem treated on the same ward during the same calendar months of the previous year, when there was no psychiatric consultant present.

Levitan and Kornfeld reported that their patients stayed in the hospital an average of twelve days *less than* patients who had not seen a psychiatrist—a statistically significant decrease over the previous "no-psychiatrist" year. This decrease occurred in spite of a trend toward longer hospital stays for other orthopedic patients during the time of the study. The psychiatrist diagnosed psychiatric conditions that interfered with healing, adjusted medications to reduce side effects that prolonged illness, and counseled family members on how to interact more rewardingly. Improving these patients' psychosocial environment enhanced their ability to cooperate with the surgical regimen, so that they recovered more completely. As a result, sixteen of the "psychiatric consultation" patients improved enough to return home, whereas only half as many of the control patients were able to avoid placement in a nursing home or other extended-care facility.

At the time of Levitan and Kornfeld's study, they estimated that a hospital bed in New York cost $200 per day, a far cry from the $3.49 rate that was in effect at the beginning of Billings' study, but unfortunately a great deal less than the cost at most hospitals in the 1990s. At the $200 rate, the decreased lengths of stay in Levitan and Kornfeld's study saved $55,200 in hospital costs during the six months of their project. In addition, $42,000 in nursing home costs were saved on patients who were able to receive follow-up at home, which was at that time about $100 per week cheaper than institutional care. Extrapolating their findings to a year, the experimenters predicted that they would have treated twice as many patients and saved almost $194,000—not a bad return on the $10,000 per year the psychiatrist was paid in part-time salary.

LIAISON PSYCHIATRY: THE BRIDGING BEGINS

In the United States, attempts to reintegrate mental health care into treatment facilities for physical illnesses began with the introduction of psychiatric wards into general hospitals around the turn of the century. Billings' group and four other groups of academic psychiatrists around the United States began consulting on general medical units in 1932. These five groups were the forerunners of a psychiatric subspecialty called "liaison psychiatry," which proliferated during the 1960s and 1970s. As the clinical arm of psychosomatic medicine, liaison psychiatry was one of the few psychiatric initiatives dedicated to reestablishing a connection with the biologically-oriented medical field by using interventions of the mind to improve the health of the physically ill.

At a time when psychiatrists treating mental patients still fell on one side or the other of the mind-body split, emphasizing medications *or* psychotherapy, liaison psychiatrists were expected to consider both mind and body in any therapeutic enterprise. During the 1980s, however, other psychiatric specialties began to catch up in transcending the barrier between mind and body. The accumulation of evidence of the effectiveness of physical therapies of the mind, and of psychological treatments of the body, has become increasingly difficult to ignore, especially when patients demand that their treatment reflect perspectives that supersede the anachronistic separation of mind and body. Just as it has become standard practice to consider possible *psychological* dimensions of medical diseases, it is now necessary for all clinicians of the mind to be able to identify *physical* as well as psychological components of mental illnesses.

No longer is liaison psychiatry the only philosophical link between mind and body. Indeed, no practitioner considered competent can ignore either realm in treating any kind of disease. Depression is accepted as at least as much a biological as a psychological phenomenon, for example, and the mind is recognized as an important influence on diseases of the body, such as cancer and heart disease. Understanding physical dimensions of the mind, psychological dimensions of the body, and interactions between the two has become the task of every physician and mental health practitioner. And undoing deceptions that view the health of the body as something separate from the health of the mind is one of the tasks of this book.

PART II

THE MIND DECEIVES
THE MIND

For every language is a foreign one and strangers we are, each to the other, all travelling incognito, even to ourselves.

—AUGUST STRINDBERG

⇔   ⇔   ⇔

THERE ALWAYS SEEMS to be something wrong with Max. One day it's his head that hurts; the next day it's his chest; back pain has kept him from sleeping for years. He has been to every specialist in the city, but no one seems to be able to make a satisfactory diagnosis. The last physician Max consulted did the most complete evaluation yet: an MRI (magnetic resonance imaging) scan of the head, a full battery of hormonal tests, a 24-hour cardiogram—even urine tests for mercury and arsenic poisoning. No abnormalities were disclosed on any test. Rather than being cheered by the good news, Max insisted that the right test still had not been done.

One doctor thought that a psychiatrist might be able to throw some light on the nature of Max's symptoms. This suggestion seemed particularly absurd to Max, who was offended by the implication that the problem was "in his head." But he did plan to see someone at the Mayo Clinic who specialized in diagnosing complicated illnesses like this one.

We have all heard about people like Max, whose persistent symptoms do not seem to have a medical cause. Some are repeatedly "reassured" that there is nothing wrong but eventually turn out to have cancer or some other disease that the doctors have missed. However, there is a large group of people, some with minor medical pathology and others with none at all, who experience significant physical disability that is the result of pathology in the mind, not in the body. The real problem in these cases is not the hidden presence of a medical illness but an inherent inability to express or even be aware of anxiety, unhappiness, or any other kind of emotional distress. Because emotions cannot be expressed directly in words, they are expressed indirectly in the form of physical sensations or changes in bodily function.

TRICKS OF THE MIND

The mind-body deception by which emotional distress and other mental phenomena are converted into bodily symptoms is called *somatization*. As is also the case in psychosomatic illnesses (such as peptic ulcer), bodily dysfunction is triggered by an underlying emotional state or conflict. Unlike psychosomatic illnesses, however, in somatization no physiological process corresponds to, or is aggravated by, the conflict: the disorder feels entirely physical but is really entirely mental. This is not a trivial deception: somatization accounts for a significant percentage of patients in the practices of most primary-care physicians and costs millions of dollars in expensive but unrewarding tests and interventions.

There are many advantages to hiding the ephemeral disquietude of the mind within the tangible folds and crevices of the body. People whose minds feel fragile, threatening, or impossibly confusing can retreat behind the reassuring substantiality of the body. Grasping at the palpable tissues of the body as an explanation for distress can be a way for an overwhelmed mind to find a foothold of meaning, no matter how precarious or deceptive.

DECEPTIVE REWARDS

At least in Western culture, physicians tend to encourage these self-deceptions. Doctors are taught to recognize the tangible, the observable, and the objective. Laboratory tests, physical findings, X-rays, and autopsy results garner far more respect than do feelings, emotions, and psychological issues. All too often patients get the message, directly or indirectly, that their illnesses are legitimate only if they are somatic.

Insurance companies, the government, and other third parties who manage payment for medical care further encourage patients to pay attention to the body while ignoring the mind. Disregarding the scientific data affirming that most mental health treatment is brief and effective, third parties typically reimburse treatment of mental disorders at a much lower rate than physical disorders. When more credibility, attention, and monetary reimbursement are accorded a backache than a depression, a patient would have to be slow indeed not to appreciate the value of presenting mental conditions in physical terms.

WINDOW TO NEW KNOWLEDGE

Somatization is not only a medically and economically important phenomenon; it is a window into the kinds of mental states that contribute to major psychiatric illnesses such as depression and major medical illnesses such as cancer. In the next two chapters, we will explore the varying forms that somatization can take: from purposeful simulation of disease, to mimicry of physical illness that occurs outside of awareness, to preoccupation with unseen malfunctions.

We will learn that somatization is one of the trickiest of deceptions, lying midway between mind and body and deceiving both. Physicians who confront the deception without understanding it come away feeling bewildered, frustrated, and incompetent. Patients who live in the grip of this deception feel helpless, miserable, and even despairing. After learning why and how somatization occurs, we will explore a plan for dealing with it that can be helpful to caretakers, families, and patients themselves.

7

Somatization Deceptions
(The Problem Is All in My Body—<u>Not</u> My Head)

MOST OF US are capable of imagining that we are ill, at least momentarily. During times of stress, after recovery from an actual illness, or when life events seem unfathomable, frightening, or confusing, it is not at all unusual to feel dizzy, get a headache or stomachache, experience shortness of breath, have heart palpitations or chest pain—and fear the worst. At some point in our lives, we all "somatize"—that is, we unconsciously express an emotional state by transforming it into a physical symptom. We take medication, stay home from work, cancel an important appointment, or otherwise alter our lives for a day or two.

Somatization symptoms can be experienced anywhere in the body and, for the most part, do not indicate serious physical pathology. Symptoms that cannot be traced to identifiable somatic problems are called "functional complaints" because they are a function of a psychological process and not a product of a structural change in the tissues of the body. For some individuals, somatization is the central experience of their lives. Virtually unaware of the ebb and flow of their subjective inner states, they recognize only changes in the body. But the fact that the origin of their bodily distress is in the mind does not mean the functional complaints are any less persistent, pervasive, and disabling.

Somatization in patients bedevils the health care system. In research summarized by psychiatrists J.I. Escobar and Z.J. Lipowski, over two-thirds of 1,000 outpatients at a medical diagnostic clinic were not medically ill. In a large health maintenance organization, almost 27 percent of all patients being treated for chronic physical complaints showed no evidence of organic disease, nor did almost one-quarter of a group of hospitalized medical patients. Astounding as it may seem, between 30 and *80* percent of people who consult physicians do so because of functional complaints. As psychiatrist A.J. Barsky notes, it is not surprising that the most common diagnosis made in general practice is "nonsickness"!

The "career somatizer" presents the physician with a futile task: to utilize the vast resources of modern medical technology in the hopes of locating and treating a physical problem that, not having any physical substrate, will never show up on any X-ray or blood test. When the usual studies reveal no disease, the patient insists on still more sophisticated tests. If the doctor refuses, the patient is insulted, fearful, or—in the ultimate threat to the physician's self-confidence—litigious. However, if the physician agrees to continue to search in the body for something that is not there, the outcome is, at best, humorous but ineffective and, at worst, deadly.

For example, a thirty-year-old woman was convinced that chronic headaches were symptoms of a brain tumor. The usual tests and X-rays showed no evidence of a tumor, but the patient's belief was unshaken. An MRI scan could not be performed for technical reasons, but a computerized tomography (CT) scan showed a questionable area in a part of the brain that could not possibly explain the patient's symptoms. The patient became even more insistent that the tumor be identified, and in desperation her neurologist recommended an arteriogram, a test in which dye is injected into the major arteries of the neck. This test is risky and can cause spasm of those arteries, resulting in stroke or even death. Nothing bad happened as a result of the test, but nothing good happened either: it was negative. A review of the CT scan then revealed that the "finding" was a smudge on the film.

Having fired the last remaining gun in his diagnostic armamentarium, the neurologist had to regroup. He reviewed the history of the "tumor" with the patient, and then asked her what *she* thought was causing the tumor they couldn't find. The patient replied, as if it were a matter of obvious fact, that the tumor was caused by an atomic ray being fired at her from a space ship that had been targeting her for years. At first she thought that the space ship was in her imagination, but when she saw an article about alien abductions in a popular tabloid, she took this as an omen that her belief was indeed correct. Her suspicions were confirmed when she noticed that radiation leaking out of the tumor would melt snow on the side of the street corresponding to her headache, but not on the opposite side.

This patient had not appeared to be psychotic in her many discussions with her doctor, perhaps because they had focused solely on concrete topics of symptoms and tests. And why hadn't the doctor asked the crucial question earlier? For this physician, the possibility of a mental dimension to physical symptoms was remote. If the patient did not have a neurological illness, what would she be doing in his office? The patient, who was aware of this bias, knew that she needed help but also knew that if she did not describe her illness in the language of the body, the neurologist would lose interest in the problem and send her immediately to a psychiatrist. This, of course, would have been appropriate, but the patient did not think much of psychiatrists: they dealt with unreal problems, and she knew that her condition was only too real, even if it could not be seen. She therefore went along with the deception that a disease of the body is real but that the disease of the mind, which was really crippling her, was not real.

WHEN IS A PHYSICAL SYMPTOM *TRULY* A PHYSICAL SYMPTOM?

It can be very difficult to tell the difference between undiagnosed physical symptoms that are caused by an undiscovered medical illness and those that are due to somatization. Bodily symptoms that surface in the context of emotional stress, or that are clearly *symbolic* of an obvious psychological conflict, are often functional rather than structural. Still, this can be a difficult call, since many physical illnesses are precipitated by emotional stress, and almost everything has symbolic meaning to someone. In addition, since people tend to do more of what they usually do when they are under stress, somatization may be enhanced by the stress of a medical illness, producing a dramatic increase in functional complaints that obscure the symptoms of the underlying medical condition.

An additional bit of information that can help tip the diagnostic scale one way or the other is whether the person is willing to consider an emotional component to the illness. Patients with medical or surgical illnesses are often only too eager to agree that the problem could be psychological—after all, far fewer people die of anxiety than cancer. Somatizers, for whom the mind is much more dangerous than the body, are more threatened by the prospect that their symptoms could be mental in origin than by the possibility of even a fatal medical illness.

Excluding environmentally influenced disorders, such as allergies, toxic reactions, and asthma, symptoms that are consistently better or worse in one psychosocial context than in another are likely to be rooted in emotional factors. For example, back pain that is excruciating only when a person's spouse is around is more likely to be amplified by psychological forces than pain that is made worse by lifting. Somatization is also often at work in people who have always had one kind of physical complaint or another, such as chronic stomachaches in childhood, incapacitating headaches during adolescence, and chest pain that began at age twenty. The same is true when an illness predictably gets worse just when it should be improving, a situation that will be discussed in more detail a little later in this section.

Dramatic or exaggerated descriptions of severe pain (e.g., "the pain is like a hot poker in my eye") may seem to be legitimate, but few people who are experiencing pure pain, with no trace of somatization, use such language. Pain that comes purely from medical illness, such as the pain of metastatic cancer, may be experienced in different organ systems but because it is difficult to pay attention to two competing stimuli at the same time, such pain is usually more compelling in one site than another. Conversely, pain that is experienced with equal intensity in two places at the same time, such as unbearable headache and incapacitating back pain, is more likely to reflect a psychological component.

It is important to remember, however, that just as physicians can overlook the emotional component in an endless search for a nonexistent physical aberration, so too can they make the reverse mistake: being deceived into thinking that the symptoms of a patient who has obvious emotional problems could not possibly be coming from the body. This point was dramatically demonstrated in the case of a fifty-five-year-old man referred to a psychiatrist for evaluation of chronic abdominal pain for which no organic cause had been demonstrated, even after exploratory surgery. The man acknowledged that he was depressed and readily agreed to psychiatric treatment. The depression and the pain got better, but a year after the first operation, the pain suddenly reappeared and the patient underwent a second operation. This time, the surgeons found what could not be detected a year earlier: cancer of the pancreas. Four months later, the patient was dead of the disease.

Exactly one year after this man had died, his sister consulted her brother's psychiatrist for help in coping with her lingering grief. One symptom of her unresolved grief was abdominal pain that had developed on the day he died and that mimicked his pain exactly. She began psychotherapy and made excellent progress in resolving her feelings. Her pain improved as well—but eight months later she, too, died from pancreatic cancer!

SECONDARY SOMATIZATION

Somatization can be a process around which the entire personality is organized (*primary somatization,* discussed in the following section), or it can be just one aspect of another mental syndrome that affects many systems of the mind and body (*secondary somatization*). Psychosis or severe reactions to emotional trauma, for example, can cause mental fragmentation that feels to the overwhelmed mind of the sufferer like fragmentation of the body. This is probably why functional somatic complaints occur in more than 85 percent of acutely psychotic patients. Bodily complaints can be used in a similar manner by patients with diseases of the brain that impair mental faculties. Minor bodily dysfunction provides a concrete focus that can serve as a distraction from the frightening disruption of their mental capacities and as a way of organizing an experience that feels overwhelming.

Giving Voice to Grief

Somatization can be secondary to (i.e., one of a number of manifestations) two common psychiatric problems that may be difficult to identify in people who have trouble expressing their emotions: *grief* and *depression*. Grieving is the process through which emotional attachment to a departed loved one is gradually surrendered. Grief can be experienced as a terrible struggle between the stark reality of the loss and the deep yearning to hold onto the lost person. One manifestation of this struggle is the "identification symptom," which is a physical complaint that mimics a symptom experienced by the lost loved one. For example, a woman whose father had died of a stroke had persistent headaches on the right side, the same side on which her father's stroke had occurred. The night before these headaches began, she had a dream in which her father came back to her and "stroked" the right side of her head.

Through the identification symptom, the lost person remains an active part of the bereaved's physical identity. Only when the grieving person truly relinquishes the attachment can the symptom representing the attachment disappear. If grief does not proceed normally, the identification symptom remains; distress within the *body* calls attention to the unwillingness of the *mind* to grieve.

Unresolved grief turned out to be the cause of chronic shortness of breath suffered by a thirty-eight-year-old woman. She had no idea what might be causing the symptom, which had persisted for five years, but when a new physician asked about her family, she unwittingly provided a clue: at first she said that she had four children, but toward the end of the interview she referred to only three children. Puzzled by this discrepancy, the physician called it to the patient's attention. In a matter-of-fact manner, she mentioned that she had had a son in addition to her three daughters, but that he had died five years ago. "How did he die?" the physician asked. "He drowned," the patient replied flatly. "Can you tell me what happened?" "No," she said, "I can't remember."

The physician called in the patient's husband, who described the traumatic event. His wife had been sitting on the bank of a river watching her seven-year-old son and her brother enjoy a summer day in a small rowboat. Neither of them could swim, and suddenly the boat overturned and sank. The patient, who could not swim either, watched helplessly as they both drowned. She was inconsolable until the day of the funeral, when she decided that they were not really gone because "they were alive in heaven." She never mentioned the terrible loss again, and everyone was relieved that she seemed to feel better. The only problem was that, for the next five years, she could barely catch her breath.

As her husband related these events, which no one had talked about since the funeral, the patient began to remember them. As if struck by a bolt of lightning, she was suddenly overcome with grief. It was not difficult for her to see how being unable to breathe reflected her buried memory of the day she had lost those two precious people—they were unable to breathe when they drowned, and she couldn't catch her breath as she watched them in terror. But she was not convinced that grief was any better than shortness of breath. It was only after her family was advised about how to help her grieve that she was able to allow herself to mourn. Active grief produced intense sadness, but as it proceeded, her body stopped reliving the loss by clutching to the last memory of those whom she had lost. As her body relinquished its hold on her son and her brother, her mind was gradually able to do the same. Of course, she never gave them up completely, but she was at least able to move beyond the primitive and unchanging connection she had maintained in the past.

Depression Masked by Bodily Symptoms

Depression, a mind-body deception discussed in detail in Part III, is often masked by two kinds of physical symptoms. First, there are direct physical symptoms of depression, such as low energy, disturbed sleep, inability to concentrate, and loss of appetite. The second kind of physical symptom is the result of somatization, which produces headaches, backaches, and a panoply of minor aches and pains that the depressed person magnifies into something bad or dangerous.

Somatization *secondary to* depression can be almost impossible to distinguish from *primary* somatization. Depressed people who find it difficult or shameful to express their feelings openly may report only the somatic complaints and deny or be truly unaware of a depressed mood. At the same time, many people who are primary somatizers lead depressing lives. Both conditions are characterized by irritability, indecisiveness, pessimism, guilt, and dependent, demanding behavior. A trial of antidepressant medication is sometimes the only way to distinguish clinically between the two. Depressed patients may initially be overwhelmed by side effects, but the physical symptoms gradually resolve. When the patient is relieved of the pressure of a depressed mood that was previously contained with somatization, his somatic complaints go away and the capacity to express emotion, which had been overwhelmed by the depression, returns. In contrast, primary somatizers often feel better as soon as they start taking an antidepressant, but the improvement does not last. Just as the physician begins to feel like a hero, the patient has a dramatic setback that erases all of the previous gains. In the case of the depressed patient, the initial preoccupation with the negative aspects of the medication resolves as the antidepressant takes effect. In the case of the somatizer, an initial placebo effect is replaced by mechanisms of retreat back into illness that are described a little later in this section.

Even what appears to be chronic somatization can mask a reversible depression. For example, a forty-year-old businesswoman had been plagued by chronic fatigue, headaches, sore muscles, and backaches for as long as she could remember. She consulted numerous physicians but never got enduring relief. Even though she was not aware of feeling depressed, a doctor tried giving her an antidepressant in the slim hope that depression might be the primary process fueling the physical symptoms. To everyone's surprise, especially the patient's, she began to feel better. Her energy level increased and the aches and pains disappeared. Only when she felt better did she realize that her pervasive lack of enthusiasm and inability to enjoy life had been the result of her constant battle against a biologically ingrained enervation.

PRIMARY SOMATIZATION

Primary somatization is not a symptom of some other condition but an organizing principle of the mind. For people in whom physical illness has become a way of life, much of what they think, say, and do is clouded by fearful preoccupation with their bodies. When an emotional response is called for, a physical sensation appears instead. There may be a favorite symptom, such as a headache, a sore knee, an upset stomach, or a diffusion of suffering in multiple systems, such as fatigue, insomnia, or joint pain. Either way, the person's identity is that of a sick person whose greatest accomplishment is to endure suffering and whose most important task is to see the doctor. Attempting to reassure primary somatizers has the paradoxical effect of increasing the intensity and variety of their complaints, while agreeing that an illness is terrible and even incurable paradoxically reduces the complaints!

Primary somatization may take place on a conscious level—that is, with full awareness—or an unconscious level, automatically, without conscious awareness. Conscious and unconscious somatization can each take a number of forms, as outlined in the table below.

Table 7-1

SOMATIZATION DECEPTIONS		
SECONDARY	PRIMARY	
	Unconscious	*Conscious*
Grief	Conversion	Malingering
Depression	Hypochondriasis	Factitious disorder
	Somatization disorder	
	Pain disorder	

Unconscious Simulation of Disease

The psychiatric manual of diagnosis subdivides syndromes in which somatization is the product of an unconscious process into several subtypes according to the predominant symptoms. *Hypochondriasis* is described as a preoccupation with having a disease that does not exist, while *somatization disorder* (also called hysteria or Briquet's syndrome) involves a large number of functional symptoms in multiple organ systems over many years. *Pain disorder* is characterized by chronic functional pain, and *conversion disorder* involves sensory or motor symptoms in regions controlled by the voluntary nervous system.

The distinction between these syndromes is, to a significant extent, artificial. For example, somatization disorder is not the only condition characterized by *somatization.* Many people with chronic functional complaints are convinced that these complaints signify a specific illness, making them candidates for two official diagnoses at once. It is also not clear that patients with just one kind of functional complaint are any different from those with multiple functional complaints. One condition linked in *DSM-IV* with disorders associated with functional physical symptoms, body dysmorphic disorder (characterized by preoccupation with an imaginary or real but exaggerated abnormality of physical appearance such as skin texture or the size of one's nose), is probably not an example of somatization at all but a type of obsessional disorder. Conversion disorder, which includes symptoms or deficits involving the voluntary muscles or the five senses, has some distinguishing characteristics that will be discussed shortly. Along with the other disorders of chronic somatization, it can be included in a broad category of somatization that results from *automatic mental processes that occur outside of conscious awareness.*

Somatization Disorder

Jack is the kind of person who is prone to unconscious somatization. As a child, Jack had a hard life. His father worked long hours and had little time left to help out around the house. By the time he was ten, Jack was regularly preparing the meals to help out his mother, who suffered from arthritis. As a teenager he began to have severe headaches that impaired his academic performance, but he tried to ignore the pain. He injured his knee playing high-school football, but that did not bother him at the time, and neither did the broken arm he incurred in an automobile accident when he was twenty. But when he injured his back on the job at age thirty, he did not bounce back, as he had done in the past. In fact, each time he tried to go back to work, his back seemed to get worse.

Despite exerting tremendous effort to get better—physical therapy, anti-inflammatory medications, injections of steroids, and chiropractic manipulations—he experienced only transient periods of improvement, followed by a return of symptoms that were worse than ever before. The doctors initially recommended against surgery, because an MRI scan showed only a slightly slipped disk that would not necessarily be helped by surgery. But Jack did not agree with this opinion and insisted on an operation. A surgeon finally relented and performed the surgery, the main effect of which was to make things worse. Not only could Jack no longer work, but he could not function in his roles of husband and father. Most of his time was now spent either being *in* pain or seeking relief *from* pain. Even after the MRI findings improved, the illness remained the central focus of Jack's life. If he socialized at all, the focus of his conversation was on pain and disability.

To Jack's physician, it began to look as if Jack's symptoms had taken on a life of their own, independent of the physical pathology that might have started them. The fact that attempts to reassure Jack that his illness was not that serious had the paradoxical effect of making Jack more anxious made the physician wonder whether Jack was just trying to get attention. But this did not seem to be a likely motivation for complaints that got worse no matter what the doctor did. After all, the physician had always taken Jack seriously and had responded to every concern Jack had expressed, including the wish for surgery. If the illness was not directly proportional to disease in the patient's back, and if the complaints were not motivated by interpersonal rewards, there must be a more complex mixture of mind and body at work here. But what could it be?

Concluding that the answer to this question was beyond his competence, the physician suggested that another kind of specialist—perhaps a psychiatrist—would be better equipped to handle this problem. Jack was not relieved that he was finally being sent to the right place, only indignant that his illness was no longer considered "real." Jack then developed a severe headache unlike anything he had experienced before; it was so severe that the idea of referring him to a psychiatrist was put on hold until the cause of the headache could be investigated. The physician was now at a complete loss. Did Jack have a medical problem that was continuing to disable him, an illness that the physician had missed despite all his tests? Or was the physician being deceived by a pseudo-illness in which another symptom popped up as soon as one disappeared? The answer to this question—"Is the patient *really* ill?"—is never clear when dealing with somatization, because the fantasy of what is in the body can never be entirely separated from the truth of what is in the mind.

Conversion Disorder

One of the first somatization syndromes recognized by modern psychiatry was "conversion disorder," a condition in which an emotional conflict is removed from the mental realm by "converting" it into a physical counterpart—an alteration in sensation or motor function, such as blindness, deafness, or paralysis. Although this transferring of feelings to the body is highly purposeful, it is still unconscious. The patient is completely unaware of the dynamic connection between the sudden *physical disability* and the powerful emotions that are inducing it.

Conversion symptoms are highly symbolic ways of simultaneously hiding, expressing, and solving a threatening emotional conflict. By *symbolic* I mean that the symptoms clearly represent the specific *content* of the conflict. For example, a young woman in her senior year of college had always wanted to be a singer. However, her father, an attorney, thought she should have a legal career. She had studied hard for the law school admission test, but when she woke up on the morning of the exam, her right arm was paralyzed! While the sudden appearance of paralysis would be frightening to most people, this young woman did not seem particularly upset. This was not too difficult to understand from an outsider's perspective, since the paralysis prevented her from taking the examination but would not interfere with a singing career. In the meantime, everyone forgot about law school and instead inundated her with solicitous concern. Consciously oblivious to these rewards, she wholeheartedly rejected the suggestion that her paralysis might have an underlying psychological purpose. Proving her symptom to be a deception—albeit an unconscious one—the paralysis inexplicably vanished when her father acknowledged that she might not be suited for a legal career, after all.

Many mental health professionals incorrectly believe that conversion disorder has all but disappeared since its heyday in Freud's era. The assumption is that people are now so much more knowledgeable about the workings of the unconscious that they do not fool themselves with such an obvious subterfuge—unless they are extremely naive or culturally backward. The fact is, however, that *one out of every three women* has experienced at least one conversion symptom, albeit fleetingly. (The incidence of conversion symptoms in men has not been studied, possibly because conversion symptoms in men are more likely to be considered evidence of malingering.) Sophistication is no barrier to somatization.

The complex origins of conversion deceptions demonstrate the fluctuating border between the mental and physical realms. The immediate cause of the apparently physical symptom is a psychological mechanism, but more often than not a somatic disease lies under that. In fact, in the majority of cases involving persistent conversion symptoms, the diagnosis is changed within five years to an actual medical illness. What does this strange reversal tell us about the border between mind and body? One possibility is that the conflict that really produces the conversion is between *the unconscious perception of a bodily disease* that cannot yet be found on a test or physical examination and *the wish not to know about the illness*. By creating its own disturbance of the body, the mind can convert a real, uncontrollable physical problem into a fantasied abnormality that is under the unconscious control of the mind.

These deceptions were operating when, two weeks before her wedding day, a twenty-five-year-old woman developed incapacitating numbness and weakness in her right arm and leg, which could not be explained by the most thorough neurological evaluation. She had developed identical symptoms ten years previously, apparently in sympathy with her mother, who had injured her right arm and leg in a fall. The first episode had resolved completely when the mother recovered.

The patient, who was very dependent on her mother, was planning to marry a man who was moving to another state to take a new job. The conflict between wanting to be married and wanting to maintain the symbiotic relationship she had always enjoyed with her mother was solved by her symptoms, since the wedding had to be cancelled so that she could have a medical workup. Over the next week the symptoms disappeared, only to reappear when the wedding was rescheduled. All physical malfunction disappeared entirely when her fiancé gave up and moved without her.

Six months later, the patient's arm and leg began to feel numb again. This time, her vision was blurred, too. When the same neurological investigations that were negative before were repeated, multiple sclerosis was found.

Testimony by Accident

In conversion disorder, emotional conflict is expressed as a bodily symptom or malfunction. There are many other ways in which intolerable memories, ideas, or feelings can be relocated from the mind to the body, helping the

sufferer to avoid something that would seem unbearable if it were recognized, but at the same time isolating the hidden emotions from the curative power of the mind.

Pain in the mind may be transferred to the body in the form of a physical malfunction such as a conversion symptom, or it may be transformed into bodily action. Certain kinds of actions that symbolize or recreate a repressed conflict or memory while keeping it out of awareness could be considered a special subtype of conversion—and some forms of accidents would also fit this description.

For example, a middle-aged woman described how, throughout her adult life, she had suffered a major accident each year in the month of April. One year she broke her arm, the next year her leg. On one occasion, she was in an automobile wreck that seriously injured her back. When attempts to exercise extreme caution each April did not decrease the rate of injury, she was persuaded to enter psychotherapy. With a good deal of effort, she asked herself why she should be hurt so badly each April. And then one day, it came to her: her mother's name was *April!*

As a child with an abusive, even tormenting mother, this woman had been caught in the terrible conflict between her need for her mother, who was her only caretaker, and the terror and rage aroused by her mother's abuse. So she rationalized her mother's behavior as "not all that bad" because "many other people were much worse off" than she. In order to support this deception, which enabled her to remain attached to the only mother she had, it was necessary to "forget" much of the abuse that had occurred. Later in life she further reinforced this defensive posture by concluding that her mother had sacrificed her chance for happiness by not remarrying after her father left.

This woman's revision of her own history on the conscious level was so airtight that the truth could only be revealed by *unconscious actions taken in the external world.* Only when she began to allow into her conscious experience the injury she had suffered due to her mother's abusive actions did her "April accidents" cease. Her mind and body had concocted a remarkably literal way to communicate the truth that had been intolerable to her as a child: *April* means *injury.*

Conscious Simulation of Disease

A dramatic form of somatization occurs in individuals for whom actions not only speak louder than words but completely replace words as a means of solving conflict. These patients consciously pretend to be ill when they know they are not. Conscious simulation of disease comes in two forms: *malingering*—pretending to be ill to achieve an obvious goal—and *factitious dis-*

order, in which the only goal seems to be to deceive physicians. Malingerers are encountered in all walks of society, while people with factitious symptoms are encountered mainly in the medical system.

Studying people who purposely feign illness can be particularly informative because their behavior is more blatant, their motivations more transparent, their personalities more obvious, than those who unconsciously simulate physical disease. Yet both types of somatizing patients share a darker side that can be observed more directly in the conscious fabricator. Let us begin by looking at the conscious motivations of the more flamboyant group, the malingerers, in order to understand the unconscious motivations of the more common group of somatizers.

Malingering

Everyone has been a malingerer at some point in time. Each time you managed to convince your mother that you shouldn't be sent to school because of a stomachache you didn't have, you were malingering. In the medical world, malingering is not a diagnosis but a type of behavior enacted by certain patients. It may also serve as an accusation by attending physicians. Technically, the term refers to the fabrication of symptoms in order to obtain some clearly recognizable external goal, such as money, drugs, avoidance of military duty, or escape from legal sanctions or unwanted responsibilities. As an isolated event, malingering does not necessarily imply severe psychopathology. A single act may even be adaptive if it makes it possible for the malingerer to escape unnecessarily dangerous situations, as may occur in wartime, or if the malingerer is able to accomplish a valuable goal, as can happen under conditions of political repression.

When it is primarily a form of antisocial behavior, however, malingering is used to cheat insurance companies, obtain addicting medications, or get out of jail. The paradox of malingering behavior is that it typically involves a great deal of work, considering the amount of gain involved. Long hospitalizations, complex lies (each of which increases the risk of exposure), and painful diagnostic tests are a lot to go through to obtain drugs or money, when these goods can more easily be had by stealing. When the malingerer gets caught and loses the gain—as frequently happens, because so many hints have been dropped that even the most trusting physician becomes suspicious—it becomes apparent that there are deeper, covert motivations for malingering that have nothing to do with the tangible goal or gain.

Malingerers are unpopular for obvious reasons, but they can also have an endearing side that comes from an uncanny, dark charisma—an ability to get "under people's skins" and involve them in the confused and confusing realm of their deceptions. Typically, everyone drawn into this carefully constructed web loses the ability to distinguish fact from fiction, fabricated illness from real illness, genuine emotion from clever manipulation. Malingerers purposefully choose the body as the vehicle for securing conscious aims, yet the full picture of what is transacted is far larger *and* far less obvious— shrouded, as it is, by unconscious needs and purposes.

A recurrent theme that emerges in the malingerer is that there is no real boundary between truth and deception, wish and deed, fantasy and reality, friend and foe. Interactions with malingering patients are extremely complex—nothing really *is* what it seems to be. Clinicians working with these patients realize that what appears to be true today will be found to be a lie tomorrow. The next day that, too, will turn out to be untrue, because the core of the patient's personality is ultimately too flimsy, too ephemeral to be truly known by anyone, including the patient.

In his novella *The Nigger of the "Narcissus,"* Joseph Conrad superbly described this lack of grounding in a genuine self. At the center of Conrad's novella is James Wait, an itinerant seaman who has signed up to work as a sailor on the ship *Narcissus.* Wait is obviously a robust and powerful person who rapidly demonstrates that he can do the work of ten men, and every sailor on the *Narcissus* wants to work with him. But the "honeymoon" lasts only as long as the ship is in the harbor. No sooner does it set sail than Wait announces that he is dying of an unnamed illness. He has suddenly become so weak, he regretfully reports, that he cannot do any work, let alone his fair share.

In reaction to this abrupt switch, the crew splits into two factions. One group becomes devoted to caring for Wait, ignoring the obvious fact that he never looks sick. Manipulated by Wait's skillful use of guilt and cajoling, the sailors cater to his every wish, even as he reviles them for not doing enough. The second group is becoming increasingly suspicious of the so-called invalid, but they are unable to agree upon a strategy for confronting Wait. The two contingents of crew members become so alienated from each other, they barely speak.

Midway through the voyage, Wait reveals, through a monologue the reader is allowed to eavesdrop on, that he has been keeping two crucial secrets. The first is that for years, he has been engaging in the practice of obtaining free passage by signing on as a crew member on ships that are going in his direction—and then pretending to be ill when he is asked to do any work. His deceptions have been so masterful that he even received a bonus at the end of his last trip, even though he never did anything but complain. Like all the other crewmen he has hoodwinked, the crew members of the *Narcissus* are so gullible that, from Wait's distorted perspective, they deserve the lies he feeds them.

The second secret Wait reveals is that the first secret is a lie! Wait himself fears that underneath his facade of illness he really *is* ill. Not only is he unsure whether he is sick or well, he is also unsure whether he is a sane deceiver or a confused madman. The only way Wait can distract himself from this unbearable inner chaos is to tell one lie after another, each one as convincing as it is contradictory of the previous lie. By undermining the crew's sense of reality, he is able to make them feel crazier than he does and thus gain a temporary sense of triumphant superiority.

Evoking at will a dizzying blend of confusion and confidence, admiration and contempt, love and hate, Wait is able to unload his inner demons on those he is deceiving. He can triumph over a devastating internal sense of impotence by making himself the most powerful force on the ship. He has become so much the center of the vessel's universe that even after a life-and-death struggle against a typhoon, during which he offers no help at all, the only question on the lips of his many shipboard caretakers is, "Is Wait safe?" He, of course, is just fine, having rested up sufficiently during the storm to hurl invectives at his comrades for not checking on his safety soon enough. Even those who have come to hate him are nonetheless consumed by him and spend their time arguing about him with those who love him.

The ultimate secret, though, is as much a secret from Wait as it is from everyone else: he is *really* dying. When the cook, the shipboard oracle, divines Wait's true state of health by casting bones, Wait suddenly changes his course to the opposite tack. Where he had been too ill to do anything, he now demands to be sent back to work immediately. Just as they have responded to the rest of Wait's lies, the crew goes along with this one, too, apparently identifying with his capricious and grandiose reversal and heaping assignments on him. Wait does not tell us whether he is so frightened by the cook's divination that he tries to convince himself that he is not really sick, or whether he automatically tends to move in the opposite direction of the truth of the moment; he probably doesn't know himself.

At precisely his moment of apparently greatest health, Wait suddenly dies. Without the continuing force of his influence, the stunned crew begin to realize how thoroughly they have been caught in an intricate web of deceptions, how they willingly sacrificed their own needs, perceptions, and feelings in their confused efforts to be of help. Only after he can no longer manipulate them into action without giving them a chance to think, do they realize how readily they divided themselves into irreconcilable camps as they identified with one or another of the irreconcilable sides of Wait's mind. Once they are no longer preoccupied with whether or not he is really the sickest or the healthiest sailor on their ship, they become aware of Wait's confusion about what was really the matter with him. Most importantly, when they are no longer in a state of frantic motion induced by Wait's need to project his mental turmoil onto the sphere of bodily action, they realize how easy it is to become entangled in the destructive but fascinating inner world of the simulator of disease.

Factitious Disorder

The most deceptive of the somatization syndromes has a dry title that belies its dramatic nature. People who have "factitious disorder" will do almost *anything* to get themselves admitted to a hospital, even if it places their lives in danger. Sometimes they simply make up symptoms, but they are not beyond cutting themselves, injecting themselves with foreign substances, taking dangerous drugs, or doing anything else that not only mimics but *produces* physical disease. Unlike malingerers, factitious somatizers do not have goals that most people would find desirable. Indeed, their only goal appears to be to become a patient and bedevil the health care system.

These unfortunate patients present a barrage of false information while revealing almost nothing about their true identities—and anything they do say is likely to be a lie. As a result, more myth than fact has accumulated about this disorder in its full-blown condition. Some researchers feel that factitious symptoms are more common than is generally assumed, while others believe that the disorder has been *over*reported because the same few patients, using different names and presenting different symptoms, have been described as different patients by the many physicians who have encountered them. Some investigators propose that any physically healthy person who would *want* to have surgery must be psychotic; others conclude that a severe personality disorder must be to blame; still another group believes that factitious disorder lacks any specific signs of psychopathology that would clearly distinguish it from other disorders. This lack of definitive knowledge undoubtedly reflects the capacity of people with factitious disorder to conceal their true selves from clinicians who try to study them.

Patients with factitious symptoms—many of whom are young, unmarried, and lack meaningful relationships but have a good deal of medical knowledge—dedicate their lives to gaining admission to hospital after hospital for treatment of fabricated illnesses. This can be a full-time occupation, and some patients are known to have been hospitalized more than 400 times in different states, countries, even continents. Patients may enter several hospitals in the same week, under different assumed names and with different "illnesses." Factitious patients usually get into the hospital via the emergency room, where they appear in the middle of the night when a less experienced and more fatigued physician is likely to be on duty. Between hospitalizations these patients are likely to engage in minor criminal activities, such as vagrancy, theft, drug abuse, disorderly conduct and assault, resulting in an alternate avocation as a prisoner instead of a patient. One ironic antisocial act of the factitious somatizer: stealing money to finance a trip to the next hospital—a kind of reverse malingering!

The range of factitious complaints is limited only by the daring and sophistication of the patient and the gullibility of the physician. Many patients switch back and forth between one organ system and another, and one simulation often provides grounds for later elaborations. For example, a patient may feign appendicitis by pretending to be in severe abdominal pain and covertly heating a thermometer. The patient undergoes exploratory surgery, which cures nothing (there was nothing to cure) but does cause adhesions that lead to another operation. After several unjustified operations (laparotomies), the patient's abdomen begins to look like a battlefield (which, in a sense, it is), so that it becomes easier for the patient to insist (and the doctor to believe) that subsequent acute symptoms are complications of the earlier procedures.

Nonsurgical conditions that are fabricated by these patients include self-induced vomiting, coughing up blood simulated by purposefully swallowing blood, inserting needles or broken glass all over the body, abusing anticoagulants; simulated seizures, fainting spells, or neurological abnormalities; and rashes or abscesses induced by injecting bacteria, milk, paint, or other substances under the skin.

Once in the hospital, the patient is the trickiest of deceivers. At first, enormous confidence is expressed in the physician at the same time that any attempt to help the physician arrive at an actual diagnosis is glibly evaded. The patient tells captivating but impossible stories about the illness, which no one is available to corroborate. For example, one patient with an unhealed abscess on his leg said that the wound started with an infection he had acquired in the Gulf War. He proceeded to regale his physicians with stories of his combat experience—although, it turned out, he was never in the military. Another patient, claiming to know a famous specialist who supposedly had treated him in another city, entertained his new physician with juicy stories about the expert's personality—even though the patient had never even visited that city, let alone the specialist.

In the name of an ostensible search for the cause of a nonexistent disease, the factitious patient has an incredible tolerance for pain and an unfathomable eagerness to undergo dangerous and invasive procedures. One patient reported in the literature even agreed to a lobotomy! Some factitious patients seem addicted to narcotics, but they will turn down regular narcotic injections that are contingent on staying in the hospital long enough for the physician to get to know them a little better. The gratification of secrecy and deception is apparently greater than that provided by the drug.

The factitious patient's hospitalization typically ends in tumult and dissatisfaction. The doctor's fascination with trying to discern a difficult diagnosis ends when he or she becomes suspicious of the continually revolving symptoms, when someone recognizes the patient, or when the patient is discovered in the act of self-inflicting a lesion. If the doctor does not immediately eject the patient as a charlatan, the patient walks out, either by provoking an angry confrontation or by sneaking away, only to be admitted somewhere else to repeat the cycle of deception, discovery, and abandonment. The patient has become the Flying Dutchman of medicine, sailing from doctor to doctor with insatiable needs, for which nothing satisfying can ever be done.

On the other side of the interaction, the physician begins the encounter with the factitious patient secure in the role of knowledgeable expert, whose only goal is to offer comfort and help—in return for which the physician feels a justly deserved sense of accomplishment in diagnosing and treating the problem. But the unfolding script of this challenging patient casts the doctor in a more sinister light, as he or she unwittingly takes on the role of a gullible perpetrator of disfiguring, painful, and unnecessary interventions. Realizing that the patient is feigning illness makes the physician feel even more like a failure because the physician was unable to recognize what, in retrospect, was an obvious deception. As the physician's confidence and self-esteem plummet, positive regard for the patient is replaced by guilt and shame, and then by a wish to be rid of a selfish manipulator who is a drain on precious resources and a constant reminder of the doctor's fallibility.

Like the malingerer, the factitious patient openly perverts the benevolent caretaking doctor-patient relationship with unconscious but powerful doses of hate and rejection. What does the patient hate? It is that very quality of the physician that is sought in the first place—the power to help. For the factitious patient, to *need* a physician reveals weakness but to *defeat* the physician at the medical world's own game provides a sense of triumph and power that feels much more gratifying than mere health.

One man was able to describe the thrill of this pyrrhic "victory" of defeating a doctor's attempt to help. The patient, who said that he was an artist, produced festering blisters on his skin by repeatedly injecting himself with paint. He went from doctor to doctor, baring his increasingly disfiguring lesions and receiving a variety of treatments, none of which did any good. On one occasion, he was treated with doses of adrenal steroids, which suppressed the function of his own adrenal glands, nearly killing him.

Eventually the patient became bored with the paint-induced lesions and began to rub the lesions with dirty pieces of glass until they became grossly infected. He showed up in the emergency room of another hospital and was admitted with septicemia, a potentially fatal blood infection. He was given intravenous antibiotics, which he secretly disconnected to prolong the treatment. He went into a coma; when he regained consciousness, he was left with gaping wounds. His request for narcotics seemed reasonable—until he was discovered selling them to one of the hospital attendants.

A physician asked the patient why he was so intent on defeating everyone, including himself. In a moment of candor, the patient, who liked this particular doctor, replied, "To tell you the truth [was it?], I don't really know.

But I'd rather have you be the one who is confused. I might be sick, but at least I can out-think you. If I ever truly needed a doctor for something, you might not come through for me. But there's nothing you, or anyone else, can do that I haven't done to myself. If I die, I'm the one who did it—it didn't happen *to* me."

The physician was not upset by this revelation. In fact, he was encouraged that a patient who had eluded understanding for so long was beginning to show an ability for self-reflection and insight. Bizarre or not, at least it was something to work on—a *beginning*. Perhaps with further discussion, it might be possible to understand the patient and maybe even help him change some of his behaviors. Of course, right at the moment of greatest therapeutic promise, the patient left, only to appear in another city with a new infection.

All forms of somatization, be they conscious or unconscious, use the body as a primary means of self-expression, control, interaction, and even livelihood. Dramatic somatizers "wear their motivations on their sleeves," whereas milder somatizers hide theirs under the gauze of more subtle interactions. In either case, however, the underlying mind-body dynamic remains the same: the apparent mental vacuum that seems to accompany a barrage of bodily complaints hides a secret core of terror, rage, and loss of the boundary between fantasy and reality, thought and action.

What enduring aspects of the personality allow somatizers to relocate experiences belonging to the mental realm to organs and tissues of the body? So far, no gene has been identified, no neurotransmitter discovered, that might account for the distortion of these psychological processes. Clinical experience with somatizers (but no formal research) suggests that this particular pattern of pathology emerges from the intersection of inborn temperamental inclinations with formative early-life experiences, distorting the growth of the personality in ways that are discussed in the next chapter.

8

Are Somatizers Born
or Made?

THERE WAS NOTHING really abnormal about Marjorie when she was a child. Though she was easily frustrated and had a hard time calming down when she was upset, this was not outside the normal range of emotional expression in children. Marjorie's mother, however, had such a strong need for her family to appear perfect that she was unable to tolerate any displays of temper or distress. If Marjorie got a little upset, her mother would simply ignore it. When Marjorie was calm, her mother was effusive in her displays of affection, but if there were any complaints, she would withdraw into icy aloofness. Realizing that her mother would not tolerate any anger or even disagreement, Marjorie learned not to complain. In fact, she tried to be the perfect child—and she was successful as long as nothing happened that made her feel—or at least *act*—disappointed or unhappy. There was no way she could experience even normal distress without risking emotional abandonment in a family in which *looking* good took precedence over *feeling* good.

Marjorie's physical health was generally good, but when she came down with chicken pox her mother positively doted on her. After all, a good mother is concerned when a child becomes ill. Furthermore, Marjorie's mother *understood* illness because she herself was subject to severe migraines that forced her to stay in bed with the curtains drawn for two or three days. So on the few occasions when Marjorie did get sick, no one minded if she did not function well. If she became a little irritable or withdrawn, no one held it against her. In contrast, when Marjorie was in her usual state of health, she had to be on her guard against displaying any irritability or any demands for attention that could result in withdrawal of her mother's affection and interest. Illness provided at least a temporary opportunity to feel bad without threat of reprisal from those she needed.

Early-life experiences interact with inborn temperamental inclinations, producing patterns of response that are apparent even in infancy. Some babies cry hardly at all, others quite frequently; some are docile and easily contented, others demanding and finicky; some are hypersensitive to their surroundings and tentative in their actions, while others seek out environmental stimulation, reveling in anything that is new.

There is no single "critical period" for the development of any human trait. Rather, the unique "mix" of the child's inborn disposition with parental responses, over time, is more important than any one event. However, like the early stages of development of a bodily organ, the phases during which structures of the mind first appear are more sensitive to disturbances than the later phases.* Because the mind, like the body, adds layer after layer of psychological specialization as it matures, an early "lesion" of experience or biology affects all subsequent personality development.

When somatization has become the organizing principle of the personality (as opposed to one of several symptoms of mental and emotional distress), there is rarely an early history of blatant abuse or gross deprivation. Though no formal studies of the deviations in personality development that occur in somatization have been reported, clinical experience shows that, when they were growing up, people who habitually resort to somatization had needs for nurturance that, while not always extreme, were substantially more than their caretakers could reliably meet. One result of this mismatch between the child's needs and the caretaker's ability to provide gratification is frantic attempts on the child's part to garner parental approval, the loss of which is so threatening that it remains hidden from the conscious mind. In a family environment that responds to illness but ignores emotions, the child gains a sense of personal competence only by coercing rewards (parental approval and whatever nurturance may be available) through action (illness), while an increasingly confusing mental life is pushed further and further underground. The next few sections explain how this complex process might unfold.

---

*The mind obviously does not have a physical structure, but some collections of functions, such as the self and the ego, endure in such a predictable form, over time, that it is useful to think of them as structures.

TEMPERAMENT

The reality of constitutional predispositions is evident from birth in the different ways in which infants accept soothing, tolerate stimulation, and interact with their caretakers. These differences become consolidated by two or three months of age. Based on their research, child development experts Alexander Thomas and Stella Chess developed a typology of temperament: "easy" (40 percent of children), "slow to warm up" (15 percent), "difficult" (10 percent), and combinations of the three types (35 percent). Difficult children are characterized by irregular bodily rhythms (such as eating and sleeping) and intense displays of emotion. Their moods are more likely to be negative than positive and, intolerant of frustration or change, they withdraw from unfamiliar stimuli. Less adaptable, harder to handle, and more trying, 70 percent of difficult children develop behavior problems, as opposed to only 18 percent of easy children.

GOODNESS OF FIT

Temperament alone does not shape the personality. The "goodness of fit" between the child and the parents also plays a crucial role. An infant who has an easy temperament can help even an anxious, hyperreactive parent to respond consistently. Conversely, a secure and confident parent can help a difficult child with unstable emotional reactions learn more comfortable ways of responding. However, parents with limited self-confidence and poor control of their own emotions may not have the resources to cope with the unpredictably intense activity, aggression, and emotionality of a difficult child. Overwhelmed, these parents are unable to demonstrate consistent interest in and empathy for their children, instead typically responding with anger, frustration, and withdrawal.

Temperamental mismatches may play an important role in the development of somatization. Children with difficult temperaments who do not receive sufficient empathy and guidance in learning to handle their own emotions must find other ways of coping. One way is to disconnect from their conscious awareness those emotions that their caretakers cannot tolerate, let alone help them control, in order to avoid feeling flooded and overwhelmed. Without the opportunity to struggle with and integrate conflicting thoughts and feelings—to "exercise" the mind by "working out" the emotions—the child's mind does not develop a sense of adequacy in the emotional arena. Once emotions are excluded from the psychological realm of the mind, they can only be expressed in the physical realm as action (behavior) or through the language of the body (somatization).

ATTACHMENT

The bond or attachment that develops between infant and mother falls along a continuum from secure to insecure. Ideally, of course, secure attachment occurs as the baby has repeated positive experiences with a reliably available mother. A sensitive and attuned mother accurately perceives her baby's different states of arousal, whether pleasant or unpleasant, and responds to them appropriately: she "mirrors" the pleasant states and soothes the unpleasant ones. When the mother soothes her baby in times of distress, the baby internalizes—takes in—these messages of safety and comfort and thereby learns that feelings of distress do not have to be overwhelming. However, if the mother is herself anxious, distracted, or overreactive, the baby takes in those signals as well. The result is an insecure attachment in which the child learns to be vigilant, fearfully watching for intolerable signs of emotional distance from the mother but also perpetually on the lookout for any sign that she might be available.

In adulthood, the irresistible pull toward illness serves as an unconscious pull toward the long-held fantasy of secure attachment. On this level the somatizer is asking physicians and other caretakers to play the role of the attuned mother who brings order and safety to internal chaos. Demands for medication, hospitalization, rest, comfort, or pity are really demands for a reliable, soothing attachment. Since the transaction between the doctor and the somatizing patient is so laden with the unconscious fantasy of unconditional gratification, as well as the memory of what really happened with important caretakers who did not live up to this ideal, sooner or later there is bound to be "trouble in paradise."

One of the first ways in which this hitch occurs is when the physician tries to make a diagnosis. The patient is enthusiastic at first, feeling that a diagnosis will legitimize the unconditional care for which the patient has always longed. But when diagnostic efforts do not pan out, the physician's interest starts to lag, reminding the patient of the chronic feelings of deprivation and abandonment that accompanied withdrawal of the parent's interest. Since somatization is a way of coping with deprivation in the first place, the somatization process now exacerbates in response to the physician's less than perfect enactment of the attuned parent role. Demands for more attention and caring also escalate. Continuing complaints that defy both diagnosis and treatment evoke feelings of inadequacy in the doctor, and some signs of alienation inevitably surface in the doctor's manner, creating even more panic in the patient. Eventually, the physician rejects the patient by declaring the patient "not sick," or the patient rejects the physician by declaring the physician "not competent" and goes somewhere else.

THWARTED AUTONOMY

Another piece of the somatizing puzzle can be found in the developmental period during which toddlers acquire language and start flexing their budding psychological "muscles" of independence and autonomy. *Words* make it possible for the child to communicate complex inner states with much more precision than do grunts, groans, tantrums, and smiles. Words are important not only because of the greater precision in communication they afford, but also because they allow the child to have private thoughts, perceptions, and feelings separate from other people. This is the time during which the child first begins to forge an identity that is distinct from other people; an identity—a sense of self—that is asserted vocally as well as behaviorally and that can choose to share some parts of the self and keep others private.

Once a sense of independence emerges, the drive to exercise it is as natural as the drive to eat, sleep, or gratify other needs. Words play an important role here, because the drive to become a separate person is facilitated by the capacity to say no, to oppose the will of the parent verbally as well as behaviorally. Although they are painful, the "terrible twos" are an important time in development, for it is during this period that the child learns to experience and express a separate and independent volition, which goes hand in hand with a separate and independent identity.

It almost sounds as if independence follows dependence in a linear sequence of personality maturation. However, the growth of human identity, like that of the body, moves back and forth, consolidating each forward step with a step or two backward. This is not a flaw in the line of personality development but a necessary rhythm that facilitates the integration of opposing attitudes. Dependency should never be totally discarded, nor the need for independence overlooked. Rather, the person who adapts best to the vagaries of life is adept at being assertive when necessary and also willing to lean on others when personal resources are running low or when a situation is simply too much to handle alone. For this reason, the developmental phase of *separation-individuation* includes *practicing,* when the child learns to assert independence, and *rapprochement,* when the child returns to the parent for emotional "refueling" and reassurance that parental support is still available.

It is easy to cuddle and reassure a child who is openly affectionate; it is more of a challenge to welcome a child who has just been negativistic, defiant, or argumentative. Yet most parents are not overwhelmed by the task of nurturing children who, at the same time, practice their newfound independence, sometimes in obnoxious ways that lead to such terms as the "terrible twos." However, those parents whose own psychology requires that their children remain bound to them through need and dependency are not able to tolerate the natural drive toward autonomy. To protect *themselves* from feeling abandoned, these parents may undermine any sign of independent action or thought. They might even retaliate by withdrawing emotionally, as if to prove that they did not need the child anyway and, at the same time, to frighten the child back to a dependent state.

Withdrawal of the parent's support (or outright attacks) in response to a child's attempts to act independently has important somatic and psychological consequences. Exercising independence means confronting a large and frightening world alone—a daunting task, even when parents are available to help. The danger represented by the threatened loss of the parent adds to the high level of emotional agitation that is inevitably evoked by the challenge of striking out on one's own. An adult might interpret the physiology of bodily arousal (discussed in detail in Part IV) as evidence of tension or fear, but young children, who are limited in their ability to conceptualize and communicate mental states, are more aware of bodily sensations—pain in the heart, a stomachache, dizziness, shortness of breath, or lightheadedness. Parents who are in tune with a child's developing mind can help the child to translate this disruptive internal state into words. Without this support, the psychology of the child who emerges from this developmental state may be organized around these bodily sensations rather than their interpretation by the mind.

Freud acknowledged this phase in which self-awareness is centered on physical sensations when he said that "the self is first and foremost a bodily self." When early experiences do not facilitate consolidation of an identity that includes the mind, the body readily asserts itself whenever the person is confronted by a situation calling for the psychological skills. One person who had this problem was Ellen, a twenty-five-year-old woman who had mild ulcerative colitis that had an unusual course. Some of the time, she was totally incapacitated by unbearable abdominal pain that could not be explained by actual physical pathology. At other times, she was completely pain-free and worked sixteen hours a day, despite having the same biopsy findings. Ellen lived out this odd alternation in lifestyle without ever questioning it. The pain intensified when her mother committed suicide, but Ellen still saw no connection.

Over the years, Ellen's gastroenterologist found that every treatment he tried either did not help or paradoxically made things worse. Finally, he suggested that a psychiatrist might help her to understand any reactions to her illness that might be contributing to her failure to respond better to treatment. Ellen was skeptical at first, but she agreed to give it a try when her physician reassured her that the psychiatrist would help him to work better with her. It turned out that she liked the psychiatrist, who did not suggest that her illness was "all in her head," but who was able to help her see how drastically her symptoms fluctuated.

The psychiatrist also pointed out that there had been dramatic fluctuations in her mother's attitude toward her as a child. It seemed that whenever Ellen had an upset stomach, her mother showered her with attention, but when she felt well enough to spend time with her friends, her mother became disinterested and withdrawn. Ellen remembered feeling confused and angry once she realized that she was being rewarded for illness and punished for health. She also remembered that she had not dared to feel strong enough to express her feelings, especially feelings of disagreement, lest her mother retaliate by abandoning her completely. When her mother committed suicide soon after Ellen felt good enough to start dating regularly, her lifelong fear had come true.

At the moment when Ellen began to recall the complicated mixture of attachment and resentment she had felt toward her mother, a startling thing happened. Suddenly she was unable to hear the doctor's voice! She had become completely deaf! Then something began to penetrate the silence: it was her mother's voice, and it was telling Ellen to be a good daughter and join her. Overwhelmed, Ellen began to feel faint.

Attempting to keep Ellen in the realm of mental self-reflection rather than somatic reactivity, the psychiatrist said, "If what we're talking about is overwhelming, you can walk out of my office—but there is no need to pass out."

"That's ridiculous," the patient replied. "Are you trying to tell me that I'm going deaf because I don't want to hear you?" After a brief pause Ellen conceded, "Your voice is coming in a little clearer, though. I don't know what's going on, but now my stomach really hurts."

"Tell me about the pain," the doctor suggested. And the patient did. Retreating to the familiar environment of the bodily self, Ellen rapidly buried her mother, and her complex feelings, within her symptoms.

In retreating to the safety of the bodily self, Ellen regained a familiar haven that protected her from the intolerable complexity of the mind. She also regained the illusion of secure attachment to a mother who could not live with the independence of Ellen's mind, but who would symbolically remain within Ellen's body so long as she was ill. However, using the body to hide intolerable conflicts of the mind does not make them go away. On the contrary, everything that is unacceptable or frightening is relegated to a secret self that remains hidden from the conscious mind, which is organized around physical symptoms that ward off emotions the mind has never learned to handle constructively. While attention is driven inexorably toward the bodily surface of experience, the secret, emotional self exerts its influence in many covert ways—through self-destructive behaviors, self-defeating relationships, and, at times, blatant short-circuiting of the mind, as in Ellen's case.

SELF-ESTEEM

According to the late psychoanalyst Heinz Kohut, young children develop self-esteem in two ways: through positive "mirroring" by their parents, and by their own experience of idealizing their parents. In the process of mirroring, children internalize the pleasure and appreciation their parents express toward them and their accomplishments, as when a parent says, "What a wonderful child!" We see the importance of mirroring when a parent teaches a child a new skill such as riding a bicycle. At first, the child is praised for sitting on the bike, for pedaling a few times, then for coasting for a few feet. As each new task is mastered, the child looks back to be sure that Mom or Dad is watching, and demands attention ("Look, Ma, no hands") if the parent is not watching. Once the skill is internalized, however, mirroring is no longer necessary, as the child takes more pleasure from the accomplishment itself than from parental approval.

Idealization allows a child to gain self-esteem by association. The feeling that a child has the most important or powerful father or mother makes the child feel equally important and powerful. As with mirroring, idealization becomes less necessary as self-esteem comes to depend more on an internal sense of pride than on external sources of support. However, everyone depends on an infusion of self-esteem from someone else at times of stress or life change. For example, when we learn a new skill such as skiing, it is normal to find ourselves looking to the instructor for frequent encouragement, until we finally learn the technique sufficiently to enjoy the thrill of mastering it. Similarly, when we look up to sports figures, rock stars, and other celebrities, we feel that we acquire some of their magic for ourselves. It is only when self-esteem is not internalized by the child, either because the parents did not mirror the child's accomplishments or felt uncomfortable being idealized, that excessive mirroring or idealization is sought in adulthood.

The health-care system provides many opportunities for adult somatizers to bask in the soothing if limited glow of mirroring and idealization. People with physical symptoms are the center of attention of the many personnel who are concerned about illness and, by implication, concerned about patients who have the illnesses. Patients receive a form of mirroring from those who are impressed with the extent of the lesion, the patient's ability to cope with it, or the challenge of making a diagnosis. Patients who have felt unnoticed and insignificant in their everyday lives can feel empowered by virtue of their association with important physicians, who must accommodate themselves to the exigencies of the disease. All it takes to remain the focus of attention in the medical world is to display more symptoms, and all it takes to have more control over that world is *not* to respond to treatment. By remaining ill, the patient holds onto a sick role that meets needs and resolves conflicts that feel impossible to deal with in the arena of the mind. And by robbing the physician of the power to heal, the patient who remains ill can become more powerful than the once exalted physician, whose capacity to determine the course of therapy has been usurped by the once devalued patient.

SPLITTING THE GOOD FROM THE BAD

During infancy and toddlerhood, mental states are uncomplicated and straightforward: they are either *good* or *bad,* white or black, with no shades of gray, no traces of the emotional diversity that comes with maturation. When the negative, oppositional states of mind that are essential components of the "no" phase of developing autonomy appear, the child who has not yet developed the psychological equipment to balance the two drastically different states of good and bad alternates from one state of mind to the other, like a pendulum. Parents discover this phenomenon when a child's unadulterated affection is suddenly and totally replaced by a hateful tantrum, only to be followed just as rapidly by endearing charm as the child's feelings become unqualifiedly positive again.

Under ordinary circumstances, parents are able to remain more or less consistently available as the child's developing personality bounces back and forth between its negative and positive sides. As parents bide their time during the terrible twos, the child learns an invaluable lesson: that it is possible to be angry, disappointed, or at odds with a loved one without destroying the bond between them. When bad feelings are repeatedly followed by restoration of good feelings, the bad feelings lose their power to destroy basic trust in the self and the world. Helping the child to tolerate opposing emotional states leads to a richer emotional self that can "hold" two opposing feelings at the same time.

Positive and negative states of mind do not have a chance to be integrated when parents cannot tolerate a child's developing willfulness. If parents become angry or withdrawn until the child is compliant, the negative side of the child's personality must be hidden, lest it trigger rejection or retaliation from a parent. The thoughts and feelings that are unacceptable must then be kept hidden in a place where they will not threaten the parent's fragile support. Shunting troubling emotions and thoughts to a secret reservoir keeps them from destroying positive experiences, but at a price: in order to maintain a consistently positive view of oneself and others, "bad" feelings must go into hiding before "good" ones can be experienced. When negative and positive emotions continue to be actively separated or "split" from each other, thoughts, attitudes, behaviors, and relationships that correspond to those emotions get dragged along with them. Divergent feelings never have an opportunity to influence each other, and mental experience never moves on to encompass the richness and complexity of human experience.

There is a big difference between *splitting* and *ambivalence* (mixed feelings). The person who feels ambivalent may say, "I've always been self-reliant, so I can't stand having to ask for help. Every time I take my medicine, it reminds me that I'm sick. I try to avoid taking it until I can't avoid it anymore, and then I stop it as soon as I can, so that I can pretend I'm well." This kind of statement shows that both sides of the patient's feelings about illness are being considered in the same frame of mind: "On the one hand . . . *this,* but on the other hand . . . *that.*" When the mechanism of splitting is operating, however, the two sets of feelings alternate as if they belong to different people—as when a patient declares at one moment, "There's nothing wrong with me, I feel fine," and in the next breath demands a stronger prescription because symptoms have become intolerable.

Another example: a patient places an urgent call to her physician, who is making rounds in the hospital. By the time the physician reaches the office, the patient has left two more emergency messages. But when the doctor returns the call, the patient's line is busy. The physician tries for the rest of the day to contact the patient, but the line remains busy because the patient is talking to friends about a dinner she is giving in a few weeks. The patient never calls back and never mentions her "emergency" at the next office visit. When the patient called, she was in desperate need, but a little while later her frame of mind was replaced by its exact opposite, at which point, feeling no need at all for the doctor, she forgot all about him.

The persistence of splitting as a defense mechanism has substantial repercussions for the personality. Denying negative feelings access to positive states that might temper their sting gives them even more power to destroy the good if they are ever unleashed. Left to its own devices, a secret, negative part of the mind grows ever more powerful, and its subversive influence becomes ever more destructive. The longer it remains hidden from the problem-solving capabilities of the mature mind, the more difficult it becomes to frame it and deal with it in the words of the adult, and the more likely it is to be expressed through the younger child's medium of behavior.

In the psychological literature, splitting is usually considered to be specific to a pervasive disturbance of the personality called "borderline personality disorder." However, splitting is actually a nonspecific mental mechanism that may influence experience in a number of psychiatric conditions, including schizophrenia, dissociative disorders such as multiple personality disorder, and severe forms of depression. Splitting can even be a normal protective mechanism when it is mobilized to cope with an unexpected stress. For example, patients with life-threatening medical illnesses, such as those described in Part IV, often split off frightening aspects of their experience from the mainstream of awareness in order to protect their feeling of safety. These patients may remain in the hospital and cooperate with complex and painful medical and surgical procedures at the same time that they insist that they are only mildly ill, or not sick at all! Similarly, terminally ill patients may put their affairs in order even as they make plans for events so far in the future that they cannot reasonably expect to live to participate in them. In these kinds of settings, splitting is limited to the situation that evokes it and is not a pervasive organizing principle of the personality.

THE SECRET SELF OF THE SOMATIZER

The overlap of conscious and unconscious forms of somatization discussed in Chapter 7 may be related to the interaction between *splitting*—which is an *unconscious* deception that conceals parts of the self from the personality—and *lying*—which is a *conscious* deception of others. Developmentally, the ability to keep a secret emerges around the age of nine or ten. At this point in the child's maturation process, words can be used to achieve new levels of closeness *or* to deepen the split between experience *as it is lived* and experience *as it is represented to others*. Deceiving others may be the child's way of maintaining the fragile, vulnerable boundaries around a developing sense of oneself as a distinct individual.

For adults who have long ago split off a secret self, words are used not as a means of sharing but as a vehicle for deceiving oneself into seeing the body but not the mind. Because it cannot be spoken and shared, the inner world of the mind feels empty and incomplete. Language does not serve its normal function of communicating true emotional meaning: what is real is not said, and what is said is not real. In the case of the somatizer for whom splitting is an important dynamic, the body becomes the "false self" that diverts attention away from an inner reality that is no longer available to the language of the mind. This inner reality of the secret self contains everything that is feared or unwanted. Largely unknown to the conscious mind, the secret self is a bewildering and even terrifying terrain that is concealed by a field of bodily symptoms that cover it like weeds in a deserted field.

This dichotomy between the surface and the interior is illustrated by Jake, a thirty-two-year-old man who secretly refused to take medications that were prescribed for his chronic skin condition. Jake was a brilliant man who, as conceited as he seemed to be, was secretly afraid that he could never measure up to his own grandiose fantasies about his abilities. So he never really tried, excusing his failure to succeed on the grounds that no one would give him a chance because his skin was ugly. It was his *body* that was failing him, he contended, not his mind.

As Jake experienced one failure after another, it became harder and harder to believe that there was nothing really wrong with *him*, that he was only the victim of his *body*. To reinforce this crumbling deception, Jake's focus expanded to encompass the medical world: now not only Jake's body but his *physicians* were the real source of his failure. None of them seemed to be able to do anything worthwhile. This was not surprising, since no doctor's therapy could work for a patient who did not take the medicine that was prescribed. Losing confidence in their ability to cure an apparently treatable problem, physician after physician became defensive and insecure, which caused them to make mistakes that further undermined their professional identities. Jake could easily feel superior to these blunderers, but only so long as he remained ill. Each time his skin got the better of him, he demanded new consultants and treatments, which were methodically defeated in their turn, as he continued to get everyone but himself to identify with his feeling of failure.

THE SICK ROLE

We learn early in childhood that we are treated differently when we are sick. A cough or a fever is a legitimate reason to miss school; a skinned knee warrants special attention or even a candy bar; a bad headache can exempt a teenager from an unwanted examination. As adults we have all called in sick at work or begged off attending a boring party because we were "not feeling well." These benefits of illness are part of the sick role.

Like all social roles, the sick role has consensually defined (though unwritten) rules, rights, responsibilities, and procedures. The physician controls access to the sick role by certifying who is or is not a patient. As long as the status of patient is retained, the person is permitted—and even required—to suspend normal duties and obligations while obtaining care and attention. In return, the patient is expected to cooperate with the treatment in order to leave the sick role as soon as possible.

For someone who was not cared for adequately as a child and did not learn how to get support as an adult, the sick role can be an enticing haven in an ungratifying world. As long as the illness is official, it is possible to express dependency even while maintaining a conscious posture of independence. The search for more caretaking is acceptable—and even expected—under the guise of the sick role, and the patient's true motivations remain unspoken and unthought. Remaining in the sick role also makes it possible to excuse failures in the other important roles that it supersedes, such as those of spouse, parent, or breadwinner. The sick role sturdily supports "if only" deceptions like: "*if only* I were not so ill, I could be . . . a better sexual partner . . . more successful at work . . . more patient with the kids . . . happier."

Remaining in the sick role hinges on the illness being considered legitimate, which usually depends on continuing physical distress or disability. Since technological medicine still does not consider mental disorders to be "real" illnesses, any hint that the problem is psychological endangers the sick role. Cure, which implies immediate eviction from the sick role, is an even more direct threat to people who have come to rely on this sanctioned use of the body to solve problems of the mind. The somatizer therefore faces the daunting psychological bind of consciously trying to get well while unconsciously defeating anything that might lead to termination of the sick role.

DECEPTIONS IN THE TREATMENT OF THE SOMATIZER

Attempts to override these kinds of dynamics by sheer force makes the treatment of somatization more frustrating, and costs are increased rather than decreased by limiting medical attention only to tangible signs of illness. On the other hand, treatment can be rewarding—and cost-effective—if a few common deceptions are avoided.

Deception #1: The most important step is to convince the patient that the symptoms are imaginary. Somatizers describe problems of the mind in the language of the body because they feel no connection to the mental self. Before their ability to tolerate it is strengthened, most somatizers are puzzled or overwhelmed by attempts to put them in touch with their secret mental world. Instead of getting better, their demonstrations of physical distress increase in order to restore the security of the bodily self and to protect themselves from the challenge to their claim to the sick role by the declaration that the illness is "not physical."

Deception #2: If a functional illness is not cured, nothing has happened. When the either-or world of the somatizer infects other people, they become convinced that the illness is totally mental *or* totally physical. This deception prevents the clinician from recognizing that not getting worse can be improvement.

Deception #3: There's nothing wrong with a little medication if it gets the patient to stop complaining. Medications that seem helpful or at least benign at first have a way of turning unexpectedly dangerous when they lead to addiction, withdrawal syndromes, noncompliance, or overdose under the influence of negative behaviors of the nonverbal self. We have already seen that it is impossible not to prescribe medications for somatizing patients, but it is better to consider the potential for a negative effect of a seemingly helpful intervention in advance rather than after it has reared its ugly head.

Deception #4: The somatizer is not "really" ill and should not be allowed to use up precious health-care resources. This is another version of the dichotomous deception that people without concrete physical pathology do not deserve the title of "patient." Telling the patient that physical but not mental distress is legitimate invites escalation of somatic complaints and denial of the legitimacy of diseases of the mind. In terms of lost productivity, personal suffering, doctor shopping, and treatment of crises that compel expensive interventions, keeping patients whose illnesses originate in the mind out of the health-care system uses up more resources than accepting and working with the patient's needs.

P A R T   I I I

THE BODY DECEIVES
THE MIND

One knows not whether there can be human compassion for anemia of the soul. When the pitch of life is dropped and the spirit is so put over and reversed that that only is horrible which before was sweet and worldly and of the day, the human relation disappears.

—OLIVER ONIONS

. . . from nothing else [but the brain] come joys, delights, laughter, and sports; and sorrows, griefs, despondency, and lamentations. . . . And by the same organ we become mad and delirious, and fears and terrors assail us. . . . All these things we endure from the brain when it is not healthy.

—HIPPOCRATES

The boundary between behavior and biology is arbitrary and changing. It has been imposed not by the natural contours of the discipline but by lack of knowledge.

—ERIC KANDEL

"HOW CAN YOU say I'm depressed? My only problem is the people I have to put up with!"

"I can pull myself together—all I need is a little more time."

"I don't know what's wrong with me—nothing's fun anymore."

"Of course, I'm depressed! Seeing what the world's like, you'd be crazy not to be depressed!"

We all feel down in the dumps at one time or another, and when we do, we often say we are "depressed." When this kind of depression is an expectable response to life's inevitable stresses, we endure it until things change. When "the blues" turn into the mental disorder clinicians call *depression,* there can be serious and even life-threatening consequences. There is no treatment for normal human unhappiness, but people suffering from clinical depression can expect to obtain relief, and doctors should know how to cure it.

Freud said that the goal of psychoanalysis was to replace neurotic suffering with "the misery of everyday life." How can we tell when feeling unhappy is everyday misery and when it is a clinical disorder requiring treatment? It may seem difficult to distinguish between depression that requires treatment and normal responses to life stresses that require patience. However, recent research allows us to make this distinction.

Both states are characterized by feeling sad, but clinically significant depression lasts longer, alters many basic functions of the mind and body, and can infiltrate virtually every aspect of the personality. In *DSM-IV,* a diagnosis of a major depressive episode is made when a person reports feeling depressed, tearful, discouraged, or unable to experience pleasure for at least two weeks; and when the feeling of depression and loss of pleasure are accompanied by at least four of seven additional symptoms:

- A change in weight of at least 5 percent in either direction, or an increased or decreased appetite nearly every day;
- Consistently increased or decreased amounts of sleep;
- Fatigue or loss of energy;
- Agitation or behavioral slowing that is obvious to others;
- Inappropriate or excessive feelings of worthlessness or guilt;
- Indecisiveness or difficulty thinking or concentrating;
- Recurrent thoughts of death or suicide.

While two weeks is the minimum duration of symptoms for an official diagnosis of a major depressive episode, a single "episode" may last a lifetime. Indeed, the concept of a *depressive episode*—that is, a distinct and de-marcated change from a previous way of functioning—may be difficult to apply to people for whom depression began so early and has lasted so long that it would be difficult for them to guess what it would be like to feel nor-mal.

Major depression is so common that everyone knows someone who has suffered from it, and many more people have had variants of depression with fewer symptoms that are just as disabling. Yet this most ubiquitous malady of mind and body remains a deception to many people. Depression appears to be a clear-cut problem of the mind, but it is actually the body that deceives the mind into soul-sapping twists and turns of negativism. People who are demoralized, unhappy, and withdrawn; those who are unenthusiastic, can-tankerous, and temperamental; those who are beset with worries; and even those who are compulsively hyperactive and grandiose—all may suffer from the same malfunction of basic cellular biology that ultimately alters the very structure of the brain. Depression is a clear example of a mind-body disor-der, because this fundamental biological disruption can be programmed into the cells of the body by mental as well as physical processes: the mind can change the orientation of the body, which in turn alters the course of the mind. As the next few chapters unfold, we will see how this debilitating process can occur.

DEPRESSING STATISTICS

At one time or another, most of us have worried about what will happen if we have a heart attack or get cancer. These days, informed consumers read their insurance policies carefully to see how well they will be covered if dis-aster strikes. But few worry about getting depressed or coming down with any other mental ailment, and few check their insurance policies to see if they cover treatment of depression. People just do not think that the mind is subject to the same kinds of ills as the body, or if they do, that they will need any help.

Statistics about depression debunk this deception. At any point in time, between 9 and 20 percent of the U.S. population have depressive symptoms, and between 4 and 6 percent have full-blown clinical depression; twice as many women as men get depressed. In a longitudinal study of 965 people who had never had a mental illness, researcher William Coryell and his as-sociates found that 11.8 percent became depressed within six years. The chance of having bipolar disorder, a complex type of mood disorder discussed in this section, has ranged from 1 percent to as much as 7 percent, the higher numbers probably including more subtle forms of the disorder.

The deception that depression is not a "real" and disabling illness is supported by insurance companies, most of whom provide less coverage for depression and other mental disorders than for so-called medical conditions. When people do not recognize depression as a serious condition, and when physicians are not taught how to identify it and are not paid for treating it, a tremendous public health problem is created. Fewer than one-third of the more than *30 million depressed people* in the United States receive any treatment at all, and for those who do, treatment is inadequate more often than not. Depression is twice as prevalent as coronary heart disease and cancer and costs as much in direct expenses and lost productivity ($44 billion per year) as coronary heart disease and one-third as much as cancer. Yet depression, which is highly responsive to the right therapy, is much less likely to be identified and treated than the other two conditions, which are much less curable.

Depression is encountered even more frequently in the medical setting than it is in the general population. In one study of 11,000 general medical outpatients, 20 percent met formal criteria for depression or had enough depressive symptoms to have trouble functioning. Despite the pervasive presence of depression in patients of primary-care physicians, these practitioners detect only half of the cases they encounter and have not been taught to manage the ones they do recognize. Most depressed patients in the primary-care setting never even meet a mental health specialist.

In all industrialized countries in the world, the incidence of depression has increased in every generation born after 1910. For some unknown reason, there was an abrupt jump in this growing risk for people born after 1940. It is not just that depression is being diagnosed more readily; more people are actually becoming depressed. Not only is depression becoming more common but it is also appearing at an earlier age, so that professionals are encountering more severely depressed children and adolescents.

DECEPTIVE BELIEFS

A popular deception about depression is that certain cases are "biological" while others are "psychological." The biological form, according to this line of thinking, is caused by a chemical imbalance and is treated with medicines, while the non-biological form is caused by emotional conflict and is cured by changing the personality. People who think they have a biochemical deficiency are convinced that all they need is the right kind of pill to disperse the black clouds of despondency that veil their personalities; those who believe their problem exists purely in the mental realm believe that all they need is one more round of therapy. The biological believers are offended by the suggestion that their state of mind might also have a psychological dimension, and the psychological believers are insulted by the suggestion that their woes may be as much a product of bodily chemicals as of childhood wounds. The truth is that there is no such thing as a *purely* biological depression or *purely* psychological depression. All cases of depression have both physical and mental dimensions. Psychological therapies have an impact on the body, and antidepressant medications have an impact on the mind.

THE DEPRESSIVE DECEPTION

The next several chapters address the mind-body deception of depression. This is the deception in which the body fools the mind into perceiving even minor challenges as overwhelming dangers from which the mind can only run. The more the mind flees in demoralized retreat, the more agitated the body becomes, further flooding the mind and making it feel increasingly incompetent. Unrestrained mind-body hyperactivity drives some sufferers to seek out others in efforts to decrease the agitation and feel safe, often resulting in excessive dependency. Other depressed sufferers who are afraid of dependency keep a ten-foot pole between themselves and anyone who might evoke the irresistible yearning to be cared for, mind and body. If left untreated, the pathological feedback loop between mind and body in depression can permanently distort a person's character as well as relationships with other people.

As we review the psychobiology of depression, we will see how the basic biological problem can be programmed into the brain (and the rest of the body) by two different but intersecting routes: *heredity* and *experience*. The same abnormality of mood that can be transmitted through the genes can also be burned into the body by losses, traumas, and unhealthy relationships. The significance of these dual pathways to pathological biology is profound. Either physical or mental events can inaugurate a complex chain of processes that disrupts both mental and physical resources. But the converse is also true: treatments that impact *either* side of the mind-body equation can reset the depressive processes back toward normal.

9

Depression: More Than
Just the Blues

THOSE WHO UNDERESTIMATE the complex interactions between mind and body in depression may be deceived into believing that it is a normal, expectable, existential, poetic, moral, or even healthy phenomenon. But depression is serious. And it can be deadly.

Consider the case of a seventy-year-old man who had experienced two serious depressions in the past. Everyone thought he was holding up well after the death of his wife of thirty years. Though he was sleeping very little and no longer went to the club he had visited every day for the past ten years, he explained that he had a lot to take care of in settling his wife's estate. Friends were happy for him when he remarried precipitously a few months later, but instead of enjoying the marriage he became morose, irritable, and sarcastic with his new wife, who soon became exasperated with him. She consulted her husband's personal physician, who reassured her that he was probably "just depressed" about the changes in his life and would soon get over it. A few weeks later, on the anniversary of his first marriage, the man shot himself in the head.

The physician had dismissed a major derangement of mind and body as a normal experience—and the patient paid the price. Unfortunately, this story is not unique: up to 15 percent of depressed people kill themselves, the majority within a few months of seeing their primary-care physicians. They may not volunteer their suicidal ideas, but if they are asked directly, most suicidal patients will admit their despairing thoughts. When physicians take depression seriously, suicide can almost always be prevented. When doctors believe that depression does not warrant the same attention as a "real" illness, the sufferer remains isolated and desperate, sometimes so much so that the only relief seems to be suicide.

Suicide is not the only means by which depression harms the body. Depression impairs physical functioning more than hypertension, diabetes, arthritis, or gastrointestinal, lung, or back diseases, and it causes more bodily pain than angina. If a patient has a medical or surgical illness, the general level of functioning is lower when depression is also present, and there may be a greater risk of premature death from heart disease and cancer in depressed people, especially men, and their relatives. With an increased risk of death from suicide, accidents, and medical illnesses, depressed patients have 1.7 times the mortality rate of the general population.

LIVING IN DEPRESSION

Depression has been recognized as a human woe since the time of the ancient Greeks. It was Hippocrates who, in the fourth century B.C., coined the terms *melancholia* and *mania*—terms that are still used in the official diagnostic nomenclature. Eugen Bleuler, who helped found the modern era of psychiatry, characterized depression as a profound disturbance that dampens and distorts motivation, perceptions, behavior, and spirit:

> The melancholic . . . has lost everything that was of value to him, and nevertheless he expects still worse for himself and those he loves, the worst that one can think of. . . . In many cases perceptions take on the character of strangeness, of uncanniness, and monotony; optical impressions are double dyed gray, things seem to stand crooked, and foods lack their peculiar flavor. Thinking, in itself, is not only colored by unpleasant feelings, but proceeds with difficulty, and only ideas of a painful content can be thought out. Thoughts of a pleasant content are flighty and transient, leaving no influence on deliberation and the general condition. Only with great difficulty can the patient resolve to act, and when he succeeds in making a movement, it is with great effort. . . .

Central to the experience of depression is loss of the capacity for pleasure. Work and family activities become burdens and demands rather than sources of productivity and intimacy. Excitement is blunted, sex becomes a chore, and contentment but a dim memory. In its textbook forms, depression is characterized by a lusterless lack of energy, a numbing torpor, that precludes even a possibility of effective action. Although motivation is paralyzed, the mind is provoked into working overtime by the distorted perception that even mundane types of stress are overwhelming. Living with depression is like trying to drive a car whose engine is revving at top speed, but the transmission either cannot be engaged or grinds into reverse; the driver, disoriented by the malfunctioning car, can no longer locate the destination on the map. The car continues to limp along, some cylinders working overtime and others unable to fire, until it finally runs out of gas.

The depressive sense of incapacity can so pervade thinking that the most minor negative experience is emphasized, while evidence that things are not as bad as they feel is discounted. Thoughts may be ponderously slow and unfocused when it comes to accomplishing significant goals, but endless hours are spent ruminating over minor failures and inadequacies, minute fluctuations in bodily functioning, and other people's lack of interest in one's plight. Convinced that nothing will ever improve, depressed patients do not even attempt to make things better. The result is that nothing changes, which provides even more evidence that there is no point in trying.

PERSONALITY AND MOOD

The word *personality* has numerous meanings in its common usage but a specific meaning in psychology: personality is what makes each person an individual; it is a characteristic way of interpreting and organizing information from both inner and outer worlds that provides a consistent style of self-expression and behavior. Personality is an integrated conglomerate of traits or tendencies to think, feel, and act in certain ways that manifest themselves independent of the specific circumstance. A person may be more or less dependable, more or less nervous, more or less generous, more or less sympathetic. An essential driving force of all of these traits is *mood,* the enduring tone of emotions.

Emotions motivate us to move forward or to retreat; they mobilize ideas and memories and connect them to our physiology so that we are able to respond to a changing world in ways that are predictable, understandable, and effective. Because emotions play a determining role in how we process information, what we experience emotionally exerts a strong influence on what is remembered: when we feel good, we find it easier to remember good times than bad times, and when we are unhappy, our attention is directed more readily toward unhappy memories. In a similar manner, many of the basic functions of the mind are directed by our mood: when our emotional state is positive, we have the energy and optimism to approach our problems and to enjoy relationships with other people; when we feel dejected or upset, we are more introverted, less self-confident, and less motivated.

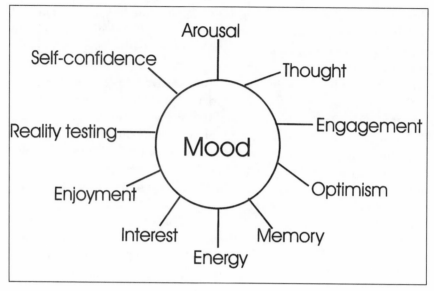

Figure 9-1.
Some mood-dependent functions

Emotional orientation is thus a major force in shaping a person's approach to life. A basically positive mood provides the psychological fuel for interest in the environment, engagement with the world, enjoyment of self and others, self-confidence, and ability to tolerate change and disappointment. A fundamentally negative mood, on the other hand, undermines adaptive abilities and acts as a damper on all aspects of the personality. Behavior becomes withdrawn and self-absorbed rather than engaging and self-expressive. Pervasive feelings of insecurity, irritability, anxiety, passivity, withdrawal, gloominess, impulsivity, and instability culminate in despondent retreat or paralyzing fearfulness. A perception of the self as flawed, undependable, and out of control prevails.

FACING THE FACTS

When I was a resident in psychiatry in 1970, I was taught that acute depression usually went away by itself: anyone who became depressed would get over it within six to twelve months, no matter what I did. The goal of whichever treatment was chosen, I was told, was to *hasten* recovery.

As I began treating depressed patients, however, I found that this conventional wisdom was rarely true. My experience was consistent with that of other clinicians and an emerging body of research. It is now known that fewer than half of all people who became depressed at some definite point in the recent past will ever get over the depression *without the right treatment.* Studies by researchers William Coryell and Martin Keller have shown that the probability of depression remitting spontaneously decreases the longer it has been present: people who have been depressed for a few months have about a 15 percent chance of not recovering; after being depressed for a year, the likelihood of remaining depressed indefinitely increases to 50 percent—and after two years of continuous depression, there is a 95 percent likelihood that depression will still be present six months later. In addition to the length of time depression has been present, factors that increase the chance of depression becoming chronic include:

- multiple depressive episodes in the past;
- feeling anxious as well as depressed;
- having a coexisting personality or medical disorder;
- having poor social support;
- experiencing substantial ongoing stress;
- having psychotic symptoms (hallucinations or delusions);
- using alcohol or illicit drugs.

Severity of depression is *not* a predictor of a poor outcome if depression is treated—but without treatment, most severe forms of depression do not go away on their own.

Many things get better with age, but depression is not one of them. As people who have been depressed grow older, the problem tends to recur more frequently, often at an escalating rate. After having been depressed once, the average person has at least a 50 percent chance of getting depressed again, but after two episodes the risk of a third is 70 percent, and after four episodes, there is a 90 percent chance of getting depressed again. Since most people have more than one episode, overall figures show that at least 75 percent—and perhaps up to 95 percent—of people who become depressed will have at least one more episode over the course of their lives.

With depression, "practice makes perfect." An important aspect of recurrences is that each new episode, in addition to repeating the symptoms of earlier episodes, *adds* new symptoms as well. Furthermore, while early episodes are often triggered by some kind of identifiable stressor—usually a loss or separation, such as the death of a spouse or going off to school—later episodes tend to occur spontaneously.

Another powerful determinant of future episodes is the residue of depressive symptoms after an episode has mostly receded. Any persistence of symptoms, even if they are mild, increases the risk of a relapse (return of the original episode) or recurrence (development of a new episode) of depression. For example, someone who no longer feels depressed but who still finds that things are not as pleasurable as they should be is more likely to suffer another full depressive episode than is someone who has no symptoms at all.

The reason why residual symptoms predict an increased risk of return of depression is that they indicate that the mind-body mechanisms that maintain depression have not fully reset themselves toward normal and therefore can be easily tilted in the direction of full-blown pathology. Conversely, when treatment completely eliminates all symptoms, the likelihood is greater that the physiology of depression has been fully corrected, so that the person will remain well. Homeostasis—the tendency of all systems of body and mind to remain in whatever state they are in most of the time (the status quo)—means that people who are depressed for a long time tend to stay depressed. Similarly, it takes more stress for people who are not prone to depression to get into a depressed state, and it is easier for them to get out of it when it does occur. By the same token, effective treatment has the potential to force the "default setting" of depression into a normal setting, restoring physiological and psychological well-being and preventing further recurrences. When therapeutic approaches are maximized, even people who have been depressed for years can expect to live comfortable and rewarding lives.

ANXIETY: A CLOSE RELATIVE

Anxiety is an integral component of depression. About 70–80 percent of depressed people are also anxious, while almost half of chronically anxious patients have clinically significant symptoms of depression. A community survey by the National Institute of Mental Health (NIMH) of randomly selected households in which no one was originally identified as a patient discovered that of those ultimately found to be depressed, 32 percent also had phobias, 31 percent had panic attacks, and 11 percent had obsessions or compulsions. Being depressed substantially increased the risk not only of having anxiety *symptoms* but also of qualifying for a formal diagnosis of an anxiety *disorder*. More than half of depressed persons are also diagnosed with panic disorder, generalized anxiety disorder, phobia, or obsessive-compulsive disorder at some time in their lives. Conversely, 40–90 percent of people with a diagnosis of panic disorder, 35–70 percent of those with social phobia, and at least half of those with generalized anxiety disorder have at least one episode of major depression.

The relationship between anxiety and depression is a complex one. We have already seen that symptoms of one often accompany the other. In addition, having symptoms of anxiety may lower the threshold for expression of a full-blown case of depression, and vice versa. Having one disorder seems to predispose the person to getting the other.

A 1989 study by researcher M. Kovacs and colleagues, which followed more than 3,000 well individuals to see whether they developed mental symptoms, found that those who later became anxious and those who later became depressed resembled each other much more than they did those who remained well or those who developed other kinds of mental problems. Other investigations (for example, those by geneticist Kenneth Kendler) show that people who are easily upset, introverted, overly dependent, unsure of themselves, and unable to tolerate stress are as likely to become anxious as they are to become depressed. Such findings, along with evidence (reviewed later in this section) that treatments for anxiety are also effective for depression and vice versa, suggest that *depression and anxiety can be different facets of the same core mechanism gone awry.*

There is also a group of people who have some symptoms of both anxiety and depressive disorders—but not enough to qualify for a diagnosis of either disorder. To describe these individuals one group of psychiatric experts proposed adding a diagnosis of "mixed anxiety-depression" to *DSM-IV.* However, the consensus was that there had not yet been a sufficient number of formal studies to justify the inclusion of this diagnosis. Nevertheless, people with mixed anxiety-depression symptoms have been found to be as impaired as patients with major depressive disorder or generalized anxiety disorder. One reason why psychiatric research into this condition is inadequate is that most patients never see a psychiatrist but are treated by primary-care physicians, who usually do not perform psychiatric research.

The presence of anxiety in people who get depressed *increases* the severity of depression and *decreases* response to treatment. Depression tends to be more chronic and produce more impairment when it is accompanied by anxiety, and the risk of suicide is also elevated. Depressed people who are anxious have more anxious people in their families, and they also have more depressed relatives. For some people, anxiety may be an indicator of a genetic contribution that makes depression more severe and treatment-resistant.

TYPES OF DEPRESSION

Depression is far from a unitary syndrome; there are many distinct forms of it, each with different symptoms, outcomes, and treatments. The early history of psychiatry's classification of depression reflects the inaccurate split between mind and body that, until recently, pervaded diagnosis in medicine. One of the first dichotomizations of depression was between "reactive" and "endogenous" subtypes. European psychiatrists originally introduced the term *reactive depression* to refer to depressed patients who were still responsive to interpersonal interactions and events, while patients with *endogenous depression* were too withdrawn and had too little energy to respond emotionally to other people.

This division lost something in the translation when it was adopted in the United States: reactive depression came to mean depression that appeared in reaction to some identifiable stress, and endogenous depression came to mean depression that did not appear to be provoked by any particular event. Insofar as patients who are capable of responding positively to the environment are often less severely depressed than those who can barely manage a feeble grimace, endogenous depression (also called "melancholic" depression) came to stand for a more severe form of depression. As time went on, reactive depression became synonymous with "neurotic" or mild depression, while the endogenous form was sometimes referred to as "psychotic" depression to emphasize severity.

These dichotomous views have been modified with experience. We now recognize that some patients who become depressed "out of the blue" have mild depressions and are responsive to their environment, while some patients who become depressed in response to stress suffer severely. When it became clear that not all severely depressed patients are psychotic (defined as having delusions or hallucinations), the two diagnostic labels, depression and psychosis, were also separated. In the current nomenclature, neurotic is not the opposite of psychotic, and endogenous is not the opposite of reactive. Any kind of depression can be mild or severe, psychotic or nonpsychotic, with biological and psychological dimensions that are variously prominent. Nevertheless, "endogenous depression" is still used synonymously with both melancholic and psychotic depression in the European literature, indicating an enduring and erroneous distinction between "biological" and "psychological" forms of the illness.

The fact that depression has both biological and psychological components has been increasingly supported by research, which has shown that (1) bodily functions are disrupted in "psychological" depressions appearing in response to obvious stressors, and (2) antidepressants cure depression that is obviously provoked by loss or other adverse events as readily as depression that appears out of the blue. In addition, the same person may have one depressive episode caused by a major trauma, another equally severe episode linked only to minor stress, and a third episode that is entirely spontaneous. The only valid distinction to make in regard to depression is in relation to its degree of severity: the more severe forms of depression, whether or not they are associated with any specific event, show more evidence of pervasive bodily disruption and require treatment with physical therapies such as medications or, in severe cases, electroconvulsive therapy.

BIPOLAR DISORDERS

The most important distinction between subtypes of depression is that of "unipolar" versus "bipolar" forms: unipolar depression is diagnosed in people who have only been depressed, while bipolar disorder is present when depression has alternated or been mixed with mood that varies in the opposite direction—in other words, when mania or hypomania has also occurred. The term *bipolar* was introduced in Europe in the 1960s as a substitute for "manic depression," to indicate that a significant number of people may experience both poles of abnormal mood and to provide a diagnosis that was less pejorative. Thus far, we have been discussing the unipolar variety.

Distinguishing between depression that is consistently characterized by low mood (unipolar) and depression in which elevated mood is also a factor (bipolar) is important clinically for two reasons. First, bipolar mood disorder tends to produce more severe and more recurrent episodes of depression than does the unipolar form. Of even greater concern, antidepressant medications that *reduce* the risk of recurrence of unipolar depression can have the opposite effect on bipolar depression.

What Is Mania?

At first glance, mania seems to be the opposite of depression. The manic person is unrealistically self-assured, outgoing, and frantically elated—not passive, withdrawn, and unbearably unhappy. Rather than brooding over imagined failures and weaknesses, the manic feels capable of accomplishing anything instantly. During manic periods, energy is boundless and sleep is unnecessary. Early in the course of a manic episode, patients whose minds and energy race ahead may make inspired decisions and do the work of an entire office. They may be captivating enough to convince others that a grandiose "pet project" actually makes sense. Inevitably, however, ideas replace each other too quickly for the person to actualize any one of them, and escalating grandiosity leads to increasingly poor judgment.

Far from being morose and slowed down, the manic is overinvolved and hyperactive, as if an inner behavioral thermostat were turned up too high. Manics can be compulsively driven by an insatiable appetite for pleasure or activity. They are the "life of the party" unless someone interferes with their plans, in which case they rapidly become sarcastic or enraged.

Manic individuals frequently walk a fine line between hilarity and disaster, as was the case for a sixty-year-old man who had experienced several attacks of mania during his lifetime. Believing that no decision he made could possibly fail, he made some astute, even brilliant, investments that gained him a fortune. When his inner genius told him that an unwise investment he was planning was the best idea he had ever had, however, he lost a fortune. During his manic periods he was charming, engaging, and insightful; but eventually his friendliness would balloon into intrusiveness, his charm sour into belligerence, and his cheer wither into forced and hollow glee.

These wild oscillations of mood had been in abeyance for several years, when the man's wife began to notice that her husband was not sleeping as much as usual. At about this time, he bought her a first-class ticket to Europe. Telling her that he had a business meeting there, he assured her that he would join her in a few days, as soon as he was prepared for the conference. Her husband was so persuasive that even remembering all the times he had gotten her out of the way to keep her from interfering with some grandiose plan did not prevent her from being convinced that the trip was a good idea.

As luck would have it, the flight was cancelled and the wife returned home. There she was greeted by the sight of a sixty-foot yacht parked on the front lawn. When she asked her husband why he had bought it, he told her that he was planning to sail from their home to Europe to meet her. The couple lived in Arizona!

Like depression, mania can have many facets. At least half of manic men and the majority of manic women and children are irritable or severely anxious rather than euphoric. Some of the time, changes in emotional tone may be overshadowed by drastic variations in energy and sleep, such as alternations between sleeping all day and still not having the energy to get out of bed, and sleeping only two or three hours and not feeling tired. In other people, manic behaviors, such as grandiose challenges of authority, pressured thrill-seeking, and compulsive spending are the most obvious expressions of a bipolar disorder. Some individuals are so uncomfortable when they feel themselves approaching a manic state that they avoid relationships and anything else that might be overstimulating.

Mania is particularly difficult to recognize in children and adolescents, in whom irritability, excessive levels of energy, hyperactivity, and racing and distracting thoughts are often confused with attention deficit disorder. Another common misdiagnosis occurs when the traits of grandiosity, impulsivity, defiance, hypersexual promiscuity, and aggression are erroneously ascribed to a personality disorder.

Hypomania is a form of mania that is serious enough to alter functioning but not so severe as to be incapacitating (*hypo* means "less than"). Hypomania is a prelude to a full-blown manic attack in some people; in others, it is a stable state that does not deteriorate into mania. People who become hypomanic but not manic are said to have a "bipolar II" mood disorder, to distinguish it from classic manic-depressive disorder (bipolar I). Hypomaniac people do not usually buy their way into bankruptcy, develop delusions of impossible powers, engage in multiple sexual encounters in a single evening, or drive down the wrong side of the road at one hundred miles per hour—but this does not mean that they do not have serious problems. They are prone to poor judgment, suicide attempts, unstable relationships, substance abuse, and impulsive decisions. In addition, they may have more rapidly recurring forms of depression that are harder to treat than depression associated with more classical bipolar I mood disorders.

People with bipolar mood disorders usually become depressed several times before manic or hypomanic behavior becomes apparent, which also makes diagnosis difficult. Nevertheless, it is crucial to decide whether the depression is bipolar or unipolar, because treatment for the two types is very different. As already noted, when given to someone with a bipolar depression, treatments for unipolar depression may have two unanticipated effects that do not occur when unipolar depression is treated with antidepressants: the antidepressants may convert depression into mania or hypomania, which is often followed by more severe depression, or they may speed up the inherent tendency of bipolar depression to come back, thereby making the depression more, rather than less, recurrent.

It has frequently been said that bipolar depression is much less common than unipolar depression (lifetime risk of about 1 percent, compared to up to 25 percent for unipolar depression). However, research by investigators Jules Angst and Janice Egeland suggests that bipolar mood disorders may occur as frequently as the unipolar forms. Bipolar mood disorders are frequently misdiagnosed for several reasons. In up to one-third of bipolar patients, the first episode of mania may occur after three episodes of depression, although the chance of becoming manic after four depressive episodes is very low. In addition, depression so influences outlook that patients who are depressed may not recall ever having felt good, let alone having been manic. As we have already seen, mania and hypomania may occur in masked forms that are not included in formal statistics.

Another common belief about bipolar disorders is that when one pole is present, the other is not (that is, a person is manic *or* depressed, but not both), a belief that is fostered by the apparent dramatic differences between the two states. However, clinical experience shows that mania and depression accompany each other at least as frequently as they alternate with each other. In a review of published studies that appeared in the *American Journal of Psychiatry* in 1992, psychiatric researcher Susan McElroy and her colleagues found that about half of manic episodes were characterized by clear-cut mixtures of depression and mania. For example, wildly elated patients may suddenly burst into tears, and patients who cannot stop their minds from racing and their bodies from accelerating out of control may commit grandiose and exhibitionistic suicides (for example, a shootout with the police). People who say that they feel profoundly depressed but do not look that bad often have a mixed element of elevated mood that sustains their capacity to look better than they feel. Depressive ruminations that race through a patient's mind at breakneck speed, intense irritability in a patient who is too depressed to move, and unbearable depression that emerges as soon as mania is treated are additional examples of mixtures of manic and depressive states. It will become apparent in Chapter 11 that, despite their apparent diversity, mania and depression, like depression and anxiety, can coexist precisely because they share a common biology (see Figure 9-2).

MANIC REPERCUSSIONS

Manic behavior is the single defining feature of bipolar disorders, but even when it is not present it has a drastic impact on the course of depression. For one thing, people with bipolar depression are more likely than those with unipolar depression to become severely depressed and to develop hallucinations and delusions. Bipolarity also results in depressions that begin earlier in life and recur more frequently. The person with bipolar depression is more likely than the unipolar patient to commit suicide and to engage in murderous as well as suicidal behavior.

"Rapid cycling" is the term used to describe bipolar patients who experience four or more episodes of depression and/or mania (or hypomania) per year, with either two weeks of normal mood in between episodes or an immediate switch from one pole to the other (e.g., directly from mania to depression) with no intervening period of normal mood. Some people develop an ultra-rapid form of cycling, in which they experience multiple recurrences of mania and depression in the course of a single day. They may wake up unable to move or think, but before too long they get a burst of energy that makes it almost impossible to sit still. Next, they are suddenly so depressed that it does not seem possible to live another hour. Then they feel fine for an hour or so, only to sink into a depressive torpor a little later. Instead of feeling elated, they feel irritable and uncomfortable. A significant number of people who develop rapid cycling also have hallucinations that may be very dramatic but, because the hallucinations do not necessarily interfere with their functioning, are not reported unless someone asks about them specifically.

Fewer than 20 percent of bipolar patients experience rapid cycling. When it is present, however, all mood changes are harder to treat. The rapid-cycling phase probably represents an acceleration of the mood swings of bipolar mood disorders—an acceleration that may be hastened by hypothyroidism (low thyroid function) or by antidepressants, the very treatments that are beneficial for patients with unipolar depression. If the antidepressants are stopped, the rapid cycling appears to remit within about five years, but, as we will see in Chapter 15, this is easier said than done.

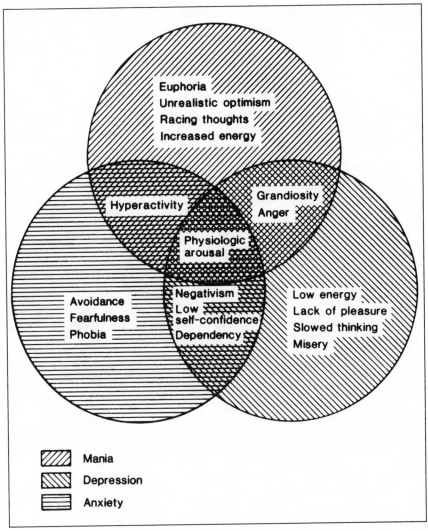

Euphoria
Unrealistic optimism
Racing thoughts
Increased energy

Hyperactivity

Grandiosity
Anger

Physiologic
arousal

Avoidance
Fearfulness
Phobia

Negativism
Low
self-confidence
Dependency

Low energy
Lack of pleasure
Slowed thinking
Misery

Mania

Depression

Anxiety

Figure 9-2.
The underlying unity of depression,
mania, and anxiety

WHAT YOU SEE IS NOT ALWAYS WHAT YOU GET

Classifying depression as bipolar or unipolar is necessary to choose the right treatment. Another classification that has significant implications for prognosis and treatment is the division of depressions into nonpsychotic and psychotic forms. In psychotic depression, depressive symptoms are accompanied by delusions (fixed, false ideas that are out of keeping with the patient's cultural or religious background) and/or hallucinations (hearing, seeing, smelling, feeling, or tasting things that are not there). Conventional wisdom holds that psychotic depression (in *DSM-IV,* major depressive episode with psychotic features) is rare because depression is frequently treated before it becomes severe enough to produce delusions or hallucinations. However, a large body of research indicates that as many as 50 percent of depressed patients have psychotic symptoms. One reason why the frequency of psychosis is underestimated is that patients either do not consider the symptoms important enough to mention or conceal them out of suspiciousness or a desire not to be considered "crazy." For their part, clinicians often do not ask patients who appear able to function about psychotic symptoms, even though some patients—especially those with bipolar depression—may have significant psychotic symptomatology without appearing to be severely impaired.

At first glance, the major subtypes of depression would appear clear-cut. Shouldn't depression obviously be bipolar or unipolar? Similarly, depressed people either hear things that are not there, or they don't. There is either a sufficient number of symptoms to justify a diagnosis of major depression, or there is not. In real life, however, such distinctions are not always that clear.

Some people who never become manic have recurrences of depression that are as rapid as those experienced by bipolar patients. Some depressed patients have symptoms, such as racing thoughts or increased interest in sex, that are usually seen in mania, but they never experience elation or anything else that seems manic. Other patients never become manic unless they take antidepressants. And how would we classify a depressed patient who was just "a little" psychotic—who occasionally hears a voice say something indecipherable or thinks that people might be plotting against him but doesn't really care? What about the 80 percent of patients with a diagnosis of dysthymic disorder (a supposedly minor form of chronic depression with fewer symptoms than major depressive disorder) who, at some point, develop an additional symptom or two and qualify for a diagnosis of major depression? Do they now have a different condition, or does the same chronic depression look different at different times?

Even within a given group, no categorical diagnosis in psychiatry is really that uniform. Some people with bipolar mood disorders have many manic episodes and some have just a few. Some patients with bipolar depression become psychotic, and so do some unipolar patients. Some depressed people are aggressive or suicidal, while others are not. Some people who are prone to depression have had traumatic experiences early in life, some have had families that misunderstood or did not care about them, and some have had highly supportive families. Some kinds of depression start early in life without any precipitant, some occur only after a major stressor, and some appear for the first time in the later years, even though earlier stressors did not trigger depression. Some depressed people abuse drugs or alcohol, and

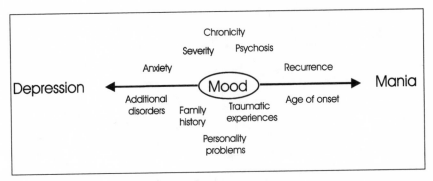

Figure 9-3.
Some dimensions of depression

some do not. Some depressed people have many depressed relatives, and others do not. Some depressions infiltrate all aspects of the personality, and some do not.

Analyzing a particular case of depression requires not only a categorical diagnosis that depends on the requisite number of specific symptoms but also a *dimensional* diagnosis that takes into account features that have a profound impact on the course and treatment response of depression. An illustration of this kind of analysis is given in Figure 9-3.

This is not to say that every depressed person is different from every other depressed person, only that there are more categories of depression and more treatment options in real-life than are listed in the textbooks.

10

Depression Invades the Mind

IS DEPRESSION CAUSED by psychological or biological factors? Mind-body experts know that there is no either/or answer to this question. Indeed, psychological and biological factors undoubtedly interact with each other, creating predispositions to depression and precipitating acute episodes. Studying the psychology of depression is difficult because even if a psychological component is consistently observed in depressed people, we cannot be sure if it is the cause or the result of the depression. It would be tempting to conclude that because a particular type of psychotherapy is an effective treatment for depression, the theory of that psychotherapy must explain why depression occurs. But what conclusion can be drawn when it turns out that the *same psychotherapy* works for different conditions that are thought to be associated with *different kinds of psychopathology*? Much of the time, we cannot be sure whether an effective psychotherapy is acting on a specific psychological set of factors that leads to depression, whether the psychotherapy has some nonspecific effect, or whether it is having an effect unforeseen by its practitioners.

Lack of certainty about whether psychological factors are the cause of depression, the result of depression, or a mixture of the two does not mean that these factors are not important. The mental side of depression is what disables people, not the physical symptoms, and anyone who holds that only the bodily component is important is deceived out of a true understanding of this condition.

DICHOTOMOUS THINKING

In Chapter 8, we saw how disallowed negative feelings can result in the *splitting* of emotional experience into dichotomized categories of good and bad. Depressed people are subject to a similar all-or-nothing style of thinking. It is not clear whether this characteristic is inherited, learned during childhood, or mobilized in adulthood in an attempt to retreat to the simpler problem-solving approaches of childhood in the face of unbearable emotions. Whatever its cause, dichotomous thinking in depression can look very much like the kind of splitting that characterizes the approach to life of people with somatization (and other) disorders, and its impact can be equally profound.

According to psychiatrist Aaron Beck, people who are prone to depression are subject to catastrophic deflation in confidence and mood because they subscribe to beliefs about themselves and the world that confront them with impossible choices. For example:

- If I'm not completely happy, then I'll be totally miserable.
- If something isn't done exactly right, then it's worthless.
- If I'm not perfect, then I'm a failure.
- If I have any bad feelings about the people I love, then it means I don't really love them.
- If I'm not in complete control, then I'm helpless.
- If I depend on anyone for anything, then I'm totally needy.

In his book on the cognitive theory of depression, Beck explains how a person whose sense of accomplishment depends on never making a mistake might conclude, after making a simple error, "I'm a total failure." Such *negative cognitions,* which are really false generalizations based on a single event, generate negative self-fulfilling prophecies. The individual who feels like a complete failure after a minor setback, for instance, then *expects* to do badly at everything else. Exerting less effort in the face of such defeatism naturally results in more failure, which only seems to confirm the negative belief.

This was the problem for an exceptionally bright thirty-five-year-old professor who believed that his contributions would make him the youngest recipient of a distinguished teaching award, usually designated for the most senior educator. Because his drive to succeed came from the belief that, if he were not considered more brilliant than everyone else, no one would respect him, the younger man was devastated when a famous older colleague received the award. Without warning, he stopped thinking of himself as the best teacher in the university and began seeing himself as the *worst*; he lost all confidence in his considerable skills and felt increasingly demoralized and depressed by the unnerving confirmations of his self-assessment that he seemed to find everywhere.

Although he was not yet as prominent as the senior associate, the professor had been an exceptionally effective teacher. Now, however, he interpreted his students' frequent questions not as a sign that they were paying attention but as an indication that they thought he did not know what he was talking about. It seemed equally obvious that students only asked to study with him because they could not find anyone better, and that when his colleagues greeted him affably, it was only because they felt sorry for him for not winning the award. He was hypervigilant in his search for any possible sign of failure and exceptionally thorough in dismissing the possibility that he had expected to achieve something that no one his age could have—or should have—achieved. His downward spiral continued; the more insecure he became, sure enough, the more mistakes he made.

Beck contends that depressed emotions are reactions to negative cognitions that arise when an event or perception activates the negative side of a person's dichotomized beliefs. Beck and many other investigators have shown that depression can be cured by cognitive psychotherapy, a type of therapy that helps patients reevaluate and correct pervasive negative thinking. This does not prove that cognitive therapy reverses the *cause* of depression, since negative cognitions also cease after treatment with antidepressants, even if negative thinking is not specifically addressed by the patient. While they may not be the clear cause of depression, cognitive distortions do comprise an essential component of the depressive experience, with predictable and debilitating consequences both for patients and for those treating them.

Most troublesome to those trying to care for depressed people is the dichotomized belief that anyone who is not completely self-reliant is irretrievably weak and dependent. Accepting any kind of help, whether it be friendly support, family or pastoral advice, psychotherapy, or medication, would be an undeniable sign of intolerable weakness. One consequence of this depressive deception is that the person does not seek treatment until the situation is desperate and then discontinues treatment as soon as symptoms improve, even a little. Taking antidepressants only when feeling overwhelmingly depressed gives the patient a false sense of self-sufficiency but then leads to the very outcome the patient is trying to avoid—persistence of the depression and the need for more treatment.

The drive behind this depressive deception of dichotomous thinking is not the basic fear of the somatizer that normal needs for nurturance will go unmet, but a fear of even the most trivial needs. For the depressed patient, self-esteem depends on being *immune* to any but the most desperate needs. And, as psychoanalyst Heinz Kohut showed in the early 1970s, the need to maintain self-esteem can be a more powerful drive than the need to be cared for.

LEARNED HELPLESSNESS

Psychologist Martin Seligman has theorized that "learned helplessness" is an important cause of acute depression. In experiments demonstrating learned helplessness, which were pioneered by Seligman, an animal is exposed to a noxious but harmless stimulus (such as a mild shock) and is prevented from escaping from the stimulus (for example, by placing the animal in a cage and administering the shock through the floor). The animal initially tries its hardest to get away, but after uselessly running back and forth a few times, it gives up, becoming passive in response to the stimulus. When conditions are changed and it becomes possible to escape (for example, when the door to the cage is opened while the shock is administered), the animal *still* remains passive. Having learned that it was helpless to change things, the animal apparently cannot unlearn this response when in a new situation. Helplessness learned in one situation tends to be transferred to any other situation involving unpleasant or challenging elements.

Learned helplessness has also been demonstrated in people. In a classical experiment, college students (the helpless subjects of many a psychology professor's experiments) were exposed to a loud noise from which they could not escape. The noise was delivered through headphones the subjects could not remove; also present was a button that, when pressed, was supposed to terminate the noise but did not work. Just like the animal subjects, the students soon stopped trying to shut off the noise. In the next phase of the experiment, they also made no effort to solve a complex intellectual problem they were all capable of solving, demonstrating that the sense of helplessness had generalized to any situation requiring effort, be it mental or physical.

Seligman feels that some cases of human depression are the result of a generalized shutting down of biological systems that mediate motivation, interest, and pleasure following exposure to repeated experiences of feeling that nothing one does can possibly have a positive impact. There is some experimental evidence to support this contention. For example, college students who have acknowledged having depressive feelings on preliminary questionnaires have been shown to develop learned helplessness in experimental settings faster than students who do not report these feelings. However, this kind of research has not been performed in patients with clinically meaningful depression, just otherwise normal students who report feelings of depression.

In animal experiments, learned helplessness can be prevented by pretreating the animals with an antidepressant, but this still does not prove an association between depression and learned helplessness, since antidepressants have many effects in addition to treatment of depression. Even if the action of antidepressants were specific in preventing learned helplessness, it could suggest that depression leads to learned helplessness as much as the reverse. While it is not possible to say that learned helplessness definitely *causes* depression, it can be said that (1) situations that make people feel helpless can bring out depression, and (2) helplessness is a common depressive symptom that frequently becomes a self-fulfilling prophecy, making whatever depression is present even worse.

GUILT

In a seminal paper entitled "Mourning and Melancholia," Freud postulated that one of the essential differences between depression and grief is that the depressed patient experiences excessive guilt, while the grief-stricken patient feels only sadness. Over the years, guilt has held up as an essential aspect of the psychology of depression, although, like every other symptom, it is just one of a number of important dimensions of the depression experience.

What do depressed people feel guilty about? One of the more common beliefs is that they themselves are to blame for not getting better, even though they have worked as hard as they can to improve. These individuals may become abjectly apologetic when they experience medication side effects and may punish themselves for the transgression of making their families unhappy. Depressed patients with delusions may blame themselves for accidents they pass on the highway, tragedies they read about in the newspaper, or other events that have nothing to do with them. Despite the importance of guilt in many cases of depression, however, Freud's assertion that guilt is a *cause* of depression has not been borne out, mainly because guilt is a ubiquitous human experience that does not clearly predispose people to depression more than to other conditions.

Guilt naturally leads to punishment in most people's minds, and the depressed person is no exception. Often, depression itself is seen as a punishment for real or imagined sins, as when a patient says, "I must have done *something* to deserve this kind of misery." The expectation of punishment is so strong in some people that they punish themselves to save others the trouble of punishing them, or because they cannot stand waiting for whatever fate might be even worse than what they are already experiencing. The ultimate punishment, of course, is suicide, which utterly nullifies the chance of things ever changing for the better.

Suicide is not the only way in which pervasive feelings of guilt can undo the positive effects of treatments for depression. Guilt was the mechanism of relapse in a forty-year-old woman who had been depressed for ten years. She eventually consented to try an antidepressant after numerous therapies had failed, not really believing that the medication would help either. Contrary to the woman's expectations, the antidepressant did begin to have a positive effect. For the first time in a very long time, she was able to relax and savor the results of her hard work. She was no longer short-tempered or chronically fatigued; in fact, she actually felt energetic throughout the day. Only when she began sleeping normally did she realize that she had not had a good night's sleep in years.

When she began to suspect that she was not imagining this dramatic change in her outlook, she stopped the medication to be sure that the effect was real. The depression came back. She tried the medication again, which worked the second time, too. This convinced her that the medication was, in fact, working—so she stopped it for good! Why? She still did not feel that she deserved to be well, and the prospect of no longer being depressed raised the fear of an even worse punishment—one she could hardly imagine— when this source of suffering was removed. It took a great deal of work for her to understand and reconsider this expectation.

LOSS

The depressive response in adulthood is frequently triggered by loss. The loss can be literal, as through death, divorce, unemployment, or relocation; partial, as when a spouse's attention is directed elsewhere or a child becomes more independent; or symbolic, as when a valued object, ideal, goal, or fantasy cannot be obtained. People who experience a loss are six times more likely to become depressed than those who do not experience a loss. It is no wonder that loss so often sets in motion the pathological response of depression: not just an internal source of grief, loss also takes away an external source of coping and comfort—be it a person or a symbolic stand-in for a person, such as wealth, an institution, or an ideal of physical perfection.

Loss can lead to depression in several ways. Disruption of any significant attachment directly produces emotional distress and loss of control of basic biological functions. For example, grief-stricken people are unable to eat or sleep. Since the security and comfort of other people help to regulate our physiology, loss of someone important adds the additional impact of removing an important source of bodily as well as emotional regulation. This "double whammy" triggers physical and psychological distress in just about anyone. When stress-response systems of the body are already vulnerable, they may be overwhelmed by the stress of loss in ways that are addressed in the next chapter.

Loss can be as disorganizing to our psychology as it is to our biology. People who depend on another person to provide them with a sense of worth, lovableness, or competence may experience the loss of that person as loss of an essential quality of the self. This perception of depletion is experienced as depression; the loss of important psychological functions leaves the person unable to tolerate the ravages of grief, let alone cope with everyday stresses.

ANGER TURNED AGAINST THE SELF

One of the more popular theories of depression is that it is the result of anger turned against the self in a person who is afraid that expressing anger toward loved ones will evoke retaliation or abandonment. According to this point of view, instead of being directed at the flesh-and-blood person, the chronically unexpressed anger is directed internally at the *images* of the other person that are stored within the patient's memory. This attack on oneself depletes the resources necessary to cope with external stress and creates feelings of intense discomfort and despair. Attacking the concept of another person stored within one's own mind can be carried out physically as well as mentally, in which case it is manifested as self-destructive behavior ranging from cutting, burning, or hitting oneself to self-starvation or overeating.

If depression were *caused* by anger turned inward, most depressed people would never seem outwardly angry. However, the reverse is actually the case: irritability is a common symptom of depression. In addition, depression—like many other conditions with interpersonal dimensions—may involve covert expressions of anger that, if consciously expressed, would feel threatening and inconsistent with the person's self-image. For example, the depressed patient who is angry at loved ones for not caring enough and at doctors for not doing enough may display persistent depression as an accusation of the doctors' failure to cure and the family's failure to cheer him up. As long as the patient is unbearably miserable, no one confronts this perpetuation of illness as a weapon; if they do, the patient who is struggling with overwhelming inner anger may up the ante by becoming suicidal.

MISERY LOVES COMPANY

When the passivity and helplessness of depression are rewarded with attention, sympathy, getting one's way, and other forms of gratification, it can be easier to be depressed than to do things for oneself. Rewards from others do not have to be positive to sustain depressive behavior in those who lack confidence in their own abilities. For some people, negative attention may be better than no attention at all.

The covert interpersonal rewards of depressive behaviors helped to entrench depression in a woman who was married to an aggressive businessman who claimed that, because he spent so much time working to support the family, he should not be required to help with any household tasks or with rearing the children. The patient had never challenged this assumption, fearing that if she became too assertive he would leave her. (In fact, he was more dependent on her than she was on him, but never testing her belief that she was the one with the greater need, she never found out the truth.) While the children were still young, she felt little conflict because they were easy and she did not mind doing all the work at home herself. But as the children entered their rebellious teenage years, she began to feel overwhelmed by responsibilities she felt ill-equipped to handle on her own. Her sense of helplessness mounted, and she began to sink into depression.

Since she felt incapable of demanding that her husband start helping out, her depression escalated to an unconscious strike. She became increasingly demoralized, making no attempt to discipline the children. They responded by staying out all night and wrecking the family car. Her husband was finally forced to do something, and he responded promptly, but as soon as things were under control he retreated to his office. Although his wife felt like a failure, she was not stupid; she quickly, if unconsciously, registered that he was more likely to become involved if she were ineffectual than if she returned to her former competent level of functioning.

Before long, she became incapable of handling any problem with the children or with the house. Her husband repeatedly took over temporarily, further reinforcing her helplessness. He began to complain with increasing bitterness about his wife's apparent ineptitude, but in remaining home to tell her how he felt, he was spending more time with her than he had in years.

Depression in this case was probably precipitated by helplessness, but it was perpetuated by learning that depression could elicit rewards that competence could not. To cure her depression, it was necessary not only to treat the specific symptoms but to convince the patient that making direct demands for involvement from her husband would produce more gratifying results. As is true of most depressed people, this patient's depression did not originate as an attempt to control her interpersonal world. However, depressive behaviors, like illness behaviors, can be maintained by people who feel incapable of influencing those around them in any other way. While depression does not originate as an attempt to control the interpersonal world, depressed behaviors—from withdrawal to suicide attempts—may be more likely to occur in people who feel incapable of influencing those around them in any other way.

DO PSYCHOLOGICAL PROBLEMS CAUSE
OR RESULT FROM DEPRESSION?

Considering the profound and pervasive alterations in mental outlook associated with depression, the view that depression is nothing more than a biological condition seems absurd. But if depression involves characteristic mental factors, does this mean that the *psychology* of depression is also the *cause* of depression? We have seen that many depressed people have trouble expressing anger toward those on whom they depend, but so do people who somatize, making this a nonspecific factor shared by both groups of patients. Similarly, depressed people tend to be overly dependent, but so are many other patients in whom inner distress activates the natural drive to seek comfort and protection from others.

In fact, it is impossible to say that any individual trait of the depressed person is specific to depression. Medically ill people can feel helpless; anxious people have negative expectations about the future; somatizers have crippling conflicts about dependency and expressing anger toward loved ones; and most people are sensitive to loss. When many of these psychological factors occur at the same time and interact with each other, we make a diagnosis of depression. But this still does not tell us whether the mental constellation of depression is only *one aspect* of a complex experience—or its *cause*.

A 1983 study by psychiatric investigator Robert Hirschfeld and colleagues, as well as a 1989 report by the same group, cast an interesting light on the "chicken and egg" question of the relationship between the mental side of depression and the entire syndrome. Using a well-validated measure of personality traits, the researchers showed that manic-depressive patients had gross psychopathology typical of their disorder when they were manic or depressed *but no measurable personality malfunctions when they were well.* In another study, depressed patients who were no longer symptomatic were found to have the same psychopathology as people who had never suffered from depression—*or even less.* Acutely anxious patients are typically dependent, emotionally unstable, introverted, and lacking in self-confidence, but after only six weeks of successful treatment of the anxiety, these personality traits were found to be substantially reduced.

Research shows that people who recover from depression become *less* dependent, passive, and hypersensitive, and *more* self-reliant, self-confident, and stable. Even if significant maladaptive character traits could be demonstrated in those who are depression-prone, these traits could still be manifestations of some underlying biological process that affects both mood and personality. The bulk of evidence suggests that individuals who are acutely depressed resemble each other during depressive periods more than they resemble each other when they are not depressed. This fascinating finding suggests that *many important aspects of depression are as much a function of the depressive state as they are of the person who becomes depressed.*

We have already seen that depression can be precipitated by a loss, but so can many other conditions, including medical illnesses. Are there any factors or traits that *do* specifically predispose one to depression? The best predictor that someone will become depressed is a history of depression in the family. The fact that the risk for developing depression is the same, whether or not the person is raised with depressed family members, suggests that *predisposing factors are inherited even more than they are learned.*

What kinds of inherited factors have the capacity to deceive the mind into accepting the negative mental orientation of depression? The next chapter introduces one answer to this question: disruption of systems in the brain that orchestrate the response of body and mind to anything perceived as dangerous.

11

Adaptation Gone Awry: Biological Dimensions of Depression

SALLY, A WOMAN in her early thirties, could not understand what was going on. Nothing had changed in her life; in fact, the business she owned was going well, as was her marriage. But despite the absence of stress, she found herself feeling increasingly morose and irritable. She began having trouble keeping track of details at work, and she had less patience for her husband, who was normally easy to get along with. She had always slept through the night but recently found herself waking up every morning at four, unable to get back to sleep. Increasingly tired during the day, she had less energy to complete her tasks and began to fall behind.

When she realized that her ability to function was definitely impaired, Sally consulted her family physician, thinking that she might have chronic fatigue syndrome. The physician could find no evidence of that, but he did elicit a history from her in which she mentioned a sufficient number of depressive symptoms to make a diagnosis of a major depressive episode. In addition to changes in mood, energy, and sleep, Sally was having difficulty concentrating, had lost interest in food, and found no enjoyment in planning her annual ski vacation.

What could have caused Sally to feel depressed? Since there was no obvious precipitant, the physician asked Sally about her use of alcohol and medications. "I just have a glass of wine with dinner, and every now and then a second glass before bed." "How often do you have that second glass of wine?" the physician asked. "During the past six months or so, perhaps four or five times a week. Work has been hard and it helps me to relax."

Surely this couldn't be enough alcohol to cause depression, could it? The physician did not think so, but it seemed easy enough to test: he asked Sally to stop drinking completely to see if this would improve her depression. Sure enough, a month after Sally had stopped drinking wine, her symptoms disappeared.

Why was Sally so prone to the depression-inducing effects of alcohol, when most people who drink a little wine do not get depressed? The only obvious risk factor was that her sister, Mallory, had also been depressed, although Mallory had become depressed after a divorce. Like Sally, Mallory had developed insomnia, irritability, low energy, and difficulty concentrating, and had lost all sense of enjoyment. When psychotherapy, focused on resolving the loss of her marriage, did not help the depression, Mallory took an antidepressant, which returned her to her normal emotional state.

Sally and her sister had experienced a similar depression, but one case was caused by a classic psychosocial stressor and the other by a physical agent. Sally's depression went away when she stopped using even a moderate amount of alcohol, while Mallory required medication even though the instigating psychological cause was resolved.

A wide array of physical factors in addition to alcohol, such as viral infections, anemia, thyroid disease, cancer, most medications, and illicit drugs, can result in depressive syndromes indistinguishable from those caused by loss or conflict. Neither Sally nor her sister were predisposed to become depressed by virtue of early experiences such as loss or helplessness, but they did share a common vulnerability that affected other people in their family. Let us now examine the kinds of risk factors that can run in families.

THE GENETICS OF DEPRESSION

Freud said that "what dimensions [a] neurosis attains depends in the first instance on the amount of the hereditary taint." In the case of depression, he was proven correct. The rate of depression in first-degree relatives (parents, siblings, children, and grandparents) of depressed individuals is more than twice that in the general population. Half-siblings have half the increased risk of full siblings of a depressed parent. If both parents are depressed, the likelihood that their child will have a similar problem increases between 50 and 75 percent.

People with more depression in the family tend to become depressed earlier in life and to develop more severe forms of depression. By the same token, people who develop depression early in life have more depressed blood relatives.

Money, religion, and politics run in families, too, but they have not yet been shown to be transmitted through the genes. Obviously, it is important to differentiate the depressing effects of being raised with depressed parents, brothers, and sisters from truly inborn influences. And once the effect of upbringing on a familial disorder were factored out, it would be necessary to differentiate between vulnerabilities that are genetic and those that are acquired during pregnancy and very early life.

Twin Studies

We saw earlier that one approach to these questions is to compare rates of depression in identical (monozygotic—one egg) twins and fraternal (dizygotic—two eggs) twins. Both kinds of twins are exposed to similar prenatal influences and grow up in the same environment, but identical twins have exactly the same genes whereas fraternal twins are like any other siblings and have about half the same genes. If a given characteristic is shared more frequently by identical than fraternal twins—technically speaking, if identical twins are "more concordant" for the characteristic—then the likelihood of an inherited rather than environmental cause of that characteristic increases dramatically.

Fraternal twins of people with depression have an 11–20 percent chance of becoming depressed themselves—a rate that approximates that for any other sibling—but 40–67 percent of identical twins of depressives become depressed. The concordance is even more striking for bipolar disorders. Fraternal twins of manic-depressive parents have a 14 percent concordance rate for developing the illness (already two to fourteen times the risk in the general population), but 72–100 percent of identical twins of manic-depressive parents become manic-depressive. The risk is the same if the twins are raised in the same household *or if they grow up separately,* further suggesting that predisposition to this disorder is inherited, not learned.

Twin studies also demonstrate an inherited component to panic disorder. Even generalized anxiety disorder, a fluctuating syndrome of overanxious responses to everyday stress, may be part of an inherited spectrum. In 1992 geneticist Kenneth Kendler reported that 1,033 pairs of female twins had increased concordance for both major depression and generalized anxiety disorder; similar results have been reported for agoraphobia and social phobia. Kendler and his group hypothesize that some common trait, which predisposes the individual to both anxiety and depression, may be inherited and that *which disorder predominates* depends on experience.

Adoption Studies

Another valuable source of information about the genetics of depression comes from studies of depressed people who were adopted soon after birth. With the exception of prenatal and perinatal events, environmental influences are provided by the adoptive family, while genes are contributed by the family of origin. A genetic factor for a given disorder is indicated if the biological family, with whom an adoptee does not interact, is more likely to have the disorder than the family that raises the adoptee.

This turns out to be the case for depression: an adoptee with a depressed biological parent is five times more likely to become depressed than an adoptee who does not have a biological parent with depression. In fact, the best predictor of the risk of depression is whether a biological parent has been depressed, *not* whether one has grown up around depressed people. This is not to say that it is fun to be raised in a depressed family—only that being exposed to depression while growing up is not more likely to make a child depressed than it is to lead to other kinds of problems. Only when there is a biological connection to a depressed relative is depression more likely to emerge.

As in other types of investigation, adoption studies suggest the presence of a particularly strong hereditary influence for manic-depressive disorders. Adopted individuals who become bipolar have more than twenty-five times the expected risk of having biological relatives who are also manic-depressive.

Gene Mapping

Those who follow popular reports of scientific advances are aware of the "human genome project," a massive effort to map the human complement of about 100,000 genes. All cells in the body have the same genes; the actual function of a given cell depends on the relatively small number of genes that are active in that cell. Any easily obtained cell, therefore, can provide DNA fragments for analysis.

As discussed in Chapter 4, current strategies for linking a gene to a particular disorder utilize inherited variability of DNA sequences from one individual to another. Variations in DNA are recognized by bacterial enzymes (called "endonucleases") that cut DNA at specific sites. The same enzymes produce different DNA fragments in different individuals, depending on the pattern of inherited recognition sites. These fragments (called "restriction fragment length polymorphisms" or RFLPs) can be differentiated through the use of various chemical approaches. Numerous DNA fragments, each containing different groups of genes, have been characterized on each chromosome. Because each enzyme cuts DNA at known points, overlapping different fragments of the same chromosome created by different enzymes eventually produce a map of the entire chromosome, identifying individual genes. Overlapping DNA fragments also make it possible to identify different alleles (versions) of the same gene.

Linkage studies determine which DNA fragments are associated with (linked to) a particular illness. Because a relatively small number of genes has been identified, most linkage is to DNA fragments, which narrows the search down to circumscribed regions of specific chromosomes but does not necessarily demonstrate the exact gene on that region. If the actual gene linked to a disease can be identified by further digestion of the fragment into identifiable pieces, it becomes possible to clone the gene and find out exactly what it does. Knowing what the abnormal protein does clarifies the pathology of the disease and makes it easier to develop treatments aimed specifically at correcting the abnormality.

There are several important problems that arise in attempting to interpret genetic linkage of psychiatric disorders. Even with careful diagnostic schemes, many disorders have overlapping symptoms, so that the same patient may receive different diagnoses at different times from different psychiatrists. In some cases, apparent linkage of a DNA fragment to one disorder may really be due to linkage to another condition, whereas lack of linkage to one diagnosis may be the result of different disorders being lumped together under one category.

Another confounding factor is that it is not clear whether linkage is in relation to the disorder per se or to some feature associated with the disorder, such as severity, recurrence, psychosis, or personality problems. For example, the common predisposition to anxiety and depression noted earlier may *not* mean that both disorders are somehow inherited together but only that there is vulnerability to excessive arousal or withdrawal in the face of stress that has different effects in different people.

Yet another methodological problem is that some cases of a given disorder may be linked to one gene, some may be linked to another gene, and some may not be associated with genetic factors at all. If cases that are associated with one gene are mistakenly lumped in with those associated with another gene or with non-genetic forms, all of which look similar clinically, linkage that actually exists may be overlooked. By the same token, a single gene may express itself in different ways under different circumstances, leading researchers to conclude there is no linkage to a particular disorder when, in fact, more than one symptom cluster is actually linked to the same gene.

Complicating matters even further is the fact that many genes have "variable penetrance," which means that they may not have the same influence in everyone. A person may carry a pathological gene but not experience its effects for one reason or another: either the person is not exposed to harmful environmental factors that would interact with the gene to produce depression or other factors are present that protect against the gene's pathological expression. Failure to find linkage between a particular gene and a type of depression does not mean that the gene does not contribute to depression, only that by itself it is not sufficient to catalyze depression at that point in the person's life. This, of course, is the case for all mental disorders in which genetic influences have been identified: genetic factors contribute to the risk of the disorder, but they do not cause the disorder by themselves.

Genes for Bipolar Disorder

Because linkage studies attempt to correlate the presence of a single DNA fragment with a single disorder, they are most likely to be helpful in disorders associated with a dominant gene with complete penetrance (i.e., only one copy of the abnormal gene is necessary to produce the disease, and everyone with the gene gets the disease). Huntington's disease, a fatal inherited neurological disorder, is a perfect example of such an illness. Another advantage of Huntington's disease for genetic research is that the same symptoms are manifested in all patients, so there is no doubt about whether the disease is present.

This is far from the case for unipolar depression, which has a familial pattern that suggests an interaction between multiple recessive genes (i.e., two copies of the abnormal gene are necessary to produce a biological abnormality), and which has different manifestations in different people. Linkage studies of bipolar disorder are more likely to be fruitful because this disorder is more clearly defined, at least in its severe form, and because certain cases run in consecutive generations, suggesting a dominant pattern of inheritance.

Studies of Chromosome 11

It is helpful to perform genetic linkage studies on homogenous populations who do not have as much genetic diversity as a randomly selected group of people and therefore are less likely to dilute evidence of linkage. One such group is the Old Order Amish, who are descended from a small group of common progenitors and to this day do not marry outside of their Order. In a careful study of an Amish population, researcher Janice Egeland found that a specific RFLP from chromosome 11 was linked to bipolar disorder. Presumably, this DNA fragment would contain the gene that is associated with bipolar illness. Since the same DNA fragment could be identified in every Amish person who was bipolar but was not found in any person who was not bipolar, it appeared that this fragment was transmitted from generation to generation, along with bipolar illness. No other version of this fragment of chromosome 11, and no other fragment of chromosome 11 or any other chromosome studied, was associated with bipolar disorder in this particular population.

Gene mapping studies by researchers S. Hodgkinson, M. Baron, and their colleagues of three Icelandic and three North American bipolar families, published in the same issue of the prestigious journal *Nature* that carried the Egeland article, found *no* association between bipolar disorder and the region of chromosome 11 that was identified in the Amish study. The most likely explanation of this discrepancy seemed to be that the same disorder could be associated with different genotypes in different populations. There was more confusion when, a few years later, the Egeland group published the results of an extension of their original study in the same journal. In the new report the linkage between the fragment on chromosome 11 and bipolar disorder had disappeared, as evidenced by the fact that two subjects who showed no evidence of being bipolar in the first investigation had become symptomatic, and neither of them had the identifying DNA fragment. The statistical analysis was so complex that changing the status of these two individuals wiped out the significant association of the chromosomal marker with bipolar disorder!

The new results complicated but did not invalidate the initial finding of a linkage between the chromosome 11 marker and bipolar illness. In all likelihood, some cases of bipolar disorder in the Amish *are* linked to a gene on chromosome 11. Other cases probably are linked to different genes. A gene that conveys risk of bipolar illness may be inherited in some people, while it may be the result of spontaneous mutation in others. Some bipolar patients may have *no* genetic risk at all but develop changes in gene *expression* after being exposed to severe trauma or overstimulation, leading to the same vulnerabilities that other people inherit. In any given population, different varieties of bipolar disorder—those that are severe versus those that are mild, those with many recurrences versus those with just a few—are probably as different genetically as they are clinically.

Studies of the X-Chromosome

Linkage of bipolar disorder to the X-chromosome has been more consistently demonstrated. Characteristics linked to the X-chromosome tend to be transmitted from mother to son but not from father to son, because boys, who have an X- and a Y-chromosome, receive the X-chromosome from their mothers and the Y-chromosome, which determines male sex, from their fathers. Since males have only one X-chromosome, one copy of an abnormal gene can produce a pathological effect. While bipolar disorder can be transmitted from father to son through a gene on an autosomal (non-sex) chromosome, mother-to-son transmission is much more common.

DNA fragments on the X-chromosome have not yet been studied by researchers investigating genetic underpinnings of bipolar disorder. So far, their investigations have centered on establishing linkage of bipolar disorder to physical traits known to be carried on the X-chromosome. Two of these traits, color blindness and deficiency of an enzyme called "glucose-6-phosphate dehydrogenase" (G6PD), have repeatedly been found in certain populations of bipolar males. Using these markers, some form of X-linkage has been observed in Jewish, Middle Eastern, Mediterranean, and Asian communities that share the same gene pool.

Even within these populations, different genes on the X-chromosome may produce the same syndrome. For example, in one study four out of five Israeli families with a high proportion of bipolar members provided evidence for linkage to G6PD deficiency, but in another report a group of Belgian bipolar families demonstrated linkage to a coagulation factor that lies on a different segment of the X-chromosome.

Overall, it has been estimated that about one-third of bipolar individuals carry some sort of X-linked gene for the disorder. Wherever the gene is located, it appears to be dominant, because only one copy of the gene is necessary to develop the disorder. Northern European populations, who do not have the same ancestors as Mediterranean populations, have demonstrated non-X-linked patterns of bipolar inheritance. Bipolar disorder that develops "out of the blue" in people with no bipolar relatives may be the result of genes with high rates of spontaneous mutation or to the alteration of gene expression by experience, providing a psychological route to the physiology of a disordered mood.

Genes Don't Have the Last Word

The fact that different genes on different chromosomes can be associated with the same clinical phenomenon suggests that in depression there may be a complex physiological process that can be influenced at multiple points but with the same final result. For example, a gene in one person may function abnormally by stimulating the production of an aberrant protein in the brain. Another gene in someone else may function abnormally by failing to stimulate a normal function. A third gene may have a completely different action at some other link in a biochemical chain. While all bipolar mood disorders with a genetic component involve mood swings and changes in sleep and energy, different genetic forms may differ significantly in severity of mood swings, associated symptoms (such as psychosis or aggressive behavior), frequency of recurrences, and response to treatment.

Although gene mapping and family studies suggest that there is a genetic factor in at least some forms of depression, it would be erroneous to conclude that depression is necessarily inherited. Even in the first Amish study showing inherited linkages, only about 60 percent of individuals who had the bipolar DNA fragment actually developed the disorder. The absence of depression in significant numbers of people with a gene for depression can be due either to the *presence* of factors that block the gene's influence or to the *absence* of factors needed to elicit the gene's expression.

There is also evidence that genes for depression have "variable expressivity," which means that the condition will vary in its manifestations as a result of variable influence of the gene. Therefore, it is not depression itself that is inherited, only the susceptibility to it. Whether that susceptibility is expressed, intensified, modified, inhibited, or suppressed depends on the interaction of genetic vulnerabilities with a host of factors residing in the body, the mind, and the environment. As we review the biology of depression, we will see that these interactions go in both directions.

ABNORMALITIES IN BIOLOGICAL RHYTHMS

How do *genetic* factors result in predispositions to *mental* aberrations? In the case of depression, the basic flaw that is created in the body involves a fundamental misalignment of stress-response systems. As we examine some of these systems, we will see how they can reset the orientation of the mind.

Nothing in life is constant. Nature follows endless cycles of activity and rest, and the systems of the body must match these cycles to engage the environment when the need for action is greatest and recharge when the environment provides breathing room. In depression, these cycles are altered, leaving systems of the body out of synch with one another.

Cycles of biological activity in the body may recur as frequently as every second (for example, brain waves and heartbeat) or as infrequently as once a year (seasonal changes in activity and mood) or even longer. Many important functions have a circadian (about twenty-four hours) rhythm, including sleep patterns, hormone secretion, body temperature, susceptibility to bacteria, and even likelihood of death during surgery.

Biological rhythms are generated by groups of neurons called "oscillators" located in the hypothalamus deep in the brain. This central location makes it possible for the oscillators to influence each other, send messages to multiple systems, and receive diverse kinds of feedback from all over the body and the brain. Patterns of arousal, alertness, body temperature, heart rate, glandular secretion, motivation, emotionality, and motor activity can then be coordinated to match the momentary requirements of the environment.

Influences that *entrain* bodily rhythms (synchronize them to external cues) are called *zeitgebers* (in German, "time givers"). A variety of events, from meals to social interactions to activities, can serve as zeitgebers. One of the most potent zeitgebers for the sleep–wake cycle is bright light. Exposure to properly timed light (of at least one-fourth the intensity of sunlight) can reset the sleep-wake cycle by twelve hours within just a few days. Information about light reaches the brain via a tract from the retina of the eye to a receptor deep within the hypothalamus.

Two pacemakers in the brain have been reasonably well studied. The one that drives the sleep-wake cycle is called the "weak oscillator" because it is easily entrained to environmental cues and can be overridden by conscious intention, as in the decision to stay up all night. The other pacemaker is called the "strong oscillator" because it is more resistant to being reset. The strong oscillator controls rhythms of body temperature, hormone secretion, mental performance, and timing of rapid eye movement (REM) sleep. Because it is the dominant rhythm generator, changes in the function of the strong oscillator can change the relationship of many biological rhythms to each other and to the external environment.

In addition to their coordination with environmental cues, the two oscillators must be synchronized with each other in order to maximize the efficiency of the body's response to the environment. When they are out of phase (desynchronized) with each other or with the environment, as occurs with jet lag and work-shift changes, the desynchronization of bodily response is perceived as unpleasant and disorienting.

In many cases of depression, both oscillators are turned forward (phase-advanced), putting them out of phase with external demands and often with each other. Hormone secretion, body temperature, and production of a stress-response neurotransmitter called norepinephrine—all of which vary over the course of the day under the influence of the strong oscillator—may reach their peaks earlier than normal in depression. It is as if an internal perception of danger were accelerating circadian rhythms to propel the body into action sooner than would be appropriate, given the usual zeitgebers.

Phase-advance of the sleep-wake cycle results in disruption in sleep rhythms such that restorative stages of sleep are preempted by a shift to REM or dreaming sleep. This is why depressed people feel tired during the day, even if they sleep excessively. Normally, REM sleep begins 70–110 minutes after falling asleep; it lasts a relatively short time and is then replaced by slow-wave (restful) sleep. As the night progresses, REM reappears more frequently and lasts longer, with diminishing periods of slow-wave sleep in-between. Most slow-wave sleep occurs earlier in the night, while REM cycles become progressively more frequent as morning approaches, with the greatest amount of REM at the end of the sleep cycle.

In depression, the first REM period develops early—40–50 minutes into the sleep cycle, and sometimes as soon as 15 minutes. Not only does REM begin too soon ("decreased REM latency"), but more REM appears during the first part of the night, allowing less time for the more restorative, slow-wave sleep that should be present at this point. There are also more eye movements during REM periods (increased REM density), suggesting that REM sleep is more intense and produces more interruptions of total sleep, contributing to the sense of daytime exhaustion.

At least one of these sleep abnormalities is found in 90 percent of depressed patients and in a significant number of manic patients. The combination of decreased sleep efficiency (decreased ability to stay asleep), decreased REM latency, and increased REM density is a more reliable biological marker of depression than any one abnormality alone. REM latency is shortest in patients with bipolar and psychotic depressions, in which case a person may begin dreaming even before falling asleep.

However, decreased REM latency, though more marked in more severe forms of depression, may actually predict a better prognosis. In addition, the degree to which REM latency increases toward normal at the beginning of treatment can predict how much better the patient will be a month later. People start to remember their dreams again at this point, because dreaming occurs closer to the time of awakening.

Biological rhythms such as the sleep-wake cycle may also be retarded or phase-delayed in depression, as if the body had given up on preparing for danger and slowed down instead. The phase changes, which occur irrespective of environmental cues in depression, indicate that cycles of mental and physical activity are being regulated by an inner timetable that is inappropriately turned ahead, set back, or in some way desynchronized. In essence, depression superimposes its own rhythm on normal cycles.

THE ADRENAL STRESS-RESPONSE SYSTEM AND THE DEXAMETHASONE SUPPRESSION TEST

For many years we have known that severe cases of depression are accompanied by an increased secretion of cortisol, one of the stress hormones (corticosteroids) produced by the adrenal gland. Cortisol is released during the fight-flight phase of the stress response, along with epinephrine and norepinephrine, which are members of a group of substances—"catecholamines"—that are produced in a different region of the adrenal gland and also in the brain. The catecholamines prepare the body for immediate action by increasing blood flow to muscles and mobilizing emergency energy reserves. In contrast, the corticosteroids provide more long-term adaptation to stress by preparing for tissue damage, modulating the immune response, ensuring continuing energy supplies, retaining fluid to compensate for blood loss, and possibly influencing mood.

Cortisol synthesis is controlled by hormones located in the hypothalamus and the pituitary, which are specialized parts of the brain that together with the adrenal gland form a two-way information loop called the hypothalamic-pituitary-adrenal axis. The amount of cortisol made available to the body is carefully regulated by the brain's estimate of how much is needed—a process known as "feedback inhibition": when the pituitary and the hypothalamus register rising blood levels of cortisol, they reduce the release of hormones that stimulate cortisol secretion. Because the body does not always need the same amount of cortisol, there is daily variation in its secretion. Cortisol levels are normally highest early in the morning in preparation for the day's activities and lowest at night, when the body is more likely to be at rest. During times of stress the brain anticipates that cortisol will be needed continuously and in increased amounts, so it dampens the normal cues for inhibition. As a result, cortisol is secreted at a constant, rather than a varying, rate and levels rapidly build. Ordinarily only life-threatening dangers provoke this drastic resetting of the hypothalamic-pituitary-adrenal interchange axis.

Although the depressed person appears lusterless and lethargic, physiologically there is the same kind of hyperactivity that occurs when the body is activated to respond to some major threat. Amounts of circulating cortisol are increased so that the body is kept in a state of continuous mobilization. The physiological mobilization persists even during sleep, suggesting that it is not the conscious perception of danger that is responsible for the changes but an automatic bodily response.

This change in cortisol regulation can be demonstrated with a test known as the dexamethasone suppression test (DST). This test utilizes the fact that the brain circuits controlling cortisol secretion can also be influenced by synthetic substances that chemically resemble cortisol. One such substance is dexamethasone, a short-acting adrenal steroid used to treat shock and certain kinds of inflammation and swelling.

Dexamethasone looks just like cortisol to the brain but not to the laboratory tests for cortisol. When dexamethasone is ingested, the hypothalamus and pituitary respond to what appears to be excess amounts of cortisol by telling the adrenal gland to decrease the amount of cortisol that is secreted, resulting in *suppression* of cortisol production on the DST. By measuring cortisol levels the day after administering dexamethasone, one can assess the brain's ability to respond to apparently rising cortisol levels by shutting down cortisol production. A depressed brain ignores the cue to reduce cortisol production, resulting in *nonsuppression* of cortisol on the DST.

Making the Invisible Visible

About 40–50 percent of all depressed patients show nonsuppression on this test. The frequency of positive results is higher (as much as 70 percent) in bipolar patients, patients with psychotic depression, and depressed people who make serious suicide attempts. Manic patients also exhibit DST non-suppression, as do people who have recently lost weight or are physically ill, under very acute stress, elderly, demented, or taking medications that alter DST metabolism. There is a 10–30 percent rate of DST nonsuppression in people with panic disorder, but other forms of anxiety and schizophrenia, which can produce as much or more distress as depression, usually are not associated with nonsuppression.

After the DST suppression test was introduced, many physicians and patients alike hoped it would prove to be a concrete means of identifying a condition that had seemed nebulous and insubstantial. Occasionally, this hope is realized, as occurred for a thirty-year-old woman who wanted to settle down but could never find the right partner. She told her psychiatrist that no matter how caring and considerate they seemed at first, every man she dated turned out to be unfaithful. She was dissatisfied and frustrated with her situation, but she did not seem particularly depressed.

With the help of psychotherapy, the woman was able to understand why she unconsciously sought out men who were bound to be disappointing. This insight helped her to avoid men who were clearly not interested in a committed relationship, but she still could not find anyone suitable. She understood that she did not look hard enough for a better partner because she believed that nobody worthwhile would ever love her. Her knowledge of these conflicts continued to expand, but her relationships did not benefit.

One day the patient saw a television program about the DST. Fascinated, she asked her psychiatrist to order the test. Viewing her problem to be purely psychological in nature, the psychiatrist could see no reason for the test, but the patient insisted and he agreed. To his surprise, the test showed nonsuppression. He thought there had to be a laboratory error and had the test repeated. This time, the woman's post-dexamethasone cortisol level was even *higher,* further confirming the results of the first test. A thorough investigation of possible medical causes of nonsuppression was unrevealing.

The psychiatrist still did not think that his patient was truly depressed. But the patient, who felt that nothing else had helped her, argued for a trial of medication. Skeptical, the psychiatrist agreed.

For the first few weeks, nothing happened. Then, just at the time when antidepressants usually begin to take effect, the patient began to notice a change, not in her conflicts per se, but in how she *reacted* to them. "I didn't realize how easily I just give up when I'm faced with a conflict," she said. "Whenever I meet someone who might be good for me, I start to feel that it won't work out and I just stop trying. This medicine seems to help me stick with it longer—I seem to trust myself more."

With her tendency to withdraw from emotional challenges now receding, the patient made more rapid strides in her psychotherapy. Six months later, she met a man whom she married a year later. She still had a tendency to avoid confronting her husband when he ignored her needs, but eventually she would address the problem head-on, and he responded well to her directness.

The woman had felt so good for so long that she thought she no longer needed the medication. Since the DST had stood her in good stead, she repeated the test, and it was still positive. But since she had no problems at all, she decided to stop the antidepressant anyway. Three months later, she realized that her old patterns had returned: she was no longer asserting herself and was starting to feel pessimistic about whether she and her husband would ever resolve their differences. Realizing what was going on, she resumed taking the medication, and within a few weeks she stopped feeling overwhelmed and demoralized by the slights and insecurities that are inherent in any relationship and once again began communicating more effectively with her husband.

Gaining Legitimacy

Physicians who become depressed can be the worst patients of all, staunchly believing that if the problem cannot be identified in a test tube, it doesn't exist. Without an "objective" illness to hang their depressive hat on, they feel ashamed of seeking treatment and do so only if they are forced into it by becoming suicidal or totally disabled. A test like the DST can legitimize the need to be treated for such individuals.

A paradoxical example of this problem was presented by a physician who consulted a psychiatrist because of intense, disabling anxiety whenever he attended a dying patient. The trouble had begun suddenly on the tenth anniversary of his father's death. The physician was a very insightful person who spoke at great length about his feelings for his father. Unfortunately, this did not have much effect on his anxiety, which by now was preventing him from working with any seriously ill patient. Since depression and anxiety are so intimately related, the physician's psychiatrist repeatedly asked about the presence of depressive symptoms, but the physician consistently denied having any.

When it became clear that psychological treatment alone was not particularly helpful, the psychiatrist performed a DST, which showed nonsuppression. Confronted with this "proof" that he must be depressed, the physician now admitted that he had been waking up at three in the morning, took no interest in pleasurable activities, and had lost fifteen pounds in the preceding two months. He had not disclosed this information earlier because he wanted his problem to be "just" psychological—something in the realm of an existential disturbance. Any evidence of a biological disturbance might signify that he was "really sick."

The physician-patient's attitude toward the DST was useful in clarifying the depressive deception he held that either he suffered from a purely psychological conflict that required only a mental treatment or he was biologically mentally ill. When he confronted this deception openly, he had to agree that the biological and psychological aspects of his state of being were not necessarily two poles at opposite ends of a spectrum, so much as different facets of the same condition. Finally acknowledging that taking an antidepressant was not necessarily a sign that he was a failure as a person, he did so. Within two months, his symptoms were gone and he was back to work. After three more months his DST had become normal and the medication was stopped. He went on to resolve his feelings about the loss of his father and had no further problems.

OTHER SIGNS OF BODILY ACTIVATION

In depressed patients, the regulation of thyroid hormone (along with several other hormonal systems) is altered in a manner similar to that of cortisol. Like cortisol, the synthesis of thyroid hormone is regulated by the hypothalamus and the pituitary in accordance with the level of thyroid in the blood and the needs of the body. The relation between thyroid function and depression is a complex one. Low thyroid function (hypothyroidism) is more common in depressed than nondepressed individuals and is frequently found in bipolar patients who have very rapid mood swings (rapid cycling). However, evidence of hyperactivity of the circuit consisting of the thyroid, the pituitary, and the hypothalamus, in the absence of actual thyroid disease, is a primary marker of depression. This abnormality can be identified by a specialized test of the hypothalamic–pituitary–thyroid axis called the thyrotropin releasing hormone (TRH) stimulation test. Whereas the DST involves suppressing brain centers that control the secretion of cortisol by the adrenal gland, the TRH stimulation test is performed by administering an artificial version of the hypothalamic hormone (TRH) that stimulates the pituitary to release thyroid stimulating hormone (TSH), which in turn activates the thyroid.

When TRH stimulates the pituitary, the level of TSH in the blood rises by a discrete amount. In depression, however, the rise in TSH after TRH administration is blunted or subnormal. A blunted TRH test usually indicates that the thyroid gland is hyperactive; in response, pituitary functioning is turned down in an attempt to bring thyroid hormone concentrations back into the normal range. Thyroid hormone levels are not actually increased in depression, but the pituitary acts as if they were. It is as if the hypothalamic-pituitary-thyroid axis were attempting to reset itself in the direction of hyperactivity but could not quite bring thyroid hormone levels into an abnormal range.

About one-third of depressed patients (not necessarily the same ones who have abnormal DSTs) have an abnormal TRH test. Like the dexamethasone test, the specificity of the thyroid test is around 90 percent; in other words, only 10 percent of otherwise healthy people who show these abnormal results are *not* depressed. Interestingly, these results are seen in some individuals who are not depressed themselves but have family histories of depression.

Since the thyroid plays an important role in making energy available to deal with stress, overactivation of both the adrenal and thyroid systems suggests that depressive physiology involves *mobilization for danger.* Furthermore, the immune response, as measured by the activity of blood cells (lymphocytes) that attack foreign invaders, is inhibited in depression, as it is in states of grief and helplessness (a topic we will return to in Part IV). All of these changes suggest that the body has shifted its orientation away from conserving energy, as it does in safer and more quiescent periods, toward overutilizing its reserves, as if to meet some severe threat. The fact that the danger exists only in the depressed person's mind does not make the physiology any less potent.

BIOLOGICAL TEST DECEPTIONS

Not long after the first psychiatric reports of the DST, psychiatrists began to order the test routinely to screen for depression. Unfortunately, the justification for this approach was more emotional than scientific. For patients, a laboratory test for depression would legitimize as a "chemical imbalance" a problem that before was considered to be a personal failing. Physicians in general practice would have a way to quantify subtle and complex emotional problems in the same manner that they could measure diabetes and infections. And psychiatrists, long the outcasts of the medical profession because of their intangible diseases and treatments, would finally have a test—just like those used by other doctors—that proved they were "real" doctors.

These hopes for the DST were understandable but deceptive. A few cases of depression can be successfully identified when the DST is used in patients with ambiguous symptoms; but when it is used to screen for depression in the same way in which a blood sugar level might be used to screen for diabetes, all that usually happens is that the psychiatrist appears scientific and the laboratory makes money! Statistical realities make it very unlikely that tests such as the DST will ever be useful as screening devices for depression.

Consider a random sample of one hundred people. The greatest number that can be expected to be depressed at any one time is about five to ten (the highest reported prevalence of depression in the general population at any point in time); at most, 50 percent, or five, of these individuals will have an abnormal DST. If just another five of the hundred being tested have one of the other numerous physical conditions that can produce DST nonsuppression, or if they are slower to absorb dexamethasone or faster to metabolize it, the same number of nondepressed as depressed people will have a positive DST. Half of the ten abnormal tests would be due to depression—but *which* half? There would be as many people with a positive test who had some condition other than depression as there would be people with a positive test who were depressed! And there would be no way to determine by the laboratory test how many of the ninety suppressors were depressed and how many were not.

Even when used to clarify the diagnosis in people who are already depressed, the DST has limitations. Pregnancy, alcohol, many medications, severe stress, even being in the hospital can produce DST nonsuppression. To make matters worse, 5 percent of nondepressed healthy individuals have a positive DST (probably because of variations in dexamethasone metabolism). Furthermore, the value of a positive DST in people who are clearly depressed is limited, since it does not predict whether a biological treatment is more or less likely to be helpful.

Does this mean that the DST should be consigned to the dustbin of medical history? Not necessarily. In depressed people who happen to be nonsuppressors in the first place, if nonsuppression continues after the patient responds to treatment (like the woman described earlier in this chapter), it means there is a greater risk (although not a certainty) that depression will return if the treatment is discontinued. A very high cortisol level following administration of dexamethasone to a patient known to be depressed increases the likelihood that psychotic symptoms are present. And there are always those times when a positive DST convinces a patient or a physician to consider the biological as well as the psychological side of depression. Hopefully, this application of the DST will become antiquated when people no longer need official certification that depression *always* has a physical dimension, whether the laboratory can measure it or not.

Given today's high level of technology, it is not surprising that many other biological tests have been administered to depressed patients, and some of them reveal interesting findings. For example, magnetic resonance imaging (MRI) studies of brain structure demonstrate abnormalities in white matter in older depressed patients with refractory depression and in bipolar patients. While gratifying to the researcher, such tests are not of much use to the practitioner because they are not specific to depression (they are also seen in schizophrenia and a number of other conditions) and cannot be used diagnostically. Since similar white matter abnormalities are seen in cases of hypertension and disorders of blood vessels of the brain, it might be thought that the MRI would be useful to "rule out" possible complicating medical illnesses, but these conditions are more readily identified by a thorough history and physical examination. While laboratory tests are useful in exploring the biological dimension of depression and other mental disorders, they cannot be used clinically to diagnose depression or decide on a treatment.

Considering how biological tests in psychiatry are developed, these limitations are hardly surprising. The validity of a test like the DST is established by determining how often it is positive in people whose diagnoses are already established by a clinical interview. It is therefore impossible for any laboratory test to be better at making a diagnosis than the clinical evaluation to which it is referenced! Another problem with attempts to transfer biological test results from the laboratory directly to the clinic is that the abnormal findings we hear about—whether on a blood test, an EEG, or an MRI—are usually obtained from small numbers of patients and are only abnormal in comparison to a small number of carefully screened normal subjects. In most cases, the power of the test to distinguish between different psychiatric disorders that are directly compared to each other, or to predict response to a given treatment, is not tested.

Such limitations are really no different from the limitations of any medical test. For example, no reasonable clinician would order an EEG to screen for epilepsy on every patient who has ever fainted. Many epileptics have normal EEGs, despite having periodic abnormal brain functioning, and 5 percent of healthy people have abnormal EEGs. This does not mean that the EEG is not useful when the test is used appropriately. It is only when clinicians rely on laboratory results alone to confirm their thinking that they are disappointed when a biological test does not do more than it is designed to do.

The history of biological tests for depression is a history of transition from one kind of deception to another. In the past, biomedical scientists insisted that, because it could not be measured by the available technology, depression was too intangible to be considered a "real" illness. Many mental health specialists agreed with this deception and paid attention only to the mental dimension of depression. Once it became clear that there was an observable physiology of depression, the pendulum swung to the other extreme. Medical aspects of depression came under more intensive study, and many psychiatrists began to shift their allegiance from idealizing their own therapeutic instincts to idealizing laboratory tests. If a patient had a positive biological test result, that patient was depressed, regardless of what symptoms might be present. And by implication, the lack of a positive test result made the mental disorder suspect, just as patients in general medicine with negative test results are considered not to be *really* ill.

Some people suffering from mental disorders, eager to join the ranks of legitimate patienthood, jumped on the biological bandwagon. One leader of a prominent self-help organization, for example, was outraged when a local psychiatric hospital stopped routinely ordering an expensive urine test for depression because it had been shown in replication studies to be unreliable. "Even if the test is no good," he insisted, "we should go on performing it, because we need it to show that our illnesses are deserving of respect." The test had become more than a test for depression; it had become a test of the legitimacy of the illness—and of the patient.

Like all absolute statements in medicine, the all-or-nothing belief in the power of the test tube to reveal "truth" is deceptive. Biological tests are a window into *some* of the *possible* bodily dimensions of depression; they are not the doorway into the entire "house" of depression. If we expect more from the current state of knowledge than a pointer in the right direction, we can only be deceived.

Although biological tests have not revolutionized clinical diagnosis and treatment, they have provided important information. As we have seen, one common finding in biological studies of depression is that the body behaves as though it were preparing itself for some terrible threat, which the mind is deceived into believing is impossible to overcome. Some fundamental shift in the way in which the brain orients the mind and body toward the challenges of life has resulted in arousal that is at the same time excessive and ineffective. To understand how this awesome deception takes place, it is necessary to understand a little about the functions of the brain that are likely to be involved.

12

How the Brain Deceives
the Mind

JERRY HAS NO appetite, and he cannot sleep through the night. Even on those few occasions when he sleeps for fourteen hours, he feels fatigued. He seems to be in a constant state of tension, completely unable to calm himself down. Even the mundane challenge of asking his boss for a raise, which was promised but not implemented due to an administrative oversight, seems unbearably threatening. In regard to this, and many other aspects of his daily life, Jerry knows what he has to do, but he cannot muster the sense of purpose to do it.

The first time Jerry got depressed, it surfaced after his father's death and took about a year to resolve. This time, his depression does not have an obvious cause and after two years nothing has changed. What has happened to Jerry? Why is this depression so inexplicable and so deeply entrenched? This chapter explores the roots of depression in the tissues of the body.

VIEWS FROM THE PAST

Theories that link a disordered mind to a malfunctioning brain have been in existence for as long as people have been attempting to understand mental problems. As early as the fourth century B.C., Hippocrates wrote that mood depends on a balance between the four "bodily humours"—blood, phlegm, yellow bile, and black bile. He proposed that the brains of depressed people were excessively influenced by black bile, which was thought to be secreted by the spleen. Since the spleen occupied a position in the body analogous to the position of Saturn in the heavens, it was believed that those born under the sign of Saturn were prone to depression. These ideas are the basis of references to bad-tempered or morose people as being "full of spleen," "saturnine," "bilious," or "phlegmatic."

The conviction that there must be some inborn physiological alteration to explain the pervasive shift of perception and mood that occurs in depression has persevered over the centuries. For example, Eugen Bleuler observed that "many affective disturbances come, as it were, from within, from the physiology of the brain and the general chemism." Herman Boerhaave, a prominent Dutch physician of the eighteenth century, argued that depression was caused by "nervous and melancholy juices." Nineteenth-century American psychologist and philosopher William James thought that changes in mood must be accompanied by some form of "chemical action," although he admitted that "little is known of its exact nature."

James also pointed out that the subjective, unobservable experiences that are collectively called *thinking* and *feeling* are a function of the brain, just as seeing is a function of the eyes and walking is a function of the legs. Until recently, much more was known about how the eyes and legs work than about the intricacies of the deeper regions of the brain, making it easier to appreciate the connection between experience and physiology in ophthalmology and neurology than in psychiatry. Now, however, technological advances have made it possible to observe how depression affects the "humours" and "melancholy juices" of the twentieth century—what we now call *neurotransmitters, receptors,* and *intracellular messengers.*

THE BRAIN, THE MIND, AND THE EMOTIONS

Reason, memory, emotion, fantasy—the most complicated and intangible of mental functions—are as deeply ingrained in human biology as the pumping of the heart or the contraction of the muscles, for the simple reason that they are equally important components of adaptation. Memory makes it possible to compare present to past situations and anticipate dangers; emotion motivates a response; fantasy facilitates imagining the consequences of one or another course of action; and reason provides the best way to handle the myriad of threats that are encountered in life.

The ability to respond to a threat is a biological necessity. But what determines whether a stimulus is registered as threatening? When perceptual and cognitive circuits in the cerebral cortex process new information, they compare it with previous experiences via their connections to memory systems deep in the brain. Any stimulus that resembles an experience already labeled as threatening, as well as anything that is difficult to recognize and categorize, is initially registered as a threat by the brain. The awareness of danger can arise from an external perception, such as a car turning suddenly in one's path; it may come from within, in the form of an uncomfortable memory or a "forbidden" idea; or it may stem from unprovoked hyperactivity of stress-response systems in the brain.

Emotion is the "fuel" that can activate the mind and body in two major directions: *arousal* or *withdrawal*. Feelings of anticipation, excitement, enthusiasm, fear, or anger arouse us to meet a challenge, whereas weariness, sadness, discouragement, and related feelings cause us to withdraw to conserve energy and replenish inner resources. The neurological seat of emotions is the *limbic system,* a collection of interrelated regions deep in the brain. Limbic connections with the prefrontal cortex, the area of complex intellectual operations, provide pathways by which thoughts influence emotions, and vice versa. Additional limbic connections with the hypothalamus (which regulates hormones, biological rhythms, and the autonomic nervous system) permit emotional states to have a direct impact on bodily activity.

All of these connections are bidirectional. For example, the *perception* of danger in the frontal lobe evokes *emotions* of fear or anger, which motivate *behaviors* of fight or flight, which in turn fuel *mental attitudes* of attack or withdrawal. The impact of these emotions on the hypothalamus is to increase the secretion of stress hormones such as the catecholamines, and to shift biological rhythms in the direction of activation rather than quiescence. Conversely, spontaneous hyperactivity of the limbic system, as occurs in some kinds of epilepsy, induces fear and anxious expectation, as does an infusion of catecholamines.

SENSE OF SELF

Emerging from this ineffable blending of core bodily processes, emotions, and thoughts is the central organizer of mental experience: the sense of self. An invisible "web" of perceptions, feelings, and cognitions defines the boundaries of each individual, providing interconnection, cohesion, and purpose to all mental processes. A positive sense of self generates confidence that any situation can be handled, if not physically then at least mentally. In turn, this general sense of control generates psychological states of comfort, pleasure, security, enthusiasm, well-being, and biologically balanced states of alertness and moderate arousal (to seek further positive stimulation and ward off negative influences). In contrast, a negative sense of self generates psychological states of insecurity, fear, despair, and biological states of hypervigilance and chronic arousal that do not diminish in the absence of stress.

The psychology of the self is linked to the neurobiology of deep regions in the brain, which have far-ranging functions: they control motivational states, emotions, appetite, and rhythms of physical and mental activity (including sleeping and waking) and can be thought of as forming a matrix of background activity in which more specific functions are embedded (see Figure 12–1). This matrix sets the overall tone of the many circuits that interact with it, much as the contrast setting in a television determines the range of more specific tuning functions, such as brightness and focus. The interaction of these deep cerebral systems with each other and with higher cortical regions determines the degree to which a stimulus (whether from inside or outside the self) arouses brain and body, whether the emotional tone of arousal is positive or negative, whether movement will be toward or away from the stimulus, and whether that movement will be executed in a smooth or a disorganized manner.

Motivational states (such as interest, excitement, aggression, or despair) tend to be cohesive and dependable because transitions between them are regulated by homeostatic mechanisms within single neurons and within connections between neurons. When these regulatory processes break down, one mind-body state may be evoked by a stimulus that should lead to a different state, and one state may be replaced unpredictably by another that has no adaptive relationship to it. For example, a challenge that should evoke interest, excitement, and mild activation of the stress–response system may instead produce paralyzing anxiety or incapacitating withdrawal. Since the neuronal systems that underlie mind-body states are collections of individual neurons, the mental deception of depression ultimately depends on derailments of the regulation of the neuron.

INTRODUCING, THE NEURON

Each system of the brain is comprised of a collection of neurons. There are more than 100 *billion* neurons in the brain, each one of which interacts with 1,000–3,000 other neurons, making for more connections between neurons than there are stars in the galaxy! Although each of us is born with all the neurons we will ever have, the newborn's brain is only one-quarter the size of the adult's. The brain grows in size as new connections (synapses) form and the neurons themselves get bigger.

The activity of growing some connections between neurons while dis-

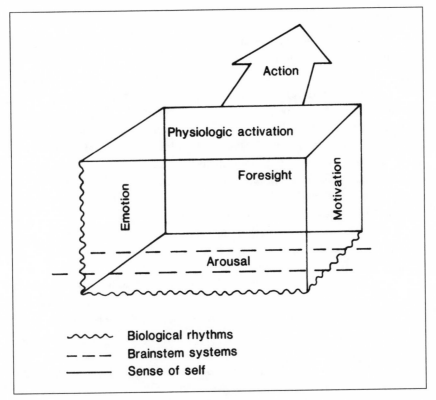

Figure 12-1.
Neurobiological systems supporting
adaptation to challenge

carding others depends on information coming into the brain *as it develops.* As a result, a brain that develops in an environment rich in information will have more neuronal connections than one that develops in an unstimulating environment. There is an evolutionary reason for this: the fact that brain development is partly dependent on the environment makes it possible for the brain to adjust to the world in which it finds itself. "Head Start" programs are designed to enrich sensory and intellectual input in order to counteract the effects of environmental deprivation on brain growth in disadvantaged children.

Neurons are organized into complex systems that process information along a host of pathways more sophisticated than the most high powered computer. To begin to make sense of the complexities of the function of these systems in depression, we will examine (1) the activity of individual neurons, (2) the combined action of groups of neurons, and finally, (3) the regulation of information transfer among neurons.

Life as a Neuron

A neuron or nerve cell consists of a cell body (or "soma") and two kinds of extensions that connect to other neurons: *axons,* which transmit messages to neighboring neurons, and *dendrites,* which receive messages (Figure 12-2). Each neuron is a kind of living factory that generates electrical energy to transmit information. This transmission is not characterized by the kind of stable outflow of electrical energy that comes from a discharging battery but rather is the product of endless cycles of buildup and release—something like a telegraph key that sends continually changing messages through brief on-off signals. Varying the frequency and location of the "Morse code" of neuronal signaling makes it possible for brain centers that mediate motivation, emotion, thinking, hypothalamic function, and other states involved in mood disorders to coordinate their activities with each other.

Neurons generate their minute electrical currents by producing flows ("fluxes") of electrically charged elements called *ions,* analogous to the way a dam generates electricity when water flows over its spillway. Just as water must be raised to a sufficient height before its energy of movement can be converted to electrical energy, oppositely charged ions must be separated before the natural tendency of positive charges to move toward negative charges provides enough ionic movement to generate a flow of electrical energy. The neuron accomplishes this task by pumping out more positively charged ions than negatively charged ions to the space outside the neuron (the extracellular space). The separation of oppositely charged ions places the neuron at rest, a state called *polarization.*

Opposites Attract

When a neuron receives a signal from another neuron, positive ions outside the neuron are allowed access to the neuron's interior through minute holes in the cell membrane called *ion channels.* Positively charged sodium and calcium ions move from the chemical bath in the extracellular space into the neuron's interior, because ions tend to move toward areas of opposite electrical charge ("opposites attract") and toward areas in which their concentration is lower (forcing sodium and calcium ions out of the neuron during polarization lowers their concentration in the interior). The sudden burst of ionic movement when ion channels are opened depolarizes the neuron (i.e., reverses the negative charge inside the neuron), producing a brief electrical burst of energy called an *action potential,* which activates the neuron to carry out its assigned task. Each segment of the axon is depolarized by the previous segment, causing the action potential to move down the length of the axon until it reaches the end of the neuron, where it causes the release of a chemical signal that activates the next neuron in the chain to depolarize.

If the neuron could not reset itself, the "Morse code" of neuronal infor-

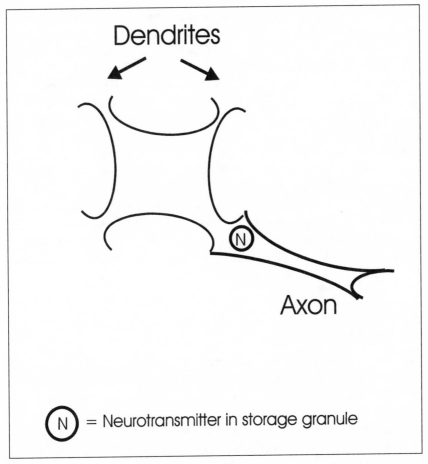

Figure 12-2.
The neuron

mation transfer would contain only one dot. The action potential ends when positive ions are pumped out of the neuron to reestablish the resting predominance of negative charges and thus repolarize the neuron. The cycle of depolarization and repolarization is so rapid that the action potential recurs about 200 times *per second,* permitting very complex modulations of messages to be sent between neurons.

HOW NEURONS INTERACT

The Synapse

Most neurons are not in actual physical contact with each other. Instead, they communicate across a small space called a *synapse,* which consists of a presynaptic (on the sending side) and a postsynaptic (on the receiving side) neuron (Figure 12-3). The synapse between the two neurons makes it possible for the electrochemical mechanisms of each neuron to flow beyond cellular boundaries and influence the thousands of other neurons with which the synapse connects. This highly complex flow of information is possible because the synapse is far more than an association between only two neurons; it is a way station or junction box between *thousands* of presynaptic and postsynaptic neurons.

There are millions of neuronal associations present at birth and formed during early development that are not active until they are "switched on" by appropriate experiences that provide *synchronized stimulation of both sides of the synapse.* Just as *Hermissenda* learns a new skill when a presynaptic neuron that sends a signal about light forms a connection with a postsynaptic neuron that makes the foot contract, people learn new constellations of thoughts and feelings when multiple presynaptic neurons for information input learn to activate multiple postsynaptic neurons for information output.

Neurotransmitters

The electrical energy generated by the neuron is an essential first step in a cascade of reactions that activates other neurons, mobilizing systems in the brain that regulate our emotions and thoughts. The action potential is not strong enough to jump across the synapse, which is just as well. If the action potential were like a spark that could leap to the next neuron down the line, the kind of information it could transmit would be limited to an on/off or yes/no statement.

Instead, connections between neurons are made by means of chemical signals called *neurotransmitters.* While the action potential is a rapid and efficient means of transmitting information *down a single neuron,* neurotransmitters have two important advantages in communicating *between neurons:* First, they can reach more than one postsynaptic neuron at the same time, and second, the impact of different neurotransmitters can converge at one postsynaptic neuron, permitting the integration of highly complex messages.

Neurotransmitters are synthesized (produced) in the neuron, transported down the axon, and stored in specialized storage granules at the end of the axon. During the action potential, calcium ions, entering the neuron from the extracellular space or released from storage sites inside the cell, function as a kind of magnet, drawing the storage granules toward the cell membrane. When the granules touch the end of the neuron, they open up, releasing their contents into the synapse. The neurotransmitter then floats from its "home" in the presynaptic neuron, crossing the biochemical "soup" that

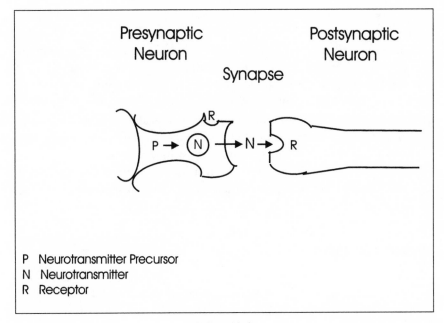

Figure 12-3.
The synapse

bathes the synapse, arriving at the cell on the other side of the synapse, the postsynaptic neuron.

At this point, the neurotransmitter interacts with its receptor in the cell membrane to produce a reaction that either stimulates or inhibits the postsynaptic neuron. Receptors are specialized regions of neurons (both presynaptic and postsynaptic) that carry the neurotransmitter's signal to the neuron. As is true of the action potential, neurotransmitter action must be terminated rapidly so that discrete, variable messages can be sent from one neuron to another. This is accomplished by uptake of the neurotransmitter back into the presynaptic neuron, where it is reinserted into storage granules that can be used for the next round of release. The ebb and flow of neurotransmitters, driven by an endlessly regenerating action potential, create the ever-changing messages of neuronal systems of the mind.

When neurotransmitter research is presented in the media, it is implied that there are only a few crucial neurotransmitters, each acting as a single circuit that produces a single function—much like a light switch connects a wire from a single power source to a single bulb. Although this is far from the truth, when we discuss the actions of neurotransmitters on psychobiological functions, we will address each transmitter system in turn, as if each neurotransmitter did, in fact, work in a separate circuit. This more simplistic approach will facilitate learning about neurotransmitters. We then move beyond this view to understand functions that transcend individual chemical transmitters.

There are perhaps *three hundred* brain substances that act as neurotransmitters, and each one of these has multiple receptors—some as many as twenty. As noted earlier, neurotransmitters and their receptors interact with each other, resulting in billions of associations between neurons. Scientists tell us that certain treatments for depression specifically affect one or another neurotransmitter, but this is only in a test tube. In the human being, anything that acts on one neurotransmitter must inevitably have an impact on the other neurotransmitters with which it interacts. But unless we look at one neurotransmitter at a time, we will not be able to appreciate the overall picture.

Biogenic Amines

Neurotransmitters that are believed to mediate mental and emotional processes can be grouped into several categories. The best known and most thoroughly researched of these are the biogenic (i.e., biologically active) amines, originating in regions deep in the brain and connecting with centers that control the stress response as well as those that mediate emotion and thought. Brain biogenic amines include norepinephrine, serotonin, dopamine, histamine, and acetylcholine. Rather than transmitting a specific message, such as the signal to contract a muscle or to feel an emotion, these neurotransmitters tell neurons *how* to process information by, for example, intensifying or muting the response to danger.

Norepinephrine is a stress-response transmitter that alerts and mobilizes the brain and body. Its function is to decrease spontaneous background firing of neurons in order to make them more responsive to specific stimulation. This shift narrows attention and heightens our alertness to the possibility of a threat, creating a readiness-to-act mode. Automatically we begin searching through memories of past activities for the right behavior in the new or threatening situation, while cardiovascular, hormonal, and metabolic reserves are mobilized. The actions of norepinephrine in activating mind and body are supported by *dopamine,* a transmitter in the brain that regulates the experience of pleasure and the initiation and coordination of mental and physical movement and stimulates the body to interact physically with threatening or novel situations.

From an evolutionary standpoint, *serotonin* is the oldest neurotransmitter (it is also found in primitive organisms, such as the snail). The many connections of serotonin-containing neurons allow this neurotransmitter to be involved in the regulation of numerous basic psychobiological functions, including appetite, sexual interest, sleep, pain perception, bodily rhythms, mood, and thought. Serotonin also appears to play a significant role in the regulation of impulsivity and the unpremeditated kind of aggression that arises abruptly in response to frustration. Serotonin often works in the opposite direction of norepinephrine, transmitting soothing signals of calm and rest that stabilize emotional responses.

A transmitter that modulates behavior in still another way is *acetylcholine,* which mediates behavioral withdrawal and inhibition. Whereas serotonin helps us to calm and organize our mental resources in adaptive ways that allow us to interact with a stressor, acetylcholine provokes us to retreat from it to wait for a time when we have more resources to mobilize. As a neurotransmitter involved in memory, acetylcholine may also play a role in encoding negative perceptions and memories.

Receptors and Second Messengers

Neurotransmitters are too big to actually enter the neuron. Instead, their "messages" are received by receptors on the cell membrane. Receptors are like locks and each neurotransmitter is like a key that can open a particular lock. The locks opened by each key may overlap in some aspects and differ in others. Because the complex interactions between neurons and their neurotransmitters are modulated by receptors, understanding receptors and their signaling mechanisms reveals more about the physiology of mood disorders than the study of individual neurotransmitters.

When a neurotransmitter meets the receptor that best fits it, a change occurs in the shape of the receptor, which brings proteins in the cell membrane into contact with enzymes that attack them, resulting in a chemical reaction. (The most common reaction involves a protein, which is linked to a wide variety of receptors, called the guanine nucleotide binding or G-protein. G-protein contains its own enzyme, which breaks the protein into components that activate further chemical reactions.) These reactions allow compounds attached to the receptor to interact with each other, resulting in the mobilization of a group of ions and small molecules that are collectively referred to as "second messengers" (neurotransmitters are the "first messengers"). Three classes of second messengers have been identified: cyclic adenosine 3'5'-monophosphate (cAMP), which is produced by the action of the enzyme adenyl cyclase on the ubiquitous energy molecule adenosine triphosphate (ATP); a group of breakdown products from a combination of protein and fatty tissue called the phosphatidylinositol (PI) system; and the calcium ion (Ca^{2+}) (Figure 12-4). The purpose of the second messenger is to tell a cell to carry out some specific action. There are too many neurons to count, and perhaps hundreds of transmitters and thousands of receptors, but it takes just a few second messengers to regulate a great diversity of cel-

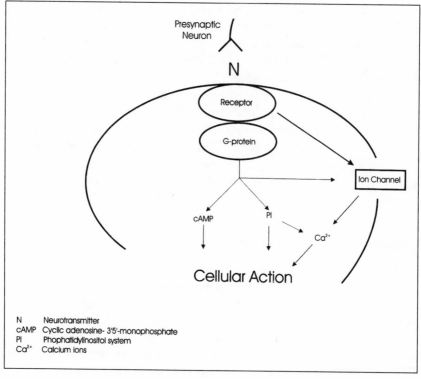

Presynaptic
Neuron

N

Receptor

G-protein

Ion Channel

cAMP   PI

Ca^{2+}

Cellular Action

N	Neurotransmitter
cAMP	Cyclic adenosine- 3'5'-monophosphate
PI	Phophatidylinositol system
Ca^{2+}	Calcium ions

Figure 12-4.
Receptors and second messengers

lular processes, including all of those that drive the systems of the mind. If we think of communications between neurons as analogous to a telephone system, each neuron can dial a variety of numbers to reach its neighbors, and each receiver may be subject to thousands of calls at a time. The cellular switchboard of second messengers integrates this complicated information, producing a unified signal that tells the neuron on the other side of the line what to do.

Interactions among second-messenger systems allow neurons to "summarize" the influence of the many neurotransmitters that act on them and to interpret the net result of activating many different receptors that have contradictory actions. The precise result of these interactions depends on which second messengers are produced by which receptors at which phase of the cell cycle. Each of the second messengers may inhibit, enhance, or modify the effect of the others on the action a neuron takes when it is activated. Cellular reactions stimulated by second messengers stop when the messenger is inactivated by reactions that are set in motion at the time the messenger is turned on.

The Gene Link

Action potentials, neurotransmitters, receptors, and second messengers obey fundamental laws that orchestrate the activities not only of the mind, not only of the brain, but of the entire body. Neurotransmitters are not just localized signals between neurons: they exist elsewhere in the body, where they coordinate activities related to the mental functions that they mediate in the brain.

For example, norepinephrine is the transmitter of alarm. When transmission of norepinephrine is at a high level, our minds prepare for danger. We are vigilant, frightened, angry, ready to attack or run. In the sympathetic nervous system, which connects the brain to the heart, blood vessels, and adrenal glands, norepinephrine makes the heart beat fast, raises blood pressure, and shifts blood flow to organs of action, such as the muscles. In the adrenal gland, norepinephrine is one of the stress hormones that stimulates the heart to pump blood more forcefully as well as faster. A single substance, therefore, communicates the same message throughout the body.

Neurotransmitter molecules have similar actions throughout the body because they use the same second-messenger systems in whatever cell they act. A transmitter tells a neuron to fire itself up by the same means that it tells a blood vessel to squeeze itself shut. These same second-messenger changes, which are stimulated by substances external to the neuron, can alter the type of messenger ribonucleic acid (messenger-RNA) that is produced from DNA, so that *the structure of the neuron is permanently altered.* In other words, second messengers have the potential to induce enduring changes in the structure of systems elsewhere in the body.

THE DEPRESSION CONNECTION

This interconnection among the basic functions of all cells means that a change in one of these functions can reverberate throughout the body. What does all this have to do with depression? Depression is accompanied by an increased risk of migraine headaches, hypertension, heart disease, and possibly cancer. Are these separate illnesses that all happen to cluster in the same person because of some sweeping genetic susceptibility? Possibly, although this seems like quite a reach. A more cogent explanation is that the same malfunction in cellular signaling, which in the brain alters the regulation of mood, in small arteries causes excessive contraction that elevates blood pressure. Excessive activity of a type of blood cell called the platelet, which plays an integral role in regulating blood vessel tone, could lead to inordinate contraction followed by overcompensatory dilatation, producing migraine headaches. Overactive adrenal function in depression may be a kind of stress response, or it could be the result of a hyperactive second-messenger signal in the part of the brain that tells the pituitary how much cortisol is needed. In white blood cells, the same disruption of normal signaling could impair those cells' ability to fight infection and cancer. Signals within cells, therefore, may be one of the forces that literally unifies mind and body.

Disruption of Synaptic Homeostasis

So far, we have discussed the synapse as a one-way flow of communication between neurons, in which the presynaptic neuron tells the postsynaptic neuron what to do. In reality, communication between these two neurons is *bidirectional:* the postsynaptic neuron "talks back" to the presynaptic neuron, telling it that the message has been received, so that the presynaptic neuron can stop signaling. Just as the presynaptic neuron communicates with neurotransmitters, the postsynaptic neuron releases a chemical substance that diffuses back to the receptors on the presynaptic neuron. (The best studied of these is nitric oxide, a gas released by neurons that dissolves readily in the surrounding fluid.) At the same time, neurotransmitters released by the presynaptic neuron float not only toward postsynaptic receptors but also back to receptors on their home base, the presynaptic neuron. These particular receptors, called *autoreceptors,* tell the presynaptic neuron that it has made enough neurotransmitter and can cut back on its activity. Both kinds of feedback ensure that the amount of transmitter—and therefore the flow of information—does not escalate out of control.

These regulatory processes are part of a general tendency of all biological systems to maintain *homeostasis* or stability. Neurons have many other homeostatic mechanisms, all of which serve to stabilize synaptic communication. One of the more enduring of these mechanisms involves resetting the number and sensitivity of receptors on both sides of the synapse, so that the overall transfer of information remains constant. Receptors are continually broken down and regenerated in response to ever-changing needs—like sand castles on a beach that are repeatedly washed away and rebuilt, depending on the weather, the tides, and the energy of small children. The capacity of receptors to regenerate themselves is no different from the ability of bone marrow to make new blood cells to replace old ones, or of skin to shed its superficial level of cells as replacement cells become available.

Receptors, like every other component of the body, are constructed in accordance with a blueprint set by DNA. But as we saw in Chapter 4, instructions to the neuron from that blueprint (which are transmitted by messenger-RNA) can be altered by neurotransmitters, an action that is mediated by second messengers. As neurons in the synapse signal each other at a constant rate, second messengers (resulting from these signals) produce new generations of receptors, ion channels, and other structures that regulate neuronal activity and that are constructed in response to the level of activity that has been present over time. In this way, a temporary state of the synapse can become enduring.

What clinical implications derive from the capacity of this two-way communication in the synapse to induce more or less permanent changes in neuronal structure and function? If the synapses that mediate mood have been normal for long periods of time, an acute stress that attempts to perturb synaptic activity will be countered by homeostatic mechanisms that reset neuronal communication back to the baseline state. In other words, people who have not been depressed tend not to become depressed, and when they do, the depression is easy to treat.

Loss of a loved one, for example, will trigger a state of arousal driven by increased norepinephrine activity, among other things. If the "default setting" of the synapses is normal, however, restitutive processes will diminish the arousal and the accompanying acute emotional state. In physiological terms, the postsynaptic neuron responds to rising norepinephrine levels by reducing the number of norepinephrine receptors as well as their responsivity to the neurotransmitter. At the same time, autoreceptors signal the presynaptic neuron to reduce norepinephrine release. The overall level of arousal is skewed only temporarily. The person experiencing the loss will feel grief, but other things being equal, the response will not degenerate into depression. Or, if depression does occur, once it is resolved, the synapses will return to their baseline healthy state.

However, in people who have been chronically or recurrently depressed, the synapses involved in emotional regulation have spent so much time in an aberrant state that this is now *their* default state, and homeostatic mechanisms resist attempts to move them to normal levels of activity. We have already seen that, even when it improves with treatment, depression that has been chronic or recurrent returns as soon as the treatment is withdrawn, presumably because synapses reset themselves to their baseline *abnormal* settings. In fact, synapses that function abnormally at baseline may work so hard at overcoming treatments that attempt to normalize them that their setting rebounds when the treatment is removed—much as a jack-in-the-box springs up when the lid holding it down is released—leading to a worsening, rather than just a return, of symptoms.

Learning through Kindling

Neurons learn to change their level of activity in many ways. One important mechanism is called *kindling* because it involves progressive increases in electrical excitability in response to less and less stimulation. The brain learns to treat something as important enough to pay attention to not only because it is overwhelmingly intense but also because it occurs at the right frequency. Because the process of kindling has been used to explain important clinical phenomena, we should know a little more about it.

Although its action is inferred in humans, kindling has only been studied in animals, especially primates. In a typical kindling experiment, a region of the brain (the limbic system seems most susceptible) is briefly but repeatedly exposed to a stimulus that makes the neurons in that region discharge (i.e., depolarize). The usual kindling stimulus is a very small electrical current or a chemical (cocaine is the most potent example) that activates neurons. The stimulus is applied directly to a targeted area of the brain through a tiny incision that has no effect on brain function. The amount of electricity or chemical administered is too small and the duration of stimulation too brief to directly affect anything other than the tiny collection of targeted neurons. The activity of neurons in the area to which the stimulus is applied, as well as elsewhere in the brain, is measured with an EEG.

The first time the stimulus is applied, it provokes local depolarization of neurons by altering neurotransmitter release or the permeability of the cell membrane to positive ions. The next time the stimulus is reapplied, the same process occurs. But after several exposures to the stimulus, something unexpected happens: the neuronal response to each stimulation begins to increase. The small depolarization that occurred initially is replaced by a larger and larger discharge of more and more neurons. If the experiment is continued, the depolarization spreads to neurons adjacent to those being stimulated and eventually to more distant sites. In addition, progressively less stimulation is needed to provoke a greater response, until finally neurons begin to discharge on their own, without any stimulation at all. Increased responsiveness to existing stimuli, as well as spontaneous discharge of large groups of neurons, continues for a long time—sometimes indefinitely—even if the stimulus is never reapplied. Kindling is more likely to have a permanent effect if it occurs early in life and if it involves multiple exposures to the kindling stimulus. However, the kindling response can occur at any time and in response to only a single intense stimulus.

Obviously, kindling experiments like these would never be applied to people. However, certain clinical situations appear to be manifestations of kindling. One such situation is posttraumatic epilepsy, a condition in which seizures develop years after a head injury. One explanation for the delayed onset of seizures is that the scar tissue in the region of the brain that was injured generates a small but abnormal electrical current that repeatedly stimulates neighboring neurons. Over time, repeated applications of this minute stimulation kindles increasing excitability into adjacent neurons. Once these neurons become hyperactive, they kindle their neighbors, until a large group of neurons begins to depolarize all at once, leading to the massive outflow of excitation that produces a seizure.

Researcher Robert Post has speculated that the physiology of abnormal mood may act as a stimulus that kindles overstimulation in the emotional centers of the brain (but does not spread to other areas that would produce seizures). Supporting this possibility is the observation that early episodes of mania and depression are usually precipitated by an observable stressor such as a loss, separation (e.g., going away to school), or some kind of uncontrollable circumstance. As time passes, depressive and manic episodes can be provoked by increasingly minor sources of stress, as if the brain were learning to function more and more abnormally with less and less provocation. Eventually, abnormal moods are less likely to be caused by loss than they are to cause loss—as fewer people are able to tolerate the depressed or manic person. The progression of mania from mildly euphoric levels to more complex and treatment-resistant states is reminiscent of the progression that occurs in kindling, when less and less stimulation is needed to produce more intense, generalized, and spontaneous abnormalities of neuronal function.

It has been observed that bipolar people often have several widely spaced episodes of depression before they become manic. After their first manic episode, however, they have more severe mania and more rapid recurrences of depression. This phenomenon could indicate that mania is a "better" kindling stimulus than depression. If so, inadvertently inducing mania in a patient by erroneously prescribing antidepressants could worsen the long-term course of a bipolar mood disorder—and, conversely, avoiding mania may be crucial to gaining better control of the mood disorder.

Kindling and life experience can interact in ways that imprint abnormal moods into the personality as well as the brain. For example, repeated experiences with helplessness or loss may kindle the pathophysiology of depression into key synapses. As mood centers in the brain slip into this abnormal state more readily, new mental frameworks arise that deceive the mind into a pervasively negative outlook. As subsequent challenges are handled with less and less effectiveness, the brain is exposed to more of the very experiences that kindle persistently abnormal moods. In the next chapter, we will examine the changes wrought in the synapses as a result of kindling and how these changes can be repaired.

13

How the Body Deceives the Mind

WHEN DOCTORS TELL depressed patients, "You have a chemical deficiency," they are restating the first biochemical hypothesis about the cause of depression: that activity of the neurotransmitter norepinephrine is too low in depressed people. This idea was originally proposed when it was noted that the first medications introduced as antidepressants blocked the reuptake of norepinephrine after it is released into the synapse, thereby prolonging its action. Investigators reasoned that, since antidepressants seemed to increase norepinephrine activity, this neurotransmitter must be low in people with depression, accounting for the inability of depressed people to mobilize themselves.

This hypothesis seemed to be supported by observations that substances that deplete norepinephrine in the brain (the antihypertensive medicine reserpine is a common example) worsen depression and bring on new depressive episodes in people who are susceptible to becoming depressed in the first place (but not those who are not subject to spontaneous depression). It seemed equally reasonable to suppose that the excess activation of mania must be due to too much norepinephrine, especially since L–dopa, a drug used to treat Parkinson's disease that elevates dopamine and norepinephrine activity, can induce mania.

One additional source of support for the "too little-depression/too much-mania" hypothesis came from the learned helplessness experiments (described in Chapter 10). Biochemical studies showed that norepinephrine is depleted during the early phases of learned helplessness. Artificially reducing norepinephrine further worsens the learned helplessness, whereas increasing the levels of neurotransmitter prevents learned helplessness from developing. When an animal that has been exposed to an inescapable stress becomes familiar with the situation and stops acting helpless, breakdown of norepinephrine slows down and synthesis speeds up, reestablishing amounts at the synapse at the usual operating levels. Such findings, which were summarized in a 1985 article by J.A. Jesberger and J.S. Richardson, suggest that loss of norepinephrine reduces the organism's ability to mobilize a stress response, and that restoration of the neurotransmitter resets the stress-response system.

Separation Depression

Another model of depression was demonstrated by experiments with infant monkeys who develop depression when they are separated from their mothers (described in detail in Chapter 17). Like learned helplessness, animal separation depression is accompanied by diminished brain levels of norepinephrine, with the lowest levels occurring in animals with the greatest behavioral signs of despair. And like learned helplessness, separation depression is *aggravated* by substances that *deplete* norepinephrine. In these experiments, loss of an important attachment appears to lead to loss of an important neurotransmitter in the brain. Once these circuits stop functioning normally, it becomes more and more difficult to activate mind and body.

Serotonin Deficiencies

For a while it was thought that levels in the urine and spinal fluid of MHPG (3-methoxy-4-hydroxy-phenylglycol), a norepinephrine metabolite, were decreased in depression, especially in bipolar depression. However, the results were so influenced by activity and diet that they were difficult to interpret. As further research on norepinephrine activity in depression proved even more contradictory, researchers began to examine other neurotransmitter systems.

Investigations of serotonin in depression seemed much more promising. A variety of measures of serotonin activity in the blood and spinal fluid have consistently been found to be lower in depressed than in nondepressed people. Depression seems to be more severe, with a greater risk of suicide, if spinal fluid levels of 5-HIAA (5-hydroxyindolacetic acid), an important serotonin metabolite, are low. Autopsies on the brains of depressed people who have died of various causes, including suicide, have shown fewer receptors for serotonin, possibly suggesting that there was less serotonin in their systems.

Serotonin mediates calm states that are the antithesis of depressive over-stimulation and repressed rage. It is also involved in the regulation of arousal, appetitive functions, aggression, and biological rhythms. As a result, some investigators have modified the "too little/too much" norepinephrine hypothesis to read that loss of serotonin regulation contributes to inability to calm oneself, excessive aggression (including aggression directed toward the self), disturbed appetites for food, sex, and life in general, and disruption of biological rhythms. When norepinephrine function is also lost, the energizing response that depends on this transmitter is lost and withdrawal and depression predominate. Excesses of norepinephrine, on the other hand, were proposed to cause the random hyperactivity of mania.

Back to the Drawing Board

Even with serotonin thrown in for good luck, the hypothesis that too little norepinephrine equals depression and too much norepinephrine equals mania turns out to be a deception. For one thing, most research has measured levels of neurotransmitter metabolites in the blood, which, to a significant extent, reflect neurotransmitter activity *outside the brain*. Cerebrospinal fluid levels come a little closer to reflecting changes in the brain, but they still are not a measure of the precise regulation of tiny neurotransmitter concentrations in the brain's synapses. Research (such as the autopsy studies) showing decreased numbers of neurotransmitter receptors or uptake pump molecules could be interpreted as evidence of insufficient neurotransmitter activity, but such a conclusion is not inevitable. An equally plausible explanation is that neurotransmitter levels have increased and that their receptors have turned themselves *down* to compensate for the change.

The problem with neurotransmitter theories is not just that the data can be interpreted in different ways: the data themselves can come out differently at different times. For example, norepinephrine activity has been found to be *elevated,* not reduced, in depression, especially when anxiety is also present. Since norepinephrine is necessary for arousal and behavioral activation, elevated norepinephrine activity would be consistent with other biological findings indicating a hyperactive stress response in depression. DST non-suppression, hyperactivity of the thyroid axis, and phase advances of biological rhythms, for example, indicate that stress–response systems are turning themselves up to meet extreme stress; it is only behavior that is shut down.

It is also misleading to conclude that, because antidepressants increase synaptic levels of norepinephrine, the problem in depression is *not enough* norepinephrine in the synapse. This line of thinking is like saying that, because aspirin can cause gastrointestinal bleeding, the cause of headaches is too much blood in the intestinal tract! Some effective antidepressants influence serotonin but not norepinephrine, some act only on dopamine, and a few have no known effect on any neurotransmitter. There are also many substances that increase brain norepinephrine levels but are of no use in depression.

Yet another complication in understanding the effect of antidepressants on norepinephrine (and other neurotransmitters) is that, although the increase in the synapse is immediate, the person taking the antidepressant feels no therapeutic effect for several weeks. When an antidepressant increases synaptic levels of norepinephrine, it activates the sympathetic nervous system, producing side effects such as jitteriness, insomnia, or sweating. Any therapeutic result of norepinephrine probably results from a decrease, or at least stabilization, of this transmitter system, bringing arousal down to controllable levels, thereby facilitating, rather than paralyzing, effective action.

Research identifying elevated levels of norepinephrine in depression, should not be interpreted simplistically either. The results of norepinephrine research have probably been contradictory because blood and cerebrospinal fluid levels of norepinephrine metabolites in depression are neither consistently high nor low, but *sometimes* shoot up too high and *sometimes* fall too low. Mild stresses provoke excessive bursts of the transmitter, while inadequate rises occur in response to meaningful stresses. It is as if the norepinephrine "thermostat" has lost its capacity to remain at the right setting. It runs too hot when the extra heat is not needed, and when more heat *is* required, it cannot muster enough power. Rather than enforcing a unitary effect toward higher *or* lower neurotransmitter levels, antidepressants may be more likely to return the thermostat to its correct setting, bringing neurotransmitter activity back from wild oscillations into line with normal physiological variation.

The evidence supporting deficient levels of serotonin in depression seems a little more solid; the only catch is that this deficiency is probably not specific to depression. Only about 40 percent of depressed people have biochemical evidence of low serotonin function, and those with evidence of a central serotonin deficiency are mainly people who are suicidal, especially if suicide attempts have been violent (for example, by hanging or shooting). This finding is not even specific to suicide. It is correlated with any form of impulsive aggression, whether it is directed inwardly in the form of suicide or outwardly in the form of unpredictable assaultiveness. Evidence of low serotonin activity has been found in suicidal people with any diagnosis, impulsive firesetters, violent felons, and other people who are in poor control of their impulses—but *not* in people who engage in *premeditated* violent or antisocial behavior. Similarly, interference with serotonin metabolism in animals leads to aggression and hyperarousal more frequently than behavioral depression. This is because serotonin helps to regulate the sudden, unexpected outbursts of aggression that can arise in response to minor frustration or distress.

We have already seen that serotonin also participates in the regulation of many other functions of the mind and body, such as appetite, sleep, biological rhythms, thought processes, and mood. These functions are abnormal in depression, and medications that act on serotonin levels have antidepressant properties. But the same functions may also be abnormal in conditions as varied as anxiety disorders, schizophrenia, bulimia, obsessive-compulsive disorder, and personality disorders, to name a few, and medications acting on the same neurotransmitter may be useful for all of these conditions. Therefore, while serotonin-related malfunctions may be an important component of mood disorders, they are not the only component in these conditions, and they are not limited to mood disorders.

The major conceptual problem with single neurotransmitter theories of depression is that all of the neurotransmitters implicated in depression interact with each other, many with overlapping functions, so that an isolated change in one or two neurotransmitters seems most unlikely. Furthermore, a single neurotransmitter has more than one effect, depending on which of its receptors are activated and how its receptors interact with receptors for other neurotransmitters. Most important, neurotransmitters mediate psychobiological *functions,* not diagnoses. Since a syndrome like depression consists of a collection of functions, many of them overlapping, studies of the relationships between neurotransmitter systems may define specific disorders better than studies of single neurotransmitters. A few studies using this approach suggest that depression is associated with the loss of normal interaction among norepinephrine, serotonin, and dopamine metabolites. No predictable change in any one transmitter occurs in response to treatment, but there is a greater concordance among levels of all three. This kind of work indicates that depression is the result of a disorder in the overall cohesiveness of systems involved in responding to danger and that the cohesiveness and coordination among systems is increased by treatment.

RECEPTOR CHANGES IN DEPRESSION

When researchers realized that the increase in synaptic concentrations of neurotransmitters produced by antidepressants occurred far sooner than the person experienced any therapeutic benefit, a search began to identify those biochemical changes that correspond with the onset of the antidepressant effect. It was found that after about a month—the time it usually takes for an antidepressant to begin working—neurons reduce the number ("down-regulation") and sensitivity (desensitization) of some norepinephrine and serotonin receptors. In other words, the *receptor effect* of antidepressants could be more therapeutically relevant than the *neurotransmitter effect,* especially since the specific message of any neurotransmitter depends on which receptor receives it.

Suicide Studies

One strategy for examining receptor changes in depression is to study receptors in the brains of depressed people who have died of suicide or other causes. In one study, autopsies revealed that the brains of suicide patients showed increases in one type of norepinephrine receptor (the beta receptor), one type of serotonin receptor (the $5HT_2$ receptor), or both, compared with brains of people who did not die of suicide. These receptor changes may have occurred to compensate for decreased levels of norepinephrine and/or serotonin in depression, or they may have been primary alterations with repercussions of their own. In addition, the receptor changes may have been linked to nonspecific factors associated with suicide rather than being specific to depression (in which case they would be found in anyone who died of suicide, not just depressed suicides). Still another possibility: they may have been a function of anxiety, which may be more prominent in suicidal depressed patients. All in all, there is no justification for comfortable conclusions at this point—only possibilities and speculations.

Autoreceptor Malfunctions

The advent of new imaging technologies, such as positron emission tomography (PET), which make it possible to visualize receptors in the living brain, may one day revolutionize the study of the receptors involved in depression. However, PET research has not yet involved visualization of most of the receptors thought to be affected in depression. Most relevant receptor research in living people has involved administering drugs that stimulate specific receptors and then measuring biochemical changes that are thought to be related to the actions of those receptors.

One set of experiments has used drugs that either block (yohimbine) or stimulate (clonidine) the autoreceptor for norepinephrine, located on the presynaptic neuron, a receptor that normally shuts down norepinephrine release when concentrations reach sufficient levels in the synapse. In depressed subjects, this particular autoreceptor seems to be underresponsive to *both* procedures: to stimulation by clonidine and inhibition by yohimbine. This finding suggests that the autoreceptor's capacity to provide appropriate feedback control of norepinephrine in the synapse has been impaired. Loss of the regulatory function of the autoreceptor could contribute to erratic, excessive release followed by inappropriate shutdown in response to normal challenges.

Receptors on Strike

Another method of studying receptors in depressed people is to examine cells that are easily obtained from the blood, such as lymphocyte cells. Such cells may not reflect exactly what is going on in the brain, but if they reflect generalized processes, or if they respond to signals from the brain as they circulate through it, changes in blood cells may be valid markers of changes in the central nervous system. Examination of the lymphocyte, a type of white blood cell, has revealed that a type of norepinephrine receptor (the beta, and possibly an alpha, receptor) turns itself down in depression. It is possible that hyperactivity of norepinephrine-driven stress-response systems in depression overstimulates these receptors, causing them to decrease their numbers in an attempt to maintain homeostasis. The finding that antidepressants further down-regulate beta receptors does not necessarily contradict the receptor changes noted in depression. Antidepressants turn down the stress response as they exert their therapeutic effect; one mechanism by which this might be accomplished is the reduction of receptor responsiveness to stress hormones. Perhaps the antidepressant facilitates the body's attempt to compensate for excessive activation of norepinephrine systems.

The interpretation of the fairly consistent finding that a specific serotonin receptor ($5HT_2$) is underactive in platelets of depressed patients is less obvious. One possibility is that this receptor, which mediates states such as depressed mood, anxiety, and disordered thinking, is not transmitting enough information in the depressed brain. Another explanation is that the receptor has been turned down to try to compensate for excessive activity of some other system that is flooding it. Whatever the ultimate reason turns out to be, the main message for consumers of mental health research is that a change in a single neurotransmitter receptor only explains part of the complex syndrome of depression; the overall balance of receptor systems is likely to be more important than a change in any one receptor.

SECOND MESSENGER CHANGES IN DEPRESSION

Norepinephrine and serotonin are not the only neurotransmitter/receptor systems implicated in depression and mania. Activity of dopamine, a neurotransmitter that mediates the initiation and organization of movement and behavior as well as the experience of pleasure, appears to be low in depression and excessive in mania. Hyperactive dopamine transmission (as occurs when amphetamines are administered, for example) can induce both psychosis and mania, and psychotic forms of mania and depression could be associated with hypertrophy of a dopamine subsystem. Hyperactivity of acetylcholine could mediate some of the withdrawal of depression, and inadequate activity of endogenous opioids (endorphins) could be partly responsible for failure to experience pleasure. Hypothalamic hormones like corticotropin-releasing hormone (which helps to regulate cortisol metabolism) and thyrotropin-releasing hormone (which helps to regulate thyroid function) also function in the brain, where they act as *neuromodulators*, altering the responsiveness of receptors to the classical neurotransmitters. Abnormalities of these and other neuromodulators could change receptor responses to a number of neurotransmitters.

It seems unlikely that the activity of all these neurotransmitters and receptors would spontaneously change at the same time in depression, or that medications that improve mood happen to act on different systems in different people. A simpler interpretation is that there is dysfunction in a basic mechanism by which cells *throughout the body* coordinate activity of diverse neurotransmitters and integrate information from their receptors. This dysfunction would have to occur somewhere in the path of cellular information processing, which goes from receptors to key branches of the second messenger system, including our old friend, the calcium ion.

Calcium Ions, Front and Center

Alterations in the calcium ion signal have been demonstrated by my group at the University of Colorado in cases of bipolar disorder. Calcium ions stimulate a host of cellular activities when their concentration is increased in two ways: when they are released from the interior of the cell where they are stored in an inactive state, and when calcium channels open to let the ions into cells from the bloodstream. We initially studied platelets—blood cells responsible for clotting and the constriction of blood vessels—because their function is similar in many ways to that of the neuron, and they arise from the same embryonic tissue as the nervous system. When the platelet is stimulated, calcium ion concentrations rise as a signal to the cell to perform its action—which, in this case, is to aggregate.

At rest, concentrations of free calcium ions within the platelet are elevated in mania; when the platelet is stimulated, the increase in calcium ion signaling that occurs is also hyperactive. Similar changes have been observed in the activity of lymphocytes, possibly in red blood cells, and a type of skin cell. These changes are present during active illness but not when the bipolar patient is well—regardless of the treatment that produces a remission—suggesting that mania is associated with hyperactivity of at least one mechanism involved in regulating cellular function. It is true that the change is in a peripheral cell, but at least the same thing is observed in different kinds of cells.

In a number of studies, the same degree of elevation of free calcium ions that is seen in mania has been found in bipolar but not unipolar depression. This finding has two potential implications. First, in bipolar individuals the same kind of cellular hyperactivity may be present in both manic and depressive states. At first glance, this may seem odd, but it explains a common clinical phenomenon: mania and depression are frequently present *at the same time* (for example, a person experiences depression with racing thoughts or suicidal mania), and when they are distinct states, they can replace each other with lightning speed. How could two biochemically opposite states occur together, unless similar increases in signaling—by calcium or some other cellular messenger—accelerate certain processes and turn others off? Calcium ions can do this because of a unique property: moderate elevations of free calcium ion concentration within cells stimulate cellular activity, while further elevations inhibit the same action. Indeed, the same increase in intracellular calcium ion levels can activate the cell at one point and suppress it at another.

In some studies, elevated calcium second messenger activity has been found in bipolar but not unipolar mood disorders; in the few studies in which the same finding is noted in unipolar patients, they are not out of the period of risk of developing mania. It seems reasonable that bipolar and unipolar depression would be different physiologically, since they are different clinically. Another interesting finding is greater variability in levels of platelet free calcium ion concentrations in bipolar patients than unipolar patients and normal people. Some bipolar patients have very high levels, some have moderately elevated levels, and some have normal results. This kind of biological variability is entirely consistent with the clinical heterogeneity of bipolar disorders: some patients have severe symptoms, some have mild ones; some are psychotic, some are not; some have many episodes, some have few; some respond to lithium, and others require different treatments.

Further second messenger research in bipolar disorders has been consistent enough with these observations to encourage scientists to look beyond individual or even groups of neurotransmitter systems and delve further into the basic mechanisms of the cell. For example, Israeli researcher Sofia Avissar and colleagues have found that a key link between receptors and the calcium signal is hyperactive in bipolar patients. The link, a component of the receptor called a G protein, responds excessively to a variety of stimuli. When it is stimulated, the G protein sets in motion the biochemical events that mobilize calcium ions to drive the cell to action, so a hyperactive G protein would lead to increased calcium mobilization. Not only are these findings consistent with each other, but they are consistent with research about the effects of treatments for bipolar disorder on cellular signaling.

Treatment of Mood, Treatment of the Cell

A second messenger theory of bipolarity holds that a primary increase in cellular signaling, ending with the calcium ion, produces mixtures and rapid alternations of mental states driven by neuronal systems that are turned up too much or slowed down too much. If the hypothesis is correct, medications that turn down this signaling mechanism should stabilize both the chaotic fluctuations of cellular action and the chaotic fluctuations in mood that they produce. Sure enough, when lithium is incubated in a test tube with platelets from patients with mania or bipolar depression, the elevated calcium level decreases to normal values. Nothing happens when lithium is incubated with platelets from normal individuals, indicating that the effect is on hyperactive and not normal intracellular signaling. Research by the Avissar group suggests that normalization of calcium ion levels within cells could result from normalization of the hyperactive G protein that they have found in cells of bipolar patients.

What happens when lithium is incubated in the patient rather than a test tube? The same thing. When bipolar patients with elevated platelet calcium levels are treated with lithium, their moods normalize and so does the level of calcium ions in their platelets. Other treatments for bipolar mood disorders, including ECT, have the same effect. The fact that something that is not even a medication also normalizes cellular signaling suggests that this is not just an accidental biochemical interaction of a drug with the cell.

The capacity of lithium (and probably other medications for bipolar disorder) to stabilize calcium ion concentrations explains another puzzling clinical phenomenon: lithium can be an effective treatment for depression as well as mania. If mania is a state of excess neurotransmitter or receptor activity and depression is the reverse, how could lithium turn these functions down in one condition and up in the other? On the other hand, if both disorders depend on hyperactive second messenger signaling that can produce increases, decreases, or mixtures of the two in the responsiveness of neurons in different parts of the brain, anything that normalizes the basic cellular "fault" will normalize emotions, thoughts, and behaviors that are driven in chaotic directions by this fault.

THE DECEPTION OF BIOCHEMICAL STUDIES

The wealth of information currently emerging about the physical aspects of depression is fascinating, but it can also be deceiving. The most important deception is to mistake the current state of knowledge for established fact, when in reality there are many gaps and inconsistencies. Frequently, these gaps are filled prematurely by practitioners eager for scientific knowledge to guide them, by patients eager for a concrete answer to why they suffer so much, and by researchers whose funding and reputations depend on how convincing their data and hypotheses sound. Whenever people become so attached to theories that they can no longer afford to consider the possibility that the theories might be wrong, knowledge is replaced by deception.

Attempting to translate sophisticated biochemical research directly into human medical terms is even more deceptive than using the DST to screen for depression. At least the DST was studied in large clinical populations. Most neurotransmitter, receptor, and second messenger research not performed in animals has been conducted in small numbers of carefully selected human subjects, usually in tertiary care centers like medical schools and the National Institutes of Health. Whether these patients bear any relationship to patients seen in everyday practice is an open question. Even if their conditions were similar, the results cannot be directly applied to clinical practice because there are no established "norms" for any of the values measured. When a simple blood count is obtained, the physician knows whether it is normal or abnormal by comparing it to pooled values from thousands of patients whose blood counts have been measured by a standardized technology in universal use. In research protocols, measurements differ in how technicians perform the tests, which is why results in patients are compared with those from a small number of matched controls rather than a large body of normative data. Therefore, results obtained in one laboratory may not be the same as those obtained in another—or even those obtained in the same laboratory at another time.

While many research studies demonstrate that depression has a biological side, that does not mean that depression is biological. To dismiss the psychology of depression as nothing more than the result of disordered physiology is to miss the two-way interaction between mind and body that allows the mind to reset bodily processes, which in turn influence the orientation of the mind. Given how much knowledge has accumulated about both the biology and psychology of depression, it is finally possible to understand how the body deceives the mind into depression, and then how the mind, in turn, solidifies the deception by altering the mechanisms of the synapse.

THE BODILY DECEPTION OF DEPRESSION

How can research about the mechanisms of depression be summarized? One piece of evidence that is well verified is that excessive mobilization of stress-response systems of the brain lead to mental interpretations of everyday challenges as overwhelming threats. This deceptive perception of danger comes from the lack of coordination among neurotransmitters that control vegetative function, arousal, energy planning, appetites, biological rhythms, and action. Erratic biochemical arousal in the brain translates into hyperactive but useless rumination about how insurmountable everything seems. Then, as arousal systems burn out or are shut down, the mind responds to dampened physiology by becoming withdrawn, immobilized, and lethargic (Figure 13-1).

The deception of impotence in the face of manageable challenge is based in the disorganization of multiple neurotransmitter systems. Uncoordinated arousal driven by norepinephrine is intensified by lowered levels of serotonin, and loss of serotonin function releases agitation, anguish, intrusive thought, and self-destructiveness, as well as baseline biological functions, from normal regulation. Without the coordinated input of action neurotransmitters such as dopamine, which would provide adequate direction to arousal, there is no constructive psychological or behavioral outlet for the sense of inner turmoil. Malfunction of other neurotransmitter systems—for example, acetylcholine, endorphins, and a type of neurotransmitter called an excitotoxin that mediates learning at low levels of activity and damage to neurons at higher levels—adds withdrawal, a heightened sense of pain, and inability to concentrate and remember. The resulting deceptive mixture of arousal and withdrawal is then spread throughout bodily systems by commonly shared cellular mechanisms that *overstimulate the physiology* of action but *inhibit the psychology* of action.

In unipolar depression, these abnormalities in cellular processes seem to be more stable, in that they produce *consistent* symptoms of lowered mood, energy, and thought. In bipolar states, cellular mechanisms swing back and forth between inhibition and excitation. As a neurotransmitter is required, intracellular messengers that are responsible for regulating its release make the initial response excessive. Mechanisms intended to keep signaling between neurons at constant levels are driven by the same hyperactive second messengers and therefore are also excessive, causing the synapse to slow down too much.

Since communication within the synapse has become inaccurate, the system cannot respond appropriately to the decrease in signal, and once again it turns itself back on too strongly. The result: an endless cycle of extremes of stimulation and inhibition, with grandiose overestimation of inner strengths and boundless energy abruptly replacing lethargic inadequacy. Sensing the loss of regulated and consistent reactions to danger, the mind starts doubting itself and looks toward external sources of regulation of a stress response that feels impossible to predict or control from within.

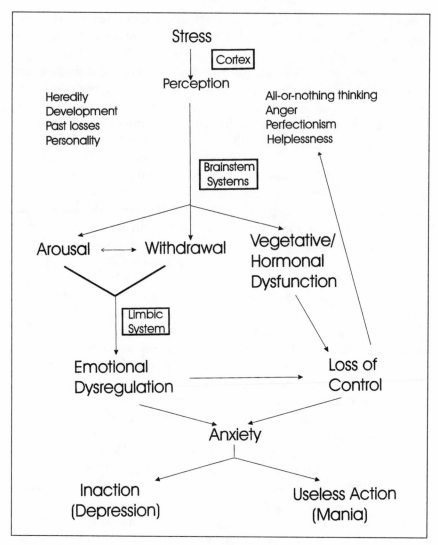

Figure 13-1.
The psychobiology of mood disorders

THE MIND-BODY MERRY-GO-ROUND: HOW THE
MIND TEACHES THE BODY TO DECEIVE THE MIND

Paradoxically, the instability of the body's stress responses, which deceives the mind out of its ability to solve problems efficiently and confidently, does not always originate in unprovoked oscillations of regulatory systems of the body. The overall contribution of innate factors to the risk of unipolar depression is, at most, 50 percent, which is about the same as for coronary heart disease, stroke, and peptic ulcer; the remaining vulnerability to depression depends on life experience. Even when genetic factors are important, they do not simply set the responsiveness of the nervous system in an abnormal direction: their contribution to depression also involves increasing the likelihood that a person will get into situations and relationships that provoke depression. For example, some people who are inherently prone to becoming overstimulated may repeatedly place themselves in overstimulating situations in order to create a level of excitement that is strong enough to be noticeable above the baseline level of arousal. Bipolar people may also seek out excitement to give themselves the illusion that their wild oscillations of mood are purposeful. However, as more arousal is provoked by each of these situations, mood instability becomes programmed more permanently into the repertoire of the synapse. Other individuals with this kind of vulnerability may limit their exposure to situations they sense will be overstimulating by keeping their distance from people. Having few meaningful attachments, they are more vulnerable to the disrupting effects of loss of any of relationship. Since the synapse learns to change its baseline setting in response to each of these situations—by altering the message from the genes from which receptors and other synaptic components are constructed—experience can influence heredity as much as heredity influences experience.

Temperament

One important way in which the risk of depression is inherited is through the range of responses to mental and interpersonal events that are programmed into the synapse. As we saw in Chapter 8, *temperament* refers to those response styles, present early in life, that have their foundation in the innate network of synaptic connections. Unstable temperament is evident as early as eighteen months of age in the children of manic-depressives, who already demonstrate avoidance, withdrawal, and emotional volatility. While this kind of temperament is probably a marker of inborn instability of mood-regulating synapses, in and of itself it does not inevitably predict later illness.

Temperamental inclinations can become magnified into serious mental illness if synaptic dysregulation, built into the synapse by the genes, is severe, or if this genetic impairment is aggravated by specific experiences. Certain substances, especially stimulants, cocaine, and alcohol, directly alter mood-regulating systems, and this alteration may persist for long periods of time after the substance is no longer being used. This is why people who abuse cocaine, which is extremely potent in kindling abnormal mood, often have severe and treatment-resistant mood disorders. Kindling may also play a role when intense or stressful experiences, which trigger excessive physiological stimulation or inhibition, convert minor instabilities into wilder response patterns—which neurons in turn learn to make part of their repertoire. On the other hand, positive experiences can reinforce stable synaptic settings and add new ones that strengthen an inherently weak system.

Emotional Trauma

Even if no inherent abnormality exists to begin with, repeated traumatic experience can program depressed, anxious, or overstimulated responses into the nervous system. Helplessness, retreat, and giving up can become routine reactions to any kind of stress in someone who is subjected to repeated abuse, with no access to support, or assistance with problem-solving. Similarly, intense and inappropriate stimulation of anger, excitement, or sexuality can kindle these emotional states into synapses of mood regulation, so that maladaptive emotions and behavior become automatic. In such an environment neuronal circuits for healthy, active responses to threat atrophy, as they receive no consistent activation by experience.

Depressive Feedback

Depression itself can condition even more impaired functioning into the synapse for two reasons. First, the physiology of depression can serve as a kindling stimulus, so that each time it is present it evokes a more profound and widespread depressive response with less and less provocation. In addition, depressive negativism, withdrawal, dependency, sensitivity to loss, and inability to achieve and enjoy create a wealth of negative experiences, from unstable relationships to loss of status and self-esteem, which induce more depressive responses in synapses. The facts that bipolar states are even more recurrent than unipolar states and that mood swings worsen after the first episode of mania suggest that mania may be a more potent behavioral sensitizer than depression, so that even one manic experience can condition instability into the synapse, which is then reinforced by the dramatic social consequences of having become manic.

THE "MOVING TARGET" OF DEPRESSION

The evolving interaction between accumulating experiences of abnormal mood and escalating vulnerabilities in the nervous system makes the mind-body deception of depression a dynamic disorder rather than something that is either present or absent in the same way across the life span. In the words of researcher Robert Post, "The neurobiology of [mood] disorders is a moving target and changes as a function of the longitudinal course of illness."

When depression or mania first appears, it is usually in response to an external stressor, such as the loss of a loved one, some other kind of separation such as starting school or moving away from home, or a situation that evokes acute feelings of helplessness or agitation. The degree to which such events cause depression depends on their severity, inherent predisposing factors, and external supports that might help "splint" an otherwise unstable response style.

For example, a person with a moody, irritable, volatile temperament may weather separations and traumas without developing more profound mood swings if parents or other sources of support can bolster unstable neuronal systems of emotional response. However, if parents are out of tune with the child's needs or are too upset to respond—or, worse yet, if their threats of abandonment further strain the child's unstable emotional response—what might be a routine loss or stress can evoke escalating dysregulation of multiple bodily systems.

In the Short Run

Early in the course of a mood disorder acute changes in neurotransmitters, receptors, and second messengers, set off by losses and other major stressors, may be reversed simply by changing the situation. When the situation cannot be undone, it is often at least possible to provide help mastering the situation psychologically, for example, by expressing and resolving feelings of grief or worry rather than suppressing them to the point where they feel insurmountable. When these approaches are not fully effective, one of the specific brief psychotherapies for depression is as likely to reset mind and body back toward normal as an antidepressant. Major personality problems have not yet developed that would require more complicated or prolonged psychotherapy, and synaptic changes are simple enough that a single antidepressant is all that is needed.

A first episode of depression, even when it resolves fully and there are no personality problems to begin with, creates self-doubt and worry about whether the depression could come back. The drive to use other people as mood stabilizers, as well as the natural tendency of anyone who is in pain and feels out of control to seek help, adds an increased urge to lean on others, or at least to have them around if something else happens. People whose experiences with unreliable caretakers or whose needs for support feel insatiable may flee this urge and develop the kind of unrealistic pseudo-independence described in Chapter 7, which then predisposes them to complete breakdown of their defenses when they finally become aware of their needs. Usually, however, after early episodes the impact of depression on the personality is as reversible as the depression itself.

In the Long Run

The situation becomes more complex with recurrences of depression. As initial depressive episodes sensitize synapses to enter abnormal states more readily and homeostatic mechanisms are mobilized to keep them there, recurrences of depression become more spontaneous and persistent. The social and personal consequences of these recurrences create an increasingly negative mind set, as the person's self-concept as a capable and dependable person is displaced by a growing feeling of incompetence and unreliability. Once the depressive response becomes built into the neurons that mediate emotions, the vicious circle of negative outlook, hypersensitivity to the ordinary stresses of life, and a tendency to provoke negative reactions from others creates a persistent distorting influence on all psychological and biological processes.

At this point, environmental changes and support do not help as much as they once did, because both the psychology and the physiology of depression have acquired a life of their own. Just as internal homeostasis has altered the "default" setting of the synapse, interpersonal homeostasis has reset the patient's relationship with the world. Family members and other important people may have become frustrated by the patient's negativism and react with equal negativism; when the negativism is manifested as repeated threats of suicide, they may even dare the patient to end the suspense and get it over with. Some patients turn to alcohol or other mood-altering substances, which provide a fleeting sense of comfort but longer-term aggravation of the synaptic pathology.

These psychological and behavioral consequences of chronic depression require more aggressive psychosocial therapies. Unless the substance abuse is treated, therapy for depression is not likely to be successful, because the substance will counteract any benefits that the therapy might have. Since conflicts with loved ones accentuate the threat of loss and disrupt interactions that could have a stabilizing effect on the patient's mood, it becomes as necessary to treat disturbed relationships as disturbed individuals. Continuation of "depressogenic" relationships and ongoing failure to get control of depression result in increasing demoralization that makes it even harder to try to get better as time goes on. If depression lasts long enough, a depressive outlook comes to feel like a core element of the personality that persists even when the depression is cured. In this case, more aggressive forms of psychotherapy are necessary to help the patient develop an identity that is not organized around being depressed.

At the same time that the depressed person's personality and relationships have become more complicated, so has the physiology of depression. Through the effects of second messengers on transcription of the message

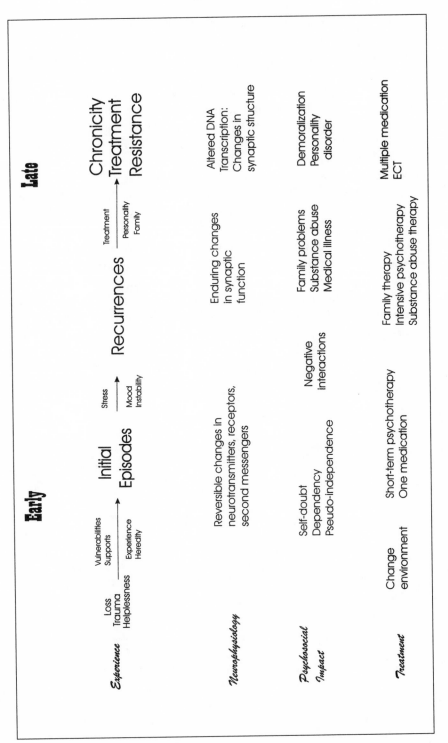

Figure 13-2.
The evolution of mood disorders

from DNA to messenger RNA, the structure of cellular machinery is changed permanently and multiple interacting elements of cellular function are recruited to abnormal levels of activity. A single treatment aimed at just one of these systems is less likely to work and combinations of medications, sometimes along with electroconvulsive therapy, are necessary to produce a remission. When medications are developed that can correct second messenger abnormalities directly or that can reset the transcription of DNA to messenger RNA, these may prove even more effective for the refractory stage of chronic depression. Regardless of the treatment, however, when depression has become the default state of the synapse as well as of the mind, stopping the treatment once the patient is better is likely to result in a return or even an increase in symptoms, as suppressed synaptic pathology rebounds.

The moral of this psychobiological story? *The longer depression is allowed to persist or recur, the harder it is to treat.* Conversely, vigorous early treatment prevents depressive psychophysiology from becoming ingrained into body and mind. The therapies discussed in the next chapter not only stop the suffering caused by this mind–body deception but also keep it from becoming a way of life.

14

A Consumer's Guide to Psychological Treatments for Depression

A RICH MYTHOLOGY and a lucrative industry have grown up around the field of psychotherapy in the years since World War II. Between 250 and 400 official varieties have been developed, each one touted by its more fervent practitioners as the definitive cure. However, much of the research into the effectiveness of these treatments is deceptive. It has been repeatedly demonstrated that 80 percent of the time, the average person receiving any kind of psychotherapy is better off than not—but it does not matter how long the therapy lasts, who does it, or what kind of therapy it is! In addition, most published psychotherapy studies have involved mildly ill patients or virtually normal college students treated by inexperienced therapists. The relevance of much of the psychotherapy literature to evaluating clinical realities is therefore open to question.

The research is more reliable for psychotherapies specifically designed for depression. There are four psychotherapies commonly used for depression: "dynamic" psychotherapy derived from psychoanalysis, cognitive therapy, interpersonal therapy, and behavior therapy.

OVERVIEW OF THE THERAPEUTIC MARKETPLACE

Psychoanalytic Therapy

The best known psychotherapy for depression is psychoanalysis, a long-term, intensive form of treatment whose goal is to uncover unconscious conflicts that are being expressed as depression. This is accomplished by encouraging a relationship with the therapist that brings up feelings from earlier, important relationships. There is a nice description of psychoanalytic theory in the popular Stephen King book, *The Eyes of the Dragon:*

> People's minds, particularly the minds of children, are like wells—deep wells full of sweet water. And sometimes, when a particular thought is too unpleasant to bear, the person who has that thought will lock it into a heavy box and throw it into that well. He listens for the splash . . . and then the box is gone. Except it is not, of course. Not really . . . even the deepest well has a bottom, and just because a thing is out of sight does not mean that it is gone. It is still there, resting at the bottom. And . . . the caskets those evil, frightening ideas are buried in may rot, and the nastiness inside may leak out after awhile and poison the water . . . and when the well of the mind is badly poisoned, we call the result insanity.

It is the goal of psychoanalysis to uncover the buried caskets by encouraging their resurfacing in the relationship with the analyst. In the case of depression, the caskets contain rage, grief, self-hatred, a futile search for identity—all of those emotions that are too overwhelming for the conscious mind to tolerate. In psychoanalysis, the process of bringing these hidden emotions to the surface, where they can finally be resolved, is supposedly facilitated by lying on a couch and being unable to see the analyst, who is quiet during most of the session. By saying whatever comes to mind (free association), an attempt is made to get around the ever vigilant censor that shifts disturbing but important thoughts, memories, and emotions away from conscious awareness. With the help of the analyst's interpretations, even the most random idea may be followed through its twists and turns, back to its unconscious source. Once the unconscious poisons of depression are brought to light, they can be drained away by the power of rational adult thought.

The average psychoanalysis takes three to seven years, and for some people, psychoanalysis seems endless as new secrets continue to emerge. While the kind of self-knowledge that results can be useful in personal development, no responsible practitioner would recommend psychoanalysis as the sole treatment for depression. As noted previously, depression may remit without treatment within a year, and psychotherapies designed for depression are effective within twelve sessions. It has been argued that a thorough analysis might prevent recurrences of depression, but there is no evidence that this is so. Indeed, focusing attention on emotions that stir up impaired stress-response systems can *increase* the previous sense of being overwhelmed and inadequate. Furthermore, exploring every experience from the past can make the depressed person feel more self-involved and unavailable to solve today's challenges. And when such massive effort does not cure the depression, feelings of helplessness and failure increase.

Dynamic Psychotherapies

Dynamic psychotherapies are based on the same insight-oriented principles as psychoanalysis but are shorter and less intensive. These therapies focus more on the problem that brought the patient to treatment than on unraveling every conflict from the past, regardless of its lack of relation to the presenting complaint. Feelings about the therapist are discussed when they illustrate a specific point about other, current relationships or when negative reactions threaten to disrupt the treatment. Therapy may be as brief as a session or two or as long as several years. Since many depressed people do as well with a brief as with a prolonged approach, it seems sensible to choose the extended form only if one of the shorter versions have not been helpful.

Even though they were not developed specifically for this disorder, the dynamic psychotherapies are probably the most commonly used psychological treatments for depression. Practice guidelines published in the *American Journal of Psychiatry* in 1993 suggest that dynamic psychotherapy be considered when depression is accompanied by feelings of chronic emptiness, harsh self-expectations, a history of abuse, loss or separation in childhood, chronic interpersonal conflicts, or a full-blown personality disorder. However, it is important for the consumer of long-term dynamic therapies to be aware that there has only been one valid investigation of their effectiveness in treating depression and that structured, time-limited therapies may be as effective and less expensive in uncomplicated forms of depression.

Combo Plate: Therapy Plus Medication?

Two psychotherapies were designed specifically for depression—cognitive therapy and interpersonal therapy. Both are time-limited (twelve to sixteen sessions, sometimes with intermittent and extended follow-up) and adhere to a structured, standardized method in which therapists are formally trained. Homework assignments follow each session, and the process and goals of therapy are well-defined. Behavior therapy, which shares many of these characteristics, was not designed as a treatment for depression, but it has been applied alone and in combination with cognitive therapy to depressed patients.

Cognitive therapy, cognitive-behavioral therapy, and interpersonal therapy have been subjected to a number of careful investigations that have compared these therapies with medication and with each other. In general, the findings indicate that psychological interventions can be equivalent to biological interventions in milder forms of depression.

A recent multi-center study of treatments for depression by the National Institute of Mental Health summarized the formal research of psychotherapies for depression. In this study, unipolar nonpsychotic depressed patients received a sixteen-week course of one of the following: (1) placebo medication plus "clinical management" (supportive psychotherapy), (2) imipramine (Tofranil) plus clinical management, (3) interpersonal therapy, or (4) cognitive-behavioral therapy. For mildly depressed patients, active treatments (conditions 2, 3, 4) were no more effective than condition number one—placebo plus clinical management. For patients with more severe depression, imipramine plus clinical management was found to be consistently superior. The outcome with interpersonal therapy or cognitive-behavioral therapy was better than placebo but not as good as with imipramine. These results suggest that therapeutic support without medication or a specific psychotherapy may be effective for mild depression, whereas more severely depressed patients do best with the addition of antidepressants. It is likely that psychotherapies designed specifically for depression will play an important role in the treatment of more severely depressed people, but not the *only* role. In fact, for most people, the combination of antidepressants and psychotherapy is more effective than either treatment alone. Now let's take a look at the specific psychotherapies commonly used as treatments for depression.

COGNITIVE THERAPY

Cognitive therapy is based on the premise that the negative emotions of depression are reactions to negative thinking. Patient and therapist work together to identify persistent negative thoughts, correct the pervasive beliefs that generate these thoughts, and develop more realistic assumptions. For example, after keeping track of what he was thinking at the moment he began to feel depressed, a man might realize that the feeling started after he began thinking that "nobody loves me" when he was greeted without enthusiasm upon returning home from work. The negative thought was the natural consequence of the false assumption that "if my wife and kids aren't always happy to see me, it means they don't love me."

The first step in reversing such negative conclusions is to generate an alternative explanation of the man's observation that his family did not seem happy to see him. For example, family members might have had something else on their minds, or they might have been happy to see him but not demonstrated it in the way he expected. Even if they were angry at him, it would still not mean that they do not love him. The patient learns to examine underlying all-or-nothing beliefs (in this case, "either my loved ones are completely devoted to me or they don't care at all") and thereby gain a broader, more reality-based perspective.

Cognitive therapy is as effective as imipramine for milder unipolar forms of depression; in addition, the rate of relapse is lower two years after a course of cognitive therapy than it is after a solo course of antidepressants. However, if the antidepressant is continued, the relapse rate on the medication is lower. A one-year follow-up showed that with continued intermittent treatment, gains of the cognitive therapy were maintained, and without medication. Some therapists use this result to demonstrate that cognitive therapy is better than antidepressants because it does not have to be continued to prevent relapse. However, patients who require ongoing treatment with antidepressants probably represent a different group than those who can discontinue the medication without suffering relapses—and the latter group may also be those who can stop cognitive therapy without relapse.

INTERPERSONAL THERAPY

Interpersonal therapy is based on the theory that depression signals an inability to handle a loss or some aspect of an ongoing relationship. Treatment offers a structured, problem-solving approach to four basic interpersonal issues believed to play a role in causing depression: (1) unresolved grief, (2) disputes between partners about roles and responsibilities in the relationship, (3) transitions to new roles such as parenthood or retirement, and (4) lack of the communication skills that are necessary to sustain a relationship.

Insofar as dynamic psychotherapy and interpersonal therapy both emphasize expressing emotions that arise in the context of important relationships, some practitioners of the dynamic approach contend that interpersonal therapy is just another variation of their approach. However, there are several important differences. The focus of interpersonal therapy is exclusively on the present; there are no attempts to explore conflicts from the past or stimulate feelings about the therapist that might reflect past relationships. Through formal assignments, interpersonal therapy helps patients to identify explicit goals related to whichever of the four basic interpersonal problems is felt to be present. Role-playing is used to help patients acquire new interpersonal skills, and structured discussions and contracts between partners are used to clarify their expectations of each other. Unlike dynamic psychotherapy, interpersonal therapy follows a structured approach outlined in a manual and uses explicit homework assignments. As with cognitive therapy, interpersonal therapy has been shown to be as effective as imipramine for uncomplicated depression, at least in some studies.

A form of interpersonal therapy is now being investigated as a possible treatment for bipolar depression by psychologist David Miklowitz of the University of Colorado. Because it is clear that psychotherapy alone is not successful in treating bipolar states, these investigators are studying the benefits of *adding,* rather than substituting, interpersonal therapy, to anti-manic drugs. Interpersonal therapy for bipolar disorder is based on the observation that two types of stresses can induce mania: loss (or the threat of it), and desynchronization of biological rhythms, especially the sleep-wake cycle. The therapeutic process involves the standard interpersonal approach to stabilizing relationships that can then help to stabilize mood. The sleep-wake cycle is stabilized by having patients go to sleep and wake up at the same time each day. Establishing a regular time of waking up can be facilitated by brief exposure to artificial bright light of the kind that is used to treat seasonal affective disorder. Too much light therapy can make a bipolar person manic, but the right duration and timing can help to stabilize the sleep-wake cycle and, with it, mood swings. Miklowitz has also found that regulating the timing of other important *zeitgebers,* such as mealtimes and routine activities, can help to regulate mood.

BEHAVIORAL AND
COGNITIVE-BEHAVIORAL THERAPIES

Behavior therapy applies several behavioral principles to the experience of depression. First, the significant loss—be it of a person, job, or home—produces not only grief but also loss of a primary "reinforcer" (reward) that has helped sustain healthy behavior. Without the reinforcer, there is nothing to stimulate the positive behavior. Undesirable, depressive behaviors may then be reinforced by "rewarding" the person with sympathy and release from normal responsibilities.

Another behavioral explanation of depression is that it is a form of learned helplessness: the person has formative experiences in which his or her behavior did not have any predictable effect on the environment and, as a consequence, develops the generalized belief that nothing is likely to have any effect.

The behavioral approach consists of systematically ignoring depressive behaviors such as self-blame, passivity, and pessimism, while rewarding behaviors that are inconsistent with depression, such as activity, experiencing pleasure, and solving problems. Rewards can include anything the patient appears to seek out—from attention, to praise, to being permitted to withdraw or complain, to money. In addition, patients are taught adaptive behaviors, such as getting along with other people and being more assertive, that will net them more consistent rewards than being depressed.

Learned helplessness is combatted by giving patients small, particular tasks that gradually increase in complexity. For example, the person who feels hopeless about ever finding a job is first given the task of getting a newspaper. The next task is to look at the want ads, and only later is a list of possible jobs drawn up and one letter of application written. Each positive experience reinforces a feeling of accomplishment, which, in turn, makes the next task easier. Behavior therapy has been shown to be an effective treatment for depression, although it has not been compared with an antidepressant medication.

When behavioral techniques are combined with cognitive approaches, the result is called "cognitive-behavioral therapy" (CBT). For example, the therapist might clarify the patient's belief, "If I express any dissatisfaction with loved ones, I will be rejected," and then institute an "experiment" in which the patient is encouraged to disagree slightly with something a family member believes. When nothing bad happens, the patient is taught additional ways of expressing disagreement and is rewarded for trying them out. As more practice is logged and appropriate assertiveness is praised, continued self-ratings of mood and degree of belief in the negative assumption are charted to demonstrate improvement to the patient.

In one study, CBT was found to be effective for patients who were more severely depressed than those enrolled in other psychotherapy research. However, even if they improve, more severely depressed patients are less likely to have a complete remission of depression with psychotherapy alone. With this population, indefinite continuation of the psychotherapy may prevent relapse, as is true of medications.

NO PSYCHOTHERAPY

Is it ever appropriate for someone who is depressed *not* to receive psychotherapy? In some uncomplicated cases, antidepressants reverse all of the mental manifestations of depression and no further treatment is needed. If complete remission of symptoms does not occur, the patient who thinks that a medication is all that is necessary should reconsider the need for more comprehensive treatment. When a person adamantly continues to refuse any type of psychological exploration, insisting that the problem is "purely biochemical," that person is under the sway of a mind-body deception in which the body is viewed as deserving attention but the mind is not. Adopting this deception at least allows the patient to accept some form of treatment (medication), but it also incites avoidance and fear of anything that seems mental or emotional, thus forcing any such issue into a secret region where it cannot be corrected.

We have already seen the debilitating effects on the personality of repeated or chronic experiences with depression. There may be a pattern of personality traits, involving dependency, obsessionality, insecurity, and self-denigration, that must be addressed in psychological terms if the depression is to be resolved permanently. Yet there are also some people who do worse with any form of psychotherapy than without it. These are people for whom depression is just one of multiple symptoms, who have had chronically empty, unsatisfying, destructive, manipulative relationships. Any close interaction requiring trust arouses emotions that they are incapable of managing. Instead they become overwhelmed with rage, fear, and a wish to destroy whatever help they may be receiving from the therapist. The shorter and more structured the therapy, the less opportunity there is for the benefits to be eroded by the fear and hatred that emerges in the intimacy of a therapeutic relationship.

In recent years, an increasing awareness of the enduring impact of childhood trauma has led to psychotherapeutic efforts directed at recovering memories of early abuse. This focus on recovery of past traumatic events has become a common component of many psychotherapies. Since a significant number of severely depressed and bipolar patients were abused as children, it is often used in their treatment. There is a good deal of controversy about whether recall of traumatic events in therapy is at all reliable. But even when it is, that does not mean it is necessarily advisable to direct therapeutic efforts toward repressed memories. Any strong or painful emotion is amplified by depression and mania; like an amplifier on a stereo receiver with the volume turned up as far as it will go, these painful emotions can produce unbearable internal "noise" that makes integrative thought impossible. Working harder on recovering the memories produces more distress without any more resolution, making the patient feel increasingly incompetent, overwhelmed, and hopeless about ever making progress. Rather than having to deal with childhood issues in order to feel less depressed, it is necessary to resolve the depression in order to deal with childhood issues, if this is still necessary once the patient can tolerate it.

MIND-BODY MECHANISMS OF PSYCHOTHERAPY

Some therapists who practice one or another form of psychotherapy claim that their brand is *the* treatment for depression. But if such drastically different methods—some focusing on behavior, others on thoughts, and still others on feelings—are all successful, how could there be only *one* correct therapy? The fact that a particular psychotherapeutic approach proves to be effective does not necessarily mean that the theory behind it is correct. For example, cognitive therapy is based on the theory that negative thinking causes depression and so aims to teach the person more realistic, less pessimistic patterns of thinking. This shift in thinking does occur during the course of cognitive-structured treatment. However, negative thinking also lessens significantly when depression is treated by antidepressants, even if the patient's view of the world is never specifically addressed. What practitioners of a successful therapy believe to be helpful may or may not be the active ingredient.

What *do* the different psychotherapies for depression have in common? The actual theoretical orientation may be less important than the overriding experience in which patient and therapist agree on a particular explanation as a way of understanding and controlling a confusing and frightening world. In the course of the therapeutic sessions, the patient learns communication skills that are helpful in everyday life and practices those skills outside the office—in essence, exercising new, healthier patterns of neuronal interaction in the brain. The person then receives positive feedback for his or her new ways of behaving in important relationships. As stress-response systems are "splinted" by the therapeutic relationship, synaptic regulatory mechanisms are repeatedly stabilized, so that they can eventually function normally on their own. As the patient gradually internalizes the therapist's support as an ever-present inner resource, he or she begins to move toward a more independent stance.

CHOOSING A PSYCHOTHERAPIST

Since the therapeutic relationship is such an important curative factor, successful psychotherapy depends as much on the match between therapist and patient as it does on any particular theory or technique. If the patient does not like or trust the therapist, it is highly unlikely that the therapy will be helpful. The same is true if the therapist can find nothing to like, or at least respect, in the patient. As noted, since treatment methods as diverse as psychodynamic, cognitive, behavioral, and interpersonal therapies can all benefit the same kind of depression, the specific theory about the cause and appropriate treatment of depression is probably less important than agreement between therapist and patient on a range of plausible explanations. If there are irreconcilable differences in their views of the problem, the patient will not comply with the treatment and the therapist will become increasingly frustrated. Therapeutic antagonism will accentuate rather than heal arousal mechanisms.

Given the current state of our knowledge, any therapist who insists that there is only one way to treat depression psychologically is too inflexible or poorly informed to be able to offer the range of therapies that may be necessary to produce a remission. A therapist who informs depressed patients that psychotherapy must continue for a long period of time to resolve personality traits that lead to or result from depression, without first determining how many maladaptive traits disappear as the depression gets better, is unaware that longstanding symptoms do not necessarily require longstanding treatment. The therapist who discourages all patients from taking antidepressants on the grounds that they do not really work, are "only good for symptom relief," or interfere with psychotherapy, is even more uninformed.

The competent psychotherapist should not be expected to know how to perform every valid technique. However, competence *does* include awareness that there are a number of effective approaches to the same problem— as well as some approaches that are unacceptable. Before the patient makes a commitment to a particular course of treatment, the responsible therapist should offer information about possible alternatives, even if the therapist does not offer them. A therapist who is not skilled in a particular method that a patient needs or prefers should willingly refer the patient to someone able to provide that treatment. The patient is then free to choose the approach that seems best. No one should continue in psychotherapy with a therapist who is unwilling to change or add treatments as the situation requires, who is not quick to seek consultation whenever improvement does not occur as expected, and most of all, who is reluctant or unwilling to admit mistakes.

THE MIND-BODY DICHOTOMY STILL
REARS ITS HEAD

Despite evidence that antidepressants improve psychological functioning and that psychotherapy can alter biology, some clinicians persist in viewing psychotherapies as achieving purely mental results and medications as treatments for purely biological disorders. This kind of polarization between mind and body encourages the continuation of a host of deceptions about the treatment of depression. One of the most common deceptions is that by producing rapid symptom relief medications undermine the person's motivation to remain in psychotherapy. No one would deny that it is necessary to be bothered by a problem to want to change it, but the idea that medications sabotage psychotherapy because they make patients feel better seems more like a psychologized version of the Puritan ethic than a scientific principle.

The idea that taking antidepressants makes patients feel that they are too sick for insight to help them, or that they are not interesting enough to the therapist, is a stepchild of the deception that psychotherapy is the "real" treatment for depression, while medications are an admission of failure. Perhaps this is a modern-day version of the medieval Christian duality that only the mind contained the potential for perfection, while the body remained forever flawed. People who subscribe to this deception typically believe that it is necessary to resolve all unconscious conflicts in order to resolve depression; medications, of course, do not get to the "real" cause of the problem. They do not consider the possibility that healing the physiological aspects of the depression might make it much easier to overcome the unconscious conflicts.

The fact is that medications appropriately prescribed facilitate rather than inhibit psychotherapy. Antidepressants correct the underlying erratic functioning of neuronal systems, which have distorted or hidden psychological resources, allowing the work of psychotherapy to proceed. The only real threat may be to the therapist—if the pace of psychotherapy is accelerated sufficiently by the antidepressant, further psychotherapy may be unnecessary!

This is what happened to a man who had been seeing a psychiatrist twice a week for two years to work on his inability to make a commitment to a woman. He had achieved great insight into his fear of closeness and several times seemed to be on the verge of establishing a lasting relationship. Each time, however, he became hostile at this tender juncture, and his behavior convinced the woman to leave him.

These setbacks provided more grist for the therapeutic mill. Even though the man seemed to have a fairly accurate understanding of the reasons underlying his fear of intimacy, continued probing always revealed more issues that needed to be addressed. After the fourth time he broke up with a woman who seemed ideal for him, he began wondering if he really needed still more information or if he had to *do* something with the information he had.

The psychiatrist finally began to wonder if the patient's inevitable drive to end relationships might reflect a depression-based surrender in the face of the psychological threat of intimacy. Although the patient seemed more annoyed and sarcastic than sad, he never really enjoyed anything, and, lo and behold, he had a brother and a grandfather who had been diagnosed as depressed. If the patient's inability to solve a clear-cut psychological problem reflected a milder version of what his relatives suffered from—a misalignment of the mind related to a malfunction in the synapse—an antidepressant might just be the ticket.

Six weeks after beginning the medication, the patient's attitude began to change. He was still worried about whether he could trust any woman, but he no longer became engulfed by his own negativity when he thought about his primary worry: that anyone he really cared about would eventually discover his many failings and leave him. He also no longer bristled with hostility the moment he realized that he was starting to feel close to a woman who had the power to hurt him. The conscious effort he put into mastering his tendency to drive away those he cared for, combined with the stabilizing effect of the medication, began to pay off, and he married and began a family a year later.

For a few months after he got married, the patient continued to attend psychotherapy sessions religiously. He had come to feel reasonably comfortable with the dangers of intimacy, but it still seemed important to him to reiterate the same fears he seemed to have mastered. Finally, the psychiatrist asked the patient why he was still coming for treatment when he was doing so well. "You've helped me so much," patient replied, "that I didn't want you to think I didn't need you anymore!"

Psychopharmacologists hold similarly deceptive beliefs about psychotherapy. Some believe that since depression has roots in a disturbed biology, psychotherapy is the superficial treatment and antidepressants are the "real" cure. These experts contend that the reward of being the center of the therapist's attention is more addicting than any medication and creates a powerful motivation to continue to have problems in order to remain in therapy. Like their colleagues who devalue medication, these psychopharmacologists ignore growing evidence that for any complex or recurrent form of depression, psychotherapy *and* antidepressants have additive effects, and treatment with either one alone leads to relapse and only partial improvement.

No matter how intimately biological and psychological processes intersect at the level of the synapse, increasingly they are separated and dichotomized by economic trends in mental health practice. As psychiatrists have increasingly identified themselves as physicians with a biomedical orientation toward their specialty, they have spent more of their time prescribing medicines. At the same time that it has been necessary to spend more time keeping up with advances in psychopharmacology, managed-care companies have come to the conclusion that psychotherapy is cheaper when it is provided by non-medical practitioners. As a result, it is now unusual for psychotherapy and pharmacotherapy to be provided by the same professional.

While psychiatrists manage medications, psychologists, psychiatric social workers, and other therapists have assumed increasing responsibility for psychological interventions. Since there are more psychologists than psychiatrists, and twice as many clinical social workers as psychologists, not to mention many other kinds of mental health practitioners, there are plenty of opportunities to receive psychotherapy from someone other than psychiatrists.

Depressed patients still receive both medications and psychotherapy under these circumstances, but they get them from different practitioners, who may or may not coordinate their care. More than 210,000 patients per month are treated with this kind of arrangement in private practice, and most mental health centers, health maintenance organizations, and managed–care programs follow this model. With increasing frequency, antidepressant prescriptions for many less severely depressed patients and a significant number of those with more severe illnesses are written by non–psychiatric physicians (usually an internist or family physician) working in conjunction with a psychologist or social worker.

Perhaps one of the strangest splits between medication and psychotherapy is enforced when psychiatrists who conduct psychoanalysis or intensive psychotherapy ask another psychiatrist to prescribe medication. The reasoning given is that psychoanalytic psychiatrists do not want to take an active role that might alter the patient's transference feelings. In reality, many of these psychiatrists are intimidated by the science of pharmacology and do not want to take responsibility for the physiological aspects of patients' conflicts.

Do these arrangements for dividing the biological and psychological aspects of care actually save money and result in more efficient care? No one really knows, and as long as those paying for mental health treatment *think* that this arrangement is cost-effective, they may not want to spend the money to verify it one way or the other. One reality is becoming clear, however: unless physicians, psychiatrists, and other mental health practitioners keep in close contact, the separation between mental and physical treatments will only widen. The therapist is unable to make adjustments in medication that might facilitate psychotherapy, and the physician is unaware of subtleties of mental function that might be affected one way or the other by the medication. Practitioners are virtually *required* to focus on only one side of the mind-body equation of depression, remaining convinced that the other side is relatively unimportant or, if it has importance, is someone else's responsibility.

TREATMENT DECEPTIONS

Practitioners of all mental health disciplines are subject to a number of deceptions about psychotherapy, which they frequently pass on to their patients. Relying on the therapist for information about treatment, patients naturally accept the deception as fact. These deceptions are commonly applied to the psychotherapy of depression, although they are not limited to this disorder. Knowledge of common deceptions will prepare therapists and patients for the best use of psychotherapy under most circumstances.

Deception #1: It is neither necessary nor possible to study psychotherapy in a scientific manner. During the time that psychoanalysis and related psychotherapies were the dominant psychological treatments, therapists considered it so obvious that these treatments were effective that they saw no need to study them objectively. In addition, it was assumed that any attempt to measure psychotherapy outcomes either would be too intrusive for patients or would alter the results so much as to make them meaningless.

Such objections have not been substantiated over the years. A variety of reliable and valid techniques have been developed to study psychotherapy. Rating scales completed by patients, therapists, and "significant others" measure depressive symptoms, social function, and other aspects of adaptation. The development of specific psychotherapies for depression that use standardized interventions has greatly facilitated formal research. Even direct observations of sessions, either by reviewing transcripts or videotapes or by actually watching treatment through a one-way mirror, does not disrupt treatment. As with any form of research, patients have been willing to participate in these kinds of studies to advance knowledge in the field and help future patients.

Over 475 psychotherapy studies, including those involving depression, have been published using these and other methodologies. These studies tell us that "because I think so" is no longer an adequate answer to the question "how do you know that your treatment is effective?"

Deception #2: The longer the treatment, the better. The common prejudice that most people need years of treatment to root out hidden problems, even if depression is no longer present, is not borne out by the facts: of all patients seeking psychotherapy, 15 percent improve before they attend their first session. After just eight sessions 50 percent are recovered; 75 percent are well after 26 sessions (or six months of weekly psychotherapy). Most outpatient psychotherapy is concluded in less than fifteen visits, and the average number of visits for all psychotherapy is five. A standard course of cognitive or interpersonal therapy takes twelve to fifteen sessions. Long-term psychotherapy may be necessary for deeply ingrained personality problems, but in many instances short-term psychotherapy is as effective and its results are as enduring. On the other hand, the benefits of even the most prolonged psychotherapy tend to deteriorate over time, and even the most well-analyzed individual is not protected from the inherent tendency of depression to recur.

Deception #3: If depression isn't gone within twelve sessions, there must be something wrong with the treatment. Controlled studies show that cognitive and interpersonal psychotherapies are effective within twelve sessions, but these studies have not included patients with severe, complicated, psychotic, chronic, or bipolar depression. Experience shows that more complicated cases of depression do not respond to the briefer psychotherapies. In addition, many patients still have some depressive symptoms after a course of focused psychotherapy for depression, and when recovery is not complete, depression is more likely to return without more treatment. People with recurrent episodes or incomplete remissions also often benefit from continued psychotherapy. The informed consumer must walk a line between the two deceptions of remaining indefinitely in psychotherapy that might *feel* useful but does not help the depression, on the one hand, and dropping out of ongoing psychotherapy for complicated forms of depression before it has a chance to complete its task, on the other.

Deception #4: Once the depression improves, treatment is over. Just because many years of psychotherapy may be no more effective for an acute episode of depression than twelve weeks of interpersonal or cognitive-behavioral therapy does not mean that therapy ends for good after those twelve weeks. It is becoming clear that the treatment of depression is a life-span proposition, because without treatment depression returns repeatedly and becomes more severe with each new episode. Just as continuing antidepressants after remission of depression prevents relapse (return of the original episode) and recurrence (development of a new episode), periodic "maintenance" psychotherapy helps to keep people out of depression after a remission. It may be reasonable to end the therapeutic relationship after recovery from a single episode of uncomplicated depression, but after several episodes, or after one episode that was either severe or bipolar, it is a good idea to continue occasional meetings with the therapist to identify and treat any early return of symptoms that the patient may overlook and minimize.

Deception #5: It doesn't matter who does the therapy or what kind of therapy it is. It is often assumed that anyone who hangs out a "therapist" shingle must know how to provide psychotherapy for depression. The truth is that it takes more than a license to be a competent therapist. Just as the responsible pharmacologist must keep abreast of new medications and new findings, the responsible psychotherapist must remain knowledgeable about new therapies that are found to be effective for depression, as well as evidence that the old treatments are not as good as was once thought. We have also seen that the generic kind of psychotherapy that digs into repressed experiences from long in the past may help some depressed patients resolve longstanding conflicts but has not been shown to be an effective treatment for depression itself. Indeed, this approach may make some depressed patients feel worse. Anyone who is told by a therapist to continue looking into the past when the present remains overwhelmingly depressing should obtain a consultation from a therapist who specializes in treating depression.

ADVICE TO THE FAMILIES OF DEPRESSED PEOPLE

More often than not, depression is a family affair. Like all humans, people with depressive tendencies seek out this similar traits in others. When they marry, they pass on the risk of depression to their children in their genes and through their behavior. Even when specific depressive symptoms have resolved, mothers who have recovered from depression tend to be unhappy, disorganized, tense, inconsistent, and inadequately responsive to their children. If their children have also inherited the neuronal patterns for depression, the mother's inability to bolster her child's fragile physiology will only increase the likelihood of depression manifesting in the child. Severely depressed parents cannot muster enough energy or confidence to provide even basic emotional sustenance. They also tend to subject their children to criticism, hostility, rejection, and threats of separation. These stresses can produce a continual perception of danger in the child, which then elicits the inborn tendency in the synapse to react excessively and unpredictably to anything that feels threatening. Day by day, depressive responses are encoded in the brain—and, therefore, into the mind.

Many children of depressed parents are negatively affected by the interaction between their unstable home environment and their unstable neuronal environment. As many as 50 percent of children whose parents have emotional disorders qualify for a diagnosis of depression; up to 75 percent of these warrant one or more additional diagnoses, which may include mania, behavioral disorders, school problems, drug abuse, suicide attempts, and accident proneness. Anxiety becomes evident even before depression and persists after a depressive episode in 40-75 percent of these children.

Children of depressed parents become ill earlier (around twelve or thirteen years of age) than depressed children whose parents are not depressed; they also become depressed at a younger age than *their* parents were when *they* became depressed. As these children grow up, their depressions last longer and are more severe. Because of the greater synaptic instability produced by the compounding factors of heredity and early upbringing, a relatively low level of stress may be necessary to trigger the depressive response.

Parents who wish to protect their children from these risks should not deceive themselves into thinking that children are not "really" affected by tensions and conflicts within the family. Even infants and toddlers become distressed and aggressive when their parents fight. When a parent becomes depressed, children often become depressed too, especially if the parent cannot function reliably in the parental role and expresses negative feelings toward the children. The children's depression will then become an additional dimension of the parent's depression.

What are such parents to do? Most important is the admission that they are depressed and in need of help. They should not be ashamed and should teach their children, by example, that there is nothing wrong with getting help. Insisting that it is better to "fight the battle alone" than to seek help from others is really to hold onto one's pride at the expense of one's health. This lesson will not be lost on a child who becomes depressed.

Appropriate treatment can often resolve even severe discord and hostility in a family that has been crippled by depression in one or both parents. In those rare instances in which therapy does not help, it may be wiser to consider a separation. Continued criticism and anger expose the children to more harmful threats of loss than an actual separation that is amicable or at least civil (especially if parents are able to consider the needs of the children above their own needs to hurt each other).

Even in the most stable marriages, parents can still reduce inherent vulnerabilities in their children by minimizing experiences that lead to erratic or defeated emotional responses. Responding promptly when a child is upset helps to soothe synaptic circuitry. In contrast, expecting the child to "learn self-control" or "cry it out" only teaches emotional circuits to respond with escalating intensity. It is impossible and undesirable to avoid *all* stress, but children should be taught that help is readily available for those challenges they cannot cope with alone. If help is predictably available from a trusted parent who is calm and in control, the child's developing synapses are protected from the overstimulation that could trigger their inherited vulnerabilities. Just as there is no shame in a depressed adult getting help, there is nothing wrong with providing a little additional "splinting" when a child's fragile, self-soothing mechanisms have become temporarily overwhelmed.

When nothing seems to work, parents should not feel ashamed to seek early treatment for their depressed child. If it is true that depression becomes more severe the more frequently it recurs, early treatment may well reduce the risk of serious problems later in life. Vigorous treatment early in life may teach inherently unstable neuronal systems of the brain to function normally. Treatment may be simpler and more readily effective before additional abnormalities have been encoded into the nervous system and the personality.

Loss of one kind or another is an inevitable experience in every family. Be it a pet or a family member, when loss does occur, it is important that the family at risk for depression—indeed, that any family—express grief openly. Suppressing sadness for fear of upsetting the children only teaches them to repress and deny their feelings instead of dealing with them. Requiring children to ignore their emotions places additional pressure on stress-response systems, which are forced into increasingly impaired functioning in response to their burden. Grief, anger, and other normal emotions diminish when they are expressed openly. Encouraging children to put their feelings into words reduces the need for buried physiological reactivity in the neuronal circuits of the brain, because in the mind the emotions have been detoxified by parental acceptance and support. Even if opportunities to prevent depression earlier in life are missed, there are always other opportunities to resolve it. The cure may come through the body; it may come through the mind. Whatever the route, a change wrought in one dimension endures in the other.

This truth was illustrated by a young woman who came from a family that was full of mental problems. Two of her grandparents were chronically depressed, as was her brother. Her parents, who fought constantly, were alcoholics. The family had to move repeatedly because they could not pay their bills. She at least could say that she had never been physically or sexually abused; nevertheless, the only real affection she received while growing up had come from a grandmother who was unaccountably stable.

For a time in early adulthood, it seemed as if heredity and early upbringing would have irreparable effects on this woman's personality. She began to suffer fits of intense insecurity and hopelessness, which she tried unsuccessfully to obliterate through the use of drugs and attachments to men who did not love her. Eventually, she suffered a complete nervous breakdown and ended up in a mental hospital.

Some innate strength, which she had either been born with or had learned from her grandmother, helped this woman to seek out the few people in the hospital who had something positive to offer. For their part, the psychiatric staff recognized her potential and were able to communicate their optimism to her. They vigorously confronted the way in which she sought out negative experiences to confirm her self-fulfilling prophecy that she would never be happy.

At first, evaluating her life was difficult for her to do; she would easily become demoralized, pessimistic, and overwhelmed when contemplating how to change her lifelong self-destructive behaviors. Periodically, she sought comfort in her familiar if negative addictive sources of soothing. An antidepressant muted the intensity of her defeatism. As her mood began to lift, it became possible for her to examine and change some of the beliefs she had developed about herself. With each success she became more confident in her ability to deal with problems within herself or in her relationships. This outcome was the result of extended psychotherapy focused on her habitual patterns of negative thinking, of making "bad things" happen before they occurred spontaneously, and of fantasizing that if she were as unhappy as her parents, they might one day reward her by becoming the kind of parents they had not been in childhood. Through the combined effects of medication and intensive investigation of her ways of thinking about herself and others, she was able to stabilize the neuronal circuits of her brain and consciously develop a new, positive orientation of her mind. She never became depressed again.

For this woman, adverse childhood experiences were amplified by genetic vulnerabilities in the brain to produce an enduring derailment of mental function that could be cured by a combination of mind-body interventions. In Part IV we will learn how the impact of an experience can be so amplified by the mind that the body suffers serious—and sometimes fatal—injuries. The same interactions of psychological and biological therapies considered in the next two chapters that cure the mind-body deception of depression can also cure the mind-body deceptions of heart disease and immune malfunction considered in the final section of the book.

15

A Consumer's Guide to Biological
Antidepressant Therapies

BECAUSE DEPRESSION HAS both biological and psychological components, treatment may be biological, psychological, or both. *Physical treatments*
of depression directly restore neuronal ability to respond appropriately to the
normal challenges of everyday life. *Psychotherapies* correct synaptic malfunctions by addressing maladaptive thinking, interactions, and behaviors that perpetuate the depressed state. It is often possible to treat uncomplicated first
episodes of unipolar depression successfully with one treatment or the other;
but recurrent, chronic, severe, psychotic, and bipolar kinds of depression must
be approached from a perspective that encompasses both body and mind, if
a positive outcome is to endure. Although physical and psychological interventions are discussed separately in this and the previous chapter, *psychological treatments affect biology, just as biological treatments affect psychology.*

Most psychotherapies and medications for depression are not nearly as specific as you might expect them to be; in addition to relieving depression,
they are also effective for anxiety, several other psychiatric conditions, and a
number of medical disorders. Electroconvulsive therapy (ECT) can help depression, mania, catatonia, some cases of schizophrenia, Parkinson's disease,
delirium, and even intractable epilepsy. As we have seen, it is also true that
any therapy that improves unipolar depression can induce mania in bipolar
individuals. The capacity to induce mania applies not only to antidepressant
medicines but to anything that has an antidepressant effect, including bright

light, manipulation of the sleep cycle, and psychotherapy. We will learn that this effect is far from benign.

TYPES OF ANTIDEPRESSANTS

In 1957, the first antidepressant medication—imipramine (Tofranil)—was introduced in the United States.* As a derivative of the antipsychotic drug chlorpromazine (Thorazine), imipramine was synthesized in an attempt to find better treatments for psychosis. It turned out that it was not very effective for psychosis but it did seem to brighten mood. Frank J. Ayd, a pioneer of modern psychopharmacology, describes the first report by a chemist of this new clinical application:

> Systematic trials [of imipramine] . . . have shown that the substance is particularly efficacious for depressive states. The effect . . . can usually be seen from the external appearance of the patient. The depressed, sad face disappears and gives place to a joyous, happy, smiling countenance. The patients show a more upright bearing, are more lively in their gestures, again take part in a more active social life, take up an activity, and usually of their own accord leave their bed much earlier. . . . The ability to be happy, and interest in the family and in work are restored, [and] positive ideas and a capacity to make decisions again become evident.

This report inspired a small group of biologically-oriented psychiatrists to begin using antidepressants in their practices. Still, it was some time before the tremendous benefits of the medication were recognized by the mental health community at large. In 1980, more than twenty years after imipramine was introduced, approximately ten antidepressants were on the market and about one-quarter of all visits to psychiatrists included a prescription for one of these medications. By the end of the decade, the use of antidepressants by psychiatrists had increased by more than 75 percent. Currently even more antidepressants are prescribed by primary-care physicians, who write 70 percent of all antidepressant prescriptions. During the 1990s, the use of antidepressants has been routinely integrated into the practices of many nonpsychiatric practitioners (such as clinical social workers, psychologists, and marital and family therapists) for whom primary-care physicians or psychiatrists write the prescriptions.

---

*All commercial medications have a generic name. Many medications are also sold under brand names (e.g., the generic name for Prozac is "fluoxetine"). When the patent expires, other drug companies may sell the same medication under the generic name or a different brand name.

A Few Facts about Antidepressants

Antidepressants are divided into several classes, depending on their chemical structure and some of their known actions (see Table 15-1). Although much is known about the pharmacological action of these drugs, it is deceptive to conclude that a given action accounts for the therapeutic effect. For example, the *tricyclic antidepressants* (TCAs) (so named because they have a three-carbon ring structure; tetracyclics have four carbon rings) block uptake of norepinephrine and/or serotonin into the presynaptic neuron, making more neurotransmitter available in the synapse. The *serotonin reuptake inhibitors* (SSRIs), a group of antidepressants with diverse chemical structures, all block serotonin reuptake. However, inhibition of neurotransmitter reuptake predicts side effects (e.g., increased synaptic norepinephrine causes jitteriness and sweating, and increased synaptic serotonin causes nausea, headaches, and sexual dysfunction) much better than therapeutic effects.

Some medications that are antidepressants have no known neurotransmitter effect and some have paradoxical effects. For example, tianeptine, which has a tricyclic structure, *enhances* serotonin reuptake, thus *reducing* synaptic concentrations of serotonin; yet it is just as effective an antidepressant as the serotonin reuptake inhibitors. Similarly, the *monoamine oxidase inhibitors* (MAOIs) inhibit an enzyme called monoamine oxidase that breaks down norepinephrine and serotonin, but this seems to be an indicator of special efficacy in certain kinds of depression rather than a mechanism of action, since there is nothing special about this particular means of increasing the availability of the two neurotransmitters. Insofar as depression involves simultaneous malfunctions of so many neurotransmitter systems at the same time, it seems more likely that, regardless of their specific neurotransmitter effect in a test tube, *all antidepressants restore equilibrium between multiple systems in ways that are not yet fully understood.*

Media and manufacturer hype notwithstanding, all antidepressant medications are equally effective in treating depression and, with the exception of bupropion (Wellbutrin), all antidepressants seem to be useful for different forms of anxiety as well as for depression. Differences in side-effect profiles help physicians choose one antidepressant over another for a specific patient. For example, because serotonin reduces aggressive outbursts, a serotonin reuptake inhibitor may be useful for depressed people with high levels of irritability, while the sedating effect of a medication like imipramine or one of the newer antidepressants like nefazodone (Serzone) makes these antidepressants desirable for the treatment of depressed people who cannot fall asleep. On the other hand, the tricyclic antidepressants tend to have cardiac effects that are problematic for patients with heart block, while the serotonin reuptake inhibitors can make migraine headaches worse. Because no

Table 15-1

ANTIDEPRESSANTS IN USE IN THE UNITED STATES

Class	Generic Name	Trade Name	Usual Dose (mg)	Special Uses in Depression	Other Uses	Common Side Effects
TCAs	Amitriptyline	Elavil	150–300	• Severe depression • Depression and panic • Depression with insomnia • Panic disorder	• Migraine headaches • Chronic pain	• Dry mouth • Blurred vision • Dizziness • Weight gain • Sedation • Arousal
	Nortriptyline	Pamelor	75–150			
	Protriptyline	Vivactil	15–40		• Sleep apnea	
	Imipramine	Tofranil	150–300		• Migraine headaches • Chronic pain • Enuresis • Attention deficit disorder	
	Desipramine	Norpramin	150–300			
	Clomipramine	Anafranil	100–250		• Obsessive–compulsive disorder	
	Trimipramine	Surmontil	150–300		• Allergies • Peptic ulcer	
	Doxepin	Sinequan	100–300			
	Amoxapine	Asendin	150–600	• Psychotic depression		• Parkinsonism • Tardive dyskinesia • Seizures
SGAs	Maprotiline	Ludiomil	150–225	*See* TCAs	*See* TCAs	• Seizures
	Trazodone	Desyrel	200–600	• Severe depression • Depression with insomnia	• Aggressive outbursts • Insomnia	• Sedation • Priapism with impotence
	Bupropion	Welbutrin	200–450	• Depression with Parkinson's disease • ?Bipolar depression		• Seizures • Arousal

Class	Generic	Brand	Dose	Depression use	Other uses	Side effects
SSRIs	Fluoxetine	Prozac	5–60	• Depression with intrusive thoughts • Depression with difficulty tolerating other medicines	• Obsessive-compulsive disorder • Posttraumatic stress disorder • Bulimia • Exhibitionism	• Sexual dysfunction • Headache • Gastrointestinal distress • Jitteriness
	Sertraline	Zoloft	100–200			
	Paroxetine	Paxil	10–40			
	Fluvoxamine	Luvox	100–200			
FGAs	Nefazodone	Serzone	200–600	• Severe and psychotic depression	• Migraine headaches • ?Memory loss	• Sedation • Dizziness
	Venlafaxine	Effexor	200–375	• Treatment resistant depression	• Memory loss	• Arousal • Hypertension
	Mitrazepine	Remeron	30–70	• Inability to tolerate other medications	• ?Migraine headaches	• Sedation
MAOIs	Phenelzine	Nardil	45–90	• Atypical depression • Depression with anxiety	• Panic disorder	• Dizziness on standing • Dangerous interactions with some foods and medicines • Sexual Dysfunction
	Isocaroxazid*	Marplan	10–40			
	Tranylcypromine	Parnate	30–80			
	Selegiline	Eldepryl	20–40		• Parkinson's disease	

TCAs = tricyclic antidepressants;
SGAs = second generation antidepressants;
SSRIs = selective serotonin reuptake inhibitors;
FGAs = fourth generation antidepressants;
MAOIs = monoamine oxidase inhibitors.

*Withdrawn from market but still available on case-by-case basis from manufacturer.

single antidepressant is best for everyone (and because people are more interested in buying antidepressants than they used to be), new antidepressants
continue to be developed.

About 60–70 percent of depressed patients respond to a given antidepressant medication. (It takes as long as four to six weeks, and even longer
in cases of severe and psychotic depression, for antidepressants to exert their
maximum effect.) These who do not improve on one medication often get
better with a different one or with a combination of medicines. Researcher
James Kocsis found that people who had been chronically depressed an average of twenty-seven years were essentially cured by antidepressants and remained so at a three-year follow-up *if they remained on the medication.*

When antidepressants are compared to placebo (sugar pills) in controlled
research, the active medication is always more effective, proving that it is not
necessary *to believe in* antidepressants for them to work. However, the response
to placebo can be as high as 40 percent. Those mental health experts who
do not think that antidepressants add anything meaningful to the treatment
of depression contend that the difference between the response rate to
placebo and active medication is too small to justify the widespread use of
antidepressants. This contention is a deception. In the first place, a placebo
response can be distinguished from an antidepressant effect in that it appears
abruptly in the first two weeks of treatment and does not last more than three
months. A true antidepressant response appears more gradually, usually during the third to fifth week of treatment, and is much more enduring. In addition, the high placebo response rate *only* applies to the first few weeks of
treatment. A favorable response to placebo is seen only in mildly to moderately depressed outpatients, especially those whose sleep, appetite, and other
physical functions are not affected. Patients with severe, bipolar, or psychotic
depression do not respond to placebo, and neither do people with milder
forms of chronic depression.

WHO NEEDS AN ANTIDEPRESSANT?

A single episode of unipolar depression that is not too severe and is not accompanied by psychotic symptoms may get better without any specific therapy. However, as already noted, the longer a person remains depressed, the
less the likelihood that depression will go away by itself. Indeed, only 5 percent of people who have experienced two years of depression improve without some kind of treatment. A time limit also applies to depression treated
with psychotherapy alone. Since psychotherapies for mild to moderate depression have generally been shown to be effective within twelve sessions,
any therapy that takes longer than this should be considered ineffective, un-

less there are complicating circumstances. When proven psychotherapeutic approaches to depression do not work as expected, it is time to consider adding an antidepressant.

Chronic, severe, psychotic, and bipolar depressions warrant consideration of medication right off the bat. A depressed person who has (or had) family members with depression, or related conditions such as alcoholism or suicide attempts, may be more likely to require an antidepressant, as is a patient with prominent vegetative symptoms such as disturbances of appetite, sleep, or energy. An antidepressant should always be considered when depression recurs after a successful course of psychotherapy.

Antidepressants can also be useful for some people who do not meet normal criteria for a depressive disorder. If depression is embedded in chronic dissatisfaction, pessimism, crankiness or misanthropy, biological therapies may moderate the perpetually negative orientation and attachment to misery and despair that make it impossible to use psychological insight to move forward. It is then easier to gain distance from feelings that seem unmanageable and untangle the complex web of deceptions that comprise the depressive stalemate.

The Prozac Deception

A recent deception about the impact of antidepressants on the personality is the notion of "cosmetic psychopharmacology." This term, which was coined by psychiatrist Peter Kramer in his bestselling book *Listening to Prozac,* refers to the use of Prozac (fluoxetine) to make normal people feel happier, more productive, and better adjusted. Antidepressants improve mood, energy, and thinking *in a depressed person,* but they are *not* "mood elevators"—they do not produce euphoria or make people with a normal mood happier. In fact, there is no scientific or clinical evidence that antidepressants produce anything but side effects in the absence of depression (or some other disorder shown to respond to these medicines).

Some people without overt signs of depression experience improvement in their daily level of functioning when they take an antidepressant. Many of these individuals, however, have subclinical forms of depression manifested by such symptoms as low energy, lagging motivation, some apathy, and a general lack of pleasure. Until they realize how much better they feel on the antidepressant, people with hidden depression that masquerades as everyday problems of living may not think they are depressed, because they assume that everyone feels the same or that they are experiencing nothing more than a "normal" reaction to everyday drudgery. The few people who are not depressed at all in the first place who feel great when they take Prozac are most likely experiencing a placebo effect enhanced by the stimulating effect of the medication. The fact that Prozac and the other antidepressants convert depressed to normal mood but do not convert normal to better mood means that these medications are not the miraculous answer to the "misery of every-day life," but it also means that they are not agents of "mind control."

Why, then, do so many people want to take Prozac—or a similar drug of the same class? For one thing, most of the new selective serotonin reuptake inhibitors (SSRIs) are taken just once a day, as opposed to antidepressants that need to be taken a few times a day. Another feature that makes Prozac-like drugs seem appealing is that they have fewer side effects than the older tricyclic antidepressants (TCAs) like imipramine, and marketing of these medications has made it seem that they have virtually no side effects. Real life, of course, has turned out to be much more complicated. SSRI doses may require careful adjustment, which is sometimes made more difficult by the limited number of dosage sizes that are available. Doses do not always remain constant, either: some patients who respond well to a given dose of Prozac need a higher dose a little later; some months after that, the medica-tion may stop working again and the dose may need to be *lowered* to restore efficacy. And as is true of any new medication, the more experience is gained with the SSRIs, the more we are learning about potential adverse effects. For example, it was initially reported that about 1 percent of patients taking Prozac developed sexual dysfunction, but as more people have taken the SSRIs for longer periods of time, the estimate has been revised upward to as high as 40 percent.

Does the overvaluation of the new antidepressants help to dispel the stigma that has stood in the way of people seeking treatment for depression? It would, if one could count on the pendulum of cultural attitudes toward technologies of the mind to swing just one way. However, the "Prozac pen-dulum" has already swung from its high point of being featured on the cover of *Newsweek* to a low point of being the subject of highly publicized law-suits against the manufacturer, alleging that the medication made people homicidal (none of these lawsuits was ever won). The problem with unre-alistic idealization of anything is that it is replaced by unrealistic devaluation when it does not turn out to be perfect.

What is the truth about Prozac and the other SSRIs? Prozac is unques-tionably an effective antidepressant, and it is usually well tolerated; but it is no more effective than any other antidepressant and no better tolerated than the other SSRIs. The four SSRIs that are currently on the U.S. market (flu-oxetine [Prozac], sertraline [Zoloft], paroxetine [Paxil], fluvoxamine [Luvox]) differ in the degree to which they are stimulating or sedating, the length of time they remain in the body, and their interactions with other medications, but not in their clinical effects. Because serotonin participates in the regula-tion of so many basic psychobiological functions, all the serotonin reuptake inhibitors are useful for a number of conditions in which these functions are disordered, such as anxiety disorders, posttraumatic stress disorder, eating disorders, unpremeditated violent outbursts in patients with brain damage and personality disorders, and obsessive-compulsive disorder.

Does Prozac make people homicidal or suicidal? All of the research on large populations of patients taking this drug indicates that it *decreases* suicidal and aggressive behavior, as would be expected of any antidepressant; in addition, all SSRIs decrease aggression turned outward or against the self, regardless of diagnosis. But if this is so, what can we make of reports that a small number of patients feel *more* depressed or aggressive while taking Prozac? The most likely explanation is that these patients have bipolar, not unipolar, depression. As we have already seen, antidepressants can rapidly induce mania or hypomania, which is usually manifested as irritability and impulsivity rather than elation when it is caused by an antidepressant. When unexpected profound irritability is provoked by an antidepressant, it may really be this kind of uncomfortable hypomania. Although antidepressants may improve bipolar depression initially, as synapses attempt to override the mood-elevating effect of the medication a more severe rebound of depression may occur that drives mood even further downward. Prozac may be a little more likely than other antidepressants to produce these effects because it is more activating or because its effect lasts longer. Or, the problem may simply have been noticed more frequently with Prozac because more people take this medication and everyone is interested in how it works.

PRESCRIBING ANTIDEPRESSANTS

It is ironic that, at the same time people who are not really depressed want to take Prozac, many people who truly need antidepressants do not receive them. There are many reasons for undertreatment of depression with antidepressants. Ignoring all scientific evidence of their efficacy, some clinicians still do not "believe in" antidepressants. Other mental health practitioners are afraid that antidepressants will sap the motivation for psychotherapy, as if psychotherapy were the "real" cure for depression, while medications just cover up symptoms. They support this point of view with studies showing a higher relapse rate of depression after withdrawal of medication than after completion of psychotherapy. However, this is a deceptive interpretation of the findings. Patients who respond to psychotherapy alone have problems that are *less severe* and *less pervasive* than those who participate in the antidepressant studies. The higher relapse rate after medications, therefore, is more likely to reflect the inherent chronicity of the depression cases that receive these treatments. In addition, some studies reporting lasting improvement after psychotherapy involve people who had some depressive symptoms but did not have a full clinical syndrome of depression.

Many of these ideas are really derived from the notion that working hard on psychological problems is more virtuous than getting better without too much suffering along the way. This attitude values the process of psychotherapy more than its purpose—to help the sufferer. If a medication facilitates this goal, is it anything other than a deception to disdain its usefulness because it has not been associated with enough pain? If depression is cured by an antidepressant, what is the virtue in continuing psychotherapy that is no longer necessary?

These days, many more physicians do prescribe antidepressants—but often in inadequate doses. For example, in a survey by Rhode Island psychiatrist Martin Keller and his associates of 6,829 patients who were given antidepressants, only *2 percent* of clinically depressed people were receiving an adequate dose. Why does this occur? Sometimes it is a compromise between not wanting to use the medication at all and giving it correctly. Sometimes it is the result of the misinformed belief that lower doses of any medication are always better. If these kinds of ideas are predicated on the belief that there is no point in maximizing the medication because it will not work anyway, the expectation is likely to be fulfilled when the inadequate dose is ineffective.

Unnecessary reluctance to use medications properly is illustrated by the psychiatrist who decided to "admit defeat" and prescribe an antidepressant when a depressed patient did not improve after two years of talking about the reasons why she was depressed. Having had little experience with these medications, the psychiatrist assumed that they would probably not help; but he did respect their side effects enough to be afraid of using a therapeutic dose. Instead he prescribed one low-dose pill a day, when the usual dose was six to eight times that amount. Four weeks later, the doctor concluded that medication was not the answer either, just as he had known all along. His pessimism was contagious. For the patient, the prospect of more of the same treatment that had brought no relief, with no new approaches in sight, made her feel unbearably hopeless. Seeing no way out, she made a serious suicide attempt and nearly died.

In desperation, the psychiatrist consulted an expert in psychopharmacology who might know about some sophisticated new medicine that would work better. However, the consultant simply recommended increasing the dose of the antidepressant! It did not seem possible that something so trivial could help, but the psychiatrist complied. Three weeks later, the patient noticed that she had begun sleeping through the night. Two weeks after that, her mind was noticeably less frozen, her energy was returning to normal, and life was beginning to look enjoyable for the first time in years. With her mind unfrozen by the antidepressant, psychotherapy took off. Two months later, she felt that therapy had been completed.

Patients' Deceptions

Even when clinicians appreciate the role of antidepressants in the treatment of depression, all too often patients refuse to take them. Many believe that only someone who is "really" sick should take a medication. Some see taking a pill as a sign of weakness, or their families may have convinced them that they should be able to "pull themselves together" without leaning on a prescription. Both of these deceptions are based on the all-or-nothing deception that if a problem is not solved entirely on one's own, it is not really solved at all. People who would rather feel strong than well proudly reject antidepressants on the grounds that it is showing too much weakness to get help in a form as tangible as a pill. These individuals trade medications that could give them real relief for the illusion of being in control that is sustained by their exertions to feel better on their own.

Many people are afraid that antidepressant drugs are addicting (they are not). Fear of depending on anything or anyone outside themselves for any length of time leads some patients to take antidepressants "as needed," skipping the medication on a day when they feel good and taking twice as much when they feel worse. This schedule perpetuates the deception that antidepressants are not helpful, since the medications are only effective when they are taken regularly and in the right doses.

Not a few depressed patients feel too unworthy or frightened of a substantial change in their lives to take the risk that the medication actually might help. Hopelessness, inability to wait any longer for the medication to begin working, and intolerance of side effects also contribute to the 50 percent rate of medication nonadherence (failure to comply with medication instructions) in depression.

Lethal Ignorance

One way of maintaining the depressive deception of self-sufficiency is by prescribing treatment for oneself. The most popular self-treatment is alcohol. Feeling more relaxed right after a drink but more depressed the next day, the depressed drinker engages in the self-deception that the substance is the only reward in an otherwise colorless life. The deception is supported when alcohol perpetuates depression and interferes with the therapeutic action of antidepressants, making the brief alcohol-induced euphoria seem the only thing that helps.

While treating substance abuse is often a necessary first step in curing depression, it can be deceptive to assume that every depressed drinker is an alcoholic. The potentially lethal consequences of seeing only one part of the complex interaction of traits that is depression is illustrated by the case of a thirty-five-year-old man who became severely depressed after his wife died. He began hearing her voice telling him that she would not have died if he had been a better husband, but she would forgive him if he were to kill himself and join her. To drown out this unbearable hallucination, he began drinking heavily. Before long, he was consuming a fifth of vodka a day.

After he was picked up by the police for public drunkenness, the man was placed in a cell to dry out. As the sedating effect of the alcohol wore off, his hallucinations once again became prominent. He was such a heavy drinker by this time that everyone assumed his hallucinations were withdrawal symptoms (delirium tremens—the "DTs") and he was sent to an alcoholism center. He was relieved that someone was finally intervening to help him, but he viewed his drinking as the treatment rather than the disease.

When he was told that his problems would go away if he would only stop drinking, he asked whether he needed other treatments, too. No, he was told: if he just stopped drinking, he would stop having hallucinations. His therapist knew he was depressed but assumed that this was another effect of the alcohol. But the patient's own experience of himself was more extensive than his therapist's experience of him, and he knew that the hallucinations, and the depression, would not go away. Without being offered any help for the underlying problem, he went back to his old standby as soon as he was released from the treatment unit.

Escalating a treatment that was aggravating the very depression it was temporarily suppressing, he was arrested again for public drunkenness.

Now that he had a reputation as an alcoholic, he was promptly sent back to the alcohol center, with the same result. The third time he was arrested, he was interviewed by a psychiatric consultant, who found out why the patient had begun drinking and prescribed an antidepressant and an antipsychotic medication. These turned out to be much more effective than vodka: the hallucinations stopped completely and the patient began to face his grief for the first time.

Despite this improvement, the man was firmly established in the mental health system as an alcoholic. He was referred back to the alcohol center, where the staff viewed antidepressants as another kind of crutch, ultimately no better than alcohol. The medications were stopped, and the man rapidly became more depressed. He visited a local mental health center, which referred him back for alcoholism therapy. He killed himself the next day.

The Need for Maintenance Treatment

Although medications reset abnormal synaptic functioning in depression, the more deeply ingrained the physiological pattern has become, the more likely it is to return when the medication is withdrawn. There is excellent evidence that people who have been depressed are less likely to get depressed again *if they continue to take antidepressants.* That is why chronic and recurrent forms of unipolar depression often require ongoing treatment to prevent relapses.

At one time it was thought that four to six months of treatment after a person feels well were sufficient to prevent relapses of unipolar depression. However, a prospective study (by University of Pittsburgh researchers David Kupfer and Ellen Frank) of people going through a third episode of unipolar depression who were successfully treated with antidepressants found that the depression tended to return whenever the medication was stopped or even reduced in dosage over five years of follow-up. A longer study may well find that stopping an antidepressant *at any point* leads to relapse. To return to the analogy of a thermostat for emotional regulation that cannot remain at the correct setting by itself, the hope is that after the medication has reset the thermostat, it will learn to maintain the corrected adjustment. However, the more time the thermostat has spent in an abnormal setting, the more likely it is to slip back to it whenever the external regulation is withdrawn.

These findings, and clinical experience, suggest that anyone who has had two previous recurrences of unipolar depression should take an antidepressant for at least five years, and probably indefinitely. What about someone with a first or second episode? In the absence of any definitive data, all we can do is weigh clinical knowledge about the potential risks and benefits of continuing or stopping the medication. If the depression was no more than a moderate disruption of an otherwise stable lifestyle, it is reasonable to gradually withdraw the medication between six months and a year after the depression has completely remitted. However, if an episode of depression was severe or psychotic, if it was present for a long time, or if it had serious consequences such as a suicide attempt or disruption of a marriage or job, the risks of continuing the antidepressant indefinitely are much less than the risks of stopping it and risking another, potentially more catastrophic episode.

Conventional wisdom holds that if an antidepressant is withdrawn and depression returns, the same medication will be just as effective when it is restarted. In real life, however, this is not always the case. Not only may the depression be more severe and complicated when it returns, but the antidepressant may not work anymore. One possible explanation for this disturbing phenomenon lies in the now familiar concept of synaptic homeostasis. For the patient with persistent depression, synapses that regulate mood have been in an abnormal state long enough for this abnormal setting to become their usual state. Medication may nudge the synapse toward normal communication, but because this is so different from the usual synaptic function, the synapse works to overcome the therapeutic effect and restore its usual pathological mode (possibly through alterations in transcription of DNA that alter the actual structure of the synapse). As we discussed in Chapter 13, while the medication is present, it suppresses such restorative mechanisms, but when it is withdrawn there is a rebound of abnormal mood that is even more severe as it escapes suppression and is no longer responsive to the same treatment. This observation makes it even more imperative to deal with the fact that many depressed people have a hard enough time getting themselves to take medication when they absolutely cannot avoid it, let alone when the medicine is only necessary to prevent a return of symptoms that are no longer present.

ALTERNATIVE PHYSICAL TREATMENTS FOR DEPRESSION

No psychiatric treatment arouses more emotion in the public, and no treatment is more mired in deception, than electroconvulsive therapy (ECT). The history of convulsive therapy, or treatment involving the induction of a convulsion, was covered briefly in Chapter 5. As we saw in that chapter, the Nobel Prize was awarded for the development of ECT as a treatment for schizophrenia, although it turned out to be a highly effective treatment for depression, mania, and catatonia.

ECT involves the passage of a brief (less than a second) electrical stimulus through the head to induce an electrical seizure in the brain that lasts about a minute. During the procedure, the patient is given a general anesthetic and a muscle relaxant, making it possible to administer adequate amounts of oxygen and to prevent contraction of muscles throughout the body that could cause skeletal injury. These precautions make ECT a safe as well as effective treatment. Its most important adverse effect is transient confusion and memory loss, which occurs in about 50 percent of patients. However, claims that ECT causes permanent brain damage are erroneous. If anything, intellectual capacity tends to *improve* after ECT, because the treatment reverses the cognitive impairment caused by depression. Brain imaging techniques, studies of neuronal elements released when the brain is injured, and even autopsies of people who have received thousands of ECT treatments over the years (at a time when medications to prevent relapse were not available or could not be tolerated) and who died of old age, do not reveal any objective evidence of brain damage. Research suggests that, in order for brain damage to occur, ECT would have to be administered three times a day without anesthesia and muscle relaxants. If administered in conjunction with anesthesia and muscle relaxants, electroconvulsive seizures lasting more *three hours* would be necessary to injure the brain.

A small percentage of people who have undergone ECT feel that their ability to think and remember has been permanently impaired. However, when their cognitive abilities are tested, no abnormalities can be found. This may mean that they have sustained brain damage that cannot be measured. It is equally possible that their cognitive problems represent residual symptoms of depression that have not responded to he ECT. Patients who complain of brain damage after ECT usually are still depressed, and they may have a refractory form of depression, a marker of which is cognitive malfunction. Since some patients who are referred for ECT have evidence of disease of the blood vessels of their brains before they receive the treatment, it is possible that they have a neurological component of the depression that makes it less likely to respond to ECT (or anything else) and that is sensitive to being aggravated by ECT.

Although ECT is commonly viewed as an outmoded treatment by the public, between 50,000 and 100,000 patients receive it each year. Nevertheless, this is only a fraction of the millions of people who receive antidepressants. If ECT is so effective and safe, why isn't it used more frequently? For one thing, most psychiatrists reserve ECT for patients who do not respond to medications or have intolerable side effects to them. In addition, ECT is usually not considered for milder forms of depression, which are routinely treated with antidepressants. The most important impediment to more widespread use of ECT, though, is the stigma that continues to surround it. When most people think about ECT, the first thing that comes to mind is that it was used to punish Jack Nicholson in *One Flew Over the Cuckoo's Nest,* or that people on talk shows say that ECT ruined their lives. The stigma of ECT is so strong that the city of Berkeley, California, passed an ordinance against its use. The ordinance was overturned because it was unconstitutional, but more importantly, all available data show that for medically healthy people the risk of ECT is less than the risk of having a baby; the only hazard is from the ancillary use of brief general anesthesia, not the electric current. ECT is only clearly dangerous for patients with brain tumors and those who have recently had a heart attack (myocardial infarction).

Sleep Deprivation Therapy

The theory that abnormalities of biological rhythms underlie depression led to attempts to treat depression by manipulating the sleep–wake cycle. Since half of depressed patients feel better after being kept up all night, or at least for that part of the night during which most REM sleep occurs, one approach to altering the sleep–wake cycle is sleep deprivation. The only problem with this approach is that depression returns, sometimes with more force, when patients make up for the lost sleep the next night or even with a brief nap. Some researchers have tried isolating REM sleep only as target for deprivation. This method also can improve mood almost immediately, but again, the symptoms return after recovery sleep.

Changing the sleep-wake cycle itself is more consistently helpful, but it is not very practical for many people because it requires changing the time of going to sleep and waking up in the opposite direction from the change that has occurred during depression. As noted previously, some depressed patients experience phase *delays* of the sleep-wake cycle; that is, they fall asleep and wake up later than is appropriate to the timing of their days. They do not feel sleepy until late at night and so either stay up or go to bed but cannot sleep. They then have trouble waking up in the morning and feel sleepy until later in the day. Other depressed patients with phase-*advanced* sleep-wake cycles become sleepy early in the evening and wake up in the middle of the night, unable to get back to sleep.

If the phase change in depression is a nidus around which biological rhythms connected with the stress response become disjointed, correcting it might force other biological systems back into alignment. A phase advance is reversed by first following the brain's cue for the sleep-wake cycle. For example, if the patient starts to feel sleepy at 6:00 P.M., that becomes the initial bedtime. The patient then goes to bed a half-hour to an hour later each night and wakes up that much later each morning, until sleep is in phase with environmental cues.

Because the sleep-wake cycle is slightly longer than the 24-hour day, it can only be manipulated by expanding it. A phase delay cannot be reversed by going to bed *earlier*, which would only shorten the cycle. Instead, it is necessary to go to bed later and later, until the time of going to sleep has gone around the clock to the right bedtime. Such manipulations must be done one-half to one hour at a time and are facilitated by *zeitgebers*, such as exposure to bright light upon awakening.

Physical approaches to depression that are nonpharmacologic in nature reinforce experience with medications in demonstrating that interventions of the body can cure problems of the mind. They are also important proof that with ingenuity and perseverance, it is almost always possible to think of something that will help a depressed person. Whenever people feel like giving up on a depressed patient, it is worth remembering that this attitude is more likely to reflect identification with the patient's hopelessness than an accurate assessment of the situation.

PHARMACOLOGY OF BIPOLAR DEPRESSION

If continuing antidepressants keeps people from getting depressed again, shouldn't everyone who has suffered from recurrent depression take an antidepressant? In cases of bipolar depression, this rule can be deceptive because, no matter how helpful they may be in the short run, antidepressants have the potential to make the mood disorder worse in two ways when taken chronically: they can bring on mania or hypomania, and they can increase rather than decrease the number of depressive recurrences.

How Sure Can We Be That Antidepressants Induce Mania and Cause Recurrences of Depression?

Because bipolar disorder involves episodes of both mania and depression, it is difficult to know with absolute certainty whether a manic episode in a bipolar patient taking an antidepressant is caused by the antidepressant or whether it would have occurred anyway. As a result, debate continues over the question of how frequently antidepressants induce mania in bipolar people. A 1992 review by researcher F. Rouillon of 15 studies involving just under 200 bipolar depressed patients showed that, after variable periods of time, 51 percent of those taking an antidepressant alone became manic, compared with 21 percent of those given lithium, 28 percent of patients taking a combination of lithium and an antidepressant, and 23 percent of patients taking a placebo.

Reviewing this and other published work, National Institute of Mental Health researchers Lori Altshuler and Robert Post estimated that about half of all manic episodes occurring in bipolar patients taking antidepressants were clearly caused by the antidepressant, while the other half seemed to be attributable to the natural course of bipolar illness. Altshuler and Post then conducted a long-term study in which they charted mood swings of 51 bipolar patients who had not responded well to lithium. The majority (82 percent) of patients switched from depression to mania or hypomania while taking antidepressants, but only 35 percent of the patients experienced the manic episodes within eight weeks of starting the antidepressant—a criterion the authors chose as suggesting a causal relationship between the antidepressant and the mania.

Of patients in this study who took antidepressants for at least six months, 26 percent developed more rapid recurrences of depression and mania, judged to be caused by the antidepressant, most within two months of starting it. In most cases, mood swings became less frequent within two to five months of stopping the antidepressant. Patients who had antidepressant-induced mania were almost five times more likely to experience accelerated cycles of depression and mania. Because this research group used very stringent criteria for determining that an antidepressant caused mania or more mood swings, it seems reasonable to assume that the cumulative effect of antidepressants on mood cycling may be even more profound than is indicated by this research.

Anything that works as an antidepressant—not just medications—can induce mania or hypomania in bipolar people, and if Altschuler's findings hold true, also more rapid mood swings. Sleep deprivation, bright light, ECT, and psychotherapy can all have this negative effect. Even lithium, which can produce remission in some cases of bipolar depression, has been known to induce mania. The small amount of research that has been done on this topic suggests that the risk of mania or hypomania is reduced by taking a mood stabilizing medication, like lithium, along with the antidepressant, but the protection is far from absolute. Even combinations of mood-stabilizing medications may not always protect against antidepressant-induced mania and mood swings. Antidepressants therefore are more complicated to use for bipolar than for unipolar depression.

Since lithium by itself is sometimes an effective antidepressant in bipolar depression, many psychiatrists prescribe it (or another mood stabilizer) without an antidepressant. Unfortunately, lithium is often better at filtering out highs in a person's mood than it is at getting rid of the lows. As a result, manic symptoms like irritability, racing thoughts, inability to sleep, hyperactivity, and impulsive behavior may go away, but the patient is left feeling sluggish and depressed. Adding an antidepressant at this point may treat the residual depressive symptoms and leave the patient well, but continuing it too long may override the mood stabilizer and produce mania, or it may speed up the inherent tendency of depression to come back.

You might be wondering what's so bad about a little mania (for ease of discussion, only the term *mania* is used, but *hypomania* is also a possibility.) For one thing, impaired judgment and irritability often cause more problems than they resolve. In addition, excessive elevation of mood is usually followed by an "overshoot" of compensatory mechanisms that produces a more severe depression, perhaps because the brain can regulate mood downward better than upward. In addition, careful longitudinal evaluations of bipolar individuals show that they often have several episodes of depression before their first manic spell. Once mania makes its debut, depressive episodes recur more frequently and with greater severity, followed by more mania. Since mood *elevation* appears to be a more potent behavioral sensitizer than depression, eliciting mania by unwittingly prescribing an antidepressant may make the patient's mood more unstable, and this instability may persist long after the antidepressant is withdrawn. Rapid cycling is like a boulder rolling downhill. It may take a good deal of effort to get it rolling, but once it is rolling, it will keep going even though no one is pushing it anymore. Of course, the same thing may happen without an antidepressant, but antidepressants may hasten or instigate the process in some people. In either case, early treatment of mania may prevent mood destabilization.

Antidepressants and Rapid Cycling

Antidepressants taken by bipolar patients for prolonged periods of time may provoke rapid recurrences of mania and depression, or they may produce a state that looks like chronic depression but is really one of continuous cycling, which was mentioned earlier. Because the person almost always feels bad, the many mood swings of "ultra rapid cycling" often are not obvious. The impression of continuous depression leads to increases or changes in antidepressant medication, which improve a given episode of depression but are inevitably followed by rebound into more depression or mania. Each brief positive response is followed by more negative recurrences, increasing rather than decreasing misery. Thanks to the process of kindling, with each successive episode of abnormal mood, synapses learn to fall into an abnormal state with greater ease. The more that instability becomes the natural state of the synapse, the more difficult it becomes to maintain normal neuronal communication with any treatment.

Mood Stabilizers

The best way to treat mania and prevent mood swings is with mood-stabilizing treatments. Lithium is the best studied of these medications. Two anticonvulsants (medications used to treat epilepsy)—carbamazepine (Tegretol) and valproic acid (Depakote or Depakene)—have also been used rather widely to treat bipolar disorder. Verapamil (Calan, Isoptin), a medication that stabilizes hyperactive intracellular signaling by the calcium ion, seems to be effective in the treatment of mania about as frequently as lithium, although it is not as well studied as the other mood stabilizers. All of these alternatives to lithium have been shown to control mania. Although they have not been studied extensively as mood stabilizers—that is, as preventive measures against recurrences of abnormal mood—clinical experience suggests that they serve this function as well. This is an extremely important point, since it may be easier to *prevent* recurrences of bipolar depression than to treat them when they occur. As with unipolar depression, ECT is the most effective treatment for bipolar depression.

As is true of the antidepressants—or any effective medication, for that matter—mood-stabilizing drugs are not without their problems. For one thing, they all have the potential for significant side effects and require much closer monitoring than the antidepressants. For example, among a fairly long list of possible adverse effects, lithium can cause weight gain, difficulty concentrating, thyroid dysfunction, and possibly kidney problems. Carbamazepine can cause unsteadiness, oversedation and confusion; valproic acid can cause sedation, weight gain, and gastrointestinal distress; and verapamil can produce constipation, headaches, and dizziness. Blood tests are necessary to adjust the doses of lithium, carbamazepine, and valproic acid, and to screen for adverse effects.

Clinicians and patients must also take into account the fact that the outcome of treatment with these medicines is as complex as their side-effect profile. For example, lithium was initially believed to be effective in about 70 percent of manic patients, but more recent experience, summarized by Robert Post, suggests that between one-fifth and two-thirds of bipolar patients on lithium eventually have recurrences of mania or depression. Another problem is that people who initially have a good response to lithium may develop tolerance to its mood-stabilizing action, especially if they stop the medication and then restart it. Perhaps as lithium begins to force the machinery of the cell into a more stable setting, the cell attempts to override the positive effect and restore the homeostasis it has learned so well; eventually, it succeeds. Tolerance has also been reported with carbamazepine and is likely to occur with the other mood stabilizers.

The rebound effect may explain another recent disturbing observation. In evaluating the results of published studies, psychopharmacologists Ross Baldessarini, Theresa Suppes, and their colleagues found that bipolar patients who had responded well to lithium for at least three years and then stopped taking the medication experienced recurrences of mania and depression sooner than if they never had taken lithium in the first place. Although lithium was clearly helpful in stabilizing mood, withdrawing it may have allowed the body to rebound so strongly that the illness proceeded at an even faster pace. When it does, cellular pathology may have become so much more complex that the same medication that worked initially may no longer be effective.

Serious Implications

There are three important implications of these findings for patients and their families. First, the decision to take mood-stabilizing treatments may be a lasting one. Continuing the medication for prolonged periods of time may reduce the risk of accelerating mood problems as well as the illness rebound and tolerance to treatment that can occur when medication is discontinued and then restarted. Second, early, vigorous treatment of bipolar mood disorders may prevent the drift of mood into states that become harder and harder to treat.

The third, and perhaps most important, implication bears directly on the second: early treatment of bipolar mood disorders can prevent later clinical deterioration and treatment resistance. By the same token, mistaking bipolar disorder for unipolar depression or attention deficit hyperactivity disorder (ADHD) and treating it with antidepressants or stimulants can provoke mania, rapid mood swings, and complicated mixed states in vulnerable individuals. We saw earlier that depression is becoming more frequent and is starting at a younger age. Society is also seeing more hyperactive and violent states in younger patients, and clinicians are encountering more cases of rapid cycling and chronically unstable mood. Some of the apparent increase in severe mood disorders may be a function of better recognition. However, many clinicians feel that they are truly encountering more patients with unstable and treatment-resistant mood disorders. More often than not, these individuals have been treated with antidepressants for early episodes of depression, or with stimulant medications for ADHD.

These are common diagnostic errors because many younger bipolar patients have symptoms similar to people with unipolar depression or ADHD. For example, the majority of bipolar individuals get depressed before they become manic, and the diagnosis may only be obvious when an antidepressant eventually induces mania (or it occurs spontaneously). Even when mania does develop early in life, it is characterized by irritability, anxiety, and emotional discomfort rather than euphoria, making it difficult to recognize and easy to misdiagnose.

The overlap between an early onset bipolar disorder and ADHD can be even more confusing. Both conditions are characterized by hyperactivity, irritability, and impulsive behavior. Bipolar people have trouble concentrating because their minds race and jump unpredictably from one topic to another. Because stimulants like methylphenidate (Ritalin) and dextroamphetamine (Dexedrine) are thought of as specific therapies for ADHD, improvement on these medicines is often considered to be evidence of ADHD. However, stimulants can improve *anyone's* attention, which is why college students take them to study and truck drivers take them on long hauls. Some bipolar patients may report feeling better on stimulants because the medications are reducing chronic depression mixed with irritability. It may come as more of a surprise that stimulants, which are inherently activating, can produce the same paradoxical sedation and calming in bipolar people, and any child, that occur in people with ADHD. For unclear reasons, some manic patients fall asleep after taking a stimulant, and some bipolar people drink coffee to get themselves to sleep. Eventually, however, stimulants act just like anything else with antidepressant properties: they produce more recurrences of mania and depression in bipolar children and adolescents. Since the mania is manifested as irritability, evidence of mood destabilization is mistaken for more symptoms of ADHD, and the stimulant is increased or changed, making the long-term problem even worse.

Now that people do not feel as stigmatized by taking antidepressants and stimulants, some younger patients may be treated too readily with these medications. When this is the case, they may show even more irritability, grandiose defiance of authority, mood swings, and depression. While it has not been proven that this overmedicating occurs, physicians and parents may want to exercise careful diagnostic scrutiny before giving these drugs to children who do not clearly qualify for them. Such caution is particularly needed in regard to antidepressants, the effective use of which in childhood and adolescent depression is not clearly established.

Deciding whether or not depression, attention problems, and/or hyperactivity are due to a bipolar mood disorder is far from easy when the child has not yet become obviously manic, or when manic symptoms are mixed with depression or expressed as behavioral problems. However, there are several clues that should raise suspicion about the possibility that the problem is really bipolar. Characteristics obviously associated with bipolar disorder are worth looking for first. Periods of not needing to sleep accompanied by high levels of energy and activity, racing thoughts, and rapid speech—alternating with states of low energy and activity and excessive sleep may be easily observable. Thrill-seeking behavior is another trait of bipolar children and adolescents that is often dismissed as normal teenage rambunctiousness or, at worst, a symptom of ADHD. In reality, the behavior is more impulsive, more dramatic, more grandiose, and sometimes more suicidal. It is one thing, for example, to ride a bicycle fast; it is quite another to ride it at high speed or in front of cars and to crash it into trees just to see what will happen. Children with ADHD may climb around and jump off chairs or beds, but their motivation is not so grandiose as to make them jump off the roof because they believe that nothing can harm them, or to run in front of cars because they do not care whether they live or die. The same is true of the difference between the irritability of ADHD and that of bipolar patients. The young person with ADHD may get into the occasional fight when frustrated or upset but is not grandiose enough to fight three large opponents at the same time or to punch a teacher or a policeman.

Unless they are experiencing a toxic reaction to a stimulant, patients with ADHD do not experience hallucinations or delusions, but these symptoms are often found in bipolar patients if one takes the trouble to ask carefully about them. The underlying element of elevated mood and energy can permit these patients to keep functioning despite hearing voices calling them names or seeing threatening demons. And, as we have seen, they may not mention these symptoms because they either are not bothered by them or do not want to be considered "crazy."

Research by psychologist Michael Strober and others has suggested particular hereditary factors that can be helpful in making a diagnosis. Having three or more depressed relatives, having any bipolar relatives, or having depressed relatives in three consecutive generations increases the likelihood of bipolarity in a depressed child. Antidepressants may provoke mania in adults who never become manic on their own, but when children develop mania in response to an antidepressant, it is virtually certain that a true bipolar condition is present.

DECEPTIONS LEADING TO MEDICATION FAILURE

About 15 percent of depressed people do not respond to antidepressants. Common causes of treatment resistance include unrecognized bipolarity, psychosis, or medical illnesses, and the use of virtually any medication or nonprescription drug. Coexisting personality disorders, marital and family problems, or the presence of another condition that provokes depression also make it more difficult to cure depression. More frequently, failure to benefit from antidepressant medications is caused by deceptions held by patients, physicians, and/or therapists. Correcting these deceptions makes it possible for many depressed people to be relieved of unnecessary suffering.

Deception #1:A little medicine is better than a lot. All antidepressants must be given in sufficient dosages to be effective. The doses of some medications (e.g., lithium, carbamazepine, valproic acid, some of the tricyclic antidepressants) are adjusted by blood level. With all other antidepressants, however, the dose is increased until the patient responds or develops side effects that limit further treatment, or until the dose is beyond the recommended range. However, as we saw earlier, many physicians still prescribe inadequate doses of antidepressants. In particular, it is easy to be deceived by the SSRIs, which come in just one size and seem to require just one dose. However, using these medications is not always as simple as it seems. Fluoxetine (Prozac), for example, which physicians have been taught to prescribe in a dose of one pill (20 mg) a day, works better for some people at doses of 60 mg, and for others at doses of just 5 mg. To complicate matters further, the dosage requirement may change over time, so that a patient who responds well to 50 or 60 mg of Prozac at one point may do better on 5 or 10 mg a year or two later.

Deception #2: If the medication doesn't work right away, it never will. For all antidepressants, there is as much as a six-week time lag before the person experiences any benefit. Changing an antidepressant before this time deprives the person of an adequate clinical trial. Those who have been severely or psychotically depressed may not enjoy the full therapeutic benefit for months. People who feel better soon after starting to take an antidepressant, especially one of the activating medications like Prozac, are usually not experiencing a true early antidepressant response so much as an early increase in energy that is not exactly the same thing as an improvement in mood, but that predicts more complete benefit later *if* the patient keeps taking the medication.

Although physicians learn about the delayed onset of action of antidepressants while still in medical school, many impulsively change medications after a week or two if the patient is not feeling any better. One reason doctors do not follow the rules they learned during their training is that postgraduate education in pharmacology too often consists of brief discussions with representatives of pharmaceutical companies, whose job is to make their medicine seem appealing, not necessarily review the complexities of its use.

Deception #3: If I just wait long enough, the medication is bound to start working. While it is necessary to wait a sufficient amount of time for an antidepressant to begin to take effect, the time delay for antidepressants to "kick in" is a finite one. If the person feels only a little better after four to six weeks at a therapeutic dose (perhaps sleeping better because of the sedative effect of the medication, but not much else), it is time to change the treatment. Of course, this time limit only applies if the doctor is prescribing enough medication, and if the patient is taking it!

Deception #4: If I take the medication too regularly, I'll become addicted to it. Half of all depressed people do not take the antidepressants that are prescribed for them, some because they fear addiction. Antidepressant medications are not addictive. Some physical symptoms, as well as a rebound of depression, may appear if these medications are withdrawn abruptly, but this does not mean that physical dependence has occurred of the kind that can develop with narcotics or tranquilizers. Nor does it mean that antidepressants are associated with the "highs" or with the need to escalate the dose, as is seen with addicting medications. For people who have been chronically or recurrently depressed, stopping the antidepressant may well result in a return of the depression. This is not a minor consequence, but it is the nature of depression, not an indication of addiction. Sometimes physicians find that, no matter how many times they explain this to a patient, the patient continues to be afraid of becoming "dependent" on an antidepressant. After careful discussion, it often turns out that the real fear is one of becoming dependent on what the medication *symbolizes*—getting help from outside oneself—rather than fear of the medication itself.

Deception #5: If the medication helps, I'll cut down on my drinking. Alcohol and depression often go together for two reasons. First, the susceptibility to alcoholism can be inherited along with the susceptibility to depression. In addition, alcohol is a common self-treatment for depression because of its sedating effect, which makes it seem as if it is helping, although the longer-term effect is to produce more depression. Even a few glasses of wine a week are sufficient to perpetuate depression. To a clinician it may seem reasonable to assume that treating depression in a person who continues to drink or take drugs will reduce the motivation to continue this drug use, but it is a deception to think that the antidepressant can overcome the effect of these substances on the brain. Even more important, the patient who continues to drink while knowing that it is harmful to do so is displaying an attachment to self-destruction that will undermine any therapeutic effort if it is not confronted.

Deception #6: If one medication doesn't work, none will work. Some people respond better to one antidepressant than another, probably because of differences in inherited patterns of metabolism and in the "fit" between receptors in the brain and the structure of a particular drug. New antidepressants, such as Effexor (venlafaxine) and Serzone (nefazodone), are becoming available that may have special uses in patients who do not respond to other medicines. The MAOIs may be more effective than other classes of antidepressants for depression accompanied by anxiety, eating and sleeping too much, sensitivity to rejection, and the capacity to be cheered up temporarily by positive events; this class of medication may also be more effective for bipolar depression. A significant number of depressed patients who do not respond to an antidepressant alone do improve with the addition of one, or a number of, medicines, such as lithium, carbamazepine (Tegretol), stimulants like methylphenidate (Ritalin), a short-acting thyroid hormone called triiodothyronine (Cytomel), a drug that blocks beta receptors named pindolol, or an antianxiety medication called buspirone (Buspar). Even combinations of antidepressants (e.g., a therapeutic dose of an SSRI and a low dose of a TCA) may produce complete improvement in people who only respond partially to one of these medications. Depressed patients with delusions or hallucinations, and some with gross confusion or difficulty thinking but no clear-cut psychosis, must have an antipsychotic medication added to the antidepressant if they are to improve. More complex medication combinations (e.g., a TCA and an MAOI) can be extremely helpful when more straightforward approaches do not work.

ECT is the option that many people consider the "last resort" for refractory depression. It is true that ECT can be more effective than anything else for some patients, but it is deceptive to consider it a miracle cure. ECT improves depression in as many as 90 percent of patients who have had inadequate trials of medication, usually because they could not tolerate full therapeutic doses or were not prescribed enough medication. However, the response rate has recently been found to be only 50 percent in patients who have had adequate doses of antidepressants, suggesting that treatment resistance can be a generic feature of a patient and not restricted to just one therapy. The positive side of this equation is that medication combinations can be effective when ECT is not, and that combinations of medications and ECT can be more effective than either one alone.

The fact that combining medications is helpful in many cases suggests that treatment-resistant depression may represent a complex mixture of receptor and second-messenger malfunctions requiring interventions aimed at more than one of them. This situation is no different from that of many other medical problems. Cancer chemotherapy, for example, routinely involves a combination of three or four drugs, and congestive heart disease is often treated with combinations of digitalis and diuretics. The need to combine treatments should not be seen as a failure but as a straightforward strategy for dealing with complex cellular pathology.

Deception #7: If I stop the antidepressant, I can always restart it if depression comes back. Sometimes antidepressants remain effective whether they are taken for a first or a later episode. However, it is being found with increasing frequency that a medication that worked perfectly well at one point no longer has any effect when it is used for a subsequent episode. It may be that the physiology of the new episode is different, or the medication itself may change later treatment response. As was described earlier for lithium, when antidepressants suppress abnormal cellular processes, those processes may rebound with such intensity that the medication no longer can normalize it. The interaction of kindling, changes in gene expression, and adverse experience with the mood disorder, over time, may even make medications that have been continually effective stop working after a period of time. The bottom line is, the decision to discontinue an antidepressant is a serious one.

Deception #8: Anyone can prescribe an antidepressant. With the introduction of newer antidepressants that can be prescribed in a dose of just one or two pills, non-psychiatric physicians, who have not had special training in pharmacology, have come to feel that it is not particularly difficult to use these medications. Recently, some non-medical therapists, especially a group of psychologists, have argued that if they prescribed medications, it would eradicate the problem of dividing biological and psychological treatments between two different practitioners. A virtual battle over this issue has erupted. Psychiatrists argue that a medical degree is necessary to prescribe medications, and psychologists counter that most of the medical training psychiatrists receive either is not relevant to prescribing medications, is forgotten soon after graduation, or can be learned in special courses without exposure to other medical training, making a highly complex issue seem deceptively simple.

This debate is more than a mere turf war, for it reflects the deceptive core of conceptualizations regarding mental disorders. Concluding that because a medication *seems* simple it *is* simple ignores the complexities both of medications and the disorders for which they are prescribed. To ignore the great potential for harm as well as good in these medications is to adopt the deception that medicines for mental disorders, like the disorders themselves, are not that "real." We are continually learning more about adverse physical effects of psychiatric medications and about dangerous interactions with other medicines taken at the same time for medical illnesses. These are grave considerations that concern all of us in the mental health fields—professionals and patients alike.

Deception #9: The treatment of childhood depression is no different from the treatment of depression in adults. In the face of overwhelming evidence of the efficacy of antidepressants, many people who would have considered taking antidepressants shameful are agreeing to try these medications. More depressed children and adolescents are being given antidepressants, too, but the evidence is weak at best that antidepressants work as well in this population as they do in adults. In fact, every controlled study of tricyclic antidepressants has demonstrated that they are no better than a placebo in children, and even less effective than a placebo in adolescents. There are a few poorly controlled studies of SSRIs in adolescents suggesting that they may be effective, but the quality of these studies is marginal. One recent but as yet unpublished study by Texas psychiatrist Graham Elmsley found that Prozac was more effective than placebo for adolescent depression, but at the end of eight weeks of treatment patients still had significant residual depressive symptoms.

Why have antidepressants not been found to be as consistently effective for children and adolescents as they have for adults? For one thing, the rate of placebo response is much higher in this group, so it is more difficult for the antidepressant to outperform a placebo. Another problem is that since there is a greater likelihood of bipolarity in younger depressed patients, some of these patients will get worse as others get better, resulting in no net benefit for the entire group. Before depression is entrenched in the nervous system, patients may be responsive enough to environmental manipulations that antidepressants do not add as much to treatment.

Deception #10: Everyone who is unhappy should take an antidepressant. In the same Keller study that found a high rate of undertreatment in people with refractory depression, one-sixth of the patients who were not getting better with antidepressants were not depressed. These people were misdiagnosed, but as we saw earlier there is probably an even larger population of people who do not have any sort of clinical disorder who are given antidepressants for "cosmetic" purposes, when there is no proof at all that this use of antidepressants is effective or safe.

Deception #11: If a patient receives an antidepressant, there is no need to talk about anything. Medication can rebalance the brain, but it is no substitute for using the mind. To decide that a pill is all that is needed is to decide that the body (the brain) is valuable but the mind is not. Those who would like to exchange a purely mentalistic approach for an equally extreme faith in biomedical technology might wish to remember the story of Antonio Egas Moniz, who won the Nobel Prize for developing the prefrontal lobotomy. Moniz was later shot by a lobotomized patient!

PART IV

THE MIND DECEIVES THE BODY

He first deceased; she for a little tried
To live without him; liked it not and died.
— Sir Henry Wotton

How fancy throws us into perturbation.
People can die by mere imagination.
— Chaucer

A heart that is joyful does good as a curer, but a spirit that is stricken makes the bones dry.
— Proverbs 17:22

⇔   ⇔   ⇔

THE MIND'S ABILITY to deceive the body out of health—and even life itself—has been recorded for centuries. In the Bible (Acts 5:1-11), Luke tells the story of Ananias and his wife, Sapphira, who lied to the apostles. The couple said that they had given all of the proceeds of the sale of their property to the apostles, but they had really kept some of the money for themselves. When Peter learned of this dishonesty, he said to Ananias, "You have not lied to men but to God."

Upon hearing these words, Ananias instantly dropped dead. When Sapphira arrived on the scene, she was also confronted by Peter, who told her that "the feet of those who have buried your husband are at the door, and they will carry you out." In response she, too, "fell down at his feet and died."

Modern history contains many examples of well-known people whose minds told their bodies when to die. When American founding father Thomas Jefferson was severely ill at age eighty-three, he declared that he wanted to live until July 4, 1826, the fiftieth anniversary of the signing of the Declaration of Independence, which, of course, he had written. He remained alive until that date and then, hearing that it was the fourth, died peacefully. Mark Twain, who was born when Halley's comet appeared in 1835, often said that he came into the world with Halley's Comet and would go out with it as well. The next time the Comet returned was in 1910, and it was in that year that Twain died.

Each of us is so intimately linked to other people that fatal mind-body deceptions often involve the mind's need for the body to remain close to someone who has died. For example, Martha Jane Camary, better known as Wild West heroine Calamity Jane, had been extremely close to Wild Bill Hickock, who died on August 2, 1876. Twenty-seven years later, Calamity Jane got sick. When she realized that it was August 2, she said, "Bury me next to Bill," and died.

The chapters in this section address syndromes of illness and death influenced by the mind that are common and relatively well-researched, as well as a few unusual varieties whose dramatic features make them interesting and instructive. Studies of these syndromes show that the mind can have a destructive influence on the body, both acutely and chronically. Research is also beginning to demonstrate the positive side of this influence: interventions of the mind can improve the body's chances of overcoming disease. The limitations as well as the practical implications of this research will be made clear, so that anyone who wants to apply principles of the mind to treat the body will not be deceived.

16

If Thoughts Could Kill:
Fatal Mind-Body Deceptions

THERE ARE TWO kinds of scientific evidence that the mind can kill the body. The first consists of anecdotal reports of healthy, or at least medically stable, people who become ill or die in the midst of a stressful or exciting event that, in itself, does not seem particularly harmful. Because the victims in these anecdotal reports were not studied prior to their demise, there is no way to be certain that their sudden illness or death was due to the state of their minds rather than their bodies. However, the association between state of mind and state of the body in these cases is so obvious that it is very difficult to avoid the conclusion that one clearly affected the other.

The second line of evidence comes from formal studies of the relation between mental and physical health in groups of subjects. As we will see, some studies have examined the high prevalence of illness and death in psychologically vulnerable populations compared with people with the same physical risk factors who, in the absence of the psychological stressors, remain healthy. In the most convincing studies, psychological risk factors are objectively measured in physically well individuals, who are then followed for many years to see if they are more likely to develop certain illnesses than subjects who are matched in every way except for specific mental factors. It requires such dedication in subjects as well as investigators to repeat physical and mental measurements over the many decades it may take for the mental influence to demonstrate its effect on the body that valid longitudinal studies of this sort are few and far between. However, the few that have been conducted offer some provocative findings.

SUDDEN DEATH UNDER STRANGE—AND EVEN HAPPY—CIRCUMSTANCES

In the early 1970s Dr. George Engel, an internist and psychoanalyst, collected a total of 170 anecdotal reports of sudden unexplained deaths and analyzed their shared features. All of the people who had died in this manner had been healthy at the time of their deaths, which occurred in the midst of some form of intense emotional experience that was too powerful to ignore or control. In 34 percent, death occurred during a time of danger or just after the danger had passed. The majority (59 percent) of deaths were associated with loss: the anniversary of a bereavement, loss of status or self-esteem, or following the threat of some other kind of real or symbolic loss. About 6 percent died during a happy ending to a protracted struggle. Engel's example of death by bereavement is illuminating:

> A 17-year-old boy collapsed and died at 6 A.M., 4 June 1970; his older brother had died at 5:12 A.M., 4 June 1969, of multiple injuries incurred in an auto accident several hours earlier. The cause of the younger boy's death was massive subarachnoid hemorrhage caused by a ruptured anterior communicating artery aneurysm.

The aneurysm could have killed this boy at any time, or it might never have burst. Why this particular moment? The fatal mind–body connection is even more compelling in some of Engel's cases, in which people with no demonstrable medical pathology died unexpectedly, presumably of cardiac arrest:

> A newspaper reporter who had for years stoutly defended the name of a high public official long since dead died suddenly at a banquet commemorating the anniversary of the latter's 101st birthday. One of the invited speakers had stunned the audience by taking the occasion to make charges about the personal life of the official being honored. The reporter rose to his feet in a vigorous defense of the man he so much admired, expressing himself with great feeling and resentment. One account claims that the truth of the charges was publicly acknowledged at the banquet, to which the reporter commented sadly, "in Adam's fall we sinned all." He died a few minutes later.

In describing another case, Engel noted that overwhelming happiness could be as fatal as overwhelming sadness: a fifty-five-year-old man died when he met his eighty-eight-year-old father after a twenty-year separation; the father then dropped dead.

Voodoo Death

People who deceive their bodies into believing it is their destiny to die provide even more dramatic illustrations of the mind's destructive power over the body. "Voodoo death" is a dramatic example that has been well-described in anthropology journals and well-publicized in movies—but also occurs right under our modern-day noses. This extreme form of mind-body deception occurs when a perfectly healthy person is killed by nothing more than a belief that death is inevitable, for example, because of a curse or prophecy, or because a dangerous taboo has been violated. People who have died of voodoo death have been autopsied and subjected to all kinds of tests, and no evidence of covert illness, suicide, or foul play has ever been found. The classic circumstances of voodoo death are described succinctly in a 1957 article by physiologist Walter Cannon, who recounts the experience of a seventeenth-century explorer in the (then) Congo:

> A young negro on a journey lodged in a friend's house for a night. The friend had prepared for their breakfast a wild hen, a food strictly banned by a rule which must be inviolably observed by the immature. The young fellow demanded whether it was indeed a wild hen, and when the host answered "No," he ate of it heartily and proceeded on his way. A few years later, when the two met again, the old friend asked the younger man if he would eat a wild hen. He answered that he had been solemnly charged by a wizard not to eat that food. Thereupon the host began to laugh and asked him why he refused it now after having eaten it at his table before. On hearing this news the negro immediately began to tremble, so greatly was he possessed by fear, and in less than twenty-four hours he was dead.

Death by Prophecy

Sophisticated people who think themselves safe from this kind of wizardry should be aware that voodoo death is not just a phenomenon of primitive cultures. When superstition intrudes into the domain of modern medicine, the most powerful of technological treatments may be rendered useless. This is what happened to a twenty-two-year-old woman described in the *Journal of Nervous and Mental Disease* in 1973, who was admitted to the hospital with chest pain and fainting associated with a heart condition that was much milder than the symptoms it was causing.

The woman had been born in the Okefenokee swamp on Friday the thirteenth. She was delivered by a midwife who had delivered two other babies on the same day. The midwife had predicted that the first child would die before her sixteenth birthday, the second before her twenty-first birthday, and the third, who was the patient, before her twenty-third birthday.

Years later, events began to bear out the prophecy. The first girl died in an automobile accident just a few days before her sixteenth birthday. The second girl seemed to have escaped the curse when she reached the age of twenty-one without incident, but when she went to a bar to celebrate her birthday, a fight broke out while she was sitting at the bar with a friend. Someone pulled a gun and she was killed by a stray bullet.

Having related this story, the patient stated with utter conviction that she knew that she would not live to be twenty-three. Her symptoms got worse and worse, even though there was no earthly reason why she should have been feeling so ill. Despite heroic efforts to save her, she died of congestive heart failure one day before her twenty-third birthday.

Psychiatrist J. L. Mathis reported a case in which "the malevolent wish of a thwarted mother" proved as powerful as "the weird incantations of a primitive shaman." The victim was a fifty-three-year-old man who, for twenty-two years, had been a joint owner with his mother of a successful nightclub. When the man expressed a desire to sell the club at a profit and start a new business, his mother disagreed and warned that "something dire" would happen to him if he tried to strike out on his own. Two days after telling her that he was going to ignore her warning, he developed asthma for the first time in his life.

The man's mother continued to resist the sale of the club but, despite his new illness, he remained adamant. On the day of the sale, she prophesied, "Something will strike you." The next day, the patient's asthma worsened considerably. He was soon having asthmatic attacks three to four times per week, which persisted despite aggressive medical therapy.

Eventually the patient regained his health and began to make plans for the future. When he called his mother to tell her that he was about to reinvest the proceeds from the sale of the club, her only reply was that he had better prepare himself for the worst. One hour later, he died of an asthma attack.

Modern-Day Sorcerers

Even the physician, who is the very embodiment of technological healing, can be as deadly as a voodoo curse to patients who believe the doctor's words have magical power. British physician Alex Comfort makes the point that "in our own society, science tends to fill the ecological niche of sorcery. We are likely to miss bewitchment, when it does occur. . . . One extremely dangerous sorcerer in our culture is the physician. . . ." Comfort illustrates the power of medical sorcery with the following case, described in 1981:

A middle-aged, polysymptomatic and robust English woman, with a long history of manipulative and neurotic behaviors, was admitted to hospital for the investigation of joint pains. In the course of study, biopsy of a solitary enlarged lymph node revealed a few malignant cells. The patient read her own notes, arranged for admission to a "home for the dying," and died suddenly two weeks later, without evident [medical] cause.

People may even act as their *own* sorcerers, generating "curses" that inexorably lead to death. Experienced clinicians have encountered patients who plan for the hour of their deaths and then proceed to die on schedule. Sometimes these patients have their own timetable for the progression of a disease, which no medical expert is able to predict.

At other times, a perfectly healthy person will accurately predict the moment of death. This was the case for a man in his seventies, reported by Engel. Returning from an exhaustive medical examination that pronounced him fit and well, he proceeded to purchase a casket and began landscaping his own burial plot. Having completed his preparations, he called his family together and began to give them all of his possessions, saying, "I don't need these anymore." Just as the last item was given away, he fell to the floor, dead.

A voodoo-like deception that death is inevitable may contribute to many "garden varieties" of our human leave-taking. For example, one study found that 85 percent of deaths following poisonous snake bites were due to cardiac arrest and not to the direct effects of the venom. Some people who commit suicide die after a sublethal overdose or a minor self-inflicted wound, apparently *believing* that the injury should be fatal. Deceived by their minds into the inevitability of death, their bodies follow suit.

THROUGH THE SCIENTIFIC LOOKING-GLASS

Isolated instances of illness or death apparently produced by the mind are captivating, even compelling, but in scientific terms they prove nothing. If certain mental states do injure the body, it is important to sort out the highly complex variables and vulnerabilities in the mind and the body in a controlled, scientific manner.

Dying on Schedule

An epidemiologic view of the ways in which beliefs can influence the timing of death is provided by a series of large studies by researcher David Phillips and his associates. In one of these studies, Phillips examined the death certificates of 2,745,149 people dying from natural causes (excluding those who died during surgery) in California from 1969-1990. Phillips found that women were most likely to die during the week after their birthdays and were least likely to die just before their birthdays, whereas men were more likely to die before, rather than after, their birthdays.

Phillips hypothesized that women tended to view birthdays as an event that is worth living for, a "lifeline" that brings attention, gifts, and the promise of more achievements in the future. Men, on the other hand, were thought to be more likely to experience birthdays as a "deadline," a marker signifying that there is one less year to live and that one has not achieved everything one hoped to achieve by this point in life. Thus terminally ill women, for whom birthdays were a lifeline, might try to hold on a little longer, allowing themselves to die after the event had passed. Conversely, men who experienced birthdays as a negative event might not be as motivated to live until the next one.

The idea that people would be able to live a little longer in order to reach an important event might seem far-fetched, especially for an event as commonplace as a birthday. Nevertheless, the Phillips group set about trying to explore their hypothesis further by examining the timing of the deaths of 390 famous Americans, reasoning that famous people would be more likely to view birthdays as a lifeline: they would receive more attention and have more accomplishments to feel good about as they looked back on the previous year, as well as more to look forward to in the coming year. The results supported Phillips' expectations: 20 percent of the famous people died shortly *after* their birthdays, suggesting that when they faced death, they hung on until their birthdays, which they presumably considered important, had passed. In contrast, Phillips found that only 3 percent of the general population died shortly following their birthdays.

Because birthdays are not important for everyone, Phillips points out that events that *are* important to a particular group may play the same role as birthdays in determining the time of death. For example, in Jewish populations the likelihood of dying was found to decrease by almost one-third just before Passover and to increase by the same amount just after that holiday, while non-Jewish mortality did not follow this pattern. The same pattern was also observed in Chinese populations in association with the symbolically important Harvest Moon Festival.

Death by Cultural Belief

To further clarify the ways in which personal symbolism as well as birthdays could influence cycles of life and death, Phillips examined California death certificates of 28,169 Chinese-Americans and 412,632 Caucasian-Americans to determine the effect of beliefs about fate on the timing of death. A belief common to the Chinese population under study was that a person's fate is influenced by the year of birth. Each year is associated with a basic element of the earth (fire, earth, metal, water, and wood), and each of these elements is linked to a specific bodily part or function (fire with the heart, for instance, and earth with lumps and tumors). In this system of thought, the element associated with a given year of birth determines susceptibility to specific diseases. For example, someone born in a fire year would be more vulnerable to heart disease, and someone born in an earth year would be more likely to get cancer later.

Phillips reasoned that people born in a fire year, who also happened to have heart disease, would see that particular illness as dictated by fate and would be more inclined to resign themselves to their disease stoically, while they would not feel as hopeless or passive in the face of cancer, a disease that was not predestined in their lives. Similarly, people with cancer who were born in an earth year would view cancer as their fate but not heart disease. The physiology of the belief that it is hopeless to try to change one's fate could interact with the physiology of the illness, leading to an earlier death than would occur in someone who was mobilized to overcome the situation.

As unlikely as it might seem, this hypothesis was confirmed for a number of diseases. As one example, Chinese patients who were born in an earth year and died from cancer lived 1.6 years *less* than cancer patients not born in an earth year. The impact of birth year on survival could not be explained by negative health habits, such as smoking. Differences in life span were also clearly linked to beliefs rather than to an actual astrological influence, since the more Chinese patients born in an earth year subscribed to traditional beliefs, the more years of life they lost to cancer. Conversely, there was little difference in age of death in non–Chinese cancer patients born in earth versus nonearth years.

The Toll of Life Events

The impact of mental states on physical health was studied from another angle by U.S. Navy researcher Richard Rahe. Rahe attempted to quantify external events that might affect a person's vulnerability to illness by developing a questionnaire called the "Schedule of Recent Experiences" (SRE). The SRE was created by asking various groups of people to rate the impact of a number of common events—some negative, some positive—such as getting married, having a baby, losing a job, or losing a spouse. Rahe found that, regardless of cultural background, most people assigned a similar number of "life change units" (LCUs) to each event when they were told that the death of a spouse would arbitrarily be given a score of 100 LCUs.

The SRE contains forty-three events grouped into four general categories. For example:

Family Events
- Death of a spouse (100)
- Divorce (73)
- Marriage (50)
- Son or daughter leaving home (29)

Personal Events
- Detention in jail (63)
- Major personal injury or illness (53)
- Outstanding personal achievement (28)
- Change in residence (20)

Work Events
- Fired from work (47)
- Retirement from work (45)
- Major change in work responsibilities (29)
- Trouble with boss (23)

Financial Events
- Major change in financial state (38)
- Mortgage or loan over $10,000 (31)
- Mortgage or loan less than $10,000 (17)

No life is stress-free, and healthy individuals report an average of 75 LCUs over a six-month period. However, Rahe and his collaborators found that an excess of stress could lead to trouble. The first application of this principle was practical: when the SRE was used to predict which members of a Seattle football team would be injured in a given season, so that steps could be taken to reduce the chance that valuable players would end up on the sidelines, it turned out that the best predictor was the amount of stress experienced *before* the season began. Players who accumulated more than 300 LCUs in a year were eight times likelier than their less stressed teammates to be injured or incapacitated during the following season.

In addition to its application in sports, the SRE has been used to predict the onset of a broad variety of illnesses in many different populations. Some studies have been *retrospective;* that is, people who are already sick are asked to enumerate the stresses they experienced in the year before becoming ill. This method is risky, because being sick influences a person's memory of past events. To overcome this objection, *prospective* studies have been conducted, in which large populations of healthy people are given the SRE and are followed for the subsequent year.

The prospective studies have produced results similar to the retrospective ones. With both methods, about half of all subjects who scored 150–300

LCUs in a year developed some sort of illness during the following year. In some cases the illness was relatively mild (the flu or a broken bone); in others, more serious conditions emerged (heart disease, cancer, or diabetes, for instance). Of those unlucky enough to experience more than 300 LCUs of stress in a year, 70 percent were ill the following year, often with more than one physical problem.

These kinds of findings should not be taken to mean that life change or stress *inevitably* increases the risk of illness. A number of studies have shown no association between stress and the onset or worsening of disease. Perhaps in these investigations people did not interpret as stressful events that others find overwhelming, or perhaps some people are more vulnerable than others to the physical impact of stress.

PSYCHOLOGICAL VULNERABILITIES TO STRESS: MIND GIVES WAY TO MATTER

Several prospective studies have investigated psychological factors that might magnify or reduce the impact of stress on the body. These kinds of longitudinal studies are important for scientific purposes because emotional well-being is measured long before any illness has begun. If a particular psychological pattern predicts illness years later, that means it is either a predisposing factor or at least a marker of some slowly developing pathological process, and not a result of the disease.

Mental Adjustment—Or Lack Thereof

One pioneering investigation was conducted by psychiatrist George Vaillant and his colleagues. Between 1942 and 1944 they enrolled 188 male college sophomores in a longitudinal study. At the start of the study, all subjects were in excellent physical health and their psychological functioning, while demonstrating a good deal of variability, was well within the normal range. Vaillant's group used questionnaires, interviews, and physical examinations periodically to reassess the subjects' physical and mental health for the next 40 years. Psychological and physical status were assessed independently of each other to avoid the possibility that knowledge of one would influence the evaluation of the other.

Vaillant found that mental adjustment during and shortly after college strongly predicted who would become chronically ill, disabled, or dead nine to thirty-five years later. Six sources of stress rendered some men much more likely than their peers to experience significant deterioration in physical health between the ages of forty-two and fifty-five:

- Disruptive or unsupportive childhoods
- Maladjustment in college
- Dissatisfaction with, or lack of progress in, careers after graduation
- Lack of means or time for vacations
- Unhappy marriages
- Frequent use of tranquilizers

Earlier *mental* health was a better predictor of later *physical* health than socioeconomic status, quality of health care, health and longevity of parents, smoking, use of alcohol, or even earlier physical health. Oddly enough, subjects whose physical health was poorer early in life were more likely to develop psychological problems when they got older, not more physical problems. General measures of *mental adjustment* turned out to be the most potent predisposing factors for *physical deterioration* of any kind, although it was not apparent exactly which of these mental/psychological factors was most important in setting the stage for later disease of the body.

Doctors Are People, Too

Carolyn B. Thomas and her associates obtained similar results when they followed 1,337 physically healthy students who were graduated from Johns Hopkins Medical School between 1948 and 1964. This study was unique in that it identified a cluster of mental characteristics that predisposed this population to the development of a specific group of illnesses years later: cancer, hypertension, heart attack, severe mental illness, and suicide. The psychological predictors—such as "neurotic" personality traits,* excessive anxiety under stress, chronic insomnia and fatigue, and lack of closeness to parents during childhood—were more important than the physical risk factors such as high blood pressure, body fat, and use of alcohol, tobacco, and coffee.

Thomas found another fascinating mental predictor of later illness in the Rorschach (ink blot) test. Certain subjects responded to the ink blots with comments about cancer, drowning, crying for help, and death. One student, for example, saw "a bat in flight, and it has tumors on the anterior wing surfaces." Years later, while in private practice, this physician developed a fatal malignancy.

Although Thomas could use psychological factors identified before students became ill to identify later illness, it was not possible to predict exactly which illness would develop or even whether it would be physical or mental. For example, students who were destined to commit suicide, become

*This term was not defined by the experimenters but apparently indicated psychological maladjustment of the kind noted by Vaillant.

mentally ill, or develop a malignant tumor all resembled each other in that they were more likely than other subjects to have had distant relationships with their parents, become pessimistic and withdrawn in response to stress, and respond to the Rorschach with comments about depression, tumors, cancer, mutilation, or death.

If pessimism, isolation, and depression set the stage for the later destruction of the body by suicide or cancer, the implications are important. Mental health clinicians have known for many years that a depressed person's inability to ask for help can eventually lead to suicide. People who feel they can or should only depend on themselves at all times may do well until they encounter one of the inevitable situations in life that require support, consultation, or assistance. Unable to find all of the resources within themselves to resolve the problem completely, and unwilling to "borrow" additional resources from someone else, they feel overwhelmed, defeated, and humiliated. A problem that could be overcome with help becomes insoluble without it. In this setting, if one is not rescued without having to ask for help, the only solution to the problem may be death, either directly through suicide or indirectly through fatal illness.

Some people who are susceptible to cancer appear to share the same aversion to receiving help as suicidal personality types. When a stress cannot be overcome alone and it feels intolerable to the person to lean on others for assistance, the result is a perception of peril and hopelessness. We have already seen how the combination of excessive danger, lack of internal resources, and inability to ask for help deceives the mind into mental disorders like depression; in subsequent chapters we will see how a similar constellation deceives the body into medical illnesses like cancer.

SOCIAL SUPPORT: THE PORT IN THE STORM

What else does stress research tell us about why one person becomes ill while another resists the debilitating effects of adverse events? One of the most crucial protective factors is *support from other people.* Social support can diminish the amount of stress encountered, reduce the impact of stress when it does occur, reinforce healthy behaviors, and have positive effects on the mind and body.

The importance of other people in reducing the unhealthy effects of stress was illustrated by a study of 170 women, aged eighteen to twenty-nine, who completed the SRE when they were thirty-two weeks into a normal first pregnancy. The subjects also evaluated their feelings about themselves and their relationships with important people in their lives, such as husbands, parents, in-laws, friends, and neighbors. Women with extensive social contacts, in whom they felt great confidence, were assigned high "social asset scores," while those who did not have many significant support people, or did not feel they could depend on those they did have, were assigned low social asset scores.

By the end of their pregnancies, 91 percent of the women who had high SRE scores and low social asset scores had had physical complications. In contrast, only a third of those with the same stress scores but better social supports had had a complicated pregnancy. Since all patients received the same prenatal care, these differences appeared to be due to the protective influences of social support.

Social Isolation Can Be Deadly

The importance of ongoing sources of social support to the preservation of health was even more compellingly demonstrated by a prospective study of 2,229 healthy men and 2,496 healthy women living in Alameda County, California. During ten years of follow-up, socially isolated men and women were 2.3 and 2.8 times respectively more likely to die of all causes than men and women of the same age who were able to maintain meaningful social relationships. The kinds of relationships that kept people alive longer were varied: marriage, ongoing contact with friends and relatives (not just *having* friends and relatives), church membership, and membership in formal or informal social groups.

The Alameda County Study found that social isolation at the beginning of the study was a better predictor of who would live and who would die than socioeconomic status, access to medical treatment and preventive health care, psychological problems, and even health-related habits, such as smoking, obesity, physical inactivity, and use of alcohol. Furthermore, the *total amount of social relatedness,* not which category of contact predominated, predicted who would be alive at the end of the study. For example, single individuals who maintained frequent contact with friends and relatives lived as long as people who were married but had few friends.

We usually think of our social network of friends and family as being *external* to us—and as being either present or absent. However, an interesting 1988 study by psychiatrist Peter Steinglass and colleagues of an Israeli village, relocated when land captured by Israel during the 1967 war was returned to Egypt, challenges this concrete notion. For these Israelis, having a network of relatives, even if they were not physically present, was more protective against the demoralization of being uprooted and relocated than the network of friends who were actually present. After being relocated to a completely different setting, in which the same friends were not available, people tended to establish new social circles that were remarkably similar to the relationships they had left behind. This study suggests that social relatedness is as much a phenomenon that occurs *within* the individual as it does *between* the individual and others. In other words, it may be the availability of other people *within one's own mind,* rather than their availability in the neighborhood, that is the most important factor in buffering the effects of stress.

It is probably not stress that kills but *the lack of capacity for relatedness in the person who confronts the stress.* To the extent that people have the capacity to borrow strength from others, the impact of any stressful event on mind and body is softened. Those who have few or no external sources of support—or cannot make use of them—are more likely to be overwhelmed by the vagaries of the world. When people do not have sustaining relationships to help them control situations that overpower their resources, their bodies as well as their minds may be subject to destructive processes that result in a variety of diseases. We will now begin to examine some of these processes.

17

Mental States That
Deceive the Body

WHAT KINDS OF bodily states kill those people who do not have sufficiently sustaining connections to others? And how do relationships keep potentially lethal physiology in check? In this chapter we will see how
attachments to other people impact bodily function. We will then revisit the
physiology of the stress response and expand our appreciation of the effects
of arousal gone awry on the activities of the body as well as those of the
mind.

ATTACHMENT

Mental states that deceive the body into physical illness, like those that deceive the mind into psychological illness, are influenced, to a great extent,
by other people. Relationships affect our ability to respond to stress for two
reasons. First, early interactions leave their indelible imprint in the form of
enduring ways of handling pressures from within and without. Second,
throughout life other people help us remain emotionally and mentally stable by giving encouragement, comfort, and the sense of belonging. Because
others have the power to stabilize us in times of stress, they also have the potential to destabilize us, creating even more stress. We will soon see that other
people can have the same lifesaving or destructive impact on the body.

In Part II we discussed how the drive to depend on others can be so powerful that people who do not trust others to meet their needs may use bodily symptoms to obtain the care they need. The drive for attachment is even more powerful. In fact, it can be even more potent than the drive for self-preservation. Attachment is a deeply ingrained biological as well as psychological force that is programmed into the genes of the body. During times of stress, we seek out "attachment figures" (those whom we trust and love) and are comforted by their presence. The threat of separation from an attachment figure is universally upsetting. Positive emotions, such as love and admiration, make people affiliate with each other, while negative emotions, such as fear and despair, are unleashed by the rupture of an attachment bond. Unpleasant emotions evoked by separation create a powerful drive to reestablish the attachment and feel good again.

Animal Research on Attachment

Because all higher animals, including humans, display similar attachment behaviors, studies of the nature of attachment in primates can tell us a great deal about attachment in people. One of the first important facts to emerge from these studies was that attachment is not the same as dependency. In Freud's day, it was thought that the drive for emotional closeness came from the gratification of appetites: early in life, so the theory went, children became attached to their parents because the parents fed and cared for them; later in life, appetites such as the sex drive and the wish to depend on someone were supposed to be the primary motivation for adult relationships. Anyone who has ever loved another person knows this is not true, but it was not until carefully designed animal studies examined the issue that scientists began to appreciate that attachment is an independent drive.

The first of these studies was done by psychologist Harry Harlow and his associates, who studied infant monkeys raised with two kinds of artificial maternal surrogates, one made of wire and one of cloth. By means of a bottle, both surrogates provided sufficient nourishment, but the wire surrogate did not have a comforting surface to which the infants could cling. If attachment were driven by nothing more than the need to be fed, animals should become equally "attached" to the cloth and the wire mother. Harlow found that infants who had been "raised" by the cloth mother preferred her, but so did infants raised by the wire mother. When confronted by something new or frightening—for example, a noisy windup toy—the wire monkey-raised infant ran immediately to the cloth monkey even though the more familiar wire mother was also available. The drive to be close to a comforting source of support, even if inanimate, seemed to be a separate drive from the drive for nourishment.

Attachment involves much more than the need to be touched, as demonstrated by the not-surprising observation that infant monkeys who have received all of their nourishment from a cloth surrogate far prefer the company of a real monkey. When the subtleties of closeness to others are added to the basics of attachment, it is seen to be such a potent drive that people, as well as animals, will forego food and other rewards in order to be with someone else.

Like many innate drives, attachment follows a developmental timetable that is dependent for its full expression on the opportunity to interact with other individuals, not just physically soothing surrogates. The relationship that is most influential in shaping the future direction of attachment is the infant's relationship with the mother (or other primary caretaker).* But as children grow older, a wide range of other attachments develop—between child and father, with peers, and then with other adults. Even inanimate objects can serve the same function as people in the mental equilibrium of the developing child, for whom a transitional object, such as a favorite blanket, stuffed toy, or doll, steadfastly held while the mother is out of view, evokes the mother's reassuring presence. In adulthood, attachment to more sophisticated transitional objects (a photograph, a good-luck charm, a song, an institution, or even a concept like patriotism) can be an equally potent stand-in for life-sustaining relationships with people. As diverse as these relationships become, they all tend to follow the pattern that characterized the earliest bond between baby and mother, a pattern that involves the body as well as the mind.

Attachment and Biology: A Reciprocal Relationship

Literally from the moment of birth, attachment involves intimate sharing of biological as well as psychological functions. When a mother awakens her infant, puts it to sleep, feeds, stimulates, and soothes, she is serving as an organizer of her baby's physiology, providing *zeitgebers* for emerging biological rhythms. Like all attachments, this interaction goes both ways: at the same time that the baby becomes attuned to the mother's biological rhythms, her rhythms become aligned with those of the baby. In fact, as early as the second day of life, cycles of activity, alertness, drowsiness, and sleep of mother and infant begin to become synchronized with each other. Animal studies expand our understanding of how completely the mother-infant relationship is a prototype for mind-body synchronization by attachment figures. For example, the infant rat's heart rate remains stable only if the infant nurses

---

*Even in kibbutzes, where children see their parents for only one or two hours a day and on the Sabbath, emotional bonds are much stronger toward the parents than toward nurses and other surrogates who spend the bulk of the day with the children and meet most of their physical needs.

regularly. Neither the presence of the mother alone nor the ingestion of milk alone controls heart rate; it is *the combination of the two* that functions as the cardiac regulator.

Physical contact continues throughout life to have the potential to regulate cardiac function in people as well as animals, especially when the heart is unstable. As a result, abnormal cardiac rhythms can be stabilized with just the touch of another person. Stabilized cardiac patients may develop a recurrence of abnormal cardiac function when they are transferred from the intensive care unit, where they have received a great deal of touching in the course of their care, to the unfamiliar setting of an open medical ward, where caretaking is far more infrequent.

Many bodily functions are regulated by the presence of soothing attachments. Memory, attentiveness, body temperature, sleep patterns, hormonal cycles, pain tolerance, and emotional state are just a few of the complex life processes that are influenced by relationships with other people. (For example, it has even been observed that the menstrual cycles of women living together [e.g., in dormitories] adjust to the same timetable.) The notion of independence, of total self-sufficiency, therefore, is a deception. Only with continued input from others are we able to "tune" our physiology as well as our psychology. Just as losing someone important can make the mind incapable of coping with everyday challenges to its integrity, it can also make the body unable to cope with everyday attacks on *its* integrity.

Measuring the Pain of Separation

Just as attachment regulates mind and body, loss of an important bond with another person creates a terrible instability in both domains. Separation and loss are disruptive for three reasons. First, they evoke grief—a state in which the mind is disrupted by an anguished but fruitless search for the lost person, and the body is disrupted by the stress response. The stress response is further intensified by being alone, which makes everything feel more dangerous than when someone else is around to offer support, help, and protection. (In fact, one of the most important adaptive advantages of attachment is that any stress is easier to handle in a group than alone.) At the same time, the loss itself has robbed the sufferer of a crucial source of psychobiological regulation that could splint mind and body during this stressful time.

Dr. Martin Reite, a psychiatrist at the University of Colorado, developed a device that can be implanted in a simple and non-traumatic surgical procedure to study the ways in which separation ruptures physiological homeostasis in primates. Since the physiology of attachment and separation reactions does not appear measurably different in the two species, information from primate studies can be applied to human beings.

Two experimental models of primate separation have been used. The first involves separation of an infant monkey from its mother. The second involves separation of a monkey from a peer with whom it has been raised as an alternative attachment figure. Both peer and mother-infant separations produce similar reactions, although the reaction of an infant separated from its mother is more intense, and both are eerily similar to separation reactions in human infants that are discussed later in this chapter. Animal separation experiments make it possible to study the physiologic mechanisms by which loss can make the body vulnerable to the kinds of medical catastrophes that were described in the last chapter and the equally pervasive cardiac and immune system malfunctions discussed in subsequent chapters.

The response of an infant monkey to separation follows a three-phase sequence: protest, depression, and reunion.

FIGHT-FLIGHT: THE PHYSIOLOGY OF PROTEST

Immediately after being separated from an important attachment figure, the primate infant enters a phase of *protest,* in which it screams, paces back and forth, and looks desperately around, obviously searching for the mother. Protest is an inevitable consequence of loss of the regulatory function of the mother on the infant's physiology and the threat of facing alone a world too complex for the infant to manage. The major adaptive advantage of the frantic activity of protest is to increase the infant's chance of being found by a mother who has temporarily lost track of her baby.

The hyperactive *behavior* of the protest phase is paralleled by equally hyperactive *physiology.* Heart rate dramatically increases and levels of stress hormones that prepare for action are high. Resting body temperature is elevated, indicating heightened metabolic activity. Changes in sleep patterns reflect increased arousal and decreased ability to rest. Since energy mobilization and stress-response systems are as hyperactive when the infant sits still as when it is active, the physiological activation is more than just a counterpart to frantic behavior. In primate species in which another adult "adopts" an infant that has been separated from its mother, protest behavior quiets down when the infant is cuddled by the surrogate, but the physiology of protest does not abate until the infant is reunited with its mother.

Protest is a special example of the body's preparation for danger that we first encountered in Part III. In that section, we saw that the perception of danger is a function of the degree to which a situation is unfamiliar, resembles previously unresolved stresses, or overwhelms adaptive capabilities. We now know that a sense of isolation or lack of support will also make any challenge feel more dangerous. The physiology of the stress response involves arousal and hypervigilance, which is a starting point for mental disorders like anxiety and depression as well as the physical disorders that will be considered later in this section. Just as it stimulates mental activity, arousal stimulates the body to prepare for physical action to overcome whatever threat is being faced. And just as mental activity can work against itself when it is overstimulated, physical activation can turn against the body when it loses its capacity to regulate itself.

The neurology of the stress response begins with the registration of danger in the frontal lobes of the brain, which compare current information to stored data about past experiences and plan a solution to the perceived problem. The perception of danger activates alerting centers like the locus coeruleus that orient the mind to expect and look for anything that might be a threat. Mobilization of action by emotions such as anger and fear, which provide the motivation to attack or run away from a stress, is provided by the limbic system. The news of danger that has emotional consequences is transmitted to the hypothalamus, the way-station between the central nervous system and the rest of the body. The hypothalamus controls hormonal responses, such as those of the adrenal and thyroid glands, that are overly activated in depression and many other syndromes involving an excessive stress response. One of the most important "arms" of the hypothalamus is a branch of the nervous system called the autonomic nervous system.

The Sympathetic Nervous System

The autonomic nervous system plays an essential role in all stress reactions, including the protest phase of separation. The sympathetic nervous system, one of its two major divisions, provides the physiologic fuel necessary to engage or escape from a stressful situation. The emotional, psychological, behavioral, and physiological mobilization that occurs when this branch is activated in response to a threat is called the "fight-flight" response.

System-wide Alert
Among other activities, sympathetic activation increases the rate and strength of cardiac contraction, dilates blood vessels that supply muscles, and constricts vessels that supply less involved organs, such as the skin and gastrointestinal tract. As a result, more blood is circulated, and more of the blood that circulates goes to the organs that need it most during an acute threat. In addition, breathing centers are stimulated to increase the rate and depth of respiration so that more oxygen can be extracted from the blood. Hyperventilation facilitates oxygen transport and increases excitability of the nervous system—but can also impair concentration.

Hormonal Help

The sympathetic nervous system also stimulates the adrenal gland to secrete a number of hormones that provide *energy* for the action systems of the body and *protection* from the effects of injury. One class of adrenal stress hormones is the catecholamines, which include epinephrine (adrenalin) and norepinephrine (noradrenalin). Important actions of the catecholamines include stimulating the heart, raising blood pressure, and activating metabolic pathways that increase levels of metabolic fuels, such as sugar and fats. Norepinephrine also acts as a neurotransmitter in the locus coeruleus, an area of the brain that produces alertness and vigilance, adding a sense of mental arousal and readiness to the fight–flight response.

During the fight–flight response, hypersecretion of a class of hormones produced in a region of the adrenal gland called the adrenal cortex, the corticosteroids (e.g., cortisol), prepares the body for the longer-term consequences of danger by suppressing the immune response, which could be activated by damaged tissue that is perceived by the body's defenses as foreign. Cortisol also alters blood pressure, availability of metabolic energy, and mood in a direction that facilitates problem-solving.

The purpose of the fight–flight response is to mobilize the organism either to engage, or run away from, some explicit threat. In human beings, this goal is facilitated by connections between (1) the parts of the brain that mediate thinking and feeling; (2) effectors of external action, such as the muscles and cardiovascular system; (3) effectors of internal action, such as the hypothalamus; and (4) brain centers that facilitate the retrieval of memories and emotions useful in developing strategies for overcoming the present threat. The same connections mediate the perception of danger in response to a memory, fantasy, or imagined possibility, activating the fight–flight response to the same degree as would a struggle with a tangible antagonist. *The perception of psychological danger therefore has the same power over the body as the perception of physical danger.*

The Parasympathetic Nervous System

The fight–flight response must be turned off if the consequences of continued physiological activation are not to become a greater stress than the original danger. Even when the threat persists, it is important to have a mechanism to control the fight–flight response and prevent depletion or destruction of bodily resources. The *conservation-withdrawal* response counterbalances the fight–flight response and is also called into play in any situation in which it is necessary to withdraw from a threat that is impossible to overcome, thus conserving energy until the situation changes. (A familiar example is hibernation, which slows down metabolism and heat production in order to reduce the expenditure of energy below the meager amount that the environment can supply.)

System-wide Shutdown

Like fight-flight, conservation-withdrawal is mediated by nerves and hormones. The nerves involved in this process are in the branch of the autonomic nervous system called the parasympathetic nervous system, which includes the vagus nerve (it gets its name from its wanderings from the brain stem to the heart, the gastrointestinal tract, and other regions scattered all over the body). The parasympathetic nervous system slows the heart, makes the gastrointestinal tract less active, reduces energy production and body temperature, and alters daily rhythms of immune function, brain-wave patterns, and the sleep-wake cycle, among others. Acetylcholine, a neurotransmitter of memory as well as the parasympathetic nervous system, changes the orientation of the brain away from engagement with danger and toward retreat.

Like the fight-flight response, conservation-withdrawal is a stress response that can be observed in many species. For example, if a wild rodent is exposed to a hawk or hungry snake from which it cannot escape, the rodent exhibits a brief period of agitation and increased heart rate, followed by complete immobility and unresponsiveness. In this catatonic state, body temperature decreases dramatically and heart rate drops to 30 beats per minute from a normal level of 210.

Overkill

Such drastic enervation is adaptive if it keeps a predator from noticing its victim. However, this potentially useful mechanism becomes dangerous if it keeps the organism from taking action when necessary. Rodents in an extreme state of conservation-withdrawal do nothing when they are actually attacked. Instead, they just sit unmoving, their hearts slowing to a standstill if the predator does not get them first.

Just as the fight-flight response must be terminated when it is no longer appropriate to the situation, mechanisms exist for ending the conservation-withdrawal response before it becomes a destructive reaction. One way to achieve this goal is to force the animal to act (for example, by forcefully dragging it away from the predator), in which case it immediately comes back to life and the physiology of conservation-withdrawal is abolished.

Out of Mind, Out of Body

The power of the mind to deceive the body into or out of the fight-flight response has many practical applications. In everyday life we are continually confronted with real and symbolic dangers, the meaning of which depends more on our mental perceptions than the explicit nature of the threat. An examination, a social engagement, or a meeting, for example, can be a challenge, a minor annoyance, or an overwhelming trauma, depending on how it is interpreted. Mild hypervigilance is helpful in these settings—but terror, a racing heart, trembling hands, and other manifestations of fight-flight can be distracting and even destructive. These manifestations of fight-flight can be brought under control through relaxation techniques, meditation, hypnosis, or simply putting the idea out of one's mind—in other words, *denial*.

The capacity of the mind to activate as well as deactivate the fight-flight phase of the stress response was demonstrated in a study of sport parachutists as they prepared to make their first jump. They were initially frightened by the prospect of jumping out of a plane for the first time—who wouldn't be? Their bodies automatically prepared for the danger: dry mouths, rapid breathing, pounding hearts, and elevated blood pressure were the norm. A few would-be parachutists responded to their own agitation by deciding not to jump. The rest, however, convinced themselves that jumping was really not so dangerous, a "conviction" that calmed their physiology and allowed them to go through with the adventure.

Anyone but another parachutist would probably consider this an example of denial, the mental mechanism whereby we are able to ignore some important aspect of external or internal reality. The interesting result of the parachutists' self-imposed mental deception was that all physiologic evidence of the fight-flight response abruptly disappeared, along with the perception of danger—even though the objective threat remained the same. This particular mind-body adaptation proved effective, since all subjects reached the ground safely. (The number who jumped again was not reported.)

If effective physical or mental action fails to disengage the fight-flight response, its persistence may exhaust rather than mobilize physical and emotional resources. For example, if violent activity and vocalizations of separated primates do not attract the mother back to them, chances are that she is too far away or too busy with something else to respond. At this point, hyperactivity becomes a liability if it attracts a predator. Because of these dangers, nature has evolved a time limit to the protest phase. In infant monkeys, the limit is one or two days. In human infants who are at least six months old, protest upon separation from the mother lasts from a few hours to as long as one week. In both species, protest is followed by a phase that seems to represent the emergence of conservation-withdrawal.

SEPARATION DEPRESSION

In studies of infant monkeys separated from their mothers, researchers I. Charles Kaufman and L.A. Rosenblum note that the infants "seemed largely disengaged from the environment and appeared to derive little comfort from the presence of others." Human infants separated from their mothers behave the same way: they curl into a fetal position and refuse to interact with anyone. Though physically capable of moving around, they do so only when forced, and even then, they seem to be moving in slow motion. Such behavior has adaptive value for wild creatures: it allows them to remain less visible, to conserve energy and body heat, and to evoke protective behaviors in available adults until the mother returns.

A glance at Figure 17.1 makes it obvious why this phase is called "separation depression." However, although separated infants of any species, including humans, look sad, it is not known if the sadness of infant separation depression is anything like the complex mental state of adult depression. One important similarity is that, like depressed adults, infants with separation depression become disengaged from the world around them, even if other sources of support are available. An extreme version of human separation depression known as "marasmus" (hospitalism), in which infants who do not have contact with their mothers (or meaningful substitutes) for a prolonged period of time become inconsolable, can have a fatal outcome. Even though sufficient attention is paid to their physical needs, these infants become increasingly withdrawn and unresponsive, refusing nourishment (or not benefiting from it), until they literally die from infection or cardiac arrest.

Conservation-Withdrawal

The behavioral slowing that characterizes adult depression is probably one manifestation of conservation-withdrawal that, as we saw in Part III, is mixed with arousal. In infant separation depression there appears to be a more clear-cut change in physiology from the fight–flight of protest to a more pure state of conservation-withdrawal. Heart rate is slowed, sometimes dangerously. Body temperature is also low, even if the infant is cuddled, indicating a primary disturbance of temperature regulation, not just the loss of body heat because there is no mother to hold the baby. Immune function, brain wave patterns, and the sleep–wake cycle are altered, as are other bodily rhythms. As with any aspect of normal physiology, these and other aspects of conservation-withdrawal can be adaptive to the extent that they allow the infant to hang on until things get better, but if they become excessive, the consequences can be dire. For example, Reite found that the hearts of a few infants in the throws of separation depression slowed to a complete halt.

REUNION

The third phase of the separation reaction is reunion—or the hope for it. In animal research, if mother and infant are reunited within a certain period of

Figure 17-1.
Separation depression

time, they cling to each other, fiercely resisting further attempts at separating them. When they are finally reassured of each other's presence, they resume their normal activities. The physiology of fight-flight and conservation-withdrawal persists for a while after the infant's behavior has returned to normal, but before too long this, too, has resolved.

British researcher John Bowlby observed that in human infants, the physical and psychological consequences of separation can be reversed if the mother and infant are reunited within three to five months. However, if separation continues much beyond this point, or if previous separations have made the infant less tolerant of the mother, *normal functioning may never be restored*. Protest and withdrawal stop and the infant regains its normal level of activity, but once the baby has accommodated itself to the loss and relinquished the attachment, it may become indifferent or even hostile to the mother, never regaining genuine affection for her. Other childhood attachments may be formed, but they do not approximate the original, deep attachment to the mother.

Building on the work of René Spitz, a renowned developmental psychiatrist, Bowlby found that hospitalized infants who are kept away from their mothers for extended periods of time seem to resent the mothers or, worse yet, not to recognize them at all. After a prolonged period of reacquaintance, many finally warm up, but some never seem to feel the same. Even some young patients who are hospitalized for just a few days, during which they have no contact with their mothers, are distant when reunited.

Spitz, who practiced for many years at the University of Colorado, suggested that adverse outcomes of mother-infant separations could be averted by allowing parents to have unrestricted access to their hospitalized infants. Lola Lubchenko, a pediatrician who was influenced by Spitz, saw to it that unlimited visiting hours were instituted at the University of Colorado hospital. This has become such a standard of practice everywhere that many pediatricians do not remember that efforts to preserve the parent-infant bond were considered neurotic, until objective research showed that the practice of sending parents home until their children were discharged was ill-advised and even dangerous.

FANTASY IS JUST LIKE REALITY WHEN IT COMES TO SEPARATION AND REUNION

Studies of infant separation show that the mental side of separation reactions can be enduring and that the physical side can kill. What are the implications for adults? As our minds grow, we are able to substitute thoughts and memories of other people for the people themselves, just as we can create symbolic stand-ins for loved ones that are every bit as potent as the actual person. Because our bodies treat these substitutes like any other source of attachment, when we lose them—even if the loss is through disappointment or a change in our thinking rather than through separation—the physiology of fight-flight and conservation-withdrawal can be elicited, with effects ranging from mildly uncomfortable to fatal. By the same token, the drive to hold onto substitutes for other people can be as powerful as the drive to hold onto the people themselves.

In fact, the drive to reestablish a bond that was disrupted involuntarily can last a lifetime, even when there is no possibility of reunion. People who have lost a parent through divorce or death may harbor a never-ending yearning to rejoin the parent. The hope that it is possible to be reunited with a dead parent drives some individuals to pursue death through suicide or risk-taking behavior, in the belief that when they die they will at last be reunited with the lost parent.

The driving power of the need to be reunited with the lost beloved was tragically illustrated by Elvis Presley. Elvis was extremely attached to his mother. Inconsolable when she died at age forty-two on August 14, 1958, he exclaimed, "My life has ended!" He spent the next nineteen years searching for her through various occult experiments. When his many attempts to contact her were met with failure, he became more frantic in his self-destructive use of drugs and food. We will never know whether he was consciously trying to join his mother, when, on August 6, 1977, at the age of forty-two, he died from an "accidental" overdose.

The fantasy of reunion can propel people to dedicate their lives to finding someone they have never known. Searches by adoptees or birth parents for the biological parent or child are now a common phenomena. Equally common but perhaps less obvious are people who take on a characteristic or mannerism—often, a dramatic or a destructive one—of lost parents in order to remain close to them.

A particularly poignant example of attempting to repair a past loss through manipulation of current circumstances was presented by a man who would provoke his wife until she finally left him. Then he would beg her to return, and eventually she would give in. The glow of the joyful reunion would last a month or two, after which the cycle would begin again. This man's mother had died when he was seven years old, just old enough for him to have many happy memories of her. He nurtured the secret hope that if only he could create the perfect reconciliation with his wife, it would feel like the reunion he fantasized but could never have with his mother. The drive for reunion was so great that the pain of repeated separations from a wife he loved was worth the dream that the separation from his mother would one day come to an end.

ATTACHMENT AND SEPARATION
THROUGHOUT THE LIFE SPAN

The drive for attachment and the physiology of separation are not only important in infancy: they continue to be driving forces of human function and malfunction throughout life. The psychophysiology of the infant separation reaction is recapitulated in adult grief, and as we learned earlier, grief is more intense and more difficult to handle if losses earlier in life have primed the mind to feel more overwhelmed and the body to respond with more severe mixtures of arousal and withdrawal. We will see in the next two chapters that fight-flight and conservation-withdrawal associated with real and imagined loss can be even more deadly in adulthood than in infancy.

Although the psychophysiology of separation is similar in infancy and adulthood, the capacity of the adult mind for fantasy and for the manipulation of mental representations of attachment figures makes for more complex forms of grief and more sophisticated ways of dealing with it. We have already seen what a potent tool denial can be in dealing with emergency reactions to normal stress, and denial is naturally brought to bear whenever emotions seem unbearable, including in the face of acute grief. However, while denial can abort the physiology of *acute* stress, it is not nearly as effective at ameliorating *chronic* arousal—the physiologic pressure is just too great. By the same token, it takes mania or global emotional numbing to sustain over time the deception that grief is not present, and even more massive effort to sustain the deception that a loss has not occurred. For example, Queen Victoria of England, after her husband Prince Albert's untimely death at age forty-two, deceived herself into acting as though he had not really died. Just as she had done when he was alive, she laid out his clothes every day for the rest of her life, as though he would return.

The determined denier can keep grief hidden for a lifetime. But like anything else that is relegated to the unconscious, in the long run grief does not go away; it just exerts its influence in secret. Stored away in that part of the mind that keeps deceptions alive, grief remains as potent as the day the person died. This very timelessness makes it possible for the right intervention to bring the grief to light and allow it to run its course years after the loss occurred.

Chronic Separation Reactions and Depression

The physiology of grief can be as unending as its psychology when active grieving is put off. In people who are prone to depression, conditions of arousal and withdrawal are readily amplified by inherently unstable stress responses to induce a new depressive episode. (In the next two chapters we will see that if the bodily vulnerability lies in the cardiac or immune systems, those systems will break down instead.) The interaction between separation reactions and depression can become a vicious circle when unresolved loss evokes the psychophysiology of depression, which in turn amplifies the emotions of grief to a point that becomes too intolerable to resolve. As with all mind-body deceptions, however, there is always an opportunity to intervene.

This was the case for forty-one-year-old Justin, who suffered inexplicable and severe depressions at ages thirty-two, thirty-six, and thirty-eight. The acute episodes resolved after about a year, but he was left with a chronic feeling of emptiness and dissatisfaction. He loved his children, but he had always distrusted his wife, although she never gave him any obvious reason to do so. His chronic low-grade suffering did not motivate Justin to seek treatment, as he believed that a strong person "keeps a stiff upper lip." However, out of curiosity he enrolled in a research project on depression. The research psychiatrist was struck by a blatant association: Justin had become depressed for the first time at his oldest daughter's tenth birthday party; the second episode began when his next oldest daughter reached the age of ten; and he had slumped into a much deeper depression, from which he never really recovered at all, when his third child turned ten. The patient had not noticed the correlation between his depressions and his children's tenth birthdays until the psychiatrist mentioned it.

When Justin was asked whether anything special had happened to *him* at the age of ten, he remembered something that he had not thought about in many years.

"It was on my tenth birthday that my father left. He and my mother had never gotten along, and when she disapproved of his buying a gun for my birthday, it was one fight too many—and he walked out. The last time I ever saw him was when he said goodbye that day. He said that he would come back to see me, but he and my mother argued about visitation and, before they could work it out, he had a heart attack and died! I never saw him again after he drove off that day. My mother blamed him for all of our problems and refused to talk about him. So I figured, what's the point of thinking about it; it won't get me anywhere."

In the course of this discussion, it became obvious that Justin's depression reappeared each time one of his children reached the age at which he had lost his father: apparently their tenth birthdays reawakened the emotion of losing his father, minus the actual memory of the loss. Justin was almost a believer, but one thing puzzled him: "If my children's birthdays remind me so much of my own tenth year," he asked, "why was my last depression so much worse than the first two?" "Is your third child a boy?" the psychiatrist asked. "Why, yes," Justin answered, "and now that I think of it, my son does remind me of myself more than my daughters do."

Now Justin was faced with a dilemma. He had a fourth child—a son— who was nine, and his chronic depression was already starting to deepen. "I guess I'm doomed to go through it again—worse than ever, probably, since I was also the youngest of four children." "Maybe there's another alternative," suggested the psychiatrist. "Why not let your grief into the open, all at once, instead of continuing to hide it and relive it through your children?"

Justin did not think that expressing his grief would help. "It won't change the past." "No," the psychiatrist agreed, "but it *could* change the future. You've had the *emotions* of grief without the *memories* for years. If you just allow the process its due, it will run its course and you'll be done with it." Unconvinced, Justin retorted, "How am I supposed to do that? I never could before."

But Justin's conviction, however heartfelt, was a deception. He had never grieved because there had never been anyone to help him with it. Psychologically he had not matured past the moment his father had left the family. Secretly, he viewed himself as someone who would never get any support for his feelings. However, the truth was that his wife, his children, and his doctor were there to help him now. With their support, he was able to relive the loss of his father. The tears, the fear, the helplessness, the sense of betrayal by his mother—the one person who could have helped him—all the feelings he had kept hidden from himself could surface now that support was available to help him tolerate the emotions of the past.

Several months later, Justin celebrated his younger son's tenth birthday. Instead of depression, he felt only nostalgia that his father could not have been with him to share the happiness he now truly felt for his family.

BEYOND GRIEF: HELPLESSNESS AND HOPELESSNESS

The more we look at reactions to separation, such as grief, the more obvious it becomes that the availability of other people is a crucial factor in determining whether this particular type of stress response gets resolved. Other people are important not only because they provide external sources of regulation of mind and body but also because they increase our sense of competence in coping with any danger. A number of other factors are crucial in determining whether we overcome loss and the myriad of other stresses to which we are subject, or whether the stresses overcome us.

Any kind of stress is less disruptive of mind and body if it feels like it can be controlled. The opposite of a sense of mastery is *helplessness,* the belief that one can take no actions to overcome a challenge. However, while helplessness implies that the individual does not have the resources to cope with a perceived danger, there is at least the *possibility* that support could become available from some external source. Compounding a feeling of helplessness with the conviction that no one else is available results in *hopelessness,* a state in which one's own efforts seem to have no effect and no help appears forthcoming from anywhere else.

Martin E.P. Seligman, whose research on helplessness was discussed in Chapter 10, has observed that

> . . . when an organism has experienced trauma it cannot control, its motivation to respond in the face of later trauma wanes. Moreover, even if it does respond, and the response succeeds in producing relief, it has trouble learning, perceiving and believing that the response worked. Finally, its emotional balance is disturbed . . .

Learned helplessness experiments show that the mind's naturally active orientation toward overcoming stress can be deceived into a globally negative and passive state by repeated experiences with uncontrollable circumstances, even when they are benign. Apparently, the expectation that nothing can be done to change the present generalizes to the expectation that nothing can be done to change the future. The outcome of a challenge is seen as a function of luck, fate, or someone else's intervention—not one's inherent abilities. No attempt is made to overcome a new challenge and, sure enough, the challenge is not overcome.

Not everyone succumbs to learned helplessness, however. While some people stop trying to solve any problem after one uncontrollable experience, others have repeated encounters with uncontrollable situations and are still ready to take over the next situation that presents possibilities of a solution. One factor that determines whether learned helplessness will develop is the belief system that the individual brings to the uncontrollable situation. People who lack confidence in their ability to control their everyday lives are more likely to become globally helpless in response to one uncontrollable event. Learned helplessness is also more likely to develop if the expectation is conveyed that a problem can only be solved by luck and not by skill. In all likelihood, temperamental inclinations toward excessive arousal may also predispose a person to feeling an overwhelming lack of control when confronted with even mildly challenging situations.

Since helplessness is readily overcome when someone else is available to help with problem solving or, as in the animal learned helplessness experiments, to physically force the subject to start taking adaptive action, the availability of other people plays a central role in reducing feelings of helplessness and the intense states of arousal that accompany them. The finding described in Chapter 16 that the *perception* of available social networks facilitates adaptation to the stress of being uprooted and moved to a new home more than the actual availability of those networks is another example of the ways in which the power of the mind to conjure up protective attachments frees us from the need to have someone physically present to combat helplessness. A memory of a real person, a fantasy about someone who might be available at some point, or one of the many concepts that can be used as substitutions for people—all can protect against feelings of helplessness and the resulting mobilization of arousal and escalating deterioration of problem-solving abilities. Conversely, lack of external supports when internal skills seem inadequate not only fosters more helplessness but also drives the mind toward the more deadly cousin of helplessness: *hopelessness.*

Helplessness is the deception that the resources to solve a problem do not exist within the individual. The sense of helplessness triggers excessive fight-flight response because the perceived threat is accentuated by the fear that it cannot be mastered. The *potential* for help, however, maintains a level of activation that keeps the body going, even if it is in an inefficient state, until control can be regained. In contrast, hopelessness is a state in which the perception of insurmountable danger is intensified by the belief that it cannot be overcome *by anyone.* Lacking the belief that the situation will change, or that the person or someone else will think of something, the predominant physiology becomes one of conservation-withdrawal: the body's way of lying low when it seems impossible to overcome a threat of any sort.

PHYSICAL CONCOMITANTS OF
HELPLESSNESS AND HOPELESSNESS

Fight-flight and conservation-withdrawal responses have been retained in animals and humans because under certain circumstances, such as when an infant is separated from its mother for relatively brief periods of time, it promotes survival. However, the stresses of modern life, so many of which are symbolic, and the nature of modern relationships, so many of which are complex, promote situations in which these stress reactions may continue unresolved at excessive levels for excessive periods of time. The last chapter introduced a few situations in which stress in the absence of supportive relationships seemed to work against the health and even the life of the individual. We can now begin to understand these fatal outcomes as the result of maladaptive twists and turns of the psychophysiology of activation and withdrawal.

A powerful description of the deadly effects of helplessness and hopelessness on the body comes from psychologist Bruno Bettelheim, who was interred by the Germans in a concentration camp in the early years of the Nazi regime, until his release was secured by international pressure. Bettelheim found that the Nazis did not have to kill everyone directly; some prisoners just gave up and died:

> Prisoners who came to believe the repeated statements of the guards—
> that there was no hope for them, that they would never leave the camp
> except as a corpse—who came to feel that their environment was one over
> which they could exercise no influence whatever, these prisoners were, in
> a literal sense, walking corpses.

The deadly impact of giving up is well-known to laboratory workers and animal trainers who must restrain recently captured wild animals. Many of these animals are able to adapt to what must be frighteningly unfamiliar and aversive captivity; but some, apparently feeling completely unable to regain their freedom or cope with their new state, expire the first time they are handled.

One of the classic demonstrations of the physical effects of hopelessness in animals was performed by physiologist Curt Richter. Richter noted that, when placed in a water-filled cylinder, laboratory rats immediately entered a state of fight-flight in which they swam for sixty to eighty hours before even coming close to drowning. When their whiskers were clipped, however, they became exhausted about 20 hours sooner. More surprisingly, as soon as they were placed in the water, a few animals dove right to the bottom and died. A rat's whiskers have nothing to do with swimming, but they are an important sensory organ that help the animal to judge the width of its body in confined spaces and therefore to adapt to unfamiliar situations.

Next, Richter studied wild Norwegian rats, a particularly fierce and independent breed. Normally these rats were excellent swimmers. However, if their whiskers were clipped, they all died within one to fifteen minutes after being immersed in the water. Some did not even live long enough to be placed in the swimming tank: they died in the experimenter's hand while their whiskers were being clipped.

The sequence of events that led to death in these animals was remarkable. There was a brief period of fight-flight, as would be expected in response to any stressful situation. But before long the rats' heart rates began a relentless decline, along with their respiratory rates and body temperatures, until their hearts slowed to a stop and the rats sank to the bottom—dead of cardiac arrest, not drowning. This abrupt switch to conservation-withdrawal apparently destabilized the cardiovascular response to stress, stopping the heart instead of mobilizing it.

Richter reasoned that clipping the rats' whiskers deprived them of a crucial adaptive mechanism that was particularly important when they were confronted with the unfamiliar danger of the swimming tank, with which previous experience had not taught them to cope. Not being able to predict, overcome, or escape from the threat, or to relate it to past experience, the loss of another coping mechanism—even though it was not directly related to the threat—appeared to deprive the rats of "confidence" that some kind of solution could be found. As a result, the fight-flight response was abruptly replaced by a hopelessness-like state that triggered the sudden and destabilizing switch from stimulation to slowing of the heart. The impact of losing their whiskers was not as drastic for the domesticated laboratory rats, because they were used to being handled and presumably did not experience the situation as so foreign that they were completely unprepared for it and could only feel hopeless.

To prove this hypothesis, Richter showed that cardiac death could be prevented by holding the wild rats briefly and then freeing them a few times, or by removing them from the water for a few seconds before their hearts began to slow, but not long enough for them to rest, and then returning them to the cylinder. This experience appeared to have taught the rats that the stress was not endless and perhaps familiarized them sufficiently with the situation so that it was not as alien and unpredictable. In response, the rats exhibited continued fight-flight response rather than cardiac slowing, and were able to swim longer than ever without tiring.

In these experiments, the mental states of helplessness and hopelessness, like that of separation depression, were severe enough to deceive the heart out of its normal coordinated response to danger via its connections to the brain. In people, these same mental states can deceive bodily systems such as the cardiovascular and immune systems out of their normal protective function, as we will see in the next two chapters.

18

Heart-Stopping Thoughts: Cardiac Mind-Body Deceptions

INTIMATE COMMUNICATION BETWEEN the brain and the heart make it possible for perceptions of a changing environment to be transmitted to the cardiovascular system, so that appropriate adjustments can be made. As with all mind-body connections, the mind conveys to the heart a *perception* of the need to increase or decrease its activity. The impact of this perception is the same whether it is accurate or inaccurate. In either case, the mind is able to speed up the heart, as in flight-fight, or slow it to a stop, as occurred with Richter's rats.

One dramatic example of this connection is the story of an unnamed man reported by psychiatrist L.J. Saul. A forty-five-year-old man found himself in a situation that was so unbearable that he felt it necessary to move to another town. Circumstances changed just before he was to leave, making it impossible for the move to be carried out as he had planned. He left anyway, not knowing what on earth he would do when he reached the new town—but unable to stay where he was.

Traveling by train to the new city with a friend, the man complained bitterly about the hopelessness of his dilemma. The train stopped at a station midway between the old and the new town, and the man walked out on the platform to try to figure out what to do. In a state of extreme agitation and ambivalence, all he could conclude about his situation was that he could not go forward and he could not go back. As the conductor called "All aboard," and before the shocked eyes of his friend, the man had a cardiac arrest and died.

To understand how this kind of catastrophe could occur, it is necessary to appreciate that the rate and rhythm of the heart (the heartbeat) are strongly influenced by the nerves and hormones that carry the messages of fight-flight and conservation-withdrawal throughout the body. In addition, metabolic changes that energize the body during the stress response can alter the blood supply to the heart and the tone of blood vessels, producing a narrowing and spasm of the vessels that supply the heart (coronary arteries), hyperactivity of diverse small arteries, and hypertension (high blood pressure). How the heartbeat, the blood supply to the heart, and blood pressure are affected by stress is discussed in the next few sections.

HOW THE HEART BEATS

The heart is a hollow muscle whose job is to circulate blood throughout the body. Figure 18.1 illustrates the four chambers to the heart—two atria and two ventricles. Blood that has circulated through the body, giving oxygen to tissues and receiving metabolic products, returns to the heart through the right atrium, which fills as the heart starts to relax. Further relaxation of the heart, along with contraction of the right atrium, forces blood into the right ventricle. As the right ventricle contracts, it sends blood through the lungs, where oxygen is added and carbon dioxide is removed. From the lungs, oxygenated blood is pulled into the left atrium, which then conducts blood to the left ventricle, whose job it is to pump blood back to the body.

Normal activity of the heart depends on three specialized tissues: muscle cells, pacemaker cells, and conduction cells. *Muscle cells* contract in unison, moving blood through the body. *Pacemaker cells* generate the signal to contract, which is transmitted in sequence by *conduction cells* to different regions of cardiac muscle.

Ions of Energy

The same electrochemical mechanisms of polarization and depolarization that prevail in neurons underlie the action of specialized cardiac pacemaker and conductor cells, once again demonstrating the unity of basic cellular processes. As in the brain, movements of ions (charged elements) in and out of these cardiac cells produce the resting state of polarization and the sudden reversal of electrical charge—depolarization—that activates cellular functions. Like neurons, cardiac pacemaker and conduction cells reset themselves (repolarize) after each depolarization, so that they can make themselves ready to be stimulated again and transmit the next signal to contract to the muscle cells of the heart. Ordinarily, this produces an orderly sequence of signal, contraction, and rest that proceeds from pacemaker cells, through the conduction cells, to the heart muscle itself. If conduction cells receive another signal very early in the process of repolarization, they will not respond. However, if a new signal to contract is received by conduction cells when they are far enough along in the repolarization process to respond but before they are prepared to transmit it normally to heart muscle, an abnormal heartbeat may result—the significance of which will soon become apparent.

Pacemaker and Conduction Cells

Pacemaker cells are responsible for generating the signal that tells the heart to contract and send blood to the body. To achieve this goal, they depolarize spontaneously about every six-tenths of a second by means of a continuous "leak" of positive ions that gradually decreases the negative internal charge of the cells until they reach the threshold for depolarization. This capacity for automatic depolarization is called "automaticity."

One important feature of both conduction and pacemaker cells that lays the groundwork for some dangerous mind–heart deceptions is the fact that these cells have the capacity for automaticity, but the rate at which they depolarize spontaneously is slower the further they are from the region that normally determines heart rate. If they receive a signal from an area that is closer to the primary pacemaker, they will be made to depolarize at a faster rate than they would depolarize on their own, and the automaticity is suppressed. If, however, the journey of the signal for depolarization down conduction pathways is delayed—either because it is generated too slowly or because its transit is interrupted—the automaticity of conduction pathway cells is no longer suppressed and they begin acting like pacemakers themselves. The capacity of conduction cells to drive the heartbeat when the primary signal fails allows the heart to keep beating, but the news is not all good: heartbeats that originate in conduction cells may be too slow to provide adequate blood flow, and they are prone to deteriorating into rhythms that are too rapid to be efficient or are completely ineffective.

Transmission of the Cardiac Impulse

The term *heart rate* refers to the speed with which the heart contracts. The term *cardiac rhythm* refers to the type of organization of the heart beat as measured by the electrocardiogram (EKG), which traces the conduction of the electrical signal from the primary pacemaker to the ventricles (pumping chambers of the heart). Under normal circumstances, the signal for the heartbeat is generated about sixty to eighty times per minute by pacemaker cells in the dominant pacemaker of the heart, the sinoatrial (SA) node, a col-

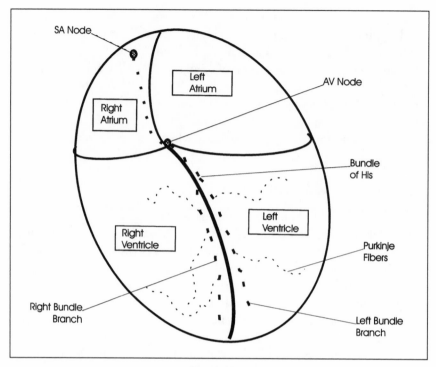

Figure 18-1.
The cardiac conduction system

lection of cells located at the top of the right atrium (see Figure 18.1). As the impulse generated in the SA node is conducted along pathways in the atria, it causes the muscle cells of the right atrium to contract. The stimulus to contract moves through the right atrium to the left atrium, which contracts after a short delay, just as *it* receives blood from the body.

The next stop for the electrical impulse generated from the SA node is the atrioventricular (AV) node, located at the juncture of the atria and the ventricles, where the signal to contract is delayed a little less than two-tenths of a second. It then proceeds to a bundle of conduction fibers called the Bundle of His (pronounced *hiss*) that runs along the wall between the two ventricles and then divides into two bundle branches, one for each ventricle. Individual conduction fibers (called Purkinje fibers) branch out over both ventricles, providing an organized signal to contract on schedule.

BAD RATES AND RHYTHMS

Disruption of any of the points along the complex path of an organized heartbeat can produce abnormalities of cardiac rate and rhythm. An *abnor-*

mal heart rate may be too slow (bradycardia) or too fast (tachycardia). Slowing of the heart rate may be caused by abnormalities of the SA node or interference with the conduction of the cardiac impulse from the SA node to the rest of the heart. The vagus nerve, which we met when we discussed the parasympathetic nervous system, decelerates the heart by slowing the rate of the SA node and by slowing conduction of the signal through the AV node. In contrast, the heart rate can be accelerated by the hormones and nerves of the sympathetic nervous system. If the heart slows down too much, it cannot pump enough blood to meet the demands of the body. Pumping of blood also becomes insufficient when the heart speeds up too much, because there is not enough time for the ventricles to fill before the next beat. Obviously, inadequate blood flow deprives bodily tissues of oxygen and nutrients, creating varying degrees of injury depending on the degree to which blood flow is reduced. Another dangerous effect of bradycardia is that when the signal to the rest of the heart from the SA node falls below the spontaneous rate of depolarization of conduction tissue down the line, abnormal heartbeats are generated in that tissue.

Rhythmic Dangers

Abnormal rhythms, called "arrhythmias," can originate anywhere in the conduction system, from the AV node to Purkinje's fibers. They can also take many forms, all resulting in loss of coordination between the atria and the ventricles, or even within each chamber of the heart. At best, abnormal heartbeats result in poorly coordinated contractions and inefficient delivery of blood to the body. At worst, they make it impossible for the heart to work at all. Most important for our purposes, certain abnormal rhythms are likely to be associated with imbalances in the mind-body responses of fight-flight and conservation-withdrawal and are of particular relevance to a study of fatal mind-heart deceptions.

Ectopic beats are premature heart beats that originate somewhere other than the SA node; they are manifestations of an early increase in automaticity of conduction tissue down the road from the SA node. This may occur because the SA node has slowed below the inherent rate of spontaneous depolarization of conduction tissue, or because conduction cells are being stimulated excessively—usually by the fight-flight stress hormones, epinephrine and norepinephrine, which accelerate heart rate by speeding up depolarization of pacemaker and conduction cells. Damaged cardiac tissue is especially prone to producing ectopic beats and other evidence of excessive automaticity, as is cardiac tissue containing two parallel conduction pathways, one with a slower conduction rate than the other. Depolarization proceeds down both branches at the same time but reaches the end of one branch before the other branch has finished depolarizing. The impulse that is accelerating the branch still depolarizing reaches some conduction cells at the "vulnerable period"—a point before the cell is fully repolarized, when stimulation makes it depolarize earlier and in a less organized manner than when it is stimulated after complete repolarization.

On occasion, everyone has ectopic beats of one kind or another. These are usually experienced as "skipping a beat" because the ectopic beat occurs early and is followed by a pause, while the conduction system is temporarily unresponsive to further stimulation. By themselves, ectopic beats are not harmful, but if they occur frequently enough, they can stimulate adjacent conduction tissue during the vulnerable period. The result is widespread and persistent abnormal depolarizations that destabilize the entire heart.

One of these more severe arrhythmias is *ventricular tachycardia,* a series of ectopic premature beats originating in the ventricles (premature ventricular contractions) and occurring in rapid sequence. The premature contractions can be generated in different ectopic locations, making them very unpredictable and uncoordinated. Because contraction of the ventricles is not coordinated with the beating of the atria or even with return of blood to the heart, the ventricles may contract when they do not contain much blood, thereby severely limiting the delivery of blood to the body. In addition, conduction tissue throughout the ventricles is depolarizing so rapidly and unpredictably that the likelihood of further deterioration of the heartbeat due to inappropriate restimulation is much greater.

The most dreaded complication of this kind of process is *ventricular fibrillation,* which occurs when there is no organized heartbeat at all and each cardiac muscle cell depolarizes independently. With heart muscles acting in complete independence of each other, the heart loses its coordinated action and cannot pump any blood; unconsciousness occurs almost immediately. Death follows rapidly if ventricular fibrillation is not corrected.

How the Brain Produces Arrhythmias

Neural pathways connecting the brain to pacemaker and conduction cells make it possible for changes in mental function to alter heart rate and rhythm to an extent ranging from the annoying to the deadly. Because the fight-flight response accelerates the rate of depolarization of pacemaker tissue and the excitability of conduction tissue, our hearts race and we have palpitations when we are frightened or angry—a bothersome but not a terribly serious experience. However, if the vessels supplying the heart (coronary arteries) are narrowed or prone to spasm, the metabolic needs of an accelerated heartbeat can exceed the capacity of coronary arteries to supply it, and cardiac tissue may become "ischemic" or damaged by an insufficient supply of oxygen. Under stressful conditions, ischemic tissue is more vulnerable to ectopic beats and the deterioration of simpler arrhythmias into tachycardia and ventricular fibrillation, leading to increasingly dangerous instability of cardiac rhythm.

The conservation-withdrawal response affects the heart as potently as fight-flight. The vagus nerve—the major source of input from the parasympathetic nervous system to the heart—decelerates the heart by slowing the spontaneous rate of depolarization of the SA node and slowing the conduction through the AV node to the rest of the heart. Ordinarily, there is nothing wrong with a slow heart rate, but if the vagal signal is excessive, it can stop depolarization of the SA node or slow transmission through the AV node so completely that the ventricles stop beating (asystole). This is a more common mechanism of sudden death in animals than humans. In people, too much vagal influence usually leads to escape rhythms that ultimately deteriorate into ventricular fibrillation or other dangerous arrhythmias.

While either fight-flight or conservation-withdrawal responses can produce arrhythmias, abnormal rhythms are even more likely to occur when both the sympathetic and the parasympathetic systems are hyperactive at the same time. An everyday example of this phenomenon occurs in highly conditioned athletes whose baseline heart rates are slow due to the strong tone of the vagus nerve. Strenuous exercise elevates heart rate by accelerating sympathetic nervous system input to the heart and increasing the levels of catecholamines, such as epinephrine. When the exercise ceases, the vagus nerve quickly drives the rate of depolarization of the SA node back to its slow baseline. However, catecholamines, which are metabolized more slowly than the rate at which the stress response resets itself, take longer to return to their resting levels. Until their levels drop, the heart is vulnerable to arrhythmias that arise when the resting rate is not fast enough to suppress the ectopic rhythms that are induced by continued elevated levels of catecholamines. A "cool down" period keeps the rate of the SA node fast enough to prevent conduction tissue from escaping its drive and then being stimulated to arrhythmia by the catecholamines that remain circulating in the bloodstream until they are metabolized away.

Researchers have attempted to investigate the ways in which mixtures of factors that speed up and slow down heart rate can destabilize the human heart. In a study by cardiologist Bernard Lown and his colleagues, healthy control subjects and patients recovering from heart attacks were placed in a dark, soundproofed room. When the door was suddenly opened, the healthy subjects all experienced transient increases in heart rate, as might be expected in anyone who was startled. Heart rate in some of the patients also sped up briefly, but other patients' hearts paradoxically *decelerated,* indicating inappropriate influence of the vagus nerve. A year and a half later, all of the patients who had recorded significant decreases in heart rate in response to the startle had died of cardiac arrest. The experiment itself was not harmful, but it seems to have illuminated an imbalance between fight-flight and conservation-withdrawal responses that was predictive of later vulnerability to cardiac death, possibly by the same mechanism.

CAN THE MIND STOP THE HEART?

The most drastic example of how the mind can deceive the heart is cardiac arrest, the complete cessation of heartbeat. Cardiac arrest is the leading cause of death in the industrialized world, killing more than 1,000 people each day in the United States alone. Three-fourths of the cases of cardiac arrest are caused by ventricular fibrillation, which produces completely disorganized depolarization of cardiac muscle fibers, so that the heart quivers but does not generate any effective contractions. Cardiac arrest may also result from asystole (absence of any electrical activity in the heart) and "electromechanical dissociation," which is the absence of effective contraction under conditions of normal electrical activity. Electromechanical dissociation is not an arrhythmia but a failure of a normally beating heart to pump effectively. The net effect of pump failure and the two kinds of arrhythmias is the same, but their treatment differs significantly. Cardiac arrest is different from heart attack or "myocardial infarction," the death of heart tissue caused by insufficient blood flow. However, when a heart attack is massive enough to prevent the heart from pumping effectively or to damage conduction tissue so that ventricular fibrillation, asystole, or electromechanical dissociation occur, cardiac arrest is likely to follow.

About 20 percent of cardiac arrests occur at the time of a heart attack. Three-fourths of people who are successfully resuscitated from a bout of ventricular fibrillation are found to have disease of the coronary arteries, the blood vessels that supply the heart. However, the link between heart attack and cardiac arrest is far from obvious. The risk of another cardiac arrest is more than ten times greater in people who have been rescuscitated from ventricular fibrillation and who do not show evidence of a heart attack than in those who show evidence of heart attack at the time of the ventricular fibrillation episode. This odd statistic probably means that when cardiac arrest is a complication of heart attack, the risk dissipates once the acute cause of ischemic damage to the heart is effectively treated. When the cause of cardiac arrest is not obvious, it is more difficult to identify and treat and possibly lies in more complex pathology of the conduction system.

Risk Factors for Cardiac Arrest

One interesting psychosocial risk factor for sudden cardiac death is having less than a twelfth-grade education. Perhaps the reason for the increased risk in this group is that, without sufficient education, it is more difficult to feel successful and in control in a complex, technologically-oriented society. The result would be an ongoing imbalance in the stress-response systems: there would be greater vulnerability to a slowing of the heart (conservation-withdrawal) due to hopelessness and to ectopic beats evoked by stress (fight-flight).

Stress in the midst of depression can be another heart-stopping combination. Studies have shown that 20 percent of cardiac arrests occur in people who have been depressed and are in the midst of coping with a stressful situation that evokes anxiety or anger. Apparently, the stress triggers fight-flight response, arousing the person out of the conservation-withdrawal state of their depression. This hyperactive combination of stress-response states may produce tachyarrhythmias that degenerate into ventricular fibrillation.

As we saw in Part III, depression produces a similar unstable combination of arousal and withdrawal. Since 15–20 percent of people who suffer heart attacks become depressed, the risk of fatal arrhythmia in depressed heart-attack patients may be greater than in heart-attack patients who are not depressed. Although not all reports have been conclusive, three prospective studies have suggested that the mind may have an even more deadly influence on a heart that is already damaged.

For example, a 1985 study reported in the *Journal of Affective Disorders* followed 351 heart-attack patients who had ventricular arrhythmias. Over the subsequent year, patients who had shown high levels of depression in the first two months after the heart attack had a greater risk of death or cardiac arrests (which were not fatal because they were resuscitated). The increased incidence of life-threatening arrhythmias in the depressed group could not be explained by any additional physical risk factors.

In a second study, this one published in 1993 in the *Journal of the American Medical Association,* 222 patients were interviewed within fifteen days following episodes of heart attack. Regardless of medical variables, such as the severity of heart disease, patients with depressive symptoms present for less than two weeks were *five times* more likely to die as non-depressed patients over the next six months. A 1984 study by researcher W. Ruberman and colleagues showed that neither clinical nor social variables, such as low educational level or living alone, explained an increased risk of death in almost 15 percent of 555 depressed European male patients in the six months following their heart attacks.

Obviously, no one would want to participate in a study to investigate how the mind can produce fatal arrhythmias under stressful conditions. However, a few patients have been under observation when their hearts were stopped by arrhythmias. One of these patients, reported by A. Rozanski, developed progressive cardiac slowing—until his heart actually stopped—whenever he listened to a particular passage from *Fox's Book of Martyrs* about tortures inflicted on heretics.

Another apparently healthy man, whose case was reported in the *The New England Journal of Medicine,* was rough-housing with his children when the doorbell rang. He looked up, said "I'm sorry," and had a cardiac arrest. Luckily, his wife, a nurse, was able to resuscitate him. Subsequently, he developed ventricular fibrillation whenever he even thought about family conflicts. Apparently the conflicts induced a fight-flight response that overstimulated his heart at the same time that he felt helpless to resolve the conflicts. Even high doses of antiarrhythmic drugs could not prevent this outcome. However, when he was taught to reduce his stressful response through meditation, the life-threatening arrhythmia stopped. No specific heart disease was ever found.

A group of researchers from the University of Southern California had the opportunity to investigate the capacity of a universally stressful experience—in this case, the January 1994 Northridge earthquake that decimated sections of Los Angeles at 4:31 in the morning—to induce fatal arrhythmias in a large population. On the day of the earthquake, twenty-four people died of cardiac arrest, five times the average mortality rate from this cause; most of the deaths occurred within an hour of the event. Over the next week, the number of people dying of cardiac arrest decreased to a lower than average value, suggesting that fewer people who were at risk of sudden cardiac death at that time were still alive. Only three of the sudden deaths occurred during physical exertion, the rest being attributable to the emotional stress of the event. There was also a 35 percent increase in the number of hospitalizations for heart attacks. The investigators extrapolated from these findings to estimate that more than 40 percent of sudden cardiac deaths are precipitated by a stressful event.

CAN THE MIND CAUSE CORONARY HEART DISEASE?

The majority of people who die of cardiac arrest have obvious or covert coronary artery disease that makes the conduction system vulnerable to arrhythmia under stressful conditions. In addition to creating the acute insult that stops the heart, can the mind create the vulnerability in the blood supply to the heart that sets the stage for sudden death? No one can prevent earthquakes, let alone the other stressors to which we are always subjected, and no one can predict sudden cardiac death. But if the mind contributes to the accumulating damage to the heart that makes sudden cardiac death more likely, correcting mental risk factors might reduce the risk of coronary heart disease and, ultimately, of heart attacks and sudden death.

Of the many risk factors for coronary heart disease that have been identified, only one—heredity—is impossible to change. The others, such as obesity, smoking, hypertension, diabetes, and high cholesterol levels, are reversible or at least manageable. Many people now exercise more, eat low-fat foods, watch their weight, and avoid even indirect exposure to cigarette smoke. However, these known physical factors account for *less than half* of the total risk for coronary heart disease, and leaving out the other half of the equation may be a dangerous deception.

Cultural Clashes of the Heart

One important non-physical contributor to coronary heart disease is cultural stress. During the decades since World War I, as the United States has become more industrialized, the incidence of coronary heart disease has been steadily increasing. This influence is even more striking considering that the established physical risk factors were higher *before* industrialization, when people were more sedentary, ate more fat, and did not treat hypertension. The incidence of coronary heart disease in the Southeastern United States, which had lagged behind the rest of the country in moving into the industrialized age, has only recently escalated, along with the growth of industry in that region. Yet, even though France is an industrialized country, there seems to be something about its culture that is less stressful: French men have *one-third* the risk of coronary heart disease as American men, despite dietary habits that should make them *more* vulnerable.

The influence of psychosocial factors on the heart becomes readily apparent in people who move from one culture to another. For example, Japanese men who move to the United States and become assimilated into Western culture have a rate of coronary heart disease that is three to five times as great as that of men who remain in Japan. However, Japanese men who move to the United States *but retain their cultural values* do not show an increased rate of heart disease. The increased risk is not attributable to changes in diet, smoking, blood pressure, or cholesterol level. Instead, it appears that immersion in a new environment, together with the loss of familiar cultural anchors, affects overall physiology in a way that makes culturally displaced people more vulnerable to disease of the coronary arteries.

Type-A Behavior and the Heart

The best known psychosocial risk factor for coronary heart disease is the "type-A personality," first proposed by cardiologists Meyer Friedman and Ray Rosenman. The history of the type-A concept is the history of an idea that was initially rejected, then embraced as gospel, and then—like any one-dimensional concept—found to be partly deceptive.

The type-A personality profile is a cluster of behaviors and response styles thought to be associated with an increased risk of coronary heart disease. The type-A person is ambitious, aggressive, hypervigilant, competitive, and impatient; he or she generally has tense muscles, speaks rapidly and emphatically, engages in fast-paced activity, and feels highly pressured and rushed. Meeting a deadline does not bring relief, only a need to meet the next deadline. Anger and irritability are central to the type-A personality, but not anxiety or depression. In contrast, type-B individuals have a more relaxed approach to stressful situations, without the tension, anger, or frantic pace of type-A people.

In the first study of the type-A personality as a coronary risk factor in 1960 by the Western Collaborative Group Study, 3,154 middle-aged men were classified as either type A or type B. In 1969, type A's were found to be twice as likely as type B's to have developed coronary heart disease and were more likely to die of it. If they suffered a heart attack during the study period, type A's were also more likely to have another one. The increased coronary risk was independent of all the standard physical risk factors.

Later research on type-A traits has been more contradictory. Some studies showed that type A's had more extensive coronary heart disease, but a 1988 study, which attempted to replicate the original findings in 2,200 people, reported that the type-A syndrome was only correlated with coronary heart disease in people under the age of fifty-five and was a poorer predictor than smoking or cholesterol levels. Two large studies, the Multiple Risk Factor Intervention Trial and the Aspirin Myocardial Infarction Study, found no relationship between type-A behavior and the risk of developing coronary heart disease.

Even the Western Collaborative Group Study did not stand the test of time. When the original group of subjects was followed from 1969 to 1983, the association between type-A traits and coronary heart disease not only disappeared but reversed direction! After longer follow-up, type A's were no more likely than type B's to die in the twenty-four hours following a heart attack, and long-term survival of type A's was *better* than type B's. The same type-A subjects who seemed to be at higher risk fourteen years earlier ended up being *half as likely* to die of coronary heart disease than the type-B subjects.

How could these new findings be explained? Did type-A subjects change their personalities or get better treatment as time went on? There was no evidence that either of these occurred. Was there a subgroup of higher-risk type A's who died off during the first part of the study? No clear differences could be found between the type A's who had a better cardiac outcome in 1983 and those who were more likely to die in 1969. The type-A story was turning out to be less straightforward than it originally seemed.

Attempting to untangle these contradictions, researchers wondered if one key element of the type-A personality—and not the entire cluster of traits—might be the direct link to coronary heart disease. If so, only populations in whom this element—whatever it was—was more prominent would display a marked association between coronary heart disease and type-A personality. The traits of time pressure (frantic pace) and anxiety seemed to be reasonable possibilities, but they appeared to be less clearly correlated than hostility with coronary heart disease as risk factors independent of the entire type-A cluster.

Type-A Behavior, Hostility, and the Heart

A study of 2,000 people found no association between type-A personality and the severity of coronary heart disease; however, the study did show that hostility, combined with a tendency to turn anger inward, did predict severity of coronary heart disease and identified those who had had heart attacks. In a prospective study of 1,877 healthy men, those who had higher hostility ratings on psychological testing were one and a half times more likely than their less hostile peers to die of coronary heart disease twenty years later.

Further prospective research has shown the same association between hostility and coronary heart disease in doctors and lawyers. In one such investigation, a personality measurement was administered to a group of medical students. By the time they had reached their mid-fifties, 14 percent of the physicians who had scored high on hostility ratings on the original personality test had died of coronary heart disease, compared with only 2 percent of those who had shown low hostility ratings at the beginning of the study. When the health of 118 law students was assessed 25 years after taking a similar personality test, those with high hostility scores were four to five and a half times as likely as those with low hostility scores to have died of coronary disease. Whether or not uncontrolled hostility actually was responsible for the increased risk of serious coronary heart disease, it at least seemed to be a marker of risk in these studies. However, this did not prove to be the case in a thirty-three-year follow-up of 1,339 college students, in whom high hostility scores did *not* predict coronary heart disease. It remains to be established whether these contradictory findings signify that hostility is not a reliable predictor of coronary heart disease or that its impact varies in different populations.

The type of hostility thought to be associated with coronary heart disease has three qualities: a cynical mistrust of people's motives, frequent anger, and—contrary to popular wisdom—the open expression of hostility (rather than hostility turned inward) without regard for the feelings of others. (An example of type-A hostility might be loudly counting the number of items in the cart of the person at the front of the express line in the grocery store, to make it known that he or she is one item over the limit.) Although this finding has remained fairly consistent, it is still unclear whether hostility is a cause of coronary heart disease, a marker of risk, or a manifestation of hyperactive physiology that produces both an irritable personality and an irritable heart.

It would be a repetition of the original type-A deception to assert that every hostile person is at increased risk of developing coronary heart disease. Whether this, or any other trait, changes physiology depends on its interaction with a host of forces in the individual and the environment. For example, the aggressive, driven, type-A executive may be less prone to helplessness and hopelessness in a competitive environment than the type-B executive who does not thrive as easily on competition and pressure. On the other hand, a type-A factory worker with a tenth-grade education, whose options for advancement are limited, may become more frustrated and hostile as the drive to forge onward is blocked, while a type-B coworker may be more appropriately matched psychologically, and therefore physiologically, to this setting. It is only in settings in which the type-A drive is maladaptive that excessive hostility and arousal begin to erode the heart.

The nature of relationships in a person's life also plays a role in determining the impact of type-A traits on physiology. Type-A people who are more self-involved or socially isolated have fewer resources to fall back on and therefore must depend entirely on themselves to fulfill their competitive motivations. When they encounter a problem that they cannot solve entirely on their own, they are unable to ask for the help they need—which makes them more likely to fail. If they are as reluctant to ask for help from friends and loved ones as they are from colleagues, they have no external supports to moderate the physiology of arousal that occurs in response to feeling increasingly frustrated, angry, and overwhelmed. As a result, the risk of coronary heart disease is greater in isolated and self-involved type A's than in those who have more attachments and therefore more help in controlling their reactions to failure and stress.

Type-A Behavior and the Arteries

Type-A traits gain the potential to damage the heart when they provoke unrestrained fight-flight responses: for example, the competitive, driven, type-A individual who responds to an obstacle by compulsively intensifying efforts to overcome it rather than adapting ambitions and desires to the constraints of reality. Mind and body continue to be activated to try to overcome the source of stress, but on those occasions when nothing constructive happens, the fight-flight response persists. In this context, unrestrained hostility may be a manifestation of unresolved fight-flight responses rather than a primary mediator of cardiac damage in Type-A people.

There are two mechanisms by which a chronic fight-flight response can compromise the blood supply to the heart. First, the sympathetic nervous system has direct connections to blood vessels that can make blood vessels everywhere, including the heart, contract. If the coronary vessels are already partially occluded, the blood supply to the heart may be reduced below the level that is necessary to sustain the muscle. The result is reduced blood flow to heart muscle (myocardial ischemia), which may not be felt at the moment but can be harmful over time.

Stress-induced constriction in coronary arteries and veins was demonstrated in an experiment reported in 1988 in the *New England Journal of Medicine* in which healthy people were asked to perform a number of mental tasks, ranging from reading a neutral passage in a book to the more stressful assignment of giving a speech about their most embarrassing experience. No change in cardiac function was observed following the benign mental tasks, but when the subjects had to reveal their weaknesses in public, coronary blood flow acutely decreased—presumably due to the effects on coronary vessels of the increased arousal associated with the stress response. There was no pain, but the efficiency of cardiac contraction was transiently reduced by the inhibition of blood flow during the stressful experience. This kind of decrease in ventricular motion caused by diminished blood flow is not harmful if it occurs from time to time, but if it continues over extended periods of time, it could contribute to ongoing cardiac malfunction. A similar process could explain some aspects of the cardiac risk Type-A people experience who are in a chronic state of fight-flight.

The second mechanism by which chronic fight-flight responses can cause coronary heart disease is by metabolic changes that clog the coronary arteries. Type-A individuals secrete more stress hormones, such as cortisol and epinephrine, in response to even mild stress, and these hormones can elevate cholesterol levels to a degree that could contribute to coronary atherosclerosis (hardening of the arteries). In addition, elevated levels of epinephrine increase the tendency of blood platelets to aggregate, which can form clots in coronary arteries. Activated platelets also release substances that can cause spasm of the vessels through which they pass.

Chronic fight-flight responses might impair the blood supply to the cardiac conduction system, making it vulnerable to arrhythmia when it is subject to the complicated physiology of acute stress in, for example, a type-A man who is perpetually angry and disappointed that his contributions are not recognized. Rather than developing strategies for overcoming setbacks, he broods for hours about how he will get back at those who have let him down. Chronic arousal, fueled by a mixture of anger and helplessness, turn up the "gain" of the sympathetic nervous system, making platelets more likely to aggregate and blood vessels more likely to constrict. Over time, areas of narrowing develop in coronary vessels, further aggravating the compromise of blood flow that occurs when the coronary vessels constrict in response to the stress of feeling overwhelmed or annoyed.

No single episode of cardiac ischemia is dangerous in itself but the cumulative effect is to injure the conduction system, making it more likely to depolarize during the critical period when it is stimulated by stress hormones and the sympathetic nervous system. One day, the man in our above example encounters a situation that provokes arousal that is more intense than usual; perhaps he has a favorite project that is rejected by the boss, or a relationship he has counted on for emotional sustenance is unexpectedly terminated. In such instances, the response of acute arousal, which accelerates the rate of depolarization of conduction tissue, runs headlong into the conservation-withdrawal response of hopelessness, which has slowed the drive from the SA node. The damaged system responds with an alternating heart rate that is slowed and then accelerated, which eventually deteriorates into ventricular fibrillation and cardiac arrest.

Knowing about the sequence of processes involved in coronary heart disease and sudden cardiac death makes it possible to develop strategies that help the mind to protect, rather than deceive, the heart. These strategies can be combined with those protecting another important bodily system that can be deceived by the stress response: the immune system.

19

Strategic Confusions: Immune System Deceptions

DARYL WENT THROUGH the first thirty years of his life without ever taking even a few hours off for illness. Recently, however, he has been getting sick constantly. First he got the flu for the first time. Then he caught a bad cold that he found very difficult to shake. He was well for a while, but before long he developed another viral illness. Daryl began to worry that he might have chronic fatigue syndrome or, worse yet, AIDS, but extensive testing showed only the acute viral syndromes. Even though he was in no immediate danger, Daryl was having a truly miserable year.

What made this year different? A year before he began catching one virus after another, Daryl's mother had died. His father had a hard time with the loss, and Daryl felt responsible for offering all the support he could. This left him no time to think about what *he* felt, and he had no opportunity to grieve the loss himself. Instead, he became depressed. In some cases depression lowers the threshold for experiencing physical symptoms without any actual biological basis, but in Daryl's case depression had lowered the threshold for developing actual medical illnesses. In this chapter, we will learn the mechanisms by which mental states can alter the capacity of the immune system, the body's most important protective agent against an invasion by disease from within and without.

The immune system is a diffuse collection of cells. Some of these cells are organized in certain organs, some circulate in the bloodstream, and some are carried by special vessels for immune cells called "lymphatics." The immune system protects the entire body against invasion by infectious agents such as bacteria and viruses, cancer cells, altered or damaged tissue, and anything else that is identified as foreign. Failures of the immune system cause persistent and severe infections, which is what happens when the AIDS virus suppresses the immune system, allowing infections to develop that the body would normally overcome. Suppression of the immune system may also allow some cancers to grow beyond the body's capacity to suppress them, which is why anticancer drugs that suppress immune cells sometimes permit a second cancer to escape suppression and grow. If the immune system is too active, on the other hand, it can destroy normal tissue, as occurs in diseases like systemic lupus erythematosus and diabetes mellitus.

This chapter describes the immune system and its association with cancer and various infections. We will see how integral the nervous system is to immune function, and how connections between the brain and the immune system make it possible for each to influence the other. We will discuss ways in which adverse mental states can act on the immune system to produce adverse physical states, and we will explore ways to use the mind that benefit the body.

THE ABC'S OF THE IMMUNE SYSTEM

Immune cells circulate in the bloodstream and lymphatics to every nook and cranny of the body. Mobilized from the thymus gland and the spleen, these cells collect in the lymph nodes, where antibodies are produced. Lymph nodes are located throughout the body; under the jaw and arms, for example, we know them as "swollen glands" when they are enlarged.

Immune cells must distinguish the body's tissues (self) from foreign cells such as viruses and bacteria (non-self) and then inactivate, remove, or destroy the non-self cells without damaging the body's own tissue. Molecules that are recognized as foreign and can stimulate an immune response are called "antigens." Antigen molecules can be found on almost anything—a cell in the bloodstream or body, a bacterium or virus, a fragment of tissue or a chemical.

Depending on the nature of the invader, a different type of immune response is catalyzed. *Humoral immunity* involves the secretion of antibodies that attack (non-self) foreign substances, such as bacteria or other toxins, *outside* the body's own cells. *Cell-mediated immunity* directly destroys invaders that reside *within* the body's cells, such as viruses as well as altered self cells such as tumor cells. Both branches of the immune response facilitate each other; indeed, one branch often requires assistance from the other in order to function normally.

Research over the past two decades has revealed the immense complexity of the immune system. To reduce this complexity to manageable units, we will examine the cells of the immune system, its antibodies, how the immune system is able to recognize so many different kinds of invaders, and the process of the immune response. It will then be easier to understand the points at which the mind can influence this rich and varied system.

As we learn about each different type of cell, however, it is important to bear in mind that it is only possible to separate elements of the immune system in a test tube. In a person, the containment of the simplest antigen is the end result of a cooperative effort of multiple elements, integrated by a host of substances, any of which may be affected by the brain. Other components of the immune system may compensate for what seems to be an important alteration in the laboratory, or a subtle change in function of a single aspect of the immune response may realign the entire system.

Immune Cells

Lymphocytes
Two kinds of cells, "lymphocytes" and "accessory cells," directly carry the immune response to foreign cells or altered self cells. Lymphocytes are blood cells that come in three varieties. *B lymphocytes* produce antibodies (discussed below), store the memory of previous encounters with a foreign substance that stimulated antibody production, and help to regulate the immune response.

T lymphocytes have varying assignments. "Killer" T cells directly attack cells that are infected with viruses or other parasites as well as cells that have been altered, usually by cancer. Killer T cells also release molecules that speed up the natural death of cells, stimulate other immune cells, and kill tumor cells. Other T cells act as regulators of the immune response. "Helper" T lymphocytes, for example, guide B cells to the appropriate site and help them to generate antibodies or promote inflammation. Helper T cells also stimulate accessory cells, which contain foreign protein fragments, to kill the internal invader. For example, one type of helper T cell encourages accessory cells to kill a bacterium that invades the interior of host cells. Another type of helper T cell gives signals that turn off the immune response so that it does not continue indefinitely. And, like B lymphocytes, memory T cells carry the memory of contact with a foreign substance for future reference.

A third type of lymphocyte is called the "natural killer" (NK) cell. NK cells directly attack the same kinds of invaders as killer T cells. However, unlike killer T lymphocytes—and every other immune cell—the NK cell does not have to recognize specific types of foreign material (antigens) and does not have to be previously sensitized to an antigen in order to go into action. Since NK cells are not limited by this specificity, they are able to respond more rapidly than other branches of the immune system and therefore constitute the first line of defense against tumors and viruses.

Macrophages and MHC Molecules

One of the key accessory cells, the macrophage, plays a crucial role in the recognition of foreign material. Like many other cells, the macrophage interior contains a molecule called the "major histocompatibility complex" (MHC) molecule, which tells whether tissue (histo) is compatible with the self. The MHC molecule is most important in identifying self cells that have been modified by foreign invaders such as viruses. The MHC molecule contains a groove into which fragments of proteins (peptides) fit. In healthy cells, the groove is occupied by a "self" peptide, which inactivates the MHC. If a bacterium, virus, or some other invader gets into the cell, it eventually encounters an MHC molecule and displaces the self peptide. The activated MHC molecule then carries the attached foreign peptide to the cell surface, where it can be recognized by lymphocytes.

In the case of the macrophage, an inflammatory T cell is activated when it recognizes the altered MHC molecule on the cell surface. Once the T cell is activated, it tells the macrophage to destroy the invader. In similar fashion, MHC molecules within B lymphocytes bind fragments of a foreign antigen that are carried into the lymphocyte by antibodies bound to the surface of the lymphocyte. The altered MHC molecules then wander back to the lymphocyte surface, where they are recognized by helper T cells that tell the B cells to divide and begin making antibodies to that antigen, which in turn are released into the body's environment.

Antibodies

Antibodies ("immunoglobulins") are complex molecules secreted by B lymphocytes that attack foreign substances outside of cells. Antibodies are particularly effective against certain bacteria, like staphylococcus, pneumococcus, and streptococcus. These bacteria are familiar to us as common causes of skin infections and pneumonia (not to mention the dreaded "flesh-eating" disease that has been in the news recently). Antibodies also neutralize the toxins produced by bacteria, such as those that cause botulism and diphtheria. Antibodies help to prevent viral reinfection as long as the virus is outside host cells, but because antibodies do not enter cells, they cannot attack infectious agents (for example, the tuberculosis bacterium) that establish themselves within host cells.

In addition to being released into the bloodstream to attack antigens directly, antibodies on the surface of B cells serve as receptors that recognize specific antigens (T lymphocytes have receptors of identical structure that recognize the same antigens, but the entire T cell attacks the antigen). Each

B lymphocyte has only one antibody, and each antibody recognizes only one antigen, with which it shares a very specific structural "fit."

When an antibody on the surface of a B lymphocyte encounters an antigen that fits it, the B cell is stimulated to divide so that enough antibodies can be made to neutralize the invader. After being stimulated, each B cell can release more than 10 million antibody molecules in a single hour. Antibodies then circulate in the bloodstream until they encounter more copies of the same antigen. If the antigen is on a foreign cell, such as a virus or bacterium, the antibody immobilizes it until a macrophage can arrive. The antibody secretes a coating over the antigen that makes the cell on which the antibody resides easier to ingest; if the antigen is on a toxin, the coating detoxifies it.

The binding of an antibody to the antigen it recognizes activates the production of a blood enzyme called "complement." The enzyme was so named because it complements the action of antibodies in destroying invaders. Complement may directly destroy cells like bacteria, or it may attract macrophages and other cells that ingest the invader. Self cells have proteins that inactivate complement so that it attacks foreign material.

It might seem sensible for us to manufacture antibodies as we need them, much as medications are manufactured for specific illnesses. However, while the body can rearrange existing antibodies, it is unable to make new ones from scratch. As a result, we are born with all the antibodies we will ever have. Luckily, there are so many inborn antibodies—about *100 million* of them—that it is highly likely that there will be a match for each of the numerous invaders that will be encountered in each person's lifetime. Unfortunately, microbes evolve faster than the organisms they attack, making it possible to develop new antigens that are able to evade even millions of the more slowly evolving immune defenses. Over the course of human evolution, billions of foreign antigens have appeared, far exceeding the number of defending antibodies that were programmed into our genes. New invaders that have antigens on their surfaces that do not match any of our antibodies have the potential to run rampant through our bodies. If they are also highly virulent, like the Ebola virus, they devastate individuals but do not produce large epidemics because people infected with them die without having a chance to pass them on. If the invader is like the HIV virus and takes longer to kill, however, it has the potential to spread like a wildfire, evading the immune defenses of everyone who catches it.

Since there are only 100,000 genes, the millions of antibodies we do possess could not possibly all be included in our genetic code. Yet all antibodies are the products of genes. How can we have more antibodies than genes? And how can antibodies foresee antigens that will be encountered in the future?

The answer lies in the structure of antibodies and the genes that produce them. Each antibody molecule consists of four parts—two identical heavy (H) chains and two identical light (L) chains (heavy chains weigh more than light chains) connected by bridging segments (Figure 19-1). Unlike most molecules, which are the product of a single gene, the antibody is assembled from the products of four different genes. Within a lymphocyte that is responsible for a particular antibody, the four "subgenes" link up to form one complete gene that produces the final antibody. A total of 4,800 genes can be assembled to make up the four segments of the H chain, and 400 genes can be assembled to make L chains. When the two types of genes are combined, a total of *1,920,000* (4,800 x 400) different types of antibodies are possible.

This is just the starting point for the number of antibody genes it is possible to assemble. By inserting small gene fragments where the major genes for antibody chains are joined, many more new antibodies can be produced. In addition, when a lymphocyte encounters an antigen that only loosely matches available antibodies, the natural rate of mutation of antibody genes may increase as much as 100,000 times. This greatly magnifies the chance that a variant will be produced that better fits the new antigen. The mutation that best fits the unfamiliar antigen is then retained in genetic memory in order to provide a more effective response the next time the antigen is encountered. The only kind of invader to which the body could not respond at all would be one whose antigens do not look anything like the antibodies the body is capable of assembling.

Cell-Mediated Immunity

Antibodies are highly effective at neutralizing antigens outside of cells. However, they are unable to enter cells and therefore cannot attack intracellular invaders such as viruses. Even when they are in the bloodstream, viruses present another problem: they can change their outer coating rapidly to avoid recognition by antibodies. Their inner proteins, on the other hand, mutate much more slowly, if at all, because these proteins are necessary for survival of the virus. When the virus reproduces itself inside a host cell, the core protein can be picked up by the MHC molecule, enabling immune cells that encounter the host cell to recognize the change in its antigenic structure.

To deal with intracellular invaders and with self cells whose surfaces are altered by cancer or other basic changes in structure that antibodies cannot attack, we have evolved another system of defense: cells that attack the antigens. As already mentioned, this branch of the cellular military is comprised of killer T cells, NK cells, and macrophages. These cells recognize antigens in similar ways, and they often coordinate their attack with other arms of the immune response.

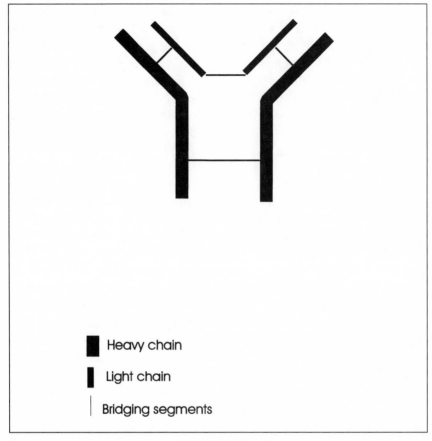

Figure 19-1.
Antibody structure

How do the millions of immune cells communicate with each other and the rest of the body? Since there are too many immune cells to be connected by nerves, chemicals that float through the bloodstream must be used for communication. One class of chemical messengers of the immune system is called the "cytokines."

Cytokines

Cytokines are chemicals produced by cells that stimulate other cells. Cytokines produced by lymphocytes are called "lymphokines," while cytokines that come from macrophages are called "monokines." Macrophages begin the immune response by releasing their cytokines; lymphocytes develop the capacity to secrete their cytokines when they are stimulated by antigens.

One type of cytokine is the family of interleukins, and one type of interleukin—interleukin-1—is released by macrophages that have captured an antigen. Interleukin-1 relays this message to B and T lymphocytes, which respond by multiplying. (Some interleukins reduce the immune response by slowing down the activation of lymphocytes.) Another group of cytokines—the interferons—are released by T lymphocytes and enhance the body's antiviral response by stimulating T cells, B cells, NK cells, and macrophages.

The interferons are a group of cytokines released by T lymphocytes and a type of structural cell called a fibroblast. By stimulating T cells, B cells, NK cells, and macrophages, interferons inhibit reproduction of viruses within cells and attract cells that digest viruses, enhancing the body's antiviral response. The capacity of various types of interferons to stimulate the immune response has led to trials of their use in a number of diseases. There is both good news and bad news from these trials: interferon may decrease the severity of diseases like multiple sclerosis, but immune system-brain connections make for a high frequency of depression as a side effect.

Because cytokines circulate in the bloodstream, they are a major route for communication between the immune system and the rest of the body. For example, interleukin-1 dilates blood vessels and induces fever, sleep, and loss of appetite through actions on the hypothalamus, while effects elsewhere produce muscle pain and gastrointestinal disturbances. This is one reason why people with infections *feel* sick. Interleukin-1 also stimulates the release of hormones from the pituitary gland as well as production of substances that lower the pain threshold. In excessive amounts, it can work against the body by producing inflammation of joints, hardening of the arteries, and even growth of leukemia cells. Interleukin-1 appears to be one substance that contributes to autoimmune diseases (the immune system attacks self cells), such as rheumatoid arthritis (immune attacks on the joints) and diabetes mellitus (immune attacks on the pancreas).

HOW AN IMMUNE RESPONSE OCCURS

The complex system of cytokines, antibodies, and immune cells provides extraordinary protection; at the same time, its very complexity provides numerous points at which the immune response may be enhanced or reduced by influences from the central nervous system. Some of the major steps in the immune response that are subject to this influence are presented in Figure 19-2 and summarized in the next few sections.

Recognition

The first step in the immune response is recognizing the presence of a foreign antigen (such as a microbe or toxin) or a self antigen (cells that have

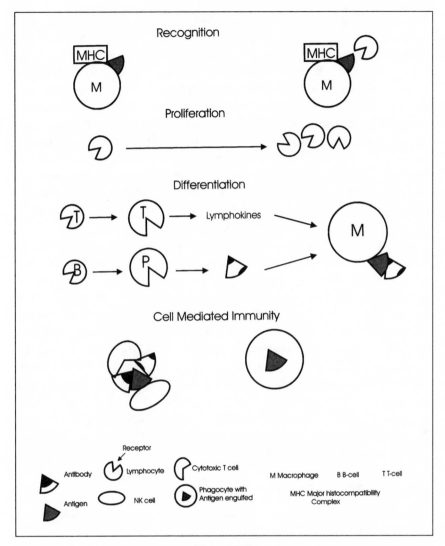

Figure 19-2.
The immune response

been altered by tissue damage or malignant transformation). Recognition usually begins when a macrophage compares the antigen with a self (major histocompatibility complex) molecule and presents the comparison to a lymphocyte. Antigen recognition most frequently occurs in organs that contain large numbers of immune cells, such as the spleen and lymph nodes. Some of the antigens become trapped in the cellular mesh of these organs, where at least one of them encounters a patrolling lymphocyte, circulating through the blood, that happens to have a receptor that is close enough to the structure of the antigen to interact with it.

Because there are so many different kinds of antigens and so many potential antibodies and T-cell receptors, only a few of the vast number of different lymphocytes in the circulation are capable of recognizing an antigen that the body has not yet encountered. It may take a while before one of the few lymphocytes capable of interacting with a new antigen runs into it, and then the initial response is weak: the lone lymphocyte that finally recognizes the antigen must refine its receptor and then reproduce in sufficient numbers to make a group (clone) of the same cells in sufficient numbers to mount a meaningful defense. The lymphocyte also needs time to grow into a more mature cell that actually conducts the attack on the antigen. These processes may require one to two weeks, which is why immunization to an antigen, such as the rubella (German measles) virus or pneumonia bacteria, takes several weeks to become effective in preventing infection.

Whether the antigen is destroyed after its first encounter with the correct antibody or lymphocyte depends on the relative numbers of each. Following the initial interaction, the size of the lymphocyte clone for that particular antigen decreases, but a significant number of lymphocytes that have learned to recognize the antigen continues to circulate for extended periods of time—sometimes for life—as "memory cells." The next time the memory cells encounter this particular antigen, the increased number of precisely matched cells will respond with much greater speed and force. This is why immunity is greater after a second or "booster" exposure to an antigen than after the first exposure, and why children have more colds when they start school than they do after continued exposure to the same viruses. Immune memory provides a mechanism by which early experience continues to affect immunity indefinitely.

Activation and Proliferation

Once a lymphocyte recognizes an antigen, it is activated to divide rapidly into clones of cells with the receptor for that antigen, while lymphocytes with different receptors remain at rest (Figure 19-2). During multiplication, lymphocyte DNA may mutate at an increased rate so that subsequent generations will have a better fit for the antigen. In addition to forming a clone of specifically responsive cells, proliferation of B lymphocytes activates the complement system, which helps to prepare the antigen for processing and attracts phagocytes (cells that engulf and digest foreign material) to attack the antigen.

Differentiation

Before an activated lymphocyte can attack an antigen, it must differentiate into a larger cell (described at the end of this section) that is capable of antibody secretion or cytotoxicity (cell killing). Macrophages that have recognized an antigen play a key role in this process by secreting interleukin-1, which activates T cells. T cells then release interleukin-2 (T-cell growth factor) that makes other T cells proliferate, B-cell growth factor that makes B cells increase in size, and B-cell differentiation factor, which facilitates differentiation of activated B lymphocytes into cells that perform the actual function of releasing antibodies or directly attacking invading cells. Helper T cells that have been activated by the same antigen that is recognized by the B cell further enhance proliferation and differentiation of B cells into clones with antibodies for that antigen.

Once the signal from the macrophage has helped B cells to recognize an antigen, they differentiate into plasma cells, which are the cells that actually release the antibody. Each plasma cell produces an antibody that is a copy of its lymphocyte's receptor for one and only one antigen. T lymphocytes that have recognized an antigen grow into larger T cells that carry out specific helper, suppressor, or cytotoxic functions and secrete lymphokines. One of these lymphokines, aptly named "migration inhibition factor," inhibits the random movement of macrophages, keeping them in the region of activated T cells that secrete this lymphokine so that they may assist in the immune response. The ability of macrophages to destroy material is then enhanced by gamma interferon, a member of the interferon family.

Antibody Production

We already know that antibodies are secreted by plasma cells, which are grown-up B lymphocytes. Each plasma cell produces only one antibody directed against a specific antigen, and all copies of that B cell in a clone produce exactly the same antibody. As they circulate in the blood or in bodily secretions, antibodies coat invaders carrying the specific antigen with which they can react, making it possible for macrophages and related cells to identify, engulf, and digest the foreigner.

Cytotoxicity

Cytotoxicity, the essential characteristic of cell-mediated immunity, involves the containment and destruction of viruses, some bacteria, and cancer cells. The "soldiers" of the cytotoxicity unit include T cells, NK cells, and macrophages that ingest infectious agents and tissue fragments. Digestion of invaders by macrophages is facilitated by coating their antigens with antibody. Recall that cytotoxic T cells destroy target cells only after being activated by an antigen that has been presented by a B cell or a macrophage, whereas natural killer cells do so without having to recognize a specific antigen.

Cellular immunity is activated when a macrophage presents a passing helper T cell with the antigen it has caught. In response, the T cell releases cytokines that increase the capacity of the macrophage to destroy the invader it is holding and that also stimulate the macrophage to produce cytokines of its own. One of these, *tumor necrosis factor,* inhibits reproduction of viruses within cells, attracts cells that digest viruses, stimulates other immune cells, and increases the natural rate at which cancer cells die.

Cellular Cooperation and Regulation of Immunity

One result of having so many different kinds of immune cells is that a sophisticated and flexible response is possible to a wide range of invaders from without and within (Figure 19-3). Central to the regulation of this response is the helper T cell. Through its lymphokines, the helper T cell facilitates the growth and differentiation of B and T lymphocytes. Interferon, which is also secreted by helper T cells, attracts NK cells to foreign tissue as a rapid first line of defense. Helper T cells also release macrophage activation factor and migration inhibition factor, which activate macrophages and keep them in the vicinity of an invader. In turn, helper T cells are activated by macrophages and B lymphocytes when they present the combination of foreign and self antigens, and by macrophages when they secrete interleukin-1, which stimulates the helper T cell to grow and secrete its own lymphokines.

Even as the immune response is instigated, processes are set in motion to shut it off so that it will not continue after it is no longer needed. Suppressor T cells, like other immune cells with the same antigen receptor, are turned on by the helper T cells that are activated when an antigen is recognized. Suppressor T cells secrete suppressor factors that directly inhibit further proliferation and differentiation of B and cytotoxic T cells. At the same time, the positive effect of helper T lymphocytes is gradually reduced.

HOW THE BRAIN INFLUENCES IMMUNITY

Because the brain processes information from the body's interior as well as the environment, it is the ideal organ for integrating the diverse elements of immunity with each other and with other bodily systems. As a result, stimulation and lesions of different parts of the brain can profoundly alter the immune response. This kind of control depends on two kinds of connections. Nerves connect the brain directly to immune organs like the spleen, thymus, and lymph nodes. However, since immune cells circulate throughout the body, additional means of transmitting information between the brain

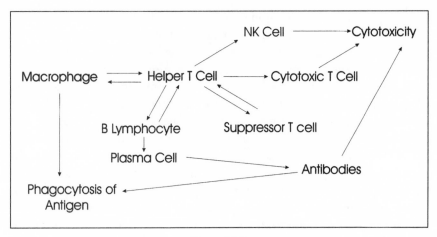

Figure 19-3.
Some interactions between immune cells

and the immune system have had to evolve. One method of communication involves hormones and neurotransmitters that interact with lymphocyte receptors. Neurotransmitters of alerting systems, such as norepinephrine, decrease lymphocyte responsiveness during acute stress. Endorphins stimulate some aspects of immune function and suppress others; prolactin, a hormone produced by the pituitary gland, suppresses lymphocyte proliferation; and melatonin, a hormone produced in the pineal gland, can enhance immunity in some circumstances. These kinds of signals to the immune system are slower than signals from the autonomic nervous system that produce sudden changes in cardiac function, but they are no less influential.

The immune system communicates with the brain directly as well as in the bloodstream and tissues. As they circulate through the brain, immune cells are influenced not only by neurotransmitters but by cytokines produced by glial cells, a type of structural cell that provides part of the matrix in which brain neurons are embedded. Glial cells, which are derived from the same tissue as macrophages, produce interleukins and tumor necrosis factor when they are activated by antigens. Some neurons can also make interleukin-1, which stimulates the growth of more glial cells and attracts macrophages to a site of injury or infection.

The immune system is capable of "talking back" to the brain, so that when lymphocytes encounter an antigen the rate of neuronal firing in certain areas of the hypothalamus increases, as does the activity of the pituitary and adrenal glands. In addition to their role as effectors of the immune response, then, lymphocytes function as scouts for the brain, reporting their encounters with antigens throughout the body by sending chemical signals. These "reports" are sent in the form of substances (endorphins, growth hormone, corticotropin releasing hormone, ACTH, and TRH) that serve as neuro-transmitters in the brain as well as hormones and immune modulators in the body. When the brain receives signals from these lymphocytes, it coordinates emotional and hormonal responses to the situation that altered immunity.

The action of neurotransmitters produced by immune cells is augmented by lymphokines, which can act as neurotransmitters when they are secreted by lymphocytes passing through the brain. The appearance of cytokines like interleukin-1 in alerting centers of the brain stimulates the sympathetic nervous system to suppress various aspects of the immune response. Interferon increases deep sleep, which may promote healing rest during infection. Cytokines probably produce some of the behavioral disturbances associated with strong immune responses that were described earlier and, in excessive amounts, may contribute to the brain damage associated with the response to infection with HIV and the agent of Lyme disease.

One of the most important functions of feedback loops between the brain and immune system is to keep the immune response from getting out of hand. This intricate communication system can be thrown out of balance by excessive or prolonged bouts of stress, which cause the brain to give the signal for the release of cortisol. As an important hormone of the stress-response system, cortisol inhibits immune cell function on many levels. The brain, therefore, is recruited almost immediately into the process of controlling the activity of the immune system. These connections also provide a route by which the brain can inhibit immunity on its own.

Learned Immune Suppression

That immune suppression could be conditioned in the laboratory was demonstrated as early as 1926. More recent studies by immunologist Robert Ader and his colleagues have replicated this observation. They paired an anticancer drug called cyclophosphamide, which both tastes bad and suppresses antibody production, with saccharine, which seems to have a desirable taste for animals as well as people but by itself has no effect on the immune system. Animals given saccharine along with the cyclophosphamide began to avoid the saccharine as if it had acquired a bad taste. At the same time, their immune systems stopped making antibodies in response to injected foreign cells, just as it did with cyclophosphamide. Saccharine, which in itself has no effect whatsoever on the immune system, had *acquired* immunosuppressive properties. The capacity to suppress immunity was retained even after saccharine was no longer paired with cyclophosphamide, and after saccharine had lost its association with the bad taste of the drug. Many studies have verified that pairing an inactive substance such as saccharine with an immunosuppressive substance causes the inactive compound to acquire the ability to suppress immunity. How does the neutral material become an immunosuppressant? The answer is that the brain records the effect of the active drug and transfers it to the neutral one. In other words, *the brain's ability to learn—to make and remember new associations—provides a route by which the mind can deceive the body out of its own immune response.*

How the Brain Anticipates Danger and Suppresses Immunity

Stress, especially if it is uncontrollable, has been shown to reduce the activity of many arms of the immune response. Immune suppression in the face of danger should have protective value: any threat carries with it the risk of injury, and injured tissue may be sufficiently altered to be recognized as foreign by the immune system. Bodily injury during a physical attack would carry with it the risk of additional injury by the body's own defenses, unless immune protection could be suspended until the acute danger has passed.

The advantage of having the brain play a role in coordinating the immune response is that it is able to anticipate danger and prepare for it. This means that the *idea* of danger can be as influential as actual physical stress in altering immune responsiveness, as is true for the effects of the stress response on the heart. For example, relatives of patients with Alzheimer's disease have been found to have lowered numbers of lymphocytes, and NK-cell activity predictably goes down in students taking examinations. Conversely, relief of stress can have a positive effect, as was illustrated in one study when the response of lymphocytes to an antigen nearly doubled a week after a group of gay men were told that they did not have the HIV virus.

Stressful experiences evoke the fight-flight response, which can suppress immunity by a number of mechanisms. This action is mediated to a significant effect by adrenal stress hormones, such as cortisol and epinephrine, but there must be other way-stations from the brain to the immune system, since removal of the adrenal glands does not prevent stress-induced immune suppression. When we are under intense stress, these various mechanisms can deplete immune cells and prevent us from fighting infection, which may be why we are more likely to get sick at these times.

Hyperactivity of the vagus nerve, one of the major effectors of the conservation-withdrawal response, can also suppress immunity. The same kinds of mixtures of fight-flight/conservation-withdrawal responses that injure the heart therefore can injure the immune systems.

It is not the threat itself but how it is experienced that determines its impact on the immune system. For example, salivary levels of an antibody called IgA, which may act as a barrier against invasion, fall in response to stress, but the decrease persists only in those who cannot cope with the stress. The interaction between stress and coping skills was found by psychiatrist Sam Perry

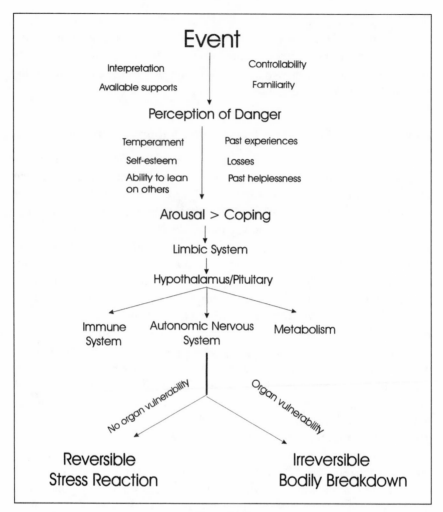

Figure 19-4.
The mind deceives the body

to have practical implications in a study of men who were positive for the HIV virus but had not yet manifested any symptoms. As everyone knows, one of the more important markers of overall status in HIV disease is the number of helper T cells. In this study, all men faced the same stress of knowing they were HIV-positive. However, those who had low levels of other life stressors and who coped actively with events in their lives had the most helper T cells. Those with high levels of stress, to which they had become resigned, had the fewest helper T cells. Those who coped actively with high levels of stress had better helper T cell counts than those who did not, and passive copers who were not under much stress also had intermediate helper T cell counts.

Animal studies suggest that when hopelessness compounds the effects of the fight-flight response with the additional immunosuppressant action of conservation-withdrawal, there is even more impairment of immunity. Conversely, a sense of familiarity, predictability, and controllability of a threat decreases the intensity of the fight-flight response and protects against immunosuppression. Moderate chronic stress, to which it is possible to adapt, may even enhance the immune response.

We have seen repeatedly that other people facilitate our physical and mental abilities to cope and adapt. Minimizing immune suppression is no exception. In a study of forty-eight medical students (a population almost as captive for experiments as laboratory animals and psychology undergraduates) immunized with hepatitis vaccine, those who reported poor social support had a delayed antibody response to the vaccine (although after a booster shot was administered, their antibodies were as adequate as those with supportive relationships). An investigation by psychoimmunology researcher J.K. Kielcot-Glaser showed that exposing medical students to the well-known stress of an important examination resulted in suppression of lymphocyte responsiveness and cell-mediated immunity against viruses in those who reported feeling lonely during the year prior to the examination but not in those who were in dependable relationships.

Separation and Loss as a Potent Stress to the Immune System

The impact of loss on the immune system involves not only the direct effect of the stress itself but also the excessive arousal that comes from losing an interpersonal source of psychological and physical regulation. One experimental manifestation of the impact of this excess arousal on immune function is that during separation depression, infant monkeys demonstrate decreased T-lymphocyte proliferation and reduced NK-cell activity in response to presentation of a substance called a mitogen (an experimental antigen) that stimulates growth of immune cells.

Decreased lymphocyte responsiveness in separated animals may continue long after mother and infant have been reunited. In fact, blunted lymphocyte proliferation has been observed at age five in monkeys who underwent separation from their mothers or peers during the first year of life. After immune functioning finally returns to normal, it often decreases again upon subsequent separations. Conversely, handling infant rats for just three minutes a day enhanced their immune response to unfamiliar antigens when they were grown. Such findings suggest that *losses early in life can sensitize the immune system to inappropriate suppression in response to a separation in adulthood.* Conversely, positive experiences in infant animals seem to enhance their immune response to unfamiliar antigens when they are grown.

Researchers have investigated the immunosuppressive effect of separation in humans as well. Psychiatrist Joe Calabrese found that NK-cell activity and lymphocyte proliferation gradually became depressed following bereavement. These deficits appeared to be most marked when the protest phase had been complicated by the behavioral and emotional depression of grief. As the depression deepened, lymphocyte responsiveness and numbers of helper T cells decreased markedly. The mixture of arousal and withdrawal seemed to be the most potent suppressor of immune functioning during grief.

In one interesting prospective study by Stephen Schleifer, the husbands of 15 women being treated for terminal breast cancer were followed while their wives were undergoing treatment and following their deaths. There was no change in the husbands' immune systems while their wives were alive, even though the men were extremely upset. However, during the first two months of bereavement, lymphocyte responsiveness declined, although the absolute numbers of lymphocytes remained the same. Gaining familiarity with the idea of loss during the prolonged stress of the spouse's illness apparently did not protect against the impact of the actual loss. Lymphocyte functioning gradually returned to normal over the next ten months in most subjects, but a few men had deficits that persisted beyond the first year of bereavement.

In this and similar studies, the extent of immune suppression was not correlated with levels of cortisol, a fact that is important because it shows that the effect of loss on the immune system is not simply a function of higher levels of stress hormones like cortisol, which are known to suppress immune cell function.

Depression and Immunity

As with any source of stress, it is probably not bereavement itself but the capacity to cope with it that influences the amount of immune suppression. People who cannot adapt to a loss become depressed, and the more depression is present following a loss, the greater the reduction of lymphocyte and NK-cell function. It is therefore not surprising that NK-cell activity is lower in individuals confronting adverse events who are already depressed or anxious than in those with the same problems who do not have these symptoms.

What is the effect of major depression—which, as we have seen, is a state of arousal mixed with hopelessness—on the immune system? A few studies have reported reduced ability of lymphocytes to proliferate, decreased NK-cell activity, or decreased numbers of cytotoxic T cells in depressed patients compared with controls. However, as Marvin Stein, one of the pioneers in the study of brain–immune system connections, pointed out several years ago, fourteen of twenty-two studies of immune function in major depressive disorder did not find any reliable alteration of immune function. In one experiment that addressed many of the weaknesses of other studies (for example, lumping together patients of different ages with different kinds of depression), Stephen Schleifer found only two changes in immune function in depressed patients: reduced proliferation of lymphocytes in more severely depressed patients and lack of the increase in lymphocyte proliferation in response to a mitogen that normally occurs with increasing age. When changes in one aspect or another of immune function have been found in other studies of depression, they also have been limited to older and more severely depressed patients. However, one study of forty-three severely depressed men noted the startling finding that those with the *fewest* depressive symptoms had the *most* inhibition of lymphocyte proliferation!

A study of 270 men infected with the HIV virus but without symptoms found that the presence of depression predicted a more rapid decrease in helper T-cell counts over time than in HIV-positive men who were not depressed. Conversely, a study of 221 HIV-positive men by psychiatrist Samuel Perry, an expert on AIDS, showed no effect of depression on lymphocyte activity or clinical outcome over the course of a year; there was also no relationship between T-cell counts and stress, depression, social support, or reactions to illness over the year of follow-up. All of this shows that we do understand more about how stress and depression produce changes in the test tube than in human beings!

CAN THE MIND DECEIVE THE IMMUNE SYSTEM INTO ILLNESS?

Scientific evidence suggests that changes in immune function associated with stress and depression do not alter susceptibility to disease as directly as, say, smoking leads to lung cancer or exposure to HIV results in the development of AIDS. One reason for this discrepancy is that only one aspect of immune function is measured at a time, but there is so much redundancy and interaction in the immune system that a single change can have unpredictable clinical ramifications. Another important issue is that health and disease are multifaceted states: even in the case of a severe injury, the outcome of any single insult to the body's defenses does not have a linear effect on overall condition.

What does appear to be the case is that mental factors do not act alone but rather amplify or attenuate other risk factors. A state of excellent bodily health may mitigate any impairment of immune protection against infection and cancer that might be promoted by negative mental states. On the other end of the spectrum, it may be impossible for mental factors to make advanced bodily disease any worse than it already is. It is probably only when some vulnerability is present in a person who is exposed to moderate doses of infectious or tumor-producing agents that psychological influences on immunity make the difference between health and disease.

Stress, Coping, and Infection

Most people have had the experience of coming down with colds, the flu, cold sores, or aggravations of chronic infections like genital herpes when they are upset or overwhelmed. A number of studies support the folk wisdom that common infections are more frequent in people experiencing chronic mental stress. This is a mundane problem, but it has implications for how to make ourselves less vulnerable when one of the infectious diseases that plague us is going around.

As with most effects of stress on the body, it is not so much the existence of the stressor as it is the ability to cope with it that determines why one person exposed to a virus becomes ill while someone else does not. For example, students with high expectations who do not perform well in school are more likely to get infectious mononucleosis than students who perform at the same level but do not expect as much of themselves. Students facing the same examination are more likely to contract acute viral illnesses if they experience anxiety, depression, and helplessness than if they feel a sense of confidence. Increased susceptibility to infection in people who feel that they are not in control of a stress is correlated with the usual measures of immunosuppression, such as reduced NK-cell activity and lymphocyte proliferation.

An experiment demonstrating the interaction of stress and illness was performed by psychologist S. Cohen and his colleagues. Cohen housed normal subjects in a controlled environment and compiled a composite "stress index" that included assessments of negative life events during the past year, a perception of being under stress, and a negative emotional reaction to the stress. When he exposed subjects to the virus that causes the common cold, he found that 74 percent of those who had a low stress index developed some signs of infection, and 27 percent got an actual cold. In contrast, 90 percent of those with a high stress index became infected and 47 percent got a cold. Reacting negatively to the perception of stress was correlated with becoming ill, while the number of stressful events was correlated with the number of symptoms when illness actually occurred, suggesting that *susceptibility to illness and severity of illness may involve two different processes.*

CANCER AND IMMUNITY

It is in the nature of all living cells to renew themselves by multiplying. Cancer is the result of loss of control of this process. In the vast majority of cases, there is no single cause of cancer. Instead, several crucial elements must fall into place before a malignancy can emerge. This is why cancer takes a long time to develop, and why there is plenty of time for many factors—perhaps even psychological ones—to influence its outcome.

One contributing factor to the cancer process is a physical agent called a "carcinogen." Common carcinogens include cigarette smoke, asbestos, ionizing radiation, dietary factors, and chemicals. Recognizing the carcinogenic power of sunlight has made dermatologists recommend that people stay out of the sun (though this recommendation is often ignored). Numerous viruses have been shown to cause tumors in animals, and a smaller number—most notably, the Ebstein-Barr virus, the hepatitis B virus, and the human T cell leukemia/lymphoma virus—are known to cause cancer in people. Once they get into the body, some carcinogens are activated to forms that actually produce cancer, and others are inactivated. Excessive activity of the first process or inadequate activity of the second can increase carcinogenic effects. Cancer-causing agents act by altering cellular DNA, producing a mutant cell with two important characteristics: excessive growth and altered self antigens.

The answer lies in the common pathway of all cellular activity—the ongoing signals that tell cells how to act: DNA. Most tumor-producing agents act by changing genes that play a crucial role in cellular regulation. At least one hundred such genes have been identified. These genes belong to two broad classes: *oncogenes* and *tumor suppressor genes.* Dangerous abnormalities in both classes of genes can be produced by carcinogens, or they can be inherited or occur spontaneously.

Oncogenes

Viruses may carry foreign oncogenes into the body. Most of the time, however, oncogenes are the result of transformation of normal genes, called "proto-oncogenes," which produce proteins that are involved in cellular growth and survival. These proto-oncogenes have the potential to alter the activity of many other genes involved in the basic activity of the cell. Some proto-oncogenes produce a type of protein that carries signals from many types of receptors to activate their cells.

Carcinogens increase the likelihood that proto-oncogenes will be converted to oncogenes by one of three processes. Mutation is one such process. In addition, as DNA strands twist around themselves when cells divide, one gene may fuse with another to produce a new oncogene. Finally, DNA contains enormous amounts of information, and when it duplicates itself during cell division, errors in copying a "letter" or two of the complex "paragraphs" spelled out by a gene are not uncommon. Most of the time, these errors do not affect the overall function of the gene, but if they occur at a crucial location, they may produce a gene whose function is altered slightly yet significantly.

To illustrate how subtle alterations in proto-oncogene structure can contribute to cancer, a gene called the Ras oncogene (named after a type of tumor) produces a protein that is necessary for the normal function of cells with receptors. Changing a single base (a molecular building block of DNA) makes the gene turn normal cells into cancer cells; the abnormal version of the Ras oncogene has been found in cells from 40-50 percent of people with colorectal cancer. Another example: the "Philadelphia chromosome," which is formed by the undesirable fusion of a region on chromosome 22 and a proto-oncogene on chromosome 9, contains an oncogene that is found in virtually all cases of chronic myelocytic leukemia, suggesting that this oncogene—produced by a mistaken overlap between two chromosomes—contributes to one form of leukemia.

Tumor Suppressor Genes

The other type of gene involved in the production of cancer is the *tumor suppressor gene*. Tumor suppressor genes normally code for proteins that keep DNA from replicating inappropriately. These proteins restrain cell division and facilitate the death of aging or abnormal cells. Like oncogenes, tumor suppressor genes can lose their normal function through mutation, changing of bases, rearrangement of the gene when the cell divides, or merging of one chromosome with another during cellular replication. A type of tumor suppressor gene called "multiple tumor suppressor gene" (MTS1) seems to be involved in restraining multiple kinds of cells: mutations that make it nonfunctional have been found in almost 50 percent of cases of malignant melanoma and cancer of the lung, brain, and breast.

Another interesting tumor suppressor gene is the p53 gene, which speeds up in cancer cells a process, called "apoptosis," of aging and death inherent in all cells, especially when the cancer cells become closely grouped together (as will be described shortly). Since cancer chemotherapy kills cancer cells by inducing apoptosis, cells with intact p53 genes are more responsive to chemotherapy, while those with p53 mutations are more resistant to it.

Because the regulation of cell growth is so complex, it takes five to ten sequential mutations in oncogenes and tumor suppressor genes to produce cells that are capable of becoming malignant—capable of invading regions in which they are formed and then spreading throughout the body. Chromosomes contain enzymes that allow DNA to repair itself, and a series of mutations or other carcinogenic alterations in DNA are only successful when DNA repair is inefficient.

Once a cell has escaped the basic mechanisms of growth regulation, it must "escape" its location in order to grow into a tumor (a large collection of cells), spread locally, and then metastasize—travel through the bloodstream to establish a foothold in distant sites. Once a ball of malignant cells reaches a certain size (about a tenth of a millimeter, or around a million cells), the tumor's blood supply is no longer sufficient to keep all the cells alive; apoptosis, mediated by the p53 gene, is triggered by the low oxygen supply in the middle of the tumor. At this point in the advancement of the disease, cancer cells that have a normal p53 gene will die, while those with p53 mutations will continue to grow. It is the loss of oxygen supply as the tumor begins to grow that actually stimulates the growth of cancer cells by killing off the weaker cells and allowing those without the p53 gene, which are more malignant, to outnumber them. As these more aggressive cells continue to divide, they pass their new genetic abnormalities onto new cells, which accumulate even more abnormalities that allow them to continue to grow.

Cancer cells that grow locally are not nearly as dangerous as those that metastasize throughout the body. The process of metastasis begins when the evolution of mutations in cancer cells includes the activation of genes that secrete substances that attract blood vessels. This provides nutrients to the growing tumor as well as a route of entry into the bloodstream. Further changes in DNA lead to the production of enzymes that can break down the connections between blood vessel cells, so that the growing cancer cells can squeeze into the new vessels and spread throughout the body. By the time the cancer begins to spread, then, it has undergone many generations of change, each successive change making it more aggressive and more resistant to treatment. One implication of this process is that, like mood disorders, cancer is easier to treat earlier in its course than it is once it has acquired a complex series of genetic changes that enable it to spread and grow and make it more resistant to therapy.

Immune Surveillance Theory

The same genetic alterations that turn normal cells into cancer cells produce changes in cellular proteins that can cause them to be recognized as non-self by the immune system. The *immune surveillance* theory holds that while a tumor is in its early stages of development, it may be possible for immune cells to contain and destroy it. It has been proposed that immune surveillance is a first line of defense against the many tumors that arise over the course of a person's lifetime but are not given a chance to get to the aggressive stage. Natural killer cells, which respond more rapidly than other immune cells (because it is not necessary for them to have had previous experience with a foreign antigen), may be the first immune cells to interact with an emerging cancer. Immune surveillance would be expected to be effective until cell growth becomes too extensive; once a tumor reaches a critical size, no attack from the immune system is likely to be effective.

Given the inevitable failures of gene replication during cellular division and the numerous carcinogens and viruses in the environment, changes in DNA leading to unrestrained cellular growth are common enough that all of us produce cancer cells from time to time that must be destroyed by the immune system before they have a chance to gain a foothold. But when the functioning of the immune system is reduced, the risk of cancer is increased. And mental as well as physical processes that suppress immune functioning could put some people at risk of cancer.

The evidence that immune suppression can lead to cancer is abundant. For example, patients who take immunosuppressant drugs to control rejection of organ transplants have an increased risk of developing leukemia, lymphoma, and skin cancer—all of which are cancers of cells that normally divide rapidly and are more subject to errors in oncogenes and tumor suppressor genes. There is also a slightly increased risk of cancer of the lung, breast, colon, uterus, and prostate glands, which also have cells that "turn over" rapidly. AIDS patients, who have severe reduction of immune function, frequently develop Kaposi's sarcoma, an otherwise rare malignant skin cancer. However, while some cancers do seem to escape control in immunosuppressed people, *most* do not. It seems probable that the immune system, which evolved to fight infection, has acquired some capacity to fight cancer cells, too, though not as efficiently. To the extent that immune surveillance does play a role in preventing cancer, it cannot be the only factor. This may explain why mental states that suppress the immune system may contribute to cancer but have yet to be shown to be the only, or even the most important, element.

DEPRESSION, HOPELESSNESS, AND CANCER

The kind of depressed mental function that modern science has shown impairs immunity has, for centuries, been thought to increase vulnerability to cancer. In 200 A.D., Greek physician Claudius Galen observed that depressed, melancholic, phlegmatic, and grief-stricken people were more prone to cancer than less troubled individuals. In the nineteenth century, James Paget stated in his authoritative text, *Surgical Pathology,* that

> . . . the cases are so frequent in which deep anxiety, deferred hope and disappointment are quickly followed by the growth and increase of cancer that we can hardly doubt that mental depression is a weighty addition to the other influences favoring the development of the cancerous constitution.

Contemporary research into psychological contributors to cancer has taken a number of directions. Psychiatrist Lawrence LeShan conducted intensive psychotherapy with hundreds of cancer patients and found that they were more likely than people without cancer to have weak or nonexistent relationships and to feel hopeless about ever leading meaningful lives. Compared with physically healthy psychotherapy patients, the cancer patients were more likely to give up and withdraw than to mobilize themselves psychologically. In a retrospective study, LeShan found that 72 percent of cancer patients, compared with only 10 percent of controls, had suffered a significant loss a few months to eight years before cancer was discovered. Cancer patients were also more likely to have lost a parent in childhood, making the later losses, which were more closely associated with the development of cancer, more difficult to handle.

Because LeShan knew which patients in his studies had cancer and which did not, he could have unconsciously skewed the results as he collected them. Researchers R.L. Horne and R.S. Picard attempted to avoid this source of potential bias by predicting the presence of lung cancer based on a psychological profile but no medical information. In this study, a scale rating the combination of childhood instability, marital problems, difficulties on the job, lack of plans for the future, and a significant loss during the past five years was as accurate as a history of smoking in predicting the presence of lung cancer.

An association between loss and cancer was also found in a study by T. J. Jacobs and E. Charles comparing twenty-five children with cancer with twenty-five children of the same ages and gender who had had only minor physical illnesses. The cancer patients were five times as likely as the controls to have lost a family member other than a parent (e.g., a grandparent, sibling, or other relative). Even more striking, during the year prior to the onset of illness, the parents of cancer patients were almost three times as likely as the parents of controls to have separated, and cancer patients' families were five times as likely as families of controls to have moved.

Concluding from studies of patients who are already ill that mental states associated with the cancer actually caused the cancer is obviously risky. If a cancer patient reports having felt hopeless prior to falling ill, how is one to be sure that the memory is not colored by the depressing knowledge of having cancer? Another problem is that since cancer does not become clinically apparent until months to years after malignant changes begin in individual cells, it is difficult to determine whether hopelessness or loss were experienced at a point in the cancer process that contributed to the actual onset of the disease. Even if emotions did play a causal role in the development of cancer, it would be necessary to determine whether they exerted a direct action on bodily defenses or whether secondary behaviors in response to the emotions, such as smoking or failure to seek early medical treatment, were really responsible.

The best way to verify that emotional or psychological states predispose to the development of cancer is to measure mental states in a population of healthy people and follow them through the initiation of the disease process to see whether subjects with the proposed pathogenic mental state but the same health habits are more likely than those without it to get sick. However, cancer is rare enough and the carcinogenic process sufficiently prolonged that it would be necessary to follow an extremely large and randomly selected group for a very long time before enough people with the predisposing emotion developed the disease to draw any conclusions other than that a few individuals who develop cancer happen to have a particular mental constellation. While this approach has the advantage of greater statistical reliability, it is prohibitively expensive to perform the kind of in-depth mental evaluation that researchers like LeShan were able to do with patients they interview or treat. It is therefore necessary to combine larger epidemiologic studies with smaller, more detailed psychological investigations to get a complete view of mind-body interactions in cancer.

One prospective study that had interesting results was Carolyn B. Thomas' project, which was described earlier. Thomas found that during medical school, physicians who developed cancer many years later, like those who ultimately committed suicide, showed lack of closeness to their families and a propensity for pessimism. A prospective study by psychologist P. J. Dattore and colleagues of 2,500 individuals who underwent extensive personality testing found that, regardless of the kind of physical care they took of themselves, subjects who were "depressive" on the initial evaluation were more likely than non-depressive subjects to develop cancer twenty years later.

In a similar prospective investigation of 2,020 men working for the Western Electric Company, those with high depression scores on a standardized psychological test called the Minnesota Multiphasic Personality Inventory (MMPI) had twice the risk of death from cancer seventeen years after the initial evaluation as those with low depression scores. Conversely, a ten-to-fourteen-year follow-up of a different sample found no association between depression scores and the later development of breast cancer. Two other studies found no relationship between various measures of depressive symptoms and the development of cancer over seventeen years in 6,848 people, and over ten years in 6,400 individuals. Each of these studies employed only one type of assessment of depressive symptoms without considering the *diagnosis* of depression. They also employed a one-dimensional view of depression as a risk factor, without looking at the interaction between depression and other mental factors and between mental and physical contributions to later illness. None of these studies addressed the question of whether mental factors had more of an influence on the course of cancer once it developed than on the onset of the disease.

On one occasion when these kinds of complexities were considered, the results suggested that depression might be more of a cofactor than a primary risk factor for cancer. For example, in 169 of 2,264 people given a depression scale who eventually developed cancer, there was no relationship between high depression scores and the later development of cancer. However, depression seemed to increase the carcinogenicity of smoking, so that the two together were associated with a greater risk of cancer than either one alone. If the immune surveillance theory is correct, depression might inhibit the recognition and destruction of early small tumors promoted by smoking.

As noted, a more comprehensive evaluation of the kind of mental state that might influence susceptibility to cancer has not been conducted because to do so is financially impossible. If a physical marker could be identified that would distinguish people who are prone to develop cancer, however, then the total number of subjects who have to be studied would be reduced to a manageable number. Psychiatrists Arthur Schmale and Harold Iker used this strategy when they evaluated forty otherwise healthy women whose only abnormality was an atypical Pap smear that may be an early warning of cancer of the cervix but is also associated with benign changes in cervical cells. Only a biopsy can establish the diagnosis. Prior to the biopsy, the investigators conducted an in-depth psychological evaluation to determine the degree of hopelessness experienced by each subject. They predicted that cancer would be found only if a woman had felt hopeless during the previous six months, or if she was prone to hopelessness when confronted with loss of self-esteem or loss of an important social role.

After Schmale and Iker recorded their predictions of who would and would not have cancer, the biopsies were performed. The results bore out the researchers' projections in both directions in 78 percent of the patients, much more than would have been expected by chance. In a replication of this study, another group found that the number of words referring to hopelessness and depression expressed by subjects in interviews conducted shortly before cervical biopsies were conducted was highly accurate in predicting the presence of cancer.

The somber presence of hopelessness and related experiences of loss and depression have also distinguished patients with other cancers. For example, without examining the patients and having no medical information—only responses on a psychosocial questionnaire—C. B. Bahnson was able to distinguish between forty patients with breast cancer and forty healthy subjects 96 percent of the time. Factors that most successfully identified cancer patients were recent loss of a family member, feelings of isolation, and inability to express anger openly.

Chronic suppression of anger was also shown to differentiate women awaiting breast biopsies who turned out to have breast cancer from those with benign lumps. As in Schmale and Iker's study, the psychological variable (suppression of anger) was assessed before the biopsies, ruling out the possibility of a reaction to the knowledge of being sick. In another report the same trait predicted whether women with newly diagnosed breast cancer developed metastases within the next year.

Negative psychological states that have been correlated with the presence of cancer diagnosed *after* mental status is evaluated could not be reactions to conscious awareness of the disease. However, this does not necessarily mean that the psychological state was responsible for the illness. Even if there is no conscious awareness of cancer, subtle changes in physiology may make it possible to sense the presence of the disease unconsciously. The tumor may also secrete substances that alter mood and outlook. Pancreatic cancer, lymphomas, and leukemias are well-known examples of malignancies that can induce depressive symptoms long before there is any other evidence of the disease. Another possibility is that the same process that causes cancer has a direct effect on the brain, undermining mental defenses at the same time that it depresses immune surveillance or repair of altered DNA. Furthermore, since depressed people can be difficult to tolerate, friends and loved ones may withdraw, adding *loss* to the interaction. Thus depression, hopelessness, or even loss could be the *result* of cancer rather than its cause.

Loss, depressive tendencies, and a low threshold for feeling hopeless may not be proven factors in the pathogenesis of cancer, but they are recurrent themes—as they are in heart disease. Indeed, lack or loss of social support has been associated with a risk of cancer or heart disease equivalent to that of smoking or having high cholesterol levels. The fact that the same set of forces—loss in the context of shaky psychological resources and a propensity to feel overwhelmed and hopeless—can contribute to such different illnesses is another example of the nonspecificity that was discussed in Part I. If we assume that inherited or acquired vulnerabilities determine which illness develops, and even whether the illness is mental or physical, our interest will turn to the ways in which loss can disrupt our bodily as well as our psychological defenses.

THE MORTALITY OF BEREAVEMENT

Loss of a loved one has a terrible impact on mind and body. Statistics report that almost half of those who have lost a spouse are unable to function normally a year following the loss, and 20 percent are in extremely poor mental and physical health. The risk of suicide is increased *250 percent* in the recently bereaved, and a major mental illness is six times more likely to develop after bereavement than after any other kind of stress. Years after the death of a spouse, many widows and widowers still keep to themselves, and some never take a chance on another relationship.

The most common mental complication of grief is depression, which is more likely to develop (1) when the bereaved has no close friend or relative to assist in coping with the painful feelings; (2) if the bereaved is emotionally unable to lean on those who are available; (3) if other people tell the bereaved not to think about the loss (i.e., they encourage excessive denial); (4) if the lost relationship was complicated by chronic anger, ambivalence, or guilt; (5) if the death was by suicide; or (6) if the bereaved is predisposed to depression by genetic factors or prior unresolved losses.

The physical consequences of bereavement, especially when it is complicated by depression, are substantial. The health of about two-thirds of widows declines in the year following loss of their spouses. People who lose a spouse are twice as likely to die of natural causes during the following year than married people in the same initial state of health who do not suffer a loss. At least half of the excess mortality rates associated with bereavement is due to heart disease; the rest is from cancer, infections, and the same illness that killed the spouse, even when that illness was not contagious. Widowers have substantially higher morality rates than widows (or men whose wives are still alive).

Of the numerous reports that document an increase in mortality following the death of a spouse, the most dramatic findings were those of W. D. Rees and S.G. Lutkins, who studied the entire population of a small town (2,350 individuals) in Wales over a number of years. Of this sample, 371 died during the study period, leaving 903 close relatives to mourn them. Everyone who lost a relative was matched with someone in a neighboring town who had not been bereaved, and the subsequent health of both bereaved subject and non-bereaved subjects was observed from the time the loss was experienced.

Rees and Lutkins found an amazing sevenfold increase in the risk of dying in the bereaved relatives: 11.6 percent of the bereaved died during the year following the loss of a family member, while only 1.6 percent of the non-bereaved subjects succumbed during the same period. People who lost a spouse, as opposed to some other relative, had the highest mortality rate— *ten times* the rate of the non-bereaved. The increased risk of death in the bereaved was not as pronounced if the loved one died at home or in the hospital, but it was much greater if the loved one died in a site other than the home or hospital such as a field, on a road, or in a shop.

Critics of the Rees and Lutkins study have suggested that the drastic differences in mortality rates they noted reflected the accidental selection of a control group that was so unusually healthy that the bereaved sample seemed at exceptionally high risk by comparison. However, even though other studies have not found the physical risk of bereavement to be quite as high, most have confirmed that loss—at least of a spouse—can be fatal. In a nine-year follow-up of 4,486 widowers over the age of fifty-five, for example, pioneering bereavement researcher Colin Parkes found a 40 percent increase in the chance of dying, especially of heart disease, during the first six months of bereavement. As has been found in most other studies, the increased risk of bereavement-induced mortality declined after six-to-twelve months.

The risk of bereavement may depend on the degree to which mind and body can borrow resiliency from other people. A comparison of the parents of all 2,518 Israeli soldiers killed in the 1973 Yom Kippur war with the parents of 1,128 Israeli men of the same age who died in automobile accidents from 1971–1975 found that, during the ten years following the loss, there was no greater overall mortality than in the rest of the Israeli population. However, parents who were widowed or divorced at the time their sons died were at greater risk of dying themselves. Apparently, the married parents were protected from the physical impact of the loss of their sons by their mutual support.

All of these studies indicate that there is an increased risk of death during the first six-to-twelve months following the loss of a loved one, with a second slight increase in mortality a few years later for widowers (but not widows). The research further shows that death from bereavement seems to be a direct result of the impact of loss on the body rather than a consequence of behaviors that might increase risk, such as poor health habits or not seeking medical treatment. The mechanisms of bereavement death seem to involve deception of cardiac and immune defenses by the physiologic consequences of excessive and unpredictable mixtures of arousal and withdrawal in psychologically vulnerable individuals.

People who are prone to depression and hopelessness, people who cannot tolerate anger and hostility, self-destructive people, lonely people, those who have no one to lean on, and those who refuse to rely on anyone who is available—these are the people whose mental defenses are likely to fail when a major attachment is lost. At this time, preexisting vulnerabilities in the heart or immune system can be overwhelmed by the physical aspects of grief. An approach to dealing with this mind–body interaction is presented in the next chapter.

20

Using the Mind to Heal the Body

CARDIOVASCULAR AND IMMUNE deceptions begin when anger, grief, hopelessness, and related states evoke useless mobilization of the body. It simplifies understanding each side of the deception to discuss the psychological and biological sides separately. However, the mental vulnerabilities that undo the body may themselves be subject to physical influences, just as physical vulnerabilities may be conditioned by repeated mental stress. *Neither side really exists in the absence of the other.*

The mental side of the deception begins when the mind perceives a danger to mental or physical integrity. The threat may be objective, such as the loss of a job, or it may come from the emergence of unbidden, forbidden memories or wishes. The next step in the process of deception occurs when mental defenses fail to keep the response to the threat within a range of intensity that is sufficient to stimulate problem-solving but not so powerful that emotional arousal becomes uncontrollable and coping skills become paralyzed. Failure of the mind's defenses may occur as a result of their inherent weakness or their susceptibility to becoming unhinged by a specific event or conflict.

DECEPTION OF MENTAL DEFENSES

Some events are so catastrophic that there would have to be something wrong with anyone who appeared to have no trouble coping with them. Most of the time, however, threat is as much a function of the mind as it is a tangible product of external reality. A situation that might not be inherently overwhelming may be devastating to a person for whom it is reminiscent of a past trauma that could not be mastered or in whom it stimulates overpowering unconscious conflicts. The controllability as well as the meaning of the stress also determines the degree of response: a relatively benign situation that feels impossible to predict or control can be more stressful than a more dangerous situation that feels controllable or at least predictable. Because unconscious threats are unknown, they are uncontrollable and can have substantial power to disrupt mental competence.

It is not just the degree to which a stressor is interpreted as dangerous but the capacity of the mind to develop constructive solutions that determine how disorganizing the experience will be. People who feel competent and are able to tolerate uncertainty and conflict without ignoring them or taking immediate action are less likely to feel overwhelmed by any problem. Likewise, people who are self-confident enough to ask for help, without feeling humiliated or totally helpless, are able to "borrow" resources to withstand the stress without placing an excessive burden on bodily systems.

On the other end of the spectrum are people who are prone to feelings of helplessness, hopelessness, grief, rage, anger, anxiety, withdrawal, or despair in response even to everyday types of stress. Such overreactivity may be built into the mind by inborn depressive or anxious dispositions, or by early experiences of loss, abuse, or unsupportive caretakers. Still another possibility: it may come from putting all of one's emotional eggs into one basket, so to speak, depending so totally on another person to regulate mind and body that any threat to the integrity of the relationship feels to the mind like overwhelming danger, which in turn overstimulates the body.

As we have seen, bereavement is the greatest danger to even the most resilient mind because the loss of a loved one is a double trauma: the loss itself is a huge source of stress, and the one person who formerly helped the bereaved cope with stresses like this is no longer there. Children, whose mental strengths are not fully developed and whose bodily regulation is not yet entirely stable, need an adult who can modulate the impact of the loss on both mind and body. Without such help, early loss can have lasting repercussions. Fearful, dependent, or avoidant attachment patterns may be imprinted in the brain, and kindling of overstimulated but still immature neurons may lead later to massive overreactions to losses.

Death of a spouse or separation from a parent have been the most thoroughly studied forms of loss, but experience dictates that symbolic mental representations of loss have the same potential to deceive the body out of its health. The memory of, or the hope for, another person can be as real as the actual person in sustaining mental and physical well-being and the loss of either can be equally disruptive. An ideology, a belief, dedication to a cause, or a fantasy can also serve as targets of attachment if they have enormous emotional meaning that can sustain mental and physical homeostasis. By the same token, losing these stand-ins for more tangible attachment figures— whether because of disillusionment, a change of philosophy, or being thrown out of a special interest group—can be just as real a threat to mental and physical integrity as any other form of bereavement.

In many cases, acute pressures that finally overwhelm mental defenses are a consequence of the same psychological dynamics that created vulnerabilities to these situations in the first place. For example, people who work their hardest to push away those they need because they are afraid they will be abandoned, no matter what they do, are more likely to actually suffer the fate they fear the most—and to be overwhelmed when it occurs. People who become totally dependent on one other person are more likely to be devastated if the relationship changes or ends. People who become enraged at the slightest frustration respond with escalating anger to every life circumstance until they cannot modulate their emotions at all. The psychophysiology of these chronic, persistent overreactions exhausts the mental reserves that are necessary to respond to the inevitable overpowering loss or the final hopeless frustration that pushes the compromised heart or immune system beyond its fragile boundaries into the realm of illness or death.

DECEPTION OF BODILY DEFENSES

When the mind cannot find a way to overcome, move beyond, or at least forget what feels like a fundamental threat to its existence, the body begins to mobilize. The body cannot tell the difference between the *perception* and the *reality* of danger and therefore prepares to meet the challenge with arousal and withdrawal mechanisms, in sequence or combination. As activation of stress-response systems is shifted from the mind to the body, the body's vulnerabilities must be tested in the same crucible that has overpowered the mind.

When mental defenses initially break down in a healthy person, mobilization is not necessarily dangerous. Heart beat may be rapid and somewhat unstable, blood pressure may go up for a while; low-level biochemical evidence of immune suppression may show up in the laboratory that does not really compromise the ability to resist infection. However, the situation is different when vulnerabilities have been programmed into stress-response systems by heredity, early experience, or chronic stress. In these cases, severe or enduring disruptions of bodily defenses may emerge as a result of the mind's excessive activation. Depending on the location of the bodily vulnerability, the result may be an emerging disturbance of coronary vessel activity that predisposes to coronary heart disease or sudden death, or a defect in immune surveillance that allows early cancer cells to gain a foothold and grow.

There are several points in both cardiac and immune disease processes at which interventions directed at the mind may help to protect the body. Mental interventions have been attempted to prevent the long-term consequences of medical mind-body deceptions and to treat them once they arise. Some of these are more supported by research than others, but even if they are based on unsubstantiated inferences or educated guesses, they are worth a try—if only because they make people active participants in the process of preventing and combatting disease, thereby replacing helplessness with mastery.

PSYCHOSOCIAL APPROACHES TO ACUTE CARDIAC DISEASE

People who are basically healthy have little to fear from the physiology of acute stress and should not add to their worries the fear that they will die if they become too upset. However, people with recent ischemic damage to the heart, such as patients on coronary care units, may be vulnerable to the impact of the fight-flight response, especially if too much emotional arousal occurs within a larger context of excessive conservation-withdrawal response or prior damage to the conduction system of the heart. Warning signs of possible vulnerability to untoward cardiac response when under stress include a history of fainting, excessive cardiovascular responses (for example, frequent palpitations) to stress, a family history of sudden death, or a previous episode of cardiac arrest, especially in the absence of clear-cut coronary heart disease. How can high-risk individuals minimize the impact of an acutely stressful event on their hearts?

Maximize Relaxation

There are a number of obvious ways to minimize the physiology of arrhythmia described in Chapter 18: relaxation training, hypnosis, biofeedback, meditation—any type of technique that teaches the mind to focus on relaxation and create a sense of calm and control, leaving less room for worries that arouse the fight-flight response. For acutely ill patients or those whose activities must be restricted, an added bonus to these approaches is that the mind learns to function as an active agent in controlling reactions to the illness at a time when the body must be passive, which actually enhances the sense of mental control. In addition to these mental techniques, antianxiety medications can be used liberally by anxious acute coronary patients if there is no medical contraindication.

Denial Redeemed

Since *denial* of an emotion blocks the physiologic effects of that emotion, at least in the short run, it can be a useful means of reducing acute stress on the heart. Right after a coronary event, it is probably healthier not to pay too much attention to the significance of it! It is better for patients to be encouraged to think about how well they are doing, how much they have improved since yesterday, and how soon they will be back on their feet. There will be plenty of time to worry about the future, once the acute situation has been resolved and the heart is less vulnerable to the ravages of the fight-flight.

The observations of Harvard psychiatrists Ned Cassem and the late Tom Hackett demonstrate the survival value of denial after a heart attack. Hackett and Cassem identified three types of emotional response in patients recovering from heart attacks on a coronary care unit (CCU). One group, the non-deniers, experienced intense fear about the prospects of surviving the event. This group viewed the cardiac monitor as a potential harbinger of death that was just waiting for a chance to signal the end.

Patients in the second group, who were called intermediate deniers, were somewhat concerned but had confidence that their physicians would be able to save them if anything bad happened; the only way in which they expressed any significant worry was in the form of bad dreams. The third group consisted of the major deniers. These patients were not aware of being at all upset about finding themselves on a CCU. Not only did they not have any bad dreams, but some of them had even forgotten having been in the bed next to a patient who had had a cardiac arrest and died!

Denial proved to be a healthy trait. The major deniers were significantly less likely to die than non-deniers with the exact same severity of disease; intermediate deniers had an intermediate risk of death on the CCU. It is always possible that the non-deniers were somehow more aware of a hidden factor that increased their risk of death and that the major deniers were more confident because of an unconscious perception that they were in better shape physically; but if there was such a physical factor, it was too subtle to be identified. It seemed more likely to the investigators that denial of the danger reduced anxiety, and with it, the physiology of the fight–flight response, which had a more adverse impact on those who were less adept at denial.

Like everything else in medicine, denial in acutely ill patients has its down side. In fact, denial that chest pain signals a heart attack probably accounts for a significant proportion of the 60 percent of cardiac arrests that occur outside the hospital. In addition, while denial as an emergency measure may enhance survival during acute cardiac illness, later it can be as hazardous as fear. The patient who denies the seriousness of the disease so completely as to see no need to take medications, change diet or lifestyle, and take other steps to reduce the risk of a recurrence is in more, rather than less, long-term danger. The ideal attitude is feeling a sense of confidence in coping with the illness, while neither being overwhelmed by, or completely denying, the full reality.

People who believe in the power of the mind over the body may want to get started, as rapidly as possible, delving into problems and behaviors that might have set the stage for a heart attack. They are correct that it is essential to solve emotional problems that, if left unaddressed, could be a source of ongoing physical arousal with potential adverse effects. However, uncovering unconscious conflicts may also arouse anxiety that could be life-threatening while the heart is still vulnerable. Since feeling familiar with the contents of one's own mind diminishes the dangers that its "secrets" will be perceived as dangerous, introspection in manageable "doses" can prevent the stress-response system from outstripping insight.

Stay in Control

Since helplessness intensifies anxiety while a sense of mastery reduces it, the more sense of control a person feels, the less anxiety and arousal will be evoked by any situation. Even when it is not possible to be in physical control, as is usually the case with a severe illness, some degree of mental control is always possible. For example, taking an active part in treatment planning promotes a greater sense of control than passively waiting for something to happen. Patients need to feel at least some sense of ownership of the therapeutic enterprise.

When modern American medicine was in its paternalistic heyday, health-care providers thought that patients would worry less if they let the professionals take care of everything without bothering them with too many facts or choices. However, it is now appreciated that no medical judgment is infallible. It is not only healthy to involve patients in medical decision-making, it is highly advisable—since the patient may be as likely to make the right choice as the physician. After all, it is the patient who must live with the results when the physician goes home at night and leaves the illness with the patient.

Minimize Separations

Separation from loved ones increases the impact of all other stresses, including the anxiety caused by the separation itself, because, as we have seen, it removes the psychobiological regulation of stress-response systems that is provided by another trusted person. This additional burden on cardiac rate and rhythm can be reduced by not restricting visiting hours for acutely ill patients. Indeed, it is essential to mobilize everyone who might bolster the patient's psychological and therefore physical defenses. This may include types of support that seem taxing to the hospital staff but are beneficial to the patient. For example, it might seem that the executive who demands twenty-four-hour access to a secretary will be more stressed if his demands are granted; however, continued immersion in the job may provide familiar people and routines that are more reassuring than they are stressful.

Increase Social Support

The availability of friends, family, and symbolic substitutes for human attachments, such as work, can help to shore up an unstable cardiovascular system. But what if nobody else is available or the patient does not make use of the supports that do exist? In this case, comprehensive medical treatment may have to address social as well as physiologic deficits to improve long-term outcome.

It may not take a complex intervention to enhance patients' use of social networks. This was demonstrated in a study by Richard Rahe and his colleagues, who provided a mere six sessions of education, group discussion, and support to patients recovering from heart attacks. After the group ended, patients reported no change in their level of satisfaction with life, and they forgot all the information about their illnesses they had learned during the group sessions. However, they did spend more time with their families and less time at work, and they felt less pressured to meet tight schedules. Over the next four years, patients who had been in the group were compared with heart attack patients who received no more than the standard treatment. No one who had a recurrent heart attack or sudden cardiac death had been in the group; in fact, all of the group-support patients remained well. Even when patients' lives remained stressful, support—first in the group and later in the family—appeared to protect their hearts.

There is some evidence that changing the type-A pattern of behaviors may improve the outcome of heart disease. For instance, in a prospective study called the Recurrent Coronary Prevention Project, patients who had suffered a heart attack were randomly assigned to a treatment plan involving counseling about diet, medication, and other health issues, or to a treatment plan that provided counseling plus help in modifying type-A behaviors. During the first four and a half years of follow-up, 7.2 percent of the counseling-only group died of cardiac disease, compared with 5.2 percent of the group that received therapy for type-A behaviors. A more impressive finding was that almost twice as many patients in the first group, which received no type-A therapy, had another heart attack during the same period.

A similar small study in Sweden found that one year after a heart attack, patients who received therapy for type-A behavior as well as regular counseling had greater reductions in blood cholesterol levels and less responsiveness of the heart to stress than those who received counseling only.

PSYCHOSOCIAL APPROACHES TO CANCER

Many treatments have been introduced for the hopelessness, helplessness, loss, and negative emotional states that have been thought to impair bodily defenses against cancer. Some of these treatments have been subjected to the scrutiny of scientific research, some remain unstudied but may still be helpful, and some are downright deceptions. We will consider treatments in each of these categories.

Sustain Hope

Who could bear to treat people with terminal illnesses and not have hope? Even if the disease could not be cured, it would be impossible to work effectively without the hope that the remainder of the patient's life would be free of pain, that others would share the burden, that the illness would have some meaning. Not to have a hope that something positive will come from the experience cheats the patient and burns out the doctor. If it does not hasten the end, it will at least make it more unpleasant.

What can a cancer patient really hope for? To hold out the promise of a cure when none is on the horizon is a cruel deception that ultimately undercuts rather than fosters hope, because it is based on a dishonest doctor-patient relationship that makes it impossible to trust anything positive the physician truthfully has to offer. But there is always something for which to hope: that the illness can be borne with dignity; that something can be learned from it; that life does not have to end while the patient is alive; that someone cares. As in all human experience, realistic hope comes from sustaining relationships, including the relationship with the physician, who nurtures the sense of attachment that is the source of the drive to strive for important goals.

Can hope sustain life? Consider the case of a sixty-year-old woman with metastatic cancer that developed a year after the death of her father. She had been very close to him but could not mourn because there was no one else to whom she felt she could talk about her feelings. Her family, who were no better at grieving, treated her as if she were already dead once she got sick, leaving her even more isolated from attachments that might replace her father as a physical and mental regulator and help her both to grieve and to confront her own illness. She was undergoing chemotherapy, but she had not seen any tangible results and did not believe that she would. Even if the treatment did work, she wondered if it would be better to die and be reunited with her father than to face a prolonged struggle with the illness by herself.

When she developed intractable nausea from the chemotherapy, the patient decided that her only real hope lay in a rapid death that would spare her any more misery and loneliness. She refused further treatment, and when she did not die immediately, she began planning suicide. She told her physician that this was the only "goal" it seemed possible for her to achieve.

The patient's physician was not deceived into ignoring the other side of this negative orientation. Even though she believed that her situation was hopeless, if she did not have the secret hope that someone else might cajole her out of this state of mind, she would not have communicated her desperation so effectively. Responding positively to her negative communication, he insisted that he would not give up and would not allow the patient to give up, either. The illness might turn out well or badly; it might have its setbacks and defeats; but they would face it together.

The patient was skeptical, but she was willing to give the physician the benefit of the doubt—at least temporarily. She agreed not to kill herself for the moment, with the understanding that she could always fall back on that solution if nothing else worked. The next step was to make the chemotherapy more tolerable. The medications usually used to treat nausea from chemotherapy did not work very well, but she agreed to try hypnosis to increase her comfort, and as it turned out, she got excellent results. Many people think that hypnosis requires passivity and submission, but in fact it involves active mental concentration that can be mastered like any technical skill, further increasing one's overall proficiency in dealing with life. Learning hypnosis gave her a more active role in the process of dealing with her illness *and* made it possible for her to resume chemotherapy.

Once she experienced a little more sense of control, the patient agreed that perhaps it might be possible to reverse her family's withdrawal from her. She invited them to visit the doctor, who helped her to point out to them that they were pulling away out of an attempt to avoid having to grieve later. It turned out that they had never handled loss differently because no one had ever suggested that they should. With a little open discussion, they decided that they had nothing to lose by trying to express their fears. The illness was divided into a series of workable challenges for each upcoming physical and mental issue. With each milestone—her first week back on chemotherapy, her first talk with the family, her first vacation—she became more hopeful about being able to reach the next step and was less preoccupied with what lay at the end of the path.

Two years later, the patient felt so well that she began to believe that the cancer might be gone. At that point, a growth was found in her abdomen that was thought to be another metastasis of the cancer. This time, it was the patient who reassured the physician. Taking him by the hand, she reminded him that they had overcome many obstacles, and this would be no different. Sure enough, the growth turned out to be a benign cyst. Fifteen years later, the patient is in perfect health. She still sees her doctor regularly, though, to renew the lifesaving attachment.

Maintain a Sense of Competency

Many people experience a serious illness as something that has taken away their sense of control over their lives. Yet in many ways, it is up to the patient to decide who is in control: the patient or the disease. Obviously, attempting to overcome the entire illness all at once would be an overwhelming task likely to increase helplessness, probably further suppress physical defenses, and certainly make life miserable. On the other hand, splitting the threat of the illness into a series of goals makes it possible to overcome each one in turn. Conquering each task builds confidence that the next task can be mastered, too.

The first principle in regaining a sense of competence is to realize that it is easier to deal with a problem in *manageable* units. The second is to have someone to turn to when inner resources begin to sag. Attachments not only nourish hope, they bolster confidence; people feel much less overwhelmed and can try harder if they know that someone will be there to pick up the slack. It does not necessarily matter where the help comes from, only that the patient can trust that it will be available when needed.

A study showing that strategies to increase mastery may have a beneficial physical effect was reported in 1993 by psychiatrist F. I. Fawzy. Beginning three months after surgical removal of a malignant melanoma (an aggressive form of skin cancer) that was not followed by chemotherapy, half of sixty-eight patients were assigned to six weekly ninety-minute group therapy sessions, and half were not. The goal of the group was to help patients cope better with the disease by educating them about it, teaching relaxation techniques, and helping them deal with their families' reactions. The intervention seemed to achieve its goal over its brief duration, since active coping increased and mood improved in the group patients.

As in the Spiegel study, no effect on physical status was noted while the group was in effect and right after it ended. However, over the next five to six years—with no further psychological treatment—only three of the thirty-four group patients had died of the melanoma, compared with ten of thirty-four patients in the control group. The group patients also had half the rate of recurrence of the cancer. The significantly lower risk of recurrence and death in the group patients could not be explained by differences in severity of the initial lesion. However, patients with more active coping skills at the beginning of the study were less likely to have a recurrence of melanoma after it was removed, and patients whose coping skills increased during the study had better survival. In contrast to Hackett and Cassem's cardiac study, patients with *less* distress at the beginning of the study—which Fawzy thought reflected more *denial* of the seriousness of the situation—did worse over the course of the study.

How could such a brief psychological maneuver have prolonged patients' time free of disease and helped them to live longer? Tests showed that NK cell activity was enhanced in group patients but not controls, although helper T cell counts remained unchanged. Could NK cell surveillance of new melanoma cells have been enhanced? Was creation of oncogenes corrected by signals from neurotransmitters, which had been stabilized by relationships with other group members? Or did patients just learn to stay out of the sun? Moderate arousal facilitates rather than suppresses immune function, and Fawzy believes that patients learned to mobilize themselves adequately but not excessively by virtue of feeling more in control of the illness. This conclusion bears much more study, since the number of patients was small and the benefit almost too dramatic to be credible. Nonetheless, Fawzy's advice to patients is well-taken: "Don't minimize. Mobilize!"

Strengthen Relationships

The effectiveness of maintaining relationships and fostering hope can only be proven scientifically by prospective controlled studies. Such a study was reported in the prestigious journal *Lancet* in 1989 by Stanford University psychiatrist David Spiegel. In Spiegel's study, a ninety-minute group therapy session was added to the medical treatment of fifty patients with metastatic breast cancer; thirty-six patients with breast cancer of similar severity did not receive the group therapy. Therapy sessions consisted of discussions of strategies for coping with cancer, instructions in the use of self-hypnosis for pain, encouragement to be more assertive with physicians, stress management, social support, and grieving losses, especially of group members who had died.

Spiegel's main interest was in demonstrating that the group could improve quality of life in cancer patients; he did not expect the group therapy to have any impact on physical outcome. To his surprise, patients who were not in a group lived about nineteen months after the study began, while those who received the group intervention lived almost thirty-seven months—almost twice as long. The prolonged survival of the group patients only began to manifest itself a year after the group ended and could not be explained by differences in illness severity between group and non-group (control) patients. Not only were the group and non-group patients similar in medical factors, but there was no difference between them in scores on a comprehensive battery of psychological tests performed before the group began.

What effect did the groups have? At the end of the group sessions, group patients had better moods, fewer phobic symptoms, and half the pain of the control patients. Any of this mental benefit could have translated into improved immune defenses and DNA repair. These factors may have been facilitated by learning to have better relationships with physicians, who in turn were more motivated to treat the patients as vigorously as possible. Positive attachments to group members and enhanced relationships with families were probably relevant as well, as was learning to be appropriately assertive.

Since no measures of immune function were obtained, the possibility of any direct action on biology is just speculative. However, a 1990 study by J. L. Richardson and his colleagues tended to confirm a positive medical effect of a group intervention. Patients with lymphoma and leukemia (types of blood cancer) were randomly assigned to a control condition (no additional treatment) or to one of three groups involving education, home visits, and social support in addition to routine medical care. Control patients had significantly shorter survival times.

Any attachment to a process, force, belief, or person that extends beyond the borders of the individual's illness may engender enough hope to push the body into more positive equilibrium. The therapeutic power of a relationship in the context of a life-threatening illness was demonstrated in an unusual case in which a fifty-four-year-old man developed an aggressive form of leukemia that did not respond to any treatment. His physician was forced to advise him to set his affairs in order as soon as possible. That night the patient, who was not particularly religious—although he was a devoted family man—had a dream in which an angel told him that God would help him stay alive so that he could find his faith and demonstrate its power.

Trusting in the support that was readily proffered by his family as well as the helping hand from the Almighty, the patient made plans for Thanksgiving dinner, which was three months away. Judging from every physical indicator, the physician predicted that it would be remarkable if the patient lived half that time. Although he felt quite ill, the patient intended to live up to his end of the bargain made in his dream.

To the physician's amazement, the patient made it to the dinner, despite a blood count that was as abnormal as ever. By now he was feeling slightly better, and he announced that he had every intention of celebrating Christmas with his family. At Christmas time, the stunned physician learned that the patient had to live until a school play in February. In February, it was necessary to live until the children went to camp for the first time the next summer. All of this was necessary because he had not yet fully demonstrated the power of faith. The patient never thought about how long he might ultimately live; he was only interested in making it to the next deadline.

By the third Christmas, the physician was beginning to think that the patient would live forever, even though by objective standards the illness was as bad as ever. However, by that time the patient was in considerable discomfort and he had begun to feel that he had accomplished the tasks that were necessary to complete. The family had a conference and decided that everyone would be at peace if the patient's life should happen to come to an end. No one had a sense of giving up, only of having achieved the major goals of their trial and of having come to peace with the illness and its inevitable outcome.

Shortly after this discussion, the patient had another dream. The same angel from his first dream appeared and confirmed that he had done enough to prove his faith. He could be released from his bargain whenever he chose and be with God. He reported this dream to his physician and his family in the morning, saying that he had achieved his final goal of being at peace with his Savior. The next night, he died in his sleep.

REDUCING THE LONG-TERM RISK OF CORONARY HEART DISEASE AND CANCER

What about the long-term health hazards of maladaptive psychological states? Is it possible to change circumstances and traits that could increase the risk of later physical disease? From a scientific standpoint, the answer to these questions is that nobody really knows. Although suggestions about reducing the impact of adverse mental states on the body are not based on firm scientific data, they may be worth considering until better research comes along.

Social Support

If there is one finding that repeatedly emerges from research on the psychobiology of physical disease, it is that people without interpersonal resources are more prone to the excessive stress reactions that seem to be associated with immune suppression and coronary heart disease. Simply put, relationships appear to protect us against the physiology of threat. A protective attachment does not necessarily require the continuous presence of another person; it may involve a memory, a fantasy, or a symbolic stand-in for a person, such as a cause or project.

This advice does not hold for everyone, however. Some people keep an emotional distance out of an awareness, perhaps unconscious, that relationships create more conflict for them than they solve. Perhaps they dare not trust anyone because they were betrayed or abandoned in childhood. Perhaps their sense of self is so flimsy that they fear losing their identities if they get too close to another person. Whatever the reason, if they are forced into intimacy, the relationship itself may be more of a stress than a support. Before recommending psychotherapy, groups, or other approaches to improving contact with others, it is therefore necessary to assess whether the cure might end up being worse than the disease. These individuals may benefit more from solidifying a relationship with something inhuman, such as a biofeedback machine, or enhancing their technical knowledge about the disease.

Handling Grief

Studies going back more than twenty years show that loss increases the risk of death—but for no more than a year after bereavement. However, unresolved grief at any time sets the stage for chronic depression, hopelessness, anger, and overwhelming reactions to subsequent stresses that involve or symbolize separation. Since the undying emotional attachment to someone who is not mourned blocks new attachments to the living, failure to grieve may make it harder to lean on others later in life. How can the adverse impact of continued grief on health be reduced?

For most people, bereavement creates feelings that naturally press to be expressed openly. When these emotions are shared, the sustaining presence of others helps to regulate them and to assist in the process of searching to fill the gap created by the loss. Grief may be disruptive, but dealing with it openly, in the context of a supportive relationship, keeps it from turning into depression, hypochondriasis, and actual physical disease.

It used to be thought that children were incapable of grief and should be protected from it. Parents who are afraid of their own emotions may deceive themselves into believing that they are being "strong" for their children by pretending that they do not feel bad, so that the children do not need to feel bad either. Unfortunately, children who are not encouraged to grieve openly after losing a parent, a sibling, or a friend are more likely to be sensitized to later losses than they are to be strengthened emotionally. When parents teach denial through their own behavior, they are imparting to their children a limited repertoire of mental defenses that are prone to break down under the stress of another loss. If no one in the family grieves, the child is faced with an intolerable dilemma that serves as a template for later psychopathology: either ignore a major segment of the mind or suffer the disapproval and possible loss of the rest of the family. If the family is in mourning but excludes the child from its unhappiness, the loss of their support is added to the original loss, which the child must grieve alone.

Expressing Anger

In early 1989, the news media carried a story that the type-A traits of hostility and aggression were most clearly associated with coronary heart disease. This story implied that if anger could damage the heart, it must be dangerous to get angry. People who had previously tried to learn how to express anger now decided that it was safer to repress their feelings.

The fact is that expressions of anger that are not excessive in intensity or duration may actually improve health. After all, the human body is made to take action in response to acute stress; it is only when arousal is chronically unresolved that bodily action is directed inward. When anger can be organized toward achieving a specific goal, as it is when people are taught to be assertive, the fight-flight response reaches a natural conclusion, allowing the physiology of arousal to return to normal. The autonomic nervous system is thereby taught to respond appropriately to everyday stresses and then reset itself.

Habitually keeping anger hidden may mean that it will be difficult to sustain the positive fighting mentality that creates an appropriate balance between fight-flight and conservation-withdrawal when the enemy is cancer instead of an external combatant. In other words, the best mental defense against cancer is one that promotes appropriate mobilization of immune responses instead of the kind of extended arousal that suppresses immune protection. Optimal recruitment of an immune response may explain why cancer patients who express anger openly—at the disease, at friends and family, at the doctor—have been found to survive longer than those who accept the illness passively. Recall that in Fawzy's study, patients who had recently undergone surgical removal of malignant melanoma and who were not psychologically mobilized to fight the cancer were more likely to suffer a relapse during the next year than those who anticipated a great struggle ahead of them.

What about Type-A Behavior?

Although research presented earlier suggests that modifying type-A behavior may have positive metabolic consequences in some people, reports challenging the association of type-A with coronary heart disease raise the question whether massive efforts to change these traits may be more trouble than they're worth. Trying to modify core characteristics of one's personality can be more stressful than using them as effectively as possible. The attachment of some type-A executives to their jobs—the organizing effect of devotion to work—may actually promote health, while asking them to give up lifelong patterns and adopt an unfamiliar lifestyle may create more unrestrained arousal—which equals more cardiac risk.

Perhaps a better goal than converting type-A traits into type-B traits would be to find ways of making existing traits operate more efficiently, so they will be less likely to create chronic low-grade arousal. Since hostility has appeared to hold up as a possible risk factor, this seems like a good place to start. Telling a type-A individual not to get angry may be counterproductive, since anger is a necessary mobilizing force in the life of a competitive person. It makes more sense to teach ways to get angry constructively. This involves reassessing impossible expectations and time constraints that lead to smoldering hostility as well as learning to express the anger of the moment more effectively and less diffusely. Developing more realistic and time-limited objectives also enhances feelings of control in any situation, minimizing helplessness and unrestrained arousal.

It is not only type-A individuals who benefit from learning to reduce the physiologic arousal that is an inevitable component of a hectic life-style. Anyone who is tense can benefit from learning relaxation training, hypnosis, meditation, and similar stress-reduction methods. Regular exercise is useful physically and mentally (unless it takes place too close to bedtime, in which case it may cause insomnia). Even though there is no convincing evidence that depression increases the risk of death from anything except suicide and accidents, depressed people are less likely to pay attention to their health or to comply with treatment of medical illnesses. Treating depression at least enhances cooperation with the treatment plan and quality of life, and could help to control the physiology of arousal.

DECEPTIONS IN PSYCHOLOGICAL APPROACHES TO PHYSICAL DISEASE

Psychological approaches to enhancing survival in cancer patients can all mobilize hope, enhance relationships, and build a sense of personal control. Even if they do not help the illness itself, these attainments can be of great benefit. However, they can also be deceptive.

One deception—an ironic one in a society in which mental illness is still considered shameful—is the mistaken belief that physical illness is ultimately caused by mental problems. The desire to move the illness from the body to the mind is certainly understandable. After all, one is less likely to die of depression than cancer. While strengthening mental resources is always a good idea, important deceptions can emerge from attempts to attribute too much power to the mind, just as they can evolve from having too little confidence in the mental realm.

Deception #1: Cancer is a sign of a bad attitude. Research suggesting that adverse reactions to stress can be a factor in the development or progression of cancer do not mean that these are the only factors, or even the most important ones. Placing too much emphasis on the power of the mind not only raises unrealistic expectations of its power to heal but can also create unrealistic feelings of responsibility that have the potential for doing more harm than good.

Deception #2: You must have wanted your cancer. A particularly cruel deception to which some psychosomatic experts are prone is the belief that people get sick because they are in a mental state that promotes the illness. In their enthusiasm to extend the dominion of the mind over the body, these experts have decided that pathogenic mental states may include an unconscious desire to get sick. This leap from a theory of the psychodynamics of somatization to a theory of the psychodynamics of illness onset is entirely unsupported by any empirical data. However, this is not its worst point. The idea of "personal responsibility" for illness may be an attempt to make people feel that they can control their illness by learning the reason why they "want" to be sick, but incapacitating guilt is the only real result. In addition, when efforts to "own" the disease do not result in its improvement, feelings of helplessness and failure increase the very psychophysiology that aggravates the disease.

Deception #3: If the cause is in the mind, then so is the cure. When psychological factors are found to influence the onset or course of a physical disease, it is tempting to believe that they are the only cause of the disease, and that addressing them will provide the cure. However, there is no evidence that any mental state by itself causes any medical disease. The cause of virtually all illnesses, mental and physical, involves a multitude of factors, all of which interact in complex ways: environment, hereditary, psychology, and formative experiences. Addressing any one of these may change the equation, but exactly *how* is largely unknown. Even if a mental factor did lead directly to a physical change, there is no reason to believe that changing that factor later will reverse whatever pathology has become established in the body. It is no more likely that the mind, by itself, can cure the body than that the body, by itself, can cure the mind.

The most dangerous version of the "mind over matter" deception is the assertion that mental approaches can replace proven biological treatments. When it does not reflect a cultural or spiritual belief, the idea that mental treatments by themselves can cure cancer is usually an attempt to deny the seriousness of the illness—as if to say, "If I don't need medical treatment, the disease can't be that bad." Being too afraid of admitting that cancer is a physical reality to accept physical treatments can lead to delays that permit additional changes in oncogenes and tumor suppressor genes, with more complex abnormalities that no longer respond to straightforward chemotherapy, or even to any chemotherapy.

Any prudent physician (and any prudent patient) would want to maximize the chances of curing illnesses like cancer and heart disease by including psychological approaches that have been found helpful (like group therapy and encouragement of assertiveness) in the overall treatment regimen. It is also possible to provide a sense of empowerment by including treatments that have never been subjected to controlled scientific scrutiny, such as the technique of visualizing immune cells attacking cancer cells. But if too much is expected of these approaches, intense disappointment that could cause even more stress and aggravate the cancer may result if the psychological approach fails to *cure* the disease. The physiology of hopelessness and depression may be even greater if patients blame themselves for not trying hard enough, as if they did not want the cancer to go away badly enough.

Deception #4: Stay well mentally or get sick physically. No one in their right mind would argue against mental health. But just how strong is the connection between a healthy mind and a healthy body? There are many residents of mental hospitals who wish that they had a more tangible disease like cancer or coronary disease—yet they do not come down with these or any other medical illnesses. Conversely, many people develop medical illnesses in the absence of any stress or mental abnormality. Bending over backward to avoid any conflict out of fear that it will lead to physical disease is not only unrealistic, it may *add* to the overall stress reaction when the inevitable frustrations and disappointments of life are encountered, increasing rather than decreasing whatever additional physical risk may be contributed by the mind.

Does this mean that we should not apply new findings about the mental side of physical disease until they are proven definitively? Not at all. It is just that we should not idealize any of these findings because they seem appealing, any more than we should dismiss them because they are inconsistent with established medical doctrine. Anything that amplifies hope and a connection to others can only be helpful, but *only if* it does not arouse impossible expectations that produce a sense of failure if they are not completely fulfilled.

WHAT DOES THE FUTURE HOLD?

People who are ill cannot wait for absolute proof of every treatment before they have a chance to try it, and whether it involves caring for illnesses of the mind or of the body, medical practice will always race ahead of hard data. This phenomenon will be enhanced rather than reduced in an era of exploding knowledge because every new advance opens up new areas of investigation that take years to understand fully. But no matter how drastically our current understanding will be revised in the future, one fact that will endure is that the mental and the physical must be integrated to understand any illness. The intellectual premise that mental conditions have a physical substrate and physical illnesses have a psychological dimension is no longer the unique idea of a few visionaries, but a basic tenet of human malfunction.

Disciplines as widely divergent as biochemistry and psychology, genetics and epidemiology, cell biology and artificial intelligence, electrophysiology and sociology, have become interested in the same problems. We do not yet know how to integrate all of the findings, but we can at least see that they do fit somehow. Those who practice the mental disciplines now need to be as knowledgable about treatments of the body as they are about treatments of the mind if they are not to fall behind the standard of care. Those who are used to working only with the test tube, x-ray, and pill must not dismiss scientific evidence about the impact of mental factors just because they do not want to be confused.

The most important problem for today's clinician is not lack of information about mind-body interactions, but too much information. So much knowledge is accumulating that no one can keep track of the actual data, let alone the ways in which new findings contradict, amplify, or have nothing to do with previous results. The explosion of research makes it tempting for the clinician to take a random sample of the literature, assuming that a clinical study tells the whole story of an illness or that a basic science report has direct clinical applications. But now more than ever it is necessary to reserve judgment, to want to learn more, and never to assume that one has the last word on anything. Only then will it be possible to avoid the deception of certainty in an ever-changing field.

Bibliography

References for specific studies, along with general references and suggested reading, are grouped below according to each major section of the book.

PART I

Alexander, F., and French, T.M. 1948. *Studies in Psychosomatic Medicine.* New York: The Ronald Press.

Alkon, D.L. 1987. *Memory Traces in the Brain.* New York: Cambridge University Press.

Alkon, D.L., and Woody, C.D. 1986. *Neural Mechanisms of Conditioning.* New York: Plenum Press.

Andhra, U. 1988. Combined effect of yoga and psychotherapy on management of asthma: A preliminary study. *Journal of Indian Psychology* 7:32–39.

Antonarakis, S.E. 1989. Diagnosis of genetic disorders at the DNA level. *N Engl J Med* 320:153–163.

Ayd, F. J. 1991. The early history of modern psychopharmacology. *Neuropsychopharmacology* 5:71–73.

Barchas, J.D., Elliott, G.R., Berger, P.A., et al. 1985. Research on mental illness and addictive disorders: Progress and prospects. *Am J Psychiatry* 142(suppl 7):1–40.

Baron, M. 1991. Genes, environment and psychopathology. *Biol Psychiatry* 29:1055–1057.

Baron, M., Endicott, J., and Ott, J. 1990. Genetic linkage in mental illness: Limitations and prospects. *Brit J Psychiatry* 157:645–655.

Baron, M., Hamburger, R., Sandkuyt, L.A., et al. 1990. The impact of phenotypic variation on genetic analysis: Application to X-linkage in manic-depressive illness. *Acta Psychiatr Scand* 82:196–203.

Bartfai, A., Pedersen, N.L., Asarnow, R.F., and Schalling, D. 1991. Genetic factors for the span of apprehension test: A study of normal twins. *Psychiatry Res* 38:115–124.

Benjamin, J., Li, L., Patterson, C., Greenberg, B.D., Murphy, D.L., and Hamer, D.H. 1996. Population and familial association between the D4 dopamine receptor gene and measures of novelty seeking. *Nature Genetics* 12:81–84.

Billings, E.G. August, 1941. Value of psychiatry to the general hospital. *Hospitals,* pp. 30–34.

Bouchard, T.J., Lykken, D.T., McGue, M., et al. 1990. Sources of human psychological differences: The Minnesota study of twins reared apart. *Science* 250:223–228.

Bynum, W.F., Porter, R., and Shepherd, M. 1985. *The Anatomy of Madness.* London: Tavistock Publications.

Chodoff, P. 1986. *DSM-III* and psychotherapy. *Am J Psychiatry* 143:201–203.

Cloninger, C.R., Adolfsson, R., and Svrakic, N.M. 1996. Mapping genes for human personality. *Nature Genetics* 12:3–4.

Conte, H.R., and Karasu, T.B. 1981. Psychotherapy for medically ill patients: Review and critique of controlled studies. *Psychosomatics* 22:285–315.

Cooper, A.M. 1985. Will neurobiology influence psychoanalysis? *Am J Psychiatry* 152:1395–1402.

Cooper, A.M. 1984. Psychoanalysis at one hundred: Beginnings of maturity. *J Am Psychoanal Assoc* 32:245–267.

Crow, T.J. 1991. The search for the psychosis gene. *Brit J Psychiatry* 158:611–614.

Detre, T. 1987. The future of psychiatry. *Am J Psychiatry* 144:621–625.

Deutsch, F. 1959. *On the Mysterious Leap from the Mind to the Body.* New York: International Universities Press.

Dorfman, W. 1980. "Psychosomatic" symptoms as a prelude to somatic diagnosis. *Psychosomatics* 21:799–803.

Dubovsky, S.L., Getto, C.J., Gross, S.A., and Paley, J.A. 1977. Impact on nursing care and mortality: Psychiatrists on the coronary care unit. *Psychosomatics* 18:18–27.

Dunbar, F. 1947. *Mind and Body: Psychosomatic Medicine.* New York: Random House.

Ebstein, R.P., Novick, O., Umansky, R., Priel, B., Osher, Y., Blaine, D., Bennett, E.R., Nemanov, L., Katz, M., and Belmaker, R.H. 1996. Dopamine D4 receptor (D4DR) exon III polymorphism associated with the human personality trait of novelty seeking. *Nature Genetics* 12:78–80.

Engel, G.L. 1977. The need for a new medical model: A challenge for biomedicine. *Science* 196:129–136.

Faust, D., and Miner, R.A. 1986. The empiricist and his new clothes: *DSM-III* in perspective. *Am J Psychiatry* 143:962–967.

Fischer, H.K. 1977. Personality and psychosomatic disease: A 1976 update. *Psychosomatics* 18:5–7.

Freud, S. 1925. An autobiographical study. *Standard Edition of the Complete Psychological Works of Sigmund Freud, Vol 20,* pp. 7–79. New York: W.W. Norton.

Freud, S. 1926. The question of lay analysis. *Standard Edition of the Complete Psychological Works of Sigmund Freud, Vol. 20,* pp. 178–258. New York: W.W. Norton.

Gershon, E.S., Merril, C.R., Goldin, L.R., et al. 1987. The role of molecular genetics in psychiatry. *Biol Psychiatry* 22:1388–1405.

Glymor, C., & Stalker, D. 1983. Engineers, cranks, physicians, magicians. *N Engl J Med* 308:960–963.

Gottlieb, H.J., Alperson, B.L., Koller, R., and Hockersmith, V. 1979. An innovative program for the restoration of patients with chronic back pain. *Physical Therapy* 59:996–999.

Green, E.D., and Waterston, R.H. 1991. The human genome project: Prospects and implications for clinical medicine. *JAMA* 266:1966–1975.

Grinker, R.R. 1969. An editor's farewell. *Arch Gen Psychiatry* 21:641–645.

Grob, G.N. 1991. Origins of *DSM-I:* A study in appearance and reality. *Am J Psychiatry* 148:421–431.

Hackett, T.P. 1977. The psychiatrist: In the mainstream or on the banks of medicine? *Am J Psychiatry* 134:432–433.

Hafner, H. 1985. Are mental disorders increasing over time? *Psychopathology* 18:66–81.

Hermann, H. 1985. Specificity and nonspecificity: A major problem in biologically oriented psychopathology. *Psychopathology* 18:82–87.

Hoffman, J.S. (1990). Integrating biologic and psychologic treatment: The need for a unitary model. *Psychiatric Clin N Am* 13:369–372.

Holden, C. 1987. The genetics of personality. *Science* 237:598–601.

Horowitz, M.J., Marmer, C.R., and Weiss, D.S., et al. 1986. Comprehensive analysis of change after brief dynamic psychotherapy. *Am J Psychiatry* 143:582–589.

Hu, S., Pattatucci, A.M.L., Patterson, C., Li, L., Fulker, D.W., Cherny, S.S., Kruglyak, L., Hamer, D.H. 1996. Linkage between sexual orientation and chromosome Xq28 in males but not in females. *Nature Genetics* 11:248–256.

Karasu, T.B. 1982. Psychotherapy and pharmacotherapy: Toward an integrative model. *Am J Psychiatry* 139:1102–1113.

Karasu, T.B. 1986. The specificity vs. nonspecificity dilemma: Toward identifying therapeutic change agents. *Am J Psychiatry* 143:687–695.

Kellner, R. 1975. Psychotherapy in psychosomatic disorders. *Arch Gen Psychiatry* 32:1021–1028.

Kendler, K. 1990. Toward a scientific psychiatric nosology. *Arch Gen Psychiatry* 47:969–973.

Kety, S.S. 1974. From rationalization to reason. *Am J Psychiatry* 131:957–963.

Koran, L.M., Sox, H.C., Martin, K.I., et al. 1989. Medical evaluation of psychiatric patients. I. Results in a state mental health system. *Arch Gen Psychiatry* 49:733–740.

Koryani, E.K. 1968. Somatic illness in psychiatric patients. *Psychosomatics* 21:887–891.

Kraepelin, E. 1968. *Lectures on Clinical Psychiatry (1904)*. New York: Hafner Publishing Co.

Krakowski, A.J., and Kimbpall, C.P., eds. 1983. *Psychosomatic Medicine.* New York: Plenum Press.

Lehmann, H.E. 1986. The future of psychiatry: Progress, mutation, or self destruct? *Can J Psychiatry* 31:362–367.

Levitan, S.L., and Kornfeld, D.S. 1981. Clinical and cost benefits of liaison psychiatry. *Am J Psychiatry* 138:790–793.

Lipowski, Z.J. 1967. Review of consultation psychiatry and psychosomatic medicine. II. Clinical aspects. *Psychosom Med* 29:201–224.

Lipowski, Z.J. 1984. What does the word "psychosomatic" really mean? *Psychosom Med* 46:153–171.

Lipowski, Z.J. 1987. The interface of psychiatry and medicine: Towards integrated health care. *Can J Psychiatry* 9:743–748.

Lipowski, Z.J. 1989. Bridging mind and brain. *Lancet* 2:1091.

Lipowski, Z.J. 1989. Psychiatry: Mindless, brainless, both or neither? *Can J Psychiatry* 34:249–254.

Luborsky, L., Singer, B., and Luborsky, L. 1975. Comparative studies of psycho-therapies. *Arch Gen Psychiatry* 32:995–1008.

Ludwig, A.M. 1975. The psychiatrist as physician. *JAMA* 234:603–604.

McCarley, R.W., and Hobson, J.A. 1977. The neurobiological origins of psychoanalytic dream theory. *Am J Psychiatry* 134:1211–1221.

McKusik, V.A. 1989. Mapping and sequencing the human genome. *N Engl J Med* 320:910–915.

Michels, R. 1986. How psychoanalysis changes. *J Amer Acad Psychoanal* 14:285–296.

Miller, H.L., Coombs, D.W., Leeper, J.D., and Barto, S.N. 1984. An analysis of the effect of suicide prevention facilities on suicide rates in the United States. *Am J Public Health* 74:340–343.

Minuchin, S., Baker, L., Rosman, B.L., et al. 1975. A conceptual model of psychosomatic illness in children. *Arch Gen Psychiatry* 32:1031–1038.

Mirsky, I.A. 1957. The psychosomatic approach to the etiology of clinical disorders. *Psychosomatic Medicine* 5:424–430.

Mirsky, I.A. 1958. Physiologic, psychologic, and social determinants in the etiology of duodenal ulcer. *Am J Dig Dis* 3:285–311.

Mitchell, P., and Waters, B. 1987. Molecular biology and the funtional psychoses. *Aust NZ J Psychiatry* 21:415–418.

Mohl, P.C. 1987. Should psychotherapy be considered a biological treatment? *Psychosomatics* 28:320–326.

Moller, H.J. 1989. Efficacy of different strategies of aftercare for patients who have attempted suicide. *J Royal Soc Med* 82:643–647.

Oates, J.A., and Wood, A.J.J. 1989. The regulation of discovery and drug development. *N Engl J Med* 320:311–312.

Onnis, L., di Gennaro, A., Cespa, G., et al. 1989. The utility of family psychotherapy in chronic psychosomatic diseases: Preliminary data from research on infantile asthma. *Medicina Psicosomatica* 34:189–203.

Parlour, R.R. 1986. Reflections of a CHAMPUS: APA peer reviewer. *J Clin Psychiatry* 47:71–74.

Reiger, D.A., Boyd, J.H., Burke, J.D., et al. 1988. One-month prevalence of mental disorders in the United States. *Arch Gen Psychiatry* 45:977–986.

Robins, L.N., Helzer, J.E., Weissman, M.M., et al. 1984. Lifetime prevalance of specific psychiatric disorders in three sites. *Arch Gen Psychiatry* 41:949–958.

Romano, J. 1990. Reminiscences: 1938 and since. *Am J Psychiatry* 147:785–792.

Rutter, M. 1986. Meyerian psychobiology, personality development, and the role of life experiences. *Am J Psychiatry* 143:1077–1087.

Scarr, S., and Weinberg, R.A. 1983. The Minnesota adoption studies genetic differences and malleability. *Child Dev* 54:260–267.

Scherl, D.J., and English, J.T. 1984. Current trends in financing psychiatric services. *Psychiatric Annals* 14:332–339.

Schlesinger, H.J., Mumford, E., and Glass, G.V. 1983. Mental health treatment and medical care utilization in a fee-for service system: Outpatient mental health treatment following the onset of a chronic disease. *Am J Public Health* 73:422–429.

Schuckit, M.A. (1983). Anxiety related to medical disease. *J Clin Psychiatry* 44:, 31–37.

Schwab, J.J. 1985. Psychosomatic medicine: Its past and present. *Psychosomatics* 26:583–593.

Sifneos, P.E. 1983. Psychotherapies for psychosomatic and alexithymic patients. *Psychother Psychosom* 40:66–73.

Sjodin, I., Svedlund, J., Ottoson, J.O., and Dotevall, G. 1986. Controlled study of psychotherapy in chronic peptic ulcer disease. *Psychosomatics* 27:187–200.

Spanos, N.P., Stenstrom, R.J., and Johnston, J.C. 1988. Hypnosis, placebo, and suggestion in the treatment of warts. *Psychosomatic Medicine* 50:245–260.

Stein, M. 1986. A reconsideration of specificity in psychosomatic medicine: From olfaction to the lymphocyte. *Psychosom Med* 48:3–2.

Sternberg, D.E. 1986. Testing for physical illness in psychiatric patients. *J Clin Psychiatry* 47(1, suppl):3–9.

Stoller, R.J. 1984. Psychiatry's mind-brain dialectic, or the Mona Lisa has no eyebrows. *Am J Psychiatry* 141:554–558.

Surman, O.S., Gottlieb, S.K., Hackett, T.P., and Silverberg, E.L. 1983. Hypnosis in the treatment of warts. *Advances* 1:19–24.

Weddington, W.W. 1980. Psychogenic explanation of symptoms as a denial of physical illness. *Psychosomatics* 21:805–813.

Weiner, H., Thaler, M., Reiser, M.I., et al. 1957. Etiology of duodenal ulcer. I. Relationship of specific psychological characteristics to rate of gastric secretion. *Psychosom Med* 19:1–10.

West, L.J., and Stein, M. 1982. *Critical Issues in Behavioral Medicine.* Philadelphia: J.B. Lippincott.

Wiesel, T. 1982. Postnatal development of the visual cortex and the influence of the environment. *Nature* 299:583–592.

Wittkower, E.D., and Warnes, H. 1977. *Psychosomatic Medicine: Its Clinical Applications.* New York: Harper and Row.

Wortis, J. 1988. The history of psychiatry. *Biol Psychiatry* 23:107–108.

PART II

Abend, S.M., Porder, M.S., and Willick, M.S. 1983. *Borderline Patients: Psychoanalytic Perspectives.* New York: International Universities Press.

Adler, G. 1981. The borderline-narcissistic personality disorder continuum. *Am J Psychiatry* 138:46–50.

Adler, G. 1986. Psychotherapy of the narcissistic personality disorder patient: Two contrasting approaches. *Amer J Psychiatry* 143:430–436.

Akhtar, S., and Thomason, J.A. 1982. Overview: Narcissistic personality disorder. *Amer J Psychiatry* 139:12–20.

Angst, J., and Hochstrasser, B. 1994. Recurrent brief depression: The Zurich Study. *J Clin Psychiatry* 55 (suppl):3–9.

Asher, R. 1951. Munchausen's syndrome. *Lancet* 1:339–341.

Barker, J.C. 1962. The syndrome of hospital addiction (Munchausen's syndrome). *J Ment Sci* 108:167–182.

Barsky, A.J. 1979. Patients who amplify bodily sensations. *Ann Intern Med* 91:63–70.

Barsky, A.J., and Klerman, G.L. 1983. Overview: Hypochondriasis, bodily complaints, and somatic styles. *Am J Psychiatry* 140:273–283.

Bowlby, J. 1988. Developmental psychiatry comes of age. *Am J Psychiatry* 145:1–10.

Certcov, D., and Calvo, J. 1973. The problem of psychotherapy in psychosomatic medicine. *Psychosomatics* 14:142–146.

Cooper, A.M., and Ronningstam, E. 1992. Narcissistic personality disorder. In *American Psychiatric Press Review of Psychiatry, Vol. 11,* eds. A. Tasman, and M.B. Riba, pp. 63–78. Washington D.C.: American Psychiatric Press.

Drossman, D.A. 1978. The problem patient. *Ann Intern Med* 88:366–372.

Dubovsky, S.L. 1981. *Psychotherapeutics in Primary Care.* New York: Grune and Stratton.

Emde, R.N. 1983. The prerepresentational self and its affective core. *Psychoanal Study Child* 38:165–192.

Emde, R.N. 1988. Development terminable and interminable. *Int J Psycho-Anal* 69:23–42.

Engel, G.L. 1959. "Psychogenic" pain and the pain-prone patient. *Am J Med* 26:899–918.

Escobar, J.I., Burnaum, A., Karno, M., et al. 1987. Somatization in the community. *Arch Gen Psychiatry* 44:713–718.

Fann, W.E., and Sussex, J.N. 1976. Late effects of early dependency need deprivation: The meal ticket syndrome. *Brit J Psychiatry* 128:262–268.

Ford, C.V. 1986. The somatizing disorders. *Psychosomatics* 27:327–337.

Ford, C.V., King, B.H., and Hollender, M.H. 1988. Lies and liars: Psychiatric aspects of prevarication. *Am J Psychiatry* 145:554–562.

Frosch, J.P., ed. 1983. *Current Perspectives on Personality Disorders.* Washington D.C.: American Psychiatric Press.

Gattaz, W.F., Dressing, H., and Newer, W. 1990. Munchausen syndrome: Psychopathology and management. *Psychopathology* 23:33–39.

Giovacchini, P.L., and Boyer, L.B. 1982. *Technical Factors in the Treatment of the Severely Disturbed Patient.* New York: Jason Aronson.

Gottlieb, H.J., Alperson, B.L., Koller, R., and Hockersmith, V. 1979. An innovative program for the restoration of patients with chronic back pain. *Physical Therapy* 59:996–999.

Green, A. 1975. The analyst, symbolization, and absence in the analytic setting. *Int J Psycho-Anal* 56:1–22.

Greenspan, S., and Lourie, R.S. 1981. Developmental structuralistic approach to the classification of adaptive and pathological personality organizations: Infancy and childhood. *Am J Psychiatry* 138:725–735.

Groves, J.E. 1978. Taking care of the hateful patient. *N Engl J Med* 298: 883–887.

Higget, A., and Fonagy, P. 1992. Psychotherapy in borderline and narcisstic personality disorder. *Brit J Psychiatry* 161:23–43.

Hyler, S.E., and Sussman, N. 1981. Chronic factitious disorder with physical symptoms (The Munchausen Syndrome). *Psychiatr Clin N Amer* 4:365–377.

Kafka, E.1972. On the development of the experience of the mental self, the bodily self, and self-consciousness. *Psychoanal Study Child* 26:217–240.

Keller, M.B., Klerman, G.L., Lavori, P.W., et al. 1982. Treatment received by depressed patients. *JAMA* 248:1848–1855.

Kendell, R.E. 1988. What is a case? *Arch Gen Psychiatry* 45:374–376.

Kernberg, O.F. 1982. Psychotherapeutic treatment of borderline personalities. In *Psychiatry,* ed. L. Grinspoon, pp. 470–487. Washington D.C.: American Psychiatric Press.

Kernberg, O.F. 1984. *Severe Personality Disorders: Psychotherapeutic Strategies.* New Haven: Yale University Press.

Kernberg, O.F. 1989. An ego psychology object relations theory of the structure and treatment of pathological narcissism. *Psychiatr Clin N Amer* 12:723–729.

Klar, H., and Siever, L.J. 1985. *Biologic Response Styles: Clinical Implications.* Washington D.C.: American Psychiatric Press.

Kohut, H., and Wolf, E.S. 1978. The disorders of the self and their treatment: An outline. *Int J Psycho-Anal* 59:413–430.

Krupp, N.E. 1976. Adaptation to chronic illness. *Postgrad Med* 60:122–125.

Krystal, H. 1979. Alexithymia and psychotherapy. *Am J Psychotherapy* 33:17–31.

Kumin, I. 1985–86. Erotic horror: Desire and resistance in the psychoanalytic situation. *Int J Psychoanalytic Psychother* 11:3–20.

Lazare, A. 1981. Conversion symptoms. *N Engl J Med* 305:745–748.

Lipowski, Z.J. 1970. Physical illness, the individual, and the coping process. *Int J Psychiatry Med* 10:91–101.

Lipowski, Z.J. 1987. Somatization: Medicine's unsolved problem. *Psychosomatics* 28:294–297.

Mahler, M.S., Pine, F., and Bergman, A. 1975. *The Psychological Birth of the Human Infant.* New York: Basic Books.

Maltsberger, T., and Buie, D.H. 1974. Countertransference hate in the treatment of suicidal patients. *Arch Gen Psychiatry* 30:625–633.

Melzer, D. 1973. *Sexual States of Mind.* Edinburgh: Chimie Press.

Mumford, D.B. 1992. Emotional distress in the Hebrew Bible. Somatic or psychological? *Brit J Psychiatry* 160:92–97.

Neill, J.R., and Sandifer, M.G. 1982. The clinical approach to alexithymia: A review. *Psychosomatics* 23:1223–1231.

Nemiah, J.C. 1973. Psychology and psychosomatic illness: Reflections on theory and research methodology. *Psychother Psychosom* 22:106–111.

Nemiah, J.C., and Sifneos, P.E. 1970. Psychosomatic illness: A problem in communication. *Psychother Psychosom* 18:154–160.

Reich P., and Gottfried, L.A. 1983. Factitious disorders in a teaching hospital. *Ann Intern Med* 99:240–247.

Reid, W.H., Dorr, D., Walker, J.I., and Bonner, J.W. 1986. *Unmasking the Psychopath.* New York: W.W. Norton.

Rinsley, D.B. 1982. *Borderline and Other Self Disorders.* New York: Jason Aronson.

Rogers, S., ed. 1988. *Clinical Assessment of Malingering and Deception.* New York: The Guilford Press.

Rosenfeld, H. 1971. A clinical approach to the psychoanalytic theroy of the life and death instincts: An investigation into the aggressive aspects of narcissism. *Int J Psycho-Anal* 52:169–177.

Sander, L.W. 1982. Polarity, paradox, and the organizing process in development. In *Frontiers of Infant Psychiatry,* eds. J. Call, E. Galenson, and R. Tyson, pp. 315–327. New York: Basic Books.

Searles, H.F. 1986. *My Work with Borderline Patients.* Northvale NJ: Jason Aronson.

Shapiro, S. 1991. Affect integration in psychoanalysis: A clinical approach to self-destructive behavior. *Bull Menninger Clin* 55:363–374.

Sifneos, P.E. 1974. A reconsideration of psychodynamic mechanisms in psycho-somatic symptom formation in view of recent clinical observations. *Psychother Psychosom* 24:151–155.

Stern, D.N. 1985. *The Interpersonal World of the Infant.* New York: Basic Books.

Stone, M.H. 1980. *The Borderline Syndromes.* New York: McGraw-Hill.

Stone, M.H. 1992. Treatment of severe personality disorders. In *American Psychiatric Press Review of Psychiatry, Vol. 11,* eds. A. Tasman, and M.B. Riba, pp. 98–114. Washington D.C.: American Psychiatric Press.

Svrakic, D.M. 1985. Emotional features of narcissistic personality disorder. *Amer J Psychiatry* 142:720–724.

Thomas, A., and Chess, S. Genesis and evolution of behavioral disorders: From infancy to adult life. *Am J Psychiatry* 141:1–9.

Twaddle, A.C. 1972. The concepts of the sick role and illness behavior. *Adv Psychosom Med* 8:162–179.

Vaillant, G.E. 1981. Dangers of psychotherapy in the treatment of alcoholism. In *Dynamic Approaches to the Understanding and Treatment of Alcoholism,* eds. M.H. Bean, and N.E. Zinberg, pp. 36–54. New York: Free Press.

Vaillant, G.E., and Schnurr, P. 1988. What is a case? A 45-year study of psychiatric impairment within a college sample selected for mental health. *Arch Gen Psychiatry* 45:313–319.

Wise, T.N. 1992. The somatizing patient. *Ann Clin Psychiatry* 4:9–16.

Wolff, H.H. 1973. Psychotherapy: Its place in psychosomatic management. *Psychother Psychosom* 22:233–249.

PART III

Akiskal, H.S. 1980. External validating criteria for psychiatric diagnosis: Their application in affective disorders. *J Clin Psychiatry* 41:6–15.

Akiskal, H.S. 1983. Dysthymic disorder: Psychopathology of proposed chronic depressive subtypes. *Am J Psychiatry* 140:11–20.

Akiskal, H.S. 1984. The interface of chronic depression with personality and anxiety disorders. *Psychopharmacol Bull* 20:393–398.

Akiskal, H.S. 1992. Depression in cyclothymic and related temperaments: Clinical and pharmacologic considerations. *J Clin Psychiatry Monograph* 10:37–43.

Akiskal, H.S., Cassano, G.B., Musetti, L., Perugi, G., Tundo, A., and Mignani, V. 1989. Psychopathology, temperament, and past course in primary major depressions. 1. Review of evidence for a bipolar spectrum. *Psychopathology* 22:268–277.

Akiskal, H.S., and McKinney, W.T. 1975. Overview of recent research in depression. *Arch Gen Psychiatry* 32:285–301.

Altamura, A.C., and Percudani, M. 1993. The use of antidepressants for long-term treatment of recurrent depression: Rationale, current methodologies, and future directions. *J Clin Psychiatry* 54(8, suppl):29–37.

Altshuler, L.I., Post, R.M., Leverich, G.S., Mikalauskas, K., Rosoff, A., and Ackerman, L. 1995. Antidepressant-induced mania and cycle acceleration: A controversy revisited. *Am J Psychiatry* 152:1130–1138.

American Psychiatric Association: Practice guideline for major depressive disorder in adults. 1993. *Am J Psychiatry* 150(4, suppl):1–23.

Angst, J. 1978. The course of affective disorders. II. Typology of bipolar manic-depressive illness. *Arch Psychiatr Nervenkr* 228:65–73.

Angst, J., Merikangas, K., Scheiddeger, P., and Wicki, W. 1990. Recurrent brief depression: A new subtype of affective disorder. *J Affective Disord* 19:87–98.

Arana, G.W., Barrera, P.J., Cohen, B.M., et al. 1983. The dexamethasone suppression test in psychotic disorders. *Am J Psychiatry* 140:1521–1523.

Arieti, S., and Bemporad, J.R. 1980. The psychological organization of depression. *Am J Psychiatry* 137:1360–1365.

Avery, D., and Winokur, G. 1976. Mortality in depressed patients treated with electroconvulsive therapy and antidepressants. *Arch Gen Psychiatry* 33:1029–1037.

Avery, D.H., Khan, A., Dager, S.R., Cohen, S., Cox, G.B., and Dunner, D.L. 1991. Morning or evening bright light treatment of winter depression? *Biol Psychiatry* 29:117–126.

Ayd, F.J. 1991. The early history of modern psychopharmacology. *Neuropsychopharmacology* 5:71–84.

Barlow, D.H. 1990. Long-term outcome for patients with panic disorder treated with cognitive-behavioral therapy. *J Clin Psychiatry* 51(12, suppl A):17–23.

Baron, M., Risch, N., Hamburger, R., Mandel, B., Kushnert, S., Newman, M., Drumer, D., and Belmaker, R.H. 1987. Genetic linkage between X-chromosome markers and bipolar affective illness. *Nature* 326:289–292.

Barry, S., and Dinan, T.G. 1990. Neuroendocrine challenge tests in depression: A study of growth hormone, TRH, and cortisol release. *J Affective Disord* 18:229–234.

Beck, A.T., Jallon, S.D., Young, J.E., et al. 1985. Treatment of depression with cognitive therapy and amitriptyline. *Arch Gen Psychiatry* 42:142–148.

Belmaker, R.H. 1991. One gene per psychosis? *Biol Psychiatry* 29:415–417.

Berridge, M.J. 1985. The molecular basis of communication within the cell. *Scientific American* 253:142–152.

Berrittini, W.H. 1991. Is investment in molecular genetics worthwhile? *Biol Psychiatry* 30:213–215.

Bettelheim, B. 1983. *Freud and Man's Soul.* New York: Alfred A. Knopf.

Blacker, D., and Tsuang, M.T. 1992. Contested boundaries of bipolar disorder and the limits of categorical diagnosis in psychiatry. *Am J Psychiatry* 149:1473–1483.

Bouhuys, A.L. 1991. Towards a model of mood responses to sleep deprivation in depressed patients. *Biol Psychiatry* 29:600–612.

Boyd, J.H., and Weissman, M.M. 1981. Epidemiology of affective disorders. *Arch Gen Psychiatry* 38:1039–1046.

Breier, A., Charney, D.S., and Heninger, G.R. 1984. Major depression in patients with agoraphobia and panic disorder. *Arch Gen Psychiatry* 41:1129–1135.

Breier, A., Charney, D.S., and Heniger, G.R. 1985. The diagnostic validity of anxiety disorders and their relationship to depressive illness. *Am J Psychiatry* 142:787–797.

Callaway, E. 1992. Psychopharmacology's need for linking variables. *Biol Psychiatry* 31:1–3.

Carlson, G.A., Davenport, Y.B., and Jamison, K. 1977. A comparison of outcome in adolescent and late-onset bipolar manic-depressive illness. *Am J Psychiatry* 134:919–922.

Carlson, G.A., and Kashani, J.H. 1988. Phenomenology of major depression from childhood through adulthood: Analysis of three studies. *Am J Psychiatry* 145:1222–1225.

Carr, D.B., and Sheehan, D.V. 1984. Panic anxiety: A new biological model. *J Clin Psychiatry* 45:323–330.

Carroll, B.J. 1986. Informed use of the dexamethasone suppression test. *J Clin Psychiatry* 47(suppl):10–12.

Cassano, G.B., Akiskal, H.S., Musetti, L., Perugi, G., Soriani, A., and Migani, V. 1989. Psychopathology, temperament, and past course in primary major depressions. 2. Toward a redefinition of bipolarity with a new semistructured interview for depression. *Psychopathology* 22:278–288.

Charney, D.S., Woods, S.W., Nagy, L.M., Southwick, S.M., Krystal, J.H., and Heninger, G.R. 1990. Noradrenergic function in panic disorder. *J Clin Psychiatry* 51(12, suppl A):5–11.

Ciompi, L. 1991. Affects as central organising and integrating factors. *Brit J Psychiatry* 159:97–105.

Clayton, P.J., Grove, W.M., Coryell, W., Keller, M., Hirschfeld, R., and Fawcett, J. 1991. Follow-up and family study of anxious depression. *Am J Psychiatry* 148:1512–1517.

Coccaro, E.F. 1989. Central serotonin and impulsive aggression. *Brit J Psychiatry* 155(suppl 8):52–62.

Conte, H.R., Plutchik, R., Wild, K.V., and Karasu, T.B. 1986. Combined psychotherapy and pharmacotherapy for depression. A systematic analysis of the evidence. *Arch Gen Psychiatry* 43:471–479.

Coryell, W. 1990. DST abnormality as a predictor of course in major depression. *J Affective Disord* 19:163–169.

Coryell, W., Andreasen, N.C., Endicott, J., and Keller, M. 1987. The significance of past mania or hypomania in the course and outcome of major depression. *Am J Psychiatry* 144:309–315.

Coryell, W., Endicott, J., and Keller, M. 1990. Outcome of patients with chronic affective disorder: A five-year follow-up. *Am J Psychiatry* 147:1627–1633.

Coryell, W., Endicott, J., and Keller, M. 1992. Rapidly cycling affective disorder. *Arch Gen Psychiatry* 49:126–131.

Coryell, W., Endicott, J., Keller, M., Andreasen, N., Grove, W., Hirschfeld, R.M.A., and Scheftner, W. 1989. Bipolar affective disorder and high achievement: A familial association. *Am J Psychiatry* 146:983–988.

Coryell, W., Scheftner, W., Keller, M., Endicott, J., Maser, J., and Klerman, G.L. 1993. The enduring psychosocial consequences of mania and depression. *Am J Psychiatry* 150:720–727.

Cowdry, R.W., Gardner, D.L., O'Leary, K.M., Leibenluft, E., and Rubinow, D.R. 1991. Mood variability: A study of four groups. *Am J Psychiatry* 148:1505–1511.

Craighead, L.W., and Craighead, W.E. 1991. Behavior therapy: Recent developments. *Current Opinion in Psychiatry* 4:916–920.

Czeisler, C.A., Kronauer, R.E., Mooney, J.J., Anderson, J.L., and Allan, J.S. (1987). Biologic rhythm disorders, depression, and phototherapy. *Psychiatr Clin N Amer* 10: 687–709.

Davis, J.M. 1976. Overview: Maintenance therapy in psychiatry. II. Affective disorders. *Am J Psychiatry* 133:1–13.

DePaulo, J.R., and Simpson, S.G. 1987. Therapeutic and genetic prospects of an atypical affective disorder. *J Clin Psychopharmacol* 7:50S–54S.

Devanand, D.P., Sackeim, H.A., Lo, E.S., Cooper, T., Huttinot, G., Prudic, J., and Ross, F. 1991. Serial dexamethasone suppression tests and plasma dexamethasone levels. *Arch Gen Psychiatry* 48:525–533.

Dubovsky, S.L. 1995. Electroconvulsive therapy. In *Comprehensive Textbook of Psychiatry VI*, eds. H.I. Kaplan, and B.J. Sadock, pp. 2129–2140. Baltimore: Williams and Wilkins.

Dubovsky, S.L., and Thomas, M. 1995. Serotonergic mechanisms and current and future psychiatric practice. *J Clin Psychiatry* 56(suppl 2): 38–48.

Egeland, J.A. 1983. Bipolarity: The iceberg of affective disorders? *Compr Psychiatry* 24:337–344.

Egeland, J.A., Gerhard, D.S., Pauls, D.L., et al. 1987. Bipolar affective disorders linked to DNA markers on chromosome 11. *Nature* 326:783–787.

Elkin, I., Shea, T., Watkins, J.T., Imber, S.D., Sotsky, S.M., Collins, J.F., Glass, D.R., Pilkonis, P.A., Leber, W.R., Docherty, J.P., Fiester, S.J., and Parloff, M.B. 1989.

National Institute of Mental Health treatment of depression collaborative research program. *Arch Gen Psychiatry* 46:971–982.

Frank, E., Kupfer, D.J., Perel, J.M., Cornes, C., Jarrett, D.B., Mallinger, A.G., Thase, M.E., McEachran, A.B., and Grochocinski, V.J. 1990. Three-year outcomes for maintenance therapies in recurrent depression. *Arch Gen Psychiatry*: 1093–1099.

Freedman, D.X. 1984. Psychiatric epidemiology counts. *Arch Gen Psychiatry* 41:931–933.

Freeman, W. 1992. Chaos in psychiatry. *Biol Psychiatry* 31:1079–1081.

Freud, S. 1926. Inhibitions, symptoms, and anxiety. *Standard Edition of the Complete Psychological Works of Sigmund Freud, Vol. 20,* pp. 75–175. New York: W. W. Norton.

Friedman, S., Jones, J.C., Chernen, L., and Barlow, D.H. 1992. Suicidal ideation and suicide attempts among patients with panic disorder: A survey of two outpatient clinics. *Am J Psychiatry* 149:680–685.

Friedmann, C.T.H. 1982. *Extraordinary Disorders of Human Behavior.* New York: Plenum.

Gabbard, G.O. 1992. Psychodynamic psychotherapy in the "decade of the brain." *Am J Psychiatry* 149:991–998.

Gaensbauer, T.J., Harmon, R.J., Cytryn, L., and McKnew, D.H. 1984. Social and affective development in infants with a manic-depressive parent. *Am J Psychiatry* 141:223–229.

Ganguli, R., Reynolds, C.F., and Kupfer, D.J. 1987. Electroencephalographic sleep in young, never-medicated schizophrenics. *Arch Gen Psychiatry* 44:36–44.

Georgotas, A., McCue, R.E., and Cooper, T.B. 1989. A placebo-controlled comparison of nortriptyline and phenelzine in maintenance therapy of elderly depressed patients. *Arch Gen Psychiatry* 46:783–786.

Gershon, E.S., Hamooct, J.H., Guroff, J.J., and Nurnberger, J.I. 1987. Birth-cohort changes in manic and depressive disorders in relatives of bipolar and schizoaffective patients. *Arch Gen Psychiatry* 44:314–319.

Gershon, E.S., and Rieder, R.O. 1992. Major disorders of mind and brain. *Scientific American* 267:127–133.

Gillen, J.C. 1983. Sleep studies in affective illness. *Psychiatric Annals* 13:367–384.

Gold, P.W., Goodwin, F.K., and Chrousos, G.P. 1988. Clinical and biochemical manifestations of depression: Relation to the neurobiology of stress (in two parts). *N Engl J Med* 319:348–353 & 413–419.

Golden, R.N., and Potter, W.Z. 1986. Neurochemical and neuroendocrine dysregulation in affective disorders. *Psychiatr Clin N Amer* 9:313–325.

Goodwin, F.K., and Jamison, K.R. 1990. *Manic Depressive Illness.* New York: Oxford University Press.

Gorman, J.M., Liebowitz, M.R., Fyer, A.J., and Stein, J. 1989. A neuroanatomical hypothesis for panic disorder. *Am J Psychiatry* 146:148–161.

Greden, J.F. 1993. Antidepressant maintenance medications: When to discontinue and how to stop. *J Clin Psychiatry* 54(8,suppl):39–45.

Greenberg, D.A. 1992. There is more than one way to collect data for linkage analysis. *Arch Gen Psychiatry* 49:745–750.

Guscott, R., and Grof, P. 1991. The clinical meaning of refractory depression: A review for the clinician. *Am J Psychiatry* 148:695–704.

Harrington, R., Rutter, M., Pickles, A., and Hill, J. 1990. Adult outcomes of childhood and adolescent depression. *Arch Gen Psychiatry* 47:465–473.

Hellerstein, D.J.,Yanowitch, P., Rosenthal, J., Samstag, L.W., Maurer, M., Kasch, K., Burrows, L., Poster, M., Cantillonm, M., and Winston, A. 1993. A randomized double-blind study of fluoxetine versus placebo in the treatment of dysthymia. *Am J Psychiatry* 150:1169–1175.

Hirschfeld, R.M.A. 1981. Situational depression: Validity of the concept. *Brit J Psychiatry* 139:297–305.

Hirschfeld, R.M.A., Klerman, G.L., Clayton, P.J., et al. 1983. Assessing personality: Effects of the depressive state on trait measurement. *Am J Psychiatry* 140: 695–699.

Hirschfeld, R.M.A., Klerman, G.L., Lavori, P., et al. 1989. Premorbid personality assessments of first onset of major depression. *Arch Gen Psychiatry* 46:345–350.

Hodgkinson, S., Sherrington, R., Gurling, H., et al. 1987. Molecular genetic evidence for heterogeneity in manic depression. *Nature* 325:805–806.

Hoffman, J.S. 1990. Integrating biologic and psychologic treatment: The need for a unitary model. *Psychiatr Clin N Amer* 13:369–372.

Hokfelt, T., Johansson, O., and Goldstein, M. 1984. Chemical anatomy of the brain. *Science* 225:1326–1333.

Hollonquist, J.D., Goldberg, M.A., and Brandes, J.S. 1986. Affective disorders and circadian rhythms. *Can J Psychiatry* 31:259–268.

Hsiao, J.K., Agren, H., Bartko, J.J., et al. 1987. Monoamine neurotransmitter interactions and the prediction of antidepressant response. *Arch Gen Psychaitry* 44:1078–1083.

Hudson, J.I., Lipinski, J.F., Keck, P.E., Aizley, H.G., Lukas, S.E., Rothschild, A.J., Waternaux, C.M., and Kupfer, D.J. 1992. Polysomnographic characteristics of young manic patients. Comparison with unipolar depressed patients and normal control subjects. *Arch Gen Psychiatry* 49:378–383.

Hunt, N., Bruce-Jones, W., and Silverstone, T. 1992. Life events and relapse in bipolar affective disorder. *J Affective Disord* 25:13–20.

Hurowitz, G.I., and Liebowitz, M.R. 1993. Antidepressant-induced rapid cycling: Six case reports. *J Clin Psychopharmacol* 13:52–56.

Jesberger, J.A., and Richardson, J.S. 1985. Animal models of depression: Parallels and correlates to severe depression in humans. *Biol Psychiatry* 20:764–784.

Kahn, D. 1990. The dichotomy of drugs and psychotherapy. *Psychiatr Clin N Amer* 13:197–208.

Kandel, D.B., and Davies, M. 1986. Adult sequelae of adolescent depressive symptoms. *Arch Gen Psychiatry* 43:255–262.

Kandel, E.R. 1983. From metapsychology to molecular biology: Explorations into the nature of anxiety. *Am J Psychiatry* 140:1277–1293.

Kandel, E.R., and Schwartz, J.H. 1981. *Principles of Neural Science.* New York: Elsevier.

Karasu, T.B. 1984. Recent developments in individual psychotherapy. *Hosp Commun Psychiatry* 35:29–37.

Karasu, T.B. 1984. *The Psychiatric Therapies.* Washington D.C.: American Psychiatric Press.

Karasu, T.B. 1989. New frontiers in psychotherapy. *J Clin Psychaitry* 50:46–52.

Kasper, S., Rogers, S.L.B., Yancey, A., et al. 1989. Phototherapy in individuals with and without subsyndromal seasonal affective disorder. *Arch Gen Psychiatry* 46:837–844.

Kasper, S., Wehr, T., Bartko, J.J., et al. 1989. Epidemiological findings of seasonal changes in mood and behavior. *Arch Gen Psychiatry* 46:823–833.

Keller, M.B. 1989. Current concepts in affective disorders. *J Clin Psychiatry* 50:157–162.

Keller, M.B., Klerman, G.L., Lavori, P.W., et al. 1984. Long-term outcome of episodes of major depression. *JAMA* 252:788–792.

Keller, M.B., and Lavori, P.W. 1984. Double depression, major depression, and dysthymia: Distinct entities or different phases of a single disorder? *Psychopharmacol Bull* 20:399–409.

Keller, M.B., Lavori, P.W., Kane, J.M., Gelenberg, A.J., Rosenbaum, J.F., Walzer, E.A., and Baker, L.A. 1992. Subsyndromal symptoms in bipolar disorder. A comparison of standard and low serum levels of lithium. *Arch Gen Psychiatry* 49:371–376.

Kendler, K.S., Heath, A.C., Martin, N.G., and Eaves, L.J. 1987. Symptoms of anxiety and symptoms of depression. Same genes, different environments? *Arch Gen Psychiatry* 44:451–457.

Kendler, K.S., Kessler, R.C., Neale, M.C., Heath, A.C., and Eaves, L.J. 1993. The prediction of major depression in women: Toward an integrated etiologic model. *Am J Psychiatry* 150:1139–1148.

Kendler, K.S., Neale, M.C., Kessler, R.C., Heath, A.C., and Eaves, L.J. 1992. Major depression and generalized anxiety disorder. Same genes, (partly) diffeent environments? *Arch Gen Psychiatry* 49:716–722.

Kendler, K.S., Neale, M.C., Kessler, R.C., Heath, A.C., and Eaves, L.J. 1992. A population-based twin study of major depression in women. *Arch Gen Psychiatry* 49:257–266.

Klerman, G.L. 1988. The current age of youthful melancholia. Evidence for increase in depression among adolescents and young adults. *Brit J Psychiatry* 152:4–14.

Klerman, G.L., Lavori, P.W., Rice, J., Reich, T., Endicott, J., Andreasen, N.C., Keller, M.B., and Hirschfeld, R.M.A. 1985. Birth-cohort trends in rates of major depressive disorder among relatives of patients with affective disorder. *Arch Gen Psychiatry* 42:689–693.

Klerman, G.L., Weissman, M.M., Rounsaville, B.J., and Chevron, E.S. 1984. *Interpersonal Psychotherapy of Depression.* New York: Basic Books.

Kocsis, J.H., Sutton, B.M., and Frances, A.J. 1991. Long-term follow-up of chronic depression treated with imipramine. *J Clin Psychiatry* 52:56–59.

Kohut, H. 1971. *The Analysis of the Self.* New York: International Universities Press.

Kovacs, M., Feinberg, T.L., Crouse-Novak, M., et al. 1984. Depressive disorders in childhood. II. A longitudinal study of the risks for a subsequent major depression. *Arch Gen Psychiatry* 41:643–649.

Kupfer, D.J. 1995. Sleep research in depressive illness: Clinical implications, a tasting menu. *Biol Psychiatry* 38:39–43.

Kupfer, D.J., Frank, E., and Perel, J.M. 1989. The advantage of early treatment intervention in recurrent depression. *Arch Gen Psychiatry* 46:771–775.

Kupfer, D.J., and Freedman, D.X. 1986. Treatment for depression: "Standard" clinical practice as an unexamined topic. *Arch Gen Psychiatry* 43:509–511.

Lader, M. 1983. Behavior and anxiety: Physiological mechanisms. *J Clin Psychiatry* 44(11, sec 2):5–10.

Lasch, K., Weissman, M., Wickramaratne, and Bruce, M.L. 1990. Birth-cohort changes in the rates of mania. *Psychiatry Res* 33:31–37.

Loosen, P.T., and Prange, A.J. 1982. Serum thyrotropin response to thyrotropin releasing hormone in psychiatric patients: A review. *Am J Psychiatry* 139: 405–416.

Loranger, A.W., Lenzenweger, M.F., Gartner, A.F., Lehmann, V., Herzig, J., Zammit, G.K., Gartner, J.D., Abrams, R.C., and Young, R.C. 1991. Trait-state artifacts and the diagnosis of personality disorders. *Arch Gen Psychiatry* 48:720–728.

Lumry, A.E. 1982. MMPI state dependency during the course of bipolar psychosis. *Psychiatry Res* 7:59–64.

Maj, M., Veltro, F., Priozzi, R., Lobrace, S., Magliano, L. 1992. Pattern of recurrence of illness after recovery from an episode of major depression: A prospective study. *Am J Psychiatry* 149:795–800.

Mann, J.J., Arango, V., Marzuk, P.M., et al. 1989. Evidence for the 5-HT hypothesis of suicide: A review of post-mortem studies. *Brit J Psychiatry* 155(suppl 8): 7–14.

Markowitz, J.S., Weissman, M.M., Ouellette, R., Lish, J.D., and Klerman, G.L. 1989. Quality of life in panic disorder. *Arch Gen Psychiatry* 46:984–992.

Marmor, J. 1983. Systems thinking in psychiatry: Some theoretical and clinical implications. *Am J Psychiatry* 140:833–838.

Maziade, M., Caron, C., Cote, R., Boutin, P., and Thivierge, J. 1990. Extreme temperament and diagnosis. A study in a psychiatric sample of consecutive children. *Arch Gen Psychiatry* 47:477–484.

McElroy, S.L., Keck, P.E., Pope, H.G., Hudson, J.I., Faedda, G.I., and Swann, A.C. 1992. Clinical and research implications of the diagnosis of dysphoric or mixed mania or hypomania. *Am J Psychiatry* 149:1633–1644.

Miklowitz, D.J., Goldstein, M.J., Nuechterlein, K.H., Snyder, K.S., and Mintz, J. 1988. Family factors and the course of bipolar disorder. *Arch Gen Psychiatry* 45:225–231.

Moore-Ede, M.C., Czeisler, C.A., and Richardson, G.S. 1983. Circadian timekeeping in health and disease. *N Engl J Med* 309:469–476 & 530–535.

Mullan, M.J., and Murray, R.M. 1989. The impact of molecular genetics on our understanding of the psychoses. *Brit J Psychiatry* 154:591–595.

Nasrallah, H.A. 1991. Neurodevelopmental aspects of bipolar affective disorder. *Biol Psychiatry* 29:1–2.

Olfson, M., and Klerman, G.L. 1993. Trends in the prescription of antidepressants by office-based psychiatrists. *Am J Psychiatry* 150:571–577.

Pauls, D.L., Morton, L.A., and Egeland, J.A. 1992. Risks of affective illness among first-degree relatives of bipolar I old-order Amish probands. *Arch Gen Psychiatry* 49:703–708.

Paykel, E.S. 1989. Treatment of depression. The relevance of research for clinical practice. *Brit J Psychiatry* 155:754–763.

Perry, J.C. 1985. Depression and borderline personality disorder: Lifetime prevalence at interview and longitudinal course of symptoms. *Am J Psychiatry* 142:15–21.

Perry, J.C. 1992. Problems and considerations in the valid assessment of personality disorders. *Am J Psychiatry* 149:1645–1653.

Pitts, F.N. 1984. Recent research on the DST. *J Clin Psychiatry* 45:380–381.

Plath, S. 1982. *The Journals of Sylvia Plath.* New York: Dial Press.

Post, R.M. 1982. Kindling and carbamazepine in affective illness. *J Nerv Ment Dis* 170:717–724.

Post, R.M. 1992. Transduction of psychosocial stress into the neurobiology of recurrent affective disorder. *Am J Psychiatry* 149:999–1010.

Post, R.M., Rubinow, D.R., and Ballenger, J.C. 1986. Conditioning and sensitization in the longitudinal course of affective illness. *Brit J Psychiatry* 149:191–201.

Price, R.A., Kidd, K.K., and Weissman, M.M. 1987. Early onset (under age 30 years) and panic disorder as markers for etiologic homogeneity in major depression. *Arch Gen Psychiatry* 44:434–440.

Prien, R.F., Carpenter, L.L., and Kupfer, D.J. 1991. The definition and operational criteria for treatment outcome of major depressive disorder. *Arch Gen Psychiatry* 48:796–800.

Quitkin, F.M., Stewart, J.W., McGrath, P.J., Nunes, E., Ocepek-Welikson, K., Tricamo, E., Rabkin, J.G., Ross, D., and Klein, D.F. 1993. Loss of drug effects during continuation therapy. *Am J Psychiatry* 150:562–565.

Reich, J. 1991. Avoidant and dependent personality traits in relatives of patients with panic disorder, patients with dependent personality disorder, and normal controls. *Psychiatry Res* 39:89–98.

Reich, J., Noyes, R., Coryell, W., and O'Gorman, T.W. 1986. The effect of state anxiety on personality measurement. *Am J Psychiatry* 143:760–763.

Reich, J., Noyes, R., Hirschfeld, R., et al. 1987. State and personality in depression and panic patients. *Am J Psychiatry* 144:181–187.

Restak, R. 1984. *The Brain.* New York: Bantam Books.

Rice, J., Reich, T., Andreasen, N.C., Endicott, J., van Eedewegh, M., Fishman, B., Hirschfeld, R.M.A., and Klerman, G.L. 1987. The familial transmission of bipolar illness. *Arch Gen Psychiatry* 44:441–447.

Robertson, M. 1987. Molecular genetics of the mind. *Nature* 325:755.

Roth, M., Gurney, C., Gavside, R.F., and Kerr, T.A. 1972. Studies in the classification of affective disorders: The relationship between anxiety states and depressive illness. *Brit J Psychiatry* 121:147–161.

Roy, A., DeJong, J., and Linnoila, M. 1989. Cerebrospinal fluid monoamine metabolites and suicidal behavior in depressed patients. *Arch Gen Psychiatry* 46:609–612.

Rudd, M.D., Dahm, P.F., and Rajab, M.H. 1993. Diagnostic comorbidity in persons with suicidal ideation and behavior. *Am J Psychiatry* 150:928–934.

Rutter, M., Izard, C.E., and Read, P.B., eds. 1986. *Depression in Young People: Developmental and Clinical Perspectives.* New York: Guilford Press.

Ryan, N.D., Puig-Antich, J., Ambosinis, P., et al. 1987. The clinical picture of major depression in children and adolescents. *Arch Gen Psychiatry* 44:854–861.

Sapolsky, R.M. 1989. Hypercortisolism among socially subordinate wild baboons originates at the CNS level. *Arch Gen Psychiatry* 46:1047–1051.

Sapolsky, R.M., and Plotsky, P.M. 1990. Hypercortisolism and its possibly neural bases. *Biol Psychiatry* 27:937–952.

Schatzberg, A.F. 1982. Toward a biochemical classification of depressive disorders. *Am J Psychiatry* 139:471–474.

Schuckit, M.A. 1983. Anxiety related to medical disease. *J Clin Psychiatry* 44(11, sec 2):31–36.

Seligman, M.E.P. 1975. *Helplessness: On Depression, Development, and Death.* San Francisco: W.H. Freeman and Co.

Sergeant, J.K., Bruce, M.L., Florio, L.P., and Weissman, M.M. 1990. Factors associated with one-year outcome of major depression in the community. *Arch Gen Psychiatry* 47:519–526.

Shapiro, M.F., Lehman, A.F., and Greenfield, S. 1983. Biases in the laboratory diagnosis of depression in medical practice. *Arch Intern Med* 143: 2085–2088.

Siever, L.J., and Davis, K.L. 1985. Overview: Toward a dysregulation hypothesis of depression. *Am J Psychiatry* 142:1017–1031.

Silverman, J.S., Silverman, J.A., and Eardley, D.A. 1984. Do maladaptive attitudes cause depression? *Arch Gen Psychiatry* 41:28–30.

Silverstone, T., and Romans-Clarkson, S. 1989. Bipolar affective disorder: Causes and prevention of relapse. *Brit J Psychiatry* 154:321–335.

Simons, A.D., Garfield, S.L., and Murphy, G.E. 1984. The process of change in cognitive therapy and pharmacotherapy for depression. *Arch Gen Psychiatry* 41:45–51.

Simons, A.D., Murphy, G.E., Levine, J.L., and Wetzel, R.D. 1986. Cognitive therapy and pharmacotherapy for depression. *Arch Gen Psychiatry* 43:43–48.

Simpson, S.G., Folstein, S.E., Meyers, D.A., McMahon, F.J., Brusco, D.M., and dePaulo, J.R. 1993. Bipolar II: The most common bipolar phenotype? *Am J Psychiatry* 150:901–903.

Solomon, R.L., Rich, C.L., and Darko, D.F. 1990. Antidepressant treatment and the occurrence of mania in bipolar patients admitted for depression. *J Affective Disord* 18:253–257.

Somoza, E., and Mossman, D. 1990. Optimizing REM latency as a diagnostic test for depression using receiver operating characteristic analysis and information theory. *Biol Psychiatry* 27:990–1006.

Starkstein, S.E., Fedoroff, P., Berthier, M.L., and Robinson, R.G. 1991. Manic-depressive and pure manic states after brain lesions. *Biol Psychiatry* 29:149–158.

Stewart, J.W., McGrath, P.J., and Quitkin, F.M. 1992. Can mildly depressed outpatients with atypical depression benefit from antidepressants? *Am J Psychiatry* 149:615–619.

Strober, M., and Carlson, G. 1982. Bipolar illness in adolescents with major depression. *Arch Gen Psychiatry* 39:549–555.

Strober, M., Morrell, W., Lampert, C., and Burroughs, J. 1990. Relapse following discontinuation of lithium maintenance therapy in adolescents with bipolar I illness: A naturalistic study. *Am J Psychiatry* 147:457–461.

Suomi, S.J., Seaman, S.F., Lewis, J.K., et al. 1978. Effects of imipramine treatment of separation-induced social disorders in rhesus monkeys. *Arch Gen Psychiatry* 35:321–325.

Swaab, D.F. 1982. Neuropeptides: Their distribution and function in the brain. *Prog Brain Res* 55:97–122.

Taylor, M.A. 1992. Are schizophrenia and affective disorder related? A selective literature review. *Am J Psychiatry* 149:22–32.

Taylor, M.A., Berenbaum, S.A., Jampala, V.C., and Cloninger, C.R. 1993. Are schizophrenia and affective disorder related? Preliminary data from a family study. *Am J Psychiatry* 150:278–285.

Thase, M.E., and Simons, A.D. 1992. Cognitive behavior therapy and relapse of nonbipolar depression: Parallels with pharmacotherapy. *Psychopharmacol Bull* 28:117–122.

Thase, M.E., Simons, A.D., Cahalane, J., McGeary, J., and Harden, T. 1991. Severity of depression and response to cognitive behavior therapy. *Am J Psychiatry* 148:784–789.

Thase, M.E., Simons, A.D., McGeary, J., Cahalane, J.F., Hughes, C., Harden, T., and Friedman, E. 1992. Relapse after cognitive behavior therapy of depression: Potential implications for longer courses of treatment. *Am J Psychiatry* 149:1046–1052.

Torgensen, S. 1983. Genetic factors in anxiety disorders. *Arch Gen Psychiatry* 40:1085–1089.

Vaillant, G.E., Roston, D., and McHugo, G.J. 1992. An intriguing association between ancestral mortality and male affective disorder. *Arch Gen Psychiatry* 49:709–715.

van Praag, H.M. 1990. The *DSM-IV* (depression) classification: To be or not to be? *J Nerv Ment Dis* 178:147–149.

van Praag, H.M. 1990. Two-tier diagnosing in psychiatry. *Psychiatry Res* 34:1–11.

Verhoeven, W.M.A., and van Praag, H.M. 1980. Neuropeptides and their potential clinical significance. *Adv Biol Psychiatry* 5:20–45.

von Zerssen, D.V., and Doerr, P. 1980. The role of the hypothalamic-pituitary-adrenocortical system in psychiatric disorders. *Adv Biol Psychiatry* 5:85–106.

Watts, C.A.H. 1984. Depressive disorders in the community: The scene in Great Britain, 1965-1984. *J Clin Psychiatry* 45:70–77.

Wehr, T.A. 1990. Manipulations of sleep and phototherapy: Nonpharmacological alternatives in the treatment of depression. *Clin Neuropharmacol* 13:S54–S65.

Wehr, T.A., and Goodwin, F.K. 1987. Can antidepressants cause mania and worsen the course of affective illness? *Am J Psychiatry* 144:1403–1411.

Wehr, T.A., Sack, D.A., and Rosenthal, N.E. 1987. Sleep reduction as a final common pathway in the genesis of mania. *Am J Psychiatry* 144:201–204.

Wehr, T.A., Sack, D.A., Rosenthal, N.E., and Cowdry, R.W. 1988. Rapid cycling affective disorder: Contributing factors and treatment responses in 51 patients. *Am J Psychiatry* 145:179–184.

Weissman, M.M., Gammon, G.D., John, K., et al. 1987. Children of depressed parents. *Arch Gen Psychiatry* 44:847–853.

Weissman, M.M., Klerman, G.L., Markowitz, J.S., and Ouellette, R. 1989. Suicidal ideation and suicide attempts in panic disorder and attacks. *N Enl J Med* 321:1209–1214.

Weissman, M.M., Klerman, G.L., Prusoff, B.A., et al. 1981. Depressed outpatients. Results one year after therapy with drugs and/or interpersonal therapy. *Arch Gen Psychiatry* 38:51–55.

Weissman, M.M., Wickramaritne, P., Merikangas, K.B., et al. 1984. Onset of major depression in early adulthood. *Arch Gen Psychiatry* 41:1136–1139.

Wender, P.H., Kety, S.S., Rosenthal, D., et al. 1986. Psychiatric disorders in the biological and adoptive families of adopted individuals with affective disorders. *Arch Gen Psychiatry* 43:923–929.

Wheelis, A. 1971. *The End of the Modern Age.* New York: Basic Books.

Whybrow, P.C., Akiskal, H.S., and Mckinney, W.T. 1984. *Mood Disorders: Toward a New Psychobiology.* New York: Plenum Press.

Winokur, G., Coryell, W., Endicott, J., and Akiskal, H. 1993. Further distinctions between manic-depressive illness (bipolar disorder) and primary depressive disorder (unipolar depression). *Am J Psychiatry* 150:1176–1181.

Winokur, G., Coryell, W., Keller, M., Endicott, J., and Akiskal, H. 1993. A prospective follow-up of patients with bipolar and primary unipolar affective disorder. *Arch Gen Psychiatry* 50:457–465.

PART IV

Abramson, L.Y., Seligman, M.E.P., and Teasdale, J.D. 1978. Learned helplessness in humans: Critique and reformulation. *J Abnorm Psychology* 87:49–74.

Adamson, J.D., and Schmale, A.H. 1965. Object loss, giving up, and the onset of psychiatric disease. *Psychosom Med* 27:557–576.

Ader, R. 1981. *Psychoneuroimmunology.* New York: Academic Press.

Aleksandrowicz, D.R. 1961. Fire and its aftermath on a geriatric ward. *Bull Menn Clin* 25:23–32.

Andrewes, D. 1992. The effect of psychotherapy on patients with cancer or coronary heart disease. *Current Opinion in Psychiatry* 5:380–384.

Avery, D., and Winokur, G. 1976. Mortality in depressed patients treated with electroconvulsive therapy and antidepressants. *Arch Gen Psychiatry* 33:1029–1037.

Bahnson, C.B. 1980. Stress and cancer: The state of the art. *Psychosomatics* 21:975–981.

Belitsky, R., and Jacobs, S. 1986. Bereavement, attachment theory and mental disorders. *Psychiatr Ann* 16:276–280.

Bennett, M.I., and Bennett, M.B. 1984. The uses of hopelessness. *Am J Psychiatry* 141:559–562.

Bennett, P., and Carroll, D. 1994. Psychophysiological and psychosocial processes in cardiovascular function and disease. *Current Opinion in Psychiatry* 7: 498–501.

Berkman, L.F., and Syme, S.L. 1979. Social networks, host resistance, and mortality: A nine-year follow-up study of Alameda county residents. *Am J Epidemiol* 109:186–204.

Bettelheim, B. 1980. *Surviving and Other Essays.* New York: Bantage Books.

Binik, Y.M., Theriault, G., and Shustack, B. 1977. Sudden death in the laboratory rat: Cardiac function, sensory and experiential factors in swimming deaths. *Psychosom Med* 39:82–91.

Borysenko, M., and Borysenko, J. 1982. Stress, behavior and immunity: Animal models and mediating mechanisms. *Gen Hosp Psychiatry* 4:59–67.

Bower, B. 1991. Questions of mind over immunity. *Science News* 139:216–217.

Bowlby, J. 1969. *Attachment and Loss. Vol I. Attachment.* London: Hogarth Press.

Bowlby, J. 1973. *Attachment and Loss. Vol II. Separation.* New York: Basic Books.

Bowlby, J. 1980. *Attachment and Loss. Vol III. Loss, Sadness, and Depression.* New York: Basic Books.

Calabrese, J.R., Kling, M.A., and Gold, P.W. 1987. Alterations in immuno-competence during stress, bereavement and depression: Focus on neuroendocrine regulation. *Am J Psychiatry* 144:1123–1134.

Cannon, W.B. 1957. "Voodoo" death. *Psychosom Med* 19:182–190.

Chrousos, G.P., and Gold, P.W. 1992. The concepts of stress and stress system disorders. *JAMA* 267:1244–1252.

Cohen, S., Tyrell, D.A.J., and Smith, A.P. 1993. Negative life events, perceived stress, negative affect, and susceptibility to the common cold. *J Pers Social Psychology* 64:131–140.

Comfort, A. 1981. Sorcery and sudden death. *J Roy Soc Med* 74:332–333.

Darko, D.F., Gillin, J.C., Risch, S.C., et al. 1988. Immune cells and the hypothalamic-pituitary axis in major depression. *Psychiatry Res* 25:173–179.

Darko, D.F., Lucas, A.H., Gillin, J.C., et al. 1988. Cellular immunity and the hypothalamic-pituitary axis in major affective disorder: A preliminary study. *Psychiatry Res* 25:1–9.

Darwin, C. 1965. *The Expression of the Emotions in Man and Animals.* Chicago: University of Chicago Press.

Dattore, P.J., Shoutz, F.C., and Lolafaye, C. 1980. Premorbid personality differentiation of cancer and noncancer groups: A test of the hypothesis of cancer proneness. *J Consulting Clin Psychol* 48:388–394.

Dembroski, T.M., MacDougall, J.M., Williams, E.B., et al. 1985. Components of type A, hostility, and anger in relationship. *Psychosom Med* 47:219–233.

Dillon, K.M., Minchoff, B., and Baker, K.H. 1985–6. Positive emotional states and enhancement of the immune system. *Int J Psychiatry Med* 15:13–17.

Dimsdale, J.E. 1977. Emotional causes of sudden death. *Am J Psychiatry* 134:1361–1365.

Dunn, A.J. 1989. Psychoneuroimmunology for the psychoneuroendocrinologist: A review of animal studies of nervous system-immune system interactions. *Psychoneuroendocrinology* 14:251–274.

Engel, G.L. 1971. Sudden and rapid death during psychological stress. Folklore or folk wisdom? *Ann Intern Med* 77:771–782.

Epstein, G., Weitz, L., Roback, H., et al. 1978. Research on bereavement: Selective and critical review. *Compr Psychiatry* 16:537–545.

Evans, D.L., Folds, J.D., Pettino, J.M., et al. 1992. Circulating natural killer cell phenotypes in men and women with major depression. *Arch Gen Psychiatry* 49:388–395.

Fauci, A.S., Lane, C., and Volkman, D.J. 1983. Activation and regulation of human immune responses: Implications in normal and disease states. *Ann Intern Med* 99:61–75.

Fawzy, F.I., Fawzy, N.W., Hyun, C.S., et al. 1993. Malignant melanoma. Effects of an early structured psychiatric intervention, coping, and affective state on recurrence and survival six years later. *Arch Gen Psychiatry* 50:681–689.

Fox, B.H. 1978. Premorbid psychological factors as related to cancer incidence. *J Behav Med* 1:45–132.

Frazure-Smith, N., Lesperance, F., and Talajic, M. 1993. Depression following myocardial infarction. Impact on six-month survival. *JAMA* 270:1819–1825.

Fricchione, G.L., and Vlay, S.C. 1986. Psychiatric aspects of patients with malignant ventricular arrhythmias. *Am J Psychiatry* 143:1518–1526.

Friend, S.H., Drvja, T.P., and Weinberg, R.A. 1988. Oncogenes and tumor-suppressing genes. *N Engl J Med* 318:618–622.

Green, W.A., Goldstein, S., and Moss, A.J. 1972. Psychosocial aspects of sudden death. *Arch Intern Med* 129:725–731.

Greer, S. 1979. Psychological enquiry: A contribution to cancer research. *Psychol Med* 9:81–89.

Hackett, T.P. 1985. Depression following myocardial infarction. *Psychosomatics* 26(suppl):23–30.

Hartel, G. 1982. Neurogenic and psychological factors in coronary heart disease: An introductory overview. *Acta Med Scan* 660(suppl):7–11.

Hearn, M.D., Murray, D.M., and Luepker, R.V. 1989. Hostility, coronary heart disease, and total mortality: A 33-year follow-up study of university students. *J Behav Med* 12:105–120.

Heisel, J.S., Locke, S.E., Kraus, L.J., and Williams, R.M. 1986. Natural killer cell activity and MMPI scores of a cohort of college students. *Am J Psychiatry* 143:1382–1386.

Henry, J.P. 1984. On the triggering mechanism of vasovagal syncope. *Psychosom Med* 46:91–93.

Hofer, M.A. 1970. Cardiac and respiratory function during sudden prolonged immobility in wild rodents. *Psychosom Med* 32:633–647.

Hofer, M.A. 1984. Relationships as regulators: A psychobiological perspective. *Psychosom Med* 46:173–179.

Holden, C. 1978. Cancer and the mind: How are they connected? *Science* 200:1363–1369.

Hopkin, K. 1996. Tumor evolution: Survival of the fittest cells. *Journal of NIH Research* 8:37–41.

Horne, R.L., and Picard, R.S. 1979. Psychosocial risk factors for lung cancer. *Psychosm Med* 41:503–514.

Irwin, M., Daniels, M., Bloom, E.T., et al. 1987. Life events, depressive symptoms and immune function. *Am J Psychiatry* 144:437–441.

Irwin, M., Daniels, M., and Weiner, H. 1987. Immune and neuroendocrine changes during bereavement. *Psychiatr Clin N Amer* 10:449–464.

Jacobs, S., and Ostfeld, A. 1977. An epidemiologic review of the mortality of bereavement. *Psychosom Med* 39:344–357.

Jacobs, T.J., and Charles, E. 1980. Life events and the occurrence of cancer in children. *Psychosom Med* 42:11–23.

Janeway, C.A. 1993. How the immune system recognizes invaders. *Scientific American* 269:72–79.

Jefferson, J.W. 1985. Biologic treatment of depression in cardiac patients. *Psychosomatics* 26(suppl):31–38.

Kaplan, B.H., Cassel, J.C., and Gore, S. 1977. Social support and health. *Medical Care* 15:47–58.

Kaufman, I.C., and Rosenblum, L.A. 1967. The reaction to separation in infant monkeys: Anaclitic depression and conservation-withdrawal. *Psychosom Med* 29:648–675.

Kielcolt-Glaser, J.K., Garner, W., Speicher, C., et al. 1984. Psychosocial modifiers of immunocompetence in medical students. *Psychosom Med* 46:7–13.

Kiecolt-Glaser, J.K., and Glaser, R. 1986. Psychological influences on immunity. *Psychosomatics* 27:621–637.

Kinzler, K.W., and Vogelstein, B. 1994. Clinical implications of basic research. Cancer therapy meets p53. *N Engl J Med* 331:49–50.

Kostis, J.B., Rosen, R.C., Brondolo, E., et al. 1992. Superiority of nonpharmacologic therapy compared to propranolol and placebo in men with mild hypertension: A randomized prospective trial. *Am Heart J* 123:466–473.

Kraemer, G.W., Ebert, M.H., Lake, C.R., and McKinney, W.T. 1984. Cerebrospinal fluid measures of neurotransmitter changes associated with pharmacological alteration of the despair response to social separation in rhesus monkeys. *Psychiatry Res* 11:305–315.

Laudenslager, M.L., Capitano, J.P., and Reite, M.L. 1985. Possible effects of early separation experiences on subsequent immune function in adult Macaque monkeys. *Am J Psychiatry* 142:862–864.

Laudenslager, M.L., and Reite, M.L. 1984. Losses and separations. Immunological consequences and health implications. In *Review of Personality and Social Psychology, 5,* P. Shaver, ed., pp. 285–312. Beverly Hills: Sage Publications.

Laudenslager, M.L., Reite, M., and Harbeck, R.J. 1982. Suppressed immune response in infant monkeys associated with maternal separation. *Beh Neural Biol* 36:40–48.

Legault, S.E., Joffe, R.T., and Armstrong, P.W. 1992. Psychiatric morbidity during the early phase of coronary care for myocardial infarction: Association with cardiac diagnosis and outcome. *Can J Psychiatry* 37:316–324.

Leor, J., Poole, W.K., and Kloner, R.A. 1996. Sudden cardiac death triggered by an earthquake. *N Engl J Med* 334:413–419.

LeShan, L. 1966. An emotional life-history pattern associated with neoplastic disease. *Ann NY Acad Sci* 125:780–793.

Levav, I., Friedlander, Y., Kark, J.D., and Peritz, E. 1988. An epidemiologic study of mortality among bereaved parents. *N Engl J Med* 319:457–461.

Levine, S., and Wiener, S.G. 1988. Psychoendocrine aspects of mother-infant relationships in nonhuman primates. *Psychoneuroendocrinology* 13:143–154.

Locke, S.E. 1982. Stress, adaptation, and immunity: Studies in humans. *Gen Hosp Psychiatry* 4:49–58.

Lown, B., Desilva, R.A., Reich, P., et al. 1980. Psychophysiologic factors in sudden cardiac death. *Am J Psychiatry* 137:1325–1335.

Lyketsos, C.G., Hoover, D.R., Guccione, M., et al. 1993. Depressive symptoms as predictors of medical outcomes in HIV infection. *JAMA* 270:2563–2567.

MagPhil, P.L.G., and Thomas, C.B. 1981. Themes of interaction in medical students' Rorshach responses as predictors of midlife health or disease. *Psychosom Med* 43:215–225.

Markowitz, J.H., Matthews, K.A., Kannel, W.B., et al. 1993. Psychological predictors of hypertension in the Framingham Study. *JAMA* 270:2439–2443.

Mathis, J.L. 1964. A sophisticated version of voodoo death. *Psychosom Med* 26:104–107.

McKinney, W.T. 1986. Primate separation studies: Relevance to bereavement. *Psychiatr Ann* 16:281–287.

Monjan, A.A., and Collector, M.I. 1977. Stress-induced modulation of the immune response. *Science* 196:307–308.

Morris, P.L.P., Robinson, R.G., Andrzejewski, P., et al. 1993. Association of depression with 10-year poststroke mortality. *Am J Psychiatry* 150:124–129.

Muller, J.E., and Verrier, R.L. 1996. Triggering of sudden death—lessons from an earthquake. *N Engl J Med* 334:460–461.

Myerson, A. 1994. The attitude of neurologists, psychiatrists, and psychologists towards psychoanalysis. *Am J Psychiatry* 151(Sesquicentennial Supplement):48–54 (originally published in November 1939).

Nossal, G.J.V. 1987. Current concepts: Immunology. *N Engl J Med* 316:1320–1325.

Nossal, G.J.V. 1993. Life, death and the immune system. *Scientific American* 269:52–63.

Parens, H., and Saul, L.J. 1971. *Dependence in Man.* New York: International Universities Press.

Parkes, C.M. 1964. Effects of bereavement on physical and mental health: A study of the medical records of widowers. *Brit Med J* 2:274–279.

Parkes, C.M. 1971. *Bereavement.* New York: International Universities Press.

Parkes, C.M., Benjamin, B., and Fitzgerald, R.G. 1969. Broken heart: A statistical study of increased mortality among widowers. *Brit Med J* 1:740–743.

Parkes, C.M., and Brown, R.J. 1972. Health after bereavement: A controlled study of young Boston widows and widowers. *Psychosom Med* 34:449–460.

Perera, F.P. 1996. Uncovering new clues to cancer risk. *Scientific American* 274:54–62.

Perry, S., Fishman, B., Jacobsberg, L., and Frances, A. 1992. Relationships over one year between lymphocyte subsets and psychosocial variables among adults with infection by human immunodeficiency virus. *Arch Gen Psychiatry* 49:396–401.

Pettingale, K.W., Greer, S., and Tee, D.E.H. 1977. Serum IGA and emotional expression in breast cancer patients. *J Psychosom Res* 21:395–399.

Phillips, D.P., Ruth, T.E., and Wagner, L.M. 1993. Psychology and survival. *Lancet* 342:1142–1144.

Phillips, D.P., Van Voorhees, C.A., and Ruth, T.E. 1992. The birthday: Lifeline or deadline? *Psychosom Med* 54:532–542.

Rabins, P.V., Harvis, K., and Koven, S. 1985. High fatality rates of late life depression associated with cardiovascular disease. *J Affective Disord* 9:165–167.

Ragland, D.R., and Brand, R.J. 1988. Type A behavior and mortality from coronary heart disease. *N Engl J Med* 318:65–69.

Rahe, R.H. 1972. Subjects' recent life changes and their near-future illness reports. *Ann Clin Res* 4:250–262.

Rahe, R.H. 1972. Subjects' recent life changes and their near-future illness susceptibility. *Adv Psychosom Med* 8:2–19.

Rahe, R.H., Ward, H.W., and Hayes, V. 1979. Brief group therapy in myocardial infarction. *Psychosom Med* 41:229–242.

Rees, W.D., and Lutkins, S.G. 1967. Mortality of bereavement. *Brit Med J* 4:13–16.

Reichlin, S. 1993. Neuroendocrine-immune interactions. *N Engl J Med* 329:1246–1253.

Reite, M.L., and Field, T., eds. 1985. *The Psychobiology of Attachment and Separation.* New York: Academic Press.

Richardson, J.L., Zarnegar, Z., Bisno, B., and Levine, A. 1990. Psychosocial status at initiation of cancer treatment and survival. *J Psychosom Res* 34:189–201.

Richter, C.P. 1957. On the phenomenon of sudden death in animals and man. *Psychosom Med* 19:191–198.

Riley, V. 1975. Mouse mammary tumors: Alteration of incidence as apparant function of stress. *Science* 189:465–467.

Ritz, J. 1989. The role of natural killer cells in immune surveillance. *N Engl J Med* 320:1748–1749.

Rogentine, G.N., Van Kammen, D.P., Fox, B.H., et al. 1979. Psychological factors in the prognosis of malignant melanoma: A prospective study. *Psychosom Med* 41:647–656.

Rogers, M.P., Dubey, D., and Reich, P. 1979. The influence of the psyche and the brain on immunity and disease susceptibility. *Psychosom Med* 41:147–162.

Rogers, M.P., and Reich, P. 1988. On the health consequences of bereavement. *N Engl J Med* 319:510–511.

Romano, J. 1994. Reminiscences: 1938 and since. *Am J Psychiatry* 151(Sesquicentennial Supplement):83–90.

Rosenblum, L.A., and Paully, G.S. 1987. Primate models of separation-induced depression. *Psychiatr Clin N Amer* 10:437–445.

Rosenman, R.H. 1984. Some relationships of the type A behavior pattern to coronary heart disease. *J Clin Psychiatry Monograph* 2:3–6.

Rosenman, R.H. 1985. The impact of anxiety on the cardiovascular system. *Psychosomatics* 26(suppl):6–15.

Rozanski, A., Bairey, C.N., Krantz, D.S., et al. 1988. Mental stress and the induction of silent myocardial ischemia in patients with coronary artery disease. *N Engl J Med* 318:1005–1012.

Ruberman, W., Weinblatt, E., Goldberg, G., and Chandhary, B. 1984. Psychosocial influences on mortality after myocardial infarctionl. *N Engl J Med* 311:552–559.

Russek, L.G., King, S.H., Russek, S.J., and Russek, H.I. 1990. The Harvard Mastery of Stress Study 35-year follow-up: Prognostic significance of patterns of psychophysiological arousal and adaptation. *Psychosom Med* 52:271–285.

Saul, L.J. 1966. Sudden death at impasse. *Psychoanal Forum* 1:88–89.

Schiele, B.C. 1946. Psychosomatic medicine and psychiatry. *Dis Nerv System* 7:101–107.

Schleifer, S.J., Keller, S.E., Camerino, M., et al. 1983. Suppression of lymphocyte stimulation following bereavement. *JAMA* 250:374–378.

Schmale, A.H., and Engel, G.L. 1967. The giving up-given up complex illustrated on film. *Arch Gen Psychiatry* 17: 135–145.

Schmale, A.H., and Iker, H.P. 1966. The affect of hopelessness and the development of cancer. *Psychosom Med* 28:714–720.

Schrader, P.L., Pontzer, R., and Engel, T.R. 1983. A case of being scared to death. *Arch Intern Med* 143:1793–1794.

Schwartz, P.J. 1984. Stress and sudden cardiac death: The role of the autonomic nervous system. *J Clin Psychiatry Monograph* 2:7–13.

Siltanen, P. 1978. Life changes and sudden coronary death. *Adv Cardiol* 25:47–60.

Sklar, L.S., and Anisman, H. 1981. Stress and cancer. *Psychol Bull* 89:369–406.

Solomon, G.F. 1987. Psychoneuroimmunology: Interactions between central nervous system and immune system. *J Neurosci Res* 18:1–9.

Sorensen, T.I.A., Nielsen, G.G., Andersen, P.K., and Teasdale, T.W. 1988. Genetic and environmental influences on premature death in adult adoptees. *N Engl J Med* 318:727–732.

Spiegel, D. 1990. Can psychotherapy prolong cancer survival? *Psychosomatics* 31:361–366.

Spiegel, D. 1991. Psychosocial aspects of cancer. *Curr Opinion Psychiatry* 4:889–897.

Spiegel, D., Bloom, J., Kraemer, H.C., and Gottheil, E. 1989. Effect of psychosocial treatment on survival of patients with metastatic breast cancer. *Lancet* 2:888–891.

Stein, M. 1989. Stress, depression and the immune system. *J Clin Psychiatry* 50:5(Suppl):35–40.

Stein, M., Miller, A.H., and Trestman, R.L. 1991. Depression, the immune system, and health and illness: Findings in search of meaning. *Arch Gen Psychiatry* 48:171–177.

Stein, M., Schiavi, R.C., and Camerino, M. 1976. Influence of brain and behavior on the immune system. *Science* 191:435–439.

Steinglass, P., Weisstub, E., and De-Nour, A.K. 1988. Perceived personal networks as mediators of stress reactions. *Am J Psychiatry* 145:1259–1264.

Steinman, L. 1993. Autoimmune disease. *Scientific American* 269:106–115.

Sternberg, E.M., Chrousos, G.P., Wilder, R.L., and Gold, P.W. 1992. The stress response and the regulation of inflammatory disease. *Ann Intern Med* 117:854–866.

Stotland, E. 1969. *The Psychology of Hope.* New York: Jossey-Bass.

Talbott, E., Kuller, L.H., Perper, J., et al. 1981. Sudden unexpected death in women. *Am J Epidemiol* 114:671–682.

Thomas, C.B. 1976. Precursors of premature disease and death. *Ann Intern Med* 85:653–658.

Thomas, C.B., and Duszynski, K.R. 1974. Closeness to parents and the family constellation in a prospective study of five disease states. *Johns Hopkins Med J* 134:251–270.

Thomas, C.B., and Greenstreet, R.L. 1973. Psychological characteristics in youth as predictors of five disease states: Suicide, mental illness, hypertension, coronary heart disease, and tumor. *Johns Hopkins Med J* 132:16–40.

Thomas, C.B., Ross, D.C., Brown, B.S., et al. 1973. A prospective study of the Rorschachs of suicides: The predictive potential of pathological content. *Johns Hopkins Med J* 132:334–353.

Tobin, J.J., and Friedman, J. 1983. Spirits, shamans, and nightmare death. *Am J Orthopsychiatry* 53:439–448.

Vaillant, G.E. 1978. Natural history of male psychological health. IV: What kinds of men do not get psychosomatic illness? *Psychosom Med* 40:420–431.

Vaillant, G.E. 1979. Natural history of male psychological health: Effects of mental health on physical health. *N Engl J Med* 301:1249–1254.

Van der Kolk, B., Greenberg, M., Boyd, H., and Krystal, J. 1985. Inescapable shock, neurotransmitters, and addiction to trauma: Toward a psychobiology of post-traumatic stress. *Biol Psychiatry* 20:314–325.

Verrier, R.L., and Lown, B. 1982. Experimental studies of psychophysiologic factors in sudden cardiac death. *Acta Med Scand* 660(suppl):57–68.

Villar, J., Farnot, U., Barros, F., et al. 1992. A randomized trial of psychosocial support during high-risk pregnancies. *N Engl J Med* 327:1266–1271.

Vogelstein, B., Fearon, E.R., Hamilton, S.R., et al. 1988. Genetic alterations during colorectal-tumor development. *N Engl J Med* 319:525–532.

Ward, A.W.M. 1976. Mortality of bereavement. *Brit Med J* 1:700–702.

Weisman, A.D., and Hackett, T.P. 1961. Prediliction to death. *Psychosom Med* 23:232–256.

Weiss, J.M., Sundar, S.K., Becker, K.J., and Cierpial, M.A. 1989. Behavioral and neural influences on cellular immune responses: Effects of stress and interleukin-1. *J Clin Psychiatry* 50:5(suppl):43–53.

Wendkos, M.H. 1979. *Sudden Death and Psychiatric Illness.* New York: Spectrum Publications.

West, M., Livesley, W.J., Reiffer, L., and Sheldon, A. 1986. The place of attachment in the life events model of stress and illness. *Can J Psychiatry* 31:202–207.

Wintrob, R.M. 1973. The influence of others: Witchcraft and rootwork as explanations of behavioral disturbances. *J Nerv Ment Dis* 156:318–326.

Wolf, S. 1967. The bradycardia of the dive reflex: A possible mechanism of sudden death. *Conditional Reflex* 2:88–95.

Zipes, D.P., Heger, J.J., and Prystowsky, E.N. 1981. Sudden cardiac death. *Am J Med* 70:1151–1154.

Zonderman, A.B., Costa, P.T., and McCrae, R.R. 1989. Depression as a risk for cancer morbidity and mortality in a nationally representative sample. *JAMA* 262:1191–1195.

Index